Japan

Chris Taylor
Nicko Goncharoff
Mason Florence
Christian Rowthorn

Japan

6th edition

Published by

Lonely Planet Publications
Head Office: PO Box 617, Hawthorn, Vic 3122, Australia
Branches: 150 Linden St, Oakland, CA 94607, USA
10a Spring Place, London NW5 3BH, UK
1 rue du Dahomey, 75011 Paris, France

Printed by
The Bookmaker Pty Ltd
Printed in China on plantation forest, acid free paper

Script Typeset by
Yoshiharu Abe

Photographs by

Front cover: Mason Florence

Glenn Beanland	Nicko Goncharoff	Matthias Ley	Anthony Weersing
Robert Charlton	Chris Hindle	Martin Moos	Ingo Westner
Thomas Daniell	Alan Holtzman	Chris Taylor	Tony Wheeler
Mason Florence	Richard I'Anson	Alex Thompson	Jeff Williams

First Published
October 1981

This Edition
October 1997

Although the authors and publisher have tried to make the information as accurate as possible, they accept no responsibility for any loss, injury or inconvenience sustained by any person using this book.

National Library of Australia Cataloguing in Publication Data

Taylor, Chris
Japan – a travel survival kit

6th ed.
Includes index.
ISBN 0 86442 4930

1.Japan – Guidebooks. I. Goncharoff, Nicko. II. Florence, Mason. III. Rowthorn, Chris. IV. Title.
(Series: Lonely Planet travel survival kit)

915.20449

text & maps © Lonely Planet 1997
Tokyo Subway Network reproduced by kind permission of Teito Rapid Transit Authority
photos © photographers as indicated 1997
climate charts compiled from information supplied by Patrick J Tyson, © Patrick J Tyson, 1997

Chris Taylor

Chris grew up in England and Australia, but has spent much of the past decade in Asia – notably Tokyo and more recently Taipei. He has contributed to Lonely Planet's *China*, *Malaysia, Singapore & Brunei*, *Indonesia* and *South-East Asia* guides, and is the author of the *Tibet* guide, *Tokyo* city guide and *Mandarin* phrasebook. He works as a freelance writer out of Taiwan; his stories have appeared in numerous magazines and newspapers.

Nicko Goncharoff

Escaping from New York at age 17, Nicko found his true home while attending university in Colorado, though he promptly left it after graduation for a brief stint in Taiwan. Eight years and numerous jobs later he found himself still in Asia, writing for a financial-news wire service in Hong Kong. Sensing his sanity was slipping away, he traded his suit for hiking boots, and joined the Lonely Planet team to work on the 5th edition of *China*. He has also written a city guide for *Hong Kong*. He now calls Boulder, Colorado his home, during the few weeks of the year that he's there.

Mason Florence

Since graduating from the University of Colorado in 1990, Mason has worked as a Kyoto-based photo-journalist. When not traipsing through the Japanese countryside seeking remnants of traditional life, he disappears into South-East Asia where he explores and documents the indigenous peoples and cultures of the region. Mason's articles and photographs have appeared in numerous books, newspapers and magazines worldwide.

Christian Rowthorn

Chris was born in England and grew up in the USA. After graduating from college, he worked a variety of lame jobs before quitting Generation X to become an ex-pat. He moved to Japan in 1992 and worked as an English teacher before becoming a regional correspondent for the *Japan Times*. He presently lives in Kyoto and travels whenever possible in Asia.

From the Authors

Chris Taylor In Tokyo, thanks to Andrew Marshall and Kibo. Thanks to Japan residents who joined me for a beer or went out of their way to give me their views and tips on what to do. Thanks also to all the Japanese who were courteous and helped out the annoying *gaijin* with never-ending questions. Special thanks to the folks at the Tokyo TIC.

Nicko Goncharoff Many, many thanks to Rieko Suda, who went above and beyond the call on countless occasions. Thanks also to Yuko and Bruce for their hospitality. MaryBeth Maslowski at JNTO took time to help me out, as did the staff at the Sapporo International Communications Plaza. Thanks also to the folks at United Airlines for their time and patience.

Mason Florence I would like to express my gratitude to the countless people who assisted along the way and the staff at the various TICs. Special thanks to Junji Sugita and Kazuhiko Miyazaki for all of their tireless help, and also to Cameron Hay of the *Japan Times* and Dara Levine (who braved the most primitive camping in rural Shikoku). And heartfelt thanks to the Goto family, and my own, for their patience.

Christian Rowthorn Chris wishes to thank, first and foremost, Cameron Hay. He also wishes to thank Chiori Matsunaga, Paul Carty, Anthony Weersing, Denise Wallace, Alex Kerr, Hiroko and Reishi Tayama, Michael Donohue, Ingo Westner, Robert Singer, Lucas Sabien, Siska Brutsaert, Michelle Gorsuch, Deng Yan, Nicholas Lutyens-Humfrey, Chris and Chihiro Everett, Matthias Ley and Thomas Daniell.

This Book

The first three editions of this book were written by Ian L McQueen. The 4th edition was rewritten by Chris Taylor, Robert Strauss and Tony Wheeler. Chris Taylor updated the 5th edition. The 6th edition was updated by Chris Taylor, Nicko Goncharoff, Mason Florence and Chris Rowthorn.

From the Publisher

This edition was coordinated in the Melbourne office by Chris Wyness with the help of Megan Fraser. Additional editing was done by Greg Alford, Peter Cruttenden, Michelle Coxall, Liz Filleul, Paul Harding, Sharan Kaur, Anne Mulvaney and Carolyn Papworth. Yoshiharu Abe helped proof and input the script. The design and mapping was done by Sally Gerdan, Chris Love, Anthony Phelan and Rachael Scott. Ann Jeffree took

the book through layout and drew many of the illustrations. Trudi Canavan drew the illustrations for the food section and Mic Looby drew the chapter ends. David Kemp and Adam McCrow designed the cover. Special thanks to Suntory Restaurant in Melbourne for their assistance with the Food Section.

Warning & Request

Things change – prices go up, schedules change, good places go bad and bad places go bankrupt – nothing stays the same. So, if you find things better or worse, recently opened or long since closed, please tell us and help make the next edition even more accurate and useful.

We value all of the feedback we receive from travellers. Julie Young coordinates a small team who read and acknowledge every letter, postcard and email, and ensure that every morsel of information finds its way to the appropriate authors, editors and publishers. Everyone who writes to us will find their name in the next edition of the appropriate guide and will also receive a free subscription to our quarterly newsletter, *Planet Talk*. The very best contributions will be rewarded with a free Lonely Planet guide.

Excerpts from your correspondence may appear in updates (which we add to the end pages of reprints); new editions of this guide; in our newsletter, *Planet Talk*; or in the Postcards section of our Web site – so please let us know if you don't want your letter published or your name acknowledged.

Thanks

Many thanks to the travellers who used the last edition and wrote to us with helpful hints, useful advice and interesting anecdotes. Your names appear on page 862.

Contents

Map Legend

BOUNDARIES

.... International Boundary

.... Prefecture Boundary

AREA FEATURES

.... Parks

.... Built-Up Area

.... Pedestrian Mall

.... Market

.... Cemetery

.... Reef

.... Beach

HYDROGRAPHIC FEATURES

.... Coastline

.... River, Creek

.... Rapids, Waterfalls

.... Lake, Intermittent Lake

.... Canal, Swamp

ROUTES

.... Freeway or Expressway

.... Highway

.... Major Road

.... Unsealed Road or Track

.... City Road

.... City Street

.... JR Railway, Station

.... Shinkansen Railway, Station

.... Private Railway, Station

.... Underground Railway

.... Chairlift or Ropeway

.... Subway, Station

.... Tram, Tram Stop

.... Walking Track

.... Walking Tour

.... Four Wheel Drive Track

.... Ferry Route

.... Bus Route

SYMBOLS

✪ CAPITAL		.... National Capital
◉ Capital		.... Regional Capital
◍ CITY		.... Major City
● City		.... City
● Town		.... Town
● Village		.... Village
■	▼	.... Place to Stay, Place to Eat
☕	♟	.... Cafe, Pub or Bar
✉	☎	.... Post Office, Telephone
❶	❻	.... Tourist Information, Bank
◕	🅿	.... Transport, Parking
🏛	⛫	.... Museum, Youth Hostel
⚏	🅰	Caravan Park, Camping Ground
✛	✚	.... Church, Cathedral
卍	🔯	Buddhist Temple, Shinto Shrine

✪	★	.... Hospital, Police Station
◔	✿	.... Embassy, Gardens
✈	✝	.... Airport, Airfield
▭	◣	.... Swimming Pool, Dive Site
❖	🐃	.... Shopping Centre, Zoo
🏛	▮	.... Stately Home, Monument
♣	◙	.... Castle, Tomb
⌒	A25	.... Cave, Route Number
▲	※	.... Mountain or Hill, Lookout
🏮	⚲	.... Lighthouse, Shipwreck
)(	◎	.... Pass, Spring
➐	⚡	.... Beach, Surf Beach
∴	⚘	.... Ruins, Ski Field
		.... Ancient or City Wall
		.... Cliff or Escarpment, Tunnel

Note: not all symbols displayed above appear in this book

Introduction

Contemporary Japan is a land of extremes. But then, arguably, it has always been that way. After centuries of bloodshed and social upheaval as warlords struggled to gain control of the nation, the country was shut tight from 1600 to 1867 under a policy of *sakoku* or 'national seclusion'. The arrival of Commodore Perry's 'black ships' in 1853 set Japan's fastness a-jitter with speculation about the changing world outside its locked doors, and by 1868 the doors had been flung open, an emperor was restored to his throne and the Japanese rushed to greet an incoming tide of Western technology and ideas that would turn their traditional world upside down.

Today, after having their economy and country ravaged by WWII and having spectacularly bounced back to become an economic superpower, it's surprising just how much of that traditional world still lingers. It's this, as much as anything else, that gives the visitor the sensation of having strayed into a land of startling opposites, a land where suburban sprawl gives way to the sensuous contours of a temple roof, where rustic red-lantern restaurants nestle in the shadow of the high-rise future.

The extremes never end. You could splurge your life savings on a week in Tokyo, but then again you could just as easily maintain a diet of youth hostels and country inns, filling yourself up in cheap noodle shops, and come away spending no more than you would on a holiday at home. Cities such as Tokyo and Osaka can sometimes seem like congested, hi-tech visions of the future, but the national parks of Hokkaidō and the alps of central Honshū offer some sparsely populated vistas that very few foreigners set their eyes on.

All this, perhaps, is to add to the mythology of Japan, a country which is the subject of more gullible and misguided musings than any other place in the world. The best way to approach Japan is by discarding your preconceptions. Somewhere between the elegant formality of Japanese manners and the candid, sometimes boisterous exchanges that take place over a few drinks, between the sanitised shopping malls and the unexpected rural festival, everyone finds their own vision of Japan. Come with an open mind and be prepared to be surprised.

Facts about the Country

HISTORY
Prehistory

The origin of Japan's earliest inhabitants is obscure. There was certainly emigration via land bridges that once connected Japan with Siberia and Korea, but it is also thought that seafaring migrants from Polynesia may have landed on Kyūshū and Okinawa. The truth is probably that the Japanese are a result of emigration from Siberia in the north, China and Korea to the west and perhaps Polynesian stock from the south.

The first recorded signs of civilisation in Japan are found in the Neolithic period around 10,000 BC. This is called the Jōmon (Cord Mark) period after the discovery of pottery fragments with cord marks. The people at this time lived as fishers, hunters and food-gatherers.

This period was gradually superseded by the Yayoi era, which dates from around 300 BC, and is named after the site where pottery fragments were found near modern Tokyo. The Yayoi people are considered to have had a strong connection with Korea and their most important developments were the wet cultivation of rice and the use of bronze and iron implements.

The period following the Yayoi era has been called the Kofun (Burial Mound) period by archaeologists who discovered thousands of grave mounds concentrated mostly in central and western Japan. Judging by their size and elaborate construction, these mounds must have required immense resources of labour. It seems likely that the custom of building these tombs was eclipsed by the arrival of Buddhism, which favoured cremation.

As more and more settlements banded together to defend their land, groups became larger until, by 300 AD, the Yamato kingdom had loosely unified the nation through conquest or alliance. The Yamato leaders claimed descent from the sun goddess, Amaterasu, and introduced the title of emperor *(tennō)* around the 5th century.

Historical Periods	
Historical Periods	*Date*
Jomon	10,000-300 BC
Yayoi	300 BC-300 AD
Kofun	300-710
Nara	710-794
Heian	794-1185
Kamakura	1185-1333
Muromachi	1333-1576
Momoyama	1576-1600
Edo	1600-1867
Meiji	1868-1912
Taishō	1912-1926
Shōwa	1926-1989
Heisei	1989 to the present

Buddhism & Early Chinese Influence

In the mid-6th century, Buddhism was introduced from China via the Korean kingdom of Paekche. The decline of the Yamato court was halted by Prince Shōtoku (573-620), who set up a constitution and laid the guidelines for a centralised state headed by a single ruler. He also instituted Buddhism as a state religion.

Despite family feuds and coups d'état, subsequent rulers continued to reform the country's administration and laws. Previously, it had been the custom to avoid the pollution of imperial death by changing the site of the capital for each successive emperor, however, in 710 this long-held custom was altered and the capital was shifted to Nara, where it remained for the next 75 years.

During the Nara period (710-794) there was strong promotion of Buddhism, particularly under Emperor Shōmu, who ordered construction of the Tōdai-ji Temple and the casting of its Daibutsu (Great Buddha) as supreme guardian deity of the nation. Both the temple and its image of Buddha can still be seen in Nara.

Heian Period (794-1185) – Establishment of a Native Culture

By the end of the 8th century, the Buddhist clergy in Nara had become so politically meddlesome that Emperor Kammu decided to sever the ties between Buddhism and government by moving the capital. The site eventually chosen was Heian (modern-day Kyoto).

Like Nara, Heian was modelled on Chang-an (present-day Xi'an), the capital of the Tang dynasty in China, and it was to continue as the capital of Japan until 1868. It was a period that saw a great flourishing in the arts and important developments in religious thinking, as ideas and institutions imported from China were adapted to the needs of their new homeland.

Rivalry between Buddhism and Shinto, the traditional religion of Japan, was reduced by presenting Shinto deities as manifestations of Buddha. Religion was assigned a role separated from politics, and Japanese monks returning from China established two new sects, Tendai and Shingon, which became the mainstays of Japanese Buddhism.

With the conquest of the Ainu (Japan's original inhabitants) in the early 9th century, Japan's borders were extended to the tip of Northern Honshū. However, the emperors began to devote more time to leisure and scholarly pursuit and less time to government. This created an opening for a noble family called Fujiwara to capture important court posts and become the chief power brokers, a role the family was able to maintain for several centuries.

The Heian period is considered the apogee of Japanese courtly elegance, but out in the provinces a new power was on the rise, that of the *samurai* or 'warrior class', which built up its own armed forces and readily turned to arms to defend its autonomy. Samurai families moved into the capital, where they muscled in on the court.

The corrupt Fujiwara were eventually eclipsed by the Taira clan, who ruled briefly before being ousted by the Minamoto family (also known as the Genji) at the battle of Dannoura (Shimonoseki) in 1185.

Kamakura Period (1185-1333) – Domination through Military Rule

After assuming the rank of *shogun* (military leader), Minamoto Yoritomo set up his headquarters in Kamakura, while the emperor remained the nominal ruler in Kyoto. It was the beginning of a long period of feudal rule by successive samurai families. In fact, this feudal system was effectively to linger on until imperial power was restored in 1868.

Yoritomo purged members of his own family who stood in his way, but after his death in 1199 (he died after falling from his horse), his wife's family (the Hōjō) eliminated all of Yoritomo's potential successors and became the true wielders of power behind the figureheads of shoguns and warrior lords.

During this era, the popularity of Buddhism spread to all levels of society. From the late 12th century, Japanese monks returning from China introduced a new sect, Zen, the austerity of which offered a particular appeal to the samurai class.

The Mongols, under their leader Kublai Khan, reached Korea in 1259 and sent envoys to Japan seeking Japanese submission. In response, the envoys were expelled. The Mongols reacted by sending an invasion fleet which arrived near present-day Fukuoka in 1274. This first attack was only just repulsed with a little help from a typhoon. Further envoys from Kublai Khan were promptly beheaded.

In 1281, the Mongols dispatched a huge army of over 100,000 soldiers to Japan for a second attempt at invasion. After an initial success, the Mongol fleet was almost completely destroyed by yet another typhoon. Ever since, this lucky typhoon has been known to the Japanese as the *kamikaze* (divine wind) – a name later given to the suicide pilots of WWII who vainly attempted to repulse another invasion.

Although the Kamakura government emerged victorious, it was unable to pay its soldiers and lost the support of the warrior class. Buddhist temples also put in a claim for prayer services intended to whip up the divine wind. Emperor Go-Daigo led an unsuccessful rebellion against the government and was exiled to the Oki Islands near Matsue, where he waited a year before trying again. The second attempt successfully toppled the government.

Muromachi Period (1333-1576) – Country at War

Emperor Go-Daigo refused to reward his warriors, favouring the aristocracy and priesthood instead. This led to the revolt of

Samurai

The prime duty of a samurai was to give faithful service to his feudal lord. In fact, the origin of the term samurai is closely linked to a word meaning 'to serve', and this can be seen in the kanji for the word. Over the centuries, the samurai established a code of conduct which came to be known as Bushidō (the Way of the Warrior). This code was drawn from Confucianism, Shinto and Buddhism.

Confucianism required the samurai to show absolute loyalty to his lord; towards the oppressed he was expected to show benevolence and exercise justice. Subterfuge was to be despised, as were all commercial and financial transactions. A real samurai had endless endurance, total self-control, spoke only the truth and displayed no emotion. Since his honour was his life, disgrace and shame were to be avoided above all else and all insults were to be avenged.

From Buddhism, the samurai learnt the lesson that life is impermanent, a handy reason to face death with serenity. Shinto provided the samurai with patriotic beliefs in the divine status both of the emperor and of Japan, the abode of the gods.

Ritual suicide, *(seppuku* or *harakiri)*, to which Japanese Buddhism conveniently turned a blind eye, was an accepted means to avoid dishonour. This grisly 'procedure' required the samurai to ritually disembowel himself before a helpful aide, who then drew his sword and lopped off the samurai's head. One reason for this ritual was the requirement that a samurai should never surrender but always go down fighting. Since surrender was considered a disgrace, prisoners received scant mercy. During WWII this attitude was reflected in Japanese treatment of prisoners of war – still a source of bitter memories for those involved.

In slack moments when he wasn't fighting, the samurai dressed simply but was easily recognisable by his triangular *eboshi*, a hat made from rigid black cloth.

The samurai's standard battle dress or armour (usually made of leather or lacquered steel) consisted of a breastplate, a similar covering for his back, a steel helmet with a visor and more body armour for his shoulders and lower body. Samurai weaponry – his pride and joy – included a bow and arrows (in a quiver), swords and a dagger – and he wasn't complete without his trusty steed.

Before entering the fray, a samurai was expected to be freshly washed and groomed and some even added a dash of perfume! The classic samurai battle took the form of duelling between individuals rather than the clashing of massed armies.

Not all samurai were good warriors adhering to their code of conduct: portrayals of samurai indulging in double-crossing, subterfuge or outright cowardice became popular themes in Japanese theatre. ■

Samurai battle helmet

Takauji Ashikaga, who had previously changed sides to support Emperor Go-Daigo. Ashikaga defeated Go-Daigo at Kyoto, then installed a new emperor and appointed himself shogun; the Ashikaga family later settled at Muromachi, a part of Kyoto. Go-Daigo escaped to set up a rival court at Yoshino, a mountainous region near Nara. Rivalry between the two courts continued for 60 years until the Ashikaga made a promise (which was not kept) that the imperial lines would alternate.

The Ashikaga ruled with gradually diminishing effectiveness in a land slipping steadily into civil war and chaos. Despite this, there was a flourishing of those arts now considered typically Japanese such as landscape painting, classical nō drama, flower arranging *(ikebana)* and the tea ceremony *(chanoyu)*. Many of Kyoto's famous gardens date from this period as do such well-known monuments as the Kinkaku-ji (Golden Temple) and Ginkaku-ji (Silver Temple). Formal trade relations were reopened with Ming China and Korea, although Japanese piracy remained a bone of contention between both sides.

The Ōnin War, which broke out in 1467, developed into a full-scale civil war and marked the rapid decline of the Ashikaga family. *Daimyō* (domain lords) and local leaders fought for power in bitter territorial disputes that were to last for a century. This period, from 1467 to around the start of the Momoyama period in 1576, is known as the Warring States period.

Momoyama Period (1576-1600) – Return to Unity

In 1568 Oda Nobunaga, the son of a daimyō, seized power from the imperial court in Kyoto and used his military genius to initiate a process of pacification and unification in central Japan. His efforts were cut short when he was betrayed by one of his own generals, Akechi Mitsuhide, in 1582. Under attack from Mitsuhide and seeing all was lost, he disembowelled himself in Kyoto's Honnō-ji Temple.

Nobunaga was succeeded by his ablest commander, Toyotomi Hideyoshi, who was reputedly the son of a farmer, although his origins are not clear. His diminutive size and pop-eyed features earned him the nickname of Saru-san (Mr Monkey). Hideyoshi extended unification so that by 1590 the whole country was under his rule. He then became fascinated with grandiose schemes to invade China and Korea. The first invasion was repulsed in 1593 and the second was aborted on the death of Hideyoshi in 1598.

The arts of this period are noted for their boisterous use of colour and gold-leaf embellishment. There was also a vogue for building castles on a flamboyant scale; the most impressive example was Osaka-jō Castle, which reputedly required three years of labour by up to 100,000 men.

The Christian Century (1543-1640)

In the mid-16th century, when the Europeans first made their appearance, there was little authority over foreign trade. The first Portuguese to be shipwrecked off southern Kyūshū in 1543 found a most appreciative Japanese reception for their skills in making firearms, which were soon spread throughout the region. The Jesuit missionary Francis Xavier arrived in Kagoshima in 1549 and was followed by more missionaries who quickly converted local lords keen to profit from foreign trade and assistance with military supplies. The new religion spread rapidly, gaining several hundred thousand converts, particularly in Nagasaki.

At first, Nobunaga saw the advantages of trading with Europeans and tolerated the arrival of Christianity as a counterbalance to Buddhism. Once Hideyoshi had assumed power, however, this tolerance gradually gave way to the suspicion of subversion by an alien religion which was deemed a threat to his rule. Edicts against Christianity were followed in 1597 by the crucifixion of 26 foreign priests and Japanese believers.

Proscription and persecution of Christianity continued under the Tokugawa government until it reached its peak in 1637 with the ferocious quelling by the authorities of the Christian-led Shimabara Rebellion. This brought the Christian century to an abrupt close, although the religion continued to be practised in secret until it was officially allowed to resurface at the end of the 19th century.

Edo or Tokugawa Period (1600-1867) – Peace & Seclusion

The supporters of Hideyoshi's young heir, Toyotomi Hideyori, were defeated in 1600 by his former ally, Tokugawa Ieyasu, at the battle of Sekigahara. Ieyasu set up his field headquarters *(bakufu)* at Edo, now Tokyo, and assumed the title of shogun; the emperor and court continued to exercise purely nominal authority in Kyoto.

A strict political regime was introduced. The Tokugawa family, besides retaining large estates, also took control of major cities, ports and mines; the remainder of the country was allocated to autonomous daimyō. In descending order of importance, society consisted of the nobility, who had nominal power; the daimyō and their warriors (samurai); the farmers; and at the bottom of the list, artisans and merchants. To ensure political security, the daimyō were required to make ceremonial visits to Edo every alternate year, and their wives and children were kept in permanent residence in Edo as virtual hostages of the government. The cost of this constant movement and the family ties in Edo made it difficult for the daimyō to remain anything but loyal. At the lower end of society, farmers were subject to a severe system of rules which dictated in minutest detail their food, clothing and housing. Social mobility from one class to another was blocked; social standing was determined by birth.

Under Tokugawa rule, Japan entered a period of national seclusion *(sakoku)*. Japanese were forbidden on pain of death to travel to or return from overseas or to trade abroad. Only the Dutch, Chinese and Koreans were allowed to remain and they were placed under strict supervision; the Dutch were confined to Dejima Island near Nagasaki and their contacts restricted to merchants and prostitutes.

The rigid emphasis of these times on submitting unquestioningly to rules of obedience and loyalty has lasted to the present day. One effect of strict rule during the Tokugawa period was to create an atmosphere of relative peace and security in which the arts excelled. There were great advances, for example, in *haiku* poetry, *bunraku* puppet plays and *kabuki* theatre. Weaving, pottery, ceramics and lacquerware became famous for their refined quality.

By the turn of the 19th century, the Tokugawa government was facing stagnation and corruption. Famines and poverty among the peasants and samurai further weakened the system. Foreign ships started to probe Japan's isolation with increasing insistence and the Japanese soon realised that their outmoded defences were ineffectual. Russian contacts in the north were followed by British and American visits. In 1853, Commodore Matthew Perry of the US Navy arrived with a squadron of 'black ships' to demand the opening of Japan to trade. Other countries moved in to demand the opening of treaty ports and the relaxation of restrictions on trade barriers.

A surge of antigovernment feeling among the Japanese followed. The Tokugawa government was accused of failing to defend Japan against foreigners and of neglecting the national reconstruction necessary for Japan to meet the west on equal terms. In 1867 the ruling shogun, Keiki, resigned and the Emperor Meiji resumed control of state affairs.

Meiji Restoration (1868-1912) – Emergence from Isolation

The initial stages of this restoration were resisted in a state of virtual civil war. The abolition of the shogunate (military government) was followed by the surrender of the daimyō, whose lands were divided into the prefectures that exist today. Edo became Japan's new capital and was renamed Tokyo (Eastern Capital). The government became centralised again and western-style ministries were appointed for specific tasks. A series of revolts by the samurai against the erosion of their status culminated in the Saigō Uprising, when they were finally beaten and stripped of their power.

Despite nationalist support for the emperor under the slogan of *sonnō-jōi* (revere the emperor, repel the barbarians), the new government soon realised it would have to meet the west on its own terms. Under the slogan *fukoku kyōhei* (rich country, strong military), the economy underwent a crash course in westernisation and industrialisation. An influx of western experts was encouraged and Japanese students were sent abroad to acquire expertise in modern technologies. In 1889, Japan created a western-style constitution which, like the military revival, owed much to Prussian influences.

By the 1890s, government leaders were concerned by the spread of liberal western ideas and encouraged a swing back to nationalism and traditional values.

Japan's growing confidence was demonstrated by the abolition of foreign treaty rights and by the ease with which it trounced China in the Sino-Japanese War (1894-5). The subsequent treaty recognised Korean independence and ceded Taiwan to Japan. Friction with Russia led to the Russo-Japanese

War (1904-05), in which the Japanese army attacked the Russians in Manchuria and Korea. The Japanese navy stunned the Russians by inflicting a crushing defeat on their Baltic fleet at the battle of Tsu-shima Island. For the first time, the Japanese were able to consider that they had drawn level with the western powers.

Industrialisation & Asian Dominance
On his death in 1912, the Emperor Meiji was succeeded by his son, Yoshihito, whose period of rule was named the Taishō era. The later stages of his life were dogged by ill-health that was probably attributable to meningitis.

When WWI broke out, Japan sided against Germany but did not become deeply involved in the conflict. While the Allies were occupied with war, the Japanese took the opportunity, through shipping and trade, to expand their economy at top speed. At the same time, a strong foothold was gained in China, thereby giving Japan a dominant position in Asia.

Social unrest led the government to pursue a more democratic, liberal line; the right to vote was extended and Japan joined the League of Nations in 1920. Under the influence of the *zaibatsu* (financial cliques of industrialists and bankers), a moderate and pacific foreign policy was followed.

Nationalism & the Pursuit of Empire
The Shōwa era commenced when Emperor Hirohito ascended to the throne in 1926. He had toured extensively in Europe, mixed with European nobility and developed a liking for the British lifestyle.

A rising tide of nationalism was quickened by the world economic depression that began in 1930. Popular unrest was marked by plots to overthrow the government and political assassinations. This led to a strong increase in the power of the militarists, who approved the invasion of Manchuria in 1931 and the installation of a Japanese puppet regime, Manchukuo. In 1933, Japan withdrew from the League of Nations and, in 1937, entered into full-scale hostilities against China.

Emperor Meiji oversaw Japan's modernisation.

As the leader of a new order for Asia, Japan signed a tripartite pact with Germany and Italy in 1940. The Japanese military leaders saw their main opponents to this new order for Asia, the so-called 'Greater East Asia Co-prosperity Sphere', in the USA.

World War II

When diplomatic attempts to gain US neutrality failed, the Japanese launched themselves into WWII with a surprise attack on Pearl Harbor on 7 December 1941.

At first, Japan scored rapid successes, pushing its battle fronts across to India, down to the fringes of Australia and out into the mid-Pacific. The Battle of Midway opened the US counterattack, puncturing Japanese naval superiority and turning the tide of the war against Japan. Exhausted by submarine blockade and aerial bombing, by 1945 Japan had been driven back on all fronts. In August of the same year, the declaration of war by the Soviet Union and the atomic bombs dropped by the USA on Hiroshima and Nagasaki proved to be the final straws: Emperor Hirohito announced unconditional surrender.

Having surrendered, Japan was occupied by Allied forces under the command of General Douglas MacArthur. The chief aim was a thorough reform of Japanese government through demilitarisation, the trial of war criminals and the weeding out of militarists or ultranationalists from the government. A new constitution was introduced which dismantled the political power of the emperor, who completely stunned his subjects by publicly renouncing any claim to divine origins. This left him with the status of a mere figurehead.

The occupation was terminated in 1952, although the island of Okinawa was only returned to Japan in 1972.

Postwar Reconstruction

At the end of the war, the Japanese economy was in ruins and inflation was rampant. A programme of recovery provided loans, restricted imports and encouraged capital investment and personal saving.

By the late '50s, trade was again flourishing and the economy continued to expand rapidly. From textiles and the manufacture of labour-intensive goods such as cameras, the Japanese 'economic miracle' branched out into virtually every sector of economic activity. Economic recession and inflation surfaced in 1974 and again in 1980, mostly as a result of steep price hikes for imported oil on which Japan is dependent. But despite these setbacks, Japan became the world's most successful export economy, generating massive trade surpluses and dominating such fields as electronics, robotics, computer technology, car production and banking.

The Giant Falters

For a long time, Japan seemed unstoppable. The term Japan Inc came to be used with suspicion by commentators who saw Japan as some huge well-oiled machine. It seemed a nation of unassailable job security and endless economic growth.

But with the arrival of the '90s, the old certainties seemed to vanish. Japan's legendary economic growth slowed to a virtual standstill. In 1993, after 38 years at the helm, the conservative Liberal Democratic Party (LDP) succumbed to a spate of scandals and was swept out of power by an eight-party coalition of reformers. In January 1995 a massive earthquake struck Kōbe: government reactions were slow and confused; Japan's much vaunted earthquake preparedness was shattered. And to top it all off, just a couple of months later a millennial cult with doomsday ambitions engineered a poison gas attack on the Tokyo subway system.

Japan-watchers had a field day. None of it was as bad as it looked, of course. Within a year the LDP was back in government, and elections in 1996 tentatively reaffirmed the LDP as Japan's government by backing LDP prime-ministerial candidate, Hashimoto Ryūtaro. The economy too is regaining buoyancy. True, unemployment is running at an all-time high, but 3.5% is a high that many other rich economies would happily live with.

One thing that observers do agree about is that Japan is changing. The life-time employment system is a thing of the past, the corporate world is being forced to open its doors to international market forces, elections are being fought around the issue of dismantling Japan's creaky government bureaucracy, and the once cosy system of political kickbacks and backroom deals that characterised business and government is finding less and less favour among Japanese voters.

GEOGRAPHY

Japan is an island nation. Much of its cultural heritage has been drawn from nearby Asian countries, but it is this 'apartness' from the Asian mainland that is defining for many Japanese. Both China and Korea are close enough to have been decisive influences, but at the same time they are too distant to have dominated Japan.

Japan has not always been physically isolated. At the end of the last Ice Age, around 10,000 years ago, the level of the sea rose enough to flood a land bridge connecting Japan with the mainland. Today, Japan consists of a chain of islands that rides the back of a 3000 km long arc of mountains along the eastern rim of the Asian continent. It stretches from around 25°N at the southern islands of Okinawa to 45°N at the northern end of Hokkaidō; cities at comparable latitudes would be Miami or Cairo in the south and Montreal or Milan in the north. Japan's total land area is 377,435 sq km, and more than 80% of it is mountainous.

Japan consists of some 1000 small islands and four major ones: Honshū (slightly larger than Britain), Hokkaidō, Kyūshū and Shikoku. Okinawa, the largest and most significant of Japan's many smaller islands, is about halfway along an archipelago that stretches from the western tip of Honshū almost all the way to Taiwan. It is far enough from the rest of Japan to have developed a culture that differs from that of the 'mainland' in many respects.

GEOLOGY

If Japanese culture has been influenced by isolation, it has equally been shaped by the country's mountainous topography. Many of the mountains are volcanic (more than 40 of which are presently active), thereby blessing the islands with numerous hot springs and spectacular scenery, and at the same time bringing the danger of frequent eruptions and intense seismic activity. Indeed, the rough and tumble of earthquakes, volcanic eruptions and *tsunami* (tidal waves), along with a monsoonal climate, has perhaps contributed to Japanese industriousness. The Japanese are used to rebuilding their world every 20 or 30 years.

Japan has the dubious distinction of being one of the most seismically active regions of the world. It is calculated that the country gets around 1000 earthquakes a year, most of them too small to notice without sophisticated seismic equipment. This seismic activity is particularly concentrated in the Kantō region, in which Tokyo is situated. Tokyo is on the receiving end of a monster tremor about every 60 years. The last biggie measured 8.2 on the Richter scale and occurred in 1923, so another big one is overdue.

CLIMATE

The combination of Japan's mountainous territory and the length of the archipelago (covering 22° of latitude) makes for a complex climate. There are big climatic differences between Hokkaidō in the north, which has short summers and long winters with heavy snowfalls, and the southern Ryūkyū Islands, which enjoy a subtropical climate. At the same time, Japan's proximity to the continental landmass also has significant climatic implications, producing a high degree of seasonal variation.

In the winter months (December to February), cold, dry air masses from Siberia move down over Japan, where they meet warmer, moister air masses from the Pacific. The resulting precipitation results in huge snowfalls on Japan's western side. The eastern side of Japan receives less snow but can still get very cold; Tokyo has colder average January temperatures than Reykjavík in Iceland, but snow, when it does fall on the capital, rarely lasts long.

The summer months (June to August) are

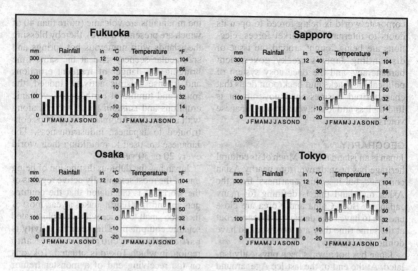

dominated by warm, moist air currents from the Pacific, and produce high temperatures and humidity throughout most of Japan. In the early part of summer there is a rainy season lasting a few weeks that starts in the south and gradually works its way northwards. Further heavy rains can occur in late summer when the country is visited by typhoons bringing torrential rains and strong winds that can have devastating effects, particularly on coastal regions.

In contrast to the extremes of summer and winter, spring and autumn are comparatively mild. Rainfall is relatively low and the days are often clear.

ECOLOGY & ENVIRONMENT

Japan was the first Asian nation to industrialise. It has also been one of the most successful at cleaning up the resulting mess, though problems remain. In the early post-war years, when Japan was frantically rebuilding its economy, there was widespread public ignorance of the problems of pollution. Government did little to enlighten the public.

Industrial pollution reached its worst from the mid-'60s to the mid-'70s. But public awareness of the issue had already been awakened by an outbreak of what came to be called Minamata disease (after the town of the same name), in which up to 6000 people were affected by organomercury poisoning in 1953. It was not until 1968 that the government officially acknowledged the cause of the disease.

By the late '60s public consciousness had reached levels that the government could only ignore at its risk. Laws were passed to curb air and water pollution. These have been reasonably successful, though critics are quick to point out that whereas toxic matter has been mostly removed from Japanese waters organic pollution remains a problem. Similarly, controls on air pollution have had mixed results: photochemical smog emerged as a problem in Tokyo in the early '70s; it remains a problem and now affects other urban centres around Japan.

In 1972 the government passed the Nature Conservation Law, which aimed to protect the natural environment and provide recreational space for the public. National parks, quasi-national parks and prefectural parks were established, and it appears that such measures have been successful in raising wildlife numbers.

Japan & Ecology

In the ecologically conscious 'green' 1990s Japan is frequently cast as an international vandal, slaughtering whales and dolphins, hacking down rainforests and polluting the ocean and atmosphere, all in the name of the rising yen. There's more than a little truth to it.

There's a low level of concern in Japan about environmental issues, particularly when it comes to Japanese activities which do not have an effect on life within Japan itself. The international environmental organisation Greenpeace has made great efforts to focus world attention on whaling and driftnet fishing. In Japan itself, the Japan Tropical Forest Action Network (JATAN) is working hard to raise consciousness within the country about exploitation of tropical rainforests.

Driftnet Fishing For several years before it became an international *cause célèbre* the nations of the Pacific had been complaining bitterly about driftnet fishing – 'strip mining the ocean' as one critic described it. The technique is simple, the devastation dramatic – you simply drag a fine net between two boats. The net is typically about 15 metres deep and the two boats hauling it can be up to 50 km apart! It's been aptly named a 'wall of death' because the driftnets catch not only the tuna they're set for but everything else which gets in the way from turtles and dolphins to sea birds and sharks. Although these creatures are not wanted, they die anyway.

It's been calculated that up to half of the catch in driftnets is unwanted and the effect on the balance of ocean life can be terrible. Following a storm of international protest, Japan has cut its driftnet fleet by one-third although Taiwan, the other chief culprit, is still using driftnets. There have been accusations that Japanese aid to the tiny South Pacific nations most at risk from the depredation of driftnet fishing has been used as a lever to silence complaints.

Packaging One example of Japan's lack of environmental concern (which every visitor will soon be aware of) is the Japanese penchant for overpackaging. At a time when most Western nations are trying to cut back on packaging, in Japan it's full speed ahead to wrap things in the largest possible number of layers of paper, plastic and cardboard, all tied together with string and bows.

Rainforests Japan is the world's largest consumer of tropical rainforest timber. The terrible destruction wrought upon the rainforests of the Malaysian states of Sabah and Sarawak has principally been to supply Japan. Apart from the large-scale destruction of the forests (where minimal regeneration takes place), the logging also silts up rivers and kills fish.

Most of the logging activity is conducted by the big Japanese trading companies and 70% to 80% of the timber ends up as plywood, most of which is used for concrete formwork moulds and then destroyed. Rainforest and coastal mangrove forests have also been wiped out to supply Japanese woodchipping operations.

Recycling Recycling is a two-sided coin in Japan. On one side, many household disposables, such as glass bottles, are efficiently recycled. On the other side, Japan is the throwaway society *par excellence*. The severe *shaken* vehicle inspection system encourages car owners to scrap their cars and buy new ones; cars more than a few years old are a rare sight on Japanese roads. There's little demand for second-hand goods and appliances, and consumer equipment is quickly scrapped to be replaced by the latest model. Stories abound of resident *gaijin* setting up house with Japanese throwaways. Around almost any big city railway station there will be tangled heaps of perfectly good bicycles, abandoned by their users.

Turtles Dolphins and whales are not the only creatures to fall prey to the Japanese economy. It's estimated that every year 30,000 hawksbill turtles, an endangered species, are killed to provide Japan with 30 tonnes of turtle shell.

Waribashi Japan's vast number of restaurants almost all provide their customers with disposable chopsticks or *waribashi*. Forests fall in order to supply these one-use only utensils.

Whales The international outcry against whaling has cut the whaling nations down to just three – Iceland, Norway and Japan. When the Japanese finally agreed to halt whaling they reserved the right to kill 300 minke whales a year for 'scientific research'. After they've been 'researched' they end up as restaurant whale meat. ∎

FLORA & FAUNA

Flora

The latitudinal spread of the islands of Japan makes for a wide diversity of flora and fauna. The Ryūkyū and Ogasawara island groups in the far south are subtropical, and flora and fauna in this region is related to that found on the Malaysian peninsula. Mainland Japan (Honshū, Kyūshū and Shikoku), on the other hand, shows more similarities with Korea and China, while sub-arctic northern and central Hokkaidō has features of its own.

The flora of Japan today is not what the Japanese saw hundreds of years ago. This is not just because much of Japan's natural landscape has succumbed to modern urban culture, but because much of Japan's flora is naturalised, not indigenous. It is thought that some 200 to 500 plant species have been introduced to Japan since the Meiji period (1868-1912), mainly from Europe but with the USA becoming a major source in recent years. Japanese gardens laid out in the Edo period and earlier represent a good opportunity to see native Japanese flora even if you aren't seeing it as it might have naturally flourished.

Much of Japan was once heavily forested. The cool-temperate zones of central and northern Honshū and southern Hokkaidō were home to broad-leaved deciduous forests and still are to a certain extent. Nevertheless, largescale deforestation is a feature of contemporary Japan. Pollution and acid rain have also taken their toll. Fortunately, the sheer inaccessibility of much of Japan's mountainous topography has preserved areas of great natural beauty – in particular the alpine regions of central Honshū as well as the lovely natural parks of Hokkaidō.

Fauna

Japan's one-time conjunction with the Asian continent has led to the migration of animals from Korea and China, and the fauna of Japan has much in common with these regions, though there are species that are unique to Japan, such as the Japanese giant salamander and the Japanese macaque. In the Ryūkyū island group, which has been separated from the mainland longer than the rest of Japan, there are examples of fauna (for example the Iriomote cat) that are classified by experts as 'living fossils'.

Japan's largest carnivorous mammals are its bears. Two species are found in Japan – the *higuma* (brown bear) of Hokkaidō and the *tsukinowaguma* (Asiatic brown bear) of Honshū, Shikoku and Kyūshū. The brown bear can grow to a height of two metres and weigh up to 400 kg. The Asiatic brown bear is smaller at an average height of 1.4 metres and a weight of 200 kg.

The Japanese macaque is a medium-sized monkey that is found in Honshū, Shikoku and Kyūshū. They average around 60 cm in length and have a short tail. The last survey of their numbers was taken in 1962, at which time there were some 30,000. They are found in groups of 20 to 150 members.

The Japanese macaque is also known as the snow monkey. Even though their thick coats effectively protect them from the extreme cold, troupes of these monkeys can be seen enjoying the warming effects of a hot spring in Central Honshū.

Endangered Species

A survey carried out in 1986 by the Environment Agency found that 136 species of mammals were in need of protection and that 15 species were already extinct. Endangered species include the Iriomote cat, the Tsushima cat, Blakiston's fish owl and the Japanese river otter.

National Parks

Japan has 28 national parks *(kokuritsu kōen)* and 55 quasi-national parks *(kokutei kōen)*. Ranging from the far south (Iriomote National Park is the southernmost of Japan's national parks) to the northern tip of Hokkaidō (Rishiri-Rebun-Sarobetsu National Park), the parks represent an effort to preserve as much as possible of Japan's natural environment. The parks are administered either directly (in the case of national parks) or indirectly (in the case of quasi-national parks) by the Environment Agency of the Prime Minister's Office.

The highest concentration of national parks and quasi-national parks is in the Tōhoku (Northern Honshū) and Hokkaidō regions, where population density is relatively low. But there are also national parks and quasi-national parks (Chichibu-Tama and Nikkō) within easy striking distance of Tokyo. The largest of Japan's national parks is the Inland Sea National Park (Seto Naikai Kokuritsu-Kōen), which extends some 400 km east to west, reaches a maximum width of 70 km and encompasses over 1000 islands.

GOVERNMENT & POLITICS

Japan's governmental system is more similar to the British parliamentary system than the American presidential one. Just as the British parliament has two houses, so the Japanese Diet has the lower House of Representatives and the upper House of Councillors. The party that controls the majority of seats in the Diet is the party in power and has the right to appoint the prime minister – usually the party's president. The prime minister then appoints his cabinet, which is usually entirely constituted of Diet members.

Like the UK's royal family, the emperor plays a ceremonial figurehead role but, perhaps even more than his British counterpart, he still commands a great deal of respect and deference. The emperor has a curious position in Japan. For centuries under the shogunate his role was purely symbolic. The Meiji Restoration 'restored' the emperor to real power, or at least it was supposed to. In fact it merely brought him out of the closet, dusted him off and gave him a new figurehead position. The close of WWII brought further changes when it was announced that the emperor was no longer divine; despite this, he still has enormous importance in Japan.

In terms of the mechanics of political power, from its formation in 1955, the Liberal Democratic Party (LDP), the conservative party in Japanese politics, has been nearly continuously in power, shaking off scandal after scandal. Elections in 1993 pushed the LDP out into the cold for a brief spell, but today it is back in control again – albeit with diminished power.

Democracy Japanese-style has been prone to scandals, matching all the regular influence-buying and favour-repaying scandals of western democracies and managing to add a few local versions of its own. The Lockheed scandal of the '70s (in which the prime minister took large bribes to ensure that All Nippon Airways (ANA) bought Lockheed Tristar aircraft) was eclipsed by the Recruit Cosmos affair of the late '80s (in which all sorts of LDP politicians from the prime minister down accepted all sorts of bribes). In the early '90s Shin Kanemaru, the doyen of LDP backroom politics, was convicted of evading tax on stashed-away election funds amounting to over US$9 million.

Many Japanese blamed the electoral system for Japan's money politics. Electoral reform has been a top agenda in recent years. Changes include a cap on raising campaign funds (which once reached astronomical amounts), changing of electoral boundaries and the abolition of the old multi-member constituencies (in which vote-buying was rife).

Geographical, Political & Administrative Divisions

Japan is divided up into nine political regions (see map) and further subdivided into 47 smaller divisions. Prefectures or *ken* make up 43 of these divisions, and they are written as 'Okayama-ken' or 'Chiba-ken'. The remaining four are Hokkaidō, which is a *dō* (district); Tokyo-to, which is a *to* (metropolis); and Osaka-fu and Kyoto-fu, which are *fu* (urban prefectures). Each of the three city areas incorporates the named city but is otherwise similar in land area to a ken.

There are other traditional names for regions of the country. Thus, Chūgoku or Western Honshū, consists of the San-in or north coast region and the San-yō or south coast region. Other traditional names you may come across in tourist literature or other sources include Hokuriku (Fukui, Ishikawa and Toyama prefectures), Sanriku (Aomori, Iwate and Miyagi), Shin-etsu (Nagano and Niigata) and Tokai (Aichi, Gifu, Mie and Shizuoka). In addition, the Tokyo area is often referred to as Kantō, while the area around Osaka is known as Kansai or Kinki.

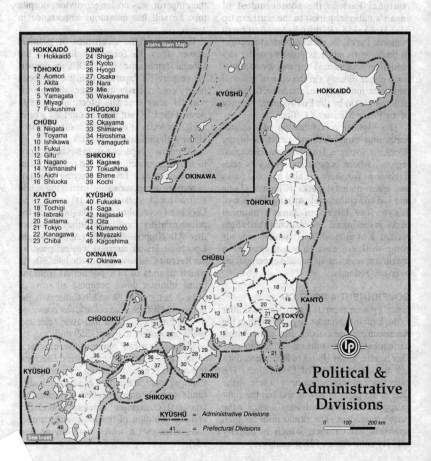

HOKKAIDŌ
1 Hokkaidō

TŌHOKU
2 Aomori
3 Akita
4 Iwate
5 Yamagata
6 Miyagi
7 Fukushima

CHŪBU
8 Niigata
9 Toyama
10 Ishikawa
11 Fukui
12 Gifu
13 Nagano
14 Yamanashi
15 Aichi
16 Shiuoka

KANTŌ
17 Gumma
18 Tochigi
19 Iabraki
20 Saitama
21 Tokyo
22 Kanagawa
23 Chiba

KINKI
24 Shiga
25 Kyoto
26 Hyogo
27 Osaka
28 Nara
29 Mie
30 Wakayama

CHŪGOKU
31 Tottori
32 Okayama
33 Shimane
34 Hiroshima
35 Yamaguchi

SHIKOKU
36 Kagawa
37 Tokushima
38 Ehime
39 Kochi

KYŪSHŪ
40 Fukuoka
41 Saga
42 Nagasaki
43 Oita
44 Kumamoto
45 Miyazaki
46 Kagoshima

OKINAWA
47 Okinawa

Joins Main Map

KYŪSHŪ
46
OKINAWA
47

HOKKAIDŌ
1

TŌHOKU
CHŪBU
KANTŌ
TOKYO
CHŪGOKU
KINKI
SHIKOKU
KYŪSHŪ

Political & Administrative Divisions

KYŪSHŪ = *Administrative Divisions*
41 = *Prefectural Divisions*

0   100   200 km

See Inset

ECONOMY

The Japanese economic phenomenon is a rags to riches story that has left commentators around the world searching for its whys and wherefores. Indeed, Japan's postwar economic success has taken so many people by surprise that there has been a tendency to overemphasise the scale of Japan's achievements. It's worth bearing in mind that while Japanese exports are extremely visible, they still account for less than 10% of the nation's GNP. Japanese industrial and real-estate investment in the USA, a controversial issue, is still on a far smaller scale than similar investment by countries such as Britain and Canada.

Still, in the short space of just 40 or so years, Japan has gone from a defeated nation to the world's largest creditor nation. The reason for this success is complex, but to a large part it can be credited to the industriousness of the Japanese, to export orientation of the economy, controls on imports and the shifting fortunes of the yen.

At the end of WWII, the Japanese economy was devastated. The MacArthur occupation government restored the competitiveness of Japanese products by drastically devaluing the yen. From a prewar yen-dollar exchange rate of ¥4 to US$1, the yen plummeted to ¥360 to US$1. Before long, Japanese products were filling the 'cheap and nasty' bins of supermarkets and stores around the world.

It might have stayed that way except that Japanese industry reinvested profits into research and development, so that by the mid-70s Japan was filing more patents than the USA. The Japanese began to make products that were not just cheap but good too. Even a potentially disastrous event such as the unstable oil prices of the 1970s, which vastly increased the costs of Japan's imported energy needs, conspired to cooperate with Japanese export ambitions. It pushed the yen down further still, increasing the competitiveness of Japanese goods, and made Japanese fuel-efficient cars suddenly seem a lot more attractive than they had been before.

Faced with an increasingly successful export economy, the US Reagan government introduced the Yen-Dollar Agreement in 1984. The yen was internationalised, and in theory this was to force up the value of the yen and make Japanese products more expensive. What wasn't taken into account was Japan's immense savings reserves and the willingness of Japanese industry to tighten belts and endure hardship. Rise the yen did, but as the yen doubled in value so did Japanese reserves of savings. Japanese industry countered with investments that offset the losses in exports. When the yen shouldered its way to an all-time postwar high of ¥130 to US$1, exports increased in price by just 20%, and the Japanese economy became stronger than ever.

One of the traditional reasons for Japan's much vaunted trade surpluses with its trading partners has been not merely the volume of its exports but also the low level of its imports. For a long time Japan's imports could be accounted for mostly by its energy requirements, of which it imports more than 80%. This situation – like many others in Japan – is changing. A combination of the high yen and consumer dissatisfaction with exorbitant retail prices has led to what some are calling a 'discount revolution'. Discount operations are bypassing Japan's legendary multilayered distribution network and passing on the benefits to consumers. Even that final bastion of Japanese protectionism – rice – has come under attack. Japanese can now dine on Californian rice, which is said to be indistinguishable from the Japanese variety and which is four times cheaper in the US than Japanese rice is at home.

Bubble Economy

If you read anything about the Japanese economy, you will come across terms like discount revolution, which is fairly self-explanatory, and bubble economy, which isn't. What is this bubble economy? In essence it refers to the credit boom of the late 1980s, when Japanese companies enjoyed the combined fruits of escalating property values, a bullish stock market and low-interest borrowings.

In January 1990 the Tokyo stock market began to slide. By October of the same year it had lost 48% of its value. The bubble had sprung a leak. In 1991, Japanese banks, hit by the fall in stock market values, could no longer afford to be so free with their money: they raised interest rates. Many speculative ventures initiated with cheap capital had to be cut back. Households hit by the rise in interest rates were forced to rein in their spending.

Japan is still recovering. The economic downturn has changed the Japanese workplace and the political system; it has challenged Japan's government bureaucracies and has shaken up the Japanese financial system. It is still unknown how much money in bad loans the Japanese banks will have to write off – so far it has been around ¥10,000 billion. Critics say this is just the beginning, and that even more profound changes will be required in the transition to a mature economy.

POPULATION & PEOPLE

Japan has a population of around 126 million people (the eighth largest in the world) and, with 75% of it concentrated in urban centres, population density is extremely high. Areas such as the Tokyo-Yokohama-Kawasaki

conurbation are so densely populated that they have almost ceased to be separate cities, running into each other and forming a huge urban sprawl which, if considered as a whole, would constitute the world's largest city.

While this high urban population density is tough on the Japanese, it has the advantage of leaving other parts of the country reasonably sparsely populated. Travellers visiting Japan are still able to enjoy large national parks, mountainous regions and, in places like Hokkaidō, near wilderness.

The other notable feature of Japan's population is its ethnic and cultural homogeneity. This is particularly striking for visitors from the USA, Australia and other nations whose countries are host to populations of considerable ethnic and cultural diversity. The Japanese have ensured that only a small number of foreigners settle in their country. Inhabitants of non-Japanese origin crept over the 1% mark for the first time in 1993. The vast majority of these are Koreans, but the newcomers who are pushing up the numbers of foreigners are largely foreign workers seeking a share in the economic miracle.

Imported Cars

Who says the Japanese don't import cars? It may be 'coals to Newcastle' and, compared to the local industry, the proportion of imported vehicles is indeed small, yet 5% of the Japanese market is still a lot of cars. BMW appears to be the most common imported nameplate. Spend long enough on Japanese expressways and you'll come away with the impression that every BMW comes complete with an 'ignore all speed limits' permit so drivers can imagine they're zooming down the autobahn to Munich. It's popularly rumoured that BMW make more money in Japan than they do in the USA.

Other German makes – Mercedes, Porsche – get a good show and you'll also see Saabs, plenty of Volvos, a few Fiats, quite a few hot Peugeot 205 GTis and a surprising number of Jaguars, Bentleys and Rolls-Royces. Believe it or not, the other major-selling European car is the good old British Mini. Minis have a huge cult following in Japan, which has developed to such an extent that more Minis are now sold in Japan than in the UK (sales almost match the combined sales in Japan of all US cars!). In a country where cars seem to be redesigned every six months, many of the Minis are sold as the 'Mini Thirty', with a notation on the side announcing that the design has barely altered since 1959.

All manner of oddities also find a market in Japan, although, no doubt, they're only brought out for a drive on the odd sunny Sunday. I saw a Ferrari Testa Rossa in Kyoto, and in Yamaguchi a flawless Lotus 7, complete with mini aero-screens and two samurai pilots in WWI leather flying helmets and aviator goggles.

Tony Wheeler

For outsiders, Koreans are an invisible minority. Indeed, even the Japanese themselves have no way of knowing that someone is of Korean descent if he or she adopts a Japanese name. Nevertheless, Japanese-born Koreans, who in some cases speak no language other than Japanese, were only very recently released from the obligation to carry thumb-printed ID cards at all times, and still face discrimination in the work place and other aspects of their daily lives.

Other ethnic groupings include the Chinese and a wide cross section of foreigners hitching a ride on the Japanese economic juggernaut. Groups such as the Ainu have been reduced to very small numbers and are today found almost only in reservations on Hokkaidō.

Burakumin

The burakumin are a mysterious minority. They are racially the same as other Japanese, and yet history has made them an outcast class. Traditionally, the burakumin belonged to communities whose work brought them into contact with the contamination of death – taboo in both Shinto and Buddhism.

There are thought to be around three million hereditary burakumin nowadays. While the conditions of modern Japan have long since rendered the burakumin distinction obsolete, it continues to exercise influence in such important aspects of Japanese social life as work and marriage. It is common knowledge, though rarely alluded to, that information about any given individual's possible burakumin origin is available to anyone (generally employers and prospective fathers-in-law) who is prepared to make certain discreet investigations. Many Japanese dislike discussing this topic with foreigners, and unless you are on very familiar terms or in enlightened company it is probably bad taste to bring it up.

Ainu

The indigenous population of Hokkaidō originally included a variety of ethnic groups, but they are now generally referred to collectively as Ainu. In Ainu language, the word 'Ainu' means man (male or human being). There is a possible link between the Ainu and the people known in ancient records as 'hairy people' who once lived in Tōhoku. Although there is a heavier growth of body hair and a tendency towards lighter skin colouring, the physical differences between Ainu and Japanese are slight; intermarriage has further reduced these differences.

The Ainu population is thought to be around 25,000; almost half of this number live in the Hidaka district, south-east of Sapporo. Intermarriage with Japanese has become so common, it's calculated that there are now probably less than 200 pure-blooded Ainu left.

Culturally, the Ainu have suffered a fate similar to the American Indians. The Ainu have made some efforts recently to rekindle pride in their culture, but the absence of a written language means that when the old folks die they also take with them a rich tradition of *yukar* or 'epic poems', folktales and songs. The Japanese still exercise racial discrimination against the Ainu (most of

An Ainu elder, of the indigenous people of Hokkaidō.

whom speak Japanese). The Ainu, however, lack the land or the finance to compete with the Japanese who have settled on Hokkaidō.

Japanese tourists seem comfortable at seeing the Ainu culture debased by pseudo 'Ainu villages' with Disneyland surroundings and souvenir shops selling tacky carvings. The old Ainu festivals and shamanic rites are 'acted' by listless, elderly Ainu. These tourist circuses can be intensely depressing – they are often combined with caged bears in zoos, a sight equally depressing, symbolic of the freedom lost by the Ainu.

If you want to see how the Ainu wish to portray themselves, make a point of visiting the Ainu Museum (not the souvenir shop ghetto) in Shiraoi, which has excellent displays and sells a catalogue sensitively compiled by the Shiraoi Institute for the Preservation of Ainu Culture, Wakakusa 2-3-4, Shiraoi, Hokkaidō 059-09.

Ageing Japan

Foreign observers looking for signs of change in the Japanese economic powerhouse frequently focus their attention on the changing age make-up of the population. WWII left Japan with a very young population and, at that time, the average life span was also relatively short compared to advanced western nations. A low birth rate and an average life span which is now the longest in the world is turning that age make-up right around. From being a nation of youngsters Japan is rapidly becoming a nation of oldsters. Other advanced nations are facing the same problem as the postwar baby boomers enter middle age, but nowhere is the change so dramatic as in Japan. Inevitably, such demographic change will have a major influence on the economy in coming decades.

EDUCATION

Among the many things that surprise visitors to Japan is the leniency with which very young children are treated. Volumes have been written on this subject; the general consensus is that the Japanese see the early years of childhood as a blissful Eden, a period of gloriously spoiled dependency that prefaces the harsh socialisation of the Japanese education system.

At an age as young as three or four the party is over: children then enter the nurseries that start preparing them for one of the most gruelling education systems in the world. Competition is fierce from the beginning, since getting into the right school can mean an important head start when it comes to the university exams. These exams, of legendary difficulty, are so demanding that any student preparing for them and getting more than four hours sleep a night, is said to have no hope of passing.

To help coach students through the exams, evening schools have sprung up and are often more successful in teaching the school curriculum than the schools themselves. Students who fail to gain entry to the university of their choice frequently spend one or two years repeating the final year of school and sitting the exams again. These students, known as *rōnin*, or 'masterless samurai', are in a kind of limbo between the school education system and the higher education system, the key to employment in Japan.

The intense pressure of this system derives in no small part from the fact that 12 years of education culminates in just two examinations that effectively determine the future of the examinee. One exam is sat by all Japanese final-year high school students on the same day; the other exam is specific to the university the student wishes to attend.

Once exams have been completed and a student gains a university place, it is time to let loose a little. University or college is considered a transitional stage between the world of education and employment, a stage in which one spends more time in drinking bouts with other students than in the halls of higher learning. In a sense the university years, for those who make it, are similar to the early years of childhood. All kinds of antics are looked upon indulgently as the excesses of youth. Some have seen a pattern in this – an alternation between extreme pressure and almost complete relaxation – which is mirrored in many aspects of Japanese social life.

As in other parts of the world, the Japanese education system processes male and female students differently. The top universities are dominated by male students, with many female students opting for two-year college courses, often in topics seen as useful training for family life, such as child psychology.

SOCIETY & CONDUCT

The Japanese are so convinced that they are different from everyone else that it's easy to become infected and start agreeing with them. A complex mythology of uniqueness has accrued around the Japanese, and one of the challenges of discovering Japan for yourself is putting the myths straight.

The Group

One of the most cherished ideas about the Japanese is that the group is more important than the individual. The image of loyal company workers bellowing out the company anthem and attending collective exercise sessions is synonymous with Japan Inc – itself a corporate metaphor.

It's easy to fall into the spirit of such images and start seeing Japan's business-suited crowds as members of a collectivised society that rigorously suppresses individual tendencies. If this happens, it's useful to remember that the Japanese are no less individual than their western counterparts – they experience the same frustrations and joys, and complain about their work conditions, the way their boss treats them and so on, just as we do. The difference is, that while these individual concerns have a place, they are less likely to be seen as defining.

The tension between group and individual interest has been a rich source of inspiration for Japanese art. Traditional values see conflict between *honne*, the individual's personal views, and *tatemae*, the views that are demanded by the individual's position in the group. The same difference is expressed in the terms *ninjō* – human feelings – and *giri* – social obligations. Salaried workers who spend long hours at the office away from the families they love are giving priority to giri over ninjō.

At this point the argument tends to disintegrate into psychobabble. But one thing is certain, and that is that the Japanese are great joiners: clubs and associations are hugely popular, and the responsibilities that come with a job or a position are taken very seriously indeed.

Men & Women

The clichéd view of Japanese women as passive homebodies holds little water these days. As with everything else in contemporary Japan, women's roles are in flux. Women are marrying later, working longer and assuming more prominent roles in public life.

Traditional Japanese society circumscribed the woman's role to the home, where as housekeeper she wielded considerable power, collecting the husband's pay and allocating it to various domestic needs. Even in the early Meiji period, however, the ideal was rarely matched by reality: labour shortfalls often resulted in women taking on factory work even though legally they were relegated to the same category as the 'deformed and mentally incompetent'.

The contemporary situation, as might be expected, is complex. There are of course those who stick to established roles. They tend to opt for shorter college courses, often at women's colleges, and see education as an asset in the marriage market; once married they leave bread-earning to their husbands. But in the '90s such women are probably in the minority: a survey in 1990 found that over 70% of women in their 40s worked.

The stereotypes are still alive and kicking, however. Switch on a Japanese TV and you will soon see the traditional male-female dynamic. The male host invariably has a female shadow whose job it is to agree with everything he says, make astonished gasps at his erudition and to giggle politely behind a raised hand at his off-the-cuff witty remarks. These *sō desu* girls, as they're known, are a common feature of countless aspects of Japanese daily life. It's *de rigueur* for all companies to employ a bevy of nubile OLs, or 'office ladies', whose tasks include chiming a chorus of falsetto 'welcomes' to visitors, making cups of tea and generally adding a personal touch to an otherwise stolid male atmosphere.

Perhaps most disturbing for western women visiting Japan is the way in which women feature in so much of the male-oriented mass culture. It's not so much a problem of women being depicted as sex objects, which most western women would at least be accustomed to in their own countries, but the fact that in comic strips, magazines and movies, women are often shown as brutalised, passive victims in bizarre, sado-masochistic rites. Some disturbing conclusions could be drawn from much of the output of the Japanese media – at the very least it could be said that popular

Japanese male sexuality has a very sadistic edge to it.

While these fantasies are disturbing, it is possible to take refuge in the thought that they *are* fantasies, and women are in fact a great deal safer in Japan than they are in other parts of the world. Harassment, when it does occur, is usually furtive, occurring in crowded areas such as trains; however, with direct confrontation, almost all Japanese men will be shamed into withdrawing the groping hand.

The Japanese & Gaijin

As a foreign visitor to Japan, you are a *gaijin*, literally, an 'outside person'. Some foreigners insist (correctly in fact) that the term *gaikokujin* (literally, 'outside country

Urban Anthropology

Visitors to Japan expecting to find a nation of suit-wearing conformists are often shocked at the sheer variety of types they discover. Indeed, in places like Tokyo's Shibuya or Osaka's Shinsaibashi, ordinary street traffic on a Friday night approaches a kind of gaudy street theatre. People-watching in such places is half the fun of being there. The following guide delineates some of the more common types.

Salarymen – just what you'd expect: businessmen, always clad in suits, often in matching groups.

Office Ladies – also known as OL's, these women may be secretaries but may equally be women who do the same work as their male bosses for half the pay. OL's usually travel in small groups wearing matching uniforms of skirts, white blouses and vests.

Ojōsans – young women, usually college students or graduates, middle class and headed for marriage to young salarymen. Ojōsans dress conservatively, with the exception of the occasional mini-skirt.

Yanquis – pronounced 'yankees', they prefer brown or blond hair, sport flashy clothes and have a portable phone permanently glued to their ear. Yanquis often work in the construction industry, where their taste for loud clothes is expressed in brightly coloured *nikka-bokka* pants (from the English word Knickerbocker).

Chimpiras – often yanquis who've taken rebellion a step further and hope to attract the attention of yakuza gangsters and be asked to join the gang – junior yakuza.

Bosozoku – motorcycle gangs – more dyed hair and flashy clothes. A typical night is spent loudly revving their motorcycle engines and speeding off tailed by the police, who never catch them. Like chimpira, some of the wilder bosozoku go on to become yakuza.

Yakuza – the real thing. They used to stand out, with tight 'punch-perms' and loud suits, but modern yakuza are hardly noticeable, except perhaps for their swagger and black Mercedes with tinted windows.

Ike-ike Onna – young women who fancy day-glo mini-skirts, dyed brown hair, dark suntans and expensive handbags. Sometimes referred to as *o-mizu*, as in 'mizu-shōbai', the so-called water trade (reflecting the fact that many ike-ike onna work in hostess bars, massage parlours and the like).

Ko Garu – *ko*, from the Japanese word for high school, *kōko*, and *garu* from the English word 'girl': a high school girl who dresses like an ike-ike onna, often seen talking on a portable phone.

Chanelah – a young woman who leans strongly toward Chanel goods, particularly expensive handbags with gold straps – perhaps the world's most dedicated shoppers. ∎

person') is more polite than the contraction gaijin, but the latter is so widely used that you will be knocking your head against a brick wall trying to change it.

Away from the big cities it's not unusual to hear whispered exclamations of *gaijin da* ('it's a foreigner!'); even in suburban Tokyo, where gaijin are a dime a dozen, many school children are still unable to resist erupting into giggles at the sight of a foreign face.

Long-term visitors to Japan are prone to an ongoing love-hate relationship, which frequently shifts sides. After being initially overwhelmed by Japanese courtesy, many foreigners, who feel that they have been in Japan long enough to deserve a more intimate footing with the culture, come to the conclusion that Japanese politeness and helpfulness mask a morbid ethnocentricity. Everybody has to deal with this in their own way, but fortunately for the short-term visitor, the polite and friendly nature of most contacts with the Japanese is likely to be the main impression.

The best advice to the Japan visitor is to enjoy Japanese courtesy and leave its more sinister implications for long-term residents to fret over. Excessive politeness does have a distancing effect, but when you're lost in a crowded city the invariable polite offer of assistance is a godsend. And, whatever the long-timers say, most visitors to Japan come away with miracle stories of Japanese courtesy: the hitchhikers who are treated to lunch and taken kilometres off their host's original route to be deposited at their destination; the traveller who arrives too late at the bank to change money and, standing miserably outside the closed doors, is offered a loan by a passer-by.

Etiquette

One of the most enduring western notions about Japan is that of Japanese courtesy and rigid social etiquette. With a little sensitivity, however, there is little chance of mortally offending anyone.

To be sure, many things are different: the Japanese bow and indulge in a ritualised exchange of *meishi* (business cards) when

Shoes are not worn inside a Japanese home.

they meet; they exchange their shoes for uncomfortable plastic slippers before entering the home; and social occasions involve sitting on the floor in positions that will put the legs of an ill-bred foreigner to sleep within five minutes. But, overall, most of the complex aspects of Japanese social interaction are functions of the language and only pose problems for the advanced student who's trying to get as close to the culture as possible.

Sitting When socialising with the Japanese or visiting them in their homes, sitting on the floor for extended periods of time can be painful for many foreigners. Sit with your legs beneath you for as long as possible and then, if you *must* stretch your legs out, do so discreetly without pointing them in anyone's direction. Pointing your feet (the lowest part of the body, literally) at people, even inadvertently, is bad form throughout Asia.

Bowing When you meet Japanese, it's polite to bow slightly from the waist and incline your head. Actually, the rule is that the deepness of a Japanese bow depends on the status (relative to oneself) of the person to whom one is bowing. When A has higher status than B, it is important that B's bow is deeper than A's. As the bows take place simultaneously, it is often incumbent on B to give a quick, surreptitious glance in the direction of A's exalted presence to determine that his or her bow is indeed lower than A's. Fortunately, no-one expects foreigners to carry on like this, and nowadays, many Japanese have taken to shaking hands, though the bow is still the most important mark of respect.

Business Cards If you are going to be working in Japan, get some business cards made up: without them, you'll be a nobody. All introductions and meetings in Japan involve an exchange of business cards – handing out yours to the right people can make things happen; not having a card looks bad. Cards should be handed over, and accepted, with some ceremony, studied carefully and referred to often. It's polite to accept a card with two hands. Do not simply stuff a proffered card into your pocket. Also, never write anything on a card you are given.

Gift Giving The exchange of gifts, the return of one kindness with another, is an important part of Japanese social life. If you visit somebody at their home, you should bring them a gift. It needn't be anything big – chocolates or flowers, much the same things that are used as gifts in the west, will do. Ideally, bring something from your own country. Gifts used for cementing friendships and for paying off small obligations are usually small and unostentatious. Where money is given it is presented in an envelope.

As a foreigner, it's quite likely that people will sometimes want to give you gifts 'for your travels'. You may not be able to reciprocate in these situations. The polite thing to do is to refuse a couple of times when the gift is offered. The other party will probably keep pushing as long as you keep refusing. A couple of refusals are enough not to seem too grasping before making off with your spoils.

Flattery What passes for flattery in the west is often perceived as quite natural in Japan. The Japanese rarely pass up the opportunity to praise each other in company. The foreigner who has made an effort to learn a few sentences of Japanese or to get by with chopsticks is likely to receive regular dollops of praise. The correct response to praise is to decline it with something like 'Not at all' *(sono koto dewa arimasen)*. Try to reciprocate if you can.

Directness Japanese do not make a virtue out of being direct. Indeed, directness is seen as vulgar. The Japanese prefer to feel their

Omiyage

Gifts are the grease that keeps the wheels of Japanese society turning. A gift can serve as a token of appreciation, a sign of respect, a guarantee of continued favour or even a bribe (see Japanese politics).

Perhaps the most troublesome and time-consuming gift of all is the omiyage – a souvenir given to friends, family and co-workers upon return from travel. In most Japanese companies, leaving for a vacation naturally entails a sense of shame, of letting down the team. To make up for this betrayal, an armful of omiyage is required. Of course, shopping for all these gifts can eat up an entire vacation (particularly a Japanese vacation, which usually lasts only a few days anyway).

Ever resourceful, the Japanese have come up with a unique solution to this problem – the train station regional speciality store. These stores are located in the passageways around big-city train stations. In the space of a few hundred metres you can pick up crab from Hokkaido, dolls from Kyushu and pickled vegetables from Shikoku. Even if everybody knows that their souvenir was picked up at the local train station, the obligation is fulfilled and everybody is happy.

Recently, these stores have sprung up in airports, selling goods from Japan's favourite international destinations: Hawaii, Disneyworld and Paris.

People have also thought of new ways to make use of goods purchased at these stores. Apparently, gifts purchased at train station speciality stores are commonly used as alibis – after a weekend spent at the local love hotel with a secretary, a gift purchased at a regional speciality store is proof that a wayward boss was actually on a business trip. ■

CHRIS TAYLOR

CHRIS TAYLOR

CHRIS TAYLOR

CHRIS TAYLOR

RICHARD I'ANSON

MARTIN MOOS

A: Geisha
B: Japanese hippy
C: Sanja Festival, Sensō-ji Temple
D: School children
E: Gion Matsuri Festival
F: Shinto priest

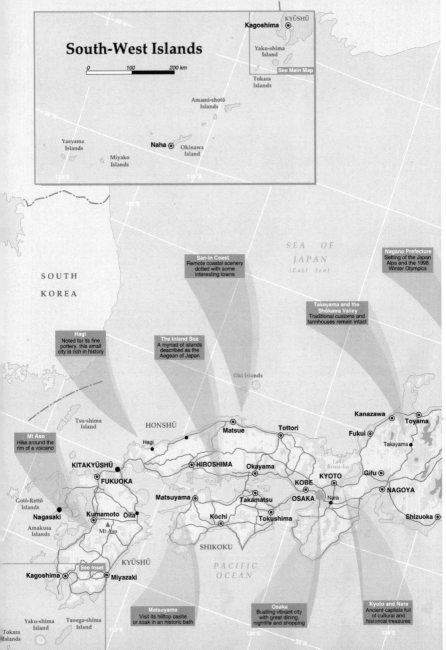

South-West Islands

KYŪSHŪ

Kagoshima

Yaku-shima Island

Tokara Islands

Amami-shotō Islands

Yaeyama Islands

Miyako Islands

Naha · Okinawa Island

See Main Map

0   100   200 km

NORTH KOREA

RUSSIA

SOUTH KOREA

San-in Coast
Remote coastal scenery dotted with some interesting towns

SEA OF JAPAN
(East Sea)

Nagano Prefecture
Setting of the Japan Alps and the 1998 Winter Olympics

Takayama and the Shōkawa Valley
Traditional customs and farmhouses remain intact

Hagi
Noted for its fine pottery, this small city is rich in history

The Inland Sea
A myriad of islands described as the Aegean of Japan

Oki Islands

Tsu-shima Island

Mt Aso
Hike around the rim of a volcano

HONSHŪ

Hagi

Matsue

Tottori

Kanazawa

Toyama

Fukui

KITAKYŪSHŪ

HIROSHIMA

Okayama

KYOTO

Gifu

Takayama

FUKUOKA

Lake Biwa-ko

NAGOYA

Gotō-Rettō Islands

Matsuyama

Takamatsu

KOBE

Nagasaki

Kumamoto Ōita

OSAKA

Nara

Shizuoka

Amakusa Islands

Mt Aso

Kōchi

Tokushima

SHIKOKU

Matsuyama
Visit its hilltop castle or soak in an historic bath

Osaka
Bustling vibrant city with great dining, nightlife and shopping

Kyoto and Nara
Ancient capitals full of cultural and historical treasures

KYŪSHŪ

See Inset

PACIFIC OCEAN

Kagoshima   Miyazaki

Yaku-shima Island

Tanega-shima Island

Tokara Islands

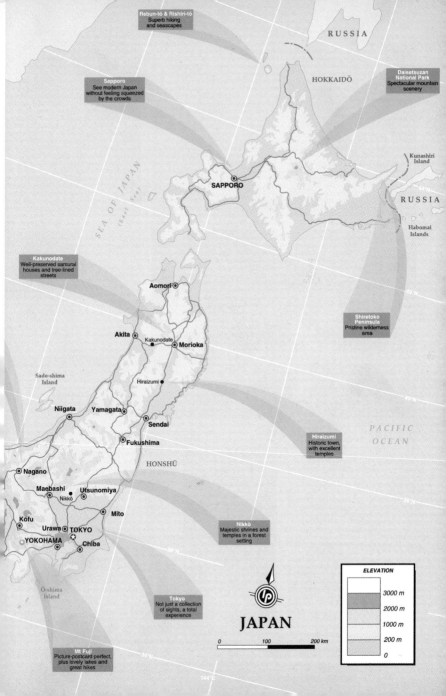

RUSSIA

HOKKAIDŌ

Rebun-tō & Rishiri-tō
Superb hiking
and seascapes

Daisetsuzan
National Park
Spectacular mountain
scenery

Sapporo
See modern Japan
without feeling squeezed
by the crowds

SAPPORO

Kunashiri
Island

RUSSIA

Habomai
Islands

SEA OF JAPAN
(EAST SEA)

Kakunodate
Well-preserved samurai
houses and tree-lined
streets

Aomori

Shiretoko
Peninsula
Pristine wilderness
area

Akita

Kakunodate

Morioka

Hiraizumi

Sado-shima
Island

Niigata

Yamagata

Sendai

PACIFIC
OCEAN

Fukushima

Hiraizumi
Historic town,
with excellent
temples

Nagano

HONSHŪ

Maebashi

Utsunomiya

Nikko

Kōfu

Mito

Urawa

TOKYO

YOKOHAMA

Chiba

Nikkō
Majestic shrines and
temples in a forest
setting

Ō-shima
Island

Tokyo
Not just a collection
of sights, a total
experience

JAPAN

0   100   200 km

Mt Fuji
Picture-postcard perfect,
plus lovely lakes and
great hikes

ELEVATION

3000 m

2000 m

1000 m

200 m

0

144°E

CHRIS TAYLOR

CHRIS TAYLOR

CHRIS TAYLOR

CHRIS TAYLOR

CHRIS TAYLOR

CHRIS TAYLOR

CHRIS TAYLOR

A	B	C
	D	E
F	G	

A: Torii
B: Raked gravel garden, Kyoto
C: Kasa (umbrella)
D: Temple calling cards

E: Cherry blossom
F: Shin-kyō Bridge, Nikkō
G: Temple doors

way through a situation when dealing with others. There is an expression for this that translates as 'stomach talk' – where both sides tentatively edge around an issue, feeling out the other's point of view until it is clear which direction negotiations can go. This can often result in what for many westerners is a seemingly interminable toing and froing that only ever seems to yield ambiguous results. But don't be deceived, the Japanese can usually read the situation just as clearly as if both sides were clearly stating their interests.

Try to avoid direct statements that may be seen as confrontational. If someone ventures an opinion, however stupid it may seem, try not to crush it with a 'No, I disagree completely,' or something similar.

Calls of Nature It's not unusual to find men urinating in crowded streets, and public toilets are occasionally unsegregated. On the other hand, the public use of handkerchiefs for blowing your nose is definitely frowned upon. A Japanese student related with an air of genuine disgust how, on a train, he had seen a beautiful western girl take a hankie from her handbag and blow her nose into it. 'How could such a beautiful girl have such bad manners?' he wondered. The polite thing to do if you have a cold in public is to keep sniffing (an admirable sign of self-restraint in Japanese eyes) until you can get to some private place to do your business.

Avoiding Offence
Japanese are tolerant of foreigner's customs for the most part; there's little chance of committing any grave faux pas. But there are certain situations where it is important to follow Japanese example. Shoes should be removed, for example, when entering a Japanese home or entering a tatami room of any kind – Japanese will not make allowances for foreign customs in this case.

Bathing in Japan also conforms to fairly strict rules and you should follow them. Whether it's a Japanese-style bath or an onsen, remember that the actual washing

takes place before entering the water. Showers or faucets are provided for this purpose. Baths and onsen are for soaking in after you have washed.

As in other parts of Asia, the respectful way to indicate for someone to approach you is by waving your fingers with the palm downwards. As a westerner you can offer your hand when you meet someone for the first time, though if you want to add a Japanese touch to the proceedings you can make a slight bow, which is the traditional Japanese greeting.

Japanese don't eat food in the street unless there are seats provided to do so. Ice creams are an exception to this rule. It's up to you whether you want to abide by this custom: no-one's going to be particularly upset if they see you wandering down the street munching on a Big Mac.

Meeting the Japanese
Your opportunities to meet the Japanese will depend a great deal on the way you travel. Obviously, if you're on a whirlwind tour of Japan, stopping in a different destination every night, you're going to have fewer opportunities to meet locals than the traveller who spends some months working in Tokyo or Osaka and then a month or so seeing the country. But even for those on a tight schedule, meeting the Japanese is not impossible due to the thoughtful provision of such programmes as the home visit system (described later in this section).

The following pointers apply to formal situations. If you take to going to bars in Japan, you're likely to meet young Japanese people for whom little of the traditional etiquette applies. In informal settings (especially after a few drinks) young Japanese can be surprisingly forward in making contact. Generally all it takes is a smile and a nod to be brought into conversation.

Shyness There are quite a lot of shy Japanese out there. When it comes to meeting foreigners many are embarrassed that their English is not up to scratch. The possibility of responding inappropriately makes some

Japanese nervous, particularly in situations they've not been trained to deal with, such as a foreigner speaking to them in English or in halting Japanese. If you need to make casual contact with a Japanese, say, to ask directions, it is always best to appear calm and relaxed and smile as you talk.

Nowadays, particularly in the big cities, more and more Japanese are becoming accustomed to dealing with foreigners. The school system is using foreign teachers as assistants for teaching English and many students attend private English-language schools where they regularly have contact with gaijin. The result is that levels of foreign-language expertise and confidence in dealing with ambassadors from the outside world are on the rise in Japan.

Home Visit System The home visit system is publicised in JNTO pamphlets and gives visitors to some of Japan's larger cities the opportunity to visit a Japanese family in their home.

Visits take place in the evening and, while dinner is usually not served, the hosts will often provide tea and sweets. It is polite to bring a small gift with you when you visit to show your appreciation of your hosts' thoughtfulness and hospitality.

Home visits can be organised in the following cities:

Tokyo	☎ 03-3502-1461
Yokohama	☎ 045-641-4759
Kyoto	☎ 075-752-3511
Osaka	☎ 06-345-2189
Kōbe	☎ 078-303-1010
Nagoya	☎ 052-581-0100
Sapporo	☎ 011-211-3341
Okayama	☎ 086-222-0457
Hiroshima	☎ 082-247-9715
Fukuoka	☎ 092-733-2220
Nagasaki	☎ 0958-22-9690
Kumamoto	☎ 096-328-2111
Kagoshima	☎ 0992-24-1111

Conversation Lounges The conversation lounge is a uniquely Japanese institution that gives members an opportunity to meet foreigners in an informal setting. Generally,

Japanese pay a fee to participate for an evening, while foreigners are admitted free. The lounge is usually a coffee-shop setup, though occasionally, as in Mickey House in Tokyo, alcohol is served. Lounges are almost always an excellent place to meet and talk with Japanese people who have an interest in the world outside their own country. For more information about conversation lounges, check the English-language magazines and the Tokyo chapter of this book.

RELIGION

In many respects, the term 'religion' can be misleading for westerners when it is applied to either Japan or China. In the west and in Islam, religion is connected with the idea of an exclusive faith. Religions in Japan, for the most part, are not exclusive of each other.

Shinto (the native 'religion' of Japan), Buddhism (a much travelled foreign import originating in India), Confucianism (a Chinese import that is less a religion than a code of ethics), and even Christianity all play a role in contemporary Japanese social life, and are defining in some way of the Japanese world view. If you are sceptical of the inclusion of Christianity, you need only attend a Japanese wedding to find certain Christian elements mingling happily with more traditional practices.

Shinto and Buddhism, the major religions in Japan, have coexisted for many centuries in relative harmony. A notable break in this amicable relationship occurred during the Meiji period, when nationalist fervour introduced 'State Shinto' as the state religion. Severe restraints were placed on Buddhism, which came under attack from nationalist zealots. The balance was restored with the abolition of State Shinto after the Allied occupation in 1945.

Shinto

Shinto is an indigenous religion that acquired its name, 'the way of the gods', to distinguish it from Buddhism, a later import. It seems to have grown out of an awe for manifestations of nature that included the sun, water, rock formations, trees and even sounds. All such manifestations were felt to have their god *(kami)*, a belief that led to a complex pantheon of gods and a rich mythology. In particularly sacred spots, shrines were erected. Important to Shinto is the concept of purification before entering such sacred domains.

Shinto is a religion without a founder and without a canon; indeed it is not a religion in the sense that you could convert to it. In a sense Shinto is an expression of the Japaneseness of the Japanese. It encompasses myths of the origin of Japan and the Japanese people, beliefs and practices in local communities and the highly structured rituals associated with the imperial family. Until 1945, Shinto belief dictated that the emperor was a kami, or divine being.

Japanese Myths The chief sources for Japanese myth are the *Kojiki* (Records of Ancient Matters; 712) and the *Nihon Shoki* (Chronicle of Japan; 720). The myths contained in these works have much in common with those of neighbouring countries and the South-East Asian and Mongolian area.

The creation of Japan is ascribed to Izanagi-no-Mikoto and Izanami-no-Mikoto. Standing on the Floating Bridge of Heaven, they dipped the Heavenly Jewelled Spear into the ocean. Brine dripped from the spear and created the island of Onogoro-jima, where the two were married. Izanami gave birth to the islands of Japan and to its deities.

Izanami gave birth to 35 gods, but in giving birth to the fire deity she was burned and died. Izanagi ventured into the Land of the Dead (Yomi-no-Kuni). He found Izanami horribly transfigured by death, and in her shame she joined the Eighty Ugly Females to pursue him. He escaped only by blocking the entry to Yomi with a huge boulder, thus separating the lands of the living and the dead. On his return to the Land of the Living, Izanami purified himself in a stream. This act created more deities, the three most important being Amaterasu Ōmikami (the sun goddess, from whom the

imperial family later claimed descent), Tsukuyomi-no-Mikoto (the moon god) and Susano-ō-no-Mikoto (the god of oceans).

According to the legend, Amaterasu ruled the High Plain of Heaven and Susano-ō was given charge of the oceans. Susano-ō missed his mother and stormed around causing general destruction for which he was exiled by his father. In a fit of pique, Susano-ō visited his sister and they had such a quarrel that Amaterasu rushed off to hide in a cave, plunging the world into darkness. All the gods assembled round the cave entrance to find a way to make Amaterasu return.

Finally, Ame-no-Uzume-no-Mikoto performed a ribald dance causing much laughter among the onlookers. Amaterasu, attracted by the commotion, peeped out of her cave and was quickly hauled out to restore light to the High Plain of Heaven. The site of these events is near Takachihō in Kyūshū. Susano-ō was deprived of his beard, toenails and fingernails and banished to earth, where he landed in Korea before heading to Izumo in Japan.

Okuninushi, a descendant of Susano-ō, took control of Japan, but passed it on to Ninigi, a grandson of Amaterasu. Myth merges into history with Ninigi's grandson, Jimmu, who became the first emperor of Japan. Amaterasu is credited with having supplied the emperor with the Three Treasures (mirror, sword and jewel) – symbols of the emperor's authority.

Shinto & Buddhism With the introduction of Buddhism in the 6th century, the Japanese formed a connection between the religions by considering Buddha as a kami (spirit god) from neighbouring China. In the 8th century the kami were included in Buddhist temples as protectors of the Buddhas. Assimilation progressed with the belief that kami, like human beings, were subject to the suffering of rebirth and similarly in need of Buddhist intercession to achieve liberation from this cycle. Buddhist temples were built close to Shinto shrines and Buddhist *sutras* (collections of dialogues and discourses) were recited for the kami.

Later, the kami were considered incarnations of Bodhisattvas (Buddhas who delay liberation to help others). Buddhist statues were included on Shinto altars or statues of kami were made to represent Buddhist priests.

State Shinto There had been something of a revival of interest in Shinto during the Edo period, particularly by neo-Confucian scholars interested in Japan's past. Some of them called for a return to imperial rule, with Shinto as the state religion. This is exactly what happened with the advent of the Meiji Restoration.

During the Meiji period, Shinto shrines were supported by the government, Shinto doctrines were taught in school and the religion became increasingly nationalistic. It was a relatively brief affair. After Japan's WWII defeat, the Allied forces dismantled the mechanisms of State Shinto and forced the emperor to refute his divine status, a principal tenet of Shinto.

The main training centres for priests are Kokugakuin University in Tokyo and Kōgakukan University in Ise. Marriage is allowed and most of the posts are hereditary, mainly held by men.

Shinto Rites & Festivals These events are important components of Japanese life. For newborn children the first shrine visit occurs on the 30th or 100th day after birth. On 15 November, the Shichigosan rite is celebrated by taking children aged seven (shichi), five (go) and three (san) to the shrine to be blessed. Seijin-no-Hi, the day of adulthood, is celebrated on 15 January by young people who have reached the age of 20.

Virtually all marriages are performed according to Shinto ritual by taking a vow before the kami. Funerals, however, are almost always Buddhist. Both religions coexist equably in traditional Japanese homes, where there are two altars: a Shinto *kamidana* (a shelf shrine) and a Buddhist *butsudan* (Buddha stand).

Shinto also plays a role in professional and daily life. A new car can be blessed for accident-free driving, a purification rite is often held for a building site or the shell of a new building, and completed buildings are similarly blessed. One of the most common purification rites is *oharai*, when the priest waves a wand to which are attached thin strips of paper.

Amulets are popular purchases at Japan's shrines. *Omamori*, special talismans, are purchased at shrines to ensure good luck or ward off evil – taxi-drivers often have a 'traffic-safety' one dangling from the rear-view mirror. Votive plaques (*ema*) made of wood with a picture on one side and a blank space on the other are also common. On the blank side visitors write a wish, for instance, success in exams, luck in finding a sweetheart or safe delivery of a healthy child. Dozens of these plaques can be seen attached to boards in the shrine precincts.

Fortunes (*omikuji*) are selected by drawing a bamboo stick at random from a box and picking out a fortune slip according to the number indicated on the stick. Luck is classified as *dai-kichi* (great good fortune); *kichi* (good fortune); *shō-kichi* (middling good fortune); and *kyō* (bad luck). If you like the fortune slip you've been given, you can take it home. If you've drawn bad luck, you can tie it to the branch of a tree in the shrine grounds – presumably some other force can then worry about it.

The *kannushi* (chief priest) of the shrine is responsible for religious rites and the administration of the shrine. The priests dress in blue and white; on special occasions they don more ornate clothes and wear an *eboshi* (a black cap with a protruding, folded tip). The *miko* (shrine maidens) dress in red and white. The ceremonial *kagura* dances performed by the miko can be traced back to shamanistic trances.

Shinto *matsuri* (festivals) occur on an annual or occasional basis and are classed as grand, middle-size or minor. In divine processions, a ceremonial palanquin (*mikoshi*) is paraded on the shoulders of participants. Other rites include *misogi* (water purification), tug-of-war, archery, horse-racing, sumo (wrestling), gagaku (sacred music) and lion dances.

Although there are hundreds of Shinto festivals throughout the year, a selection of the most interesting or spectacular ones might include:

Onta Matsuri
first Sunday in February at Asuka
Tagata Hōnen-sai
15 March at Tagata-jinja Shrine
Hana-taue
first Sunday in June at Chiyoda
Nachi-no Hi Matsuri
14 July at Kumano Nachi Taisha
Osore-zan Taisai
20-24 July on Mt Osore-zan
Oyama-sankei
first day of the eighth lunar month at Hirosaki
Takachihō-no-Yo-Kagura
late November to early February around Takachiho
On-matsuri
16-18 December in Nara

Buddhism

Japanese Buddhism has adapted along individual lines with some decisive variances from other forms of the religion.

Origins of Buddhism The founder of Buddhism, Siddhartha Gautama, was born around 563 BC at Lumbini on the border of present-day Nepal and India.

In his 20s, Prince Siddhartha left his wife and newborn son to follow the path of an ascetic. Despite studying under several masters, he remained dissatisfied and spent another six years undergoing the most severe austerities. During this period he gave a graphic account of himself: 'Because of so little nourishment, all my bones became like some withered creepers with knotted joints; my buttocks like a buffalo's hoof; my backbone protruding like a string of balls...' Realising that this was not the right path for him, he gave up fasting and decided to follow his own path to enlightenment. He sat crosslegged under a Bodhi tree at Bodhgaya and went into deep meditation for 49 days. During the night of the full moon in May, at the age of 35, he became 'the enlightened' or 'awakened one'.

Shortly afterwards, Buddha delivered his first sermon, 'Setting in Motion the Wheel of Truth', at Deer Park near Sarnath. Then,

Zen Buddhism

The most famous brand of Japanese Buddhism actually arose in China, though its origins lie in India. The word Zen is the Japanese reading of the Chinese *chan*. Legend has it that Bodidharma, a 6th-century Indian monk, introduced Zen to China, but most historians credit this to Huineng (618-907), a Chinese monk.

It took another 200 years for Zen to take root in Japan. It did so in two major schools: Rinzai and Sōtō. The differences between the schools are not easily explained, but at a simple level the Sōtō school places more emphasis on seated meditation *(zazen)*, and the Rinzai school on riddles *(kōan)*. The object of meditative practice for both schools is enlightenment *(satori)*.

The practice of zazen has its roots in Indian yoga. Its posture is the lotus position: the legs are crossed and tucked beneath the sitter, the back ramrod straight, the breathing rhythmical. The idea is to block out all sensation and empty the mind of thought – much harder than you might imagine if you've never tried it. Buddha images are often in the lotus position.

A kōan is a riddle that lacks a rational answer. Most of them are set pieces that owe their existence to the early evolution of Zen in China. In the course of meditating on an insoluble problem, the mind eventually returns to a form of primal consciousness. The most famous kōan was created by the Japanese monk Hakuin: 'What is the sound of one hand clapping?' Fans of *The Simpsons* will already know the answer to this one, and are already enlightened.

Although Zen emphasises the direct, intuitive approach to enlightenment rather than rational analysis, there are dozens of books available on the subject. Two favourites are *Zen & Japanese Culture* (Princeton University Press, 1971) by D T Suzuki and *Zen Flesh, Zen Bones* (Penguin Books, London, 1971) compiled by Paul Reps. ■

as the number of his followers grew, he founded a monastic community and codified the principles according to which the monks should live. The Buddha continued to preach and travel for 45 years until his death at the age of 80 in 483 BC. To his followers, Buddha was also known as Sakyamuni (the sage of the Sakya clan or 'Shaka' in Japanese). Buddhists believe that he is one of the many Buddhas who appeared in the past and that more will appear in the future.

Approximately 140 years after Buddha's death, the Buddhist community diverged into two schools: Hinayana (the Lesser Vehicle) and Mahayana (the Greater Vehicle). The essential difference between the two was that Hinayana supported those who strove for the salvation of the individual, whereas Mahayana supported those who strove for the salvation of all beings. Hinayana prospered in South India and later spread to Sri Lanka, Burma, Thailand, Cambodia, Indonesia and Malaysia. Mahayana spread to inner Asia, Mongolia, Siberia, Japan, China and Tibet.

The basis of Buddhism is that all suffering in life comes from the overindulgence of our desires. Suppression of our sensual desires will eventually lead to a state of nirvana where desire is extinct and we are free from its delusion.

Buddha, who was not a god and did not even claim to be the only enlightened one, felt that the way to nirvana was to follow an eight-fold path of right behaviour and thinking.

Development of Buddhism in Japan Buddhism was introduced to Japan via Korea in the 6th century. Shōtoku Taishi, acknowledged as the 'father of Japanese Buddhism', drew heavily on Chinese culture to form a centralised state and gave official recognition to Buddhism by constructing temples in and around the capital. Horyū-ji Temple, close to Nara, is the most celebrated temple in Japan from this period.

Nara Period The establishment of the first permanent capital at Heijō-kyō (present-day Nara) in 710 also marked the consolidation of Buddhism and Chinese culture in Japan.

In 741, Emperor Shōmu issued a decree for a network of state temples (Kokubun-ji) to be established in each province. The centrepiece of this network was Tōdai-ji Temple, with its gigantic Vairocana Buddha (Daibutsu).

Nara Buddhism revolved around six schools – Ritsu, Jōjitsu, Kusha, Sanron, Hossō and Kegon – which covered the whole range of Buddhist thought as received from China. Three of these schools have continued to this day: the Kegon school, based at the Tōdai-ji Temple; the Hossō school, based at the Kōfuku-ji Temple and Yakushi-ji Temple; and the Ritsu school, based at the Tōshōdai-ji Temple.

Heian Period In 794, the capital was moved from Nara to Heian-kyō (present-day Kyoto). During the Heian period, political power drifted away from centralised government into the hands of aristocrats and their clans, who became a major source of Buddhist support.

The new schools, which introduced Mikkyō (Esoteric Buddhism) from China, were founded by separate leaders on sacred mountains away from the orthodox pressures of the Nara schools.

The Tendai school (derived from a Chinese school on Mt Tian-tai in China) was founded by Saichō (762-822), also known as Dengyō Daishi, who established a base at the Enryaku-ji Temple on Mt Hiei-zan, near Kyoto.

Saichō travelled to Mt Tian-tai in China, where he studied meditation and the Lotus Sutra. On his return, he expanded his studies to include Zen meditation and Tantric ritual. The Tendai school was only officially recognised a few days after his death, but the Enryaku-ji Temple developed into one of Japan's key Buddhist centres and was the source of all the important schools (Pure Land, Zen and Nichiren) in the following Kamakura period.

The Shingon school (derived from the Chinese term for mantra) was established by

Kūkai (714-835), often referred to as Kōbō Daishi, at the Kongōbu-ji Temple on Mt Kōya-san and the Tō-ji Temple in Kyoto.

Kūkai trained for government service but decided at the age of 18 to switch his studies from Confucianism and Taoism to Buddhism. He travelled as part of a mission to Chang-an (present-day Xian) in China, where he immersed himself in Esoteric Buddhism. On his return, he made a broad impact on cultural life, not only spreading and sponsoring the study of Mikkyō, but also compiling the first Chinese-Japanese dictionary and the *hiragana* syllabary which made it much easier for Japanese to put their language into writing.

During this period, assimilation with Shinto continued. Many shrine temples *(jingū-ji)* were built for Buddhist rituals in the grounds of Shinto shrines. Theories were propounded which held the Shinto kami to be manifestations of Buddhas or Bodhisattvas. The collapse of law and order during these times inspired a general feeling of pessimism in society and encouraged belief in the Mappō or End of the Law theory, which predicted an age of darkness with a decline in Buddhist religion. This set the stage for subsequent Buddhist schools to introduce the notion of Buddhist saviour figures such as Amida.

Kamakura Period In this period, marked by savage clan warfare and the transfer of the capital to Kamakura, three schools emerged from Tendai tradition.

The Jōdo (Pure Land) school, founded by Hōnen (1133-1212), shunned scholasticism in favour of the Nembutsu, a simple prayer that required the believer to recite Namu Amida Butsu or 'Hail Amida Buddha' as a path to salvation. This 'no-frills' approach – easy to practise, easy to understand – was popular with the common folk.

Shinran (1173-1262), a disciple of Hōnen, took a more radical step with his master's teaching and broke away to form the Jōdo Shin (True Pure Land) school. The core belief of this school considered that Amida had *already* saved everyone and hence to

recite the Nembutsu was an expression of gratitude, not a petition for salvation.

The Nichiren school bears the name of its founder, Nichiren (1222-82), a fiery character who spurned traditional teachings to embrace the Lotus Sutra as the 'right' teaching. Followers learned to recite Namu Myōhō Rengekyō or 'Hail the Miraculous Law of the Lotus Sutra'. Nichiren's strident demands for religious reform of government caused antagonism all round and he was frequently booted into exile.

The Nichiren school increased its influence in later centuries; the now famous Hokke-ikki uprising in the 15th century was led by Nichiren adherents. Many of the new religious movements in present-day Japan – Sōka Gakkai for example – can be linked to Nichiren.

Later Developments During the Tokugawa period (1600-1867), Buddhism was consolidated as a state institution. When the shogunate banned Christianity, a parallel regulation rigidly required every Japanese to become a certified member of the local temple.

During the Meiji period, Shinto was given priority and separated from Buddhism, which suffered a backlash of resentment. Today, Buddhism prospers in Japan both in the form of traditional schools and in a variety of new movements.

Buddhist Gods There are dozens of gods in the Japanese Buddhist pantheon. Images vary from temple to temple, depending on the religious schools or period of construction, but three of the most common images are those of Shaka (Sanskrit: Sakyamuni), the Historical Buddha; Amida (Sanskrit: Amitabha), the Buddha of the Western Paradise and Miroku (Sanskrit: Maitreya), the Buddha of the Future.

Kannon (Sanskrit: Avalokitesvara) is the 'one who hears their cries' and is available in no less than 33 different versions, including the goddess of mercy, a female form popular with expectant mothers. When Christianity was banned, Japanese believers ingeniously kept faith with the Holy Virgin by creating a clone 'Maria Kannon'.

Jizō is often depicted as a monk with a staff in one hand and a jewel in the other. Pieces of clothing or red bibs draped around Jizō figures are an attempt to cover the souls of dead children. According to legend, this patron of travellers, children and expectant mothers helps the souls of dead children perform their task of building walls of pebbles on the banks of Sai-no-kawara, the river of the underworld. Believers place stones on or around Jizō statues as additional help.

For information on Buddhist temples see Architecture in the special Arts section.

Shugendō

This somewhat offbeat Buddhist school incorporates ancient Shamanistic rites, Shinto beliefs and ascetic Buddhist traditions. The founder was En-no-Gyōja, to whom legendary powers of exorcism and magic are ascribed. He is credited with the enlightenment of kami (spirit gods), converting them to *gongen* (manifestations of Buddhas). Practitioners of Shugendō, called *yamabushi* (mountain priests), train both body and spirit with arduous exercises in the mountains.

Until the Meiji era, many of Japan's mountains were the domain of yamabushi who proved popular with the locals for their skills in sorcery and exorcism. During the Meiji era, Shinto was elevated to a state religion and Shugendō was barred as being culturally debased. Today, yamabushi are more common on tourist brochures than in the flesh, but Shugendō survives on mountains such as Dewa Sanzan and Omine-san.

Confucianism

Although Confucianism is essentially a code of ethics, it has exerted a strong enough influence to become part of Japanese religion. Confucianism entered Japan via Korea in the 5th century. To regulate social behaviour, Confucius took the family unit as his starting point and stressed the importance of the five human relationships: master and subject, father and son, elder brother and younger brother, husband and wife, friend and friend.

The strict observance of this social 'pecking order', radiating from individual families to encompass the whole of society, has evolved over centuries to become a core concept in Japanese life. The influence of Confucianism can be seen in such disparate examples as the absolute loyalty demanded in Bushidō (the code of the samurai), the extreme allegiance to the emperor in WWII, the low status of women, and the hierarchical ties in modern Japanese companies.

Folklore & Gods

Japan has a curious medley of folk gods. Common ones include the following:

Shichifuku-jin are the seven gods of luck – a happy band of well-wishers plucked from Indian, Chinese and Japanese sources. Their images are popular at New Year, when they are, more often than not, depicted as a group on a treasure ship *(takarabune)*.

Ebisu is the patron of seafarers and a symbol for prosperity in business. He carries a fishing rod with a large red, sea bream dangling on the line and can be recognised by his beaming, bearded face.

Bishamon is the god of war. He wears a helmet, a suit of armour and brandishes a spear. As a protector of Buddhism, he can be seen carrying a pagoda.

Daikoku, the god of wealth, has a bag full of treasures slung over his left shoulder and a lucky mallet in his right hand.

Benzaiten is the goddess of art, skilled in eloquence, music, literature and wisdom. She holds a Japanese mandolin (biwa) and is often escorted by a sea snake.

Fukurokuju looks after wealth and longevity. He has a bald, dome-shaped head, and a dumpy body and wears long, flowing robes.

Jurojin also covers longevity. He sports a distinguished white beard and holds a cane to which is attached a scroll listing the life span of all living beings.

Hotei, the god of happiness, is instantly recognisable (in Japan and elsewhere in Asia) by his large paunch and Cheshire-cat grin. Originally a Chinese beggar priest, he is the only god in this group whose antecedents can be traced to a human being. His bulging bag provides for the needy and is never empty.

A variety of fabulous creatures inhabit Japanese folklore and crop up regularly in shops, festivals and shrines:

Tanuki is often translated as 'badger', but bears a closer resemblance to a North American raccoon. Like the fox, the tanuki is thought of as a mischievous creature and is credited with supernatural powers, but is more a figure of fun than the fox. Statues usually depict the tanuki in an upright position with straw headgear and clasping a bottle of sake.

Kitsune is a fox, but for the Japanese it also has strong connections with the supernatural and is worshipped in Japan at over 30,000 Inari shrines as the messenger of the harvest god. The Fushimi Inari Taisha Shrine near Kyoto is the largest of its kind and is crammed with fox statues.

Maneki-neko, the Beckoning Cat, is a very common sight outside shops or restaurants. The raised left paw attracts customers and their money.

Tengu are mountain goblins with a capricious nature, sometimes abducting children, sometimes returning those who were missing. Their unmistakable feature is a long nose, like a proboscis.

Kappa are amphibious creatures about the size of a 12 or 13 year old boy and have webbed hands and feet. They have a reputation for mischief, such as dragging horses into rivers or stealing cucumbers. The source of their power is a depression on top of their heads which must always contain water. A crafty method to outwit a kappa is to bow to it. When the kappa – Japanese to the core – bows back, it empties the water from its head and loses its power. The alternatives are not pleasant. Kappa are said to enjoy ripping out their victim's liver through the anus!

Christianity

Portuguese missionaries introduced Christianity to Japan in the 16th century. In 1549, Francis Xavier landed at Kagoshima, on Kyūshū. At first, the feudal lords (daimyō) seemed eager to convert together with their subjects. However, the motivation was probably less a question of faith and more an interest in gaining trade advantages.

The initial tolerance shown by Oda Nobunaga was soon reversed by his successor, Toyotomi Hideyoshi, who considered the Jesuits a colonial threat. The religion was banned in 1587 and 26 Christians were crucified in Nagasaki 10 years later. After expelling the remaining missionaries in 1614, Japan clammed up to the outside world

for several centuries. During this time a small number of Christians kept their faith active as a type of 'back-room Buddhism'. Christian missions were allowed back at an early stage during the Meiji era to build churches and found hospitals and schools, many of which still exist.

Despite these efforts, Christianity has not met with wide acceptance among the Japanese who tend to feel more at home with Shinto and Buddhism. The number of Christians in Japan is a very small portion of the population – possibly one million.

New Religions

A variety of new religions has taken root in Japan. They cover a wide range of beliefs from founder cults to faith healing. Easily the largest of these new religions is Sōka Gakkai (Creative Education Society). Founded in the '30s, it follows Nichiren's teachings and numbers over 20 million followers. (The Clean Government Party (Komeito) was founded in 1964 as a political offshoot of Sōka Gakkai, but now tends to play down the association. It is the second-largest opposition party and, as its name implies, takes a dim view of corruption.)

The emergence of the Aum Shinrikyō and its 1995 subway gas attack in downtown Tokyo has drawn attention to the dangers of cult activities in Japan.

LANGUAGE

It is something of a cliché that Japanese spend years studying English and end up unable to string a coherent English sentence together. This is partly due to the language-teaching techniques employed in Japanese classrooms, but it also reflects the difficulty of translation. Structurally, Japanese and English are so different that word-for-word translations will often produce almost incomprehensible sentences.

Grammar

To English speakers, Japanese language patterns often seem to be back to front and lacking in essential information. For example, where an English speaker would say 'I'm going to the shop' a Japanese speaker would say 'shop to going', omitting the subject pronoun (I) altogether and putting the verb at the end of the sentence. To make matters worse, many moods which are indicated at the beginning of a sentence in English occur at the end of a sentence in Japanese, as in the Japanese sentence 'Japan to going if' – 'if you're going to Japan'.

Fortunately for visitors to Japan, it's not all bad news. Unlike other languages in the region (Chinese, Vietnamese and Thai among others), Japanese is not tonal and the pronunciation system is fairly easy to master. In fact, with a little effort, getting together a repertoire of travellers' phrases should be no trouble – the only problem will be understanding what people say back to you.

Writing

Japanese has one of the most complex writing systems in the world, using three different scripts (four if you include the increasingly used Roman script *romaji*). The most difficult of the three, for foreigners and Japanese alike, is *kanji*, the ideographic script developed by the Chinese. Not only do you have to learn a couple of thousand of them, but unlike Chinese many Japanese kanji have wildly variant pronunciations depending on context.

Because of the differences between Chinese grammar and Japanese grammar, kanji had to be supplemented with an alphabet of syllables, or a syllabary, known as *hiragana*. And there is yet another syllabary that is used largely for representing foreign-loan words such as **terebi** (TV) and **femunisuto** (feminist); this script is known as *katakana*. If you're serious about learning to read Japanese you will have to set aside several years.

If you're thinking of tackling the Japanese writing system before you go or while you're in Japan, your best bet would be to start with hiragana or katakana. Both syllabaries have 48 characters each, and can be learned within a week – it will take at least a month to consolidate them though. You can practise your katakana on restaurant menus, where

such things as **kōhii** (coffee) and **keiki** (cake) are frequently found, and practise your hiragana on train journeys, as station names are indicated in hiragana.

Romanisation

The romaji used in this book follows the Hepburn system of romanisation. Macrons are used to indicate long vowels. Most place names will use a combination of romaji and English – the romaji suffix will in most cases be separated from the proper name by a hyphen and followed by its English translation. For example: Tōdai-ji Temple (**ji** is the romaji word for temple); Shimabara-hantō Peninsula (**hantō** means peninsula) and Ise-jingū Shrine (**jingū** means shrine). These suffixes, however, will not be hyphenated when they are not followed by a direct English translation: for example, Suizenji Garden (the **ji** for temple will not be hyphenated) and Oshima-kōen Park (the **shima** for island will not be hyphenated).

Language Guides

Japanese phrasebook (Lonely Planet, 1994) offers a convenient collection of survival words and phrases for your trip to Japan. Tae Moriyama's *The Practical Guide to Japanese Signs* (Kodansha, 1987) is a convenient introduction to some commonly encountered Japanese signs. It not only identifies them but explains how they came about and has been followed by a second volume.

The popularity of Japanese studies has spawned an incredible number of specialist publications. Some of them are quirky enough to make them worth browsing through or taking home as an off-beat souvenir, even if you have nothing but a casual acquaintance with the language. Check out Kodansha's Power Japanese series as a starter – *Gone Fishin'* and *How to Sound Intelligent in Japanese* are good examples. Phrasebooks are also available on everything from Japanese slang to lovemaking.

The following selection of Japanese phrases will see you through some of the more common situations experienced by travellers to Japan. For a more comprehensive guide to making yourself understood in Japan, try Lonely Planet's *Japanese phrasebook*.

Pronunciation

The following as in British pronunciation.

a   as the 'a' in 'father'
e   as the 'e' in 'get'
i   as the 'i' in 'macaroni'
o   as the 'o' in 'lot'
u   as the 'u' in 'flu'

Vowels appearing in this book with a macron (or bar) over them (ā, ē, ō, ū) are pronounced in the same way as standard vowels except that the sound is held twice as long. You need to take care with this as vowel length can change the meaning of a word: *yuki* means 'snow', while *yūki* means 'bravery'.

Consonants are generally pronounced as in English, with the following exceptions:

f   this sound is produced by pursing the lips and blowing lightly
g   as the 'g' in 'goal' at the start of a word; and nasalised as the 'ng' in 'sing' in the middle of a word
r   more like an 'l' than an 'r'

Basics

The all-purpose title **san** is used after a name as an honorific and is the equivalent of Mr, Miss, Mrs and Ms.

Yes.
  hai   はい。
No.
  iie   いいえ。
OK.
  daijōbu/ōkē   だいじょうぶ。／オーケー。
No.
  chigaimasu   違います。
  (disagreement)
No.
  chotto chigaimasu ちょっと違います。
  (disagreement; less emphatic)
Please.
  dōzo   どうぞ。
  (when offering something)

Please.
  o-negai shimasu お願いします。
  (when asking for something)
Excuse me.
  sumimasen   すみません。
  (to attract attention)
I'm sorry.
  gomen nasai/   ごめんなさい。／
  sumimasen   すみません。
Thank you.
  dōmo arigatō どうもありがとう。
Thank you very much.
  dōmo arigatō どうもありがとう
  gozaimashita ございました。
Thanks. (informal)
  dōmo   どうも。
What?
  nani   なに？
When?
  itsu   いつ？
Where?
  doko   どこ？
Who?
  dare   だれ？
How many?
  ikutsu   いくつ？
How much?
  ikura   いくら？

Greetings & Civilities

Good morning.
  o-hayō gozaimasu おはようございます。
Good afternoon.
  konnichiwa   こんにちは。
Good evening.
  kombanwa   こんばんわ。
Goodbye.
  sayōnara   さようなら。
See you later.
  dewa mata   ではまた。

I am disturbing you. (entering a room)
  o-jama shimasu/shitsurei shimasu
  おじゃまします。／失礼します。
Thanks for taking care of me. (when leaving)
  o-sewa ni narimashita
  お世話になりました。
This is Mr/Mrs/Ms (Smith).
  kochira wa (Sumisu) san desu
  こちらは（スミス）さんです。

My name is (Smith).
watashi wa (Sumisu) desu
私は（スミス）です。

Pleased to meet you.
dōzo yoroshiku
どうぞよろしく。

Take care.
ki o tsukete kudasai
気をつけてください。

Have a good trip.
yoi go-ryokō o
よい御旅行を。

Please give my regards to Mr/Mrs/Ms Suzuki.
Suzuki san ni yoroshiku o-tsutae kudasai
鈴木さんによろしくお伝え下さい。

Sorry to keep you waiting.
taihen o-matase shimashita
たいへんお待たせしました。

Small Talk

How are you?
o-genki desuka?
お元気ですか。

Fine.
ē, okagesamade
ええ、おかげさまで

Please say it again more slowly.
mō ichidō, yukkuri itte kudasai
もう一度、ゆっくり言ってください。

What is this called?
kore wa nan-to iimasuka?
これは何といいますか。

Where are you from?
o-kuni wa doko desuka?
お国はどこですか。

It's up to you. (when asked to make a choice)
o-makase shimasu
お任せします。

Is it OK to take a photo?
shashin o totte mo ii desuka?
写真を撮ってもいいですか。

I don't understand.
wakarimasen
わかりません。

Can you speak English?
eigo ga dekimasu ka?
英語ができますか。

I cannot speak Japanese.
nihongo wa dekimasen
日本語はできません。

Please speak in English/Japanese.
(eigo)/(nihongo) de hanashite kudasai
（英語）／（日本語）で話してください。

Is there an interpreter?
tsūyaku wa imasuka?
通訳はいますか。

Please write in Japanese/English.
(nihongo)/(eigo) de kaite kudasai
（日本語）／（英語）で書いてください。

Just a minute.
chotto matte kudasai
ちょっと待ってください。

Nationality

Australia
ōsutoraria　オーストラリア

Canada
kanada　カナダ

China
chūgoku　中国

Denmark
denmāku　デンマーク

France
furansu　フランス

Germany
doitsu　ドイツ

Holland
oranda　オランダ

Hong Kong
hon kon　香港

India
indo　インド

Indonesia
indoneshia　インドネシア

Italy
itaria　イタリア

Japan
nihon　日本

Korea
kankoku　韓国

Malaysia
marēshia　マレーシア

New Zealand
nyūjiirando　ニュージーランド

Philippines
firipin　フィリピン

Singapore
shingapōru　シンガポール

Sweden
suēden　スウェーデン

Switzerland
   suisu スイス

Thailand
   tai タイ

UK
   igirisu イギリス

USA
   amerika アメリカ

Are you (American)?
   anata wa (america-jin) desu ka?
   あなたは（アメリカ人）ですか。

I am not (American), I am (French).
   watashi wa (america-jin) dewa arimasen,
   watashi wa (furansu-jin) desu
   私は（アメリカ人）ではありません。
   私は（フランス人）です。

I come from (Hong Kong).
   watashi wa (hon kon) kara kimashita.
   私は（香港）から来ました。

Accommodation

Where is ...?
   ... wa, doko desuka?
   …は、どこですか。

Do you have any vacancies?
   aita heya wa arimasuka?
   あいた部屋はありますか。

I don't have a reservation.
   yoyaku wa shite imasen
   予約はしていません。

How much is it per person?
   hitori ikura desuka?
   ひとりいくらですか。

Does it include (breakfast)/(a meal)?
   (chōshoku)/(shokuji) wa tsuite imasuka?
   （朝食）／（食事）はついていますか。

I'm going to stay for (one night)/(two nights).
   (hito ban)/(futa ban) tomarimasu
   （一晩）／（二晩）泊まります。

Can I leave my luggage here?
   nimotsu o azukatte itadakemasen ka?
   荷物をあずかっていただけませんか。

hotel
   hoteru ホテル

Japanese-style inn
   ryokan 旅館

youth hostel
   yūsu hosuteru ユースホステル

private lodge
   minshiku 民宿

single room
   shinguru rūmu シングルルーム

double room
   daburu rūmu ダブルルーム

twin room
   tsuin rūmu ツインルーム

Japanese-style room
   washitsu 和室

western-style room
   yōshitsu 洋室

(western) bed
   beddo ベッド

Japanese-style bath
   o-furo お風呂

room with a (western-style) bath
   basu tsuki no heya バス付きの部屋

Getting Around

How much is the fare to ...?
   ... made, ikura desuka?
   …まで、いくらですか。

Does this go to ...?
   kore wa ... e ikimasuka?
   これは…へ行きますか。

Is the next station ...?
   tsugi no eki wa ... desuka?
   つぎの駅は…ですか。

Please tell me when we get to ...
   ... ni tsuitara oshiete kudasai
   …に着いたら教えてください。

Where is the ... exit?
   ... guchi wa doko desuka?
   …口はどこですか。

east
   higashi 東

west
   nishi 西

north
   kita 北

south
   minami 南

left
   hidari 左

right
   migi 右

straight ahead
   massugu まっすぐ

Do you have an English subway map?
eigo no chikatetsu no chizu ga arimasuka?
英語の地下鉄の地図がありますか。

Where is this address?
kono jūsho wa doko desuka?
この住所はどこですか。

Excuse me please, can you help me?
sumimasen ga, oshiete kudasaimasenka?
すみませんが、教えてくださいませんか。

I'd like to go to ...
... ni ikitai desu
…に行きたいです。

How do I get to ...?
... e wa dono yō ni ikeba ii desu ka?
…へはどのように行けばいいですか。

Could you write down the address for me?
jūsho o kaite itadake masen ka?
住所を書いていただけませんか。

Please stop here.
koko ni tomete kudasai
ここに止めてください。

aeroplane
hikōki 飛行機

bus
basu バス

subway
chikatetsu 地下鉄

train
densha 電車

taxi
takushii タクシー

airport
kūkō 空港

bus stop
basu tei バス停

station
eki 駅

ticket office
kippu uriba 切符売場

Green Window
midori no madoguchi みどりの窓口

travel centre
ryokō sentā 旅行センター

entrance
iriguchi 入口

exit
deguchi 出口

left-luggage office
ichiji azukarijo 一時預り所

ticket
kippu 切符

one way
kata-michi 片道

return
ōfuku 往復

non-smoking seat
kin-en seki 禁煙席

window seat
mado-gawa no seki 窓側の席

bank
ginkō 銀行

post office
yūbinkyoku 郵便局

GPO
chūō yūbinkyoku 中央郵便局

phone
denwa 電話

public phone
kōshū denwa 公衆電話

toilet
o-tearai お手洗い

police box
kōban 交番

Emergencies

Help me!
tasukete! 助けて！

Watch out!
ki o tsukete! 気をつけて！

Thief!
dorobō! どろぼう！

Call the police!
keisatsu o yonde kudasai!
警察を呼んでください！

Call a doctor!
isha o yonde kudasai!
医者を呼んでください！

Food

Do you have an English menu?
eigo no menyū wa arimasuka?
英語のメニューはありますか。

I would like the set menu please.
setto menyū o o-negai shimasu
セットメニューをお願いします。

I'm a vegetarian.
watashi wa saishoku-shugisha desu
私は菜食主義者です。

Do you have any vegetarian meals?
saishoku-shugi ryōri wa arimasuka?
菜食主義料理はありますか。

What do you recommend?
o-susume wa nan desuka?
おすすめは何ですか。

This is delicious.
oishii desu
おいしいです。

Please bring the bill.
o-kanjō onegai shimasu
お勘定お願いします。

breakfast		
chōshoku/asa gohan	朝食／朝ご飯	
lunch		
ranchi/hiru gohan	ランチ／昼ご飯	
dinner		
yūshoku/ban gohan	夕食／晩ご飯	
Chinese food		
chūgoku ryōri	中国料理	
Buddhist vegetarian food		
shōjin ryōri	精進料理	
Japanese food		
nihon ryōri/ washoku	日本料理／和食	
western dishes		
yōshoku	洋食	
restaurant		
resutoran	レストラン	
cafeteria		
shokudō	食堂	
quality Japanese restaurant		
ryōtei	料亭	
coffee shop		
kohii shoppu/ kissaten	コーヒーショップ／喫茶店	
bar		
bā	バー	
pub		
izakaya	居酒屋	

Shopping

How much is this?
kore wa ikura desuka?
これはいくらですか。

It's too expensive.
taka-sugimasu
高すぎます。

Can you give me a discount?
waribiki dekimasu ka?
割引できますか。

I'm just looking.
miru dake desu
見るだけです。

Please give me this/that.
(kore)/(sore) o kudasai
（これ）／（それ）をください。

Can I have a receipt?
ryōshūsho o kudasai
領収書をください。

cheap		
yasui	安い	
expensive		
takai	高い	
big		
ōkii	大きい	
small		
chisai	小さい	
shop		
mise	店	
supermarket		
sūpā	スーパー	
bookshop		
honya	本屋	
camera shop		
shashinya	写真屋	
department store		
depāto	デパート	

Health

How do you feel?
kibun wa ikaga desuka?
気分はいかがですか。

I don't feel well.
kibun ga warui desu
気分が悪いです。

It hurts here.
koko ga itai desu
ここが痛いです。

I have asthma.
watashi wa zensoku desu
私は喘息です。

I have diarrhoea.
geri o shite imasu
下痢をしています。

I have a toothache.
ha ga itamimasu
歯が痛みます。
I have a cold.
kaze o hikimashita
風邪をひきました。
I'm allergic to antibiotics/penicillin.
kōsei busshitsu/penishirin ni arerugii desu
抗生物質／ペニシリンにアレルギーです。

hospital
byōin　　　　　　病院
doctor
isha　　　　　　医者
dentist
ha-isha　　　　　歯医者
pharmacy
yakkyoku　　　　薬局
constipation
bempi　　　　　　便秘
diabetes
tōnyōbyō　　　　糖尿病
fever
netsu　　　　　　熱
food poisoning
shoku chūdoku　食中毒
hay fever
kafun shō　　　　花粉症
indigestion
shōka furyō　　　消化不良
migrane
henzutsū　　　　偏頭痛
condom
kondōmu　　　　コンドーム
aspirin
asupirin　　　　アスピリン
tampons
tampon　　　　　タンポン
contraceptive
piru　　　　　　　ピル
antiseptic
shōdoku　　　　消毒

Days
today
kyō　　　　　　今日
tomorrow
ashita　　　　　明日
yesterday
kinō　　　　　　きのう
Sunday
nichiyōbi　　　日曜日
Monday
getsuyōbi　　　月曜日
Tuesday
kayōbi　　　　火曜日
Wednesday
suiyōbi　　　　水曜日
Thursday
mokuyōbi　　　木曜日
Friday
kinyōbi　　　　金曜日
Saturday
doyōbi　　　　土曜日

Numbers

0	*zero/rē*	〇
1	*ichi*	一
2	*ni*	二
3	*san*	三
4	*yon/shi*	四
5	*go*	五
6	*roku*	六
7	*nana/shichi*	七
8	*hachi*	八
9	*kyū/ku*	九
10	*jū*	十
11	*jūichi*	十一
12	*jūni*	十二
20	*nijū*	二十
21	*nijūichi*	二十一
30	*sanjū*	三十
100	*hyaku*	百
200	*nihyaku*	二百
1000	*sen*	千
5000	*gosen*	五千
10,000	*ichiman*	一万
20,000	*niman*	二万
100,000	*jūman*	十万
1,000,000	*hyakuman*	百万

Japanese Arts

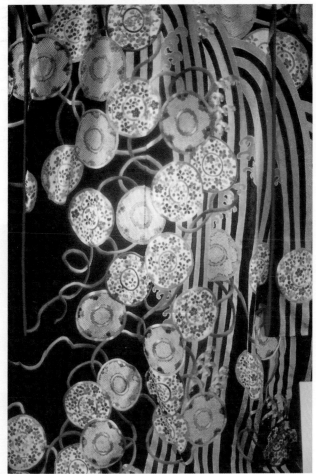

INGO WESTNER

The wealth of modern Japan is founded on the ability to absorb influences from the outside world and use them to create something distinctly Japanese. The art of Japan is founded on very much the same ability. Essentially, Japanese art is the result of this ability coupled with a tremendous native technical facility.

Until the last century, the main influences on Japanese art came from the nearby countries of China and Korea. While Japan was still living in the Stone Age, China had a well developed, technological culture. It is hardly surprising then, that when frequent contact was established between the two countries, Japan would be hungry for whatever skills and knowledge the Chinese had to give. In borrowing many aspects of Chinese culture, Japan also absorbed influences from such distant countries as Persia, Afghanistan and even ancient Rome, since China maintained an active trade with these countries along the Silk Road. Perhaps the most important influence of all came from India, via China, in the form of Buddhism, which entered Japan in the 6th century AD.

All these outside influences notwithstanding, the Japanese add something of their own to their art. There is a fascination with the ephemeral, with the unadorned, with forms that echo the randomness of nature. A gift for caricature is also present, from early Zen ink paintings right up to the *manga* (or comics) of contemporary Japan. There is a wildness and passion in some works which is less evident in the art of China. An interest in the grotesque or the bizarre is also often visible in many works of Japanese art, from Buddhist scrolls depicting the horrors of hell to the highly stylised depictions of body parts in the *ukiyo-e* wood-block prints of the Edo period.

When asked to define their aesthetic principles, Japanese reach for words like *wabi, sabi* and *shibui*. These concepts tend to overlap, and

Previous page: Embroidered kimono detail

Stone torii gate – the act of passing through is said to purify the soul of devotees before they enter the shrine's inner grounds

MATTHIAS LEY

are often used more emotively than descriptively. Together they refer to a kind of rustic simplicity and to a restrained, quiet and cultivated sense of beauty. Such ideals can be found in the measured proceedings of the tea ceremony (among other things). But they are by no means the final say on a long and vibrant artistic tradition that continues to seek new inspirations and produce new forms.

Art Periods

 Since Japanese art is heavily influenced by mainland culture, it is natural that the evolution of Japanese art continuously reflects the state of relations between Japan, China and Korea. During periods of frequent contact, new ideas and techniques were rapidly assimilated, resulting in art which was sometimes indistinguishable from that of the mainland. During periods of isolation, native ideas and sensibilities were allowed to come to the fore and Japanese art developed its own personality.

Japanese archaeologists have unearthed large numbers of artefacts from Japan's earliest historical periods. The Jōmon period (10,000-300 BC) takes its name from the decorative 'coiled rope' pottery produced by Japan's early hunters and gatherers. Similarly, the Yayoi period (300 BC-300 AD), which saw the introduction of wet-rice farming and bronze and iron use from the mainland, has left many examples of simple, refined earthenware pottery and clay figurines. The Kofun period (300-710 AD) is named after the *kofun* – the round or keyhole-shaped burial mounds of Japan's earliest emperors. *Haniwa* (clay ring) earthenware cylinders and sculptures, some as tall as 1.5m, surrounded these burial mounds.

The Asuka (552-645) and Hakuhō (645-710) periods mark an important turning point. The arrival of Mahayana (or Greater Vehicle) Buddhism introduced religious themes that would inspire Japanese art for over five hundred years. The earliest works of sculpture were produced by Korean artisans – notable examples can be seen at Hōryū-ji Temple in Nara and Kōryū-ji Temple in Kyoto – but by the Nara period (710-794) a golden age of Japanese sculpture had arrived. Japanese sculptors produced such masterpieces as the Shō-Kannon statue and the Yakushi Triad (both on display at Yakushi-ji Temple in southern Nara) as well as the Ganjin statue at Nara's Tōshōdai-ji Temple. Also during this period, outstanding religious murals were painted, very much in the vein of Indian religious cave paintings.

It was difficult in these early days for Japan to shrug off the influence of China. But by the early Heian period (794-1185), as Tang-dynasty China faltered and Japan distanced itself from its mainland neighbour, a truly native culture began to emerge. For Japanese, this period is the apogee of elegant courtly life. The imperial capital moved from Nara to Heian (modern-day Kyoto). The literary arts flourished. The break with Chinese tradition can be seen in the development of the 31-syllable *waka* poem, precursor to the 17-syllable *haiku*, and in narrative epics like *Genji Monogatari* (The Tale of Genji) by Murasaki Shikibu. In the visual arts, *Yamato-e* (Japanese painting) broke with Chinese landscape tradition by depicting court scenes on folding panels. The graceful lines of Byōdō-in Temple in Kyoto, one of the few remaining structures from this period, are also testament to the beauty of Heian architecture.

After a period of brutal internal warfare a military government was established in Kamakura. The early art of the Kamakura period (1185-1333) was filled with a wild energy, though later art of the period became more subdued under the influence of a military government which eschewed vibrancy in art for a more spartan aesthetic. During this period, Zen became popular in Japan. Its disavowal of Buddha images gave rise to a new tradition of human portraits and statues and marked the beginning of a secularisation of art which would gain momentum in the following centuries.

In 1336, the centre of power moved back to Kyoto. During the Muromachi period (1333-1576), Zen had an enormous impact on the arts in Japan, exemplified by the ink paintings of Sesshū, the tea ceremony of Sen no Rikyū and the garden of Kyoto's Ginkaku-ji Temple. The period was marked by a spirit of contemplation. However, in 1467, the 11-year Ōnin War broke out, which essentially destroyed the country. This 'brush with the void' left a deep impact on Japan, and the idea of wabi, or stark simplicity, was born.

After another period of internal struggle, a powerful shogun, Toyotomi Hideyoshi, took control and presided over an era of unprecedented grandeur and flamboyance in the arts. The new elite encouraged artists to produce elaborate works to decorate their palaces. The Momoyama period (1576-1600) was typified by huge gardens, gilded screen paintings and brilliant textile work. Also during this period, the first westerners arrived, bringing with them technology and treasures unlike anything seen in Japan before.

During the following Edo period (1600-1867), Japan shut itself off from the world and the Japanese arts coalesced into the forms by which they are known today. With the rise of the merchant class, art was no longer the province of emperors and nobles and this had a tonic effect on Japanese artists, who now could sell their work to a much wider audience. The most important development during this time was the wood-block print depicting the 'floating world' of Edo courtesans and *kabuki* actors. Ukiyo-e paintings mark the end of a long progression in Japanese art, which began with depictions of the Buddha and ended up with depictions of normal people in everyday situations.

From the Meiji Restoration the arts in Japan have been revolutionised by contact with the west. As was the case with early Chinese influences, Japanese artists have swiftly moved from imitation to innovation: from film to fashion, architecture to literature, Japanese artists have made and continue to make unique international contributions.

Sacred cedar tree – designated in Shinto by a plaited straw rope (shimenawa) and strips of white paper (gohei)

MASON FLORENCE

Religious Sculpture

Fine art in Japan begins with the introduction of Mahayana Buddhism in the 6th century AD. At this time, the nation turned its nascent artistic skill, already manifest in its production of fine pottery and metalwork, to the production of Buddhist images. Early works of this time are heavily continental in influence, many of them actually made by Korean or Chinese immigrants. These sculptors were brought over specially from the mainland to furnish Japan's new temples with Buddhist images. Later, when contacts with China evaporated during the late Heian era, native sculpture techniques were allowed to flourish and a distinct Japanese style began to appear.

INGO WESTNER

The Vajisravana statue, one of the fearsome heavenly beings, standing guard at Tō-ji Temple, Kyoto

A knowledge of the different types of Buddhist sculptures found in Japanese temples is a good step to understanding Buddhism itself. The images fall into four main groups, each of which represents a different level of being in the Buddhist cosmology. This cosmology, of course, comes to Japan from India, via China and Korea, and Japanese Buddhist art naturally reflects this varied inheritance.

At the head of Japanese Buddhism's hierarchy of deities are *nyorai*, or Buddhas. These are beings who have attained enlightenment and freed themselves from the cycle of rebirth. Nyorai images are most conspicuous by their simple robes, a lump on the head symbolising wisdom and a head of tight 'snail shell' curls. The major nyorai are: Shaka (the Historical Buddha), recognisable by one hand raised in a preaching gesture; Yakushi (the Healing Buddha), with one hand also raised in a preaching gesture and the other hand clutching a vial of medicine; Amida (the Buddha of Western Paradise or of Light), usually seen sitting with knuckles together in a meditative posture; and Dainichi (the Cosmic Buddha), usually portrayed in princely attire, sitting with one hand clasped around a raised finger of the other hand (a sexual gesture indicating the unity of being). Nyorai are usually portrayed with two bodhisattvas in a triad configuration.

After Buddhas, the next most important beings are *bosatsu* (bodhisattvas). These are beings who have put off their own personal entry into nirvana in order to help others attain enlightenment. Images of bosatsu are more human in appearance than nyorai and most easily distinguished from the latter by a topknot of hair or a crowned headpiece, sometimes with smaller figures built into the crown. The most common bosatsu in Japanese temples is Kannon, the goddess of mercy. Also common, both in temples and scattered around the countryside, are images of Jizō, the bodhisattva assigned to save travellers and children. Jizō are often depicted carrying children in their arms.

Lustrous bronze sculpture of a meditating Buddha, Tenmangū Shrine, Kyoto

CHRIS TAYLOR

The next group of beings are not native to Buddhism, but were borrowed from Hinduism to serve particular purposes in the Buddhist cosmology. These beings are called *ten* (heavenly beings or devas). While some appear as beastly ogres, others are human in appearance. The most common of these are *niō* (guardians) which are often found in the gates leading up to temples. The giant Kongō guardians at Nara's Toōdai-ji Temple are perhaps the most famous of these images.

Finally, there are the *myō-ō* (kings of wisdom or light). These beings serve as protectors of Buddhism and were introduced to Japan along with esoteric Buddhism in the 9th century. The most common myō-ō image is Fudō Myō-ō who is usually depicted as a wrathful being clutching an upright sword.

MATTHIAS LEY

Gilt statue of Amida, the meditative nyorai, sculpted in the Heian style (circa 1600) – Alex Kerr Collection

Architecture

Shrines Shinto, the indigenous religion of Japan, translates as the 'way of the gods'. Japanese *kami* (gods) inhabit all natural phenomena – from towering volcanoes to curiously misshapen rocks – and the earliest Shinto shrines were simply sacred places marked off with a special plaited rope called a *shimenawa* and strips of white paper *(gohei)*. From this rope evolved fences and eventually the *torii* gates that are now one of the most obvious features of a shrine.

Shrine buildings come in many varieties, but the architecture of most of them probably evolved from the storehouses and dwellings of prehistoric Japan: many of their now ornamental features were once functional in nature. Pairs of stone lion-like creatures called *komainu* often flank the main path to a shrine; one usually has its mouth open in a roar and the other has its mouth closed. Further along the approach is an ablution basin *(chōzuya)* where visitors use the ladle *(hishaku)* to rinse both hands before pouring water into a cupped hand to rinse their mouths. The shrine's main building is the *honden*, which enshrines the resident kami. The honden is off-limits to layfolk, and only occasionally entered by Shinto priests. In front of the honden is the *haiden*, or hall of worship. In smaller shrines, these may share one roof. In front of the haiden is an offering box *(saisen-bako)*, above which hangs a gong and a long piece of rope. Visitors throw a coin into the box, then sound the gong twice, make two deep bows, clap loudly twice, bow again twice (once deeply, once lightly) and then step back to the side.

Shrine maiden at Mie dressed in the traditional vermilion pleated trousers

The oldest Japanese shrines were built in a 'pure' native style. But with the introduction of Buddhism in the 6th century AD, shrine buildings started to incorporate elements of Chinese temple architecture. The 'pure' style is marked by features such as natural wood columns and walls (as opposed to red and white), *chigi* (horns) protruding over the ridge of the roof, and free-standing columns that support the ridge of the

Built in 1895 as a replica of the imperial palace that existed in Heian times, Kyoto's Heian Jingū Shrine shows architectural influences from the Tang dynasty, China

roof at either gabled end. Look too for *katsuogi* – short logs that lay horizontally across the ridge of the roof.

Perhaps the most stunning example of a pre-Buddhist, Japanese-style shrine is Naikū Shrine, which forms part of the Ise-jingū Grand Shrine at Ise. Other notable Shinto shrines include Izumo Taisha near Matsue, and Meiji-jingū and Yasukuni-jinja in Tokyo.

Temples Buddhist temples can be found the length and breadth of Japan. Along with the religion itself, Japan imported from China and Korea the architecture used in Buddhist temples. Temples are divided into three broad architectural categories: *wayō*, or Japanese-style; *daibutsuyō*, or Great Buddha style; and *karayō*, or Chinese style.

In early Japanese temples, the principal structure was the pagoda, a building that evolved from the Indian stupa (a reliquary for enshrining sacred remains of the Buddha). The Japanese variety, a graceful terraced structure of roofs capped with a spire, is Chinese-influenced. In time the pagoda became just one of many buildings that typically could be found in a temple complex.

MASON FLORENCE

Kyoto's Gingaku-ji Temple, built in the 15th century as a villa for an Ashikaga shogun, has one of Japan's oldest tea huts, an attractive pond setting and a meticulously raked dry garden comprising two unusual mounds of white sand

Temples vary widely in their construction, depending on the type of school and the historical era of construction. A selection of the finest Buddhist temples would include many in and around Kyoto, Nara and Kōya-san as well as Eihei-ji Temple (near Fukui) in Chūbu; the Chūson-ji Temple (Hiraizumi) in Tōhoku; Zenkō-ji Temple in Nagano; and, close to Tokyo, the temple complexes of Nikkō and Kamakura.

Main Temple Buildings

While some differences exist between the temples of Japan's various schools of Buddhism, most temple compounds contain the following basic structures:

Pagoda – This is a tower-like structure based on the Indian stupa which is believed to house a relic (such as a bone or a tooth) of the Historical Buddha. While these were the focal point of early Japanese temples, in later temples they are often relegated to the periphery.

Kondō or **Hondō** – This is the main hall of the temple and is often found at the centre of the compound. Housed within this structure are the main images of the Buddha as well as other elements of a Buddhist altar. The central image often has offerings of incense sticks, food or flowers placed before it. This is where worship takes place and lay people are sometimes excluded from entry on all but special occasions.

Kōdō – This is the lecture hall where monks gather to study and recite scriptures. It is often beside the main hall.

Mon – This means gate and refers to both the large outer gate of the temple *(daimon)* and the smaller inner gate *(chūmon)*. Housed within these gates you will sometimes find two fierce-looking guardian figures *(niō)*.

Kyōzō – This is the *sutra* repository which is used to store the sacred scriptures of the temple. Often built in the shape of a log cabin on stilts, this structure is designed to maintain a constant internal temperature to guard the sutras against decay.

Other Structures – On the periphery of the compound you will also find the monks' daily living areas, like the dining hall and the dormitory. Other halls, particularly in the grander temples, exhibit temple treasures. Of course, now that many temples are operated as business concerns, you will also find a temple office. Talismans and fortunes are often on sale in these offices. ■

A secluded setting for meditators – small mountain hut in remote Aomori

MASON FLORENCE

Castles The first Japanese castles were simple mountain forts which relied more on natural terrain than on structural innovations for defence. The great disadvantage of such structures was that they were as inaccessible to those defending them as to the enemy they were defending against.

The 'plain's castle' *(hira-jiro)*, the kind mostly seen in Japan today, evolved from the fortified residences of chieftains built on flatter terrain. By the Momoyama period, castle architecture had reached a level of great sophistication, producing masterworks of impregnability and grace, such as Himeji-jō, Osaka-jō and Fushimi-jō castles. Defences became ever more elaborate, with the addition of stone walls, moats, earthworks and labyrinthine mazes of halls and tunnels within the castles. Around the castles grew *jōka-machi* – castle towns.

The central feature of the castle was the *tenshu*, a tower or keep. The larger castles, such as Himeji-jō, had several tenshu ranged around the central one, and the various gates were also mounted with fortifications. The buildings atop stone ramparts were mostly built of wood, but the wood was covered with plaster to protect it against fire and firearms.

The wide-ranging wars of the 16th and 17th centuries left Japan with a huge number of castles. In 1615 the Edo government, seeking to rein in the power of local *daimyō* (domain lords), ordered that there be only one castle to each domain. In the years of peace that followed the castle fell into disuse. Their fortunes have revived in the 20th century thanks to mass tourism.

INGO WESTNER

Fortified by an elaborate system of high walls and moats, five-storeyed Himeji-jō Castle is a classic example of a military stronghold in Tokugawa Japan

Houses With the exception of the northern island of Hokkaidō, traditional Japanese houses are built with the broiling heat of summer in mind. They are made of flimsy materials designed to take advantage of even the slightest breeze. The reasoning behind this is that it is easier to bundle up in winter than it is to cool down in summer. Before the advent of air-conditioning, this was certainly the case. Another reason behind the gossamer construction of Japanese houses is the relative frequency of earthquakes in the country, which precludes the use of heavier building materials such as stone or brick.

A particularly traditional type of Japanese house is the *machiya* (townhouse) built by merchants in cities like Kyoto and Tokyo. Until very recently, the older neighbourhoods of Kyoto and some areas of Tokyo were lined with neat, narrow rows of these houses, but most have fallen victim to the current frenzy of construction. These days, the best place to see machiya is in eastern Kyoto, near Kiyomizu-dera Temple. Takayama, as well as the post towns along the Kiso Valley, are also good spots to

The narrow exterior of a Kyoto townhouse – its fine window detail, designed to let in light and air but maintain privacy, is typical of machiya architecture

THOMAS DANIELL

view traditional machiya architecture. The more elegant mansions of the noble classes and warriors, with their elaborate receiving rooms, sculptured gardens and tea huts, can also be viewed in places like Kyoto, Nara and Kanazawa and former feudal cities scattered around Japan.

Farmhouses The most distinctive type of Japanese farmhouse is the thatched roof *gasshō-zukuri*, so named for the shape of the rafters which resemble a pair of praying hands. While such farmhouses look cosy and romantic, one must remember that they were often home for up to 40 people and occasionally farm animals as well. Furthermore, the lack of windows, black floorboards and soot-covered ceiling guaranteed a cave-like atmosphere. The only weapon against this darkness was a fire built in a central fireplace in the floor known as an *irori*, which also provided warmth in the cooler months and hot coals for cooking. Multi-storey farmhouses were also built to house silkworms for silk production (particularly prevalent during the Meiji era) in the airy upper gables.

MASON FLORENCE

Traditional farmhouses, capped by thick, high-pitched thatched roofs, in Miyama-cho, Kyoto

Kura Japan's traditional *kura* (storehouses) are instantly recognisable by their white plaster walls. The use of a thick coat of plaster was not merely decorative but was designed to protect the building and the valuables stored inside from the frequent fires which plagued Japanese cities. The plaster seems to have done its job, and many kura survive to this day in villages like Imai-cho in Nara, Kurashiki in Western Honshū and Kitakata in Northern Honshū.

Gardens

Unlike European gardens, you won't find flowers, water fountains and flowing streams in Japanese gardens; grass rarely makes an appearance. No matter how random a Japanese garden looks – with its mossy rocks, gnarled roots, haphazard paving and paths that meander like a daydream – it is meticulously planned, right down to the last pebble. In the best Japanese gardens there is an exquisite 'compositional' quality, and no component is without a nuance of meaning. Even features that lay outside the garden may influence the layout – *shakkei*, or borrowed scenery, may make use of distant hills or a river, even the cone of a volcano. One example of this is the garden at Shūgaku-in Imperial Villa in Kyoto, which uses mountains 10 km distant as elements in its composition.

Japanese gardens fall into four basic types: *funa asobi* (pleasure boat style), *shūyū* (stroll style), *kanshō* (contemplative style) and *kaiyū* (many pleasure style).

The funa asobi garden is centred on a large pond used for pleasure boating. The best views are from the water. In the Heian period, such gardens were often built around noble mansions, the most outstanding remaining example being the garden which surrounds Byōdō-in Temple in southern Kyoto.

The finely manicured, wandering moss garden of Taizo-in subtemple – Myōshin Temple, Kyoto

ANTHONY WEERSING

The shūyū garden is intended to be viewed from a winding path, allowing the garden to unfold and reveal itself in stages and from different vantages. Popular during the Heian, Kamakura and Muromachi periods, shūyū gardens can be found around many noble mansions and temples from those eras. A celebrated example is at Ginkaku-ji Temple in Kyoto.

The kanshō garden should be viewed from one place; Zen rock gardens, the rock and raked gravel spaces that are also known as *kare sansui*, or dry mountain stream gardens, are an example of this sort. The kanshō garden is designed to facilitate contemplation: such a garden can be viewed over and over again without yielding to any one 'interpretation' of its meaning. The most famous kanshō garden of all is at Kyoto's Ryoan-ji Temple.

Lastly, the kaiyū, or many pleasure garden, features many small gardens surrounding a central pond, often incorporating a teahouse. The structure of this garden, like the stroll garden, lends itself to being explored on foot, and provides the viewer with a variety of changing scenes, many built as miniature landscapes. The most famous kaiyū garden is at the Katsura Rikyū Imperial Villa in western Kyoto.

THOMAS DANIELL

A classic rock and raked gravel garden at Tōfuku-ji Temple, Kyoto

Fine Arts

Painting The techniques and materials used in the early stages of Japanese painting owed much to Chinese influence. But by the end of the Heian period, the emphasis on religious themes painted according to Chinese conventions gave way to a purely Japanese style of painting. Known as Yamato-e, this style covered indigenous subjects and was frequently used in scroll paintings and on screens.

Ink paintings *(suiboku-ga* or *sumi-e)* by Chinese Zen artists were introduced to Japan during the Muromachi period and copied by Japanese artists, who produced hanging pictures *(kakemono)*, scrolls *(emaki)* and decorated screens and sliding doors.

During the Momoyama period, Japan's daimyō flaunted their wealth and power by commissioning artists who painted in flamboyant colours and embellished with copious gold leaf. The most popular themes depicted Japanese nature (plants, trees and seasons) or characters from Chinese legends. The Kanō school was the most famous of such painting styles.

Western techniques of painting, including the use of oils, were introduced during the 16th century by the Jesuits. Japanese painters who combined western and Japanese styles sometimes produced interesting results: portraits of westerners thoughtfully included an oriental incline to the eyes.

MATTHIAS LEY

Detail from a painted fusuma (sliding panel) – Tenryu-ji Temple, Kyoto

The Edo period was marked by the enthusiastic patronage of a wide range of painting styles. The Kanō school continued to be in demand for the depiction of subjects connected with Confucianism, mythical Chinese creatures or scenes from nature. The Tosa school, whose members followed the Yamato-e style of painting, was kept busy with commissions from the nobility to paint scenes from the ancient classics of Japanese literature.

The Rimpa school not only absorbed the style of other schools (Chinese, Kanō and Tosa), but progressed beyond their conventions to produce strikingly original decorative painting. The works of art produced by a trio of outstanding artists from this school (Tawaraya Sōtatsu, Hon'ami Kōetsu and Ogata Kōrin) rank among the finest of this period.

Irezumi

Japanese *irezumi*-tattooing – is widely considered the best of its kind. In feudal times, the authorities tattooed criminals, thus stigmatising them as 'branded'. In due course, those who had been tattooed exhibited a kind of defiant pride in their markings, which set them apart from others in society.

Japanese tattoos, usually completed in blue and red natural dyes, often cover the whole body with intricate designs featuring auspicious animals, flowers, Buddhist deities or subjects drawn from Japanese folktales.

As a sop to foreign sensibilities, tattooing was banned during the Meiji era, but was promptly reinstated after the Prince of Wales (later to become the UK's King George V) took a liking to the art and had a rampant dragon inscribed on his arm in 1881.

Nowadays, many ordinary Japanese shun tattoos; it is a fair assumption that any Japanese you see flaunting tattoos are either Yakuza (Japanese mafia types) or have connections with the shady side of society. ■

Calligraphy *Shōdō* ('the way of writing') is one of Japan's most valued arts, cultivated by nobles, priests and samurai alike and still studied by Japanese schoolchildren today as *shūji*.

Like the characters of the Japanese language itself, the art of shodō was imported from China. In the Heian period, a distinctly Japanese style of shodō evolved called *wayō*. This is more fluid and cursive than the purely Chinese style, which is referred to as *karayō*. The Chinese style remained popular in Japan even after the Heian period among Zen priests and the literati.

In both Chinese and Japanese shodō there are three important types. Most common is *kaisho*, or block-style script. Due to its clarity, this style is favoured in the media and in applications where readability is a must. *Gyōsho*, or running hand, is semi-cursive, and often used in informal correspondence. *Sōsho*, or grass hand, is a truly cursive style. Sōsho abbreviates and links the characters together to create a flowing, graceful effect; it is popular for calligraphy.

Ukiyo-e If there is one art form that westerners instantly associate with Japan, it is the ukiyo-e, or wood-block print. Ukiyo-e ('pictures of the floating world') comes from the term 'ukiyo' – a Buddhist metaphor for the transient world of fleeting pleasures. The subjects chosen by artists were characters and scenes from the 'floating world' of the entertainment quarters in Edo (modern-day Tokyo), Kyoto and Osaka.

Hanging scroll in the wayō style, reading 'Praise to the god of Tenmangu' (god of calligraphy), by Prince Shoren-in (16th century) – Alex Kerr Collection

The floating world, centred in pleasure districts like Edo's Yoshiwara, was a topsy-turvy kingdom, an inversion of all the usual social hierarchies that were held in place by the power of the Tokugawa shogunate. Here, money counted for more than rank, actors and artists were the arbiters of style, and prostitutes elevated their art to such a level that their social and artistic accomplishments matched those of the ladies of noble families. Added to this was an element of spectacle. Both kabuki and sumo, with their ritualised visual opulence, found large popular audiences in this period.

The vivid colours, novel composition and flowing lines of ukiyo-e caused great excitement in the west, sparking a vogue which a French art critic dubbed 'Japonisme'. Ukiyo-e became a key influence on impressionist (for example, Toulouse-Lautrec, Manet and Degas) and post-impressionist artists. But among the Japanese the prints were hardly given more than passing consideration – millions were produced annually in Edo. They were cheap items, often thrown away or used as wrapping paper for pottery. For many years, the Japanese continued to be perplexed by the keen interest foreigners took in this art form which they considered of ephemeral value.

The first prints of ukiyo-e were made in black and white in the early 17th century; the technique for colour printing was only developed in the middle of the 18th century. The success of a publisher lay in close cooperation between the artist, engraver and printer through all stages of production.

The first stage required the artist *(eshi)* to draw a design on transparent paper and indicate the colouring needed. The engraver *(horishi)* then pasted the design face down on a block of cherry wood and carved out the lines of the design in relief. The printer *(surishi)* inked the block and took a proof. Each colour required a separate block; it was up to the printer to use his skill to obtain accurate alignment and subtle colour effects that depended on the colour mixture and pressure applied.

The reputed founder of ukiyo-e is Iwa Matabei. The genre was later developed by Hishikawa Moronobu, who rose to fame with his illustrations for erotic tales. His wood-block prints of scenes from the entertainment district of Yoshiwara introduced the theme of *bijin-e* (paint-

MATTHIAS LEY

ings of beautiful women), which later became a standard subject. Early themes also covered scenes from the theatre (including the actors) and the erotic *shunga*. Kitagawa Utamarō is famed for his bijin-e which emphasise the erotic and sensual beauty of his subjects. All that is known about Tōshūsai Sharaku, a painting prodigy whose life is a mystery, is that he produced 145 superb portraits of kabuki actors between 1794 and 1795.

Towards the end of the Edo period, two painters produced outstanding works in this art genre. Katsushika Hokusai was a prolific artist who observed his fellow inhabitants of Edo with a keen sense of humour. His most famous works include manga (cartoons), *Fugaku Sanjūrokkei* (Thirty-Six Views of Mt Fuji) and *Fugaku Hyakkei* (One Hundred Views of Mt Fuji). As Hokusai approached the end of his life – he died at the age of 89 – he delighted in signing his works with the pen name *gakyōrōjin* (literally, 'old man mad with painting').

Andō Hiroshige followed Hokusai, specialising in landscapes, although he also created splendid prints of plants and birds. His most celebrated works include *Tōkaidō Gojūsan-tsugi* (Fifty-Three Stations of the Tōkaidō), *Meisho Edo Hyakukei* (One Hundred Views of Famous Places in Edo) and *Omi Hakkei* (Eight Views of Omi) – Omi is now known as Lake Biwa-ko.

The sliding panels and doors of aristocratic mansions were often decorated with elaborate landcape paintings – Confucian scholars, reclusive monks, curly-maned lions, pine trees and exotic birds were common themes

ANTHONY WEERSING

Crafts

Craftworkers have always enjoyed the same esteem accorded artists and their works prized as highly as works of fine art. Indeed, the whole distinction between art and craft is quite artificial in Japan, as many crafts are produced purely as works of art (lacquerware, for example) and many works of art are made to be used in daily life (painted screens). The following is a brief survey of the major crafts of Japan.

Ceramics & Pottery Ceramic art in Japan is usually considered to have started around the 13th century with the introduction of Chinese ceramic techniques and the founding of a kiln in 1242 at Seto in Aichi by Tōshirō. The Japanese term for pottery and porcelain, *setomono* (literally, 'things from Seto'), clearly derives from this still thriving ceramics centre.

During the following century, five more kilns were established: Tokoname, Shigaraki, Bizen, Echizen and Tamba. Together with Seto, these were known as the 'Six Ancient Kilns' and acquired a reputation for high-quality stoneware.

The popularity of the tea ceremony in the 16th century stimulated developments in ceramics. The great tea masters, Furuta Oribe and Sen no Rikyū, promoted production of exquisite Oribe and Shino wares in Gifu. The powerful shogun Toyotomi Hideyoshi, who thought nothing of plastering the walls of his tearoom with gold, encouraged the master potter Chōjiro to create works of art from clay found near Hideyoshi's palace. Chōjiro was allowed to embellish the tea bowls he created with the character *raku* (enjoyment). This was the beginning of Kyoto's famous *raku-yaki* style of pottery. Tea bowls became highly prized objects commanding stupendous prices. Even today, connoisseurs of the tradition of the tea ceremony are happy to shell out as much as US$30,000 for the right tea bowl.

Hideyoshi's invasion of Korea at the end of the 16th century was a

Living National Treasures

Beat Takeshi, an irreverent local comedian, once presented himself at the Agency for Cultural Affairs with a request that he be designated a 'Living National Treasure'. He was unsuccessful. But he wasn't attempting the impossible. In Japan it is not a requirement that you be an inanimate work of art to be designated a national treasure.

'Living National Treasure' has a nice ring to it and would certainly look impressive on a *meishi* (business card). How do you become one? Well, for a start, you need to be Japanese. Secondly you need to be involved in the traditional arts, crafts or performing arts of Japan, more specifically to be a 'Bearer of Important Intangible Cultural Assets', which is, for the record, how Living National Treasures are more properly addressed.

Living National Treasures first came into being in 1955 as a result of the 1950 Law for the Protection of Cultural Assets. It is difficult to see how appointing people Living National Treasures protects them in any way (perhaps there are 'no touching' laws) but, by 1990, 97 individuals had been officially 'treasured' in the fields of *kabuki*, *nō*, *bunraku* and traditional music and dance, and a further 92 in the fields of Japanese crafts such as ceramics, paper making, weaving and lacquer. New appointments and new categories are made annually. Perhaps Beat still has a chance. ■

military disaster, but it proved to be a boon to Japanese ceramics when captured Korean potters introduced Japan to the art of manufacturing porcelain. In 1598, a Korean master potter, Ri Sampei, built the first porcelain kiln at Arita in Kyūshū.

During the Edo period, many daimyō encouraged the founding of kilns and the production of superbly designed ceramic articles. The climbing kiln *(noborigama)* was widely used. Constructed on a slope, the kiln had as many as 20 chambers and the capability to achieve temperatures as high as 1400°C.

During the Meiji period, ceramics waned in popularity, but were later included in a general revival of interest in *mingei-hin* (folk arts) headed by Yanagi Sōetsu, who encouraged famous potters such as Kawai Kanjirō, Tomimoto Kenkichi and Hamada Shōji. The English potter Bernard Leach studied in Japan under Hamada and contributed to the folk-art revival. On his return to Cornwall in England, Leach maintained his interest in Japanese ceramics and promoted their appreciation in the west.

There are now over 100 pottery centres in Japan with large numbers of artisans producing everything from exclusive tea utensils to souvenir badgers *(tanuki)*. Department stores regularly organise exhibitions of ceramics. Master potters are highly revered and the government designates the finest as 'Living National Treasures'.

The Tourist Information Center's (TIC) useful *Ceramic Art & Crafts in Japan* leaflet is published by the Japan National Tourist Organization (JNTO) and provides full details of pottery centres, kilns and pottery fairs in Japan.

Lacquerware The Japanese have been using lacquer to protect and enhance the beauty of wood since the Jōmon period. In the Meiji era, lacquerware became very popular abroad and remains one of Japan's best known products. Known in Japan as *shikki* or *nurimono*, lacquerware is made using the sap from the lacquer tree *(urushi* in Japanese). Raw lacquer is actually toxic and causes a severe irritation of the skin in

Modern Shigaraki-yaki piece from Shiga – a style once favoured by tea master Sen no Rikkyū (1522-91) for crafting tea bowls

ANTHONY WEERSING

those who have not developed an immunity. Once hardened, however, it becomes inert and extraordinarily durable. The most common colour of lacquer is an amber or brown colour, but additives have been used to produce black, violet, blue, yellow and even white lacquer. In the better pieces, multiple layers of lacquer are painstakingly applied and left to dry, and finally polished to a luxurious shine.

Japanese artisans have devised various ways to further enhance the beauty of lacquer. The most common method is called *maki-e* which was developed in the 8th century. Here, silver and gold powders are sprinkled onto the liquid lacquer to form a picture. After the lacquer dries, another coat of lacquer is applied to seal the picture. The final effect is often dazzling and some of the better pieces of maki-e lacquerware are now national treasures.

ANTHONY WEERSING

Finely crafted hair ornaments with coloured lacquer and elaborate gold inlay

Famous Ceramic Centres

Arita-yaki (Arita, Kyūshū) – Arita porcelain is still produced in the town where the first Japanese porcelain was made. In the mid-17th century, the Dutch East India Company exported these wares to Europe, where they were soon copied in ceramics factories such as those of the Germans (Meissen), the Dutch (Delft) and the English (Worcester). It is commonly known to westerners as 'Imari' after the name of the port from which it was shipped. The Kakiemon style uses designs of birds and flowers in bright colours. Another popular style is executed in blue and white and incorporates scenes from legends and daily life.

Satsuma-yaki (Kagoshima, Kyūshū) – The most common style of this porcelain has a white, cloudy, cracked glaze enamelled with gold, red, green and blue.

Karatsu-yaki (Karatsu, Kyūshū) – Karatsu, near Fukuoka in northern Kyūshū, produces tea ceremony utensils which are Korean in style and have a characteristic greyish, crackled glaze.

Hagi-yaki (Hagi, Honshū) – The town of Hagi in Western Honshū is renowned for Hagi-yaki, a type of porcelain made with a pallid yellow or pinkish crackled glaze.

Bizen-yaki (Bizen, Honshū) – The ancient ceramics centre of Bizen in Okayama-ken is famed for its chunky, unglazed bowls which turn red through oxidation. Bizen also produces roofing tiles.

Mashiko-yaki (Mashiko, Honshū) – The town of Mashiko in Tochigi-ken, Northern Honshū, is renowned as a folk craft centre producing wares with a distinctive reddish glaze.

Mino-yaki (Toki, Honshū) – From Toki in Gifu-ken in Central Honshū come pieces executed in the Oribe style which have a greenish glaze and are decorated with creatures and flowers; the Shino style, greatly prized by connoisseurs of tea utensils, employs a heavy white glaze.

Temmoku-yaki (Seto, Honshū) – Seto city in Aichi-ken, Central Honshū, has a long tradition as a ceramics centre. The standard product is ash-glazed, heavy stoneware, but Seto also produces special ceramic wares such as *temmoku*, an ancient Chinese style which uses a brown and black glaze.

Kiyomizu-yaki (Kyoto, Honshū) – The approach road to the Kiyomizu-dera Temple in Kyoto is lined with shops selling Kiyomizu-yaki, a style of pottery which can be enamelled, blue-painted or red-painted.

Kutani-yaki (Ishikawa, Honshū) – The porcelain from Ishikawa-ken in Central Honshū is usually green or painted. ■

Washi *Washi*, traditional Japanese handmade paper, was introduced from China in the 5th century. Its golden age was the Heian era, when washi was highly prized by members of the Kyoto court for writing poetry and diaries. Colours were added to produce patterns (silver and gold leaf was often applied), and sometimes paper was made to especially complement the mood of a particular poem. Washi continued to be made in large quantities until the introduction of western paper in the 1870s. After that time, the number of families involved in papermaking plummeted to only 851 in 1973.

Recently, washi has enjoyed something of a revival and a large variety of colourful, patterned paper is available in speciality stores, including one (Kakimoto Washi) in Kyoto which sells washi for use in computer printers.

Textiles Textiles have always played an important role in Japanese society: the fabric used in a kimono was an indication of class status. Until the introduction of cotton to Japan in the 16th century, Japanese textiles were made mostly of bast fibres or silk. Of all Japanese textiles, intricately embroidered brocades have always been the most highly prized, but sumptuary laws imposed on the merchant class in the Edo period prohibited the wearing of such kimonos. To circumvent these laws, new techniques of kimono decoration were devised – the most important being the technique of *yūzen* dyeing. In this technique, rice-paste is applied to the fabric like a stencil to prevent a colour from bleeding onto other areas of the fabric. By repeatedly changing the pattern of the rice-paste, very complex designs can be achieved.

At the other end of the spectrum, *aizome* (the technique of dyeing fabrics in vats of fermented indigo plants) gave Japan one of its most distinctive colours. Used traditionally in making hardy work clothes for the fields, Japan's beautiful indigo-blue can still be seen in many modern-day textile goods.

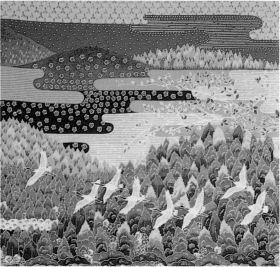

Highly decorated sheet of washi paper – not only functional, it's also durable and quite beautiful

ANTHONY WEERSING

Carpentry If jade is the perfect medium for the expression of the Chinese artistic genius, then for the Japanese it is wood. Perhaps nowhere in the world has the art of joinery been lifted to such high levels as it has in Japan.

This genius for joinery translates well to the art of cabinetry. Particularly prized by collectors of Japanese antiques are chests called *tansu*. Perhaps the most prized of all tansu is the *kaidan dansu*, so named because it resembles a flight of stairs ('kaidan' is the Japanese word for stairs). These are becoming increasingly difficult to find, but determined hunting at flea markets and antique stores may still turn up the occasional good piece; but don't expect any bargains.

ANTHONY WEERSING

Tansu piece with washi-covered panels

Dolls Dolls have played a part in Japanese society from prehistoric times, when the rites of burial demanded that clay figures be buried along with the dead. During the Kofun period of ancient Japan, burial mounds of emperors and nobles were usually surrounded by hundreds of haniwa clay figures, some in human form.

Today, dolls still figure prominently in two Japanese festivals: the Hina Matsuri (Doll Festival), held on 3 March, when girls display ornamental *hina-ningyō* dolls on tiered platforms as part of the festivities; and on Children's Day, held of 5 May, when both boys and girls display special dolls.

Some of the more common dolls today are: *daruma dolls*, which are based on the figure of Bodhidarma, who brought Buddhism to China from India; *gosho-ningyō dolls*, chubby plaster dolls sometimes dressed as figures in *nō* dramas; *kyō-ningyō dolls*, elaborate dolls made in Kyoto, dressed in fine brocade fabrics; *kiku-ningyō dolls*, large dolls covered by real chrysanthemum flowers; and *ishō-ningyō dolls*, which is a general term for elaborately costumed dolls, sometimes based on kabuki characters.

Bamboo Crafts Japanese bamboo baskets are among the finest in the world, and are remarkable for their complexity and delicacy (as well as their price). Tools used in the tea ceremony, like ladles and tea whisks, are also made of bamboo and make interesting souvenirs. Be careful when buying bamboo crafts in Japan as many are not Japanese at all, but cheap imitations imported from other parts of Asia.

ANTHONY WEERSING

The elegant look of a kyō-ningyō

Bonsai A skill imported from China during the Kamakura era, Bonsai is the artificial dwarfing of trees, or the miniaturisation of nature.

Bonsai trees are carefully clipped and their roots pruned to keep their dwarf dimensions. Some specimens have been handed down over generations and are extremely valuable. A related art is *bonkei*, which is the technique of reproducing nature on a small tray using moss, clay, sand, etc.

TIC offices can provide further information on where to find or practice bonsai. Large hotels or department stores often have bonsai displays. Devotees of the art should make the 30 minute trip outside Tokyo to visit the Bonsai Village at Bonsai-machi, Ōmiya, Saitama.

Flower Arrangement

Ikebana, the art of flower arranging, developed in the 15th century and can be grouped into four main styles: *rikka* (standing flowers), *nageire* (throwing-in), *shōkai* (living flowers) and *moribana* (heaped flowers). There are several thousand different schools at present, the top three of which are Ikenobō, Ōhara and Sōgetsu, but they share one aim: to arrange flowers to represent heaven, earth and humanity. Ikebana displays were originally used as part of the tea ceremony but can now be found in private homes – in the *tokonoma* (alcove for displays) – and even in large hotels.

Apart from its cultural associations, ikebana is also a lucrative business – its schools have millions of students, including many young women who view proficiency in the art as a means to improve their marriage prospects.

To find out more about courses for foreigners, contact Ikebana International (☎ 03-3293-8188), Ochanomizu Square Building, 1-6 Surugadai, Kanda, Chiyoda-ku, Tokyo. Some schools provide instruction in English; prices start around ¥3000 an hour.

Tea Ceremony

Chanoyu, also known as *sadō*, or 'the way of tea', dates back to the Nara period, when it was used by meditating Buddhist monks to promote alertness. By the 14th century it had developed into a highly elaborate and expensive pursuit for the aristocracy.

The turning point for the tea ceremony took place in the 16th century. Sen no Rikkyū (1522-91) established a spartan aesthetic, using utensils that echoed the irregularities of the natural world. Other tea masters took different approaches, and today the tea ceremony can be divided into the three Senke schools (Ura, Omote and Mushakoji) and other influential schools such as Enshu, Yabunouchi and Sohen.

The traditional setting for the tea ceremony is a thatched teahouse in the setting of a landscaped garden. The preparation and drinking of the tea is conducted according to a highly stylised etiquette and the mental discipline involved was once an essential part of the training of a samurai warrior. Novices tend to find the proceedings fatiguing, and connoisseurs maintain that full appreciation of the art takes years of training and reflection.

For a demonstration of chanoyu in Tokyo or Kyoto ask for details at the TIC or check with the large hotels; prices for a basic session start at ¥1000. A classic treatment of this subject, written with precision and devotion, is *The Book of Tea* (Dover Publications, New York, 1964) by Okakura Kakuzō.

Performing Arts

The two most famous Japanese theatrical traditions are kabuki and nō. Both are fascinating, but without a great deal of prior study, don't expect to understand much of the proceedings. This is not a major problem as both forms work well on the level of spectacle. Even native Japanese speakers have difficulties understanding the archaic Japanese used in traditional theatre, so although you may have spent the last few years diligently working on your Japanese, it probably won't be much use to you. Fortunately, some theatres in Tokyo and Kyoto (the two places where you are most likely to see kabuki or nō) have programmes with a synopsis of the play in English, and headphones are sometimes available for a commentary in English.

The best source for details of performances is the TIC in Tokyo or Kyoto. Some local publications such as *Tokyo Journal*, *Tour Companion* in Kyoto and *Kansai Time Out* also publish theatre information. If you want to watch drama productions on TV in Tokyo, check the programme on channels 1 and 3. If you want to delve deeper into the subject the following publications may be useful: *The Kabuki Handbook* by Aubrey & Giovanna Halford (Tuttle, New York, 1979); *The Nō Plays of Japan* by Arthur Waley (Tuttle, Tokyo, 1976); *A Guide to Nō* by PG O'Neill (Hinoki Shōten, Tokyo & Kyoto, 1954); *A Guide to Kyōgen* by Don Kenny (Hinoki Shōten, Tokyo & Kyoto, 1968); or *The Bunraku Handbook* by Hironaga Shuzaburō (Maison des Arts, Tokyo, 1976).

Kabuki The origins of kabuki lie in the early 17th century, when it was known as *kabuki odori*, which can be loosely translated as avant-garde dance. Its first exponent was a maiden of Izumo Taisha Shrine who led a troupe of women dancers to raise funds for the shrine. It quickly caught on and was soon being performed with prostitutes in the lead roles. With performances plumbing ever greater depths of lewdness, the Tokugawa government banned women from the kabuki stage. The women were promptly replaced with attractive young men of no less availability. The exasperated authorities issued yet another decree, this time commanding that kabuki roles be taken by older men.

This move had a profound effect on kabuki. The roles played by these older male actors required greater artistry to be brought off credibly. The result was that, while remaining a popular art form that gave expression to popular themes, kabuki also metamorphosed into a serious art form, with the more famous of its practitioners becoming the stuff of which legends are made.

Kabuki is a theatre of spectacle, of larger-than-life gestures, and as such employs opulent sets, a boom-crash orchestra and a ramp through the audience that allows important actors to get the most mileage out of

---

The Art of the Dropped Word

Rakugo, the Chinese character for which literally means 'the dropped word', is the art of comic narrative that dates back to the late 16th century. It is thought to have emerged from the warlord practice of including comic storytellers in their retinues for light amusement, similar to the European tradition of the court jester. By the 1670s, however, professional performers had found an audience in the emerging urban cultures of major cities such as Edo (modern-day Tokyo). Rakugo underwent a process of refinement and a corresponding elevation in status as the years passed, and in 1791 the first permanent rakugo performance venue was established in Edo. By the mid-19th century, the performance art had grown so popular that there were 200 halls in Edo alone. The assault of new media entertainments in the 20th century has reduced the number of Tokyo halls drastically, though performances can still be seen on TV and in a few remaining rakugo venues, and heard on the radio from time to time.

Rakugo is delivered by a solitary performer seated on a cushion in the centre of a propless stage. Performers are unaccompanied, except for a brief musical flourish of *shamisen*, flute and drums, which announce their entrance and exit. Vocal mimicry (from the voices of characters to natural sounds such as the gurgling of water) and facial contortions are used to comic and dramatic effect throughout the storytelling, which is drawn from a small established repertoire of rakugo plots. Like *kabuki* drama, where the performer rules supreme, the prestige of rakugo raconteurs draws not on the story they tell but on the way they tell it, their digressions, the unexpected details that bring an old tale to life.

Why is it called 'the dropped word'? The name refers to the conclusion of a rakugo tale, which culminates in a punch line, known in Japanese as *ochi*. Ochi is a Japanese reading of the Chinese character *raku* – 'drop'. ■

their melodramatically stylised entrances and exits. Initially, it featured plebeian versions of nō classics but, as this displeased the Tokugawa government, kabuki was compelled to develop a canon of its own. It did so by drawing on disparate themes, both modern and historical. For the most part kabuki deals with feudal tragedies of divided loyalties, of the struggle between duty and inner feelings; the latter has produced a large body of work on the theme of love suicides.

Unlike the theatre of the west, the playwright is not the applauded champion of kabuki. The play is merely a vehicle for the genius of the actor; he is remembered long after the writer who put the words in his mouth is forgotten.

The main kabuki theatres in Japan are the Kabuki-za and National theatres in Tokyo, the Minami-za Theater in Kyoto and the Shin Kabuki-za Theater in Osaka.

Nō Nō is an older form of theatre than kabuki, dating back some 600 years. It seems to have evolved as a cross-pollination between both indigenous Shinto-related dance and mime traditions, and dance forms that had their origins elsewhere in Asia. It was adopted as a courtly performing art, and in this capacity underwent numerous refinements.

Masked nō character – the mask is so highly crafted that, when tilted at different angles under lights, it conveys the mood of the character

MASON FLORENCE

The result was an essentially religious theatre whose aesthetic codes were defined by the austerities and the minimalism of Zen. Unlike the spectacle of kabuki, the power of nō lies in understatement. And in this respect – its use of masks as a mode of expression and the bleak emptiness of the sets, directing all attention to the performers – nō has been a form of Japanese theatre that has fascinated western artists searching for a more elementally powerful theatre in which to express themselves. Of these, perhaps the most famous is WB Yeats.

One of the most interesting aspects of nō is the formalised structure of its plays. Two performers alone are vital to its presentation – the one who watches *(waki)* and the one who acts *(shite)*. Remembering that nō is a theatre of masks, it is the role of the one who watches to, as it were, demask the one who acts. The reason is that the shite is not who he or she seems. Usually the shite is a ghost whose spirit has lingered on in a particular place because of some tragedy that took place in the past. The recognition, the demasking by the waki, gives way to the second act, in which the shite dances a re-enactment of the tragedy, and reveals his or her true identity.

Whether this is a kind of cathartic liberation or a sorrowful celebration of the lingering pain of the tragedy is partly dependent on whether the story is a happy one or not. It also depends on how you interpret the sometimes quite bizarre but nevertheless spell-binding proceedings of the nō performance.

For nō, the main theatres are the National Nō, Kanze Nōgaku-dō and Tessenkai Nōgaku Institute theatres in Tokyo, the Kongō Nōgaku-dō Theatre and Kanze Nōgaku-dō Kaikan in Kyoto and the Osaka Nō Kaikan in Osaka.

MATTHIAS LEY

Unlike heavily costumed nō and kabuki actors, butō perfomers usually appear near nude or smeared by white or coloured body paint

Kyōgen *Kyōgen* is a comic drama that evolved hand in hand with nō. It originally served as an interlude, a little light relief within the more serious business of a nō play, but came to stand on its own and is now more often performed separately between two different nō plays. Unlike the heavily symbolic nō, kyōgen draws on the real world for its subject matter and is acted in colloquial Japanese. The subjects of its satire are often samurai, depraved priests and faithless women – the performers are without masks and a chorus often accompanies.

Performances are often held at the major nō theatres, such as the ones mentioned above.

Bunraku Like kabuki, *bunraku* developed in the Edo period. It is Japan's professional puppet theatre, using puppets that are a half to two-thirds life-size and hand-held and controlled by three puppeteers dressed in black robes and usually hooded. The puppeteers often make little attempt to hide their presence, which can seem obtrusive until you get used to concentrating on the puppets rather than their manipulators. On a raised dais near the stage, a narrator *(tayū)* tells the story and provides the voices for individual characters, while musical accompaniment is provided by the three-stringed *shamisen*.

The main bunraku theatres are the National Theater in Tokyo, Gion Corner in Kyoto and the Asahiza and National Bunraku theatres in Osaka.

Butō *Butō* is Japanese experimental/avant-garde dance which was born in the '60s and has received considerable international acclaim. Butō dancers perform nearly nude, with loincloths and body paint. Movement is slow, drawn-out and occasionally grotesque. The exaggerated expressions of butō are intended to express the emotions of the dancers and choreographer in the most direct way possible. While this may not be to everyone's liking, it is, in some ways, more accessible that other types of Japanese performance art, as all meaning is conveyed with physical movement.

Unfortunately for those interested in seeing butō performed, most butō troupes are small, underground affairs. The best way to find out if there are any shows going on during your visit is to check with the TIC.

Music

Ancient Music *Gagaku* is the 'elegant' music of the Japanese imperial court which was derived from Chinese models. It flourished between the 8th and 12th centuries, then declined for several centuries until it became part of a revival of interest in national traditions during the Meiji period.

Court orchestras were divided into two sections with formally prescribed functions. The orchestra of the 'right' dressed in green, blue or yellow and played Korean music. The orchestra of the 'left' dressed in red and played Chinese, Indian or Japanese music. The repertoire of an orchestra included *kangen* (instrumental) pieces and *bugaku* (dance) pieces.

Nowadays, a gagaku ensemble usually consists of 16 players performing on drums and kettle drums, string instruments such as the *biwa* (lute) and *koto* (plucked zither) and wind instruments such as the *hichiriki* (Japanese oboe) and various types of flute.

Traditional Instruments There are several traditional Japanese instruments which continue to play a part in Japanese life, both publicly and privately. Some are used in orchestras or the theatre, while others are used for solo performances.

The shamisen is a three-stringed instrument resembling a banjo with an extended neck. It was very popular during the Edo period, particularly in the entertainment districts of Osaka and Edo. It is still used as formal accompaniment in Japanese theatre (kabuki and bunraku), and the ability to perform on the shamisen remains one of the essential skills of a geisha.

The koto is a type of plucked zither with 13 strings. It was adapted from a Chinese instrument before the 8th century and the number of strings gradually increased from five to 13. A bass koto, with 17 strings, has since been created this century – leading to an even greater musical range for this ancient instrument.

MATTHIAS LEY

Shamisen musicians performing in Gion, Kyoto's famed geisha quarter

The biwa, which resembles a lute, was also derived from a Chinese instrument and appeared in Japan in the 8th century. It was played by travelling musicians, often blind, who recited Buddhist *sutras* (collections of dialogues and discourses) to the accompaniment of the instrument. During the Heian period, the biwa was used in court orchestras. In the succeeding Kamakura period, storytellers created a different style for the biwa to accompany tales from medieval war epics, the most famous of which are the *Tales of Heike*. Although biwa ballads were in vogue during the 16th century, the instrument later fell out of favour. More recently, the composer Takemitsu Tōru has found a new niche for the biwa in a western orchestra.

The *shakuhachi* is a wind instrument imported from China in the 7th century. Its name derives from the length of the instrument measured in traditional Japanese units: one *shaku* and eight *hachi* sun (totaling 54 cm). The shakuhachi was popularised by wandering Komusō monks in the 16th and 17th centuries, who played it as a means to enlightenment as they walked alone through the woods. Even today, the sound of the shakuhachi conjures up in the minds of the Japanese an image of lonely monks and dark forests.

Taiko refers to any of a number of large Japanese drums often played at festivals or in parades. Perhaps most famous of all taiko drum music is performed daily from 1 April to 3 November on Sado-ga-shima Island, near Niigata. The drummers who perform this music train year-round to endure the rigours of playing these enormous drums. Check with the TIC about occasional special taiko festivals which are held on the island.

Modern Music Japan has the second-largest domestic record market in the world. More than any other nation in Asia, the Japanese have taken to western music and you can meet fans of everything and everybody from Bach fugues to acid jazz, from Ry Cooder to Iggy Pop. Even if you don't speak any Japanese, you can at least sit around with young Japanese and swap the names of bands you like.

Tokyo in particular is very much on the live-music circuit and is a good place to catch up with everything from symphonies to the latest indie bands. The best place to get information on who's going to be in town is *Tokyo Journal* in Tokyo and *Kansai Time Out* in the Kansai region.

An overwhelming feature of the local music scene is the *aidoru* or idol singer. Generally untalented, the popularity of idols is generated largely through media appearances and is centred on a cute, girl-next-door image – something akin to the Kylie phenomenon that swept the western music scene in the early '90s.

The predominance of imitation of western styles is probably the main reason why very few Japanese acts have had any popularity in the west. Exceptions are performers like Kitarō, whose oriental synthesised sounds have had considerable success, and Sakamoto Ryūichi, a former member of Yellow Magic Orchestra and creator of the music for *The Last Emperor*. Orqesta de la Luz, a salsa band composed entirely of Japanese musicians, regularly plays to ecstatic Hispanic audiences at stadium-sized venues across the USA and Latin America. When its latest CD went

MASON FLORENCE

Okinawan music maverick Kina Shōkichi, performing in Okinawa

CHRIS TAYLOR

Japan's drummers, admired for their high energy levels – traditional taiko player or modern-day rock percussionist

on sale at Tower Records in New York, the entire stock was sold out within three hours. In 1993 they became the first group ever to receive an award for Cultural Achievement from the United Nations. Still, no Japanese act has as yet been able to match the success of one Sakamoto Kyū, who made it to the top of the American hit parade in 1963 singing 'Sukiyaki'.

Little known in his own country, one musician who is held in high esteem by many western musicians is Kina Shōkichi. He has been a major force in the popularisation of indigenous Okinawan music. His electric-traditional crossovers make for fascinating, often haunting listening. The Tsugaru-hantō Peninsula, at the tip of Tōhoku in Northern Honshū, has its own brand of music called Tsugaru-jamisen, which is a fun combination of racing banjos and wailing songs.

Literature

Like the other arts, Japanese literature has always been heavily influenced by outside sources. For most of Japan's history, this influence came from China. Japan's first real literature, the *Kojiki* (Record of Ancient Matters) and *Nihon Shoki* (Chronicle of Japan) were written in the 8th century in emulation of Chinese accounts of their nation's history. It was only during times of relative isolation from the mainland that Japanese literature developed its own voice.

Interestingly, much of Japan's early literature was written by women. One reason for this was that men wrote in imported Chinese characters, while women wrote in Japanese script *(hiragana)*. Thus, while the men were busy copying Chinese styles and texts, the women of the country were producing the first authentic Japanese literature. Among these early female authors is Murasaki Shikibu, who wrote one of Japan's all time classics, *Genji Monogatari* (The Tale of Genji). Now available in translation, this novel documents the intrigues and romances of early Japanese court life. Although it is perhaps Japan's most important work of literature, its extreme length probably limits its appeal to all but the most ardent Japanophile.

The Narrow Road to the Deep North is a famous travel classic by the revered Japanese poet Matsuo Bashō. *Kokoro*, by Natsume Sōseki, is a modern classic depicting the conflict between old and new Japan in the mind and heart of an aged scholar. The modern and the traditional also clash in the lives of two couples in *Some Prefer Nettles* by Tanizaki Junichirō. *The Makioka Sisters*, also by Tanizaki, is a famous family chronicle that has been likened to a modern-day *Tale of Genji*. Ibuse Masuji's *Black Rain* is a response to Japan's defeat in WWII. (Although made into a film in Japan, the book bears no relation to the Hollywood movie of the same name.)

Snow Country by Kawabata Yasunari is a famous story set in Japan's northern regions. Endō Shūsaku's *Silence* is a historical story of the plight of Japanese Christians following Tokugawa Ieyasu's unification of the country.

Mishima Yukio's *The Golden Pavilion* reconstructs the life of a novice monk who burned down Kyoto's golden Kingaku-ji Temple in 1950. Although Mishima is probably the most controversial of Japan's modern writers and is considered unrepresentative of Japanese culture by many Japanese, his work still makes for very interesting reading. Abe Kōbō's *Woman of the Dunes* is a classic tale by one of Japan's more respected avant-garde writers.

Of course not all Japanese fiction can be classified as literature. Murakami Ryū's *Almost Transparent Blue* is strictly sex and drugs and was a blockbuster in the Japan of the '70s. Murakami has written another provocative bestseller for the '90s in *Coin Locker Babies*. Murakami Haruki is another bestselling author; novels available in English include *A Wild Sheep Chase* and *Dance, Dance, Dance* – both touch on sheep and Hokkaidō. Banana Yoshimoto has had unaccountable international success for her *Kitchen*.

Ōe Kenzaburō is Japan's Nobel laureate. Look out for *Pluck the Buds, Shoot the Kids* – which must rate alongside Mishima's *The Sailor Who Fell from Grace with the Sea* as one of the best titles in modern Japanese fiction – and his semi-autobiographical *A Personal Matter*, about how the birth of a brain-damaged child affects his father.

Bashō

Matsuo Bashō, the father of haiku poetry, wielded the sword before picking up the pen. Born in Ueno, Mie Prefecture, in 1644 to a samurai family, the young Bashō studied the arts of war in preparation for becoming a samurai. He swore loyalty to a local lord and would have gone on to become a regular fighting man if it had not been for two unforeseen events. First, the lord to whom Bashō had sworn loyalty was something of an aesthete and took to instructing his protege in the art of poetry. Second, the lord passed away while Bashō was only 22. After the death of his lord, instead of finding another master, Bashō set out for Kyoto in search of culture and excitement.

After some time spent among the literati of the capital, Bashō moved to Edō (Tokyo) where he refined his poetry and gained enough recognition to support himself as a teacher of haiku. In the fall of 1684, Bashō embarked on a voyage westward, hoping to quell an inner restlessness which had plagued him in the city. This was to be the first of the major voyages which would became the hallmark of his poetic life.

Back in Edo, Bashō studied Zen under a teacher by the name of Butchō. Zen philosophy had a deep impact on his work, and many comparisons have been made between his haiku and Zen koans (short riddles intended to bring about a sudden flash of insight in the listener). Indeed, the best of Bashō's haikus have the effect of a Zen koan on the listener – a rare case of a word being worth a thousand pictures.

Bashō was also influenced by the natural philosophy of the Chinese sage Chang-tzu, from whom he learned a way of looking at nature uncritically – seeing the 'just-so-ness' of each object. Later, he developed his own poetic principle which he called 'sabi,' usually translated as a kind of spare, lonely beauty. This lonely beauty is perhaps better experienced than explained, a good example being a haiku he wrote in Arano:

on a withered branch
a crow is perched
an autumn evening

Bashō embarked on three more poetic pilgrimages in his life and was in the midst of a fourth when he fell sick and died in Osaka in 1694. His ceaseless peregrination certainly qualifies Bashō as the poet laureate of the traveler, to whom he addressed this haiku:

traveller's heart
never settled long in one place
like a portable fire

After his death, Bashō's disciples went on to popularize the art of haiku and today haiku is the best known of Japan's literary arts. For those who would like to delve deeper into Bashō's haiku, the most comprehensive books on the subject are *Bashō's Haiku, Volumes I and II* by Toshiharu Oseko. ■

Film

At the time cinema first developed in the west, Japan was in the throes of the Meiji Restoration and was enthusiastically embracing everything associated with modernity. Motion pictures were first imported in 1896 and, in characteristic Japanese fashion, they were making their own by 1899. Until the advent of talkies, dialogue and general explanation of what was going on was provided by the *benshi*, a live commentator. This was necessary for foreign films but the benshi quickly became as important a part of the cinematic experience as the film itself.

At first, Japanese films were merely cinematic versions of traditional theatrical performances, but the Tokyo earthquake in 1923 prompted a split between period films or *jidaigeki* and new *gendaigeki* films, which followed modern themes. The more realistic storylines of the new films soon reflected back on the traditional films with the introduction of *shin jidaigeki* or 'new period films'. During this era, samurai themes became an enduring staple of Japanese cinema.

As the government became increasingly authoritarian in the years leading up to WWII, cinema was largely put to propaganda purposes. After the war, feudal films with their emphasis on blind loyalty and martial ability were banned by the Allied authorities, but cinematic energy soon turned to new pursuits, including animated films, monster movies and comedies.

The '50s are generally thought of as the golden age of Japanese cinema. Directors like Kurosawa Akira led Japanese cinema onto the international stage when his *Rashōmon* (1950) took the top prize at the Venice Film Festival in 1951. Kurosawa continued his success and emerged as Japan's most influential director. His *Shichinin-no-Samurai* (Seven Samurai; 1954) gained the ultimate accolade when it was shamelessly ripped off by the Hollywood blockbuster *The Magnificent Seven*. Other Kurosawa classics include *Yōjimbō* (1961), the tale of a masterless samurai who single-handedly cleans up a small town bedevilled by two warring gangs, and *Ran* (1985), an epic historical film. Kurosawa still commands a high reputation among western directors, though his recent films (he is now over 80) like *Yume* (Dreams; 1990) and *Madadoyo* (1993) have not been particularly well received in the west.

In the '70s and '80s Japanese cinema retreated before the onslaught of international movie making, in part because of the failure to develop new independent film-making companies in an era when big production companies were losing their clout worldwide. Recently, however, there have been a number of independently produced Japanese films which have had some art-house success in the west and serve as a good introduction, not just to Japanese cinema, but to modern Japan itself.

Itami Jūzō's *Tampopo* (1985) is a wonderful comedy weaving vignettes on the themes of food and sex into a story about a Japanese noodle restaurant – 'Zen and the art of noodle making' as one critic described it. From the same director comes *Marusa-no-Onna* (A Taxing Woman; 1988), an amusing insight into taxation, Japanese-style. The latter was so popular in Japan that it has spawned an equally amusing sequel: *A Taxing Woman 2*.

Donald Richie's *Japanese Cinema – An Introduction* (Oxford University Press, Hong Kong, 1990) is brief, but useful for the beginner.

Facts for the Visitor

PLANNING
When to Go
For the Japanese, each of the seasons has its pleasures (spring, with its clear skies and cherry blossoms, is probably the most celebrated), but for the visitor the best times to visit are the more climatically stable seasons of spring and autumn.

The only drawback of spring (March to May) – an otherwise magnificent time to be in Japan – is that the cherry blossom season is a holiday period for the Japanese, and many of the more popular travel destinations tend to be flooded with Japanese tourists, who head out of the cities in droves. Popular tourist attractions become congested at this time of year, and it is wise to book ahead for your accommodation.

If it's the cherry blossoms you want to see, bear in mind that the blossoms are notoriously fickle, blooming any time from early to late April. Moreover, when the blossoms do come, their moment of glory is brief, lasting generally a mere week. Still, if you're going to be travelling in Japan during April, chances are you'll come across cherry blossoms somewhere, as they creep slowly across Japan beginning in the south and making their way northwards (their progress is followed obsessively on all the TV channels).

Autumn (September to November) is an equally good time to travel, with pleasant temperatures and fantastic autumn colours out in the country – the shrines and temples of historical centres such as Kamakura or Kyoto look stunning against a backdrop of autumn leaves.

Travelling in either winter or summer is a mixed bag. Mid-winter (December to February) weather can be bitterly cold, particularly on the Japan Sea side of Honshū and Hokkaidō, while the sticky summer months (June to August) can turn even the briefest excursion out of the air conditioning into a soup bath. On the plus side, you will generally find major tourist attractions to be quieter at this time of the year.

All things considered, the ideal trip to Japan would see you in Hokkaidō and Northern Honshū during the height of summer; in southern Honshū, Kyūshū and Shikoku from late summer to early autumn; and in Central Honshū during autumn. Peak holiday seasons, particularly the late April to early May 'Golden Week' and the mid-summer O-bon festival can cause travel problems. See the Holidays & Festivals section for details.

Maps
The best maps for Japan are more readily available in Japan than they are overseas. Good English maps are readily available in major cities such as Tokyo and Osaka.

The JNTO's free *Tourist Map of Japan* is a reasonable 1:2,000,000 English-language map of the whole country which is quite adequate for general route planning. Both Shobunsha and Kodansha (two Japanese publishers) publish a series of bilingual fold-out maps with prices ranging from around ¥700.

The *Japan Road Atlas* (Shobunsha, Tokyo, ¥2890) covers all of Japan at 1:250,000 except for Hokkaidō, which is covered at 1:600,000. Most towns are shown in kanji (Japanese script) as well as romaji (Roman script). However, mountains, passes, lakes, rivers and so on are only shown in romaji, and it is not unsual for small towns and villages to be left off altogether. Despite these drawbacks, the atlas is the best mapping available for detailed exploration of the country, both by car and rail, as every railway station less bulky should pick up a copy of the *Bilingual Atlas of Japan* (Kodansha, 1992).

Japan Guide Maps (JGM) produces a series of English-language maps covering the whole country area by area; the map of Kyūshū, at 1:500,000, is typical. Although they're not bad, these maps are not as good as equivalent Japanese-language maps, which are often free. Check the Service &

Parking Area (SAPA) maps which are available free at expressway service centres.

Giveaway town maps may also have enough romaji detail to make them useable for non-Japanese speakers, however, much of this mapping is often wildly exaggerated in scale and appearance. Stylised maps, where all roads are completely straight and all corners right angles, are very common.

What to Bring

The number one rule in Japan, as anywhere else, is travel light. Bulky luggage can be a hassle in Japan, as there is often only day-pack-size coin lockers in which to store it.

What clothing you bring will depend not only on the season, but on where you are planning to go. Japan extends a long way from north to south: the north of Hokkaidō can be under deep snow at the same time as the Okinawa Islands are basking in tropical sunshine. And if you're going anywhere near the mountains, you'll need good, cold-weather gear at most times of the year, even in the height of summer if you're intent on climbing Mt Fuji. Generally, however, Japan's climate is somewhat similar to that of continental USA; while it can get icy in winter, high summer is definitely T-shirt weather and much of the year is pleasantly mild.

There is a distinct wet season between June and July, but rain is a possibility at any time of year, and an umbrella is well worth having. Almost every shop and hotel in Japan seems to have an umbrella stand outside, often with a neat locking arrangement so umbrellas can be stowed safely.

Unless you're in Japan on business, you are unlikely to meet situations where 'coat and tie' standards are enforced; casual clothing is all you'll need. Also, laundrettes are reasonably common, so you can count on recirculating your wardrobe fairly regularly. Some hotels, hostels and other accommodation have laundry facilities for their guests' use.

The same rule, but underlined, applies to shoes. If your feet are big, make sure your shoes will outlast your stay in Japan. Choose them carefully – you want shoes which are not only comfortable for walking but which

are also easy to slip on and off for the frequent indoor occasions where they must be abandoned. Remember that slippers are almost always provided for indoor and bathroom use, so you don't really need to bring anything other than your outdoor shoes. Bring a towel – even in an expensive ryokan, a towel is not necessarily provided or it may be of a size westerners will consider more like a washcloth. Most hotels and ryokan will supply a *yukata*, that all-purpose Japanese 'dressing gown', but not always and it's such a vital piece of apparel that you should buy yourself one as soon as possible. They make a fine souvenir of Japan.

SUGGESTED ITINERARIES

Given the high costs of touring Japan, most travellers keep to fairly tight itineraries. Fortunately, with a little forethought this is easy to do: Japan's excellent road and rail network allow you to get around quickly, and public transport unfailingly runs to schedule. If you want to see as much of Japan as possible in a short time, don't forget to organise a JR Rail Pass before you go – see the Getting Around chapter for details.

Tokyo-Kyoto

The Tokyo-Kyoto route is the most popular Japan primer. For first-time visitors with only a week or so to look around, a few days in Tokyo sampling the modern Japanese experience and four or five days in the Kansai region exploring the historical sites of Kyoto and Nara is a recommended option. It allows you take in some of Japan's most famous attractions while not attempting to cover too much ground. The journey between Tokyo and Kyoto might be broken half-way at Nagoya in order to take an overnight trip to Takayama, a delightful rural town.

Tokyo & South-West

Travellers with more time to spend in Japan tend to head west and south before considering Northern Honshū and Hokkaidō. The reason is that Kansai, Western Honshū and Kyūshū are richer in sights than the northern regions of Japan. If you're a nature buff, you should consider dropping these regions in favour of the Japan Alps and Northern Honshū and Hokkaidō, where there is superb hiking.

Assuming you fly into Tokyo, it's worth spending a few days exploring the city before heading off to the Kansai area (notably Kyoto and Nara). A possible side trip en-route would be to Takayama from Nagoya and then on to Kanazawa, a culturally interesting city that gets neglected by many travellers. An interesting overnight trip out of Kyoto or Osaka is to the Buddhist mountain sanctuary of Kōya-san – temple accommodation is available here.

From Kansai, many Rail Pass travellers take a shinkansen straight down to Fukuoka in Kyūshū. Fukuoka is not a major attraction – though the nearby town of Dazaifu is pleasant – and can be safely skipped if you're pressed for time in favour of Nagasaki, a city with an interesting cosmopolitan history and a moving and fascinating museum about the atomic blast of 1945 that levelled the city. From Nagasaki it is possible to do a loop through northern Kyūshū that takes in Kumamoto, the volcanic Mt Aso (some good hiking in this area) and the penultimate in tacky hot spring resorts, Beppu. To the south is the balmy port city of Kagoshima, complete with an ash-spewing volcanic island just offshore.

The fastest way to return to Kansai or Tokyo is by shinkansen along the Inland Sea side of Western Honshū. Possible stopovers include Hiroshima and Himeji, a famous castle town. From Okayama, the seldom visited island of Shikoku is easily accessible. The Japan Sea side of Western Honshū is less touristed and more rural – notable attractions are the shrine at Izumo and the small cities of Matsue and Tottori.

Tokyo/Kansai & Northern Japan

A good approach to northern Japan from either Tokyo or Kansai is via Matsumoto and Nagano, which are excellent bases for hikes and visits to rural communities such as Kamikōchi. From Nagano, you might travel up to Niigata and from there to the seldom visited Sado-ga-Shima Island. On the other side of Honshū, the city of Sendai provides easy access to Matsushima, one of Japan's most celebrated scenic outlooks.

Highlights north of Sendai include Hiraizumi, a cultural centre that is worth a layover, and Aoyama, of little interest in itself but good as a base for visits to the Towada-Hachimantai National Park: Lake Towado-ko is one of the most picturesque in all Japan.

From Aomori to Hokkaidō by train involves a journey through the world's longest underwater tunnel. Hakodate is a pleasant port city. Sapporo is the capital of Hokkaidō; it's a prosperous and orderly city with a number of minor but worthwhile attractions and lively nightlife. The annual February snow festival is one of Japan's major winter drawcards. Elsewhere around Hokkaidō the attractions are mostly for lovers of outdoor pursuits such as hiking and skiing. Daisetsuzan National Park and Shikotsu-Toya National Park are two popular destinations.

TOURIST OFFICES

The Japan National Tourist Organisation (JNTO) produces a great deal of literature, which is available both from its overseas and TIC offices (see below). Publications include *Your Guide to Japan*, a handy booklet giving information on places of interest, calendar events and travel data; the *Tourist Map of Japan* and *Your Travelling Companion Japan* – *with tips for budget travel*, which has money-saving tips on travel, accommodation and places to eat. Also worth picking up is *The Tourist's Handbook – practical ways to solve your language problems*, which aims to do just what it says. Most publications are available in English and, in some cases, other European and Asian languages. Separate brochures are available on a number of important tourist destinations. The JNTO also has an Internet homepage which features travel updates: http://www.jnto.go.jp.

Local Tourist Offices

JNTO operates four Tourist Information Centers (TIC):

Kansai international airport
Passenger Terminal Building, 1st floor, Kansai international airport, Izumi-Sano, Osaka 549; open 9 am to 9 pm daily, year-round (☎0724-56-6025)
Kyoto
1st Floor, Kyoto Tower Building, Higashi-Shiokoji-chō, Shimogyo-ku, Kyoto 600; open from 9 am to 5 pm weekdays, and from 9 am to noon on Saturday; closed on Sunday and national holidays (☎075-371-5649)
Tokyo
B1F, Tokyo International Forum, 3-5-1, Marunouchi, Chiyoda-ku, Tokyo 100; open from 9 am to 5 pm weekdays, and from 9 am to noon on Saturday; closed on Sunday and national holidays (☎03-3201-3331)
Tokyo international airport (Narita)
Passenger Terminal 2, 1st floor, Narita airport, Chiba 282; open from 9 am to 8 pm daily, year-round (☎0476-34-6251)

TIC offices have counters for making some hotel or ryokan reservations, but cannot make transport bookings; they can, however, direct you to agencies which can, such as the Japan Travel Bureau (JTB) or the Nippon Travel Agency (NTA). 'Teletourist' is a round-the-clock taped information service on current events in town operated by the TIC's Tokyo (☎03-3503-2911) and Kyoto (☎075-361-2911) offices. JNTO also operates Goodwill Guides, a volunteer programme with over 30,000 members who wear a blue and white badge with a dove and globe logo.

Japan Travel-Phone JNTO operates a nationwide toll-free phone service available from 9 am to 5 pm, seven days a week. The main aim is to provide assistance for visitors unable to get to the TIC offices in Tokyo or Kyoto. To contact an English-speaking travel expert, call ☎0088-22-2800; in Tokyo call ☎03-3502-1461, and in Kyoto ☎075-3502-1461. You can also use this service to help with language problems when you're stuck in a hopeless linguistic muddle.

Tourist Information System JNTO's Tourist Information System is an attempt to provide English language tourist information throughout Japan (82 offices in 52 cities at the last count). It doesn't always work, unfortunately, though the staff at these offices will generally have some English-language information to hand out to you even if their English is limited to 'haro'.

Other Information Offices Away from Tokyo or Kyoto there are information offices (annai-jo) in almost all the major railway stations but the further you venture into outlying regions, the less chance you have of finding English-speaking staff. If you want a licensed, professional tourist guide try TIC, a large travel agency such as JTB, or phone the Japan Guide Association in Tokyo on ☎03-3213-2706.

Tourist Offices Abroad
JNTO has a number of overseas offices including the following:

Australia
Level 33, The Chifley Tower, 2 Chifley Square, Sydney, NSW 2000 (☎(02) 9232-4522)
Canada
165 University Ave, Toronto, Ontario M5H 3B8 (☎(416) 366-7140)
France
4-8 rue Sainte-Anne, 75001 Paris (☎01-42-96-20-29)
Germany
Kaiserstrasse 11, 60311 Frankfurt am Main 1 (☎(069) 20353)
Hong Kong
Suite 3704-05, 37th Floor, Dorset House, Taikoo Place, Quarry Bay (☎2968-5688)
South Korea
10th Floor, Press Centre Building, 25 Taipyongno 1-ga, Chung-gu, Seoul (☎(02) 732-7525)
Switzerland
13 rue de Berne, 1201 Geneva (☎(022) 731-81-40)
Thailand
Wall Street Tower Building, 33/61, Suriwong Rd, Bangkok 10500 (☎(02) 233-5108)
UK
Heathcoat House, 20 Savile Row, London W1X 1AE (☎(0171) 734-9638)
USA
Chicago: 401 North Michigan Ave, IL 60611 (☎(312) 222-0874)
Los Angeles: 624 South Grand Ave, Suite 1611, CA 90017 (☎(213) 623-1952)
New York: One Rockefeller Plaza, Suite 1250, NY 10020 (☎(212) 757-5640)
San Francisco: 360 Post St, Suite 601, CA 94108 (☎(415) 989-7140)

VISAS & DOCUMENTS
Passport

A passport is essential. If yours is within a few months of expiry, get a new one now – many countries will not issue a visa if your passport has less than six months of validity remaining. Be sure too that your passport still has several empty pages for visa, entry and exit stamps. Even in modern Japan, losing a passport is a hassle. It's sensible to keep a photocopy of the information page of your passport in a separate place from your passport; at the very least ensure that you carry some photo ID apart from your passport.

Visas

Tourist and business visitors of many nationalities are not required to obtain a visa if staying in Japan less than 90 days. Visits involving employment or other remunerated activity require an appropriate visa.

Stays of up to six months are permitted for citizens of Austria, Germany, Ireland, Mexico, Switzerland and the UK. Stays of up to three months are permitted for citizens of Argentina, Belgium, Canada, Denmark, Finland, France, Iceland, Israel, Italy, Netherlands, New Zealand, Norway, Singapore, Spain, Sweden, the USA and a number of other countries.

Visitors from Australia and South Africa are among those nationals requiring a visa. This is usually issued free, but passport photographs are required and a return or onward ticket must be shown. Visas are valid for 90 days.

Visa Extensions It has become difficult to extend visas. With the exception of nationals of the few countries whose reciprocal visa exemptions allow for stays of six months, 90 days is the limit for most visitors. Those who do apply should obtain two copies of an Application for Extension of Stay (available at Immigration Bureaus), a letter stating the reasons for the extension (along with any supporting documentation you may have) and your passport. There is a processing fee of ¥4000. Many long-term visitors to Japan get around the extension problem by briefly leaving the country, usually going to Hong

Kong, South Korea or Taiwan; however, the immigration officials can be very difficult when they return.

Working Holiday Visas Australians, Canadians and New Zealanders between the ages of 18 and 25 (the age limit can be pushed up to 30) can apply for a working holiday visa. This visa allows a six month stay and two six-month extensions. The visa's aim is to enable young people to travel extensively during their stay and for this reason employment is supposed to be part time or temporary, although in practice, many people work full time.

A working holiday visa is much easier to obtain than a proper visa and is popular with Japanese employers as it can save them a great deal of inconvenience. Single applicants must have the equivalent of A$2500 of funds and a married couple $A3500, and all applicants must have an onward ticket from Japan.

Working Visas The ever-increasing number of foreigners clamouring for a role in the Asian economic miracle has prompted much stricter visa requirements for Japan. There are legal employment categories for foreigners that specify standards of experience and qualifications. Working visas must be organised outside Japan.

Arriving in Japan and looking for a job is quite a tough proposition these days, though people still do it. It is necessary for your prospective employer to obtain a Certificate of Eligibility. Without it you are not able to work legally. It takes 90 days to issue, and you will be required to apply for a work visa with the certificate at an embassy or consulate overseas, not in Japan itself.

Alien Registration Card

Anyone, and this includes tourists, who stays for more than 90 days is required to obtain an Alien Registration Card. This card can be obtained at the municipal office of the city, town or ward in which you're living but moving to another area requires that you re-register within 14 days.

You must carry your Alien Registration

Card at all times as the police can stop you and ask to see the card. If you don't have the card, you will be taken back to the station and will have to wait there until someone fetches it for you.

Photocopies

Although Japan is a very safe country to travel in, it's still a good idea to keep photocopies of vital documents separate from the originals – if anything goes missing, a photocopy makes it much easier to replace. A further precaution is to leave copies of documents with someone at home. Documents you should consider photocopying include your passport (the data pages), air tickets, birth certificate and educational certificates. Similarly, keep records of all credit card numbers and the serial numbers of travellers' cheques. Last of all, experienced travellers generally carry an emergency stash of funds separately from the rest of their money. Just how much this should be in Japan, however, can be difficult to say – anything less than US$100 won't go very far.

Onward Tickets

As is the case in most Asian countries nowadays, nobody is checking whether travellers have onward tickets at Japanese customs. If you look particularly desperate, you may be asked to show that you have sufficient funds to finance your visit and fly out of the country.

Travel Insurance

Even in a country as safe as Japan, you should arrange for a travel insurance policy that covers theft, property loss and medical expenses. Theft may be very rare, but in the event of serious medical problems or an accident, it is unlikely that your travel expenses would meet the bill in Japan.

There are a wide variety of travel insurance policies available, and it is wise to check with a reliable travel agent about which will best suit you in Japan and other countries in the region. The policies handled by STA travel (which has branches in Japan) are usually good value.

Wherever you buy your travel insurance, always check the small print:

- Some policies specifically exclude 'dangerous activities' such as scuba diving and motorcycling. If you are going to be diving or riding a motorbike in Japan, check that your policy covers you.
- Check as to whether your medical coverage requires you to pay first and claim later; if this is the case you will need to keep all documentation.

Driving Licence

To drive in Japan, you will need an international licence backed up by your national licence. See the Car section of the Getting Around chapter for more details.

Hostel Cards

Youth hostel accommodation is plentiful in Japan. See the Youth Hostels entry of the Accommodation section in this chapter for information about obtaining cards.

Student & Youth Cards

Japan is one of the few places left in Asia where a student card can be useful. Officially, you should be carrying an ISIC card to qualify for a discount (usually for entry to sights), but in practice you will often find that any youth or student card will do the trick.

Seniors' Cards

Discounting for seniors is not a common practice in Japan, and generally seniors' cards will not be particularly useful. In some cases, however, discounting is available on the trains if you are over 65. Proof of age should be enough to qualify for discounts of this kind.

International Health Certificate

Japan is more scrupulous about the risks of travellers arriving from countries where there is a risk of becoming infected with yellow fever or an epidemic of, say, cholera. If you are arriving from a high-risk area, it would be a good idea to come prepared with an International Health Certificate that indicates you have had all the necessary jabs.

Other Documents

Extra passport photographs are easy to organise in Japan. Those arriving on a working holiday visa should bring their educational certificates and work references.

EMBASSIES
Japanese Embassies Abroad

Visas for Japan are available through Japanese embassies and consulates, including the following:

Australia
112 Empire Circuit, Yarralumla, Canberra, ACT 2600 (☎ (02) 6273-3244); there are also consulates in Brisbane (☎ (07) 3221-5188), Melbourne (☎ (03) 9639-3244), Perth (☎ (08) 9321-3455), Sydney (☎ (02) 9231-3455).

Canada
255 Sussex Drive, Ottawa, Ontario K1N 9E6 (☎ (613) 241-8541); there are also consulates in Edmonton (☎ (403) 422-3752), Montreal (☎ (514) 866-3429), Toronto (☎ (416) 363-7038), Vancouver (☎ (604) 684-5868)

France
7 Ave Hoche, 75008-Paris (☎ 01-48-88-62-00)

Germany
Godesberger Allee 102-104, 53175 Bonn (☎ (0228) 81910)

Hong Kong
47th Floor, One Exchange Square, 8 Connaught Place, Central (☎ 2522-1184)

Ireland
Nutley Building, Merrion Centre, Nutley Lane, Dublin 4 (☎ (1) 269-4033)

Israel
Asia House, 4 Weizman St, 64 239 Tel-Aviv (☎ 695-7292)

New Zealand
7th Floor, Norwich Insurance House, 3-11 Hunter St, Wellington 1 (☎ (04) 473-1540); there is also a consulate in Auckland (☎ (09) 303-4106)

Singapore
16 Nassim Rd, Singapore 1025 (☎ 235-8855)

Thailand
1674 New Petchburi Rd, Bangkok 10310 (☎ 02-252-6151)

UK
43-46 Grosvenor St, London W1X OBA (☎ (0171) 465-6500)

USA
2520 Massachusetts Ave, NW Washington DC 20008-2869 (☎ (202) 939-6700); there are also consulates in Anchorage (☎ (907) 279-8428), Atlanta (☎ (404) 892-2700), Boston (☎ (617) 973-9772), Chicago (☎ (312) 280-0400), Honolulu (☎ (808) 536-2226), Houston (☎ (713) 652-2977), Kansas City (☎ (816) 471-0111), Los Angeles (☎ (213) 617-6700), New Orleans (☎ (504) 529-2101), New York (212) 371-8222), Portland (☎ (503) 221-1811), San Francisco (☎ (415) 777-3533)

Foreign Embassies in Japan

See the Tokyo chapter for a list of foreign embassies.

CUSTOMS

Customs allowances include the usual tobacco products, three 760 ml bottles of alcoholic beverages, 57 grams of perfume and gifts and souvenirs up to a value of ¥200,000 or its equivalent. The alcohol and tobacco allowances only apply for those who are 20 or older. Spirits have come down in price in Japan over recent years, but a good bottle of duty-free will still be appreciated as a gift; there is no possibility of reselling it for profit. The penalties for importing drugs are very severe.

Most western men's magazines (not to mention pornography) would probably qualify for confiscation by Customs officers: although less stringently enforced than it once was, it is still illegal to possess magazines or videos which display pubic hair.

There are no limits on the import of foreign or Japanese currency. The export of foreign currency is also unlimited but a ¥5 million limit exists for Japanese currency.

MONEY
Costs

However you look at it, Japan is a very expensive place to travel. A skeleton daily budget, assuming you stay at the cheapest places (¥2200 per night in a hostel), eat modestly (¥1500) and spend ¥1500 on short-distance travel works out at ¥5000 (US$50). Add at least ¥1000 for extras like snacks, drinks, admission fees and entertainment. More expensive accommodation costs around ¥4200 to ¥5500 for a *minshuku* (Japanese-style B&B), cheap ryokan or business hotel.

Food costs can be kept within reasonable limits by taking set meals. A fixed 'morning service' breakfast (*mōningu sābisu* or *setto*) is available in most coffee shops for around ¥350. At lunch time there are set meals (*teishoku*) for about ¥650. Cheap noodle places, often found at stations or in department stores, charge around ¥300 for a filling bowl of noodles. For an evening meal, there's the option of a set course again or a single order – ¥600 to ¥700 should cover this. Average prices at youth hostels are ¥450 for a Japanese breakfast and ¥700 for dinner.

Transport is a major expense, although there are ways to limit the damage. The Japan Rail Pass is well worth the money if you intend to travel widely in a short space of time. Overnight buses are cheaper than the train, and enable you to save on accommodation. Hitching is not only easy, it also puts you in touch with a cross section of Japanese society. If you want to avoid emptying your wallet at an alarming rate, you should only use taxis as a last resort. Most cities in Japan have fast, efficient public transport, so you rarely need taxis anyway.

Carrying Money

The Japanese are used to a very low crime rate and often carry wads of cash for the almost sacred ritual of cash payment. Foreign travellers in Japan can safely copy the cash habit, but should still take the usual precautions – don't, for example, leave large amounts of cash in your back pocket; always keep your travellers' cheques, credit cards, etc, in a safe place.

Money Transfers

If you are having money sent to a bank in Japan, make sure you know *exactly* where the funds are going: the bank, branch and location. Telex or telegraphic transfers are much faster, though more expensive, than mail transfers. A credit-card cash advance (see Credit Cards) is a worthwhile alternative. American Express transfers require a trusty friend back home.

Bank & Post Office Accounts

Banking operations have been cautiously modernised over the last few years in Japan

– good news for the customers who have had to put up with a creaky system. Surprisingly, for a hi-tech country like Japan, the present cosy arrangement between the banks discourages competition and encourages inefficiency and expensive bank charges for simple things like paying a bill. Interest rates on deposits – in most cases very low at present – are to be linked to market rates and raised to appropriate levels. At least Japanese banks now turn on their ATMs at weekends.

Opening a bank account is not an option for visitors on a tourist visa (most banks simply won't let you do it; others may require that you only withdraw money from the branch in which you opened your account). Some travellers, however, open a post office savings account (*yūbin chokin*) at the main post office in one of the major cities; this allows you to withdraw funds from any post office. You should be able to get things started by using the following Japanese phrase: *yūbin chokin no kōza o tsukutte kudasai* (I would like to open a post office savings account).

Credit Cards

The use of credit cards is becoming more widespread in Japan, but outside major cities, cash still reigns supreme. American Express, Visa, MasterCard and Diners Club are the most widely accepted international cards. The main offices are:

American Express
American Express Tower, 4-30-16 Ogikubo, Suginami-ku, Tokyo (☎ 3220-6100)
Diners Club
Senshu Building, 1-13-7 Shibuya, Shibuya-ku, Tokyo (☎ 3499-1311)
MasterCard
Dai Tokyo Kasai Shinjuku Building, 16th Floor, 3-25-3 Yoyogi, Shibuya-ku (☎ 5350-8051)
Visa
Imperial Tower, 11th Floor, 1-1-1 Uchisaiwai-chō, Chiyoda-ku (☎ 5251-0633)

Be warned, finding a bank or an ATM that will allow you a cash advance on your credit card is rarely easy.

Currency

The currency in Japan is the *yen* (¥) and banknotes and coins are easily identifiable. There are ¥1, ¥5, ¥10, ¥50, ¥100 and ¥500 coins; ¥1000, ¥5000 and ¥10,000 banknotes. The ¥1 coin is an aluminium lightweight, the ¥5 and ¥50 coins have a hole in the middle.

Currency Exchange

All major currencies are accepted by banks in Japan. The currencies of neighbouring Taiwan and Korea, however, are not easy to offload – change NT dollars and Korean won into yen or US dollars before arriving in Japan.

As of mid 1997 currency exchange rates were:

Australia	A$1	=	¥86.60
Canada	C$1	=	¥83
Germany	DM1	=	¥66.80
Hong Kong	HK$1	=	¥14.80
New Zealand	NZ$1	=	¥78.07
Singapore	S$1	=	¥80.06
United Kingdom	UK£1	=	¥191.03
Unites States	US$1	=	¥115.03

Changing Money

You can change cash or travellers' cheques at an 'Authorised Foreign Exchange Bank' (signs are always displayed in English) or at some of the large hotels and stores. These are easy to find in cities, but much less common elsewhere. The safest and most practical way to carry your money is in travellers' cheques, which also provide slightly more favourable rates.

Banking Hours

As a general rule, always change more money than you think you will need. Banking hours are Monday to Friday, 9 am to 3 pm, closed on Saturday, Sunday and national holidays. Japan may be a hi-tech place, but to change money you have to show your passport, fill in forms and (sometimes) wait until your number is called, all of which can take anything up to half an hour. If you're caught cashless outside regular banking hours, try a large department store or major hotel.

Automatic telling machines (ATM) are now widespread throughout Japan, but are closed on Sunday. Commercial districts often have ATMs operating on weekends and late at night; some of these also provide international access.

Tipping & Bargaining

There is little of either in Japan. If you want to show your gratitude to someone, give them a gift rather than a tip. Bargaining is largely restricted to discount electronics districts, where a polite request will often bring the price down by around 10%.

Consumer Taxes

Unfortunately, Japan does have a 5% consumer tax, introduced in 1989 and extremely unpopular with the Japanese public. If you eat at expensive restaurants and stay at 1st class accommodation you will encounter a service charge – a disguised form of tipping – which varies from 10% to 15%. A local tax of 3% is added for restaurant bills exceeding ¥5000 or for hotel bills exceeding ¥10,000. This means it is sometimes cheaper to ask for separate bills. At onsen (hot-spring) resorts, a separate onsen tax applies. This is usually 3% and applies at cheap accommodation, even youth hostels.

POST & COMMUNICATIONS

The symbol for post offices is a white and red T with a bar across the top. Red mailboxes are for ordinary mail, blue ones for special delivery. The Japanese postal system is reliable and efficient and, for regular postcards and airmail letters, not markedly more expensive than other advanced countries.

Addresses

In Japan, finding a place from its address can be a near impossibility, even for the Japanese. The problem is twofold: firstly, the address is given by an area rather than a street; and secondly, the numbers are not necessarily consecutive: prior to the mid-50s numbers were assigned by date of construction. During the occupation after WWII, an attempt was made to bring some 'logic' to Japanese addresses, and many streets were assigned names, but the Japanese reverted to their own system as soon as the Americans left.

To find an address, the usual process is to ask directions – even taxi drivers often have to do this. The numerous local police boxes are there, in part, to give directions. Businesses often include a small map in their advertisements or on their business cards to show their location.

Starting from the largest area and working down to an individual address, first comes the *ken* (prefecture) as in Okayama-ken or Akita-ken. Four areas in Japan do not follow this rule – Tokyo-to, Kyoto-fu, Osaka-fu (those cities and the areas around them) and the island of Hokkaidō. After the prefecture comes the *shi* or city. Thus Okayama city in Okayama Prefecture is properly Okayama-shi, Okayama-ken. In country areas, there are also *gun*, which are like counties, and *mura* or 'villages'.

Large cities are then subdivided first into *ku* (wards), then into *chō* or *machi* and then into *chōme*, an area of just a few blocks. The chōme is the smallest division, so an address like 4-4 3-chōme should locate the actual place you want. For the poor gaijin, the system often seems to be changed back and forth without rhyme or reason and an address like 2-4-8 Nishi Meguro can also be written 4-8 Nishi Meguro 2-chōme. The building number is either a single numeric or a hyphenated double numeric. When there are three hyphenated numerics the first one is the chōme, so 1-2-3 is building 2-3 in 1-chōme.

You can buy maps which show every building in every chōme and there are often streetside signs indicating building locations, but they are very hard to interpret.

Postal Rates

The airmail rate for postcards is ¥70 to any overseas destination; aerograms cost ¥80. Letters weighing less than 10 grams are ¥80 to other countries within Asia, ¥100 to North America or Oceania (including Australia and New Zealand) and ¥120 to Europe, Africa and South America.

Sending Mail

District post offices (the main post office in a ward or *ku*), are normally open from 8 am to 7 pm on weekdays, 8 am to 3 pm on Saturday and 9 am to 12.30 pm on Sunday and public holidays. Local post offices are open 9 am to 5 pm on weekdays and 9 am to 1 pm on Saturday. Main post offices in the larger cities may have some counters open 24 hours a day.

Mail can be sent to Japan, from Japan or within Japan when addressed in western (romaji) script, but it should, of course, be written as clearly as possible.

Receiving Mail

Although any post office will hold mail for collection, the poste restante idea is not well known and can cause confusion in smaller places. It is probably better to have mail addressed to you at a larger central post office. Letters are usually only held for 30 days before being returned to sender. When inquiring about mail for collection ask for *kyoku dome yūbin*.

Some embassies will hold mail for their nationals; check before you depart. Unless it's a five-star hotel or a place that is particularly popular with foreigners, hotels and hostels are not such a good idea in Japan. Another possibility is American Express, which will hold mail for their cardholders or users of American Express travellers' cheques. Normally, mail will be held for 30 days only unless marked 'Please hold for arrival'. American Express has offices in most major Japanese cities – check for the latest addresses with your nearest American Express office or with the Tokyo head office – see the Credit Cards entry above.

Telephone

The Japanese public telephone system is very well developed; there are a great many public phones and they work almost 100% of the time. It is very unusual to see a vandalised phone in Japan. Local calls cost ¥10 for three minutes; long-distance or overseas calls require a handful of coins which are used up as the call progresses; any unused coins are returned.

Most payphones will also accept prepaid phonecards *(terefon kādo)*, though by the time you have this book in your hands probably not for international calls. It's much easier to buy one of these than worry about having coins to hand; they are readily available from vending machines, telephone company card outlets and many shops in ¥500 and ¥1000 denominations. Phonecards are magnetically encoded, and after each call a small hole is punched to show how much value remains. The phone also displays the remaining value of your card when you insert it. Since they come in a huge variety of designs, card collecting is a popular activity.

International Calls At the time of writing, a new international phonecard system was being introduced: the KDD Superworld Card, which provides ¥3200 worth of calls for ¥3000. Unlike conventional phonecards, this one operates via a 'secret' number that lasts as long as the charge remains on the card; there is no need to insert the card into a phone, and KDD were promising international calls from *any* touch-tone phone.

Also available are blue and chrome credit card phones, though these are extremely rare – you may come across them occasionally in airport lounges, at big hotels and in some of

the Welcome Inn group ryokans. AT&T Calling Cards can be used on all Japanese phones by dialling ☎ 0055; direct calls to the USA can be made by calling ☎ 0039-111, the phone number you are calling in the USA and then your AT&T Calling Card number.

To place an international call through the operator, dial ☎ 0051 – international operators all seem to speak English. To make the call yourself, simply dial ☎ 001 (KDD), 0041 (ITJ) or 0061 (IDC) (rates between these three companies vary very little) then the international country code, the local code and the number. KDD's ☎ 002 international access number provides an automatic callback in English and Japanese with the price of the call you have just made. Another option is to dial 0039 for home country direct which takes you straight through to a local operator in the country dialled. You can then make a reverse-charge (collect) call or a credit card call with a telephone credit card valid in the destination country.

In some hotels or other tourist locations, you may find a home country direct phone where you simply press the button labelled USA, UK, Canada, Australia, NZ or wherever to be put through to your operator.

Dialling codes include:

Country	Direct Dial	Home Country Direct
Australia	001-61	0039-611
Canada	001-1	0039-161
Hong Kong	001-852	0039-852
Netherlands	001-31	0039-311
New Zealand	001-64	0039-641
Singapore	001-65	0039-651
Taiwan	001-886	0039-886
UK	001-44	0039-441
USA	001-1	0039-111*

* For mainland USA you can also dial 0039-121, for Hawaii you can also dial 0039-181

Fax & Telegraph

Japan may be an economic miracle but getting a fax out of the place can still be a real hassle. Most post offices do not offer fax services, and large hotels generally do not

Japan Area Codes
The country code for Japan is 81. The area codes for some of the main cities are:

Tokyo	03	Hiroshima	082
Yokohama	045	Matsuyama	0899
Narita	0476	Fukuoka	092
Nagoya	052	Nagasaki	0958
Osaka	06	Sendai	022

allow you to use their facilities unless you are a guest. Telegraph services are available in the GPOs of Japanese cities.

Email

Compuserve and America Online subscribers can pick up their email via local numbers in Japan. Check with your server before you leave for Japan access numbers. Don't expect to find internet cafes outside the major cities of Tokyo and Osaka. Many of the grey IDD public phones in Japan have a jack that allows you to log on.

BOOKS

There's no need to stock up on books, particularly books about Japan, before you leave home (although it would definitely be cheaper to do it this way). If you're passing through Tokyo there are bookshops with excellent selections of books on all aspects of Japanese culture. Outside Tokyo, the choice of foreign-language books is not as good, though many larger cities will have a branch of Kinokuniya and/or Maruzen with a foreign section. In the back blocks, however, you may be hard pressed to find anything in English other than the occasional newspaper and copy of *Time*.

Most of the following books should be available in Tokyo in paperback:

Travel

Travel books about Japan often end up turning into extended reflections on the oddness or uniqueness of the Japanese. One writer who does not fall prey to this temptation is Alan Booth. *The Roads to Sata* (Penguin) is the best of his writings about Japan, and traces a four month journey on foot from the northern tip of Hokkaidō to Sata, the southern tip of Kyūshū. Booth's *Looking for the Lost – Journeys Through a Vanishing Japan* (Kodansha) was his last book, and again recounts walks in rural Japan.

The *Inland Sea* (Weatherhill) by Donald Richie is another memorable Japanese travelogue, this time about a journey through the little-visited islands between Western Honshū and Shikoku.

Oliver Statler's *Japanese Inn* is an excellent introduction to Japanese history, as seen from the perspective of a post town. He has also penned a fascinating account of a walking tour of the Shikoku temple circuit in *Japanese Pilgrimage* (Picador).

Okubo Diary (Stanford University Press), by the British anthropologist Brian Moeran, is a memoir of his stay in a tiny Kyūshū village. *Unbeaten Tracks in Japan* (Virago Books) by Isabella Bird recounts the 'off the beaten track' travels of a doughty Victorian-era lady and includes an interesting account of the dying Ainu culture in Hokkaidō.

The Japan Travel Bureau (JTB) produces an illustrated book series with pocket-sized books covering various aspects of Japan including lifestyle, eating, festivals, the salaryman, Kyoto, Nikkō and other subjects in a bouncy, highly visual style.

If you want more detail about Tokyo than can be provided in this book, Lonely Planet's *Tokyo city guide* is the book to get.

History

Those looking for a brief and readable account of how modern Japan got to be the way it is should grab a copy of Ann Waswo's *Modern Japanese Society – (1868-1994)* (Oxford University Press). It is a no-nonsense round-up of recent events that has little truck with the accepted cliches, and in this sense it makes for a refreshing read. Other recommended reads in a similar vein include Richard Storey's *A History of Modern Japan* (Penguin) and *The Japanese Achievement* (Sidgwick & Jackson, 1990) by Hugh Cortazzi which spans earliest Japanese history to the present.

Japan: A Short Cultural History (Stanford University Press) by George B Sansom, though written some 40 years ago, is still among the best wide-ranging introductions to Japanese history. Sansom is also author of the more scholarly, three-volume *A History of Japan* (Stanford University Press). Those who get hooked should seek out the six-volume *Cambridge History of Japan*.

Edward Seidensticker's *Low City, High City* (Knopf) traces the history of Tokyo from 1867 to 1923 – the tumultuous years from the Edo period to the great earthquake. *Tokyo Rising: The City Since the Great Earthquake* (Knopf) continues the story from the '20s, through the destruction of WWII and the period of explosive growth to today's super city status. Paul Waley's *City of Stories* (Weatherhill) is another good historical account of Tokyo.

Religion

The role of religion in Japanese society is a complex one, but there are several good primers that are readily available in good Japanese bookshops. The best of these include: *Japanese Religion: A Cultural Perspective* by Robert S Elwood & Richard Pilgrim (Prentice-Hall); *Religions of Japan – Many Traditions within One Sacred Way* by H Byron Earhart (Harper & Row); and *Japanese Religion – A Survey by the Agency for Cultural Affairs* (Kodansha)

Probably the best introduction to Zen, which after all is the Buddhist sect that gets the most foreign attention, is *Zen & Japanese Culture* by Daisetsu T Suzuki (Routledge & Kegan Paul). Peter Matthiessen, author of the *Snow Leopard* and many other fine books, gives a personal account of his Zen experiences in Japan and elsewhere in *Nine Headed Dragon River* (Shambala).

The Cult at the End of the World – the Incredible Story of Aum (Arrow), by David E Kaplan & Andrew Marshall, as its subtitle helpfully explains, tells the incredible story of the Aum cult. This extremely readable piece of investigative journalism follows Shoko Asahara's journey from small-time charismatic to the head of a cult that attempted to bring the world to its knees by gassing central Tokyo.

Culture & Society

Inside Japan (Penguin), by Peter Tasker, is still an excellent wide-ranging introduction to modern Japanese culture, society and the economy, even if the changes of the last 10 years since it was written are starting to date

some of its observations. Much more dated, but still hanging in there, Ruth Benedict's *The Chrysanthemum & the Sword* (Tuttle) was the groundbreaking study of Japanese culture and attitudes written in the USA during WWII. Remarkably, Benedict was a cultural anthropologist who had never visited Japan or studied the language. Her book has been translated into Japanese and remains something of a classic despite the difficult circumstances under which it was written.

The Japanese Today (Belknap) by Edwin O Reischauer, is a standard textbook on Japanese society and a useful primer for anyone planning to spend time in Japan.

Business

There is no shortage of books that purport to describe the secrets of Japanese business, far more than we can possibly hope to do justice to here. *The Art of Japanese Management – Applications for American Executives* (Simon & Schuster) has been around for a while now, but is still considered a good introduction. For a more critical account, check out *Japan in the Passing Lane – An Insider's Account of Life in a Japanese Auto Factory* by Satoshi Kamata (Pantheon).

For nuts and bolts information there are several surveys of Japanese companies available. The *Japan Company Handbook* detailing listed companies is published quarterly in two sections by Toyo Keizai Inc. *Nippon 1997* is an annual statistical publication published by JETRO. Other annual publications also available include: *Survey of Japanese Corporations Overseas* (Toyo Keizai), *Japan Trade Directory* (JETRO), *Japan Economic Almanac* (The Nikkei Weekly), and *Japan: An International Comparison* (Keizai Koho Center, or Japan Institute for Social and Economic Affairs).

Those thinking seriously of doing business in Japan might like to seek out *Setting Up an Office in Japan* (American Chamber of Commerce in Japan), *Setting Up and Operating a Business in Japan* by Helen Thian (Tuttle), or *Setting Up Enterprises in Japan – Guidelines on Investment, Taxation and Legal Regulations* (JETRO). JETRO's

Investment Japan – A Directory of Institutions and Firms Offering Assistance to People Seeking to Set Up a Business in Japan is a particularly comprehensive listing of useful contacts across all industries.

The *City Source English Telephone Directory* is another essential reference source. It has over 1000 pages of telephone numbers and a wealth of useful practical information. The Nippon Telegraph & Telephone (NTT) English Information Service (☎ 3201-1010) will tell you the address of the nearest NTT office, where you can pick up a free copy. Similarly useful is the *Japan Yellow Pages* published by Japan Yellow Pages Ltd (☎ 3239-3501).

General

Among the more interesting recent books to appear about Japan is Ian Buruma's *Wages of Guilt – Memories of War in Germany & Japan* (Littlebrown). It explores the effects of Japan's (and Germany's) involvement in WWII on the contemporary psyche of the nation. Ian Buruma is also the author of one of the best introductions to Japan's sleazy 'water trade' and the overall cultural implications of what goes on there in *A Japanese Mirror* (Penguin). See the Religion entry above for information on *The Cult at the End of the World*, for another offbeat look at Japan.

Lost Japan (Lonely Planet Journeys), by Alex Kerr, was originally written in Japanese and draws on the author's experiences in Japan over 30 years. He explores the ritualised world of Kabuki, retraces his initiation into Tokyo's boardrooms, and exposes the environmental and cultural destruction that is the other face of contemporary Japan. The book won Japan's prestigious Shincho Gakugei Literature Prize in 1994.

In the Realm of a Dying Emperor (Vintage), by Norma Field, is a lyrical combination of memoir and reportage, as the author's past mingles with her account of three Japanese whose lives have been lived at odds with mainstream Japanese society. It gives pause to thought for all those who see Japanese culture as monolithic and de-individualising. Karl Taro Greenfield attempts the same in his racy *Speedtribes – Children of the Japanese Bubble*, a book which stretches the reader's credulity somewhat, but still makes for an entertaining foray into the drug-peddling, computer-hacking underworld of disaffected Japanese youth.

Jonathan Rauch's *Outnation – A Search for the Soul of Japan* (Littlebrown) is an intelligent and penetrating account of his six months in Japan. Pico Iyer's *The Lady and the Monk* (Vintage) is an unabashed romanticisation of Japan (mainly Kyoto) by a writer whose primary strength is as an essayist. It still makes for a great read, even if you might want to balance some of his reflections with the reality of modern Japan. One of the earliest writers to grapple with the difficulty of presenting Japan to a foreign audience was Lafcadio Hearn. *Writings From Japan* (Penguin) is a good sampler that follows Hearn's deepening affection for the country he visited and never left.

A book that gets many recommendations is *Max Danger – the Adventures of an Ex-Pat in Tokyo* (Tuttle). The book has quite a following in Japan. David Morley's *Pictures From the Watertrade* (Flamingo) is a novelistic account of a love affair with Japan.

For a comprehensive rundown on literary works from and about Japan complete with extracts, look out for *Traveller's Literary Companion – Japan*, edited by Harry Guest (Passport Books). It's full of fascinating morsels that lead on to more substantial discoveries.

The two volumes of *Discover Japan – Words, Customs & Concepts* (Kodansha) were originally published as *A Hundred Things Japanese* and *A Hundred More Things Japanese* and consist of a series of short essays on things Japanese by a wide variety of writers.

Bookshops

Most major Japanese cities will have a branch of Maruzen or Kinokuniya, both of which usually stock a reasonable selection of English-language books. Outside Tokyo, Osaka and Kyoto, you are unlikely to find books in foreign languages other than English.

NEWSPAPERS & MAGAZINES

Some interesting facts about the Japanese newspaper industry: there are more than 160 local and national newspaper companies in Japan, some of the larger ones producing morning and evening editions of the same paper; a 1991 survey found that over 52 million newspapers are sold daily in Japan, 1.24 for every household; Japan's most popular paper, the *Yomiuri Shimbun*, has the largest circulation in the world, pulling in around 10 million readers daily. You'll probably need a stiff drink after that.

On the English-language front, Japan produces several good newspapers and a small clutch of decent magazines. You can get these, along with the big-name foreign magazines like *Time* and *Newsweek*, in most major urban centres. Out in the country, there won't be anything but Japanese publications. In Okinawa, Kyūshū and Hokkaidō, the English dailies normally arrive a day late.

The *Japan Times*, with its good international news section and unbiased coverage of local Japanese news, is read by most newcomers looking for work because of its employment section – the Monday edition has the most extensive listings. The paper costs ¥160. The *Daily Yomiuri* rates alongside the *Japan Times* in its coverage of local and international news, and is particularly worth picking up on Saturday when a 'World Report' from the *Los Angeles Times* is included, and on Sunday when it has an eight-page supplement, 'View From Europe', culled from the British *Independent*.

The *Mainichi Daily News* is another good English-language newspaper widely available in Tokyo and its environs. If you oversleep and miss the morning papers, the *Asahi Evening News* is not bad – look out for the Entertainment section on Thursday if you're in Tokyo. All these newspapers can be picked up from newsstands in the major cities, particularly at railway stations, or at hotels that cater to foreign tourists and businesspeople.

Foreign magazines and newspapers are available in the major bookshops, though they tend to be very expensive. US magazines such as *Newsweek* and *Time* are popular and widely available despite a ¥700 (US$7) cover price. For the more specialist magazines, you'll need to visit the big bookshops in Tokyo, Osaka and Kyoto.

The Japanese also publish a number of magazines in English, mainly for their ever-growing English-speaking community. Most of these magazines are a kind of community service, providing information on theatres and cinemas, details about various cultural events as well as classifieds for anything from marriage partners to used cars. The Tokyo-based *Tokyo Journal* is the pick of the crowd with its comprehensive listings and informative, readable articles on local cultural and topical issues.

Kansai Time Out, produced in the Kansai region around Osaka, has excellent information and listings of use to both foreign visitors and residents. In the Nagoya area, *Eyes* is a useful listings magazine.

Students of Japanese should look out for *Nihongo Journal* and the *Hiragana Times*, monthly bilingual magazines for Japanese learners. The *Nihongo Journal* is particularly good, having an accompanying tape for pronunciation and listening comprehension practice and good listings of Japanese-language schools. Both magazines require that you have acquired the rudiments of Japanese and can at least read hiragana and a smattering of kanji.

RADIO & TV

The common consensus is that Japanese radio is dismal, mainly because it places far more emphasis on DJ jive than it does on music. Given the quality of Japanese pop music, this might be just as well. For English-language broadcasts, the possibilities are pretty much limited to the appallingly banal US armed services' Far East Network (FEN).

Even the FM stations are fairly uninspiring, though the situation is better in Tokyo than elsewhere in Japan. Tokyo's J-WAVE and Inter FM are both worth a listen, even if the chances that you will become a devoted regular are very slim. In the end, a good supply of tapes and a Walkman is required if music is essential to your sanity.

Like radio, most TV is inaccessible to the non-Japanese speaker. Even if you do speak the language, there's still not a great deal worth watching: inane variety shows are the order of the day. TVs can be fitted with an adapter so that certain English-language programmes and movies can be received in either Japanese or English. The Japanese Broadcasting Corporation (NHK) even broadcasts a nightly bilingual news report. Japanese TV news is not particularly exciting, and the simultaneous interpreting tends to be halting, but it's better than being cut off from the news altogether.

Finally, many Japanese hotel rooms will have a pay cable TV with video channels. It is unlikely that English-language movies will be available except for the porn channel which usually needs no translation.

VIDEO SYSTEMS

Japan is the world's leading producer of VCRs and video recorders. The local system is the American NTSC standard. If you are using a PAL or SECAM system video camera, bring your own video cartridges with you. In areas like Tokyo's Akihabara, where duty-free electronics items are on sale, it is possible to buy video equipment that switches between the three systems.

PHOTOGRAPHY & VIDEO
Film & Equipment

The Japanese are a nation of photographers. No social occasion is complete without a few snaps and an exchange of the photos taken at the last get-together. This, combined with the fact that the Japanese are major producers of camera equipment and film, means there is no problem obtaining photographic equipment or print film. Slide film is readily available but cheaper in other places around Asia.

A 36 exposure Kodachrome 64 slide film costs about ¥850 without processing; Fuji slide film, such as Velvia and Provia, is similarly priced. The very popular disposable cameras are even sold from vending machines. They typically cost from ¥1000 to ¥2000; more expensive ones have a built-in flash.

Processing

Processing print film is fast and economical in Japan, although the standards are not always the best and prices vary (¥2000 for a 36 exposure film is typical). In the big cities it is usually possible to have Fuji or Sakura slide film processed within 24 hours (¥1000 for 36 exposures) and the final results appear to be of a consistently high standard.

Kodachrome slide film, however, can only be processed by the Imagica Kodak depot in Ginza, Tokyo but the processing is fast (24 hours) and the results are good. There is no problem honouring pre-paid Kodachrome film either. Away from Tokyo, send Kodachrome film to: Far East Laboratories Ltd, 2-14-1 Higashi Gotanda, Shinagawa-ku, Tokyo.

Video

Properly used, a video can give a fascinating record of your travels. Think about how it differs from still photography; use it to pan around everyday scenes that perhaps would not be worth photographing. Of course you can use a video camera to record all the moments you would on a still camera too – the sunsets and the fabulous views. Remember also that video 'flows', which means that you can shoot countryside rolling past a train window for example. It's best not to get too carried away with the movement idea though; try and film in long takes and avoid bouncing around.

Video cameras these days have remarkably sensitive microphones. Watch out for ambient noise. Filming by the side of the road can result in disastrously noisy sound effects.

Remember that a video camera, like a still camera, is an obtrusive instrument and, even in shutter-happy Japan, not everyone appreciates having one stuffed in their face. Always ask first.

Highlights of Japan

MASON FLORENCE

Previous page: Miyajima's famous floating torii gate

Top: Sky building at dusk, Osaka

Middle: Three-colour Pond, Bandai skyline drive, Fukushima

Bottom: Bridges at Katsura Imperial Villa, Kyoto

With the notable exception of Mt Fuji, few visitors to Japan have many preconceptions of any highlight they definitely do not want to miss – there is no Japanese equivalent of the Taj Mahal, Statue of Liberty, Sydney Opera House or Eiffel Tower. Nevertheless, Japan is crammed with attractions.

Castles

Japan seems to have an abundance of castles. Few of them are originals, however, and even the copies represent a small proportion of the number that once littered the country. In the 17th century, the Tokugawa shogunate decreed that each domain maintain just one castle, which led to the destruction of many minor castles; others burnt down or fell into ruin. In 1873, the sixth year of the Meiji era, the government, in a paroxysm of anti-feudalism, ordered that another 144 castles be destroyed, leaving 39 originals. By the end of WWII this had further been reduced to 12.

The 1960s saw an enormous spate of castle reconstructions, but these were all rebuilt like Hollywood movie sets – authentic when viewed from a distance but constructed from very 'unfeudal' concrete and steel.

By general agreement, the greatest surviving castle is Himeji-jō. Combining elegance and impregnability it soars above the plain it was built on, earning it the name 'White Egret'. It's an easy day trip from Kyoto. Running a close second place is Shikoku's Matsuyama-jō Castle.

Matsumoto-jō Castle in Central Honshū is another fascinating Japanese castle that has withstood the march of the years remarkably well. Hirosaki-jō Castle is not quite in the same league as the others, but it does have the added attraction of a well preserved samurai quarter.

Conveniently near Kyoto are the pretty lakeside Hikone-jō and the small Inuyama-jō castles. Elsewhere, Matsue-jō Castle has a fine setting and some interesting nearby streets. Bitchū-Matsuyama Castle at Takahashi represents an earlier era, hidden away on a high hilltop rather than standing proudly at the centre of its town. Kumamoto-jō Castle in Kyūshū is a modern reconstruction, but its design is very interesting and the museum has informative displays about castle construction. Edo Castle was once the largest castle in the world; today its huge moats and walls surround the Tokyo Imperial Palace.

ALLAN HOLTZMAN

The classic lines of Himeji-jō – built by warlord Toyotomi Hideyoshi in 1580

Gardens

Japan is famed for its beautiful gardens, and whether they are the larger Edo 'stroll gardens' or the small contemplative Zen gardens, there is always an exquisite attention to detail. The Japanese love to rate things: the 'big three' in the garden category are the Kairaku-en (Mito), the Kenroku-en (Kanazawa) and the Kōraku-en (Okayama). Not all visitors are likely to agree with the official listings; Mito, for example, simply has lots of lawn.

Kyoto has almost too many gardens to mention, including gardens that virtually define the rock garden and the Zen *kare-sansui*, or dry-landscape garden. Among the best smaller Zen gardens outside Kyoto are the beautiful Kōmyō-ji at Dazaifu, the Jōei-ji in Yamaguchi and the Raikyū-ji at Takahashi.

Other large gardens include the Ritsurin-kōen in Takamatsu, the Suizenji-kōen with its miniature Mt Fuji in Kumamoto and the Iso-teien in Kagoshima with a real smoking volcano as borrowed scenery. Hikone has the very beautiful Genkyū-en Garden and one of Japan's few surviving original castles. The Sankei-en Park in Yokohama is also very fine.

Scenery & Natural Attractions

Expressways, railways, factories, skyscrapers and a teeming population would scarcely seem to leave room for natural attractions. Yet, despite the population density, Japan is a mountainous country with many areas of great natural beauty.

Just as the Japanese rate the three best gardens, they also rate the three best views. These are the 'floating' torii of Miya-jima Island (see the Shrines section), the long sandspit of Amanohashidate and the bay of Matsushima, with its pine-covered islands. The misty, island-dotted waters of the Inland Sea would also have to be one of the most beautiful sights.

Some of the most spectacular mountain scenery in Japan is found in Nagano-ken (Kamikōchi and Hakuba) and northern Gifu-ken (Takayama and the Shōkawa Valley region).

Mt Fuji, the much climbed symbol of Japan, can actually seem like

Mt Tsurugi-dake – the northern backbone of the Japan Alps

ANTHONY WEERSING

Hot Springs

The islands of Japan are blessed with a natural abundance of rumbling, underground thermal activity, and centuries of tapping these sources has created one of the country's greatest pleasures – *onsen*.

With more than 2000 onsen to choose from, no other culture seems so obsessed with bathing as to have cultivated the activity to such a fine art. The baths are found just about everywhere; from pristine, remote retreats to kitschy, overdeveloped spa towns and from city centres to seasides, riverbanks and rural mountain tops.

While famed commercial resorts, such as Dōgo Onsen in Shikoku and Beppu in Kyūshū, provide a good introduction to onsen, the effort it takes to seek out less touristed springs will prove to be worthwhile.

What distinguishes onsen-yu from regular bath water is its varied content of natural gases and minerals. There is a wide variety of springs to discover: indoor tubs, outdoor *rotenburo*, cascading waterfall tubs, jungle tubs, sand baths, mud baths, and even chances to parley with bathing monkeys (if the mixed bathing tubs (*kon-yoku*) aren't exciting enough). For the truly adventurous, there are remote springs deep in the mountains. Naturally these involve a bit more effort to get to – and to dig out if you're in snow country – and in most cases are just about impossible to find without the help of a local guide.

Many of the country's best tubs are crafted from the ultimate in bath woods, *hinoki* (cypress), prized for its pleasant aroma. Other baths commonly feature stone construction.

While soaking in onsen water is known to relieve physical ailments (from skin disorders, arthritis and rheumatism to more unmentionable torments like constipation and haemorrhoids), the majority of people go to simply have their bodies, and their minds, soothed and relaxed. Visiting an onsen is often just part of a greater excursion, be it staying at a traditional country inn or hiking though the alps, but can frequently end up being the best part of a trip.

Clearly not every onsen is alike and choosing the right one to visit can often make or break the experience. Just because it says onsen, don't assume you're headed for nirvana. Hot springs can prove to be very hit and miss and need to be chosen carefully. Aside from the many springs described in this book, there are two excellent books in English devoted exclusively to hot springs, both full of interesting facts and tidbits, and worth seeking out for anyone looking to onsen-hop their way through Japan.

A Guide to Japanese Hot Springs by Anne Hotta with Yoko Ishiguro (Kodansha, 1986) details over 160 springs, and *Japan's Hidden Hot Springs* by Robert Neff (Tuttle, 1995) takes an even more selective approach in introducing onsen and memorable inns located off the conventional tourist routes. Otherwise, as with all else when travelling, simple word of mouth can often lead you to the best tub.

So whether it's being buried up to the neck in a thermally heated sand bath, soaking in a pool in the middle of a remote forest, or luxuriating in a glitzy resort, the onsen experience is one of Japan's greatest treasures. For those who make the effort, a visit to an onsen can prove to be one of the highlights of a journey through Japan. ■

MASON FLORENCE

One of Beppu's infamous sand baths – said to bring relief to all those aches and pains

Shinjuku station at rush hour when you get close up, but from a distance it's as beautiful as it has ever been. Mt Bandai-san and its lakes in the Tōhoku region offer more superb scenery.

Hokkaidō, the second-largest but least densely populated island, offers wonderful mountain scenery around Lake Mashu-ko in the Daisetsuzan National Park and around Tōya-ko and Shikotsu-ko lakes in the west. The Shiretoko-hantō and Shakotan-hantō peninsulas have fine coastal scenery. If you can get in an extra few days on Hokkaidō, the islands of Rishiri-tō and Rebun-tō in the north offer superb hiking.

Kyūshū has some wonderful volcanic scenery, particularly in the immense caldera of Mt Aso, the bleak, volcano-studded Kirishima National Park, and rumbling Sakurajima near Kagoshima. At the extreme western end of the country, Iriomote-jima Island has dense jungle and good scuba diving.

Historical Japan

Feudal castles are not the only symbols of 'old Japan' which have disappeared over the years. The destruction of WWII, the Japanese penchant for knocking down the old and putting up the new, plus the often flimsy and inflammable construction of so many old Japanese buildings have combined to leave few reminders of an earlier Japan. Apart from temples, shrines and castles, there are some reminders of the country's history.

Hakodate, in Hokkaidō, is a fascinating old port town with some very interesting Meiji period western-style buildings. Similar buildings can be seen in the port towns of Nagasaki and Kōbe. Hakone, near Tokyo, was a post town on the Tōkaidō Highway and preserves a short stretch of that road. Tsumago and Magome also maintain a post town atmosphere.

Takayama, north of Nagoya, has many fine old buildings and a farmhouse village (Hida Folk Village) consisting of more than a dozen houses of the *gasshō-zukuri* or 'hands in prayer' architectural style. The houses were all dismantled and reconstructed as a village after a huge dam was built in the region. Similar farmhouse villages can be found at Kawasaki and Takamatsu. Kanazawa, which escaped bombing during WWII, is another town with many reminders of an earlier era.

Kurashiki is famed for its canal district and old warehouses, many of which have been converted into museums. Further along the San-yō coast is Tomo-no-Ura, a small port you can explore by bicycle. On the opposite San-in coast, the town of Hagi exemplifies the kind of contradiction so typical of Japan. While the town is famous for its role in the ending of the Edo era and the beginning of the Meiji Restoration, it is also famous for its finely preserved Edo period buildings. Uchiko in Shikoku has a single old street where wealthy wax merchants once lived. The small town of Chiran, near Kagoshima in southern Kyūshū, has an old street of well-preserved samurai buildings and a kamikaze museum.

Shrines

Shrines are the focus of Japan's indigenous Shinto faith. They come in many styles, but there are clues that distinguish shrines from Buddhist temples. Generally, a red torii gate (or perhaps a series of them) marks the entrance to a shrine; inside the entrance you will find a *temizuya* – a small pavilion with a basin for ritual purification of the hands and mouth. Shrines are known as *jinja*, though you will also come across the terms *jingū* and *gū*.

The three great shrine centres are Ise, Nikkō and Izumo Taisha. Ise has the imperial shrine to Amaterasu, the mythical ancestor of the Japanese imperial line. Nikkō has the shrine to Tokugawa Ieyasu, founder of the Tokugawa shogunate. Izumo Taisha has the largest and, it is claimed, oldest shrine hall in Japan. Kyoto is, of course, particularly well endowed with impressive shrines.

Other important or interesting shrines include the very popular Meiji-jingū Shrine in Tokyo, the Itsukushima-jinja with its much photographed floating torii on Miya-jima Island and the hilltop Kotohira-gū Shrine in Shikoku. Kyūshū has two particularly interesting shrines. The Tenman-gū Shrine at Dazaifu near Fukuoka is dedicated to the legendary Sugawara-no-Michizane, who was exiled there from Kyoto. Just outside Takachiho the Ama-no-Iwato-jinja has the very cave where the sun goddess Amaterasu once hid. In Northern Honshū, you can see shrines frequented by worshippers of Shugendō in the spectacular surroundings of the sacred mountains of Dewa Sanzan, near Tsuruoka.

Temples

Distinguishing a Buddhist temple from a Shinto shrine is simply a matter of examining the entrance. While shrines are entered through an arched torii, a temple (*tera* or *ji*) is entered through a gateway, usually flanked by guardian figures. The most important temples in Japan are found in Kyoto and Nara and the surrounding Kansai region.

Important Kyoto temples include the Daitoku-ji, with its gardens; the ancient Kiyomizu-dera with its superb hillside site; the 13th-century Sanjūsangen-dō and the Tō-ji, founded by Kōbō Daishi. Nara has the fine Tōshōdai-ji and the Tōdai-ji, with its Great Buddha. Also in the Kansai region is Kōbō Daishi's

NICKO GONCHAROFF

Natural wood columns and hanging ropes of a typical shrine – Koganeyama-jinja, Kinkazan Island in Miyagi

---

Amusing Japan

Beyond the intriguing allure of traditional Japan – the temples, shrines, sumo and sushi bars – there is a large number of unconventional attractions, some of which are just mildly peculiar while others are downright bizarre! Including eat-your-heart-out-Disney vigour with a notorious ability to imitate and replicate, Japan offers everything from Wild West dude ranches to a string of Eiffel Towers found throughout the country.

Beyond the standard amusement parks like Tokyo Disneyland and Eiga Mura (movie village), a Universal Studios-type film complex in Kyoto, there are a myriad of possibilities just slightly out of the ordinary Japan itinerary. Tours, some of which are conducted in English, are offered by all four of the major breweries (Kirin, Asahi, Sapporo and Suntory) as well as by various makers of indigenous delicacies such as sake, soy sauce and even Japanese pickles (*tsukemono*). In addition, there is an ever-growing number of opportunities for visitors to experience different local arts and crafts hands-on, from paper making to throwing your own pottery.

If those activities don't interest you then perhaps you would rather take in a visit to the Tokyo stock exchange, play a game of pachinko, or experience the virtual-reality rides at a high-tech game centre. And if those don't grab you then what about trying the instant mini photo/sticker machines which have swept the nation.

Then there is an array of sights which aim to offer the convenience of being able to tour other countries without actually having to leave Japan. In recent years an astounding network of theme parks have popped up, modelled after fashionable countries, and each elaborately done to the very last detail (minus language barriers and the long list of fears Japanese potentially face when they do travel abroad). No effort or expense has been spared in creating these virtual nations; everything from the arts, architecture and culinary offerings to the country's fauna are there to add that authentic touch. If all of that weren't enough, the parks even hire citizens from the respective countries to work in these re-created nations.

---

mountaintop Kōya-san, the wonderful Hōryū-ji and the Byōdō-in in Uji, one of the most famous buildings in Japan.

Close to Tokyo, Kamakura offers some of the best temple tramping in Japan; Kōtoku-in Temple has the best known giant Buddha statue in Japan. Although the 88 temples in Kōbō Daishi's circuit of Shikoku have no great significance individually; taken together they represent the most important pilgrimage route in Japan. The Kōsan-ji, at nearby Setoda in the Inland Sea, is a Disneyland of temples – all modern reproductions of important temples crammed together in one location. Onomichi, on the Honshū coast near Setoda, has an interesting temple walk.

Modern Japan

Ancient temples and shrines, feudal castles and Zen gardens are all very well, but Japan is also the land of *pachinko* parlours, love hotels, robot-operated production lines and multi-storey buildings filled with nothing but bars. It's also the only place in the world to have suffered atomic destruction. The atomic bomb museums at Hiroshima and Nagasaki should not be avoided.

Hiroshima is also a good place to see the modern Japanese industrial machine in peak form. It's easy to arrange a factory visit at many centres in Japan, but the huge Mazda car factory

The most illustrious of these (and perhaps the one most worth visiting) is Nagasaki's Huis ten Bosch, which could even fool a Dutch person into believing that they are travelling in 19th century Holland. With genuine windmills and canals, and tall ships similar to those on which the first Europeans arrived at Nagasaki, it is truly an impressive sight. Then there is Parque Espana, a Spain theme park in Kansai, Canada and Germany villages in Hokkaidō, and the Turkey Culture Village at Niigata in Northern Honshū.

Japan also plays host to a number of curious 'around the world in an hour' attractions. In both suburban Tokyo and on Awaji Island there are groupings of world famous buildings and monuments including exact replicas of India's Taj Mahal and Pisa's leaning tower, although all of these have been thoughtfully scaled down to a quarter of their original size. Elsewhere there are several Eiffel Towers and even a replica of the USA's Mt Rushmore, which is a third the size of the original.

It is, however, not just foreign cultural icons that Japan has set out to perfect. In recent years it seems that re-creating its own natural attractions has even found a niche. While indoor rock-climbing facilities and Tokyo's all-season ski dome may serve some practical purpose, Kyūshū's Seagaia resort nearly defies explanation. The massive Ocean Dome, just a stone's throw from bona fide surf and sandy beaches along the Miyazaki-ken coastline, is an enormous indoor beach resort complete with a permanent blue sky, squeaky clean sand, an ocean of simulated waves and a sunroof.

Often the greatest mysteries of these curious attractions lie in their locations, frequently far enough off the beaten track to leave you wondering just who in the world could have dreamed them up. One of the best examples of this is the well publicised Orochi Loop in Western Honshū's rural Shimane-ken, so named for its stunning resemblance to the shape of a coiling snake. The Orochi Loop, in fact, is simply a highway off-ramp, but that didn't stop officials from billing it as a 'must see' attraction and even going to the trouble of shaving off the top of a nearby mountain top to facilitate convenient viewing. ■

in Hiroshima is certainly worth a visit. After work, the Japanese salary-men head for the huge entertainment districts, where the neon burns bright and the bill at the end of the evening would bankrupt the average Third World country. Even if you don't venture inside a single bar, these colourful areas are fascinating to wander around. Interesting ones include Tokyo's up-market Roppongi area and, in the Shinjuku district, the decidedly raunchier Kabuki-chō area. Shinjuku in Tokyo is also 'modern Japan' at its most modern; with two million people passing through its railway station every day, Shinjuku is probably the busiest place in the world.

Osaka's Namba district is another good example of a busy entertainment district, while Nakasu Island in Fukuoka is said to have a higher concentration of bars than anywhere else in Japan – hence the world? If you travel north in search of bars and nightlife, go to the Kokubun-chō district in Sendai and the Susukino district in Sapporo, Hokkaidō.

The Japanese passion for hot springs (onsen) is well documented and, in many places, is a very tasteful and ritualistic activity. In others, it is most definitely not. The spa town of Beppu in Kyūshū is the Las Vegas of onsen towns with bright lights and bad taste in full swing.

Love hotels are another side of Japan and it's surprising that an enterprising publisher hasn't yet produced a coffee-table book on love hotel architecture. In some places there are major enclaves of love hotels – the Dōgenzaka area of Tokyo's Shibuya district is a good example.

TIME

Despite Japan's east-west distance, the country is all on the same time, nine hours ahead of Greenwich Mean Time (GMT). Thus, when it is noon in Japan, it is 5 pm the previous day in Honolulu, 7 pm the previous day in San Francisco, and 10 pm the previous day in New York, 3 am in London, 11 am in Hong Kong, 1 pm in Sydney, and 3 pm in Auckland. Daylight-saving time is not used in Japan. Times are usually expressed on a 24-hour clock.

ELECTRICITY
Voltage & Cycle

The Japanese electric current is 100V AC, an odd voltage found almost nowhere else in the world. Furthermore, Tokyo and eastern Japan are on 50 Hz, western Japan including Nagoya, Kyoto and Osaka is on 60 Hz. Most North American electrical items, designed to run on 117V, will function reasonably well on Japanese current.

Plugs & Sockets

Japanese plugs are flat two pin, identical to North American plugs.

WEIGHTS & MEASURES

Japan uses the international metric system. One odd exception is the size of rooms, which is often given in tatami mat measurements known as jō. Tatami sizes vary regionally in Japan, which tends to complicate things. In Tokyo a tatami mat measures 1.76 by 0.88 metres, while in Kyoto a mat measures 1.91 by 0.96 metres (see the Long-Term Accommodation section later in this chapter for more on tatami mat measurement).

LAUNDRY

Some youth hostels and ryokan have washing facilities, but failing this the best option is to seek out a *koin rōndori* (coin laundry). In suburban Japan there is almost always one with easy walking distance. Costs range from ¥200 to ¥300 for a load of washing and ¥100 for every seven to 10 minutes of drying time. Those staying in business hotels or more up-market accommodation can use the hotel laundry service, though it will cost more than doing it yourself.

HEALTH

Travel health depends on your predeparture preparations, your day-to-day health care while travelling and how you handle any medical problem or emergency that does develop. However, looking after your health in Japan should pose few problems since hygiene standards are high and medical facilities widely available, though expensive. The average life expectancy among the Japanese is now 80 years for women and 74 for men, a sure sign that they are doing something right.

Travel Health Guides

There are a number of useful books on travel health:

Staying Healthy in Asia, Africa & Latin America (Moon Publications). Probably the best all-round guide to carry, as it's compact but very detailed and well organised.

Travellers' Health, Dr Richard Dawood (Oxford University Press). Comprehensive, easy to read, authoritative and also highly recommended, although it's rather large to lug around.

Where There is No Doctor, David Werner (Hesperian Foundation). A very detailed guide intended for someone, like a Peace Corps worker, going to work in an undeveloped country, rather than for the average traveller.

Travel with Children, Maureen Wheeler (Lonely Planet Publications). Includes advice on travel health for younger children.

Predeparture Preparations

Health Insurance A travel-insurance policy to cover theft, property loss and medical problems is a wise idea. With such a wide variety of policies available, it may be best to consult your travel agent for recommendations. The international student travel policies handled by STA Travel or other student travel organisations are usually good value. Some policies offer a choice between lower and higher medical expense options; choose the high-cost option for Japan. Check the small print.

Some policies specifically exclude 'dangerous activities' which can include scuba diving, motorcycling, even trekking. If such activities are on your agenda you don't want that sort of policy. A locally acquired motorcycle licence may not be valid under your policy.

You may prefer a policy which pays doctors or hospitals direct rather than you having to pay on the spot and claim later. If you have to claim later make sure you keep all documentation. Some policies ask you to call back (reverse charges) to a centre in your home country where an immediate assessment of your problem is made.

Check if the policy covers ambulances or an emergency flight home. If you have to stretch out you will need two seats and somebody has to pay for them!

Medical Kit A small medical kit is a good thing to carry even though most items will usually be readily available in Japan. Your kit could include:

- Aspirin or paracetamol – for pain or fever
- Antihistamine (such as Benadryl) – useful as a decongestant for colds, allergies, to ease the itch from insect bites or stings or to help prevent motion sickness. Antihistamines may cause sedation and interact with alcohol so care should be taken when using them.
- Imodium or Lomotil – for stomach upsets
- Rehydration mixture for treatment of severe diarrhoea. This is particularly important if travelling with children, but is recommended for everyone
- Antiseptic such as povidone – iodine (eg Betadine) for cuts and scratches
- Calamine lotion – to ease irritation from bites or stings
- Bandages and Band-aids
- Scissors, tweezers and a thermometer (mercury thermometers are prohibited by airlines)
- Insect repellent, sunscreen (can be difficult to find in Japan), and chapstick

Health Preparations Make sure you're healthy before you start travelling. Dental treatment in Japan is expensive. If you're short-sighted bring a spare pair of glasses and your prescription. If you require a particular medication bring an adequate supply as it may not be available in Japan, but also remember to bring the prescription – it may be illegal in Japan. Another idea, if you need particular medication, is to bring the packaging showing the generic rather than the brand name (which may not be available locally), as it will make getting replacements easier.

Immunisations No immunisations are required or necessary for Japan.

Basic Rules

Care in what you eat and drink is the most important health rule; stomach upsets are the most likely travel health problem (between 30% and 50% of travellers in a two-week stay experience this), but such problems are unusual in Japan.

Water Tap water is safe to drink all over Japan, but drinking from mountain streams should be done with caution. On Rebuntō Island (Hokkaidō), travellers have been warned that the springs could be contaminated with fox faeces, which contain tapeworm cysts. There have been reports of the schistosomiasis parasite still lurking in the countryside in rice paddies or stagnant water – avoid wading around barefoot in these places.

Food Hygiene in Japan rarely causes complaints. Most of the raw food can be eaten without health worries, although raw freshwater fish and raw wild boar meat should be avoided. The consumption of *fugu* (globefish) – not for the budget traveller – can famously result in death, but the dangers are absurdly exaggerated. (See the Food section for more details.)

Medical Problems & Treatment

Motion Sickness Eating lightly before and during a trip will reduce the chances of motion sickness. If you are prone to motion sickness, try to find a place that minimises disturbance – near the wing on aircraft, close to midships on boats or near the centre on buses. Fresh air usually helps, reading and cigarette smoke don't. Commercial antimotion-sickness preparations, which can cause drowsiness, have to be taken before the trip commences. Ginger is a natural preventative and is available in capsule form.

Sexually Transmitted Diseases Gonorrhoea and syphilis are the most common of these diseases; sores, blisters or rashes around the genitals, discharges or pain when urinating are common symptoms. Symptoms may be less marked or not observed at all in women. Syphilis symptoms eventually disappear completely but the disease continues and can cause severe problems in later years. While abstinence is the only 100% preventative, using condoms is also effective. The treatment of gonorrhoea and syphilis is by antibiotics.

There are numerous other sexually transmitted diseases, for most of which effective treatment is available. However, there is no cure for herpes and there is also currently no cure for AIDS.

HIV/AIDS HIV, the Human Immunodeficiency Virus, may develop into AIDS, Acquired Immune Deficiency Syndrome. HIV is a major problem in many countries. Any exposure to blood, blood products or bodily fluids may put the individual at risk. The disease is often transmitted through sexual contact or dirty needles – vaccinations, acupuncture, tattooing and ear or nose (or any other) piercing can be potentially just as dangerous as intravenous drug use. HIV/AIDs can also be spread through infected blood transmission. You may want to take a couple of syringes with you, in case of emergency.

Environmental Hazards
Sunburn Sunburn is generally only a problem in the summer months in Japan, but if you're hiking at high altitudes it can be a risk at almost any time of year. Use a sunscreen, hat and barrier cream for your nose and lips. Calamine lotion is good for mild sunburn.

Protect your eyes with good quality sunglasses, particularly if you will be near water, sand or snow.

Prickly Heat Prickly heat is an itchy rash caused by excessive perspiration trapped under the skin. Keeping cool but bathing often, using a mild talcum powder or opting for air-conditioning may help you acclimatise.

Fungal Infections Fungal infections, which occur with greater frequency in hot weather, are most likely to occur on the scalp, between the toes or fingers, in the groin and on the body (ringworm). You get ringworm, which is a fungal infection not a worm, from infected animals or by walking on damp areas, like shower floors.

To prevent fungal infections wear loose, comfortable clothes, avoid artificial fibres, wash frequently and dry carefully. If you do get an infection, wash the infected area daily with a disinfectant or medicated soap and water, and rinse and dry well. Apply an antifungal cream or powder like Tinaderm. Try to expose the infected area to air or sunlight as much as possible, and wash all towels and underwear in hot water as well as changing them often.

Women's Health
Gynaecological Problems Sexually transmitted diseases are a major cause of vaginal problems. Symptoms include a smelly discharge, painful intercourse and sometimes a burning sensation when urinating. Male sexual partners must also be treated. Medical attention should be sought and remember in addition to these diseases, HIV or hepatitis B may also be acquired during exposure. Besides abstinence, the best thing is to practise safe sex using condoms.

Antibiotic use, synthetic underwear, sweating and contraceptive pills can lead to fungal vaginal infections when travelling in hot climates. Maintaining good personal hygiene, and loose-fitting clothes and cotton underwear will help to prevent these infections.

Fungal infection, characterised by a rash, itch and discharge, can be treated with a vinegar or lemon-juice douche, or with yoghurt. Nystatin, miconazole or clotrimazole pessaries or vaginal cream are the usual treatment.

Pregnancy Most miscarriages occur during the first three months of pregnancy, so this is the most risky time to travel as far as your own health is concerned. Miscarriage is not uncommon, and can occasionally lead to severe bleeding. The last three months should also be spent within reasonable distance of good medical care. A baby born as early as 24 weeks stands a chance of survival, but only in a good modern hospital. Pregnant women should avoid all unnecessary medication, but vaccinations and malarial prophylactics should still be taken where possible. Additional care should be taken to prevent illness and particular attention should be paid to diet and nutrition. Alcohol and nicotine, for example, should be avoided.

Contraception

Although oral contraceptives are available from clinics specialising in medical care for foreigners, it is preferable to bring adequate supplies with you. Only in 1990 was the marketing of oral contraceptives officially authorised in Japan, and even now the low-dosage varieties widely available in the west are hard to get hold of. Meanwhile the condom reigns supreme. Condoms are widely available in Japan, but generally only locally produced varieties, which tend to be small and made with very thin rubber – a dangerous combination when you consider the HIV-AIDS threat. It's a good idea to bring your own, or buy foreign made condoms at the American Pharmacy in Hibiya, Tokyo. There are also two branches of the condom shop, Condomania, in Tokyo's Roppongi and Harajuku. Both have a wide variety of condoms.

Medical Assistance

The TIC has lists of English-speaking hospitals and doctors in the large cities. Dental care is widely available at steep prices. If you need a medicine not readily available in Japanese pharmacies try the American Pharmacy (☎ 03-3271-4034) close to the Yuraku-chō TIC in Tokyo. A peculiarity of the Japanese medical system is that most drugs are supplied not by pharmacies but by doctors. Critics say that as a result, doctors are prone to over-prescribe and choose the most expensive drugs.

Emergencies Emergency services in Japan will usually only react fast if you speak Japanese. Try the Tokyo English Lifeline (TELL; ☎ 03-3403-7106) for emergency assistance in English. The Japan Helpline (☎ 03-0120-461-997) is an emergency number which operates 24 hours a day, seven days a week. Don't clog the line unless you really do have an emergency.

Counselling & Advice Adjusting to life in Japan can be tough but there are several places to turn for help. The TELL phone service provides confidential and anonymous help. If they don't have the right answers at hand, they can pass you on to someone who might. Tokyo Tapes (☎ 03-3262-0224) has a wide variety of tapes available to help you deal with problems.

TOILETS

In Japan you will come across both western style toilets and Asian squat toilets, though generally squat toilets are on the way out – you rarely find them in modern buildings or in homes. When you are compelled to squat, the correct position is facing the hood, away from the door. This is the opposite to squat

Condoms

If you arrive in Tokyo unprepared, look out for the Condomania stores in Roppongi (appropriately) and Harajuku. These places are always crowded so, if you're the shy type, making that embarrassing purchase might be something of an ordeal – but then again why else would you be in there? Condomania stocks everything from Small Pecker ('protection for the little guy') to Peter Meter ('the rubber that's also a ruler'); not to mention Lickety Sticks (in four flavours – caffeine-free also available) and Nose Condoms ('for the safe practice of brown nosing'). No sniggering please, this is serious business. ■

toilets in most other places in Asia. Make sure the contents of your pockets don't spill out. Toilet paper isn't always provided so carry tissues with you. In homes and ryokan, separate toilet slippers are often provided just inside the toilet door. These are for use in the toilet only, so remember to change out of them when you leave.

It's quite common to see men urinating in public – the unspoken rule is that it's OK providing it's at night and you've been drinking. Women don't enjoy the same freedom. Public toilets are free in Japan. The kanji script for 'toilet' is 手洗い, for 'men' is 男, and for 'women' is 女.

WOMEN TRAVELLERS

The major concern of women travellers in many countries – 'Will I be physically safe?' – is not a worry in Japan. Overall, it is a very safe country to travel in and crimes against women are rare. Jam-packed rush-hour subways or buses can still bring out the worst in the Japanese male, however. When movement is impossible, roving hands are sometimes at work and women often put up with this interference because, in Japan, it would simply be impolite or unseemly to make a fuss. In most cases a loud complaint will shame the perpetrator into withdrawing his hand. Failing this, some women visitors suggest the offending hand should be grabbed, held up and the whereabouts of its owner inquired about.

There are some aspects of Japanese life which are not anti-female but certainly strike women as peculiar on first encounter. Public toilets, for example, are not always sex segregated although there may be doors labelled male and female. It can be a real shock to a western woman when she enters the door marked 'women' and finds a row of urinals with men lined up at them. It's an equal shock to the unprepared western male when he steps back from a urinal and finds women all around him.

Women's roles in the Japanese mass media are something that many western women find difficult to accept. This ranges from advertising that some would describe as 'sexist' to *manga* (comics) and other magazines where women are often portrayed in what almost anyone would have to agree are wildly exploitative situations. Such magazines are widely read by men in trains and other public places, and it can be disconcerting to find yourself seated next to someone reading one.

GAY & LESBIAN TRAVELLERS

Tokyo, being the big city it is, has an active gay scene, with clubs and support groups and a small but lively gay quarter. Outside Tokyo, however, Japan remains reasonably conservative. Even if the particular provincial city you are in has a gay scene, you will find it difficult to break into unless you spend considerable time in the place or have some local contact who can show you around. Same-sex couples probably won't encounter too many problems travelling in Japan. You will be given twin rooms as opposed to doubles, and it would be sensible to simply accept this and not cause a fuss demanding a double, which will only embarrass your host, particularly in the smaller ryokan. Some women report that they have been shooed away from love hotels, and in provincial Japan men may encounter the same treatment.

Organisations

It may be worth writing to International (Gay) Friends (☎03-5693-4569) in Tokyo before you go to Japan. The postal address is 1F Passport, CPO Box 180, Tokyo 100-91.

On the Internet the following organisations may be of help when you are planning your trip:

Hyper Stag
    http://www.gavie.or.jp/jp/hpstag/index.html
GayNet Japan
    http://www.gnj.or.jp/gaynet/
OutRageous Tokyo
    http://shrine.cyber.ad.jp/darrell/outr/home/outr
    -home.html
Planet Rainbow
    http://www.kt.rim.or.jp/rainbow/

DISABLED TRAVELLERS

As Asian countries go, Japan is probably the most considerate for the disabled. An example is the musical pedestrian lights that grace most intersections, another the raised bumps on railway platforms that are there for guidance – not to trip over when you're drunk. Many modern buildings nowadays feature access ramps. Elsewhere, however, you can expect little in the way of facilities.

Manga – Japanese Comics

It's a well-known fact that in comparisons of mathematical ability, Japanese high school students regularly show up better than their peers in other advanced nations. What is not so well known is that Japanese students would also come out well ahead in their consumption of comic books. In fact, the Japanese are the world's number one consumers of comic books (*manga*).

Manga is a catch-all word covering cartoons, magazine and newspaper comic strips and the comic books which take up so much space in so many Japanese shops. A Japanese comic book is rarely a slim volume (weekly comics as thick as phone directories are not unusual) and there's a version to appeal to every market niche. The text will always be in Japanese but there's usually an English subtitle on the front cover announcing at whom it's aimed, whether it's a 'Lady's Comic', a 'Comic for Business Boys' or even an 'Exciting Comic for Men', (for 'exciting' read 'soft-core porn').

Japanese comic-strip artists (there are thousands of them to cater for the insatiable demand) are often as well known and as wealthy as pop stars. There's no question that it's a big business: *Shōnen Jump*, the most

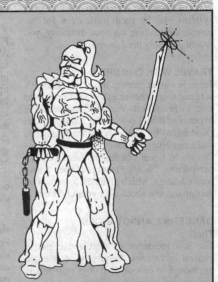

popular comic, has weekly sales which top four million copies. It's also an inventive business. Japanese comic artists pioneered multi-panel movements, perspectives which brought the reader into the action, close-ups, curious angles and a host of movie-like techniques. Along with inventiveness came recognition in the form of annual awards, regular reviews and serious critiques.

The curious westerner leafing through a manga may be somewhat surprised at the explicitness of the action. Japanese censors may black out the pubic hair in imported copies of *Playboy*, but it certainly all hangs out when it comes to comic books. Even the 'Lady's Comics' may give you a few surprises with their sexual activity. But manga also tackle very serious subjects: *jitsuma manga* ('practical comics') and *benkyō manga* ('study comics') actually set out to teach everything from high school subjects to international finance.

The ready acceptance of the dark side of so many manga would seem to indicate an avid interest in areas that are repressed in daily Japanese life. Of course (so the Japanese reasoning goes), it's only natural that adults should want to recapture something of their childhood by turning to comics after 11 hours in the office. And while we may level an accusing finger at the violence and sexual content of the manga, we also have to acknowledge that Japan is still probably the safest place in the world to walk the streets at night.

Those interested in Japanese comics can join the crowds leafing through recent issues in bookshops. Many smaller hotels, hostels and ryokan will have stacks of old issues for their guests' amusements. *Japan Inc* (University of California Press, Berkeley, 1988) by Shōtarō Ishinomori, is an English translation of a popular manga series on international finance and Japanese-US trade relations; it also contains an interesting introductory history of manga. ■

While there are dangers – such as the virtual non-existence of pedestrian paths – probably the best way to consider Japan is as a congested, fast-moving version of home. It is safer and politer than anywhere else in Asia, and even drivers of vehicles tend to be courteous. Problems, if they do arise, are likely to occur in the big cities, where the press of commuters on the public transport systems can be hard work even for the nimble: depending on your disability, you would probably need assistance.

TRAVEL WITH CHILDREN

Japan is a great place to travel with kids. It's safe and there's never a shortage of places to keep them amused – the only drawback is the expense of it all. Look out for *Japan for Kids* (Kodansha) by Diane Wiltshire Kanagawa and Jeane Huey Erickson, an excellent introduction to Japan's highlights from a child's perspective. Lonely Planet publishes *Travel with Children*, which gives the lowdown on getting out and about with your children.

DANGERS & ANNOYANCES
Theft
The low incidence of theft and crime in general in Japan is frequently commented on, though of course, theft does exist and its rarity is no reason for carelessness. In airports and on the crowded Tokyo rail network it's sensible to take the normal precautions, but there's no need for paranoia.

Lost and found services do seem to work; if you leave something behind on a train or other transport, it's always worth inquiring if it has been turned in.

Earthquakes
Japan is a very earthquake-prone country, although most can only be detected by sensitive instrumentation. If you experience a strong earthquake, head for a doorway or supporting pillar. Small rooms, like a bathroom or cupboard, are often stronger than large rooms but even a table or desk can provide some protection from falling debris. Of course, it is better to be outside than inside,

but keep away from buildings because of the danger of falling glass or other debris.

All Japanese hotels have maps indicating emergency exits, and local wards have emergency evacuation areas (fires frequently follow major earthquakes). In the event of a major earthquake, stay calm and follow the locals, who should be heading for a designated safe area.

Fire
Although modern hotels are subject to high safety standards, traditional Japanese buildings with their wooden construction and tightly packed surroundings can be real fire traps. Fortunately, most old buildings are small places where you are unlikely to be trapped on the 40th floor, but it's wise to check fire exits and escapes. Onsen (hot-spring/spa) centres, where buildings are often traditional in design with floors covered in grass tatami mats and where much drunken revelry takes place, can pose particular dangers.

Beaches & Swimming
Few public beaches have lifeguards and summer weekends bring many drowning accidents. Watch for undertows or other dangers. Severe sunburn is possible in Japan, just as in more obviously 'hot' places. However, as yet, the Japanese seem unaware of the dangers of overexposure. Bring a good sunblock lotion if you are going to be outdoors for long hours in the summer.

Noise
In Japanese cities the assault on the auditory senses can be overwhelming, so it's no wonder so many pedestrians are plugged in to Walkmans. Pedestrian crossings are serenaded by electronic playtime music, loudspeaker systems broadcast muzak or advertisements, bus passengers are bombarded with running commentaries in Mickey Mouse tones and accommodation may include TVs turned up full volume in dining rooms or lounges. Earplugs can help.

The Yakuza

The yakuza, perhaps because they are often referred to as the 'Japanese Mafia', are much misunderstood by foreign visitors to Japan. Enjoying deep penetration into Japanese society, powerful right-wing political support, operating as vast syndicates with interests in everything from real estate to hospitals (plus, of course, obvious business activities such as prostitution, drugs and gambling), the yakuza is a highly organised and widely tolerated component of Japan's hierarchical society.

The yakuza occupy (at least nominally) a lowly position in this hierarchy, but they compensate for this with a bravado that looks to historical antecedents. Many yakuza see themselves as custodians of honour and chivalry, traditional values that are all but vanished in contemporary Japan. Japan's ultra-nationalist right – which also looks for a return to 'traditional values' – enjoys yakuza support, and the black propaganda vans you will encounter cruising urban Japan are often driven by yakuza.

There are thought to be close to 90,000 yakuza members in Japan and yakuza earnings are probably over US$10 billion annually. The largest of the groups is the Yamaguchi-gumi, based in Kōbe. It claims over 20,000 'employees' and pulls in about a fifth of total yakuza annual earnings.

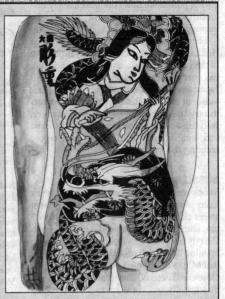

How do you pick a yakuza? Short-cropped permed hair is à la mode amongst the lower orders. Those with money often drive a US *yakuzamobile* (nobody else fancies US cars very much). Yakuza will also affect an arrogant swagger *(iburi)* and a gruff manner of speech *(aragoto)*. A bodyful of tattoos is *de rigeur* (cherry blossoms signify the brief but cheerful life of an ardent criminal), but don't forget to look out for that telling detail: failure in one's obligations to the group is punished by the amputation of a little finger at the first joint. Repeated convictions move to the next joint and so on until, presumably, there are no fingers left – a sign of the honourable but bumbling custodian of Japan's samurai past. ∎

Size

Even medium-sized foreigners need to mind their head in Japanese dwellings, though, in some homes, padded bags attached to the top of door frames acknowledge the problem. The western frame may find it hard to fit into some seats and those with long legs will often find themselves wedged tight. Toilets in cramped accommodation necessitate contortions and careful aim.

Wildlife

Japan is hardly a high danger region when it comes to wildlife, although in Okinawa Prefecture much fuss is made about the 'deadly *habu*' snake. To avoid an unhappy encounter with a deadly habu, don't go traipsing barefoot through the undergrowth. Snake bites do not cause instantaneous death and antivenenes are available. Keep the victim calm and still, wrap the bitten limb tightly, as you would for a sprained ankle, and then attach a splint to immobilise it. Then seek medical help, if possible with the dead snake for identification. Don't attempt to catch the snake if there is any remote possibility of being bitten again. Tourniquets and sucking out the poison are now comprehensively discredited. On the mainland islands the *mamushi* is also poisonous.

There are still bears in remote areas of Hokkaidō and they can be fiercely protective of their cubs. Foxes, also found in Hokkaidō, can carry diseases and should be avoided. Japan also has wasps, mosquitoes and other biting or stinging insects but not in extraordinary numbers or of unusual danger. Jellyfish and other marine dangers also exist and local advice should be heeded before entering the water.

BUSINESS HOURS

Shops are typically open seven days a week from around 10 am to 8 pm. Department stores close slightly earlier, usually 6.30 or 7 pm, and also close one weekday each week. If a city has several major department stores, opening hours will probably be organised so that Mitsukoshi closes on Monday, Daimaru closes on Tuesday, and so on. Large companies usually work a 9 am to 5 pm five-day week, and some also operate on Saturday morning. (See the Money section for banking hours and the Post & Communications section for post office hours.)

PUBLIC HOLIDAYS & SPECIAL EVENTS

Japan has 13 national holidays. When a public holiday falls on a Sunday, the following Monday is taken as a holiday. You can expect a total sell-out for travel and lodging during the New Year (29 December to 6 January), Golden Week (27 April to 6 May) and mid-August.

Japan's public holidays are:

Ganjitsu
  (New Year's Day) 1 January
Seijin-no-hi
  (Adult's Day) 15 January
Kenkoku Kinen-no-bi
  (National Foundation Day) 11 February
Shumbun-no-hi
  (Spring Equinox) 21 March (approximately)
Midori-no-hi
  (Green Day) 29 April

Kempō Kinem-bi
  (Constitution Day) 3 May
Kodomo-no-hi
  (Children's Day) 5 May
Keirō-no-hi
  (Respect-for-the-Aged Day) 15 September
Shūbun-no-hi
  (Autumn Equinox) 23 September (approximately)
Taiiku-no-hi
  (Sports Day) 10 October
Bunka-no-hi
  (Culture Day) 3 November
Kinrō Kansha-no-hi
  (Labour Thanksgiving Day) 23 November
Tennō Tanjōbi
  (Emperor's Birthday) 23 December

National Festivals & Events

Japan has a large number of festivals, or *matsuri*, and annual events. Japanese festivals are mainly of Shinto origin and related to the seasonal planting, growing and harvesting of rice. Annual events, on the other hand, are often Buddhist imports from China or more recent imports from the west, as in Valentine's day.

Shōgatsu (New Year)
  1-3 January. New Year celebrations include much eating and drinking, visits to shrines or temples and the paying of respects to relatives and business associates.
Seijin-no-hi (Adult's Day)
  15 January. Ceremonies are held for boys and girls who have reached the age of majority (20). To celebrate the end of winter and drive out evil spirits, the Japanese indulge in *setsubun* or bean throwing while chanting '*fuku wa uchi oni wa soto*' (in with good fortune, out with the devils).
Hina Matsuri (Doll Festival)
  3 March. During this festival old dolls are displayed and young girls are presented with special dolls *(hina)* which represent ancient figures from the imperial court.
Knickers Giving Day
  14 March. This is a slightly bizarre recent addition to the collection of festivals in Japan. The idea is that men should reciprocate the gift of chocolates on 14 February, St Valentine's Day, with a gift of panties for their lady!
Hanami (Blossom Viewing)
  February – April. The Japanese delight in the brief blossom-viewing seasons. The usual sequence is plum in February, peach in March and cherry in late March or early April.

O Higan (Equinoctial Week)
> March and September. At this time, family graves are visited and temples hold memorial services for the dead.

Golden Week
> 29 April-5 May. Golden Week is so called because it takes in Green Day (29 April), Constitution Day (3 May) and Children's Day (5 May). This is definitely not a time to be on the move since transport and lodging in popular holiday areas can be booked solid.

Kodomo-no-hi (Children's Day)
> 5 May. This is a holiday dedicated to children, especially boys. Families fly paper streamers of carp *(koi)*, which symbolise male strength.

Tanabata Matsuri (Star Festival)
> 7 July. The two stars Vega and Altair meet in the Milky Way on this night. According to a myth (originally Chinese), a princess and a peasant shepherd were forbidden to meet, but this was the only time in the year when the two star-crossed lovers could organise a tryst. Children copy out poems on streamers and love poems are written on banners that are hung out on display. An especially ornate version of this festival is celebrated from 6 to 8 August in Sendai.

O Bon (Festival of the Dead)
> 13-16 July and August. According to Buddhist tradition, this is a time when ancestors return to earth. Lanterns are lit and floated on rivers, lakes or the sea to signify the return of the departed to the underworld. Since most Japanese try to return to their native village at this time of year, this is one of the most crowded times of year to travel or look for accommodation.

Shichi-Go-San (Seven-Five-Three Festival)
> 15 November. Traditionally, this is a festival in honour of girls who are aged three and seven and boys who are five. Children are dressed in their finest clothes and taken to shrines or temples where prayers are offered for good fortune.

Local Festivals

Japan has plenty of local matsuri (festivals) that take place throughout the year. Kyoto, Nara and Tokyo are especially famous for local festivals, but elsewhere too there are special matsuri which often involve the display of *mikoshi* (portable shrines). The religion section includes details of major Shinto matsuri.

Festival details are also provided throughout this book under relevant sections for individual cities or regions. The TIC in Tokyo and Kyoto provide up-to-date listings of festivals and should have a useful JNTO

leaflet entitled *Annual Events in Japan*. If you do base a visit around festivals, remember that accommodation can be swamped by visitors from all over the country, so book well in advance.

The highlights of Japan's festivals are as follows:

Wakakusayama Turf Burning Festival
> 15 January. Participants dress in traditional warrior-monk attire while they burn turf; Wakakusayama, Nara, Kansai.

Sapporo Snow Festival
> Early February. Fantastic ice sculptures are the attraction of this very popular annual event – book ahead for accommodation; Sapporo, Hokkaidō

Hachinohe Emburi Festival
> 17-20 February. Rice-planting dances are held to honour the god of the rice harvest, Inari; Hachinohe, Aomori prefecture.

Omizutori
> 12-13 March. Ceremonial torch bearing, while monks make offerings of water to Kannon; Tōdai-ji Temple, Nara, Kansai.

ACTIVITIES
Cycling

Although much of Japan is mountainous, the coastal regions are popular with cyclists. See the Getting Around chapter for more information about cycling in Japan. See also the Accommodation section of this chapter for information about cycling terminals.

Hiking

The Japanese are keen hikers, and many of the national parks of Japan have hiking routes. Local maps are almost always available in youth hostels and nearby minshuku, but they are only rarely in English. Around Tokyo, the popular hiking areas are Nikkō and the Chichibu-Tama National Park. If you want to get away from it all, Gumma prefecture offers hikes on which you are very unlikely to happen across other foreigners. In the Kansai region, Nara has some pleasant hikes.

Japan comes into its own as a hiking destination in the Central Alps, in Northern Honshū and in Hokkaidō. In these less populated and mountainous regions of Japan, there may be the added incentive of an onsen soak at the end of a long day's walk. Hikers who get up into the mountains see a side of Japan that few gaijin ever experience.

Golf

Golf equals prestige in Japan. If you want to set foot on a green, a fat wallet and corporate clout are handy assets. Membership fees are rarely less than US$5000, can easily reach US$25,000 and often soar higher. Of course it is usually the company that takes out corporate membership and thus pays for its employees to go golfing. Green fees usually start at around US$100 a day. Real golf courses have recently prompted an environmental backlash as Japanese non-golfers have raised a storm of protest against more and more of the countryside being converted to golf courses.

Skiing

Skiing developed in Japan in the 1950s and there are now more than 300 ski resorts, many with high-standard runs and snowmaking equipment. The majority of resorts are concentrated on the island of Honshū, where the crowds are huge, the vertical drops rarely more than 400m and all runs start at altitudes of less than 2000m. Snow cover in southern and eastern Honshū is generally adequate, but can be sparse and icy.

Skiers on Hokkaidō, however, can look forward to powder skiing that matches anything in the European Alps or North American Rockies. Niseko and Furano, two of Hokkaidō's best resorts, have excellent facilities (Niseko has 43 lifts) and neither suffers from extreme crowding.

JNTO's *Skiing in Japan* pamphlet covers 20 resorts on Honshū and Hokkaidō with travel information, ski season dates, accommodation details, resort facilities and costs. Japan Airlines offers special ski tour packages including air fares, transportation, meals and accommodation.

Skiing is normally possible from December to April, though the season can be shorter in some of Honshū's lower-altitude resorts. Akakura, which is within easy reach of

Tokyo, is known for its deep snow that thaws quickly by the end of March. Shiga and Zaō, on Honshū, are best for early April skiing. The best time for cross-country skiing is March or April, when the snow is firmer and deeper; January and February are often very cold and stormy.

Resort accommodation ranges from hostels to expensive hotels but is heavily booked during the ski season. Many resorts are sited at hot springs and double as onsen or bathing spas. Avoid weekends and holidays when lift lines are long and accommodation and transportation are heavily booked.

Lift passes cost ¥2600 to ¥4200 a day. Daily rental of skis, stocks and boots can cost up to ¥5000 but finding larger-size ski boots may be difficult. Equipment can only be hired at resorts and is usually old and of a low standard; advanced equipment for the more experienced skier is rare. Since clothing cannot be hired, and second-hand gear is very hard to find, it's advisable to bring your own equipment. For those with plenty of cash it is possible to buy it in Japan – many ski shops hold sales from September to November and package-deal bargains can be found with skis, bindings and stocks included. Tokyo's Jimbōchō, Shinjuku, Shibiya and Ikebukuro areas have good ski shops.

As well as downhill skiing, Japan also offers good terrain for cross-country skiing and touring, especially in the Hakodate region of Hokkaidō – a good way to get away from the crowds. The Japanese are very hospitable and foreigners are welcome to join in races and festivities organised by the local authorities. One of the most famous is the Sapporo Marathon cross-country ski race.

Diving

The Okinawan islands, or more particularly the Yaeyama island group, in the far southwest of Japan are popular among Japanese as watersports destinations. As you would expect, diving in Japan is expensive. Typical rates are ¥12,000 per day. Courses for beginners are available in places like Ishigaki and Iriomote islands, but starting costs are around ¥80,000. Instruction will be in Japanese.

COURSES

There are courses for almost every aspect of Japanese culture. The Tokyo Tourist Information Centre (TIC) has a wealth of information material available. Applicants for cultural visas should note that attendance at 20 class hours per week are required. Those wishing to work while studying need to apply for permission to do so.

Japanese Language

The TIC leaflet *Japanese & Japanese Studies* lists government-accredited schools which belong to the Association of International Education. The association can also be contacted directly (☎ 03-3485-6827). Also available at the TIC is *The Guide to Japanese Career & Vocational Schools*. It has an extensive list of vocational and language schools, as well as details of the Monbusho Japanese Government Scholarship. *Nihongo Journal* is an excellent monthly language magazine for students of Japanese, and advertises Japanese language schools.

Costs at private Japanese-language schools vary enormously depending on the school's status and facilities. There is usually an application fee of ¥5000 to ¥30,000, plus an administration charge of ¥50,000 to ¥100,000 and then the annual tuition fees of ¥350,000 to ¥600,000. Add accommodation and food, and it is easy to see that studying is not a viable option for most people unless they also have an opportunity to work.

Martial Arts

Aikidō, judo, karate and kendō can be studied in Japan. Less popular disciplines, such as *kyūdō* (Japanese archery) and sumo, also attract devotees from overseas. Relevant addresses include:

All-Japan Judo Federation, c/o Kodokan, 1-16-30 Kasuga, Bukyō-ku, Tokyo (☎ 03-3818-9580)

Amateur Archery Federation of Japan, Kishi Memorial Hall, 4th Floor, 1-1-1 Jinan, Shibuya-ku, Tokyo (☎ 03-3481-2387)

International Aikidō Federation, 17-18 Wakamatsu-chō, Shinjuku-ku, Tokyo (☎ 03-3203-9236)

Japan Kendō Federation, c/o Nippon Budokan, 2-3 Kitanomaru-kōen, Chiyoda-ku, Tokyo (☎ 03-3211-5804/5)

Nihon Sumo Kyokai, c/o Kokugikan Sumo Hall, 1-3-28 Yokoami, Sumida-ku, Tokyo (☎ 03-3623-5111)

World Union of Karate-dō Organisation, 4th Floor, Sempaku Shinkokai Building, 1-15-16 Toranomon, Minato-ku, Tokyo (☎ 03-3503-6640)

WORK

There is always debate about how difficult it is to find work in Japan, but one thing most foreigners in Japan agree on is that it is harder than it used to be. The Japanese economy has been through a prolonged downturn and Japanese employers have become more discriminating.

The largest number of foreign workers in Japan these days are from less developed countries. They take on work that the Japanese themselves no longer have a taste for. Building sites and restaurants are just two areas that have become increasingly dominated by (often illegal) foreign workers. Most users of this book are more likely to be doing work the Japanese *can't* do – English teaching and foreign modelling for example.

Finding casual work is certainly still possible, particularly if you look neat and tidy. (Appearances are *very* important in Japan, suit and tie for the men please, businesslike dresses for the women.) But you will need to be determined, and you should have a sizeable sum of money to carry you through while you are looking for work, and possibly to get you out of the country if you don't find any (it happens). Many foreigners who have set up in Japan over the last few years maintain that a figure of around US$5000 or more is necessary to make a go of it in Japan. People do it with less, but they are taking the risk of ending up penniless and homeless before they find a job.

Once upon a time, blonde hair and blue eyes were all that was needed for an English-teaching job; nowadays real qualifications are essential. Be wary of anyone who is prepared to employ you without qualifications – there are some very exploitative deals, especially in Tokyo.

English Teaching

Teaching has always been the easiest job for native-English-speaking foreigners to find. This is definitely no longer the case. Unless you have the basic minimum of a university degree, it would be foolish to roll up in Japan in the hope that a teaching job will come your way. Even qualified teachers sometimes have difficulty finding work. Consider lining up a job before arriving in Japan. Big schools, like Nova for example, now have recruitment programmes in the USA and the UK – US and British English being the two preferred accents for teaching.

Australians, New Zealanders and Canadians, who can take advantage of the Japan working holiday visa (see Visas), are in a slightly better position. Schools are happier about taking on unqualified teachers if they don't have to bother with sponsoring a teacher for a work visa. Nevertheless, Australian and New Zealand (to a lesser extent Canadian) accents are considered less desirable than US and British accents and this can be an impediment to getting a job in one of the better schools. Many working holiday visa recipients find themselves working for small, unreliable outfits.

Private Schools The Monday edition of the *Japan Times* is the best place to look for teaching jobs. Some larger schools rely on direct inquiries from would-be teachers.

Tokyo is the easiest place to find teaching jobs; schools across Japan advertise or recruit in the capital. Heading straight to another of Japan's major population centres (say Osaka, Fukuoka, Hiroshima or Sapporo), where there are smaller numbers of competing gaijin, is also a good bet.

Check the fine print carefully once you have an offer. Find out how many hours you will teach, whether class preparation time is included and whether you get sick leave and paid holidays. Find out how and when you will be paid and if the school will sponsor your visa. It's worth checking with other foreign staff to find how they are treated. Check also whether your school is prepared to serve as a guarantor in the event that you rent an apartment.

Government Schools The JET programme provides 2000 teaching assistant positions for foreign teachers. The job operates on a yearly contract and will have to be organised in your home country. The programme gets very good reports from many of the teachers involved with it.

Teachers employed by the JET programme are known as Assistant English Teachers (AETs). Although you will have to apply in your home country in order to work as an AET with JET, it's worth bearing in mind that many local governments in Japan are also employing AETs for their schools. Such work can be obtained in Japan without having to go home.

International Schools Big cities like Tokyo and Yokohama with large foreign populations have a number of international schools for the children of foreign residents. Work is available for experienced, western-trained teachers in all disciplines and the schools will usually organise your visa.

Rewriting

Since the general standard of translation in Japan ranges from bad to comical, transforming 'Japlish' into English has become a big industry. Technical documents and manuals pose particular problems and, ideally, visitors hoping to work as translators should also have the appropriate technical knowledge. Rewriting work is harder to come by than teaching but try the *Japan Times*. Office jobs usually pay ¥2000 to ¥3000 per hour.

Hostessing

Most company expense accounts stretch to the odd night at a hostess club, where the women pour drinks for salarymen, listen to their troubles and generally provide an amiable atmosphere. Hostessing has been described as 'psychological prostitution', but there is no pressure to grant sexual favours; it's more a matter of slipping on the mask, making light conversation, perhaps giggling at the occasional innuendoes.

Working visas are not issued for hostessing – it's an illegal activity to which the authorities seem to turn a blind eye. An introduction is usually required, but at any gaijin house there will usually be women working in this field. Rates for western women working as hostesses typically range from ¥2000 to ¥3000 per hour (plus tips), with bonuses for bringing customers to the club. An ability to speak Japanese is an asset, but not essential – many Japanese salarymen want to practise their English with a hostess.

Modelling

Modelling jobs for foreigners are increasingly dominated by professional models; you will need a proper portfolio of photographs. Non-professionals are more likely to pick up casual work as extras in advertising or film.

ACCOMMODATION

Japan offers an interesting diversity of accommodation styles, particularly for those with some money to throw around – a budget room is almost a contradiction in terms in Japan. Where they do occur, the best deals are to be found in Japanese-style accommodation.

Youth hostels are the bottom of the range. The average cost is ¥2400 to ¥2600. But by staying only at youth hostels, you will also cut yourself off from an essential part of the Japan experience. Try to vary your accommodation routine, and include at least one night at a traditional ryokan (Japanese-style inn), a *shukubō* (temple lodging) and a minshuku (Japanese B&B).

Cheap places to stay are often further out of town, which can mean an expensive taxi ride if you arrive late. If you get really stuck in the late hours, the nearest *kōban* (police box) should be able to point you in the right direction for a place to stay. Business hotels are often conveniently close to the station, but you're generally looking at an absolute minimum of ¥5000 in one of these. Capsule hotels or love hotels are useful late-night alternatives.

Reservations

Generally, it is quite feasible to look for a room when you arrive in a new town, though reservations are best made a few days in advance. During peak holiday seasons, you should book as far ahead as possible, particularly if you have a special choice. Out of season, calling a day in advance is usually sufficient.

The information offices (annai-jo) at main railway stations can usually help with reservations, and are often open until about 6.30 pm or later. Even if you are travelling by car, the railway station is a good first stop in town for information, reservations and even cheap car parking. The Japanese run their accommodation according to an established rhythm which favours checkouts at around 10 am and check-ins between 5 and 7 pm; unannounced latecomers disturb their pattern.

Making phone reservations in English is usually possible in most major cities. Providing you speak clearly and simply, there will usually be someone around who can get the gist of what you want.

But there will also be frequent occasions when hotel staff understand no English. If you really get stuck, try asking the desk staff at the last place you stayed to phone your reservation through.

It is possible to make bookings at the TIC offices in Tokyo and Kyoto. JNTO offices abroad and TIC offices in Tokyo and Kyoto stock some useful magazines, such as *Reasonable Accommodations in Japan*, which has details of 200 hotels, ryokan and business hotels in 50 major cities in Japan. Other useful publications include *Directory of Welcome Inns*, a very extensive listing, and *Japanese Inn Group*, which has a number of ryokan throughout Japan that are used to dealing with foreigners.

Gaijin Houses

This is the cheapest category of accommodation, especially for long-term stays, but you should be prepared for basic dorms or shared tatami rooms and probably a communal kitchen. Prices for the cheapest houses start around ¥1800 per night. Some places offer reductions for stays longer than a month.

Gaijin houses are only found in Tokyo and Kyoto. They advertise in publications such as *Tokyo Journal*, *Kansai Time Out* and *Kyoto Visitor's Guide*. TIC offices do not provide information on gaijin houses; many of them are illegal.

Youth Hostels

For budget travellers youth hostels are best, and it is quite feasible to plan an entire itinerary using them. By far the best source of information on hostels is the (Japan) *Youth Hostel Handbook* available for ¥580 from the Japan Youth Hostel Association (JYHA) (☎ 03-3288-1417), Suidobashi Nishi-guchi Kaikan, 2-20-7, Misaki-chō, Chiyoda-ku, Tokyo 101.

Branch offices in Tokyo which stock the handbook and can supply information are in the 2nd level basement of Sogo department store, Yūraku-chō (two minutes on foot from TIC); the 4th floor of the Keiō department store, Shinjuku; and the 7th floor of the Seibu department store, Ikebukuro. Many hostels throughout Japan also sell the handbook.

The *Youth Hostels Map of Japan* is a useful map with one-line entries for each hostel on the reverse. It's published jointly with JNTO, and is available free from JNTO and TICs in Japan.

The JYHA handbook is mostly in Japanese, though there is some English at the front in the symbol key and on the locator map keys. The hostels on each map are identified by name (in kanji) and a page number. Each hostel is accompanied by a mini-map, photo, address in Japanese, fax and phone details, a row of symbols, access instructions in Japanese, open dates, bed numbers and prices for bed and meals.

By looking at the photos and the symbols it is quite easy to single out hostels which might be interesting. The reversed swastika symbol means that the hostel is a temple. Pay careful attention to the closing and opening dates: many hostels – particularly those in rural areas – close over New Year or shut down in the winter. For the musically inclined, the handbook even has a page with the words and music for the 'Youth Hostel Song'.

The *Youth Hostel Map of Japan* has hostel addresses in English, but it can still be a struggle trying to work out a romaji version of the address. The *IYHF Handbook* has a ridiculously skimpy set of entries for Japan and is not worth considering for a Japan trip.

Youth Hostel Categories There are various categories of youth hostel in Japan: JYHA hostels, privately run and government-subsidised hostels, ryokan hostels and hostels run by youth organisations, shrines and temples. In general, the atmosphere is more relaxed at privately run hostels, ryokan and religious establishments; the other hostels can sometimes feel as if they are being run as military camps.

Membership & Regulations You can stay at over 70 municipal hostels without a youth-hostel membership card. Elsewhere, you will need a JYHA membership card or one from an affiliate of the International Youth Hostel Federation (IYHF), otherwise you must pay an extra charge. It is much simpler if you become a member in your own country, as JYHA registration requires that members have lived in Japan for a year, have an Alien Registration Card and pay a ¥2000 joining fee.

Nonmembers must pay an additional ¥600 per night for a 'welcome stamp'. Six welcome stamps plus a photograph entitles you to an IYHF International Guest Card valid worldwide for the rest of the year. If you purchase all six stamps at once the price is reduced to ¥2800, a saving of ¥800.

Youth hostel membership has a minimum age limit of four years but no maximum age – you will meet plenty of Japanese seniors and often a few foreign ones approaching their 70s as well.

Hostel charges currently average ¥2400 per night; some also add the 5% consumption tax *(shōhizei)*. Private rooms are also available in some hostels at ¥3500 per night upwards. Average prices for meals are ¥450 for breakfast and ¥750 for dinner. Although official regulations state that you can only stay at one hostel for three consecutive nights, this probably depends on the season.

Almost all hostels require you to use a regulation sleeping sheet which you can rent for ¥100 if you do not have your own. As a friendly gesture, some hostels have introduced a special reduction – sometimes as much as ¥500 per night – for foreign hostellers.

Hostellers are expected to check in between 3 and 8 pm. Checkout is usually required before 10 am and dormitories are closed between 10 am and 3 pm. Bath time is usually between 5 and 9 pm, dinner time is between 6 and 7.30 pm, breakfast time is between 7 and 8 am.

Hostel Food The food at hostels varies widely: some places provide stodgy and unimaginative fare while others pull out all the stops to offer excellent value. At consecutive hostels in Hokkaidō, you may be served a luscious Jenghis Khan hotpot one night, sukiyaki the next and sashimi the following night – all accompanied by copious complimentary beer.

The hostel breakfast is usually Japanese style, for which it takes a little time to acquire a taste. Many travellers skip *natto* (fermented soybeans), *nōre* (seaweed) and raw egg and head off in search of a *mōningu* set breakfast of coffee, toast and a boiled egg from a nearby coffee shop. It can even work out cheaper doing it this way. Many hostels now allow alcohol on the premises. Some require you to help with the washing-up, others prefer to keep you out of the kitchen.

Reservations Advance reservations are essential for the New Year holiday weeks, March, the late April/early May Golden Week, and July and August. You should state the arrival date and time, number of nights, number and sex of the people for whom beds are to be reserved and the meals required. When corresponding from abroad *always* include two International Reply Coupons.

In Japan, computer bookings can be made in Tokyo and Osaka and increasing numbers of youth hostels are plugging into the system. Some hostels also have fax numbers. For confirmation, return postage-paid postcards are available from post offices or to make things even simpler, use the pre-printed cards available from JYHA headquarters in Tokyo.

Telephone bookings are fine if you can muster enough Japanese. One way to simplify things is to ask a Japanese, perhaps a fellow hosteller or a member of the youth hostel staff, to make the booking for you.

Out of season you can probably get away with booking a day or so in advance. Hostels definitely prefer you to phone, even if it's from across the street, rather than simply rolling up without warning. If you arrive without warning, you shouldn't expect any meals.

Advantages & Disadvantages Youth hostels are comfortable, inexpensive by Japanese standards, and usually good sources of information when used as a base for touring. They are also a good way to meet Japanese travellers and other foreigners. By carefully studying the JYHA handbook, you can select interesting places and weed out possible duds. Many hostels have superb sites: some are farms, remote temples, outstanding private homes or elegant inns.

Some hostels, however, have very early closing hours, often 9 pm, and a routine strongly reminiscent of school or perhaps even prison. In the high season you are likely to encounter waves of school children or throngs of students. Some hostels organise meetings in the evening with games, songs and dances, which any resident gaijin may find difficult to decline. The novelty of these can wear thin. If you are reliant on public transport, access to some youth hostels is complicated and time-consuming.

Shukubō
Staying in a shukubō or temple lodging is one way to experience another facet of traditional Japan. Sometimes you are allocated a simple room in the temple precincts and left to your own devices. You may also be allowed to participate in prayers, services or zazen meditation. At many temples the meals are vegetarian *(shōjin ryōri)*.

The TICs in Tokyo and Kyoto both produce leaflets on temple lodgings in their regions. Kōya-san, a renowned religious centre, includes over 50 shukubō and is one of the best places in Japan to try this type of accommodation.

Over 70 youth hostels are temples or shrines – look for the reverse swastika symbol in the JYHA handbook. The suffixes -ji or -in are also clues that the hostel is a temple.

Toho & Mitsubachi

The Toho network is a diverse collection of places which have banded loosely together offering a more flexible alternative to youth hostels at a reasonable price. Most of the 70 places are in Hokkaidō, although there are a few in northern and central Japan. The emphasis seems to be on informal hospitality, outdoor pursuits, and accommodation with original architecture such as log cabins. Some members of Toho function as rider houses (*mitsubachi*) which offer reasonable accommodation to those touring on motorcycles. The main drawback (or attraction for some travellers) of these places is that most of them are difficult to reach. English is rarely spoken.

Prices average ¥3500 per person per night, without meals, or ¥4200 with two meals. A list of Network members is available, in Japanese only, for ¥150 plus postage. The list is published by Mr Shinpei Koshika (☎ 011-271-2668), Sukkarakan, South 3 West 8, Chūō-ku, Sapporo 060, Hokkaidō. You will need to know some Japanese to make the most of this list. An English version of this booklet is reportedly being produced.

Cycling Terminals

Cycling terminals (*saikuringu tāminaru*) provide low-priced accommodation of the bunk-bed or tatami-mat variety and are usually found in scenic areas suited to cycling. If you don't have your own bike, you can rent one at the terminal.

At around ¥2500 per person per night or ¥4000 including two meals, terminal prices compare favourably with those of a youth hostel. For more information contact the Japan Bicycle Promotion Institute (☎ 03-3583-5444), Nihon Jitensha Kaikan Building, 1-9-3 Akasaka, Minato-ku, Tokyo.

Camping Grounds & Mountain Huts

Camping is one of the cheapest forms of accommodation, but official camping grounds are often only open during the Japanese 'camping season' (July and August), when you can expect an avalanche of students. Facilities range from bare essentials to deluxe. JNTO publishes *Camping in Japan*, a limited selection of camping grounds with details of prices and facilities.

In some restricted areas and national parks, camping wild is forbidden, but elsewhere, foreigners have reported consistent success. Even if there is no officially designated camping ground, campers are often directed to the nearest large patch of grass. Provided you set up camp late in the afternoon and leave early, nobody seems to mind, though it would be common courtesy to ask permission first (assuming you can find the person responsible). Public toilets, usually spotless, and water taps are very common, even in remote parts of Japan.

The best areas for camping are Hokkaidō, the Japan Alps, Tōhoku and Okinawa.

Mountain huts are common in many of the hiking and climbing areas. Unoccupied huts provide a free roof over your head. Other huts, in the Japan Alps for example, are run privately and offer bed and board (two meals) at around ¥5000 per person.

Kokuminshukusha

Kokuminshukusha (people's lodges) are government institutions offering affordable accommodation in scenic areas. Prices average ¥5500 to ¥6500 per person per night including two meals.

Kokumin Kyūka Mura

National vacation villages or *kokumin kyūka mura* are also government sponsored and many offer camping or sports facilities in national parks. Prices are similar to those of the people's lodges.

Kaikan

Kaikan (literally 'meeting hall') is hotel-style accommodation sponsored by government or public organisations. Nonmembers are often accepted. A typical price per person per night is around ¥6000, including two meals.

Minshuku

A minshuku is usually a family-run private lodging, rather like a B&B in Europe or the USA. Minshuku can be found throughout Japan and offer one way to peep into daily Japanese life. The average price per person per night with two meals is around ¥5500. You are expected to lay out and put away your bedding and bring your own towel.

JNTO publishes a booklet, *Minshukus in Japan*, which lists details of about 300 minshuku. The Japan Minshuku Association (☎ 03-3364-1855), Sukegawa Building, 4-10-15, Takadanobaba, Shinjuku-ku Tokyo, has a leaflet in English describing the minshuku concept and providing advice on staying at one; a list of minshuku is also available. The Japan Minshuku Center (☎ 03-3216-6556), Tokyo Kōtsū Kaikan Building, 21 Yūraku-chō, Chiyoda-ku, Tokyo 100 can help with computer bookings; a similar office operates in Kyoto. Some of the places listed in the Japanese Inn Group's handy little booklet (see the following Ryokan section) are really minshuku rather than ryokan. The line between the two accommodation categories can be fuzzy.

Ryokan

For a taste of traditional Japanese life, a stay at a ryokan is mandatory (see Staying at a Ryokan). Ryokan range from ultra-exclusive establishments (priced accordingly and available only to guests bearing a personal recommendation) to reasonably priced places with a homy atmosphere, and there are corresponding fluctuations in what you get for your money. Prices start around ¥4000 (per person, per night) for a 'no-frills' ryokan without meals. For a classier ryokan, expect prices to start at ¥8000. Exclusive establishments – Kyoto is a prime centre for these – charge ¥25,000 and often much more.

Ryokan owners prefer to charge on a room and board (breakfast and dinner) per person basis. If, like many foreigners, you find yourself overwhelmed by the unusual offerings

of a Japanese breakfast, it should be possible to have dinner only, but in many ryokan, opting out of both meals is unacceptable. The bill is reduced by about 10% if you decline breakfast.

A 10% to 20% service charge is added to your bill. If the total charge for accommodation, food, drink and other services per person per night is ¥10,000 or less, a 3% tax applies – a bill over ¥10,000 attracts 6% tax. Tipping is not expected.

Ryokan Guides & Addresses The Welcome Inn Reservation Centre (☎ 03-3211-4201), 9th floor, Kōtsū Kaikan Building, 2-10-1 Yūraku-chō, Chiyoda-ku, Tokyo 100, publishes regional guides to ryokan and hotels that welcome foreigners. The *Directory of Welcome Inns* pamphlets are available at TICs, where bookings can also be made. Room rates range from ¥4000.

JNTO publishes the *Japan Ryokan Guide*, a listing of government-registered members of the Japan Ryokan Association (JRA). Prices start around ¥8000 and rise to astronomical heights.

Pensions

Pensions are usually run by young couples offering western-style accommodation based on the European pension concept, and many offer sports and leisure facilities. They are common in rural areas. Pensions seem to specialise in quaint names like Pension Fruit Juice, Pension Pheasant or Pension Morning Salada and often have decidedly quaint decor as well, sometimes like a romantic Japanese dream of a European country cottage.

Prices average ¥6000 per person per night or ¥8500 including two meals. Food is often excellent, typically a French dinner and an American breakfast. JNTO publishes *Pensions in Japan*, a selection of pensions all over Japan.

Capsule Hotels

In the '70s, the Japanese architect Kurokawa Kisho, came up with the idea of modifying a shipping container to hold a bed, bath and all 'mod cons'. A site was found for his construction which can still be seen on the outskirts of Tokyo's Ginza area.

Capsule hotels *(capseru hoteru)* have reduced the original concept to a capsule measuring two metres by one metre by one metre – about the size of a coffin. Inside is a bed, a TV, a reading light, a radio and an alarm clock. Personal belongings are kept in a locker room.

This type of hotel is common in the major cities and often caters to travellers who have partied too hard to make it home or have missed the last train. There are a few for women only, but the majority are only for men. Some capsule hotels have the added attraction of a sauna.

An average price is ¥3800 per night or ¥1400 for a three hour stay. You could try one as a novelty, but it's not an experience recommended to those who easily become claustrophobic.

Business Hotels

These are economical and practical places geared to the single traveller, usually lesser-ranking business types who want somewhere close to the station. Rooms are clean, western style, just big enough for you to turn around in and include a miniature bath/WC unit. A standard fitting for the stressed businessman is a coin-operated TV with a porno channel. Vending machines replace room service.

Staying at a Ryokan

On arrival at the ryokan, you leave your shoes at the entrance, don a pair of slippers, and are shown by a maid to your room, which has a *tatami* (reed mat) floor. Slippers are taken off before entering tatami rooms. Instead of using numbers, rooms are named after auspicious flowers, plants or trees.

The interior of the room will contain an alcove *(tokonoma)*, probably decorated with a flower display or a calligraphy scroll. One side of the room will contain a cupboard with sliding doors for the bedding; the other side will have sliding screens covered with rice paper and perhaps open onto a veranda with a garden view.

The room maid then serves tea with a sweet on a low table surrounded by cushions *(zabuton)* in the centre of the room. At the same time you are asked to sign the register. A tray is provided with a towel, cotton robe *(yukata)* and belt *(obi)* which you put on before taking your bath. Remember to wear the left side over the right – the reverse order is used for dressing the dead. In colder weather, there will also be an outer jacket *(tanzen)*. Your clothes can be put away in a closet or left on a hanger.

Dressed in your yukata, you will be shown to the bath *(o-furo)*. At some ryokan, there are rooms with private baths, but the communal ones are often designed with 'natural' pools or a window looking out into a garden. Bathing is communal, but sexes are segregated. Make sure you can differentiate between the bathroom signs for men 男 and women 女 – although ryokan used to catering for foreigners will often have signs in English. Many inns will have family bathrooms for couples or families.

Dressed in your yukata after your bath, you return to your room where the maid will have laid out dinner – in some ryokan, dinner is provided in a separate room but you still wear your yukata for dining. Dinner usually includes standard dishes such as miso soup, pickles *(tsukemono)*, vegetables in vinegar *(sunomono)*, hors d'oeuvres *(zensai)*, fish – either grilled or raw (sashimi), and perhaps tempura and a stew. There will also be bowls for rice, dips and sauces. Depending on the price, meals at a ryokan can become flamboyant displays of local cuisine or refined arrangements of *kaiseki* (a cuisine which obeys strict rules of form and etiquette for every detail of the meal and setting).

After dinner, while you are pottering around or out for a stroll admiring the garden, the maid will clear the dishes and prepare your bedding. A mattress is placed on the tatami floor and a quilt put on top. In colder weather, you can also add a blanket *(mōfu)*.

In the morning, the maid will knock to make sure you are awake and then come in to put away the bedding before serving breakfast – sometimes this is served in a separate room. Breakfast usually consists of pickles, dried seaweed *(nori)*, raw egg, dried fish, miso soup and rice. It can take a while for foreign stomachs to accept this novel fare early in the morning.

The Japanese tendency is to make the procedure at a ryokan seem rather rarefied for foreign comprehension and some ryokan are wary of accepting foreign guests. However, once you've grasped the basics, it really isn't that hard to fit in. ∎

Cheap single rooms can sometimes be found for ¥4500, though the average rate is around ¥6000; most business hotels also have twin rooms; doubles are rare. Cheaper business hotels usually do not have a service charge, though places costing ¥7000 or more often add a 10% charge.

The Japan Business Hotel Association at 43 Kanda-Higashi, Matsusita-chō, Chiyoda-ku, Tokyo, publishes the *Business Hotel Guide*, a handy pamphlet which lists business hotels throughout Japan along with phone numbers, prices, addresses and access details. Ask for a copy at JNTO or TIC. The Japanese version is useful if you need to give directions to a taxi driver – match up the phone numbers in the Japanese and English versions. Popular business hotel chains include Green Hotel found near so many railway stations, Sun Route, Washington, Tōkyū Inns and Hokke Club. The Hokke Club hotels are unusual in their conveniently early check-in and late checkout times. Most Japanese hotels kick you out by 10 or 11 am and won't let you check in until 3 or 4 pm.

Hotels

Deluxe and 1st class hotels offering the usual array of frills and comforts have sprung up in most of Japan's major cities and are comparable to the best in the USA and Europe. Singles start around ¥8000 and rise to a cool ¥20,000 or way beyond if you fancy a suite. The Japan Hotel Association has 445 government-registered members, all neatly listed in an informative JNTO leaflet, *Hotels in Japan*.

Some of the leading hotel chains, such as ANA Hotels, Holiday Inns, The New Otani Hotels, Prince Hotels and Tōkyū Hotels have overseas offices. Bookings can also be made through the overseas offices of major Japanese travel agencies such as Japan Travel Bureau (JTB), Kintetsu International, Tōkyū Tourist Corporation, Nippon Travel Agency (NTA) and Japan Air Lines (JAL). Most of these agencies also have schemes for discount hotel coupons such as JTB's 'Sunrise Super Saver', NTA's 'NTA Hotel Pass' or JAL's 'Room & Rail'.

Expect to pay 10% or more as a service charge plus a 5% consumer tax; add another 3% local tax if the bill exceeds ¥10,000. Asking for separate bills for meals can sometimes reduce the tax paid.

Love Hotels

Love hotels are one of the wild cards of Japanese accommodation. They are there as a short-time base for couples to enjoy some privacy. Customers are not necessarily singles in search of sex; the hotels are also used by married couples, who often lack space at home for relaxing together.

To find one on the street, just look for flamboyant facades with rococo architecture, turrets, battlements and imitation statuary. The design of the hotels emphasises discretion: entrances and exits are kept separate; keys are provided through a small opening without contact between desk clerk and guest; photos of the rooms are displayed to make the choice easy for the customer. There's often a discreetly curtained parking area so your car cannot be seen once inside.

The rooms can fulfil most fantasies, with themes ranging from harem extravaganza to sci-fi. Further choices can include vibrating beds, wall-to-wall mirrors, bondage equipment and video recorders to recall the experience (don't forget to take the video cassette with you when you leave).

Charges on an hourly basis are at a peak during the day and early evening. Love hotels are of more interest to foreign visitors after 10 pm, when it's possible to stay the night for about ¥5000 per room (rather than per person), but you should check out early enough in the morning to avoid a return to peak-hour rates. Outside love hotels there will usually be a sign in Japanese (occasionally in English) announcing the rates for a 'rest' (usually two hours) or a 'stay' (overnight).

Long-Term Accommodation

If you're intending to stay longer in Japan, a job offer which appears lucrative at first sight may seem markedly less so when you work out your rent and other living costs. Ideally, you can avoid many hassles by negotiating decent accommodation as part of your work contract.

If at all possible, get a Japanese to help you with your search and negotiations since Japanese landlords are notoriously wary of foreign tenants and often prefer to do business with a local go-between. If you are on good terms with a Japanese friend, this person may offer to act as a *hoshō-nin* (guarantor). This represents considerable commitment and the guarantor's *hanko* (seal) is usually required on your rental contract.

A pitfall which is often overlooked is that you may have to lay out four, possibly as much as seven months' rent *in advance*. For starters, there's one to two months' rent payable as *reikin* (key money). This is a non-refundable gift that goes into the pocket of the landlord. Then there's a *shikikin* (damage deposit) of one to three months' rent. This is refundable at a later date as long as both sides agree there's no damage. Avoid later squabbles over shikikin by making duplicate inventories, signed by both parties, before you move in. The *fudōsan-ya* (estate agent) will of course want *tesūryō* – one month's rent as a non-refundable handling fee. Finally, you have to pay *maekin* which is one month's rent in advance and is also non-refundable.

These high, up-front costs are cogent reasons why foreigners looking for long-term employment in Japan should arrive with a sizeable financial float. This will allow more time to choose a decent job and avoid the scenario – assuming your stay was mostly motivated by financial gain – of leaving Japan with very little to show for your stay and an embittered feeling about the place.

Standard contracts often run for two years and some *ōya-san* (landowners) may require the additional payment of maintenance fees and fire insurance. When *kōshin* (renewal) comes up, you should expect a raise in your *yachin* (monthly rent). When you decide to move on, make absolutely sure you give notice *at least* one month in advance. Otherwise you will be landed with payment of an extra month's rent.

What to Look For It's usually best for budget travellers to find their feet in a gaijin house before putting out feelers for other accommodation. Inner city rentals are obviously high, as are those for chic suburban areas. Commuting costs often reduce the apparent gain of lower rental costs outside town and you may not like your nightlife being curtailed by transport timetables.

At the top end of the housing market are *manshon*, which are modern concrete condominiums or rental apartments. At the lower end are *danchi*, functional concrete blocks of public flats, which are sought after by those with moderate or low incomes.

Japanese are often amazed at the spaciousness of western housing, since the average Japanese family in the city makes do with much less space in their apartment. If you want a house or apartment similar to urban sizes in the west, you can expect to pay several million yen a month.

In major cities like Tokyo and Kyoto, gaijin houses are the cheapest options for long-term stays, but you should be prepared for basic dorms or shared tatami rooms and a communal kitchen. Prices for the cheapest houses start around ¥1600 per night. If you negotiate for a monthly price, you may be able to reduce the rent to ¥30,000 per month.

Where to Look There are several methods to hunt for housing – it depends what you want and how long you intend to stay.

Asking other foreigners at work or play in schools, clubs, bars, gaijin houses, etc is one way of locating long-term accommodation. If you strike lucky, you may find somebody leaving the country or moving on who is willing to dump their job contacts, housing and effects in one friendly package.

Notice boards are another good source and are often found at tourist information offices, international clubs, conversation clubs, etc. Even if there's nothing on the board, ask someone in charge for a few tips.

Regional and city magazines aimed at foreigners often have classified ads offering or seeking accommodation. In Tokyo, you should look at *Tokyo Journal*, *Tokyo Flea Market* or *Tokyo Classifieds*; for the Kansai area (Osaka, Kōbe, Kyoto, Nara) you should peruse *Kansai Time Out*. There are plenty of other magazines all over Japan with suitable ads. TIC or the local tourist office should know which publications are best, particularly if you decide to live somewhere more remote like Hokkaidō or Okinawa.

Newspapers also have classified ads for rentals. The Friday edition of the *Japan Times* is a good example. If you want to get an idea of long-term accommodation costs before travelling to Japan, pick up a copy of this edition. JNTO offices and Japanese embassies usually have back copies lying around.

Common abbreviations in rental ads include K – kitchen, D – dining room, L – living room, UB – unit bath (combined bath and toilet). An ad specifying 3LDK, for example, means three bedrooms and one living room combined with dining kitchen. The size of rooms is usually given in standard tatami mat measurements, known as *jō*. There are several tatami sizes, but as a general rule of thumb, one tatami mat equals one jō which is 1.8 metres by 0.9 metres (1.62 sq metres). A room described as being 4.5 jō, for example, is 7.29 sq metres: a medium-sized room by Japanese standards but poky by western standards.

Using a fudōsan-ya (estate agent) is the most expensive option and really only feasible if you intend to stay a long time and need to determine exactly the type and location of your housing. English-language magazines such as *Tokyo Journal* and *Kansai Time Out* carry ads from estate agents specialising in accommodation for foreigners.

Additional Costs Before you sign your contract, ask the landlord for precise details about gas, electricity and water. Check if a telephone is already installed since installation of a new telephone is a costly business. You can expect to pay around ¥75,000 but you've then purchased the right to have a phone line anywhere in Japan. This right is negotiable, either privately or through private agencies which deal in phone rights. If you move and want to take your phone line with you, the charge for transferral is around ¥13,000.

Japan is introducing schemes for recycling garbage: in some cities residents are asked to separate it into *moeru-gomi* (burnable), *moenai-gomi* (non-burnable), and *shigen-gomi* (recyclable). If you hear a noisy truck grinding through your area with a loudspeaker announcing '*chirigami kōkan*', your area will have a system to save used newspapers and magazines. In return for your used newspapers and magazines, you will be given rolls of toilet paper and garbage liners.

ENTERTAINMENT

Japan offers visitors a wealth of entertainment opportunities including everything from traditional performances of kabuki to rock and roll bars. Tokyo, Osaka and Kyoto are the best places for entertainment, traditional or otherwise, but provincial cities and rural tourist destinations often turn up a surprise find.

The only complaint most visitors have with entertainment in Japan is the expense involved. Cinema tickets, for example, range from ¥1800 to ¥2000, which probably makes Japan the most expensive place in the world to catch a movie. Live music prices are also high, ranging from around ¥1500 for a local act to ¥6000 and upwards for international stars.

Cinemas

If you are willing to fork out a fistful of yen for your movie-going pleasure, Japan's major cities (in particular Tokyo) offer the opportunity to catch up with everything from the latest Hollywood blockbusters to rare art-house releases. In Tokyo, the best place to find out what's playing where is *Tokyo Journal*. Screening times are indicated, and the magazine also includes useful maps for finding the cinemas. *Kansai Time Out* has info on movie screenings for the Kansai area (Osaka, Kyoto and Kōbe), and in the Nagoya area *Eyes* does the same thing.

Clubs & Discos

Before you think about heading off to a club, bear in mind that you are probably going to be hit for a ¥4000 to ¥5000 cover charge. This will usually include two or three drinks, but it still makes for an expensive night of dancing. In the big cities like Tokyo, Osaka, Kyoto, Fukuoka and Sapporo there are usually a few bars around with no cover charge that have dancing on Friday and Saturday nights.

Traditional Entertainment

Kabuki is one of the most popular traditional entertainments, and the best place to see it is Tokyo. This is true too of nō, though tickets tend to sell out quickly and performance schedules vary – check with the TIC. Bunraku is an Osaka tradition. In Kyoto there are tourist performances that include a little of everything, including kyogen – comic interludes – and gagaku – court orchestral music. Such performances, it must be said, are touristy.

Geisha entertainment is too expensive for most travellers. Some operators offer 'geisha night tours' of Tokyo, but such activities are only for those with little sensitivity to the feeling of being processed through a cultural event. The real thing will cost around ¥50,000 per head (or more) and will require introductions.

Live Houses & Bars

Live houses and bars are the cheapest nightlife option for travellers and foreign residents in Japan. It's well worth making a point of at least calling into one 'gaijin bar' while you are in Japan. For many travellers it will be their best opportunity to meet young Japanese in an informal setting.

Very few of the gaijin bars recommended in this book have entry charges, and where they do they are usually the price of a drink ticket just to ensure that you do spend some money while you are there. Drink prices generally average out at ¥500 for a beer to ¥700 for spirits.

Live houses are venues for local bands and are often worth checking out. Performances tend to start and finish early (say 7.30 to 10 pm). Keep an eye on magazines like *Tokyo Journal* and *Kansai Time Out*.

SPECTATOR SPORT
Sumo

Sumo, Japanese wrestling, is a simple sport; it's the ritual surrounding it that is complicated. The rules of the game are deceptively simple – the *higashi* (east) wrestler tries either to push his *nishi* (west) opponent out of the ring or unbalance him so that some part of his body other than his feet touch the ground. The 4.55 metre diameter ring *(dohyō)* is on a raised platform, much like a boxing ring, but there the similarity ends. Sumo matches do not go 10 rounds, they are brief and often spectacular and the ritual and build up to the brief encounter is just as important as the clash itself.

There are no weight classes in sumo; they're all big, and in lookalike Japan, sumo wrestlers certainly stand out. Gargantuan bulk is the order of the day and sumo wrestlers achieve their pigged-out look through diet (or lack of it from the weight-watcher's point of view). Large quantities of an especially fattening stew called *chankonabe* are supplemented with esoteric activities, such as masseurs who manipulate the wrestler's intestines so they can pack more food in. Would-be sumo wrestlers, usually 15-year-olds from rural areas, traditionally join one of the 28 *heya* (stables) of wrestlers, often run by retired fighters, and work their way up through the ranks.

Sumo still retains traces of its connections to Shinto fertility rites, including the shrine-like roof which hangs over the ring and the referee or *gyōji* in his wizard-like outfit. It is said that the dagger worn by the referee was to allow him to commit instant seppuku if he made a bad refereeing decision! The wrestlers wear a *mawashi* with a broad leather belt; it's rather like a *fundoshi*, the traditional loincloth drawn between the buttocks. A good grasp on the belt is a favourite hold but there are 48 recognised holds and throws.

The pre-game preliminaries often last far longer than the actual struggle, as the opponents first hurl salt into the dohyō to purify it and then put great effort into psyching each other out with malevolent looks and baleful stares. A series of false starts often follows before two immovable objects finally collide with an earth-shaking wallop. Sometimes that initial collision is enough to tip one of them out of the ring but usually there's a brief interlude of pushing, shoving, lifting and tripping. Sometimes neither opponent is able to get a grip on the other and they stand there, slapping at each other like two angry, and very overweight, infants.

The Tokyo sumo stables are in Ryōgoku, near the new Kokugikan sumo arena. Six major sumo tournaments (basho) are held each year: January (Tokyo – Kokugikan Stadium), March (Osaka – Furitsu Taiikaikan Gymnasium), May (Tokyo – Kokugikan Stadium), July (Nagoya – Aichi Kenritsu Taiikukan Gymnasium), September (Tokyo – Kokugikan Stadium) and November (Fukuoka – Kokusai Center Sogo Hall).

At a basho, prices start at ¥1000 for a basic bench seat at the back, but if you can afford ¥7000 for a balcony seat, you will not only be closer to the action but will also be able to delve deep into the mysteries of the refreshment bag that comes with the ticket. Ringside seats are highly prized and virtually unobtainable unless you have inside contacts. Tune in to Far East Network (FEN) on 810 kHz for simultaneous radio coverage of the action in English. TV coverage is extensive and most of the English-language newspapers devote a section to sumo.

Each basho commences on the Sunday closest to the 10th of the month and lasts a fortnight, during which each wrestler competes in one bout a day. The big crowds arrive in the late afternoon to watch the top-ranking wrestlers; the earlier part of the day is reserved for the lower-ranking fighters.

If you want to see a sumo bout, but arrive in Japan at a time when no basho is being held, you can visit one of the sumo stables to watch training. JNTO publishes a leaflet entitled Traditional Sports which has a sumo section with full details of tournaments, purchase of tickets, visits to sumo stables and even a bibliography of books and magazines in English on the subject. Contact TIC for more information.

Wrestlers who reach the rank of yokozuna or 'grand champion' become celebrity figures in Japan. With the exception of several Hawaiians, very few foreigners have successfully made the big time in this sport. And what happens to a retired sumo wrestler? Well he loses weight, cuts his hair and returns to Japanese anonymity; many sumo wrestlers experience severe heart problems later in their lives.

Baseball

Sumo wrestling may be the most Japanese sporting activity, but baseball is Japan's number one sport both for spectators and participants. Baseball bounced into Japan in 1873 with a US teacher, Horace Wilson, who taught at Tokyo University. There have been professional teams since the 1930s and, just as in the USA, there are little-league teams, school teams, work teams and 'bunch of friends in the local park' teams. At the professional level, however, baseball is big business and the nightly televised games draw huge audiences.

Despite the similarity to American baseball – even many of the terms (double play, first base, home run) are carried straight over without translation – baseball has been cleverly altered to fit the Japanese mood. Read Robert Whiting's You've Got to Have Wa (Macmillan, New York, 1989) for the full story on baseball Japanese-style. Even the Japanese emphasis on the group over the individual has played its part in fitting baseball into the Japanese mould and wa means something like 'team spirit'.

Japanese professional baseball is divided into two leagues: Central and Pacific. Each league has six teams, which are usually given really original names such as Tigers or Giants (although the Hiroshima Carp do sound distinctly Japanese) and are mostly supported or owned by big businesses. Each team is allowed two gaijin players, usually Americans past their prime or facing some sort of contractual difficulty in the USA. They often have trouble adapting to the Japanese requirements that they be just another member of the team, not rock the boat and definitely not show up the local stars!

The season lasts from April to October and

is followed by the Japan Series, a seven-match contest between the top two teams. In Tokyo, the centre of the baseball universe is Kōrakuen Stadium. Expect to pay around ¥700 for a basic seat.

The All-Japan High School Baseball Championship Tournaments are taken very seriously in Japan. These are the major annual sporting events when the flower of youthful vitality goes on display. During August, when the summer tournament is in progress, baseball seems to be the only topic on everybody's mind.

Martial Arts

Japan is renowned for its martial arts, many of which filtered through from China and were then adapted by the Japanese. During feudal times, these arts were highly valued by ruling families as a means of buttressing their power.

After WWII, martial arts were perceived as contributing to the aggressive stance which had led to hostilities and their teaching was discouraged. Within a decade, however, they had returned to favour and are now popular both in Japan and abroad.

For more information contact the TIC or the associations listed in the Martial Arts section of Studying in Japan in this chapter. JNTO also publishes a leaflet entitled *Traditional Sports*, which covers this subject.

Kendō *Kendō*, or the 'way of the sword', is the oldest of the martial arts and was favoured by the samurai to acquire skills in using swords as well as to develop mental poise. Today, it is practised with a bamboo stave and protective body armour, gauntlets and a face mask. The winner of a bout succeeds in landing blows to the face, arms, upper body or throat of an opponent.

Iaijutsu, the art of drawing a sword, is closely related to kendō. One of the few martial arts developed specifically for women was the art of wielding *naginata*, a type of halberd.

Karate Karate (literally, 'empty hands') may have originated in India, but was refined in China and travelled from there to Okinawa, where it took hold as a local martial art. It

began in the 14th century and only continued on to the rest of Japan in the first half of this century. For this reason it is not considered a traditional Japanese martial art.

The emphasis is on unarmed combat, as the name of the sport implies. Blows are delivered with the fists or feet. For optimum performance, all movements require intense discipline of the mind. There are two methods of practising karate. The first is *kumite*, when two or more people spar together. The second is *kata*, when one person performs formal exercises.

Aikidō The roots of this solely defensive art can be traced to the Minamoto clan in the 10th century, but the modern form of *aikidō* was started in the 1920s by Ueshiba Morihei.

Aikidō draws on many different techniques, including shinto, karate and kendō. Breathing and meditation form an integral part of training, as does the concentration on movement derived from classical Japanese dance and the awareness of *ki* (life force or will) flowing from the fingertips.

Judo This is probably the most well known martial art; it has become a popular sport worldwide and regularly features in the Olympic Games.

The origins of this art are found in *jūjutsu*, a means of self defence favoured by the samurai, which was modernised into judo (the 'gentle way') by Kano Jigoro in 1882. The basic principles and subtle skills of the art lie in defeating opponents simply by redirecting the opponents' strength against themselves.

Soccer

Japan's J-League comprises 16 teams. Excitement about the sport has died since the inaugural year of 1993, when it seemed that soccer was poised to sweep away all other sports and become a national obsession. The sport is still popular, though, and the ruling that teams are allowed to employ up to five foreign players means that some of the world's best goal scorers are lifting the standards of play. In Tokyo, matches are played at the National Stadium.

Japanese Cuisine

MASON FLORENCE

Previous page: Restaurant specialising in crab cuisine, Osaka

Top: Tempura

Middle: Yakitori

Bottom: Unajū

FOOD

Those familiar with Japanese food know that eating is half the fun of being in Japan. Even if you've already tried some of Japan's better known specialities, you're likely to be surprised by how delicious the original article is when served on its home turf. More importantly, the adventurous eater will be delighted to find that Japanese food is far more than just the sushi, tempura and sukiyaki for which it is best known in other countries. Indeed, it could be eminently possible to spend a month here and sample a different speciality restaurant each night.

This variety is fairly new to Japan. Until the beginning of this century, Japanese food was spartan at best (at least among the farming masses) and the typical meal consisted of a bowl of rice, some miso soup, a few pickled vegetables and, if one was lucky, some preserved fish. As a Buddhist nation, meat was not eaten until the Meiji Restoration of 1868. Even then, it took some getting used to: early accounts of Japan's first foreign residents are rife with horrified stories of the grotesque dietary practices of 'the barbarians' – including the 'unthinkable' consumption of milk.

These days the Japanese have gone to the opposite extreme and have heartily embraced foreign cuisine. Unfortunately this often means a glut of fast-food restaurants in the downtown areas of most cities. In fact, there are so many McDonald's that the president of McDonald's Japan once remarked that it was only a matter of time before Japanese youth start growing blonde hair!

Those in search of a truly Japanese experience will probably want to avoid such fast-food emporiums to sample some of Japan's more authentic cuisine. Luckily this is quite easy to do, although some may balk at charging into an unfamiliar restaurant where both the language

Zaru soba noodles – to sample one of Japan's most traditional foods, head to a soba-ya for a fortifying, nutritious bowl of freshly made buckwheat noodles.

Eating in a Japanese Restaurant

When you enter a restaurant in Japan, you'll be greeted with a hearty *'Irasshaimase!'* ('Welcome!'). In all but the most casual places the waiter or waitress will next ask you *'Nan-mei sama?'* ('How many people?'). Answer with your fingers, which is what the Japanese do. You will then be led to a table, a place at the counter or a tatami-mat room.

At this point you will be given an *oshibori* (a hot towel), a cup of tea and a menu. The oshibori is for wiping your hands and face. When you're done with it, just roll it up and leave it next to your place. Now comes the hard part: ordering. If you don't read Japanese you can use the romanised translations in this book to help you, or direct the waiter's attention to the Japanese script. If this doesn't work there are two phrases which may help: *'O-susume wa nan desu ka?'* ('What do you recommend?') and *'O-makase shimasu'* ('Please decide for me'). If you're still having problems, you can try pointing at other diners' food or, if the restaurant has them, dragging the waiter outside to point at the plastic food models in the window.

When you've finished eating, you can signal for the bill by crossing one index finger over the other to form the sign of an 'x'. This is the standard sign for 'cheque please'. You can also say *'O-kanjō kudasai'*. Remember there is no tipping in Japan and tea is free of charge. Usually you will be given a bill to take to the cashier at the front of the restaurant. At more up-market places, the host of the party will discreetly excuse him or herself to pay before the group leaves. Unlike some places in the west, one doesn't usually leave cash on the table by way of payment. Only the bigger and more international places take credit cards, so cash is always the surer option.

When leaving, it is polite to say to the restaurant staff, *'Gochisō-sama deshita'* which means, 'It was a real feast'. ∎

and the menu are likely to be incomprehensible. The best way to get over this fear is to familiarise yourself with the main types of Japanese restaurants so that you have some idea of what's on offer and how to order it. Those timid of heart should take solace in the fact that the Japanese will go to extraordinary lengths to understand what you want and will help you to order.

With the exception of *shokudō* (all around eateries) *and izakaya* (drinking restaurants), most Japanese restaurants are speciality restaurants serving only one type of cuisine. This naturally makes for delicious eating, but does limit your choice. The following will introduce the main types of Japanese restaurants, along with the most common dishes served. With a little courage and effort you will soon discover that Japan is a gourmet paradise where good food is taken seriously.

Shokudō

A shokudō, or 'eating place', is the most common type of restaurant in Japan, found near train stations, tourist spots and just about any other place where people congregate. Easily distinguished by the presence of plastic models in the window, these inexpensive places usually serve a variety of Japanese *(washoku)* and western *(yoshoku)* foods. At lunch, and sometimes dinner, the easiest way to order at a shokudō is to order a *teishoku*, or set course meal (sometimes also called *ranchi setto*, lunch set, or *kōsu*). This usually includes a main dish of meat or fish, a bowl of rice, miso (soy-bean paste) soup, shredded cabbage and a few Japanese pickles called *tsukemono*. In addition, most shokudō serve a fairly standard selection of *donburi-mono* (rice dishes) and *menrui* (noodle dishes). When you order noodles, you can choose between *soba* and *udon* noodles, both of which are served with a variety of toppings. If

Soy beans (daizu) – the nutritious base for an endless variety of Japanese foods – soy sauce, miso, tofu and the smelly nattō.

you're at a loss as to what to order, simply tell the waiter *kyō-no-ranchi* (today's lunch) and they'll do the rest. Expect to spend about ¥800 to ¥1000 for a meal at a shokudō. Some of the more common dishes are:

Rice Dishes

katsu-don	カツ丼	a bowl of rice topped with a fried pork cutlet
oyako-don	親子丼	a bowl of rice topped with egg and chicken
niku-don	肉丼	a bowl of rice topped with thin slices of cooked beef
ten-don	天丼	a bowl of rice topped with tempura shrimp and vegetables

Noodle Dishes
(Add 'soba' or 'udon' to the following when ordering)

kake	かけそば／うどん	plain noodles in broth
kitsune	きつねそば／うどん	noodles with fried tofu
tempura	天ぷらそば／うどん	noodles with tempura shrimp
tsukimi	月見そば／うどん	noodles with raw egg on top

Izakaya

An izakaya is the Japanese equivalent of a pub. It's a good place to visit when you want a casual meal, a wide selection of food, a hearty atmosphere and, of course, plenty of beer and sake. When you enter an izakaya, you are given the choice of sitting around the counter, at a table or on a tatami-mat floor. You usually order a bit at a time, choosing from a selection of typical Japanese foods like yakitori, sashimi and grilled fish, as well as Japanese interpretations of western foods like french fries and beef stew.

Izakaya can be identified by their rustic facades, and the red lanterns outside their doors bearing the Chinese characters for izakaya. Since izakaya food is casual drinking fare, it is usually fairly inexpensive. Depending on how much you drink, you can expect to get away with ¥2500 to ¥5000 per person.

In addition to the following dishes, refer to the yakitori and sushi & sashimi sections later on for additional choices.

agedashi-dōfu	揚げだし豆腐	deep fried tofu in a fish stock soup
jaga-batā	ジャガバター	baked potatoes with butter
niku-jaga	肉じゃが	beef and potato stew
shio-yaki-zakana	塩焼魚	a whole fish grilled with salt
yaki-onigiri	焼きおにぎり	a triangle of grilled rice with yakitori sauce
poteto furai	ポテトフライ	french fries
chiizu-age	チーズ揚げ	deep fried cheese
hiya-yakko	冷奴	a cold block of tofu with soy sauce and scallions
tsuna sarada	ツナサラダ	tuna salad over cabbage
yaki-soba	焼きそば	fried noodles with meat and vegetables
kata yaki-soba	固焼きそば	hard fried noodles with meat and vegetables
sashimi mori-awase	刺身盛り合せ	a selection of sliced sashimi

Pickled plums – served with almost every meal, the ubiquitous umeboshi has been appreciated by the Japanese for its health-giving properties for hundreds of years.

Robatayaki

Similar to an izakaya, a *robatayaki* is a rustic drinking restaurant serving a wide variety of foods grilled over charcoal. The name means 'hearth-side cooking' and every effort is made to re-create the atmosphere of an old country house – which was always centred around a large hearth or *irori*. Eating at a robatayaki restaurant is a feast for the eyes as well as the taste buds: you sit around a counter with the food spread out in front of you on a layer of ice, behind which is a large charcoal grill. You don't need a word of Japanese to order, just point at whatever looks good. The chef will grill your selection and then pass it to you on a long wooden paddle – grab your food quickly before he snatches it back. Some of the best robatayaki chefs are real performers and make a show of cooking the food and serving customers. You'll wonder how no-one winds up getting injured by flying food.

The fare at a robatayaki restaurant is largely the same as that at an izakaya. They have menus, but no-one uses them – just point and eat. The drink of choice is beer or sake. Expect to spend about ¥3000 per head. Not as common as izayaka, robatayaki usually have rustic wooden facades modelled on traditional Japanese farmhouses.

Okonomiyaki

The name means 'cook what you like', and an *okonomiyaki* restaurant provides you with an inexpensive opportunity to do just that. Sometimes described as Japanese pizza or pancake, the resemblance is in form only. At an okonomiyaki restaurant you sit around a *teppan* (an iron hotplate) armed with a spatula and chopsticks to cook your choice of meat, seafood and vegetables in a cabbage and vegetable batter.

Some places will do most of the cooking and bring the nearly finished product over to your hotplate for you to season with bonito flakes *(katsuo bushi)*, soy sauce *(shōyu)*, parsley, Japanese Worcestershire-style sauce and mayonnaise. Cheaper places will simply hand you a bowl filled with the ingredients and expect you to cook it for yourself. If this happens, don't panic. First, mix the batter and filling thoroughly, then place it on the hot grill, flattening it into a pancake shape. After five minutes or so, use the spatulas to flip it and cook for another five minutes. Then dig in.

Most okonomiyaki places also serve *yaki-soba* (fried noodles) and *yasai-itame* (stir-fried vegetables). All of this is washed down with mugs of draft beer. One final word: don't worry too much about preparation of the food – as a foreigner you'll be expected to be inept and the waiter will keep a sharp eye on you to make sure no real disasters occur.

mikkusu okonomiyaki	ミックスお好み焼き	mixed fillings of seafood, meat and vegetables
modan-yaki	モダン焼き	okonomiyaki with fried egg
gyū okonomiyaki	牛お好み焼き	beef okonomiyaki
yasai okonomiyaki	野菜お好み焼き	vegetable okonomiyaki
negi okonomiyaki	ネギお好み焼き	thin okonomiyaki with scallions

Shiso – high in vitamins, this aromatic Japanese herb adds a fresh and minty flavour to many seafood dishes and salad dressings.

Yakitori

Yakitori means skewers of grilled chicken, a popular after-work meal. Yakitori is not so much a full meal as it is an accompaniment for beer and sake. At a yakitori restaurant you sit around a counter with the other patrons and watch the chef grill your selections over charcoal. The best way to eat here is to order a few skewers of several varieties and then order seconds of the ones you really like. Ordering can be a little confusing since one serving often means two or three skewers (be careful – the price listed on the menu is usually that of a single skewer).

In summer, the beverage of choice at a yakitori restaurant is beer or cold sake, while in winter it is hot sake). A few drinks and enough skewers to fill you up should run from ¥3000 to ¥4000 per person. Yakitori restaurants are usually small places, often near train stations, and are best identified by a red lantern outside and the smell of grilling chicken.

yakitori	やきとり	plain, grilled white meat
hasami/negima	はさみ／ねぎま	pieces of white meat alternating with leek
sasami	ささみ	skinless chicken breast pieces
kawa	かわ	chicken skin
tsukune	つくね	chicken meat balls
gyū-niku	牛肉	pieces of beef
rebā	レバ	chicken livers
tebasaki	手羽先	chicken wings
shiitake	しいたけ	Japanese mushrooms
piiman	ピーマン	small green peppers
tama-negi	たまねぎ	round, white onions
yaki-onigiri	焼きおにぎり	a triangle of rice grilled with yakitori sauce

Sushi & Sashimi

Like yakitori, sushi is considered an accompaniment for beer and sake. Nonetheless, both the Japanese and foreigners often make a meal of it and it's one of the healthiest meals around. Although sushi is now popular in the west, few foreigners are prepared for the delicacy and taste of the real thing. Without a doubt, this is one dish that the visitor to Japan should sample at least once.

There are two main types of sushi: *nigiri-zushi* (served on a small bed of rice – the most common variety) and *maki-zushi* (served in a seaweed roll). Lesser known varieties include *chirashi-zushi* (a layer of rice covered in egg and fish toppings), *oshi-zushi* (fish pressed in a mould over rice) and *inari-zushi* (rice in a pocket of sweet, fried tofu). Whatever kind of sushi you try, it will be served with lightly vinegared rice. In the case of nigiri-zushi and maki-zushi, it will contain a bit of *wasabi* (hot, green horseradish).

Sushi is not difficult to order. If you sit at the counter of a sushi restaurant you can simply point at what you want, as most of the selections are visible in a refrigerated glass case between you and the sushi chef. You can also order à la carte from the menu. When ordering, you usually order *ichi-nin mae* (one portion), which usually means two pieces of sushi. Be careful since the price on the menu will be that of only one piece. If ordering à la carte is too daunting, you can take care of your whole order with one or two words by ordering an assortment plate of nigiri-zushi called a *mori-awase*. These usually come in three grades: *futsū nigiri* (regular nigiri), *jō nigiri* (special nigiri) and *toku-jō nigiri* (extra special nigiri). The difference is in the type of fish used. Most mori-awase contain six or seven pieces of sushi. Of course you can order fish without the rice, in which case it is called sashimi.

Before popping the sushi into your mouth, dip it in *shōyu* (soy sauce) which you pour from a small decanter into a low dish specially provided for the purpose. If you're not good at using chopsticks, don't worry, sushi is one of the few foods in Japan that is perfectly acceptable to eat with your hands. Slices of pickled ginger *(gari)* will also be served to help

Wasabi (horseradish) – the fresh wasabi root, traditionally grown in clear mountain streams, is grated into a paste and served as a fiery seasoning to cool dishes like sushi.

refresh the palate. The beverage of choice with sushi is beer or sake (hot in the winter and cold in the summer), with a cup of green tea at the end of the meal.

Be warned that a good sushi restaurant can cost upwards of ¥10,000, while an average place can run to ¥3000 to ¥5000 per person. One way to sample the joy of sushi on the cheap is to try an automatic sushi place, usually called *kaiten-zushi*, where the sushi is served on a conveyor belt which runs along a counter. Here you simply reach up and grab whatever looks good (which certainly takes the pain out of ordering). You're charged according to how many plates of sushi you've eaten. Plates are colour-coded according to their price and the cost is written either somewhere on the plate itself or on a sign on the wall. You can usually fill yourself up in one of these places for ¥1000 to ¥2000 per person.

Automatic sushi places are often distinguished by miniature conveyor belts in the window while regular sushi restaurants often can be identified by fishtanks in the window or a white lantern with the characters for sushi written in black letters.

Daikon sprouts (kaiware daikon) – with their fresh, pungent taste, these sprouts are often used to garnish Japanese-style salads and sushi dishes such as nori-maki.

ama-ebi	甘海老	sweet shrimp
awabi	あわび	abalone
ebi	海老	prawn or shrimp
hamachi	はまち	yellowtail
ika	いか	squid
ikura	イクラ	salmon roe
kai-bashira	貝柱	scallop
kani	かに	crab
katsuo	かつお	bonito
maguro	まぐろ	tuna
tai	鯛	sea bream
tamago	たまご	sweetened egg
toro	とろ	the choicest cut of fatty tuna belly, very expensive
unagi	うなぎ	eel with a sweet sauce
uni	うに	sea urchin roe

Sukiyaki & Shabu-shabu

Restaurants usually specialise in both these dishes. Popular in the west, sukiyaki is a favourite of most foreign visitors to Japan. When made with high-quality beef, like Kōbe beef, it is a sublime experience. Sukiyaki consists of thin slices of beef cooked in a broth of soy sauce, sugar and sake and is accompanied by a variety of vegetables and tofu. After cooking, all the ingredients are dipped in raw egg (the heat of the ingredients tends to lightly cook the egg) before being eaten.

Shabu-shabu consists of thin slices of beef and vegetables cooked by swirling the ingredients in a light broth and then dipping them in a variety of special sesame seed and citrus-based sauces. Both of these dishes are prepared in a pot over a fire at your private table, but you needn't fret about preparation – the waiter or waitress will usually help you get started and then keep a close watch as you proceed. The key is to take your time and add the ingredients a little at a time, savouring the flavours as you go.

Sukiyaki and shabu-shabu restaurants usually have a traditional Japanese decor and sometimes a picture of a cow to help you recognise them. Ordering is not difficult. Simply say sukiyaki or shabu-shabu and indicate how many people's worth of food is required. Expect to pay between ¥3000 to ¥10,000 per person.

Okra ('lady's fingers') – served raw in salads or lightly cooked in soups, this olive-green, star-shaped vegetable has quite an unusual slippery texture.

Tempura

One of the most famous of all Japanese foods, tempura is not actually Japanese at all, but was borrowed from the Portuguese traders in the 16th century. Since then, the Japanese have transformed it into something uniquely their own. Good tempura is portions of fish, prawns and vegetables cooked in fluffy, non-greasy batter.

When you sit down at a tempura restaurant, you will be given a small bowl filled with a light brown sauce *(ten-tsuyu)* and a plate of grated *daikon* radish; you mix this into the sauce. Dip each piece of tempura into this sauce before eating it. Tempura is best when it's hot, so don't wait too long – use the sauce to cool each piece and dig in.

While it's possible to order à la carte, most diners choose to order a teishoku (full set), which includes rice, miso soup and Japanese pickles. Some tempura restaurants also offer courses of tempura which include different numbers of tempura pieces.

Expect to pay between ¥2000 and ¥10,000 for a full tempura meal. Finding these restaurants is tricky as they have no distinctive facade or decor. If you look through the window you'll see customers around the counter watching the chefs as they work over large woks filled with oil.

Eating Etiquette

When it comes to eating in Japan, there is quite a number of implicit rules, but they're fairly easy to remember. If you're worried about putting your foot in it, relax – the Japanese almost expect foreigners to make fools of themselves in formal situations and are unlikely to be offended as long as you follow the standard rules of politeness in your own country.

Among the more important eating 'rules' are those regarding chopsticks. Sticking them upright in your rice is considered bad form – that's how rice is offered to the dead! It's also bad form to pass food from your chopsticks to someone else's – another Buddhist funeral rite which involves passing the remains of the cremated deceased among members of the family using chopsticks.

It's worth remembering that a lot of effort has gone into the preparation of the food so don't pour soy sauce all over it (especially the rice) and don't mix it up with your chopsticks. Also, if possible, eat everything you are given. And don't forget to slurp your noodles!

When eating with other people, especially when you're a guest, it is polite to say *'Itadakimasu'* (literally, 'I will receive') before digging in. This is as close as the Japanese come to saying grace. Similarly, at the end of the meal, you should thank your host by saying *'Gochisō-sama deshita'* which means, 'It was a real feast'.

When drinking with Japanese remember that it is bad form to fill your own drink; fill the glass of the person next to you and wait for them to reciprocate. Filling your own glass amounts to admitting to everyone at the table that you're an alcoholic. It is polite to raise your glass a little off the table while it is being filled. Once everyone's glass has been filled, the usual starting signal is a chorus of *'kampai'* which means 'cheers!'. Constant topping up means a bottomless glass – just put your hand over your glass if you've had enough.

There is also a definite etiquette to bill-paying. If someone invites you to eat or drink with them, they will be paying. Even among groups eating together it is unusual for bills to be split. The exception to this is found among young people and close friends and is called *warikan* (each person paying their own share). Generally, at the end of the meal something of a struggle will ensue to see who gets the privilege of paying the bill. If this happens, it is polite to at least make an effort to pay the bill – it is extremely unlikely that your Japanese 'hosts' will acquiesce. ■

Daikon radish – rich in enzymes which are known to aid digestion, the long, white Japanese radish is used in innumerable Japanese dishes. Freshly grated, it adds a refreshing, tangy taste to the dipping sauces served with tempura and soba noodles.

Rāmen

The Japanese imported this dish from China and put their own spin on it to make what is one of the world's most delicious fast foods. Rāmen dishes are big bowls of noodles in a meat broth served with a variety of toppings, such as sliced pork, bean sprouts and leeks. In some restaurants, particularly in Kansai, you may be asked if you'd prefer *kotteri* (thick) or *assari* (thin) soup. Other than this, ordering is simple: just sidle up to the counter and say 'rāmen', or ask for any of the other choices usually on offer (a list follows). Expect to pay between ¥500 and ¥900 for a bowl. Since rāmen is originally Chinese food, some rāmen restaurants also serve *chāhan* or *yaki-meshi* (fried rice), *gyōza* (dumplings) and *kara-age* (deep-fried chicken pieces).

Rāmen restaurants are easily distinguished by their long counters lined with customers hunched over steaming bowls. You can also hear a rāmen shop – it is considered polite to slurp the noodles and aficionados claim that slurping brings out the full flavour of the broth.

rāmen	ラーメン	standard issue, the cheapest item on the menu – soup and noodles with a sprinkling of meat and vegetables
chāshū-men	チャーシュー麺	rāmen topped with slices of roasted pork
wantan-men	ワンタン麺	rāmen with meat dumplings
miso-rāmen	みそラーメン	rāmen with miso-flavoured broth
chānpon-men	ちゃんぽん麺	Nagasaki-style rāmen with assorted vegetables and meat in the broth

Soba & Udon

Soba and udon are Japan's answer to Chinese-style rāmen. Soba noodles are thin, brown, buckwheat noodles, while udon noodles are thick, white, wheat noodles. Most Japanese noodle shops serve both soba and udon prepared in a variety of ways. Noodles are usually served in a bowl containing a light, bonito-flavoured broth, but you can also order them served cold and piled on a bamboo screen with a cold broth for dipping. By far the most popular type of cold noodles is *zaru soba*, which is served with bits of seaweed *(nori)* on top. If you order these noodles you'll receive a small plate of wasabi and sliced scallions – put these into the cup of broth and eat the noodles by dipping them in this mixture. At the end of your meal, the waiter will give you some hot broth to mix with the leftover sauce which you drink like a kind of tea. As with rāmen, you should feel free to slurp as loudly as you please.

Soba and udon places are usually quite cheap (about ¥900), but some fancy places can be significantly more expensive (the decor is a good indication of the price).

Add 'soba' or 'udon' to the following four dishes when ordering:

Mountain yam (yama-imo) – when grated, this vegetable becomes an oozing, starchy mass. It is often served on top of soba noodles or mixed deliciously with wasabi, soy sauce and cubes of fresh red tuna.

kake	かけそば／うどん	plain noodles in broth
kitsune	きつねそば／うどん	noodles with slices of fried tofu
tempura	天ぷらそば／うどん	noodles with tempura shrimp
tsukimi	月見そば／うどん	noodles with raw egg on top (literally 'moon viewing')
zaru soba	ざるそば	cold noodles with seaweed strips served on a bamboo tray

Unagi

Unagi is Japanese for eel, an expensive and popular delicacy in Japan. Even if you can't stand the creature back home, you owe it to yourself to try unagi at least once while in Japan. It's cooked over hot coals and brushed with a rich sauce made from soy sauce and sake. Full unagi dinners can be quite expensive, but many unagi restaurants offer *unagi bentō* (boxed lunches) and lunch sets for around ¥1500. Most unagi restaurants display plastic models of their unagi sets in their front windows and have barrels of live eels to entice passers-by.

unagi teishoku	うなぎ定食	full-set unagi meal with rice, grilled eel, eel-liver soup and pickles
unadon	うな丼	grilled eel over a bowl of rice
unajū	うな重	*grilled eel over a flat tray of rice (larger than unadon)*
kabayaki	蒲焼き	skewers of grilled eel without rice

Nabemono

A *nabe* is a large cast-iron cooking pot and the term *nabemono* refers to any of a variety of dishes cooked in these pots. Like sukiyaki and shabu-shabu, nabemono are cooked at your table on a small gas burner or a clay *habachi*. Eating nabemono is a participatory experience, with each diner putting in ingredients from trays of prepared, raw food. The most famous nabemono is called *chanko-nabe*, the high-calorie stew eaten by sumo wrestlers during training. Chanko-nabe restaurants are often run by retired sumo wrestlers and the walls of such restaurants are often festooned with sumo arcana.

Since nabemono are filling and hot, they are usually eaten in winter. They are also popular as banquet and party dishes since the eating of a nabe dish is a very communal experience. It is difficult to pick out a nabe restaurant – the best way is to ask a Japanese friend for a recommendation.

Lotus root (renkon) – appreciated for its firm and crisp texture, slices of this root are often added to pots of steaming nabe or deep-fried as tempura.

chanko-nabe	ちゃんこ鍋	sumo wrestler's stew of meat and vegetables
botan-nabe	ぼたん鍋	wild boar stew with vegetables
yose-nabe	寄せ鍋	seafood and chicken stew with vegetables

Fungi Heaven

Whatever season, you'll always find a wonderful range of mushrooms *(kinoko)* in Japan. From the highly acclaimed (and pricey) *matsutake* that hits up-market restaurant tables in autumn, to the rich flavour of the *shiitake*, the pleasant texture of the *shimeji* or the subtle taste of the long, white *enoki*, Japan is a virtual paradise for the mushroom-lover. ■

Fugu

The deadly *fugu*, or pufferfish, is eaten more for the thrill than the taste. It's actually rather bland – most people liken the taste to chicken – but acclaimed for its fine texture. Nonetheless, if you have the money to lay out for a fugu dinner (around ¥10,000), it makes a good 'been there, done that' story back home.

Although the danger of fugu poisoning is negligible, some Japanese joke that you should always let the other person try the first piece – if they are still talking after five minutes, consider it safe and have some yourself. If you need a shot of liquid courage to get started, try a glass of *hirezake* (toasted fugu tail in hot sake) – the traditional accompaniment to a fugu dinner.

Fugu is a seasonal delicacy best eaten in winter. Fugu restaurants usually serve only fugu and can be identified by a picture of a fugu on the sign out the front.

fugu teishoku	ふぐ定食	a set course of fugu served several ways, plus rice and soup
fugu chiri	ふぐちり	a stew made from fugu and vegetables
fugu sashimi	ふぐ刺身	thinly sliced raw fugu
yaki fugu	焼きふぐ	fugu grilled on an habachi at your table

Tonkatsu

Although it's held in low esteem abroad, the Japanese have figured out a way to prepare pork that rivals the best steak. *Tonkatsu* is a deep-fried breaded pork cutlet served with a special sauce, usually as part of a set meal *(tonkatsu teishoku)*. Even if you shy away from pork at home, you ought to try this dish once while you're here – you'll probably be pleasantly surprised.

Tonkatsu is served both at speciality restaurants and at shokudō. Naturally, the best tonkatsu is to be found at the speciality places, where a full set will run from ¥1500 to ¥2500. When ordering, you can choose between *rōsu*, a fatter cut and *hire*, a leaner cut of pork.

tonkatsu teishoku	とんかつ定食	a full set meal of tonkatsu, rice, miso soup and shredded cabbage
minchi katsu	ミンチカツ	minced pork cutlet
kushikatsu	串カツ	deep-fried pork and vegetables on skewers

Kushiage & Kushikatsu

Dieters beware, this is the fried food to beat all fried foods. *Kushiage* and *kushikatsu* are deep-fried skewers of meat, seafood and vegetables eaten as an accompaniment to beer. Kushi means skewer and if it can be fitted on to a skewer, it's probably on the menu. Cabbage is often eaten with the meal to ease the guilt of eating all that grease.

You order kushiage and kushikatsu by the skewer (one skewer is *ippon*, but you can always use your fingers to indicate the number). Like yakitori, this food is popular with after-work salarymen and students and is therefore fairly inexpensive, though up-market places exist. Expect to pay from ¥2000 to ¥5000 for a full meal and a couple of beers. Not

Burdock (gobō) – this high-fibre root is often sliced, lightly cooked and dressed with a nutty vinaigrette of soy sauce and sesame seeds.

particularly distinctive in appearance, the best way to find a kushiage and kushikatsu place is to ask a Japanese friend.

ebi	えび	shrimp
ika	いか	squid
renkon	レンコン	lotus root
tama-negi	たまねぎ	white onion
gyū-niku	牛肉	beef pieces
shiitake	しいたけ	Japanese mushrooms
ginnan	銀杏	ginkgo nuts
imo	いも	potato

Kaiseki

Kaiseki is the pinnacle of Japanese cuisine where ingredients, preparation, setting and presentation come together to create a dining experience quite unlike any other. Born as an adjunct to the tea ceremony, kaiseki is a largely vegetarian affair (though fish is often served, meat never appears on the kaiseki menu). One usually eats kaiseki in the private room of a *ryōtei* (an especially elegant style of traditional restaurant), often overlooking a private, tranquil garden. The meal is served in several small courses, giving one the opportunity to admire the plates and bowls which are carefully chosen to complement the food and seasons. Rice is eaten last (usually with an assortment of pickles) and the drink of choice is sake or beer.

Sansho – used whole or finely ground, the fresh young sprigs from the sansho (prickly ash) tree are added to enhance the subtle taste of many Japanese dishes.

This all comes at a steep price – a good kaiseki dinner costs upwards of ¥10,000 per person. One way to sample the delights of kaiseki without breaking the bank is to visit a kaiseki restaurant for lunch. Most places offer a lunchbox (*bentō*) containing a sampling of their dinner fare for around ¥2500.

Unfortunately for foreigners, kaiseki restaurants can be intimidating places to enter. If possible, bring along a Japanese friend or ask a Japanese friend to call ahead and make arrangements. There is usually only one set course, but some places offer a choice of three courses – graded *take* (regular), *matsu* (special) and *ume* (extra-special).

Japanese Sweets

Although most restaurants don't serve dessert (plates of sliced fruit are usually served at the end of a meal in Japan), there is no lack of sweets in Japan. Most sweets (known generically as *wagashi)* are sold in speciality stores for you to eat at home. Many of the more delicate-looking ones are made to balance the strong, bitter taste of the special *matcha* tea served during the tea ceremony.

Although pleasant to look at, some westerners find Japanese sweets unappealing – perhaps because many of them contain a sweet red bean paste called *anko*. This unusual filling turns up in even the most innocuous looking pastries. But don't let anyone make up your mind for you: try a Japanese sweet for yourself. Who knows, you may be a member of that small minority of foreigners who really love them.

Red radish (aka-kabu) – its vivid colour, fresh taste and crisp texture make it an ideal garnish.

With such a wide variety of sweets it's difficult to specify names. However, you'll probably find many variations on the anko-covered-by-glutinous rice theme *(mochi)*. Another sweet to look out for is the *yōkan* – a sweet, bean jelly slice. For confectionery aficiondos, however, Kyoto is undisputedly the place to head.

Sweet shops are easy to spot; they usually have open fronts with their wares laid out in wooden trays to entice passers-by. Buying sweets is simple – just point at what you want and indicate how many you'd like with your fingers.

Eating on the Cheap

Japan can be an expensive place to eat, however, with a little effort you should be able to get away with a daily food budget of ¥1800, perhaps less.

Like anywhere else, the cheapest way to fill yourself up in Japan is to do your own cooking. Unfortunately, apart from some youth hostels, there are not many places where this is possible. If you're really strapped, however, you can fix instant noodles just about anywhere. Failing that, you can purchase food from supermarkets and convenience stores which involves little or no preparation.

If you have to stick to restaurants, there are a variety of options. Fast food is an obvious contender, but most people haven't come all the way to Japan to eat what they can get at home. Your best bet is probably the humble shokudō. This is where your average working man eats his lunch and maybe his dinner. Noodle and rice dishes in such places usually start at around ¥550. A good option is the lunch set (ranchi setto) served at shokudō, coffee shops and many other restaurants. They usually start at ¥600.

Another possible option is the cafeterias of major universities, many of which are open to all and serve government-subsidised meals for around ¥500.

O-bentō (boxed lunch)
– sold in tiny street
take-aways, bustling
department stores and
on station platforms, the
o-bentō serves as a
handy, cheap and
nutritious meal of rice,
seafood, meat and
vegetables.

DRINKS

Alcohol

Drinking is the glue that holds Japanese society together. It is practised by almost every adult, male or female, and a good number of teenagers (alcohol is sold from vending machines and under-age drinking is not nearly as frowned upon as it is in some countries). Going out for a few rounds after work with co-workers is both the joy and bane of the Japanese salaryman's life. After a few drinks, Japanese workers feel secure enough to vent their frustrations and speak their minds, confident that all will be forgiven by the time they arrive at the office in the morning. Occasionally, Japanese drinking crosses the boundary between good-natured fun and ugly inebriation, as anyone who has been in a public park during cherry blossom season can attest. However, drunkenness rarely leads to violence in Japan, so the visitor does not have to be overly concerned.

Beer Introduced at the end of last century, beer *(biiru)* is now the favourite tipple of the Japanese. The quality is generally excellent and the most popular type is the light lager, although recently some breweries have been experimenting with darker brews. The major breweries are Kirin, Asahi, Sapporo and Suntory. Beer is dispensed everywhere, from vending machines to beer halls and even in some temple lodgings. A standard can of beer from a vending machine is about ¥250, although some of the monstrous cans cost over ¥1000. At bars, a beer starts at ¥500 and climbs upward depending on the establishment. Draft beer *(nama biiru)* is widely available, as are imported beers.

Sake Rice wine has been brewed for centuries in Japan. Once restricted to imperial brewers, it was later produced at temples and shrines across the country. In recent years, consumption of beer has overtaken that of sake, but it's still a standard item in homes, restaurants and drinking places. Large casks of sake are often seen piled up as offerings outside temples and shrines, and it plays an important part in most celebrations and festivals.

Most westerners come to Japan with a bad image of sake; the result of having consumed low grade brands overseas. Although it won't appeal to all palates, some of the higher grades are actually very good and a trip to a restaurant specialising in sake is a great way to sample some of the better brews.

There are several major types of sake, including *nigori* (cloudy), *nama* (unrefined) and regular, clear sake. Of these, the clear sake is by far the most common. Clear sake is usually divided into three grades: *tokkyū* (premium), *ikkyū* (first grade) and *nikkyū* (second grade). Nikkyū is the routine choice. These are further divided into *karakuchi* (dry) and *amakuchi* (sweet). Apart from the national brewing giants, there are thousands of provincial brewers producing local brews called *jizake*.

Sake is served *atsukan* (warm) and *reishū* (cold), the former being more popular in the winter. When you order sake, it will usually be served in a small flask called a *tokkuri*. These come in two sizes, so you should specify whether you want an *ichigo* (small) or a *nigo* (large). From these flasks you pour the sake into small ceramic cups called *o-choko* or *sakazuki*. Another way to sample sake is to drink it from a small wooden box called a *masu*, with a bit of salt at the rim.

Tokkuri bottles – coming in all shapes and sizes, many restaurants and sake brewers design their own.

However you drink it, with a 17% alcohol content, sake is likely to go right to your head, particularly the warm stuff. After a few bouts with sake you'll come to understand why the Japanese drink it in such small cups. Particularly memorable is a real sake hangover born of too much cheap sake. The best advice is not to indulge the day before you have to get on a plane.

Shōchū For those looking for a quick and cheap escape route from their sorrows, *shōchū* is the answer. It's a distilled spirit, with an alcohol content of about 30%, which has been resurrected from its previous low-class esteem (it was used as a disinfectant in the Edo period) to the status of a trendy drink. You can drink it as a *oyu-wari* (with hot water) or as a *chūhai* (a highball with soda and lemon). A 720ml bottle sells for about ¥600 which makes it a relatively cheap option compared to other spirits.

Wine, Imported Drinks & Whiskey Japanese wines are available from areas such as Yamanashi, Nagano, Tōhoku and Hokkaidō. Standard wines are often blended with imports from South America or Eastern Europe. The major producers are Suntory, Mann's and Mercian. Prices are high – expect to pay at least ¥1000 for a bottle of something drinkable.

Imported wines are often stocked by large liquor stores or department stores in the cities. Bargains are sometimes available at ¥600, but most of the imports are considerably more expensive.

Prices of imported spirits have been coming down in recent years and bargain liquor stores have been popping up in the bigger cities. However, if you really like imported spirits, it is probably a good idea to pick up a duty-free bottle or two on your way through the airport.

Whiskey is available at most drinking establishments and is usually drunk *mizu-wari* (with water and ice) or *onzarokku* (on the rocks). Local brands, such as Suntory and Nikka, are sensibly priced and most measure up to foreign standards. Expensive foreign labels are popular as gifts.

Most other imported spirits can be had at drinking establishments in Japan. Bars with a large foreign clientele, including hotel bars, can usually mix anything at your request. If not, they will certainly tailor a drink to your specifications.

Drinking Places What you pay for your drink depends on where you drink and, in the case of a hostess bar, with whom you drink. As a rule, hostess bars are the most expensive places to drink (up to ¥10,000 per drink), followed by up-market traditional Japanese bars, hotel bars, beer halls and casual pubs. If you are not sure about a place, ask about prices and cover charges before sitting down. As a rule, if you are served a small snack with your first round, you'll be paying a cover charge (usually a few hundred yen, but sometimes much more).

Izakaya and *yakitori-ya* are cheap places for beer, sake and food in a casual atmosphere resembling that of a pub. *Aka-chōchin*, which display a red lantern outside the premises, are similar pubs for the working man – down-to-earth in price and decor. All Japanese cities, whether large or small, will have a few informal pubs with reasonable prices. Such places are popular with young Japanese and resident gaijin, who usually refer to such places as 'gaijin bars'. In summer, many department stores open up beer gardens on the roof. They are a popular spot to cool off with an inexpensive beer. Many rooftop gardens offer all-you-can-eat/drink specials for around ¥3000 per person. Beer halls are affordable and popular places to swill your beer in a faux-German atmosphere.

The bars which are found in their hundreds, jammed into tiny rooms of large buildings in the entertainment districts of many cities, are often used by their customers as a type of club – if you drop in unexpectedly the reception may be cool or, more likely, you'll simply be told that they're full. Hostess bars are inevitably expensive, often exorbitant and, without

Salmon roe (ikura) – as an appetiser to accompany sake, this is often served with freshly grated daikon radish and a dash of soy sauce.

an introduction, best avoided. They cater mainly to those entertaining on business accounts. Hostesses pamper customers with compliments or lend a sympathetic ear to their problems. The best way to visit is in the company of a Japanese friend who knows the routine – and may pick up the tab.

Japan, of course, is also where karaoke got its beginnings. If you've never sung in a karaoke bar, it's worth a try at least once. The uninitiated usually find that a few stiff drinks beforehand helps. Customers sing to the accompaniment of taped music and, as the evening wears on, voices get progressively more ragged. Sobbing, mournful *enka* (folk ballads) are the norm, although more and more western hits are finding their way into karaoke 'menus'. If you visit a karaoke place with a Japanese friend, it's unlikely that you'll escape without singing at least one song – a version of *Yesterday* or *My Way* will usually satisfy the crowd.

Nonalcoholic Drinks

Most of the drinks you're used to at home will be available in Japan, with a few colourfully named additions like Pocari Sweat and Calpis Water. One convenient aspect of Japan is the presence of drink machines on virtually every street corner, and at ¥110 refreshment is rarely more than a few steps away.

Coffee & Tea Coffee *(kōhii)* tends to be expensive in Japan, costing between ¥350 and ¥500 a cup, with some places charging up to ¥1000. A cheap alternative is some of the newer chains of coffee restaurants like Doutor or Pronto or donut shops like Mr Donut (which offers free refills). An even cheaper alternative is a can of coffee, hot or cold, from a vending machine. Although unpleasantly sweet, at ¥110, the price is hard to beat.

When ordering coffee at a coffee shop in Japan, you'll be asked whether you like it *hotto* (hot) or *aisu* (cold). Black tea also comes hot or cold, with *miruku* (milk) or *remon* (lemon). A good way to start a day of sightseeing in Japan is with a *mōningu setto* (morning set) of tea or coffee, toast and eggs, which costs around ¥350. The following are some of the more common drinks available in *kissaten* (Japanese coffee shops).

kōhii	コーヒー	regular coffee
burendo kōhii	ブレンドコーヒー	blended coffee, fairly strong
american kōhii	アメリカンコーヒー	weak coffee
kōcha	紅茶	black, British-style tea
kafe ōre	カフェオーレ	café au lait, hot or cold
orenji jūsu	オレンジジュース	orange juice

Japanese Tea Unlike black tea which westerners are familiar with, Japanese tea is green and contains a lot of vitamin C and caffeine. The powdered form used in the tea ceremony is called *matcha* and is drunk after being whipped into a frothy consistency. The more common form is leafy green tea *(o-cha)*, which is drunk after being steeped in a pot. While *sencha* is one popular variety of green tea, most restaurants will serve a free cup of brownish tea called *bancha*. In summer a cold beverage called *mugicha* (roasted barley tea) is served in private homes.

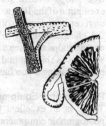

Fancy flourishes – a feast for the eyes as well as the taste buds, Japanese cuisine is characterised by decorative swirls of fruit and vegetable.

Although not particularly popular in the west, Japanese tea is very healthy and refreshing and is said by some to prevent cancer. Most department stores carry a wide selection of Japanese teas.

THINGS TO BUY

The Japanese are obsessive shoppers, and consequently everything from tiny speciality shops to some of the world's largest and most luxurious department stores give visitors ample opportunity to empty their pockets before going home. True, some items are overpriced, but many things, including electronic gear like cameras and video cameras, are much cheaper than you might expect. The current high value of the yen means that you are unlikely to come up with prices for such things that are competitive with prices in Hong Kong and Singapore, however.

As well as all the electronic gadgetry available in Japan, there is a wide range of traditional crafts to choose from, though for good stuff you're really going to be spending big money. It pays to shop around if you have anything particular in mind. The big department stores, which often have the best selections of Japanese gift items, can vary enormously in their prices from one store to another. In some shops, you are paying for extras such as the high level of service (a feature of all Japanese shops anyway), location and interior decor, all of which are very important to the well-heeled Japanese but lesser considerations to the traveller looking for a bargain.

Tax-Free Shopping

Shopping tax-free in Japan is not necessarily the bargain you might expect. Although tax-free shops enable foreigners to get an exemption of the 10% to 30% sales tax levied on most items, these still may not always be the cheapest places to shop. Other bulk-buying shops are often a better deal. The best advice is to shop around and compare prices before making a purchase.

Photographic Equipment

Tokyo is an excellent hunting ground for photographic equipment. Almost all the big-name brands in camera equipment are Japanese, and for these locally produced items, prices can be very competitive. The prices for accessories, such as motor drives and flash units, can even be competitive with Singapore and Hong Kong. In addition, shopping in Japan presents the shopper with none of the rip-off risks that abound in other Asian discount capitals.

As always, be prepared to shop around. Tokyo's Shinjuku area (see the Tokyo chapter) is the best place for buying camera equipment, although Ginza too has a good selection of camera shops. Second-hand camera equipment is worth checking out too. In Tokyo, both Shinjuku and Ginza have a fair number of second-hand shops where camera and lens quality is usually very good and prices are around half what you would pay for new equipment.

Electronic Equipment & Hi-Fi

Much of the electrical gadgetry on sale in Japan is designed for Japan's curious power supply (100V at 50 or 60 Hz) and will usually require a transformer for use overseas. Other problems include the incompatibility of Japanese TVs, video recorders and FM radios with foreign models. The safest bet is to go for export models – the prices may be slightly higher, but in the long run you'll save the expense of converting the equipment to suit the conditions in your own country. Two places to look for export models are the International Arcade in Ginza and the big LAOX store in Akihabara, Tokyo.

For battery-operated items such as Walkmans and Diskmans, scout around the hundreds of electrical shops in Tokyo's Akihabara. Some bargaining (don't get too carried away – this is not Bombay) will bring prices down around 10% or so.

Computers

Computers and accessories are expensive in Japan. Unless you're resident in Japan and have no choice, save your computer purchases for elsewhere.

Music & Instruments

From CDs to electric guitars, musical equipment can be cheaper in Japan than elsewhere. At branches of Tower Records, Virgin Megastore and HMV Records (at least one of these, and possibly all three will be found in cities all over Japan) imported US CDs range between ¥1750 and ¥2200. Japanese CDs average around ¥2300, although you can occasionally come across real bargains. Wave, located in Tokyo's Roppongi, Shibuya and Ikebukuro districts, has excellent selections of both Japanese and western music in CD, LP and tape format.

The Japanese are great music lovers and, consequently, there are plenty of musical equipment shops in all the major cities. Bargains can usually be had on Japanese-made instruments, while foreign-made ones will generally be more expensive than they are in other parts of the world. For example, a Japanese-assembled Fender guitar will be about half the price of the same US-assembled model. For musical equipment, it is usually possible to negotiate lower prices than those marked.

Pearls
The Japanese firm Mikimoto developed the technique of producing cultured pearls by artificially introducing an irritant into the pearl oyster. Pearls and pearl jewellery are still popular buys for foreign visitors, but it would be wise to check prices in your own country. Size, quality and colour will all have a bearing on the price. Toba, in the Ise area (Kansai region) is a centre for the production of cultured pearls.

Cars, Motorcycles & Bicycles
Information on purchasing these vehicles can be found in the Getting Around chapter.

Clothes
Japanese-made clothes and shoes are excellent quality and needn't cost the earth. In up-market and fashionable districts, most of the clothes shops are exclusive boutiques with exclusive prices. In less fashionable areas, there are countless retail outlets for an industry providing economical, mass-produced versions of designer clothes. In such shops, it is possible to pick up a suit for around ¥12,000 – perfect if you're a newly arrived English-language teacher with a backpack full of travel-soiled jeans and T-shirts.

Toys
Tokyo has some remarkable toy shops. See the Tokyo chapter for detail. Elsewhere, look out for some of the traditional wooden toys produced as regional specialities – they make good souvenirs for adults and children alike.

Japanese Arts & Crafts
As well as all the hi-tech knick-knacks produced by the Japanese, it is also possible to go home loaded down with Japanese traditional arts & crafts. Anything from carp banners to kimono can make good souvenirs for the converted Japanophile.

Ningyō *Ningyō* (Japanese dolls) are usually intended for display, not for playing with. Often quite exquisite, with coiffured hair and dressed in kimono, they make excellent souvenirs or gifts. Also available are the *gogatsu-ningyō*, dolls dressed in samurai suits used as gifts on Boy's Day. The most famous dolls are made in Kyoto and are known as *kyō-ningyō*.

Ningyō can be bought in tourist shops, department stores and special doll shops. In Tokyo (see the Tokyo chapter) Asakusa-bashi's Edo-dōri is well known for its many doll shops.

Japanese dolls come in many different shapes and sizes, and each has a different purpose.

Kasa *Kasa* (Japanese umbrellas) are another classic souvenir item. They come in two forms: *higasa*, which are made of paper, cotton or silk and serve as a sunshade; and *bangasa*, which are made of oiled paper and keep the rain off. Again, department stores and tourist shops are your best bet for finding kasa.

Koinobori *Koinobori* are the carp banners that you see flying from poles in Japan. The carp is much revered for its tenacity and perseverance, but you might like the banners for their simple elegance. They're available from Shibuya's Oriental Bazaar in Tokyo and are occasionally sold in tourist shops.

Katana *Katana* (Japanese swords) make a fantastic souvenir – it's just that good ones are going to cost more than all your other travel expenses put together! The reason for their expense is both the mystique attached to them as the symbols of samurai power and the great care that went into making them. Sword shops that sell the real thing will also stock *tsuba*, sword guards, and complete sets of samurai armour. Department stores, on the other hand, stock realistic (to the untrained eye at least) imitations at affordable prices.

Shikki *Shikki* (lacquerware) is another Japanese craft that has been mastered to a superlative degree. The lacquer-making process, involving as many as 15 layers of lacquer, is used to create objects as diverse as dishes and furniture. As you might expect, examples of good lacquerware cannot be had for a song, but smaller items can be bought at affordable prices from department stores. Popular, easily transportable items include bowls, trays and small boxes.

Washi *Washi* (Japanese paper) has been famous for more than 1000 years as the finest hand-made paper in the world. Special shops stock sheets of washi and products made from it, such as notebooks, wallets and so on. As they're generally inexpensive and light, washi products make excellent gifts and souvenirs. Again, you'll find them in the big department stores. Tokyo's Ginza also has a large washi shop in the same building as the Contax Gallery (see the Central Tokyo map in the Tokyo chapter).

Stoneware & Porcelain The difference between stoneware and porcelain is in the firing process. Stoneware is fired at temperatures of between 600°C and 900°C and is frequently admired for its earthiness and imperfections. Porcelain, on the other hand, is fired at much higher temperatures (1300°C to 1400°C) and is transformed into a glass-like substance in the process. Imperfections in porcelain are considered just that – imperfections – and are discarded.

Numerous pottery villages still exist in various parts of Japan. Many of them feature pottery museums and working kilns which can be visited. Of course, it is also possible to buy examples of stoneware and porcelain. Not too far from Tokyo is Mashiko (see the Around Tokyo section); in Western Honshū is Imbe, near Okayama, famed for its *bizen-yaki* pottery; in the Kansai region is Tamba Sasayama, with its Tamba pottery; in Kyūshū, the home of Japanese pottery,

Tsuba (hand guards for samurai swords) became miniature works of art, sculpted with symbols such as this Buddhist guardian figure.

Koishiwara, Karatsu, Imari and Arita are all sources of different pottery styles.

Ukiyo-e Ukiyo-e wood-block prints (literally 'pictures from the floating world'), originally were not an art form. Wood-block printing originated in the 18th century as one of Japan's earliest manifestations of mass culture and, as such, was used in advertising and posters. The name derives from a Buddhist term indicating the transient world of daily pleasures, ukiyo-e uniquely depicting such things as street scenes, actors and courtesans.

Today, tourist shops in Japan stock modern reproductions of the work of famous ukiyo-e masters such as Hokusai whose scenes of Mt Fuji are favourites. It is also possible to come across originals by lesser-known artists at prices ranging from ¥5000 to ¥40,000. Try the Oriental Bazaar in Shibuya, Tokyo if you're looking for reasonably priced originals. In Ginza, Tokyo, there are a couple of galleries that stock contemporary wood-block prints – many of them deal with very modern themes and are strikingly innovative.

Kimono & Yukata Kimono are seldom worn by Japanese women nowadays. Indeed, most young Japanese women would have no idea how to dress themselves in a kimono. Still, they are worn occasionally, mostly on ceremonial occasions such as a school graduation or wedding day.

For most non-Japanese, the cost of a kimono is prohibitively expensive. For a 'bottom of the range' kimono, prices start at around ¥60,000 and soar to ¥1 million or more. The best option for those interested in owning their own kimono is to look for an antique silk kimono in places like Shibuya's Oriental Bazaar in Tokyo. Alternatively, if you're in Japan during March or September, these are the months that the Daimaru store has sales of its rental kimono. Be warned, however, these sales are also popular with local Japanese.

For those not in the kimono league, another option might be to look for a yukata (the cotton bathrobes worn in ryokan). These have a distinctively Japanese look and are not only affordable (from around ¥3500 up) but also highly useable.

Getting There & Away

Flying into Tokyo is only one of a diverse range of ways of getting to Japan and only a tiny part of the whole story. For a start there are many other airports in Japan, some of which make better entry points than Tokyo's inconvenient Narita international airport. It's also possible to arrive in Japan by sea from a number of nearby countries, particularly South Korea. Japan can also serve as the starting or finishing point for the popular Trans-Siberian Railway trip across Russia.

AIR

There are flights to Japan from all over the world, usually to Tokyo but also to a number of other Japanese airports. Although Tokyo may seem the obvious arrival and departure point in Japan, for many visitors this may not be the case. If, for example, you were travelling from Tokyo to western Japan then out to Hong Kong or Australia, it could be much more convenient to fly out of, say, Fukuoka rather than backtrack all the way to Tokyo.

Arriving in Japan

Airports There are international airports on the main island of Honshū (Nagoya, Niigata, Osaka and Tokyo), Kyūshū (Fukuoka, Kagoshima, Kumamoto and Nagasaki), Okinawa (Naha) and Hokkaidō (Sapporo).

Tokyo Narita international airport gets a lot of flak. It's a big, impersonal place, and even worse it's more than 60 km from central Tokyo. Airport bus services take 1½ hours at the best of times. Train services are faster. But unless you've got direct access to a major bank's central vault, don't even consider taking a taxi. (See the Getting Around section of the Tokyo chapter for more details on airport transport.)

Airport transport isn't the end of the Tokyo horror story. Narita is not a particularly user-friendly airport and immigration formalities can be extremely slow and tedious. When you finally do reach Tokyo,

the city itself is big, expensive and may seem overwhelmingly confusing. All in all, if you can plan your arrival elsewhere in Japan, then do so.

There is one exception to this tale of woe. When Narita international airport opened, China Airlines (along with most domestic airlines flights) stayed at the convenient old Haneda airport. This was because Air China (mainland China) did not want to fly to the same airport as China Airlines (Taiwan). Consequently, visitors preferring to make Tokyo their entry point can avoid the hassles of Narita international airport by flying China Airlines to Haneda airport instead.

Osaka Almost all of Osaka's international flights now go via the new Kansai international airport.

Kansai International Airport Kansai international airport is the first Japanese airport to function 24 hours a day. It serves the key Kansai cities of Kyoto, Osaka and Kōbe. Airport transport to any of these cities is fast and reliable.

Nagoya Nagoya may have few attractions in its own right, but it's conveniently located between Tokyo and Osaka. From Nagoya, flights connect with Australia, Canada, China, Guam, Hong Kong, Indonesia, Malaysia, New Zealand, the Philippines, Singapore, South Korea, Taiwan, Thailand and the USA.

Fukuoka Fukuoka, at the northern end of Kyūshū, is the major arrival point for Western Japan. The airport, conveniently located near the city, has flight connections with Australia, North America and a number of Asian destinations.

Naha Okinawa Island, south-west of the main islands of Japan, is a convenient arrival or departure point for Hong Kong and

Taiwan. There are also connections with Guam and the USA.

Niigata Niigata, north of Tokyo, is connected with Seoul in South Korea and with Irkutsk, Vladivostok and Khabarovsk in Russia. From Khabarovsk, the Trans-Siberian Express and Aeroflot operate to Moscow. A *shinkansen* (bullet train) line connects Niigata with Tokyo.

Other Airports On the island of Kyūshū, Kagoshima airport has flights to Hong Kong, Kumamoto airport has flights to South Korea, and Nagasaki has flights to Shanghai and Seoul.

On Hokkaidō, Sapporo airport has connections with South Korea.

North America
West coast flights to Japan go straight across the Pacific and take about 10 hours. From the east coast, flights usually take the northern route over Alaska – the new nonstop flights take about 13 hours. The big time change on the trans-Pacific flights is a sure-fire recipe for jet lag and there's also a date change as you cross the International Date Line.

Seven-day advance purchase return fares are US$910 to US$1125 from the west coast (depending on the season) and US$1150 to US$1370 from the east. Regular economy fares are much higher – US$875 to US$940 (one way) from the west coast, US$1195 to US$1295 from the east coast.

Better deals are available if you shop around. From the east coast, return fares as low as US$750 to US$880 and one-way fares of US$749 are possible. From the west coast, fares can drop to between US$550 and US$690 with carriers such as Canadian Airlines International and Korean Airlines. Flights on Korean Airlines are often routed through Seoul, those on Canadian through Vancouver.

United Airlines is usually not quite as competitive in terms of fares: low-season return prices start at around US$700. But it's hard to beat for convenience and availability, with two direct flights daily to Tokyo from both San Francisco and Los Angeles. There are also direct flights to Osaka daily from both cities. Another advantage in flying United is their good frequent-flyer program: a return flight to Japan can help you rack up a healthy number of miles toward a free ticket.

Fares from Canada are similar to those from the USA. Canadian Airlines International, which operates out of Vancouver, often matches or beats the best fares available from the USA. Travel Cuts, the Canadian student travel organisation, offers one-way Vancouver-Tokyo flights from C$800 and returns from C$1000 or more depending on the season.

Check the Sunday travel sections of papers like the *Los Angeles Times* or the *New York Times* for travel bargains. Council Travel and STA Travel are two good discount operations specialising in student fares and other cheap deals. They have offices all across North America. Another travel agent worth calling is Overseas Tours (☎ 800-323-8777), 199 California Drive, Suite 188, Millbrae, CA 94030. Its reliable, consistently digs up good fares, and can arrange mail-order purchases using cheques or money orders.

Europe
Most direct flights between Europe and Japan fly into Tokyo but some continue to Kansai. Flight times vary widely depending on the route taken. The most direct route is across Scandinavia and Russia. Since Russia became hard up for cash, there have been far more flights taking this route as the Russians have opened their airspace in return for hefty fees.

The fastest nonstop London-Tokyo flights on the Russian route take just under 12 hours. Flights that stop in Moscow take an extra 2½ hours. Finnair's Helsinki-Tokyo flight over the North Pole and the Bering Strait takes 13½ hours. Before the Russians opened their skies, the popular route was via Anchorage, Alaska. Some flights still operate that way and take about 17 hours, including the Anchorage stopover. Finally, there are the old trans-Asian routes across the Middle East and South Asia, which take anything from 18 to 30 hours depending on the number of stops en route.

Return economy air fares between London and Tokyo are around UK£1000 and are valid for 14 days to three months. A ticket valid for a year away costs about UK£1300. Although a wide variety of cheaper deals are available, generally, the lower the price, the less convenient the route. Expect to pay

around UK£900 to UK£1000 for a one-year valid return ticket with a good airline via a fast route. For a less convenient trans-Asian route, count on UK£700 or lower and about half that for one-way tickets.

In London, STA Travel (☎ 0171-937 9962) at 86 Old Brompton Rd, London SW7 3LQ or 117 Euston Rd, London NW1 2SX; Trailfinders (☎ 0171-938 3366) at 46 Earls Court Rd and at 194 Kensington High St, London W8 7RG (☎ 0171-938 3444) and

Air Travel Glossary

Apex Apex, or 'advance purchase excursion' is a discounted ticket which must be paid for in advance. There are penalties if you wish to change it.

Baggage Allowance This will be written on your ticket: usually one 20 kg item to go in the hold, plus one item of hand luggage.

Bucket Shop An unbonded travel agency specialising in discounted airline tickets.

Bumped Just because you have a confirmed seat doesn't mean you're going to get on the plane – see Overbooking.

Cancellation Penalties If you have to cancel or change an Apex ticket there are often heavy penalties involved; insurance can sometimes be taken out against these penalties. Some airlines impose penalties on regular tickets as well, particularly against 'no show' passengers.

Check In Airlines ask you to check in a certain time ahead of the flight departure (usually 1½ hours on international flights). If you fail to check in on time and the flight is overbooked the airline can cancel your booking and give your seat to somebody else.

Confirmation Having a ticket written out with the flight and date you want doesn't mean you have a seat until the agent has checked with the airline that your status is 'OK' or confirmed. Meanwhile you could just be 'on request'.

Discounted Tickets There are two types of discounted fares – officially discounted (see Promotional Fares) and unofficially discounted. The lowest prices often carry drawbacks – like flying with unpopular airlines, inconvenient schedules, or unpleasant routes and connections. A discounted ticket can save you other things than money – you may be able to pay Apex prices without the associated Apex advance booking and other requirements. Discounted tickets only exist where there is fierce competition.

Full Fares Airlines traditionally offer first class (coded F), business class (coded J) and economy class (coded Y) tickets. These days there are so many promotional and discounted fares available from the regular economy class that few passengers pay full economy fare.

Lost Tickets If you lose your airline ticket an airline will usually treat it like a travellers' cheque and, after enquiries, issue you with another one. Legally, however, an airline is entitled to treat it like cash and if you lose it then it's gone forever. Take good care of your tickets.

No Shows No shows are passengers who fail to show up for their flight, sometimes due to unexpected delays or disasters, sometimes due to simply forgetting, sometimes because they made more than one booking and didn't bother to cancel the one they didn't want. Full-fare passengers who fail to turn up are sometimes entitled to travel on a later flight. The rest of us are penalised (see Cancellation Penalties).

On Request An unconfirmed booking for a flight, see Confirmation.

Open Jaws A return ticket where you fly out to one place but return from another. If available this can save you backtracking to your arrival point.

Travel Bug (☎ 0161-721 4000) all offer rock-bottom return flights to Tokyo and can also put together interesting Round-the-World routes incorporating Tokyo on the itinerary. The weekly listings magazine *Time Out* or the various giveaway papers are good places to look for travel bargains but take care with shonky bucket shops and prices that seem too low to believe. The really cheap fares will probably involve cash-strapped Eastern European or Middle

Eastern airlines and may involve complicated transfers and long waits along the way.

The Far East Travel Centre (FETC) (☎ 0171-734 9318) at 3 Lower John St, London W1A 4XE, specialises in Korean Airline ticketing and can fly you from London Gatwick via Seoul to your choice of Nagasaki, Nagoya, Osaka, Sapporo and Tokyo. This is a good option for visitors who don't want to take the conventional Tokyo route.

Overbooking Airlines hate to fly empty seats and since every flight has some passengers who fail to show up (*see* No Shows) airlines often book more passengers than they have seats. Usually the excess passengers balance those who fail to show up but occasionally somebody gets bumped. If this happens guess who it is most likely to be? The passengers who check in late.

Promotional Fares Officially discounted fares like Apex fares which are available from travel agents or direct from the airline.

Reconfirmation At least 72 hours prior to departure time of an onward or return flight you must contact the airline and 'reconfirm' that you intend to be on the flight. If you don't do this the airline can delete your name from the passenger list and you could lose your seat. You don't have to reconfirm the first flight on your itinerary or if your stopover is less than 72 hours. It doesn't hurt to reconfirm more than once.

Restrictions Discounted tickets often have various restrictions on them – advance purchase is the most usual one (*see* Apex). Others are restrictions on the minimum and maximum period you must be away, such as a minimum of 14 days or a maximum of one year. *See* Cancellation Penalties.

Standby A discounted ticket where you only fly if there is a seat free at the last moment. Standby fares are usually only available on domestic routes.

Tickets Out An entry requirement for many countries is that you have an onward or return ticket, in other words, a ticket out of the country. If you're not sure what you intend to do next, the easiest solution is to buy the cheapest onward ticket to a neighbouring country or a ticket from a reliable airline which can later be refunded if you do not use it.

Transferred Tickets Airline tickets cannot be transferred from one person to another. Travellers sometimes try to sell the return half of their ticket, but officials can ask you to prove that you are the person named on the ticket. This is unlikely to happen on domestic flights; on an international flight tickets may be compared with passports.

Travel Agencies Travel agencies vary widely and you should ensure you use one that suits your needs. Some simply handle tours while full-service agencies handle everything from tours and tickets to car rental and hotel bookings. A good one will do all these things and can save you a lot of money but if all you want is a ticket at the lowest possible price, then you really need an agency specialising in discounted tickets. A discounted ticket agency, however, may not be useful for other things, like hotel bookings.

Travel Periods Some officially discounted fares, Apex fares in particular, vary with the time of year. There is often a low (off-peak) season and a high (peak) season. Sometimes there's an intermediate or shoulder season as well. At peak times, when everyone wants to fly, not only will the officially discounted fares be higher but so will unofficially discounted fares or there may simply be no discounted tickets available. Usually the fare depends on your outward flight – if you depart in the high season and return in the low season, you pay the high-season fare. ■

The Japan Centre (☎ 0171-437 6445) 66-68 Brewer St, London W1R 3PJ, handles all sorts of ticket permutations. Its basement has a shop section (☎ 0171-439 8035) with books and assorted Japanese paraphernalia as well as a Japanese restaurant with reasonable prices. It's worth a visit for a taste of Japan.

An alternative route to Japan from Europe is to fly to Hong Kong and buy an onward ticket from one of Hong Kong's very competitive travel agencies. London-Hong Kong flights are much more competitively priced than London-Tokyo ones. If you have to go to Hong Kong en route to Tokyo, a London-Hong Kong-London ticket plus a Hong Kong-Tokyo-Hong Kong ticket can work out much cheaper than a London-Hong Kong-Tokyo-London ticket.

London remains one of the best places in Europe to purchase keenly priced airline tickets although Amsterdam is also very good.

Australia

The cheapest fares between Australia and Japan are generally with Garuda; one-way/return fares start at around A$850/1250. Fares with Garuda allow a stopover in Bali

Japan Air Lines (JAL), All Nippon Airways (ANA) and Qantas all have direct flights between Australia and Japan. You can fly from most Australian state capitals to Tokyo, Osaka, Nagoya and Fukuoka. There's only a one hour time change between Australia and Japan and a direct Sydney-Tokyo flight takes about nine hours.

A return excursion Sydney-Tokyo fare is around A$1650, valid for four months. If you have a working holiday visa, the validity is extended to one year. STA Travel offices or the numerous Flight Centres are good places to look for discount ticket deals.

New Zealand

Air New Zealand and Japan Air Lines each fly Auckland-Tokyo three times weekly (about 11 hours flying time); return fares start from NZ$1550 (low season) and NZ$1750 (high season). Air Pacific flies Auckland-Tokyo twice weekly via Fiji (stops permitted) for about NZ$1722.

Asia

Most Asian nations have air links with Japan. South Korea is particularly popular because it's used by many travellers as a place to take a short holiday from Japan when their visas are close to expiring. The immigration authorities treat travellers returning to Japan after a short break in South Korea with great suspicion. Hong Kong has traditionally been popular as a bargain basement for airline ticketing, but prices are no longer as cheap as they once were.

Many carriers fly Bangkok-Japan, and the competitive pressures mean frequent price changes. Typical fares include Bangkok-Tokyo on United Airlines (one-way/return 9900/11,900 Baht) and Bangkok-Taipei-Tokyo on China Airlines (8900/14,500 Baht).

South Korea Numerous flights link Seoul and Pusan with cities in Japan but the cheapest travel is by ferry. (See the following Sea section for information on sea-travel bargains between Korea and Japan.)

Hong Kong There are direct flights between Hong Kong and a number of cities in Japan, though the biggest choice and best deals will be to Tokyo. Agents like the Hong Kong Student Travel Bureau or Phoenix Travel can offer one-way tickets from around HK$2300 to HK$2900, and return tickets from HK$3000 to HK$5000, depending on the period of validity. Discounted tickets are generally only available on flights to Narita, Kansai and Nagoya, although Dragon Air flies to Kagoshima at competitive rates (HK$3000 return).

Taiwan Agents handling discounted tickets advertise in the English-language *China News* and *China Post*. There are flights from Taipei to Fukuoka, Naha, Osaka or Tokyo. If you are stopping off in Taiwan between Hong Kong and Japan, check on China Air tickets, which allow a stop-over in Taipei before continuing on to Tokyo's very convenient Haneda airport.

Flights also operate between Kaohsiung and Osaka or Tokyo.

China Air China has several flights a week from Beijing to Tokyo and Kansai, via Shanghai. Japan Airlines (JAL) flies from Beijing and Shanghai to Tokyo, Osaka and Nagasaki. There are flights between Dalian and Fukuoka/Tokyo on All Nippon Airways. China Northwest Airlines flies from Nagoya to Xi'an, once a week.

Chinese visas obtained in Japan are outrageously expensive – US$80 to US$120 depending on which agent you use. You'll save money if you can obtain the visa elsewhere, but as Chinese tourist visas are only valid for one to three months from date of issue it's useless to obtain one too far in advance.

Other Asian Centres There are regular flights between Japan and other major centres like Manila, Bangkok, Kuala Lumpur, Singapore and Jakarta. Some of the cheapest deals between Europe and Japan will be via South Asia – Bangladesh Biman will fly you from London to Dhaka to Tokyo at about the lowest price going.

Other Regions
There are also flights between Japan and South America, Africa and the Middle East.

Round-the-World & Circle Pacific Tickets

Round-the-World (RTW) fares are put together by two or more airlines and allow you to make a circuit of the world using their combined routes. A typical RTW ticket is valid for one year, allows unlimited stopovers along the way and costs about £1400, A$3500 or US$2700. An example, including Tokyo in Japan, would be a British Airways/United Airways combination flying London-New York-Tokyo-Singapore-London. A South Pacific version of the ticket might take you London-New York-Los Angeles-Tahiti-Sydney-Tokyo-London. There are many versions involving different combinations of airlines and routes. Generally, routes which stay north of the equator are a little cheaper than routes that include countries like Australia or South America.

Circle Pacific fares are a similar idea and

allow you to make a circuit of the Pacific. A typical combination is Los Angeles-Tokyo-Bangkok-Sydney-Auckland-Honolulu-Los Angeles (US$2188). Sydney can generally be interchanged with most Australian east coast capitals or Cairns.

Enterprising travel agents put together their own RTW and Circle Pacific fares at much lower prices than the joint airline deals but, of course, the cheapest fares will involve unpopular airlines and less popular routes. It's possible to put together a RTW from London for as little as UK£700. Travel agents in London have also come up with another variation on these combination fares – the Circle Asia fare. A possible route would include London-Hong Kong-Tokyo-Manila-Singapore-Bangkok-London.

SEA
South Korea
South Korea is the closest country to Japan and a very popular visa-renewal point. Many long-term visitors to Japan who are teaching English or who are engaged in some other kind of work, drop over to Korea when their permitted period of stay in Japan is about to expire, then come back to start a fresh stay. Expect to have your passport rigorously inspected.

Pusan-Shimonoseki This popular ferry service is the cheapest route between South Korea and Japan. Daily departures with the Kampur Ferry Service's vessels *Kampu* or *Pukwan* leave Pusan at 6 pm and arrive in Shimonoseki at 8.30 am the next morning. One-way fares start from about US$65 for students, continue up through US$85 for an open tatami-matted area and peak at US$140 for a cabin. There's a 10% discount on return fares and children under six travel free. Fares for children aged six to 12 are half price. (See the Shimonoseki section of the Western Honshū chapter for more details.)

Pusan-Fukuoka There is both an ultra-fast hydrofoil service and a ferry service running between Pusan and Fukuoka. The JK Line Hydrofoil, which takes just three hours, costs around US$120 one way, US$220 return. The service operates daily. Costs for the Camellia-line ferry service, which takes around 15 hours, are US$85 one way, US$120 return.

China

The Japan-China International Ferry service connects Shanghai and Osaka/Kōbe. The ship departs once weekly, one week to Osaka and the next week to Kōbe, and takes two days. Off-season it's near empty, but can be crowded during summer. A 2nd-class ticket is around US$180. The Shanghai Ferry service connects Osaka and Shanghai on a weekly basis. Tickets are similarly priced. There are also ships from Nagasaki to Shanghai every Thursday.

Ships from Kōbe to Tanggu (near Tianjin) leave from Kōbe every Thursday at noon, arriving in Tanggu the next day. Economy/1st-class tickets cost US$200/300. The food on this boat gets poor reviews so bring a few emergency munchies. Tickets can be bought in Tianjin from the shipping office (☎ 31-2243) at 89 Munan Dao, Heping District. In Kōbe, the office is at the port (☎ 078-321-5791).

Taiwan

A weekly ferry operates between Taiwan and Okinawa, sometimes via Ishigaki and Miyako in Okinawa Prefecture. The Taiwan port alternates between Keelung and Kaohsiung. Departure from Okinawa is on Thursday or Friday; departure from Taiwan is usually on Monday. The trip takes 16 to 19 hours. Fares from Okinawa range from ¥15,600 economy class to ¥24,300 1st class; fares are slightly cheaper from Taiwan than from Japan.

You can buy tickets from travel agents in your port of departure, but you can also buy them direct from the ferry company, Arimura Sangyo, which has an office in Naha (☎ 0988-64-0087) and Osaka (☎ 02-424 8151). In Taiwan you can buy tickets from Yeong An Maritime Company (☎ 02-771-5911) in Taipei, or in Kaohsiung (☎ 07-551-0281) and Keelung (☎ 02-424-8151).

Other Places

For travellers intending to take the Trans-Siberian Railway to Moscow, there's a weekly ferry service between Yokohama and the Russian port of Nakhodka near Vladivostok.

TRANS-SIBERIAN RAILWAY

A little-used option of approaching or leaving Japan is the Trans-Siberian Railway. It won't be particularly attractive to those looking at getting out of Japan in a hurry – visas and bookings take time – but for those with time to spare and an interest in avoiding expensive flights, it might be an attractive option.

There are three Trans-Siberian Railway routings, one of which is to travel directly across Russia followed by a flight from either Vladivostok or Khabarovsk – an expensive routing. The cheaper options are the Chinese Trans-Mongolia and Russian Trans-Manchuria routings, which both end in China, from where there are ferry connections to Japan via Tianjin and Shanghai.

Information on ferry connections between Japan and China is included in the Sea section of this chapter. Air connections with Vladivostok and Khabarovsk are via Niigata in Northern Honshū. Discounted tickets are not available on these flights and they both cost ¥65,000 one way, ¥128,000 return – not cheap. There are also ferry connections between Nakhoda (near Vladivostok) and Niigata.

Travel between China and Japan is cheaper by ferry. Air connections between the two countries remain very expensive – one of the cheapest options is Fukuoka-Shanghai (¥42,000 one way, ¥87,600 return) with China Air.

For more information on using this route contact national tourist agencies such as the Japan National Tourist Organisation (JNTO), China International Travel Service (CITS), Intourist (Russia) or Ibusz (Hungary). In Japan the Tourist Information Centres (TIC) in Tokyo and Kyoto and the Japan-Soviet Tourist Bureau (JSTB) should have more information. The JSTB has offices in Tokyo (☎ 03-3432-6161) and Osaka (☎ 06-531-7416).

More detailed information is also available in a good number of publications – see Robert Strauss' *Trans-Siberian Handbook* (Compass Publications, 1993) in particular. Those making their way to Japan via China (or vice versa) should pick up a copy of Lonely Planet's *China – a travel survival kit* which has invaluable information on travel in China as well as information on Trans-Siberian travel.

LEAVING JAPAN

The availability of discounted tickets in Japan has improved greatly over the last few years. The average Japanese travel agent still tends to charge its clients the earth, but in Japan's major cities there is an increasing number of agents that provide tickets for price-conscious foreigners.

Worthy of a special mention is STA Travel, which is computerised and can organise tickets efficiently (many Japanese agents are not and can't). For information on STA Travel and other discount agents check with local gaijin-oriented magazines. In Tokyo, the best place to look is *Tokyo Journal*. In the Kansai Region (Kyoto, Osaka and Kōbe) check with *Kansai Time Out*.

Departure Tax

Kansai international airport charges a departure tax of ¥2650 and Tokyo's Narita international airport charges a departure tax of ¥2040. Departure tax is not charged at the other international airports.

WARNING

This chapter is particularly vulnerable to change – prices for international travel are volatile, routes are introduced and cancelled, schedules change, special deals come and go, and rules and visa requirements are amended. Airlines and governments seem to take a perverse pleasure in making price structures and regulations as complicated as possible. You should check directly with the airline or travel agent to make sure you understand how a fare (and ticket you may buy) works. In addition, the travel industry is highly competitive and there are many lurks and perks. The upshot of this is that you should get opinions, quotes and advice from as many airlines and travel agents as possible before you part with your hard-earned cash. The details given in this chapter should be regarded as pointers and are not a substitute for careful, up-to-date research.

Getting Around

Japan has an enormous variety of travel possibilities and, like everything else in Japan, its transport network is extremely well organised. The Japanese are used to departures and arrivals timed to the minute and they plan trips with schedules that require split-second timing.

TIMETABLES

In many popular areas of Japan, transport schedules are so frequent that timetables hardly matter – does it really make any difference if the train departs at 10.30 or 10.40 am? If, however, you really want to know what goes where and when, then you need a *jikokuhyō* or 'book of timetables'.

These come in a variety of forms, including a completely comprehensive monthly *ōki-jikokuhyō*, which lists just about every passenger vehicle that moves. This can be useful if you're exploring the back blocks of Japan and need to know about buses to remote villages or ferries between small islands. The drawbacks? It's the size and weight of a telephone directory and is completely in Japanese. Deciphering a 1000-page kanji timetable is not most people's idea of fun travel! In any case, the ōki-jikokuhyō is always available at stations (often tied to the ticket-office counter with a piece of string) and at most ryokan, youth hostels, minshuku and other accommodation.

An easier alternative is the Japan Travel Bureau's (JTB) *Mini-Timetable* which costs ¥310 and is issued monthly. It's about the size of a pocket dictionary and lists JR

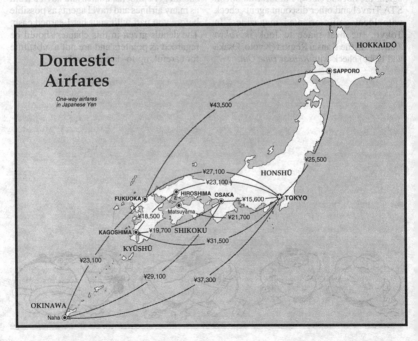

Domestic Airfares

One-way airfares in Japanese Yen

HOKKAIDŌ
SAPPORO
¥43,500
¥25,500
HONSHŪ
¥27,100
¥23,100
¥15,600
TOKYO
FUKUOKA
HIROSHIMA OSAKA
Matsuyama
¥18,500
¥21,700
KAGOSHIMA ¥19,700 SHIKOKU
¥31,500
KYŪSHŪ
¥23,100
¥29,100
¥37,300
OKINAWA
Naha

shinkansen services, limited and ordinary expresses, intercity and express trains in the Tokyo, Nagoya and Osaka areas, limited express services on the main private lines, expressway buses and all the domestic airline schedules. Other advantages of the mini guide are that it has some explanations in English and place names are shown in romaji on maps and main timetables. You're still going to have to do some deciphering of kanji but even a short-stay visitor should find this no problem.

TRAVEL AGENCIES

Information and tickets can also be obtained from travel agencies, of which there are a great number in Japan. Nearly every railway station of any size will have at least one travel agency in the station building to handle all sorts of bookings in addition to train services. The JTB is the big daddy of Japanese travel agencies.

DISCOUNT TICKETS

There are some agencies that deal in discounted tickets both for international and domestic travel. Typical savings on shinkansen tickets are around 20%, which is good news for long-term residents who are not eligible for Japan Rail Passes. Discount ticket agencies are found in the major cities and these agencies sometimes advertise in the English-language journals produced for long-term residents. (See the Tokyo chapter for details of discounters in that city.)

BAGGAGE FORWARDING

The average traveller should have no problems stowing their luggage on Japanese trains – there's capacious storage space overhead. But if you have too much baggage, highly efficient forwarding services are available.

AIR

Rail travel has such a pervasive image in Japan that it's easy to forget there's a dense network of air routes. In many cases, flying can be much faster than even shinkansen rail travel and not that much more expensive. Flying is also an efficient way to travel from the main islands to the any small islands around the coast of Japan. As well as numerous small local operators, there are five major domestic airlines.

Local Air Services

Japan Air Lines (JAL) is the major international carrier and also has a domestic network linking the major cities. All Nippon Airways (ANA) is the second largest international carrier and operates a more extensive domestic system. Japan Air Systems (JAS) only does a couple of overseas routes but flies to many destinations in Japan. Air Nippon Koku (ANK) and South-West Airlines (SWAL) are smaller domestic carriers. ANK links many smaller towns all over Japan while SWAL is particularly good for connections through Okinawa and the other South-West Islands.

The Domestic Airfares Chart shows some of the major connections and the one-way fares. There's a 10% discount on round-trip fares if the return flight is made within seven to 10 days. The airlines have some weird and wonderful discounts if you know what to ask for. JAL, for example, has a women's group discount available for groups of three or more women. Or a husband and wife discount if their combined age totals 88 or more!

If you're flying to or from Tokyo, note that most domestic airlines use the convenient Haneda airport, while all international flights, except those with China Airlines, use Narita. If you're flying to Tokyo to make an international connection out of Nrita it would be rather embarrassing to end up at Haneda – make sure you're on one of the less frequent domestic Narita flights or that you have plenty of time (around three hours) to make the transfer from Haneda to Narita.

TRAIN

As in India, rail is *the* way to travel in Japan but there are few other similarities. Japanese rail travel is usually fast, frequent, clean, comfortable and often very expensive. The services range from small local lines to the shinkansen super-expresses or 'bullet trains' which have become a symbol of modern Japan.

Railway Stations

Railway stations in Japan are usually very well equipped. The main station is often literally the 'town centre' and in many cases will be part of a large shopping centre with a wide variety of restaurants, bars, fast-food outlets and other facilities.

Meals The Japanese railway system is not renowned for its high-class cuisine, though you may find that the shinkansen dining cars turn out pretty good food. Anyway, you certainly won't starve, as apart from the dining cars, there are snacks, drinks, ice creams and meals sold from the aisles. A good bet is to come prepared with a *bentō* (boxed lunch). At almost every station there will be a shop selling bentō, typically for ¥1000 or less. Some towns and stations have a particular bentō speciality.

Left Luggage Only major stations have left-luggage facilities but there are almost always coin-operated storage lockers which cost ¥100 to ¥500 per day, depending on their size. The lockers work until midnight (not for 24 hours) so, after that time, you have to insert more money before your key will work. If your bag is simply too large to fit in the locker, look suitably dumbfounded and ask *Tenimotsu azukai doko desuka?* ('Where

is the left-luggage office?'). If you are directed back to the lockers, just point at your oversized luggage, shake your head and say *Ōki-sugi masu!* ('It's too big for the locker!').

Japan Railways

Japan Railways (JR) is actually a number of separate private railway systems which provide one linked service. For the railway user, JR gives every impression of being a single operation which indeed it was for more than a century.

In 1987, it was decided that the accumulated losses of the government-run JNR (JR's predecessor) had simply gone too far and the government privatised it. To most Japanese, JR is known as *kokutetsu* – *koku* means 'national', *tetsu* means 'line' or literally 'iron', short for 'iron road'.

The JR system covers the country from one end to the other and also provides local services around major cities like Tokyo and Osaka. There is more than 20,000 km of railway line and about 20,000 services daily. In many cities, the JR central station forms the hub of the town centre, and is surrounded by hotels, restaurants, entertainment areas, bus services, car rental agencies, travel agencies, airline offices and the like. Shinkansen lines are totally separate from the regular railways and, in some places, the shinkansen stations are a fair distance from the regular

Ekiben – Lunch in Locomotion

Ekiben are one of those delightful Japanese institutions. A contraction of the words *eki* (railway station) and *bentō* (lunch box), every railway station worth its salt has an ekiben stand, and some stations are famous for their ekiben.

Legend has it that the first ekiben were served in 1885 at Utsunomiya station, not far from Tokyo. Back in those days an ekiben was a humble offering – pickles and rice balls were standard fare. How times change. There are close to 3000 varieties nowadays; stations vie with each other to produce ever more delectable take-away lunch boxes. It must be said, not all of them are successful, and anyone who makes a habit of eating ekiben on their travels is going to come across the occasional dud.

However, as a rule standards are high. This is no surprise because Japanese are obsessive gourmets; some of them travel the country just to savour a regional speciality, and a particular station along the way might be favoured for its mushroom or marinated boar or trout ekiben. Prices are reasonable, once you get used to the idea that you're not buying a hastily flung-together take-out. Famous ekiben tend to range from ¥1000 upwards, although cheaper ones are often available on trains. ■

JR station. JR also operate buses and ferries, and ticketing can combine more than one form of transport.

Private Railways

The private railway lines usually operate short routes, often no more than 100 km in length. In many cases they service resort areas from a major city. The local commuter services are often on private railway lines. The Kansai region around Kōbe, Kyoto, Nagoya, Nara and Osaka is an area particularly well served by private railway lines.

Unlike JR stations, the private line stations do not usually form the central focus of a town. In Tokyo, the various private lines into the city all terminate on the Yamanote loop which forms a neat outer ring around central Tokyo.

Shinkansen

The fastest and best known train services in Japan are the 'bullet trains'. Nobody knows them by that name in Japan, they're simply called shinkansen or super-expresses. Shinkansen translates as 'new trunk line'. The shinkansen reach speeds of up to 270 km/h, running on continuously welded lines which totally eliminate the old railway clickety-clack of wheels rolling over joints. The Nozomi super express shinkansen is the fastest shinkansen service. They are still not as fast as the high-speed trains in France, but the Japanese service has established an incredible record for speed, reliability and safety. In more than 30 years of operation, there has never been a fatality.

The shinkansen service efficiency starts even before you board the train. Your ticket indicates your carriage and seat number, and platform signs indicate where you should stand for that carriage entrance. The train pulls in precisely to the scheduled minute and, sure enough, the carriage door you want is right beside where you're standing. Your departure from the train is equally well organised. As you approach the station, a recorded voice announces, in English and Japanese, that you will soon be arriving and should make your way to the door as the stop will be a short one.

On each shinkansen route, there are two types of services: a faster express service stopping at a limited number of stations and a slower service stopping at all shinkansen stations. There is no difference in fare. There are, however, regular and Green Car (1st class) carriages. If you don't share the Japanese passion for cigarettes, there are a limited number of non-smoking carriages *(kin-en-sha)*; request one when booking. Unreserved carriages will always be available, even on the shinkansen, but at peak holiday periods they can be very crowded and you may have to stand for the entire trip.

Shinkansen Routes There are four shinkansen routes, all starting from Tokyo. One runs via Nagoya, Kyoto, Osaka and Hiroshima to Shimonoseki at the western end of Honshū and on to Fukuoka/Hakata on the northern coast of Kyūshū. Another runs via Sendai to Morioka, almost at the northeastern end of Honshū; at Fukushima it branches off to Yamagata, creating a third line. The fourth line runs north from Tokyo to Niigata on the north coast of central Honshū.

Tokyo-Osaka-Hakata The Tōkaidō line runs from Tokyo to Osaka and contiues to Fukuoka/Hakata as the San-yō line. Three types of trains run on this route – the Hikari (Light), the Kodama (Echo) and the new Nozumi. The difference lies in the speed and the number of stops – while the Hikari stops only at Nagoya and Kyoto on the Tokyo-Osaka run, the Kodama stops at all the shinkansen stations. The Nozumi also stops at Nagoya and Kyoto, but does the trip around 20 minutes quicker. From Tokyo to Kyoto, the Nozumi service takes around two hours and 20 minutes, the Hikari two hours and 40 minutes, and the Kodama four hours. All the way to Hakata from Tokyo takes five hours by Nozumi, six hours by Hikari.

Most westbound Hikari services continue beyond Osaka but stops vary from one departure to the next, so check your schedule carefully. There's a similar pattern eastbound from Hakata: some Hikari services terminate in Osaka, others continue on to Tokyo.

Kodama services usually operate shorter segments along the Tokyo-Osaka-Hakata route. For example, Tokyo-Osaka, Osaka-Hakata, Osaka-Hiroshima, Hiroshima-Hakata, or the reverse.

Departures from Tokyo or Osaka are generally every 10 to 15 minutes from around 6 am to 11 pm, and all arrivals are before midnight. Services use the Tokyo central station. On a clear day, the Tokyo-Kyoto shinkansen run provides fine views of Mt Fuji – the shinkansen train passing by with Mt Fuji in the background being a favourite travel brochure picture.

Tokyo-Sendai-Morioka-Yamagata The Tōhoku line would have continued all the way to Sapporo on Hokkaidō if costs had not aborted that plan. There are three services: two of them – the Yamabiko, which is the express, and the Aoba, which is the local train – travel to Morioka or one of the main stops en route (Fukushima or Sendai); the third is the Tsubasa, which travels via Fukushima to Yamagata.

Depending on the stops, Yamabiko trains take as little as 1¾ hours to Sendai or 2½ to three hours and 20 minutes to Morioka. Except for a few late evening services which terminate at Fukushima, the Aoba services all terminate in Sendai and take about 2½ hours.

Direct Tsubasa services from Tokyo to Yamagata are extremely rare, but some Yamabiko services (approximately once every 1½ hours) allow connections to Tsubasa trains at Fukushima. The entire trip from Tokyo to Yamagata takes around 2½ hours.

There are more than 50 departures from Tokyo's Tokyo and Ueno stations every day, roughly half going all the way to Morioka and the rest terminating at Sendai or Fukushima. The scenery on this route is not as impressive as on the Tokyo-Osaka-Hakata route.

Tokyo-Niigata The Jōetsu line is frequently held up as a prime example of Japanese political corruption. Niigata is not really of sufficient importance to require a shinkansen railway line so passenger usage has always been relatively low. To make matters worse,

the route had to tunnel straight through the mountainous spine of Honshū, which made it a very expensive project. So why did it get built? Because Niigata was the home town of Prime Minister Kakuei Tanaka, whose political activities also included taking a couple of million US dollars in bribe money from Lockheed Aircraft!

There are about 45 departures a day from Tokyo or Ueno stations, more than 30 going all the way to Niigata. The express services are known as Asahi (Sunrise), the slower ones as Toki (Crane). The Tokyo-Niigata trip takes from one hour 50 minutes to two hours 20 minutes.

Travellers on the Trans-Siberian Railway through Russia will arrive at Niigata if flying to Japan from Khabarovsk or Vladivostok in Russia.

Other Train Services

While the shinkansen routes run most of the length of Honshū, a network of JR lines, supplemented by a scattering of shorter private lines, cover much of the rest of Japan. Although these services are efficient, they are nowhere near as fast as the shinkansen, and typically take about twice as long. (See the following section on Classes for more information about non-shinkansen trains.)

Even slower than the regular trains, but enormously popular nevertheless, are JR's steam locomotive (SL) services. After retiring its last steam trains in 1975, JR has now revived several services as special holiday attractions. On the Yamaguchi line from Ogōri to Tsuwano in Western Honshū, there's a steam train service operating throughout the summer and autumn months. Other SL services operate on the Hōhi line from Kumamoto to Mt Aso in Kyūshū and on the private Oigawa line from Kanaya, near Shizuoka, about 200 km south-west of Tokyo, to Senzu. SL services are very popular, so make enquiries and reservations well ahead of time.

Classes

All JR trains, including the shinkansen, have regular and Green Car (1st class) carriages.

The seating is slightly more spacious in 1st class, but most people will find the regular carriages quite OK.

The slowest trains stopping at all stations are called *futsū*. A step up from this is the 'ordinary express' or *kyūkō* which stops at only a limited number of stations. A variation on the kyūkō trains is the *kaisoku* or 'rapid' services. Finally, the fastest regular (non-shinkansen) trains are the *tokkyū* or 'limited express' services.

The longer the route, the more likely you are to find faster train services. Local futsū trains are mainly limited to routes of less than 100 km. In the back blocks of Japan these local trains are called *donko* and may well operate with older equipment than the main-line trains.

Reservations

Tickets can be bought at any JR station to any other JR station. Tickets for local services are usually dispensed from a vending machine but for longer distances you must go to a ticket window. For reservations, complicated tickets, Japan Rail Pass validations and the like, you will need a JR Travel Service Center. These are found at Narita airport and at the main JR stations in Hakata, Hiroshima, Kyoto, Kumamoto, Nagoya, Niigata, Nishi-Kagoshima, Osaka, Sapporo, Sendai, Shimonoseki, Tokyo (Tokyo, Ueno, Ikebukuro, Shinjuku and Shibuya stations), and Yokohama. Large stations that don't have a Travel Service Center will have a Green Window ticket counter – *Midori-no-Madoguchi* or *Guriin Uindō*. Any major station should have these counters with their green band across the glass.

Major travel agencies in Japan also sell reserved-seat tickets, and you can buy shinkansen tickets through JAL offices overseas if you will be flying JAL to Japan.

On futsū services, there are no reserved seats. On the faster kyūkō, tokkyū and shinkansen services you can choose to travel reserved or unreserved. However, if you travel unreserved, there's always the risk of not getting a seat and having to stand, possibly for the entire trip. This is a particular danger at weekends, peak travel seasons and on holidays. Reserved-seat tickets can be bought any time from a month in advance to the day of departure.

Validity & Stopovers Your ticket is valid for two days for a 100 to 200 km trip, with an extra day for each extra 200 km. During that time, you can make as many stopovers as you want so long as the ticket distance is more than 100 km. You cannot stop in Fukuoka, Hiroshima, Kitakyūshū, Kōbe, Kyoto, Nagoya, Osaka, Tokyo, Sapporo, Sendai or Yokohama if your ticket also starts or finishes in one of those cities. In other words, if you bought an Osaka-Kitakyūshū ticket you could not stop at Hiroshima but you could stop at other smaller stations along the way. Additional surcharges are on a per-trip basis, so that every time you break your journey, you must pay the relevant surcharge for the next sector. Therefore, if you're planning a multi-stop trip, you're better off getting a simple futsū ticket and paying express surcharges to the conductor as you go along.

Costs

Basic fares can easily be calculated from a straightforward distance/fare table in the JNTO *Railway Timetable*. Rural lines have a slightly higher fare structure than trunk lines. Shinkansen fares are simply the basic fare plus a super-express distance surcharge. Shinkansen tickets show the three figures – total, basic fare and shinkansen surcharge. (See the following Surcharges section.) Typical basic fares from Tokyo or Ueno, though not including the new Nozomi super express, are:

Tokyo or Ueno	Distance (km)	Futsū	Shinkansen
Fukushima	273	¥4530	¥8330
Hakata	1177	¥13,180	¥21,300
Hiroshima	895	¥11,120	¥17,700
Kyoto	514	¥7830	¥12,970
Morioka	535	¥8030	¥15,370
Nagoya	366	¥5970	¥10,380
Niigata	334	¥5360	¥9880
Okayama	733	¥9990	¥16,050
Osaka	553	¥8340	¥13,480
Sendai	352	¥5670	¥10,190
Shimonoseki	1089	¥12,570	¥20,690

Surcharges Various surcharges are applied to the base-level fares, starting with a ¥500 fee for a reserved seat. The shinkansen fares include this fee, so deduct ¥500 for the cost of travelling by shinkansen in an unreserved carriage. Some surcharges vary with the season – see Travel Seasons later in this section. Above the basic futsū fare, the surcharge for kyūkō (ordinary express) and tokkyū (limited express) services are:

Distance (Up to)	Kyūkō Surcharge	Tokkyū Surcharge
50 km	¥520	¥720
100 km	¥720	¥1130
150 km	¥930	¥1750
200 km	¥1030	¥2060
300 km	¥1240	¥2270
400 km	¥1240	¥2470
600 km	¥1240	¥2780
600 km +	¥1240	¥3090

The express surcharges (but not the shinkansen super-express surcharge) can be paid to the train conductor. There's an additional surcharge for Green Car (1st class) travel. Further surcharges apply for overnight sleepers and these vary with the berth type from ¥5150 for a regular three-tier bunk, ¥6180 to ¥10,300 for various types of two-tier bunks, and up to ¥13,100 to ¥16,850 for a standard or 'royal' compartment. Note that there are no sleepers on the shinkansen services as none of these runs overnight. Japan Rail Pass users must still pay the sleeper surcharge. Sleeper services mainly operate on trains from Tokyo or Osaka to destinations in Western Honshū and Kyūshū.

The Nozomi super express has higher surcharges than other shinkansen and cannot be used with a Japan Rail Pass. As a guideline, the surcharge for Tokyo-Nagoya is ¥5160 as opposed to ¥4410 by other shinkansen; for Tokyo-Hakata ¥9920 as opposed to ¥8120 by other shinkansen.

Travel Seasons Some of the fare surcharges are different during the off-peak and peak seasons as opposed to the rest of the year. Off-peak dates are between 16 January and 28 February, all of June and September, and from 1 November to 20 December, except Friday, Saturday, Sunday, national holidays and the day before national holidays. Peak season dates are 28 April to 6 May (Golden Week), 21 July to 31 August, 25 December to 10 January and 21 March to 5 April. During these peak seasons, travelling is very difficult and trains are heavily booked. The rest of the year is 'normal season'! On shinkansen services, for example, offer a ¥200 discount during the off-peak season or charge a ¥200 surcharge during the peak season.

Discounts & Special Fares If you buy a return ticket for a trip which is more than 600 km each way, you qualify for a 20% discount on the return leg. You can also get coupons for discounted accommodation and tours combined with your rail travel. There's even a JR prepaid card which you can use for ticket vending machines to gain a 6% or 7% discount on the larger denomination cards.

There are a number of excursion tickets, known as shūyū-ken or furii (Japanese for 'free') kippu. A waido shūyū-ken or 'wide excursion ticket' takes you to your destination and back and gives you unlimited JR local travel in the destination area. There are waido shūyū-ken available to travel from Tokyo to Hokkaidō and then around Hokkaidō for up to 20 days. A Kyūshū or Shikoku waido shūyū-ken gets you to and from either island and gives you 20 days of travel around them. You can even go to Kyūshū one way by rail and one way by ferry.

Variations include a mini shūyū-ken (a shorter time span, smaller area waido shūyū-ken), a rutō shūyū-ken (a multi-stop ticket along a certain route) and an ippan shūyū-ken (a sort of do-it-yourself return ticket with certain stops). One interesting variation is a five day seishun jūhachi kippu, literally a 'Youth 18 Ticket'. The latter are theoretically aimed at Japanese university students and are only available during university vacation periods (2 February to 20 April, 20 July to 10 September, 10 December to 20 January).

Still, it seems that many foreign residents have successfully used these tickets, even if they look a few years the wrong side of 18.

Basically, they allow you to buy five train tickets to anywhere in Japan for ¥11,300. The only catches are that you can only travel on local trains and each ticket must be used within 24 hours. However, even if you only use one to go to Kyoto and back from Tokyo (with a few side trips thrown in), you'll be saving money.

Japan Rail Pass

One of Japan's few travel bargains is the unlimited travel Japan Rail Pass. The pass lets you use any JR services for seven days for ¥27,800, 14 days for ¥44,200 or 21 days for ¥56,600. Green Car (1st class) passes are ¥37,000, ¥60,000 and ¥78,000 respectively. Children aged six to 11 get a 50% discount. The pass cannot be used for the new super express Nozomi shinkansen service, but is OK for everything else. The only additional surcharge levied on the Japan Rail Pass is for overnight sleepers. Since a reserved seat Tokyo-Kyoto shinkansen ticket costs ¥12,970, you only have to travel Tokyo-Kyoto-Tokyo to make a seven day pass come close to paying off.

The pass can only be bought overseas and cannot be used by foreign residents in Japan. The clock starts to tick on the pass as soon as you validate it, which can be done at certain major railway stations or even at the JR counter at Narita airport if you're intending to jump on a JR train immediately. Don't validate it if you're just going into Tokyo and intend to hang around the city for a few days. The pass is valid *only* on JR services; you will still have to pay for private railway services.

Schedules & Information

The most complete timetables can be found in the *jikokuhyō* (timetable books) but JNTO produces a handy English-language *Railway Timetable* booklet which explains a great deal about the railway services in Japan and gives timetables for the shinkansen services, JR limited expresses and major private lines. If your visit to Japan is a short one and you will not be straying far from the major tourist destinations, this booklet may well be all you need.

The TIC offices at Narita airport, Tokyo and Kyoto can also supply information on specific schedules. Major JR stations all have JR train information counters, but English speakers are rarely available.

If you need to know anything about JR – time schedules, fares, fastest routings, lost baggage, discounts on rail travel, hotels and car rental – call the JR East-Infoline in Tokyo on ☎ 03-3423-0111. The service is available in English and operates from 10 am to 6 pm, Monday to Friday, but not on holidays.

BUS

In addition to its local city bus services, Japan also has a comprehensive network of long-distance buses. These 'highway buses' are nowhere near as fast as the shinkansen and heavy traffic can delay them even further, but the fares are comparable with those of the local train (futsū) without any reservation or express surcharges. The trip between Tokyo and Sendai, for example, takes about two hours by shinkansen, four hours by limited express and nearly eight hours by bus. Tokyo-Kyoto is less than three hours by shinkansen and more than eight hours by bus.

Bus services have been growing in recent years, partly because of the gradual extension of the expressway network, partly because of the closing of uneconomical JR lines and partly because of escalating rail fares. Of course, there are also many places in Japan where railways do not run and bus travel is the only public transport option.

The main intercity bus services run on the expressways and usually stop at expressway bus stops where local transport is available to adjacent centres. The main expressway bus route runs between Tokyo, Nagoya, Kyoto and Osaka and stops are made at each city's main railway station. There are also overnight services and the comfortable reclining seats are better for a night's sleep than sitting up in an overnight train.

Bookings can be made through JTB offices or at the Green Window in large JR stations. The Japan Rail Pass is valid on some highway buses although, of course, the shinkansen would be far preferable! Note, however, that the storage racks on most buses are generally too small for backpacks. Other popular bus services include routes from Tokyo to Sendai, Yamagata and Hirosaki in Northern Honshū and to Niigata and areas around Mt Fuji in Central Honshū. There are extensive networks from Osaka and Hiroshima into areas of Western Honshū and around the smaller islands of Hokkaidō, Kyūshū and Shikoku.

Night Services

An option that is becoming increasingly popular among travellers is the network of night buses. They are relatively cheap, spacious (allowing room to stretch out and get some sleep) and save on a night's accommodation. They typically leave at around 10 or 11 pm and arrive the following day at around 6 or 7 am.

Costs

Some typical prices out of Tokyo include:

Destination	Fare
Aomori	¥10,000
Hakata	¥15,000
Hiroshima	¥11,840
Kyoto	¥8030
Nagoya	¥6500
Niigata	¥5150
Osaka	¥8450
Sendai	¥6100

CAR

One of the common myths about travel in Japan is that it's virtually impossible for a gaijin to travel by car: the roads are narrow and congested making travel incredibly slow; getting lost forever is a constant fear since the signs are in Japanese; the driving is suicidal; fuel is prohibitively expensive; parking is impossible; and foreigners are altogether better off sticking to the trains.

None of this is necessarily true. Of course, driving in Tokyo is a near impossibility but not many visitors rent cars to get around New York or London either. The roads are actually fairly well signposted in English so, on the major roads, getting lost is unlikely. The

minor roads are more likely to test your navigational ability but as Japan is compact, you can never be lost for long. The driving is a long way from suicidal – polite and cautious is probably a better description. Fuel is expensive but no more so than most of Europe, in fact it's cheaper than many countries in Europe. As for parking, it is rarely free, but neither is it impossibly expensive.

All in all, driving in Japan is quite feasible, even for the just mildly adventurous. In some areas of the country it can prove much more convenient than other forms of travel and, between a group of people (two adults and a couple of children for example), it can also prove quite economical. You will certainly see more of the country than all but the most energetic public transport users.

On the Road

Licence You will need an International Driving Permit backed up by your own national licence. The international permit is issued by your national automobile association and costs around US$5. Make sure it's endorsed for cars and motorcycles if you're licensed for both.

Foreign licences and International Driving Permits are only valid in Japan for six months. If you are staying longer you will have to get a Japanese licence from the licence office *(shikenjo)*. You need your own licence, passport photos, Alien Registration Card or Certificate of Residence, the fee and there's also a simple eyesight test to pass.

Fuel There's no shortage of petrol (gas) stations, the cost of petrol is about ¥150 to ¥160 per litre (about US$5 per US gallon) and the driveway service will bring a tear to the eye of any driver who resents the western trend to self-service. In Japan, not only does your windscreen get washed but you may even find your floor mats being laundered and the whole staff coming out, at the trot, to usher you back into the traffic and bow respectfully as you depart.

Maps & Navigation Get yourself a copy of the *Japan Road Atlas* (Shobunsha, Tokyo,

1990, ¥2890). It's all in romaji with sufficient names in kanji to make navigation possible even off the major roads. If you're really intent on making your way through the back blocks, a Japanese map will prove useful even if your knowledge of kanji is nil. When you really get lost, a signposted junction will offer some clues if you've got a good map to compare the symbols. The Metropolitan Expressway Public Corporation produces a free *Metropolitan Expressway Map* for the Tokyo region.

These days, there is a great deal of signposting in romaji so getting around is not a great feat. Road route numbers also help; for example, if you know you want to follow Route 9 until you get to Route 36 the frequent roadside numbers make navigation child's play. If you are attempting tricky navigation, use your maps imaginatively – watch out for the railway line, the rivers, the landmarks. They're all useful ways of locating yourself when you can't read the signs. Bring a compass, you'll often find it useful and, if you really get lost, Japan's compact size will always come to the rescue – head generally north and you will hit the main road or the coast in 20 km.

If you're a member of an automobile association in your home country you're eligible for reciprocal rights at the Japan Automobile Federation (JAF). Its office is directly opposite the entrance to the Tokyo Tower at 3-5-8 Shiba-kōen, Minato-ku, Tokyo 105. The JAF has a variety of publications, including a useful *Rules of the Road* book and will make up strip maps for its members.

Road Rules

Driving in Japan is on the left – like most other countries in the region stretching from India, through South-East Asia and down through Australia and the Pacific. One of the minor curiosities about this is that when the Japanese buy imported cars they like them to be really different – to have the steering wheel on the left side. This might have some sort of logic to it with German or US cars (they drive on the right) but none whatsoever with British cars (like the Japanese, the British drive on the left). Nevertheless, most Jaguars, Rolls-Royces and Minis sold in Japan will be left-hand drive. Apart from being on the wrong side of the road from the European or North American perspective, there are no real problems with driving in Japan. There are no unusual rules or interpretations of them and most signposts follow international conventions. The JAF has an English-language *Rules of the Road* book for ¥1860 (slightly discounted if you're a member of an overseas association). See the previous Maps & Navigation section for more about the JAF.

You see very little evidence of the police on Japanese roads; they're simply not there most of the time. I did see a taxi driver grabbed for running a red light in Kyoto once, but I never saw a speed trap and on most roads, there's very little opportunity to break the speed limit anyway. On the expressways, lots of cars exceed the speed limit and on one occasion I saw a police car cruising sedately along the inside lane at more-or-less the limit, while cars whizzed by at something above it. When speed traps *are* used, they will probably be on the one nice open stretch of road where the speed limit is way below the speed most people will be inclined to travel.

Tony Wheeler

Speed traps, however, are notorious in Hokkaidō and their presence is advertised in a strange manner: the incredibly rusty hulk of what was once a police car is simply mounted on a pedestal beside the road. Passing drivers nonchalantly activate their hi-tech radar detector defence systems and accelerate. Hokkaidō is definitely one of those places in Japan where you not only need to make use of a car, but you can also really enjoy yourself.

Robert Strauss

A blind eye may be turned to moderate speeding but for drinking and driving you get locked up and the key is thrown away. Don't do it.

Rental

There are a lot of car rental companies in Japan and although you'll find many of them represented at Narita airport, renting a car at Narita to drive into Tokyo is absolutely not a good idea. Heading off in the opposite direction towards Hokkaidō makes a lot more sense. Car rental offices cluster round railway stations and the best way to use rent-a-cars in Japan is to take a train for the long-distance part of your trip, then rent a car when you get to the area you want to explore. For example, the northern (San-in) coast of Western Honshū is a good place to drive – but don't drive there from Tokyo, take the train to Kyoto and rent a car there.

Japanese car rental companies are set up for this type of operation and offer lots of short-term rates – such as for people who just want a car for half a day. However, they're not much good at one-way rentals; you're always going to get hit for a repositioning charge and if the car has to be brought back from another island, the cost can be very high indeed. Typical one-way charges within the island of Honshū are ¥6000 for 100 km and ¥2400 for each additional 50 km. It makes a lot of sense to make your trip a loop one and return the car to the original renting office. Some of the main Japanese car rental companies and their Tokyo phone numbers are:

Car Rental Company	Telephone
Budget	☎ 03-3263-6321
Nippon	☎ 03-3485-7196
Nissan	☎ 03-3587-4123
Toyota	☎ 03-3264-0100

Rental costs are generally a flat rate including unlimited km. Typical rental rates for a small car (a Toyota Starlet or Mazda 121 – one step up from the Japanese microcars) is ¥8000 to ¥9000 for the first day and ¥5500 to ¥7000 per day thereafter. Move up a bracket (a Mazda 323 or Toyota Corolla) and you're looking at ¥10,000 to ¥13,500 for the first day and ¥8000 to ¥9000 thereafter. On top of the rental charge there's a ¥1000 per day insurance cost. Of course, you can also rent luxury cars, sports cars, even imported cars, but why give yourself headaches you don't need? Something easy to park is probably the best thing to have in Japan.

It's also worth bearing in mind that rental costs go up during peak seasons – 28 April to 6 May, 20 July to 31 August, and 28 December to 5 January. The increase can make quite a difference to costs. A car that costs ¥8800 a day usually will go up to ¥9700 during any of the peak seasons.

Communication can be a major problem when renting a car, although waving your driving licence and credit card and pointing at a picture of the type of car you want to rent usually makes it pretty clear what you want. Some of the offices will have a rent-a-car phrasebook with questions you might need to ask in English. Nippon Rent-a-Car even has an 'English-speaking desk' (☎ 03-3485-7196) where you can ring for assistance in English.

Check over your car carefully – perhaps it's an expectation that cars will only be used locally, but rental cars in Japan don't seem to be checked as thoroughly as those in the west. Check that all the tyres are in good order and that the jack and tool kit are in place.

Apart from maps and a phrasebook, other essentials are a compass (see Maps & Navigation in the previous On the Road section) and your favourite cassette tapes. Non-Japanese speakers will find very little to listen to on Japanese radio and the cassettes will help pass time in traffic jams. A Japanese-language tape is a good idea if you're keen to learn some Japanese as you drive.

Your rented car will, incidentally, almost certainly be white. Like refrigerators and washing machines, cars in Japan seem to be looked upon as white goods – 80% or 90% of the cars on the road are white, the exception being hot-shots in red sports cars and a few members of the avant-garde who drive black or grey cars.

Purchase

Since few foreign tourists drive themselves around Japan, the manufacturers have never promoted the overseas delivery options which are so popular with expensive European cars. Presumably, it could be done if you really wanted to. Long-term visitors or residents are more likely to be looking for a second-hand vehicle to use while in Japan and sell on departure. However, think carefully before making this decision. There are so many drawbacks to running a car in Japan's crowded cities that the alternative of renting a car on the odd occasion when you really need one may be preferable.

Buying used cars in Japan is subject to the same pitfalls as in most other places in the world, but the stringent safety inspections mean that you're unlikely to buy an unsafe vehicle. Once it's three years old, every car has to go through a *shaken* (inspection) every two years which is so severe that it quickly becomes cheaper to junk your car and buy another. The shaken costs about ¥100,000 and once the car reaches nine years of age it has to be inspected every year. This is the major reason you see so few old cars on the road in Japan. A car approaching an unpassable shaken drops in value very rapidly and, if you can find one, could make a good short-term purchase.

Another obstacle to buying a car in Japan is that you must have an off-street parking place before you can complete the registration formalities. Exemption from this requirement is one reason why the little microcars are so popular in Japan. To qualify as a microcar, a vehicle must have an engine of less than 660 cc, be less than 140 cm wide and less than 330 cm long.

Language is likely to be the major handicap in buying a car, so it's very useful to have a Japanese speaker to help with the negotiations. Foreign residents often sell their cars through the English-language papers.

Types of Roads
When & Where to Drive If you're going to drive yourself in Japan, do it sensibly. There's absolutely no reason to drive in the big cities or to drive in the heavily built-up areas like the San-yō coast of Western Honshū. If you're simply going from town A to town B and then stopping for a while, you're much better off taking the train.

In the less urbanised areas, however, a car can be useful. The northern San-in coast of Western Honshū, for example, is a world apart from the congested southern coast and slow public transport makes a car a much more attractive option. Hokkaidō is another good area for a drive-yourself trip. There are many areas where a car can be useful for a short excursion into the surrounding countryside, such as the loop from Kagoshima in Kyūshū down to Chiran and Ibusuki on the Satsuma Peninsula, or for a couple of days to make a circuit of (say) Okinawa Island. Car rental companies cater to this with short rental periods of a day or half day.

Expressways The expressway system will get you from one end of the country to another but it is not particularly extensive. Also, since all the expressways charge tolls, it is uniformly expensive – about ¥27 a km. Tokyo to Kyoto, for example, will cost about ¥9000 in tolls. This does have the benefit of keeping most people off the expressways so they are often delightfully uncrowded. The speed limit on expressways is 80 km/h but seems to be uniformly ignored. At a steady 100 km/h, you will still find as many cars overtaking you as you overtake, some of them going very fast indeed.

There are good rest stops and service centres at regular intervals. A prepaid highway card, available from tollbooths or at the service areas, saves you having to carry so much cash and gives you a 4% to 8% discount in the larger card denominations. Exits are usually fairly well signposted in romaji but make sure you know the name of your exit as it may not necessarily be the same as the city you're heading towards.

Other Roads On Japan's lesser roads, the speed limit is usually 50 km/h, and you can often drive for hours without ever getting up to that speed! The roads are narrow, traffic is usually heavy, opportunities to overtake are limited and often no-overtaking restrictions apply in the few areas where you could overtake safely. Sometimes you never seem to get out of built-up areas and the heavy traffic and frequent traffic lights can make covering 300 km in a long day's drive quite a feat. It's worth contemplating that just after WWII, only 1.5% of the roads in Japan were paved.

Generally, however, the traffic does keep moving, slow though that movement may be. The further you travel from the main highways, the more interesting the countryside becomes. Occasionally you'll come to stretches which are a wonderful surprise. Along a beautiful winding mountain road without a car in sight, it's easy to appreciate why the Japanese have come to make such nice sports cars.

Parking

Along with congestion and navigational difficulties, the impossibility of finding a parking space is the other major myth about driving in Japan. While there are few places you can park for free and roadside parking is virtually nonexistent, finding a place to park is usually not too difficult and the cost is rarely excessive.

Parking meters are rare and when they do exist are often a distinct technological step beyond what we have in the west. One type has an electronic 'eye' to detect if your car is still sitting there when your time is up. If so, a light on top of the meter then starts to flash to alert a passing meter inspector to come and issue the ticket! Even more sinister are the meters which lock your car in place. When your time's up a barrier rises up between the front and back wheels and you cannot move the car until you've paid the fine directly into the meter! Under normal circumstances, meters usually cost ¥100 for each half hour.

Off-street parking is usually in car parks – often very small ones with an attendant in a booth who records your licence plate number on arrival and charges you when you leave. Sometimes you have to leave the keys with the attendant. The charge might be ¥200 or ¥300 an hour but if you can read the small print, you may get a pleasant surprise or a nasty shock. Sometimes the first half hour or hour is free, particularly at railway station car parks. At some car parks the rate increases dramatically after, say, three hours to discourage long-term car parking. Unfortunately, it takes a lot of Japanese small print to discover these regulations. Even in big city multi-storey car parks, the charges are rarely as high as in equivalent car parks in, say, Australia or the USA.

Railway station car parks are usually a good bet, as they are conveniently central

and reasonably priced. Watch for interesting car parking technology, particularly the rotating vertical conveyer belts where your car disappears into a sort of filing cabinet. Car parking spaces seem to be zealously guarded and many daytime car parks are chained up at night to prevent anyone getting a free space for the evening.

In one city I saw a series of meters which operated from 7 am to 7 pm. So they were free after 7 pm, right? No way. For no visible reason, after 7 pm it was 'no parking'!
Tony Wheeler

MOTORCYCLE

Japan is the home of the modern motorcycle and you certainly see a lot of them on the road. Once upon a time they were all small displacement machines but now there are plenty of larger motorcycles as well. During the holidays you will see many groups of touring motorcyclists and, as usual in Japan, they will all be superbly equipped with shiny new motorcycles, efficient carriers and panniers, expensive riding leathers and, when the inevitable rain comes down, excellent rainproof gear.

Buying or Renting a Motorcycle

If you enjoy motorcycles and you're staying long enough to make buying and selling a motorcycle worthwhile, then this can be a great way of getting around the country. A motorcycle provides the advantages of your own transport without the automotive drawback of finding a place to park. Nor do you suffer so badly from the congested traffic.

Although Japan is famed for its large-capacity road burners, these bikes are less popular in Japan for a number of reasons including outright restrictions on the sale of machines over 750 cc. The motorcycle licence-testing procedure also varies with the size of machine and before you can get a licence for a 750 cc motorcycle, you must prove you can lift one up after it has fallen over! Not surprisingly, this cuts down on the number of potential big motorcycle riders.

The 400 cc machines are the most popular large motorcycles in Japan but, for general touring, a 250 cc machine is probably the best bet. Apart from being quite large enough for a compact country like Japan, machines up to 250 cc are also exempt from the expensive shaken (inspections).

Smaller machines are banned from expressways and are generally less suitable for long-distance touring but people have ridden from one end of Japan to another on little 50 cc 'step-thrus'. An advantage of these is that you can ride them with just a driving licence, and don't need to get a motorcycle licence.

Buying a new machine is no problem, though you will find a better choice of large capacity machines in the big cities. Used motorcycles are often not much cheaper than new ones and, unless you buy from another gaijin, you will face the usual language problems in finding and buying one. Because of the small demand for large motorcycles, their prices tend to drop more steeply than small ones, but on the other hand, the popularity of the 250 cc class means these machines hold their value better. As with

everything else in Japan, you rarely see a motorcycle more than a couple of years old.

There are numerous used motorcycle dealers around Ueno station in Tokyo, on the streets parallel to Shōwa-dōri and north of the Ueno subway station. Some of these larger dealers actually employ gaijin salespeople who speak Japanese and English. Corin Motors (☎ 03-3841-4112) is a collection of nearly 20 motorcycle shops along Korin-chō, a block from the Disneyland bus exit. They're open from 9 am to 7 pm, Monday to Saturday. As with used cars the English-language papers and magazines are a good place to look for a foreigner's motorcycle for sale.

Renting a motorcycle for long-distance touring is not as easy as renting a car, although small scooters are available in many places for local sightseeing.

On the Road

As with car driving, your overseas licence and International Driving Permit are all you need to ride a motorcycle in Japan. Crash

---

Bent on Bikes

Just as expensive European cars have carved out a lucrative market in Japan, so have foreign motorcycles. The occasional Italian Ducati or Moto-Guzzi, German BMW or British Triumph can be seen among the throngs of Kawahondazukis, but the real foreign standout is the Harley-Davidson. Japanese motorcyclists have a real passion for 'hogs' and many HD riders even have their bikes kitted out like the California Highway Patrol and ride them in what looks like a US police uniform!

Old motorcycles also have a following, though you rarely see them on the road. There are Japanese magazines for vintage motorcycle enthusiasts and from the number of for-sale advertisements for old motorcycles, there must be many carefully restored machines hidden away – older Japanese ones as well as European and US collectors' items. Corin Motors in Ueno (see Buying or Renting a Motorcycle) has a small museum of old motorcycles while the Honda showroom, beside the Aoyama Itchōme subway station, displays some old Honda racing motorcycles including Mike Hailwood's beautiful six-cylinder Honda of the mid-'60s. ∎

helmets are compulsory and you should also ensure your riding gear is adequate to cope with the weather, particularly rain. For much of the year the climate is ideal for motorcycle touring but when it rains it really rains.

Touring equipment – bags, panniers, carrier racks, straps and the like – are all readily available from dealers. Remember to pack clothing in plastic bags to ensure it stays dry, even if you don't. An adequate supply of tools and a puncture repair kit can prove invaluable.

Riding in Japan is no more dangerous than anywhere else in the world, which is to say it is not very safe and great care should be taken at all times. Japan has the full range of worldwide motorcycle hazards from single-minded taxi drivers to unexpected changes in road surface, heedless car-door openers to runaway dogs.

BICYCLE

Exploring Japan by bicycle is perfectly feasible. Although the slow average speed of traffic on Japanese roads is no problem for a bike rider, pedalling along in a constant stream of heavy traffic is no fun at all. Reportedly, the Japan Cycling Association warns cyclists not to ride more than 100 km per day because of the danger from car exhaust fumes. Japanese cyclists seem to have a higher tolerance of heavy traffic and doggedly follow routes down recommended major highways. Tunnels can be an unnerving experience at first.

Cycling in Japan

In 1899, the British adventurer John Foster Frazer, cycling across the country en route from Europe to the USA, declared Japan 'the wheelman's paradise'. Foster may not have had to contend with the traffic on Route 1 or the bewildering complexities of Tokyo's expressways, but his original judgement remains sound. Japan is still a great country to explore on two wheels.

Unchanged since Foster's day are the topography and the climate, both important considerations for the would-be bicycle tourer. Japan's topographic wild card is its mountains. Even the coastal roads can have their hilly moments. (I cursed a former edition of this book atop a very large hill on the Niigata coastline for describing the area as 'ideal for cycling' – well, perhaps it was and my legs weren't.)

The Tōkaidō coastline, stretching south-west from Tokyo through Nagoya and past Osaka, is mostly flat, but it is also polluted, congested and unrelievedly boring. Avoid Route 1 at all costs. On the other hand, the Japan Sea coastline – windswept, sometimes hilly but rarely congested – is a cyclist's delight. It provides the cyclist with good roads, abundant wildlife and some of the freshest seafood in Japan. Hokkaidō, Shikoku and Kyūshū offer more of the same on even quieter roads.

That said, my own favourite cycling territory is in the mountains of Central Honshū – hard work but rewarded by spectacular scenery, delicious hot springs in which to soothe aching bones and, best of all, a glimpse of rural Japan that few city dwellers get a chance to see.

Climatic conditions require some serious consideration, particularly for cyclists planning a lengthy tour of Japan. Winter is something of a mixed bag. November and December are often sunny though cold and can be good months for touring Japan's coastal regions. In January and February, however, snowfalls, rain and cold conditions make much of Japan – particularly the Japan Alps, Northern Honshū and Hokkaidō – unattractive to all but the most masochistic of cyclists. Summer, on the other hand, is swelteringly hot and humid, a good time to stick to the coast or the cooler latitudes of Hokkaidō.

The rainy season is best avoided for obvious reasons. While it generally arrives in May and lingers for just a few weeks, it can't always be relied on to end on time, as I discovered on one sodden trip from Niigata to Kyoto. Typhoons blow up with immense ferocity in late summer and can play havoc with a tight itinerary. This leaves spring and autumn, the best seasons to be cycling in Japan: both are blessed with cool weather and minimal rainfall and see the Japanese countryside at its best.

The single biggest frustration for the cyclist in Japan is probably the lack of Romanised street names. This situation is improving gradually, but it can still be maddeningly difficult to find your way out of urban centres onto the road of your choice. (On one memorable occasion I managed a 90 minute circumnavigation of the Kanazawa ring road that brought me back to where I'd started.) A handy way of avoiding such confusion and the frustration of inner-city traffic is to put your bike on a train. To do this, a carry bag is required. Specialist carry bags, known in Japanese as *rinko bukuro* or *rinko baggu*,

The secret of enjoyable touring is to get off the busy main highways and onto the minor roads. This requires careful route planning, good maps and either some ability with kanji or the patience to decipher country road signs, where romaji is much less likely to be used. Favourite touring areas for foreign cyclists include Kyūshū, Shikoku, the Japan Alps (if you like gradients!), the Noto-hantō Peninsula and definitely Hokkaidō. Valiant Japanese cyclists have been known to ride as far up Mt Fuji as the road permitted and then shouldered their steeds so that they could conquer the peak together.

There's no point in fighting your way out of big cities by bicycle. Put your bike on the train or bus and get out to the country before you start pedalling. To take a bicycle on a train you may be required to use a bicycle carrying bag: they're available from good bicycle shops.

The Maps & Navigation section for car travel earlier in this chapter also applies to bicycles but there is also a series of Bridgestone *saikuringu mapu* (cycling maps). They identify many places in romaji as well as kanji but, as yet, only cover part of the country in Central Honshū. The cycling maps show where bicycles can be rented, identify special bicycle tracks and accommodation which is popular with cyclists and even show steep road gradients.

The Japan Bicycle Promotion Institute (Nihon Jitensha Kaikon Biru) (☎ 03-3583-5444) is also known as the Bicycle Cultural

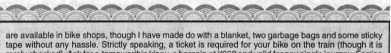

are available in bike shops, though I have made do with a blanket, two garbage bags and some sticky tape without any hassle. Strictly speaking, a ticket is required for your bike on the train (though it is rarely checked). Ask for a *temawarihin kippu*, a bargain at ¥260 and valid for any single journey. Ferries are also an opportunity to rest aching legs, and taking your bike aboard is no problem, though sometimes an extra charge will be required.

The best machine for touring Japan is a lightweight touring road machine or else a suitably equipped hybrid or cross bike. While mountain bikes are all the rage they are hardly required for Japan's well-paved roads. If you do bring a mountain bike, be sure to fit slimmer profile, preferably slick tyres, unless you're planning to spend all your time on mountain trails. Bikes with suspension forks require too much maintenance to consider as viable touring machines.

Perhaps the most important question for the cyclist looking at a holiday in Japan is costs. However you look at it, Japan is not cheap. Try to bring your own bike and accessories – even though Japan produces some of the world's best cycling equipment, prices will be cheaper at home. Camping is a good antidote to Japan's high accommodation costs, and many cyclists sustain themselves on a diet of instant noodles and sandwiches. Bear in mind, however, that after a long rainy day a comfortable inn with home cooking becomes a great temptation and it's easy to stray from a tight budget. Worst of all, if you're really pinching the pennies you'll never get into the bars, restaurants and hot springs where you can meet the Japanese at their most relaxed and welcoming. Even if you're planning to camp out and eat cheaply, it would be wise to budget US$30 per day.

Japan is a reasonably safe country to cycle in but, on a cautionary note, accidents happen more frequently than you might imagine. Comprehensive insurance is a must, as is a decent lightweight helmet. Also, despite Japan's reputation as a crime-free country, bicycles do get stolen, and of late professional gangs of bike thieves have been targeting big cities, especially around railway stations. I have lost no less than three expensive bikes over the last eight years. Bring a lock.

An essential purchase for those planning to tour Japan by bike is a copy of *Cycling Japan* (Kodansha, 1993), edited by Brian Harrell, long-term Japan resident and bike expert who also publishes the useful newsletter *Oizake* (Tailwind), another useful source of information (available for US$15 annually from B Harrell, 2-24-3 Tomigaya, Shibuya-ku, Tokyo, ☎ 03-3485-0471).

Cycling Japan is packed with information on everything from where to buy a large-frame bike to insurance policies to the best *onsen* accommodation. The rest of the book suggests itineraries, from Hokkaidō to Kyūshū. For off-road aficionados the wilderness of the Oku-Shiga forest trail sounds particularly inviting, not least because it passes through the Shiojiri vineyards. Fill your drink bottle with a Honshū muscat or or a drop of chardonnay?

John Ashburne

Centre and is across from the US Embassy at 1-9-3 Akasaka, Minato-ku, Tokyo. The institute has a museum and is a useful source of information about the special inns for cyclists (cycling terminals or *saikuringu terminaru*), maps, routes and types of bicycles suitable for foreign dimensions.

Useful Japanese phrases for cyclists include *Kanazawa ... yuki wa kono michi desuka?* ('Is this the route to ... Kanazawa?') and *Chizu o kaite kudasai* ('Draw a map, please').

Purchase & Rental

If you already have some experience of bicycle touring you will, no doubt, have your own bicycle and should bring this with you. Most airlines these days will accommodate bikes, sometimes as part of your baggage allowance, sometimes free. Often, all you have to do is remove the pedals before handing it over.

If you want to buy a bicycle in Japan, it is possible but nowhere near as simple as you might think. A glance at the bicycle park at any big railway station – or simply at the bicycle-clogged streets and sidewalks around the station – will reveal that lots of Japanese ride bikes. But very few of them are anything you would want to ride more than a few km. Despite all the high-tech Japanese bicycle equipment exported to the west, 10-speed touring bikes and modern mountain bikes are conspicuous by their absence in Japan. The vast majority of bicycles you see around the cities are utilitarian single-speed machines; cleaner and more modern versions of the heavy single-speed clunkers you find all over China or India.

This doesn't mean you can't find bicycles suitable for touring, it's just that you have to search them out. Even when you find an outlet handling multi-geared bikes, you should buy with care since they're likely to be built for the average-size Japanese rather than the average-size gaijin. If you're short to average it may not be a problem, but a tall gaijin is liable to have real trouble finding a big enough machine. Specialist dealers are one place to look, bicycle shops near US

military bases are another but easiest of all is to bring your own bicycle with you.

A number of adventure travel companies operate bicycle tours in Japan. It is not easy to rent a touring bike for a long trip but, in many towns, you can rent bicycles to explore the town. Look for bicycle-rental outlets near the railway station; typical charges are around ¥200 per hour or ¥800 for a day. In many towns, a bicycle is absolutely the ideal way to get around. In the mountain town of Tsuwano in Western Honshū, for example, it seems like there are more bicycles available for rent than there can ever be visitors to rent them. Also in Western Honshū, between Okayama and Kurashiki, there's an excellent half-day cross country bicycle path and a one-way rental system.

Many youth hostels have bicycles to rent – there's a symbol identifying them in the (Japan) *Youth Hostel Handbook*. The cycling inns found in various locations around the country (see the Accommodation section in the Facts for the Visitor chapter) also rent bicycles.

Many foreigners who have just arrived in Japan, on seeing the piles of discarded bicycles that litter most Japanese cities, make the assumption that you can just pick one up and ride into the sunset. Theoretically, yes ... but Japan doesn't really work that way. About the only thing that a Japanese police officer on a beat is diligent about is checking bike registrations. If you get picked up with a bike that is not registered in your name, you'll be hauled down to the local kōban and have to wait while they trace the original owner and check the bike in question wasn't stolen. There's a strong likelihood that the bike will be returned to the dump afterwards.

HITCHING

Hitching is never entirely safe in any country in the world, and we don't recommend it. Travellers who decide to hitch should understand that they are taking a small but potentially serious risk. But many people do choose to hitch, and the advice that follows should help to make their journeys as fast and safe as possible.

Japan can be an excellent country for hitchhiking, though this may partly be because so few Japanese hitchhike and gaijin with their thumbs out are also a very rare sight. Many hitchhikers have tales of extraordinary kindness from motorists who have picked them up. There are equally numerous tales of motorists who think the hitchhiker has simply lost his or her way to the nearest railway station, and accordingly takes them there.

The rules for hitchhiking are similar to anywhere else in the world. Make it clear where you want to go – carry cardboard and a marker pen to write in kanji the name of your destination. Write it in romaji as well, as a car-driving gaijin may just be coming by. Look for a good place to hitch; it's no good starting from the middle of town though, unfortunately, in Japan many towns only seem to end as they merge into the next one. Expressway entrance roads are probably your best bet. A woman should never hitch alone, even in Japan.

Truck drivers are particularly good bets for long-distance travel as they often head out on the expressways at night. If a driver is exiting before your intended destination, try to get dropped off at one of the expressway service centres. The Service Area Parking Area (SAPA) guide maps (☎ 03-3403-9111 in Tokyo) are excellent for hitchers. They're available free from expressway service areas and show full details of each interchange (IC) and rest stop – important orientation points if you have a limited knowledge of Japanese.

In Japan, as anywhere else in the world, it's a hitchhiker's duty to entertain. Although the language gap can make that difficult, get out your phrasebook and try and use at least some Japanese.

Be prepared to reciprocate kindnesses. You may find your driver will insist on buying you food or drinks at a rest stop; it's polite if you can offer fruit, rice crackers or even cigarettes in return.

WALKING

There are many opportunities for hiking and mountain climbing in Japan but few visitors

set out to get from place to place on foot. Alan Booth did, all the way from Hokkaidō to Kyūshū and wrote of the four month journey in *The Roads to Sata*.

It would be quite feasible to base an itinerary on walks, preferably out of season to avoid the day-trippers. JNTO publishes a *Combined Mini-Travel Series* with ideas on walks in Japan, including: *Walking Tour Courses in Tokyo*; *Walking Tour Courses in Nara*; and *Walking Tour Courses in Kyoto*. *Hiking in Japan* by Paul Hunt (Kodansha, Tokyo & London, 1988) has excellent walking suggestions throughout the country.

The Oirase Valley walk, near Lake Towada-ko (Tōhoku) is very pleasant. In the Japan Alps region, Kamikōchi is one of several bases for walks; and Takayama has a pleasant extended walking trail for several hours round the temple district. In the Kiso Valley, there's a very good walk between Magome and Tsumago.

In the Japan Alps and Hokkaidō, it's quite easy to break down hikes into smaller walks. On Rebun-tō Island, at the northern tip of Hokkaidō, there is plenty of scope to spend several days doing different walks in spectacular scenery, and the same applies to the other Hokkaidō national parks, especially Daisetsuzan. Shikoku has some fine walks, particularly up Mt Ishizuchi-san. In Kyūshū there are some excellent walks through areas of volcanic activity, such as on the Ebinokōgen Plateau near Mt Kirishima-yama.

BOAT

Japan is an island nation and there are a great many ferry services both between islands and between ports on the same island. Ferries can be an excellent way of getting from one place to another and seeing parts of Japan you might otherwise miss. Taking a ferry between Osaka (Honshū) and Beppu (Kyūshū), for example, is a good way of getting to Kyūshū and (if you choose the right departure time) seeing some of the Inland Sea on the way.

The routes vary widely from two-hour services between adjacent islands to 1½-day trips in what are in fact small ocean liners.

The cheapest fares on the longer trips are in tatami-mat rooms where you simply unroll your futon on the floor and hope, if the ship is crowded, that your fellow passengers aren't too intent on knocking back the booze all night. In this basic class, fares will usually be lower than equivalent land travel but there are also more expensive private cabins. Bicycles can always be brought along and most ferries also carry cars and motorcycles.

There are long-distance routes from Hokkaidō to Honshū and many services from Osaka and Tokyo to ports all over Japan, but the densest network of ferry routes connects Kyūshū, Shikoku and the southern (San-yō) coast of Western Honshū, across the waters of the Inland Sea. Apart from services connecting A to B, there are many cruise ships operating in these waters. Ferries also connect the mainland islands with the many smaller islands off the coast and those dotted down to Okinawa and beyond to Taiwan.

Information on ferry routes, schedules and fares can be found in the comprehensive ōki-jikokuhyō timetable and on information sheets from TIC offices. Ask for a copy of the Japan Long Distance Ferry Association's excellent English-language brochure. Some ferry services and their lowest fares include:

From Hokkaidō to Honshū	Fare
Muroran to Oarai	¥9570
Otaru to Maizuru	¥6590
Otaru to Niigata	¥5150
Otaru to Tsuruga	¥6590
Tomakomai to Nagoya	¥15,450
Tomakomai to Ōarai	¥9570
Tomakomai to Sendai	¥8850

From Tokyo	Fare
to Kōchi (Shikoku)	¥13,910
to Kokura (Kyūshū)	¥12,000
to Kushiro (Hokkaidō)	¥14,420
to Nachi-Katsuura (Honshū)	¥9060
to Naha (Okinawa)	¥19,670
to Tokushima (Shikoku)	¥8200
to Tomakomai (Hokkaidō)	¥11,840

From Osaka	Fare
to Beppu (Kyūshū)	¥6900
to Imabari (Shikoku)	¥4500
to Kagoshima (Kyūshū)	¥10,300

to Kōchi (Shikoku)	¥4530
to Matsuyama (Shikoku)	¥4430
to Naha (Okinawa)	¥15,450
to Shin-Moji (Kyūshū)	¥4840
to Takamatsu (Shikoku)	¥2780

From Honshū	Fare
Hiroshima to Beppu (Kyūshū)	¥3600
Kawasaki to Hyuga (Kyūshū)	¥17,720
Kōbe to Hyuga (Kyūshū)	¥7620
Kōbe to Kokura (Kyūshū)	¥4840
Kōbe to Matsuyama (Shikoku)	¥3500
Kōbe to Naha (Okinawa)	¥15,450
Kōbe to Oita (Kyūshū)	¥5050
Nagoya to Sendai (Honshū)	¥9580

From Kyūshū	Fare
Hakata to Naha (Okinawa)	¥12,970
Kagoshima to Naha (Okinawa)	¥11,840
Kokura to Matsuyama (Shikoku)	¥3500

LOCAL TRANSPORT

All the major cities offer a wide variety of public transport. In many cities you can get day passes for unlimited travel on bus, tram or subway systems. The pass is called a 'one day open ticket' or a *furii kippu*, though, of course, it's not free. If you're staying for an extended period in one city, commuter passes are available for regular travel.

Train & Subway

Several cities, especially Osaka and Tokyo, have mass transit rail systems comprising a loop line around the city centre and radial lines into the central stations and the subway system. Subway systems operate in Fukuoka, Kōbe, Kyoto, Nagoya, Osaka, Sapporo, Sendai, Tokyo and Yokohama. They are usually the fastest and most convenient ways of getting around the city.

For subways and local trains you will probably have to buy your ticket from a machine. Usually they're relatively easy to understand even if you cannot read kanji since there will be a diagram explaining the routes, and from this you can find what your fare should be. However, if you can't work the fare out, an easy solution is to buy a ticket for the lowest fare on the machine. When you finish your trip, go to the *ryōkin seisanjo* or fare adjustment office before you reach the exit gate and pay the excess. JR train and subway stations not only have their names posted above the platform in kanji and romaji but also the names of the preceding and following stations.

Bus

Almost every Japanese city will have a bus service but it's usually the most difficult public transport system for gaijin to use. The destination names will almost inevitably be in kanji (the popular tourist town of Nikkō is a rare exception) and often there are no numbers to identify which bus you want. Buses are also subject to the usual traffic delays.

Fares are either paid to the driver on entering or as you leave the bus and usually operate on one of two systems. In Tokyo and some other cities, there's a flat fare irrespective of distance. In the other system, you take a ticket as you board which indicates the zone number at your starting point. When you get off, an electric sign at the front of the bus indicates the fare charged at that point for each starting zone number. You simply pay the driver the fare that matches your zone number. Drivers usually cannot change more than ¥1000 but there is often a change machine in the bus.

In almost any town of even remote tourist interest, there will be *teiki kankō basu* (tour buses), usually operating from the main railway station. The tour will be conducted entirely in Japanese and may well go to some locations of little interest. However, in places where the attractions are widespread or hard to reach by public transport, tours can be a good bet.

Tram

A number of cities have tram routes – particularly Nagasaki, Kumamoto and Kagoshima in Kyūshū, Kōchi and Matsuyama in Shikoku and Hakodate in Hokkaidō. These are excellent ways of getting around as they combine many of the advantages of bus travel (particularly the good views) with those of subways (it's easy to work out where you're going). Fares work on similar systems to bus travel and there are also unlimited-travel day tickets available.

Taxi

Taxis are convenient but expensive and are found in even quite small towns; the railway station is the best place to start looking. Drivers are often reluctant to stop and pick you up near a station taxi stand, so either wait at the correct spot for a taxi off the rank or walk a couple of streets away. Fares vary very little throughout the country – flagfall (posted on the nearside windows) is ¥600 to ¥660 for the first two km, after which it's around ¥100 for each 350m (approximately). There's also a time charge if the speed drops below 10 km/h. A red light means the taxi is available, a green light means there's an additional night time surcharge, a yellow light means the cab is on a call.

Don't whistle for a taxi, a straightforward wave should bring one politely to a halt. Don't open the door when it stops, the driver does that with a remote release. He (if there are women taxi drivers in Japan they are very rare) will also shut the door when you leave the taxi.

Drivers are normally as polite as anybody else in Japan but, like the majority of Japanese, they are not linguists. If you can't tell the driver where you want to go, it's useful to have the name written down in Japanese. At hotel front desks there will usually be business cards complete with name and location, which are used for just this purpose. Note that business names, including hotels, are often quite different in Japanese and English.

Taxi drivers have just as much trouble finding Japanese addresses as anyone else. Just because you've gone round the block five times does not necessarily mean your driver is a country boy fresh in from the sticks. Asking directions and stopping at police boxes for help in finding the address is standard practice.

Tipping is not usually done unless you've got a lot of bags or your destination has been particularly difficult to find. A 20% surcharge is added after 11 pm or for taxis summoned by radio. Like many other places in the world, taxis in Japan seem to dissolve and disappear when rained upon.

Tokyo

東京

Japan's capital city is a place of vast proportions. Like London or Paris or Bombay or Bangkok, you might spend a lifetime exploring it and never run out of new things to discover. Granted, the larger picture is sometimes depressing – shoebox housing estates and office blocks traversed by overhead expressways crowded with trucks, buses and commuting Toyotas. But at street level the attentive eye is rewarded with an almost miraculous plethora of fabulous detail. And, more than anywhere else in Japan, Tokyo is where the old and the new collide: not a small part of Tokyo's fascination reposes in the tensions between the urgent rhythms of 20th century consumer culture and the quieter moments that linger from other, older traditions.

While Tokyo sports some of the world's biggest and most lavish department stores, the average Tokyo suburb hasn't fallen prey to supermarket culture. Suburban streets are lined with tiny specialist shops and restaurants, most of which stay open late into the night. Close to the soaring office blocks in the business districts and commercial centres are entertainment quarters – mazes of blazing neon offering an intoxicating escape from the drudgery of the commute-and-work regimen that is the lot of Tokyo's surging crowds of office workers. In the shadow of the overhead expressways and the office blocks exist pockets of another Tokyo – an old wooden house, a kimono shop, a Japanese inn, an old lady in kimono and *geta* sweeping the pavement outside her home with a straw broom.

As might be expected of a city that has established itself as one of the economic powerhouses of the modern world, what confronts the visitor more than anything else is the sheer level of energy in Tokyo. On the busy train lines, even at 11 pm on a Monday there is standing room only. Crowds sweep you up, carry you in their wake, and a barrage of noise assaults you at every turn. Train drivers assume strange, masked voices to advise you of the stops. On escalators, female announc-

HIGHLIGHTS

◆ Wander the streets of Shinjuku, home to Tokyo's busiest railway station and rowdiest entertainment quarter along with some of the best shopping and dining in the country

◆ Retreat to the calm of Meiji-jingū Shrine, one of Japan's finest

◆ Dip into the old-world hustle and bustle of Asakusa's Sensō-ji Temple, probably the liveliest place of Buddhist worship in all Japan

◆ Spend a day in Ueno-kōen Park exploring the museums – the Tokyo National Museum has the biggest collection of Japanese art in the world

◆ Make a visit to the Ginza complete by seeing a performance of kabuki

TOKYO

ers who sound like chirping birds ask you to stand within the yellow lines. Shops blare out their personal anthems into the crowded streets, traffic lights and vending machines play digitised melodies, and politicians drive the streets in cars fitted with loudspeakers, thanking constituents for having voted for them in the recent elections.

CHRIS TAYLOR

RICHARD I'ANSON

CHRIS TAYLOR

TONY WHEELER

CHRIS TAYLOR

CHRIS TAYLOR

THOMAS DANIELL

A	B	C
	D	E
F	G	

A: Yasukuni-jinja Shrine
B: Monk, Sensō-ji Temple
C: Tokyo Tower
D: Prayer tablets, Ueno-kōen Park

E: Akihabara
F: Sanja Festival, Sensō-ji Temple
G: Shibuya at night

Tokyo

Tokyo International Exhibition Center

Wangan Expwy

Shuto Expwy No 9

Harumi-dōri

Tsukiji Fish Market

Shin-ōhashi-dōri

Shōwa-dōri

Chūō-dōri

Hamarikyū Garden

Port of Tokyo

Rainbow Bridge

See Central Tokyo Map

Hibiya Park

Shuto Expwy No 1

Hibiya-dōri

World Trade Centre

Zōjō-ji Temple

Tokyo Grand Hotel

Tokyo Prince Hotel

Shiba Park

Tokyo Tower

See Akasaka Map

Swedish Embassy

Australian Embassy

Daiichi Keihin

Sengaku-ji Temple

Canadian Embassy

Asia Centre of Japan

See Roppongi & Nishi-Azabu Map

South Korean Embassy

Takanawa Prince Hotel

Shinagawa Prince Hotel

Pt. Arisugawa Memorial Park

German Embassy

French Embassy

Aoyama Cemetery

Nezu Museum of Art

Sakurada-dōri

National Park Nature Study

Jingū Gaien Garden

Aoyama-dōri

See Harajuku & Aoyama Map

Shuto Expwy No 3

Shuto Expwy No 2

Yebisu Garden Place

Rinshi-no-mori Park

Meiji-jingū Shrine

Yoyogi-kōen Park

New Zealand Embassy

See Shibuya Map

0   0.5   1 km

N

Tokyo Transport

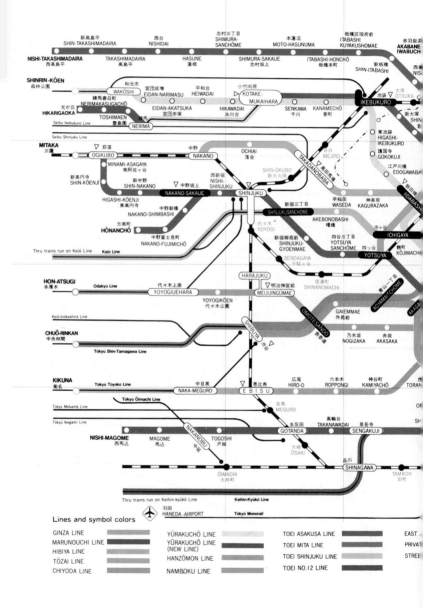

Lines and symbol colors

GINZA LINE	YŪRAKUCHŌ LINE	TOEI ASAKUSA LINE
MARUNOUCHI LINE	YŪRAKUCHŌ LINE (NEW LINE)	TOEI MITA LINE
HIBIYA LINE	HANZŌMON LINE	TOEI SHINJUKU LINE
TŌZAI LINE	NAMBOKU LINE	TOEI NO.12 LINE
CHIYODA LINE		

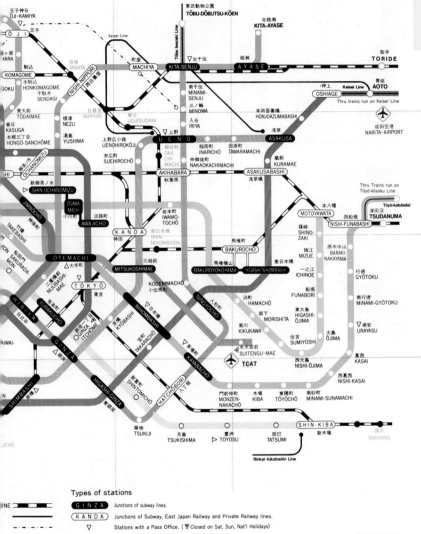

Types of stations

▬▬▬▬	GINZA — Junctions of subway lines.
▬▬▬▬	KANDA — Junctions of Subway, East Japan Railway and Private Railway lines.
▽	Stations with a Pass Office. (▽ Closed on Sat. Sun, Nat'l Holidays)

© Jun. 1996 TRTA

CHRIS TAYLOR

CHRIS TAYLOR

TONY WHEELER

NICKO GONCHAROFF

JEFF WILLIAMS

A: Lantern, Sensō-ji Temple, Asakusa
B: Pipers, Sanja Festival, Sensō-ji Temple, Asakusa
C: Prayer tablets, Sensō-ji Temple, Asakusa
D: Tokyo Metropolitan Government Offices, designed by Tange Kenzō
E: Colourful character

In fact, some of the best sights Tokyo has to offer are often not the kind of things you can put in a guidebook. They jump out at you unexpectedly on a crowded street: the woman dressed in traditional kimono buying a hamburger at McDonald's; and the Buddhist monk with an alms bowl, standing serenely in the midst of jostling crowds of shoppers in Ginza. Tokyo is a living city. It is less a collection of sights than an experience.

HISTORY

Tokyo is something of a miracle; a city that has literally risen from the ashes (the result of US aerial bombing at the end of WWII) to become one of the world's leading economic centres.

Tokyo used to be known as Edo (literally 'gate of the river'), so named for its location at the mouth of the Sumida-gawa River. The city first became historically significant in 1603, when Tokugawa Ieyasu established his shogunate (military government) there. From a sleepy backwater town, Edo grew into a city from which the Tokugawa clan governed the whole of Japan. By the late 18th century it had become the most populous city in the world. When the Tokugawa clan fell from power and the authority of the emperor was restored in 1868, the emperor and the capital were moved from Kyoto to Edo, and the city became Tokyo (Eastern Capital).

After 250 years of isolation imposed by the Tokugawa Shogunate, Tokyo set about transforming itself into a modern metropolis. Remarkably, it has been successful in achieving this in spite of two major disasters that, in each case, practically levelled the whole city – the great earthquake and ensuing fires of 1923, and the US air raids of 1944 and 1945.

Not much of the old Japan is left in Tokyo. Indeed, given the violence of the city's history – the periodic conflagrations (known to the locals as the 'flowers of Edo'), the earthquakes and the destruction brought about through war – it's a wonder that anything is left at all. What you find today is a uniquely Japanese version of a 21st century city. In short, if you're looking for traditional Japan you're better off heading for Kyoto or Kamakura, where recent history has been kinder to the traditional past. Tokyo is a place you visit to see the Japanese success story in action.

ORIENTATION

Tokyo is a vast conurbation spreading out across the Kantō Plain from Tokyo-wan Bay. But for visitors nearly everything of interest lies either on or within the JR Yamanote line, the rail loop that circles central Tokyo. In Edo times, Yamanote referred to 'Uptown'; the estates and residences of feudal barons, the military aristocracy and other members of the elite of Edo society in the hilly regions of Edo. Shitamachi, or 'Downtown', was home to the working classes, merchants and artisans. Even today the distinction persists, with the areas west of Ginza being the more modernised, housing the commercial and business centres of modern Tokyo, and the areas east of Ginza, centred in Asakusa, retaining more of the character of old Edo.

Essential for finding your way around Tokyo is a map of Tokyo's subway and Japan Railways (JR) network. The JR Yamanote line does a loop through Tokyo, above ground, that takes you through most of the important centres of the city, both Yamanote and, to a lesser extent, Shitamachi. It is actually possible to do the trip very cheaply, because buying a ticket to the next station for ¥120 doesn't stop you going in the less direct of the two possible directions and taking in the whole city on the way.

Starting in Ueno, two stops to the south is Akihabara, the discount electronics capital of Tokyo. Continuing in the same direction, you come to Kanda, which is near Tokyo's second-hand bookshop district, Jimbō-chō. The next stops are Tokyo station, close to the Marunouchi office district, and Yūraku-chō station, a short walk from Ginza. From there, trains continue through to the teen-oriented, fashionable shopping areas of Shibuya and Harajuku. Another two stops on is Shinjuku, a massive shopping, entertainment and business district. Between Shinjuku and Ueno the train passes through Ikebukuro (really a down-market version of Shinjuku) and Nippori, one of the few areas left in Tokyo where you can find buildings that have survived Tokyo's 20th century calamities.

Maps

A *Tourist Map of Tokyo* is available from the TIC (see the following Tourist Offices section of this chapter). *New Tokyo – A Bilingual Atlas* (Kodansha) is a book of maps that prospective residents of the city will find useful. English bookshops in Tokyo also stock a number of excellent foldout maps by local publishers. The *Rail Map of the Tokyo Area* and *Bilingual Map of Tokyo*, are both extremely good, as is the *Bilingual Map of the Tokyo Metropolitan Area* – all are published by Shobunsha. If you want to get serious about tackling Tokyo, pick up a copy of *Tokyo Rail & Road Atlas: A Bilingual Guide* (Kodansha), an 80-page atlas guide to the city.

Guidebooks

There are a number of publications that might supplement the one you have in your hands, particularly if you are planning to become a resident of Tokyo. For a light-hearted look at the city, Don Morton and Naoko Tsunoi's *The Best of Tokyo* (Tuttle) has recently come out in an updated edition with recommendations ranging variously from 'best traditional Japanese dolls' to 'best toilet'. For a comprehensive pocket-sized guide to Tokyo, Lonely Planet publishes *Tokyo city guide*.

Jean Pearce's *Footloose in Tokyo* (John Weatherhill) and *More Footloose in Tokyo* (John Weatherhill) are excellent guides to exploring Tokyo on foot. Even if you don't follow Pearce's routes, her introductions to some of Tokyo's most important areas make for interesting background reading. The first book is the more 'essential' of the two.

Gary Walters' *Day Walks Near Tokyo* (Kodansha International) covers 25 countryside trails, most of which can be reached from central Tokyo in an hour.

INFORMATION
Tourist Offices

In the new Tokyo International Forum is the Tourist Information Center, (TIC; ☎ 03-3201-3331), the single best source of information about Tokyo and the rest of Japan available in Tokyo. The Tokyo office is the best of the five TICs (two in Narita airport, one in Kyoto and one in Kansai international airport) run by the Japan National Tourist Organization (JNTO). It has an enormous range of information for travellers who know how to ask the right questions and, unlike the Kyoto centre, has no limit on the time you can spend harassing the staff.

While you can take a large number of brochures for yourself at the TIC, bear in mind that there is a lot more available for those who ask. Besides travel information, the centre also has information for those with specialised interests in Japan – anything from martial arts to the tea ceremony or Japanese paper making.

The TIC is located one floor below ground level in the Tokyo International Forum which is next to the Yūraku-chō station and the Sogō department store. Opening hours are Monday to Friday from 9 am to 5 pm and Saturday from 9 am to noon; closed Sunday and public holidays.

Immigration Office

The Tokyo Regional Immigration Bureau is best reached from Ōtemachi subway station on the Chiyoda line. Take the C2 exit, cross the street at the corner and turn left. Walk past the Japan Development building; the immigration bureau is the next building on your right.

Foreign Embassies

Most countries have embassies in Tokyo, though visas are generally expensive in Japan.

Australia
   2-1-14 Mita, Minato-ku (☎ 03-5232-4111)
Austria
   1-1-20 Moto Azabu, Minato-ku (☎ 03-3451-8281)
Belgium
   5-4 Niban-chō, Chiyoda-ku (☎ 03-3262-0191)

Canada
7-3-38 Akasaka, Minato-ku (☎ 03-3408-2101)
China
3-4-33 Moto Azabu, Minato-ku (☎ 03-3403-3380)
Denmark
29-6 Sarugaku-chō, Shibuya-ku
(☎ 03-3496-3001)
France
4-11-44 Minami Azabu, Minato-ku
(☎ 03-5420-8800)
Germany
4-5-10 Minami Azabu, Minato-ku
(☎ 03-3473-0151)
India
2-2-11 Kudan Minami, Chiyoda-ku
(☎ 03-3262-2391)
Indonesia
5-2-9 Higashi Gotanda, Shinagawa-ku
(☎ 03-3441-4201)
Ireland
8-7 Sanban-chō, Chiyoda-ku (☎ 03-3263-0695)
Israel
3 Niban-chō, Chiyoda-ku (☎ 03-3264-0911)
Italy
2-5-4 Mita, Minato-ku (☎ 03-3453-5291)
Laos
3-3-22 Nishi Azabu, Minato-ku (☎ 03-5411-2291)
Malaysia
20 Nampeidai-chō, Shibuya-ku (☎ 03-3476-3840)
Myanmar (Burma)
4-8-26 Kita Shinagawa, Shinagawa-ku
(☎ 03-3441-9291)
Nepal
7-14-9 Todoroki, Setagaya-ku (☎ 03-3705-5558)
New Zealand
20-40 Kamiyama-chō, Shibuya-ku
(☎ 03-3467-2271)
Norway
5-12-2 Minami-Azabu, Minato-ku
(☎ 03-3440-2611)
Philippines
11-24 Nampeidai-chō, Shibuya-ku
(☎ 03-3496-2731)
Russian Federation
2-1-1 Azabudai, Minato-ku (☎ 03-3583-4224)
Singapore
5-12-3 Roppongi, Minato-ku (☎ 03-3586-9111)
South Korea
1-2-5 Minami-Azabu, Minato-ku (☎ 03-3452-7611)
Spain
1-3-29 Roppongi, Minato-ku (☎ 03-3583-8531)
Sri Lanka
1-14-1 Akasaka, Minato-ku (☎ 03-3585-7431)
Sweden
1-10-3 Roppongi, Minato-ku (☎ 03-5562-5050)
Switzerland
5-9-12 Minami Azabu, Minato-ku
(☎ 03-3473-0121)

Taiwan (Association of East Asian Relations)
5-20-2, Shirogane-dai, Minato-ku, Tokyo
(☎ 03-3280-7811)
Thailand
3-14-6 Kami Osaki, Shinagawa-ku
(☎ 03-3441-7352)
UK
1 Ichiban-chō, Chiyoda-ku (☎ 03-3265-5511)
USA
1-10-5 Akasaka, Minato-ku (☎ 03-3224-5000)
Vietnam
50-11 Moto Yoyogi-chō, Shibuya-ku
(☎ 03-3466-3311)

Money

Banks are open Monday to Friday from 9 am to 3 pm. Look for the 'Foreign Exchange' sign outside. The exchange procedure can take up to 15 minutes.

Credit Cards Credit cards have become much more common in Tokyo over recent years. Finding an ATM that will give you a cash advance on an international credit card, however, is nobody's idea of fun.

American Express For reporting theft of your card or other problems, American Express has a 24 hour toll-free number: ☎ 0120-376-199. There are four American Express offices in Tokyo:

American Express Tower, 4-30-16 Ogikubo, Suginami-ku, Tokyo 167-01 (☎ 03-3220-6010)
Shinjuku Gomeikan Building, 1 Floor, 3-3-9 Shinjuku, Shinjuku-ku, Tokyo 160 (☎ 03-3352-1555)
Toranomon Mitsui Building, 3-8-1 Kasumigaseki, Chiyoda-ku, Tokyo 100 (☎ 03-3508-2400)
Yūraku-chō Denki Building, South 1 Floor, 1-7-1 Yūraku-chō, Chiyoda-ku, Tokyo 100 (☎ 03-3214-0068)

Other Cards Diners Club (☎ 03-3499-1311), JCB Card (☎ 03-3294-8111), MasterCard (☎ 03-5350-8051) and Visa (☎ 03-5251-0633l; in an emergency ☎ 0120-133173). All have offices in Tokyo.

Post & Communications

Postal Services Look for the red and white T with a bar across the top. Post boxes have two slots: the red-lettered slot is for Tokyo mail and the blue-lettered one is for mail going to other destinations. The Tokyo central post office (☎ 03-3241-4891) is next to Tokyo station in the Tokyo station plaza, Chiyoda-ku. Poste restante mail will be held there for 30 days. It should be addressed as follows:

Jane **SMITH**
Poste Restante
Central Post Office
Tokyo, JAPAN

International parcels and registered mail can be sent from the Tokyo international post office next to Ōtemachi subway station.

Telephone Almost all public telephones in Tokyo these days take prepaid phonecards, though to make an international call (look out for the grey IDD phones) you will need a KDD Superworld Card (*sūpā wārudo kādo*), which should be available from 7-Elevens and other convenience stores.

There is an English-language directory assistance service (☎ 03-3201-1010) available Monday to Saturday from 10 am to 7 pm. Long-term visitors should pick up a copy of *Townpage English Telephone Directory*. It has around 1000 pages of telephone numbers and is available free from any Nippon Telegraph & Telephone (NTT) office. Ring the NTT English Information Service (☎ 03-3201-1010) for the address of the nearest NTT office.

The area code for Tokyo is ☎ 03.

Fax The Kokusai Denshin Denwa (KDD) international telegraph office (☎ 3275-4343), one block north of Ōtemachi subway station, has fax and telex facilities. The Shinjuku KDD (☎ 3347-5000) close to the south exit of Shinjuku station can also handle faxes. Faxes can be sent from 9 am to 6 pm Monday to Friday; to 5 pm on Saturday.

Budget travellers, particularly those staying at the Kimi Ryokan (see Places to Stay), can use the Kimi Information Center, not far from the ryokan. You have to pay a registration fee of ¥2000, but after this you

pay the fax charges individually. The centre will also receive faxes for you.

Email The Internet cafe phenomenon has come to Tokyo but whether it's here to stay is another question. See the Places to Eat section of this chapter for details of some of the more popular places at the time of writing.

Travel Agencies
In Tokyo there are a number of travel agencies where English is spoken and where discounting on flights and domestic travel is the norm. For an idea of current prices check the daily English language newspapers or *Tokyo Journal*.

One of the most reliable operators is STA Travel, which has three Tokyo offices: Ikebukuro (☎ 5391-2922); Yotsuya (☎ 5269-0751); and Shibuya (☎ 5485-8380). Another long-standing agent worth trying is Across Traveller's Bureau, which also has three Tokyo offices: Ikebukuro (☎ 5391-2871); Shinjuku (☎ 3340-6741); and Shibuya (☎ 5467-0077).

Bookshops
Kinokuniya (☎ 3354-0131) in Shinjuku, on Shinjuku-dōri, has a good selection of English-language fiction and general titles on the 6th floor, including an extensive selection of books and other aids for learning Japanese. There is also a limited selection of books in other European languages – mainly French and German. Kinokuniya is a good place to stock up on guidebooks if you are continuing to other parts of the world. It's closed on the third Wednesday of every month.

Maruzen (☎ 3272-7211) in Nihombashi near Ginza has a collection of books almost equal to Kinokuniya's and is always a lot quieter. This is also Japan's oldest western bookshop, established in 1869. Take the Takashimaya department store exit at Nihombashi subway station and look for Maruzen on the other side of the road. It's closed on Sunday.

The 3rd floor of Jena (☎ 3571-2980) in Ginza doesn't have quite the range of some other foreign-language bookshops but it does have a good selection of fiction and art books, and stocks a large number of newspapers and magazines. It's closed on public holidays.

A new addition to the scene is Tower Books (☎ 3496-3661), on the 7th floor of the new Tower Records building in Shibuya. Not only does this place have an extensive selection of English books, it also has a fabulous array of magazines and newspapers from around the world; prices for magazines are considerably cheaper than elsewhere around town. It's open daily.

Some other notable English bookshops around Tokyo include Biblos (☎ 3200-4531), across from JR Takadanobaba station; the Aoyama Book Center (☎ 3442-1651), next to Roppongi subway station; Wise Owl (☎ 5391-2960), on the 4th floor of the Shineido Bookshop in Ikebukuro; and the Yaesu Book Center (☎ 3281-1811), next to JR Tokyo station in Nihombashi.

Tokyo's traditional bookshop area is Jimbō-chō. Although most of the bookshops in this area cater only to those who read Japanese, there are a couple of foreign-language bookshops. The best is Kitazawa Shoten (☎ 3263-0011), which has an excellent academic selection on the ground floor and second-hand books on the 2nd floor – don't expect any bargains. If you exit from Jimbō-chō subway station on Yasukuni-dōri and set off westwards in the direction of Ichigaya, Kitazawa is about 50m away on the left.

Libraries

The National Diet Library (☎ 3581-2331) is the largest library in Japan, with 1.3 million books in western languages. Books have to be requested on a special form. The library is close to Nagata-chō subway station on the Yūraku-chō and Hanzomon lines and is open Monday to Saturday from 9.30 am to 5 pm.

The British Council (☎ 3235-8031), in Iidabashi, has a library of books and magazines. It's open Monday to Friday from 10 am to 8 pm. The American Center (☎ 3436-0901), in Shiba-kōen, has a similar setup. It's open Monday to Friday from 10.30 am to 6.30 pm.

The Japan Foundation Library (☎ 3263-4504) is close to Kojimachi station on the Yūraku-chō line. It has some 30,000 English-language publications and is only open to foreigners. It's open from 9.30 am to 5 pm, closed Sunday and Monday.

For languages other than English, the Bibliotheque de la Maison Franco-Japonaise (☎ 3291-1144) is open from 10 am to noon, 1 to 6 pm, closed Saturday, and is close to Ochanomizu station on the JR Chūō line. The Goethe Institute Tokyo Bibliotek (☎ 3583-7280), with around 15,000 volumes, is open daily from noon to 6 pm (8 pm on Friday) and closed on weekends. It is close to Aoyama Itchōme station on the Ginza line.

In Ginza, the World Magazine Gallery (☎ 3545-7227) has a good selection of magazines from all corners of the world. It's open 11 am to 7 pm, closed on Sunday.

Newspapers & Magazines

Tokyo has a wealth of English-language magazines covering local events, entertainment and cultural listings. The pick of the pack is undoubtedly *Tokyo Journal*, and its Cityscope section alone is worth ¥600 a month for its comprehensive listings of movies, plays, concerts, art exhibitions and unclassifiable 'events'. Look out for it in English-language bookshops.

Check out the Tokyo TIC for giveaway listings magazines. These come and go, but are of a muchness, featuring advertising for expensive foreign-oriented restaurants and shows and a smattering of practical information and event listings. *Tokyo Tour Guide* is one of the better giveaways. It comes out monthly. *Tokyo Day & Night* is another monthly freebie; its one saving grace is its colour maps.

Clubs & Conversation Lounges

Once a popular window into the foreign world for Japanese, conversation clubs seem a little tired nowadays. Still, a few linger on, and if you're new to Japan they can represent a good opportunity to meet local Japanese as well as other foreigners.

Mickey House (☎ 3209-9686) is an 'English bar' that offers free coffee and tea as well as reasonably priced beer and food. Entry is free for foreigners. It's mainly regulars but you won't find it a closed scene. Take the main exit at JR Takadanobaba, turn right on to Waseda-dōri and look for the Tōzai line subway station entrance on your left; Mickey House is on the 4th floor of the Yashiro building, not far away – it's difficult to find the first time. It's open from 5 to 11 pm, closed Sunday.

Associations

The following is just a selection of what's available. Those with more specialised interests should check with the TIC or the classified pages of *Tokyo Journal*.

Amnesty International (☎ 3203-1050)

Asiatic Society of Japan has monthly meetings (☎ 3586-1548)

Beta Sigma Phi is an international women's group with social events (☎ 0471-75-8444)

Buddhist English Academy has regular meetings; call them for a schedule (☎ 3342-6605)

Gay & Lesbian Educational Equity holds meetings and workshops on ridding society of 'homophobia/heterosexism' (☎ 3722-7615)

International House of Japan is a prestigious association that runs academic seminars and is able to provide accommodation to its members at reasonable rates, although membership is expensive (¥200,000) and requires two nominations from members (☎ 3470-4611)

Japan Association of Translators meets the third Saturday of every month (fax 044-433-2962)

Japan Foundation has, among other things, library classes and free screenings of Japanese films with English subtitles – a real rarity in Japan (☎ 3263-4503)

Medical Services

The TIC has a list of clinics and hospitals where English is spoken in Tokyo. Note that clinics in Tokyo are expensive, charging upwards of ¥6000 for a consultation.

Probably the best choice is the Tokyo Medical & Surgical Clinic (☎ 3436-3028), close to Kamiya-chō and Shiba-kōen subway stations. It's open 9 am to 5 pm weekdays, 9 am to 1 pm Saturday; there's a 24 hour emergency service available.

The International Clinic (☎ 3583-7831) in Roppongi is another clinic with English-speaking staff. It is open from 9 am to 5 pm Monday to Friday, 9 am to noon on Saturday.

International Pharmacies It's often difficult to find what you need in Japanese pharmacies. The American Pharmacy (☎ 3271-4034) is just around the corner from the TIC, near Yūraku-chō station and Hibiya subway station, and is open Monday to Saturday from 9 am to 7 pm. Another option is the pharmacy at the National Azabu Supermarket (☎ 3442-3181), close to Hiro-o subway station.

Emergency

Emergency numbers are: police ☎ 110; fire ☎ 119. English speakers should be available. If not, ring Japan Helpline (☎ 0120-461-997), an emergency number that operates 24 hours a day, seven days a week. For information on your nearest medical treatment centre, ring the information desk of the Tokyo Fire Department (☎ 3212-2323).

Dangers & Annoyances

Tokyo can be annoying at times but it is rarely dangerous. If possible, avoid the rail network at peak hours – around 8 to 9.30 am and 5 to 7 pm – when the surging crowds would try anyone's patience. The noise can be aggravating in some of the busy commercial districts.

Earthquakes Tokyo's last big earthquake was in 1923. There is no certainty that the city is due for another big one but, as Kōbe recently discovered, a violent tremor can do a lot of damage in a short space of time. Check the locations of emergency exits in your hotel and be aware of earthquake safety procedures (see the Earthquakes section in the Facts for the Visitor chapter). If an earthquake occurs, the Japanese Broadcasting Corporation (NHK) will broadcast information and instructions in English on all its TV and radio networks. Tune to channel 1 on your TV, or to NHK (639 kHz AM) or FEN (810 kHz AM) on your radio.

Tokyo Architectural Treats

Tokyo is by no means teeming with interesting architecture: most of the city is dull. It grew too quickly, it was flattened by an earthquake in 1923 and then again by Allied bombing in WWII, and real value has always reposed in land, not buildings: architecture has tended to be utilitarian, designed to be replaced after a couple of decades of use. But there are some fabulous structures scattered across town for those who wish to look for them.

The one overwhelming architectural feature of modern Tokyo is the Tokyo Metropolitan Expressway – 220 km of it girds the city. For most of us it is such an eyesore that it tends to get overlooked. But as Noriyuki Tajima points out in his wonderful pocket guide *Tokyo – A Guide to Recent Architecture*: 'The scale and monumentality, weight and strength of the expressway – like ancient Roman city walls – easily overwhelms any of the city's buildings, and striking contrasts are formed against its backdrop.' Take a look at how the expressway interacts with street scenes in central Tokyo (particularly Yūraku-chō and Nihombashi) and you'll see what he means.

The most famous of Japan's homegrown architects is Tange Kenzō. His Tokyo Metropolitan Government Offices in Shinjuku may look sinister, and have been criticised as totalitarian, but they are a remarkable achievement and pull in large numbers of visitors daily (around 6000). Those with an interest in Tange's work should also look out for the United Nations University, close to Omotesandō subway station.

Peter Eisenman has made some avant-garde contributions to Tokyo's urban landscape. The NC building is perhaps the most interesting. It embodies the movement of tectonic plates and the transient nature of Tokyo architecture: the result is a structure caught in the moment of collapse, all angles at odds with each other, as if one had given a child a felt tip and asked them to design a building for you. The building is close to Shin-Koiwa station on the JR Sōbu line.

In central Tokyo, the Tokyo International Forum was the product of an international competition. The result is a glass and steel ocean liner with a miracle of a hall – pedestrian walkways are planned to link Yūraku-chō and Tokyo stations via the forum. The new Edo-Tokyo museum in Ryōgoku is a bizarre structure that you can't help but marvel at, particularly as you stand in the sprawling plaza that surrounds it – the Star Wars connotations seem to strike everyone. The Spiral building in Aoyama is an interior treat, and a long-time favourite with Tokyo residents.

Visitors to Asakusa in search of 'lost Japan' might pause and take a look at the Super Dry Hall, an eccentric Philippe Starck design that celebrates Asahi beer with an upside-down building with what looks to be a golden turnip on its bottom (head) – the 'golden flame' represents the frothy head of a beer. The interior is as remarkable as the exterior.

Lastly, see the Shibuya Walking Tour in this chapter for some more architectural highlights: notably the Bunkamura, the Humax Pavilion and Shibuya Beam. ∎

CENTRAL TOKYO
Imperial Palace 皇居

The Imperial Palace is the home of Japan's emperor and the imperial family. The palace itself is closed to the public for all but two days of the year, 2 January (New Year's Day) and 23 December (the emperor's birthday). Still, it is possible to wander around its outskirts and visit the gardens, where you can at least get a view of the palace with the Nijū-bashi Bridge in the foreground.

The present palace was completed in 1968. It replaced the palace built in 1888, which was destroyed by Allied bombing in WWII. The palace occupies the site of Edo-jō Castle, from which the Tokugawa Shogunate ruled all Japan. In its time the castle was the largest in the world, though apart from the massive moat and walls, virtually nothing remains of it today.

It is an easy walk from Tokyo station, or Hibiya or Nijūbashi-mae subway stations, to the Nijū-bashi Bridge. The walk involves crossing Babasaki Moat and the expansive Imperial Palace plaza. The vantage point, which is popular with photographers, gives you a picture-postcard view of the palace peeking over its fortifications, with the Nijū-bashi Bridge in the foreground.

Imperial Palace East Garden 皇居東御苑

The Imperial Palace East Garden is the only quarter of the Imperial Palace proper that is open to the public. To enter go through the

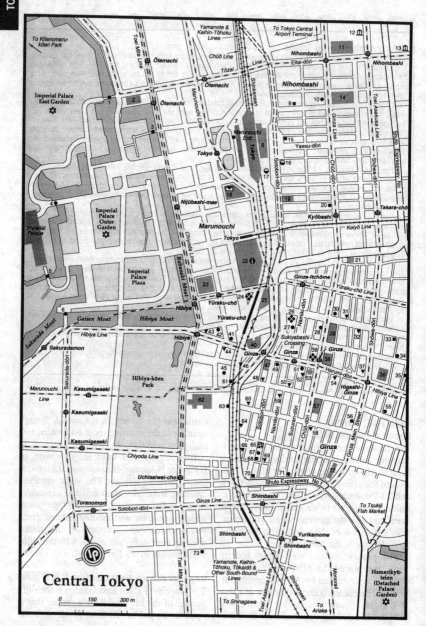

Central Tokyo

0   150   300 m

PLACES TO STAY
2 Palace Hotel
　パレス　ホテル
7 Tokyo Station Hotel
　東京ステーションホテル
9 Yaesu Terminal Hotel
　八重洲ターミナルホテル
15 Business Hotel Heimat
　ビジネスホテル
　ハイマート
21 Hotel Seiyo Ginza
　ホテル西洋銀座
33 Hotel Ginza Dai-ei
　ホテル銀座ダイエー
35 Hotel Atami-sō
　ホテル熱海荘
55 Ginza Tōkyū Hotel
　銀座東急ホテル
56 Ginza Tōbu Hotel
　銀座東武ホテル
62 Imperial Hotel
　帝国ホテル
68 Ginza Nikkō Hotel
　銀座日航ホテル
70 Ginza International Hotel
　銀座国際ホテル
72 Ginza Dai-Ichi Hotel
　銀座第一ホテル
73 Sun Hotel Shimbashi
　サンホテル新橋

PLACES TO EAT
31 Volks
32 Tenya
　天屋
37 Nair's
43 Saigon
44 Dondo
46 Yakitori Alley
　焼き鳥屋
48 Ginza Palmy Building
50 New Torigin
　ニュー鳥ぎん
52 Pilsen Beer Hall
54 Maharaja Indian
58 Sapporo Lion Beer Hall
59 Ten'ichi
　天一
60 Doutor Coffee
64 Sapporo Restaurant
　Indonesia

66 Sushi-sei
　寿司清
69 Kyubei
　久兵衛

OTHER
1 Ōte-mon Gate
　大手門
3 Wadakura-mon Gate
　和田蔵門
4 Sakashita-mon Gate
　坂下門
5 Nijū-bashi Bridge
　二重橋
6 Sakurada-mon Gate
　桜田門
8 Daimaru Department
　Store
　大丸百貨店
10 Maruzen Bookshop
　丸善書店
11 Tōkyū Department Store
　東急百貨店
12 Kite Museum
　凧の博物館
13 Yamatane Museum of Art
　山種美術館
14 Takashimaya
　Department Store
　高島屋
16 Airport Limousine Bus
　Stop
　空港リムジンバス
17 JR Highway Bus Terminal
　JRハイウェイバスのりば
18 Tokyo Station Plaza;
　Central Post Office
　東京中央郵便局
19 Yaesu Book Center
　八重洲ブックセンター
20 Meidiya International
　Supermarket
　明治屋
22 Tokyo International
　Forum; TIC
　東京国際フォーラム
23 Imperial Theatre
　帝国劇場
24 Sogō Department Store
　そごう百貨店
25 Kōtsū Building
　交通会館

26 Printemps Department
　Store
　プランタン百貨店
27 Kodak Imagica
　コダックイマジカ
28 Nikon Gallery
　ニコンギャラリー
29 Matsuya Department
　Store
　松屋百貨店
30 Ito-ya Stationery Shop
　伊東屋
34 World Magazine Gallery
36 Kabuki-za Theatre
　歌舞伎座
38 Mitsukoshi
　Department Store
　三越百貨店
39 Wakō Department
　Store
　和光百貨店
40 Hankyū & Seibu
　Department Stores
　阪急／西武百貨店
41 American Express
42 American Pharmacy
　アメリカンファーマシー
45 Hibiya Chanter;
　L'Attresco
　日比谷シャンテ
47 Hankyū Department
　Store
　阪急百貨店
49 Sony Building
　ソニービル
51 Jena Bookshop
　イエナ洋書店
53 Mitsubishi Building
　三菱ビル
57 Matsuzakaya
　Department Store
　松坂屋百貨店
61 Nishi-Ginza
　Electric Center
　西銀座電力センター
63 International Arcade
65 Hachikan-jinja Shrine
　八幡神社
67 Takumi Souvenirs
　たくみ土産物店
71 Hakuhinkan Toy Park
　博品館

Ōte-mon Gate, a 10 minute walk north of the Nijū-bashi Bridge. This was once the principal gate of Edo-jō Castle; the garden itself lies at what was once the heart of the old castle. Entry is free. It is open from 9 am to 4 pm (last entry at 3 pm); closed Monday and Friday.

Kitanomaru-kōen Park 北の丸公園

Kitanomaru-kōen Park itself is unremarkable. Nevertheless, it does have a couple of worthwhile museums. You can get there from Kudanshita or Takebashi subway stations. Alternatively, if you're walking from the Imperial Palace East Garden, take the Kitahanebashi-mon Gate, turn left and look for Kitanomaru-kōen Park on your right.

Science Foundation Museum A definite second place after Ueno's National Science Museum or even the Tepco Science Museum in Shibuya, the Science Foundation Museum is not a major attraction. For science buffs, however, it does cover a lot of ground over its five floors, and children will enjoy it. Don't expect too much English, though an English booklet is available with your ticket. Entry is ¥600. The museum is open daily from 9.30 am to 4 pm.

National Museum of Modern Art The permanent exhibition features Japanese art from the Meiji period onwards. It's worth checking to see if any special exhibitions are being held. Entry is ¥515. The museum is open from 10 am to 5 pm, closed Monday. Your admission ticket (hold on to the stub) gives you free admission to the Craft Museum.

Craft Museum An annexe of the National Museum of Modern Art, this museum houses crafts such as ceramics, lacquerware and dolls. Entry is ¥515. The museum is open from 10 am to 5 pm, closed Monday.

Yasukuni-jinja Shrine 靖国神社

If you take the Tayasu-mon Gate exit (just past the Budokan) of Kitanomaru-kōen Park, across the road and to your left is the Yasukuni-jinja Shrine, the Shrine for Establishing Peace in the Empire. Dedicated to

Japan's 2.4 million war dead since 1853, it is the most controversial shrine in all Japan.

The Japanese constitutional separation of religion and politics and renunciation of militarism didn't stop a group of class-A war criminals being enshrined here in 1979; it also doesn't stop annual visits by politicians on the anniversary of Japan's defeat in WW II (15 August). The loudest protests are from Japan's Asian neighbours, who suffered most from Japanese aggression. This is not to say you should boycott the shrine; it is well worth a visit. Black vans blasting right-wing propaganda (in Japanese) are often there to remind you where you are, however.

Yūshūkan Museum Next to the Yasukuni-jinja Shrine is the Yūshūkan Museum, with treasures from the Yasukuni-jinja Shrine and other items commemorating Japanese war dead. There are limited English explanations, but an English pamphlet is available. Interesting exhibits include the long torpedo in the large exhibition hall which is actually a *kaiten*, or 'human torpedo', a submarine version of the kamikaze. There are displays of military uniforms, samurai armour and a 'panorama of the Divine Thunderbolt Corps in final attack mode at Okinawa'. Admission is ¥200, and the museum is open daily from 9 am to 5 pm.

Ginza 銀座

Ginza is the shopping area in Tokyo that *everyone* has heard of. Back in the 1870s, Ginza was one of the first areas to modernise, featuring a large number of novel (for Tokyoites of that time) western-style brick buildings. Ginza was also home to Tokyo's first department stores and other harbingers of the modern world such as gas lamps.

Today, other shopping districts rival Ginza in opulence, vitality and popularity, but Ginza retains a distinct snob value. It is still the place to go and be seen emptying the contents of your wallet. If you are an impecunious traveller, on the other hand, Ginza is still an interesting area to browse in: the galleries at least are usually free and there are discount coffee shops and fast-food joints to take a break in.

The best place to start your exploration of Ginza is the Sukiyabashi Crossing, which is a 10 minute walk from the Imperial Palace. Alternatively, take the Sukiyabashi Crossing exit at Ginza subway station.

Museums There are no major museums in Ginza. The Yamatane Museum of Art, on the 8th Floor of the Yamatane building, is devoted to modern Japanese art. Entry is ¥600. It's open from 10 am to 5 pm; closed Monday.

The Kite Museum is a tiny place stuffed with kites (several thousand of them), and there may even be a craftsperson making kites. The museum is on the 5th floor above the Tameikan Restaurant. Entry is ¥300. It's open from 11 am to 5 pm; closed Sunday.

Showrooms Only Sony maintains a showroom in Ginza these days, which is a pity. The Sony Plaza (☎ 3573-2371) is on Sukiyabashi Crossing. The building hosts a fascinating walk-through display of Sony's many products, and you're free to fiddle with many of the items.

Galleries Ginza is overflowing with galleries, many of them so small that they can be viewed in two or three minutes. Others feature work by unknown artists who have hired the exhibition space themselves. Wander around and visit any galleries that seem particularly interesting. They are scattered throughout Ginza but are concentrated in the area south of Harumi-dōri, between Ginza-dōri and Chūō-dōri.

The Idemitsu Art Museum holds Japanese and Chinese art and is famous for its collection of work by the Zen monk Sengai. It's a five minute walk from either Hibiya or Yūraku-chō stations, on the 9th floor of the Kokusai building, next door to the Imperial Theatre. Admission is ¥500, and it is open from 10 am to 5 pm; closed Monday.

Probably the best of the photographic galleries in the area are the Nikon Gallery (☎ 3572-5756), the Contax Gallery (☎ 3572-1921) and the Canon Photo House Ginza (☎ 3573-7821). They're sponsored by the respective camera companies and have free, changing exhibits.

The Nikon Gallery is on the 3rd floor of the Matsushima Gankyōten building, opposite the Matsuya department store on Chūō-dōri, and is open from Tuesday to Sunday from 10 am to 6 pm.

The Contax Gallery is on the 5th floor of the building next door to the Sanai building on Chūō-dōri; there is no English sign at ground level. Admission is free, and it is open from Tuesday to Sunday from 10.30 am to 7 pm.

The Canon Photo House is on one of the side streets between Chūō-dōri and Shōwa-dōri and is open from 10 am to 6 pm daily except Sunday.

Kabuki-za Theatre Even if you don't plan to attend a kabuki performance, it's worth taking a look at the Kabuki-za Theatre (☎ 3541-3131). Performances take place twice daily (usually from 11.30 am and from 4.30 pm) and tickets range from ¥2000 to ¥14,000, depending on the seat. If you only want to see part of a performance you can ask about a restricted ticket for the 4th floor for ¥700 to ¥1400. For ¥600, plus a deposit of ¥1000, you can get an earphone guide that explains the kabuki performance in English as you watch – it is not available with restricted tickets. For phone bookings, ring at least a day ahead; the theatre won't take bookings for the same day.

Tsukiji Fish Market　築地魚市場
This is where all that sushi and sashimi turns up after it has been fished out of the sea. The day begins very early, with the arrival of fish and its wholesale auctioning. The wholesale market is not open to the general public, which is probably a blessing, given that you'd have to be there before 5 am to see the action. You are free to visit the outer market and wander around the stalls that are set up by wholesalers and intermediaries to sell directly to restaurants, retail stores and other buyers. It is a fun place to visit, and you don't have to arrive *that* early: as long as you're there sometime before 8 am there'll be some-

thing going on. Watch out for your shoes – there's a lot of muck and water on the floor.

The done thing is to top off your visit with a sushi breakfast in one of the nearby sushi shops. There are plenty of places on the right as you walk from the market back to Tsukiji subway station. The market is closed on Sunday and public holidays.

AKIHABARA 秋葉原

Akihabara is Tokyo's discount electrical and electronics centre, with countless shops ranging from tiny specialist stores to electrical department stores. You could go there with no intention of buying anything and within half an hour find half a dozen things that you couldn't possibly live without.

The range of products is mind boggling, but before you rush into making any purchases, remember that most Japanese companies use the domestic market as a testing ground. Many products end their days there without ever making it onto overseas markets. This may pose difficulties if you take something home and later need to have a fault repaired. Also, the voltage for which the product was made may not be the same as that available in your home country. Some larger stores (Laox is a reliable option) have tax-free sections with export models for sale.

While prices may be competitive with those you are used to at home, it's unusual to find prices that match those of dealers in Hong Kong or Singapore. You should be able to knock another 10% off the marked prices by bargaining, though this is often not the case with the tax-free items in the bigger stores. To find the shops, take the Electric Town exit of Akihabara station. You'll see the sign on the platform if you come in on the JR Yamanote line.

UENO 上野

Ueno is worlds away from trend-setting Tokyo districts like Shibuya and Ginza. It has long been seen as a terminus for rustic job-seekers from the deep north of Honshū, and there's a decidedly tatty air about some corners of the area. Still, Ueno is not without charm, and Ueno-kōen Park has some of

Japan's best museums and galleries. The park is also famous as Tokyo's most popular site for *hanami* (cherry blossom viewing) when the blossoms come out in early to mid-April. Note, that this *doesn't* make Ueno-kōen the *best* place to see the blossoms (see Shinjuku-gyoen Park in the Shinjuku section later for an altogether quieter hanami spot).

Ueno-kōen Park 上野公園

Ueno Hill was the site of a last-ditch defence of the Tokugawa Shogunate by about 2000 Tokugawa loyalists in 1868. They were duly dispatched by the imperial army, and the new Meiji government decreed that Ueno Hill would be transformed into Tokyo's first public park. Today, Ueno-kōen Park may not be the best of Tokyo's parks, but it certainly packs in more attractions than any of the others.

Saigō Takamori Statue This slightly unusual statue of a samurai walking his dog, near the southern entrance to the park, is a favourite meeting place. Saigō Takamori started out on the side of the Meiji Restoration but ended up ritually disembowelling himself in defeated opposition to it. The turnabout in his loyalties occurred when the Meiji government withdrew the powers of the military class to which he belonged. See Kagoshima in the Kyūshū chapter for more about Saigō Takamori.

Tokyo National Museum The Tokyo National Museum is the one museum in Tokyo that is worth going out of your way to visit. Not only is it Japan's largest museum, housing some 87,000 items, it also has the world's largest collection of Japanese art. Only a portion of the museum's huge collection is displayed at any one time. Entry is ¥400. The museum is open from 9 am to 4 pm; closed Monday.

The museum has four galleries, the most important of which is the Main Gallery. It's straight ahead as you enter, and houses a very impressive collection of Japanese art, from sculpture and swords to lacquerware and calligraphy. The Gallery of Eastern Antiquities, to the right of the ticket booth, has a collection of art and archaeological finds from all of Asia east of Egypt. The Hyōkeikan, to the left of the ticket booth, has a collection of Japanese archaeological finds. There is a room devoted to artefacts used by the Ainu people, the indigenous ethnic group of Japan who now live only in Hokkaidō.

Finally, there is the Gallery of Hōryūji Treasures, which is only open on Thursday, and then only 'weather permitting'. The exhibits (masks, scrolls, etc) are from the Hōryū-ji Temple in Nara. Because they are more than 1000 years old, the building often remains closed if it's raining or humid.

National Museum of Western Art The National Museum of Western Art has an impressive permanent collection and is also frequently host to special exhibits on loan from other museums of international repute. There is a special emphasis on the French impressionists, with originals by Rodin, including 'The Thinker', and paintings and sketches by, among others, Renoir and Monet. Entry is ¥400. The museum is open from 9.30 am to 4.30 pm; closed Monday.

Tokyo Metropolitan Museum of Art The Metropolitan Museum of Art has a number of different galleries that run temporary displays of contemporary Japanese art. Galleries feature both western-style art such as oil paintings and Japanese-style art such as sumi-e (ink brush) and ikebana (flower arranging). The admission charge varies according to the exhibition, but entry to the museum itself is free, and there are often interesting displays with no admission charge. It's open from 9 am to 5 pm; closed Monday.

National Science Museum The National Science Museum is a massive free-for-all packed with all kinds of scientific goodies. There is something on everything here – from space technology to plate tectonics. Not all the exhibits are labelled in English, but an English pamphlet is available for ¥300. Entry is ¥400. The museum is open from 9 am to 4 pm; closed Monday.

Shitamachi History Museum The Shitamachi History Museum re-creates life in Edo's Shitamachi, the plebeian downtown quarters of old Tokyo. Exhibits include a merchant's shop, a sweet shop, the home and business of a copper-boiler maker, and a tenement house; take off your shoes and look around inside. Upstairs, the museum exhibits utensils and items from the daily life of the average Shitamachi resident. You are free to

The Flowers of Edo

Today there is little left of Shitamachi, and the only way to get some idea of the circumstances in which the lower classes of old Edo lived is by visiting somewhere like Ueno's Shitamachi Fūzoku Shiryōkan (History Museum). Edo was a city of wood, and the natural stained-wood frontages and dark tiled roofs gave the city an attractiveness that is little in evidence in modern Tokyo. Nevertheless, the poor lived in horribly crowded conditions, in flimsy wooden constructions, often with earthen floors. Conflagrations regularly swept great swaths across the congested wooden buildings of the city. In a perverse attempt to make the best of misfortune, Edo dwellers almost seemed to take pride in the fires that periodically purged their city, calling them *Edo-no-hana*, or 'flowers of Edo'.

The flowers of Edo occurred with such frequency that it has been estimated that any Shitamachi structure could reckon on a life span of around 20 years, often less, before it would be destroyed by fire. Preventive measures included building houses that could be completely sealed: with the approach of a fire, the house would be sealed and left with candles burning inside, starving the interior of oxygen. Private fire brigades operated with standard bearers who would stake their territory close to a burning building and exact payment if they managed to save it.

Modern building techniques have eliminated most of 'Edo's flowers' but you can still see the occasional wooden structure that has miraculously survived into the late 20th century. ∎

TOKYO

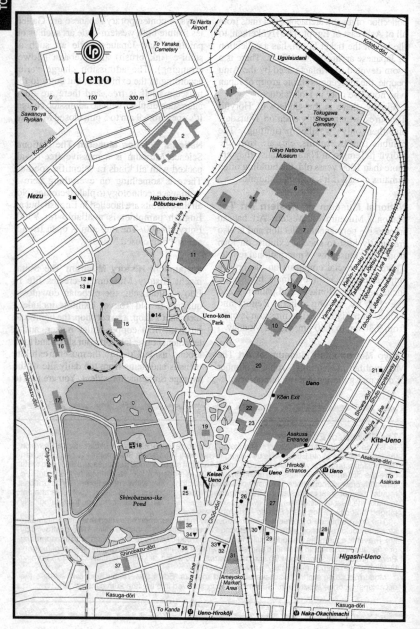

Ueno

0   150   300 m

To Yanaka Cemetery

To Narita Airport

Kototoi-dōri

Uguisudani

To Sawanoya Ryokan

Tokugawa Shogun Cemetery

Kototoi-dōri

Tokyo National Museum

Nezu

Hakubutsu-kan-Dōbutsu-en

Keisei Line

Ueno-kōen Park

Keihin-Tōhoku Line
Takasaki & Jōetsu Line
Tōhoku Main Line & Jōban Line

Monorail

Yamanote & Tōhoku & Jōetsu Shinkansen

Ueno

Shinobazu-dōri

Chiyoda Line

Kōen Exit

Ueno

Shōwa-dōri
Hibiya Line
Shuto Expressway No 1

Asakusa Entrance

Kita-Ueno

Keisei Ueno

Asakusa-dōri

To Asakusa

Hirokōji Entrance

Ueno

Ueno

Shinobazuno-ike Pond

Chūō-dōri

Higashi-Ueno

Shinobazu-dōri

Ginza Line

Ameyoko Market Area

Kasuga-dōri

To Kanda

Ueno-Hirokōji

Kasuga-dōri

Naka-Okachimachi

pick many of them up and have a closer look. Entry is ¥200. It's open from 9.30 am to 4 pm; closed Monday.

Ueno Zoo Established in 1882, Ueno zoo was the first of its kind in Japan. It's a good outing if you have children; otherwise, it can be safely dropped from a busy itinerary. Among the Japanese the zoo is very popular for its pandas (not on view on Friday). Entry is ¥400. The zoo is open daily from 9.30 am to 4 pm.

Tōshō-gū Shrine Dating from 1651, this shrine, like its counterpart in Nikkō, is dedicated to Tokugawa Ieyasu, who unified Japan. Entry is ¥100. The shrine is open daily from 9 am to 5.30 pm; from 9 am to 4.30 pm in winter.

Ameyoko-chō Arcade   アメ横
Ameyoko-chō was famous as a black-market district after WWII, and is still a lively shopping area where many bargains can be found. Shopkeepers are much less restrained than

PLACES TO STAY		OTHER		16	Ueno Zoo
3	Ryokan Katsutarō 旅館勝太郎	1	Kanei-ji Temple 寛永寺		上野動物園
12	Hotel Ohgasio 鴎外荘	2	Tokyo University of Fine Arts 東京芸大	17	Aquarium 水族館
13	Suigetsu Hotel 酔月ホテル	4	Gallery of Hōryū-ji Treasures 法隆寺宝物館	18	Benzaiten Temple 弁財天
21	Hotel Green Capital ホテルグリーン キャピタル	5	Hyōkeikan Main Gallery 表慶館	19	Kiyomizu Kannon-dō Temple 清水観音堂
25	Kinuya Hotel きぬやホテル	6	Main Gallery 東京国立博物館	20	Tokyo Metropolitan Festival Hall 東京文化会館
28	Hotel Sun Targas ホテル サン・ターガス	7	Gallery of Eastern Antiquities 東洋館	22	Japan Art Academy 芸術院会館
29	Ueno Capsule Kimeya Hotel 上野カプセル きめやホテル	8	Rinno-ji Temple 輪王寺	23	Ueno-no-Mori Art Museum 上野の森美術館
37	Hotel Parkside ホテルパークサイド	9	National Science Museum 国立科学博物館	24	Saigō Takamori Statue 西郷隆盛銅像
PLACES TO EAT		10	National Museum of Western Art 国立西洋美術館	26	Ameyayoko-chō Arcade アメヤ横丁
30	Ueno Yabu Soba 上野藪蕎麦	11	Tokyo Metropolitan Museum of Art 東京都美術館	27	Marui Department Store 丸井百貨店
32	Doutor Coffee			31	Ameyoko Centre Building アメ横センタービル
33	Samrat	14	Five Storeyed Pagoda 五重塔		
34	McDonald's			35	Shitamachi History Museum 下町風俗資料館
36	Izu-ei 伊豆栄	15	Tōshō-gū Shrine 東照宮		

elsewhere in Tokyo, attracting customers with raucous cries that rattle down the crowded alleyways like the trains overhead. Look for the big romaji sign opposite Ueno station.

AROUND UENO

Korin-chō   上野バイク街

See the Motorcycle section of the Getting Around chapter for information about the busy Korin-chō area, or Ueno Baiku-gai (Bike St), the motorcycle shopping centre in the shadow of Ueno station. There's an interesting motorcycle museum on the 3rd and 4th floor of the clothing shop of Corin Motors.

Kappabashi-dōri   カッパ橋道具街

Just two stops from the Ueno subway station on the Ginza line, at Tawaramachi, is Kappabashi-dōri. This is where you go if you're setting up a restaurant. You can get flags that advertise the food in your restaurant, personalised cushions, crockery and most importantly, all the plastic food you need. Whether you want a plate of spaghetti bolognese complete with an upright fork, a steak and chips, a lurid pizza or a bowl of ramen, it's all there. Items aren't particularly cheap, but some of them are very convincing and could make unusual Japanese mementos.

Kappabashi-dōri is five minutes walk from any of the Tawaramachi subway station's exits.

ASAKUSA   浅草

Long considered the heart of old downtown, Asakusa is an interesting area to explore on foot. The big attraction is Sensō-ji Temple, also known as Asakusa Kannon-dō Temple. In Edo times, Asakusa was a halfway stop between the city and its most infamous pleasure district, Yoshiwara. In time, however, Asakusa developed into a pleasure quarter in its own right, eventually becoming the centre for that most loved of Edo entertainments, kabuki. In the very shadow of Sensō-ji a fairground spirit prevailed and a whole range of very secular entertainments were provided, from kabuki theatres to brothels.

When Japan ended its self-imposed isolation with the commencement of the Meiji Restoration, it was in Asakusa that the first

cinemas opened, in Asakusa that the first music halls appeared and in Asakusa's Teikoku Gekijo Theatre (Imperial Theatre) that western opera was first performed before Japanese audiences. It was also in Asakusa that another western cultural export to the Japanese – the striptease – was introduced. A few clubs still operate in the area.

Unfortunately, Asakusa never quite recovered from the bombing at the end of WWII. Although Sensō-ji was rebuilt, other areas of Tokyo assumed Asakusa's role of the pleasure district. Asakusa may be one of the few areas of Tokyo to have retained something of the spirit of Shitamachi (the old downtown), but the bright lights have shifted elsewhere – notably to Shinjuku.

Sensō-ji Temple   浅草寺

Sensō-ji enshrines a golden image of the Buddhist Kannon, goddess of mercy, which according to legend was miraculously fished out of the nearby Sumida-gawa River by two fishermen in 628. The image has remained on the spot ever since, through successive rebuildings of the temple. The present temple dates from 1950.

If you approach Sensō-ji from Asakusa subway station, the entrance is via Kaminari-mon Gate (Thunder Gate). The gate's protector gods are: Fūjin, the god of wind, on the right; and Raijin, the god of thunder, on the left.

Straight ahead is Nakamise-dōri, the temple precinct's shopping street, where everything from tourist trinkets to genuine Edo-style crafts is sold. There's even a shop selling wigs to be worn with a kimono. Try the *sembei* (crackers) that a few shops specialise in – you'll have to queue, though, as they are very popular with Japanese visitors.

Nakamise-dōri leads to the main temple compound. Whether the ancient image of Kannon actually exists is a secret – it's not on public display. Not that this stops a steady stream of worshippers making their way to the top of the stairs to bow and clap. In front of the temple is a large incense cauldron: the smoke is said to be health bestowing, and you will see visitors rubbing it into their bodies through their clothes.

Dempō-in Garden 伝法院

To the left of the temple precinct is **Dempō-in Garden**. Although it is not open to the public, it is possible to obtain a ticket by calling in to the main office to the left of the Sensō-ji's five-storeyed pagoda. The garden is one of Tokyo's best, containing a picturesque pond and a replica of a famous Kyoto teahouse. It's closed on Sunday and holidays.

Sumida-gawa River Cruise It may not be the most scenic river cruise you've ever experienced, but the *suijō basu*, or 'water bus' is a great way to get to or from Asakusa.

The cruise departs from next to Asakusa's Azuma Bridge and goes to Hamarikyū-teien Garden, Hinode Pier and Odaiba Seaside Park. Probably the best option is to buy a ticket to Hamarikyū-teien Garden for ¥720

Shitamachi Walking Tour

The backstreets of Asakusa offer some of Tokyo's few opportunities to experience something of the flavour of old Shitamachi. The difference between Asakusa and other more modern districts of Tokyo is apparent as soon as you enter Nakamise-dōri, the gaudy, touristy shopping thoroughfare that leads into the precincts of **Sensō-ji Temple**.

Exit Sensō-ji Temple the way you entered it: through the Hōzō-mon Gate at the temple end of Nakamise-dōri. Turn right and follow the road around the perimeter of the temple grounds. **Chingo-dō Temple** is on the right, next door to the back entrance to Dempō-in Garden. More than anything else, the temple is an interesting oddity. Chingo-dō was founded in 1883 as a refuge for the 'raccoon dogs' that inhabited the Sensō-ji grounds – it obviously didn't do them much good as they're not much in evidence these days. A small flea market often sets up outside the temple, and the stalls may carry interesting festival accessories.

Follow the road and bear right and you come to an arcade lined with shops selling traditional items, including yukata and kimono. Farther along is the **Hanayashiki amusement park**. It hasn't got a lot to recommend it, unless you are overcome by a hankering to risk your life on one of the fairly rickety-looking rides. The Panorama Hall inside displays historical photographs of Asakusa. Hanayashiki is open seven days a week; the entrance fee is ¥700 for adults and ¥400 for children (rides range from ¥200 to ¥500).

The area around the amusement park was once the **Rokku cinema district**. It's difficult to imagine this area as a glamourous entertainment district, but that's what it was. The only cinemas left nowadays sport sad billboards advertising soft porn. The Furansu-za, probably Tokyo's oldest operating strip joint, also lurks in this area. Close by (next door to the Big Boy restaurant) is the **Rox Building**, a shopping centre that is notable for its failure to return Rokku to some of its previous grandeur. The nearby **Asakusa Engei Hall** is one of Tokyo's few remaining venues for performances of *rakugo*, the comic storytelling tradition.

Ahead is another arcade, taken up mostly by Japanese restaurants specialising in tempura and so on. However, worth a look are the traditional sembei-making shops. These savoury crackers are a popular traditional snack, and in some of these shops (as on Nakamise-dōri) you can watch them being made.

The arcade takes you back onto Kamanarimon-dōri, which has some good Japanese restaurants (see the Places to Eat section). Turn right here and cross over Kokusai-dōri. Following the small residential street that leads to Kappabashi-dōri, to your left is an area that is riddled with temples. The largest is **Tokyo Hongan-ji Temple**; it's on the right just before you reach Kappabashi-dōri.

Kappabashi-dōri Ave is Tokyo's wholesale restaurant supplies area. This makes for a more interesting walk than you might think, and can be a good source of off-the-wall souvenirs. Kappabashi-dōri is chock-a-block with shops selling plastic food, bamboo cooking utensils, noren, customised cushions and even the red lanterns (*chōchin*) that light the back alleys of Tokyo by night. Turn right into Kappabashi-dōri and walk up the road a few blocks, then cross Kappabashi-dōri and make your way back.

The landmark that tells you you've reached the end of your Shitamachi tour and done the rounds of the plastic foodshops is the **Niimi Building**, which is crowned with an enormous chef's head – you can't miss it. A few minutes down the road to your left is Tawarimachi subway station on the Ginza line. ■

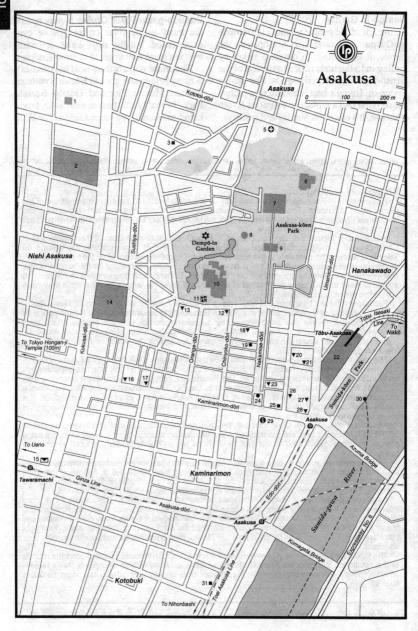

Asakusa

0   100   200 m

Asakusa

Kototoi-dōri

1

Nishi Asakusa

Sushiya-dōri

2

3

4

5

6

7

8

Dempō-in
Garden

Asakusa-kōen
Park

9

10

11

13

12

14

Kokusai-dōri

To Tokyo Hongan-ji
Temple (100m)

Orange-dōri

Chinyoko-dōri

Nakamise-dōri

18

19

20

21

16   17

23

24

25

26

27

28

Kaminarimon-dōri

Umamich-dōri

Hanakawado

Tōbu Isesaki
Line

To
Nikkō

Tōbu-Asakusa

22

Sumida-kōen   Park

30

Azuma Bridge

29

Asakusa

To Ueno

15

Tawaramachi

Ginza Line

Kaminarimon

Asakusa-dōri

Asakusa

Edo-dōri

Sumida-gawa   River

Komagata Bridge

Expressway No 6

Kotobuki

31

Toei Asakusa Line

To Nihonbashi

(the ticket includes the ¥200 entry fee for the garden). After looking around the garden it is possible to walk into Ginza in about 10 to 15 minutes. Boats leave every 20 to 30 minutes from 9.30 am to 6.15 pm and cost ¥520 to Hamarikyū-teien Garden, ¥560 to Hinode Pier and ¥960 to Odaiba Seaside Park.

SHINJUKU 新宿

If you had only a day in Tokyo and wanted to dive headfirst into the modern Japanese phenomenon, Shinjuku would be the place to go. Nearly everything that makes Tokyo interesting rubs elbows here: high-class department stores, discount shopping arcades, flashing neon, government offices, swarming push-and-shove crowds, street-side video screens, stand-up noodle bars, hostess clubs, tucked-away shrines and sleazy strip bars.

Shinjuku is a sprawling business, commercial and entertainment centre that never lets up. Approximately two million people a day pass through the station alone, making it one of the busiest in the world. On the western side of the station is Tokyo's highest concentration of skyscrapers, and presiding over them Tange Kenzō's Tokyo Metropolitan Government Offices, massive awe-inspiring structures. The eastern side of the station – the more interesting by far – is a warren of department stores, restaurants, boutiques, neon and sleaze.

PLACES TO STAY
2 Asakusa View Hotel
   浅草ビューホテル
3 Sukeroku-no-yado
   Sadachiyo Bekkan
   助六の宿、
   貞千代別館
19 Ryokan Asakusa
   Shigetsa
   旅館三河屋別館
25 Asakusa Plaza Hotel
   浅草プラザホテル
31 Hotel Towa
   ホテルTOWA

PLACES TO EAT
12 Daikokuya
   大黒屋
13 La Mentei Rāmen
   ラーメン亭
16 Tenya
   天屋
17 Owariya
   尾張屋
18 Japanese Inn
   Shigetsu
   旅館指月

20 Tatsumiya
   辰巳屋
21 McDonald's
23 Tonkya
   とんきゃ
26 Ramen House
   Asakusa
   ラーメンハウス浅草
27 KFC
28 Kamiya Bar
   神谷バー

OTHER
1 Banryo-ji Temple
   万隆寺
4 Hanayashiki
   Amusement
   Park
   花やしき遊園地
5 Sensō-ji Hospital
   浅草寺病院
6 Asakusa-jinja Shrine
   浅草神社
7 Sensō-ji Temple
   浅草寺

8 Five Storeyed
   Pagoda
   五重塔
9 Hōzō-mon Gate
   宝蔵門
10 Dempō-in Temple
   伝法院
11 Chingo-dō Temple
   鎮護寺
14 Rox Building
   ロックスビル
15 Post Office
   郵便局
22 Matsuya Department
   Store
   松屋百貨店
24 Kaminari-mon Gate
   雷門
29 Asakusa Tourist
   Information Center
   浅草文化観光
   センター
30 Sumida-gawa River
   Cruise
   墨田川水上バス

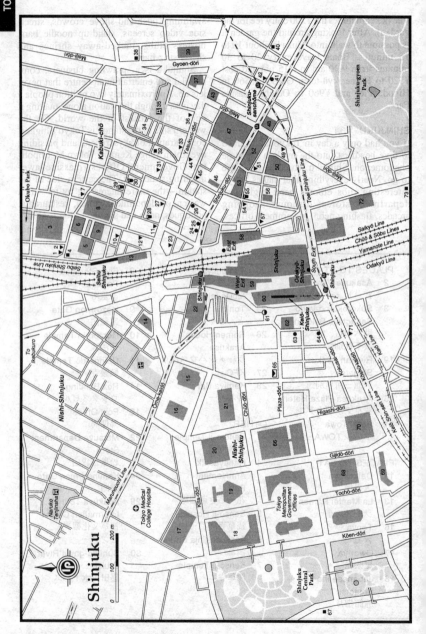

Shinjuku

0   100   200 m

Meiji-dōri

Gyoen-dōri

Shinjuku-gyoen
Park

Kabuki-chō

Shinjuku-
sanchōme

Ōkubo Park

Meiji-dōri

Yasukuni-dōri

Toei Shinjuku Line

Shinjuku-dōri

Seibu
Shinjuku Line

Seibu Shinjuku Line

Saikyō Line
Chūō & Sōbu Lines
Yamanote Line
Ōdakyū Line

East
Exit

Shinjuku

Odakyū-
Shinjuku

South Exit

Shinjuku

Nishi-Shinjuku

To
Ikebukuro

West
Exit

Keiō-
Shinjuku

Keiō Line

Keiō Line

Naruko
Tenjinsha

Marunouchi Line

Kōshū-kaidō

Kokusai-dōri

Keiō Shin-sen Line

Tokyo Medical
College Hospital

Nishi-
Shinjuku

Chūō-dōri

Plaza-dōri

Higashi-dōri

Gijidō-dōri

Ōme-kaidō

Kita-dōri

Tokyo
Metropolitan
Government
Offices

Tochō-dōri

Kōen-dōri

Shinjuku
Central
Park

PLACES TO STAY

4 Green Plaza Shinjuku
(Capsule Hotel)
グリーンプラザ新宿

13 Shinjuku Prince Hotel
新宿プリンスホテル

14 Star Hotel Tokyo
スターホテル東京

17 Tokyo Hilton International
東京ヒルトンホテル

18 Century Hyatt Hotel
センチュリーハイアット
ホテル

32 Shinjuku-ku Capsule
Hotel
新宿区カプセルホテル

38 Hotel Sun Lite Shinjuku
ホテルサンライト新宿

40 Winning Inn Shinjuku
(Capsule Hotel)
ウィニングイン新宿

56 Central Hotel
セントラルホテル

66 Keio Plaza
Inter-Continental Hotel
京王プラザインターコン
チネンタルホテル

67 Shinjuku New City Hotel
新宿ニューシティホテル

69 Shinjuku Washington
Hotel
新宿ワシントンホテル

73 Shinjuku Park Hotel
新宿パークホテル

PLACES TO EAT

1 Pekin Chinese
Restaurant
北京飯店

2 Tainan Taami
台南台湾レストラン

7 Tokyo Kaisen Ichiba
東京海鮮市場

10 Kaiten-zushi
回転寿司

11 Yōrōnotaki
養老の滝

12 Ban Thai

23 Ibuki
伊吹

27 Tōkaien
東海苑

31 Yatai Mura
(Street Food Stalls)
屋台村

33 Hofbräuhaus Beer Hall

36 Oriental Wave

42 Istanbul

44 Irohaniheto
いろはにほへと

45 El Borracho

49 Daikokuya
大黒屋

51 Tsunahachi
つな八

57 Suehiro
スエヒロ

71 Rose de Sahara

OTHER

3 Hygeai Shopping Centre

5 Shinjuku Tōkyū
Bunka Kaikan
新宿東急文化会館

6 Liquid Room

8 Koma Theatre
コマ劇場

9 Shinjuku Joy Cinema
新宿ジョイシネマ

15 Kasai Kaijō Building
火災海上ビル

16 Shinjuku Nomura
Building
新宿野村ビル

19 Shinjuku Sumitomo
Building
新宿住友ビル

20 Shinjuku Mitsui Building
新宿三井ビル

21 Shinjuku Centre Building
新宿センタービル

22 Odakyū Department
Store
小田急百貨店

24 Studio Alta Building
スタジオアルタビル

25 Konika Plaza

26 Kirin City

28 Catalyst

29 Rock Bar Mother

30 Rockin' Chair

34 Golden Gai
ゴールデン街

35 Hanazono-jinja Shrine
花園神社

37 Marui Men's
丸井メンズ

39 Isetan Park City
パークシティ伊勢丹

41 Rolling Stone

43 Minami Sports

46 Kinokuniya Bookshop
紀伊国屋書店

47 Isetan Department Store
伊勢丹百貨店

48 Marui Men's
丸井メンズ

50 Mitsukoshi South
三越南館

52 Mitsukoshi Department
Store
三越百貨店

53 Marui Department Store;
Virgin Megastore
丸井百貨店／
ヴァージンメガストア

54 Tower Records

58 My City Department Store
マイシティ

59 Odakyū Department Store
小田急百貨店

60 Keiō Department Store
京王百貨店

61 Airport Limousine Bus Stop
空港リムジンバス乗り場

62 Highway Bus Terminal
高速バスターミナル

63 Yodobashi Camera
ヨドバシカメラ

64 Sakuraya Camera
カメラのサクラヤ

65 Post Office
郵便局

68 Shinjuku NS Building
新宿 NS ビル

70 KDD Building
KDD ビル

72 Takashimaya Times
Square
タカシマヤタイムズ
スクエア

West Side 新宿西口

Shinjuku's west side is mainly administrative, but the area behind the Keiō department store is home to Tokyo's largest camera stores: Yodobashi Camera and Sakuraya Camera. Yodobashi Camera has practically everything you could possibly want that relates to photography, including a huge stock of film, darkroom equipment, tripods, cameras, lenses and other accessories. Its prices are usually very reasonable. Yodo-bashi even has a limited selection of second-hand photographic equipment. This area is also the best place to seek out computer equipment.

Elsewhere, the attractions of Shinjuku's west side are mainly the interiors of buildings and the lookout at the Tokyo Metropolitan Government Offices.

Shinjuku NS Building The interior of this building is hollow, featuring a 1600 sq metre atrium illuminated by sunlight which comes in through the glass roof. Overhead, at 110m, is a 'sky bridge'. The atrium itself features a 29m pendulum clock that is listed in the *Guinness Book of Records* as the largest in the world. The 29th and 30th floors have a large number of restaurants, including a branch of the Spaghetti Factory. On the 5th floor, you can browse through the showrooms of the Japanese computer companies in the OA Center.

Shinjuku Sumitomo Building The Sumitomo building bills itself as 'a building that's actually a city', a concept that the Japanese seem to find particularly appealing (Sunshine City in Ikebukuro is another 'city' building). Like the Shinjuku NS building, the Sumitomo building has a hollow core. The ground floor and the basement feature a 'jewel palace' (a jewellery shopping mall) and a general shopping centre. There is a free observation platform on the 51st floor.

Pentax Forum On the 1st floor of the Shinjuku Mitsui building is the Pentax Forum (☎ 3348-2941), a must for photography buffs. The exhibition space has changing exhibits by photographers sponsored by

Pentax. Undoubtedly, the best part of the Pentax Forum, however, is the vast array of Pentax cameras, lenses and other optical equipment on display. It is completely hands-on – you can snap away with the cameras and use the huge 1000 mm lenses to look through the windows of the neighbouring buildings. Entry is free. It's open daily from 10.30 am to 7 pm.

Metropolitan Government Offices Altogether there are three towering blocks, the centrepiece of which had a brief spell of glory as the tallest building in Japan before it was promptly knocked from pole position by the Yokohama Landmark Tower. The buildings were designed by Tange Kenzō, and whatever your feelings about them you'll have to agree that they are something of a marvel. Head up to the 45th floor of the No 1 building for a fantastic free view of the Tokyo skyline; open 9 am to 5 pm (until 7 pm on weekends); closed Monday and public holidays.

East Side 新宿東口

Shinjuku's east side is an area to wander through and get lost in rather than an area in which to search out particular sights.

Kabuki-chō Tokyo's most notorious red-light district lies east of Seibu Shinjuku station, north of Yasukuni-dōri. It's a safe area to stroll around, and most of what goes on is very much off limits to foreigners. There are, however, several strip clubs in the area that are frequented by foreigners (at least one of them occasionally advertises in the tourist magazines), though you can figure on spending around ¥5000 if you wander into one of these places. Further explorations of Kabuki-chō's seedy offerings will require a Japanese escort or exceptional Japanese-language skills.

This is one of the world's more imaginative red-light areas, with 'soaplands' (massage parlours), love hotels, peep shows, pink cabarets ('pink' is the Japanese equivalent of 'blue' in English), porno video booths and strip shows that involve audience participation. The streets here are all crackling neon and drunken salarymen. High-pitched female voices wail out invitations to their establishments through distorting sound systems, and Japanese punks earn a few extra yen passing out advertisements for *tere kura* ('telephone clubs'), where an hourly fee buys a list of girls' telephone numbers.

Kabuki-chō is not wall-to-wall sex; there are also some very straight entertainment options, including cinemas and some of the best restaurants in Tokyo.

Hanazono-jinja Shrine Nestled in the shadow of Kabuki-chō is this quiet, unassuming shrine. It only takes around 10 minutes to stroll around the grounds, but it's a fine place to sit down and take a break. You hardly know you are in Shinjuku. The shrine is particularly pleasant when it's lit up in the evening.

Shinjuku-gyoen Park This park is one of Tokyo's best escapes, and at 144 acres, one of Tokyo's largest parks. It dates back to 1906 and was designed as a European-style park, though a Japanese garden is also included. Other features are a French garden, a hothouse containing tropical plants and, near the hothouse, a pond containing giant carp. Admission is ¥200. The park is open from 9 am to 4.30 pm; closed Monday.

IKEBUKURO 池袋
Traditionally Shinjuku's poor cousin, Ikebukuro has been treated to something of a facelift in recent years. Agreed, it shouldn't be high on a busy itinerary, but it's worth noting that its attractions include two of the world's largest department stores (Seibu and Tōbu – but the world's largest is Yokohama Seibu), one of the tallest buildings in Asia (the Sunshine City building), the second-busiest station in Tokyo, the world's largest automobile showroom (Toyota Amlux), and the escalator experience of a lifetime (Tokyo Metropolitan Art Space). Like Shinjuku, Ikebukuro divides into an east side and a west side.

East Side　池袋東口
Sunshine City Billed as a 'city in a building', Sunshine City is essentially 60 floors of office space and shopping malls, with a few overpriced cultural and entertainment options thrown in. If you've got ¥620 to burn, you can take a lift to the lookout on the 60th floor and gaze out on Tokyo's murky skyline.

Not in the Sunshine City building itself but in the Bunka Kaikan building of Sunshine City is the **Ancient Orient Museum**. Admission is ¥500. It's open daily from 10 am to 4.30 pm, closed Monday, and is strictly for those with a special interest in ancient odds and ends such as coins and beads.

Also of interest to some might be the **Sunshine Planetarium** (¥800) and the **Sunshine International Aquarium** (¥1600).

Toyota Amlux Even if you are not an auto buff, this place has to be seen to be believed – Japanese hi-tech at its best. There are auto display areas, features on auto production, good historical displays, and a unique sensurround, smellorama cinema. But best of all is the building itself, with its subterranean lighting and ambient sound effects. Entry is free. It is open from 11 am to 8 pm weekdays, and from 10 am to 7.30 pm weekends; closed Monday.

Department Stores Just why Ikebukuro should have two of the world's largest department stores is an unfathomable mystery. Tōbu is the bigger of the two, but Seibu (for many years the world's biggest) still feels bigger and busier. You can easily spend an entire afternoon just wandering around the basement food floor of Seibu sampling the little titbits on offer. The 12th floor has an art museum and the top floor is restaurant city, with something like 50 restaurants, many of them offering great lunch specials, almost all of them sporting food-relief queues at lunch-time. Tōbu closes Wednesday, Seibu on Thursday.

Art Galleries In the annexe of the Seibu department store is the Sezon Museum of Art, which has changing art exhibits, usually of a very high standard. In Tōbu's Metropolitan Plaza is the Tōbu Art Museum, which also features changing art exhibits.

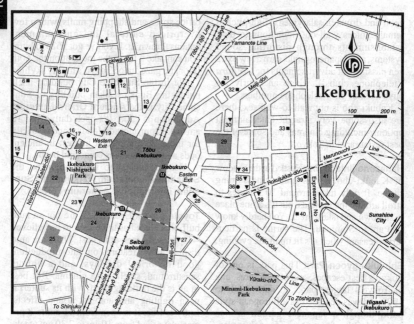

Ikebukuro

West Side   池袋西口

There's not really a lot to see on the west side,
but anyone who hasn't been to Ikebukuro for
a couple of years should check out the area
between the Tokyo Metropolitan Art Space
and the southern end of the station. The
Metropolitan Plaza building is packed with
classy boutiques, restaurants and a massive
HMV Records (6th floor – great browsing).
Just across the road is the **Spice 2** building,
which does a repeat performance of the Metropolitan Plaza.

Tokyo Metropolitan Art Space Part of the
'Tokyo Renaissance' plan launched by the
Department of Education, this huge cultural
bunker was plonked down just where Tokyo
needed it most – on the west side of Ikebukuro. Designed to host performance art, the
building has four halls. Those without a
ticket for anything should treat themselves to
the soaring escalator ride – it doesn't get
much more exciting than this in Ikebukuro!

AROUND IKEBUKURO
Rikugi-en Garden   六義園

Just three stops from Ikebukuro, near the JR
Komagome station (Yamanote line), is
Rikugi-en Garden. It's a 25 acre Edo-style
kaiyū, or 'many pleasure' garden. The landscaped views here evoke famous scenes
from Chinese and Japanese literature (good
luck finding them). The garden was established in the late 17th century by Yanagisawa
Yoshiyasu, and after falling into disuse, it
was restored by the founder of the Mitsubishi
group, Iwasaki Yataro. Entry is ¥200. It's
open from 9 am to 5 pm; closed Monday.

HARAJUKU & AOYAMA   原宿・青山

Harajuku and Aoyama are Tokyo in loafers.
They're pleasant areas to stroll in and watch
locals spend their money in boutiques and
bistros. The big attraction for foreign visitors
used to be the Sunday sub-culture parade at
Yoyogi-kōen Park. The authorities have put
a stop to that, and Yoyogi-kōen nowadays is

just an average park. But Harajuku and Aoyama still have a lot going for them. Takeshita-dōri still swarms with bubble-gum teenagers shopping for illiterate T-shirts and fish-neck stockings; Omote-sandō, with its alfresco cafes and boutiques, is still the closest Tokyo gets to Paris; the bistro alleys of Aoyama sport some of the best international cuisine in town; and Meiji-jingū Shrine is Tokyo's most splendid shrine.

Meiji-jingū Shrine 明治神宮
Completed in 1920, Meiji-jingū was built in memory of Emperor Meiji and Empress Shōken, under whose rule Japan ended its long isolation from the outside world. Unfortunately, like much else in Tokyo, the shrine was destroyed in the bombing at the end of WWII. Rebuilding was completed in 1958.

Meiji-jingū might be a reconstruction of the original, but unlike so many of Japan's post-

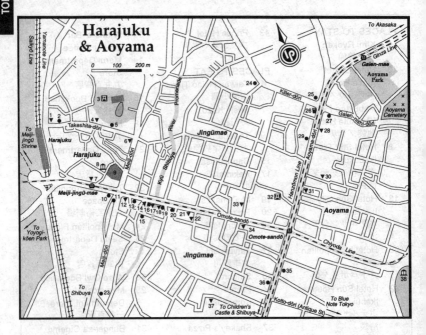

war reconstructions, it is altogether authentic. The shrine itself was built with Japanese cypress, while the cypress for the huge torii gates came from Alishan in Taiwan.

Meiji-jingū-gyoen Garden This garden offers peaceful strolls, being almost deserted on weekdays. It's particularly beautiful in June, when the irises are in bloom. Entry is ¥300. The garden is open daily from 9 am to 5 pm (4 pm from November to February).

Meiji-jingū Treasure Museum As you approach the Meiji-jingū Shrine, there are so many signs indicating the way to the treasure museum that you tend to feel obliged to go there. In fact, the collection of items from the lives of the emperor and empress is a minor attraction. It includes official garments, portraits and other imperial odds and ends. Admission is ¥500. It is open daily from 9 am to 4.30 pm; closed on the third Friday of each month.

Yoyogi-kōen Park　代々木公園
This is not one of Tokyo's best, but at 133 acres its wooded grounds make for a relaxing walk. The Sunday performances of live music, mime and dance are now a thing of the past, though two or three bands may set up of an afternoon, weather permitting.

Ota Memorial Art Museum
太田記念美術館
The Ota Memorial Art Museum has an excellent collection of ukiyo-e wood-block prints and offers a good opportunity to see works by Japanese masters of the art, including Hiroshige. Entry is ¥800. It's open daily from 10.30 am to 5.30 pm (generally closed from the 25th to the end of the month).

Nezu Fine Art Museum　根津美術館
This well-known collection of Japanese art includes paintings, calligraphy and sculpture. Also on display are Chinese and Korean art exhibits, and teahouses where tea ceremonies

PLACES TO EAT		34	Hanae Mori Building;	19	Vivre 21
1	McDonald's		L'Orangerie	20	Oriental Bazaar
4	Shūtarō		モリハナエビル	23	Crocodile
	しゅうたろう	37	Las Chicas	24	Watarium Gallery
6	Son of the Dragon			25	Bell Commons
	Chinese Restaurant	**OTHER**		26	Pylon
	龍子中華料理店	2	Taurus Vintage	27	Japan Traditional
7	Stage Y2		Clothing		Craft Centre
12	Lotteria	3	Tōgō-jinja Shrine		日本伝統工芸
14	Cafe de Rope		東郷神社		センター
17	Shakey's Pizza	5	Get Back	29	Cycland (Cycling)
18	Häagen Dazs	8	Ota Memorial	31	Kiss
	Ice Cream		Art Museum	32	Zenkō-ji Temple
21	Genroku		太田記念美術館		善光寺
	元禄	9	Laforet	35	Cay; Spiral Building
22	Bamboo Cafe	10	Chicago Thrift Shop	36	Kinokuniya
28	Tony Roma's;	11	Condomania		International
	Doutor Coffee	13	Body Shop		Supermarket
30	Bordeaux Cellar	15	Oh God; Zest		紀ノ国屋
33	Brasserie Flo	16	Kiddyland	38	Nezu Fine Art
			子供の城		Museum
					根津美術館

are performed. Most people seem to visit more for the expansive gardens – they're beautiful – than the displays, which alone hardly justify the high entry charge of ¥1000. It's open from 9.30 am to 4.30 pm; closed Monday.

Children's Castle 子供の城

Children's Castle (☎ 3797-5666) is not so much an amusement park as an activities centre for kids. Featured are play rooms, AV rooms, a swimming pool (children only), library, computer room and so on. Activities cost ¥400-500. It's open from 12.30 pm to 5.30 pm weekdays, and 10 am to 5.30 am weekends; closed Monday.

Galleries

Aoyama is packed with tiny galleries, most of which are free. Up Killer-dōri, in particular, look out for Watarium (☎ 3402-3001), an adventuristic display space with a great art bookshop and probably the best supply of postcards in Tokyo. It's open 11 am to 7 pm;

closed Monday. The futuristic Spiral Garden (☎ 3498-1171) features changing exhibits, shows, dining and live music. It's open 11 am to 8 pm daily.

Kotto-dōri, or 'Antique Street' as it's called in the tourist literature, is a good place to seek out both galleries and souvenirs.

SHIBUYA 渋谷

Shibuya is a bustling, youth-oriented shopping district where its easy to get the feeling that everyone over the age of 35 is turned back to Ueno or Ikebukuro at the station. Like Shinjuku, Shibuya is not exactly rich in sights but it is a good area to stroll around and there's some of the best department store browsing to be had in all Tokyo.

Tepco Electric Energy Museum 電力館

Even if you had to pay to get in here (you don't), the Tepco Electric Energy Museum would still be worth a visit. It may be seven floors of advertising for the Tokyo Electric

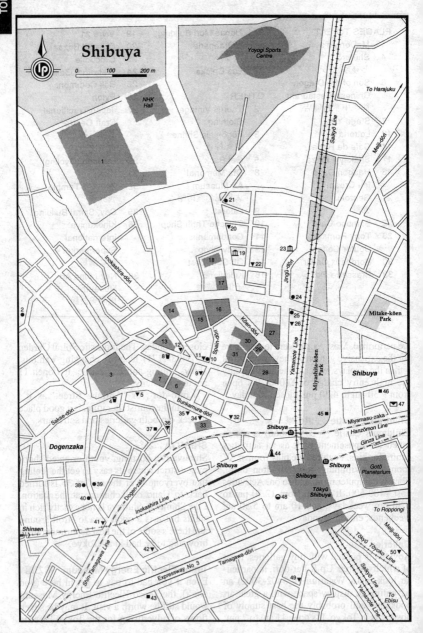

Shibuya

0   100   200 m

NHK Hall — 1

Yoyogi Sports Centre

To Harajuku

Inokashira-dōri

Kōen-dōri

Spain-dōri

Bunkamura-dōri

Sakae-dōri

Dogenzaka

Shinsen

Dogen-zaka

Shin-Tamagawa Line

Inokashira Line

Expressway No 3

Tamagawa-dōri

Meiji-dōri

Saikyō Line

Yamanote Line

Jingū-dōri

Miyashita-kōen Park

Mitake-kōen Park

Shibuya

Miyamasu-zaka

Hanzōmon Line

Ginza Line

Shibuya

Gotō Planetarium

Tōkyū Shibuya

To Roppongi

Shibuya

Tōkyō Tōyoko Line

Saikyō Line

Yamanote Line

To Ebisu

PLACES TO STAY		41	Healthy Boutique	23	Tepco Electric

PLACES TO STAY
- 18 Shibuya Tōbu Hotel
  渋谷東武ホテル
- 37 Hotel Ivy Flat
  ホテルアイビー
  フラット
- 43 Hotel Sun Route
  Shibuya
  ホテルサンルート
  渋谷
- 45 Shibuya Tōkyū Inn
  渋谷東急イン
- 46 Shibuya Business
  Hotel
  渋谷ビジネスホテル

PLACES TO EAT
- 5 Bougainvillea
- 9 Samrat
- 11 Victoria Station
- 12 Ryūnohige
- 20 Siam Thai
- 22 Jūnikagetsu
  Restaurant Building
- 26 Suehiro
  末広
- 32 Only Malaysia
- 34 Tamakyū
  玉久
- 35 Warung I Balinese
- 36 Reikyō
  麗郷

- 41 Healthy Boutique
- 42 Tainan Taami
  台南担仔麺
- 49 Kantipur
- 50 Only Malaysia

OTHER
- 1 NHK Broadcasting
  Centre; Tenji Plaza
  NHK放送センター
- 2 Kanze Nō-gakudō
  Theatre
  観世能楽堂
- 3 Tōkyū Department
  Store
  東急百貨店
- 4 Bar, Isn't It?
- 6 One-Oh-Nine
  Building
- 7 One-Oh-Nine '30s
- 8 Club Quattro
- 10 Octopus Army
- 13 The Beam
- 14 Tōkyū Hands
  東急ハンズ
- 15 Parco Part III
- 16 Parco Part I
- 17 Parco Part II
- 19 Tobacco & Salt
  Museum
  たばこと塩の博物館
- 21 Eggman

- 23 Tepco Electric
  Energy Museum
  電力館
- 24 Bic Camera
- 25 Tower Records
- 27 Marui Department
  Store
  丸井百貨店
- 28 Seibu Department
  Store
  西武百貨店
- 29 Disney Store;
  Humax Pavilion
- 30 Seibu Seed
  西武シード
- 31 Loft Department
  Store; Wave Record
  Shop
  ロフト百貨店／
  ウェーブレコード店
- 33 109 Building
- 38 On Air West
- 39 On Air East
- 40 Dr Jeekhan's
- 44 Hachikō Statue
  ハチコー像
- 47 Shibuya Post Office
  渋谷郵便局
- 48 South Exit Bus
  Station
  南出口バス停

Power Co, but it's all presented so dynamically, and the displays cover such a wide variety of themes that it's impossible to hold this against the place. Anything and everything associated with electricity gets the treatment. Kids will love it. It's open from 10.30 am to 6.30 pm; closed Wednesday.

Gotō Planetarium 五島プラネタリウム
Directly to the east of Shibuya station on the 8th floor of the Tōkyū Bunka Kaikan cinema complex, the great drawback of the Gotō Planetarium is the fact that it is all in Japanese. All the

same, the heaven's projected onto the 20m overhead dome look very impressive. Entry is ¥900. It's open from 11.10 am to 6 pm, and from 10.30 am on weekends; closed Monday.

Love Hotel Hill
Take the main road to the left of the Hachikō plaza, and at the top of the hill, on the side streets that run off the main road, is a concentration of love hotels catering to all tastes. The buildings alone are interesting, as they represent a broad range of architectural pastiches, from miniature Gothic castles to

Middle-Eastern temples. It's OK to wander in and take a look. Just inside the entrance there should be a screen with illuminated pictures of the various rooms available. You select a room by pressing the button underneath a room's picture and proceeding to the cashier. Prices for an all-night stay start at around ¥7500.

This area is gradually being invaded by other entertainment options such as alfresco cafes, restaurants, performance halls and so

Shibuya Walking Tour

The first stop on anyone's tour of Shibuya is clearly signposted in Shibuya station. Take the Hachikō exit to see a diminutive bronze statue of the dog, **Hachikō**. This is Shibuya's most popular meeting spot so expect to see a couple of hundred people milling around looking for friends in the crowd. As for the dog, the story goes that he waited for his master every day at Shibuya station for 10 years, apparently unaware that his master had died at work one day and wasn't coming home anymore, *ever*. This is the kind of dogged loyalty (so to speak) that strikes a chord in Japanese hearts. Hachikō was rewarded with a statue.

Opposite Hachikō, roads radiate in every direction. The pedestrian crossing here must be one of the busiest in the world. To get your bearings look for the **109 Building** pinned between Bunkamura-dōri, to the right, and Dogen-zaka (*zaka* means 'slope' or 'hill') to the left. Take Bunkamori-dōri. The 109 building isn't worth a visit unless you want to do some boutique shopping, but keep your eyes to the left and look for a ramshackle wooden structure that cocks a defiant thumb at the massive commercial shrines that surround it. This popular *izakaya* (Japanese pub) is called **Tamakyū** (see Places to Eat in this chapter). It has entered legend as the restaurant that refused to budge when the rest of the area sold out to big business: Tokyo residents have been heard to say that it's the one that deserves the statue not the dog at the station.

Farther up, on the other side of the road, is the One-Oh-Nine Building, with a branch of HMV (complete with resident British DJ). At the top of the road is the **Tōkyū Bunkamura**. The name means 'cultural village', and the lobby, designed by Jean Michel-Wilmotte, aims to conjure up an air of Continental elegance – 'Parisian chic' was the expression used at the time of the building's construction. The Bunkamura has performance halls, cinemas, a bookshop and a museum with changing exhibits in the basement.

A walk around the Bunkamura and back eastward takes you into the maze-like heart of Shibuya. From Club Quattro, one of Tokyo's premier live venues, the lanes to the right are a warren of bars, specialist shops, and restaurants. Look out for Shibuya Beam, a building that gets rubbished as an architectural example of Shibuya's crass commercialism – it's a bizarre meeting of mismatched hi-tech themes and fun for it.

Where the road forks (see Places to Eat for information about Ryū-no-Hige, a good Taiwanese restaurant), double back and head up to **Tōkyū Hands**, a Tokyo institution with a mind-boggling eight floors of do-it-yourself supplies, hobby items, hardware, toys and other bizarre oddments.

Up the hill, the second lane on the right runs between Parco I and III. The enormous **Parco I, II and III** complex is touted by some as Tokyo's ultimate shopping experience. Take a look at the art galleries: Parco I has the Clifford Gallery and the Parco Gallery on the 8th floor, and on the 6th floor of Parco II is Exposure. The lane continues down into Spain-dōri; not that there's anything particularly Spanish about it. It's Shibuya's equivalent of Takeshita-dōri in Harajuku: a teeny shopping street with a few coffee shops and fast-food barns thrown in. Look out for **Octopus Army**, the kitschy store that sums the area up, on the lower corner of Spain-dōri.

Turn left at the bottom of Spain-dōri and take the second lane on the left. Here you'll find the enormous **Seibu department store** complex. Up the lane is **Loft** and the Shibuya branch of **Wave**, both of which are run by Seibu. Loft is a youth-oriented department store full of bric-a-brac and juvenilia – good browsing – and Wave is the Japanese version of the Virgin megastores and HMV.

If you can't face another department store (likely), several minutes up the road is the **Tobacco & Salt Museum**, another of those quirky Tokyo museums. There are diagrams and exhibits showing the history of tobacco use and production (salt gets the same treatment). There's not much in the way of English explanations, but you get an English pamphlet with your ¥100 entry charge. The museum is open from 10 am to 6 pm, closed Monday.

Behind the museum, on Jingū-dōri, is the new and massive **Tower Records** building. As well as CDs, videos, multi-media products and T-shirts, the store stocks Tokyo's best range of imported magazines at the cheapest prices in town. From here it is possible to walk to Harajuku along Meiji-dōri in around half an hour; alternatively walk south to Shibuya station. ■

on. Dr Jeekhan's is an up-market video-game parlour, of a kind that is quite common in Tokyo and elsewhere nowadays; among other things, you might dress up in a space-suit and shoot aliens with a laser gun. Payment is by way of debit cards (¥6000 to ¥10,000). Just down the road is the On Air Theatre (east and west branches are on either side of the road), which has a streetside cafe.

AKASAKA 赤坂
Akasaka is home to Tokyo's heaviest concentration of top-notch hotels and a good selection of mid-range restaurants. Its sights, however, are low-key.

Hie-jinja Shrine 日枝神社
The hilltop shrine of Hie-jinja was undergoing renovations at the time of writing, and its famous 'tunnel' of bright orange torii (the main reason to visit) had disappeared altogether.

Hotel Sights
Some of Akasaka's luxury hotels are sights in themselves. The Hotel New Otani, for example, has preserved part of a 400-year-old garden that was once the property of a Tokugawa regent. For views over the area (forget the expensive Tokyo tower), the ANA Hotel Tokyo and the Akasaka Prince Hotel both offer skyline spectacles from their lofty upper reaches.

Aoyama-dōri 青山通り
Aoyama-dōri runs from Akasaka down to Shibuya, taking in the Akasaka Palace grounds (not a major attraction) and Harajuku en route. About halfway between Akasaka and Aoyama-Itchōme station on the left-hand side is the Sōgetsu Kaikan building, head of the **Sōgetsu school of avant-garde flower arrangement**. If you have even a passing interest in ikebana, this is an interesting place to visit. There are displays, a bookshop, and even a budget coffee shop.

On the 6th floor of the same building is the **Sōgetsu Art Museum**, notable for its highly idiosyncratic and eclectic collection of art treasures from across the centuries and the four corners of the globe. Exhibits range

from Indian Buddhas to works by Matisse. Admission is ¥500. It's open from 10 am to 5 pm; closed Sunday.

ROPPONGI 六本木
Roppongi is restaurants and nightlife, but mainly nightlife. There's no compelling reason to visit by day, though there are a couple of nearby tourist attractions.

Tokyo Tower 東京タワー
Tokyo's Eiffel Tower lookalike is more impressive from a distance; up close, the 330m tower is a tourist trap. The Grand Observation Platform (¥800) is only 150m high; if you want to peer through the smog at Tokyo's uninspiring skyline from 250m up, it will cost you a further ¥600 to get to the Special Observation Platform. The tower also features an overpriced aquarium (¥800), a wax museum (¥750), the Holographic Mystery Zone (¥300) and showrooms.

The tower is a fair trudge from Roppongi; take the Hibiya subway line one stop to Kamiya-chō station. The observation platforms are open daily from 9 am to 8 pm from 16 March to 15 November, until 9 pm in August, until 6 pm the rest of the year.

Zōjō-ji Temple 増上寺
Behind the Tokyo Tower is this former family temple of the Tokugawas. It has had a calamitous history, even by Tokyo's standards, having been rebuilt three times in recent history, most recently in 1974. It's still a pleasant place to visit if you're in the vicinity of the tower. The main gates date from 1605 and are included among the nation's 'Important Cultural Properties'. On the grounds there is a large collection of statues of Jizō, the patron saint of travellers and the souls of departed children.

OTHER ATTRACTIONS
Parks & Gardens
Although the Japanese purport to be ardent lovers of nature and see this as one of the qualities that distinguishes them from other races, Tokyo, like many other Japanese cities, is not particularly green and has a

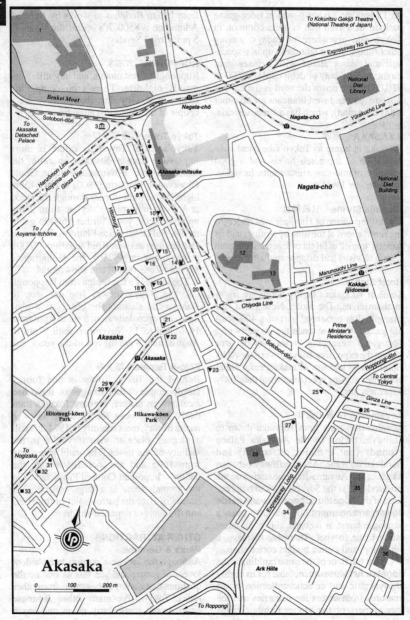

To Kokuritsu Gekijō Theatre
(National Theatre of Japan)

Expressway No 4

National Diet
Library

Benkei Moat

Nagata-chō

Sotobori-dōri

To
Akasaka
Detached
Palace

Nagata-chō

Yūrakuchō Line

Hanzōmon Line

Aoyama-dōri

Ginza Line

Akasaka-mitsuke

Nagata-chō

National Diet
Building

Hitsugi-dōri

To
Aoyama-Itchōme

Marunouchi Line

Kokkai-
jijidomae

Chiyoda Line

Akasaka

Prime
Minister's
Residence

Sotobori-dōri

Roppongi-dōri

Akasaka

To Central
Tokyo

Ginza Line

Hitotsugi-kōen
Park

Hikawa-kōen
Park

To
Nogizaka

Expressway Loop Line

Ark Hills

Akasaka

0   100   200 m

To Roppongi

shortage of park space. If you've been hitting the bitumen and haven't seen a tree for days, try the following parks.

Hibiya-kōen Park This park is not one of Tokyo's best but it is close to Ginza and makes a reasonably quiet retreat from the boutiques and department stores.

Koishikawa Kōraku-en Garden Next to the Kōraku-en amusement park and Tokyo Dome, this has to be one of the best and least-visited (by foreigners at least) gardens in Tokyo. It is a stroll garden with a strong Chinese influence, and was established in the mid-17th century. Entry is ¥200. It's open from 9 am to 4.30 pm; closed Monday.

Hamarikyū-teien Garden Often referred to in English as the Detached Palace Garden, a visit can be combined either with a visit to Ginza or, via the Sumida-gawa River Cruise, with a visit to Asakusa (see the Asakusa section of this chapter). The garden has walks, ponds and teahouses. Entry is ¥200. It is open from 9 am to 4.30 pm; closed Monday.

Museums & Galleries
There's an enormous number of museums and galleries in Tokyo. In many cases their exhibits are small and specialised and the admission charges prohibitively expensive for travellers with a limited budget and a tight schedule. For a more complete listing, get hold of the TIC's *Museums & Art Galleries* pamphlet. Better still, look out for *Tokyo Museums – A Complete Guide* (Tuttle) by Thomas & Ellen Flannigan, which covers everything from the Tombstone Museum to the Button Museum.

PLACES TO STAY	PLACES TO EAT	OTHER
1 Hotel New Otani ホテルニュー大谷	6 Shakey's Pizza	3 Suntory Museum of Art サントリー美術館
2 Akasaka Prince Hotel 赤坂プリンスホテル	7 Subway Sandwiches	
	8 Mughal	4 Tōkyū Plaza 東急プラザ
5 Akasaka Tōkyū Hotel 赤坂東急ホテル	9 Tenichi 天一	12 Hie-jinja Shrine 日枝神社
13 Capitol Tōkyū Hotel キャピタル東急 ホテル	10 Pizzeria/Trattoria Marumo	14 Goose Bar
	11 Moti	20 Tofuya
17 Capsule Hotel Fontaine Akasaka キャプセルホテル フォンテーン赤坂	15 Sushi-sei 寿司清	24 Akasaka Sakuradō (Dolls) 赤坂桜堂
	16 Victoria Station	26 Inachu Lacquerware いなちゅう漆器
31 Capsule Inn Akasaka キャプセルイン赤坂	18 Tenya 天屋	27 Doutor Coffee
32 Hotel Yōkū Akasaka ホテル陽光赤坂	19 Capricciosa	28 Laforet Museum; Akasaka Twin Tower ラフォーレ ミュージアム／ 赤坂ツインタワー
33 Marroad Inn Akasaka マロードイン赤坂	21 KFC	
	22 Moti	
34 ANA Hotel Tokyo ANA ホテル東京	23 Mugyōdon	
	25 Tony Roma's	35 USA Embassy アメリカ大使館
36 Hotel Ōkura ホテル大倉	29 Aozai	
	30 Yakitori Luis	

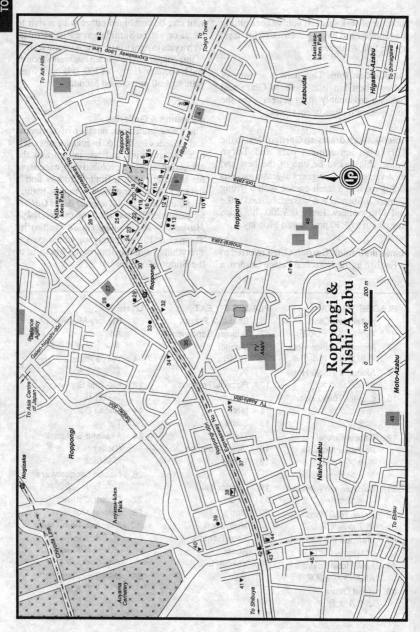

Roppongi & Nishi-Azabu

PLACES TO STAY

1   Roppongi Prince
    Hotel
    六本木プリンス
    ホテル
2   Hotel Marroad
    Roppongi
    ホテルマロウド
    六本木
27 Hotel Ibis; Moti
    ホテルアイビス

PLACES TO EAT

7   Hamburger Inn
8   Bikkuri Sushi
    びっくり寿司
10 Spago; Fukuzushi
    スパゴ／福寿司
11 Hard Rock Café;
    Tony Roma's
12 McDonald's
15 Bellini's Pizza
    Kitchen
16 Moti Darbar
17 Kushisuke
    串助
19 Seryna

23 Tsubohachi
    つぼ八
24 Tainan Taami
    台南担仔麺
26 Il Bianco
30 Almond
31 Sicilia
32 Moti
34 Bengawan Solo
36 Kantipur
37 Maenam
40 Cyberia (Internet
    Cafe)
41 La Escondida
43 Hobson's
45 Casa Monnon

OTHER

3   Roppongi Pit Inn
4   Axis Building
5   Déja Vu
6   Gas Panic
9   Roi Building;
    Paddy Foley's
13 Cavern Club
14 Kento's
18 Charleston

20 Lexington Queen
21 Bar, Isn't It?
22 Motown House
25 Square Building
28 Velfarre
29 Bauhaus
33 Meidiya International
    Supermarket
    明治屋
35 Wave
38 Nishi-Azabu Post
    Office
    西麻布郵便局
39 Yellow
42 Nishi-Azabu
    Crossing
    西麻布交差点
44 328 (San-Nippa)
46 Chinese Embassy
    中国大使館
47 Swedish Centre;
    Stockholm
48 International House
    of Japan
    国際文化会館

Edo-Tokyo Museum This is the best of Tokyo's new museums without a doubt. Just the building itself, which looks like it has been spirited from the set of *Star Wars*, is a wonder. The Nihombashi Bridge divides this vast display into re-creations of Edo period Tokyo and Meiji period Tokyo. Entry is ¥500. It's open from 10 am to 6 pm (9 pm on Friday); closed Monday. The museum is close to Ryōgoku station on the JR Sōbu line, and can be combined with a visit to the Sumo Museum.

Sumo Museum Close to the main entrance to Kokugikan Sumo Stadium, the Sumo Museum is quite a treat, but unfortunately there is nothing in the way of English explanations. Entry is free. It is open weekdays

from 9.30 am to 4.30 pm. See the Edo-Tokyo Museum for getting there.

Tokyo Metropolitan Museum of Photography Japan's first large-scale museum devoted entirely to photography is in new premises in the Ebisu Garden Palace. The emphasis is on Japanese photography, but international work is also displayed. Entry is ¥500. It is open from 10 am to 6 pm (8 pm Thursday and Friday); closed Monday. From JR Ebisu station take the covered walkway to Ebisu Garden Palace, which is basically a shopping mall established by the Ebisu brewery.

Tokyo Metropolitan Teien Museum This museum lacks a permanent display of its own, but the building itself was designed by French architect Henri Rapin and it lies in pleasant gardens. Take the east exit of Meguro, walk straight ahead along Meguro-dōri for around five minutes and look out for the museum on the left. Entry is usually ¥600 (depending on the exhibition). It's open from 10 am to 6 pm; closed the second and fourth Wednesday of the month.

Amusement Parks

Tokyo Disneyland Only the Japanese signs reveal that you're a long way from Orange County – Tokyo Disneyland is a near-perfect replica of the Anaheim, California, original. A few rides may be in slightly different locations, but basically you turn left from the entrance to Adventureland, head straight on to Fantasyland or turn right to Tomorrowland.

Its opening hours vary seasonally from 8.30 am to 10 pm in summer and 10 am to 6 pm in winter, but phone ☎ 0473-54-0001 to be sure. It's open daily, except for about a dozen days a year (most of them in January) when it is closed all day. A variety of tickets are available, including an all-inclusive 'passport' which gives you unlimited access to all the rides for ¥5100 (children aged 12 to 17, ¥4500; those aged 4 to 11, ¥3500). As at the original Disneyland, there are often long queues at popular rides (30 minutes to one hour is normal). Crowds are usually lighter in the mornings and heavier on weekends and holidays.

There is now a direct train service to Disneyland from JR Tokyo station: take the Keiyō line to Maihama station (¥210; 15 minutes). A variety of shuttle buses also run from Tokyo (¥600), Ueno (¥600) and Yokohama (¥1000) stations, from Narita (¥2000) and Haneda (¥700) airports and from the various nearby Disneyland hotels.

Tokyo Disneyland also has a ticket office (☎ 3201-3511) on the 1st floor of the north wing of the Denki building next to JR Yūraku-chō station. It's open daily from 10 am to 6.30 pm; closed Sunday and national holidays.

Kōraku-en Amusement Park Next to the

Kōraku-en subway station on the Marunouchi subway line, the Kōraku-en Amusement Park (☎ 3817-6098) is of the old rattle-and-shake school, and is popular precisely for that reason. The 'Ultra Twister' roller coaster ride takes first prize for most visitors. Geopolis is a new hi-tech addition to the amusement park, with attractions like the Geopanic indoor roller coaster and Zombie Zone.

Entry is ¥1400 for adults, ¥700 for children, and most rides are ¥600. Opening hours vary seasonally, but the core hours are 10 am to 8 pm, closed the second and fourth Tuesday of the month.

Sesame Place If you are travelling with very young children, Sesame Place (☎ 0425-95-1152) is a good low-tech option. Based on the Sesame Street TV series, the attractions are interactive and safe for children. Entry is ¥2100 for adults, ¥2600 for children (from three to 12 years).

To get there, take the JR Musahi Itsukaichi line to Akigawa station, and take a Summerland bus to the Summerland bus stop. Change there for a shuttle bus to Sesame Place.

ORGANISED TOURS

If you simply *must* join a tour, first stop should be the TIC, which has comprehensive listings of what's available. The options are unfortunately universally staid and predictable.

Probably the widest range of organised tours is available from JTB's Sunrise Tours (☎ 5620-9500). Both morning and afternoon tours are available, as well as tours for those with more specialised interests; industrial tours and village life and crafts tours are examples. The Japan Gray Line (☎ 3433-5745) also runs tours. Costs hover around ¥10,000 to ¥11,000 for an all-day tour with lunch.

Night tours are a popular alternative to the standard run of sights. Possibilities include kabuki night tours with meals and geisha shows and 'adults only' tours, which include a topless revue.

SPECIAL EVENTS
Tokyo's main festivals are:

Ganjitsu (New Year's Day)
1 January. This is the one day in the year (well, the night before is, anyway) that the trains run all night. It is customary for Japanese to visit Buddhist and Shinto shrines to pray for luck in the coming year. For a look at the action, head to Meiji-jingū Shrine, Sensō-ji Temple or the Yasukuni-jinja Shrine. The day after New Year's Day is one of the two occasions each year when the Imperial Palace is open to the public and the imperial couple display themselves before adoring crowds. Enter the inner gardens by the Nijū-bashi Bridge between 9 am and 3.30 pm.

Dezome-shiki
6 January. Firemen dressed in Edo-period costumes put on a parade involving acrobatic stunts on top of bamboo ladders. The parade takes place on Chūō-dōri in Harumi from 10 am onwards.

Seijin-no-hi (Adult's Day)
15 January. Those who turn 20 get a national holiday for reaching the age when they are legally able to drink and smoke. A traditional display of archery is held at Meiji-jingū Shrine.

Setsubun
3 or 4 February. Throughout Japan, beans are scattered from the inside of a building outwards, which is the direction it is hoped the 'devils' will take, and from the outside inwards, which is the direction that good luck is meant to take. In Tokyo, ceremonies are held at Zōjō-ji Temple, Kanda-jinja Shrine and Sensō-ji Temple. Sensō-ji Temple offers the added attraction of a classical dance.

The golden dragon dance, held at the Sensō-ji Temple, is part of the Kinryū-no-Mai festival.

Hari-kuyō
Early February. Check with the TIC for the dates of this typically quirky Japanese festival held for pins and needles that have been broken in the preceding year. At Sensō-ji Temple, women lay their pins and needles to rest by 'burying' them in tofu and radishes.

Hina Matsuri (Doll Festival)
3 March. Throughout Japan, girls display miniature imperial figures on shelves covered with red cloth. From about mid-February onwards, a doll fair is held in Asakusabashi – check with the TIC for exact details.

Kinryū-no-Mai
18 March. A golden dragon dance is held at Sensō-ji Temple to celebrate the discovery of the golden image of Kannon that now rests there. Two or three dances are performed during the day.

Hanami (Blossom Viewing)
Early to mid-April. This is one festival you can't help hearing about if you happen to be in Japan at the time. Interest in the progress of the sakura (cherry blossoms) verges on a national obsession, with panoramic views of famous cherry blossom viewing parks and close ups of the blooms themselves taking up as much TV viewing time as major sports events do in other parts of the world. In Tokyo, *the* place to go for hanami is Ueno-kōen Park; if you want some peace, however, go to Shinjuku-gyoen Park, where the blooms are better and the crowds smaller. Other famous spots around Tokyo include Yasukuni-jinja Shrine and Koishikawa Kōraku-en Garden.

Hana Matsuri (Buddha's Birthday)
8 April. Celebrations are held at Buddhist temples all over Japan. In Tokyo, celebrations take place at Sensō-ji Temple and Zōjō-ji Temple, among others.

Ueno Tōshō-gū Taisai
17 April. Ceremonies, traditional music and dance are held at Ueno's Tōshō-gū Shrine in memory of Tokugawa Ieyasu.

Kanda Matsuri
Mid-May. This festival is held on odd-numbered years on the Saturday and Sunday closest to 15 May and is a traditional Edo festival that celebrates a Tokugawa battle victory. A whole range of activities take place at Kanda-jinja Shrine.

Sanja Matsuri
May. On the 3rd Friday, Saturday and Sunday of May, at Sensō-ji Temple in Asakusa, up to 100 mikoshi carried by participants dressed in traditional clothes are paraded through the area in the vicinity of the temple.

Sannō-sai
10 to 16 June. Street stalls, traditional music and dancing, and processions of mikoshi are all part of this Edo Festival, held at Sannō Hie-jinja Shrine, near Akasaka-Mitsuke subway station.

O Bon

13 to 15 July. This festival takes place at a time when, according to Buddhist belief, the dead briefly revisit the earth. Dances are held and lanterns lighted in their memory. In Tokyo *bon odori* dances are held in different locations around town.

Sumida-gawa Hanabi Taikai

Last Saturday of July. The biggest fireworks display of its kind in Tokyo is held on the Sumida-gawa River in Asakusa.

Tsukudajima Sumiyoshi-jinja Matsuri

Sunday closest to 7 July. There are several three-day festivals that take place in Tokyo every three years. In this one, activities centre around the Sumiyoshi-jinja Shrine, with dragon dances and mikoshi parades among other things. The next festival will take place in 1992. The Sumiyoshi-jinja Shrine is across the Sumida-gawa River (via the Tsukuda-ōhashi Bridge) from Tsukiji subway station on the Hibiya line.

Fukagawa Hachiman Matsuri

15 August. In this, another triennial, three-day Edo festival, foolhardy mikoshi-bearers charge through eight km of frenzied crowds who dash water on them. The action takes place at Tomioka Hachiman-gū Shrine, next to Monzen-Naka-chō subway station on the Tōzai line.

Ningyō-kuyō

25 September. Childless couples make offerings of dolls to Kannon in the hope that she will bless them with children. More interesting for spectators is the ceremonial burning by priests of all the dolls that remain from previous years. It takes place at Kiyomizu-dō Temple in Ueno Park from 2 pm to 3.30 pm.

Furusato Tokyo Matsuri (Metropolitan Citizen's Day)

First Saturday and Sunday in October. A wide range of activities are held at different locations around town. In particular, check out Asakusa's Sensō-ji Temple and Ueno-kōen Park.

Oeshiki

12 October. This festival is held in commemoration of Nichiren (1222 to 1282), founder of the Nichiren sect of Buddhism. On the night of the 12th, people bearing large lanterns and paper flower arrangements make their way to Hommon-ji Temple. The nearest station is Ikegami station on the Tōkyū Ikegami line.

Kanda Furuihon Ichi

27 October to 3 November. A huge sale of second-hand books is held in the Jimbō-chō area. There are 30% reductions on books. Go to the Jimbō-chō intersection and start your explorations there (see the Bookshops section of this chapter).

Meiji Reidaisai

30 October to 3 November. A series of events is held at Meiji-jingū Shrine in commemoration of the Meiji emperor's birthday. Particularly interesting to watch are displays of horseback archery in traditional clothes. Other events include classical music and dance.

Shichi-go-san (Seven-Five-Three Festival)

15 November. As the title implies, this is for children aged seven, five and three. The children (boys aged five and girls aged three and seven) make a colourful sight, as they are dressed in traditional clothes and taken to different shrines around town, notably Meiji-jingū Shrine, Yasukuni-jinja Shrine and Sannō Hie-jinja Shrine.

Gishi-sai

14 December. The day's events commemorate the deaths of the 47 rōnin (masterless samurai) who committed seppuku after avenging the death of their master. The activities involve a parade of warriors to Sengaku-ji Temple – the rōnin's burial place – and a memorial service from 7.30 pm onwards. The temple is directly west of Sengaku-ji subway station on the TOEI Asakusa line.

PLACES TO STAY

There are few places in the world more expensive than Tokyo when it comes to accommodation. If you can afford five-star rates, then you'll have no shortage of opulent retreats to choose from. Everyone else will be looking at ways to limit the damage.

As is the case elsewhere around Japan, you have a choice of hotels, business hotels, ryokan, youth hostels and gaijin houses. Where you end up will mainly be determined by budget. Hotels are expensive however you look at it. Business hotels are a good compromise solution, with rates in Tokyo from ¥6000 to ¥7000. Ryokan are better still, if you can make a few concessions to Japanese etiquette, with rates from around ¥4500. At youth hostels and at gaijin houses you can get single rates down to ¥2500 per night (which is about as low as it gets in Tokyo), with just two caveats: the youth hostels impose an early evening curfew; the gaijin houses are generally way out in the boondocks and only take long-termers.

Places to Stay – bottom end

If it's imperative that you find inexpensive accommodation, be certain to make a booking before you arrive. Flying into Narita (particularly on a night-flight) without accommodation lined up can be nightmarish.

Youth Hostels Tokyo has two youth hostels: the *Tokyo International Youth Hostel* (☎ 3235-1107) in Iidabashi; and the *Yoyogi Youth Hostel* (☎ 3467-9163). The usual regulations apply – you have to be out of the building between 10 am and 3 pm (10 am and 5 pm at Yoyogi) and you have to be in by 10 pm; the latter is a real drawback in a late night city like Tokyo. There's a three night limit to your stay and the hostels can often be booked right out during peak holiday periods.

The Tokyo International Youth Hostel doesn't require that you be a member but does ask that you book ahead and provide some identification (a passport will do) when you arrive. To get there, exit from Iidabashi station (either JR or subway) and look for the tallest building in sight (it's long, thin and glass fronted). Rates vary seasonally, but are ¥2900 per person per night most of the year. A sleeping sheet costs ¥150 for three nights. The Narita airport TIC has a step-by-step instruction sheet on how to get to the hostel from the airport most cheaply.

The Yoyogi Youth Hostel requires that you be a youth hostel member to stay and charges ¥2800. There are no meals available, but there are cooking facilities. To get there, take the Odakyū line to Sangūbashi station and walk towards the Meiji-jingū Shrine gardens. The hostel is enclosed in a fenced compound – not a former prison camp but the National Olympics Memorial Youth Center – in building No 14. Staff may let you exceed the three night limit if it is not crowded.

Ryokan The *Kimi Ryokan* (☎ 3971-3766) is a popular long-runner with a good location and inexpensive Japanese-style rooms. Of all the ryokan in Tokyo, the Kimi has the most convivial lounge area, and there's a notice board too. Be sure to book ahead; there's nearly always a waiting list. The Kimi is on the west side of Ikebukuro station. Prices range from ¥3500 (there are only three of these and they're rarely free) to ¥4300 for singles, from ¥7000 to ¥8000 for doubles and from ¥7500 for twins.

The *Asia Center of Japan* (☎ 3402-6111), near Aoyama-Itchōme subway station

(Ginza line), is a popular option in the upper-budget category. This is another place that attracts many long-term stayers, and even though it's a lot bigger than the Kimi, it's still often fully booked. The station is under the easily recognisable Aoyama Twin Tower building on Aoyama-dōri. Walk past the building towards Akasaka-Mitsuke, turn right (towards Roppongi) and the Asia Centre is a short walk up the third street on the left. Rooms have pay TV, and singles cost from ¥4900, twins/doubles from ¥6400. Rooms with bathrooms are significantly more expensive.

Not far out of Shinjuku on the Marunouchi subway line is *Shin-Nakano Lodge* (☎ 3381-4886). Singles without bathroom cost ¥4400 and there are also doubles with bath for ¥9000. Both western and Japanese-style rooms are available, but the Japanese rooms are cheaper. Make sure you specify what you want and confirm the price when you book. At Shin-Nakano station take the No 1 exit; turn left at the park and follow the road to the four-way intersection (there's a hardware shop on the corner); turn right here and look for the lodge on the right.

Close to the JR Gotanda station on the Yamanote line is the *Ryokan Sansui-sō* (☎ 3441-7475). This is not the greatest of locations, but it's only a few stops from Shibuya, the nearest main railway terminus. Take the east exit. Turn right, take the first right after the big Tōkyū department store and then the first left. Turn left and then right, walk past the bowling centre and look for the sign on the right directing you down the side street to the ryokan. Prices for singles/doubles without bath are ¥4900/ 8600; doubles with bath cost ¥9000; triples without bath cost ¥12,000.

Ueno may be a bit of a trek from the bright lights, but it's a good sightseeing base and there are several budget ryokan in the area. The *Sawanoya Ryokan* (☎ 3822-2251) is within walking distance of Nezu subway station on the Chiyoda line (see the Ueno map). If you're coming from Narita international airport, it will probably be easier and just as cheap if there are more than one of you to catch a taxi from Ueno station. Singles cost ¥4500 to ¥4800; doubles cost ¥8400 without bath and ¥9000 with; triples cost ¥11,400 without bath and ¥12,900 with.

Ryokan Katsutarō (☎ 3821-9808) is another option in the vicinity. Singles, doubles & triples cost ¥4500, 8400 & 12,300 without bath; doubles/triples with bath cost ¥9000/13,200. Not far away is the larger *Suigetsu Hotel* (☎ 3822-9611), which has a laundrette and rooms with private bathrooms. You can also change money there. Singles/doubles cost ¥6500/11,400, triples cost ¥14,400

One stop away from Ueno on the JR Yamanote line (Uguisudani station) is the *Sakura Ryokan* (☎ 3876-8118). Take the southern exit and turn left. Pass the Iriya subway station exits on the left – the Sakura Ryokan is on the right-hand side of the second street on your left. If you're exiting from Iriya subway station on the Hibiya line, you take the No 1 exit and then turn left. Singles/doubles without bath cost ¥5000/9000; triples cost from ¥12,000 to ¥13,500. There are also western-style rooms available with bath from ¥6000 for a single.

Three stops away from Ueno on the Ginza line is Asakusa, which also has a few reasonably priced ryokan. *Ryokan Asakusa Shigetsu* (☎ 3843-2345) is just around the corner from the Sensō-ji Temple, an interesting area. From Kaminari-mon Gate, walk in the direction of Sensō-ji Temple and look for the ryokan on a sidestreet to the left – there's a toy shop and a shoe shop on the corner. The ryokan is on the left-hand side of the road. Singles/doubles with bath start at ¥6000/13,000.

In Nishi Asakusa (near Tawaramachi subway station, which is one stop away from Asakusa on the Ginza line) is the *Kikuya Ryokan* (☎ 3841-6404/4051). It's just off Kappabashi-dōri and prices are ¥4800/8000 for singles/doubles; triples cost ¥12,000. This ryokan gets good reports as a quiet and friendly place to stay.

A place that verges on belonging to the gaijin house category is *Apple House* (☎ 0422-51-2277). The advantage of this place is that it is big and has three branches

all close to each other. Rates can be paid on a night-by-night basis (which is not possible in most gaijin houses) and the guesthouse has good facilities (kitchen, laundry, fax, satellite TV, etc). Rates vary depending on how long you stay, but reckon on ¥3000 to ¥3500 for a single, less if you're prepared to share. Long-term discounts are available.

To get to Apple House take the Chūō line from Shinjuku station (platform No 10) to Higashi Koganei station and ring the guesthouse. Somebody will come to the station and meet you. Ring to make sure they actually have a vacancy before you go all the way out there.

Capsule Hotels Capsule hotels are strictly a male domain and you find them wherever there are large numbers of salarymen, bars, hostess clubs and other drains for company expense accounts. Close to the western exit of Ikebukuro station is the *Ikebukuro Plaza* (☎ 3590-7770), which costs ¥4000 per night. An even cheaper option is the *Capsule Kimeya Hotel* (☎ 3971-8751), where capsules cost ¥3090. It's over on the east side of Ikebukuro, not far from Sunshine City.

Shinjuku is another good area for capsule hotels. Right in the heart of Kabuki-chō, Shinjuku's infamous red-light district, is the *Shinjuku-ku Capsule Hotel* (☎ 3232-1110). It's open from 5 pm to 10 am and costs ¥4100. See the Shinjuku map for a couple of other capsule hotels.

Gaijin Houses Gaijin Houses are more an option for those planning to stay long-term in Tokyo. Some gaijin houses offer nightly or weekly rates, but many of them are geared to foreigners working in Tokyo and charge by the month. If you just want a cheap place to crash and don't mind commuting into town to do your sightseeing, try ringing around the gaijin houses when you get to Tokyo.

Long-termers can expect to pay from ¥40,000 to ¥70,000 a month for a bed in a shared room, with no deposits or key money required. Watch out for rip-offs, and always have a good look at a place before forking out a month's rent – some gaijin houses in Tokyo are noisy fleapits. Facilities are sometimes ridiculously limited – one shower and toilet for 40 people is a typical shock-horror story. This kind of thing is OK for a while, but if you're going to be based in Tokyo for an extended period, you'll probably want to start looking for something better.

The following is a selection of some of the longer-running gaijin houses in Tokyo. Check the latest issue of *Tokyo Journal* or *Tokyo Classified* for more. Unless otherwise indicated, the prices given here are per person per month. Daily and weekly rates are only given where they apply.

English House: shared rooms ¥38,000; private singles/doubles ¥60,000; Musashi Nakahara (Nambu line) (☎ 044-411-4511)
Friendship House: shared rooms from ¥9500 per week, private rooms ¥59,500 to ¥90,000 per month; four locations, including Kichijōji (JR) (☎ 3327-3179/3765-2288)
Liberty House: shared rooms from ¥35,000 per month, private from ¥59,000; four locations including Waseda and Shin-Ōkubo (☎ 5272-7238)
Sakura House: private singles from ¥51,000 to ¥65,000; Nishi-Magome (Tōkyū line) (☎ 3754-3112)
Sun Academy: private singles from ¥60,000; two branches, Musashi Shinjo (Nambu line) (☎ 044-798-5401/411-4511)
Taihei House: share rooms from ¥35,000; private from ¥45,000; Komagome (JR Yamanote line) (☎ 3940-4705)
Villa Paradiso: singles ¥2300 per day, ¥59,000 to ¥61,000 per month; Tama Plaza (Shintamagawa line) (☎ 045-911-1184)

Places to Stay – middle

Hotels Mid-range hotels in Tokyo mean business hotels. There's little to distinguish one from another, however, their chief drawcard is convenience. In Tokyo, business hotels generally cost from ¥6500/11,000 for a single/double; anything cheaper than this and you've either struck a bargain or are in a dump. Rooms come with a built-in bathroom (shower, bath and toilet), a telephone, pay TV and other features like disposable toothbrushes and shaving equipment. Always check what time your hotel locks its doors before heading out at night. Some hotels stay open all night, but many lock up at midnight or 1 am.

An adventurous late-night alternative is a love hotel. These can be found in any of Tokyo's entertainment districts – particularly in Shinjuku, Shibuya, Roppongi and Ikebukuro. All-night rooms range in price from about ¥7000 to ¥8000, but 'all night' doesn't start until 10 or 11 pm, when the regular hour-by-hour customers have run out of energy.

Central Tokyo Hotels in central Tokyo are expensive for obvious reasons. You'll find similar standards at cheaper rates elsewhere around town.

Business Hotel Heimat: singles/doubles ¥6700/9000; across from the Nihombashi exit of JR Tokyo station (☎ 3273-9411)
Ginza Capitol Hotel: singles ¥9100; twins ¥14,800; two minutes from Tsukiji subway station (☎ 3543-8211)
Ginza International Hotel: singles/doubles ¥13,000/ 19,000; two minutes from Shimbashi station (☎ 3574-1121)
Hotel Atami-sō: singles ¥11,300; twins ¥21,000; two minutes from Higashi-Ginza subway station (☎ 3541-3621)
Hotel Ginza Dai-ei: singles ¥11,000; doubles or twins ¥18,000; one minute from Higashi-Ginza subway station (☎ 3545-1111)
Sun Hotel Shimbashi: singles ¥8400; twins ¥14,000; three minutes from Shimbashi station (☎ 3591-3351)
Tokyo City Hotel: singles/doubles ¥8800/12,500; twins ¥13,000; two minutes from Mitsukoshi-mae station (☎ 3270-7671)
Yaesu Terminal Hotel: singles/doubles ¥10,800/ 17,200; one minute from the JR Tokyo station (☎ 3281-3771)

Ueno & Asakusa The cheaper ryokan in these areas are better value, but if they're all full, the business hotels are generally cheaper than those in other areas around Tokyo.

Asakusa Plaza Hotel: singles/doubles ¥6700/10,500; next to Asakusa subway station (☎ 3845-2621)
Hotel Green Capital: singles/twins ¥7500/11,500; next to JR Ueno station (☎ 3842-2411)
Hotel Parkside: singles/doubles ¥9300/16,500; near Ueno's Shinobazu Pond (☎ 3836-5711)
Hotel Sun Targas: singles/twins ¥7400/10,400; five minutes walk from Ueno station (☎ 3833-8686)
Hotel Towa: singles from ¥8600; doubles ¥11,000; five minutes walk from Asakusa subway station (☎ 3843-0108)
Kinuya Hotel: singles/doubles ¥6700/10,800; next to Keisei Ueno station (☎ 3833-1911)

Shinjuku Shinjuku is a good hunting ground for business hotels that cater to foreigners.

Hotel Sun Lite Shinjuku: singles from ¥8600 to ¥9500; twins from ¥14,200 to ¥16,000; doubles from ¥12,000 to ¥15,000; 10 minutes from the east exit of Shinjuku station (☎ 3356-0391)

Shinjuku New City Hotel: singles/doubles from ¥8900/18,200; twins from ¥14,900; 10 minutes from the west exit of Shinjuku station, behind Shinjuku Central Park (Shinjuku Chūō-kōen) (☎ 3375-6511)

Shinjuku Park Hotel: singles from ¥9000; twins from ¥18,000; doubles from ¥17,000; seven minutes from the south exit of Shinjuku station (☎ 3356-0241)

Shinjuku Washington Hotel: singles/doubles ¥11,639/17,510; 10 minutes from the west exit of Shinjuku station (☎ 3343-3111)

Star Hotel Tokyo: singles/doubles ¥9000/17,300; three minutes from the west exit of Shinjuku station (☎ 3361-1111)

Hotel Sun Route: singles/doubles ¥9500/14,000; five minutes from the south exit of Shinjuku station (☎ 3375-3211)

Ikebukuro There are innumerable business and love hotels in the Ikebukuro area, as well as some of the most popular cheaper ryokan.

Dai-Ichi Inn Ikebukuro: singles/doubles from ¥8300/16,000; close to the east exit of Ikebukuro station (☎ 3986-1221)

Hotel Grand Business: singles ¥7500 to ¥8000; twins ¥12,000 to ¥12,600; five minutes from the east exit of Ikebukuro station (☎ 3984-5121)

Hotel Happokaku: singles from ¥6000; doubles/twins from ¥10,000; close to east exit of Ikebukuro station (☎ 3982-1181)

Ikebukuro Royal Hotel: singles from ¥5500 to ¥8500; doubles from ¥9800 to ¥12,000; five minutes from the west exit of Ikebukuro station (☎ 5396-0333)

Hotel Sun City Ikebukuro: singles from ¥7500; doubles/twins from ¥11,000; close to the west exit of Ikebukuro station (☎ 3986-1101)

Hotel Sun Route Ikebukuro: singles from ¥8700; doubles/twins from ¥14,400/15,400; five minutes north of the east exit of Ikebukuro station (☎ 3980-1911)

Shibuya Shibuya is an expensive area to base yourself in. If you're looking for more inexpensive business hotels, Ueno, Ikebukuro and even Shinjuku represent much better value for money. The following hotels are all within easy striking distance of Shibuya station.

Hotel Ivy Flat: singles ¥10,200; twins ¥16,300; five minutes from the Hachikō exit of Shibuya station (☎ 3770-1122)

Hotel Sun Route Shibuya: singles from ¥6700; doubles/twins ¥13,000/17,500; five minutes from Shibuya station on the south side of the expressway (☎ 3464-6411)

Shanpia Hotel Aoyama: singles/doubles ¥10,300/17,000; five minutes from the Hachi-kō exit of Shibuya station (☎ 3407-2111)

Shibuya Business Hotel: singles/doubles ¥8400/12,100; two minutes from the east exit of Shibuya station (☎ 3409-9300)

Shibuya Tōkyū Inn: singles from ¥14,600 to ¥15,600; doubles/twins ¥21,200/22,600; one minute from the east exit of Shibuya station (☎ 3498-0109)

Shibuya Tōbu Hotel: singles from ¥11,800; doubles/twins from ¥16,400/20,000; five minutes northwest from Shibuya station (☎ 3476-0111)

Roppongi & Akasaka These are good areas to be based in if you want access to central Tokyo and a lively nightlife (it's possible to walk down to Roppongi from Akasaka). Like Shibuya, Akasaka and Roppongi are not areas in which you are going to find any accommodation bargains.

Hotel Ibis: singles/doubles ¥15,000/23,000; two minutes from Roppongi subway station (☎ 3403-4411)

Marroad Inn Akasaka: singles/doubles from ¥9600/10,600; five minutes from Akasaka subway station (☎ 3585-7611)

Shanpia Hotel Akasaka: singles ¥9990; twins ¥16,890; four minutes from Akasaka subway station (☎ 3586-0811)

Toshi Centre Hotel: singles from ¥6400; twins ¥11,600; seven minutes from Akasaka-Mitsuke subway station (☎ 3265-8211)

Places to Stay – top end

Although Tokyo is one of the world's most expensive cities, its top-end hotels are no more expensive than similar hotels anywhere else, and you get Japan's legendary high standard of service.

Top-end hotels are naturally found mostly in central Tokyo. Given that all such hotels have very high standards, location should be a prime factor in deciding where you stay. The Imperial Palace and Ginza areas have a certain snob appeal, but the Akasaka area, which combines a good central location with nearby entertainment options, would be an equally good choice. The west side of Shinjuku station has a concentration of top-notch hotels, and is a good area in which to see Tokyo at its liveliest.

Among Tokyo's best are: the *Hotel Seiyo Ginza*, which also happens to be the most expensive; the *Akasaka Prince*; the *New Otani; and the Hotel Ōkura*. The *Imperial Hotel* in central Tokyo is probably the best known hotel in the city. The following prices are for the least expensive rooms available in each hotel.

Akasaka Prince Hotel: singles ¥24,000; doubles/twins ¥36,000/32,000; next to Nagata-chō subway station (☎ 3234-1111; fax 3262-5163)

Akasaka Tōkyū Hotel: singles ¥19,000; doubles/twins ¥32,000/29,000; next to Nagata-chō or Akasaka-mitsuke subway stations (☎ 3580-2311; fax 3580-6066)

ANA Hotel Tokyo: singles ¥23,000; doubles/twins ¥29,000; near Akasaka subway station (☎ 3505-1111; fax 3505-1155)

Asakusa View Hotel: singles ¥15,000; doubles/twins ¥21,000/28,000; 10 minutes from Asakusa subway station (☎ 3847-1111; fax 3842-2117)

Capitol Tōkyū Hotel: singles ¥23,000; doubles/twins ¥35,500; near Nagata-chō subway station (☎ 3581-4511; fax 3581-5822)

Century Hyatt Tokyo: singles ¥22,000; doubles/twins ¥29,000/32,000; west exit of Shinjuku station (☎ 3349-0111; fax 3344-5575)

Dai-Ichi Hotel Tokyo: singles ¥27,000; doubles/twins ¥38,000/34,000; close to Shimbashi station (☎ 3501-4411; fax 3595-2634)

Ginza Dai-Ichi Hotel: singles ¥15,000; doubles/twins ¥25,000/23,000; near Higashi-Ginza and Shimbashi stations (☎ 3542-5311; fax 3542-3030)

Ginza Tōbu Tokyo Renaissance Hotel: singles ¥17,000; doubles/twins ¥28,000; close to Higashi-Ginza subway station (☎ 3546-0111; fax 3546-0111)

Ginza Tōkyū Hotel: singles ¥17,500; doubles/twins ¥29,800; near Higashi-Ginza station (☎ 3541-2411; fax 3541-6622)

Hotel Metropolitan: singles ¥16,500; doubles/twins ¥21,500; near the west exit of Ikebukuro station (☎ 3980-1111; fax 3980-5600)

Hotel Ōkura: singles ¥28,500; doubles/twins ¥37,000/40,000; near Kamiya-chō subway station (☎ 3582-0111; 3582-3707)

Hotel New Otani: singles ¥25,500; doubles/twins ¥32,500/32,500; near Nagata-chō subway station (☎ 3265-1111; 3221-2619)

Hotel Seiyo Ginza: singles ¥48,000; twins ¥65,000; 10 minutes from Higashi-Ginza subway station (☎ 3535-1111; fax 3535-1110)

Imperial Hotel: doubles/twins ¥39,000; near Hibiya-kōen Park (☎ 3504-1111; 3581-9146)

Keiō Plaza Inter-Continental Hotel: singles ¥16,000; doubles/twins ¥24,000; near west exit of Shinjuku station (☎ 3344-0111; 3345-8269)

Le Pacific Meridien Tokyo: singles ¥21,000; doubles/twins ¥25,000; close to Shinagawa station (☎ 3445-6711; fax 3445-5733)

Palace Hotel: singles ¥22,000; doubles/twins ¥32,000/28,000; near Tokyo station and Ōtemachi subway station (☎ 3211-5211; fax 3211-6987)

Roppongi Prince Hotel: singles ¥19,500; doubles/twins ¥24,500/23,000; close to Roppongi subway station (☎ 3587-1111; fax 3587-0770).

Takanawa Prince Hotel: singles ¥20,000; doubles/twins ¥25,000/24,000; near Shinagawa station (☎ 3447-1111; 3446-0849)

Tokyo Hilton International: doubles/twins ¥27,000; near Shinjuku station (☎ 3344-5111; fax 3342-6094)

Tokyo Station Hotel: singles ¥13,000; twins ¥17,000; doubles ¥19,000; in JR Tokyo station (☎ 3231-2511; fax 3231-3513)

PLACES TO EAT

Tokyo can lay claim to being Asia's most cosmopolitan city on many fronts, but none more so than its restaurant scene. Scanning the food section of a recent *Tokyo Journal*, 160 restaurants are reviewed: the entries begin with *Oz Cafe* (a Sydney-style cafe with a 'breezy patio') and end with *Ichioku* (a pioneering *mukokuseki* restaurant that does a good tofu steak).

Not that Tokyo is all trendy international and ethnic cuisines at chalked-up prices. There's a multitude of dining spots out there, ranging from exclusive Japanese and foreign restaurants to inexpensive slurp-'em-back noodle stands. And in all but the very cheapest and most exclusive restaurants, plastic food window displays tell you the basics – what's to eat and how much it costs.

You rarely have to look far for a restaurant in Tokyo, but at busy times of the day finding one without a queue outside it can be difficult. Check out the basements and upper floors of the big department stores for *resutoran-gai* ('restaurant streets') – these invariably have a good selection of Japanese, Chinese and Italian restaurants with inexpensive lunch-time specials. Railway stations are the home of Chinese noodle ramen shops, obentō (boxed meals) stands and curry rice restaurants. Big commercial districts like the east side of Shinjuku simply brim with restaurants – everything from revolving sushi to pizza.

During the day, the best eating areas are the big shopping districts like Shibuya, Shinjuku, Harajuku and Ginza. Shinjuku could well take the prize as Tokyo's best daytime gourmet experience, though it's no slouch by night either. The Ueno and Ikebukuro areas, where many travellers stay, abound in small Japanese and Chinese noodle bars, and Ikebukuro has an increasing number of up-market alternatives these days, including French, Italian and Vietnamese restaurants. Don't forget that Aoyama and Roppongi are not just nightclubs – they have some of the best eating out in Tokyo.

If you are going to be in Tokyo for some time, pick up a copy of John Kennerdell's *Tokyo Restaurant Guide* (Yohan) or Rick Kennedy's *Good Tokyo Restaurants*. The *Tokyo Journal* runs a consistently ground-breaking restaurant guide; it's a great source for off-beat dining ideas.

The following section on cuisine first describes restaurants serving Japanese food by area. Places serving international cuisine are listed by area in the Other Cuisines section and are then described more fully under separate cuisine sections.

Japanese

Central Tokyo & Ginza If you are even remotely on a budget, Ginza is best avoided as a place to eat out in the evening. During the day it's a different story. There are some very economical lunch-time teishoku deals to be had in the department stores. A couple of good options are: *Restaurant City*, on the 8th floor of the Matsuya department store; the 2nd basement level of the Matsuzakaya department store; and the basement floors of the Ginza Palmy building.

For a taste of pre-economic-miracle Tokyo, it's worth taking a look around Yūrakuchō's *Yakitori Alley*. This under-the-tracks litter of scruffy bars is gradually being squeezed out by more genteel establish-

ments, but what's left is still old-time earthy Tokyo at its best – figure on spending ¥1500 per head on beer and some yakitori.

On the subject of beer and rowdiness, Ginza is a good place to dip into Japanese beer hall culture. This is not a purist's idea of Japanese cuisine – beer halls are the kind of place you find sashimi and french fries sharing the same menu – but the beer hall has its place staked out in the Japanese culinary landscape. The *Sapporo Lion Beer Hall* (☎ 3571-2590) is the biggest, and a good place to start. The extensive menu includes everything from Japanese snacks to German sausages – food and beers will set you back from ¥2000 to ¥2500. It's open from 11.30 am to 10.15 pm daily. *Pilsen* (☎ 3571-3443) works better on the ambience front, but the food is a shade less palatable.

Just south of Harumi-dōri is *New Torigin* (☎ 3571-3333), hidden away down a very narrow back alley but signposted in English. There's an English menu too, and this authentic, very popular little place does excellent yakitori at ¥120 to ¥200 per stick and the steamed rice dish known as Kamameshi at ¥700. A complete meal with a beer costs about ¥1500.

Of course, Ginza is the place for establishment up-market dining too. Assuming you want to splash out, *Ten'ichi* (☎ 3571-1949) is *the* place for tempura: from ¥7000 for lunch; from ¥8000 for dinner. There are numerous branches of *Sushi-sei* (☎ 3572-4770) around town, but the Ginza branch is the flagship. This is not the *best* Tokyo has to offer, but for reliable sushi at affordable mid-range prices (say, ¥4000 per head), it's a good choice.

It's possible to find inexpensive Japanese food for people on the run in Ginza. The area across from American Express has a decent revolving sushi restaurant and several noodle shops. You will find more revolving sushi shops in Ginza itself. Also worth keeping an eye out for is *Tenya*, the tendon (tempura and rice) chain that has rice and tempura dishes from ¥490.

Ueno & Asakusa Although the occasional pizza place or Indian restaurant makes an appearance, you're better off sticking to Japanese food in these older parts of Tokyo. In both Ueno and Asakusa, you're never far from a cheap ramen or tonkatsu restaurant. Some of the better restaurants tend to be uncompromisingly Japanese – don't bother asking for the English menu.

For lunch-time meals in Ueno, Ameyoko Arcade is a good place to start. There's nothing remarkable in here and it's pointless making recommendations, but there's a reasonable number of snackeries with plastic food displays. Ueno station is another possibility – again no prizes for excellence, but inexpensive and wholesome enough. For lunch or dinner, try *Ueno Yabu Soba* (☎ 3831-4728) in the Ameyoko area; this friendly and authentic soba restaurant has a colour-photo menu to help customers choose from the reasonably priced soba and udon noodle dishes on offer.

Honke Ponta (☎ 2831-2351) is a Tokyo institution: the city's oldest tonkatsu restaurant. It's open for lunch and dinner, but you need to be there early for the latter as it closes at 8 pm. The menu is diverse, but the thing to order is the tonkatsu, which is ¥2500. Honke Ponta is closed Monday.

In Asakusa, the area between Sensō-ji Temple and Kaminarimon-dōri is the best place to seek out Japanese food. On Kaminarimon-dōri itself *Tenya*, a branch of the mod-con tendon chain, has tempura and rice dishes from ¥490. A bit further up the road towards Asakusa subway station, *Owariya* (no English sign) is a classy soba shop, with dishes ranging from ¥1100. To the right of the entrance to Sensō-ji Temple is *Tonkya*, a small, family-run tonkatsu establishment (closed Thursday), where you can eat well from ¥700. To the left is a branch of *Yoshinoya*, a chain that can be found all over Tokyo, specialising in very inexpensive gyūdon (beef and rice). Just outside the temple precincts, look out for the cheapest ramen in Asakusa (possibly in all of Tokyo) at *La Mentei* – ¥280 for a bowl.

Tatsumiya (☎ 3842-7373) is an old Edo-period restaurant, full of very interesting bric-a-brac, that specialises in nabe ryōri

('stew', or literally 'pot cuisine') during the winter months. Prices for this speciality average ¥2500. At midday, bentō are available for ¥850. Evening courses that allow you to sample a wide range of goodies will cost ¥4200. Tatsumiya is closed on Monday.

Daikokuya (☎ 3844-1111) is another period piece, having lingered in Asakusa for over a century. Its ebi-tendon (prawn tempura with rice) is celebrated and costs ¥1700. It's closed Sunday.

Close to Asakusa subway station is *Kamiya Bar* (☎ 3841-5400), said to be the oldest bar in Japan. There's a beer hall on the ground floor where you order and pay for beer and food as you enter. Upstairs, both western and Japanese food are served. Kamiya is renowned for a cocktail of its own invention called denki buran – the *buran* stands for brandy – and it comes in two varieties, 60 and 80 proof. Kamiya is closed on Tuesday.

Ikebukuro Ikebukuro is perhaps not the place for a serious Japanese meal but there are plenty of fine places to fill up in. At lunch-time, don't forget to check out the restaurant floors in Seibu, Tōbu and Marui department stores – hundreds of restaurants to choose from and nearly every one sporting a queue!

The busy shopping area on the east side of the station is where Ikebukuro comes into its own. Look out for revolving sushi restaurants *(Taiyuzushi* and *Komazushi* are two popular ones), ramen shops and izakaya (the red lanterns outside are a giveaway).

Yōrōnotaki (there's no English sign but it's a huge place and hard to miss), next to the Metropolitan Plaza on the west side of the station, is a chainstore izakaya (there are hundreds of branches all over Japan). The food is reliable, the beer's cheap and there's an illustrated menu for easy ordering.

Shinjuku Shinjuku is the busiest and most energetic commuter junction in Tokyo, and there are a vast number of restaurants around the station and in the east-side entertainment area. The large numbers of businessmen and young people here make Shinjuku a good place to eat out at night and sample some of the places that specialise in beer and snacks – after all, enough snacks soon become a meal.

The east side of the station is the best place to seek out something to eat. Behind Mitsukoshi department store is a favourite for tempura, *Tsunahachi* (☎ 3352-1012). It's

not exactly cheap (sets around ¥2000) and long queues are the rule, but it's worth both the wait and the money. Not far away is the lively *Daikokuya* (☎ 3352-2671), a popular student hang-out. It has all-you-can-eat deals (yaki-niku ¥1500, shabu-shabu and sukiyaki ¥1950; add ¥1000 and it's all you can drink too).

A Quick Guide to International Cuisine in Tokyo

Central Tokyo & Ginza Ginza has an excellent range of international cuisine, but bear in mind that most of it is very pricey. The following list includes a few more reasonably priced options:

Indian – *Maharaja, Nair's*
Italian – *L'Affresco*

Ueno & Asakusa If you're determined to avoid Japanese food there are plenty of fast-food specialists, but fewer foreign restaurants in the Ueno and Asakusa areas. *Samrat* and *Maharaja* in Ueno serve good Indian food.

Ikebukuro Not quite the backwater it used to be, Ikebukuro has some good French, Italian and even Vietnamese food.

Chinese – *Pekintei*
French – *Chez Kibeau*
German – *Munchen*
Italian – *Pizzeria Capri, Capricciosa*
Vietnamese – *Saigon*

Shinjuku As well as a wide variety of Japanese restaurants and fast-food centres there are also some superb places for foreign food in Shinjuku; the Kabuki-chō area to the east of the station has countless restaurants of all types.

Cambodian – *Angkor Wat* (in Yoyogi)
Chinese – *Tokyo Kaisen Ichiba, Oriental Wave*
German – *Hofbräuhaus Beer Hall*
Korean – *Tōkaien*
Taiwanese – *Tainan Taami*
Thai – *Ban Thai, Kao Keng*

Harajuku & Aoyama These are trendy areas and most of the international restaurants are out of the price range of the average budget traveller. However, there are some good coffee shops to sit around in, and watch the fashionable world pass by.

American – *Tony Roma's*

Cafes – *Stage ¥2, Cafe de Rope, Bamboo Cafe, Cafe des Pres, Cafe La Fleur, Cafe Häagen Dazs, Las Chicas*
Chinese – *Son of the Dragon*
French – *L'Orangerie, Bordeaux Cellar, Brasserie Flo*

Shibuya Shibuya has numerous fast-food restaurants and places serving a wide variety of international cuisines.

American – *Victoria Station*
Balinese – *Warung I*
Chinese – *Reikyō, Ryūnohige*
Indian – *Samrat*
Malaysian – *Only Malaysia*
Nepalese – *Kantipur*
Taiwanese – *Tainan Taami*
Vegetarian – *Shizenkan, Healthy Boutique*

Akasaka Akasaka is one of the best places to eat out in Tokyo. Most of the restaurants are in a compact enclave between Sotobori-dōri and Hitotsugi-dōri.

American – *Subway Sandwiches, Tony Roma's, Victoria Station*
Indian – *Moti* (two branches), *Mughal, Taj*
Italian – *Pizzeria/Trattoria Marumo*
Korean – *Mugyōdon*
Vietnamese – *Aozai*

Roppongi & Nishi-Azabu There's great dining in Roppongi. Prices are high, but not universally so.

American – *Hamburger Inn, Spago, Tony Roma's, Victoria Station*
Indian – *Moti, Samrat*
Indonesian – *Bengawan Solo*
Italian – *Capricciosa, Sicilia, Bellini's Pizza Kitchen*
Mexican – *Casa Monnon, La Escondida*
Taiwanese – *Tainan Taami*
Thai – *Maenam, Rice Terrace* ■

In a similar vein to Daikokuya is *Irohanihoheto* (☎ 3359-1682). This is another izakaya chain that is popular with students. It's on Yasukuni-dōri on the 6th floor of the Piccadilly movie house. *Ibuki* (☎ 3342-4787) is an old-style sukiyaki and shabu-shabu restaurant that is accustomed to gaijin. A sukiyaki course is ¥2500, while shabu-shabu is ¥3200. There's an inexpensive revolving sushi restaurant almost next door.

Don't forget to plunge into Kabuki-chō and check out the back lanes (particularly on the Seibu Shijuku station side) for interesting restaurants. The area is littered with them, all with plastic food displays in the outside windows.

Harajuku & Aoyama Affordable Japanese restaurants in Harajuku include *Genroku* (☎ 3498-3968), on Omote-sandō. There are branches of this revolving sushi shop in most of Tokyo's commercial districts, but the Harajuku branch is probably the best. Servings start at ¥130 a plate.

On Takeshita-dōri, *Shūtarō* (☎ 3402-7366) is a tonkatsu and katsudon specialist; most dishes are around the ¥1000 mark. *Maisen* (☎ 3470-0071) is famous for its tonkatsu, and tends to get busy at lunchtime; it's down near the Hanae Mori building and is open daily.

Aoyama is packed with bistros and continental diners, but Japanese restaurants are few and far between. *Mominoko House* (☎ 3405-9144) barely scrapes in as Japanese – it's more health food really. For vegetarian Japanese in an arty living room environment, it's a good spot for either lunch or dinner – expect ¥1500 to ¥2000 per head. It's closed Sunday.

Shibuya Take the briefest of looks around Shibuya, and it will probably occur to you that there must be a lot of restaurants lurking in all those department stores. There are. Try the 7th floor of Parco 1 or the 8th floor of the One-Oh-Nine building. The *Jūnikagetsu* (meaning '12 months' for all you language students) restaurant building is a department store that dispenses with shopping altogether and just collects a bunch of restaurants together.

The adventurous (you will need some Japanese) should show their support to *Tamakyū* (☎ 3461-4803), the creaking little pile of timber that refused to be budged by the 109 building; it's about the only non-shiny thing left in Shibuya these days. Inside is a lively little izakaya, not one of Tokyo's best, but not bad. Expect to pay ¥2000 to ¥2500 with drinks.

The Shibuya branch of *Shabuzen* (☎ 3485-0800) is a roomy venue for splashing out on some shabu-shabu. For ¥3300 it's an all-you-can-eat deal; spend an extra ¥1000 and you get Japanese beef. For up-market yakitori, *Nambantei* has branches the world over; the Shibuya branch (☎ 3498-0940) is on the 2nd floor of the Tōkyū Bunka Kaikan building. Dinner courses are from around ¥3000.

Akasaka The Akasaka/Roppongi area is packed with excellent Japanese restaurants, though bear in mind that bargains are few and far between.

In Akasaka, take a stroll in the streets running off and parallel to Sotoburi-dōri. In this neighbourhood there are branches of expensive restaurant chains such as *Tenichi*, where set-course tempura in opulent surroundings starts at ¥6500, or *Sushi-sei*, a branch of the famous sushi chain where costs of around ¥4000 per head are the norm. For a good inexpensive lunch try *Kushinobō* (☎ 3586-7390), a kushiage specialist that is highly recommended. Dinner courses cost from ¥2500.

If the idea of a tofu restaurant is a new one, you would be surprised at just how many of them there are in Tokyo. *Tōfuya* (☎ 3582-1028) is the perfect introduction to a cuisine that too many visitors miss out on – some Japanese would be helpful here. For straight izakaya dining, *Yakitori Luis* (☎ 3585-4197), close to Akasaka subway station, is a popular yakitori place where prices start at ¥200 per snack.

Roppongi Roppongi has some of Tokyo's most expensive Japanese dining. To be sure, the occasional greasy-spoon ramen shop or smoky izakaya materialises here and there, but it's the wining, dining jetset that many of Roppongi's more well known Japanese restaurants are aimed at.

If you *really* want to splash out, Roppongi's memorable top-end Japanese restaurants include: *Fukuzushi* (☎ 3402-4116), a sushi/sashimi restaurant with a good cocktail bar; *Seryna* (☎ 3403-6211), for teppanyaki, shabu-shabu and suki-yaki; and *Inakaya* (☎ 3405-9866), probably Tokyo's most expensive robotayaki.

Not so expensive, and a long-time favourite for Roppongi revellers is *Bikkuri Sushi*, a late-night revolving sushi that's seen it all. Another place that stays open late (until 5 am) and is used to stray gaijin falling in through the door is *Tsubohachi*, a small yakitori bar.

Other Cuisines

There's a fabulous range of Italian, French, Chinese, Indian and other cuisines available in Tokyo these days. The bistro experience is as much a part of everyday Tokyo as the izakaya is. Budget travellers will have to watch costs since international food – with the exception of the fast-food barns – is always more expensive than the cheapest local dishes.

Fast Food Most of the budget-priced Japanese and Chinese restaurants serve their food just as quickly and often more cheaply than the fast-food chains, but if you simply can't do without a Big Mac or a Shakey's pizza, Tokyo won't deprive you of the pleasure.

Most of the major fast-food chains have muscled in on the lucrative Japanese market. *Shakey's Pizza*, *KFC* and *McDonald's* seem to have a branch next to every railway station in Tokyo. The McDonald's phenomenon has spawned some Japanese variations on the same theme such as *Mos Burger*, *Lotteria* and *Love Burger*, to name a few.

Also worth seeking out are the Japanese food chains like *Yoshinoya* (with gyūdon – beef and rice – dishes) and *Tenya* (with tendon – tempura and rice – dishes).

Discount coffee shops are another good fast-food option. The major chain is *Doutor* (look for the yellow and brown signs). Doutor sells coffee from ¥190 and German hotdogs for ¥190. You can put together a good lunch, including a ¥150 piece of cake, for around ¥550 – not bad in Tokyo. *Pronto* is another inexpensive chain. The *Mister Donut* places are good for an economical donut, orange juice and coffee breakfast.

American *Victoria Station* is a chain with branches in Roppongi (☎ 3479-4601) and Shibuya (☎ 3463-52880) among others. It serves ribs and roast beef, but it's the do-it-yourself, all-you-can-eat salads that have made it famous among foreign residents. *Tony Roma's* is an expensive charcoal ribs specialist, and is generally more popular with Japanese than with foreigners. It has branches in Aoyama (☎ 3479-5214), Akasaka (☎ 3585-4478) and Roppongi (☎ 3408-2748). *Subway* is a much less pricey alternative, and has branches serving subs all over town nowadays – even in Ginza.

For inexpensive hamburgers and fries in an authentic diner setting, the *Hamburger Inn* (☎ 3485-8980) in Roppongi has been around forever; it's just around the corner from the Gas Panic complex and is open all night. For a noisier, flashier hamburger experience, the *Hard Rock Cafe* (☎ 3408-7018) has a branch in Roppongi too – they're everywhere, from Beijing to Bali, these days.

British British-style pubs are a popular import and Tokyo has no shortage of them. *1066* (☎ 3719-9059) in Naka-Meguro has hearty English food (roast lunch on Sunday) and British beer on tap. There is also live folk music regularly – the entrance fee includes a banquet.

Cafe Restaurants *Las Chicas* (☎ 3407-6865), in Aoyama, is so popular they say they are turning the Japanese gourmet reviewers away (Lonely Planet is a different matter). Check the place out at lunch, when African meals make an appearance in one of the rooms (it's a warren in there), and inexpensive cafe meals are available outside. The members-only club is upstairs, where you'll also find a hair boutique called the Sin Den and a studio where musical types toil away at the latest sounds. There's even a computer where you can log on. It's a unique concoction. Evening meals – Continental – are popular.

Parisien-style cafes are the thing in Harajuku these days – it's probably the only part of Tokyo you would want to be seated gazing out into the street. *Cafe des Pres* (☎ 5411-3721) looks for all the world as if it has been snatched from Paris and plonked down on Omote-sandō. It has prices to match too – ¥620 for a coffee. Lunch courses cost ¥2500; dinner prices go through the roof. *Cafe La Fleur* (☎ 3486-0176), not far away on Aoyama-dōri, is a similar setup, though slightly cheaper. *Cafe Häagen Dazs* (☎ 5467-0747) was there before any of the others, and is a great place to watch the Harajuku crowds.

Cambodian A long runner, *Angkor Wat* (☎ 3370-3019) is still doing an excellent job of promoting one of the world's more obscure cuisines. The staff are friendly and speak Japanese, Mandarin, Khmer and some English – there's always someone who can steer you to the right spicy salad or coconut soup.

To get to Angkor Wat, take the Yamanote line to JR Yoyogi station. Take the east exit, cross the road, walk straight ahead and after about 100m look for Angkor Wat in a lane on your right.

Chinese Tokyo residents in the know have a soft spot for *Tainan Taami*. This is Taiwanese food as it should be – small, inexpensive servings, lots of noise, steam and stir-fry aromas, and consistently reliable standards. There are branches in Roppongi (☎ 3408-2111), Suidobashi (☎ 3263-4530), Ginza (☎ 3571-3624) and Shibuya (☎ 3464-7544), but the pick of the bunch is the Shinjuku branch (☎ 3232-8839), located in the nether regions of Kabuki-chō – appropriately, it stays open late.

Also in Kabuki-chō is the *Tokyo Kaisen Ichiba* (☎ 35273-8301), literally the 'Seafood Market'. You can not miss the building, a girder and glass construction with a fish market downstairs. Upstairs, you get to eat the fish. This place has slightly up-market prices but simply picking the cheapest things on the menu at random (around ¥1200 per serve) will provide some delicious surprises. There's an English menu.

Oriental Wave (☎ 3202-0121), located in Shinjuku, is really the Tokyo Daihanten, Japan's biggest Chinese restaurant. For the

Tokyo's Internet Cafes

It would be wrong to say that Internet cafes have taken Tokyo by storm, but there are good number of them about. There will probably be more by the time this book is in print. The trend in Tokyo – and this it must be said is a healthy one – is less towards the fully-fledged Internet cafe than towards the cafe with a couple of connected computers in it.

Examples of the latter include *Cafe des Près* (☎ 5411-3721), on Omote-sandō, Harajuku, which has a couple of IBMs and a connection fee of ¥500 for 30 minutes. *Las Chicas* (☎ 3407-6863), in Aoyama, has a single Mac which diners can use for free. *Kiss* (☎ 3401-8165), also has a Mac that can be used free if you're using the cafe.

The Sony building in Ginza has computers you can log on with, or alternatively check out *Pulse Point* (☎ 3289-0132), on the 4th floor, where you can lunch on bagels and log on either with Macs or IBMs – the cost is ¥500 for 30 minutes.

Cyberia (☎ 3423-0318), in Nishi Azabu, has over 10 IBMs, offers lessons, you can receive your email, and cappuccino is on tap. Costs are ¥500 for 30 minutes. If you can find the Yoshida building in Roppongi, the *IAC Internet Surf Shop* (☎ 5561-9339) has the same rates and besides the inevitable cappuccino it serves beer too.

For those who want to get serious about the Internet, *YuMeDi Akihabara* (☎ 5296-5581) has over 100 Macs and 30 IBMs. This place charges ¥1500 for the day, but unfortunately you can only send email, not receive it. ■

most part it's an unremarkable multistorey diner of the sort beloved by expatriate Chinese the world over. The exception is the 3rd floor yum cha hall. This is one of the few places in Tokyo where correct yum cha form is observed by having the food brought around on trolleys.

In Harajuku, close to the lower end of Takashita-dōri, is *Son of the Dragon*, or *Ryūnoko*, a small, divey Sichuan restaurant that's perhaps not quite the real thing but close enough for Tokyo.

Shibuya has a couple of long-time favourites: *Ryūnohige* (☎ 3461-5347) and *Reikyō* (☎ 3461-4220). Both are Taiwanese run (again) and thoroughly Chinese – it's the diners who make ambience not the decor. Figure on around ¥2000 to ¥3000 (with drinks) for dinner, ¥800 for lunch. Reikyō is closed Thursday.

French There's no shortage of surprisingly good mid-range French restaurants in Tokyo. It's just a pity that so many require a guide on the first visit.

Pas À Pas (☎ 3357-7888) is a tiny, informal place that resembles a living room more than a restaurant; as is frequently pointed out, it revolutionised French dining in the city by offering the real thing without pomp and ceremony at reasonable prices. You can order any combination of starter, main course and dessert for ¥1000 at lunch, ¥2500 at dinner. To get there, take the Marunouchi line to Yotsuya-Sanchōme subway station, take the Yotsuya-Sanchōme exit, turn right, walk past the Marusho bookshop, cross the road and take the second street on the left. *Pas À Pas* is a few doors down on the left on the 2nd floor.

Aoyama probably has the best selection of French restaurants in Tokyo. *Bordeaux Cellar* (☎ 5410-4507), as the name suggests, is best known for its wine list (a good selection available by the glass), but the meals won't disappoint. Figure on ¥3000 to ¥4000 for meals; most wines range from ¥2000 to ¥4000 per bottle. Bordeaux Cellar is closed on Sunday. *Brasserie Flo* (☎ 5474-0611) is modelled on a Montparnasse original, and is one of the few French restaurants around

that's open for breakfast (¥600 from 8 am). Dinner courses hover at around ¥4000.

Another affordable French restaurant is Ikebukuro's *Chez Kibeau* (☎ 3987-6666), a home-style place run by Kibo, owner of the Kimi Ryokan. Anyone staying at the Kimi can pick up a map from reception for getting there. Main courses range from around ¥1500.

Harajuku's Hanae Mori building (5th floor) is home to *L'Orangerie* (☎ 3407-7461), which has long been lauded as offering Tokyo's best Sunday brunch buffet (11.30 am to 3.30 pm). At ¥3965, however, it won't be the cheapest brunch of your life.

Indian Indian has been a fixture on the Tokyo restaurant scene for a long time. *Maharaja*, which has branches all over Tokyo, is a good stop for lunch in Ginza (☎ 3572-7196). Evening meals range from ¥2000, but it has good lunch-time specials from ¥900 and an excellent tandoori mixed grill for ¥1250. The Shibuya branch is on the 8th floor of the 109 building.

Also in Ginza, *Nair's* (☎ 3541-7196) is a Tokyo institution, dating back to the early 1950s. Be prepared to queue for curries that are not necessarily authentic (foreign reviewers of restaurants steadfastly ignore the place), but indisputably unique and very interesting. It's closed on Tuesday. The Restaurant City floor of Ikebukuro's Seibu also has a branch.

Moti has two branches in Roppongi (☎ 3479-1939) and two more in Akasaka (☎ 3582-3620, 3584-6640). Moti is unquestionably Tokyo's favourite Indian restaurant chain, and the food is always worth waiting in line for. Check out the (reasonably) new branch in Roppongi, *Moti Darbar* (☎ 5410-6871). All have good lunchtime sets (from around ¥900), and evening meals from around ¥2500 per head.

Samrat is essentially a chain of Moti clones; at least they're cheaper. Branches to look out for include Ueno (☎ 3568-3226) Shibuya (☎ 3496-9410) and Roppongi (☎ 3478-5877). Lunchtime is good for chicken, mutton or vegetable curry with rice and naan for ¥850. Main courses average ¥1500.

Indonesian *Bengawan Solo* (☎ 3403-3031) in Roppongi was one of Tokyo's first 'ethnic' restaurants and it's still going strong. *Warung I* (☎ 3464-9795) in Shibuya is a popular Balinese restaurant. The restaurant itself is not at ground level, but at least the English sign is.

Italian Italian is so popular that pasta and pizza are virtually Japanese staples these days. Every department store has an Italian restaurant, and every shopping district has dozens of them.

In the Ginza area you can splash out on a Venetian-style lunch at *L'Affresco* (☎ 3581-7421). The restaurant interior looks like something out of *Roman Holiday*, but that's part of the fun. Lunch courses are ¥3000, dinner around ¥5000.

In Akasaka, *Marumo* (☎ 3585-5371) is much better than it looks from the outside. Note in particular the lunch sets, from ¥800, which fill the place up between noon and 2 pm. Evening main courses range from around ¥1200. In Roppongi, a long-time runner is *Sicilia* (☎ 3405-4653). Look for the queue snaking out on to the street. Figure on spending around ¥2500 per head.

Another Roppongi favourite is *Bellini's Pizza Kitchen* (☎ 3470-5650). It's more Californian than Italian, but the wood-fired pizza is indeed good, and in the summer the open front makes for great people watching.

The *Capricciosa* chain cannot go unmentioned, if only for the famous size of their servings. Every dish is enough for two: the ideal is for three people to order two dishes (average ¥1300 per dish). There are branches in Roppongi, Shibuya, Shinjuku, Takadanobaba, Ikebukuro, and just about everywhere.

Korean Every neighbourhood has its Korean yakiniku restaurant, and they're often such convivial places to knock back a few beers over some sizzling beef that you wonder why anyone bothers with the real thing. A good place to find out is *Mugyōdon* (☎ 3586-6478), a boisterous, smoky place in Akasaka that sees as many Korean customers as Japanese.

Tōkaien (☎ 3200-2924) is a nine-floor monster on Yasukuni-dōri, Shinjuku. Japanese,

Mandarin, Korean, and even a little English are spoken here. Reckon on about ¥2000 per head on any of the first four floors. The upper floors have banquets and are more exclusive.

Malaysian *Only Malaysia* (☎ 3496-1177) is no longer the only one in town; it has opened a second branch on the other side of Shibuya station – see the Shibuya map. It's easy to miss the sign at ground level, so look carefully.

Malay-chan (☎ 5391-7638) just creeps in as a recommendation, and mainly as a place for lunch if you happen to find yourself on the wrong side of the tracks in Ikebukuro. The lunch deals come in big servings at around ¥750 to ¥850.

Mexican Local expats will all have their favourites, but for starters head down to Nishi-Azabu. *Casa Monnon* (☎ 3499-2559) is a small, intimate space where you can knock back some home-cooked Mexican. Nearby *La Escondida* (☎ 3486-0330) is something special, with troubadours, regional specialities, and (of course) prices to match.

For real American tacos and burritos, the *Zest* chain is worth a recommendation. Prices are reasonable. Look out for branches in Harajuku (☎ 3499-0293), Roppongi (☎ 3478-0222) and Nishi-Azabu (☎ 3400-3985).

Thai Thai restaurants are undoubtedly Tokyo's South-East Asian favourite, and they're everywhere. Not that popularity means low prices.

Ban Thai (☎ 3207-0068) in Shinjuku was the restaurant that started it all. It no longer has the buzz it had back when it was the only place in town serving decent Thai food, but it's still there and the menu is virtually unchanged. It's on the 3rd floor of the Dai-Ichi Metro building.

Also in Shinjuku's Kabuki-chō is the *yatai-mura* (the street stall village), a small enclave of Thai, Filipino and Chinese stalls catering to the area's foreign workers. It has a good Thai stall *(Kao Keng)*. It has expanded operations upstairs and the menu is in Japanese as well as Thai – the friendly staff will help you with your order. It's strictly an after 9 pm thing.

Maenam (☎ 3404-4745) is that most unlikely of things, a late-night Thai diner cum cocktail bar – in Roppongi of course. Prices are much more reasonable than you'd expect; it's open until 4 am. But the pick of the Thai restaurants in this area is *Rice Terrace* (☎ 3498-6271) down in Nishi-Azabu, next to the Aoyama cemetery. It's a charming place, and the food is spot on. Figure on ¥3000 upwards with drinks.

Turkish *Istanbul* (☎ 3226-5929) is another of those pioneering ethnic restaurants that is still going strong. It's a hole-in-the-wall outfit in Shinjuku san-chōme, an interesting, much-neglected area in itself. Follow the chef's suggestions if you're a newcomer.

Vegetarian For a people who famously subsisted on rice, vegetables and the occasional fish (if they were lucky) pre-Meiji Restoration, the Japanese are a very carnivorous people these days. In Tokyo the situation is looking up for vegetarians, but it has been a long time coming.

You'll find most of the health and vegetarian restaurants lurking up dingy flights of stairs in areas such as Ogikubo, Shimo Kitazawa, Nakano and Kōenji. One place that doesn't require a compass and an aerial survey map to find is *Shinzenkan II* (☎ 3486-0281) in Shibuya. It's nothing to get excited about and it's definitely more a lunch place than an evening place (it closes at 8 pm anyway), but it serves a good daily special with brown rice. Also in Shibuya is *Healthy Boutique* (☎ 3476-0591), which has vegetarian lunch sets from ¥800.

The TIC has a pamphlet with a list of vegetarian and health restaurants. The problem is finding them.

Vietnamese *Saigon* (☎ 3989-0255), on the east side of Ikebukuro station, attracts a good number of foreign diners, is inexpensive and not that difficult to find (there's an English sign). Surprisingly enough – given its location – it is one of Tokyo's best Vietnamese restaurants.

ENTERTAINMENT

Tokyo is very much the centre of the Japanese world and has the best of everything. On the nightlife front, there are those who maintain that Osaka is more cutting edge, but then Osaka offers nowhere near the diversity of entertainment options that Tokyo does: traditional entertainment such as kabuki; avant garde theatre; countless cinemas; live houses; pubs and bars.

Kabuki

The simplest way to see kabuki in Tokyo is at the *Kabuki-za Theatre* (☎ 3541-3131) in Ginza. Performances and times vary from month to month, so you'll need to check with the TIC or with the theatre directly for programme information. Earphone guides providing 'comments and explanations' in

Kabuki is a blend of music, dance, mime, and spectacular staging and costuming.

English are available for ¥600. Prices for tickets vary from ¥2000 to ¥14,000, depending on how keen you are to see the stage.

Kabuki performances can be quite a marathon, lasting from 4½ to five hours. If you're not up to it, you can get tickets for the 4th floor for less than ¥1000 and watch only part of the show but earphone guides are not available in these seats. Fourth-floor tickets can be bought on the day of the performance. There are generally two performances daily, starting at around 11 am and 4 pm.

Japan's national theatre, *Kokuritsu Gekijō Theatre* (☎ 3265-7411), also has kabuki performances, with seat prices ranging from ¥1200 to ¥7200. Again, earphone guides are available. Check with the TIC or the theatre for performance times.

Nō

Nō performances are held at various locations around Tokyo. Tickets will cost between ¥3000 and ¥10,000, and it's best to get them at the theatre itself. Check with the TIC or the appropriate theatre for times.

The *Kanze Nō-gakudō Theatre* (☎ 3469-6241) is about a 10 to 15 minute walk from Shibuya station. The *Ginza Nō-gakudō* (☎ 3571-0197) (Ginza Nō Stage) is about a 10 minute walk from Ginza subway station, on Sotobori-dōri. The *Kokuritsu Nō-gakudō* (☎ 3423-1331) (National Nō Theatre) is in Sendagaya. Exit Sendagaya station in the direction of Shinjuku on the left and follow the road which hugs the railway tracks; the theatre is on the left.

Bunraku

Osaka is the home of bunraku, but performances do take place in Tokyo several times a year at the *Kokuritsu Gekijō Theatre* (☎ 3265-7411). Check with the TIC or the theatre for information.

Tea Ceremonies

A few hotels in Tokyo hold tea ceremonies which you can observe and occasionally participate in for a fee of about ¥1000. The *Hotel New Otani* (☎ 3265-1111) has ceremonies on its 7th floor on Thursday, Friday and

Saturday from 11 am to noon and 1 to 4 pm. Ring them before you go to make sure the show hasn't been booked out. The *Hotel Okura* (☎ 3582-0111) and the *Imperial Hotel* (☎ 3504-1111) also hold daily tea ceremonies.

Music

Check the latest issue of *Tokyo Journal* for who's playing around town. Tokyo is the only city in Asia where you have the luxury of perhaps seeing up and coming performers playing in an intimate venue. Name acts performing when we were last in town included Joe Sample, Napalm Death, Honeycrack, Elvis Costello & the Attractions, 60ft Dolls, Sting, the Sex Pistols, Lou Reed, Lush, Stevie Wonder and Color Me Badd. Ticket prices generally range from ¥5000 to ¥8000 depending on the performer and the venue.

Live Music Tokyo's homegrown live music scene is disappointing given how vibrant the city is in other quarters.

Overseas and local acts perform regularly at *Club Quattro* (☎ 3477-8750) and *On Air West* (☎ 5458-4646) in Shibuya and at the *Liquid Room* (☎ 3200-6811) in Shinjuku. These are places you book tickets for, however, not places you just turn up at in the hope of catching a good live act.

In Harajuku, *Crocodile* (☎ 3499-5205) has live music seven nights a week. There's usually a ¥2000 cover with one drink. It's a spacious place with room for dancing if the music allows it. In Aoyama, *Cay* (☎ 3498-5790) is a venue that combines Thai food and live music – very expensive, with the combined meal and music charge coming in at between ¥7000 and ¥10,000.

Loft (☎ 3365-0698) in Shinjuku is a Tokyo institution. Had they been Japanese, the Rolling Stones would have played here long before they cut their first single. It's smoky, loud and lots of fun on a good night.

Down Ebisu, just up the road from Wendy's, on the west side of the station, is *Milk* (☎ 5458-2826), which has live music on Thursday and Friday nights. Check out the kitchen – there's no food but it's a great place to chat and sip on a G&T in between sets.

Roppongi is the place for 'oldies-but-goodies'. The *Cavern Club* (☎ 3405-5207) hosts flawless I-wanna-hold-your-hand covers by four Japanese mop-heads; cover is ¥1300. *Kento's* (☎ 3401-5755) features '50s standards; live music cover is ¥1300. Forget the '50s, forget the Beatles, *Bauhaus* (☎ 3403-0092) is the place for '70s and '80s rock covers; cover is ¥1800 with one drink. Bauhaus is on the 6th floor of the Wada building.

Jazz Jazz has a serious following in Tokyo. For listings of performances, check the latest issue of *Tokyo Journal*.

Tokyo's big-name jazz venue is *Blue Note Tokyo* (☎ 3407-5781) in Aoyama; a cover charge of between ¥6000 and ¥10,000 keeps the riff-raff away and jazz aficionados within spitting distance of the greats of jazz. The *Shinjuku Pit Inn* (☎ 3354-2024) is another serious venue, though less likely to feature famous overseas acts than Blue Note; a cover of ¥3000 is the usual. The *Roppongi Pit Inn* (☎ 3585-1063) is another likely spot.

Other Nightlife

There has been an explosion of new bars and clubs over the last couple of years in Tokyo, making the job of coming up with specific recommendations ever more difficult. The following is a run down of popular bars and clubs in the livelier entertainment districts of Tokyo. If you're serious about nightlife, pick up a copy of Tokyo Journal's very comprehensive *Tokyo Nightlife Guide* (Yohan).

Shinjuku Shinjuku doesn't yield up its secrets as readily as other, more gaijin-oriented parts of entertainment Tokyo. And when you do stumble across something, it often falls into the quirky category. Still, Shinjuku is highly underrated as an area for a night out.

Dubliners is a recent arrival; look for it on the 2nd floor above the Lion Beer Hall. It's a good spot for an early evening get together, with live Irish folk music and Guinness on tap. Probably Shinjuku's most popular expat evening hangout at the time of writing, it's also

worth a visit at lunch time, when Irish stews and the like are available at teishoku prices.

Catalyst (☎ 3209-4102) is a classy spot, with a bar (drinks ¥500), dance space and lounge. It's open from 8 pm to 5 am; there's a ¥2000 cover including two drinks on the weekends. Other bars in the vicinity include *Rock Bar Mother*, a tiny basement bar with an extensive CD collection and a friendly crowd, *Shuffle Beat* and *Rockin' Chair*, both of which are rather more sedate spots for a drink.

You may not like *Rolling Stone* (☎ 3354-7347) – it's a grubby, low-life kind of place – but it's been there forever and it still manages to pull in the crowds on Friday and Saturday nights; there's a ¥1000 cover.

The *Liquid Room* (see the Live Houses entry above) has occasional events – look out for notices in *Tokyo Journal* and in the big CD stores around town.

Aoyama Aoyama is like Roppongi only cool. There's not much you can say about the clubs in this part of town; you're either part of the scene or you're not.

One place you don't need too much of an attitude for is *Apollo* (☎ 3478-6007). You will need to be elderly, however: no women under 20; no men under 25. It's very much a professional singles kind of place; cover is ¥2500 with two drinks.

At the time of writing the hottest club in Aoyama was *Pylon* (☎ 3478-1870). It usually features guest DJs playing a mix of soul, hip hop, jazz funk and so on, and is open Friday from midnight to 5 am and Saturday from 10 pm; cover is ¥2500 with two drinks. It's in the basement of a building also inhabited by a Wendy's.

Shibuya There's always been a dearth of decent places for a drink in Shibuya. The new *Bar, Isn't It?* up by the Bunkamura has remedied that. It's the same formula that allowed them to take first Kansai and then Roppongi by storm; cavernous dimensions and an enlightened pricing policy – *everything* is ¥500. It's amazing how busy this place gets by 9.30 pm, even mid-week.

Cave (☎ 3780-0715) is an interesting late

night option, particularly if Bar, Isn't It? is just too overwhelmingly gaijin. There are a couple of dance spaces and a bar somewhere in the inky darkness of this place – find them. It's open from 10 pm, and entry is ¥2500 with two drinks.

Ebisu Ebisu used to be mainly a locals scene, but it's changing rapidly. See the Live Music entry above for information on *Milk*, one of the more interesting new clubs in Tokyo. Also in the same building as Milk is *What the Dickens* (☎ 3780-2099), a British pub that does away with twee attempts at tradition and just creates a big hearty space, with Guinness and Bass on tap.

Roppongi There's always conjecture as to whether Roppongi has overdosed on the sleaze factor, drifted into a no-return spiral of violence; or whether, simply, the crowds are just heading elsewhere. The fact is, Roppongi is livelier than ever. Some of the old perennials have gone out of business or are feeling the pinch, but others – like Gas Panic – are doing a booming business. No matter what the critics say, Roppongi is still *the* place to check out the Tokyo nightlife scene.

Starting with the bars – and there's an awful lot of them – the smart thing to do if you arrive in Roppongi before, say, 11 pm is to linger on the sleazy Almond Cafe corner and collect flyers for bars that are opening or closing down and having drink specials as a result. Alternatively, head to somewhere like *Bar, Isn't It?* (☎ 3746-1598). It's big and cheap, and you can even get a snack before moving on. The *Gas Panic Miller Bar* (☎ 3746-1017) has a happy hour from 5 to 8 pm, when beers cost just ¥300. *Motown House* (☎ 5474-4605) has survived on the same formula forever: a long bar; expensive drinks; and a knowledgeable but unadventurous DJ. Think of it as a salaried version of Gas Panic. Speaking of which – from humble beginnings as a raunchy rival to Déja Vu, Gas Panic has emerged as the king of

Roppongi sleaze. Nowadays there's the Miller Bar at ground level, and clubs upstairs and downstairs. Five minutes walk away is *Gas Panic Club* (☎ 3402-7054), which is essentially a meat market on steroids. With the 'gangsta rap' sounds', jumbo-size bouncers and in-your-face bar staff, violence forever feels as close as a tap on the shoulder. On Friday and Saturday nights there's groping room only.

If the crowds at Gas Panic are too much for you, stroll next door to *Déjà Vu* (☎ 3403-8777), an altogether quieter scene. The *Charleston* (☎ 3402-0372) used to have a certain reputation but it cleaned up its act years ago and is now a pleasant spot for a pizza and a few drinks. Better still is *Charleston & Sons* (☎ 3479-0595), with its alfresco drinking and dining just around the corner from the Hard Rock Cafe. This is the perfect place for a late night pizza (¥1000) – it's open until 5 am. *Paddy Foley's* (☎ 3423-2250) is an authentic-looking Irish pub with Guinness on tap and a convivial crowd. Get here early enough and you may even be able to hear yourself speak – a rarity in Roppongi. On the club front, *Velfarre* (☎ 3746-0055) is Roppongi's disco Hilton. Dance clubs don't get much bigger, flashier or better behaved than this place. And the odd thing is it's only open until midnight – by 9 pm it's packed. There's a ¥4000 cover for women, ¥5000 for men (¥500 extra Friday and Saturday nights) with three drinks. If you've got the money and you want to see just how far Tokyo will go for a good time, check it out.

For other Roppongi clubs, check the latest issue of *Tokyo Journal* (the scene is forever changing). A few reliable options include *Yellow* (☎ 3479-0690), once avant-garde and now an interesting inky space to dance in (look for the plain yellow sign outside; cover ¥2000 to ¥3500); *328 (San-Nippa)* (☎ 3401-4968), which can always be counted on for an interesting mix of people and great music (more a bar than a club, but people dance all the same); and *Lexington Queen* (☎ 3401-1661), one of Roppongi's first discos and still the place that every visiting celebrity ends up in (they must think Tokyo is caught in a Saturday Night Fever time warp) – easy to knock, the Lex sticks by a winning formula and Roppongi wouldn't be the same without it.

SPECTATOR SPORT
Sumo
Sumo tournaments at Tokyo's *Ryōgoku Kokugikan Stadium* (☎ 3866-8700) in Ryōgoku take place in January, May and September and last 15 days. The best seats are all bought up by those with the right connections, but balcony seats are usually available from ¥6000 and bench seats at the back for about ¥1000. If you don't mind standing, you can get in for around ¥500. Tickets can be bought up to a month prior to the tournament, or simply turn up on the day. The stadium is adjacent to Ryōgoku station on the northern side of the railway tracks.

Baseball
Although soccer has made some headway in recent years, baseball remains Japan's most popular team sport. There are two professional leagues, the Central and the Pacific. The baseball season runs from April until the end of October. The two main places to see baseball in Tokyo are as follows:

Tokyo Dome (the Big Egg): next to Kōrakuen Amusement Park (☎ 3811-2111)
Jingū Kyūjo: close to JR Shitanomachi station (☎ 3404-8999)

THINGS TO BUY
Despite the prevailing exchange rates, the determined shopper can still come up with bargains in Tokyo. Naturally, the best one-stop shopping options are the department stores, which stock virtually everything, including souvenirs. Unless a major sale is on, however, department stores are expensive places to shop.

Flea Markets
Although flea markets sound like promising places to shop for interesting antiques and souvenirs, bear in mind that this is Tokyo and there are unlikely to be any real bargains. At the very least, take a look at somewhere like the Oriental Bazaar (see the following Antiques & Souvenirs section) and make a note of prices before embarking on a flea market shopping spree. Tokyo's main flea markets are as follows:

Iidabashi Antique Market – 6 am to 6 pm on the first Saturday of every month; Central Plaza, Ramura building close to Iidabashi JR and subway stations
Tōgō-jinja Shrine – 4 am to 4 pm on the first Sunday of each month; JR Harajuku station
Nogi-jinja Shrine – dawn to dusk on the second Sunday of each month; from Nogi-zaka subway station on the Chiyoda line – the shrine is on Gaien-higashi-dōri
Hanazono-jinja Shrine – 7 am to 5 pm on the second and third Sunday of every month; close to Isetan department store on the east side of Shinjuku station
Roppongi – 8 am to 8 pm on the fourth Thursday and Friday of every month; in front of the Roy building, close to Roppongi subway station;

Antiques & Souvenirs
One of the best places to look for antiques and interesting souvenirs is in the basement of the Hanae Mori building (☎ 3406-1021) in Harajuku. There are more than 30 antique shops there. Not far from the Hanae Mori building, the Oriental Bazaar (☎ 3400-3933) is open every day except Thursday and is an interesting place to rummage through. It has a wide range of good souvenirs – fans, folding screens, pottery, etc – some at very affordable prices.

For straight souvenir shopping, the International Arcade south of Yūrakuchō station in central Tokyo is one of the best places to go. Some of the stuff here is tacky, but there are also worthwhile purchases such as reproductions of wood-block prints. Asakusa's Nakamise-dōri at Sensō-ji Temple is another area with interesting souvenirs.

The Tokyo Antique Fair takes place three times a year and brings together more than 200 antique dealers. The schedule for this event changes annually, but for information on the schedule you can ring Mr Iwasaki (☎ 3950-0871) – he speaks English.

Everywhere Vendors

There are no prizes for guessing that Japan has the largest number of vending machines per capita in the world. You cannot walk for five minutes without bumping into one. A major reason must be that in crime-free Japan they go unmolested. In most civilised countries, plonking a beer vending machine down on a suburban street corner would be unthinkable.

There are thought to be around 4.5 million vending machines in Japan, and demand is still growing. A Japanese cartoon showed the future. A company official exhorts employees to work harder to meet the growing need for vending machines, and in the next frame the answer is unveiled – a huge vending-machine vending machine.

You can buy almost anything from vending machines. Soft drinks, coffee and cigarettes are the most common vending machine products, but beer vending machines are also reasonably common. Other less common machines sell goods ranging from rice and vegetables to neckties and computer software. Condom vending machines can sometimes be found outside pharmacies, and pornography (magazines and videos) can be found in some areas.

Probably the most controversial vending machine venture in recent years has been for the sale of used panties. Ostensibly once owned and worn by female high-school students, the panties come in vacuum-sealed packs of three (with a photo of the erstwhile owner) and are targeted at the average fetishistic man about town. The cost? Around ¥3000 to ¥5000, making them the perfect, reasonably priced Japanese souvenir for the folks at home. ■

Japanese Dolls

Edo-dōri, next to JR Asakusabashi station, is the place to go if you're interested in Japanese dolls. Both sides of the road have large numbers of shops specialising in traditional as well as contemporary Japanese dolls.

Photographic Equipment

Check the Shinjuku section for information on the big camera stores there. Ginza's Harumi-dōri is another place for photographic equipment – there are several second-hand photographic shops where Japanese gear can often be bought at good prices.

Clothes

There are no hard and fast rules when it comes to clothes shopping. Even areas like Ginza may offer heavily discounted prices on some items. For general off-the-rack wear, Shinjuku and Shibuya are good areas to shop around and compare prices.

The department stores are good places to start looking. Seibu, Isetan, Marui and Parco are more middle-ground – a good mix of youth and mature casual wear. Stores such as Takashimaya, Matsuzakaya and Mitsukoshi are more conservative. In Shibuya, in particular, note the three Parco stores and Seed, a Seibu spinoff that brings a host of boutiques together under one roof. February and August are the months for massive department store sales. If you're in Tokyo at this time of the year be sure to check out prices.

Areas like Harajuku, Aoyama and Nishi-Azabu are the best places for specialised boutiques.

Music

Given the number of massive CD emporia in Tokyo these days, it's worth a quick run down. For a while it seemed that Tower, the original discount CD supermarket was going to be marginalised by the less cluttered, hipper Virgin and HMV stores. Tower has struck back with a massive new store in Shibuya – even if you're not a music lover, the 7th floor bookshop is worth a look. Note that imported CDs are *cheaper* than the local pressings. Prices range from ¥1590 to around ¥2190.

Kids' Stuff

Japanese are particularly creative when it comes to finding things to keep their kids occupied, and Tokyo has some great toy shops. Even if you don't have any children of your own, some of the shops make for fun browsing. Places to take a look at are Loft in Shibuya and Kiddyland in Harajuku. The latter has five floors of stuff that your kids would probably be better off not knowing about. The biggest toy shop in Japan (the world?) is in Ginza. Hakuhinkan Toy Park even has a child-oriented theatre and restaurants on its upper floors. You can probably leave your kids in one of these places and take a permanent vacation – they won't notice ... really!

GETTING THERE & AWAY
Air

With the exception of China Airlines, all international airlines touch down at Narita airport rather than at the more conveniently located Haneda airport. Narita has had a controversial history, its construction having met with some considerable opposition from farmers it displaced, and from student radicals. Even today, it is very security conscious which can slow down progress in and out of the airport.

Arrival Immigration and customs procedures are usually straightforward, although they can be time consuming for non-Japanese. Note that Japanese customs officials are probably the most scrupulous in Asia; backpackers arriving from anywhere remotely third-worldish (the Philippines, Thailand, etc) can expect some questions and perhaps a thorough search. Don't carry anything you shouldn't be carrying. You can change money in the customs hall after having cleared customs or in the arrival hall. The rates will be the same as those offered in town.

Narita has two terminals, No 1 and No 2. This doesn't complicate things too much as both have railway stations that are connected to JR and Keisei lines. The one you arrive at will depend on the airline you are flying with. Both terminals have clear English signposting for limousine bus and train services.

Departure Be sure to check which terminal your flight leaves from, and give yourself plenty of time to get out to Narita. There is a ¥2000 departure tax at Narita.

Airline Offices Following is a list of the major airline offices in Tokyo.

Aeroflot
    No 2 Matsuda Building, 3-4-8 Toranomon, Minato-ku (☎ 3434-9671)
Air China (formerly CAAC)
    2-5-2 Toranomon, Minato-ku (☎ 5251-0711)
Air France
    New Aoyama Building, West 15th floor, 1-1-1 Minami Aoyama, Minato-ku (☎ 3475-2211)
Air India
    Hibiya Park Building, 1-8-1 Yūraku-chō, Chiyoda-ku (☎ 3214-7631)
Air Lanka
    Dowa Building, 7-2-22 Ginza, Chūō-ku (☎ 3573-4261)
Air New Zealand
    Shin Kokusai Building, 3-4-1 Marunouchi, Chiyoda-ku (☎ 3287-1641)
Alitalia
    Tokyo Club Building, 3-2-6 Kasumigaseki, Chiyoda-ku (☎ 3580-2242)
All Nippon Airways (ANA)
    Kasumigaseki Building, 3-2-5 Kasumigaseki, Chiyoda-ku (☎ 3272-1212)
American Airlines
    Nichirei Higashi-Ginza Building, 6-19-20, Chiyoda-ku (☎ 3248-2011)
Asiana Airways
    Ark Mori Building, 1-12-32, Akasaka, Minato-ku (☎ 3582-6600)
Bangladesh Biman
    Kotobuki Building, 2-5-21 Tonranomon, Minato-ku (☎ 3593-1252)
British Airways
    Sanshin Building, 1-4-1 Yūraku-chō, Chiyoda-ku (☎ 3593-8811)
Canadian Airlines International
    Hibiya Park Building, 1-8-1 Yūraku-chō, Chiyoda-ku (☎ 3281-7426)
Cathay Pacific
    Toho Twin Tower Building, 1-5-2 Yūraku-chō, Chiyoda-ku (☎ 3504-1531)
China Airlines
    Sumitomo Building, 1-12-16 Shiba Daimon, Minato-ku (☎ 3436-1661)
Continental Micronesia Airlines
    Sanno Grand Building, 2-14-2 Nagata-chō, Chiyoda-ku (☎ 3508-6411)
Delta Airlines
    Kioicho Building, Kioicho, Chiyoda-ku (☎ 5275-7000)
Dragon Air
    1-5-2 Yūraku-chō, Chiyoda-ku (☎ 3506-8361)
Finnair
    NK Building, 2-14-2 Kōjimachi, Chūō-ku (☎ 3222-6801)

Garuda Indonesian Airways
    Kasumigaseki Building, 3-2-5 Kasumigaseki, Chiyoda-ku (☎ 3593-1181)

Japan Airlines (JAL)
    2-2 Kanda Surugadai, Chiyoda-ku (☎ 5489-1111)

Japan Air System (JAS)
    4-47 Ōtamachi, Naka-ku. Yokohama (☎ 045-212-2111)

Japan Asia Airways
    1-10-7 Dōgenzaka, Shibuya-ku (☎ 5489-5411)

KLM
    Yūraku-chō Denki Building, 1-7-1 Yūraku-chō, Chiyoda-ku (☎ 3216-0771)

Korean Air
    Tokyo KAL Building, 3-4-15 Shiba, Minato-ku (☎ 5443-3311)

Lufthansa
    3-1-13 Shiba-Kōen, Minato-ku (☎ 3578-6700)

Malaysian Airlines (MAS)
    Hankyū International Express Building, 3-3 Shimbashi, Minato-ku (☎ 3503-5961)

Northwest Airlines
    5-12-12 Toranomon, Minato-ku (☎ 3533-6000)

Philippine Airlines
    Hibiya Mitsui Building, 1-1-2 Yūrakuchō, Chiyoda-ku (☎ 3593-2421)

Qantas
    Urban Toranomon Building, 1-16-4 Toranomon (☎ 3593-7000)

Sabena Belgian World Airlines
    Building 2-2-19 Akasaka, Minato-ku (☎ 3585-6151)

Scandinavian Airlines (SAS)
    1-22-12 Toranomon, Minato-ku (☎ 3503-8101)

Singapore Airlines
    Yūraku-chō Building 709, 1-10-1 Yūraku-chō, Chiyoda-ku (☎ 3213-3431)

Swissair
    Hibiya Park Building, 1-8-1 Yūraku-chō, Chiyoda-ku (☎ 3212-1011)

Thai Airways International
    Asahi Seimei Hibiya Building, 1-5-1 Yūraku-chō, Chiyoda-ku (☎ 3503-3311)

United Airlines
    Kokusai Building, 3-1-1 Marunouchi, Chiyoda-ku (☎ 3817-4411)

Virgin Atlantic Airways
    5-2-1 Minami Aoyama, Minato-ku (☎ 3499-8811)

Train

All major JR lines radiate from Tokyo station; northbound trains stop at Ueno station, which like Tokyo station is conveniently on the JR Yamanote line. Private lines – which are often cheaper and quicker for making day trips out of Tokyo – start at various stations around Tokyo. With the exception of the Tōbu Nikkō line, which starts in Asakusa, all private lines originate somewhere on the Yamanote line.

Shinkansen There are three shinkansen lines that connect Tokyo with the rest of Japan: the Tōkaidō line passes through Central Honshū, changing its name along the way to the San-yō line before terminating at Hakata in Northern Kyūshū; the Tōhoku line runs north-east via Utsunomiya and Sendai as far as Morioka, with the Yamagata branch heading from Fukushima to Yamagata; and the Jōetsu line runs north to Niigata. Of these lines, the one most likely to be used by visitors to Japan is the Tōkaidō line, as it passes through Kyoto and Osaka in the Kansai region. All three shinkansen lines start at Tokyo station, though the Tōhoku and Jōetsu lines make a stop at Ueno station.

Other JR Lines As well as the Tōkaidō shinkansen line there is a Tōkaidō line servicing the same areas but stopping at all the stations that the shinkansen zips through without so much as a toot of its horn. Trains start at Tokyo station and pass through Shimbashi and Shinagawa stations on their way out of town. There are express services to Yokohama and the Izu-hantō Peninsula, via Atami, and from there trains continue to Nagoya, Kyoto and Osaka.

Northbound trains start in Ueno. The Takasaki line goes to Kumagaya and Takasaki, with onward connections from Takasaki to Niigata. The Tōhoku line follows the Takasaki line as far north as Ōmiya, from where it heads to the far north of Honshū via Sendai and Aomori. Getting to Sendai without paying any express surcharges will involve changes at Utsunomiya and Fukushima. Overnight services also operate for those intent on saving the expense of a night's accommodation.

Private Lines The private lines generally service Tokyo's sprawling suburbia and very few of them go to any areas that visitors to Japan would care to visit. Still, where private lines do pass through tourist areas, they are usually a cheaper option than the JR lines. Particularly good bargains are the Tōkyū Tōyoko line, running between Shibuya station and Yokohama; the Odakyū line, running from Shinjuku to Odawara and the Hakone region; the Tōbu Nikkō line, running from Asakusa to Nikkō; and the Seibu Shinjuku line from Ikebukuro to Kawagoe.

Bus

Generally long-distance buses are little or no cheaper than the trains but are sometimes a good alternative for long-distance trips to areas serviced by expressways. The buses will often run direct, so that you can relax instead of watching for your stop as you would have to do on an ordinary train service.

There are a number of express buses running between Tokyo, Kyoto and Osaka. Overnight buses leave at 10 pm from Tokyo station and arrive at Kyoto and Osaka between 6 and 7 am the following day. They cost from ¥8000 to ¥8500. The buses are a JR service and can be booked at one of the Green Windows in a JR station. Direct buses also run from Tokyo station to Nara and Kōbe. And from Shinjuku station there are buses running to the Fuji and Hakone regions, including, for Mt Fuji climbers, direct services to the fifth station, from where you have to walk.

Ferry

A ferry journey can be a great way to get from Tokyo to other parts of the country. Fares are not too expensive (by Japanese standards anyway) and there is the advantage that you save the expense of a night or two's accommodation.

From Tokyo, there are long-distance ferry services to Kushiro (☎ 5400-6080) and Tomakomai (☎ 3578-1127) in Hokkaidō (2nd class ¥14,420 and ¥11,840 respectively); to Kōchi (☎ 3578-1127) (2nd class ¥10,500) and Tokushima (☎ 3567-0971) (2nd class ¥8200) in Shikoku; to Kokura (☎ 3567-0971) in Northern Kyūshū (2nd

class ¥12,000); and to Naha (☎ 3273-8911 or 3281-1831) on Okinawa (¥19,670).

Departures may not always be frequent (usually once every two or three days for long-distance services) and ferries are sometimes fully booked well in advance, so it pays to make inquiries early. The numbers given above for ferry companies will require some Japanese-language skills or the assistance of a Japanese speaker. If you have problems, contact the TIC at Narita or in Tokyo.

GETTING AROUND

Tokyo has an excellent public transport system. Everything of note is conveniently close to a subway or JR station. Bus services are difficult to use if you don't read kanji, but the average visitor to Tokyo won't need the buses anyway.

Narita Airport

Narita international airport is 66 km from central Tokyo, and is used by almost all the international airlines but only by a small number of domestic operators. Travel time into Tokyo will take from 50 minutes to 1½ hours or more, depending on your mode of transport and destination in town.

Depending on where you're going, it is generally cheaper and faster to travel into Tokyo by train than by limousine bus. Rail users will probably need to change trains somewhere, and this can be confusing on a jetlagged first visit. Limousine buses provide a hassle-free direct route to a number of Tokyo's top hotels, and for some visitors this convenience is decisive.

Train There are three rail services between both terminals at Narita airport and Tokyo: the private Keisei line; the JR Narita Express (N'EX); and the Narita airport service. The Keisei service runs into Nippori and Ueno, from either of which you can change on to the Yamanote line for access to Ikebukuro, Shinjuku and other destinations. N'EX and the Narita airport service run into Tokyo (from where you can change to almost anywhere). N'EX also runs to Shinjuku, Ikebukuro and Yokohama.

The Keisei line has two services: the Keisei Skyliner, which will get you to Ueno in 60 minutes for ¥1880, and the Keisei limited express, which does the trip in 71 minutes and costs ¥980. Limited express services are much more frequent than the Skyliner, and what's another 11 minutes?

The N'EX services are fast, extremely comfortable and include amenities like drink dispensing machines and telephones. To Tokyo station takes 53 minutes and costs ¥2890; to Shinjuku station takes 79 minutes and costs ¥3050; to Ikebukuro station takes 94 minutes and costs ¥3050; and to Yokohama station takes 90 minutes and costs ¥4100. N'EX services run approximately half hourly between 7 am and 10 pm, but Ikebukuro services are very infrequent; in most cases you will be better off heading to Shinjuku and taking the Yamanote line from there. Seats are reserved only, but can be bought immediately before departure if they are available.

Narita airport rapid trains take 90 minutes and cost ¥1260 to Tokyo. Trains only run approximately once an hour.

Limousine Bus Limousine bus ticket offices are clearly marked with the sign 'Limousine' at Narita. Don't be misled by the name because they're just ordinary buses and take 1½ to two hours (depending on the traffic) to travel between Narita airport and a number of major hotels around Tokyo. Check departure times before buying your ticket, as services are not all that frequent. The fare to hotels in eastern Tokyo is ¥2800, while to Ikebukuro, Akasaka, Ginza, Shiba, Shinagawa, Shinjuku or Haneda airport it is ¥2900. There is also a bus service straight to Yokohama, which costs ¥3300 and takes around two hours.

TCAT From 6.15 am to 8.50 pm limousine buses also run every 15 minutes to Narita from the Tokyo City Air Terminal (TCAT) and cost ¥2700. The TCAT is next to Suitengu-mae subway station on the Hanzōmon line in Nihombashi. There is also a frequent shuttle bus service between the

TCAT and Tokyo station, costing ¥200 and departing from the Yaesu side at Tokyo station (look for the signs). If you are leaving Tokyo, you can check in your luggage at the TCAT before taking the bus out to the airport. Some travellers swear by this service.

Haneda Airport
Most domestic flights and China Airlines (Taiwan) flights use the convenient Haneda airport.

Getting from Haneda airport to Tokyo is a simple matter of taking the monorail to Hamamatsu-chō station on the JR Yamanote line. The trip takes just under 20 minutes; trains leave every 10 minutes and cost ¥270. Taxis to places around central Tokyo will cost around ¥6000. There's a regular bus service between Haneda and the TCAT that takes around 30 minutes. Limousine buses also connect Haneda with TCAT (¥900), Ikebukuro and Shinjuku (¥1100).

There is a direct bus service between Haneda and Narita (¥2900), which can take up to two hours depending on the traffic. The alternative is to take the monorail in to Tokyo, and then connect with one of the Narita services running from various stations on the Yamanote line (see the preceding Train section).

Train
Tokyo has a crowded but otherwise awesome railway network. Between the JR and private above-ground lines and the private subway lines, you can get to almost anywhere in town quickly and not all that expensively. Unfortunately it all shuts down somewhere between midnight and 1 am and doesn't start up again until 5 or 6 am the next day, but this at least allows the taxi drivers to make some money.

Avoiding Tokyo's rush hour is not often possible. Things tend to quieten down between 10 am and 4 pm, when travelling around Tokyo can actually be quite pleasant, but before 9.30 am and from about 4.30 pm onwards there are likely to be cheek-to-jowl crowds on all the major train lines. Note that after 10 pm most passengers are in various degrees of intoxication. It helps.

JR Lines Undoubtedly, the most useful line in Tokyo is the JR Yamanote line, which does a 35 km loop around the city, taking in most of the important areas. You can do the whole circuit in an hour for the ¥120 minimum fare – a great introduction to the city. Another useful above-ground JR route is the Chūō line, which cuts across the centre of town between Shinjuku and Akihabara. Tickets are transferable on all JR lines.

The major JR stations of Tokyo, Shibuya, Shinjuku, Ikebukuro and Ueno are massive places with thronging crowds and never enough English signposting. Just working out how to buy a ticket can drive a newcomer to the edge of madness. Always stay cool. If it's a JR train you're taking, look for the JR sign and the rows of vending machines. If you don't know the fare, put in ¥120 and punch the top left-hand button (the one with no price on it). When you get to your destination you can pay the balance at the ticket gate. English signposting points the way to the railway platforms.

If you get tired of fumbling for change every time you buy a ticket, the JR system offers the option of 'orange cards'. The cards are available in denominations of ¥1000, ¥3000 and ¥5000. Fares are automatically deducted from the cards when you use them in the orange-card vending machines.

Subway Lines Apart from the JR Yamanote and Chūō lines, there are 12 subway lines (13 if you include the Yūrakuchō New Line), of which eight are TRTA lines and four are TOEI lines. This is not particularly important to remember, as the subway services are essentially the same, have good connections from one to the other and allow for ticket transfer between the two systems. Train lines are colour-coded on the excellent maps that are available free at subway stations and tourist information counters around town.

Ticket prices start at ¥160 for short hops, but if your trip involves a change of train you can be sure it will cost ¥180. As with the JR system, if you are in doubt at all (there are still subway stations in Tokyo where the subway pricing maps are only in Japanese), buy a ticket for ¥160 and upgrade if necessary at your destination.

The subway equivalent of the JR Orange card is the SF Metro card. It comes in denominations of ¥1000, ¥3000 and ¥5000 and can be used directly in the automatic ticket gates or used to buy tickets.

Discount Tickets There are no massively discounted tickets available for travel around Tokyo, but if you're moving around a lot you can save some yen. Probably the best deal is the Tokyo Combination Ticket, which allows travel on any subway, tram, Toei bus or JR train in the metropolitan area until the last train of the day. It costs ¥1560 and is available from subway and JR stations and even post offices.

Bus
Many Tokyo residents and visitors spend a considerable amount of time in the city without ever using the bus network. This is partly because the train services are so good and partly because the buses are much more difficult to use. In addition, buses are at the mercy of Tokyo's sluggish traffic flow. Services also tend to finish fairly early in the evening, making them a pretty poor alternative all round.

Pick up a copy of the free *Toei Bus Route Guide* from the TIC if you are planning to use the bus network. When using the buses, it's useful to have the name of your destination written in Japanese so that you can either show the driver or match up the kanji yourself with that on the route map. Fares are paid as you enter the bus, and it's a flat ¥200 for city destinations.

Taxi
Taxis are so expensive that you should only use them when there is no alternative. Rates start at ¥680, which gives you two km (1½ km after 11 pm), after which the meter starts to clock up an additional ¥90 for every

347m; you also click up ¥90 for every two minutes you sit idly gazing at the scenery in a typical Tokyo traffic jam.

Tram

Tokyo's only remaining tram (streetcar) service (the Toden Arakawa line) runs from opposite Ōtsuka station on the JR Yamanote line. It passes the Sunshine City building in Ikebukuro, heads on to Zoshigaya and then terminates in Waseda, not far from Waseda University. The line is perhaps worth using for a visit to Zoshigaya, an old residential area under threat from Tokyo's rapacious property developers. There are a number of small temples in the area, as well as Zoshigaya cemetery, the final resting place of Lafcadio Hearn and Natsume Sōseki.

Around Tokyo

東京の附近

Tokyo itself may be a tangle of expressways and railway lines, a congested sprawl of high-rises, department stores and housing estates, but an hour or so by rail is all you need to reach some of Japan's most famous sights. Apart from the Ogasawara Islands, all the attractions in this chapter can be visited as day trips from Tokyo, although in some cases it would be worth staying away overnight.

Foremost among the historical attractions around Tokyo are Kamakura and Nikkō, both of which rate highly among Japan's must-sees. Hakone and the Mt Fuji region provide views of Mt Fuji, though you should be aware that the right weather conditions are crucial.

Most of the other sights around Tokyo are less interesting for short-term visitors, despite heavy promotion by the Tourist Information Center (TIC). For long-term residents, areas like the Izu-hantō Peninsula and the Bōsō-hantō Peninsula are pleasant retreats from Tokyo, but cater largely to the needs of Japanese tourists and, to many foreign visitors, may seem like a never-ending succession of entry fees, roped walkways and orderly queues.

This chapter begins with places to the far west of Tokyo and moves clockwise, finishing with the Izu Seven Islands to the south-east and the Ogasawara Islands further south.

Izu-hantō Peninsula
伊豆半島

The Izu-hantō Peninsula, west of Tokyo, is noted for its abundant hot springs and serves as a popular get-away for Tokyo residents. In fact, official sources quote the peninsula as Japan's most popular resort and holiday area. Anyone who knows Japan will realise that this is a warning – stay away during peak

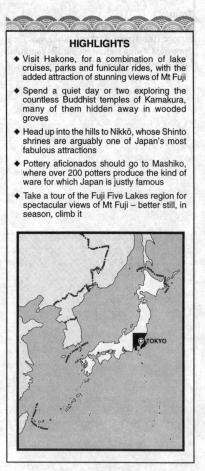

HIGHLIGHTS

◆ Visit Hakone, for a combination of lake cruises, parks and funicular rides, with the added attraction of stunning views of Mt Fuji

◆ Spend a quiet day or two exploring the countless Buddhist temples of Kamakura, many of them hidden away in wooded groves

◆ Head up into the hills to Nikkō, whose Shinto shrines are arguably one of Japan's most fabulous attractions

◆ Pottery aficionados should go to Mashiko, where over 200 potters produce the kind of ware for which Japan is justly famous

◆ Take a tour of the Fuji Five Lakes region for spectacular views of Mt Fuji – better still, in season, climb it

holiday periods. Besides, apart from some attractive coastline scenery there is little on the peninsula to attract short-term visitors to Japan. There are no outstanding destinations and travel costs to and around the area mount up very quickly.

Although it's possible to get around the

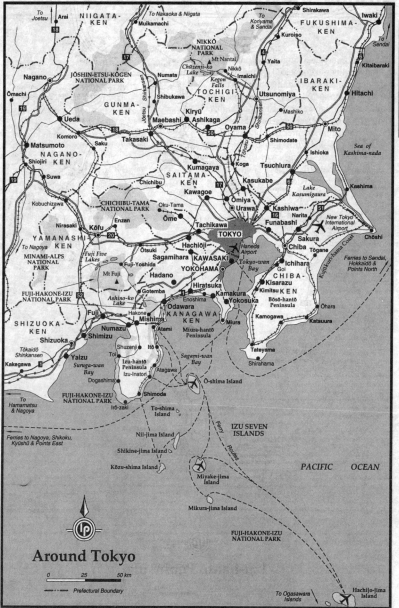

Around Tokyo

0   25   50 km

- - - - Prefectural Boundary

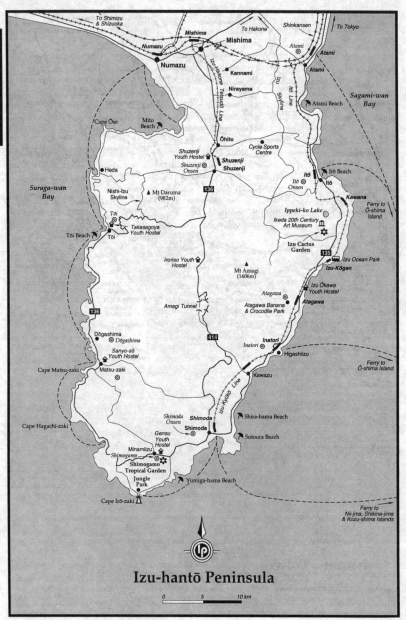

Izu-hantō Peninsula

| 0 | 5 | 10 km |

peninsula in one long and hurried day, it's better to stay overnight at a halfway point, such as Shimoda. The ideal accommodation of course is going to be an onsen hotel (where the hot-spring water is piped into segregated bathing areas in the hotel), but realistically this is going to be out of the price range of many travellers. Fortunately, many of the minshuku and ryokan around the peninsula also have onsen bathing areas and can provide a futon at more affordable rates.

A suggested itinerary for the peninsula circuit is to start at Atami – a hot-spring resort town whose name means 'hot sea' – and travel down the east coast to Shimoda. From there you can cut across to Dogashima on the west coast and travel up to Mishima or Numazu, where there are railway stations with direct access to Tokyo. There are frequent and reliable bus services between all the main towns on the peninsula, and some of the towns are also serviced by ferries.

ATAMI 熱海

Atami is a touristy hot-spring resort. Its easy access from Tokyo by shinkansen makes it an expensive place to spend the night. Head down to Itō or Shimoda if you are looking for cheaper accommodation and less tourist development.

There is a tourist information centre (☎ 0557-81-6002) at Atami railway station that can help you with finding accommodation; there should be an English speaker on hand.

MOA Art Museum　ＭＯＡ美術館

Atami's prime attraction is the MOA Art Museum. The museum, housed in the world headquarters of the Church of World Messianity, has a collection of Japanese and Chinese art that includes a few 'national treasures' and a good number of 'important cultural properties'. The museum is open from 9.30 am to 4.30 pm and closed on Thursday. Admission is a very hefty ¥1500. The museum is about 10 minutes by bus north of Atami station – take the bus from the No 4 bus stand outside the station to the last stop (MOA bijitsukan, ¥140).

Izusan-jinja Shrine　伊豆山神社

About 10 minutes to the north of Atami station by bus, this is not an important shrine, but it's situated in tranquil and expansive grounds. There is also a local history museum which is open 9 am to 3.30 pm daily (except Monday). Entry is ¥150. Take a bus from No 4 bus stand and get off at Izusan-jinja-mae (¥170).

Places to Stay

Atami is an expensive place to spend the night. Most hotels quote rates that include two meals and, with the exception of the occasional minshuku, all have hot-spring water piped in for bathing. Most places are about a km south of Atami station in the beachfront area. In this area you can find the *Atami Kinjō-kan* (☎ 0557-81-6261) which has rates starting at ¥19,500 per person including two meals. The *Pension Kurotake* (☎ 0557-67-1828) is a more reasonable option, with per-person rates of ¥9000 to ¥13,000.

Getting There & Away

An ordinary Tōkaidō line train from Tokyo station will get you to Atami in one hour and 50 minutes for ¥1850. A limited express (the Odoriko) will shave 20 minutes off this time, but is considerably more expensive at ¥3990 – just ¥10 less than the shinkansen in fact which takes only 55 minutes. Ordinary trains leave Tokyo every 40 minutes during the day. It is also possible to approach Atami via Shinjuku by taking the Odakyū line to Odawara (one hour and 10 minutes, ¥1550), and then connecting with the Tōkaidō line to Atami (20 minutes, ¥390).

ITŌ 伊東

Itō is another hot-spring resort and is famous as the place where Anjin-san (William Adams), the hero of James Clavell's *Shogun*, built a ship for the Tokugawa Shogunate. The nearby attractions of Lake Ippeki-ko, Ikeda 20th Century Art Museum and Izu Cactus Garden can all be visited by taking a bus from the No 10 stop outside Itō station. It is also possible to continue on to Atagawa by train and visit the Atagawa Banana & Crocodile Park (open daily from 8.30 am to 5 pm; entry ¥900), a theme park that seems eccentric even by Japanese standards.

Itō station has a tourist information centre (☎ 0557-37-6105) at the beachfront, close to where the bay cruises leave from.

Lake Ippeki-ko 一碧湖

All the tourist literature refers to it as 'gourd-shaped' which for the record means it's roughly circular. Lake Ippeki-ko is around four km in circumference and is a pleasant enough spot. There's boat hire on the lake – 30 minutes for ¥600. To get there, take a bus from either the No 5 or 10 bus stop outside Itō station. The 25 minute journey costs ¥470. Lake Ippeki-ko can be combined easily with a visit to the Ikeda 20th Century Art Museum.

Ikeda 20th Century Art Museum 池田20世紀美術館

The Ikeda 20th Century Art Museum has a collection of paintings and sculptures by Matisse, Picasso, Dali and others. The museum is 25 minutes from Itō station and is open daily from 10 am to 4.30 pm. Admission is ¥800. To get there, take the same buses as for Lake Ippeki-ko and get off at Ikeda Bijitsukan. The trip costs ¥530.

Izu Ocean Park 伊豆海洋公園

The Izu Ocean Park (ask for *Izu Kaiyō-kōen*) has 12 natural swimming pools, as well as facilities for snorkelling and scuba diving. It's 45 minutes by bus from Itō. Admission is just ¥300, but use of the pools costs ¥1550.

Special Events

On the first Sunday of July (from 10 am), Itō holds the Tarai-nori Kyōsō, a race down the Matsu-kawa River in washtubs using rice scoops as oars. There is nothing in the way of traditional costumes and the like.

Places to Stay

The *Itō Youth Hostel* (☎ 0557-45-0224) costs from ¥2570 depending on the season. Some English is spoken here, and there are

bicycles for rent. From Itō station take an Ōshima bus for 15 minutes to the Shōgyō Gakkō-mae stop, from where it's a further one km walk. The *Business Hotel Itō* (☎ 0557-36-1515) is one of the cheapest deals in town: singles/twins are ¥5150/9270. Look for it, a four-storey building, around 300m east of the railway station, close to the waterfront.

Other accommodation options can be found in the numerous pensions that exist out of town. The Lake Ippeki-ko area is good for pensions: *Pension Itōsansō* (☎ 0557-36-4454) has rooms from ¥7500. Most of the other pensions range from ¥9000 per night. There is also a host of accommodation possibilities in the Izu Kōgen (plateau) area which is easily accessible from Izu Kōgen station. If you don't mind spending ¥7000 to ¥8000 on a room, there will be plenty of places to choose from.

Getting There & Away

Itō is about 25 minutes from Atami station on the JR Itō line and the cost is ¥310. Atami station has English signposting for Itō trains. The JR limited express (tokkyū) 'Odoriko' service also runs from Tokyo station to Itō, taking one hour and 45 minutes and costing ¥4300. Direct ordinary trains from Tokyo station are quite a bit cheaper at ¥2160 and take about two hours and 10 minutes.

SHIMODA 下田

If you only have time for one town on the peninsula, make it Shimoda, the most pleasant of the hot-spring resorts. Shimoda is famous as the residence of the American Townsend Harris, the first western diplomat to live in Japan. The Treaty of Kanagawa, which resulted from Commodore Perry's visit, ended Japan's centuries of self-imposed isolation by opening the ports of Shimoda and Hakodate to US ships and establishing a consulate in Shimoda in 1856.

There is a small information centre (☎ 0558-22-1531) across from the station, but no English is spoken. Staff will help you book accommodation.

Ryōsen-ji & Chōraku-ji Temples
了仙寺・長楽寺

About a 25 minute walk south of Shimoda station is Ryōsen-ji Temple, famous as the site of another treaty, supplementary to the Treaty of Kanagawa, signed by Commodore Perry and representatives of the Tokugawa Shogunate. Today the temple is less interesting than its next-door neighbour, Chōraku-ji Temple, which has a **sex museum** featuring a collection of erotic knick-knacks – pickled turnips with suggestive shapes and stones with vagina-like orifices in them. This odd museum is open from 8.30 am to 5 pm daily and admission is ¥500.

The museum also has a series of pictures depicting the tragic life of the courtesan Okichi-san. The story goes that Okichi-san was forced to give up the man she loved in order to attend to the needs of the barbarian Harris. When he left (he was in Japan for just five years), she was stigmatised by her relationship with him, driving her to drink and suicide. Okichi-san is routinely sentimentalised as a sacrifice to internationalism.

Hōfuku-ji Temple   宝福寺

On the way to Ryōsen-ji Temple is Hōfuku-ji Temple which has a museum (¥300) that memorialises the life of Okichi-san and includes scenes from the various movie adaptations of her life.

Mt Nesugata-yama   寝姿山

Directly in front of Shimoda station is Mt Nesugata-yama. Cablecars run up to a park every 10 minutes. The park has a photography museum, a small temple, good views of Shimoda and Shimoda Bay and a reasonably priced restaurant. A return cablecar trip, including admission to the park, costs ¥1200. The park is open from 9 am to 5.30 pm.

Bay Cruises

From the Shimoda harbour area, there are numerous bay cruises. Most popular with the Japanese is a 'Black Ship' cruise which departs every 40 minutes (approximately) from 9.40 am to 3.30 pm and costs ¥900 for a 20 minute spin around the bay.

Three boats a day (9.40 and 11.20 am, and 1.25 pm) leave on a Cape Irō-zaki course. You can leave the boat at Irō-zaki and travel on by bus or stay on the boat to return to Shimoda. One-way tickets to Irō-zaki cost ¥1500 and the trip takes 40 minutes.

Special Events

From 16 to 18 May, the Kuro-fune Matsuri (Black Ship Festival) is held in Shimoda. It commemorates the first landing of Commodore Perry with parades and fireworks displays.

Places to Stay & Eat

As in the other peninsula resort towns, there is a wealth of accommodation in Shimoda, most of it overpriced. The *Gensu Youth Hostel* (☎ 0558-62-0035) is 25 minutes by bus from town (from the No 2 bus stand outside Shimoda station) and has beds for ¥2800. Even further from town is the *Amagi Harris Court Youth Hostel* (☎ 0558-35-7253) which is around five km inland from Kawazu station, between Itō and Shimoda. It has beds for ¥2800. You can get there from Kawazu station by boarding a Shuzenji-bound bus and getting off at the first stop after Yukano Onsen. There are hiking trails and waterfalls in this area.

For budget minshuku as well as koku-minshukusha, check with the information centre across from the station – rooms should be available for ¥5000 to ¥7000, without meals. For up-market onsen hotels, the best hunting ground is east of the station in the area that fronts onto Shimoda Bay. The *Kurofune Hotel* (☎ 0558-22-1234) is one of the better hotels in this area and charges ¥22,000 per person, with two meals.

There is reasonably inexpensive business hotel accommodation in the *Station Hotel Shimoda* (☎ 0558-22-8885), right next to the station. Singles/twins cost ¥5800/11,500. Also not far from the station is the affordable *Kokuminshukusha New Shimoda* (☎ 0558-23-0222), a pleasant place that costs ¥6900 per person, with two meals. Minshuku around town include *Shimoda-ya* and also *Shimizu-ya*.

Getting There & Away

Shimoda is as far as you can go by train on the Izu-hantō Peninsula; the limited express from Tokyo station takes two hours and 45 minutes and costs ¥6150. Alternatively, take an Izu Kyūkō line train from Itō station for ¥1440; the trip takes about an hour. There are a few express services each day from Atami station, but the express surcharge makes them expensive.

Bus platform No 5 in front of the station is for buses going to Dōgashima, while platform No 7 is for those bound for Shuzenji.

SHIMOGAMO HOT SPRING 下加茂温泉

The Shimogamo area is another place to loll around in hot water, but as it's off the railway line it's less developed than other onsen areas around the peninsula. Buses run to the area from in front of Shimoda station. There's plenty of accommodation along the Aono-gawa River, including the *Minshuku Fukuya* (☎ 0558-62-1003) which has rates from ¥7000 to ¥7500 per person, with two meals. Not far from here is the Yumiga-hama Beach – an excellent beach by Japanese standards.

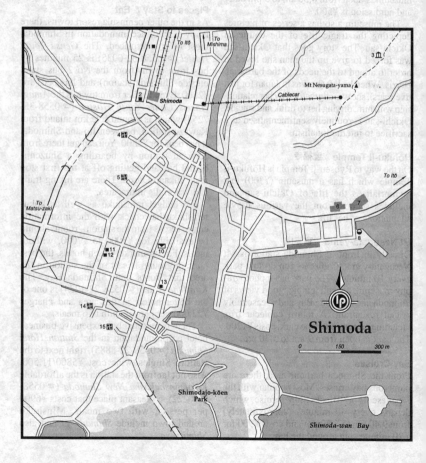

Shimoda

CAPE IRŌ-ZAKI   石廊崎

Cape Irō-zaki, the southernmost point of the peninsula, is noted for its cliffs and lighthouse. It also has a jungle park, a tropical garden and some fairly good beaches. If that sounds appealing, you can get to the cape by bus or boat (see the Bay Cruises entry of the Shimoda section) from Shimoda. Buses from Shimoda to the Irō-zaki lighthouse take around 55 minutes and cost ¥890.

CAPE MATSU-ZAKI   松崎

The attraction of Matsu-zaki is its collection of around 200 traditional houses with

1	Kokuminshukusha New Shimoda 国民宿舎ニュー下田
2	Station Hotel Shimoda ステーションホテル下田
3	Photography Museum 写真とカメラの記念館
4	Tōden-ji Temple 稲田寺
5	Hōfuku-ji Temple 宝福寺
6	Fujiya Hotel 富士屋ホテル
7	Hotel Kurofune 黒船ホテル
8	Bay Cruises 遊覧船
9	Morning Fish Market 海の朝市
10	Shimoda Post Office 下田郵便局
11	Shimizu-ya (Minshuku) 清水屋
12	Shimoda-ya (Minshuku) 下田屋
13	Matsumoto Ryokan 松本旅館
14	Ryōsen-ji Temple 了仙寺
15	Chōraku-ji Temple 長楽寺

namako-kabe walls – diamond-shaped tiles set in plaster. They are concentrated in the south of town, over the river, particularly in the area around the tourist information centre (☎ 0558-42-2540) which itself is in a delightful namako-kabe house.

Places to Stay

The Sanyo-sō Youth Hostel (☎ 0558-42-0408) has beds for ¥2800. The hostel is a good couple of km to the east of town; take a Shimoda-bound bus and get off at the Yūsu-hosteru-mae bus stop.

Getting There & Away

Buses from Shimoda to Dōgashima pass through Matsu-zaki. The fare from Shimoda is ¥1170; from Dōgashima ¥490. High-speed ferries also travel from Matsu-zaki to Dōgashima (¥420), Toi (¥1540), Heda (¥1950) and Numaza (¥3290).

DŌGASHIMA   堂ヶ島

From Shimoda, it's a picturesque bus journey to Dōgashima, on the other side of the peninsula. There are no breathtaking views, but the hilly countryside and narrow road that winds its way past fields and through small rural townships make for an interesting trip. Along the way is Cape Matsuzaki, recommended for its traditional-style Japanese houses and quiet sandy beach.

The main attractions at Dōgashima – a touristy but pleasant place to wander around – are the unusual **rock formations** that line the seashore. The frequent boat trips available include a visit to the town's famous shoreline cave – a hole in the roof lets in light. A 20 minute trip costs ¥900. Paths from the right of the jetty follow the cliffs to the hole in the cave roof.

Getting There & Away

Buses to Dōgashima (¥1290) leave from platform No 5 in front of Shimoda station. In Dōgashima buses leave from opposite the jetty. Buses to Shuzenji (¥2030) leave from stop No 2.

High-speed ferries are also available to Numazu (one hour and 15 minutes, ¥3090) which is connected with Tokyo by the Tōkaidō line; there are six departures a day from 10 am to 4.45 pm. Boats also go to Toi (25 minutes, ¥820). From Toi, it is possible to continue to Heda and Shuzenji by bus or take another boat to Numazu.

HEDA 戸田

North of Dōgashima is the small town of Heda – by Izu standards a relatively untouristed beach town. To get there from Dōgashima, you may need to change buses at Toi; and if you are travelling on the Dōgashima-Numaza high-speed ferry, you will need to change boats at Toi; Dōgashima to Heda costs ¥1530 by boat. Tōkai buses run between Shuzenji and Heda, taking around one hour and costing ¥1100.

The *Takasagoya Youth Hostel* (☎ 0558-98-0200) is in the nearby town of Toi; beds cost ¥2600.

SHUZENJI 修善寺

Shuzenji is another hot-spring resort. It is connected to the Tōkaidō line by the Izu-Hakone Tetsudō line, making it, along with Atami, one of the two main entry points to the peninsula. The Shuzenji onsen area, where you'll find ryokan accommodation, shops, restaurants and Shuzenji's few attractions, is around 10 minutes by bus from the station.

Shuzen-ji Temple is around 2½ km south-west of the railway station. It's by no means a major attraction, but is worth a look. It dates back to 807 AD and is said to have been founded by Kōbō Daishi. The present structure dates from 1489. The Treasure Hall costs ¥300 to enter. Also nearby is the **Shigetsu-den Hall**, a minor attraction. Take a Tōkai or Izu-Hakone bus from stand No 1 or 2 outside Shuzenji station. Ask for Shuzenji Onsen.

The *Shuzenji Youth Hostel* (☎ 0558-72-1222) is a 15 minute bus ride from Shuzenji station. Take a bus from the No 6 stand at Shuzenji station bus terminal to the new town guchi stop. The hostel is closed from 18 to 22 January and from 30 May to 3 June.

Getting There & Away

From Tokyo access to Shuzenji is via Mishima on the Tōkaidō line (see the Mishima entry below). Izu-Hakone Tetsudō trains from Mishima to Shuzenji take around 25 minutes and cost ¥490; trains run approximately hourly from 9 am to 5 pm. Buses from Shuzenji to Shimoda take around two hours and cost ¥2070.

MISHIMA 三島

Mishima, on the Tōkaidō line, was once an important post town on the old Tōkaidō highway. You might pause here, before heading into the Izu-hantō Peninsula or back to Tokyo, to take a look at Rakuju-en Garden and Mishima-taisha Shrine.

There is an information centre (☎ 0559-71-3338) in front of the station, but there are unlikely to be any English speakers on hand.

Rakuju-en Garden

Just a two or three minute walk south of Mishima station, Rakuju-en Garden is a Meiji-era stroll garden. The pond has its source at Mt Fuji, as did the scattered volcanic rocks. Also in the garden is a small shrine and a folkcraft museum. Entry to the garden is ¥300. It's open from 9 am to 5.30 pm; closed Monday.

Mishima-taisha Shrine
Mishima-taisha is the most important shrine on the Izu-hantō peninsula and is set in wooded environs. There is quite a small treasure hall with Kamukura-era exhibits on display; entry to the hall is ¥300. The shrine is around a five minute walk from the south-east gate of Rakuju-en Garden.

Special Events

Mishima-taisha Shrine is the venue for an annual festival involving horseback archery and parades of floats from 15 to 17 August.

Getting There & Away

A Tōkaidō line shinkansen from Tokyo takes one hour and five minutes to get to Mishima and costs ¥4310. Ordinary trains take twice as long and cost ¥2160. See the Shuzenji entry for information on getting there.

It's only 10 minutes by train from Mishima to Numazu, from where it is possible to continue into the Izu-hantō Peninsula by boat or by bus (see the Dōgashima section of this chapter for details).

SHIMIZU & SHIZUOKA　清水・静岡
West of Mishima, and also on the Tōkaidō line, is the town of Shimizu and the city of Shizuoka. Pre-Meiji Shōgun Tokugawa Ieyasu 'retired' to Shizuoka, and the **Kunōzan Tōshō-gū Shrine** in Shimizu has a number of his possessions in its treasure house. Only moats and ramparts mark the site of **Shizuoka Castle**, destroyed during WWII, but the town also boasts the interesting prehistoric site of **Toro Iseki** which dates from the Yayoi period (see the History section in the Facts about the Country chapter). The site museum displays the artefacts excavated here and there are reconstructions of Yayoi dwellings. The site is about 2½ km south-east of the JR station.

Hakone　箱根

If the weather cooperates and Mt Fuji is clearly visible, the Hakone region can make a wonderful day trip out of Tokyo. You can enjoy cablecar rides, visit an open-air museum, poke around smelly, volcanic hot springs and cruise Lake Ashino-ko. The weather, however, is crucial, for without Mt Fuji hovering in the background much of what Hakone has to offer diminishes in interest.

An interesting loop through the region takes you from Tokyo by train and toy train to Gōra; then by funicular and cablecar up Mt Sōun-zan and down to Tōgendai by Lake Ashino-ko; by boat around the lake to Moto-Hakone, where you can walk a short stretch of the Edo era Tōkaidō highway; and from there by bus back to Odawara, where you catch the train to Tokyo. (If you're feeling energetic, you can spend 3½ hours walking the old highway back to Hakone-Yumoto which is on the Tokyo line.)

ODAWARA　小田原
Odawara is billed in the tourist literature as an 'old castle town', which it is; the only problem is that the castle, like many of Japan's castles, is an uninspiring reconstruction of the original. That said, the castle is worth visiting during the cherry blossom season, as there are some 1000 *sakura* trees planted on the grounds. The castle and surrounding park area is a 10 minute walk south-east of Odawara station and admission is ¥250. It's open from 9 am to 4.30 daily. There is very little else of interest in the town which is principally a transit point for Hakone.

HAKONE-YUMOTO　箱根湯元
Yumoto is Hakone's most popular hot-spring resort. It's possible to stop off en route between Odawara and Gōra, but also consider approaching the town on foot from Moto-Hakone via the old Tōkaidō hiking course (see the Moto-Hakone entry later in this section).

Hakone-Yumoto sports all the touristy paraphernalia of a typical onsen town and, if this is new to you, it makes for an interesting stroll in itself. The chief cultural attraction is **Sōun-ji Temple**, a Rinzai sect temple.

HAKONE OPEN-AIR ART MUSEUM
彫刻の森美術館
The Hakone Open-Air Art Museum is next to Chōkoku-no-Mori station, one stop before Gōra station.

The focus is on western and Japanese 19th and 20th century sculpture. Artists exhibited include Bourdelle, Despiau, Rodin and Moore. There are also a couple of indoor exhibits, including a Picasso collection.

Admission is a hefty ¥1500 and the Hakone 'free pass' (see Getting Around later in this section for details) is *not* accepted, though it will earn you a discount. The museum is open from 9 am to 5 pm between March and October; during the rest of the year it closes at 4 pm.

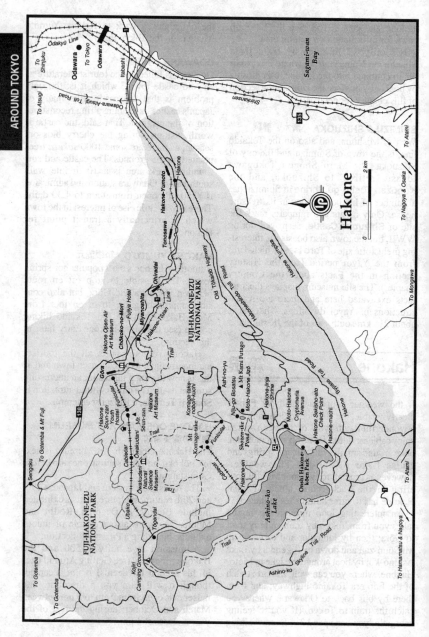

Hakone

GŌRA 強羅

Gōra is the terminus of the Hakone-Tōzan line and the starting point for the funicular and cablecar trip to Tōgendai on Lake Ashino-ko. The town also has a couple of its own attractions which may be of minor interest to travellers. If you are in this area between 11.30 am and 2.30 pm, check out the **Gyōza Center**, a famous dumpling shop with nine kinds of *gyōza* or dumplings – ¥500 is enough to fill you up.

Gōra-kōen Park 強羅公園

Just a short walk beside the funicular tracks up Mt Sōun-zan is Gōra-kōen Park. There is a French Rock Garden, seasonal flowers, alpine and tropical plants. Entry is ¥820. The park is open from 9 am to 9 pm from 21 July to 21 August; during the rest of the year it closes at 5 pm.

Hakone Art Museum 箱根美術館

Further up the hill, 10 minutes from Gōra station, the Hakone Art Museum has a moss garden and a highly rated collection of ceramics from Japan and China. Entry is ¥800. It is open from 9 am to 4.30 pm; closed Thursday.

MT SŌUN-ZAN & ŌWAKUDANI
早雲山・大涌谷

From Gōra, continue to the summit of Mt Soun-zan by funicular (10 minutes, ¥400). If you don't have a Hakone 'free pass' (see the following Getting Around section), tickets are sold at the booth to the right of the platform exit.

Mt Sōun-zan is the starting point for what the Japanese refer to as a 'ropeway', a 30 minute, four km cablecar ride to Tōgendai (one way ¥1300; return ¥2300). On the way, the gondolas pass through Ōwakudani. Get out here and take a look around the volcanic hot springs – the gondolas pass by every 52 seconds, so you can continue your journey whenever you like. In fine weather Mt Fuji looks fabulous from here.

Ōwakudani is a volcanic cauldron of steam, bubbling mud and mysterious smells. The black, boiled eggs on sale here are cooked in the boiling mud – they're good for you. Next to the cablecar stop, there's a building with restaurants, souvenir shops and a reasonably priced stand-up noodle bar. The restaurant has a good lunch selection.

The **Ōwakudani Natural Science Museum** has displays relating to the geography and natural history of Hakone. Entry is ¥400; it's open daily from 9 am to 4.30 pm.

LAKE ASHINO-KO 芦ノ湖

Lake Ashino-ko is touted as the primary attraction of the Hakone region, but it's Mt Fuji, with its snow-clad slopes glimmering on the water, that lends the lake its poetry. And unfortunately the venerable mountain is frequently hidden behind a dirty grey bank of clouds. If so, you have the consolation of a ferry trip across the lake and a postcard of the view.

At Kojiri, Moto-Hakone and Hakone, you can hire rowing boats (¥500 to ¥600 per half hour) or pedal boats (¥1500 per half hour). The truly indolent can take chauffeur-driven motor boats for a ¥6000 jaunt around the lake. See the following Getting Around section for more details about lake transport.

MT KOMAGA-TAKE 駒ケ岳

Mt Komaga-take is a good place from which to get a view of the lake and Mt Fuji. From Tōgendai, boats run to Hakone-en, from where a cablecar (¥610 one way, ¥1030 return) goes to the top. You can leave the mountain by the same route or by a five minute funicular descent (¥360 one way, ¥620 return) to Komaga-take-nobori-kuchi. Buses run from there to Hakone Machi (¥340), Hakone-Yumoto (¥540) and to Odawara (¥770).

Rock Carvings 元箱根石仏群

Not far from Mt Komaga-take-nobori-kuchi are a group of Buddhas and other figures carved in relief on rocks that lay between Mt Komaga-take and Mt Kami Futago. They date from the Kamakura era (1192 to 1333) and still look very good despite the battering from the elements they must have received in the intervening centuries. On one side of the road is the Niju-go Bosatsu, a rock carved with numerous Buddha figures. Across the road, the Moto-Hakone Jizō – patron saint of travellers and souls of departed children – is the largest of a number of rock carvings.

To get there from the funicular, turn right and follow the road down until you reach a T-junction. Turn left here and then left again; the carvings are around 400m up the road.

MOTO-HAKONE 元箱根

Moto-Hakone is a pleasant spot with a few places where you can eat or get an overpriced cup of coffee. There are a couple of interesting sights within easy walking distance of the jetty.

Hakone-jinja Shrine 箱根神社

It's impossible to miss Hakone-jinja Shrine, with its red torii rising from the lake. Walk around the lake towards the *torii* (entrance gate); huge cedars line the path to the shrine which is in a wooded grove. The shrine is very atmospheric. There is a treasure hall on the grounds. It is open from 9.30 am to 4 pm and costs ¥300.

Cryptomeria Ave 旧街道杉並木

Cryptomeria Ave or 'Sugi-namiki' is a two km path between Moto-Hakone and Hakone-machi lined with cryptomeria trees planted more than 360 years ago. The path runs behind the lakeside road used by the buses and other traffic.

Old Tōkaidō Highway 旧東海道石畳

Up the hill from the lakeside Moto-Hakone bus stop is the old Tōkaidō highway, the road that once linked the ancient capital Kyoto with Edo, today the modern capital, Tokyo. It is possible to take a 3½ hour walk along the old road to Hakone-Yumoto station, passing the Amazake-jaya Teahouse, the Old Tōkaidō Road Museum and Sōun-ji Temple along the way.

HAKONE-MACHI 箱根町

Hakone-machi lies further around the lake beyond Moto-Hakone. Known in Japanese

as Hakone Sekisho-ato, the Hakone Check Point was operated by the Tokugawa Shogunate from 1619 to 1869 as a kind of medieval customs post between Edo and the rest of Japan. The present-day check point is a recent reproduction of the original. Further back towards Moto-Hakone is the **Hakone History Museum** which displays a small selection of samurai artifacts. It's open daily from 9 am to 4.30 pm, and admission is ¥200.

SPECIAL EVENTS

The Ashino-ko Kosui Matsuri, held on 31 July at Hakone-jinja Shrine near Moto-Hakone, features fireworks displays over Lake Ashino-ko. On 16 August, in the Hakone Daimonji-yaki Festival, torches are lit on Mt Myojoga-take so that they form the shape of the Chinese character for 'big' or 'great'. The Hakone Daimyō Gyoretsu Festival on 3 November is a re-enactment of a feudal lord's procession by 400 costumed locals.

PLACES TO STAY

Hakone's local popularity is reflected in the high price of most accommodation in the area. And with the exception of one remote (and not very easy to find) youth hostel and a couple of Welcome Inns, there's little in the way of alternatives.

To get to both the *Hakone Sengokuhara Youth Hostel* (☎ 0460-8966) and the *Fuji Hakone Guest House* (☎ 0460-4-6577) – they're in the same place – take a No 4 bus from Odawara station to Senkyōrō-mae bus stop (50 minutes). There is an English sign close by. Beds at the hostel cost ¥2800. The Guesthouse has singles from ¥5000 to ¥6000 and doubles from ¥10,000 to ¥12,000. A natural hot spa is available for bathing. The other Inn Group Hotel, *Moto Hakone Guesthouse* (☎ 0460-3-7880) is conveniently located in Moto-Hakone and has rates of ¥5000 per person.

The *Fujiya Hotel* (☎ 0460-2-2211) is one of Japan's earliest western-style hotels and highly rated on all fronts; room rates start at ¥25,000. The hotel is around 250m west of Miyanoshita station on the Hakone-Tōzan line.

GETTING THERE & AWAY

There are basically three ways of getting to the Hakone region: by the Odakyū express bus service from the Shinjuku bus terminal on the western side of Shinjuku station; by JR from Tokyo station; and by the private Odakyū line from Shinjuku station.

Train

JR trains run on the Tōkaidō line between Tokyo station and Odawara. Ordinary trains take 1½ hours, cost ¥1420 and run every 15 minutes or so. Limited express trains take one hour and 10 minutes and the express surcharge is ¥1430. Shinkansen do the journey in 42 minutes, cost ¥3570 and leave Tokyo station every 20 minutes.

From Shinjuku station the private Odakyū line runs into Hakone. Quickest and most comfortable is the Romance Car which takes one hour and 25 minutes and costs ¥1680 to Odawara or ¥1950 to Hakone Yumoto. There's also an express service which takes around 1½ hours and costs ¥830 to Odawara or ¥1100 to Hakone Yumoto.

At Odawara, it is possible to change to the Hakone-Tōzan line which takes you to Gōra (¥570). Alternatively, if you are already on the Odakyū line, you can continue on to Hakone-Yumoto and change to the Hakone-Tōzan line (¥340) by walking across the platform.

Bus

The Odakyū express bus service has the advantage of running directly into the Hakone region, to Lake Ashino-ko and to Hakone-machi for ¥1830. The disadvantage is that the bus trip is much less interesting than the combination of Romance Car, toy train (Hakone-Tōzan line), funicular, cablecar (ropeway) and ferry. Buses run from the west exit of Shinjuku station 11 times daily and take around two hours.

GETTING AROUND
Train

The Odakyū line offers a Hakone furii pasu (Hakone 'free pass') which costs ¥5400 in Shinjuku or ¥4050 in Odawara (which is the place to buy it if you are travelling on a JR Rail Pass) and allows you to use any mode of transport within the Hakone region for four days. The fare between Shinjuku and Hakone-Yumoto is also included in the pass, although you will have to pay a ¥850 surcharge if you want to take the Romance Car. This is a good deal for a Hakone circuit, as the pass will save you at least ¥1000 even on a one day visit to the region.

Bus

The Hakone-Tōzan bus company and Izu Hakone bus company service the Hakone area and between them they manage to link up most of the sights. If you finish up in Hakone-machi, Hakone-Tōzan buses run between here and Odawara for ¥1100. Hakone-en to Odawara costs ¥1200. Buses run from Moto-Hakone to Yumoto for ¥880 every half hour from 10 am to 3 pm.

Boat

Ferry services crisscross Lake Ashino-ko, running between Tōgendai, Hakone-machi and Moto-Hakone every 30 minutes or so for ¥1000. The 'Pirate Ship' has to be seen to be believed – tourist kitsch at its worst, but fun all the same.

Mt Fuji Area

Curiously, in a country where people have had such an impact on the landscape, Japan's most familiar symbol is a natural one, the perfectly symmetrical cone of Mt Fuji. Combine it with a shinkansen hurtling past and you have the essential picture-postcard Japan cliché. Apart from the mountain itself, the Mt Fuji area also has a series of attractive lakes around its northern side.

MT FUJI　富士山

Japan's highest mountain stands 3776m high and, when it's capped with snow in winter, it's a picture-postcard perfect volcanic cone. Fuji-san, as it's known in Japanese (*san* is the Chinese reading of the ideograph for

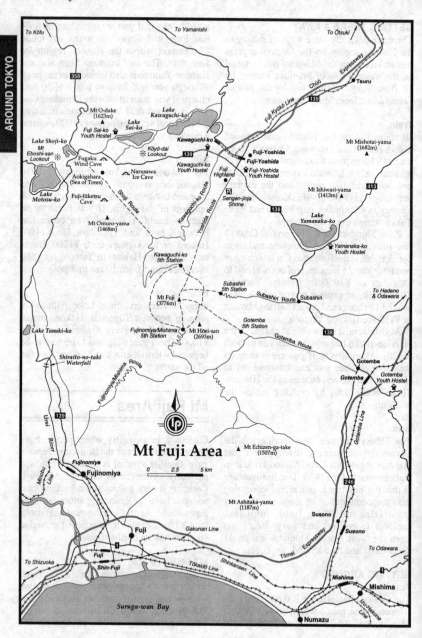

Mt Fuji Area

0   2.5   5 km

'mountain'), last blew its top in 1707 covering the streets of Tokyo with volcanic ash. On an exceptionally clear day, you can see Mt Fuji from Tokyo, 100 km away, but for much of the year you'd be pushed to see it from 100m away. Despite those wonderful postcard views, Mt Fuji is a notoriously reclusive mountain, often hidden by cloud. The views are usually best in winter and early spring, when a snow cap adds to the spectacle.

Information
Climbing Mt Fuji and *Mt Fuji & Fuji Five Lakes* brochures are available from the TIC in Tokyo, and provide exhaustive detail on transport to the mountain and how to climb it, complete with climbing schedules worked out to the minute.

During the climbing season, there is also a 24 hour taped English climbing information line on ☎ 0555-23-3000. Alternatively, contact the Fujiyoshida Tourist Information Service (☎ 0555-24-1236).

Mt Fuji Views
You can get a classic view of Mt Fuji from the shinkansen as it passes the city of Fuji. There are also good views from the Hakone area and from the Nagao Pass on the road from Hakone to Gotemba. The road that encircles the mountain offers good views, particularly near Yamanaka-ko and Sai-ko lakes.

Climbing Mt Fuji
Officially the climbing season on Fuji is July and August, and the Japanese, who love to do things 'right', pack in during those busy months. The climbing may be just as good either side of the official season, but transport services to and from the mountain are less frequent and many of the mountain huts are closed. You can actually climb Mt Fuji at any time of year, but a mid-winter ascent is strictly for experienced mountaineers.

Although everybody – from small children to grandparents – makes the ascent in season, this is a real mountain and not to be trifled with. It's just high enough for altitude sickness symptoms to be experienced and, as on any mountain, the weather on Mt Fuji can be viciously changeable. On the summit it can quickly go from clear and cold to cloudy, wet, windy, freezing cold and not just miserable but downright dangerous. Don't climb Mt Fuji without adequate clothing for cold and wet weather because even on a good day at the height of summer the temperature on top is likely to be close to freezing.

The mountain is divided into 10 'stations' from base to summit, but these days most climbers start from one of the five, fifth stations which you can reach by road. From the end of the road, it takes about 4½ hours to climb the mountain and about 2½ hours to descend. Once you're on the top, it takes about an hour to make a circuit of the crater. The Mt Fuji Weather Station on the south-western edge of the crater is on the actual summit of the mountain.

You want to reach the top at dawn – both to see the *goraiko* (sunrise) and because early morning is the time when the mountain is least likely to be shrouded in cloud. Sometimes it takes an hour or two to burn the morning mist off, however. To time your arrival for dawn you can either start up in the afternoon, stay overnight in a mountain hut and continue early in the morning, or climb the whole way at night. You do not want to arrive on the top too long before dawn, as it's likely to be very cold and windy, and if you've worked up a sweat during the climb, you'll be very uncomfortable.

Although nearly all climbers start from the fifth stations, it is possible to climb all the way up from a lower level. These low-level trails are now mainly used as short hiking routes around the base of the mountain, but gluttons for punishment could climb all the way on the Yoshida Route from Fuji-Yoshida or on the Shoji Route from near Lake Shoji-ko. There are alternative sand trails on the Kawaguchi-ko, Subashiri and Gotemba routes which you can descend very rapidly by running and *sunabashiri* (sliding), pausing from time to time to get the sand out of your shoes.

Fifth Stations There are four 'fifth stations' around Fuji and it's quite feasible to climb from one and descend to another. On the northern side of Fuji is the Kawaguchi-ko Fifth Station, at 2305m which is reached from the town of Kawaguchi-ko. This station

is particularly popular with climbers starting from Tokyo. The Yoshida route, which starts much lower down close to the town of Fuji-Yoshida, is the same as the Kawaguchi-ko route for much of the way.

The Subashiri Fifth Station is at 1980m,

Climbing Mt Fuji

I'd started out on a hot August night; at 10 pm the temperature had been around 27°C (80°F) but by 4 am it was below freezing and the wind was whistling past at what felt like hurricane speed. With a surprising number of other *gaijin* and a huge number of Japanese, I'd reached the top of Mt Fuji.

Climbing Fuji-san is definitely not heroic: in the two month 'season' as many as 180,000 people get to the top – 3000-odd every night. Nor is it that much fun – it's a bit of a dusty slog and when you get to the top it's so cold and windy that your main thought is about heading down again. But, with Fuji, the climb and the views aren't really what you do it for. To Japanese Fuji climbers, it's something of a pilgrimage; to gaijin, it's another opportunity to grapple with something uniquely Japanese.

Like many other climbers, I made my Fuji climb overnight. Although seeing the sunrise from mountaintops is a 'must do' in many places, on Fuji it is almost imperative that you arrive at dawn, as this is the one time of day when you have a good (but not guaranteed) chance of a clear view. Most of the time, the notoriously shy mountain is discreetly covered by a mantle of cloud.

So at 9.30 pm I got off the bus at the Kawaguchi-ko Fifth Station which is where the road ends and you have to start walking. I'd bought some supplies (a litre of 'Pocari Sweat' and a packet of biscuits) at a 7-eleven in the town of Kawaguchi-ko and, wearing a shirt and a coat, I was all set. The night was clear, but dark, and I was glad I'd got some new batteries for my torch before I'd left Tokyo.

My experience of climbing holy mountains is that you always get to the top too early – you work up a real sweat on the climb and then you freeze waiting for dawn. So I hung around for a while before starting out. Surprisingly, about half my fellow passengers on the bus had been gaijin, most of them a group of Americans planning on converting the Japanese to Mormonism!

By the time I reached a marker at 2390m I'd already stopped to unzip the lining from my coat, but on the rest of the climb to the top I put on more and more clothes.

Despite the daily hordes climbing the mountain, I still managed to lose the path occasionally, but by 11 pm I was past 2700m and thinking it was time to slow down even more if I wanted to avoid arriving too early. By midnight I was approaching 3000m – virtually halfway – and at this rate I was going to be at the top by 2.30 am, in line with the four hours and 35 minutes it was supposed to take, according to the tourist office leaflet! In Japan, even mountain climbing is scheduled to the minute.

It was also getting much cooler. First I added a T-shirt under my shirt, then a hat on my head, then gloves. Next I zipped the jacket lining back in place and, finally, I added a sweater to the ensemble. Although I'd started on my own, some of the other faces I met at rest stops were becoming familiar by this point and I'd fallen in with two Canadians and a Frenchman.

Huts are scattered up the mountainside, but their proprietors have been fairly cavalier about matching huts with stations: some stations have a number of huts, while others have none. The proprietors are very jealous of their facilities, and prominent signs, in English as well as Japanese, announce that even if it is pouring with rain, you can stay outside if you aren't willing to fork over the overnight fee. Fortunately, at 1.30 am we were virtually swept into one hut, probably in anticipation of the numerous bowls of *rāmen* (noodles) we would order. We hung out in this comfortable 3400m hideaway until after 3 am, when we calculated a final hour and a bit of a push would get us to the top just before the 4.30 am sunrise.

We made it and, looking back from the top, we suddenly saw hordes of climbers heading up towards us. It was no great surprise to find a souvenir shop (there is absolutely no place in Japan that tourists might get to where a souvenir shop is not already waiting for them). The sun took an interminable time to rise, but eventually it poked its head through the clouds, after which most climbers headed straight back down. I spent an hour walking around the crater rim, but I wasn't sorry to wave Fuji-san goodbye. The Japanese say you're wise to climb Fuji, but a fool to climb it twice. I've no intention of being a fool.

Tony Wheeler

and the route from there meets the Yoshida route just after the eighth station. The Gotemba Fifth Station is reached from the town of Gotemba and, at 1440m, is much lower than the other fifth stations. From the Gotemba station it takes seven to eight hours to reach the top, as opposed to the 4½ to five hours it takes on the other routes. The Fujinomiya or Mishima Fifth Station, at 2380m, is convenient for climbers coming from Nagoya, Kyoto, Osaka and western Japan. It meets the Gotemba route right at the top.

Equipment Make sure you have plenty of clothing suitable for cold and wet weather, including a hat and gloves. Bring drinking water and some snack food. If you're going to climb at night, bring a torch (flashlight). Even at night it would be difficult to get seriously lost, as the trails are very clear, but it's easy to put a foot wrong in the dark.

Mountain Huts There are 'lodges' dotted up the mountainside, but they're expensive – ¥4000 for a mattress on the floor squeezed between countless other climbers – and you don't get much opportunity to sleep anyway, as you have to be up well before dawn to start the final slog to the top. No matter how miserable the night might be, don't plan to shelter or rest in the huts without paying. The huts also prepare simple meals for their guests and for passing climbers. Camping on the mountain is not permitted.

Getting There & Away
See the following Fuji Five Lakes and Gotemba sections for transport details to Kawaguchi-ko and Gotemba, the popular arrival points for Tokyo Fuji climbers. Travellers intending to head west from the Fuji area towards Nagoya, Osaka and Kyoto can take a bus from Kawaguchi-ko or Gotemba to Mishima on the shinkansen line.

Kawaguchi-ko Route From Kawaguchi-ko, there are bus services up to the fifth station from April to mid-November. The schedule varies considerably during that period. The trip takes 55 minutes and costs

¥1700. During the peak climbing season there are buses until quite late in the evening – ideal for climbers intending to make an overnight ascent. Taxis also operate from the railway station to the fifth station for around ¥8000, plus tolls, which is not much different from the bus fare when divided among four people.

There are also direct buses from the Shinjuku bus terminal to the Kawaguchi-ko Fifth Station. These take 2½ hours and cost ¥2600. This is by far the fastest and cheapest way of getting from Tokyo to the fifth station. If you take two trains and a bus, the same trip can cost nearly ¥6000.

Subashiri Route From Subashiri, buses take 55 minutes and cost ¥1220 to the Subashiri Fifth Station. From Gotemba station they cost ¥1500.

Gotemba Route From Gotemba, buses to the Gotemba Fifth Station operate four to six times daily, but only during the climbing season. The 45 minute trip costs ¥1080.

Fujinomiya or Mishima Route The southern route up the mountain is most popular with climbers from western Japan approaching the mountain by shinkansen. Bus services run from Shin-Fuji (¥2400) and Mishima railway stations (¥2390) to the fifth station in just over two hours.

FUJI FIVE LAKES 富士五湖
The five lakes arched around the northern side of Mt Fuji are major attractions for Tokyo day-trippers and offer water sports and some good views of Mt Fuji. Very few foreign visitors to Japan make it out to the five lakes – Hakone has always been the more popular spot for views of Mt Fuji. Still, if you're planning to climb Mt Fuji, a morning or afternoon in Kawaguchi-ko and Fuji-Yoshida is worthwhile.

Yamanaka-ko is the largest of the lakes, but it doesn't offer much in the way of attractions – unless you count an enormous swan-shaped hovercraft that does 35-minute circuits of the lake for ¥900.

The town of Kawaguchi-ko is on the lake of the same name. Like Gotemba, it's a popular departure point for climbing Mt Fuji. Around 600m north of the station, on the lower eastern edge of the lake, is a cablecar (¥400 one way; ¥700 return) to the **Fuji Viewing Platform** (1104m). Buses run from the station (five minutes, ¥540).

At Fuji-Yoshida, five minutes south of Kawaguchi-ko by train, is **Sengen-jinja Shrine** which dates from 1615 (although this area is thought to have been the site of a shrine as early as 788 AD). In the days when climbing Mt Fuji was a pilgrimage and not an annual tourist event, a visit to this shrine was a necessary preliminary to the ascent. The entrance street to the shrine still has some Edo-era pilgrims' inns. From Fuji-Yoshida station take a bus to Sengen-jinja-mae (five minutes, ¥200).

The nearby **Fuji Highland** is a massive amusement park, a major attraction for day-tripping Tokyoites.

The area around the smaller Lake Sai-ko is less developed than the areas around the larger lakes. There are good views of Mt Fuji from the western end of the lake and from the **Kōyō-dai lookout** near the main road. Close to the road are the **Narusawa Ice Cave** and the **Fugaku Wind Cave**, both formed by lava flows from a prehistoric eruption of Mt Fuji. There's a bus stop at both caves or you can walk from one to the other in about 20 minutes. The **Fuji-fūketsu Cave**, further to the south, is often floored with ice.

The views of Mt Fuji from further west are not so impressive, but tiny **Lake Shoji-ko** is said to be the prettiest of the Fuji Five Lakes. Continue to Mt Eboshi-san, a one to 1½ hour climb from the road, to a lookout over what the Japanese call the **Sea of Trees** to Mt Fuji. Next is **Lake Motosu-ko**, the deepest of the lakes, while further to the south is the wide and attractive drop of the **Shiraito-no-Taki Waterfall**.

Organised Tours

In good weather, the Fuji area might be one of the few occasions in Japan that it is worth taking a tour bus. A tour bus sets off from Mishima station daily at 10 am. It takes around eight hours, visiting Gotemba, Lake Yamanaka-ko, a Fuji fifth station, the Nar-usawa ice cave, Shin-Fuji and then heads back to Mishima. It costs ¥5300. Times alter frequently, so it would be best to check with Fuji Kyūkō (☎ 0555-22-7100) before heading up there.

Places to Stay

There are a total of three youth hostels in the Fuji area: the *Fuji Yoshida* (☎ 0555-22-0533); *Kawaguchi-ko* (☎ 0555-72-1431); and *Fuji Sai-ko* (☎ 0555-82-2616). The Fuji Yoshida costs ¥2500 a night, the Kawaguchi-ko is ¥2800 and the Sai-ko is ¥2300 or ¥2450, depending on the season. The Fuji Yoshida is around one km south of Fuji Yoshida station, just off Route 139 (look out for the Lawson's on the left-hand corner if you're walking north). The Kawaguchi-ko is about 500m south-east of Kawaguchi station. The Sai-ko is on the north-eastern end of the lake of the same name, on the road that circles the lake. It conveniently has its own bus stop (Yūsu hosteru mae), and buses from Kawaguchi station take around 35 minutes (ask for Saiko Minshuku).

There are numerous hotels, ryokan, minshuku and pensions around the Fuji Five Lakes, particularly at Kawaguchi-ko. The tourist information office at the Kawaguchi-ko station can make reservations. The Japanese Inn Group is represented by the *Hotel Ashiwada* (☎ 0555-82-2321), at the western end of Lake Kawaguchi-ko, and the *Petit Hotel Ebisuya* (☎ 0555-72-0165) which is just one minute from Kawaguchi station. Rooms at the Ashiwada costs ¥7000/13,000 for singles/doubles with attached bathrooms, while those at the Ebisuya are ¥5000 per person without bathroom and ¥6000 with bathroom.

Getting There & Away

Fuji-Yoshida and Kawaguchi-ko are the two main travel centres in the Fuji Five Lakes area. Buses operate directly to Kawaguchi-ko from the Shinjuku bus terminal in the Yasuda Seimei 2nd building (stop No 50), beside the main Shinjuku station in Tokyo. The trip takes one hour and 45 minutes and there are departures up to 16 times daily at the height of the Fuji climbing season. The fare is ¥1700. Some buses continue to Yamanaka-ko and Motosu-ko lakes.

You can also get to the lakes by train, although it takes longer and costs more. JR Chūō line trains go from Shinjuku to Ōtsuki (one hour and ¥2890 by limited express; ¥1260 by local train or futsū). At Ōtsuki you cross the platform to the Fuji Kyūkō line local train which takes another hour at a cost of ¥1110 to get to Kawaguchi-ko. The train actually goes to Fuji-Yoshida first (50 minutes, ¥990), then reverses out for the final short distance to Kawaguchi-ko. On Sunday and holidays from March to November there is a direct local train from Shinjuku which takes two to 2½ hours and costs ¥2330.

From Fuji-Yoshida and Kawaguchi-ko, buses run north to Kōfu, from where you can continue north-west to Matsumoto.

Getting Around

There's a comprehensive bus network in the area, including regular buses from Fuji-Yoshida station that pass by the four smaller lakes and around the mountain to Fujinomiya (1½ hours, ¥2150) on the south-western side. From Kawaguchi-ko, there are nine to 11 buses daily making the two hour trip to Mishima (¥1470) on the shinkansen line.

North of Tokyo

North of Tokyo are the Saitama and Tochigi prefectures which include numerous places of interest, such as the old town of Kawagoe, the Chichibu-Tama National Park and the temple and shrine centre of Nikkō, one of Japan's major tourist attractions.

KAWAGOE 川越

The principal attraction in Kawagoe (population 304,000) is its warehouse merchant houses (dozōzukuri), many of which have been designated as 'national treasures'. The clay-walled buildings were built to be fireproof – by sealing them completely and leaving a candle burning inside, the buildings were starved of oxygen, leaving the fire nothing to breathe. Most of them were built after a disastrous fire swept the town in 1893 and several now operate as museums. Also in the area is **Kita-in Temple**, once a major headquarters of the Tendai sect and still an impressive sight. The Kawagoe Festival is held on 14 to 15 October; it's a boisterous affair with clashing floats and activities that go on well into the night.

Getting There & Away

The Seibu Shinjuku line from Tokyo's Seibu Shinjuku station operates to the conveniently located Hon-Kawagoe station (one hour, ¥420). Take the middle of the three roads that radiate out north of the station – most of the old buildings are along this road or on side streets off it. The Tōbu Tōjō line also runs to Kawagoe from Ikebukuro (45 minutes, ¥540), but the station is inconveniently situated a ¥1000-taxi-ride from the old part of town.

CHICHIBU-TAMA NATIONAL PARK
秩父多摩国立公園

Hikes in the Chichibu-Tama National Park are more likely to appeal to Tokyo residents than to short-term visitors to Japan. The park is divided into the Chichibu and the Oku-Tama regions – these are connected by a hiking trail that goes via Mt Mitsumine.

Chichibu Region 秩父

The Chichibu region has two walks and the famous **Chichibu-jinja Shrine** which is near Chichibu and Seibu Chichibu stations. The shorter walk starts from Yokoze station, one stop after Seibu Chichibu station. You can walk the trail as a circuit via Mt Buko-san or turn off to Urayama-guchi station via the **Hashidate Stalactite Cavern**.

Mitsumine-guchi station is the starting point for the longer walk which connects Chichibu with Oku-Tama. There is reason-

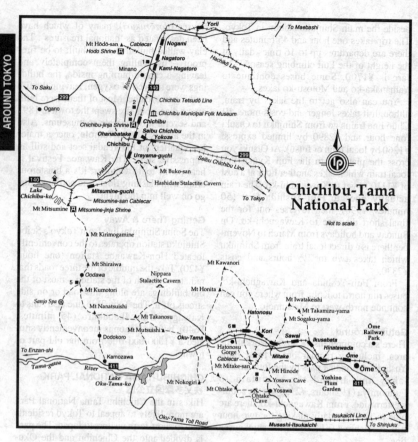

Chichibu-Tama
National Park

Not to scale

ably priced accommodation available on the trail at the *Mountain Hut Kumitori San-sō*. The trail goes past **Mitsumine-jinja Shrine**, about a 40 minute walk from the station. The shrine was founded some 2000 years ago and has long been favoured as a mountain retreat by members of the Tendai Buddhist sect. The walk takes about eight hours to Kamozawa, from where buses run to Oku-Tama station (50 minutes, ¥580).

Nagatoro Near Nagatoro station there is a rock garden and the **Nagatoro Synthetic Museum** which houses a collection of rocks

and fossils. From mid-March to mid-November, boats leave from Oyahana-bashi Bridge, 700m from Kami-Nagatoro station, to shoot the **Arakawa River rapids**. The trip lasts 50 minutes and costs ¥2600.

Places to Stay Oku-Chichibu Lake Youth Hostel (☎ 0494-55-0056) is a 15 minute walk from Lake Chichibu-ko bus stop and costs ¥2350. The *Chichibu Nagatoro SL Hotel* (☎ 0494-66-3011) is good value. It charges ¥5000 per person and is close to the Mt Hōdō-san cablecar and to Nagatoro station.

PLACES TO STAY

1 Chichibu Nagatoro SL Hotel
   秩父長瀞 SL ホテル
2 Nishichu Ryokan
   西中旅館
3 Chikujukan Ryokan
   ちくじゅかん旅館
4 Oku-Chichibu Lake Youth Hostel
   奥秩父湖ユースホステル
5 Mountain Hut Kumotori San-sō
   山小屋雲取山荘
6 People's Lodge Hatonosu-sō
   国民宿舎鳩ノ巣荘
7 Mitake Youth Hostel
   ユースホステル御嶽
8 Komadori San-sō
   駒鳥山荘

Not far from Chichibu station is the
Nishichu Ryokan (☎ 0494-22-1350), costing
¥5500 per person, with two meals. Down the
road towards Chichibu station is the more
expensive *Chikujukan Ryokan* (☎ 0494-22-
1230) which costs ¥14,000 per person, with
two meals.

Getting There & Away The cheapest and
quickest way of getting to the Chichibu area
is via the Seibu Ikebukuro line from Seibu
Ikebukuro station; ordinary services take one
hour and 48 minutes and cost ¥690. The
limited express Red Arrow service goes
direct to Seibu Chichibu station in 1½ hours
for ¥1290. Alternatively, JR trains depart
from Ueno station to Kumagaya station on
the Takasaki line (one hour and 10 minutes,
¥1090), where you will have to change to the
Chichibu Tetsudō line to continue to
Chichibu station (45 minutes, ¥720). All things
considered, unless you are travelling on a JR
rail pass, it would be cheaper to set off from
Ikebukuro even if you are based in Ueno.

Oku-Tama Region **奥多摩**
Like the Chichibu region, Oku-Tama has

some splendid mountain scenery and a few
good hiking trails.

Ōme Railway Park Steam locomotives are
on display and there is a memorial hall
housing model trains in the railway museum,
about a 15 minute walk from Ōme station. It
is open from 9 am to 4.30 pm, but closed on
Monday. Admission is ¥100.

Mitake From Mitake station it is possible to
walk via Mt Sogaku-yama and Mt Takamizu-
yama to Kori station. A shorter (one hour)
walk to Sawai station takes in Mitake Gorge
and the Gyokudo Art Museum.

Mt Mitake-san Buses run from Mitake
station to the Mt Mitake-san cablecar terminus
(¥270), from where a cablecar (one-way ¥560;
return ¥1070) takes you close to the summit.
About 30 minutes on foot from the cablecar
terminus on Mt Mitake-san is **Mitake-jinja
Shrine**, said to date back some 1200 years.

Other Attractions Buses run from Oku-
Tama station to the nearby artificial Lake
Oku-Tama-ko (¥330). The **Nippara Stalac-
tite Cavern** is 30 minutes by bus from
Oku-Tama station (¥470).

Places to Stay The *Mitake Youth Hostel*
(☎ 0428-78-8774) is very close to the Mt
Mitake-san cablecar terminus and charges
¥2600 per person. About a 15 minute walk
from the cablecar terminus in the opposite
direction from the youth hostel is the
Komadori San-sō (☎ 0428-78-8472) which
costs ¥4500 to ¥5000 per person. The
People's Lodge Hatonosu-sō (☎ 0428-85-
2340) charges ¥4500 per person or around
¥7000 with two meals, and is a short walk
from Hatonosu station.

A good alternative if you're in the area for
the hiking is the *Mountain Hut Kumitori
San-sō* (☎ 0485-23-3311), with a per-person
charge of ¥5000 with meals – there are
cheaper rates without them, but in this neck
of the woods you will need to bring your own
food or forage for berries. The hut is a few

hours up the trail that connects the Chichibu and Oku-Tama regions.

Getting There & Away You can get to Oku-Tama by taking the JR Chūō line from Shinjuku station to Tachikawa station (¥430) and changing there to the JR Ōme line which will take you on to Oku-Tama station (¥590). The first leg takes 40 minutes and the second leg 70 minutes.

NIKKŌ 日光

Nikkō is not only one of the most popular day trips from Tokyo, it's also one of Japan's major tourist attractions due to its splendid shrines and temples. It's worth trying to slot Nikkō into even the most whirlwind tour of Japan.

History

Nikkō's history as a sacred site stretches back to the middle of the 8th century, when the Buddhist priest Shōdō (735-817) established a hermitage there. For many years it was a famous training centre for Buddhist monks, before declining into obscurity. That is until it was chosen as the site for the mausoleum of Tokugawa Ieyasu, the warlord who took control of all Japan and established the shogunate which ruled for 250 years until the Meiji Restoration ended the feudal era.

Tokugawa Ieyasu was laid to rest among Nikkō's towering cedars in 1617, but it was his grandson Tokugawa Iemitsu who commenced work in 1634 on the shrine that can be seen today. The original Tōshō-gū Shrine was completely rebuilt using a huge army of some 15,000 artisans from all over Japan.

The work on the shrine and mausoleum took two years to complete and the results continue to receive mixed reviews. In contrast with the minimalism that is generally considered the essence of Japanese art, every available nook and cranny of Ieyasu's shrine and mausoleum is crowded with detail. Animals, mythical and otherwise, jostle for your attention from among the glimmering gold-leaf and red lacquerwork. The walls are decorated with intricate patterning, coloured relief carvings and paintings of, among other things, flowers, dancing girls, mythical

beasts and Chinese sages. The overall effect is more Chinese than Japanese. It's a grand spectacle no matter what the critics say.

Tōshō-gū was constructed as a memorial to a warlord who devoted his life to conquering Japan. Tokugawa Ieyasu was a man of considerable determination and was not above sacrificing a few scruples in order to achieve his aims. He is attributed with having had his wife and eldest son executed because, at a certain point, it was politically expedient for him to do so in order to ingratiate himself with other feudal powers. More than anything else, the grandeur of Nikkō is intended to inspire awe; it is a display of wealth and power by a family that for nearly three centuries was the supreme arbiter of power in Japan.

Orientation & Information

First stop in Nikkō should be the Kyōdo Center which has an excellent tourist information office (☎ 0288-53-3795). The office has a wealth of useful pamphlets and maps. There is another, less informative, tourist information office (☎ 0288-53-4511) in Tōbu-Nikkō station.

It's a 30 minute walk uphill from the JR and Tōbu stations to the shrine area. Bus No 1, 2, 3 or 4 goes to the Shin-kyō bus stop for ¥190.

Hikers should pick up a copy of *Nikko-Yumoto-Chuzenji Area Hiking Guide*. It costs ¥150, is available from some of the pensions in the area as well as at the information counters in Nikkō, and has maps and information on local flora and fauna.

Tickets Ticketing arrangements for the sights in Nikkō are more organised than they used to be, though there's still room for confusion. Basically it works like this: Rinnō-ji Temple costs ¥850; Tōshō-gū Shrine costs ¥1250; and Futara-san-jinja Shrine costs ¥300. In the interests of saving a few yen, the best idea is to buy a 'two-shrines-one-temple' ticket *(nisha-ichijikōtsū-baikan-ken)* for ¥900. This covers all three of the above sights, with the one exception that it doesn't include entry to the Nemuri-Neko (sleeping cat) in Tōshō-gū Shrine, a

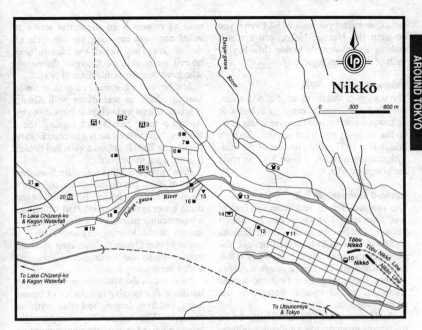

Nikkō

0   300   600 m

To Lake Chūzenji-ko
& Kegon Waterfall

To Lake Chūzenji-ko
& Kegon Waterfall

Daiya-gawa River

Daiya-gawa River

To Utsunomiya
& Tokyo

Tōbu
Nikkō

Nikkō

Tōbu Nikkō Line

Nikkō Line

PLACES TO STAY		
4	Nikkō Pension Green Age Inn 日光ペンション グリーンエイジ INN	
6	Hotel Seikoen ホテル清晃苑	
7	Nikkō Tōkan-sō Ryokan 日光ユースホステル	
8	Nikkō Tōkan-sō 日光東館荘	
9	Nikkō Youth Hostel 日光ユースホステル	
13	Nikkō Daiyagawa Youth Hostel 日光大谷川ユース ホステル	

16	Nikkō Kanaya Hotel 日光金谷ホテル
18	Turtle Inn Nikkō タートルイン日光
19	Annex Turtle Hotori-an アネックスタートル ほとり庵
21	Nikkō Green Hotel 日光グリーンホテル

PLACES TO EAT	
11	Yōrō-no-Taki 養老の滝
15	Yakitori Bar 焼き鳥屋

OTHER	
1	Taiyūn-byō Shrine 大猷院廟
2	Futara-san-jinja Shrine 二荒山神社
3	Tōshō-gū Shrine 東照宮
5	Rinnō-ji Temple 輪王寺
10	Bus Terminal バスターミナル
12	Kōdo Center
14	Post Office 郵便局
17	Shin-kyō Bridge 神橋
20	Nikkō Museum 日光博物館

sight that will set you back ¥430. Even if you do visit the Nemuri-Neko, you are still making a considerable saving than buying each of the tickets separately.

Shin-kyō Bridge 神橋

The story goes that the monk, Shōdō Shōnin, who first established a hermitage in Nikkō in 782, was carried across the river at this point on the backs of two huge serpents. Today's bridge is a 1907 reconstruction of the mid-17th century original. It costs ¥300 to cross the bridge on foot.

Rinnō-ji Temple 輪王寺

The original Tendai sect Rinnō-ji Temple was founded 1200 years ago by Shōdō Shōnin. The Sambutsu-dō (Three Buddha Hall) has huge gold-lacquered images, the most impressive of which is the *senjū* (1000 armed Kannon). The central image is Amida Nyorai, flanked by *batō* (a horse-headed Kannon), whose special domain is the animal kingdom.

The Hōmutsu-den (Treasure Hall), also on the temple grounds, has a collection of treasures associated with the temple, but admission (¥300) is not included in the two-shrines-one-temple ticket.

Tōshō-gū Shrine 東照宮

A huge stone torii marks the entrance to Tōshō-gū Shrine, while to the left is a five storey pagoda, originally dating from 1650, but reconstructed in 1818. The pagoda has no foundations and is said to contain a long suspended pole that swings like a pendulum, restoring equilibrium in the event of an earthquake.

The true entrance to the shrine is through the torii at the Omote-mon Gate, protected on either side by Deva kings. Directly through the entrance are the **Sanjinko** (Three Sacred Storehouses). On the upper storey of the last storehouse are imaginative relief carvings of elephants by an artist who famously had never seen the real thing. To the left of the entrance is the **Shinkyūsha** (Sacred Stable), a suitably plain building housing a carved white horse. The stable's

only adornment is an allegorical series of **relief carvings** depicting the life-cycle of the monkey. They include the famous 'hear no evil, see no evil, speak no evil' threesome who have become emblematic of Nikkō.

Just beyond the stable is a granite water font at which, in accordance with Shinto practice, worshippers cleanse themselves by washing their hands and rinsing their mouths. Next to the gate is a **sacred library** containing 7000 Buddhist scrolls and books; it is not open to the public.

Pass through another torii, climb another flight of stairs, and on the left and right are a drum tower and a belfry. To the left of the drum tower is the **Honji-dō Hall** which has a huge ceiling painting of a dragon in flight known as the Roaring Dragon. There's a queue to stand beneath the dragon and clap hands – do so and the dragon will respond with a perfunctory roar.

Next comes the **Yōmei-mon Gate** which bustles with a teeming multitude of Chinese sages, children, dragons and other mythical creatures. Worrying that its perfection might arouse envy in the gods, the final supporting pillar on the left-hand side was placed upside down as a deliberate error.

Through the Yōmei-mon Gate and to the right is the Nemuri-neko (Sleeping Cat). The **Sakashita-mon Gate** here opens onto a path that climbs up through towering cedars to **Ieyasu's tomb**, a relatively simple affair. If you are using the two-shrines-one-temple ticket it will cost an extra ¥430 to see the cat and the tomb. To the left of the Yōmei-mon Gate is the **Jinyōsha**, a storage depot for Nikkō's mikoshi (portable shrines) which come into action during the May and October festivals. The **Honden** (Main Hall) and the **Haiden** (Hall of Worship) can also be seen in the enclosure.

Futara-san-jinja Shrine 二荒山神社

Shōdō Shōnin founded this shrine. It's dedicated to the mountain Nantai, the mountain's consort Nyotai and their mountainous progeny Tarō. It's essentially a repeat performance of Tōshō-gū Shrine on a smaller scale, but worth a visit all the same.

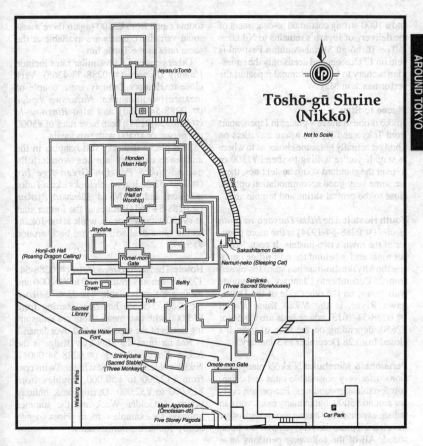

Tōshō-gū Shrine
(Nikkō)

Not to Scale

Ieyasu's Tomb

Honden
(Main Hall)

Haiden
(Hall of
Worship)

Jinyōsha

Steps

Sakashitamon Gate

Honji-dō Hall
(Roaring Dragon Ceiling)

Yōmei-mon
Gate

Nemuri-neko (Sleeping Cat)

Drum
Tower

Belfry

Sanjinko
(Three Sacred Storehouses)

Torii

Sacred
Library

Granite Water
Font

Shinkyūsha
(Sacred Stable)
('Three Monkeys')

Omote-mon Gate

Walking Paths

Main Approach
(Omotesan-dō)

Five Storey Pagoda

Car Park

Taiyūin-byō Shrine 大猷院廟

The Taiyūin-byō enshrines Ieyasu's grandson Iemitsu (1604-51) and is very much a smaller version of Tōshō-gū Shrine. The smaller size gives it a less extravagant air and it has been suggested that it is more aesthetically worthy than its larger neighbour – this is best left for the experts to quibble over. Many of the features to be seen in the Tōshō-gū are replicated on a smaller scale: the storehouses, drum tower and Chinese gate for example. The shrine also has a wonderful setting in a quiet grove of cryptomeria. Entry is included in the two-shrines-one-temple ticket.

Special Events

The Gohan Shiki on 2 April is a rice harvesting festival held at Rinnō-ji Temple in which men (in days past, samurai lords) are forced to eat great quantities of rice in a tribute to the bounty supplied by the gods. Sacred dances are also performed at the festival by priests.

On 16 and 17 April the Yayoi Matsuri – a procession of portable shrines – is held at Futāra-san-jinja Shrine.

The Tōshō-gū Shrine Grand Festival on 17 and 18 May is Nikkō's most important annual festival. It features horseback archery and a 1000-strong costumed re-enactment of the delivery of Ieyasu's remains to Nikkō.

The Tōshō-gū Shrine Autumn Festival is held on 17 October and needs only the equestrian archery to be an autumnal repeat of the performance in May.

Places to Stay

Nikkō is one of the few places in Japan, apart from Tokyo and Kyoto, where travellers on a budget actually get some choice as to where to stay. If you're willing to spend ¥1500 or so over the standard youth hostel rates, there are some very good accommodation options close to the central shrine and temple area.

Youth Hostels The *Nikkō Daiyagawa Youth Hostel* (☎ 0288-54-1974) is the more popular of the town's two hostels. It costs ¥2600 per night and is behind the post office opposite the Shyakusho-mae bus stop. It's closed from 25 December to 1 January. A 10 minute walk away, on the other side of the Daiyagawa River, is the *Nikkō Youth Hostel* (☎ 0288-54-1013) where beds are ¥2450 or ¥2650, depending on the time of year. It's closed from 28 December to 3 January.

Pensions & Minshuku Nikkō's many pensions offer very reasonable rates and clean, comfortable surroundings. Per-person costs are around ¥5000, but in many cases you can reduce expenses by sharing rooms with other travellers. Nikkō is very popular so book ahead. All of the following pensions have someone who can answer your questions in English.

One of the more popular pensions in Nikkō is the *Turtle Inn Nikkō* (☎ 0288-53-3168) with rooms from ¥3900 to ¥5000 per person without bath and from ¥4700 to ¥5800 with bath (prices vary seasonally). Meals are also available at ¥1000 for breakfast and ¥2000 for dinner. From the station, take a bus to the Sōgō-kaikan-mae bus stop, backtrack around 50m to the fork in the road and follow the river for around five minutes. Further west, over the river, but on the same road, is the *Annex Turtle Hotori-An* (☎ 0288-53-3663), where Japanese and western-style

rooms range from ¥5200 (again there's seasonal variation); meals are available at the same rates as the Turtle Inn.

Other pensions with similar rates include *Humpty Dumpty* (☎ 0288-53-4365). Very close to Humpty Dumpty are a couple of inexpensive minshuku: *Narusawa Lodge* (☎ 0288-54-1630) and also *Ringo-no-Ie* (☎ 0288-53-0131); both have rates of ¥5000 per person or ¥6500 with two meals.

Two places that take full honours in the ambience category are the wonderfully named *Nikkō Pension Green Age Inn* (☎ 0288-53-3636), which looks like a Tudor mansion, and the *Nikkō Tōkan-sō Ryokan* (☎ 0288-54-0611). Rates at the former start at ¥9800 with two meals, while at the Tōkan-sō the same deal will set you back around ¥15,000.

Hotels The *Nikkō Green Hotel* (☎ 0288-54-1756) has rooms from ¥6500 to ¥18,000 and meals are also available. The *Hotel Seikoen* (☎ 0288-53-5555) has rates starting from ¥13,000 with two meals. Both are uninspiring hotels of the type found all over Japan.

Not far from the Shin-kyō Bridge is the *Nikkō Kanaya Hotel* (☎ 0288-54-0001), Nikkō's oldest and classiest hotel. Twins cost from ¥12,000 to ¥50,000, doubles from ¥15,000 to ¥32,000. During peak holiday periods – Golden Week and the summer holidays for example – room prices soar to nearly double the normal rates.

Places to Eat

Many travellers staying in Nikkō prefer to eat at their hostel or pension, but there are also a number of places on the main road between the stations and the shrine area. Across the road from the fire station is a branch of the izakaya chain *Yōrō-no-Taki* which has cheap beer and a good selection of snacks and meals. Further up, close to the Shin-kyō Bridge, is a great little *yakitori bar* – look for the entrance scrawled with English recommendations. It seems that countless travellers have been won over by the charm of the old lady who runs this place and the great food she prepares. There's an English menu and meals start at an economical ¥300 – try the yaki-udon, a bargain at only ¥500. This place closes early at around 7 pm. In the shrine area itself there are a couple of shops selling tourist trinkets and quite reasonable food – they'll even provide an English menu if you look like you are having difficulties.

Getting There & Away

The best way to visit Nikkō is via the Tōbu-Nikkō line from Asakusa station in Tokyo. The station is in the basement of the Tōbu Department Store, but is well signposted and easy to find from the subway. Limited express trains cost ¥2690 and take one hour and 55 minutes. A reservation is required (on a quiet day you'll probably be able to organise this before boarding the train). Trains run every 30 minutes or so from 7.30 to 10 am; after 10 am they run hourly. Rapid trains require no reservation, take 15 minutes longer than the limited express and cost ¥1300. They run once an hour from 6.20 am to 4.30 pm. Tickets can be purchased at the automatic vending machines.

Travelling by JR is costly and time-consuming – it's really only of interest to those on a Japan Rail Pass. The quickest way would be to take the shinkansen from Ueno to Utsunomiya (53 minutes, ¥4510) and change there for an ordinary train (no other options) for the 45 minute, ¥720 journey to Nikkō. The trains from Utsunomiya to Nikkō leave on average once every half hour. Not all Nikkō line trains run the full distance to Nikkō – you may have to get off at an intermediate station and wait for the next Nikkō-bound train.

Nikkō-Kinugawa Free Pass Unlike the Hakone pass, the Nikkō pass doesn't pay if you are day-tripping out of Tokyo. The ticket is valid for four days, costs ¥5710 and is available from Tōbu railways in Asakusa. It includes transport from Asakusa to Nikkō (but not the express surcharge) and all bus costs between Nikkō and Chūzenji, Yumoto Onsen, Kunigawa, Kirifuri Plateau and Lake Ikari-ko (see the Around Nikkō section for more information on these destinations).

AROUND NIKKŌ

Nikkō is part of the Nikkō National Park, which covers 1402 sq km, sprawling over Fukushima, Tochigi, Gunma and Niigata prefectures. It is a mountainous area, complete with extinct volcanoes, lakes, waterfalls and marshlands. There are good hiking opportunities in the area and some remote hot-spring resorts.

The main attractions around Nikkō are Lake Chūzenji-ko, Yumoto Onsen, Kinugawa Onsen and the marshlands around Lake Ozenuma. The latter and Yumoto Onsen offer some good hiking opportunities.

Lake Chūzenji-ko　中禅寺湖

Chūzenji-ko is chiefly a scenic attraction and it's probably not worth cutting short your visit to the Nikkō shrines in order to see it. If you have plenty of time, however, then the lake and the 97m **Kegon Waterfall** are definitely worth visiting. The waterfall features an elevator (¥520 return) down to a platform where you can observe the full force of the plunging water. Also worth a visit is a third **Futara-san-jinja Shrine**, complementing the ones in the Tōshō-gū Shrine area and on Mt Nantai.

For good views of the lake and Kegon Waterfall, the Akechidaira bus stop (the stop before Chūzenji Onsen) has a cablecar up to a viewing platform (¥620 return). From this point, it is a pleasant 1.5 km walk up to the lake area. In **Chūzenji Onsen** there is another cablecar up to the **Chanoki-daira viewing platform** (¥440 one way).

As you might expect, Lake Chūzenji-ko has the usual flotilla of cruise boats all clamouring to part you from your yen. The lake, which reaches a depth of 161m, is a fabulous shade of deep blue in good weather conditions and this, along with the mountainous backdrop, makes for a pleasant cruise. An alternative to the cruises is the rowboats that are available for ¥1000 per hour.

Just by the Chūzenji Onsen cablecar is the hi-tech **Nikkō Nature Museum**. It has displays and films on the Nikkō region's flora and fauna, though none of it will be particularly accessible to those people who don't understand Japanese. Entry is ¥800 and it's open daily from 9 am to 5 pm (closed the fourth Wednesday of every month).

See the Yumoto Onsen entry for information on the Senjōgahara Hiking Course from Lake Chūzenji-ko to Yumoto.

Places to Stay The *Chūzenji Pension* (☎ 0288-55-0888) charges from ¥9500 per person, with two meals. To find it from the Nikkō-Chūzenji road, turn left at the lakeside, cross the bridge and look out for the pension on the left about 100m down the road. West of here, on the northern side of the lake, is the *Pension Friendly* (☎ 0288-55-0027), where a room with two meals costs ¥8500 per person.

Getting There & Away Buses from the Nikkō station area to Chuzenji Onsen take 50 minutes and cost ¥1100.

Yumoto Onsen　湯元温泉
From Chūzenji-ko, you might continue on to the quieter hot-spring resort of **Yumoto Onsen** by bus (30 minutes, ¥840) or alternatively you can hike there in three or four hours from Ryūzu Falls on the central northern part of Lake Chūzenji-ko.

The Chūzenji-ko-Yumoto hike takes around three hours and is known as the Senjōgahara Shizen Kenkyū-ro (literally the 'Battlefield Plateau Natural Research Road'). From Chūzenji Onsen, Yumoto-bound buses stop at Ryūzu Falls (¥250). It's not particularly challenging, but if you're doing it in the summer months bring a hat, a supply of water and cover yourself with sun protection, as there's little in the way of shade for most of the walk. The walk follows the Yu-gawa River to Lake Yumoto-ko (look out for the 75m Yu Falls in this area), where it wends around the western edge of the lake to Yumoto. From Yumoto, you can catch a bus back to Nikkō (1½ hours, ¥1650).

Kinugawa Onsen & Nikkō Edo Village　鬼怒川温泉・日光江戸村
South-east of Nikkō on the Tōbu Kinugawa line are Kinugawa Onsen and the Nikkō Edo

Village. Kinugawa is a hotel-packed onsen town that owes its existence entirely to tourism and the Japanese love of soaking in hot water. To get there from Nikkō, you will need to backtrack one station on the Tōbu line and change trains for the Tōbu Kinugawa line.

The nearby Edo Village may be of interest to those with children. It's an imaginative recreation of an Edo-period village, with samúrai quarters, a 'temple of hell', ninja displays and even a 'ninja maze' – visitors are recommended to 'call out for help' if they get trapped. The village is open daily from 9 am to 4 pm (3 pm from December to March) and entry is ¥3200. There are shuttle buses running from Kinugawa Onsen station to the village for ¥410.

Lake Ozenuma　尾瀬沼
The high marshlands (Ozegahara; 1400m) around Lake Ozenuma are the largest of their kind in Japan, covering an area of around eight sq km. The area is noted for its birdlife and wildflowers (in particular the *mizubashō* or skunk cabbage). As interesting as this area sounds, getting out there takes some determination and some Japanese language skill probably wouldn't go astray either. Public transport in this neck of the woods is woefully infrequent or absent altogether – the Japanese all have cars, after all.

The best bet for getting into the Oze region is to start from Nemuta in Gunma prefecture, rather than from Nikkō. From Nemuta station (Jōetsu line) there are regular buses to Ōshimizu (two hours, ¥2100), one of the main trailheads for hikes into the region. There are inexpensive huts to stay in on the hiking trails.

MASHIKO　益子
Mashiko is a centre for country-style pottery, with about 50 potters, some of whom you can see working at their kilns. The town achieved fame when the potter Hamada Shōji (1894-1978) settled there and, from 1930, produced his Mashiko pottery. His influence brought a legion of other potters to Mashiko, many of them foreign. The noted English potter

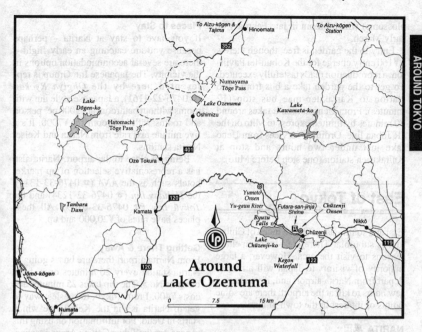

Around
Lake Ozenuma

Bernard Leach worked in Mashiko for several years.

Mashiko's kilns are spread out over quite a wide area and getting to see them requires a lot of footwork. Pick up the *Tourist Map of Mashiko* from the tourist information counter at Utsunomiya station (see the following Getting There & Away section) or from TIC in Tokyo before you go. **Hamada House** and **Tsukamoto kiln** (☎ 0285-72-3223) are recommended, but bear in mind that there are some 300 kilns in the area and you could literally spend weeks seeking them out.

Hamada House has both wood-fired kilns and modern automated contraptions, and visitors can play around with the machinery themselves. One hour introductory courses are available at Tsukamoto Kiln for ¥3570, but a reservation is required. The **Mashikoyaki Kyōhan Centre** (☎ 0285-72-4444) also has one-hour courses, but firing of any items made takes a month.

Getting There & Away

It is possible to combine Mashiko with a visit to Nikkō if you set off from Tokyo very early and use the JR route. See the Nikkō Getting There & Away section for travel details to Utsunomiya. From Utsunomiya Tōbu station, buses run regularly during the day to Mashiko, taking one hour and costing ¥1150 one way. Ask at the tourist information counter outside Utsunomiya station for instructions on getting to the bus stop and bus times. This office also has tourist maps of Mashiko.

MITO 水戸

The capital of Ibaraki prefecture, Mito (population 234,000) was once a castle town. Today its only notable attraction is **Kairaku-en Garden**, one of Japan's three most celebrated landscape gardens (the other two are Kenroku-en in Kanazawa and Kōraku-en in Okayama). The 18-acre gardens date back to 1842 and are popular for their *ume* (plum blossoms) which bloom in late February or early March.

Entry to the garden is free, though there's a ¥160 entry charge for the Kobun-tei Pavillion, a reproduction that's tastefully executed. To get to the garden take a bus from Mito station to Kairakuen-mae bus stop (12 minutes). From Ueno station it takes around 80 minutes by limited express to Mito on the JR Jōban line. Ordinary services from Ueno take just under two hours and stop at Kairaku-en station (one stop before Mito).

East of Tokyo

East and south-east of Tokyo much of Chiba-ken is suburbia. There are few compelling reasons to visit the area. However, a large majority of visitors to Japan will arrive or depart from Narita airport and, if you have a few hours to kill at the airport, there are some points of interest in the town of Narita.

NARITA 成田
If you're not going to the airport, the only real reason to go to Narita is to visit **Narita-san Shinshō-ji Temple**. While the temple was founded some 1000 years ago, the main hall is a 1968 reconstruction. The temple itself remains an important centre of the Shingon sect of Buddhism and attracts as many as 10 million visitors a year.

If you've got to kill time in the airport area, there's also the **Museum of Aeronautical Sciences** as well as the **Chiba Prefectural Botanical Garden**, both right beside the airport. There's a brochure *For Passengers Transiting at Narita* about the airport vicinity attractions, and tours are operated from the airport.

Special Events
The main festivals centred on Narita-san Shinshō-ji Temple are Setsubun, on 3 or 4 February, and the Year End Festival, on 25 December. Things get very hectic at the temple on both these occasions and a high tolerance level for crowds is a must.

Places to Stay
If you have to stay at Narita – perhaps because you are catching an early flight – there are several accommodation options in the vicinity. The Japanese Inn Group is represented here by the *Ohgiya Ryokan* (☎ 0476-22-1161), a Japanese-style inn with rooms without bathroom at ¥5000 per person and rooms with bathroom for ¥7000. It's a five minute taxi ride from Narita and Keisei Narita stations.

Being so close to the airport, Narita also has a representative selection of up-market hotels such as the *ANA* (☎ 0476-33-1311), the *Holiday Inn* (☎ 0476-32-1234) and the *Tokyū Inn* (☎ 0476-33-0109). All these places have rates of ¥20,000 and up.

Getting There & Away
From Narita airport there are buses going to Narita station every 20 minutes or so from bus gate No 5. The trip takes 25 minutes and costs ¥400. From Tokyo, the easiest way to get to Narita is via the Keisei line which starts in Ueno. For information on using this service, see the Tokyo Getting Around section.

BŌSŌ-HANTŌ PENINSULA 房総半島
The Bōsō-hantō is a popular get-away for Tokyo residents, but a low priority for foreign travellers. Swimming and beaches are chief among the attractions, but if the weather is even close to good enough for fun at the beach you can expect big crowds. **Minami Chikura Beach** and **Setohama Beach** are surfing centres in the months of July and August.

Among Japanese, the peninsula is noted for displays by **women divers** at Shira-hama and Onjuku beaches. Traditionally the women dived to the sea bottom in search of edible goodies such as shellfish and seaweed; it's a tourist event nowadays.

Places to Stay
The Bōsō-hantō Peninsula has an abundance of minshuku and youth hostels. Youth hostels include the *Kujūkurihama Youth Hostel* (☎ 0475-33-2254; ¥2800) at Awa-Amatsu,

and the *Tateyama Youth Hostel* (☎ 0470-28-0073; ¥1770) at Cape Nojima-zaki.

Getting There & Away
Train The Bōsō-hantō Peninsula can be reached on either the JR Sotobō line which runs from Tokyo to the eastern edge of the peninsula, or the JR Uchibō line which runs to the Tokyo Bay western edge of the peninsula. The two lines effectively meet at the bottom of the peninsula at Tateyama. Local trains from Tokyo station to Tateyama cost ¥2160 and take two hours and 50 minutes; limited express services take two hours and cost ¥4000.

Boat Ferries run from Kawasaki's Ukushima Port to Kisarazu approximately every 45 minutes; they take 65 minutes to Kisarazu and cost ¥1030.

Getting Around
The transport network around the peninsula is very good. Most of the beaches are serviced by JR trains; there is also a private line that cuts across the peninsula from Goi to Ōhara, as well as a good network of local buses.

South-West of Tokyo

South-west of Tokyo are the cities of Kawasaki and Yokohama which have virtually merged with the capital to create one immense urban corridor. Beyond is the fascinating old town of Kamakura, and the Miura-hantō Peninsula.

KAWASAKI 川崎
Kawasaki (population 1.17 million) is a sprawling industrial port city, partly built on land reclaimed from Tokyo Bay. Its attractions can be summed up in the **Kawasaki Daishi Temple** and the **Nihon Minka-en Garden**.

Kawasaki Daishi Temple 川崎大師
Formerly known as Heigen-ji Temple, Kawasaki Daishi temple has a long pedigree (legend has it founded in 1127) and is a little like Kawasaki's answer to Sensō-ji Temple in Asakusa, Tokyo. Like Sensō-ji, Kawasaki Daishi houses an image that was fished from the water – this time the sea. The image is one of Kōbō Daishi, the founder of the Shingon sect, to which the temple is affiliated.

The temple is well worth a visit as there are interesting shops nearby, an impressive five-storey pagoda and very few foreign tourists about – in fact you'll be lucky to see any. Entry is free.

Nihon Minka-en Garden 日本民家園
The Nihon Minka-en Garden is an open-air museum with 22 traditional Japanese buildings collected from the surrounding countryside and reassembled on one site to give visitors a glimpse of the way of life of an older Japan. Most of the structures are farmhouses, although there is also a Shinto shrine and a kabuki stage. The oldest of the buildings dates back to 1688.

Entry is ¥300. The garden is open daily from 9.30 am to 4 pm (except Monday).

Special Events
Kawasaki hosts the famous Jibeta Matsuri in which processions of costumed locals parade wooden phalluses to celebrate the vanquishing of a sharp-toothed demon. The demon had taken up residence in a fair maiden and had already emasculated two bridegrooms before a local blacksmith came up with the ingenious idea of deflowering the maiden with an iron phallus. History doesn't record the maiden's feelings about this solution, but defeat of the demon gave rise to much celebration and an annual re-enactment of the forging of the metal phallus. Freudians are welcome.

The festival takes place in the late afternoon of 15 April, starting with a procession, followed by a re-enactment of the forging and rounded off with a banquet. The action takes place close to Kawasaki Daishi station.

Getting There & Away
For the Nihon Minka-en Garden, take an Odakyū line train from Shinjuku station to Mukōgaoka-yuen station (20 minutes,

¥230). For Kawasaki Daishi Temple, take the Keihin Tōhoku line from Tokyo station to Kawasaki (20 minutes, ¥290) and change there for the Daishi line – Kawasaki Daishi station is just three stops away (¥130). From Yokohama it takes just 20 minutes to Kawasaki (¥290) on the Keihin Tōhoku line.

YOKOHAMA 横浜

The site of present-day Yokohama (population 3.22 million) was little more than mud flats 150 years ago. Today it's Japan's largest port and second largest city. Its fortunes are very much those of modern Japan. It was opened to foreign trade in 1858; in 1872 Japan's first railway line was laid, connecting the city with Tokyo; by the early 20th century the city had embarked on a course of industrialisation. Nowadays its port facilities are complemented by massive steel-making, automobile, oil-refining and chemical industries.

Effectively, Yokohama forms a vast continuous conurbation with Tokyo and in many ways it's simply a far-flung satellite of the capital city. For the Japanese, however, Yokohama's proximity to the sea and its international associations as a trading port have bestowed upon it a certain cosmopolitan sheen and made it a popular sightseeing destination.

Yokohama's main attractions are its harbour, a lively Chinatown, the Sankei-en Garden and new developments associated with the Landmark Tower.

Orientation & Information

Arriving in Yokohama can be slightly confusing. Most of the sights are quite a way from Yokohama station and it makes more sense to go to Sakuragi-chō or Kannai stations. From Sakuragi-chō station the Minato Mirai 21 development area is a five minute elevator ride away. From the Minato Mirai 21 area it's possible to walk to Yamashita Park in around 25 minutes, but it's a dull experience and you'd be better off taking a train one stop to Kannai station. The latter is close to the park, the harbour area, Chinatown and a number of other sights such as the Silk Museum and the Foreigners' Cemetery.

The Yokohama International Tourist Association (☎ 045-641-4759) and also the Kanagawa Prefectural Tourist Association (☎ 045-681-0007) are both on the ground floor of the same building that houses the Silk Museum. Both offices have at least one staff member who speaks English. The best of the give-away brochures is the *Yokohama City Guide* – *Yokohama Paradise*. The Minato Mirai 21 complex also has a tourist office, but no English is spoken.

Yokohama Station Area

The Yokohama station area is given over unrelentingly to shopping. Its only real attraction is the **Hiraki Ukiyoe Museum** which has a collection of over 8000 woodblock prints, both old and new, on the 6th floor of the Sogo department store – yes, the largest department store in the world. Entry is ¥500. The museum is open daily from 10 am to 7 pm (except Tuesday). Sogo is close to the east exit of Yokohama station.

Minato Mirai 21 みなとみらい21

This new development (the '21' stands for '21st century') just north of Sakuragi-chō station is another of those Japanese excursions into the metropolis-of-the-future theme. The whole thing won't be completed until the year 2000, but there's a fair bit to be ogled at already. One of the highlights is the new **Landmark Tower** which not only is the tallest building in Japan, but also has the world's fastest lift (45 km/hr). The inevitable viewing platform is on the 70th floor and it's open from 10 am to 9 pm (10 pm Saturday and every day during July and August); entry is ¥1000.

Clustered around the Landmark Tower are a number of ho-hum attractions. Probably the pick of the lot is the **Yokohama Maritime Museum** and *Nippon Maru* sailing ship. Entry is ¥600. It's open daily from 10 am to 5 pm (except Monday). The **Yokohama Museum of Art** is devoted to modern art and costs ¥500. It's open daily from 10 am to 5 pm (except Thursday). **Yokohama Cosmo World** is an amusement park with the world's largest ferris wheel (it also functions as a clock which probably makes it the world's largest clock as well). Entry is free, but rides range from ¥100 to ¥600. It's open from 1 to 9 pm weekdays, 11 am to 10 pm weekends and is closed on Monday. Some visitors might also want to check out the Minato Mirai 21 **Yokohama Pavilion**, a five-part complex that is fairly dull for the most part but has a miniature version of 21st century Yokohama called Yokohama Gulliver Land. The complex is open from 9 am to 5 pm daily and is free.

Yamashita-kōen Park Area　山下公園

This area, north-east of Kannai station, is traditionally Yokohama's sightseeing district. At the heart of it all is the decidedly dowdy Yamashita-kōen Park – its only genuine claim on your attention is the fact that it commands a harbourfront view.

Another possible diversion is the **Silk Museum** which takes you on a tour of the world of silk and silk production with characteristic Japanese thoroughness. Entry is ¥300. It's open daily from 9 am to 4.30 pm (except Monday). The *Hikawa Maru* is a passenger liner moored off the park and a fun attraction for kids. Entry is ¥800. The boat is open daily from 9.30 am to 9.30 pm and has a beer garden in the summer months.

Three companies operate harbour cruises from the pier next to the *Hikawa Maru*: Marine Rouge and Marine Shuttle. The Marine Shuttle is cheaper – a 40 minute cruise costs ¥900. There are also 90 minute cruises for ¥2000.

The **Marine Tower** lingers on from the early days of Japanese tourism, offering a diminutive (106m) view over the harbour for ¥700. Other relatively nearby attractions include the **Harbour View Park** and the **Foreigners' Cemetery**, whose claim to fame is 4000 dead foreigners – some interesting headstone inscriptions if your interests run in this direction.

Chinatown　中華街

Not far from the harbour area is Chinatown, or *chūkagai*, as it is known in Japanese. Chinatowns in Japan differ very little from Chinatowns elsewhere, but the main reason to head over is for lunch – see the Places to Eat section. Be warned: this place gets packed on the weekends.

Sankei-en Garden　三渓園

Sankei-en Garden was established in 1906 by a Yokohama silk merchant. The beautifully landscaped gardens feature a three storey pagoda that is 500 years old. The pagoda, along with an old villa and farmhouses, was moved to the garden.

There are separate ¥300 admission charges to the outer and inner gardens. The inner one is a fine example of traditional Japanese garden landscaping. The garden is open daily from 9 am to 4.30 pm (closed from 29 to 31 January). The No 8 bus, from the road running parallel to the harbour behind the Marine Tower, operates with less than commendable frequency. If one does happen along, ask for the Sankei-en-mae bus stop. Alternatively, locals recommend taking the train to Negishi station and changing here for a city bus bound for Sakuragi-chō (No 54, 58, 99, 101 or 108). Get off at the Honmoku stop and from here it's an easy five minute walk to the south entrance of the park.

Places to Stay

The *Kanagawa Youth Hostel* (☎ 045-241-6503) costs ¥2600 (¥2800 during summer). It's just a five minute walk from Sakuragi-chō station. For ryokan accommodation, see the information centres in the Silk Museum building. Most of them, like the *Echigoya Ryokan* (☎ 045-641-4700) where rooms cost around ¥6000 per person, are located out of town and are difficult to find.

Most other accommodation in Yokohama is aimed at business travellers or Japanese tourists and prices can be very high indeed. The *Yokohama International Seamen's Hall* (☎ 045-681-2141) is a reasonably inexpensive place that is well located; singles/doubles cost ¥5800/12,200. Very close by is the *Aster Hotel* (☎ 045-651-0141). Singles/doubles are ¥7700/14,500. The hotel is recognisable by the big dragon painted on the side of the building.

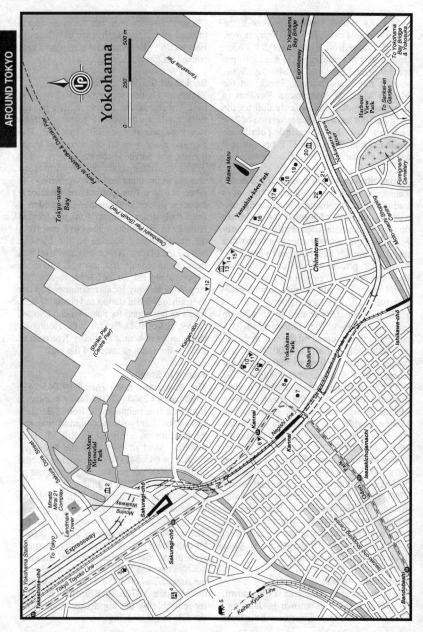

Yokohama

0   250   500 m

PLACES TO STAY		22	International	OTHER	
1	Yokohama Royal		Seamen's Hall	2	Yokohama Maritime
	Park Hotel Nikkō		横浜海員会館		Museum
	横浜ロイヤルパーク				日本丸メモリアル
	ホテル	**PLACES TO EAT**			パーク
3	Kanagawa Youth	6	Victoria Station	4	Iseyama Shrine
	Hostel	11	Baiko Emmie's		伊勢山皇大神宮
	神奈川ユース		梅香亭	5	Zoo; Nogeyama Park
	ホステル	12	Suginoki; Scandia		野毛山動物園
16	Hotel Yokohama		杉の木	7	City Hall
	ザホテル横浜	14	San Marina		市役所
17	Hotel New Grand	15	Parkside Gourmet	8	JTB
	ホテルニュー		Plaza	9	Cape Cod
	グランド			10	Bar Bar Bar; Pot Luck
18	Star Hotel Yokohama			13	Silk Museum
	スターホテル横浜				シルク博物館
21	Aster Hotel			19	Marine Tower
	アスターホテル			20	Doll Museum
					人形の家

There are a number of hotels along the harbour front facing Yamashita-kōen Park, but all of them are very expensive. The *Hotel Yokohama* (☎ 045-662-1321) is an up-market option by the waterfront with singles/doubles from ¥17,000/26,000. The *Hotel New Grand* (☎ 045-681-1841) has singles/twins from ¥10,000/28,000.

Places to Eat

Yokohama's chief gourmet attraction is its Chinatown, the only one within easy striking distance of Tokyo. Expect slowly shuffling queues at almost any time, though the weekends naturally see the area at its crowded worst. Places with good reputations include *Keika Hanten* (☎ 045-641-0051), *Katō Hanten* (☎ 045-641-0335), *Manchin Rō* (☎ 045-681-4004), *Kashō Rō* (☎ 045-681-6781) and, for dim sum (expensive), *Manchin Rō Tenshin Po* (☎ 045-681-4004), though this is just a sampling of the wide variety available.

Yokohama's reputation as a gourmet getaway does not rest on its Chinese food alone (which, after all, is not particularly authentic anyway). The area between Kannai

station and Yamashita-kōen Park is packed with bars, coffee shops and restaurants. Wander through the side streets of this area in the evening and you'll come across half a dozen interesting possibilities in no time. There are also a number of bars in this area, such as *Cape COD* and *Bar Bar Bar*. The latter has a long saloon-style bar on the 1st floor and live music upstairs.

A fascinating little place to call into is *Baiko Emmie's* (☎ 045-681-4870), with its touching sign outside promising 'English spoken'. If this place looks like it's been around for a while that's because it has. The original was established in 1924, though it moved to its current location in the '50s. Try the hayashi rice (¥750) or the curry rice (¥750). It's closed Sunday. For salads, fries and the like, call into *Pot Luck* (☎ 045-662-0525), an American-style kitchen (complete with an obligatory Budweiser sign outside); the 'trucker salad' at ¥1800 is enough for three. Another good salad stop is the branch of *Victoria Station* (☎ 045-631-0393).

The Yamashita-kōen Park area is largely western food at marked up prices, but there are some interesting restaurants and the lunch deals are generally reasonable. *Scandia* (☎ 045-201-2262), just across the road from the Silk Museum, is probably the only Danish restaurant in Japan. *Suginoki* (☎ 045-212-4143) is just around the corner and serves what it alleges to be Spanish cuisine. Prices are reasonable, but check out the plastic food display outside – it looks like it should have been changed back in the Meiji Restoration.

The Sakuragi-chō station area has a couple of spots for a snack or meal. *Becker's Hamburgers* is an American-style hamburger joint, while the *Kirin City* does cappuccino and sells cakes – a good breakfast stop.

In the Yokohama station area, try the basement mall that leads out from the station. Here you'll find the usual Japanese snackeries and a *Doutor Coffee* – always good for breakfast or lunch. The 10th floor of the Sogo department store is *Restaurant Avenue*, while also on the east side of the station is the Porta complex with a basement food centre.

Getting There & Away
Train There are numerous trains from Tokyo – the cheapest being the Tōkyū Tōyoko line from Shibuya station to Sakuragi-chō station for ¥290. The trip takes a total of 44 minutes by local train and 35 minutes by limited express (same price). Trains stop at Yokohama station on the way to Sakuragi-chō station.

The Keihin Tōhoku line goes through to Yokohama (¥440) and Kannai (¥610) stations from Tokyo and Shinagawa stations. The Tōkaidō line from Tokyo or Shinagawa stations also runs to Yokohama station, taking around 30 minutes and costing ¥470.

To Kamakura, take the Yokosuka line from Yokohama station (¥370). The Tōkaidō shinkansen stops at Shin-Yokohama station, a fair way to the north-west of town, on its way into the Kansai region. Shin-Yokohama station is connected to Yokohama, Sakuragi-chō and Kannai stations via the Yokohama line.

Getting Around
The Airport Both trains and buses connect Narita to Yokohama, but if you want to be

sure of getting to Narita at a particular time you should take the train. N'EX services between Yokohama station and Narita take 90 minutes and cost ¥4100 – you should reserve a seat. JR Airport Narita trains take two hours to do the same trip and cost ¥1850. Limousine buses travel frequently between the Yokohama City Air Terminal (YCAT) and Narita in around two hours (depending on the traffic) for ¥3300.

Bus The Blue Line double-decker bus service does a long loop through town taking in all of Yokohama's most notable moments. Buses depart from stop No 14 on the east exit of Yokohama station. A one-way ticket is ¥270, while an all day ticket is ¥600. You can hop on to the bus at any of the Blue Line bus stops around town. Elsewhere, buses around town are a standard ¥200.

AROUND YOKOHAMA
Yokohama Hakkeijima Sea Paradise
Hakkeijima Sea Paradise (☎ 045-788-8888) as its name suggests, is a vast watery amusement park. This is really a place to bring the kids, although adults too can enjoy attractions like the aquarium which really is one of the best and biggest in Japan – and that's saying something. There are watersport attractions such as the water chute and a high-speed roller coaster that zips out over the waves (the surf coaster). Indeed, as the flyers pronounce, 'so much enjoyment that one day won't be enough'.

Entry is ¥2400 for adults, ¥1400 for elementary and junior high school students and ¥700 for younger children. Hakkeijima is open from 10 am to 9 pm weekdays and 9 am to 9 pm weekdays and holidays. To get there, take a Keihin-Kyūkō line train from Yokohama station to Kanazawa Hakkei station (¥260) and from there change to the Seaside line and go to Hakkeijima (¥230).

KAMAKURA 鎌倉
The capital of Japan from 1185 to 1333, Kamakura is without a doubt the most historically rewarding day trip out of Tokyo. There are a huge number of Buddhist

Buddhism in Kamakura

The Buddhism that established itself in Japan during the 6th century belonged to the Mahayana (Greater Vehicle) school. This school maintained that enlightenment, or release from the cycle of birth and death, was available not only to those special few with the ability to unswervingly follow Buddhist precepts (the eight-fold path), but to all sentient beings. This, it was claimed, had been disclosed by the Buddha (Gautama) himself in his last sermon, the *Lotus Sutra*.

It was not until some five centuries later, during the Kamakura period, that Buddhism spread to all of Japan. Initially the Kamakura period was marked by disillusionment with the institutions of Buddhism and the monastic orders. It was widely believed that history had entered Mappō (the Later Age), a period of Buddhist decline, during which individuals would no longer be able to achieve enlightenment through their own efforts. This led to the flourishing of several alternatives to established Buddhist doctrine – notably Zen and the Pure Land school of Buddhism.

Adherents of the Pure Land school preached that in the Later Age salvation could only be achieved through devoting oneself to the transcendent Buddha Amida. Such, it was believed, was the infinite mercy of the Amida, that all who called on him sincerely would achieve salvation in the Pure Land after death. This denial of responsibility for one's own enlightenment was, in a sense, a 'soft option' and thus accounted for the sect's popularity among the lower orders of society who did not have the 'luxury' of devoting themselves to the rigours of pursuing personal enlightenment. This also contrasted with Zen, a Chinese import that strove to bring out the Buddhahood of the individual through meditative practice that sought out the empty centre of the self.

Zen, which literally means 'meditation', with its rigorous training and self-discipline, found support among an ascendant warrior class and made a considerable contribution to the evolution of the samurai ethic. Doctrinal differences on the question of whether *satori* ('enlightenment') could be attained suddenly, or whether it was a gradual process, accounted for Zen breaking into the Rinzai and Sōtō sects.

The contending schools of Pure Land and Zen, along with the views of charismatic leaders such as Nichiren, led to revitalisation of Buddhism within Japan during the Kamakura period. All the major Buddhist sects active in Japan today can trace their antecedents back to that period. ■

temples and the occasional shrine dotted around the surrounding countryside, and there are some very pleasant walks. Although Kamakura – like any other major attraction in Japan – gets packed out on weekends and holiday periods, mid-week can be very peaceful in the outlying temples.

History

In the 10th century the power of the emperor in Kyoto was largely ceremonial and real power had for some time rested in the hands of the Fujiwara clan. As the power of the Fujiwara declined, the Taira clan led by Taira Kiyomori, and the Minamoto clan led by Minamoto Yoshitomo, began an all-out struggle for supreme power. In 1159 the Taira routed the Minamoto forces.

Although many executions followed, by chance Yoshitomo's third son's life was spared and the boy was sent to spend his days in an Izu-hantō Peninsula temple. As soon as the boy, Minamoto Yoritomo, was old enough, he began to gather support for a counterattack on his clan's old rivals. In 1180 he set up his base at Kamakura, an area that shared the advantages of being far from the debilitating influences of Kyoto court life, being close to other clans loyal to the Minamoto and naturally easy to defend, and being enclosed by the sea on one side and densely wooded hills on the others.

With a series of victories over the Taira behind him, Minamoto Yoritomo was appointed shogun in 1192; he governed Japan from Kamakura. The lack of an heir after Yoritomo's death, however, gave power to the Hōjo, the family of Yoritomo's wife.

The Hōjo clan ruled Japan from Kamakura for more than a century until finally in 1333, weakened by the cost of maintaining defences against threats of attack from Kublai Khan in China, the Hōjo clan was defeated by Emperor Go-Daigo. Kyoto once again became capital.

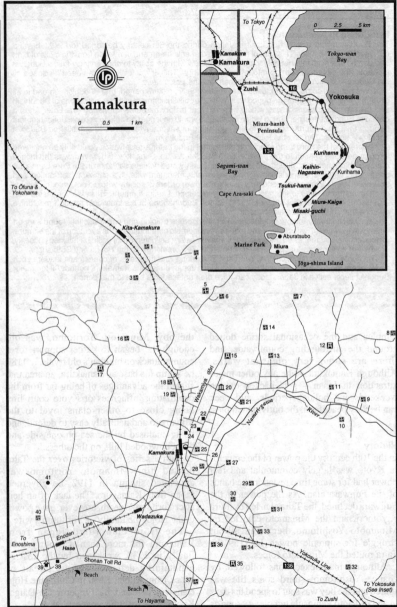

Kamakura

0   0.5   1 km

To Ōfuna & Yokohama

Kita-Kamakura

To Tokyo

Kamakura
Kamakura

Zushi

Yokosuka

Tokyo-wan Bay

0   2.5   5 km

Miura-hantō Peninsula

16

134

Sagami-wan Bay

Kurihama

Keihin-Nagasawa

Kurihama

Cape Ara-saki

Tsukui-hama

Miura-Kaiga

Misaki-guchi

Aburatsubo

Marine Park

Miura

Jōga-shima Island

Wakamiya-ōji

Namerigawa River

Kamakura

To Enoshima

Enoden Line

Yugahama

Hase

Wadazuka

Shonan Toll Rd

Beach

Beach

To Hayama

Yokosuka Line

136

To Yokosuka
(See Inset)

To Zushi

Orientation & Information

Kamakura's main attractions can be seen in a day of walking augmented by the occasional bus. Temples are usually well signposted in both English and Japanese. You can either start at Kamakura station and work your way around the area in a circle, or start north of Kamakura at Kita-Kamakura station and visit the temples between there and Kamakura on foot. The itinerary in this section follows the latter route.

The Kamakura Tourist Information Center (☎ 0467-22-3350) is just outside Kamakura station. Maps and brochures are available here and the office should also be able to help you find accommodation. The booklet *Sightseeing in Kanagawa* covers Kamakura and other sights in the region.

Engaku-ji Temple　円覚寺

Engaku-ji Temple is on the left as you exit Kita-Kamakura station. It is one of the five main Rinzai Zen temples in Kamakura. Rinzai is distinguished from the other major school of Zen Buddhism in Japan, Sōtō, by its use of riddles, stories and formal question-and-answer drills as aids to attaining enlightenment. Sōtō, on the other hand, relies more exclusively on meditation.

Engaku-ji Temple was founded in 1282, allegedly as a place where Zen monks might pray for soldiers who had lost their lives defending Japan against the second of Kublai Khan's invasion attempts. Today the only real reminder of the temple's former magnificence and antiquity is the **San-mon Gate** which is a 1780 reconstruction. At the top of the long flight of stairs through the gate is the **Engaku-ji bell**, cast in 1301 and the largest bell in Kamakura. The Main Hall inside the San-mon is quite a recent reconstruction, dating from the mid-'60s.

Entry is ¥200. The temple is open daily from 8 am to 5 pm from April to September and from 8 am to 4 pm during the rest of the year.

Tōkei-ji Temple   東慶寺

Tōkei-ji Temple, across the railway tracks from Engaku-ji Temple, is notable for its grounds as much as for the temple itself. On weekdays, when visitors are few, it can be a pleasantly relaxing place. Walk up to the cemetery and wander around.

Historically, the temple is famed as having served as a women's refuge. Women could be officially recognised as divorced after three years as nuns in the temple precincts. Today there are no nuns; the grave of the last abbess can be found in the cemetery. Entry is ¥50. The temple is open daily from 8.30 am to 5 pm.

Jōchi-ji Temple   浄智寺

A couple of minutes farther on from Tōkei-ji Temple is Jōchi-ji Temple, another temple with pleasant grounds. Founded in 1283, this is considered one of Kamakura's five great Zen temples. Entry is ¥100. It is open daily from 9 am to 4.30 pm.

Kenchō-ji Temple   建長寺

Kenchō-ji Temple is Kamakura's most important Zen temple. The grounds and the buildings are well maintained and still in use. The first of the main buildings you come to, the Buddha Hall, was moved to its present site and reassembled in 1647. The second building, the Hall of Law, is used for Zazen

meditation. Further back is the Dragon King Hall, a Chinese-style building with a garden to its rear. The temple bell, the second largest in Kamakura, has been designated a 'national treasure'. Entry is ¥200. The temple is open daily from 9 am to 4.30 pm.

Ennō-ji Temple   円応寺

Across the road from Kenchō-ji Temple is Ennō-ji Temple, distinguished primarily by its collection of statues depicting the judges of hell. Presiding over them is Emma, an ancient Hindu deity known in Sanskrit as Yama. The idea of hell and judgement became important Buddhist concepts with the rise of the Pure Land School. The temple is open daily from 10 am to 4 pm.

Hachiman-gū Shrine   八幡宮

Further down the road, where it turns towards Kamakura station, is Hachiman-gū Shrine. It was founded by Minamoto Yoriyoshi, of the same Minamoto clan that ruled Japan from Kamakura. There is some debate as to whether Hachiman, the deity to which the shrine is dedicated, has always been regarded as the god of war; his dedication may simply be a reflection of the fact that Hachiman is also the guardian deity of the Minamoto clan. Whatever the case, this Shinto shrine presents the visitor with a drastically different atmosphere to the repose of the Zen temples clustered around Kita-Kamakura station.

If you enter the shrine from the direction of Kita-Kamakura station, you are actually entering from the rear and not by the proper entrance gates. This is not a problem; after taking a look at the shrine, follow the stairs down to the square below the shrine. To the right is a gingko tree beneath which it is said that a famous political assassination was carried out in 1219, making the tree very old indeed.

At the foot of the stairs there is a dancing platform and the main avenue which runs to the entrance of the shrine. At the entrance on the left is an **arched bridge** which in times past was designated for the passage of the shogun and no-one else. The bridge is so steep that every crossing must have been quite a test of shogunal athletic prowess.

MARTIN MOOS

MASON FLORENCE

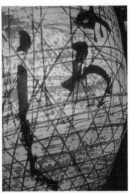
THOMAS DANIELL

MASON FLORENCE

THOMAS DANIELL

MASON FLORENCE

MASON FLORENCE

A	B
C	D	E
F	G

A: Festival floats, Kyūshū
B: Boy at Gion Festival, Kyoto
C: Red lantern
D: Traditional dancer, Naha

E: Green lanterns
F: Shinto priest, Siramine shrine, Kyoto
G: Kodo drummer, Sado-ga-shima Island

THOMAS DANIELL

CHARLOTTE HINDLE

CHRIS TAYLOR

CHRIS TAYLOR

CHRIS TAYLOR

CHRIS TAYLOR

A: Dressed for Childrens' Day
B: Climbing Mt Fuji - with bikes!
C: Doga-shima Island
D: Temple offerings
E: Edo-period costumes
F: Kanji (lit. 'Three Rivers')

National Treasure Museum To the left of the dancing platform (assuming you're continuing to walk away from the shrine) is the Kokuhō-kan, or the National Treasure Hall. This is one museum which is recommended, as it provides your only opportunity to see Kamakuran art, most of which is hidden away in the temples. Entry is ¥150. The museum is open daily except Monday from 9 am to 4 pm.

Great Buddha   大仏

The Kamakura Daibutsu (Great Buddha) was completed in 1252 and is Kamakura's most famous sight. Once housed in a huge hall, the statue today sits in the open, its home having been washed away by a tsunami in 1495. Cast in bronze and weighing close to 850 tonnes, the statue is 11.4m tall. Its construction is said to have been inspired by Yoritomo's visit to Nara (where there is another, even bigger, Buddha statue) after the Minamoto clan's victory over the rival Taira clan. Even though Kamakura's Great Buddha doesn't quite match Nara's in stature, it is commonly agreed that it is artistically superior.

The Buddha itself is the Amida Buddha (Sanskrit, Amitābha), worshipped by the followers of the Pure Land (Jōdo) sect as a figure of salvation.

To get to the Great Buddha, take a bus from the No 2, 7 or 10 bus stops in front of Kamakura station and get off at the Daibutsu-mae bus stop. Entry is ¥150. The Great Buddha is open daily from 7 am to 5.30 pm.

Hase-dera Temple   長谷寺

Not far from the Daibutsu-mae bus stop is Hase-dera Temple, also known as Hase Kannon Temple. The grounds have a garden and an interesting collection of statues of Jizō, the patron saint of the souls of departed children. Ranked like a small army of urchins, the statues are clothed to keep them warm by women who have lost children to abortion or miscarriage. The main point of interest in the grounds, however, is the Kannon statue.

Kannon (Sanskrit, Avalokiteshvara), the goddess of mercy, is the bodhisattva of infinite compassion and, along with Jizō, one of Japan's most popular Buddhist deities. The nine metre wooden carved **jūichimen** (11 faced Kannon) here is believed to be very ancient, dating from the 8th century. The 11 faces are actually one major face and 10 minor faces, the latter representing 10 stages of enlightenment. It is also commonly believed that the 11 faces allow Kannon to cast an eye in every direction, ever vigilant for those in need of her assistance.

Entry is ¥200. From October to February, Hase-dera Temple is open daily from 7 am to 4.40 pm. During the rest of the year it closes at 5.40 pm.

Other Shrines & Temples

If you're still in the mood for temple tramping, there are plenty more in and around Kamakura which has somewhere in the vicinity of 70 temples and shrines.

From the Great Buddha it is best to return to Kamakura station by bus and take another bus out to the temples in the eastern part of town. These have the advantage of being even less popular with tourists than the temples in Kita-Kamakura; they may lack the grandeur of some of Kamakura's more famous temples, but they more than make up for this with their charm. There is also a delightfully restful village-like atmosphere in the town's outer fringes.

Egara Ten-jin Shrine This Shinto shrine would not be particularly noteworthy if it were not so closely associated with academic success. Students write their academic aspirations on *ema* (small wooden plaques) which are then hung to the right of the shrine. In the grounds there's another ancient gingko tree said to be around 900 years old. Buses from stop No 6 in front of Kamakura station run out to Egara Ten-jin Shrine; get off at the Tenjin-mae bus stop.

Zuisen-ji Temple The grounds of this secluded Zen temple make for a pleasant stroll and include Zen gardens laid out by Musō Kokushi, the temple's founder. The temple is open daily from 9 am to 5 pm and has a ¥100 admission charge. It is possible to get there from Egara Ten-jin Shrine on foot in about 10 to 15 minutes; turn right where the bus turns left in front of the shrine, take the next left and keep following the road.

Sugimoto-dera Temple This interesting little temple, founded in 734 AD, is reputed to be the oldest in Kamakura. Ferocious temple guardians are poised on either side of the entrance, while the temple grounds and the thatch-roofed temple itself are littered with banners boldly announcing *Jūichimen Sugimoto Kannon* ('11 faced Kannon of Sugimoto') in Chinese characters. The temple houses three Kannon statues, though they are not in the same league as the famous statue at Hase-dera Temple.

Entry is ¥100 and the temple is open daily from 8.30 am to 4.30 pm. To get to the temple, take a bus from the No 5 stop in front of Kamakura station and get off at the Sugimoto Kannon bus stop.

Hōkoku-ji Temple Down the road (away from Kamakura station) from Sugimoto-dera Temple, on the right-hand side, is Hōkoku-ji Temple. This is a Rinzai Zen temple with quiet landscaped gardens where you can relax under a red parasol with a cup of Japanese tea. This is also one of the more active Zen temples in Kamakura, regularly holding Zazen classes for beginners. Entry is ¥100. The temple is open daily from 9 am to 4.30 pm.

Special Events
Setsubun is the bean-throwing ceremony held throughout Japan on 3 or 4 February. The best celebrations in Kamakura are at Hachiman-gū Shrine.

The Kamakura Matsuri is a week of celebrations held from the second Sunday to the third Sunday in April. It includes a wide range of activities, most of which are centred on the Hachiman-gū Shrine.

During the Bonbori Matsuri, held from 7 to 9 August, hundreds of lanterns are strung up around Hachiman-gū Shrine.

The Hachiman-gū Matsuri is held from 14 to 16 September. Festivities include a procession of mikoshi and, on the last day, a display of horseback archery.

The Menkake-gyōretsu, on 18 September, is a masked procession held at Goryō-jinja Shrine.

Places to Stay
The *Kamakura Kagetsuen Youth Hostel* (☎ 0467-25-1238) has beds at ¥2800. From Kamakura station take an Enoden train to Hase station. The hostel is around five minutes walk south-west of the station (just north of the seafront).

Not far from the youth hostel is *BB House* (☎ 0467-25-5859) which provides accommodation for women only and costs ¥5000 per person, including breakfast.

Just around the corner from Kamakura station is the *Ryokan Ushio* (☎ 0467-22-7016), where rates start at ¥5000 per person. It's a little tricky to find. Take the busy shopping street that runs parallel to the train tracks next to the station (there's a torii gate at the entrance) and take the third left. About 20m down this road you should see a sign on the left pointing into an alley. The ryokan is at the bottom of the alley.

The *City Pension Shangri La* (☎ 0467-25-6363) is nearby and has twins for ¥6000, plus four person rooms at economical rates. It's in a modern white building on the left side of the road as you walk up from the station. Just a few doors down is the expensive *Tsurugaoka Kaikan* (☎ 0467-24-1111) where costs range from ¥16,000 with two meals.

Places to Eat
The station area is cluttered with inevitable fast-food joints and coffee shops serving curry rices and Japanese-style gratins and pastas. For more palatable fare, head up into the Shopping Town street or the main road to Hachiman-gū Shrine, both of which run north-east from the station.

On the main road, look out for *Sakuraya*, just north of the Tsurugaoka Kaikan hotel. It's a no-frills Japanese lunch stop with generic dishes like katsudon and soba, but inexpensive and tasty. Just south of here is *Riccione Milano*, an Italian place that does decent pasta lunches from around ¥850.

On the Shopping Town street there's a branch of the Izakaya chain *Yōrōnotaki* on the right just after you enter from the station square; opposite is *Hirano Rāmen*, a basic little rāmen shop where the standard bowl of noodles costs ¥500. Further up the road, close to the Ryokan Ushio, is *Niraku-sō*, a good Chinese restaurant.

Getting There & Away

Yokosuka line trains run to Kamakura from Tokyo, Shimbashi and Shinagawa stations. The trip takes about 55 minutes and fares are ¥880 from Tokyo and Shimbashi and ¥760 from Shinagawa. It is also possible to catch a train from Yokohama (25 minutes, ¥320) on the Yokosuka line. If you're planning to get off at Kita-Kamakura station, it is the stop after Ōfuna.

A cheaper, but more complicated, option begins with a one hour and 15 minute ride on the Odakyū line from Shinjuku in Tokyo to Katase-Enoshima station (¥590 by express or for ¥1190 by the *Romance Car* service). When you leave the station, cross the river and turn left. Enoshima station is a 10 minute walk away and there you can catch the Enoden line to Kamakura for ¥240 (24 minutes). This is not a bad way to get to Kamakura if you were planning to take in Enoshima anyway.

It is possible to continue on to Enoshima, either via the Enoden line from Kamakura station (¥240) or by bus from stop No 9 in front of Kamakura station.

Free Pass There is a bewildering variety of 'free passes' for sightseeing in Kamakura and Enoshima, and they all represent fairly good savings. The JR Kamakura-Enoshima Free Pass is valid for two days, allows for transport on the JR between Ōfuna and Kamakura, on the Shōnan monorail between Ōfuna and Enoshima, and on the Enoden line between Fujisawa and Enoshima. From Tokyo station the pass costs ¥1900; from Yokohama station ¥1080.

Odakyū also offers a similar deal from Shinjuku station. The 'A ticket' is particularly good because it offers the added convenience of use of the buses within the Kamakura area. It costs ¥1980 from Shinjuku station and is valid for two days.

Getting Around

The transport hub for the Kamakura area is Kamakura station. A lack of English signposting makes the bus network difficult to use, but the Tourist Center should have the latest details on which stops service which destinations. Bus trips around the area cost either ¥170 or ¥190.

ENOSHIMA　江ノ島

Avoid this popular beach on weekends, when it's packed with day-trippers. At the end of the beach is a bridge to **Eno-shima Island**, where the Enoshima-jinja Shrine is reached by an 'outdoor escalator' that costs ¥270, but you *can* walk though. The shrine houses a *hadaka-benzaiten* – a nude statue of the Indian goddess of beauty. Other sights around the island include the **Enoshima Tropical Garden** which is open from 9 am to 5 pm daily and costs ¥200.

Shōnan Beach　湘南

West of Enoshima, Shōnan Beach is popular with surfers, particularly the areas around Ōsaki, Tamaishi and Yuigahama.

Getting There & Away

Buses and trains run frequently between Kamakura and Enoshima (see the Kamakura Getting There & Away section). The Tōkaidō line goes to Ōfuna station from Tokyo station at a cost of ¥760. At Ōfuna, change to the Shōnan monorail to Shōnan Enoshima station for ¥290. Alternatively, trains run on the Odakyū line from Shinjuku station to Katase-Enoshima station. The *Romance Car* takes one hour and 10 minutes and costs ¥1190, while an express takes five minutes longer and costs ¥590.

MIURA-HANTŌ PENINSULA 三浦半島

Strictly for long-term residents, the Miura-hantō Peninsula has beaches and the usual collection of overpriced, touristy marine parks, harbours and tropical gardens.

Aburatsubo Marine Park
油壺マリンパーク

This park has around 6000 fish in an aquarium that surrounds the viewer. It also offers 'synchronised swimming with girls and dolphins and laser light shows all put to music'. The park is a 15-minute bus trip from Misaki-guchi station. Entry is ¥1600 for adults and ¥800 for children. It's open from 9 am to 5 pm daily.

Joga-shima Island   城ケ島

The 35 minute trip costs ¥850. It's said that on a clear day you are able to see Mt Fuji from the boat, but you'd have to be *very* lucky. The island is actually connected to the mainland by a bridge, and buses go there from Misaki-guchi station.

Other Attractions

About five km north of Joga-shima Island, **Cape Ara-saki** has beaches with unusual rock formations. Take a bus from Misaki-guchi station to the Nagai bus stop and change for a bus to the Ara-saki bus stop. It takes about an hour to walk the **Mito-hama Beach Hiking Course** from Misaki-guchi station and back. The path takes you past a fishing village, beaches and a small shrine.

Getting There & Away

The cheapest and easiest way to the Miura-hantō Peninsula is to take the Keihin Kyūkō line from Tokyo station or Shinagawa station through to Misaki-guchi station in the south-east of the peninsula – you can get to most other destinations around the peninsula from here by train or bus. From Shinagawa the train takes one hour and 10 minutes and costs ¥880.

An alternative point of entry to the peninsula is Yokosuka which is serviced by the Yokosuka line (it passes through Kamakura) from Tokyo and Shinagawa stations. The fare is ¥1090.

Izu Seven Islands
伊豆諸島

The Izu Seven Islands are peaks of a submerged volcanic chain that projects out into the Pacific from the Izu-hantō Peninsula. There is still considerable volcanic activity. In November 1986 Mt Mihara-yama erupted and the residents of Ō-shima Island were evacuated to Tokyo.

Not so long ago the island chain was a place of exile, however, it's now a popular holiday destination for Tokyo residents. To escape the crowds, avoid the holiday periods and head for the more remote islands. Consult with the TIC in Tokyo for the latest ferry schedules and accommodation on the islands.

Ō-SHIMA ISLAND   大島

The main attraction of Ō-shima Island – at 91 sq km the largest of the group – is the active volcano **Mt Mihara-yama**. Buses run to the summit from Motomachi Port. **Oshima-kōen Park** has a natural zoo and a camping ground.

Information

The Izu Seven Islands Tourist Federation (☎ 03-3436-6955) in Tokyo has information on minshuku, and there is also the helpful Ōshima Tourist Association (☎ 04992-2-2177) which offers help to travellers.

Places to Stay

The *Umi-no-Furusatsu-mura* (☎ 04992-4-1137) camping ground is the cheapest place to stay, with pre-pitched tents at ¥4000 for six people, plus an extra ¥300 per person. There are also lodges with beds for ¥2000 per person. The *Mihara Sansō Youth Hostel* (☎ 04992-2-2735) charges ¥3100 per bed, while the *Izu Oshima People's Lodge* (☎ 04992-2-1285) costs ¥9000 per person, including two meals.

Getting There & Away

Air There are three flights a day from Tokyo to Ō-shima Island with Air Nippon Koku (ANK). The 40 minute flight costs ¥7550 one way.

Boat Ferry services run once daily to Ō-shima Island from Tokyo's Takeshiba Pier (10 minutes from Hamamatsu-chō station) and from Atami and Itō. The trip from Tokyo takes seven hours and costs ¥4140 (2nd class). From Atami it takes one hour and 10 minutes and costs ¥2380 in 2nd class. High speed services take one hour and cost ¥4800. There are also ferries from Itō (1½ hours, ¥2070).

TO-SHIMA ISLAND   利島

To-shima Island, 27 km south-west of Ō-shima Island, is the smallest of the Izu Seven Islands, with a circumference of only eight km. The island is mountainous, although its volcano is now dormant, and there are no swimming beaches. Much of the island is used for the cultivation of camellias which makes it a picturesque place to visit between December and February when the flowers are in bloom.

Places to Stay

The island has six minshuku with prices of ¥6000 to ¥6800 with two meals. For information contact the Izu Seven Islands Tourist Federation (☎ 03-3436-6955).

Getting There & Away

Ferries leave from Tokyo's Takeshiba Pier. The trip takes around nine hours and fares start at ¥4600 in 2nd class.

NII-JIMA ISLAND   新島

Nii-jima Island has an area of 23 sq km and its beaches have made it so popular that there are now over 200 minshuku on the island. Even with this abundance of accommodation, it's a good idea to ring the Niijima Tourist Association (☎ 04992-5-0048) if you're visiting during a holiday period.

The 10 hour boat trip from Tokyo's Takebashi Pier costs ¥5560 in 2nd class. There are also boats from Ō-shima and To-shima.

SHIKINE-JIMA ISLAND   式根島

Six km south of Nii-jima Island is tiny Shikine-jima Island, with an area of only 3.8 sq km. The island has swimming beaches, hot springs and plenty of accommodation.

Ferries to Shikine-jima Island depart from Takeshiba Pier daily, take 10 hours and cost ¥5560 in 2nd class. Ferries also leave from Shimoda on the Izu-hantō Peninsula. The trip takes around 3½ hours and costs ¥3100 in 2nd class.

KOZU-SHIMA ISLAND   神津島

This 18 sq km island is dominated by an extinct volcano, **Mt Tenjo**. The island also has good beaches, **Tokyo-ji Temple** and a cemetery for former exiles, including 57 feudal warriors.

Places to Stay

There are around 180 minshuku on the island with costs of around ¥8000 with meals; bookings can be made through the Kozushima Kankō Renmei (☎ 04992-8-0321), but only in Japanese.

Getting There & Away

Ferries leave from Takeshiba Pier and cost ¥5890 in 2nd class. Services from Shimoda take three hours and 40 minutes and cost ¥3100.

MIYAKE-JIMA ISLAND   三宅島

Known as Bird Island due to the 200 species of birds that live there, the island is 180 km south of Tokyo and is the third largest of the Izu Seven Islands, with a circumference of 36 km. It has a volcano, which last erupted in 1962, some good beaches, a couple of small lakes and an onsen. You can explore the island in a hired car, on a rented bicycle or you can make use of the local bus services.

Places to Stay

For reasonably priced minshuku, contact the Miyake-jima Tourist Association (☎ 04994-6-1144). There are camping grounds at Sagiga-hama, Okubo-hama and Miike-hama beaches; you'll need your own equipment, however.

Getting There & Away

By boat from Tokyo costs ¥6230 in 2nd class. There are also two flights a day with Air Nippon (☎ 03-3780-7777) for ¥9450.

MIKURA-JIMA ISLAND 御蔵島

Mikura-jima Island is only 20 km from Miyake-jima, but is not of great interest. Accommodation is limited, camping is not allowed and transport connections are infrequent.

HACHIJO-JIMA ISLAND 八丈島

Hachijo-jima Island, 290 km south of Tokyo, is the southernmost and second largest of the Izu Seven Islands (68 sq km). It has a pleasant, semi-tropical climate and is becoming increasing popular among young Japanese. Sights include the now dormant volcano, some good beaches, a botanical garden, **Tametomo-jinja Shrine** and **Sofuku-ji Temple**. Bicycles and cars can be rented.

There are some interesting local customs which are now maintained as tourist attractions, including a form of **bull-fighting** found throughout Asia in which two bulls try to push each other out of a ring. Bull fights are held daily at Jiyugaoka and admission is ¥800. The Runin Matsuri (Exile Festival) is held from 28 to 30 August with a costumed procession, drum beating and folk dancing.

Places to Stay

For accommodation information, ring the local tourist association (☎ 04996-2-1121, ext 282).

Getting There & Away

Ferries from Tokyo (via Miyake-jima) take around 10½ hours and cost ¥7800 in 2nd class. They depart daily during the summer season. Alternatively, there is a more frequent air service (six flights a day) between Haneda airport and the island with Air Nippon (☎ 03-3780-7777). The flight takes one hour and costs ¥12,650 one way.

Ogasawara Island 小笠原諸島

Although technically part of Tokyo-to, these islands are far to the south of the Izu Seven Islands. They have a climate similar to that of the Okinawa islands. Like those islands, they remained occupied by US forces until 1968, long after they had left the mainland islands.

The main group of islands includes **Chichi-jima** ('Father Island'), **Haha-jima** ('Mother Island') and **Ani-jima** islands, on which you will find a number of minshuku and where **scuba diving** is popular. Further south are the Kazan (Volcano) Islands which include **Iwo-jima** Island, one of the most famous battle sites of WWII. The island is still off limits to visitors because it contains live ammunition.

Boats to Chichi-jima Island leave approximately once a week from Tokyo, take around 28½ hours and cost ¥24,620 for 2nd class tickets. For more information ring Ogasawara Kaiun (☎ 03-3451-5171). Boats between Chichi-jima and Haha-jima take around two hours, leave daily and cost ¥3600 in 2nd class.

Central Honshū 本州の中央部

Central Japan, known in Japanese as Chūbu, extends across the area sandwiched between Tokyo and Kyoto.

This chapter covers the prefectures at the heart of the Chūbu region: Aichi-ken, Gifu-ken, Nagano-ken, Toyama-ken, Fukui-ken and Ishikawa-ken. Niigata-ken and Sado-ga-shima Island have been included in the Northern Honshū chapter and Shizuoka-ken and Yamanashi-ken are in the Around Tokyo chapter.

Chūbu divides into three geographical areas with marked differences in topography, climate and scenery. To the north, the coastal area along the Sea of Japan features rugged seascapes. The central area inland encompasses the spectacular mountain ranges and highlands of the Japan Alps, while the southern Pacific coast area is heavily industrialised, urbanised and densely populated so may not be much interest to travellers.

Transport in the southern area is excellent, with Nagoya functioning as the major transport hub and southern gateway to the region. The mountainous inland area is served by the JR Takayama line and JR Chūō line, which run roughly parallel from north to south. The main transport hubs and gateways for this area are Takayama to the west and Matsumoto to the east.

Another useful rail connection is provided by the JR Shin-etsu line which links Tokyo with Nagano. Transport in the northern area centres around the JR Hokuriku line, which follows the coast along the Sea of Japan, providing an extremely efficient link between the main transport hubs of Kanazawa and Toyama.

Bear in mind that transport outside the main cities in Chūbu, especially around the Japan Alps, is severely restricted between the months of November and May. Access to ski resorts is an obvious exception. Bus fares also tend to be ridiculously expensive: a one hour trip can cost up to ¥2000. If there are several of you interested in a day trip, renting

HIGHLIGHTS

◆ Inuyama, home to one of Japan's most well preserved castles and, in summer, ukai fishing

◆ Takayama, a small, beautiful city known for its traditional architecture and skilled wood-workers

◆ Shōkawa Valley, a remote agricultural region where traditional customs and farmhouses remain largely intact

◆ The superb mountain scenery and hiking trails of Nagano-ken's Kamikōchi and Hakuba

◆ The cultural and artistic centre of Kanazawa

◆ Noto-hantō Peninsula, offering lovely coastal scenery and fine seafood

a car may actually be the most affordable option.

The attractions of Chūbu lie in the central and northern areas, each of which can be skimmed in five days, but preferably give yourself two weeks for both if you really want to enjoy all that the region has to offer.

Nagoya　名古屋

Nagoya (population 2,150,000) is Japan's fourth largest city and centre of the Chūkyō industrial zone, Japan's third largest. Nagoya is mainly a commercial and industrial city, not a top travel destination. But the city has made a push to accommodate foreign visitors, and English-language signs make it easy to get to Nagoya's two major sights, the Nagoya-jō Castle and the Atsuta-jingū Shrine. There are some lesser attractions as well, and the city itself is fairly pleasant; a scaled-down, far more relaxed version of Tokyo. Nagoya is also a convenient transport hub for trips to Gifu and Inuyama or longer excursions into the Japan Alps.

Nagoya rose to power as a castle town during the feudal age. All three of Japan's great historical heroes, Oda Nobunaga, Toyotomi Hideyoshi and Tokugawa Ieyasu were born in the town or nearby. Tokugawa Ieyasu built Nagoya-jō Castle for one of his sons in 1610-14. Not much of the past remains, however. During WWII, the city was flattened by US aerial bombing, which also claimed most of Nagoya-jō.

Orientation

The city was completely rebuilt after WWII on a grid system with expansive avenues and side streets connecting in straight lines. This makes it easy to find one's way around the central part of the city.

From the east exit of Nagoya station, Sakura-dōri runs directly eastwards to the TV tower, a useful landmark on Hisaya-ōdōri. The area either side of Hisaya-ōdōri, south of the TV tower, is the Sakae entertainment district. Nagoya-jō Castle is north of the TV tower.

Nagoya station is vast, a city in itself. The shinkansen platforms are on the west side of the station. The Meitetsu and Kintetsu lines are on the east side of the station, which is also handy for connections with the subway system, the Meitetsu bus station and the city centre.

Information

Tourist Offices There is a Nagoya city tourist information office inside Nagoya station – take the central exit and look out for it in the middle of the hall. It has several English-language maps of the city, information on sights and accommodation, and usually at least one English-speaker behind the counter.

Better still is the Nagoya International Center (☎ 052-581-0100), which is located on the 3rd floor of the International Center (Kokusai Center) – a 10 minute walk east along Sakura-dōri. Staff here speak English (some also speak Chinese, French or Spanish), and have a wealth of information on both Nagoya and other destinations in Central Honshū. The centre has extensive lists of restaurants, bars, hotels and ryokan, though they're not allowed to make recommendations. Staff can also help arrange home visits with a Japanese family. There's also a library, TV newscasts from the USA and a bulletin board. The centre is open Tuesday to Saturday from 9 am to 8.30 pm and Sunday and holidays from 8 am to 5 pm. It is closed on Monday.

Post The main post office is a couple of minutes on foot north of Nagoya station. There is also a smaller office in the station itself, on the west side.

Books & Maps *Live Map Nagoya* is a useful colour map of the city, with hotels and sights accurately sited, while the *Goodwill Establishments Nagoya* map also includes lists of shops, restaurants and hotels where English is spoken. At the station master's office of some subway stations you can also pick up the *Nagoya City Bus and Subway System* map in English, which has just about all the information one could ask for on the local transit network.

Useful local publications with restaurant, entertainment and festival listings include *Eyes* (¥250) and *Nagoya Avenues* (¥250), both of which are published bi-monthly.

Emergency Nagoya International Center (☎ 052-581-0100) can provide all the advice needed for dealing with emergencies. There's a medical clinic (☎ 052-551-0509) in the same building. The Tachino Clinic (☎ 052-541-9130) has staff who speak English, French, German and Spanish. It's in the Dai-Nagoya building, opposite the east exit of Nagoya station.

Planning Your Itinerary

There are just a couple of significant sights in Nagoya, which can be knocked off in half a day or so. Inuyama, Gifu and Seki are within easy reach by train. Ise-jingū Shrine (see the Kansai section) and Takayama are both feasible as day trips if you make an early start, though if you have the time it would be better to stay one night at the very least.

Nagoya-jō Castle 名古屋城

Tokugawa Ieyasu built Nagoya-jō on the site of an older castle in 1610-14 for his ninth son. It was destroyed in WWII and replaced in 1959 with a ferroconcrete replica. Look out for the three-metre-long replicas of the famous *shachi-hoko*, dolphin-like sea creatures that stand at either end of the roof (and inside every souvenir shop in town).

The interior houses a museum with armour and family treasures which escaped the bombing. The castle also boasts an elevator to save you all the puff of climbing stairs. The Ninomaru Garden has a teahouse

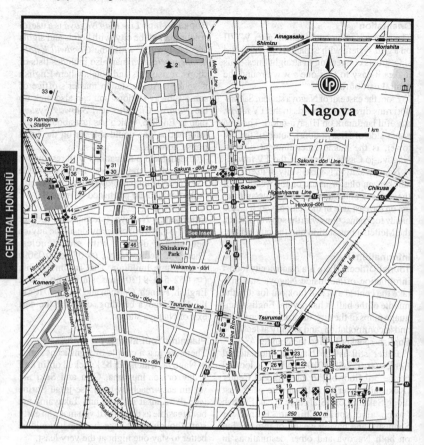

in an attractive setting in the castle grounds. Admission costs ¥500 and it's open from 9.30 am to 4.30 pm.

The castle is a five minute walk from Shiyakusho station on the Meijō subway line.

Atsuta-jingū Shrine　熱田神宮

This shrine, one of the most important in Japan, dates from the 3rd century and is said to house the *kusanagi-no-tsurugi* (the sacred sword – literally the 'grass-cutting sword'), one of the three imperial regalia (the others being the curved jewels and the sacred

mirror) of the imperial family. The sacred sword, like the other two imperial regalia, was, according to mythology, handed down to the imperial family by the goddess Amaterasu Ōmikami. Visitors aren't allowed to view the sword or any of the other imperial regalia, but don't feel too bad: no-one but the emperor and a few selected Shinto priests ever get to see them either. There is a small museum that houses various Shinto and Tokugawa-era artifacts. The shrine grounds are open daily 24 hours, while the museum is open from 9 am to 4.30 pm, closed the last Wednesday and Thursday of every month;

PLACES TO STAY

8 Nagoya Tōkyū Hotel
名古屋東急ホテル

20 International Hotel
Nagoya
名古屋国際ホテル

22 Nagoya Green Hotel
名古屋栄グリーン
ホテル

24 Sun Hotel Nagoya
サンホテル名古屋

25 Nagoya Dai-Ni
Washington Hotel
名古屋第二ワシント
ンホテル

29 Nagoya Hilton
名古屋ヒルトン

32 Kimiya Ryokan
きみや旅館

35 Hotel Sun Plaza
サンプラザホテル

36 Nagoya Dai-Ichi
Hotel
名古屋第一ホテル

38 Hotel Associa
Nagoya
Terminal
アソシア名古屋
ターミナルホテル

39 Fitness Hotel 330
Nagoya
フィットネスホテル
330名古屋

40 Hotel Castle Plaza
ホテルキャッスル
プラザ

42 Business Hotel Star
Nagoya
ビジネスホテル
3スター名古屋

43 City Hotel Nagoya
シティホテル名古屋

44 Meitetsu Grand Hotel
名鉄グランドホテル

46 Aichi-ken Seinen-
kaikan Youth Hostel
愛知県青年会館

49 Ryokan Meiryu
旅館名龍

50 Yamazen Ryokan
山善旅館

51 Marutame Ryokan
まるため旅館

PLACES TO EAT

3 Carina Pizza

7 Cafe de Crie

9 Suien
翠園中国料理

11 Tsubohachi
つぼ八

12 Lian Hua
蓮花

16 Mr Donut

17 McDonald's

18 KFC

19 Okonomishokudo-gai
お好み食堂街

21 Fujiko
富士子

23 Irohanihoheto
いろはにほへと

26 Tsubohachi
つぼ八

27 Ebisuya
えびすや

31 Yoshinoya
吉野屋

48 Santa Barbara
Restaurant and Grill

OTHER

1 Tokugawa Art
Museum
徳川美術館

2 Nagoya-jō Castle
名古屋城

4 Tōkyū Hands
Department Store
東急ハンズ

5 Nagoya TV Tower
テレビ塔

6 Aichi Arts Centre
愛知芸術文化
センター

10 Underground Cafe
(Bar)

13 Sakae Bus Station
栄バスターミナル

14 Mitsukoshi
Department Store
三越デパート

15 Marui Department
Store
丸井デパート

28 Across the Border
(Bar)

30 Nagoya International
Centre
国際センタービル

33 Noritake Craft Centre

34 Nagoya Main Post
Office
中央郵便局

37 City Bus Station
市バスターミナル

41 Nagoya Station
名古屋駅

45 Meitetsu & Kintetsu
Department Stores
名鉄デパート／
近鉄デパート

47 Matsuzakaya
Department Store
松坂屋デパート

entry to the museum is ¥300, ¥500 if there is a special exhibit being held.

From Shiyakusho subway station (close to the castle), take the Meijō line south to Jingū-nishi station (seven stops). To reach the shrine from Nagoya station, take the Meitetsu Nagoya Honsen line to Jingū-mae (four stops) and then walk west for five minutes.

Tokugawa Art Museum 徳川美術館
The collection of the Tokugawa Art Museum includes prints, calligraphy, painted scrolls, lacquerware and ceramics which previously belonged to the Tokugawa family. The museum is open from 10 am to 5 pm daily except on Monday; admission is ¥1000.

The easiest way to reach the museum is to take bus No 16 from Shiyakusho subway station (near Nagoya-jō) and get off at the Shindeki stop.

Nagoya Port Area 名古屋港周辺
Redeveloped to attract tourists, the cargo port now boasts several mildly interesting attractions. These include the hi-tech **Nagoya Port Aquarium** (one of Japan's largest), the **Port Tower**, with good views of the harbour, the **Maritime Museum** on the 3rd floor of the Port Tower and the **Fuji Antarctic Exploration Ship**. All of them can be visited with a combination ticket for ¥2000, provided you roll up before 1 pm. Just visiting the Port Tower and Maritime Museum will only set you back ¥300. Take the Meijō subway line to Nagoya-kō (Nagoya Port) subway station. The attractions are signposted in English.

Factory Tours
Nagoya is an industrial town, and there are several good tours of local factories for the commercially curious. The **Noritake Craft Center** offers a look at the production line of Japan's most well-known maker of porcelain tableware. Call ☎ 052-561-7114 to make reservations. The craft centre can be reached by taking the Higashiyama subway line to the Kamejima station.

Automobile giant Toyota Motor Corporation is east of Nagoya, and tours of its main plant in Toyota City can be arranged by calling ☎ 0565-23-3922.

Lager lovers might appreciate the chance to tour Asahi Beer's Nagoya factory (☎ 052-792-8966). The free tours are held Monday to Friday from 9.30 am to 3 pm, though it would be wise to call ahead just to make sure. To get there, take the JR Chūō line to Shin-moriyama station. From there it's about a 15 minute walk east.

Special Events
The Atsuta Festival, held on 5 June at the Atsuta-jingū Shrine, features displays of martial arts, sumo matches and fireworks.

On the first Saturday and Sunday of June, the Tennō Matsuri Festival takes place in Deki-machi. Large *karakuri* (mechanical puppets) are paraded on floats in the precincts of the Susano-o-jinja Shrine.

Nagoya Matsuri Festival, held in mid-October, is the big event of the year. It includes costume parades, processions of floats with karakuri, folk dancing, music and a parade of decorated cars.

Places to Stay
Accommodation in Nagoya is clustered largely around the station and the Sakae commercial and entertainment district. Nagoya's excellent subway system means that basing yourself in the station area is no impediment to taking an evening trip into Sakae.

Youth Hostels The *Aichi-ken Seinen-kaikan Youth Hostel* (☎ 052-221-6001) is in a good location, not too far from Nagoya station. As a result, it's the first budget place to be booked out – reserve in advance if you want to be sure of a bed. The hostel charges ¥2800 per night. Japanese-style family rooms and guest rooms are available from around ¥5100 per night. From Nagoya station (eastern exit), the hostel is a 20 minute walk south-east. Alternatively, you can take bus No 20 from the stop in front of the Toyota building and get off at the Nayabashi stop. From there, it's three minutes south on foot. Look out for the blue sign with tiny English

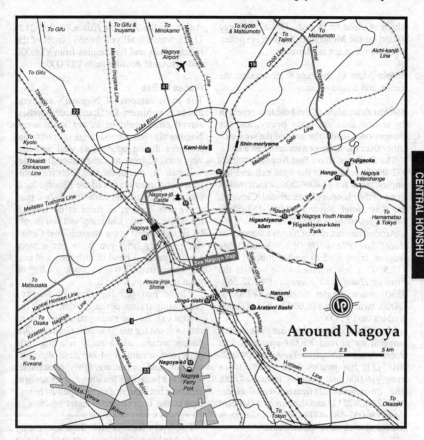

Around Nagoya

0   2.5   5 km

writing out front. The hostel is closed from 28 December to 5 January.

The *Nagoya Youth Hostel* (☎ 052-781-9845) is further out to the east of town near Higashiyama-kōen Park. The charge is ¥2200 per night, and the hostel is closed from 29 December to 3 January. From Nagoya station, take the subway on the Higashiyama line to Higashiyama-kōen station. From the No 2 exit, turn left and follow the main road, Higashiyama-dōri, to the next main intersection, where you'll see signs for the hostel.

Ryokan The *Ryokan Meiryu* (☎ 052-331-8686) is a member of the Japanese Inn Group and charges ¥5150/8240 for singles/doubles. It's centrally located, three minutes on foot from Kamimaezu subway station on the Meijō line. Just a few blocks away, the *Yamazen Ryokan* (☎ 052-321-1792) has fairly large rooms for between ¥4800 and ¥5400 per person. The owners don't speak much English, but welcome foreign guests.

Two other options with per person costs of around ¥4000 are the *Kimiya Ryokan* (☎ 052-551-0498), which is north of the Nagoya International Center building, and the *Marutame Ryokan* (☎ 052-321-7130), which is close to Higashi Betsuin subway station on the Meijō line. English is spoken at Kimiya, but not at Marutame.

Hotels Most of the hotels are around the station and Sakae areas.

Station Area Most of the business hotels in the station area are fairly pricey, and the cheaper ones tend to be around the west exit rather than the more convenient east exit.

The *Business Hotel Star Nagoya* (☎ 052-452-0033) is close to the west exit and has singles/twins for ¥5400/8200, which makes it one of the cheaper places around. Close by, the *City Hotel Nagoya* (☎ 052-452-6223) has singles/twins at ¥6000/9000.

Around the east exit of Nagoya station, the *Hotel Sun Plaza* (☎ 052-563-0691) has singles from ¥6590 and doubles from ¥12,560. A few minutes walk west is the *Fitness Hotel 330 Nagoya* (☎ 052-562-0330), where singles range from ¥7500 to ¥8000, twins from ¥12,000 to ¥14,000 and doubles cost ¥11,000.

Most of the other hotels near the east exit range from around ¥9000 upwards. The *Hotel Associa Nagoya Terminal* (☎ 052-561-3751) has singles from ¥9000, twins from ¥16,000 and doubles from ¥14,000. The enormous *Meitetsu Grand Hotel* (☎ 052-582-2211) and the *Nagoya Dai-Ichi Hotel* (☎ 052-581-4411) offer similar rates and are also close to the east exit.

Sakae Area The Sakae area is a more lively part of town to be based in terms of eating out and nightlife. One of the cheapest options around is the *Nagoya Dai-Ni Washington Hotel* (☎ 052-962-7111), which has singles from ¥5800, and twins and doubles from ¥11,600. Just across the road, the *Sun Hotel Nagoya* (☎ 052-971-2781) has singles at ¥6000 and twins at ¥9700.

The Sakae area also has a number of very up-market hotels. Probably the best is the *Nagoya Tōkyū Hotel* (☎ 052-251-2411), which has singles at ¥13,500, twins at ¥26,000 and doubles at ¥22,000. Not far from Sakae, close to Fushimi subway

station, is the *Nagoya Hilton* (☎ 052-212-1111), which is all you would expect of the Hilton chain and has singles from ¥21,000 and twins and doubles from ¥29,000.

Places to Eat

The most famous of Nagoya's regional dishes is kishimen, flat, handmade noodles, served either cold or in hot stock soup. Nagoya also has a good range of traditional Japanese dining options, as well as some very good Chinese and international dining.

Locals say one of the best spots for kishimen is the main branch of the *Ebisuya* local chain of restaurants. Ordering dishes may prove challenging, as there is no English menu, but just say 'kishimen' and you should be all right. Staff at the International Center can probably help you write out a more specific order. A bowl of kishimen will cost anywhere from ¥700 to ¥1200 depending on what ingredients are in it.

Those just passing through Nagoya (changing trains perhaps) can take the central exit for the main part of the station and look out for the basement *Gourmet One* dining arcade. It's a fairly relaxing little place with a number of Japanese-style restaurants, and prices are fairly reasonable. There is a branch of *Yoshinoya*, the excellent Japanese beef and rice chain (open 24 hours) next to the International Center building, a 10 minute walk from the station.

For lively izakaya-style Japanese eating and drinking, look out for one of the branches of the *Tsubohachi* or *Irohanihoheto* izakaya chains – figure on ¥2000 per head for dinner and drinks. The basement of the Sakaemachi building has *Okonomishokudo-gai*, a 'street' of cheap restaurants that are popular with students and other young people. One other place to look out for, close to Sakae subway station, is *Fujiko*, a somewhat dusty-looking corner stall doing a brisk business in yakitori (chicken kebabs) – squeeze into one of the three tiny tables around the back or buy it to take away.

For good Taiwanese food (an excellent and little-known cuisine), try *Lian Hua* on the east side of Sakae subway station. It has an illustrated menu and a good selection of authentic Taiwanese street stall snacks. An evening meal would come to ¥2000 to ¥2500 per head with a drink. Just around the corner is *Suien*, another authentic Chinese restaurant (this time Shanghainese) with a limited illustrated menu (some of the best stuff is in Japanese and Chinese only).

For decent Italian pizza and pasta, check out *Carina Pizza*, north of the TV tower. There is also a branch on the 9th floor of the Maruei Skyle building, part of the Maruei department store in Sakae. If running around Sakae has you in need of a jump start, the *Cafe de Crie* coffee shop can provide you with a decent cup of coffee for ¥180.

Entertainment

Nagoya, while a big city, isn't as exciting as Tokyo or Osaka, but it does have a bit of a nightlife scene and a few bars that attract an interesting mix of *gaijin* (foreigners) and Japanese. Among the more popular spots (dark and loud – not necessarily the best places to meet people) are the *Underground* and the *Underground Cafe*, which are on the 3rd and 4th floors of the same building, respectively. The Underground is basically a dance space with good soul sounds and a cover charge of ¥1000 to ¥2000 on some nights of the week, while the Underground Cafe is more of a drinking spot – both get packed on Friday and Saturday nights. However, both places also have a strict dress code – no shorts or sandals – that may prove a barrier to many travellers.

Other drinking options include *Santa Barbara Restaurant and Grill*, near the Osu Kannon subway station, and *Across the Border*, another popular gaijin hangout, not far from the Nagoya Hilton. Santa Barbara has all sorts of nightly specials (Heineken draught for ¥300 on Monday night, for example) and live music on Saturday and Sunday.

Nagoya also offers a good sampling of live jazz, rock and classical music, including some well-known Japanese and international artists. Check the Concert and Theatre section of *Eyes* to see who's playing where and when.

Things to Buy

Nagoya and the surrounding area are known for various arts & crafts such as *arimatsu-narumi shibori* (elegant tie-dying), cloisonné (enamelling on silver and copper), ceramics and *seki* blades (swords, knives, scissors etc). For information on the Noritake porcelain factory, see the Factory Tours section, above. Nagoya International Center can provide details on tours of specific factories or museums as well as shopping.

The major shopping centres are in Sakae and around Nagoya station. For souvenir items (handmade paper, pottery, tie-dyed fabric etc) you can browse in Sakae in the giant department stores such as Matsuzakaya, Marui and Mitsukoshi, or try Meitetsu, an equally vast department store next to the station.

Getting There & Away

Air Nagoya's Komaki airport is linked by air with most of Japan's major cities by All Nippon Airways (ANA), Japan Airlines (JAL) and Japan Air Systems (JAS). If you're coming from Tokyo, however, the shinkansen is much quicker, as the bus from Nagoya station to the airport takes 30 to 40 minutes.

An increasing number of international carriers are using Komaki airport, which does not suffer from the chronic congestion of Tokyo's Narita airport. Direct flights are available to Nagoya from Bangkok, Beijing, Hong Kong, Manila, Seoul, Singapore, Sydney, Taipei and Vancouver.

Train The JR shinkansen is the fastest rail service to Nagoya. The journey on the Hikari shinkansen takes about two hours from Tokyo (¥10,380), about one hour from Osaka (¥6060) and 50 minutes from Kyoto (¥5340).

Ise-shima National Park is connected with Nagoya on the Kintetsu line, which runs via Ise-shi station and Toba to Kashikojima. Nagoya to Ise takes 80 minutes (¥2280). If you want to use JR, it will take at least two hours (¥2890); take the JR Kisei line to Taki and then change for Ise.

Nara is connected with Nagoya on the Kintetsu line. Nagoya to Nara takes 2¼ hours.

For the Japan Alps and related side trips, you can take the JR Chūō line to Nagano via Matsumoto. To reach Takayama from Nagoya, take the JR Hida limited express (*tokkyū hida*), which gets you there in 2½ hours (¥5750). If you want to work in a stop at Inuyama en route, the Meitetsu Inuyama line connects with the JR Takayama line at Shin-Unuma station, across the river from Inuyama.

Inuyama is connected with Nagoya station on the Meitetsu Inuyama line. The trip takes about 30 minutes.

Gifu is connected with Nagoya station on the JR Tōkaidō Honsen line as well as the Meitetsu Nagoya line. Either way, the trip takes about 30 minutes.

Bus JR buses operate between Tokyo and Osaka with stops in Nagoya and Kyoto. The approximate times and prices to Nagoya are as follows: Tokyo – six hours, ¥5000; Kyoto – 2¾ hours, ¥2200; Osaka – 3½ hours, ¥2600.

Hitching To hitch east from Nagoya to Tokyo, or west to Kyoto or Osaka, your best bet is the Nagoya Interchange on the Tomei Expressway. Take the subway on the Higashiyama line from Nagoya station to Hongo station (13 stops) – one stop before the terminus at Fujigaoka. The interchange is a short walk east of the station.

Boat The Taiheiyo ferry (☎ 03-661-7007) runs between Nagoya and Tomakomai (Hokkaidō) via Sendai. Ferries depart from Nagoya-futō pier, which is 40 minutes by bus from the Meitetsu bus station. Alternatively, take the Meijō subway south to its terminus at Nagoya-kō station.

The 2nd class passenger fare from Nagoya to Sendai is ¥9580 and the trip takes 21 hours. There are evening departures every second day. The fare from Nagoya to Tomakomai is ¥15,450 and the full trip takes about 40 hours.

Getting Around

The Airport Express bus services run between the airport and the Meitetsu bus station (3rd floor, gate No 5). The trip takes 30 minutes and the one-way fare is ¥850. Buses also leave from in front of the Meitetsu Grand Hotel, across from the west exit of Nagoya station. Taxis also take around 30 minutes and cost about ¥4000.

Subway Nagoya has an excellent subway system with four lines, all clearly signposted in English and Japanese. The most useful lines for visitors are probably the Meijō line, Higashiyama line and the Sakura-dōri line. The last two run via Nagoya station. Fares range from ¥200 to ¥320 on all lines. If you intend to do a lot of travel by bus and subway, you can save money with a one day pass (¥850), which is available at subway stations.

Bus There is an extensive bus system but the subway is easier to handle for those with a limited grasp of Japanese. The main bus centre is the Meitetsu bus station which is on the 3rd floor of the Meitetsu department store on the south side of Nagoya station.

Southern Gifu-ken

Gifu Prefecture consists almost entirely of mountains, with the exception of the plain around the city of Gifu, the prefectural capital. In the south of the prefecture the two cities of interest to travellers are Gifu and Inuyama, which are famed for *ukai* (cormorant fishing) and easily visited as side trips from Nagoya.

SEKI 関

Seki (population 68,000) is renowned as an ancient centre for swordsmiths. It still produces a few swords, but there isn't much growth in the sword market so the emphasis of production has been switched to cutlery and razor blades (Seki produces 90% of Japan's razor blades).

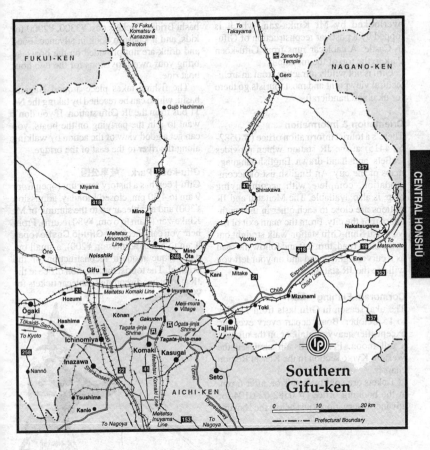

Southern Gifu-ken

0   10   20 km

Prefectural Boundary

Swordsmithing demonstrations are given on 2 January, the first Sunday of each month from March to September, the second weekend in October and the first Sunday in November. The best source of information on swordsmithing displays is the Seki Tourism Association (☎ 0575-22-3131). There are several *minshuku* (family-run lodges) and ryokan around Seki and some visitors combine a stay with an evening dinner on a boat while watching ukai, which is held from 11 May to 15 October.

The Seki Festival is held on the fourth Sunday in March, and centres around a parade of elaborate floats that winds through the town.

From Gifu, trains run on the Meitetsu Minomachi line to Seki in 50 minutes. Trains leave from the Eki-mae Shin-Gifu station, which is directly across from the main exit of the Meitetsu Shin-Gifu station. There are also buses from Gifu to Seki which take about 30 minutes.

GIFU 岐阜

Gifu (population 410,000) was hit by a colossal earthquake in 1891 and later given a thorough drubbing in WWII. The city is overlooked by Mt Kinka-zan, which is topped by a postwar reconstruction of Gifu-jō Castle. A cablecar runs from Gifu-kōen Park to the top of the mountain.

Gifu is not wildly attractive from an architectural viewpoint and most tourists go there for ukai and handicrafts.

Orientation & Information

There's a tourist information office (☎ 0582-62-4415) at the JR station which provides leaflets and hand-drawn English-language maps of the city. An English list of accommodation, complete with accompanying map, is also available. The Meitetsu and JR stations are close to each other in the southern part of the city. From the main exit of the Meitetsu Shin-Gifu station walk straight out to the main road, turn left and follow the road as it curves right: ahead and on your left you will see the JR station.

Cormorant Fishing   鵜飼い

The ukai season in Gifu lasts from 11 May to 15 October. Boats depart every evening, except after heavy rainfall, or on the night of a full moon. For details on ukai see the Western Kyoto section in the Kansai Region chapter.

Tickets are sold by hotels or, after 6 pm, at the booking office (☎ 0582-62-0104 for advance reservations) just below the Nagara-

bashi Bridge. Tickets cost ¥3300, ¥2900 for kids, and it's best to book in advance. Food and drink are not provided on the boats, so bring your own provisions for the two hour boat ride.

The fishing takes place around Nagara-bashi, which can be reached by taking the No 11 bus from the JR Gifu station. If you don't want to join the partying on the boats, you can get a good view of the action by walking along the river to the east of the bridge.

Gifu-kōen Park   岐阜公園

Gifu-kōen has a history museum (open from 9 am to 4.30 pm, closed Monday, admission ¥300) and a cablecar up to the summit of Mt Kinka-zan (8 am to 6 pm, ¥980 return). From here you can check out **Gifu-jō Castle** (open 9 am to 5 pm, admission ¥200), a small but picturesque modern reconstruction of the original. The tourist information office at the JR station has discounted cablecar tickets for ¥900.

Cormorants, attached to long leashes, catch several dozen fish in a night. A small metal ring at the base of their necks stops them from swallowing the fish.

Shōhō-ji Temple 勝法寺

The main attraction of this orange and white temple is the papier-maché Daibutsu (Great Buddha) which is nearly 14m tall and was created from about a tonne of paper sutras (prayers). Completed in 1747, the Buddha took 38 years to make. The temple is a short walk south-west of Gifu-kōen Park.

Places to Stay

Gifu has plenty of ryokan and hotels, and the information office at the station can provide a list (including a helpful map) of accommodation options.

Youth Hostel *Gifu Youth Hostel* (☎ 0582-63-6631) is perched atop a hill south of Gifu-kōen. There are several ways to get up there, but all require a walk of around two km. The recompense for the long hike is the low ¥1650 (¥1850 during July-August and December) it costs for a bed for the night.

Take the No 9 bus to Higashi Betsuin (around 15 minutes), walk toward the tunnel, and just before the entrance take the path to the right which leads uphill to the hostel. Alternatively, you can take the No 3 bus to Kashimori-kōen, where there's another trail which leads up to the hostel. Both walks will take 20 to 30 minutes. The hostel is closed from 29 December to 3 January.

Ryokan About three minutes walk from the JR Gifu station, the *Kogetsu Ryokan* (☎ 0582-63-1781) charges ¥3700 per person, excluding meals, which is about as cheap as you'll find in this part of Japan. A bit further north, the *Yamaguchiya Ryokan* (☎ 0582-63-0984) is also pretty reasonable at ¥4000 per person.

Hotels There are quite a number of business hotels in the station area. The *Grand Palace Hotel* (☎ 0582-65-4111) is directly opposite JR Gifu station and has singles/twins from ¥6000/11,000. Just east of the station, the *Miho Hotel* (☎ 0582-64-3241) has singles/doubles for ¥5000/9000.

One of the cheapest options is the *Hotel Gifu* (☎ 0582-62-1280), which has singles from ¥4000 and twins from ¥7000. There are also a number of cheaper business hotels north of the Kin-machi tram stop. The *Business Hotel Asahi* (☎ 0582-66-1919) has singles at ¥4500 and twins at ¥8000.

Things to Buy

Gifu is famous for its *kasa* (oiled paper parasols) and *chōchin* (paper lanterns), which are stocked in all the souvenir shops.

If you want to see a shop that not only sells but also makes kasa, you should visit Sakaida Honten (☎ 0582-72-3865). The shop is open daily except Sunday and holidays from 7 am to 5 pm, though it usually also shuts down from lunch time. It's a 12 minute walk south-east of JR Gifu station.

Ozeki Shōten (☎ 0582-63-0111) is a lantern factory. Visitors are not permitted into the workshop, but there's a display that explains the processes of frame building, pasting and painting. Lanterns are also on sale here. The shop is open from 9 am to 5 pm daily except Sunday and holidays. To get there, take the No 11 bus and get off at the Meiji-kōen stop. From there it's a short walk east down the main road to the factory.

Getting There & Away

From Nagoya station take the Meitetsu Nagoya line (30 minutes, ¥440) to Gifu. The JR Tōkaidō line will also get you there.

INUYAMA 犬山

The highlights of Inuyama (population 69,000) are its castle and activities such as ukai and river running. The riverside setting of the castle is quite attractive, and inspired a turn-of-the-century Japanese geologist to christen the area the 'Japan Rhine'. Nearby the beautiful Uraku-en Garden is also worth visiting for its tranquil beauty and 370 year old teahouse. Other attractions in the area include the western architecture of the Meiji-mura Village Museum and boat trips down the Kiso-gawa River.

CENTRAL HONSHŪ

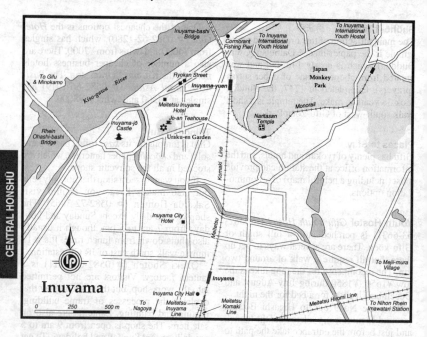

Orientation & Information

The castle and the ukai area are within easy walking distance of Inuyama-yuen station, which is one stop north of the main Inuyama station. Most of the town's restaurants and shops are closer to Inuyama station. The Inuyama Sightseeing Information Center (☎ 0568-61-1800), on the 2nd floor of Inuyama station, has English-language pamphlets and maps, and can book accommodation.

Inuyama-jō Castle 犬山城

Dating from 1440, this is Japan's oldest castle and is preserved in its original state – a relative rarity in Japan. It is also the only privately owned castle in the country, having been in the hands of the Narusune family since 1618. From the top storey of the castle, there's a fine view across the Kiso-gawa River.

The castle is a 15 minute walk west of Inuyama-yuen station. It's open daily from 9 am to 4.30 pm and entry is ¥400.

Uraku-en Garden & Jo-an Teahouse
有楽苑 ・ 如庵

Uraku-en is 300m east of Inuyama-jō Castle in a corner of the grounds of the Meitetsu Inuyama Hotel. The centre of attention in the garden is the Jo-an Teahouse, rated as one of the finest in Japan. It was constructed in 1618 in Kyoto by Oda Urakusai, a younger brother of Oda Nobunaga. Urakusai was a renowned tea master who founded his own tea ceremony school.

Admission to the teahouse costs ¥800. It's open from 9 am to 5 pm but closes an hour earlier between December and February. Remember to swap your shoes for the sandals provided next to the ticket window before traipsing through the garden.

Cormorant Fishing 鵜飼い

Ukai takes place close to Inuyama-yuen station at Inuyama-bashi Bridge. The boat dock and booking office are just east of the bridge. Tickets cost ¥2800 during July and August; ¥300 less during June and September. Book your ticket in Inuyama in the morning or call ahead and reserve tickets at the dock office (☎ 0568-61-0057) if your Japanese is up to it.

The boats set out from a dock near the southern end of the bridge next to the Inuyama-yuen station. Sailings are generally at 7 pm nightly except after heavy rainfall or on the night of a full moon. The fishing season lasts from 1 June to 30 September. For details on ukai see the Western Kyoto section of the Kansai Region chapter.

Kiso-gawa River Trip　木曽川下り

Flat-bottomed wooden boats shoot the rapids on a 13 km section of the Kiso-gawa River. The trip takes about an hour and entails little risk although you might get dampened by spray. If you want a slightly faster and noisier ride, you can take a motorised boat.

From Nagoya station take the Meitetsu Inuyama line to Inuyama station, and then change to the Meitetsu Hiromi line for the Nihon Rhein Imawatari station (¥730). From there it's a five minute bus ride to the boat dock. The fare for the boat trip is ¥3400. Call Nihon Rhine Kankō (☎ 0574-28-2727) for more details.

Japan Monkey Park
日本モンキーパーク

Unless you are really keen on monkeys or amusement park rides, you can skip this. Apart from the Japan Monkey Research Center, a zoo and a botanical garden, there's also a collection of handicrafts related to monkeys.

Admission to the park costs ¥1500. It's open from 9.30 am to 5 pm daily but closes an hour earlier from early December to mid-February. A monorail (¥300 round trip) zips you from Inuyama-yuen station to the park in four minutes.

Special Events

On the Saturday and Sunday closest to 7 and 8 April, the Inuyama Matsuri takes place at the Haritsuna-jinja Shrine. This festival dates back to 1650 and features a parade of 13 three-tiered floats decked out with lanterns. Mechanical puppets perform to music on top of the floats.

Places to Stay

If you intend to stay in Inuyama, perhaps as an extension of a ukai jaunt, you can check with the information office in the Nagoya International Center (see the earlier Nagoya section) or the Inuyama Sightseeing Information Center.

The cheapest and one of the best options in Inuyama is the *Inuyama International Youth Hostel* (☎ 0568-61-1111), about a 30 minute walk east of Inuyama-yuen station. There is no dormitory accommodation, but a very comfortable single with your own sink and toilet will only set you back ¥3600. Western-style twin rooms are ¥6200, Japanese *tatami* rooms are ¥5600. Book in advance if possible, as this place is very popular, especially in summer. The hostel is closed from 28 December to 3 January. To get there from Inuyama-yuen station, follow the road along the river north from Inuyama-bashi Bridge until you reach the first intersection (about 20 minutes). Turn right and follow the signs to the steps, which lead up the hill to the hostel. You can shorten the walk a bit by taking the monorail into the Monkey Park (¥150). After getting off, don't go into the park but instead take the exit to the left and follow the stairs down until you reach a three-way intersection. Take the road directly opposite, walk around 250m and the sign for the hostel will be on your left. The monorail runs between 8.30 am and 6 pm.

Around 300m north-west of the Inuyama station is the *Inuyama City Hotel* (☎ 0568-61-1600), which has singles at ¥6500, twins at ¥11,000 and doubles at ¥10,000. Further north again, close to the Kiso-gawa River, is the expensive *Meitetsu Inuyama Hotel* (☎ 0568-61-2211), where singles/doubles will set you back ¥12,000/17,000. Nearby is a row of six or seven ryokan facing the river: prices here start at around ¥8000 per person.

Getting There & Away

Inuyama is connected with Nagoya station via the Meitetsu Inuyama line. The ordinary express takes 35 minutes and costs ¥520. You can connect with the JR Takayama line at Shin-Unuma station, one stop north of

Inuyama-yuen. From Inuyama there are frequent trains to Gifu (30 minutes, ¥360) where you can connect with the JR Takayama and Tōkaidō lines.

AROUND INUYAMA
Meiji-mura Village Museum　明治村
In Meiji-mura, 20 minutes by bus from Inuyama, you can see more than 60 Meiji-era buildings brought together from all over Japan. The clash of architectural styles on display, both western and Japanese, provides a sense of the play of contradictions in the Meiji period, as Japan sought to transform itself into a unified modern nation and an international power. The aerial bombing of Japan late in WWII, natural disasters and unbridled modernisation have left few buildings of this era standing; this open-air museum provides a rare chance to see what's left.

Even if you chug around on the village locomotive or tram, you'll still need at least half a day to enjoy the place at an easy pace.

The village is open from 9.30 am to 5 pm daily but closes an hour earlier between November and February. Admission costs ¥1500.

A bus departs every 20 minutes from Inuyama station for the 20 minute (¥380) trip to Meiji-mura. You can also take a one hour bus ride from the Meitetsu bus station in Nagoya direct to Meiji-mura. Buses leave twice an hour. The round-trip fare is ¥1190.

Ōgata-jinja Shrine　大県神社
This shrine is dedicated to Izanami, the female Shinto deity, and draws women devotees seeking marriage or the birth of children. The precincts of the shrine contain rocks and other items resembling female genitals.

Ōgata-jinja is a 15 minute walk east of Gakuden station, to the south-west of Meiji-mura, on the Meitetsu Komaki line.

The Hime-no-Miya Grand Festival takes place on the first Sunday in March at Ogata-jinja. The local populace pray for good harvests and prosperity by parading through the streets bearing a portable shrine with replicas of female genitals.

Tagata-jinja Shrine　田県神社
This shrine is dedicated to Izanagi, the Shinto deity who is the male counterpart of Izanami. The main hall of the shrine has a side building containing a collection of phalluses of all dimensions, left as offerings by grateful worshippers.

Tagata-jinja is at Tagata-jinja-mae station, one stop further south of Gakuden station, on the Meitetsu Komaki line.

The festival of Tagata Hōnen Sai takes place on 15 March at the Tagata-jinja Shrine. Replicas of male genitals are carted around in this male complement of the Hime-no-Miya Festival.

Tajimi　多治見
Tajimi (population 94,000) has a long history as a porcelain-producing centre and is famed for its Mino ware (Mino-yaki). It remains as one of the largest porcelain-producing centres in Japan. There are two major porcelain festivals held each year, where local producers gather to display their latest creations. The Tajimi Tōki Festival is held in the second weekend of April, while the Tajimi Minoyaki Danchi Festival is held in late September/early October: the exact date changes from year to year. Check with JNTO for more details.

Close to Tajimi station (just over one km to the east) is the **Prefectural Porcelain Museum**, a small place that's open from 9 am to 4.30 pm (closed Monday). Admission is ¥200.

Tajimi is not far to the east of Meiji-mura, but unless you have your own transport it is most easily reached from Nagoya on the JR Chūō line (32 minutes, ¥640).

GERO　下呂
Gero is favoured by Japanese tourists for its hot-spring spas *(onsen)*, but its appeal is dampened by the town's sprawl of concrete buildings. The waters of the spas are reputedly beneficial for the complexion, rheumatism and athletic injuries. The town is fairly compact, making it easy to walk around and go hot-spring hopping.

Apart from its numerous spas, including

several communal open-air ones, Gero boasts its own 'hot-spring temple' – **Onsen-ji** – overlooking the town. Some travellers rave about the Takehara Bunraku performances held at **Gero Gasshō Village Folklore Museum**. The puppets are operated by one man and performances are held four to five days a week, with one or two performances daily. Admission to the museum is ¥750. Other minor attractions include the **Mine-ichigo Relics Park** and **Zenshō-ji Temple**, which is next to the station of the same name, one stop north of Gero.

Places to Stay

There are numerous ryokan and minshuku in this resort town. One of the cheapest spots is the *Katsuragawa Minshuku* (☎ 0576-25-2615), which has good rooms for ¥3650. Unfortunately there are only six of them, so it's best to call ahead. Katsuragawa is across the river and several blocks north of the railway station. On the railway side of the river, 15 minutes walk north-west of the station, the *Miyanoya Minshuku* (☎ 0576-25-2399) offers rooms and two meals for ¥6500. Both hotels have baths with onsen water piped directly in. If you're looking for a more upscale stay, the *Ogawaya Ryokan* (☎ 0576-25-2800) has both an outside onsen bath and a 25m indoor bathing pool! In addition, all rooms face out onto the river. A stay here will cost you ¥17,000 per person, which includes two meals. For more options (there are dozens) check with the Gero tourist information office, at the west exit of the railway station.

Getting There & Away

To get to Gero, take a JR Takayama line train from Gifu station or from Nagoya. The Hida limited express does the trip in around 1½ hours, and costs ¥4100.

GUJŌ HACHIMAN 郡上八幡

The main claim to fame of this town is its Gujō Odori Folk Dance Festival, held from early July to early September when the townsfolk continue nearly four centuries of tradition and let their hair down for some frenzied dancing. During the four main days of the festival (from 13 to 16 August) the dancing goes on through the night.

The town's other main attraction is Gujō Hachiman Castle, built some 400 years ago. However, the castle's historical integrity was somewhat compromised by the relatively late addition (in 1933) of the donjon. Apparently locals felt their neighbourhood fortress needed the multi-storey parapet in order to compete with the likes of Inuyama and Nagoya castles. The castle is open from 9 am to 4.30 pm, except from June to August, when it's open from 8 am to 6 pm. Admission is ¥300. From the railway station, take a bus to the Honchō bus station. The castle lies another 25 minutes by foot to the north-east.

If you decide to overnight in Gujō Hachiman, your cheapest choice is probably the *Hachiman Cycling Terminal* (☎ 0575-62-2139), a municipal minshuku which doubles as a bicycle rental shop. A room and two meals costs ¥5100. The only drawback is that it's around five km out of town. From the railway station, catch a bus to the Honchō bus station, and then get on the Meihō bus to the Chuō-bashi Bridge. From there it's a three minute walk. If you want to stay in town, the *Bizenya Ryokan* (☎ 0575-65-2068) is 10 minutes walk from the railway station along the main road, but is more expensive at ¥8500 per person, including two meals.

From Gifu, take a train to Mino Ōta (JR Takayama line), then change to the Nagaragawa line for the 90 minute trip to Gujō Hachiman.

Northern Gifu-ken

The major attractions of the mountainous Gifu Prefecture lie to the north in the Hida District, which is part of the Japan Alps. Takayama, the administrative centre of Hida, retains much of its original architecture and small-scale charm. From Takayama, you can make side trips to the spectacular mountain regions around Kamikōchi to the east (where there are numerous hot-spring resorts and

CENTRAL HONSHŪ

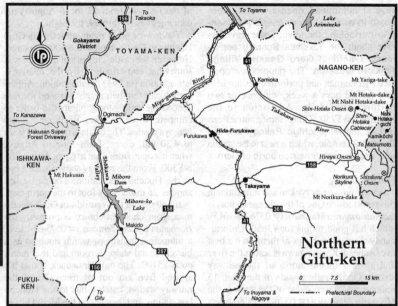

Northern Gifu-ken

CENTRAL HONSHŪ

excellent scope for short walks or long hikes) or you can visit the Shōkawa Valley for a look at rural life and architecture in remote farming villages to the west. If you go east from Takayama you can cross the Japan Alps to Matsumoto and Nagano, and if you head west, you can continue to Kanazawa.

Access to the remoter parts of Hida is restricted by severe weather conditions which often last from November to mid-May. Check first with Japan Travel-Phone (☎ 0120-44-4800, toll free) or the Takayama tourist information office if you plan to visit during the winter.

More details about the Japan Alps region can be found in the Nagano-ken section of this chapter.

TAKAYAMA 高山

Takayama (population 66,000) lies in the ancient Hida District tucked away between the mountains of the Japan Alps, and should be a high priority on any visit to Central Honshū

and the Japan Alps. Give yourself two days to enjoy the place and add a few more if you plan to use it as a base to visit the mountains.

Takayama, with its traditional inns, shops and sake breweries, is a rarity: a Japanese city (admittedly a small one) that has managed to retain something of its traditional charm. It's a small place, easily tackled on foot or by bicycle, and a good town to take a break from the more urgent rhythms of larger urban centres.

Historically, the inhabitants of Takayama have long been known for their woodworking skills: Hida carpenters were drafted to construct imperial palaces and temples in the Kyoto and Nara regions. The woodworking tradition continues to this day with the production of furniture and woodcarvings.

Takayama entered history proper in the late 16th century, when it was established as the castle town of the Kanamori family. The present layout of the town dates from this period.

The Takayama Festival, held in April and

October (see later in this section), is rated as one of the three great festivals in Japan and attracts over half a million spectators. If you plan to go to the festival and want to stay in Takayama, book your accommodation well in advance.

Orientation

All the main sights, except Hida Folk Village, are in the centre of town, a short walk from the station. The streets are arranged in a grid pattern, similar to Kyoto or Nara, and this makes it easy to find your way around. From the centre, you can continue east for 10 minutes along Kokubun-ji-dōri, which is the main street, until you reach Teramachi (Temple District) and Shiroyama-kōen Park in the Higashiyama (Eastern Mountain) District.

Hida Folk Village is a 10 minute bus ride west of the station.

Information

The Hida tourist information office (☎ 0577-32-5328), directly in front of JR Takayama station, has English-language maps and information on sights and accommodation. Also very helpful is the JNTO pamphlet *Takayama and Shirakawago*, though the office doesn't always have it in stock. The office also has English-language bus schedules for services between Takayama and Hirayu Onsen, Shin-Hotaka Onsen, Kamikōchi and Shōkawa Valley.

Those interested in Takayama festivals should ask for a pale green booklet called *Background of Takayama Festival*, and the colourful *Hida Festival Guide*, which covers festivals throughout the district. The office is open from 8.30 am to 6 pm between 1 April and 31 October. During the rest of the year it closes at 5 pm.

If you want to arrange a home visit, a home stay, or would like to arrange for a volunteer interpreter for non-Japanese languages (or even sign language) call the International Affairs Office (☎ 0577-32-3333, ext 212).

Planning Your Itinerary

Takayama makes a good base for trips into the mountains (Kamikōchi, Hirayu Onsen, Shin-Hotaka or Norikura), or to the Shōkawa Valley with its traditional farmhouses.

Sights in town include more than a dozen museums, galleries, collections and exhibitions. Collections range from wild birds, toys and lion masks to folkcraft and archaeology. A small sampling is provided in this section, but check with the information office for full details.

Walking Tour

From the station, you can complete a circular walking tour of the main sights in an hour. A walking tour of the Higashiyama District which passes through Teramachi and Shiroyama-kōen Park is also highly recommended. This walk takes about two hours, and includes nearly a dozen temples and shrines. It is particularly enjoyable in the early morning or late afternoon.

Although Hida Folk Village is itself an enjoyable place to walk around, the approach to the village from the station offers only a dreary, urban stroll – the bus ride zips you through this in 10 minutes.

Takayama-jinya　高山陣屋

Originally built in 1615 as the administrative centre for the Kanamori clan, Takayama-jinya (Historical Government House) is worth visiting to see how the authorities governed at that time. The present buildings are reconstructions dating from 1816.

As well as government offices, a rice granary and a garden, there's a torture chamber with explanatory detail.

Admission costs ¥410 and it's open daily from 8.45 am to 5 pm, April to October, and closes 30 minutes earlier during the rest of the year.

Sanmachi Suji　三町筋

This area is the centre of the old town, and consists of three streets (Ichi-no-Machi, Ni-no-Machi and San-no-Machi) lined with traditional shops, breweries, restaurants, museums and some private homes. The sake breweries are easily recognised by the round

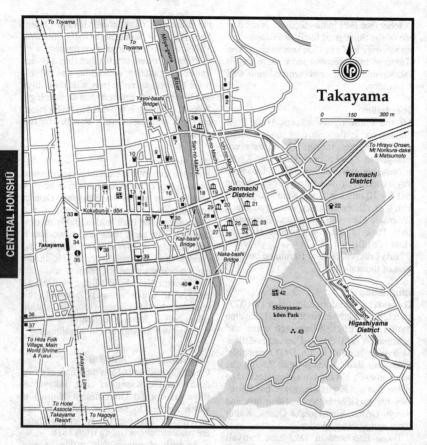

Takayama

0   150   300 m

To Toyama
To Toyama
Miya-gawa River
Yayoi-bashi Bridge
San-no-Machi
Ichi-no-Machi
Ni-no-Machi
To Hirayu Onsen, Mt Norikura-dake & Matsumoto
Teramachi District
Sanmachi District
Kokubun-ji - dōri
Takayama
Kaji-bashi Bridge
Naka-bashi Bridge
Enako-gawa River
Takayama Line
To Hida Folk Village, Main World Shrine & Fukui
To Hotel Associa Takayama Resort
To Nagoya
Shiroyama-kōen Park
Higashiyama District

basket of cedar fronds hanging above the entrance. The best plan is to stroll around without trying to see everything and thus avoid risking an overdose of museums.

Hida Archaeology Museum The Hida Archaeology Museum displays craft items and archaeological objects in a traditional house. The house was constructed with secret passages and windows in case the owners needed to make a quick exit. Admission costs ¥400 and it's open daily from 8 am to 6 pm, March to November, and closes an hour earlier from December to February.

Fujii Folkcraft Art Gallery This museum is close to the archaeology museum and displays folkcraft from Japan, China and Korea. It's in an old merchant's house. Admission costs ¥400 and opening hours are from 9 am to 5 pm daily.

Hirata Folk Art Museum The Hirata Folk Art Museum is a merchant's house dating from the turn of the century. The displays include items from everyday Japanese life. Admission costs ¥200 and it's open daily from 9 am to 5 pm.

Gallery of Traditional Japanese Toys This gallery has an exhibition of some 2000 dolls and folk toys from the 17th century to the present day. The gallery is open daily from 8.30 am to 5 pm and entry costs ¥250.

Takayama Museum of Local History This museum is devoted to the crafts and traditions of the region. Pride of place is allotted to images carved by Enshū, a woodcarving priest who wandered around the region in the

17th century. Admission costs ¥300. It's open from 8.30 am to 5 pm, closed on Monday, with the exception of the high-season summer months, when it's open daily.

Kusakabe Folk Art Museum
日下部民芸館
This museum is a fine example of a wealthy merchant's home, with the living quarters in one section and the warehouse in another. It is fitted out as it would have been if you'd walked in to talk business in the late 1890s. Admission costs ¥500. It's open daily from 9 am to 5 pm, but closes 30 minutes earlier from December to March.

Yoshijima-ke House   吉島家住宅
This house is on the same street as the Kusakabe Folk Art Museum. Although Yoshijima-ke is also a merchant's house, it has more refined architectural details such as lattice windows which provide a lighter atmosphere. It's open daily from 9 am to 4.30 pm, apart from December to February, when it closes on Tuesday; admission costs ¥500.

Lacquerware Exhibition Hall
春慶会館
If lacquerware is a specific interest, you should visit the Lacquerware Exhibition Hall (Shunkei Kaikan) (☎ 0577-32-3373), which is north-east of the station, a couple of blocks before Yayoi-bashi Bridge. More than 1000 lacquerware items are on display with an exhibit showing production techniques. The hall is open from 8.30 am to 5 pm; admission costs ¥300.

Festival Floats Exhibition Hall
屋台会館
If you can't be in Takayama for the big festivals, you can still see four of the *yatai* (festival floats) which are displayed at the Takayama Yatai Kaikan (Festival Floats Exhibition Hall) in seasonal rotation. The hall is adjacent to the grounds of the Sakurayama Hachiman-gū Shrine, where the autumn festival begins. Those yatai which are not on display are stored in tall *yatai-kura* (yatai storehouses) which can be seen in the

town. For the technically minded, a collapsible top tier allows the yatai to pass through the doors.

The yatai, some of which date from the 17th century, are spectacular creations with flamboyant carvings, metalwork and lacquerwork. The complex marionettes, manipulated by eight accomplished puppeteers using 36 strings, are capable of amazing tricks and acrobatics.

Admission to the hall costs ¥800 and includes a glossy leaflet with information about the yatai. It's open from 9 am to 4.30 pm.

Lion Mask Exhibition Hall   獅子会館
Just below the Yatai Kaikan is the Lion Mask Exhibition Hall, which has a display of over 800 lion masks and musical instruments connected with the lion dances commonly performed at festivals in central and northern Japan. There are also frequent displays of ancient mechanical puppets – a good chance for a close-up view of these marvellous gadgets in action.

Admission costs ¥600 and this includes the mechanical puppet show (displays twice an hour). The hall is open from 8.30 am to 5 pm.

Hida Kokubun-ji Temple   飛騨国分寺
The original temple was built in the 8th century, but the oldest of the present buildings dates from the 16th century. The old gingko tree beside the three-storey pagoda is impressively gnarled and in remarkably good shape considering it's believed to have stood there for 1200 years. Admission costs ¥300 and it's open from 9 am to 4 pm. The temple is a five minute walk from the station.

Teramachi & Shiroyama-kōen Park
寺町・城山公園
The best way to link these two areas in the Higashiyama District is to follow the walking trail. Teramachi has over a dozen temples (the youth hostel is in Tenshō-ji Temple) and shrines which you can wander around at your leisure before continuing to the lush greenery of the park. Various trails lead through the park and up the mountainside to the ruins of Takayama-jō Castle. As

you descend, you can take a look at Shōren-ji Temple, which was transferred to this site from the Shirakawa Valley when a dam was built there in 1960. Admission to the main hall costs ¥200.

From the temple it's a 10 minute walk back to the centre of town.

Hida Folk Village   飛驒民俗村
The Hida Minzoku-mura (Hida Folk Village) is a large open-air museum with dozens of traditional houses which once belonged to craftspeople and farmers in the Takayama region. The houses were dismantled at their original sites and rebuilt here. You should definitely include this museum in your visit to Takayama.

The admission charge (¥700) admits you to both the eastern and western sections of the village, which are connected part of the way by a pleasant walk through fields. Allow at least two hours if you want to explore the village on foot at a leisurely pace. On a fine day, there are good views across the town to the peaks of the Japan Alps. The village is open from 8.30 am to 5 pm.

The western section, called Hida-no-Sato, stretches over 10 hectares and contains a village of 12 traditional old houses and a complex of five traditional buildings with artisans demonstrating folk arts & crafts. It takes about two hours, at a leisurely pace, to follow the circular route. The displays are well presented and offer an excellent chance to see what rural life was like in previous centuries.

The eastern section of the village is centred around the Hida Minzokukan (Hida Folklore Museum) at the Minzokukan-mae bus stop. There are four buildings in the museum complex: Wakayama House, Nokubi House, Go-kura Storehouse (used for storage of rice as payment of taxes) and the Museum of Mountain Life.

To walk from the western to the eastern section, take the road downhill, and keep an eye out for the wooden sign directing you onto the path to the Minzokukan. The path winds past several fields and ends up at the Museum of Mountain Life.

Hida Folk Village is only a 20 minute walk from Takayama station, but the route through the urban sprawl is not enjoyable. Either hire a bicycle in town, or take the Hida-no-Sato bus from the bus station which takes 10 minutes to reach Hida-no-Sato and then continues downhill for a couple of minutes to Minzokukan-mae. Buses leave twice an hour from the No 2 gate. The one-way fare is ¥250. A discount ticket is available that combines both the round-trip fare and admission to the park for ¥1000, a saving of ¥200. Ask at the ticket window for the 'Hida-no-Sato setto ken'. The last bus back from the park leaves the Minzokukan-mae stop at 3.26 pm.

Markets
The asa-ichi (morning markets) take place every morning from 7 to 11 am, starting an hour earlier from April to October. The Jinya-mae Market is a small one in front of Takayama-jinya; the Miyagawa Market is larger, strung out along the east bank of the Miya-gawa River, between Kaji-bashi Bridge and Yayoi-bashi Bridge. Those in need of an early morning coffee can stop at a stand-up stall in the middle of this market for a steaming cup (¥200). The markets aren't astounding, but provide a pleasant way to start the day with a stroll past gnarled farmers at their vegetable stands and stalls selling herbs, pickles and souvenirs.

Special Events
Takayama is famed all over Japan for two major festivals which attract over half a million visitors. Book your accommodation well in advance.

Sannō Matsuri Festival takes place on 14 and 15 April. The starting point for the festival parade is Hie-jinja Shrine. A dozen yatai, decorated with carvings, dolls, colourful curtains and blinds, are drawn through the town. In the evening the floats are decked out with lanterns and the procession is accompanied by sacred music. A famous feature of the floats is the marionettes, which perform amazing antics.

Hachiman Matsuri Festival, which takes place on 9 and 10 October, is a slightly smaller version of Sannō Matsuri and starts off at the Sakurayama Hachiman-gū Shrine. If you plan to stay in Takayama for either of these festivals, you must book months in advance and expect to pay up to 20% more than you would at any other time. Alternatively, you could stay elsewhere in the region and commute to Takayama for the festivals.

Places to Stay

The tourist information office outside Takayama station can help with reservations either in Takayama or elsewhere in the region, and has lists of places to suit all budgets.

Youth Hostel *Hida Takayama Tenshō-ji Youth Hostel* (☎ 0577-32-6345) is a temple in the pleasant surroundings of Teramachi, but hostellers should be prepared to stick to a rigid routine. Punctually at 10 pm you are lulled to sleep by music and at 7 am you are awakened by the recorded twittering of birds. A bed for the night costs ¥2600, ¥3100 for nonmembers. For ¥1000 extra you can have a room to yourself, if one is available (not likely). The youth hostel is a 25 minute walk across town from the railway station. To shave 20 minutes off the walk, board the bus for Shin Hotaka and get off at the Betsuin-mae stop. The youth hostel is a five minute walk east.

Shukubō The *Rikkyoku-ji Temple* (☎ 0577-32-0519) has beds for ¥2800, though getting one may be tricky unless you speak at least some Japanese. The temple is not very distinctive, and somewhat blends in with the other buildings on the street, so keep a sharp eye out. The entrance for accommodation is on the right side of the temple: look for the sign with the green arrow on it.

Minshuku Without doubt one of the most pleasant places to stay is the *Rickshaw Inn* (☎ 0577-32-2890), a modern-style minshuku with almost a South-East Asian look to it. The owners speak English and are very friendly, and the room rates are good value for money. A bed in one of the comfortable

three or four-bed dorm rooms costs ¥3200, while Japanese-style rooms with attached bath are ¥4900 per person. Singles are available for ¥4200, ¥6000 with attached bath. The inn also has some English-language information on hand, including a useful map of nearby restaurants and bars, and an international card phone. It's about eight minutes walk from the railway station.

Close to the railway station is the *Minshuku Kuwataniya* (☎ 0577-32-5021), by far Takayama's longest-running minshuku (70 years). Per person costs are from ¥7000 which includes two meals, with dinner always featuring the famed Hida beef.

Hachibei (☎ 0577-33-0573) is a pleasantly faded, rambling place close to Hida-no-Sato Village. Take a bus to the Hida-no-Sato bus stop; from there it's an eight minute walk north. Prices start at ¥7000 per person and include two meals. Also on the western side of town, but closer to the railway station, is *Sosuke* (☎ 0577-32-0818), where you can get a room for ¥4500 per person, without meals. It's a nice enough place but is on a busy road. This can be a drawback in the summer as the owners turn off the air-conditioning around midnight, leaving you little choice but to open the window to let in air, and traffic noise.

Ryokan Most of Takayama's ryokan cost between ¥8000 and ¥15,000 per person including two meals, and in some cases you may need some Japanese before the proprietors will take you. Up in the north-east section of town, next to the Lacquerware Exhibition Hall, is the flower-festooned *Murasaki Ryokan* (☎ 0577-32-1724), which has rooms for ¥7500 per person, with two meals. Take a moment to admire the dazzling wall of flowers (200 pots worth) along the front of the building, the product of 15 years work.

In the same area, but nearer the river, is the *Sumiyoshi Ryokan* (☎ 0577-32-0228), a delightfully traditional-style place with rates from ¥8000 to ¥15,000. Straight ahead (east) from the station and just over the river is the *Ryokan Gōtō* (☎ 0577-33-0870), another traditional-style inn, with rates from ¥9000. The architecturally modern *Ryokan Seiryu* (☎ 0577-32-0448) is close to the town centre. Prices start at ¥10,000 per person including two meals.

Hotels The *New Alps Hotel* (☎ 0577-32-2888) is just a minute's walk from the station. Singles/doubles start at ¥5000/10,000, which is pretty good value. Over by the river, the *Hotel Alpha One* (☎ 0577-32-2211; the Greek character for *alpha* and the numeral '1' are on the sign outside) is another reasonably inexpensive place, with singles from ¥5100 and twins/doubles at ¥10,800/9800. Just a 10 minutes walk from the station, the *Takayama Central Hotel* (☎ 0577-35-1881) has singles at ¥5500 and twins from ¥11,000.

More up-market possibilities include the *Takayama City Hotel Four Seasons* (☎ 0577-36-0088), with singles/twins from ¥6700/12,700, and the *Takayama Green Hotel* (☎ 0577-33-5500), with twins and doubles from ¥18,000. Several km south of town lies the luxurious *Hotel Associa Takayama Resort* (☎ 0057-36-0001). All rooms boast views of the Japan Alps, and the hotel has both indoor and outdoor hot-spring baths and a tennis court. Rates start at ¥19,800 for a standard twin and climb quickly from there. A free shuttle bus runs hourly between Takayama station and the hotel.

Places to Eat

Takayama is known for several culinary treats. These include Hida-soba (buckwheat noodles with broth and vegetables), hoba-miso (miso paste cooked on a hoba leaf, often served with beef or vegetables) and sansai (mountain greens). You might also want to try mitarashi-dango (skewers of grilled rice balls seasoned with soy sauce) or shio-sembei (salty rice crackers). Hida beef, though relatively new on the culinary scene, is considered to be among the finest grades of meat in Japan.

Close to Takayama station is a *Yamamotoya*, one of many little soba places along the street where you can try Hida-soba. The restaurant also serves tempura and katsudon (fried pork chops over rice) sets from around ¥800.

Most restaurants, especially in the Sanmachi Suji, close quite early, between 7 and 9 pm. If you can't manage an earlier dinner, your best bet is to try the restaurants and izakaya closer to the railway station.

Suzuya (☎ 0577-32-2484) is a well-known restaurant with rustic decor in the centre of town, on the station side of the river. It serves all the local specialities and its teishoku (set meal) lunches are pretty good value – prices start from around ¥1000. Opening hours are from 11 am to 7.30 pm, but it's closed on Tuesday. To help you order, there's also an English menu.

For a bite of history, try *Ebisu*, a little soba restaurant in the Sanmachi Suji that has been in business for 370 years. Ordering can be a bit tricky, however, as there is no English menu. Nearby, for tofu fans only, is the *Noguchiya Tofu Restaurant*. Set lunches range from ¥700 to ¥1500, featuring numerous tasty varieties of hot and cold tofu dishes, and there's a picture menu to help with the ordering ordeal. The restaurant closes at 5 pm.

Murasaki, part of an izakaya chain, has a great atmosphere, reasonable food and drink prices and an illustrated menu for easy ordering. There's no English sign: look out for the large red sign hanging on the right side of the street.

For a complete change, you could try *Tom's Bellgins Bell* (☎ 0577-33-6507), a couple of blocks north-west of Kaji-bashi Bridge. Its amiable Swiss owner, Tom Steinmann, fulfils all those cravings for things like rósti or fondue. His pizzas are excellent, and prices start at around ¥1500.

If you're looking for a friendly place to knock back a few cold beers, the *Red Hill Pub* has an excellent selection of domestic and imported beers. It's a pretty popular spot with locals, and tends to get crowded after 11 pm, so go a bit earlier if you want a seat. *Tonio Pub* is an English-style place with Guinness on tap and reasonable prices, as far as Japanese bars go, that is.

Bunched around the old part of town are eight sake breweries with pedigrees dating back to the Edo period. Formerly, the production processes for this *jizake* (local sake) were closed to visitors, but the breweries have recently started to arrange tours and tastings from early January to the end of February only. The information office at the station can arrange for prospective foreign imbibers to join these tours.

Things to Buy

Takayama is renowned for several crafts. *Ichii ittobori* (woodcarvings) are fashioned from yew and can be seen as intricate components of the yatai floats or as figurines for sale as souvenirs. The craft of Shunkei lacquerware was introduced from Kyoto several centuries ago and is used to produce boxes, trays and flower containers. Pottery is produced in three styles ranging from the rustic Yamada-yaki to the decorative ceramics of Shibukusa-yaki. If your house feels empty, local makers of traditional furniture can help you fill it.

The Sanmachi Suji area has many shops selling handicraft items or you can browse in handicraft shops along the section of Kokubun-ji-dōri between the river and the station.

The Lacquerware Exhibition Hall (see earlier in this section), which is run by the city, has two adjacent shops with outstanding lacquerware and porcelain, and prices are generally lower than those you'll find in private shops.

Like Takayama's restaurants, many of the shops close in the early evening, usually around 7 to 8 pm.

Getting There & Away

Train Takayama is connected with Nagoya on the JR Takayama line. The Hida limited express takes around 2¼ hours (¥5750). There are eight Hida departures daily in either direction.

Express trains run from Osaka and Kyoto to Gifu or Nagoya and continue on the JR Takayama line to Takayama. The trip takes about five hours from Osaka and 30 minutes

less from Kyoto. If you are travelling on a rail pass, the best course of action would be to take a shinkansen to Nagoya and change there to the Takayama line.

Toyama is connected with Takayama on the JR Takayama line. The fastest express from Toyama takes around 1½ hours whereas the local train (*futsū*) rambles to Takayama in just under three hours.

Bus Many roads in this region close in the winter. This means that bus schedules usually only start from early May and finish in late October. For exact opening or closing dates either phone Japan Travel-Phone (☎ 0120-44-4800, toll free) or check with the tourist offices.

A bus service connects Takayama with Hirayu Onsen (one hour, ¥1500) and takes another hour (and another ¥1500) to reach Kamikōchi. Direct buses run from Takayama via Hirayu Onsen to Shin-Hotaka Onsen (¥2070) and the nearby cablecar (ropeway).

Another bus route runs on the spectacular Norikura Skyline Road connecting Norikura with Takayama in 1¾ hours.

A bus/train combination runs from Takayama via Kamikōchi to Matsumoto. Take a bus from Takayama to Kamikōchi then change to another bus for Shin-Shimashima station on the Matsumoto Dentetsu line and continue by rail to Matsumoto. For more details see the Kamikōchi section in this chapter.

Car Takayama is well situated for day trips to the Shōkawa Valley region and northern Alps resorts such as Hirayu and Shin-Hotaka. However, although these destinations are only an hour or two away, bus fares are surprisingly expensive. For example a journey up to Shin-Hotaka and back costs more than ¥4000. If there are three or four of you, it may be worth renting a car for a day or two. Eki Rent A Car System, run by JR, has an office at the railway station (0577-33-3522), and there's a branch of Nippon Rental Car west of the railway station, near the Takayama Green Hotel and Sosuke minshuku.

Mt Fuji

CHRIS TAYLOR

RICHARD I'ANSON

CHRIS TAYLOR

NICKO GONCHAROFF

MARTIN MOOS

MARTIN MOOS

A	B
C	D
E	F

A: Hida Folk Village
B: Sumo tournament, Nagoya
C: Kenroku-en Garden, Kanazawa
D: Wash basin, Takayama
E: Souvenir seller, Wajima
F: Gasshō-zukuri houses, Yokayama

Getting Around

With the exception of Hida Folk Village, the sights in Takayama can be easily covered on foot. You can amble from the station across to Higashiyama on the other side of town in 25 minutes.

Bus The bus station is on your left as you exit the station. Although the main sights in town are best seen on foot or by bicycle, the walk to Hida Folk Village is tedious and unattractive. It's preferable to use the half-hourly bus service which takes 10 minutes and costs ¥250. There isn't any bus service within Takayama to speak of, as the distances are too short.

Cycling There are several bicycle rental places near the station and in town. Rates are usually around ¥350 for the first hour, ¥200 for each additional hour and ¥1300 for the day. The youth hostel is a far better deal, charging ¥80 per hour or ¥600 for the day.

SHŌKAWA VALLEY REGION 荘川

This is one of the more interesting regions in Japan and highly recommended as a side trip from Takayama or as a short stopover en route between Takayama and Kanazawa. Although much of what you see here has been specially preserved for, and supported by, tourism, it still presents a view of rural life found in few other parts of Japan. To avoid large contingents of tourists, avoid the peak times of May, August and October.

In the 12th century, the remoteness and inaccessibility of the area is claimed to have attracted a few stragglers from the Taira clan. They sought hideaways here and on Kyūshū after their clan was virtually wiped out by the Genji clan in a brutal battle at Shimonoseki in 1185.

In the present century, construction of the gigantic Miboro Dam in the '60s submerged many of the villages. The attention this attracted to the region also drew tourists interested in the unusual architecture of the remaining villages and their remote mountain surroundings.

There are many villages and hamlets spread around the Shōkawa Valley region. Shirakawa-gō and Gokayama are two districts with dozens of specially preserved houses and are the most commonly visited by travellers.

Bus services to and around Shōkawa Valley are infrequent, so it's important to check the schedule before heading out from Takayama. Exact times change from season to season, but there are generally only two buses daily to Ogimachi. Buses from there to Gokayama are similarly limited. Bus fares are also quite expensive, so if there are several of you interested in a day trip, you may want to consider renting a car. See under Takayama for details.

Shirakawa-gō District & Ogimachi
白川郷・荻町

The Shirakawa-gō District consists of several clusters of houses in villages stretching for several km. Ogimachi, the central cluster, is the most convenient place for bus connections, tourist information and orientation. When arriving by bus, ask to get off at the Gasshō-shuraku bus stop.

Information The tourist information office (☎ 05769-6-1013) is next to the Gasshō-shuraku bus stop in the centre of Ogimachi. It's open from 9 am to 4 pm, closed Wednesday. The office has a Japanese map of the whole region including a detailed map of Ogimachi itself. An English leaflet is also available. The office can also help book accommodation, but the staff don't speak English, so you may want to arrange this from Takayama.

Tenbōdai Lookout To get your bearings, climb to the Tenbōdai lookout; from here, you'll obtain the view seen on most tourist brochures. From the Gasshō-shuraku bus stop, walk north along the main road for about 10 minutes and on your right you will see a wooded hill beside the road with a side street leading around the foot of the hill. You can either follow the side street to the top of the hill or, after walking about 10m down the side street, take the steep path on your right which gets you to the top in about 15 minutes.

CENTRAL HONSHŪ

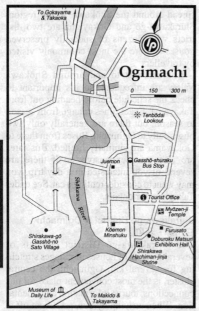

Shirakawa-gō Gasshō-no-Sato Village
白川郷合掌の里

This well-presented group of over a dozen *gasshō-zukuri* buildings was largely collected from the surrounding region during construction of the Miboro Dam, and reconstructed for display as an open-air museum. Several of the houses are used for demonstrating regional crafts such as woodwork, straw handicrafts, ceramics and painting in Chinese ink – most of these items are on sale either from the artisans or at the ticket office.

You can wander away from the houses for a pleasant stroll through the trees further up the mountain. If you don't take a picnic, you can stop at the rest house near the exit which is run by a chatty lady who offers tea, biscuits and home-made *mochi* (rice cakes) toasted over the *irori* (open hearth).

Admission costs ¥700. The village is open daily except Thursday from 8.30 am to 5 pm between April and November, from 8 am to 6 pm in August, and from 9 am to 4 pm

between December and January. To reach the entrance, you have to walk west from the main road, cross a suspension bridge over the river, and continue through a dimly lit tunnel dripping with moisture.

Myōzen-ji Temple This temple in the centre of Ogimachi has a museum displaying the traditional paraphernalia of daily life.

Admission to the museum costs ¥200 and it's open daily from 8 am to 5 pm. There are shorter opening hours during the winter.

Doburoku Matsuri Exhibition Hall This exhibition hall (Doburoku Matsuri-no-Yakata) is very close to the Shirakawa Hachiman-jinja Shrine. The hall contains displays devoted to the Doburoku Matsuri Festival, an event clearly not lacking in liquid refreshment (*doburoku* is a type of unrefined sake), which is held in mid-October at the shrine.

Admission costs ¥300 and it's open daily from 9 am to 4 pm (closed from December to April).

Museum of Daily Life If you walk for about 15 minutes from the centre of Ogimachi back along the road toward Takayama, you'll reach the Museum of Daily Life, just beyond the second bridge. On display are agricultural tools, rural crafts, equipment for the cultivation of silkworms and various household items from the past. Admission costs ¥300 and the museum is open daily, April to November, from 8 am to 6 pm. It opens one hour later in December and is closed from January to March.

Places to Stay Some of the gasshō-zukuri buildings function as minshuku and are a popular accommodation option in this region. If you don't speak Japanese, it would be a good idea to enlist the support of the tourist information office in introducing you to one. Ryokan prices start around ¥9000 per person including two meals; minshuku prices for the same deals start at around ¥7000. A couple of rustic possibilities include *Kōemon* (☎ 05769-6-1446) as well

Hida's Gasshō-Zukuri

Winter in the Hida region can get quite fierce, and inhabitants faced snow and cold long before the advent of propane heaters and 4WD vehicles. One of the most visible symbols of that adaptability is gasshō-zukuri architecture, seen in the steeply slanted straw-roofed homes that still dot the landscape around Takayama and the Shōkawa Valley.

The sharply angled roofs were designed to prevent heavy snow accumulation, a serious concern in a region where nearly all mountain roads shut down from December to April. The name gasshō comes from the Japanese word for 'praying' because the shape of the roofs was thought to resemble two hands clasped in prayer. Gasshō buildings also often featured pillars crafted from stout cedar trees to lend extra support.

The gasshō-zukuri building has become an endangered species, with most examples having been gathered together and preserved in folk villages. This sometimes means that two homes which are now neighbours were once separated by several days or weeks of travel on foot or sled. But local authorities have worked hard to re-create their natural surroundings, making it possible to imagine what life in the Hida hills might have looked like hundreds of years ago. ■

as Furusato (☎ 05769-6-1033). *Juemon* (☎ 05769-6-1053) is one minshuku which has received favourable comments from foreign visitors.

If you want the cheapest option in the area, you'll have to travel to near Gokayama. The *Etchū Gokayama Youth Hostel* (☎ 0763-67-3331) is a gasshō-zukuri house in a fairly remote location (about two km on foot from the bus stop on the main road). See the Gokayama District Places to Stay section for more information on costs and finding the hostel.

Places to Eat Breakfast and dinner are usually included in the price of your ryokan or minshuku. The main street in Ogimachi has several restaurants, including the atmospheric *Shiraogi*, which has dishes from around ¥800. For a real treat, however, try the shiraogi-teishoku, which at ¥2200 gives you a good sampling of the local cuisine.

Getting There & Away If you plan to travel in this region during the winter, you should check first on current road conditions by phoning Japan Travel-Phone (☎ 0120-44-4800, toll free) or the tourist office in Takayama.

Nagoya There is a direct JR bus, running once daily, between Nagoya and Ogimachi during the following peak seasons: from 21 April to 6 May, from 14 July to 10 November, and from 28 December to 5 January. The price for a one-way ticket is ¥4670 and the trip takes five hours. Advance bookings are recommended. Slight alterations are made to these dates every year so you should check exact details before travelling.

Another bus service is operated once a day by Nagoya Tetsudō and runs between Nagoya and Kanazawa via Ogimachi between 1 July and 12 November.

Takayama There are two daily bus connections with Ogimachi, made in two stages. The first stage is a bus service operated by Nohi bus company between Takayama and Makido (one hour, ¥1900). The second stage is a connecting bus service operated by JR between Makido and Ogimachi. The trip takes about an hour and a one-way ticket costs ¥1410 – unless, of course, you have a Japan Rail Pass. Departures from Takayama are around 8 am and 5 pm.

Kanazawa The price of a one-way ticket on the Nagoya Tetsudō service between Ogimachi and Kanazawa costs ¥2610 and the trip takes about three hours. Alternatively, take the train from Kanazawa on the JR Hokuriku line to Takaoka, then from

Takaoka station, take a bus to Ogimachi via Gokayama (2½ hours, ¥2250).

Another option is to take the train on the Jōhana line from Takaoka to Jōhana. From Jōhana there's a bus service to Ogimachi.

Getting Around Ogimachi is easily covered on foot. If you want to visit Gokayama, you will have to wait for infrequent buses or hitch.

Gokayama District 五箇山

Gokayama is just inside the boundaries of Toyama-ken, a short distance north of Ogimachi. Prior to the Edo period, the feudal lords of Kanazawa used the isolated location of Gokayama as a centre for the secretive production of gunpowder. Many of the houses open to the public in this region have displays of equipment used for making gunpowder. The construction of a road to Gokayama and the provision of electricity didn't occur until 1925.

In the Gokayama area, gasshō-zukuri houses are scattered in small groups along the valley. The following is a brief description of the sights as you travel north from Shirakawa-gō District and Ogimachi. There are bus stops at each group of houses.

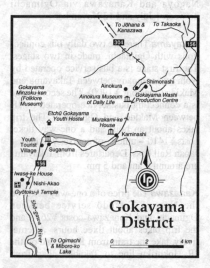

Gokayama District

To Jōhana & Kanazawa / To Takaoka
304 / 156
Shimonashi
Gokayama Minzoku-ken (Folkore Museum)
Ainokura
Ainokura Museum of Daily Life
Gokayama Washi Production Centre
Etchū Gokayama Youth Hostel
Murakami-ke House
Youth Tourist Village
Suganuma
Kaminashi
156
Iwase-ke House
Nishi-Akao
Gyōtoku-ji Temple
Shō-gawa River
To Ogimachi & Miboro-ko Lake
0   2   4 km

Nishi-Akao Nishi-Akao is about 20 minutes by bus from Ogimachi. The two attractions here are **Gyōtoku-ji Temple** (open daily 9 am to 5 pm, ¥150), and **Iwase-ke House** (open daily 8 am to 5 pm, ¥300), which was once the local centre for the production of gunpowder.

Suganuma Suganuma is four km beyond Nishi-Akao and lies just below the main road. The **Folklore Museum** consists of two houses: one displays items from traditional life; the other, across the path, is devoted to exhibits which explain the traditional techniques for gunpowder production. The combined admission charge is ¥300 and they're open daily from 9 am to 4 pm between May and November. For ¥1000 you can buy cassettes of the local music – a haunting combination of twanging stringed instruments and mournful wailing.

Close by is an attractive group of gasshō-zukuri houses that are worth strolling around. From Nishi-Akao, take a Takaoka-bound bus for the 10 minute ride to Suganuma.

Just to the south of Suganuma is a **Youth Tourist Village**. If you cross the bridge over the river and take the road to the right, you'll eventually puff your way uphill to the youth hostel (see Places to Stay).

Kaminashi Kaminashi is on the main road, four km beyond Suganuma. **Murakami-ke House** dates from 1578 and has now become an interesting museum. It is well maintained by the proud and enthusiastic owner who conducts visitors on a tour of the exhibits and then sits them down around the irori and sings local folk songs. Admission costs ¥300, and the house is open daily from 8 am to 5 pm. A detailed leaflet is provided in English.

Also close by and worth a look is **Hakusan-gū Shrine**. The main hall dates from 1502 and has been designated an Important Cultural Property.

Takaoka-bound buses from Nishi-Akao take around 15 minutes to reach Kaminashi.

Shimonashi & Ainokura Shimonashi is on the main road, four km beyond Kaminashi.

Just beyond the bus stop, there's a road on your left leading up a steep hill toward Ainokura. About 100m up this road, you reach **Gokayama Washi Production Center** on your left. The production of *washi* (Japanese paper) has been a speciality of the region for several centuries and you can see the production process here. For ¥550, you can even have a go at it yourself and keep your work of art. The centre is open daily between April and November from 8.30 am to 5 pm.

From here it takes another 25 minutes on foot, winding up the hill to reach the side street leading off to the left to Ainokura. This is an impressive village of gasshō-zukuri houses with fine views across the valley. The **Ainokura Museum of Daily Life** in the village is open from 8.30 am to 5 pm, closed on Tuesday, and charges ¥200 admission. The museum shuts down from December to April.

Places to Stay Several gasshō-zukuri houses in the Gokayama area function as minshuku. Expect to pay around ¥7000 per person for a bed and two meals. The youth hostel near Suganuma offers the most inexpensive way to stay in accommodation of this kind.

The helpful tourist information offices in Takayama and Ogimachi can assist with reservations and there is an information office in the centre of Ainokura. Advance reservations are highly recommended, particularly during the peak seasons of May, August and October.

Etchū Gokayama Youth Hostel (☎ 0763-67-3331) is a fine old gasshō-zukuri farmhouse and a great place to stay; it's only a few km off the main road. A bed for the night costs ¥2800. For ¥1000 you get a fine dinner which often includes grilled trout and sansai (mountain greens). Some travellers have found their dining experience heightened by having the privilege of washing their own dishes afterwards!

The hostel is not easy to find. The closest bus stop is at Suganuma, which is only 12 minutes by bus from Kaminashi bus stop or 25 minutes by bus from Ogimachi.

From the Suganuma bus stop on the main road, walk down the side street through the cluster of houses by the river and cross the large bridge. At the other end of the bridge, turn right and wind your way for about two km uphill until you come to the hostel, which is in a small cluster of houses perched on the mountainside. A sign in the Suganuma bus shelter advises hostellers arriving during the snowy season to phone the hostel from a nearby house to make sure the road is not blocked before attempting to walk there.

In Suganuma itself, you could also try *Yohachi* (☎ 0763-67-3205), a rambling minshuku close to the river.

In Ainokura, you have a choice of several minshuku; check with the *minshuku annai-shō* (minshuku information office), which can help with reservations.

In Kaminashi, try the *Kokuminshukusha Gokayama-sō* (☎ 0763-66-2316) which costs ¥7360 per person including two meals. The building is a bit of an architectural monstrosity, so if it's charm you're after, it might be worth looking elsewhere.

If you want to stay in Nishi-Akao, *Nakaya* (☎ 0763-67-3252) is a little ryokan with per person rates of ¥6800, including two meals.

Getting There & Away Gokayama is about 20 minutes from Ogimachi by infrequent bus. Hitching is a good way to avoid long waits for buses. Gokayama is also served by the buses running between Kanazawa and Nagoya via Ogimachi, but only from July to November. About four buses make their way through the various towns between approximately 9 am and 5 pm. For details, refer to the Ogimachi Getting There & Away section. Remember that many roads in this region are closed during the winter.

HIRAYU ONSEN 平湯温泉
This is a hot-spring resort in the Japan Alps and of primary interest to visitors as a hub for bus transport in the region. The information office (☎ 0578-9-3130) opposite the bus station has leaflets and information on hot-spring ryokan as well as a small nature trail in the area. Compared with other towns in the area, like Shin-Hotaka and Kamikōchi,

this is not all that an attractive place to stay, though there are a few nice ryokan around. *Ryosō Tsuyukusa* (☎ 0578-9-2620) has rooms for ¥7000, two meals included, and a nice, though tiny, outdoor onsen bath. *Eitarō* (0578-9-2540) is a bit fancier, as reflected in its per person rate of ¥11,000. Both places are about five minutes walk from the bus station, along the road leading to Shin-Hotaka. There is also the *Hirayu Camping Ground* (☎ 0578-9-2610), about 700m from the bus station in the direction of Takayama, which charges ¥500 for a tent site. It's often full during the summer.

Getting There & Away

Buses from Takayama to Norikura, Kami-kōchi and Shin-Hotaka Onsen all run via Hirayu Onsen (one hour, ¥1500).

There are frequent bus connections between Hirayu Onsen and Kamikōchi, but *only* from late April to late October. The trip takes 65 minutes (¥1550) and runs via Nakanoyu. The section on Kamikōchi has more details regarding combined bus/rail connections with Matsumoto.

There are bus services approximately three times a day between Norikura (Tatami-daira) and Hirayu Onsen, and as many as eight times daily during the peak season of late July to late August. The trip takes 45 minutes and costs ¥1850. The Norikura Skyline Road is *only* open from 15 May to 31 October. There are frequent bus connec-tions between Hirayu Onsen and Shin-Hotaka Onsen (35 minutes, ¥860).

SHIN-HOTAKA ONSEN   新穂高温泉

This is a hot-spring resort with the added attraction of the Shin-Hotaka cablecar, reportedly the longest of its kind in Asia, which whisks you up close to the peak of **Mt Nishi Hotaka-dake** (2908m) for a superb mountain panorama. The cablecar consists of two sections and a combined ticket costs ¥1500 one way (¥2800 round trip) and an extra ¥300 if you take your backpack. The cablecar is near the Shin-Hotaka Onsen bus station.

If you are fit, properly equipped and give yourself ample time, there are a variety of hiking options from Nishi Hotaka-guchi (the top cablecar station). One option which takes a bit less than three hours would be to hike over to **Kamikōchi**. Near the Shin-Hotaka Onsen bus station is a counter entitled 'Mountaineering Service Center', which has some maps of area hiking trails. Unfortu-nately, despite the English-language sign, none of the information is in English.

Also near the bus station, adjacent to the parking lot, is a rather spartan public onsen. During the summer it tends to be crowded with tourists, but in the off season your only company is likely to be a few weary shift workers from the electric plant across the river.

Places to Stay

This far up into the mountains, low-cost accommodation options are hard to find. Most of the minshuku and ryokan are clus-tered around the Shin-Hotaka Onsen guchi bus stop, which is a few km before the Shin-Hotaka Onsen bus station. One of the cheapest spots is the *Yamanoyado* minshuku (☎ 0578-9-2733), which charges ¥7800 per person (¥8100 in summer), including two meals. Right next door, *Komagusakan* ryokan (☎ 0578-9-2408) charges ¥8000, also with two meals. Most of the other options in the area charge between ¥12,000 and ¥16,000 per person.

There are a few more minshuku in the Naka-O Onsen area, two bus stops past Shin-Hotaka Onsen guchi. Of these, your best bet is probably *Mahoroba* (☎ 0578-9-2382), a friendly place with a very nice outdoor onsen bath and rooms for ¥8000, including two meals. If you can get a Japanese speaker to book your room for you, they can arrange to have the owner pick you up at the Naka-O guchi bus stop. Otherwise you'll have to walk a bit. Across from the bus stop is a small road leading uphill. Take it for about one km: Mahoroba is on the left side of the road, just past the (infrequently served) Naka-o Kōminkan-mae bus stop.

Up near the Shin-Hotaka Onsen bus station, the *Shin-Hotaka Campground* (☎ 0578-9-2513) has tent sites for ¥500. If you don't have a tent, they'll rent you one for the rather steep fee of ¥2000. The camping ground is only open during July and August.

Getting There & Away

There are frequent bus connections with Hirayu Onsen (35 minutes, ¥860) and Takayama (one hour 35 minutes, ¥2070). There are several buses daily to Toyama (3½ hours, ¥2380), however, you'll need to change buses at Kamioka and possibly also at Tochio Onsen. There is one direct bus around noon, but this only runs from mid-July to late August. There is also a direct bus to Nagoya (5½ hours, ¥5400) during this same period.

FURUKAWA 古川

Furukawa, on the route between Takayama and Toyama, was originally a castle town. It's quite a pleasant place to visit, particularly if you like strolling around areas with white storehouses (*kura*), old residences and shops. The main draw for Furukawa is the festival in April. If you want to attend, you should stay in Furukawa and reserve your accommodation well in advance.

One slightly confusing but important point is that the station for Furukawa is called Hida-Furukawa.

Information

Information can be obtained at the station, but you may find it easier to use the tourist information office in Takayama which can also provide maps and leaflets, and arrange reservations.

Special Events

The major annual festival is Furukawa Matsuri which is held on 19 and 20 April. The festival features squads of young men, who, dressed in loincloths (the event is also referred to as the Hadaka Matsuri or 'Naked Festival'), parade through town with a giant drum. There are also processions with large yatai similar to those used in the Takayama festivals.

Places to Stay

Hida Furukawa Youth Hostel (☎ 0577-75-2979) is about three km west of Hida-

Furukawa station (40 minutes on foot), or 1.2 km (15 minutes walk) west of Hida Hosoe station (two stops north of Hida-Furukawa). Ask for Shinrin-kōen, which is a park next to the hostel. Only 22 beds are available, so to avoid disappointment make an advance reservation. A dorm bed costs ¥3100 and bicycles are available for hire. The hostel is closed from 30 March to 10 April.

The *Ryokan Tanbo-no-Yu* (☎ 0577-73-2014) is a straightforward ryokan that costs ¥7000 per person. No English is spoken. To find the ryokan, turn right from the station, then take the third left, the first right and look out for the ryokan (a nondescript tan-coloured building with a sign outside) on the corner as the road turns to the right.

Things to Buy

Furukawa is famous for handmade candles. In the centre of town, you can visit Mishima-ya, a shop which has specialised in traditional candle-making techniques for over two centuries.

Getting There & Away

Hida-Furukawa station is three stops north of Takayama on the JR Takayama line. The trip takes 15 minutes. There are also hourly buses from Takayama station to Hida-Furukawa station (30 minutes).

Getting Around

Furukawa is small enough to stroll around, but if you want to see the surrounding countryside (or maybe puff it on up to the youth hostel) you can rent bicycles at the railway station for ¥500 for four hours, ¥1000 for the whole day.

Nagano-ken 長野県

Most of Nagano-ken consists of the northern, central and southern ranges of the Japan Alps – hence its claim to being the 'Roof of Japan'.

Nagano-ken is one of the most enjoyable regions to visit in Japan, not only for the beauty of its mountainous terrain, but also for the traditional architecture and culture which linger in many parts of the prefecture and which have been spared the industrial zoning often seen elsewhere in Japan. Agriculture is still a major source of income here, but the lack of pollution has also attracted growing numbers of companies from the electronics and precision manufacturing industries.

Included in this prefecture are several national parks and quasi-national parks which attract large numbers of campers, hikers, mountaineers and hot-spring aficionados. Several hikes in this prefecture are covered in *Hiking in Japan* by Paul Hunt. Skiers can choose from dozens of resorts during the ski season, which lasts from late December to late March.

Getting Around

Travel in the prefecture relies mainly on the JR lines which run parallel to the Japan Alps from south to north and it is this axis which dictates the itinerary for most visitors. There are two scenic routes which traverse the Japan Alps: one runs from Matsumoto via Kamikōchi to Takayama (Gifu-ken) and the other runs from Shinano-ōmachi via the Kurobe Dam to Tateyama (Toyama-ken). When making travel plans for the mountains, bear in mind that many roads are closed and bus services are stopped due to heavy snowfall from mid-October to early May. If possible try to avoid major sights and trails during peak tourist seasons (early May, July and August) when they tend to become clogged with visitors.

JNTO publishes *Japan Nagano Prefecture*, a brochure which provides concise details and mapping.

KARUIZAWA 軽井沢

Karuizawa lies at the foot of Mt Asama-yama and lays claim to being Japan's trendiest summer resort or 'holidayland'. Originally a prosperous post town on the Nakasen-dō Highway linking Tokyo and Kyoto, it was 'discovered' by Archdeacon AC Shaw in 1896 and quickly became a favourite summer retreat for the foreign community.

Since then many affluent urbanites, both foreign and Japanese, have set up summer residences and turned the place into a booming centre for outdoor pursuits such as golf, tennis, horse riding and walking. There's even a 'Ginza' shopping street duplicating all the fashionable boutiques, restaurants, shops and crowds which no city-dweller can do without. In comparison with the other attractions of Nagano-ken, this place gets a low rating, though there is some nice scenery to enjoy outside of town.

Orientation & Information

Karuizawa extends over a large area. Kyū-Karuizawa (Old Karuizawa) is the core part and is close to Karuizawa station. Naka-Karuizawa (Central Karuizawa) is several km further east.

There are tourist information offices at JR Karuizawa station (☎ 0267-42-2491), Naka-Karuizawa station (☎ 0267-45-6050) and on Karuizawa Ginza (☎ 0267-42-5538). Office hours are from 9 am to 5 pm, longer during peak season.

The JNTO brochure, *Karuizawa Heights*, has concise details and maps. The tourist offices also have colour pamphlets in English with maps of the area that include several hiking trails.

Mt Asama-yama 浅間山

Climbing is currently prohibited on Mt Asama-yama (2560m) – for good reason as it is known to have erupted at least 50 times and has been active over the last few years.

For a close look, however, you can visit **Onioshidashi Rocks**, a region of lava beds on the northern base of the mountain, where there are two gardens with lookout platforms. The **Onioshidashi Rock Garden** is open daily from 8 am to 6 pm from May to September and to 5 pm for the rest of the year; entry is ¥300.

There are buses from Karuizawa and Naka-Karuizawa stations to the lookouts (55 minutes). Get off at the Onioshidashi-en stop.

Usui Pass & Lookout 碓氷峠・見晴台

In Kyū-Karuizawa, a walking trail leads

CENTRAL HONSHŪ

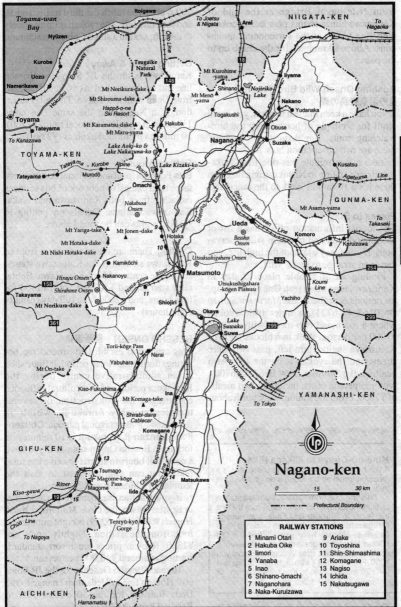

Nagano-ken

0   15   30 km

– · – · –   Prefectural Boundary

RAILWAY STATIONS

1 Minami Otari	9 Ariake
2 Hakuba Oike	10 Toyoshina
3 Iimori	11 Shin-Shimashima
4 Yanaba	12 Komagane
5 Inao	13 Nagiso
6 Shinano-ōmachi	14 Ichida
7 Naganohara	15 Nakatsugawa
8 Naka-Kuruizawa	

from Nite-bashi Bridge at the end of Karuizawa Ginza to this pass and a lookout with fine views of the surrounding mountains. Allow 80 minutes for the climb up to the pass.

Hoshino Onsen Wild Bird Sanctuary
星野温泉野鳥の森
If you have a keen interest in birds, you could stroll for a couple of hours along the bird-watching route. For dedicated 'twitchers' there are two observation huts.

Take a five minute bus ride from Naka-Karuizawa station to Nishiku-iriguchi. From there it's a 10 minute walk to the sanctuary.

Places to Stay
The tourist information office has a list of accommodation and can help with reservations. If you fancy a taste of the high life, you can even arrange to rent a villa.

Finding an affordable place to stay in Karuizawa is no mean feat. One of the cheapest options is probably the *Morikaku San-so* (☎ 0267-42-6721), a quiet little ryokan where a room and two meals will cost you ¥7000 per person. Walk two blocks north of Karuizawa station, turn left, pass two more streets and the ryokan is on the left. Also nearby is the *Shoraku-en* (☎ 0267-42-6700), with per person costs, including two meals, of ¥7800. From the station, walk north about

Mine-no-Chaya to Mikasa Hike
If you have four or five hours to spare, this is a pleasant forest amble along a delightful 10 km trail.

Take the bus from Naka-Karuizawa station to Mine-no-Chaya (25 minutes). From there a trail leads to **Shiraito-taki Falls**, continues to **Ryugaeshi-taki Falls** and then leads via Kose Onsen to Mikasa. Here you will find the Old Mikasa Hotel, now preserved as a museum. If you're interested, a stroll through it will cost you ¥300. From Mikasa it's an eight minute bus ride (or a 70 minute walk) to Karuizawa station. ■

500m until you reach the third traffic signal, and then turn left. The ryokan is immediately to the left, next to a small Chinese restaurant.

Getting There & Away
Karuizawa is on the JR Shin-etsu Honsen line and can be reached in two hours (¥4720) from Ueno station in Tokyo. The rail connection with Nagano on the same line takes 1½ hours if you do it by local train (¥1260), 50 minutes by limited express (¥2390).

Getting Around
Bus For both local and regional destinations, there is an extensive network of bus services radiating from both Karuizawa and Naka-Karuizawa stations. Details on getting to specific sights can be found above.

Cycling There are bicycle shops in front of Karuizawa station, Naka-Karuizawa station and in the centre of Kyū-Karuizawa. Rental rates start around ¥500 per hour, ¥1400 for four hours, and ¥2000 for a full day (usually eight hours).

BESSHO ONSEN 別所温泉
This town was established around the hot springs during the Heian period. It flourished as an administrative centre during the Kamakura period and this cultural influence encouraged the construction of several temples, notably **Anraku-ji**, which is renowned for its octagonal pagoda, **Chūzen-ji** and **Zenzan-ji**. Anraku-ji is 10 minutes on foot from Bessho Onsen station. If you have a couple of hours to spare for a five km rural hike, you can continue east to visit the temples of Chūzen-ji and Zenzan-ji.

If you want an inexpensive place to stay in Bessho Onsen, the *Ueda Mahoroba Youth Hostel* (☎ 0268-38-5229) is eight minutes on foot from the station. Nightly costs are ¥2800. Ryokan prices are resort standard, starting at around ¥10,000 per person.

To reach Bessho Onsen, take the JR Shin-etsu Honsen line to Ueda then change to the Ueda Railway for the 30 minute ride to Bessho Onsen (¥570).

NAGANO 長野

Nagano (population 347,000), capital of the prefecture, has been around since the Kamakura period (1185-1333), when it was a temple town centred around Zenkō-ji Temple. Zenkō-ji is still Nagano's main attraction, drawing more than four million visitors every year.

This small city will have to cope with even heavier crowds when it hosts the 1998 Winter Olympics, although many of the actual events will take place at ski resorts and newly built sporting facilities outside the city. In preparation for the games, which will be held in February 1998, the city is trying to make things easier for visitors by putting up English signs, and staffing information centres and hotels with speakers of English and other foreign languages. New hotels and restaurants are also popping up, to cash in on the two week spending spree it is hoped will put Nagano firmly on the world tourist map. But so far development has not been too overwhelming, and the city still retains a friendly small-town feeling, albeit with a cosmopolitan touch.

Nagano is also an important transport hub, providing access to the superb recreational facilities in the surrounding region. As a destination, it shouldn't be a high priority, but it's worth staying overnight here to visit Zenkō-ji and stroll around town.

Orientation & Information

JR Nagano station is at an angle to Chūō-dōri, the main road running north to Zenkō-ji Temple, and there is a slightly confusing warren of streets running out from the station and connecting with Chūō-dōri at various points. Once you've navigated these though, the rest is fairly straightforward. Chūō-dōri runs directly north, and is the main shopping area. It takes around 20 minutes on foot following Chūō-dōri to reach Zenkō-ji.

There's a brand new Nagano city tourist information centre (☎ 0262-26-5626) in the JR Nagano station. The office itself looks ready for the Olympic crowds, the staff less so. When we visited there was not an English speaker to be found, though this will no doubt change as the Olympics draw closer. The centre has some good English-language colour maps and guides to both Nagano and the surrounding areas: ask for the *Guide to Nagano City and Northern Shinano*, which has a wealth of useful facts and maps. The information centre is open daily from 9.30 am to 5.45 pm.

If the staff at the centre can't answer your queries, try the International Relations section of Nagano City Hall (☎ 0262-24-5121), which has both English and Chinese speakers on hand. Hours are 8.30 am to 5.15 pm Monday to Friday. The Association of Nagano Prefecture for Promoting International Exchange (☎ 0262-35-7186) can also help visitors, including French and German speakers. It is also open from 8.30 am to 5.15 pm Monday to Friday.

Zenkō-ji Temple 善光寺

Zenkō-ji is believed to have been founded in the 7th century, and was the home of the Ikkō Sanzon, allegedly the first Buddhist image to arrive in Japan (in 552). There have subsequently been several different stories concerning the image, which was, at times, the subject of disputes and was lost, rediscovered and finally installed again.

Although the temple buildings have been destroyed several times by fire, donations for reconstruction have always been provided by believers throughout Japan. The immense popularity of this temple stems from its liberal acceptance of believers, including women, from all Buddhist sects. The temple is affiliated with both the Tendai and Jōdo sects, and there are some 60 other Zenkō-ji temples scattered throughout Japan.

The centre of the temple complex is the Kondō (Main Hall), a reconstruction dating from 707 and a National Treasure.

Once you've entered the inner sanctum of the Kondō, you'll see a small ticket window on your left where English-language pamphlets are available. After you've bought your ticket, take off your shoes (and place them in the bag provided), then proceed through the ticket collector's entrance. At the back of the hall, you descend a flight of steps into complete darkness – the absence of light is intentional and mandatory. Keep groping your way along the right-hand side of the tunnel until you feel something heavy, moveable and metallic – the key to salvation! Continue to fumble your way along the tunnel until you see light again. It can be a bit disorienting, and people with claustrophobia may want to think twice before heading into the darkness!

The temple is about 1.5 km from JR Nagano station, at the northern end of Chūō-dōri. If you're not in the mood to walk, you can take a 10 minute bus ride to Dai-mon Gate (¥200), or go by taxi (¥900). Another option is to take the Nagano Dentetsu line from the station and get off at the third stop – Zenkōji-shita station (¥160). From there it's a 10 minute walk westward to the temple.

Courses

Travellers interested in Japanese cultural pursuits such as martial arts, traditional music and even Zen can check with any of the above information centres to arrange one day study courses. Staff will either make arrangements for you, or give you a phone number where you can speak with someone in English.

Special Events

The Gokaichō Festival is held at Zenkō-ji once every seven years from 10 April to 20 May. Millions of pilgrims attend this extravaganza, when a sacred image of Buddha, given to the emperor by a Korean king in 552, is put on display – the next festival is in 1999. The Nagano city tourist information centre has complete lists of all the various little festivals taking place throughout the year in the surrounding area.

Places to Stay

Youth Hostel The *Zenkō-ji Kyōju-in Youth Hostel* (☎ 0262-32-2768) is a temple in a side street a couple of minutes on foot east of Zenkō-ji. Matronly guidance from the manager ensures an amicable, but strict, regime. Keep

things amicable by making an advance reservation. A bed for the night is ¥2800.

Shukubō *Shukubō* (temple lodgings) are available around Zenkō-ji but only for genuine students of Zen. If you are interested, the Nagano City Hall International Relations section or the Association of Nagano Prefecture for Promoting International Exchange may be able to help.

Ryokan The *Shimizuya Ryokan* (☎ 0262-32-2672) is a cosy little place not too far from the Dai-mon Gate of Zenkō-ji. Per person

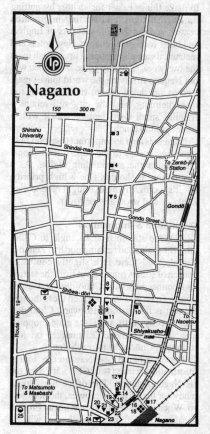

rates range from ¥8000 to ¥12,000 including two meals. There's no English sign for the ryokan, but keep a sharp eye out for a small sign posted above a cold drinks vending machine that says 'Boy Scouts of Japan Office'.

Nagano's most famous hotel is the venerable *Gohonjin Fujiya* (☎ 0262-32-1241), which looks out over Chūō-dōri and the Daimon Gate. The first hostel on the site opened its doors in the late 18th century and the same family has run the business ever since. The current building, which dates from 1923, is rather western-looking in design but still functions as a traditional Japanese inn. Rates start at ¥9000 per person with two meals, which isn't cheap, but then again isn't that expensive for 200 years worth of history and hostelry.

Hotels The station area has a number of standard business hotels. The *Nagano Dai-Ichi Hotel* (☎ 0262-28-1211) is just to the east of the station and has singles from ¥6000 to ¥6500, twins at ¥11,000 and doubles at ¥10,000. Also close to the station is the *Hotel New Nagano* (☎ 0262-27-7200), where single rooms are ¥6500, twins range from ¥12,500 to ¥14,000 and doubles (there are only two of them) are ¥12,500. Almost directly opposite the station, the *Hotel Ikemon* (☎ 0262-27-2122) is another mid-range business hotel. It has singles at ¥6000, twins at ¥10,000 and very reasonably priced (by Japanese standards) doubles at ¥8000.

One option worth considering is the *Mitsui Garden Hotel Nagoya* (☎ 0262-25-1131), which gives you an up-market stay for standard business hotel rates. Singles are ¥7500, and twins and doubles start at ¥13,500. There are also semi-doubles (a single room with a small double bed crammed in it) for ¥11,000. Other more up-market options include the *Nagano Washington Hotel* (☎ 0262-28-5111), with singles/twins from ¥7000/15,500, and the *Nagano Royal Hotel* (☎ 0262-28-2222), with singles from ¥8500 to ¥9500, and doubles and twins from ¥15,000.

CENTRAL HONSHŪ

PLACES TO STAY		
2	Zenkō-ji Kyōju-in Youth Hostel 善光寺教授院ユースホステル	
3	Gohonjin Fujiya 御本陣藤屋	
4	Shimizuya Ryokan 旅館清水屋	
10	Nagano Washington Hotel 長野ワシントンホテル	
11	Mitsui Garden Hotel Nagoya 三井ガーデンホテル長野	
13	Hotel New Nagano ホテルニューナガノ	
17	Nagano Dai-Ichi Hotel 長野第一ホテル	
22	Nagano Royal Hotel 長野ロイヤルホテル	
23	Hotel Ikemon ホテル池門	

PLACES TO EAT		
5	Ōtaya 太田屋そば	
8	Thirty's Pizza Bar	
9	Pink Elephant Ethnic Live Bar ピンクの象	
12	KFC	
15	McDonald's	
19	Kinryū Honten Chinese Restaurant 金龍本店	
20	Tsubohachi つぼ八	
21	Yōrōnotaki 養老の滝	

OTHER		
1	Zenkō-ji Temple 善光寺	
6	Central Post Office 中央郵便局	
7	Daiei Department Store ダイエーデパート	
14	Doutor Coffee	
16	Nagano Railway Station 長野駅	
18	Midori Department Store みどりデパート	
24	Post Office 郵便局	
25	Bus Station バスターミナル	

Places to Eat

Midori, a department store immediately on your right as you exit the station, has a cluster of inexpensive restaurants on the 5th floor, a good place for a quick bite to eat if you're just passing through. Prices generally range from ¥800 to ¥1200 for set meals, and the restaurants are open from 11 am to 9 pm. Also on the right side coming out of the station is *Giraffe*, a narrow little place that functions as a coffee shop by day and a bar by night. Prices are fairly cheap: a cup of coffee is ¥180, and a (modest-sized) glass of beer is ¥395. Food prices aren't too bad either. Across from the station you'll also find a branch of the *Doutor* coffee shop chain, which also charges ¥180 per cup.

On the local speciality front, Nagano is famed for its soba, and there are many restaurants around Zenkō-ji that serve the stuff up.

If you walk downhill from Dai-mon Gate along the left-hand side of Chūō-dōri, after about 300m you'll see a shop window with a mill grinding flour. This is *Ōtaya*, a restaurant which specialises in home-made soba. Prices for a soba set lunch start at around ¥680. You won't find these prices on the menu (which is in Japanese anyway) so try asking for *soba lanchi* (soba lunch) and see what you get.

Another local speciality is oyaki, little wheat buns filled with pickles, squash, radish, red bean paste and the like. There's a little stand right in front of the railway station that serves up several different tasty varieties, for around ¥130 a piece.

The izakaya chains *Yōrōnotaki* and *Tsubohachi* have branches near the station. For not-bad pizzas, head up Chūō-dōri to *Thirty's Pizza Bar*. The place itself feels more like a bar, but if you don't like the decor, it also has takeaway/delivery service, with a toll-free number for ordering, no less (☎ 0120-35-8804). It's open from 5 pm to 1 am.

For cheap Indian food, try the *Pink Elephant Ethnic Live Bar*. There's a two dish minimum after 8 pm (it is a bar after all), but dishes are only around ¥400 to ¥500 each. Drinks are standard Japanese bar prices, unfortunately.

Getting There & Away

Trains from Ueno station in Tokyo via the JR Shin-etsu Honsen line take three hours and cost ¥3810, plus a ¥2770 limited express surcharge. The JR Shinonoi line connects Nagano with Matsumoto in 70 minutes via local train (¥1090), 50 minutes via limited express (¥2720). To Nagoya it takes three hours and costs ¥4420 plus a ¥2770 limited express surcharge.

In preparation for the 1998 Winter Olympics, JR is building a new shinkansen line which will link Nagano with Tokyo in 1½ hours. At the time of writing, the new line was scheduled to open in October 1997.

Getting Around

Nagano is small enough to comfortably navigate on foot. City buses to Zenkō-ji and other local destinations leave from in front of the station.

TOGAKUSHI 戸隠

Togakushi lies north-west of Nagano and is a popular destination for hikers, particularly in late spring and during autumn. In the winter, skiers favour the slopes around Mt Menō-yama and Mt Kurohime-yama. The one hour hike to **Togakushi-Okusha Sanctuary** includes a pleasant section along a tree-lined approach. The Nagano city tourist information centre has maps that outline hiking trails in the area.

Togakushi is reached by taking a bus from Nagano to the Chūsha bus stop. For an inexpensive place to stay, there's *Togakushi Kōgen Yokokura Youth Hostel* (☎ 0262-54-2030), which is a couple of minutes from Chūsha bus stop and next to a ski slope. A bed for the night costs ¥2800. There are also quite a few ryokan in the area: prices generally start at around ¥8000 to ¥10,000 per person.

There are buses from Nagano bus station to Chūsha (¥1350), which take about an hour and run via the scenic **Togakushi Birdline Highway**. You might want to consider buying a round-trip ticket, which is valid for one week and costs ¥2400. Buses to Chūsha leave Nagano approximately once an hour between 6.50 am and 6.40 pm.

OBUSE 小布施

If you are interested in *ukiyo-e* (wood-block prints), then you should make the short trip to Obuse, north-east of Nagano, and visit the **Hokusai-kan Museum**. This museum displays a collection of ukiyo-e works by the great master of this art form, Hokusai. The display consists of 30 paintings and two festival floats. Admission costs ¥500 and it's open daily from 9 am to 4.30 pm from April to October. During the rest of the year the opening hours are from 9.30 am to 4 pm.

To reach Obuse, take the Nagano Dentetsu line from Nagano (20 minutes, ¥630). The museum is eight minutes on foot from the station. Exit the station building and walk straight ahead, crossing a small intersection, until you reach the main road. Turn right here and continue down the main road past two sets of traffic lights. About 50m after the second set of lights, take the side street to your left which leads to the museum.

YUDANAKA 湯田中

This town is famous for its hot springs, particularly those known as **Jigokudani Onsen** (Hell Valley Hot Springs), which attract monkeys keen to escape the winter chill with a hot soak.

Uotoshi Ryokan (☎ 0269-33-1215), a member of the Japanese Inn Group, charges ¥3900 to ¥4900 per person per night. The ryokan owner may offer to demonstrate *kyūdō* (Japanese archery) on request. You can either arrange to be picked up at the station or walk from there to the ryokan (seven minutes).

If you want to commune with the monkeys, try a night at *Kōraku-kan* (☎ 0269-33-4376), which is perched up a small valley next to Jigokudani Onsen. Accommodation is fairly basic for the money (¥9000 per person with two meals), as is the food, but the onsen baths are quite nice, and available 24 hours. Getting there is a bit of a trek. From the Yudanaka station take the bus to Kanbayashi Onsen (15 minutes, ¥220) and

get off at the last stop. From here walk uphill along the road about 400m until it curves 180 degrees, where you come to a large sign over a trailhead. Follow that trail for a pleasant, tree-lined 1.6 km to get to the ryokan. If you arrive during the morning carrying any bags of food, keep a sharp eye out for any marauding monkeys: some of the nasty beasts may try to snatch your goodies from you.

From Nagano, take the Nagano Dentetsu line to Yudanaka, one hour by local train (¥1110) and 40 minutes by express, which run about once an hour (¥1210). Make sure when boarding at Nagano that your train goes all the way to the Yudanaka terminus, as some trains only go as far as Nakano.

HAKUBA AREA 白馬

The town of Hakuba, north-west of Nagano, is used as an access point for outdoor activities in the nearby mountains. Skiing in the winter and hiking or mountaineering in the summer attract large numbers of visitors. The hiking trails tend to be less clogged during September and October. Even in midsummer you should be properly prepared for hiking over snow-covered terrain.

Hakuba will be hosting several events during the 1998 Winter Olympics, including the downhill giant slalom and nordic ski competitions and ski jumping. For more information about Hakuba and the surrounding region, contact the English-speaking staff at the tourist information office in Matsumoto.

Mt Shirouma-dake 白馬岳

The ascent of this mountain is a popular hike, but you should be properly prepared. There are several mountain huts which provide meals and basic accommodation along the trails.

From Hakuba station there are buses which take 40 minutes (¥960) to reach Sarukura, where the trailhead is located. From here, you can head west to climb the peak in about six hours; note that there are two huts on this route. If you don't feel like climbing the peak, you can follow the trail for about 1¾ hours as far as the Daisekkei (Great Snowy Gorge).

You could also take the trail south-west of Sarukura and do the three hour climb to **Yari Onsen**. There's an open-air hot spring here with a mountain panorama and another mountain hut, in case you feel compelled to stay.

Tsugaike Natural Park　栂池自然公園

Tsugaike Natural Park (Tsugaike Shizen-en) lies below Mt Norikura-dake in an alpine marshland. A three hour hiking trail takes in most of the park which is renowned for its alpine flora. Admission to the park is ¥300.

From Hakuba Oike station it takes an hour by bus to reach the park. During summer there are one to two buses an hour. Between June and late October there's also a bus from Hakuba station which takes about 1½ hours.

Happō-o-ne Ski Resort　八方尾根スキー場

This is a busy ski resort in the winter and a popular hiking area in the summer. From Hakuba station, a five minute bus ride takes you to Happō; from there it's an eight minute walk to the cablecar base station. From the top station of the cablecar you can use two more chair lifts, and then hike along a trail for an hour or so to Happō-ike Pond on a ridge below Mt Karamatsu-dake. From this pond you can follow a trail leading to Mt Maru-yama (one hour), continue for 1½ hours to the Karamatsu-dake San-sō (mountain hut) and then climb to the peak of **Mt Karamatsu-dake** (2696m) in about 30 minutes. The total round-trip fare for the gondola and two chair lifts is ¥2270. The main gondola runs between 8 am and 5 pm, while the chair lifts close at 4.30 pm.

Nishina Three Lakes　仁科三湖

While travelling south from Hakuba, there are three lakes (Nishina San-ko), which provide scope for some short walks. Lake Nakazuna-ko and Lake Aoki-ko are close to Yanaba station and Lake Kizaki-ko is next to Inao station.

Salt Road　塩の道

In the past, Hakuba lay on the route of the Shio-no-Michi (Salt Road) which was used to carry salt on oxen from the Sea of Japan to Matsumoto. Parts of this road still exist and there's a popular three hour hike along one section which starts at **Otari Folklore Museum** (Otari Kyodokan) – three minutes on foot from Minami Otari station – and continues via **Chikuni Suwa Shrine** before finishing at Matsuzawa-guchi. From there, it's a 15 minute bus ride to Hakuba Oike station which is two stops north of Hakuba station.

If you are thirsting for more background on salt, you could take the train further down the line to Shinano-ōmachi station and visit the Salt Museum (Shio-no-Michi Hakubutsukan).

Places to Stay

Not far from the cablecar base station at Happō-o-ne is the *Wade Ryokan* (☎ 0261-72-5552), a government-run minshuku (*kokuminshukusha*) that caters to hikers and skiers. Per person rates with two meals start at ¥7500. This place fills up quickly, so it would be wise to book ahead, for which you will probably need the help of a Japanese speaker. To get there, take the bus to Happō-o-ne ski resort from Hakuba station.

Across the road is the *Lodge Hakuba* (☎ 0261-72-3095), another hiker/skier place with similar prices. *Hajimeno Ippo* (☎ 0261-75-3527) is a minshuku which is a member of the Toho network. You'll probably need to know some Japanese and it's small, so advance reservations are a necessity. Dormitory-style accommodation costs ¥3800 per person with two meals, ¥4800 between December and May. For ¥1400 more per person you can get your own room. The minshuku is 12 minutes on foot from Iimori station (one stop south of Hakuba) and is usually closed in June and November.

Getting There & Away

Hakuba is on the JR Ōito line. From Matsumoto the trip takes about 1¾ hours by local train (¥930) and one hour by limited express (¥2060). From Shinano-ōmachi station allow 35 minutes.

Continuing north, the Ōito line eventually connects with the JR Hokuriku Honsen line at Itoigawa, which offers the options of heading north-east toward Niigata or south-west to Toyama and Kanazawa. However, at the time of writing the service between Hakuba and Itoigawa had been suspended for one year due to massive river flooding and landslides that had buried a section of the line north of Minami Otari. JR has not yet announced a date for re-opening the section, which means it may be closed for an extended period of time. Limited bus services are available that cover the gap, but they're scheduled mainly for local use. If the line is still out, it would be best to approach Hakuba from the south.

ŌMACHI 大町

The city of Ōmachi has several stations, but the one to use is called Shinano-ōmachi, which has tourist information facilities. The main reason for visiting Ōmachi is to start or finish the **Tateyama-Kurobe Alpine Route**, which is an expensive but impressive jaunt by various means of transport across the peaks between Nagano-ken and Toyama-ken. See the Toyama-ken section later in this chapter for details. If you have time to kill in Ōmachi while waiting for connections, the **Salt Museum** (Shio-no-Michi Hakubutsukan) is just five minutes on foot from the station. It's open daily (closed Wednesday from November to April) from 8.30 am to 4.30 pm and entry is ¥400.

Places to Stay

An inexpensive place to stay is the *Kizaki-ko Youth Hostel* (☎ 0261-22-1820), which is 15 minutes on foot from Shinanosazaki station (just south of Lake Kizaki-ko), two stops north of Shinano-ōmachi station. A bed for the night costs ¥2800. From the station, walk north in the direction of the lake; at the south end of the lake, turn left and look for the hostel on the right. Close to the hostel, clustered around the southern end of the lake, are numerous hotels, pensions and minshuku. If you need to overnight near the Shinano-ōmachi station, the *Omachi Station Hotel*

(☎ 0261-22-7111) has singles from ¥5200 and twins/doubles from ¥10,900/10,700. It's opposite the railway station.

Getting There & Away

Local trains on the JR Ōito line connect Ōmachi with Matsumoto in one hour (¥560). For connections with Hakuba on the same line allow 35 minutes. The main approach or departure is, of course, via the Tateyama-Kurobe Alpine Route – see the Toyama-ken section of this chapter for more details.

HOTAKA 穂高

Hotaka is a small town with a couple of interesting sights, but it's especially popular with hikers and mountaineers, who use it as a base to head into the mountains. Both the station and bicycle rental place (to your right as you exit on the east side of the station) have basic maps of the town. You can either walk around the area or rent a bicycle at ¥200 per hour. If you're staying at the youth hostel, you can also rent a bicycle there.

Rokuzan Art Museum 碌山美術館

The Rokuzan Art Museum (Rokuzan Bijutsukan) is 10 minutes on foot from the station and worth a visit. On display are sculptures by Rokuzan Ogiwara, a master sculptor whom the Japanese have claimed as the 'Rodin of the Orient'. Admission costs ¥500 and it's open from 9 am to 5 pm between April and October but closes an hour earlier during the rest of the year. It is closed on Monday.

Wasabi Farms わさび農場

Even if you're not a great fan of *wasabi* (Japanese horseradish), a visit to the Dai-ō Wasabi Farm is a good excuse to cycle or walk through fields crisscrossed with canals. The farm is the largest of its kind in Japan, and is a couple of km directly east of Hotaka station. The basic map provided at the station or at the adjacent bicycle rental office is sufficient for orientation.

Nakabusa Onsen 中房温泉

These remote hot springs are reached by bus (70 minutes) from Ariake station, one stop north of Hotaka. From here, there are several trails for extended mountain hikes. There is also accommodation if you're in the mood to get away from it all and soak for a few days (see the Places to Stay section below).

Mt Jonen-dake　常念岳

From Toyoshina station, two stops south of Hotaka, it takes 10 minutes by taxi to reach Kitakaidō, which is the start of a trail for experienced hikers to climb Mt Jonen-dake (2857m) – the ascent takes about eight hours. There are numerous options for mountain hikes extending over several days in the region, but you must be properly prepared. Hiking maps and information are available at the Hotaka, Matsumoto and Nagano tourist offices, although the more detailed maps are in Japanese.

Places to Stay

Azumino Youth Hostel (☎ 0263-83-6170) is four km west of Hotaka station (a one hour walk). A bed for the night costs ¥3100, and bicycles are available for hire. The hostel is closed from 17 January to 7 February.

Not far from Hotaka station are numerous pensions and ryokan. The *Hotaka Pension* (☎ 0263-82-4411) is just to the north of the station and has per person costs from ¥6500 including two meals. The *Shioya Ryokan* (☎ 0263-82-2012) is just to the east of the station and has similar prices.

Nestled up near Nakabusa Onsen are two places where you can take a break from the road and soak up the nourishing minerals of the local hot springs. The *Ariake-so Kokuminshukusha* (☎ 0263-35-9701) is by far the less expensive of the two, with per person rates of around ¥8500, including two meals. More luxurious is the *Nakabusa Onsen* hotel (☎ 0263-35-9704), where a room and two meals will set each of you back ¥15,500. They do offer a rate of ¥8500, but during peak periods you may have to share your room with other guests: pretty steep prices for a dorm bed. To get there, take a bus from Ariake station (one stop north of Hotaka): Nakabusa Onsen is the last stop.

Getting There & Away

Hotaka is about 30 minutes (¥310) from Matsumoto on the JR Ōito line.

MATSUMOTO　松本

Matsumoto (population 200,000) has a superb castle, and is a convenient base for exploration of the Japan Alps, which means it is swamped with backpackers and cyclists during July and August.

The city has been around at least since the 8th century, and was the castle town of the Ogasawara clan during the 14th and 15th centuries. It continued to prosper and grow in size during the Edo period (1600-1868), though somewhere along the way things seem to have slowed down. The city has a somewhat lazy, dishevelled feel to it, though the coming of the 1998 Winter Olympics will probably force the people to spruce things up a bit. All in all, the city merits an overnight stay, but not much longer.

Information

Matsumoto city tourist information office (☎ 0263-32-2814) is on your right at the bottom of the steps leading from Matsumoto station's eastern exit. The English-speaking staff can provide maps and leaflets, help with accommodation and give plenty of other travel information. The office is open daily from 9.30 am to 6 pm; 9 am to 5.30 pm during winter.

JNTO publishes two colour brochures: *Japan Matsumoto* which has good maps and *Japan Matsumoto & the Japan Alps* which provides wider regional coverage; and a concise leaflet entitled *Matsumoto & Kamikōchi*. The first two are available at the Matsumoto tourist information office.

Matsumoto-jō Castle　松本城

Even if you only spend a couple of hours in Matsumoto, make sure you see this splendid castle.

The main attraction in the castle grounds is the original three-turreted castle donjon, built circa 1595, in contrasting black and white. Steep steps and ladders lead you up through six storeys. On the lower floors there are displays of guns, bombs and gadgets to storm castles – complete with technicolour graphics, which are useful for those who can't read the Japanese descriptions. At the top, there's a fine view of the mountains. The structure includes slits and slots for archery and firearms, slatted boards to provide basic ventilation (or a means to bombard attackers) and a Tsukimi Yagura or 'Moon Viewing Pavilion', which was used as a dainty retreat for those lighter moments when the castle was not under attack.

Opening hours are from 8.30 am to 4.30 pm daily but it is closed from 29 December to 3 January. Admission to the castle costs ¥500 and is valid also for the Japan Folklore Museum. The castle is 15 minutes on foot from the station; if you take a bus, the stop for the castle is Shiyakusho-mae (¥190).

Japan Folklore Museum
日本民俗資料館

To the right of the entrance to the castle grounds is the Nihon Minzoku Shiryōkan (Japan Folklore Museum), which has exhibits on several floors relating to the archaeology, history and folklore of Matsumoto and the surrounding region. One floor is devoted to flora and fauna, while another floor displays the superb Honda collection of clocks and watches from the east and west. There are some fascinating timepieces, including a

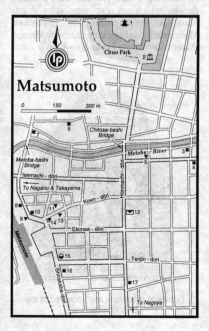

PLACES TO STAY

3	Marumo
	まるも旅館
4	Nunoya
	ぬのや旅館
6	Nishiya
	にしや旅館
7	Hotel Ōte
	ホテル大手
8	Hotel New Station
	ホテルニューステーション
10	Hotel Iidaya
	ホテル飯田屋
16	Matsumoto Tōkyū Inn
	松本東急イン
17	Matsumoto Tourist Hotel
	松本観光ホテル

PLACES TO EAT

5	Delhi
9	Sushi Snack
	寿司スナック
11	Yōrōnotaki
	養老の滝
13	Mr Donut
14	McDonald's

OTHER

1	Matsumoto-jō Castle
	松本城
2	Japan Folklore Museum
	日本民俗資料館
12	Main Post Office
	中央郵便局
15	Matsumoto Bus Station
	松本バスターミナル

Rolls Royce clock, a banjo clock and an elephant clock.

Admission to the museum is included in the price of the castle admission ticket (¥500). Opening hours for the museum are the same as those for the castle.

Japan Ukiyo-e Museum
日本浮世絵博物館

If you have an interest in ukiyo-e, this museum should be on your list. Several generations of the Sakai family have collected over 100,000 prints, paintings, screens and old books – the largest private collection of its kind in the world. English labelling is minimal, but an explanatory leaflet in English is provided. Admission is ¥900 and opening hours are from 10 am to 5 pm daily, except Monday.

Access to the museum is a real pain unless you take the eight minute taxi ride (¥1500) from the station. Otherwise you need to go from Matsumoto station on the Matsumoto Dentetsu line and get off at the fourth stop, Ōniwa (¥170). Turn left out of the tiny station office and walk about 50m up the street to a main road. Bear left again, and continue for about 300m, passing under an overpass, and then turn right at the road mirror. Carry on down this street to the traffic lights then continue straight across for another 100m. The Japan Ukiyo-e Museum is on your left. The walk from Ōniwa station to the museum takes about 20 minutes.

Utsukushigahara-kōgen Plateau
美ケ原高原

From April to mid-November, this alpine plateau is a popular excursion from Matsumoto. Buses stop at Sanjiro Bokujo (Sanjiro Ranch) and there are pleasant walks and the opportunity to see cows in pasture (a constant source of Japanese fascination) and **Utsukushigahara-kōgen Bijutsukan** (an open-air museum), which charges ¥1400 for admission. It has a bizarre series of 120 sculptures, including 'Venus of Milo in the Castle of Venus' and 'Affection Plaza', but to be honest there are likely to be few travellers who would find the exhibits worthy of the

hefty admission charge. On a clear day there are fine views of the Japan Alps from here. There is also a two day hiking trail to **Kirigamine**.

Matsumoto Dentetsu buses run up to the plateau from the Matsumoto bus station (gate No 1) in around one hour 20 minutes and cost ¥1900.

Special Events

During the Heso Matsuri (Navel Festival), held from 6 to 7 June, revellers demonstrate that Matsumoto is the navel of Japan by prancing through the streets wearing costumes that appropriately reveal their navels.

During August, the Takigi Nō Festival features *nō* theatre, by torch light, which is performed outdoors on a stage in the park below the castle.

For those interested in phallic festivals, the Dōsojin Festival is held in honour of *dōsojin* (roadside guardians) on 23 September at Utsukushigahara Onsen. Then on 3 and 4 October, Asama Onsen celebrates the Asama Hi-Matsuri, a fire festival with torch-lit parades which are accompanied by drumming. At the beginning of November, Matsumoto celebrates the Oshiro Matsuri (Matsumoto Castle Festival), which is a cul-

Roadside guardians are honoured at the Dōsojin Festival.

tural jamboree including costume parades, puppet displays and flower shows.

The tourist information office has precise dates and more information.

Places to Stay

The tourist information office at the station has lists of accommodation and can help with reservations. If your main objective is to use Matsumoto as a staging point to visit the Japan Alps, there's no real reason to stay in the town itself unless you get stranded here late in the day.

Youth Hostels *Asama Onsen Youth Hostel* (☎ 0263-46-1335) is a bit regimented and drab: it closes at 9 pm and lights go out punctually at 10 pm. But it does have the advantage of a few nice onsen baths in the neighbourhood. Beds are the standard youth hostel rate of ¥2800. The hostel is closed from 28 December to 3 January.

To reach Asama Onsen by bus from the Matsumoto bus station, there are two options: either take bus No 6 to Shita-Asama (¥240) or bus No 7 to Dai-Ichi Koko-mae (¥280). The bus ride takes 20 minutes, and the hostel is then five minutes on foot.

Ryokan For a very reasonably priced ryokan close to the station, the best bet is *Nishiya* (☎ 0263-33-4332). Some English is spoken here and per person costs are ¥3600 without meals. The place is actually more a minshuku in terms of standards, but at these prices, who's complaining?

For a more refined atmosphere, try *Marumo* (☎ 0263-32-0115), a delightful place near the Metoba River that has its own coffee shop. Rates are around ¥6000 per person including breakfast. It's quite popular with Japanese tourists, so you might want to book ahead. Around the corner is *Nunoya* (☎ 0263-32-0545), a ryokan which specialises in Mediterranean cuisine, and has slightly higher rates.

If you feel like staying outside of town, there's the *Enjyoh Bekkan* (☎ 0263-33-7233), at Utsukushigahara Onsen. This ryokan is a member of the Japanese Inn

Group, and prices start at ¥4800/9000 for singles/doubles – excluding meals. The hot-spring facilities are available day and night. A western-style breakfast is available for ¥800. From Matsumoto, take the 20 minute bus ride to Utsukushigahara Onsen and get off at the terminal. From there it's 300m to the ryokan.

Hotels There are few bargains to be had in this category. One of the cheapest business hotels around is the *Matsumoto Tourist Hotel* (☎ 0263-33-9000). It's about a 10 minute walk from the station and has a limited number of singles at ¥4900. Slightly more up-market rooms are also available at ¥7500/11,500 for singles/doubles. The *Hotel Iidaya* (☎ 0263-32-0027) is just across from the station and has singles from ¥6500 to ¥7300, and twins and doubles from ¥12,000. Just across the road is the *Hotel New Station* (☎ 0263-35-3850), which has singles from ¥6700 to ¥7200, twins from ¥11,200 to ¥14,240 and doubles at ¥11,200. Cheaper, and dingier, is the *Hotel Ōte* (☎ 0263-36-0516), which is just over the river, about a five minute walk from the station, and has singles/twins at ¥5000/9000.

More expensive hotels include the *Hotel Buena Vista* (☎ 0263-37-0111), with singles from ¥8000 to ¥11,000 and twins from ¥15,000 to ¥27,000, and the *Matsumoto Tōkyū Inn* (☎ 0263-36-0109), where singles are ¥9000, twins and doubles ¥17,000. Both are close to the station.

Places to Eat

Like Nagano, Matsumoto is renowned for its shinshū-soba, a variation on the soba theme which is eaten either hot or cold (zaru-soba) with wasabi and soy sauce. Other specialities more peculiar to the region include raw horsemeat, bee larvae, pond snails and zazamushi (crickets). Most of these are unlikely to be of interest to any but the most adventurous of travellers, but if you want to try the soba, there are a couple of shops close to the station with plastic food outside – drag the staff out and point.

On the 2nd floor of the station there is an

arcade with various restaurants offering inexpensive set meals. Alternatively, the basement of the bus station also has various cheap eateries. You can get oyaki around here too. Curry fans may want to try out the *Delhi* restaurant, on a street corner near the Metoba River. There's neither an English sign nor menu, but there are only eight different curry dishes, so you can't go too wrong. Try asking for the 'Indo curry' (mild) or the 'Karakuchi curry' (considerably more spicy). Both come with a small salad, and cold water is readily available. Next door to the Delhi is a ramen (noodle) shop that looks worth a visit.

Getting There & Away

Air Matsumoto airport has flights to Fukuoka, Hiroshima, Osaka and Sapporo.

Train From Tokyo (Shinjuku station), there are Azusa limited express services which reach Matsumoto in 2¾ hours and cost ¥3810 with a ¥2770 limited express surcharge. The fastest services on the JR Chūō Honsen line from Nagoya take 2½ hours. The JR Shinonoi line connects Matsumoto with Nagano in 55 minutes. The trip from Matsumoto to Hakuba on the JR Ōito line takes about 1½ hours.

Both train and bus travel have to be combined for the connection between Matsumoto and Kamikōchi. For more details about this see the Kamikōchi Getting There & Away section.

Bus The Matsumoto Dentetsu company runs regular buses between Matsumoto and Shinjuku in Tokyo (3¼ hours, ¥3400), Osaka (5½ hours, ¥5600) and Nagoya (3½ hours, ¥3400). All departures are from the Matsumoto bus station.

Getting Around

The castle and the city centre are easily covered on foot.

The Airport An airport shuttle bus (¥530) connects Matsumoto airport with the city centre in 25 minutes. Bus departures are timed according to flight schedules. A taxi to the airport from Matsumoto station costs ¥3420.

Bus Matsumoto bus station is diagonally across the main street to the right as you leave the east exit of the station. The terminal set-up is a mess: it's part of a large department store, which means you have to negotiate your way down to the basement and make your way through various food counters to find the door to your gate, and climb the steps to the bus stop back at ground level. Good luck.

SHIRAHONE ONSEN 白骨温泉

This is a classic hot-spring resort which has retained some traditional inns with open-air hot-spring baths in a mountain setting. Since it is close to Shin-Shimashima station, it could easily be visited as part of a trip to Kamikōchi; those with time to kill might like to test for themselves the truth of the saying that bathing here for three days ensures three years without a cold. Shirahone Onsen is also popular with hikers as a base for trails around **Norikura-kōgen Plateau**.

For a place to stay, you could try *Ōishi-kan Youth Hostel* (☎ 0263-93-2011), which is part of a ryokan, just a couple of minutes on foot from the bus station. A bed for the night is ¥2500, and the onsen bath is a bargain at ¥150. Right nearby, the *Ryokan Tsuruya* (☎ 0263-93-2101) has traditional Japanese accommodation for ¥10,000 per person, two meals included. Believe it or not, these are probably your two cheapest options.

Getting There & Away

From Matsumoto, you first travel by rail on the Matsumoto Dentetsu line to Shin-Shimashima station, then take a Matsumoto Dentetsu bus (one hour, ¥1400) to Shirahone Onsen. There are only three departures daily, around 8 am, 3 and 5 pm. Buses to Norikura-kōgen summit and to Norikura-kōgen Kyūka-mura (vacation village) also pass through Shirahone Onsen. These bus services only operate between late April and mid-November.

KAMIKŌCHI 上高地

Kamikōchi lies in the centre of the northern Japan Alps and has some of the most spectacular scenery in Japan. In the late 19th century, foreigners 'discovered' this mountainous region and coined the term 'Japan Alps'. A British missionary, Reverend Walter Weston, toiled from peak to peak and sparked Japanese interest in mountaineering as a sport. He is now honoured with his own annual festival and Kamikōchi has become a base for strollers, hikers and climbers. Remember, Kamikōchi is *closed* from November to May.

Orientation

On a fine day, the final stages of the approach to Kamikōchi on the road from Nakanoyu provide a superb mountain panorama: Taishō-ike Pond on your left, and a series of high peaks ranged in the background. From here, the road continues a short distance to the bus station, which is the furthest point to which vehicles are officially allowed in this valley. A short distance on foot beyond the bus station, the Azusa-gawa River is spanned by Kappa-bashi Bridge – at peak season, you probably only need to follow the sound of clicking shutters to find this photogenic subject. From this bridge, you can choose to follow a variety of trails.

Information

Tourist Office At the bus station, there is an information office (☎ 0263-95-2405), open from late April to mid-November only. It's geared mostly to booking accommodation, but also has leaflets and maps. It's preferable to make prior use of the tourist information offices in Takayama or Matsumoto, which have English-speaking staff.

Books & Maps JNTO publishes a leaflet entitled *Matsumoto & Kamikōchi*, which has brief details and a map of Kamikōchi. The tourist offices also have several large maps (covering Kamikōchi, Shirahone Onsen and Norikura-kōgen Plateau) which show mountain trails, average hiking times, mountain huts and lists of tourist facilities. However, they are all in Japanese. *Hiking in Japan* by Paul Hunt covers some trails in the area.

Planning Your Itinerary

If you want to avoid immense crowds, don't plan to visit between late July and late August, or during the first three weeks in October. Between June and mid-July, there's a rainy season which makes outdoor pursuits depressingly soggy.

It's perfectly feasible to visit Kamikōchi from Matsumoto or Takayama in a day, but you'll miss out on the pleasures of staying in the mountains and the opportunity to take early morning or late evening walks before the crowds appear. At the same time, accommodation is expensive: budget travellers beware.

Day Walks If you want to do level walking for short distances, without any climbing, then you should stick to the river valley. A typical three hour walk (round trip) of this kind would proceed east from Kappa-bashi Bridge along the right-hand side of the river to Myōjin-bashi Bridge (45 minutes) and then continue to Tokusawa (45 minutes) before returning. For variety, you could cross to the other side of the river at Myōjin-bashi Bridge.

West of Kappa-bashi Bridge, you can amble along the right-hand side of the river to Weston Monument (15 minutes) or keep to the left-hand side of the river and walk to Taishō-ike Pond (20 minutes). A bridge across the river between Weston Monument and Taishō-ike Pond provides variation for the walk.

Hiking There are dozens of long-distance options for hikers and climbers, varying in duration from a couple of days to a week. *Hiking in Japan* by Paul Hunt provides some ideas. The large Japanese maps of the area show routes and average hiking times between huts, major peaks and landmarks – but you've got to be able to read Japanese or get someone reliable to help decipher the maps. Favourite trails and climbs (which can mean human traffic jams on trails during peak seasons!) include Mt Yariga-take

(3180m) and Mt Hotaka-dake (3190m) – also known as Mt Oku-Hotaka-dake. Other more distant popular destinations include Nakabusa Onsen and Murodō, which is on the Tateyama-Kurobe Alpine Route.

If you want to hike between Kamikōchi and Shin-Hotaka Onsen (see Shin-Hotaka Onsen under the earlier Northern Gifu-ken section of this chapter), there's a steep trail which crosses the ridge below Mt Nishi Hotaka-dake (2909m) at Nishi Hotaka San-sō (Nishi Hotaka Mountain Cottage) and continues to Nishi Hotaka-guchi, the top station of the cablecar for Shin-Hotaka Onsen. The hike takes nearly four hours (because of a steep ascent). Softies might prefer to save an hour of sweat and do the hike in the opposite direction.

Strollers are unlikely to suffer mishap, but those heading off on long hikes or climbs should be properly prepared. Even in summer, temperatures can plummet, or the whole area can be covered in sleeting rain or blinding fog.

Special Events

On the first weekend in June, the climbing season opens with the Weston Festival,

which honours Walter Weston, the British missionary and alpinist.

Places to Stay

This is Kamikōchi's downside. Accommodation is expensive, advance reservations are essential during the peak season and the whole place shuts down from November to May. You'd be well advised to book a room before arriving in Kamikōchi; the tourist information offices at Takayama and Matsumoto are convenient since they have English-speaking staff.

There is a handful of hotels, mostly around Kappa-bashi Bridge, which is a short walk from the bus station. *Kamikōchi Nishiitoya San-sō* (☎ 0263-95-2206) is relatively expensive, with per person costs with two meals coming in at ¥13,390. It is said to be adding an annex with bunk bed accommodation: this might turn out to be a significantly cheaper option, so it's worth calling to check. Up along the river, near Myojin Pond, the *Myojinkan Ryokan* (☎ 0263-95-2036) is a bit cheaper, with per person rates of ¥10,300. The *Son-ei Kamikōchi Alpine Hotel* (☎ 0263-95-2231) is viciously expensive (¥20,000 per person), but it has some 'skiers beds' for ¥7500. This is no bargain, but it's about the cheapest you'll find in town, with the one exception of the *Konashidaira Campground* (Kamikōchi Konashidaira Kyampu-jō) (☎ 0263-95-2321), which lies across the river from the bus terminal. It has tent sites for ¥400, rental tents for ¥2000, and a few 'bungalows' for ¥6000. Further up the river, about three km north-east of Kappa-bashi Bridge, the *Tokusawa Kyampu-jō* has similar rates for tent sites and rentals.

Dotted along the trails and around the mountains are dozens of mountain cottages or mountain huts (*san-sō* or *yama-goya*), which provide two meals and a bed for an average cost of around ¥7000 per person.

Places to Eat

Most visitors either take their meals as part of their accommodation package or bring their own. Several of the hotels around Kappa-bashi Bridge have restaurants. The

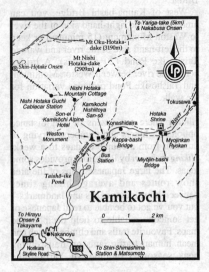

Kamikōchi

bus station has vending machines and limited facilities for buying food.

Getting There & Away

Bus services for Kamikōchi cease from mid-November to late April and the exact dates can vary. If you plan to travel at the beginning or end of this period, check first with a tourist office or call Japan Travel-Phone (☎ 0120-44-4800, toll free).

The connection between Kamikōchi and Matsumoto involves travel by train and bus. From Matsumoto, take the Matsumoto Dentetsu line to Shin-Shimashima station – don't confuse this with the station called Shimojima. The trip takes 30 minutes and the fare is ¥670. From Shin-Shimashima station take the bus via Nakanoyu to Kamikōchi (1¼ hours, ¥2050). Buses run hourly between late April and late July, more frequently from late July to late August. Hourly services resume between late August and early November, after which buses cease running altogether until late April.

From Kamikōchi you can continue by bus via Hirayu Onsen to Takayama. Between Takayama and Kamikōchi there are frequent bus connections between 7 am and around 2.30 pm, but *only* from April to October. The bus runs via Nakanoyu and you have to change to another bus at Hirayu Onsen. The full trip takes around two hours and costs ¥3050.

Between Norikura Tatami-daira (near the summit of Mt Norikura-dake) and Kamikōchi buses run via Hirayu Onsen approximately three times a day (two hours), five or six times a day in July and August. The Norikura Skyline Road is *only* open from 15 May to 31 October. The trip takes around two hours and costs ¥2950. There is one bus daily between Kamikōchi and Norikura-kōgen Plateau (¥1800), two buses a day from late July to late August. There are also one or two buses daily between Kamikōchi and Shirahone Onsen. The ride takes 45 minutes and costs ¥1500.

The road between Nakanoyu and Kamikōchi is closed to private cars: only buses and taxis are permitted, so don't rent a car if you're planning to come here.

NORIKURA-KŌGEN PLATEAU & NORIKURA ONSEN
乗鞍高原・乗鞍温泉

This alpine plateau below Mt Norikura-dake (3026m) is popular with hikers and famous for the Norikura Skyline Road (closed from November to May), a scenic bus route which leads to the Tatami-daira bus stop at the foot of the mountain. From there, a trail leads to the peak in about 40 minutes. Norikura Onsen is a hot-spring resort on the plateau and a base for skiing and hiking which is open all year round.

Places to Stay

There is a choice of accommodation including ryokan, pensions and mountain huts, most of which are grouped around the Suzuran bus stop. An inexpensive place to stay near the ski lifts is *Norikura Kōgen Youth Hostel* (☎ 0263-93-2748), which has nightly rates of ¥3100. On the way to the youth hostel, you might want to look out for the *Ryokan Mitake-sō* (☎ 0263-93-2016), an unassuming white building with a wooden annex that has rates of ¥8000 to ¥10,000 per person with two meals. Close by is the *Pension Chimunii* (Chimney Pension) (☎ 0263-93-2902), which has per person costs of ¥7500 including two meals. There aren't many rooms, so it would be wise to book ahead. All three places are near the ski-jō mae bus stop, one past the Suzuran stop.

Tatami-daira, near the summit of Mt Norikura-dake, is not an ideal place to spend the night: it's basically a big parking lot with a few well-worn trails snaking off from it to the nearby peaks. But if you get stuck up here (quite possible, given the inconvenient bus schedules), there are two ryokan with per person rates of ¥8000 to ¥10,000, including two meals. They are next to each other at the far end of the parking lot.

Getting There & Away

The bus between Norikura Tatami-daira and Takayama operates along the Norikura Skyline Road between 15 May to 31 October and usually runs via Hirayu Onsen. The ride

CENTRAL HONSHŪ

takes about 1½ hours and costs ¥2650. There are five or six buses daily between 7.30 am and 12.20 pm.

From July to mid-October, there are five to six buses a day between Norikura-kōgen and Shin-Shimashima station, where you can catch trains to Matsumoto. The trip takes about an hour and costs ¥1300 (to Suzuran). Services are suspended on Sunday and holidays.

There are also one or two buses a day between Norikura-kōgen, Shirahone Onsen and Kamikōchi. The fare from Suzuran to Kamikōchi is ¥1800.

If you are driving your own vehicle, be aware that the one-way toll for driving on the Norikura Skyline is a hefty ¥1540, and unless you plan to take the toll road onward to Matsumoto (or stay up at Tatami-daira for the rest of your life), you'll have to buy a round-trip pass for ¥3080.

KISO VALLEY REGION　木曽川

A visit to this region is highly recommended if you want to see several small towns with architecture carefully preserved from the Edo period. As a bonus, there's the opportunity to combine your visit to Magome and Tsumago with an easy walk. JNTO publishes a leaflet entitled *Kiso Valley*, which has details and maps for the region.

The thickly forested Kiso Valley lies in the south-west of Nagano-ken and is surrounded by the Japan Alps. It was traversed by the Nakasen-dō Highway, an old post road which connected Edo (present-day Tokyo) with Kyoto and provided business for the post towns en route. With the introduction of new roads and commercial centres to the north, and the later construction of the Chūō railway line, the region was effectively bypassed and the once prosperous towns went into decline. During the '60s, there was a move to preserve the original architecture of the post towns and tourism has become a major source of income.

Magome was the birthplace of a famous Japanese literary figure, Shimazaki Tōson (1872-1943). His masterpiece, *Ie* (published in English in 1976 and entitled *The Family*),

records the decline of two provincial families in the Kiso region.

On 23 November, the Fuzoku Emaki Parade is held along the old post road in Tsumago and features a procession by the townsfolk who dress in costume from the Edo period.

Magome to Tsumago Walk
馬籠から妻籠への路

Magome Magome is a small post town with rows of traditional houses and post inns (and souvenir shops, of course) lining a steep street. The town's tourist information office (☎ 0264-59-2336) is a short way up, on the right-hand side of the street. The office is open from 8.30 am to 5 pm and dispenses tourist literature as well as reserving accommodation. Close by is a museum devoted to the life and times of Shimazaki Tōson, which may be a little impenetrable for non-Japanese speakers. It's open daily from 8.30 am to 4.45 pm between April and October, with shorter hours during winter. Admission is ¥300.

To walk from Magome to Tsumago, continue toiling up the street until the houses eventually give way to a forest path which winds down to the road leading up a steep hill to Magome-kōge Pass. This initial walk from Magome to the pass takes about 45 minutes and is not particularly appealing because you spend most of your time on the road. You can cut out this first section by taking the bus between Magome and Tsumago and getting off after about 12 minutes at the pass.

There's a small shop-cum-teahouse at the top of the pass where the trail leaves the road and takes you down to the right along a pleasant route through the forest. From the teahouse to Tsumago takes just under two hours.

Tsumago Tsumago is so well preserved it feels like an open-air museum. Designated by the government as a protected area for the preservation of traditional buildings, no modern developments such as TV aerials or telephone poles are allowed to mar the scene. The tourist information office (☎ 0264-57-

3123), open from 9 am to 5 pm, is halfway down the main street. Tourist literature on Tsumago and maps are available and the staff are happy to make accommodation reservations.

About 50m beyond the post office, on the same side of the street, is the **Okuya Kyōdokan Folk Museum**, which is part of a magnificent house built like a castle. During the Edo period, felling of trees in the Kiso region was strictly controlled. In 1877, following the relaxation of these controls, the owner decided to rebuild using *hinoki* (cypress trees). Admission to the museum is ¥600, and it's open daily from 9 am to 4.45 pm.

If you continue from this house up the main street, the bus station can be reached by taking any of the side streets on your left.

Baggage Forwarding As a special service for walkers on the trail between Magome and Tsumago, the tourist offices in both villages offer a baggage-forwarding service during peak visiting seasons. For a fee of ¥500 per piece of luggage, you can have your gear forwarded. The deadline for the morning delivery is 8.30 am and for the afternoon delivery, it's 11.30 am. The service operates daily from late July to 31 August but is restricted to Saturday, Sunday and national holidays between late March and late July and September through November.

Places to Stay & Eat Both tourist information offices can help book accommodation at the numerous ryokan and minshuku in the area. Prices for a room and two meals at ryokan start at around ¥9000 while minshuku prices for a similar deal start at around ¥6500. *Minshuku Daikichi* (☎ 0264-57-2595) is a friendly place just four minutes on foot from the Tsumago bus station with per person rates of ¥7000.

Magome and Tsumago have several restaurants on their main streets. The local specialities include gohei-mochi (a rice dumpling on a stick coated with nut sauce) and sansai (mountain greens), which can be ordered as a set meal (sansai teishoku) for about ¥1000.

Getting There & Away The main railway stations on the JR Chūō line that provide access to Magome and Tsumago are Nakatsugawa station and Nagiso station respectively. Some services do not stop at these stations, which are about 12 minutes apart by limited express – check the timetable. By limited express, the trip between Nagoya and Nakatsugawa takes 55 minutes (¥2980); between Nakatsugawa and Matsumoto it takes 85 minutes (¥3600). Local trains take nearly twice as long, but cost about half as much. Direct buses also operate between Nagoya and Magome and the trip takes just under two hours. From Tokyo, take the JR Chūō line to Shiojiri, where you'll need to change for a train to Nakatsugawa. A limited express ticket for the entire trips costs ¥9550.

Buses leave hourly from outside the Nakatsugawa station for Magome (30 minutes, ¥510). There's also an infrequent bus service between Magome and Tsumago (30 minutes, ¥640). If you decide to start your walk from the Magome-kōge Pass, take this bus and get off at the bus stop at the top of the pass.

From Tsumago, you can either catch the bus to Nagiso station (10 minutes, ¥270), or if you're still in the mood to hike, walk there in 1½ hours.

Kiso-Fukushima & Mt On-take
木曽福島・御岳山

Kiso-Fukushima was an important barrier gate and checkpoint on the old post road. From the station, it takes about 20 minutes on foot to reach several old residences, museums and temples.

Mt On-take (3063m) is an active volcano – entry to the crater area is prohibited. For centuries the mountain has been considered sacred and is an important destination for pilgrims.

There are several trails to the summit. One popular trailhead is at Nakanoyu Onsen, 80 minutes by bus from Kiso-Fukushima station. From the trailhead, it takes about 3½ hours to hike to the summit. Another trailhead is at Tanohara Natural Park, 1½ hours by bus (¥2110) from Kiso-Fukushima station; from here the hike to the summit takes about three hours. Be careful to check the bus schedules before setting out: there are only two to three buses daily to each destination.

An inexpensive place to stay is *Kiso Ryōjōan Youth Hostel* (☎ 0264-23-7716), which is a short bus ride from Kiso-Fukushima station. Take the 25 minute bus ride to Ohara bus station – the hostel is three minutes on foot from there and is a useful base for hiking or sightseeing in the area. Beds at the hostel cost ¥2800. There are numerous minshuku and ryokan in Kiso-Fukushima itself, including several near the railway station. Minshuku prices start at around ¥7000 and ryokan at ¥10,000.

Kiso-Fukushima is on the JR Chūō line and limited expresses run to Nagoya in 1½ hours or to Matsumoto in 40 minutes.

Narai 奈良井

Narai is another town on the old post road with a high proportion of traditional buildings from the Edo period. It seems less exposed to large-scale tourism than Magome and Tsumago.

Orientation & Information Narai's main street extends for about one km and lies to your left as you exit the railway station.

The station information office is run by local senior citizens who go out of their way to load you down with Japanese brochures.

Things to See At intervals along the street there are five old wells which were used by thirsty travellers during the Edo period. The sake brewery is easily recognised by its basket of fronds hanging from the roof above the entrance. Continuing down the street, there are side streets on the right-hand side which lead to tranquil temples.

Many of the houses lining the main street originally functioned as inns during the heyday of the old post road; most have been turned into museums though some still operate as ryokan. Nakamura-tei House was once a shop specialising in lacquerware and

is now a museum run by a friendly proprietor. Admission costs ¥150.

At the end of the main street, you pass a temple on your left, and just beyond is the Minzoku Shiryōkan (Local History Museum), which gives a taste of what life was like before the tourists arrived. Admission costs ¥150.

If you feel like following the old post road, continue uphill for four km (about 1¾ hours) to **Torii-tōge Pass**. From there, it's another four km (1¾ hours) to the station at **Yabuhara**.

Places to Stay *Iseya* (☎ 0264-34-3051) is a minshuku housed in a traditional wooden building, with per person rates of ¥7500, including two meals. A few of the rooms are little changed from when they were originally built 170 years ago. It's about 10 minutes walk south of the railway station along the main road.

Getting There & Away Narai is on the Chūō line, about 45 minutes by local train from Matsumoto (¥560).

TENRYŪ-KYŌ GORGE & MT KOMAGA-TAKE　天竜峡・駒ヶ岳

Both Tenryū-kyō and Mt Komaga-take lie east of the Kiso Valley and are easily reached via the JR Iida line, which runs roughly parallel to the Chūō line.

The main sightseeing approach for Tenryū-kyō is a one hour boat trip down the Tenryū River and through the gorge (¥2900). Boats leave from the dock close to Tenryū-kyō station.

Mt Komaga-take (2956m) is a popular hiking destination. From Komagane station, a 55 minute bus ride (¥980) takes you up to the base station of the cablecar at Shirabi-daira. The eight minute cablecar ride (¥1130) whisks you up to Senjōjiki. From there, the hike to the peak takes about 2½ hours.

There are numerous pensions, minshuku and ryokan around the town, and several mountain huts along the trails. If you want to stay at *Komagane Youth Hostel* (☎ 0265-83-3856), from the Komagane station, take a bus bound for Suganodae for 15 minutes and get off at the Grand Hotel-mae bus stop. From there it's a 10 minute walk to the hostel, where a bed will cost you ¥2350 (¥2650 in winter).

Toyama-ken 富山県

TOYAMA 富山

Toyama (population 321,000) is a heavily industrialised city with few tourist attractions. But it does provide a convenient access point for a visit to the northern Japan Alps.

Information

The information office in Toyama station has a somewhat useful pamphlet on the Tateyama-Kurobe Alpine Route, as well as leaflets and maps (in Japanese) on other destinations such as Unazuki Onsen and Gokayama. JNTO has a leaflet entitled *Tateyama, Kurobe & Toyama* that has details on transport links and accommodation.

Places to Stay

If you have to stay in Toyama, there are plenty of business hotels just a few minutes on foot from the station. One hundred metres down the street to your right as you exit the station is the *Toyama Business Hotel* (☎ 0764-32-8090), which has singles for ¥5500 and a few twins from ¥9000 to ¥10,000. The *Hotel Alpha One Eki-Mae* (☎ 0764-33-6000) has over 270 singles at ¥5600 to ¥5800, and a smaller number of twins from ¥10,800. It's just opposite the station.

Toyama Youth Hostel (☎ 0764-37-9010) lies way out to the north-east of the city, 45 minutes by bus from the station (bus station Nos 7 and 8). Rates vary from ¥2200 to ¥2350 depending on the season.

Getting There & Away

Air Daily flights operate between Toyama and Tokyo.

Train The JR Takayama line links Toyama with Takayama in about 1½ hours by limited

express (¥3220), three hours by local train (¥1590). The Toyama Tateyama line links Toyama with Tateyama, which is the starting (or finishing) point for those travelling the Tateyama-Kurobe Alpine Route. The Toyama Chihō Tetsudō line links Toyama with Unazuki Onsen, which is the starting point for a trip up the Kurobe-kyō Gorge.

The JR Hokuriku line runs west via Takaoka (15 minutes) to Kanazawa (one hour), Kyoto (3½ hours) and Osaka (four hours). The same line runs north-east via Naoetsu (1¼ hours) to the ferry terminal for Sado-ga-shima Island and Niigata (three hours) and Aomori at the very tip of Northern Honshū.

TATEYAMA-KUROBE ALPINE ROUTE
立山黒部アルペンルート

JNTO publishes a leaflet entitled *Tateyama, Kurobe & Toyama* with details on this route, which extends between Toyama and Shinano-ōmachi. The route is divided into nine sections using various modes of transport. The best place to take a break, if only to escape the Mickey Mouse commentaries and enjoy the tremendous scenery, is Murodō. Transport buffs will want to do the lot, but some visitors find a trip from Toyama as far as Murodō is sufficient, and skip the expense of the rest. The following route description is from Toyama to Shinano-ōmachi, but travel in either direction is possible.

The season for heavy crowds of visitors is between August and late October and reservations are strongly advised for travel in these months. Better yet, avoid doing the trip during this period.

The route is closed from late November to early May. For the precise dates, which vary each year, check with a tourist office or call Japan Travel-Phone (☎ 0120-44-4800, toll free).

The Route

From Toyama station, take the chug-a-lug Toyama Tateyama line for the one hour ride (¥1100) through rural scenery to Tateyama (at an altitude of 454m). Very close to Tateyama station is *Sugita Youth Hostel* (☎ 0764-82-1754), a convenient place to stay if you are making an early start or a late

CENTRAL HONSHŪ

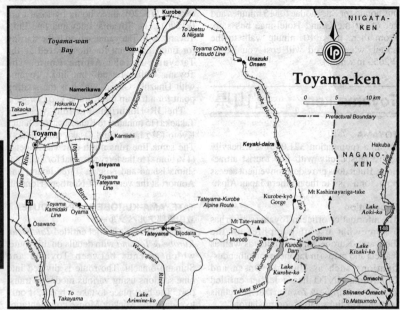

finish on the route. A bed for the night is ¥2800. There are also plenty of ryokan about. One of the more reasonable options is *Senzanso* (☎ 0764-82-1726), which charges around ¥7000/8000 per person including two meals.

From Tateyama, take the seven minute ride (¥620) in the cablecar to **Bijodaira**. From here, it's a 55 minute ride (¥1630) by bus via the alpine plateau of Midagahara to **Murodō** (altitude 2450m). You can break the trip at Midagahara and do the 15 minute walk to see **Tateyama caldera** – the largest non-active crater in Japan. The upper part of the plateau is often covered with deep snow until late into the summer – the road is kept clear by piling up the snow to form a virtual tunnel.

At Murodō, the natural beauty of the surroundings has been somewhat spoilt by a monstrous bus station to service the annual flood of visitors. From here, there are various options for short hikes. To the north, just 10

minutes away on foot, is **Mikuriga-ike Pond**. Twenty minutes further on again is **Jigokudani Onsen** (Hell Valley Hot Springs): no bathing here, unless you don't mind boiling bath water. To the east, you can hike for about two hours – including a very steep final section – to the peak of **Mt O-yama** (3003m) for an astounding panorama. For the keen long-distance hiker who has several days or even a week to spare, there are fine routes south to Kamikōchi or north to Keyaki-daira in the Kurobe-kyō Gorge.

Continuing on the route from Murodō, there's a 10 minute bus ride to Daikanbō via a tunnel dug through Mt Tate-yama. The ticket for this claustrophobic experience costs the hefty sum of ¥2060.

At **Daikanbō** you can pause to admire the view before taking the cablecar for the seven minute ride (¥1240) to Kurobe-daira, where another cablecar whisks you down in five minutes (¥820) to Kurobeko beside the vast **Kurobe Dam**.

There's a 20 minute walk from Kurobeko to the dam, where you can descend to the water for a cruise or climb up to a lookout point before taking the trolley bus to **Ogisawa** (16 minutes, ¥1240). From there, a 40 minute bus ride (¥1300) takes you down to Shinano-ōmachi station – at an altitude of 712m. From here there are frequent trains to Matsumoto (one hour), from where you can connect with trains for Tokyo, Nagoya and Nagano.

There's no denying it's a unique way to travel but not everyone will agree it's worth the cost. Transport expenses for an adult to make the 89.3 km trip from Toyama to Shinano-ōmachi add up to ¥10,010.

KUROBE-KYŌ GORGE & UNAZUKI ONSEN 黒部峡・宇奈月温泉

From Unazuki Onsen, the Kurobe Kyokoku tramcar line provides a superbly scenic alpine run past hot-spring lodges and continues up the Kurobe-kyō Gorge to Keyaki-daira. Here you can hike to an observation point for a panorama of the northern Japan Alps. Keyaki-daira is also linked with Hakuba and Murodō by trails that are suitable for seasoned hikers, properly prepared and with several days to spare.

Places to Stay

There's no shortage of luxury accommodation in this area, but there are a few reasonably priced places as well. In Unazuki, the *Etsuzan-so* (0765-62-1016) is one of the best deals around at ¥7300 per person, including two meals (generous portions). Also in Unazuki is *Kurobe-so* (☎ 0765-62-1149), a bit more pricey at ¥8200, but the higher cost gets you access to an outdoor onsen bath. In Kuronagi, which is a 28 minute ride up the gorge on the Kurobe Kyokoko line (¥470), the *Kuronagi Ryokan* (☎ 0765-62-1820) has rooms with two meals (and of course, onsen baths) for ¥8500 per person. Reservations are recommended, since these cheaper spots fill up quickly. Unless you speak Japanese, you'll probably need to enlist the help of one of the tourist offices to book a room by phone.

Getting There & Away

Take the train on the Toyama Chihō Tetsudō line from the separate terminus (next to Toyama station) to Unazuki Onsen. The trip from Toyama takes 1½ hours and the fare is ¥1650. Trains leave once an hour. If you're arriving on the JR Hokuriku line from the north, change to the Toyama Chihō Tetsudō line either at Kurobe (the stations are separate) or at Uozu (the stations are together).

When you arrive at the railway station at Unazuki Onsen, you then have to walk for five minutes to the station for the Kurobe Kyōkoku Tetsudō (tramcar line). The tramcar line only operates from early May to late November and open carriages are used on most runs. The fare from Unazuki Onsen to Keyaki-daira is ¥1410 and the trip takes 1½ hours. A surcharge is payable for travel on the daily run with enclosed carriages.

GOKAYAMA 五箇山

This remote region, famous for its gasshō-zukuri architecture, is in the south-western corner of Toyama-ken, near the border with Gifu-ken. Details on Gokayama are in the section on Shōkawa Valley; see under Northern Gifu-ken, earlier in this chapter.

Getting There & Away

To visit Gokayama, you can either take a bus from Takaoka station (one hour 50 minutes to Suganuma, ¥1700) or you can take a Jōhana line train from Toyama to Jōhana (50 minutes, ¥560) and continue from there by bus (one hour to Suganuma). Several buses run further, linking Gokayama with Ogimachi and Shirakawa-gō. From Ogimachi you can take buses to Takayama. Buses are not that frequent, so build some extra time into your itinerary.

Ishikawa-ken 石川県

This prefecture offers the visitor a nice blend of cultural/historical sights and natural beauty. Kanazawa, longtime power base of the Maeda clan, boasts several excellent museums, traditional architecture and one of Japan's most famous gardens. To the north, the Noto-Hantō Peninsula has beautiful seascapes, rolling hills and quiet fishing villages. Hakusan National Park, near the southern tip of Ishikawa, offers the chance for some fine hiking.

KANAZAWA 金沢

During the 15th century, Kanazawa (population 442,000) came under the control of an autonomous Buddhist government, but this was ousted in 1583 by Maeda Toshiie, head of the powerful Maeda clan, which continued to rule for another three centuries. The wealth acquired from rice production allowed the Maeda to patronise cultural and artistic pursuits – Kanazawa is still one of the key cultural centres in Japan.

During WWII, the absence of military targets in Kanazawa spared the city from destruction and preserved several historical and cultural sites. As the capital of Ishikawa-ken, Kanazawa has its fair share of functional urban architecture. However, it has retained some attractive features from the old city, including the famous Kenroku-en Garden.

The main sights can be seen in a day or so and side trips to the Noto-hantō Peninsula and Eihei-ji Temple in Fukui-ken are highly recommended.

Orientation

Kanazawa is a sprawling city, and the central city area is a 15 minute bus ride to the south-east of JR Kanazawa station. Fortunately the city has an excellent bus service, making it easy to get to the main sightseeing districts, which can then be covered on foot. The Katamachi District is the commercial and business hub of Kanazawa. From there it's a short walk east to Kenroku-en Garden and its surrounding attractions. The samurai houses in the Nagamachi District are a short walk west from Kohrinbo 109 department store, a useful orientation point in the centre of Katamachi. Just south of Katamachi, across the river, is the temple district of Teramachi, another interesting area to explore.

On the eastern side of Kanazawa, the hills rising behind the Higashiyama District are popular for walks and views across the city.

Information

Tourist Offices At the back of the JR ticket office in Kanazawa station is the Kanazawa tourist information office (☎ 0762-32-6200). The office has English-speaking staff and is open daily from 9 am to 6 pm.

An essential port of call for anyone planning an extended stay in Kanazawa is the International Culture Exchange Center (☎ 0762-23-9575) in the Shakyo Center close to Kenroku-en Garden. The 4th floor of the centre has an English library and a useful noticeboard.

JNTO publishes an informative leaflet entitled *Kanazawa*, which has concise information on sights, maps, timetables and lists of places to stay for Kanazawa. A local bilingual monthly newsletter, *Cosmos*, also has information on local happenings, concerts and the like. It can be found at any of the above information centres, as well as at some local bars, restaurants and shops.

Post The most convenient post office is in Kohrinbo, close to Kohrinbo 109 department store. This post office is open Monday to Friday from 9 am to 6 pm.

Bookshops For a limited selection of foreign books, you can try Maruzen or Utsunomiya bookshops, which are both in the centre of the city, near the Kohrinbo 109 department store.

Courses

Japanese-language classes are offered at the International Culture Exchange Center (see under Information, above). The Ishikawa Interhuman Network (☎ 0762-21-9901) offers classes in calligraphy, tea ceremony (*chanoyu*), flower arrangement (*ikebana*) and other cultural pursuits.

Nagamachi Samurai Houses
長町武家屋敷跡

The Nagamachi District, once inhabited by samurai, has retained a few of its winding streets and tile-roofed mud walls. **Nomura Samurai House**, though partly transplanted from outside Kanazawa, is worth a visit for its decorative garden. Admission costs ¥400 and it's open from 8.30 am to 4.30 pm.

Close by is **Yūzen Silk Center** (Saihitsu-an), where you can see the silk-dyeing process. Admission costs ¥500 and includes an English leaflet, tea and a sweet. It's open from 9 am to noon and from 1 to 4.30 pm but is closed on Thursday.

Kenroku-en Garden　兼六園

Usually billed as the star attraction of Kanazawa, Kenroku-en is also ranked by Japanese as one of their three top gardens –

the other two are Kairaku-en in Mito and Kōraku-en in Okayama.

The name of the garden *(kenroku* translates as 'combined six') refers to a renowned Chinese garden from the Sung dynasty which required six attributes for perfection, including seclusion, spaciousness, artificiality, antiquity, abundant water and broad views. In its original form, Kenroku-en formed the outer garden of Kanazawa Castle, but from the 17th century onwards it was enlarged until it reached completion in the early 19th century. The garden was opened to the public in 1871.

Kenroku-en is certainly attractive, but its fame has attracted enormous crowds which, by sheer weight of numbers, make severe inroads into the intimacy and enjoyment of the place as a garden. To escape the rush hours, try to visit early in the morning or late in the afternoon.

CENTRAL HONSHŪ

Kanazawa Walking Tour
Duration: Half or full day, depending on length
Sights: Nagamachi Samurai houses; Katamachi shopping and entertainment district; Kenroku-en Garden; Ishikawa Prefectural Art Museum; Honda Museum; Ishikawa Prefectural Museum for Traditional Products & Crafts; Higashi Geisha District; Ōmichō Market

If your legs are itching for exercise and your mind is ready for a healthy dose of culture, you can try tackling Kanazawa's sights in one fell swoop. Start with a 10 minute bus ride (for example, bus No 20, 21 or 22) from the station to the Kohrinbo bus stop. From there it's a 10 minute walk to the samurai houses in Nagamachi. You can then return to Kohrinbo and walk east for 15 minutes to Kenroku-en Garden and Seison-kaku Villa. There are plenty of relaxing spots to sit down and enjoy the scenery here and it's a good spot to take a breather.

Next door to the Seison-kaku Villa is the Ishikawa Prefectural Museum of Traditional Products & Crafts. A five minute walk south will then bring you to the Ishikawa Prefectural Art Museum, which is also close to the Honda Museum.

If, at this point, you've had your fill of sightseeing, you can catch bus No 11 or 12 back to the station, or walk back to Katamachi, if that's where you're staying. Otherwise, head north from the park to the Asano-gawa Ōhashi Bridge, cross the river, and head into the Higashi Geisha District. Keen walkers can even head past this area and up into the wooded hills of Higashiyama: there is a walking course with posted signs in English that takes you to some temples and nice views of the city.

Heading back across the bridge, a 15 minute stroll along Hyakumangoku ōdori will bring you to the Ōmichō Market, where you can wind up your day with an excellent seafood meal at one of the many little restaurants there, as long as you arrive before 8 pm, when most places close.

Of course there are numerous variations on the above route. For example, after hitting Kenroku-en, you could head back through Katamachi and then turn south to cross the river into the Teramachi temple district. And if you don't feel like walking for six to eight hours, the Kanazawa Historical Trail bus does a loop through the city that runs near almost all the major sights. See the Getting Around section for details. ∎

Admission costs ¥300 and it's open daily from 7 am to 6 pm. From 16 October to 1 March opening hours are from 8 am to 4.30 pm.

Seison-kaku Villa　成巽閣

This retirement villa, on the south-eastern edge of Kenroku-en, was built in 1863 by a Maeda lord for his mother. A visit to this stylish residence with its elegant chambers and furnishings is recommended. Admission costs ¥500 and includes a detailed explanatory leaflet in English. It's open from 8.30 am to 4.30 pm, closed on Wednesday.

Ishikawa-mon Gate

Just outside Kenroku-en, this elegant gate with its lead tiles (useful if ammunition ran short) is all that's left of Kanazawa Castle, which burnt down so many times that the locals obviously got sick of rebuilding the thing.

Ishikawa Prefectural Art Museum

This museum specialises in antique exhibits of traditional arts with special emphasis on Kutani ceramics, Japanese painting and Yūzen fabrics and costumes. The exhibits are rotated throughout the year. Admission

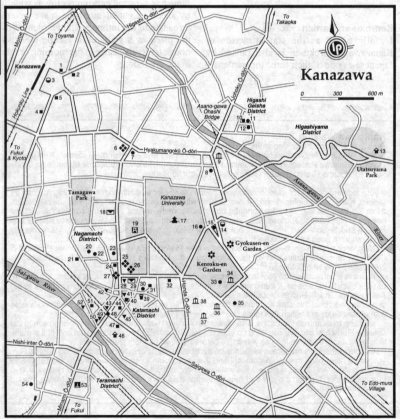

PLACES TO STAY
1 Holiday Inn
   Kanazawa
   ホリデーイン金沢
2 Kanazawa Station
   Hotel
   金沢ステーション
   ホテル
4 Kanazawa ANA Hotel
   金沢全日空ホテル
5 Garden Hotel
   Kanazawa
   ガーデンホテル金沢
10 Yōgetsu Minshuku
   民宿陽月
13 Kanazawa Youth
   Hostel
   金沢ユースホステル
21 Yamadaya
   山田家
24 Kanazawa
   Tōkyū Hotel
   金沢東急ホテル
31 Ryokan Kikunoya
32 Kanazawa Dai-Ichi
   Hotel
   金沢第一ホテル
44 Murataya Ryokan
   村田屋旅館
46 Matsui Youth Hostel
   松井ユースホステル
47 Kanazawa
   Washington Hotel
   金沢ワシントン
   ホテル
51 Kanazawa Prince
   Hotel
   金沢プリンスホテル

PLACES TO EAT
28 Mr Donut
41 McDonald's
42 Sayur
43 Tsubohachi
   つぼ八

45 Kopkunka
49 Irohanihoheto
   いろはにほへと
50 Tamazushi
52 Legian; Polé Polé Bar

OTHER
3 Hokutetsu Kankō Bus
   Company
   北鉄観光バス
   ターミナル
6 Meitetsu Marukoshi
   Department Store
   名鉄丸越スカイ
   プラザ
7 Ōmichō Market
8 Terashima Samurai
   House
   寺島応養邸
9 Ōhi Pottery Museum
   大樋美術館
11 Shima Geisha House
   志摩
12 Kaikarō
   懐華楼
14 Kenroku-en-shita Bus
   Stop
   兼六園下バス停
15 Ishikawa Local
   Products Shop
   石川県観光物産館
16 Ishikawa-mon Gate
   石川門
17 Kanazawa-jō Castle
   Ruins
   金沢城跡
18 Post Office
   郵便局
19 Oyama-jinja Shrine
   尾山神社
20 Nomura Samurai
   House
   野村家跡

22 Yūzen Silk Centre
   彩筆庵
23 Maruzen
25 Daiwa Department
   Store
   ダイワ
26 Atrio Shopping Plaza
27 Kohrinbo 109
   Department Store
   香林坊109
29 Post Office
   郵便局
30 Utsunomiya
   Bookshop
33 Seison-kaku Villa
   成巽閣
34 Ishikawa Prefectural
   Museum for
   Traditional Arts &
   Crafts
   石川県立伝統産業
   工芸館
35 Ishikawa Prefectural
   Nō Theatre
   石川県立能楽堂
36 Honda Museum
   本多蔵品館
37 Nakamura Memorial
   Museum
   中村記念美術館
38 Ishikawa Prefectural
   Art Museum
   石川県立美術館
39 Sapporo Lion Beer
   Hall
40 Doutor Coffee Shop
48 Katamachi
   Intersection
   片町交差点
53 Ninja-dera Temple
   忍者寺
54 Kutani Kosen Gama
   Kiln
   久谷光仙窯

CENTRAL HONSHŪ

costs ¥350, but more is charged for special exhibitions. It's open from 9.30 am to 5 pm.

Nakamura Memorial Museum
中村記念美術館

The Nakamura Memorial Museum is reached via a narrow flight of steps below the Ishikawa Prefectural Art Museum. The museum displays the collection of a wealthy sake brewer, Nakamura Eishun. Exhibits are changed throughout the year, but usually include tea ceremony utensils, calligraphy and traditional crafts. Admission costs ¥300 and includes green tea and a Japanese titbit. It's open from 9 am to 4.30 pm daily except Tuesday.

Honda Museum   藩老本多蔵品館

Members of the Honda family were chief retainers to the Maeda clan and this museum exhibits the family collection of armour, household utensils and works of art. The bulletproof coat and the family vase are particularly interesting. One cogent reason to visit this museum is the detailed, descriptive catalogue in English.

Admission costs ¥500. The museum is open from 9 am to 5 pm, closed on Thursday between November and February.

Gyokusen-en Garden   玉泉園

If you want to visit a delightful garden with more intimacy and less crowds than Kenroku-en, Gyokusen-en is definitely recommended. The garden dates from the Edo period and consists of several gardens rising on two levels up a steep slope. You can take tea here for an additional ¥400.

Admission costs ¥500 and includes a detailed leaflet in English. The garden is open from 9 am to 4 pm but is closed from early December to early March.

Ōhi Pottery Museum   大樋

This museum was established by Nagazaemon, who developed Ōhi pottery, a special type of slow-fired, amber glaze ceramic specifically for use in the tea ceremony. The exhibit includes examples of Nagazaemon's work. Admission costs ¥500 and the museum is open daily from 9 am to 5 pm.

The Japanese turn even the humble teapot into a work of art.

Terashima Samurai House   寺島応養邸

This is the residence of a middle-class retainer of the Maeda clan and was built in 1770. There's a peaceful garden and tea is available for ¥400 in the tea-ceremony room. Admission costs ¥300 and includes a detailed pamphlet in English. It's open from 9 am to 4 pm but is closed on Thursday.

Higashi Geisha District   ひがし茶屋街

If you follow the main road north from Terashima Samurai House and cross the Asano-gawa River, you reach the Higashi Geisha District, which was established early in the last century as a centre for geisha to entertain wealthy patrons. There are several streets still preserved with the slatted, wooden facades of the geisha houses.

A former geisha house that is open to the public is **Shima**. Admission (including the enclosed garden) costs ¥300. It's open from 9 am to 6 pm but is closed on Monday. Across the street is **Kaikarō**, a 180-year-old home that has been refurbished and had a tearoom added to it. Admission is a bit steep at ¥700, and the tea isn't cheap either, but it's a beautiful setting. Hours are also 9 am to 6 pm.

Yōgetsu is another former geisha house in this district that now functions as a minshuku – see the Places to Stay section.

Teramachi District　寺町

Teramachi stretches beside the Sai-gawa River, just south of the city centre. This old neighbourhood was established as a first line of defence, and still contains dozens of temples and narrow backstreets – a good place for a peaceful stroll. **Ninja-dera Temple**, also known as Myōryū-ji Temple, is about five minutes on foot from the river. Completed in 1643, this temple resembles a labyrinthine fortress with dozens of stairways, corridors, secret chambers, concealed tunnels and trick doors. The popular name of Ninja-dera refers to the temple's connection with *ninjutsu* (the art of stealth) and the *ninja* (practitioners of the art). Although the gadgetry is mildly interesting, mandatory reservation and a tour (conducted in Japanese) can make the visit unduly time-consuming.

Admission costs ¥700 and is by reservation (☎ 0762-41-2877) only. It's open from 9 am to noon and 1 to 4.30 pm, but closes 30 minutes earlier between December and February. For more information on the activities of the elusive ninja see the Iga-Ueno section of the Kansai chapter.

Those interested in the production of Kutani ceramics might like to visit the nearby **Kutani Kosen Gama Kiln**, which is open to the public. There is no charge for admission and it's open daily from 8.30 am to noon and from 1 to 5 pm. The kiln is in an area of the city that was once known as the Nishi Geisha District, a precinct which had similar functions to its counterpart in the eastern part of the city.

Edo-mura Village　江戸村

This is an open-air museum of transposed buildings dating from the Edo period – it's a long way from Kanazawa and you should allow at least half a day for your visit.

There are 20 buildings on display, including an inn, farmhouses, a samurai mansion and a pawnshop. One of the farmhouses has a tiny room above the entrance which housed the servants and at night the stairs were removed to stop them doing a flit.

Minibuses shuttle between Edo-mura Village

and **Danpūen**, which is a similar but smaller open-air museum concentrating on crafts.

Admission to the village costs a hefty ¥1200 and the ticket includes free transport to and from Danpūen. An explanatory English leaflet and map are provided. The village is open daily from 8 am to 5 pm.

To reach Edo-mura Village, take bus No 12 (45 minutes, ¥540) from Kanazawa station. The bus goes via Yuwaku Onsen and climbs uphill for a few more minutes before dropping you off at the palatial Haku-unrō Hotel. Walk for about 10 minutes up the hill in front of the hotel and then climb the steps on the left to reach the entrance office for Edo-mura. The minibus for Danpūen leaves from this office every 20 minutes.

Market

Ōmichō Market lies on the main bus route between the station and the Kohrinbo area in the centre of the city. The most convenient bus stop for the market is Musashi-ga-tsuji. Ōmichō Market is a warren of several hundred shops, many of which specialise in seafood. Take a break from sightseeing and just wander around here to watch market life.

Special Events

Some of the major festivals celebrated here are:

Kagatobi Dezomeshiki
　6 January. Scantily clad firemen brave the cold, imbibe sake, and demonstrate ancient firefighting skills on ladders.
Dekumawashi (Puppet Theatre Festival)
　10 to 16 February. Displays of *jōruri*, a traditional form of puppet theatre, are held in the evening at the village of Oguchi.
Asano-gawa Enyūkai
　Early April. Performances of traditional Japanese dance and music are held on the banks of the Asano-gawa River.
Hyakumangoku Matsuri
　13 to 15 June. This is the main annual festival in Kanazawa, commemorating the first time the region's rice production hit 1,000,000 *goku* (around 150,000 tonnes), under the leadership of the first Lord Maeda. The highlight is a huge parade of townsfolk dressed in costumes from the 16th century. Other events include *takigi nō* (torch-lit performances of nō drama), *tōrō*

nagashi (lanterns floated down the river at dusk) and a special tea ceremony at Kenroku-en.

Bon Odori (Folk Dancing Festival)

Mid-August. Folk dancing festivals are held in several places including the Futamata area, and the village of Hatta where the festival is called Sakata Odori.

Places to Stay

The tourist information office in the station can help with reservations for accommodation. Those thinking of staying in a business hotel should bear in mind that the station area is not particularly convenient for sightseeing in Kanazawa.

Station Area The station area has the usual abundance of business hotel accommodation. Directly in front of the station is the *Garden Hotel Kanazawa* (☎ 0762-63-3333), which has singles from ¥6300, twins from ¥12,000 and doubles from ¥11,000. Close by is the *Kanazawa Station Hotel* (☎ 0762-23-2600), where singles range from ¥6700 to ¥8000, twins from ¥12,700 to ¥15,000, and doubles from ¥11,700 to ¥15,000.

Central Kanazawa *Matsui Youth Hostel* (☎ 0762-21-0275) is small and relaxed, but closes at 10 pm. Nightly costs are ¥2800 per person in tatami-style rooms. Note that the hostel is closed from 31 December to 2 January. From the station, take a bus from terminal No 7, 8 or 9 for the 14 minute ride to the city and get off at the Katamachi bus stop. Walk a few metres back up the street to a large intersection. Turn right here, then take the second side street on your right. The hostel is halfway down this street.

Murataya Ryokan (☎ 0762-63-0455) is a member of the Japanese Inn Group. There are English signs everywhere, though not too many English speakers to accompany them. The per person rate is ¥4500 (without meals), and the price goes down a bit if there are two or three of you. To find this ryokan, follow the directions for Matsui Youth Hostel. Having turned right at the large intersection, take the first side street on your left and continue about 20m until you see the ryokan sign on your left.

Tucked away up a little lane near the Utsunomiya bookstore is *Ryokan Kikunoya* (☎ 0762-31-3547), a modest-looking place with per person rates of ¥5000, excluding meals. Over near the Nagamachi samurai houses is *Yamadaya* (☎ 0762-61-0065), where rooms can be had for ¥5300, including breakfast. Dinner costs an additional ¥2500.

On the business hotel front, most of the central Kanazawa accommodation is fairly expensive. One of the cheaper places around is the *Kanazawa Dai-Ichi Hotel* (☎ 0762-22-2011), which is just east of the Kohrinbo 109 department store, close to Kenroku-en Garden. Singles/doubles here are ¥5500/10,000. Not far from the Katamachi intersection, the *Kanazawa Prince Hotel* (☎ 0762-23-2131) is a decent mid-range place with singles from ¥6500 and twins and doubles from ¥12,000. Probably the most up-market choice in the area is the *Kanazawa Tōkyū Hotel* (☎ 0762-31-2411), next door to the Kohrinbo 109 department store, with rates from ¥12,000 for singles, ¥19,500 for twins, and ¥21,000 for doubles.

Higashiyama District *Yōgetsu Minshuku* (☎ 0762-52-0497) is a geisha house dating from the previous century. Prices start at around ¥4500 per person, without meals. The minshuku is on the same street as the Shima geisha house, about 20 minutes on foot from the station or 10 minutes by bus No 11 or 12: get off at Hashiba-chō, walk across the bridge, take the third right and walk two or three minutes.

Kanazawa Youth Hostel (☎ 0762-52-3414) is way up in the hills to the east of the city and commands a superb position. Unfortunately, this also means that access to the hostel is mighty inconvenient, unless you have your own transport – bus services are infrequent.

A dorm bed costs ¥2800 for members. Private rooms are a good deal at ¥3800 per person. The doors close at 10 pm and loudspeakers marshal the slumbering troops for breakfast in the morning. During peak season, the hostel may take members only. Bicycle rental is available.

To reach the hostel from the station, take

bus No 90 for Utatsuyama-kōen Park and get off after about 25 minutes at the Suizokukan-mae bus stop, which is virtually opposite the hostel.

Places to Eat

Kanazawa's main speciality is seafood, and it pops up everywhere: even the humble box lunches (obentō) at the railway station nearly all feature some type of fish. Oshi-zushi, a thin layer of pressed fish laid atop vinegared rice and cut into pieces, is said by some to be the precursor to modern sushi.

The station area is not particularly exciting on the dining front. The area around the Katamachi intersection in central Kanazawa offers much more variety. For quality set lunches (from around ¥800), the 4th floor of Kohrinbo 109 department store has a variety of inexpensive places to eat.

For delicious and relatively inexpensive sushi, try one of the tiny restaurants that line the walkways of Ōmichō Market. There are not many English menus to be found, but if you grab a seat at the counter you should be able to get your order across. A lot of places here also serve seafood donburi – seafood served atop a deep bowl of rice. Many places often have donburi sets (donbori teishoku), which include pickles and miso soup for around ¥800 to ¥1200. The restaurants here close around 7 to 8 pm, so it's best to make it for lunch or early supper.

Down near the Sai-gawa River in Katamachi, *Tamazushi* has earned a reputation as one of Kanazawa's best sushi restaurants. Prices, while not cheap, won't blow out your budget either. Sushi set meals range from ¥1000 to ¥2500, and a lot of individual sushi items are priced at ¥100 to ¥200 (though there are a few ¥800 picks in there too). There's no English menu, but the various sushi sets are displayed in the front window, giving you an idea of what's on offer.

The Katamachi District also has a surprising number of international restaurants. *Legian* is a popular Indonesian restaurant down by the river. It looks a little down-at-heel, but the food is good and authentic. The Patio building on the first parallel street to

the east of Katamachi-dōri has an excellent Thai restaurant, *Kopkunka*. It's not particularly cheap (Thai restaurants never are in Japan), and you should figure on around ¥2500 per head with drinks.

One place definitely worth trying is *Sayur*, a tiny place that serves organic food and drinks. Dishes are a mix of Japanese and South-East Asian cuisine, and are delicious. It also has a small but interesting selection of micro-brews and organic sake. Figure on around ¥2000 per person, including drinks.

Entertainment

Nō theatre is alive and well is Kanazawa, and performances are held fairly often (once a week during summer) at the *Ishikawa Prefectural Nō Theatre* (0762-64-2598). It is also possible to attend rehearsals free of charge. Enquire at the Kanazawa tourist information office (0762-32-6200), or check the current edition of *Cosmos* for performance times. Occasionally there are also classical music performances, featuring both Japanese and western compositions. Check with *Cosmos* to see what's on that month, and where.

Although Kanazawa is not a huge city, it has an incredible number of bars and clubs. Most are of the hole-in-the-wall variety, jam-packed into high rises in Katamachi. One place that seems to draw a good mix of gaijin and locals is *Polé Polé*. It's grungy and dark, the floor is littered with peanut shells and the music (reggae) is loud. The truly adventurous might want to order the house cocktail speciality, 'elephant wank'. If not, then there's the old standby, the 'screaming orgasm'. It's in the same building as the Indonesian restaurant Legian (same ownership as well) – walk to Legian along the river and then walk through the building to find Polé Polé.

Things to Buy

Kanazawa is a centre for traditional crafts such as *kaga yūzen* (silk dyeing), *kutani-yaki* (colourful ceramics), *kaga maki-e* (lacquerware with gold, silver or pearl overlay), woodcarving using *kiri* (paulownia) and *kinpaku* (gold leaf) – a tiny gold leaf in your tea is meant to be good for rheumatism.

For a quick view or purchase of these crafts, you can visit Kankō Bussankan (Ishikawa Local Products Shop). The tourist information office can set up visits to workshops or direct you to museums of specific interest such as the one close to the station, which specialises in the production of gold leaf.

Getting There & Away

Air Kanazawa airport (Komatsu Kūkō) has air connections with Tokyo, Sendai, Fukuoka and Sapporo. There's also an international connection with Seoul (Korea).

Train Kanazawa is linked to south-western destinations by the JR Hokuriku line: Fukui (55 minutes), Kyoto (2½ hours) and Osaka (three hours). The same line runs north-east to Takaoka (45 minutes), Toyama (one hour) and further north up the coast. To travel to Takayama (2½ hours), you need to change to the JR Takayama line at Toyama. The quickest way to travel between Tokyo and Kanazawa is by taking the Jōetsu shinkansen from Tokyo station to Nagaoka (one hour 40 minutes), and then travelling onwards by limited express to Kanazawa (three hours). The whole trip costs ¥13,510. There are two daily departures of the limited express Hakusan service from Ueno to Kanazawa. The journey takes just over six hours and costs ¥10,690.

The JR Nanao line (together with the privately run Noto Tetsudo line) connects Kanazawa with Wajima (Noto-hantō Peninsula) in 2¼ hours.

Bus There are regular bus services between Kanazawa and Tokyo (Ikebukuro, 7½ hours, ¥7700), Kyoto (four hours, ¥3990) and Nagoya (four hours, ¥3990). The Meitetsu bus service between Kanazawa and Nagoya operates from July to early November via Gokayama and Shirakawa-gō. Departures from Kanazawa are at around 9.30 am. The entire trip takes around eight hours and costs ¥6880.

Getting Around

The Airport A good bus service connects Kanazawa airport with Kanazawa station in 55 minutes (¥1050). There are one to two departures hourly from 7 am to 6 pm, and buses leave from the No 4 gate at the Hokutetsu bus station, in front of the railway station.

Bus The bus network is extensive and fares start at ¥200. From the station, bus Nos 10 and 11 will take you to the Kenroku-en-shita bus stop, a useful point if you just want to visit the main sights around Kenroku-en Garden. To ride from the station to the centre of the city, you can choose from several buses, including bus Nos 20, 21 and 30, and get off at the Kohrinbo bus stop. The bus company also operates the 'Kanazawa Historical Trail' bus, which makes a 45 minute loop through the city that passes by all the major tourist attractions. There are two to three buses per hour from 9 am to 4 pm, and you can get on them at any of the tourist attractions.

The office of the Hokutetsu Kankō bus company just outside the station sells a Kanazawa Sightseeing Pass (Kanazawa shūyū jōshaken) for ¥900 that allows unlimited travel on local buses for one day. These passes can also be bought on buses.

Bicycle Rental is available (¥1000 for the day or ¥600 for four hours) at the station, but the hills and the urban traffic snarls aren't particularly inviting. If you're still interested, head out of the railway station, turn left and walk toward the end of the building, and then left again where you'll see a small booth and lots of bicycles.

The Kanazawa Youth Hostel also has bicycles for rent (cheaper prices), but it's quite a puff returning up the hill to the hostel.

NOTO-HANTŌ PENINSULA 能登半島

For an enjoyable combination of rugged seascapes, traditional rural life and a light diet of cultural sights, this peninsula is highly recommended. Noto-hantō Peninsula is easily accessible from Kanazawa, Takaoka or Toyama. The wild, unsheltered western side of the peninsula is probably of more interest: the indented coastline of the eastern side has been heavily developed to cater to tourists, and has lost quite a bit of its charm.

Information
Kanazawa tourist information office (☎ 0762-32-6200) in JR Kanazawa station can help reserve accommodation and deal with most other queries regarding the Noto-hantō Peninsula. The office has copies of the *Easy Living Map*, which has good detail on Ishikawa Prefecture, including the peninsula. Also available are copies of the *Guide to Northern Noto*, a colourful English-language pamphlet with background on the various sights around the northern section of the peninsula.

JNTO's leaflet *Noto Peninsula* has concise information on sights, maps, timetables and lists of places to stay for the Noto-hantō Peninsula.

There are also information offices at Wajima station and Nanao station; Nanao also has its own Society to Introduce Nanao to the World (☎ 0767-53-1111), which arranges home visits.

Planning Your Itinerary
It's not really possible to do justice to the peninsula with a day trip in which you tick off all the sights in hurried procession; this leaves little time to savour the pace of rural life. A better idea might be to spend at least two nights and three days gradually working your way around the coastline, which has plenty of youth hostels, minshuku and ryokan. The rather erratic bus schedules will make rushing around the peninsula fairly difficult in any case, so you may as well just do like the locals and take it slowly.

Special Events
The Noto-hantō Peninsula has dozens of festivals throughout the year. Seihaku-sai Festival, held in Nanao from 13 to 15 May, includes a spectacular procession of festival floats. Gojinjō Daikō Nabune Festival, held in Wajima between 31 July and 1 August,

features wild drumming performed by drummers wearing demon masks and seaweed headgear. Ishizaki Hoto Festival, held in Nanao in early August, is famed for its parade of tall lantern poles.

Full details on annual festivals and events are available from the tourist information offices in Kanazawa, Wajima or Nanao.

Accommodation
The peninsula is well provided with youth hostels, minshuku and ryokan. Reservations are advisable during peak season and can be made through the Kanazawa, Wajima or Nanao tourist information offices. If you have the money, it's worth spending at least one or two nights in one of the minshuku or ryokan, especially if you're a seafood lover: most places serve up healthy portions of delicious sashimi, grilled fish and shellfish.

There are also camping grounds tucked away in a few pockets of the peninsula, although most are difficult to reach using public transportation. If you're interested in using them in summer, call ahead to see if there are any tent sites available: many places are often full in July and August.

Things to Buy
You won't have to look too far on your travels around the peninsula before seeing shops groaning with the main regional craft – lacquerware. A large proportion of the townsfolk in Wajima are engaged in producing Wajima-nuri, lacquerware renowned for its durability and rich colours.

Getting There & Away
Train The JR Nanao line runs from Kanazawa to Wakura Onsen. Here you will usually have to change to the private Noto Tetsudo line, which runs up to Wajima, and also branches off to Suzu and Takojima, near the tip of the peninsula.

If you're heading to Wajima, the way to avoid changing trains is to take one of the two daily Kanazawa-Wajima limited express trains, which go direct, make the trip in 2¼ hours and cost ¥2950. With any other train, you'll have to get off at Nanao or Wakura

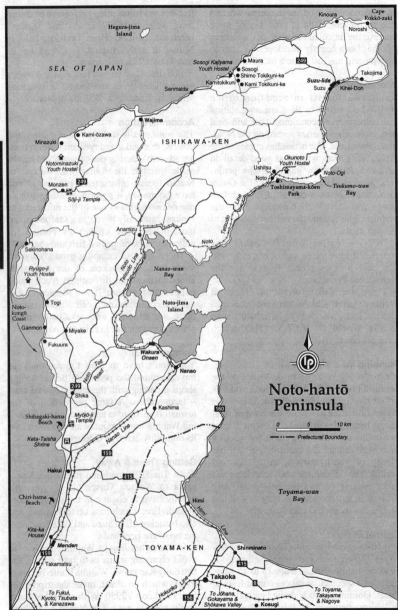

SEA OF JAPAN

Hegura-jima Island

Kinoura

Cape Rokkō-zaki

Noroshi

Maura

Sosogi Kajiyama Youth Hostel

Sosogi

Shimo Tokikuni-ke

Kamitokikuni

Kami Tokikuni-ke

Suzu-Iida

Suzu

Takojima

Kihei-Don

Senmaida

Wajima

Kami-ōzawa

ISHIKAWA-KEN

Minazuki

Notominazuki Youth Hostel

Okunoto Youth Hostel

Ushitsu

Noto-Ogi

Monzen

Noto

Toshimayama-kōen Park

Tsukumo-wan Bay

Sōji-ji Temple

Anamizu

Sekinohana

Noto

Ryūgo-ji Youth Hostel

Nanao-wan Bay

Noto-jima Island

Noto-kongō Coast

Togi

Ganmon

Miyake

Fukuura

Wakura Onsen

Shika

Nanao

Shibagaki-hama Beach

Myōjō-ji Temple

Kashima

Keta-Taisha Shrine

Nanao Line

Hakui

Chiri-hama Beach

Himi

Toyama-wan Bay

Kita-ke House

Menden

Takamatsu

Himi Line

TOYAMA-KEN

Shinminato

To Fukui, Kyoto, Tsubata & Kanazawa

Hokuriku Line

Takaoka

To Jōhana, Gokayama & Shōkawa Valley

Kosugi

To Toyama, Takayama & Nagoya

Noto-hantō Peninsula

0   5   10 km

Prefectural Boundary

Onsen to change to the Noto Tetsudo line. From here most trains from Nanao or Wakura Onsen head to Suzu-Iida, so you'll have to change trains, this time at Anamizu, and wait seven to 20 minutes for a train to Wajima.

The fare from Nanao to Wajima is ¥970, from Nanao to Suzu, ¥1520.

Bus This is more convenient than the train. Hokutetsu Kankō bus company's Okunoto express bus service runs direct between Kanazawa and Wajima, and some buses go on to Sosogi and Maura. The trip between Kanazawa and Wajima takes two hours and the ticket costs ¥2100 one way. A similar service connects Kanazawa with Suzu (2¾ hours, ¥2500). There are around eight or nine buses daily between Kanazawa and Wajima, around three daily between Kanazawa and Suzu.

Getting Around

Train The railway lines stay mainly inland on the peninsula, so they're not really useful for getting around the more interesting western and northern coastal areas. If you are using trains, Nanao, Wajima and Suzu are all possible staging points to start or finish your tour.

Bus Local buses are infrequent and it's sometimes worth the added expense to use one of the scheduled tour buses (see below) for short hops to reach more remote places.

Useful local bus lines include: Wajima to Monzen, Monzen to Anamizu, and Wajima to Ushitsu via Sosogi and Kami Tokikuni-ke. Local bus timetables are available at some tourist information offices.

Tour Buses There are regular sightseeing buses which follow a variety of routes around the peninsula. Depending on the itinerary, the ticket price includes transport, a Japanese-speaking guide, admission fees for sights, and lunch. In terms of transport, these buses are very convenient. However, the lunch is no great shakes and any pauses in the rapid-fire commentary from the guide are filled with recorded sounds ranging from jungle noises to songs and breaking waves. Ear plugs are advised.

There are many permutations, but most of the itineraries use Kanazawa or Wajima as a starting or finishing point. Some tours operate throughout the year, others only operate between March and November. Tickets for a full-day tour range from ¥5000 to ¥7000.

Cycling The peninsula should appeal to cyclists as its coastal terrain is flat, and inland there's only an occasional gradient. The camping grounds and youth hostels are spread out at convenient intervals. The tourist information offices (Kanazawa, Wajima and Nanao) have a very good map (in Japanese) entitled *Noto Hantō Rōdo Mappu*, which covers the area on a scale of 1:160,000.

Kita-ke House　喜多家

This residence of the Kita, a wealthy family which once administered over 100 villages in the region, is on the coast, about 30 minutes by bus north of Kanazawa. Kita-ke is built in local farmhouse style, and inside there are displays of weapons, ceramics, farming tools, folk art and documents. There is also a fine garden.

Admission costs ¥700 and includes a detailed leaflet in English. It's open from 8.30 am to 5 pm. To get there by train, take the JR Nanao line to Menden station, then walk for 20 minutes.

Chiri-hama Beach　千里浜

This long beach near Hakui station on the west coast has become an attraction for motorists, and at times it resembles a sandy motorway with droves of buses, motorcycles and cars roaring past the breakers, leaving a wake of plastic bags, fast-food wrappings and dead sea birds. Give this place a miss.

Keta-taisha Shrine　気多大社

This shrine, set in a wooded grove close to the sea, is believed to have been founded in the 8th century, but the architectural style of the present building dates from the 17th century. The shrine is open from 8.30 am to 4.30 pm and is just 10 minutes via the Togi-bound bus from Hakui station (approximately 10 buses run daily). Get off at the Ichinomiya bus stop (¥230). Admission costs ¥100.

Myōjō-ji Temple 妙成寺

Myōjō-ji was founded in 1294 by Nichijō, a disciple of Nichiren, as the main temple of the Myōjō-ji school of Nichiren Buddhism. The temple complex is composed of several buildings including the strikingly elegant five-storey pagoda *(gojū-no-tō)*. Admission costs ¥350 and includes an excellent English leaflet with map. It's open from 8 am to 5 pm. To reach the temple from Hakui station, take the Togi bus and get off at Takiya-guchi (18 minutes, ¥370), then walk for 15 minutes.

From the temple, it takes about 25 minutes on foot to reach **Shibagaki-hama Beach** with its small fishing community.

Noto-kongō Coast 能登金剛海岸

The stretch of rocky shoreline known as Noto-kongō extends for about 16 km between Fukūra and Sekinohana and includes a variety of rock formations such as Gammon, which resembles a large gate. Buses from Hakui station to Fukūra take just over an hour (¥920), and often you'll have to change buses at Miyake. There are around 10 buses daily to Miyake/Togi. The ride offers pleasant sea views as the road winds along the coast passing fishing villages with their protective concrete breakwaters.

Close to Monzen there's the famous **Sōji-ji Temple**, which was established in 1321 as the head temple of the Sōtō school of Zen. After a fire severely damaged the buildings in 1898, the temple was restored, but it now functions as a branch temple; the main temple has been transferred to Yokohama. Admission costs ¥300 and it's open daily from 8 am to 5 pm. To reach the temple from Anamizu station, take a 40 minute bus ride to the Sōji-ji-mae bus stop. There are buses to Monzen (¥640) every one to two hours.

Places to Stay *Notominazuki Youth Hostel* (☎ 0768-46-2022) is at Minazuki, which is 35 minutes by bus from Monzen. There's a coastal hiking trail (about 2½ hours) between Minazuki and Kami-ōzawa. Nightly costs are ¥2600. The hostel is closed from 29 December to 7 January, and from 1 October to 31 March it only operates from Thursday to Sunday.

If you're looking for a more upscale stay in Monzen, the *Tokugi Ryokan* (☎ 0768-42-0010) has rooms for ¥7000 per person, including two meals.

The *Minazuki Seishōnen Ryokōmura Campsite* (☎ 0768-46-2103) is perched on the coast in Minazuki, not too far from the Notominazuki Youth Hostel.

Wajima 輪島

Wajima is a fairly small town, but it has long been renowned as a centre for the production of lacquerware and has now become a major centre for tourism. There aren't really any beaches around, and the only real reason to stay here overnight is to catch the morning market the next day, or to use the town as a base for exploring the surrounding area.

The tourist information office at Wajima station provides English leaflets and maps and the staff can help you book accommodation.

Wajima Lacquerware Hall This hall is in the centre of town next to the Shin-bashi Bridge. The 2nd floor has a display of lacquerware production techniques, as well as some impressively aged pieces: there are a few bowls that were being swilled out of when Hideyoshi was struggling to unify Japan 500 years ago. If you're inspired, there's a shop downstairs where you can purchase some contemporary examples (not quite as appealing). Admission to the hall costs ¥200. It's open daily from 9 am to 5.30 pm.

Wajima Urushi Art Museum This museum has a significantly larger collection of lacquerware – enough to fill galleries on two floors. Pieces from around Asia as well as from Japan are on display. Admission is ¥600, and the museum is open daily from 9 am to 4.30 pm. It's about 15 minutes walk west of the railway station.

Kiriko Kaikan This hall houses the huge lacquered floats used in regional festivals. Admission costs ¥460, and it's open from 8 am to 5 pm. From the station, the hall is 20 minutes on foot or you can take the six minute bus ride from the station and get off at the Tsukada bus stop – if you're lucky enough to catch one of the infrequent buses, that is.

Hegura-jima Island Those interested in a day trip and a boat ride can take the ferry to Hegura-jima Island, which boasts a lighthouse, several shrines and no traffic. Birdwatchers flock to the island in spring and autumn. If you want to extend your island isolation by staying overnight there are plenty of minshuku. Reservations can be made in Japanese by calling ☎ 0768-22-4961.

From early April to late October, the ferry departs Wajima at 8.30 am and reaches the island at 10.20 am. The return ferry leaves at 2.30 pm. During the winter the return ferry departs at 1 pm. Weather conditions can sometimes cause sailings to be cancelled. A return ticket costs ¥3040.

Market The morning market (*asa-ichi*) takes place daily between 8 am and noon – except on the 10th and 25th of each month. Despite its touristy trappings, the market might appeal for its array of chuckling old crones dangling seaweed, fish or ridiculous tourist tat in front of shoppers and drawing attention to their wares with a cheery *Dō deska?* ('How about it?'). To find the market, walk north along the river from the Wajima Lacquerware Hall and turn right just before Iroha-bashi Bridge.

Places to Stay The tourist information office at Wajima station can help you find accommodation. Wajima has dozens of minshuku with prices starting at around ¥6500 per person and these include two meals (copious and delicious seafood). One place that might be worth a try is *Asunaro* minshuku (☎ 0768-22-0652), which is about 15 minutes on foot from the station on the other side of the Shin-bashi Bridge from the

Wajima Lacquerware Hall. Rates are ¥6500 per person, two meals included. There are several other minshuku in the area, all with similar prices.

Wajima Chōraku-ji Youth Hostel (☎ 0768-22-0663) is also in the same neighbourhood. After crossing the Shin-bashi Bridge, walk one block along the main road and then take the first turn right. At the next street turn left and walk another two minutes: the hostel is on the left side, next to a temple. Nightly rates are ¥2500. The hostel is closed from 31 December to 4 January and from 31 March to 4 April. The front door closes for the night at 10 pm.

About 15 minutes by bus to the west of town is the *Sodegahama Campground* (☎ 0768-22-2211). Take one of the Monzen-bound buses to Sodega-hama Beach.

Getting There & Away For details on getting to Wajima from Kanazawa see Getting There & Away at the beginning of the Noto-Hantō Peninsula section.

Wajima is the main transport hub for the northern section of the peninsula. The bus station is opposite the railway station. From here you can take buses along the northern coast to Sosogi, where you can change for buses to Kinoura and Cape Rokō-zakki. Bus services also link Wajima with Ushitsu on the inland coast, from where you can catch a train or bus to Tsukumo-wan Bay and Suzu. There are also buses to Monzen, on the western shore.

There are usually around eight buses daily from Wajima to Ushitsu (one hour 20 minutes, ¥1190), which pass by Sosogi (40 minutes, ¥710). Buses to Monzen (40 minutes, ¥710) leave every one to two hours.

Sosogi 曽々木

The village of Sosogi, about 10 minutes by bus from Senmaida, has a couple of attractions. After the Taira were defeated in 1185, one of the few survivors, Tokitada Taira, was exiled to this region. The Tokikuni family, which claims descent from this survivor, eventually divided into two parts and established separate family residences here.

Shimo Tokikuni-ke (Lower Tokikuni Residence), built in 1590, is a smaller version of its counterpart, but it has an attractive garden. Admission costs ¥400 and includes an English leaflet. The residence is open from 8 am to 5 pm, and opens an hour later from December to March.

Just a few minutes walk away, **Kami Tokikuni-ke** (Upper Tokikuni Residence), with its impressive thatched roof and elegant interior, was constructed early in the 19th century. Admission costs ¥400 and includes an English leaflet. It's open from 8.30 am to 6 pm, but closes an hour earlier from December to March. From Wajima station, the bus ride to Kami Tokikuni-ke takes about 40 minutes.

Places to Stay Sosogi is a pleasant, quiet spot, and not a bad choice for an overnight stay. The *Sosogi Kajiyama Youth Hostel* (☎ 0768-32-1145) is seven minutes on foot from the Sosogi-guchi bus stop. The hostel is a convenient base for walking along the nearby coastal hiking trail. A bed for the night is ¥2800.

There is a string of minshuku along the road east of the Sosogi-guchi bus stop. *Yokoiwaya* (☎ 0768-32-0603) is about 150m down the road from the bus stop (walk around the large cliff face on the inland side of the road). For ¥6500 you get a comfortable room and an outstanding seafood dinner: in most Japanese cities the dinner alone would easily cost ¥7000. If this place is full, don't worry: there are plenty of other choices in the area.

Cape Rokō-zaki 禄剛崎

The road north-east from Sosogi passes Cape Rokō-zaki and winds round the tip of the peninsula to the less dramatic scenery on its eastern coast. At the cape, you can amble up to Noroshi Lighthouse where a nearby signpost marks the distances to Vladivostok, Shanghai and Tokyo. A coastal hiking trail runs west along the cape. The scenery is nice, and during the week when the tourist buses run less frequently, the town of Noroshi reverts to its true role as a sleepy, remote

fishing village. There are some beaches in the area, but they're nothing special, being fairly rocky and somewhat polluted. But Noroshi is a good place to laze around for a few days, hike along the coast and soak up the beauty of Noto-hantō.

Places to Stay One of Noroshi's more unique accommodation options is the *Garō Minshuku Terai* (☎ 0768-86-2038). The name of the place means 'Terai's Art Gallery Minshuku', and refers to the artwork that adorns the walls and shelves of the inn. A stay here will cost you ¥6500, including two meals. Nearby, the *Rokō-zaki Lighthouse Pension* (☎ 0768-86-2030) is a pleasantly appointed European-style inn which costs ¥10,000 per person for a room and two meals.

There are several camping grounds in the area, including the *Mt Yamabushi Campground* (☎ 0768-88-2737), perched on a hilltop east of Noroshi, and *Kinoura Campsite* (☎ 0768-86-2204), near the little town of Kinoura, about eight km west of Noroshi.

Getting There & Away Cape Rokō-zaki is one of the more inconvenient places to access on the peninsula. The easiest way to get there is from Suzu, which is on the Noto Tetsudo line. From the Suzu station there are five to six JR buses to Noroshi daily between 6.30 am and 6.30 pm (¥740). There are five buses a day back to Suzu from Noroshi between 8 am and 5.30 pm.

If you're coming from Wajima, you'll first have to get a bus to Sosogi-guchi, where you then change for buses to Kinoura. There are only three of these a day (12.30, 3.45 and 5.45 pm, ¥770), and only the *first two* get you there in time to link up with a JR bus, which will then take you from Kinoura to Noroshi (¥280). On Sunday, there is only one JR bus from Kinoura to Noroshi (4.30 pm). Services back from Noroshi to Kinoura are similarly sparse, though they are better timed to allow you to catch the onward Kinoura-Sosogi bus. The above times are subject to change: check the schedule at one of the tourist information offices or at the bus station.

To avoid this logistical tap dance, you might try catching a ride with one of the tour buses run by Hokutetsu Kankō bus company, which usually leave Wajima around 8 am. Drivers may not take you, especially if the tour is full or close to it, but if you do get on, expect to pay around ¥1000 for the ride to Noroshi.

Tsukumo-wan Bay

Tsukumo-wan Bay, heavily indented and dotted with islands, is mildly scenic, but it's not really worth spending ¥750 on the boat tour despite the boat's glass bottom. From the bay, it's five minutes on foot to Noto-Ogi station, which has rail connections via Ushitsu to Kanazawa. If you want an inexpensive place to stay right next to the water, *Tsukumo-Wan Youth Hostel* (☎ 0768-74-0150) is only 15 minutes on foot from the station. A bed for the night is ¥2500. There are also plenty of ryokan and minshuku about.

Ushitsu 宇出津

The limited attractions of Ushitsu are around Toshimayama-kōen Park, which has good views out to sea. The town itself is not all that interesting, and its main function for travellers is likely to be as a transportation link. From here there are six to seven buses daily to Wajima (¥1190), which pass by Sosogiguchi (¥800).

HAKUSAN NATIONAL PARK

Travellers with a thirst for exercise (and time on their hands) may want to venture down to this national park, which is in the south-east corner of Ishikawa Prefecture and spills over into neighbouring Fukui, Toyama and Gifu prefectures. The park has several peaks reaching above 2500m, with the highest being Mt Hakusan (2702m). In the summer, hiking and scrambling uphill to catch mountain sunrises are the main activities, while in winter skiing and onsen bathing take over.

The alpine section of the park is crisscrossed with trails, offering hikes of up to 25 km in length. For hikers who are well equipped and in no hurry, there is even the possibility of making a 26 km trek from the park over to Ogimachi in Shōkawa Valley, Gifu Prefecture. However, camping is prohibited in the park except at designated camping grounds, which means you'll have to either hike very fast or break the rules.

Those looking to hike on and around the peaks are required to overnight at either Murodō Center or Nanryu Mountain Lodge. Getting to either of these requires a minimum of 3½ to five hours on foot. That doesn't stop the park from swarming with visitors, however. In the peak season of July-August, visitors are required to make reservations a week in advance if they plan to stay up here.

The area surrounding the alpine section of the park is dotted with little villages offering onsen baths, minshuku and ryokan accommodation and camping grounds.

Public transport to Hakusan consists mainly of infrequent buses between April and November, and shuts down altogether during the winter months. Before making your way down here, it would be wise to check with the tourist information office in Kanazawa on the current situation regarding transport and accommodation.

Places to Stay

In the alpine area of the park your two choices are the *Murodō Center* (☎ 07619-3-1001) and the *Nanryu Mountain Lodge* (☎ 07619-8-2022). Murodō can hold up to 750 people in its four lodges, and per person rates are ¥6100, including two meals. It is open from 1 May to 15 October, weather permitting. Nanryu is smaller (only 150 people), and has similar rates. There is also a camping ground at Nanryu, which is the only place in the alpine area where camping is permitted. There is an overnight fee of ¥300; renting a tent will cost you another ¥2200. During the peak season of July-August reservations must be made at least one week in advance for both Murodō and Nanryu.

There are several ways to hike up to both places but the closest access point is Bettōdeai. From here it's six km to Murodō (about 4½ hours walk) and five km to Nanryu

(3½ hours). You can also access the lodges from trailheads at Ichirino and Chūgū Onsen, but these involve hikes of around 20 km. See the following Getting There & Away section for details on transport to the trailheads.

Ichirino, Chūgū Onsen, Shiramine and Ichinose all have minshuku and ryokan. Per person rates with two meals start at ¥6500 and ¥8000 respectively.

There are several camping grounds in the area. *Ichinose Yaeijō* (☎ 07619-8-2716) has 20 camp sites near Ichinose, which is in turn close to the trailhead at Bettōde-ai. *Midori no Mura Campground* (☎ 07619-8-2716), near Shiramine, has tents and bungalows for rent. There is also a camping ground near Chūgū Onsen. Most of the camping grounds are only open from June to October, with the exception of the one at Nanryu Mountain Lodge, which operates year-round, if you can get to it.

Unless you speak Japanese, you'll probably need to go through the tourist information office at Kanazawa or another major city to book accommodation in any of the above places. You can also try the Shiramine Town Hall (☎ 07619-8-1001), which reportedly has one or two staff who can handle basic enquiries in English.

Getting There & Away

This is not easily done, even during the peak summer period. The main mode of transport to the Hakusan area is the Hokutetsu Kankō bus from Kanazawa station. Between 27 April and 6 May there is one bus daily to Bettōde-ai (two hours, ¥1900), leaving around 6.30 am. Frequency increases to between two and four buses a day from mid-July to mid-August, and then reverts back to one bus daily in late August. From September to mid-October, bus services are further scaled back to weekends and holidays, weather permitting.

Hokuriku Tetsudo also has several departures daily for Ichirino and Chūgū Onsen. Check with the Kanazawa tourist information office or the Hokutetsu Kankō bus company office at Kanazawa station for the latest schedule.

If you're coming from Fukui, you can take the Echizen Honsen line for the one hour ride out to Katsuyama, where you can change to a Hokuriku Tetsudo bus to Shiramine. At the time of writing, bus departures from Katsuyama to Shiramine were at 8.20 am and 7.55 pm. From Shiramine you'll have to either wait for an infrequent bus, take a taxi, or hitch a ride.

Fukui-ken　福井県

FUKUI　福井

Fukui (population 252,000), the prefectural capital, doesn't have a lot to hold the interest of most travellers. It was given quite a drubbing in 1945 during the Allied bombing, and what was left largely succumbed to a massive earthquake in 1948. It was totally rebuilt, and is now known as a major textile centre. There's no real reason to linger here, but Fukui is useful as a staging point to visit sights in the prefecture. Between 19 and 21 May, Fukui celebrates the Mikuni Festival with a parade of giant warrior dolls.

If you need to stay in Fukui, there's the rather drab *Fujin Seinen Kaikan Youth Hostel* (☎ 0776-22-5625), around 500m north-west of the station next to Chūō-kōen Park, where a bed for the night is ¥2800. Close to the east exit of Fukui station (the main exit is the west exit) is the *City Hotel Fukui* (☎ 0776-23-5300), where singles range from ¥5500 to ¥7500, twins range from ¥11,000 and doubles are ¥9500. A more upscale option is the *Hotel Akebono Bekkan* (☎ 0776-22-0506), which is a member of the Japanese Inn Group and has singles/doubles at ¥6800/8360. From the station, walk straight ahead and take the second street on the left that crosses over the river.

Fukui lies on the JR Hokuriku Honsen line: 55 minutes east is Kanazawa and 40 minutes south-west is a major railway junction at Tsuruga, which provides convenient access to Nagoya, Kyoto and Osaka.

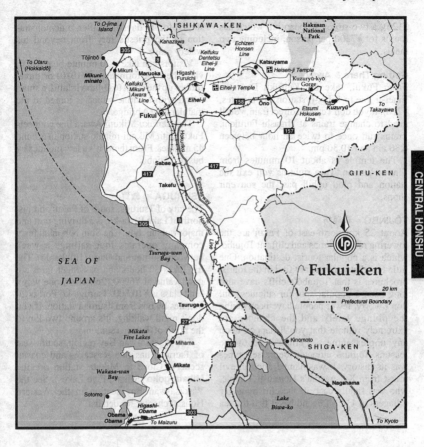

EIHEI-JI TEMPLE 永平寺

Founded in 1244 by Dōgen, Eihei-ji is now one of the two head temples of the Sōtō sect of Zen Buddhism and is ranked among the most influential centres of Zen in the world.

The temple is geared to huge numbers of visitors who come either as sightseers or for Zen training. The complex has about 70 buildings, but the standard circuit usually concentrates on the seven major buildings: *tosu* (toilet), San-mon Gate, *yokushitsu* (bath), *daikuin* (kitchen), Butsuden (Buddha Hall), Hattō (Dharma Hall) and the Sō-dō (Priests' Hall).

Normal daily admission costs ¥400. The temple is open daily from 5 am to 5 pm; however, note that the temple is frequently closed for periods varying from a week to 10 days – before you visit, check with a tourist information office or use Japan Travel-Phone (☎ 0120-44-4800, toll free).

Places to Stay

A convenient youth hostel is *Eihei-ji Monzen Yamaguchi-sō* (☎ 0776-63-3123), which is five minutes on foot from Eihei-ji station. A bed for the night is ¥2800. Near the front gate to Eihei-ji is the *Green Lodge* (☎ 0776-63-

3126), a two-storey wooden inn which has rooms for ¥7300 per person, including two meals.

Getting There & Away

From Fukui, take the Keifuku Dentetsu Eihei-ji line to Eihei-ji station (35 minutes, ¥710). If you don't catch a direct train, you'll need to change trains at Higashi-Furuichi. Trains run once to twice an hour between 6.30 am and 10.30 pm.

The temple is about 10 minutes from Eihei-ji station. Turn right as you exit the station and plod uphill past the souvenir shops.

TŌJINBŌ　東尋坊

About 25 km north-east of Fukui are the towering rock columns and cliffs at Tōjinbō, which is a popular tourist destination. One little fact that you may not find in the tourist brochures is that Tōjinbō's cliffs have also long been a popular spot for suicides. But don't worry, fewer people have been taking the plunge lately and the chances are extremely remote that you'll happen upon any unpleasantness. Perhaps one of the reasons Tōjinbō attracted depressed types was its history. It was named after an evil priest from Katsuyama's Heisen-ji Temple, who was finally cast off the cliff by angry villagers in 1182. Legend has it that the sea surged for 49 days thereafter, a demonstration of the priest's fury from beyond his watery grave.

Visitors can take a 30 minute boat trip to view the rock formations (¥1010) or travel further up the coast to **O-jima Island**, a small island with a shrine which is joined to the mainland by a bridge.

The Keifuku Mikuni Awara line connects Fukui with Mikuni-minato station in around 45 minutes. From there, it's a few minutes by bus to Tōjinbō.

TSURUGA　敦賀

The city of Tsuruga, south of Fukui and just north of Lake Biwa-ko, is a thriving port and major rail junction. The Shin Nihonkai ferry company operates four sailings a week between Tsuruga and Otaru (Hokkaidō). The trip takes 30 hours and passenger fares are good value at ¥6900 (2nd class, one way). First class is ¥10,300. Tsuruga-kō Port is 20 minutes by bus from Tsuruga station. If you don't mind walking, it's around two km to the north of Tsuruga station.

The Wakasa-wan Bay region, south-west of Tsuruga, has fine seascapes and coastal scenery. Close to Mikata station are the **Mikata-goko** (Mikata Five Lakes). See the Wakasa-wan Bay section in the Western Honshū chapter for details.

Kansai Region

関西地方

The region described as Kansai in this chapter is also known as Kinki. While the term 'Kinki' is actually a much more distinct geographical division, encompassing the prefectures of Shiga, Mie, Nara, Kyoto, Waka-yama, Osaka, Kōbe and Hyōgo, the area is more frequently referred to colloquially as Kansai, a term which means 'west of the barrier'. This 'barrier' is an allusion to the historical barrier stations or checkpoints that separated Kansai from Kantō, the area 'east of the barrier'. The barriers were located in different places through Japanese history, but finally ended up in Hakone during the rule of the Tokugawa Shogunate from Edo (contemporary Tokyo) in Kantō.

Kansai's major drawcards are of course Kyoto and Nara, but the cities of Osaka and Kōbe are also vibrant and increasingly cosmopolitan urban centres. More and more foreigners are settling in the area, and *Kansai-ben*, the local dialect, is gaining attention from foreign students of Japanese. Anyone interested in Kansai-ben should pick up a copy of Peter Tse's *Kansai Japanese* (Tuttle, 1993), a lively introduction to the dialect. With the opening of Kansai International airport in 1994, Kansai is now the first port of call for many foreigners visiting Japan. Built on an artificial island in Osaka-wan Bay, it is Japan's first 24 hour airport.

Kyoto, with its hundreds of temples and gardens, was the imperial capital between 794 and 1868, and is now a magnet for domestic and international tourism. It continues to function as the major cultural centre of Japan, but business and industry are closing in on the traditional architecture.

Nara predates Kyoto as an imperial capital and has an impressive array of temples, burial mounds and relics from early times.

Osaka and Kōbe are major centres in a sprawling industrial belt and are, for the most part, of limited interest to travellers, but even so not without their attractions. Osaka, like Tokyo, is a great place to sample Japanese

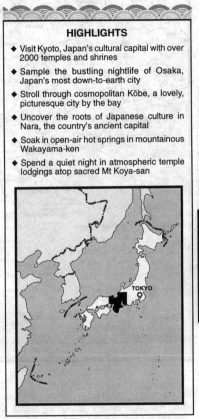

HIGHLIGHTS

- ◆ Visit Kyoto, Japan's cultural capital with over 2000 temples and shrines
- ◆ Sample the bustling nightlife of Osaka, Japan's most down-to-earth city
- ◆ Stroll through cosmopolitan Kōbe, a lovely, picturesque city by the bay
- ◆ Uncover the roots of Japanese culture in Nara, the country's ancient capital
- ◆ Soak in open-air hot springs in mountainous Wakayama-ken
- ◆ Spend a quiet night in atmospheric temple lodgings atop sacred Mt Koya-san

TOKYO

city life in all its busy, mind-boggling intensity, while Kōbe, now almost completely recovered from the disastrous earthquake of 1995, is one of Japan's most cosmopolitan and attractive cities. Himeji, just east of Kōbe, has what is probably the best of Japan's many feudal castles.

In Mie-ken the main attractions are Ise-jingū, one of Japan's most important Shinto shrines, and the lovely seascapes around the

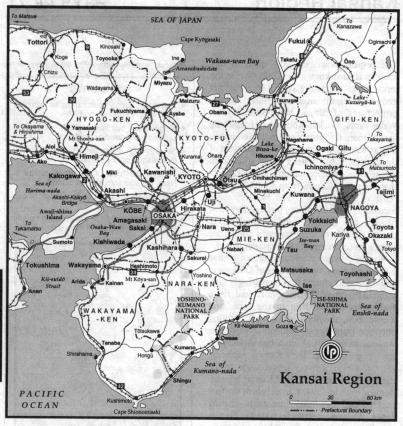

Kansai Region

Shima-hantō Peninsula. Wakayama-ken offers mountain *onsens* (hot spring baths), a rugged seacoast and the temple complex of Mt Kōya-san, one of Japan's most important Buddhist centres where travellers can stay in atmospheric temple lodgings away from the frenetic pace of big cities.

Kyoto　京都

If there are two cities in Japan that *have* to be included on anyone's Japan itinerary, they are Tokyo and Kyoto (population 1.4 million). Some of what you've seen in Tokyo, you'll see again in Kyoto – the glare of neon by night, the large-scale urban ugliness. But more than any other city in Japan, if you care to seek it out, Kyoto offers what all westerners long for of Japan – raked pebble gardens, the sensuous contours of a temple roof, the tripping step of a latter-day geisha in pursuit of a taxi.

Despite this, first impressions are likely to be something of an anticlimax. The beauty of Kyoto doesn't force itself upon the visitor. You have to seek it out. Kyoto is a city that, like the other cities of Japan, has its eyes far more firmly on the future than on the past. But, happily, it is still a city where the past lingers on: there are more than 2000 temples and shrines; a trio of palaces; and dozens of gardens and museums. Months or even years could be spent exploring Kyoto to turn up still new surprises.

The city's one major drawback is that its fame attracts huge numbers of visitors (nearly 40 million annually), particularly during holidays and festivals. The spring and autumn periods, when Kyoto is at its most beautiful, are also very busy. An early start to the day can help, but sooner or later you are going to collide with the inevitable crowds of tour groups. The best advice if this annoys you is not to spend all your time on the major attractions. Often just a short walk from the big-name sights are lesser attractions that are nearly deserted because they don't figure in the standard tour-group itinerary.

HISTORY

The Kyoto basin was first settled in the 7th century, and by 794 it had become Heian-kyō, the capital of Japan. Like Nara, a previous capital, the city was laid out in a grid pattern modelled on the Chinese Tang dynasty capital, Chang'an (contemporary Xi'an). Although the city was to serve as home to the Japanese imperial family from 794 to 1868 (when the Meiji Restoration brought the imperial family to the new capital, Tokyo), the city was not always the focus of Japanese political power. During the Kamakura period (1185-1333), Kamakura served as the national capital, and during the Edo period (1600-1867) the Tokugawa Shogunate ruled Japan from Edo – now Tokyo.

The problem was that from the 9th century the imperial family was increasingly isolated from the mechanics of political power and the country was largely ruled by military families, or shogunates. While Kyoto still remained capital in name and was the cultural focus of the nation, imperial power was for the most part symbolic and the business of running state affairs was often carried out elsewhere.

Just as imperial fortunes have waxed and waned, the fortunes of the city itself have fluctuated dramatically. In the Ōnin War (1466-67) that marked the close of the Muromachi period, the Imperial Palace and most of the city was destroyed. Much of what can be seen in Kyoto today dates from the Edo period (1600-1867). Although political power resided in Edo, Kyoto was rebuilt and flourished as a cultural, religious and economic centre. Fortunately, Kyoto was spared the aerial bombing that razed other Japanese urban centres to the ground in the closing months of WWII.

Today, even though it has seen a rapid process of industrialisation, Kyoto remains an important cultural and educational centre. It has some 20% of Japan's National Treasures and 15% of Japan's Important Cultural Properties. There are 24 museums and 37 universities and colleges scattered throughout the city. And even if the city centre looks remarkably like the centre of a dozen other large Japanese cities, a little exploration will turn up countless reminders of Kyoto's long history.

ORIENTATION

Kyoto is a fairly easy city to navigate. JR Kyoto station is in the south of the city, and from there Karasuma-dōri runs north past Higashi Hongan-ji Temple, the commercial centre of town and the Imperial Palace. The commercial and nightlife centres are between Shijō-dōri and Sanjō-dōri (to the south and north respectively) and between Kawaramachi-dōri and Karasuma-dōri (to the east and west respectively). Although some of Kyoto's major sights are in the city centre, most of Kyoto's best sightseeing is on the outskirts of the city in the eastern and western parts of town. These areas are most conveniently reached by bus. For pleasant day trips out of the city, try the Kitayama mountains or the areas west of the city around Takao, both of which are well serviced by bus and train.

Kyoto has retained a grid system based on the classical Chinese concept. This system of numbered streets running east to west and avenues running north to south makes it

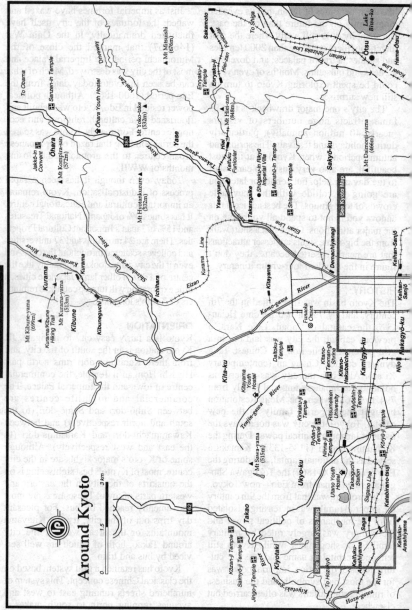

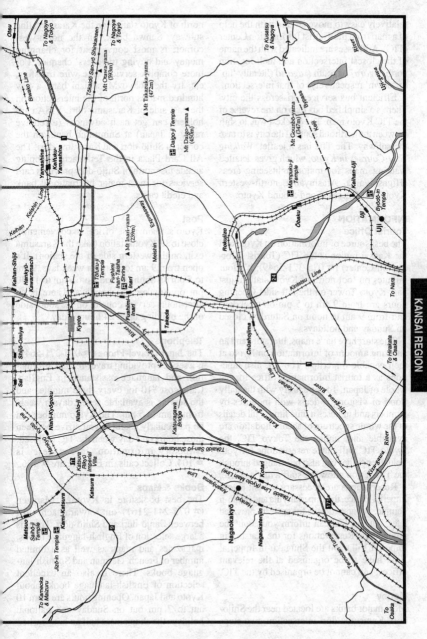

relatively easy to move around with the help of a map from the Tourist Information Center (TIC). Addresses are indicated with the name of the closest intersection and their location north *(agaru)* or south *(sagaru)* (literally 'up' or 'down' respectively) of that intersection.

Efficient bus services crisscross the city. There's a simplified bus map on the reverse of the TIC Kyoto map. The quickest way to shift between the north and south of the city is to take the subway. The TIC has a leaflet, *Walking Tour Courses in Kyoto*, which gives detailed walking maps for major sightseeing areas (Higashiyama, Arashiyama, north-western Kyoto and Ōhara) in and around Kyoto.

INFORMATION
Tourist Office
The best source of information on Kyoto and the Kansai region is the TIC (Tourist Information Center) (☎ 075-371-5649); it's four minutes on foot north of Kyoto station, just past Kyoto Tower on the left side. Opening hours are from 9 am to 5 pm on weekdays and from 9 am to noon on Saturday, closed on Sunday and holidays.

The staff here have maps, literature and an amazing amount of information on Kyoto at their capable fingertips. The TIC also functions as a tourist information office for the whole of Japan. To cope fairly with the daily flood of visitors, it deals with inquiries by numbers and imposes a time limit. Full details of the whole spectrum of accommodation are available and, unlike the Tokyo TIC, the Kyoto TIC will make reservations for you. Volunteer guides can also be arranged through the TIC if you allow the staff a day's notice.

Reservations are necessary to visit Kyoto Imperial Palace, the Imperial Villa and Saihō-ji Temple. Separate details for each are provided later, but the TIC can inform you about the procedures. Reservations for the Katsura-in Imperial Villa and the Shūgaku-in Imperial Villa have to be organised at the relevant offices, and cannot be organised by the TIC.

Money
Most major banks are located near the Shijō-dōri, Karasuma-dōri intersection, two stops north of Kyoto station on the Karasuma line subway. Sanwa bank, on the north-west corner, is most convenient for changing money and buying travellers' cheques. For more complex services like wire transfers, etc, try the Tokyo Mitsubishi bank a few hundred metres north of the intersection on the east side of Karasuma-dōri. VISA card holders can get cash advances (a relative rarity in Japan) at Sumitomo bank, on the corner of Shijō-dōri and Karasuma-dōri. The All Card Plaza in the Teramachi shopping arcade just north of Shijō-dōri provides card services for most major international bank and credit cards.

Post
Kyoto's main post office is conveniently close to JR Kyoto station (take the Karasuma exit, on the western side of the station). It's open from 9 am to 7 pm on weekdays, 9 am to 5 pm on Saturday and from 9 am to 12.30 pm on Sunday and holidays. There is an after-hours service counter on the south side of the building open 24 hours a day.

Telephone
The Japan Travel-Phone (☎ 075-371-5649) is a service providing travel-related information and language assistance in English. Calls cost ¥10 for every three minutes and the service is available seven days a week, from 9 am to 5 pm. The Kyoto number can be particularly useful if you arrive between those hours on a day when the TIC is closed. Directory information, in Japanese, is ☎ 104. Collect calls, in English, are ☎ 106.

Books & Maps
The best bookstore in Kyoto is Maruzen (☎ 075-241-2161) on Kawaramachi-dōri between Sanjō-dōri and Shijō-dōri. There is a large selection of English-language books, magazines and maps as well as a limited number of French, German and Spanish-language books. There is also an excellent selection of English-language books about Kyoto and Japan. Opening hours are from 10 am to 7 pm but on Sunday and national holidays the shop closes half an hour earlier.

Kyoto: A Contemplative Guide (Tuttle, Tokyo, 1989 reprint) by Gouverneur Mosher treats a few sights in fond detail to give a taste of the amazing variety of exploration possible in Kyoto. The transport information is long out of date, but it's the sort of book well worth reading before, during or after your stay.

Old Kyoto: A Guide to Traditional Shops, Restaurants & Inns (Kodansha, Tokyo, 1989 reprint) by Diane Durston is a must for those in search of specific Kyoto handicrafts. It also has detailed information on atmospheric old ryokan and restaurants.

Also by Diane Durston, *Kyoto, Seven Paths to the Heart of the City* (Kinzō Honda, 1987) is a good book for those interested in exploring some of Kyoto's old, traditional neighbourhoods.

For those anticipating a long stay in town, *Easy Living in Kyoto* (Kyoto City International Foundation, 1995) is available at the Kyoto International Community House (see Useful Organisations for details).

Available at the TIC just north of Kyoto station, *Tourist Map of Kyoto, Nara* fulfils most mapping needs and includes a simplified map of the subway and bus systems. *Walking Tour Courses in Kyoto* details ways to see the sights in Kyoto on foot. Also available is the *Kyoto Transportation Guide* map which has detailed information on bus routes in the city and some of the major stops written in both English and Japanese. Some find that the Japanese-only version, available at major bus stops, is more useful, as all names are written in Japanese and it is more detailed. Also at the TIC, the simply titled *Useful Information* sheet has lists of admission prices to all the main sights as well as a list of inexpensive restaurants with an accompanying map. The best map of Kyoto, intended for long-term foreign residents, is the *Guide to Kyoto* available at the Kyoto International Community House (see Useful Organisations for details).

Newspapers & Magazines
Kyoto Visitor's Guide is the best source of information on events happening in Kyoto during your visit. It's available at the TIC,

Maruzen bookstore, Kyoto International Community House and most major hotels.

Another excellent source of information on Kyoto and the rest of the Kansai area is *Kansai Time Out*, a monthly English-language listings magazine (¥300). Apart from lively articles, it has a large section of ads for employment, travel agencies, clubs, lonely hearts, etc. It's all in there from the 'Kinki Macintosh Users Group' (it's OK, they're into computers) to the Japan Animal Welfare Society (JAWS). It's available at Maruzen bookstore, the TIC or by calling ☎ 078-232-4516. *Kansai Flea Market* is a free monthly aimed at foreign residents with work and housing listings as well as entertaining personals. It's also available at Maruzen bookstore.

Those with a literary bent might want to look out for *Kyoto Journal* which publishes in-depth articles and artwork by Kyoto residents and others. It's also available at Maruzen bookstore or by calling ☎ 075-771-6111.

Medical Services
For an emergency clinic try the Kyoto Holiday Emergency Clinic (☎ 075-811-5072), and for emergency dental problems call Kyoto Holiday Emergency Dental Clinic (☎ 075-441-7173). Sakabe International Clinic (☎ 075-231-1624) also provides 24 hour emergency service.

For non-emergency medical care, the Japan Baptist Hospital (☎ 075-781-5191) usually has some English-speaking doctors on its staff. It's in north-east Kyoto; to get there take bus No 3 from Shijō Kawaramachi station and get off at the Baptist Byōin-Mae stop. It's a short walk up the hill.

Emergencies
If you need to use English and want help finding the closest suitable service, try the Japan Travel-Phone (☎ 075-371-5649) or Japan Helpline (☎ 0120461-997).

If your Japanese is proficient, the police phone number is ☎ 110, and for an ambulance dial ☎ 119.

Dangers & Annoyances

The west bank of the Kamogawa River between Sanjō-dōri and Shijō-dōri is a popular summer hang-out spot for Kyoto youth, including some wanna-be gangs. There have been several incidents of individuals or small groups of foreign men being attacked by these gangs. It's best to avoid this area on hot summer evenings. Luckily, these are isolated incidents and the rest of the city is quite safe.

Useful Organisations

The Kyoto International Community House (☎ 075-752-3010), not far from Nanzen-ji Temple, is an essential stop for those planning a long-term stay in Kyoto and can be quite useful for short-term visitors as well. Services include typewriter rental, fax (sending and receiving), and a library with maps, books, newspapers and magazines from around the world. There's also a lobby with English-language TV (CNN news generally).

Perhaps most useful for residents, however, is the noticeboard, which has messages regarding work, accommodation, sayonara sales and so on. The large, airy building is also a pleasant place to relax while on the east side of town and a good chance to meet local ex-pats and Japanese.

The Kyoto International Community House also offers free Japanese language classes as well as tea ceremony, *No* and *koto* classes for a minimal fee. Those who would like to get a taste of these subjects can sit in on a lesson for free or ¥1000 (depending on the class). If you would like to meet a Japanese family at home, you can also make arrangements through the Community House. Let them know at least one day, preferably two days in advance. While you're there you can pick up a copy of their excellent city map *Guide to Kyoto* and their *Easy Living in Kyoto* book, both of which are intended for residents.

WHEN TO GO

Kyoto is a city that has attractions at any time of the year, with the possible exception of the muggy height of summer. Spring and autumn are probably the best times to visit Kyoto, though these times are also the most popular with Japanese tour groups so the crowds can be quite severe. Winter in Kyoto is quiet and not unbearably cold, and is a viable option for those with a distinct aversion to crowds.

The ephemeral cherry blossom season *(hanami)* usually starts in April and lasts about a week. The Japanese become besotted with 'cherry blossom mania' and descend on favourite spots in hordes. The top spots for spectacular displays of blossom include the Path of Philosophy, Maruyama-kōen Park and Heian-jingū Shrine (see the Eastern Kyoto section), Arashiyama (see under Western Kyoto) and the Imperial Palace Park (see the Central Kyoto section). A good place to see the cherry blossoms without the crowds is the Kamogawa River north of Demachiyanagi station.

Autumn colours are similarly spectacular and attract huge numbers of 'leaf-gazers'. Popular viewing spots include Ōhara, Kurama and Shūgaku-in Imperial Villa (see under northern Kyoto), Sagano and Takao (western Kyoto) and Tōfuku-ji Temple (see the south-eastern Kyoto section). Perhaps the best place to enjoy the foliage away from the crowds is in the Takao region (see the Kiyotaki River Hike under Jingo-ji Temple).

PLANNING YOUR ITINERARY

Kyoto is worth considering as a base for travel in Japan. It is within easy reach of Osaka Itami airport and Kansai international airport, both of which have none of the acute overcrowding problems experienced at Tokyo's Narita international airport. As a base for travel in Kansai, Kyoto is by far the best choice, considering its wealth of accommodation and proximity to Nara, Osaka, Kobe and Wakayama Prefecture.

It is difficult to advise on a minimum itinerary for Kyoto – you should certainly consider it a 'must-see' in Japan and allocate as much time as possible for it. Take your time because there's no point in spoiling your stay by overdoing the number of sights visited. Quite apart from the sensory overload, overintensive sightseeing also entails heavy outlay on admission fees. Kyoto is particularly suited to random rambling through the backstreets.

The absolute minimum for a stay in Kyoto would be two days, in which you could just about scratch the surface by visiting the Higashiyama area in eastern Kyoto. Five days will give you time to add Arashiyama, western Kyoto and central Kyoto. Ten days would allow you to cover these areas plus northern Kyoto, southern and south-eastern Kyoto and leave a day or so for places further afield (from Kyoto you have easy access for day trips to Nara, Yoshino, Lake Biwa-ko, Ise, Himeji and Osaka) or for in-depth exploration of museums, shops and cultural pursuits.

Kyoto is also an excellent place to indulge specific cultural interests, whether they be the arts, Buddhism or folkcrafts. The best place to find information on such activities is the TIC, which is used to dealing with both ordinary and extraordinary requests. For example, details are available on Zen temples which accept foreigners, specialist museums, Japanese gardens and villas, Japanese culinary arts and natural-food outlets, traditional crafts (silks, basketry, ceramics, pottery, temple paraphernalia, paper making, etc), Japanese drama, *chanoyu* (tea ceremony) and *ikebana* (flower arranging).

A final word of advice is that it's easy to overdose on temples in Kyoto. If you don't find temples to your liking, don't visit them. Instead, go for a hike in the mountains (see the boxed asides in this section), or do some shopping in the stores around Shijō-dōri (see Things to Buy), or do some people watching on Kiyamachi-dōri. Best of all, find a good restaurant and sample some of the best food in all Japan (see Places to Eat).

CENTRAL KYOTO

Central Kyoto looks much like any other Japanese city, but there are a few major sights in the area, such as the Imperial Palace, Nijō-jō Castle and several museums.

The area around Kyoto station (just below the city centre) is a fairly dull part of town; the main sights are Nishi Hongan-ji Temple and Tō-ji Temple. For further information, be sure to use the TIC, which is a couple of minutes on foot north of the station.

Kyoto Imperial Palace　京都御所

The original Kyoto Imperial Palace was built in 794 and was replaced numerous times after destruction through fires. The present building, on a different site and smaller than the original, was constructed in 1855. Enthronement of a new emperor and other state ceremonies are still held there.

The tour guide explains details while you are led for about 50 minutes past the Shishin-den Hall, Ko Gosho (Small Palace), Tsune Gosho (Regular Palace) and the Oike-niwa (Pond Garden).

Foreigners are privileged to be given preferential access – Japanese visitors have to wait months for permission – but the Imperial Palace does not rate highly in comparison with other attractions in Kyoto.

Reservation & Admission This is organised by the Imperial Household Agency (Kunaichō) (☎ 075-211-1215), which is a short walk from Imadegawa subway station. You will have to fill out an application form and show your passport. Children should be accompanied by adults over 20 years of age (but are forbidden entry to the other three imperial properties; Katsura Rikyu, Sento Gosho and Shugakuin Rikyu). Permission to tour the Imperial Palace is usually granted the same day. Guided tours in English are given at 10 am and 2 pm from Monday to Friday and at 10 am on the third Saturday of the month (except the months of April, May, October and November, when no Saturday tours are given); you should arrive no later than 20 minutes beforehand at the Seishomon Gate. Admission is free. The tour lasts about 50 minutes.

The agency's office is open weekdays from 8.45 am to noon and from 1 to 4 pm. This office is also the place to make advance reservations to see the Sentō Gosho Palace, and the Katsura-in and Shūgaku-in imperial villas. If you want to arrange reservations from abroad or from outside of Kyoto, the

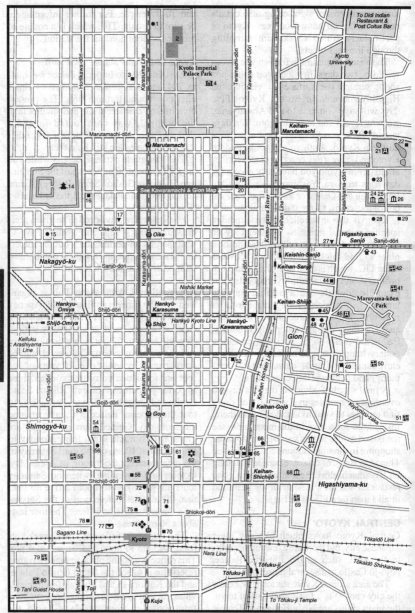

KANSAI REGION

To Didi Indian
Restaurant &
Post Coitus Bar

Kyoto
University

Kyoto Imperial
Palace Park

Keihan-
Marutamachi

Marutamachi-dōri

Marutamachi

See Kawaramachi & Gion Map

Oike

Oike-dōri

Nakagyō-ku

Sanjō-dōri

Nishiki Market

Hankyū-
Omiya

Shijō-dōri

Hankyū-
Karasuma

Shijō-Omiya

Keifuku
Arashiyama
Line

Shijō

Hankyū Kyoto Line

Hankyū-
Kawaramachi

Keishin-Sanjō

Keihan-Sanjō

Keihan-Shijō

Higashiyama-
Sanjō

Sanjō-dōri

Maruyama-kōen
Park

Gion

Shimogyō-ku

Gojō-dōri

Gojō

Keihan-Gojō

Kyōmizu-zaka

Shichijō-dōri

Keihan-
Shichijō

Higashiyama-ku

Shiokoji-dōri

Kyoto

Sagano Line

Nara Line

Tōkaidō Line

Tōfuku-ji

Tōfuku-ji

Tōkaidō Shinkansen

To Tani Guest House

Toji

Kujo

To Tōfuku-ji Temple

Horikawa-dōri

Karasuma Line

Teramachi-dōri

Kawaramachi-dōri

Kamo-gawa River

Keihan Line

Higashiyama-dōri

Karasuma-dōri

Kawaramachi-dōri

Keihan Hōnen Line

Omiya-dōri

Karasuma Line

Kintetsu Line

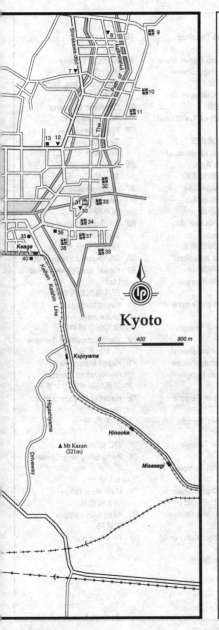

Kyoto

0   400   800 m

KANSAI REGION

PLACES TO STAY

- 3 YWCA
- 13 Sunflower Hotel
- 16 International Hotel
  Kyoto; Kyoto Kokusai
  Hotel
  京都国際ホテル
- 18 Uno House
  宇野ハウス
- 22 Three Sisters Inn
  スリーシスターズイン
- 29 Kyoto Traveler's Inn
  京都トラベラーズイン
- 36 Yachiyo Ryokan
  八千代旅館
- 40 Miyako Hotel
  都ホテル
- 43 Higashiyama Youth
  Hostel
  東山ユースホステル
- 44 Iwanami Ryokan
  岩波旅館
- 49 Uemura Ryokan
  上村旅館
- 52 Ryokan Hinomoto
  旅館ひのもと
- 53 Kyoto Tōkyū Hotel
  京都東急ホテル
- 58 Pension Station Kyoto
  ペンションステーション
  京都
- 59 Matsubaya Ryokan
  松葉屋旅館
- 60 Ryokan Kyōka
  旅館京花
- 61 Ryokan Murakamiya
  旅館村上家
- 63 Yuhara Ryokan
  ゆはら旅館
- 64 Ryokan Hiraiwa
  旅館平岩
- 65 Riverside Takase &
  Annexe Kyōka
  リバーサイド高瀬
  アネックス京花
- 70 Kyoto Century Hotel
  京都センチュリーホテル

Key continued on next page

75 Hokke Club Kyoto; Kyoto
New Hankyū Hotel
法華クラブ京都／
京都新阪急ホテル
76 Kyoto Dai-San Tower
Hotel
京都第3ホテル
78 Kyoto Grand Hotel
京都グランドホテル

PLACES TO EAT
5 Zac Baran Restaurant
ザックバラン
7 Buttercups Restaurant
8 Omen Noodles
おめん
12 Okariba
お狩り場
17 Obanzai Organic
Restaurant
おばんざい
27 Dai-kitchi Yakitori
大吉やきとり
30 Okutan
奥丹

OTHER
1 Imperial Household
Agency
宮内庁
2 Imperial Palace
京都御所
4 Sentō Gosho Palace
仙洞御所
6 Kyoto Handicraft Center
京都ハンディークラフト
センター
9 Ginkaku-ji Temple
銀閣寺
10 Hōnen-in Temple
法然院
11 Anraku-ji Temple
安楽寺
14 Nijō-jō Castle
二条城
15 Nijō-jinya
二条陣屋

19 Ippō-dō Teashop
一保堂
20 Kakimoto Paper Store
21 Heian-jingū Shrine
平安神宮
23 Kyoto Kaikan Hall
京都会館
24 Museum of Traditional
Crafts
伝統産業会館
25 National Museum of
Modern Art
国立近代美術館
26 Kyoto Municipal
Museum of Art
市立美術館
28 Kanze Kaikan Nō
Theatre
観世会館能楽堂
31 Nomura Museum
野村美術館
32 Eikan-dō Temple
永観堂
33 Chōshō-in Temple
聴松院
34 Nanzen-ji Temple
南禅寺
35 Kyoto International
Community House
37 Tenju-an Temple
天授庵
38 Nanzen-in Temple
南禅院
39 Konchi-in Temple
金地院
41 Chion-in Temple
知恩院
42 Shōren-in Temple
青蓮院
45 Kyoto Craft Center
京都クラフトセンター
46 Yasaka-jinja Shrine
八坂神社
47 Gion Kōbu Kaburen-jō
Theatre
祇園歌舞練所

48 Gion Corner
祇園コーナー
50 Kōdai-ji Temple
高台寺
51 Kiyōmizu-dera Temple
清水寺
54 Costume Museum
風俗博物館
55 Nishi Hongan-ji
Temple
西本願寺
56 Kungyoku-dō
薫玉堂
57 Higashi Hongan-ji
Temple
東本願寺
62 Kikokutei Shōsei-en
Garden
渉成園
66 Shōmen-yu Sento Bath
67 Kawai Kanjirō Memorial
Hall
河井寛次郎博物館
68 Kyoto National
Museum
京都国立博物館
69 Sanjūsangen-dō Temple
三十三間堂
71 Kyoto Minshuku
Reservation Center
京都民宿予約センター
72 Kintetsu Department
Store
近鉄デパート
73 TIC
TIC 観光案内所
74 Porta Shopping Center
ポルタショッピング
センター
77 Main Post Office
中央郵便局
79 Kanchi-in Temple
観智院
80 Tō-ji Temple
東寺

KANSAI REGION

application forms are available from JNTO offices, the TIC or direct from the Imperial Household Agency – remember to include return postage or international reply coupons.

To reach the Imperial Palace, take the subway to Imadegawa or a bus to the Karasuma-Imadegawa stop and walk south-east. The office is inside the walled park surrounding the palace.

Sentō Gosho Palace　仙洞御所
This is a few hundred metres south-east of the Kyoto Imperial Palace. Visitors must obtain advance permission from the Imperial Household Agency and be over 20 years old. Tours (in Japanese) start at 11 am and 1.30 pm. The gardens, which were laid out in 1630 by Kobori Enshū, are the main attraction.

Kyoto Imperial Palace Park　京都御苑運動広場
The Imperial Palace is surrounded by a spacious park planted with a huge variety of flowering trees and open fields. It's perfect for picnics, strolls and just about any sport you can think of. Best of all, it's free. Take some time to visit the pond at the park's southern end, with its gorgeous carp. The park is most beautiful in the plum or cherry blossom seasons (March and April, respectively). It's located between Teramachi-dōri and Karasuma-dōri (on the east and west sides) and Imadegawa-dōri and Marutamachi-dōri (on the north and south sides).

Nijō-jō Castle　二条城
This castle was built in 1603 as the official Kyoto residence of the first Tokugawa shogun, Ieyasu. The ostentatious style of construction was intended as a demonstration of Ieyasu's prestige and to signal the demise of the emperor's power. To safeguard against treachery, Ieyasu had the interior fitted with 'nightingale' floors (intruders were detected by the squeaking boards) and concealed chambers where bodyguards could keep watch.

After passing through the grand Kara-mon Gate, you enter **Ninomaru Palace** which is divided into five buildings with numerous chambers. Access to the buildings depended on rank – only those of highest rank were permitted into the inner buildings. The Ohiroma Yon-no-Ma (Fourth Chamber) has spectacular screen paintings. Don't miss the excellent Ninomaru Palace Garden which was designed by the tea master and landscape architect Kobori Enshū.

The neighbouring **Honmaru Palace** dates from the middle of last century and is only open for special viewing in the autumn.

Admission for Ninomaru Palace and garden is ¥500; it's open daily from 8.45 am until last admission at 4 pm (gates close at 5 pm). It's closed from 26 December to 4 January. A detailed fact sheet in English is provided. The Ninomaru Palace is so inundated with visitors that you have to choose your exit according to the numbered location of your shoes! While you're in the neigh-bourhood, you might want to take a look at Shinsen-en Garden, just south of the castle (outside the walls). This forlorn garden, with its small shrines and pond, is all that remains of the original Imperial Palace, abandoned in 1227.

To reach the castle, take bus No 9, 12, 50, 52, 61 or 67 to the Nijō-jō-mae stop. Alternatively you can take the subway to Oike and then walk for 12 minutes.

Pontochō　先斗町
Pontochō is a traditional centre for night entertainment in a narrow street running between the river and Kawaramachi-dōri. It's a pleasant place for a stroll in the summer if you want to observe Japanese nightlife. Many of the restaurants and teahouses which have verandas over the river tend to prefer Japanese customers but a few reasonable places can be found (check Places to Eat). The geisha houses usually control admittance of foreigners with a policy of introductions from Japanese only and astronomical charges. Many of the bars also function along similar lines. This is a good place to spot geisha and apprentice geisha (*maiko*) on their way to or from appointments. On weekend evenings, a few minutes standing at the Shi-jō end of the street usually yields a sighting or two.

KANSAI REGION

KYOTO STATION AREA
Nishi Hongan-ji Temple　西本願寺

In 1591, Hideyoshi Toyotomi built this temple, known as Hongan-ji, as a new headquarters for the Jōdo Shin-shū (True Pure Land) school of Buddhism, which had accumulated immense power. Later, Tokugawa Ieyasu saw this power as a threat and sought to weaken it by encouraging a breakaway faction of this school to found Higashi Hongan-ji (*higashi* means 'east') in 1602. The original Hongan-ji then became known as Nishi Hongan-ji (*nishi* means 'west'). It now functions as the headquarters of the Hongan-ji branch of the Jōdo Shin-shū school, with over 10,000 temples and 12 million followers worldwide.

The temple contains five buildings, featuring some of the finest examples of architecture and artistic achievement from the Azuchi-Momoyama period (1568-1600). The Daisho-in Hall has sumptuous paintings, carvings and metal ornamentation. A small garden and two nō stages are connected with the hall. The dazzling Kara-mon Gate has intricate ornamental carvings. Both the Daisho-in Hall and the Kara-mon were transported here from Fushimi-jō Castle. Reservations (preferably several days in advance) for tours should be made either at the temple office (☎ 075-371-5181) or through the TIC. The tours (in Japanese) cover some but not all of the buildings and are conducted from Monday to Friday at 10 and 11 am and 1.30 and 2.30 pm. On Saturday the tours are at 10 and 11 am. The temple is a 12 minute walk north-west of JR Kyoto station. Admission is free.

Higashi Hongan-ji Temple　東本願寺

When Tokugawa Ieyasu engineered the rift in the Jōdo Shin-shū school, he founded this temple as a competitor to Nishi Hongan-ji. Rebuilt in 1895 after a fire, it is certainly monumental in its proportions, but less impressive artistically than its counterpart. A curious item on display is a length of rope, made from hair donated by female believers, which was used to haul the timber for the reconstruction. The temple is now the head-quarters of the Ōtani branch of the Jōdo Shin-shū school.

Admission is free and the temple is open from 9 am to 4 pm. It's a five minute walk north of Kyoto station.

Tō-ji Temple　東寺

This temple was established in 794 by imperial decree to protect the city. In 818, the emperor handed over the temple to Kūkai, the founder of the Shingon school of Buddhism. Many of the temple buildings were destroyed by fire or fighting during the 15th century; most of those that remain today date from the 17th century.

The Lecture Hall (Kōdō) contains 21 images representing a Mikkyō (Esoteric Buddhism) mandala. The Main Hall (Kondō) contains statues depicting the Yakushi (Healing Buddha) trinity. In the southern part of the garden stands the five-storey pagoda which, despite having burnt down five times, was doggedly rebuilt in 1643 and is now the highest (57m) pagoda in Japan.

Kōbō-san market fair is held here on the 21st of each month. Those held in December and January are particularly lively.

Admission to the temple costs ¥500 and there is an extra charge for entry to special exhibitions. A good explanatory leaflet in English is provided. It's open from 9 am to 4.30 pm. The temple is a 15 minute walk south-west of Kyoto station.

EASTERN KYOTO　京都の東部

The eastern part of Kyoto, notably the Higashiyama (Eastern Mountains) district, merits top priority for a visit to its fine temples, peaceful walks and traditional night entertainment in Gion.

The following descriptions of places to see in eastern Kyoto begin with sights in the southern section; the sights in the northern section begin with the National Museum of Modern Art.

Allow at least a full day to cover the sights in the southern section, and another full day for the northern section. JNTO publishes a leaflet, *Walking Tour Courses in Kyoto*, which covers the whole of eastern Kyoto.

Sanjūsangen-dō Temple 三十三間堂

The original temple was built in 1164 at the request of the retired Emperor Go-shirakawa. After it burnt to the ground in 1249, a faithful copy was constructed in 1266.

The temple's name refers to the 33 *sanjūsan* (bays) between the pillars of this long, narrow building which houses 1001 statues of the Thousand-Armed Kannon (the Buddhist goddess of mercy). The largest Kannon is flanked on either side by 500 smaller Kannon images, neatly lined up in rows.

There are an awful lot of arms, but if you are picky and think the 1000-armed statues don't have the required number, then you should remember to calculate according to the nifty Buddhist mathematical formula which holds that 40 arms are the equivalent of 1000 arms, because each saves 25 worlds. Visitors also seem keen to spot resemblances to friends or family members among the hundreds of images.

At the back of the hall are 28 guardian statues with a great variety of expressive poses. The gallery at the western side of the hall is famous for the annual Tōshi-ya Festival, held on 15 January, when archers shoot arrows the length of the hall. The ceremony dates back to the Edo period when an annual contest was held to see how many arrows could be shot from the southern end to the northern end in 24 hours. The all-time record was set in 1686, when an archer successfully landed over 8000 arrows at the northern end.

The temple is open from 8 am to 5 pm (1 April to 15 November) and 9 am to 4 pm (16 November to 31 March). Admission is ¥400 and an explanatory leaflet in English is supplied.

The temple is a 15 minute walk east of Kyoto station, or you can take bus No 206 or 208 and get off at the Sanjūsangen-dō-mae stop. It's also very close to Keihan Shichi-jō station. From the station, walk straight east, up Shichijō-dōri.

Kyoto National Museum 京都国立博物館

The Kyoto National Museum is housed in two buildings opposite Sanjūsangen-dō Temple. There are excellent displays of fine arts, historical artifacts and handicrafts. The fine arts collection is especially highly rated, holding some 230 items that have been classified as National Treasures or Important Cultural Properties.

Admission costs ¥400 but note that a separate charge is made for special exhibitions. It's open daily from 9 am to 4.30 pm and is closed on Monday.

Kawai Kanjirō Memorial Hall 河井寛次郎記念館

This museum was once the home and workshop of one of Japan's most famous potters, Kawai Kanjirō. The house is built in rural style and contains examples of his work, his collection of folk art and ceramics, and his kiln.

The museum is open daily from 10 am to 5 pm. It's closed Monday and from 10 to 20 August and 24 December to 7 January. Admission costs ¥700. The hall is a 10 minute walk north of the Kyoto National Museum or you can take bus No 206 or 207 from Kyoto station and get off at the Umamachi stop.

Kiyōmizu-dera Temple 清水寺

This temple was first built in 798, but the present buildings are reconstructions dating from 1633. As an affiliate of the Hossō school of Buddhism, which originated in Nara, it has successfully survived the many intrigues of local Kyoto schools of Buddhism through the centuries and is now one of the most famous landmarks of the city. This, unfortunately, makes it a prime target for bus loads of Japanese tourists, particularly during cherry blossom season. Some travellers are also put off by the rather mercantile air of the temple – stalls selling good luck charms, fortunes and all manner of souvenirs. If you find this bothersome, head to some of the quieter temples further north.

The main hall has a huge veranda, supported on hundreds of pillars, which juts out over the hillside. Just below this hall is the Otawa waterfall where visitors drink or bathe in sacred waters which are believed to have therapeutic properties. Dotted around the precincts are other halls and shrines. At the Jishu Shrine, visitors try to ensure success in love by closing their eyes and walking about

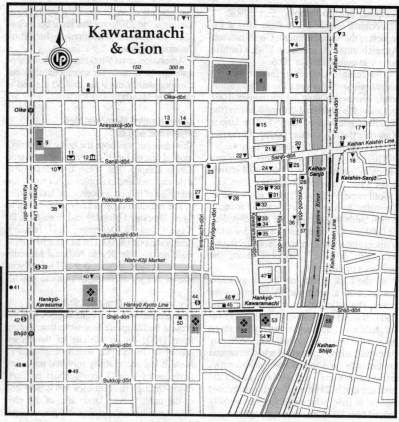

Kawaramachi & Gion

0   150   300 m

18m between a pair of stones – if you miss the stone, your desire for love won't be fulfilled!

The steep approach to the temple, known as 'Teapot Lane', is lined with shops selling Kyoto handicrafts, local snacks and souvenirs. Shopkeepers hand out samples of *yatsuhashi*, a type of dumpling filled with a sweet bean paste.

Admission to the temple costs ¥300 and it's open from 6 am to 6 pm. To get there from Kyoto station take bus No 206 and get off at either the Kiyōmizu-michi or Gojō-zaka stops. Plod up the hill for 10 minutes to reach the temple.

Sannen-zaka & Ninnen-zaka Walk
三年坂・二年坂

One of the most enjoyable strolls around the backstreets and temples of Kyoto follows a winding route between Kiyōmizu-dera Temple and Maruyama-kōen Park. If you walk down from the entrance of Kiyōmizu-dera Temple along the right-hand road (Kiyōmizu-zaka) for about 200m, you'll see a small street on your right down a flight of steps. This is **Sannen-zaka**, a street lined with old wooden houses and shops selling local pottery, food and souvenirs. There are also pleasant teahouses with gardens – it's a

KANSAI REGION

good place to relax over a bowl of steaming noodles.

Halfway down Sannen-zaka, the road bears sharp left. Follow it a short distance, then go right down a flight of steps into Ninnen-zaka, another street lined with his-

toric houses, shops and teahouses. At the end of **Ninnen-zaka**, zig-zag left then right and continue north for five minutes to reach the entrance for Kōdai-ji Temple (which is on the right up a long flight of stairs). Just before the entrance to Kōdai-ji, you can take a detour into **Ishibei-koji** street on your left – perhaps the most beautiful street in Kyoto, though it's not really a street at all but a cobbled alley surrounded on both sides by elegant, traditional Japanese inns and restaurants. For a detailed map of this area, check the TIC's *Walking Tour Courses in Kyoto*.

Kōdai-ji Temple　高台寺

Kōdai-ji was founded in 1605 by Kita-no-Mandokoro in memory of her late husband, Toyotomi Hideyoshi. The extensive grounds include gardens designed by the famed landscape architect, Kobori Enshū, and teahouses designed by the renowned master of the tea ceremony, Sen-no-Rikyū.

The temple was only recently opened to the public and is worth a look. It's open from 9 am to 5 pm and admission costs ¥500. An explanatory leaflet in English is provided.

Maruyama-kōen Park　円山公園

This park is a favourite of locals and visitors alike as a place to escape the bustle of the city centre and amble around the gardens, ponds, souvenir shops and restaurants. Peaceful paths meander through the trees and carp glide through the waters of a small pond in the centre of the park.

For two weeks in April, when the park's cherry trees come into bloom, the calm atmosphere of the park is shattered by hordes of drunken revellers. The centrepiece of it all is a massive shidarezakura cherry tree – one of the most beautiful sights in Kyoto, particularly when lit up from below at night (you'll need a long neck to see it above the heads of everyone else). For those who don't mind crowds, this is a good place to observe the Japanese at their most uninhibited. The best advice is to arrive early and claim a good spot high on the east side of the park, from which you can safely peer down on the mayhem below.

Yasaka-jinja Shrine　八坂神社

This colourful shrine is just down the hill from Maruyama-kōen Park. It's considered the guardian shrine of neighbouring Gion and is sometimes endearingly referred to as 'Gionsan'. This shrine is particularly popular as a spot for *Hatsu-mōde*, the first shrine visit of the new year. If you don't mind a stampede, come here around midnight on New Year's Eve or any of the following days. Surviving the crush is proof that you're blessed by the gods! Yasaka-jinja also sponsors Kyoto's biggest festival, Gion Matsuri (for details, see the Special Events section later in this chapter).

Gion District　祇園

Gion is the famous entertainment and geisha district on the eastern bank of the Kamogawa River. Modern architecture, congested traffic and contemporary nightlife establishments have cut a swathe through its historical beauty, but there are still some places left for an enjoyable walk.

Hanami-kōji is a street running north to south which bisects Shijō-dōri. The southern section is lined with 17th century, traditional restaurants and teahouses, many of which are exclusive establishments for geisha entertainment. If you wander around here in the late afternoon or early evening, you can often glimpse geisha or maiko (apprentice geisha) on their way to or from appointments.

At the bottom of this street you reach **Gion Corner** and the adjoining **Gion Kōbu Kaburen-jō Theatre**. For more details on these two places, see the section on Entertainment later.

If you walk from Shijō-dōri along the northern section of Hanami-kōji, you will reach Shinmonzen-dōri running east to west at the fourth intersection. Wander in either direction along this street which is packed with old houses, art galleries and shops specialising in antiques – but don't expect flea-market prices here.

For more historic buildings in a beautiful waterside setting, wander down **Shirakawa Minami-dōri** which is roughly parallel with, and one block south of, the western section of Shinmonzen-dōri.

Chion-in Temple　知恩院

Chion-in was built in 1234 on the site where Hōnen had taught and eventually fasted to death. Today it is still the headquarters of the

Jōdo school, which was founded by Hōnen, and a hive of religious activity. For visitors with a taste for the grand and glorious, this temple is sure to satisfy.

The oldest of the present buildings date back to the 17th century. The two-storey San-mon Gate at the main entrance is the largest in Japan and prepares the visitor for the massive scale of the temple. The immense main hall contains an image of Hōnen and is connected with the Dai Hōjō Hall by a 'nightingale' floor constructed to 'sing' (squeak) at every step. The massive scale of the buildings reflects the popular nature of the Jōdo school, which holds that earnest faith in the Buddha is all that is necessary to achieve salvation.

After visiting the main hall, with its fantastic gold altar, you can walk around the back of the same building to see the temple's gardens. On the way, you'll pass a darkened hall with a small statue of Amida Buddha on display – glowing eerily in the darkness. It makes a nice contrast to the splendour of the main hall.

The giant bell, cast in 1633 and weighing 74 tonnes, is the largest in Japan. The combined muscle-power of 17 monks is required to make the bell budge for the famous ceremony which rings in the new year.

The temple is open from 9 am to 4.30 pm (March to November) and from 9 am to 4 pm (December to February); admission costs ¥400. The temple is close to the northeastern corner of Maruyama-kōen Park. From Kyoto station take bus No 206 and get off at the Chion-in-mae stop or walk up (east) from the Keihan Sanjō or Shijō stations.

Shōren-in Temple 青蓮院

Shōren-in is hard to miss with its giant camphor trees growing just outside its walls. This temple was originally the residence of the chief abbot of the Tendai school. The present building dates from 1895, but the main hall has sliding screens with paintings from the 16th and 17th centuries. Often overlooked by the crowds which descend on other Higashiyama temples, this is a pleasant place to sit and think while gazing out over the beautiful gardens.

Admission to the temple costs ¥400, and it's open from 9 am to 5 pm. An explanatory leaflet in English is provided. The temple is a five minute walk north of the Chion-in Temple.

National Museum of Modern Art 国立近代美術館

This museum is renowned for its collection of contemporary Japanese ceramics and paintings. Exhibits are changed on a regular basis (check with the TIC or *Kansai Time Out* for details). Admission costs ¥400 and it's open from 9.30 am to 5 pm daily.

Kyoto Museum of Traditional Crafts 伝統産業会館

If you want a break from temple gazing, you could pop in to the Kyoto Museum of Traditional Crafts for exhibitions, demonstrations and sales of Kyoto handicrafts. It's located in the basement of the Kyoto International Exhibition Hall. Admission is free and it's open from 10 am to 6 pm, closed Monday.

Heian-jingū Shrine 平安神宮

The Heian-jingū was built in 1895 to commemorate the 1100th anniversary of the founding of Kyoto. The buildings are gaudy replicas, reduced to a two-thirds scale, of the Imperial Palace of the Heian period.

The spacious garden, with its large pond and Chinese-inspired bridge, is also meant to represent the kind that was popular in the Heian period. About 500m in front of the shrine there is a massive steel *torii* gate. Although it appears to be entirely separate from the shrine, this is actually considered the main entrance to the shrine itself.

Two major events, Jidai Matsuri (22 October) and Takigi Nō (1 to 2 June), are held here. Jidai Matsuri is described later in the Special Events section, while details for Takigi Nō are under Traditional Dance & Theatre in the later Entertainment section.

Entry to the shrine precincts is free but admission to the garden costs ¥500. It's open from 8.30 am to 5.30 pm (15 March to 31 August) though closing time can be an hour earlier during the rest of the year. Take bus No 5 from Kyoto station or Sanjō station and get off at the Jingū-michi stop or walk up from Sanjō station.

Nanzen-ji Temple 南禅寺

This is one of the most pleasant temples in all Kyoto, with its expansive grounds and numerous subtemples. It began as a retirement villa for Emperor Kameyama, but was dedicated as a Zen temple on his death in 1291. Civil war in the 15th century destroyed most of the temple; the present buildings date from the 17th century. It operates now as headquarters for the Rinzai school of Zen.

At the entrance to the temple stands the massive San-mon Gate. Steps lead up to the 2nd storey which has a fine view over the city. Beyond the gate is the Hōjō Hall with impressive screens painted with a vivid depiction of tigers. A good look at the painted screens reveals the fact that the artist never actually saw a tiger, but instead relied on accounts received from China and India. The effect is that of tiger-dog.

Within the precincts of the same building, the 'Leaping Tiger Garden' is a classic Zen garden well worth a look. While you're in the Hōjō, you can enjoy a cup of tea while sitting on *tatami* mats gazing at a small waterfall (¥400, ask at the reception desk of the Hōjō). It's an inexpensive way to get a taste of the tea ceremony in pleasant surroundings.

Perhaps the best part of Nanzen-ji is overlooked by most visitors: a small shrine hidden in a forested hollow behind the main precinct. To get there, walk up to the red brick aqueduct in front of Nanzen-in subtemple. Follow the road that parallels the aqueduct up into the hills, past a small subtemple on your left. Follow the path into the woods, past several brightly coloured torii gates until you reach a waterfall in a beautiful mountain glen. Here, pilgrims pray while standing under the waterfall, sometimes in the dead of winter. Hiking trails lead off in all directions from this point; by going due north, you'll eventually arrive at the top of Mt Daimon-ji-yama (two hours) and by going east you'll eventually get to Yamashina (also about two hours).

Admission to the temple costs ¥350,

though most of the grounds can be explored for free. It's open from 8.30 am to 5 pm. A brief explanatory leaflet in English is provided. The temple is a 10 minute walk south-east from the Heian-jingū Shrine; from Kyoto station or Sanjō station take bus No 5 and get off at the Eikan-dō-mae stop. You can also take the Keishin streetcar local from Sanjō station to Keage and walk five minutes down the hill to Nanzen-ji.

Dotted around the grounds of Nanzen-ji are several subtemples which are often skipped by the crowds and consequently easier to enjoy.

Nanzen-in Temple This subtemple is on your right when facing the Hōjō Hall – follow the path under the aqueduct. It has an attractive garden designed around a heart-shaped pond. This garden is best in the morning or around noon, when sunlight shines directly into the pond, illuminating the colourful carp. Admission costs ¥350.

Tenju-an Temple This stands at the side of the San-mon Gate, a four minute walk west of Nanzen-in Temple. Constructed in 1337, the temple has a splendid garden and a great collection of carp in its pond. A detailed leaflet in English is provided. Admission costs ¥300.

Konchi-in Temple When leaving Tenju-an Temple, turn left and continue for 100m – Konchi-in is down a small side street on the left. The stylish gardens fashioned by the master landscape designer Kobori Enshū are the main attraction. Admission costs ¥400. It's open from 8.30 am to 5 pm (March to November) but closes half an hour earlier during the rest of the year.

Nomura Museum 野村美術館

The Nomura Museum is a 10 minute walk north of Nanzen-ji Temple. Exhibits include scrolls, paintings, tea-ceremony implements and ceramics which were bequeathed by the very wealthy business magnate Tokushiki Nomura. It's open from 10 am to 4 pm (closed on Monday), and admission is ¥600.

Eikan-dō Temple 永観堂

Eikan-dō, also known as Zenrin-ji Temple, is made interesting by its varied architecture and its gardens and works of art. It was founded in 855 by the priest Shinshō, but the name was changed to Eikan-dō in the 11th century to honour the philanthropic priest Eikan.

The best approach is to follow the arrows and wander slowly along the covered walkways connecting the halls and gardens.

In the Amida-dō Hall, at the southern end of the complex, is the famous statue of Mikaeri Amida (Buddha Glancing Backwards).

There are various legends about this statue. One version maintains that Eikan was doing a dance in honour of Amida Buddha when the statue stepped down and joined in. When Eikan stopped in amazement, the Buddha looked over his shoulder and told him to keep on jiving. A more prosaic version holds that the Buddha looked back over his shoulder to admonish a monk who was lax in chanting his sutras.

On the right of this statue, there's an image of a bald priest with a superb expression of intense concentration.

From the Amida-dō Hall, head north to the end of the covered walkway. Change into the sandals provided, then climb the steep steps up the mountainside to the Taho-tō Pagoda where there's a fine view across the city.

The temple is open from 9 am to 4 pm and admission costs ¥400. An explanatory leaflet in English and a map are provided.

The Path of Philosophy 哲学の道

The Path of Philosophy (Tetsugaku-no-Michi in Japanese) has long been a favourite with contemplative strollers who follow the traffic-free route beside a canal lined with cherry trees which come into spectacular bloom in April. It only takes 30 minutes to follow the walk, which starts after Eikan-dō Temple and leads to Ginkaku-ji Temple. During the day, be prepared for crowds of tourists; a night stroll will definitely be quieter. A map of the walk is part of *Walking Tour Courses in Kyoto*, a leaflet available from the TIC or JNTO.

Hōnen-in Temple 法然院

This temple was founded in 1680 to honour Hōnen, the charismatic founder of the Jōdo school. This is a lovely, secluded temple with carefully raked gardens set back in the woods.

Entry is free. It's open from 7 am to 4 pm. The temple is a 12 minute walk from Ginkaku-ji Temple, on a side street just east

KANSAI REGION

Mt Daimonji-yama Climb
Time: two hours
Distance: five km
Major Sights: Ginkaku-ji Temple, Daimonji Yaki site

Located directly behind Ginkaku-ji Temple, Mt Daimonji-yama is the main site of the Daimon-ji Yaki fire festival. From almost anywhere in town the Chinese character for 'great' *(dai)* is visible in the middle of a bare patch on the face of this mountain. On 16 August, this character is set ablaze to guide the spirits of the dead on their journey home. The view of Kyoto from the top is unparalleled.

Take bus No 5 to the Ginkaku-ji Michi stop and walk up to Ginkaku-ji. Here, you have the option of visiting the temple or starting the hike immediately. To find the trailhead, turn left in front of the temple and head north for about 50m toward a stone *torii* (shrine gate). Just before the torii, turn right up the hill.

The trail proper starts just after a small parking lot on the right. It's a broad avenue through the trees. A few minutes of walking brings you to a red banner hanging over the trail (warning of forest fires). Soon after this you must cross a bridge to the right then continue up a smaller, switchback trail. When the trail reaches a saddle not far from the top, go to the left. You'll climb a long flight of steps before coming out at the top of the bald patch. The sunset from here is great, but bring a torch. ■

of the Path of Philosophy. Cross the bridge over the canal and follow the road uphill through the bamboo groves.

Ginkaku-ji Temple   銀閣寺

Ginkaku-ji is definitely worth seeing, but be warned that it is often swamped with bus loads of visitors jamming the narrow pathways.

In 1482, Shogun Ashikaga Yoshimasa constructed a villa here which he used as a genteel retreat from the turmoil of civil war. Although its name translates as 'Silver Pavilion', the plan to completely cover the building in silver was never carried out. After Yoshimasa's death, it was converted to a temple.

The approach to the main gate runs between tall hedges before turning sharply into the extensive grounds. Walkways lead through the gardens which include meticulously raked cones of white sand (probably symbolic interpretations of a mountain and a lake), tall pines and a pond in front of the temple. A path also leads up the mountainside through the trees.

Admission costs ¥500 and it's open from 8.30 am to 5 pm from 15 March to 30 November and from 9 am to 4.30 pm the rest of the year. An explanatory leaflet in English is provided. From Kyoto station or Sanjō station, take bus No 5 and get off at the Ginkaku-ji-mae stop. From Demachiyanagi station or Shijō station, take bus No 203 to the same stop.

NORTH-WESTERN KYOTO
京都の西北部

The north-western part of Kyoto is predominantly residential, but there are a number of superb temples with tranquil gardens in secluded precincts. For Zen fans, a visit to Daitoku-ji Temple and Ryōan-ji Temple is recommended. Kinkaku-ji Temple is another major attraction. The JNTO leaflet on walks also covers this area, but most of the walk is along unremarkable city streets.

Those who have the time and inclination to escape the tourist trail might consider a visit to the Takao District.

Daitoku-ji Temple   大徳寺

The precincts of this temple, which belongs to the Rinzai school of Zen, contain an extensive complex of 24 subtemples of which two are mentioned below, but eight are open to the public. If you want an intensive look at Zen culture, this is the place to visit, but be prepared for temples which are thriving business enterprises and often choked with visitors.

Daitoku-ji is on the eastern side of the grounds. It was founded in 1319, burnt down in the next century, and rebuilt in the 16th century. The San-mon Gate contains an image of the famous tea master, Sen-no-Rikyū, on the 2nd storey.

According to some historical sources, Toyotomi Hideyoshi was so enraged when he discovered he had been demeaning himself by walking *under* Rikyū, that he forced the master to commit *seppuku* (ritual suicide) in 1591.

Daisen-in Subtemple   大仙院

The famous Zen garden in this subtemple is worth a look – that is, of course, if you can make any progress through the crowds. The jovial abbot posed for pictures, dashed off calligraphy souvenirs at lightning speed, held up his fingers in a 'V' for victory sign and completed the act with a regal bow and a rousing 'Danke schön' to each member of a German tour group. If you arrive at 9 am, you might miss the crowds.

Kōtō-in Subtemple   高桐院

This subtemple is in the western part of the grounds. The gardens are superb.

Admission charges to the temples vary, but usually average ¥350. Those temples which accept visitors are usually open from 9 am to 5 pm. The temple bus stop is Daitoku-ji-mae. Convenient buses from Kyoto station are Nos 205 and 206. It's also not a far walk west of Kitaō-ji subway station.

Kinkaku-ji Temple   金閣寺

Kinkaku-ji, the famed 'Golden Temple', is one of Japan's best known sights. The original building was constructed in 1397 as a retirement villa for Shogun Ashikaga Yoshimitsu.

His son converted it into a temple. In 1950, a young monk consummated his obsession with the temple by burning it to the ground. The monk's story was fictionalised in Mishima Yukio's *The Golden Pavilion*.

In 1955, a full reconstruction was completed which exactly followed the original design, but the gold-foil covering was extended to the lower floors. The temple may not be to everyone's taste (the tremendous crowds just about obscure the view anyway).

The temple is open from 9 am to 5 pm and admission costs ¥400. To get there from Kyoto station, take bus No 205 and get off at the Kinkaku-ji-michi stop; bus No 59 also stops close to the temple.

Ryōan-ji Temple 竜安寺

This temple belongs to the Rinzai school of Zen and was founded in 1450. The main attraction is the garden arranged in the *kare-sansui* ('dry landscape') style. An austere collection of 15 rocks, apparently adrift in a sea of sand, is enclosed by an earthen wall. The designer, who remains unknown, provided no explanation.

The viewing platform for the garden can become packed solid but the other parts of the temple grounds are also interesting and less of a target for the crowds. Among these, the Kyoyo-chi Pond is perhaps the most beautiful, particularly in autumn. Probably the best advice at Ryōan-ji is to come as early in the day as possible.

Admission costs ¥400 and the temple is open from 8 am to 5 pm (8.30 am to 4.30 pm from December to March). From Sanjō Keihan station take bus No 59 and from Kyoto station take bus No 52.

Ninna-ji Temple 仁和寺

Ninna-ji was built in 842 and is the head temple of the Omura branch of the Shingon school of Buddhism. The present temple buildings, including a five-storey pagoda, are from the 17th century. The extensive grounds are full of cherry trees which bloom in April.

The temple is open from 9 am to 4.30 pm and admission costs ¥400. Separate entrance fees are charged for the Kondō (Main Hall) and Reihōkan (Treasure House), which is only open for the first two weeks of October. To get there, take bus No 59 from Sanjō station and get off at the Omuro Ninna-ji stop which is opposite the entrance gate. From Kyoto station take bus No 26.

Myōshin-ji Temple 妙心寺

Myōshin-ji, a vast temple complex dating back to the 14th century, belongs to the Rinzai school of Zen. There are over 40 temples but only four are open to the public.

From the north gate, follow the broad stone avenue flanked by rows of temples to the southern part of the complex. The ceiling of the Hattō (Lecture Hall) features the unnerving painting *Dragon Glaring in Eight Directions*. Admission costs ¥400 and it's open from 9.10 am to 3.40 pm.

Taizō-in Temple

This temple is in the south-western corner of the grounds. The garden is worth a visit. Admission costs ¥400 and it's open from 9 am to 5 pm.

The north gate of the Myōshin-ji Temple is an easy 10 minute walk south from Ninna-ji Temple or you can take bus No 10 from Sanjō Keihan station.

Kitano-Tenman-gū Shrine 北野天満宮

This shrine is of moderate interest, probably best visited for the market fair. The Tenjin-san market fair is held here on the 25th of each month. Those held in December and January are particularly colourful.

There's no charge for admission and it's open from 5.30 am to 6 pm. From Kyoto station, take bus No 50 and get off at the Kitano-Tenmangū-mae stop. From San-jō Keihan station, take bus No 10 to the same stop.

Kōryū-ji Temple 広隆寺

Kōryū-ji, one of the oldest temples in Japan, was founded in 622 to honour Prince Shōtoku who was an enthusiastic promoter of Buddhism.

The Hattō (Lecture Hall), to the right of the main gate, houses a magnificent trio of

9th century statues: Buddha, flanked by manifestations of Kannon.

The Reihōkan (Treasure House) contains numerous fine Buddhist statues including the Naki Miroku (Crying Miroku) and the world renowned Miroku Bosatsu which is extraordinarily expressive. A national upset occurred in 1960 when an enraptured student clasped the statue and snapped off its little finger.

The temple is open from 9 am to 5 pm (4.30 pm from December to the end of February) and admission costs ¥600. Take bus No 11 from Sanjō Keihan station, get off at the Ukyō-ku Sogo-chosha-mae stop and walk north.

Takao District　高雄

This is a secluded district tucked far away in the north-western part of Kyoto. It is famed for autumn foliage and the temples of Jingo-ji, Saimyō-ji and Kōzan-ji.

Jingo-ji Temple is the best of the three temples located in the Takao District. This mountain temple sits at the top of a long flight of stairs which stretch from the Kiyotaki River to the temple's main gate. The Kondō (Gold Hall) is the most impressive of the temple's structures, located roughly in the middle of the grounds at the top of another flight of stairs. After visiting the Kondō, head in the opposite direction along a wooded path to an open area overlooking the valley. Don't be surprised if you see people tossing small disks over the railing into the chasm below. These are *kawarakenage*, light clay disks which people throw in order to rid themselves of their bad karma. Be careful, it's addictive and at ¥100 for two it can get expensive (you can buy the disks at a nearby stall). The trick is to flick the disks very gently, convex side up, like a Frisbee. When you get it right, they sail all the way down the valley – taking all that bad karma with them (and don't worry, the clay disks are biodegradable).

To reach Jingo-ji, take bus No 8 from Sanjō Keihan station to the last stop, Takao, allowing one hour for the ride. The other two temples are within easy walking distance of

the bus stop, **Saimyō-ji** being the better of the two (five minutes north of Jingo-ji).

There are two options for bus services to Takao: an hourly JR bus which takes about an hour to reach the Takao stop from Kyoto station; and an hourly Kyoto bus from Keihan-sanjō station which also takes about an hour to reach Takao. To get to the temple, first walk down to the river then look for the steps on the other side.

Hozu River Trip　保津川下り

This ride is a great way to enjoy the beauty of Kyoto's western mountains without any strain on the legs. The river winds through steep forested mountain canyons before it arrives at its destination, Arashiyama. Between 10 March and 30 November, there are seven trips (from 9 am to 3.30 pm) daily down the Hozu River. During the winter, the number of trips is reduced to three a day and the boats are heated. There are no boat trips from 29 December to 4 January.

The ride lasts two hours and covers 16 km between Kameoka and Arashiyama through occasional sections of choppy water – a scenic jaunt with minimal danger.

The price is ¥3700 per person. The boats depart from a dock which is eight minutes on foot from Kameoka station. Kameoka is accessible by rail from Kyoto station or Ni-jō station on the JR Sagano (San-in) line. The Kyoto TIC provides an English leaflet and a photocopied timetable sheet for rail connections. The train fare from Kyoto to Kameoka is ¥390 one way by regular train (don't spend the extra for the express as it makes little difference in time).

WESTERN KYOTO　京都の西部

Arashiyama and Sagano are two districts worth a visit in this area if you feel like strolling in pleasant natural surroundings and visiting temples tucked into bamboo groves. The JNTO leaflet, *Walking Tour Courses in Kyoto*, has a rudimentary walking map for the Arashiyama area. Note that Arashiyama is wildly popular with Japanese tourists and can be packed, particularly in the cherry-blossom and maple-leaf seasons. To

Kiyotaki River Hike

Time: about two hours
Distance: about five km
Major Sights: Jingo-ji Temple, Kiyotaki-gawa River, Hozu-gawa River

This is one of the most beautiful hikes in the Kyoto area, especially in autumn, when the maples set the hillsides ablaze with colour. Start from Jingo-ji Temple (see Jingo-ji Temple for transport details). The trail begins at the bottom of the steps leading up to the temple and follows the Kiyotaki-gawa River south (downstream). After about one hour of riverside walking, you'll get to the small hamlet of Kiyotaki, with its quaint riverside inns and restaurants. Just before the town there is a trail junction which can be confusing; the trail leaves the riverside for a while and comes to a junction on a hillside. At this spot, head uphill back toward the river, not further into the woods. After passing through the town, cross over a bridge and continue downstream. The trail continues to hug the river, and passes some excellent, crystal-clear swimming holes – great on a hot summer day.

After another 30 minutes or so you'll come up to a road. Turn right, walk through the tunnel and continue along this road for another 30 minutes to reach Hozukyō station. The riverside below the bridge here is a popular summer picnic and swimming spot – bring a bathing suit and picnic basket and join the fun. From Hozukyō station you can catch a local train back to Kyoto (20 minutes, ¥230). ∎

avoid the crowds, go early on a weekday or head to some of the more offbeat spots.

Bus No 28 links Kyoto station with Arashiyama. Bus No 11 connects Keihan-sanjō station with Arashiyama. The most convenient rail connection is the 20 minute ride from Shijō-Omiya station on the Keifuku-Arashiyama line to Arashiyama station. You can also take the JR San-in line from Kyoto station or Ni-jō station and get off at JR Saga station (be careful to take only the local as the express does not stop in Arashiyama). There are several bicycle rental shops (¥600 for three hours, ¥1000 for the day) near the station, but it's more enjoyable to cover the relatively short distances between sights on foot.

Togetsu-kyō Bridge   渡月橋

Togetsu-kyō Bridge is the main landmark in Arashiyama, a couple of minutes on foot from the station. Upon arrival here, you may wonder why the Japanese make such a fuss about this place; it's not very beautiful, particularly with all the tacky shops and vending machines nearby. The best advice is to head north immediately to the quieter regions of Sagano.

This is a good spot, however, in July and August, to watch (cormorant fishing) in the evening. If you want to get close to the action, you can pay ¥1300 to join a passenger boat. The TIC can provide a leaflet and further details.

Tenryū-ji Temple   天竜寺

Tenryū-ji is one of the major temples of the Rinzai school of Zen. It was built in 1339 on the former site of Emperor Go-Daigo's villa after a priest had dreamt of a dragon rising from the nearby river. The dream was interpreted as a sign that the emperor's spirit was uneasy and the temple was constructed as appeasement – hence the name *tenryū* (heavenly dragon). The present buildings date from 1900, but the main attraction is the 14th century Zen garden.

Admission costs ¥500 and it's open from 8.30 am to 5.30 pm (April to October) and has a 5 pm closing time during the rest of the year.

Ōkōchi Sansō Villa   大河内山荘

This is the lavish home of Denjiro Ōkōchi, a famous actor in samurai films. The extensive gardens allow fine views over the city and are open to visitors. Admission costs a hefty ¥700 (including tea and a cake). The villa is a 10 minute walk through bamboo groves north of Tenryū-ji Temple.

KANSAI REGION

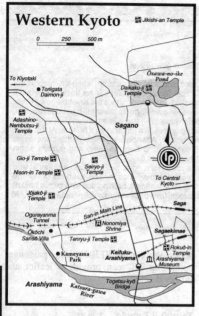

Western Kyoto

Jikishi-an Temple

0   250   500 m

To Kiyotaki

Osawa-no-ike Pond

Toriigata Daimon-ji

Daikaku-ji Temple

Adashino-Nembutsu-ji Temple

Sagano

Gio-ji Temple

Seiryo-ji Temple

Nison-in Temple

To Central Kyoto

Jōjakō-ji Temple

Saga

Ogurayanma Tunnel

San-in Main Line

Nonomiya Shrine

Okōchi Sanso Villa

Tenryu-ji Temple

Sagaekimae

Kameyama Park

Keifuku-Arashiyama

Rokuō-in Temple

Arashiyama Museum

Arashiyama

Katsura-gawa River

Togetsu-kyō Bridge

Temples North of Ōkōchi Sansō Villa

If you continue north from Ōkōchi Sansō Villa, the narrow road soon passes stone steps on your left leading up to the pleasant grounds of **Jōjakō-ji Temple**. A further 10 minutes on foot brings you to **Nison-in Temple**, which is in an attractive setting up the wooded hillside.

If you have time for a detour, there are several small temples west of Nison-in. Adashino Nembutsu-ji Temple is a rather unusual temple where the abandoned bones of paupers and destitutes without next of kin were gathered. Thousands of stone images are crammed into the temple grounds. These thousands of abandoned souls are remembered each year with candles here in the Sentō Kuyō ceremony held on the evenings of 23 and 24 August. Admission is ¥500.

Daikaku-ji Temple 大覚寺

Daikaku-ji is 25 minutes walk north-east of Nison-in Temple. It was built in the 9th

century as a palace for Emperor Saga who converted it into a temple. The present buildings date from the 16th century, but are still palatial in style with some impressive paintings. The large Osawa-no-Ike Pond was once used by the emperor for boating.

The temple is open from 9 am to 5 pm and admission costs ¥500. Close to the temple entrance are separate terminals for Kyoto-shi (Kyoto City) buses (No 28 goes to Kyoto station) and Kyoto buses (No 71 goes to Kyoto station and No 61 to Keihan-sanjō station).

SOUTH-WESTERN KYOTO
京都の西南部
Katsura Rikyū Imperial Villa 桂離宮

This villa is considered to be one of the finest examples of Japanese architecture. It was built in 1624 for the emperor's brother, Prince Toshihito. Every conceivable detail of the villa, the teahouses, the large pond with islets and the surrounding garden has been given meticulous attention.

Tours (in Japanese) start at 10 and 11 am, and 2 and 3 pm and last about 40 minutes. You should be there 20 minutes beforehand. An explanatory video is shown in the waiting room and a leaflet is provided in English. Admission is free, but you *must* make reservations through the Imperial Household Agency (see earlier details for the Kyoto Imperial Palace) and usually several weeks in advance. Visitors must be over 20 years of age.

To get to the villa from Kyoto station take bus No 33 and get off at the Katsura Rikyū-mae stop which is a five minute walk from the villa. The easiest access from the city centre is to take a Hankyū line train from Hankyū Kawaramachi station to Hankyū Katsura station which is a 15 minute walk from the villa.

Saihō-ji Temple 西芳寺

The main attraction at this temple is the heart-shaped garden, designed in 1339 by Musō Kokushi. The garden is famous for its luxuriant mossy growth – hence the temple's other name, 'Koke-dera' (Moss Temple). Visiting the temple is recommended only if you have time and patience to follow the

Cormorant Fishing

Ukai (cormorant fishing) is mentioned in Japanese historical documents as early as the 8th century. It is still common in Gifu and Kyoto prefectures, although it's largely a tourist attraction these days. The cormorants and the crew splash about; the passengers have a fun time drinking and eating.

The season lasts from May to September; the best times for fishing are moonless nights when the fish are more easily attracted to the glare of a fire in a metal basket suspended from the bow of the boat. Fishing trips are cancelled during and after heavy rain.

The cormorants, up to a dozen in number, sit on the boat, attached to long leashes. In the water, a small metal ring at the base of their necks stops them guzzling their catch. After filling their gullets with fish, they are hauled on board and obliged to disgorge the contents. Each boat usually has a crew of four to handle the birds, the boat and the fire.

The cormorant catch is usually *ayu*, a type of sweet fish, much prized by Japanese. A nifty cormorant can catch several dozen fish in a night. After completing their night's work, the cormorants are loaded into bamboo baskets in a strictly observed order of seniority – cormorants are very conscious of social ranking and will protest if this is not respected. Life expectancy for a cormorant ranges between 15 and 20 years, so they probably do have a point about seniority. ■

reservation rules. If you don't, visit nearby Jizo-in Temple to get a taste of the atmosphere of Saihō-ji without the expense or fuss.

Reservations Reservations are the only way you can visit. This is to avoid the overwhelming crowds of visitors who used to swamp the place when reservations were not required.

Send a postcard at least one week before the date you require and include details of your name, number of visitors, address in Japan, occupation, age (you must be over 18) and desired date (choice of alternative dates preferred). The address is Saihō-ji Temple, 56 Kamigaya-cho, Matsuo, Nishikyō-ku, Kyoto. Enclose a pre-stamped return post-card for a reply to your Japanese address. You might find it convenient to buy an *ōfuki-hagaki* (send and return postcard set) at a Japanese post office.

You should arrive at the time and on the date supplied by the temple office. After paying your ¥3000 'donation', you spend up to 90 minutes copying or chanting sutras or doing Zen meditation before finally being guided around the garden for 90 minutes.

Take bus No 28 from Kyoto station to the Matsuo-taisha-mae stop and walk southwest.

Jizo-in Temple

This delightful little temple could be called the 'poor man's Saihō-ji'. It's only a few minutes walk south of Saihō-ji in the same atmospheric bamboo groves. While the temple does not boast any spectacular build-ings or treasures, it has a nice moss garden and is almost completely ignored by tourists, making it a great place to sit and think. Admission is ¥400. For directions see Saihō-ji Temple.

SOUTH & SOUTH-EASTERN KYOTO
京都の南部・東南部

The district to the south of Kyoto is mostly devoted to industry (also famed for sake breweries), but Tōfuku-ji Temple and the foxy Fushimi-Inari Taisha Shrine are worth a visit.

To the south-east, Daigo-ji Temple is in rural surroundings and offers scope for a gentle hike to complement the architectural splendours. The city of Uji isn't exactly part of Kyoto, but it's easy to reach on a day trip, or as a convenient stop when travelling between Kyoto and Nara.

Tōfuku-ji Temple　東福寺

Founded in 1236 by the priest Enni, Tōfuku-ji now belongs to the Rinzai sect of Zen Buddhism. Since this temple was intended to compare with Tōdai-ji Temple and Kōfuku-ji Temple in Nara, it was given a name combining characters from the names of each of these temples.

Despite the destruction of many of the buildings by fire, this is still considered one of the five main Zen temples in Kyoto. The huge San-mon Gate is the oldest Zen main gate in Japan. The *tōsu* (lavatory) and *yokushitsu* (bathroom) date from the 14th century. The present temple complex includes 24 subtemples; at one time there were 53.

The Hōjō (Abbot's Hall) was reconstructed in 1890. The gardens, laid out in 1938, are worth a visit. As you approach the northern gardens, you cross a stream over Tsūten-kyō (Bridge to Heaven), which is a pleasant leafy spot – the foliage is renowned for its autumn colour. The northern garden has stones and moss neatly arranged in a chequerboard pattern.

The nearby **Reiun-in subtemple** receives few visitors to its attractive garden.

Admission costs ¥300 for the main temple and admission charges for the subtemples are about the same. Opening hours are from 9 am to 4 pm. English leaflets are provided.

To reach Tōfuku-ji by train, you can either take a JR train on the Nara line or a train from Keihan-sanjō station on the Keihan Honsen line. Get off at Tōfuku-ji station and walk east up the hill toward the mountains. Bus No 208 also runs from Kyoto station via Tōfuku-ji. Get off at the Tōfuku-ji-mae stop.

Fushimi-Inari Taisha Shrine 伏見稲荷大社

This intriguing shrine was dedicated to the gods of rice and sake by the Hata family in the 8th century. As the role of agriculture diminished, deities were enrolled to ensure prosperity in business. Nowadays, the shrine is one of Japan's most popular, and is the head shrine for some 30,000 Inari shrines scattered the length and breadth of Japan.

The entire complex, consisting of five shrines, sprawls across the wooded slopes of Mt Inari. A pathway wanders four km up the mountain and is lined with hundreds of red torii (arches). There are also dozens of stone foxes. The fox is considered the messenger of Inari, the god of cereals, and by extension the stone foxes, too, are often referred to as Inari. On an incidental note, the Japanese traditionally see the fox as a sacred, somewhat mysterious figure capable of 'possessing' humans – the favoured point of entry is under the fingernails. The key often seen in the fox's mouth is for the rice granary.

The walk around the upper precincts of the shrine is a pleasant day hike. It also makes for a very eerie stroll in the late afternoon and early evening, when the various graveyards and miniature shrines along the path take on a mysterious air. It's best to go with a friend at this time.

On 1 April, there is a festival at 11 am which features displays of flower arranging. On 8 April, there's a Sangyō-sai Festival with offerings and dances to ensure prosperity for national industry. During the first few days in January, thousands of festive believers pray at the shrine.

Local delicacies sold on the approach streets include barbecued sparrow and 'Inari-sushi' which is fried tofu wrapped around sweetened sushi – commonly believed to be the favourite food of the fox.

To get to the shrine from JR Kyoto station, take a JR Nara line train to Inari station. From Keihan-sanjō station on the Keihan line, get off at Fushimi-Inari station. There is no admission charge for the shrine.

Daigo-ji Temple　醍醐寺

Daigo-ji was founded in 874 by the priest Shobo who gave it the name of Daigo (ultimate essence of milk). This refers to the five periods of Buddha's teaching which were often compared to the five forms of milk prepared in India – the highest form is called 'daigo' in Japanese.

The temple was expanded into a vast complex of buildings on two levels – Shimo Daigo (Lower Daigo) and Kami Daigo (Upper Daigo). During the 15th century, the buildings on the lower level were destroyed with the sole exception of the five-storey pagoda. Built in 951, this pagoda still stands and is lovingly pointed out as the oldest of its kind in Japan and the oldest existing building in Kyoto.

In the late 16th century, Hideyoshi took a fancy to Daigo-ji and ordered extensive rebuilding. It is now one of the main temples of the Shingon school of Buddhism. To explore Daigo-ji thoroughly and leisurely, mixing hiking with temple viewing, you will need at least half a day.

Hōkō Hanami Gyōretsu Parade On the second Sunday in April, a parade called Hōkō Hanami Gyōretsu takes place in the temple precincts. This re-enacts in full period costume the cherry-blossom party which Hideyoshi held in 1598. As a result of this party, the temple's abbot was able to secure Hideyoshi's support for restoration of the dilapidated temple complex.

Sampō-in Temple This was founded as a subtemple in 1115, but received a total revamp under Hideyoshi's orders in 1598. It is now a fine example of the amazing opulence of that period. The Kanō paintings and the garden are special features.

The garden is jam-packed with about 800 stones – the Japanese mania for stones goes back a long way. The most famous stone here is Fujito-no-ishi which is linked with deception, death and a fabulous price that was spurned; it's even the subject of a nō play, *Fujito*. Admission to Sampō-in costs ¥500. It's open from 9 am to 5 pm (March to October) and closes one hour earlier during the rest of the year.

Hōju-in Treasure House This is close to the Sampō-in Temple, but is only open to the public from 1 April to 25 May and from 1 October to 25 November. Despite the massive admission fee of ¥700, it really

should not be missed if you happen to be there at the right time. The display of sculptures, scrolls, screens, miniature shrines and calligraphy is superb.

Climb to Kami Daigo From Sampō-in Temple in Shimo Daigo (Lower Daigo), walk up the large avenue of cherry trees, through the Niō-mon Gate and past the pagoda. From there you can continue for a pleasant climb through Kami Daigo (Upper Daigo), browsing through temples and shrines on the way. Allow 50 minutes to reach the top.

To get to the Daigo-ji Temple complex, take bus No 'Higashi' (east) 9 and get off at the Daigo-Sampo-in-mae stop.

Mampuku-ji Temple 黄檗山万福寺
Mampuku-ji was established as a Zen temple in 1661 by the Chinese priest Ingen. It is a rare example in Japan of a Zen temple built in the pure Chinese style of the Ming dynasty. The temple follows the Ōbaku school of Zen, which is linked to mainstream Rinzai Zen, but incorporates a wide range of Esoteric Buddhist practices.

Admission costs ¥400 and it's open from 9 am to 4.30 pm. The temple is a short walk from the two railway stations (JR Nara line and Keihan Uji line) at Ōbaku – about 30 minutes by rail from Kyoto.

Uji 宇治
Uji is a small city to the south of Kyoto. Its main claims to fame are the **Byōdō-in Temple**, tea cultivation and ukai (cormorant fishing). The stone bridge at Uji, the oldest of its kind in Japan, has been the scene of many bitter clashes in previous centuries – traffic jams seem to dominate nowadays.

Uji can be reached by rail in about 40 minutes from Kyoto on the Keihan-Uji line or JR Nara line.

Byōdō-in Temple This temple was converted from a Fujiwara villa into a Buddhist temple in 1052. The Phoenix Hall (Hōō-dō), more properly known as the Amida-dō, was built in 1053 and is the only original remaining building. The phoenix was a popular

KANSAI REGION

mythical bird in China and was revered by the Japanese as a protector of Buddha. The architecture of the building resembles the shape of the bird, and there are two bronze phoenixes perched opposite each other on the roof. The building was originally intended to represent Amida's heavenly palace in the Pure Land. This building is one of the few extant examples of Heian period architecture and its graceful lines make one wish that far more had survived the wars and fires which plagued Kyoto's past.

Inside the hall is the famous statue of Amida and 52 Bosatsu (Bodhisattvas) dating from the 11th century and attributed to the priest-sculptor, Jōchō.

The temple, complete with its reflection in a pond, is a number one attraction in Japan and draws huge crowds. For a preview without the masses, take a look at the 10 yen coin. Admission costs ¥400 and it's open from 8.30 am to 5 pm (March to November) and from 9 am to 4 pm during the rest of the year. Leaflets in English are provided.

The nearby **Hōmotsukan Treasure House** contains the original temple bell and door paintings and the original phoenix roof adornments. Admission costs ¥300 and it is only open from 1 April to 31 May and from 15 September to 23 November. Opening hours are from 9 am to 4 pm. A brief leaflet is supplied in English.

The approach street to the temple complex is lined with souvenir shops, many of which roast local tea outside. A small packet of the tea is popular as a souvenir or gift.

Between 17 June and 31 August, ukai trips are organised in the evening around 7 pm on the river near the temple. Prices start at ¥1500 per person. The TIC has a leaflet with up-to-date information on booking. More details about ukai are included in the Arashiyama section in Western Kyoto.

If you're hungry while in Uji and can't wait to get back to Kyoto to eat, the coffee shop *Shiki* (☎ 0774-24-4374), across the river from Byōdō-in, serves a good set lunch for ¥680 (with an English menu). Coffee is ¥350. It's open from 9.30 am to 6 pm, closed Wednesday. It's next to Hashi-dera Temple.

NORTHERN KYOTO 京都の北部

The area north of Kyoto provides scope for exploration of rural valleys and mountainous areas. The twin valleys of Kurama and Kibune are perhaps the most pleasant day trip in the Kyoto area, giving one the feeling of being deep in the country without the necessity of long travel. Ōhara also makes another pleasant day trip, perhaps twinned with an excursion to Mt Hiei-zan and the Enryaku-ji Temple or Shūgaku-in Rikyū Imperial Villa.

Shūgaku-in Rikyū Imperial Villa
修学院離宮

This villa, or 'detached palace', was begun in the 1650s by the abdicated emperor Go-Mizunoo, and work was continued after his death in 1680 by his daughter Akenomiya. Designed as an imperial retreat, the villa grounds are divided into three large garden areas on a hillside – lower, middle and upper. The gardens' reputation rests on their ponds, pathways and impressive use of 'borrowed scenery' in the form of the surrounding hills; the view from the Rinun-tei Teahouse in the upper garden is particularly impressive.

Tours (in Japanese) start at 9, 10 and 11 am; 1.30 and 3 pm (50 minutes). Get there early. A leaflet in English is provided.

Admission is free, but you must make reservations through the Imperial Household Agency – usually several weeks in advance (see the earlier Kyoto Imperial Palace section for details).

From Kyoto station, take bus No 5 and get off at the Shūgaku-in Rikyū-michi stop. The trip takes about an hour. From the bus stop it's a 15 minute walk to the villa. You can also take the Keihan Eizan line from Demachiyanagi station to the Shūgaku-in stop and walk east about 25 minutes toward the mountains.

Shisendō & Manshū-in Temple
詩仙堂・曼殊院

Both these sights are in the vicinity of Shūgaku-in Rikyū Imperial Villa and both are less touristy than other major sights.

Shisendō (House of Poet-Hermits) was

built in 1641 by Jōzan, a scholar of Chinese classics and a landscape architect, who wanted a place to retire at the end of his life. The garden provides relaxation – just the rhythmic 'thwack' of a bamboo *sōzu* (animal scarer) to interrupt your snooze.

Admission costs ¥400 and an English leaflet is provided; it's open from 9 am to 5 pm. The house is a five minute walk from the Ichijoji-sagarimatsu-mae bus stop on the No 5 route.

Manshū-in was originally founded by Saichō on Mt Hiei-zan, but was relocated here at the beginning of the Edo period. The architecture, works of art and garden are impressive.

The temple is open from 9 am to 5 pm and admission costs ¥500; a leaflet in English is provided. The temple is a 10 minute walk from Shūgaku-in Rikyū Imperial Villa.

Mt Hiei-zan & Enryaku-ji Temple
比叡山・延暦寺

A visit to Mt Hiei-zan and Enryaku-ji is a good way to spend half a day hiking, poking around temples and enjoying the atmosphere of a key site in Japanese history.

Enryaku-ji was founded in 788 by Saichō, the priest who established the Tenzai school of Buddhism. The Tenzai school did not receive imperial recognition until 1823, after Saichō's death. But from this time the temple continued to grow in power; at its height it possessed some 3000 temple buildings and an army of thousands of *sōhei*, or warrior monks. In 1581, Oda Nobunaga saw the temple's power as a threat to his aims to unify the nation. He destroyed most of the temple buildings along with the monks inside.

As it now stands, the temple area is divided into three sections – Tōdō, Saitō and Yokawa (of minimal interest). The Tōdō (Eastern Section) contains the Kompon Chū-dō (Primary Central Hall) which dates from 1642. Admission costs ¥400. It's open from 8.30 am to 4.30 pm (April to November) and from 9 am to 4 pm during the rest of the year. A leaflet in English is provided. This part is heavily geared to group access with large expanses of asphalt for parking.

The Saitō (Western Section) contains the Shaka-dō Hall, dating from the Kamakura period. The Saitō, with its stone paths winding through forests of tall trees, temples shrouded in mist and the sound of distant gongs, is the most atmospheric part of the temple.

Getting There & Away You can reach Mt Hiei-zan and Enryaku-ji by either train or bus. The most interesting way is the train/cablecar/ropeway route described below. If you're in a hurry or would like to save money, however, the best way is a direct bus from San-jō Keihan or Kyoto station.

Train Take the Keihan line north to the last stop, Demachiyanagi, and change to the Yase-yuen/Hiei bound Eizan line train (be careful not to board a Kurama bound train which leaves from the same platform). At Yase-yuen (the last stop), board the cablecar (nine minutes, ¥520) and then the ropeway (three minutes, ¥300) to the peak from which you can walk down to the temples.

Enraku-ji is also accessible from Saka-moto on the Lake Biwa-ko side of the mountain (take the Keihan Keishin line from Kyoto to Sakamoto, or JR from Kyoto to Eizan and walk uphill to the Sakamoto cablecar which costs ¥820).

Bus Kyoto bus Nos 17 and 18 run from Kyoto station to Ōhara in about 50 minutes. Be careful to board a tan Kyoto bus, not a green Kyoto city bus of the same number. Get off before Ōhara at the Yase-yuen bus stop. From there it's a short walk to the cablecar station (departures every half hour) where you can ascend the mountain in two stages. A combined ticket (one way) for both sections costs ¥820. The lookout at the top cablecar station has fine views across Lake Biwa-ko, though skip it if the weather is dull; entry costs ¥300.

From Keihan-sanjō station in central Kyoto, you can take Kyoto bus No 16 towards Ōhara and get off at the Yase-yuenchi bus stop.

From Kyoto station there are direct buses

to Enryaku-ji Temple and Mt Hiei-zan at 9.50, 10.45 and 11.45 am and 1.50 pm (one hour 10 minutes, ¥650). There are also direct buses from Keihan-sanjō station at 8.55, 9.35 and 11.06 am and 12.06, 1.05 and 3.05 pm (52 minutes, ¥650).

Ōhara 大原

Ōhara, a quiet farming town about 10 km north of Kyoto, provides a glimpse of old rural Japan along with picturesque Sanzen-in Temple and Jakkō-in Convent. It's most popular in autumn, when the maple leaves change colour and the mountain views are spectacular. From late October to mid-

Ōhara girl on her way
back home after gathering wood.

November avoid this area on weekends as it will be packed.

From Kyoto station, Kyoto bus Nos 17 and 18 run to Ōhara. The ride takes about an hour and costs ¥520. From Sanjō station, take Kyoto bus Nos 16 or 17 (45 minutes, ¥470). Be careful to board a tan Kyoto bus, not a green Kyoto city bus of the same number. Allow half a day for a visit, possibly twinned with an excursion to Mt Hiei-zan and the Enryaku-ji Temple. JNTO includes a basic walking map for the area in its leaflet *Walking Tour Courses in Kyoto*.

Sanzen-in Temple Founded in 784 by the priest Saicho, Sanzen-in belongs to the Tendai sect of Buddhism. Saicho, considered one of the great patriarchs of Buddhism in Japan, also founded Enraku-ji on nearby Mt Hiei. The temple's Yusei-en Garden is one of the most oft-photographed sights in Japan and rightly so. Take some time to sit on the steps of the Sin-den Hall and admire its beauty. Then head off to the Ojo-gokuraku Hall (Temple of Rebirth in Paradise) to see the impressive Amitabha trinity, a large Amida image flanked by attendants Kannon and Seishi, gods of mercy and wisdom, respectively. After this, walk up to the hydrangea garden at the back of the temple, where, in late spring and summer, you can walk among hectares of blooming hydrangea.

If you feel like a short hike after leaving the temple, head up the hill around the right side of the temple to see the oddly named (it sounds like any other waterfall) **Soundless Waterfall**. The sound of this waterfall is said to have inspired Shomyo Buddhist chanting.

If you have time, **Shorin-in Temple**, just 100m to the left of the entrance to Sanzen-in, is worth a look, if only through its admission gate, to admire its unique thatch roof.

To get to Sanzen-in, follow the signs from Ōhara's main bus stop up the hill past a long arcade of souvenir stalls. The entrance is on your left as you crest the hill. The temple is open from 8.30 am to 5.30 pm March to November and closes half an hour earlier during the rest of the year. Admission costs ¥500 and an English leaflet is provided.

Jakkō-in Convent This convent lies to the west of Ōhara. Walk out of the bus station up the road to the traffic lights, then follow the small road to the left; the temple is at the top of a steep flight of stone steps.

The history of Jakkō-in Convent is exceedingly tragic – bring a supply of hankies. The actual founding date of the convent is subject to some debate (somewhere between the 6th and 11th centuries), but it acquired fame as the nunnery which harboured Kenrei Mon'in, a lady of the Taira clan. In 1185, the Taira were soundly defeated in a sea battle with the Minamoto clan. With the entire Taira clan slaughtered or drowned, Kenrei Mon'in threw herself into the waves with her son, the infant emperor; she was fished out – the only member of the clan to survive.

She was returned to Kyoto, where she became a nun living in a bare hut until it collapsed during an earthquake. Kenrei Mon'in was accepted into Jakkō-in Temple and stayed there, immersed in prayer and sorrowful memories, until her death 27 years later.

The convent itself is quite plain, its real beauty coming from the wooded glade in which it is set. Unfortunately, like many Japanese temples, the tranquillity of the place is shattered by periodic announcements, in this case, a version of Kenrei Mon'in's tragic tale read in a melodramatic voice.

Jakkō-in is open from 9 am to 5 pm and admission costs ¥500. Perhaps it's best to climb up to the entrance gate and look from there, as the admission price is quite steep considering the small size of the convent.

Kurama & Kibune 鞍馬・貴船

Located only 30 minutes north of Kyoto on the Keihan Eizan line, Kurama and Kibune are a pair of tranquil valleys long favoured by Kyotoites as places to escape the crowds and stresses of the city below. Kurama's main attractions are its mountain temple and onsen (hot spring). Kibune, over the ridge, is a cluster of ryokan overlooking a mountain stream. Kibune is best enjoyed in the summer, when the ryokan serve dinner on platforms built over the rushing waters of Kibune-gawa River, providing welcome relief from the summer heat.

The two valleys lend themselves to being explored together. In the winter, one can start from Kibune, walk 30 minutes over the ridge, visit Kurama-dera Temple and then soak in the onsen before heading back to Kyoto. In the summer, the reverse is best; start from Kurama, walk up to the temple, then down the other side to Kibune to enjoy a meal suspended above the cool river. If you happen to be in Kyoto on the night of 22 October, be sure not to miss the Kurama-no-himatsuri Fire Festival, one of the most exciting festivals in the Kyoto area (see the Special Events section for details).

To get to Kurama and Kibune, take the Keihan Eizan line from Kyoto's Dema-chiyanagi station. For Kibune, get off at the second-to-last stop, Kibune Guchi, take a right out of the station and walk about 20 minutes up the hill. For Kurama, go to the last stop, Kurama, and walk straight out of the station. Both destinations are ¥400 and take about 30 minutes to reach.

Kyoto bus No 32 also leaves from the Demachiyanagi station to both destinations but is much slower than the train. On Sunday and national holidays from 21 March to 30 November, Kyoto bus No 95 runs in the morning from Kurama to Ōhara for those who want to visit both areas in one day. The fare is ¥390.

Kurama-dera Temple In 770 the monk Gantei left Nara's Toshodai-ji Temple in search of a wilderness sanctuary in which to meditate. Wandering in the hills north of Kyoto, he came across a white horse which led him to the valley known today as Kurama. After seeing a vision of the deity Bishamon-ten, guardian of the northern quarter of the Buddhist heaven, he established Kurama-dera in its present location, just below the peak of Mt Kurama. Originally belonging to the Tendai sect, since 1949 Kurama has been independent, describing its own brand of Buddhism as Kurama Kyō.

The entrance to the temple is just up the hill from the Keihan Eizan line's Kurama station. Admission is ¥200 and it's open every day from 9 am to 4.30 pm. A tram goes to the top for ¥100 or you can hike up (follow the main path past the tram station). The trail is worth taking if it's not too hot, as it winds through a forest of towering old-growth cedar trees. At the top, there is a courtyard dominated by the Honden (Main Hall). Behind the Honden a trail leads off to the mountain's peak.

At the top, those who want to continue to Kibune can take the descending trail down the other side. It's a 30 minute hike from the Honden of Kurama-dera to the valley floor of Kibune. On the way down there are two mountain shrines which make pleasant rest stops.

Kurama Onsen Kurama Onsen, one of the few onsens within easy reach of Kyoto, is a great way to relax after a hike. The outdoor bath, with a fine view of Mt Kurama, costs ¥1000. The inside bath costs ¥2300, but even with the use of sauna and locker thrown in, it's difficult to imagine why one would opt for the indoor bath. For both baths, buy a ticket from the machine outside the door of the main building (instructions are in Japan-

ese and English). The onsen is open daily from 10 am to 9 pm.

To get to Kurama Onsen, walk straight out of Kurama station and continue up the hill past the entrance to Kurama-dera Temple. It's about 10 minutes on the right. There's also a free shuttle bus which runs between the station and the onsen which leaves about every 30 minutes.

Kibune Kibune's main attractions are its river-top dining platforms which are open from 1 June to the end of September. In addition to these, all the ryokan in the valley are open year-round and serve as romantic escapes for travellers willing to pay mid-level ryokan prices. **Kibune Shrine**, half-way up the valley, is worth a quick look, particularly if you can ignore the plastic horse statue at its entrance. Admission is free.

From Kibune you can hike over the mountain to **Kurama-dera Mountain Temple**, along a trail which starts halfway up the valley on the east side. For details on dining and lodging in Kibune see Places to Eat and Places to Stay.

BATHS
After a day spent marching from temple to temple, nothing feels better than a good hot

---

The Japanese Bath

The Japanese bath *(o-furo)* is another ritual which has to be learnt at an early stage and, like so many other things in Japan, is initially confusing but quickly becomes second nature. The all-important rule for using a Japanese bath is that you wash *outside* the bath and use the bath itself purely for soaking. Getting into a bath unwashed, or equally dreadful, without rinsing all the soap off your body, would be a major error.

Bathing is done in the evening, before dinner; a pre-breakfast bath is thought of as distinctly strange. In a traditional inn there's no possibility of missing bath time, you will be clearly told when to bathe lest you not be washed in time for dinner. In a traditional inn or a public bath, the bathing facilities will either be communal (but sex segregated) or there will be smaller family bathing facilities for families or couples.

Take off your *yukata* or clothes in the ante-room to the bath and place them in the baskets provided. The bathroom has taps, plastic tubs (wooden ones in very traditional places) and stools along the wall. Draw up a stool to a set of taps and fill the tub from the taps or use the tub to scoop some water out of the bath itself. Sit on the stool and soap yourself. Rinse thoroughly so there's no soap or shampoo left on you, then you are ready to climb into the bath. Soak as long as you can stand the heat, then leave the bath, rinse yourself off again, dry off and don your yukata. ∎

bath. Kyoto is full of *sentos* (public baths), ranging from small neighbourhood baths with one or two tubs to massive complexes offering saunas, mineral baths and even electric baths. Both of the following baths are worth a visit and could even double as an evening's entertainment.

Funaoka Onsen

This is an old bath on Kuramaguchi-dōri, which boasts an outdoor bath and sauna, as well as some museum-quality woodcarvings in the changing room (apparently carved during Japan's invasion of Manchuria, particularly interesting for history buffs). It's open from 3 pm to 1 am, closed Tuesday. Admission is ¥320. To find it, head west on Kuramaguchi-dōri from the Kuramaguchi/Horiikawa intersection. It's on the left not far past Lawson convenience store. Look for the large rocks out front.

Shomen-yu

This is perhaps the mother of all sentos. Three storeys high, with an outdoor bath on the roof, this is your chance to try riding an elevator naked (if you haven't already had the pleasure). Everything is on a grand scale here, including the sauna which boasts a TV and room for 20. Men, don't be surprised if you spot some *yakuza* gangsters among the bathers (instantly recognisable by their tattoos). It's open from 2 pm to 1 am with the exception of Sunday when it opens at 9 am and Tuesday when it's closed. Admission is ¥320. It's south of Gojō-dōri about 300m east of the Kamogawa River. Look for the sign in English and Japanese.

ACTIVITIES

There are loads of things to do in Kyoto beside visiting temples. In addition to shopping, people watching and hiking, the following three activities are all good ways to spend a day here.

Gekkeikan Sake Brewery Tour

The town of Fushimi, just south of Kyoto, is home to 37 sake breweries, the largest of which is Gekkeikan, the world's leading producer of sake. Although most of the company's sake is now made in a modern facility in Osaka, a limited amount of handmade sake is still made in an old *kura* (warehouse) here in Fushimi.

The brewery is open from 9.30 am to 4.30 pm, closed Monday. Admission is ¥300. If you are travelling with a tour group larger than 20 people and call two weeks in advance (☎ 075-623-2001) you can arrange a guided English tour of the brewery. Otherwise, ask at the TIC about joining a tour given in Japanese. To get there, take a Keihan local train to Fushimi Momoyama station and walk five minutes south-west.

Nishijin Textile Center

In the heart of Kyoto's Nishijin textile district, this is a good place to observe the weaving of fabrics used in kimonos and their ornamental belts called *obi*. There are also displays of completed fabrics and kimonos. It's on the south-west corner of the intersection of Horiikawa-dōri and Imadegawa-dōri. It's open daily from 9 am to 5 pm and admission is free (there is a ¥360 charge for certain special kimono displays). To get there, take bus No 9 to the Horikawa-Imadegawa stop.

Kyoto International Community House Cultural Demonstrations

The Community House offers a variety of introductory courses in Japanese culture which are open to all for observation and participation. These are: The Way of Tea (tea ceremony), Thursday from 2 to 4 pm, ¥1000; The Koto (a Japanese string instrument), Wednesday from 2 to 4 pm, no fee; Introduction to No, Thursday from 10 am to noon, no fee; and Introduction to Sencha (another kind of tea ceremony), Thursday from 2 to 4 pm, ¥1000.

Call ☎ 075-752-3512 to register (English speakers are usually on hand). The Community House is in eastern Kyoto about 500m west of Nanzen-ji Temple. Take bus No 'Higashi' (east) 9 from Sanjō-Keihan station, get off at the Keage stop and walk north (downhill) along the canal. Alternately, you

Beautiful kimonos are worn for the Gion Matsuri festival in Kyoto.

can take a Keishin line local street train from Sanjō-Keihan to Keage.

ORGANISED TOURS

Some visitors on a tight schedule find it convenient to opt for an organised tour of the city allowing them to see more sights than if they had gone on their own.

Two companies, Gray Line Kyoto Nara (☎ 075-691-0903) and JTB Sunrise Tours (☎ 075-341-1413), offer almost identical morning, afternoon and all-day tours. Morning and afternoon tours cost ¥5000, while all-day tours with a buffet lunch thrown in are ¥10,600.

A more intimate tour is offered by a private English-speaking tour guide named Hajime Hirooka, who calls himself Johnny Hillwalker. He takes small groups of travellers on walking tours of the city starting from Kyoto station and covering some of the sights in central and eastern Kyoto. Per person price is ¥2000 or ¥3000 per couple, though admission prices for museums and temples are extra. Call ☎ 075-622-6803 for details.

SPECIAL EVENTS

There are hundreds of festivals (Mimatsuri) spread throughout the year. Listings can be found at the TIC or in *Kyoto Visitor's Guide*, *Kansai Time Out* or in the weekend editions of the English-language newspapers available in Japan. The following are some of the major or most spectacular festivals. These attract hordes of spectators from out of town, sometimes twice as many as the resident population, so you need to book accommodation well in advance.

Aoi Matsuri (Hollyhock Festival)
  15 May. This festival dates back to the 6th century and commemorates the successful prayers of the people for the gods to stop calamitous weather. Today, the procession involves imperial messengers in oxcarts and a retinue of 600 people dressed in traditional costume; hollyhock leaves are carried or used as decoration. The procession leaves around 10 am from the Imperial Palace and heads for Shimogamo-jinja Shrine where ceremonies take place. It sets out from here again at 2 pm and arrives at Kamigamo-jinja Shrine at 3.30 pm.

Gion Matsuri
17 July. Perhaps the most renowned of all Japanese festivals, this one reaches a climax on the 17th with a parade of over 30 floats depicting ancient themes, which are decked out in incredible finery. On the three evenings preceding the main day, people gather on Shijō-dōri, many dressed in beautiful light summer kimonos, to look at the floats and carouse from one street stall to the next.

Daimon-ji Gozan Okuribi
16 August. This festival, commonly known as Daimon-ji Yaki, is performed to bid farewell to the souls of ancestors. Enormous fires are lit on five mountains in the form of Chinese characters or other shapes. The fires are lit at 8 pm and it is best to watch from the banks of the Kamogawa River or pay for a rooftop view from a hotel.

Kurama-no-Himatsuri Fire Festival
22 October. The origins of this festival are traced back to a rite using fires to guide the gods of the nether world on their tours around this world. Portable shrines are carried through the streets and accompanied by youths with flaming torches. The festival climaxes around 10 pm in the village of Kurama which is 30 minutes by train from Kyoto station.

Jidai Matsuri (Festival of the Ages)
22 October. This festival is of recent origin, dating back to 1895. More than 2000 people, dressed in costumes ranging from the 8th century to the 19th century, parade from the Imperial Palace to Heian-jingū Shrine.

PLACES TO STAY

Kyoto has a wide range of accommodation to suit all budgets. Choices range from the finest and most expensive ryokan in Japan to youth hostels and *gaijin* houses. Bear in mind that most of the cheaper places are further out of town. You can save time spent traversing the city if you organise your accommodation around the areas of interest to you. To help with planning, the following accommodation listings have been sorted according to location and price range. Gaijin houses usually offer reduced rates if you ask for weekly or monthly terms.

The TIC offers advice, accommodation lists and helps with reservations. Two useful TIC leaflets are *Reasonable Ryokan & Minshuku in Kyoto* and *Inexpensive Accommodations in Kyoto (Dormitory-Style)*.

PLACES TO STAY – BOTTOM END
Camping

The best place for this is along the Kiyotaki-gawa River between Kiyotaki and Hozukyō (see the Kiyotaki day walk in the Western Kyoto section for details on transportation). The river is crystal clear and runs through picturesque mountains. You can camp at the river and use nearby trains or buses for the 30 minute ride into town. For bathing, you can use the river or public baths in town. All in all, this is a very pleasant, realistic option from the beginning of April to the end of October.

Central Kyoto

Uno House (☎ 075-231-7763) is a celebrated gaijin house that provides you with the dubious privilege of a real grungy accommodation experience. The attraction is the price and the absence of youth hostel regimentation. Dorm beds start at ¥1650, and private rooms range from ¥2250 to ¥5400.

Take bus No 205 or Toku 17 – make sure the kanji character for toku or 'special' (特) precedes the number – from Kyoto station (bus terminal A3) to the Kawaramachi-marutamachi-mae stop. The trip takes about 20 minutes. You can also take the city subway, get off at the Marutamachi stop and walk east for 10 minutes.

Higher standards prevail at *Tani House Annexe* (☎ 075-211-5637), but it doesn't have dorm accommodation. It has singles for ¥6500, doubles with bath and air-con for ¥6500 and triples for ¥8000. Take bus No 5 from Kyoto station (bus terminal A1) and get off at the Kawaramachi-sanjō-mae stop. The trip takes about 20 minutes.

One other place worth checking out is *Tōji An Guest House* (☎ 075-691-7017). It's around 10 minutes walk from Kyoto station, and has dorm accommodation at ¥2060. There's no curfew here, but it's often full with long-termers.

Eastern Kyoto

Higashiyama Youth Hostel (☎ 075-761-8135) is a spiffy hostel which makes an excellent base very close to the sights of

Higashiyama. For a dorm bed and two meals, the charge is ¥4500. Private rooms are available for ¥5500 per person (including two meals). Bicycle rental costs ¥1000 per day.

This hostel is very regimented but if you're the kind of person who likes being in bed by 9.30 pm (tear the following Entertainment section of this chapter out of your book), this might be just your ticket. Meals are not a highlight, so you might prefer to skip them and find something more interesting in the town centre.

To get there, take bus No 5 from Kyoto station (terminal A1) to the Higashiyama-sanjō-mae stop (20 minutes). If you're in the Sanjō station area, you can walk to the hostel in 15 minutes.

ISE Dorm (☎ 075-771-0566) provides basic accommodation (42 rooms) at rates of ¥2800 per day or from ¥48,000 per month. Facilities on offer include phone, fridge, air-con, shower and washing machine. The place is noisy, dirty and the management is rude. On the plus side, there is usually a room available and arrangements for a stay can be made very quickly. By all means, take a look at the place before you check in.

Take bus No 206 from Kyoto station (bus terminal A2) to the Kumano-jinja-mae stop. The office is down a very small alley, so ask someone for directions once you get into the general area.

North-Western Kyoto

Utano Youth Hostel (☎ 075-462-2288) is a friendly, well-organised hostel which makes a convenient base for covering the sights of north-western Kyoto.

Like the Higashiyama Youth Hostel, everything is ordered: 10 pm curfew, 10.30 pm lights-out and 6.30 am wakey-wakey. The men's bath is a large jacuzzi. There's an international phone just outside the front door. The buffet breakfast is good value for ¥500. If you want to skip the hostel supper, turn left along the main road to find several coffee shops offering cheap set meals (teishoku). Rates are ¥2650.

Ask at the hostel's front desk about postage stamps, one-day travel passes, '11 bus tickets for the price of 10', postcards and discount entry tickets (to Sanzen-in Temple, Manshu-in Temple and Movieland). There's also a meeting room with bilingual TV news, but for many travellers, fond memories are reserved for the heated toilet seats!

Take bus No 26 from Kyoto station (bus terminal C1) to the Yūsu Hosuteru-mae stop. The ride takes about 50 minutes.

Northern Kyoto

Aoi-Sō Inn (☎ 075-431-0788) has singles for ¥2000, doubles and triples for ¥7000. It's reported to be a quiet place with no evening curfew, and a coin laundry and kitchen are available. The inn is near the old Imperial Palace, a five minute walk west from subway Kuramaguchi Shin-mei (exit 2) between the Kuramaguchi Hospital buildings. Call first to check directions and vacancies.

Tani House (☎ 075-492-5489) is an old favourite for short-term and long-term visitors on a tight budget. There is a certain charm to this fine old house with its warren of rooms, jovial owners and quiet location next to Daitoku-ji Temple. Costs per night are ¥1600 for a space on the floor in a tatami room and ¥3800 to ¥4400 for a double private room. There's no curfew and free tea and coffee are provided. It can become crowded, so book ahead. Take the 45 minute ride on bus No 206 from Kyoto station (bus terminal B4) and get off at the Kenkun-jinja-mae stop.

Kitayama Youth Hostel (☎ 075-492-5345) charges ¥2800 for a dorm bed (without meals) or ¥3700 with two meals. Take bus No 6 from Kyoto station (bus terminal B4) to the Genkoan-mae stop (allow 35 minutes for the trip). Walk west past a school, turn right and continue up the hill to the hostel (five minutes on foot). This hostel is an excellent base from which to visit the rural area of Takagamine which has some fine, secluded temples such as Kōetsu-ji, Jōshō-ji and Shōden-ji.

Guest House Kyoto (☎ 075-491-0880) has single rooms at ¥2500 per day or ¥40,000 for one month. Twin rooms are ¥4000 per day or ¥50,000 for one month. Take bus No

205 from Kyoto station (bus terminal B3) to the Senbon-kitaoji-mae stop (50 minutes).

Takaya (☎ 075-431-5213) provides private rooms at ¥4000 per day or from ¥50,000 for one month. Take the subway from Kyoto station to Imadegawa station (15 minutes).

Kyoto Ōhara Youth Hostel (☎ 075-744-2528) is a long way north out of town, but the rural surroundings are a bonus if you want to relax or dawdle around Ōhara's beautiful temples. A dorm bed costs ¥2300. From Kyoto station, you can take Kyoto bus (not Kyoto city bus) Nos 17 or 18 or from Sanjō station Kyoto bus Nos 16 or 17. Get off at the To-dera stop (near To-dera Temple). Both rides take about an hour and cost around ¥500. The TIC can give precise details for other train or bus routes to get you there.

West of Kyoto Station

Tani Guest House (☎ 075-681-7437, 075-671-2627) provides a dorm bed for ¥2000 and single/double rooms for ¥2500/4500. Monthly rates are ¥35,000 to ¥55,000. This is not connected with the management of the other Tani lodgings. To get there, take the JR line to Nishioji station (five minutes), then walk for 10 minutes.

PLACES TO STAY – MIDDLE
Central Kyoto & Station Area

Ryokan *Ryokan Hiraiwa* (☎ 075-351-6748), a member of the Japanese Inn Group, is used to receiving foreigners and offers basic tatami rooms. It is conveniently close to central and eastern Kyoto. Singles/doubles cost from ¥4100/8200 and facilities include bilingual TV, air-con and coin laundry. To get there from Kyoto station you can either walk (15 minutes) or take bus Nos 205, 42 or Toku (Special) 17 – make sure the kanji for toku precedes the number – from bus terminal A3. Get off at the third stop, Kawaramachi Shomen; from there it's a five minute walk.

Ryokan Kyōka (☎ 075-371-2709), a member of the Japanese Inn Group, has 10 spacious, Japanese-style rooms. Singles cost ¥4100 and doubles cost ¥8200. If you give

advance notice, a kaiseki dinner is available for between ¥3500 and ¥5000. It's about eight minutes on foot from Kyoto station, close to the Higashi Hongan-ji Temple.

Matsubaya Ryokan (☎ 075-351-4268) is a member of the Japanese Inn Group. Prices for singles/doubles are ¥4500/9000; triples cost ¥12,600. This ryokan is also close to Higashi Hongan-ji Temple.

Ryokan Murakamiya (☎ 075-371-1260), also a member of the Japanese Inn Group, is seven minutes on foot from Kyoto station. Prices for singles are ¥4000 and doubles ¥8000.

Riverside Takase (☎ 075-351-7920) is a member of the Japanese Inn Group and has five Japanese-style rooms. The cost for singles/doubles starts at ¥3300/6600; triples cost from ¥9000. Take bus No 205 from Kyoto station (bus terminal A3) and get off at the third stop, Kawaramachi Shomen.

The recently built *Pension Station Kyoto* (☎ 075-882-6200) is a member of the Japanese Inn Group and a quiet place. Prices for singles/doubles are ¥4200/10,000. Some rooms are available with baths for a slightly higher price. The pension is an eight minute walk from the station.

Yuhara Ryokan (☎ 075-371-9583) has a family atmosphere and a riverside location popular with foreigners. Prices for singles/doubles are ¥4000/8000 without meals. It's a 15 minute walk from Kyoto station.

Ryokan Hinomoto (☎ 075-351-4563) is a member of the Japanese Inn Group with a position right in the centre of the city's nightlife action. It's a small place that is a favourite with many frequent visitors to Kyoto. Singles cost from ¥4000 to ¥5500; doubles cost from ¥8000 to ¥9000 without meals. Take bus No 17 or 205 from Kyoto station (bus terminal A3) and get off at the Kawaramachi-matsubara-mae stop.

Hotels In general, hotels work out slightly more expensive than staying in a ryokan and have far less character. Still, they are generally a lot more flexible about the hours you keep and are not without certain advantages. The following suggestions are some of the more reasonably priced business hotels in the central Kyoto region:

Hokke Club Kyoto (☎ 075-361-1251) – singles cost from ¥7000 to ¥9000; twins from ¥12,000; opposite JR Kyoto station

Karasuma Kyoto Hotel (☎ 075-371-0111) – singles cost from ¥8800; twins from ¥16,000; doubles from ¥20,000; next to Shijō subway station

Kyoto Central Inn (☎ 075-211-1666) – singles/twins cost from ¥7000/11,000; next to Kawaramachi station

Kyoto Dai-Ichi Hotel (☎ 075-661-8800) – singles/twins cost ¥6800/13,500; 10 minute walk southeast of Kyoto station

Kyoto Dai-San Tower Hotel (☎ 075-343-3111) – singles cost from ¥6500 to ¥9500; twins from ¥11,000 and doubles from ¥15,000; five minute walk from JR Kyoto station

Eastern Kyoto

Ryokan Mishima (Mishima Shrine) (☎ 075-551-0033) operates as part of a Shinto shrine and is a member of the Japanese Inn Group. Singles/doubles/triples cost ¥4000/7000/¥10,500. On request, you can fulfil your photographic fantasy by dressing up in Shinto robes. Take bus No 206 (east-bound) from Kyoto station (bus terminal A2) and get off at the Higashiyama-umamachi-mae stop.

Pension Higashiyama (☎ 075-882-1181) is a member of the Japanese Inn Group. It's a modern construction by the waterside and convenient for seeing the sights in Higashiyama. Prices for singles/doubles are ¥4200/8400; triples cost ¥12,000. For a break from Japanese breakfast, you could try the pension's American breakfast (¥800). Dinner is also available for ¥2000.

To get there, take bus No 206 from Kyoto station (bus terminal A2) for an 18 minute ride to the Chioin-mae stop.

Ryokan Ohto (☎ 075-541-7803) is a member of the Japanese Inn Group, has a riverside location and charges ¥4000 for singles and from ¥8000 for doubles. You can get there via bus Nos 206 or 208 from Kyoto station (bus terminal A2) to Shichijō Ōhashi bus stop.

Not far from Kiyōmizu-dera Temple, the *Ryokan Sieki* (☎ 075-551-4911) is yet another member of the Japanese Inn Group

and has singles for ¥4500, doubles for ¥8000 and triples from ¥11,000. It's 15 minutes from Kyoto station (bus terminal A2) by a No 206 bus; get off at Gojō-zaka bus stop.

Three Sisters Inn (Rakutō-sō) (☎ 075-761-6333) is a popular ryokan, at ease with foreign guests. Singles go from ¥4900 to ¥12,800, doubles from ¥9800 to ¥16,000. Take bus No 5 from Kyoto station and get off at the Dobutsu-en-mae stop – the inn is just to the north of Heian-jingū Shrine. *The Three Sisters Annexe* (☎ 075-761-6333), close by, is run by the same management, and has singles for ¥10,000, doubles for ¥18,000, and triples for ¥24,000.

Iwanami (☎ 075-561-7135) is a pleasant, old-fashioned ryokan with a faithful following of foreign guests. It's right in the heart of Gion on a quiet side street. Book well in advance. Prices start at ¥9500 per person including breakfast. Take bus No 206 to the Chioin mae stop.

Uemura (☎ 075-561-0377) is a beautiful little ryokan near Kiyomizu-dera Temple at ease with foreign guests. Per person prices are ¥9000 with breakfast. You'll have to book well in advance as there are only three rooms. It's on Ishibeikōji-dōri, a quaint cobblestone alley. Take bus No 206 and get off at Yasui bus stop, then walk in the direction of Kōdai-ji Temple.

Kyoto Traveller's Inn (☎ 075-771-0225) is a business hotel, very close to the Heianjingū Shrine, offering both western and Japanese-style rooms. Prices for singles/twins start at ¥5500/10,000. There's no curfew and the Green Box restaurant on the 1st floor is open until 10 pm. Take bus No 5 from Kyoto station to the Dōbutsu-en-mae stop and walk north.

Northern Kyoto

Ryokan Rakucho (☎ 075-721-2174) is a member of the Japanese Inn Group. Prices for singles/doubles are ¥4500/8000.

The quickest way to get there is to take the subway from Kyoto station to Kitaoji station, walk east across the river and then turn north at the post office. To get there by bus, take bus No 205 from Kyoto station (bus terminal A3) and get off at the Furitsu-daigaku-mae stop.

Western Kyoto

Pension Arashiyama (☎ 075-881-2294) is a member of the Japanese Inn Group. Most of the rooms in this recently opened ryokan are western style. Singles/doubles are ¥4200/8400; triples cost ¥12,000. An American breakfast is available for ¥800.

To get there, take the 30 minute ride on Kyoto bus Nos 71, 72 or 73 and get off at the Arisugawa-mae stop.

PLACES TO STAY – TOP END
Central Kyoto
Ryokan Top-end ryokan accommodation in Kyoto is, as you might expect, very expensive. Listed here are some of the ryokan that occasionally have foreign guests.

Kinmata (☎ 075-221-1039) commenced operations early in the last century and this is reflected in the original decor, interior gardens, antiques and *hinoki* (cypress) bathroom. Rooms cost from ¥25,000 to ¥40,000 per person, including two meals. Advance reservation is essential. It's in the centre of town, very close to the Nishiki-kōji market – if you can afford to stay here, the cost of a taxi will be a financial pinprick.

Hiiragiya (☎ 075-221-1136) is another elegant ryokan favoured by celebrities from around the world. Reservations are essential. For a room and two meals, per-head costs range from ¥30,000 to ¥90,000. Close by, the *Hiiragiya Annexe* (☎ 075-231-0151) also offers top-notch ryokan service and surroundings but at slightly more affordable rates. Per-head costs start at ¥16,000 with two meals.

Tawaraya (☎ 075-211-5566) has been operating for over three centuries and is classed as one of the finest places to stay in the world. Guests at this ryokan have included the imperial family and royalty from overseas. It is a classic in every sense. Reservations are essential, preferably many months ahead. Per-head costs range from ¥35,000 to ¥75,000.

Hotels The up-market ryokan experience is not for everyone, and there are a number of high-class hotels in the central district.

Hotel Fujita Kyoto (☎ 075-222-1511) – singles cost from ¥9000 to ¥17,000; twins from ¥14,500 to ¥31,000; doubles from ¥23,000 to ¥31,000; five minute walk from Marutamachi subway station

Holiday Inn Kyoto (☎ 075-721-3131) – economy double for one/two persons costs ¥10,000/13,000; holiday doubles for one/two persons ¥10,000/14,000; free shuttle bus from south exit of JR Kyoto station

International Hotel Kyoto (☎ 075-222-1111) – singles cost from ¥9000 to ¥16,000; twins from ¥14,500 to ¥31,000; doubles from ¥23,000 to ¥27,000; 15 minutes by taxi from JR Kyoto station

Kyoto Century Hotel (☎ 075-351-0111) – singles cost ¥14,000; doubles from ¥18,000; five minutes walk from JR Kyoto station

Kyoto Grand Hotel (☎ 075-341-2311) – singles cost from ¥12,000 to ¥17,000; doubles from ¥21,000 to ¥27,000; 10 minute walk from JR Kyoto station

Kyoto New Hankyū Hotel (☎ 075-343-5300) – singles cost from ¥12,000 to ¥14,000; twins from ¥17,000 to ¥25,000; doubles from ¥22,000 to ¥26,000; five minute walk from JR Kyoto station

Kyoto Tokyū Hotel (☎ 075-341-0111) – singles cost from ¥14,000; twins from ¥23,500; doubles (only six) for ¥23,500; 15 minutes by taxi from JR Kyoto station

Kyoto Hotel (☎ 075-211-5111) – enormous new hotel, singles/twins/doubles cost from ¥16,000/25,000/31,000. Five minute walk from Sanjō Keihan station

Eastern Kyoto
Yachiyo (☎ 075-771-4148) is an elegant ryokan close to Nanzen-ji Temple. Prices per person for a room and two meals range from ¥20,000 to ¥40,000.

Miyako Hotel (☎ 075-771-7111) is a graceful, western-style hotel perched up on the hills and a classic choice for visiting foreign dignitaries. The hotel surroundings stretch over 6.4 hectares of wooded hillside and landscaped gardens. For a change from western-style rooms, you could try the Japanese wing. Singles range from ¥15,000 to ¥19,000 and doubles range from ¥21,000 to ¥38,000. Higher prices prevail on weekends.

KANSAI REGION

OTHER ACCOMMODATION
Shukubō

Shukubō or temple lodgings are usually in peaceful, attractive surroundings with spartan tatami rooms, optional attendance at early morning prayer sessions and an early evening curfew. Guests use public baths near the temples. There are quite a large number of shukubō in Kyoto, but generally they are not interested in taking foreigners who cannot speak Japanese. The shukubō listed here have English speakers on hand. For more information and a list of the shukubō in Kyoto, check with the TIC, where you can also pick up a copy of their handout entitled *Shukubos in Kyoto*.

The *Myōren-ji Temple* (☎ 075-451-3527) charges ¥4000 with breakfast. Take bus No 9 from Kyoto station (bus terminal B1) to the Horikawa-Teranouchi-mae stop. This pleasant temple is used to dealing with foreign guests.

The *Hiden-in Temple* (☎ 075-561-8781) charges ¥4500 with breakfast. Take bus No 208 to the Sennyuji-michi-mae stop; another approach is to take the JR Nara line to Tōfuku-ji station.

Women-Only Accommodation

Rokuō-in Temple (☎ 075-861-1645) provides temple lodgings for women only – it's in western Kyoto, close to Rokuō-in station on the Keifuku Arashiyama line. Per-person price is ¥4500 including breakfast. Ask at the TIC for further information on these places and more ideas on the range of lodgings for women.

PLACES TO EAT

Kyoto is famed for kyō-ryōri, a local variation on kaiseki cuisine. Kaiseki features a wide range of Japanese dishes, and great attention is given to service. Sake accompanies the meal, and rice is served last. As you might expect, it's a very expensive experience. A modest kaiseki course might cost ¥6000 per person, a full spread ¥15,000, and then there are exclusive establishments where you can shell out ¥50,000 (if you are

deemed fit to make a reservation). For lesser mortals with punier budgets, some restaurants do a kaiseki bentō (boxed lunch) at lunch time (11 am to 2 pm) at prices starting around ¥2000.

Another style of cooking for which Kyoto is renowned is shōjin ryōri. This is a vegetarian cuisine (no meat, fish, eggs or dairy products are used), which was introduced from China along with Buddhism and is now available in special restaurants usually connected with temples. As it is a cuisine that has its origins in Buddhist asceticism, don't expect a hearty dig-in affair – great attention is given to presentation and dishes tend to be small tasters. Tofu plays a prominent role in the menu and for a meal of this type, prices start at ¥2000.

The TIC's *Useful Information* sheet has a list of reasonable restaurants in town, as does the *Kyoto Visitors Guide*. Another source of restaurant tips is the *IGS Kyoto Guide*, which is produced by the Kyoto Chamber of Commerce. It also includes information on shopping and hotels and is available at the TIC. For gourmet dining, the TIC's *Kyoto Gourmet Guide* may be useful, but be prepared to spend a lot. Diane Durston's book *Old Kyoto: A Guide to Traditional Shops, Restaurants & Inns* (Kodansha, 1989), available at Maruzen bookstore, would be a handy companion for extended exploration of Kyoto's culinary pleasures.

Japanese Cuisine

Central Kyoto A good place to try kaiseki cuisine is *Uzuki* (☎ 075-221-2358) on Pontochō-dōri. It's an elegant place with a great platform for riverside dining in the summer. Set kaiseki courses start at ¥5000. It's open from 5 to 11 pm, closed Wednesday. Also on Pontochō-dōri is the izakaya *Zu Zu* (☎ 075-231-0736). This is a fun place to eat and drink and there is an English menu available, although many of the items available aren't listed on it. Perhaps the best bet is to point at what other diners are eating or ask the waiter for a recommendation. The fare is sort of nouveau Japanese – things like shrimp and tofu or chicken and plum sauce. Count on spending about ¥3000 per person.

For a delicious, filling lunch of noodles or donburi (rice served with a variety of toppings) try *Toroku* (☎ 075-231-7887). Their tannin donburi (rice with egg and beef) is a good choice for ¥850, as is kitsune soba (fried tofu with noodles) for ¥550. It's often packed with office workers so the best bet is to go during off-peak hours. It's open for lunch from 11.30 am to 2.30 pm and dinner from 5 pm to 8 pm, closed Saturday evening and Sunday.

Takasebune (☎ 075-561-6040) serves a fine tempura set for lunch or dinner in a classic old Japanese house behind Hankyu department store for ¥700/1500/2000, depending on the amount of tempura you'd like. The sashimi is also good and there's a simple English menu. Lunch is served from 11 am to 3 pm and dinner from 4.30 to 9.30 pm, closed Monday.

For good sushi in lively surroundings, head to *Tomi-zushi* (☎ 075-231-3628), near the Shinkyōgoku shopping arcade. Here, you rub elbows with your neighbour, sit at a long marble counter and watch as some of the fastest sushi chefs in the land do their thing. One person can fill up here for about ¥4000. It's open from 5 pm to midnight, closed Thursday. Go early or wait in line.

Near Skaraza theatre, *Kane-yo* (☎ 075-221-2020) is a good place to try a great Japanese favourite, grilled eel. You can sit downstairs with a nice view of the waterfall or upstairs on the tatami mats. The ¥800 kane-yo donburi set is about the cheapest you'll find anywhere – and it's good. It's open daily from 11.30 am to 3 pm. Look for the barrels of live eels outside and the wooden facade.

If you've never tried automatic sushi, don't miss *Musashi Sushi* (☎ 075-231-0691), at the junction of Sanjō-dōri and Kawaramachi-dōri. Here, you sit as a parade of sushi goes sliding by on multicoloured plates. The price of each item is written on the plate itself – red plates are ¥100, orange ¥190 and green ¥290. Sure, it's not the best sushi in the world, but it makes a good story. About

¥1500 is enough to fill you up. It's open daily from 11 am to 9.30 pm. Look for the mini-sushi conveyor belt in the window.

Further west on Sanjō-dōri, diagonally across from Sanjō post office, *Biotei* (☎ 075-255-0086) is a favourite of Kyoto vegetarians. Best for lunch, they serve a daily set of Japanese vegetarian/whole food for ¥850 (the occasional bit of meat is offered as an option, but you'll be asked your preference). Lunch from 11 am to 2 pm and dinner from 5 to 8.30 pm, and it's closed Sunday and Monday. It's open from 5 pm to midnight; closed on Sunday and Monday.

Near Sanjō bridge, *Ganko Sushi* is a good place for sushi or just about anything else. It serves elegant lunch sets from ¥1000 and dinners from about ¥3000 per person (there's a picture menu to ease ordering). It's open daily from 11.30 am to 10.30 pm. Look for the large display of plastic food models in the window.

North of Oike-dōri, there are some more interesting choices. For ramen, try *Shin-shin-tei* (☎ 075-221-6202), famous for its shiro (white) miso ramen (¥600). The place isn't much to look at but the ramen is excellent. It's open from 10.30 am to 5 pm, closed Sunday.

For excellent kushi-katsu (skewers of fried meat and vegetables) try *Ōiwa* (☎ 075-231-7667), just south of the Fujita Hotel. Ordering is easy, just ask for the course (30 skewers) and say 'stop' when you're full (you'll only be charged for what you've eaten; the whole course is ¥5000). It's open from 5 to 10 pm, closed Wednesday.

A little out of the way, but good value, *Obanzai* (☎ 075-223-6623) serves an all-you-can-eat vegetarian lunch for ¥820 and dinner for ¥2060 (slightly higher on weekends). Most of the ingredients are organically grown, a rarity in this country. It's open daily from 11 am to 9 pm.

For a truly raucous Kyoto izakaya (drinking restaurant) see *A-Bar* under the entertainment section.

Eastern Kyoto Starting from Sanjō station and walking east, you'll see two good choices for yakitori. The first, on the right just after the post office is *Ichi-ban Yakitori*

(☎ 075-751-1459), where there's an English menu and a friendly young owner to help with ordering. It's open from 5 pm to midnight, closed Sunday. Just look for the yellow-and-red sign and the big lantern. Further up the street, on the left side just before Higashiyama-dōri, look for the red lanterns outside *Dai-kitchi Yakitori* (☎ 075-771-3126). Although a little brightly lit for some people's taste, the yakitori is very good and the owner is friendly. It's open daily from 5 pm to 1 am. At both places, figure on about ¥3000 per person with beer or sake.

In the Higashiyama area, tucked inside the north gate of Maruyama-kōen Park, there's a traditional restaurant called *Hiranoya Honten* (☎ 075-561-1603) which specialises in the kind of food that was typical in land-locked Kyoto before the advent of refrigeration. It's called imobō, and consists of a type of sweet potato and dried fish. All meals are served in restful, private tatami mat rooms. An English menu is available and prices for a set meal start at ¥2400. It's open daily from 10.30 am to 8 pm.

If you walk north of Nanzen-ji Temple for a couple of minutes along the Path of Philosophy, you reach *Okutan* (☎ 075-771-8709), a restaurant inside the luxurious garden of Chōshō-in Temple. This is a popular place which has specialised in vegetarian temple food for hundreds of years. A course of 'yutōfu' (bean curd cooked in a pot) together with vegetable side dishes costs ¥3000. The restaurant is open from 10.30 am to 6 pm daily except Thursday.

For an experience you won't soon forget, try *Okariba* (☎ 075-751-7790), at the east end of Marutamachi-dōri, on the north side of the Sunflower Hotel. The name means hunting lodge and the place has a rustic, woody feel. The owner is an avid hunter and fisherman who serves much of his quarry. If it crawls, walks or swims, it's probably on the menu. The inoshishi (wild boar) barbecue is a good start. Non-meat eaters can try the fresh ayu (sweet river fish). Hoba miso is worth a try just for the presentation – it's thick miso cooked on a giant leaf over a *hibachi* right at your table, with assorted vegetables for dipping. More daring options include bear meat, venison, and even horsemeat sashimi (animal lovers look elsewhere). Those in need of a boost can try the hebi-iri-sake (sake with snake in the bottle). It's said to increase one's stamina (after the hangover wears off). If the master likes you, you'll probably be served the house speciality – candied insects (they're not that bad). The rule here is, don't eat anything until the master himself has a bite. Figure on about ¥4000 per person. Okariba is open from 5 to 11 pm, closed Sunday.

About five minutes walk from Ginkaku-ji Temple, and virtually opposite the Ginkaku-ji-mae bus stop, is *Omen* (☎ 075-761-8926), a noodle shop named after the thick, white noodles (omen) it serves in a hot broth with vegetables. At ¥900, the kamaage noodles are good value and the folksy decor is interesting – one drawback is that the place is often packed solid. It's open from 11 am to 10 pm daily except Thursday.

At the bottom of Nijō-dōri, on the east side of the Kamogawa River, *Chabana* (☎ 075-751-8691) is the classic okonomiyaki joint. If you don't have a favourite, just ask for the mixed okonomiyaki (¥700). Good for a late night snack, they're open daily from 5 pm to 4 am. Look for the rotating light outside.

International Cuisine

Central Kyoto Central Kyoto, in particular the Kawaramachi area, is excellent for digging up reasonably priced alternatives to Japanese fare. To get an idea of what's available, the best starting place is Nishi-Kiyamachi-dōri (the one with a small canal running through the centre of it) and the lanes that run off it. There's a wide range of international and Japanese restaurants in this area, many with English menus.

For inexpensive Italian food, top of anyone's list should be *Capricciosa* (☎ 075-221-7496). This successful chain is renowned throughout Japan for its affordable and authentic pasta and pizza, delivered in enormous portions. Two portions here are easily enough to feed three people. The main Kyoto store is a little south of the intersection of Sanjō and

Kawaramachi streets. It's open daily from 11.30 am to 10 pm. Another place with an English menu and English-speaking staff is *Daniel's* (☎ 075-212-3268) behind Daimaru department store; during the day only pasta dishes are available, but by night the menu sports a wide variety of both pasta and pizza dishes. You can eat well here from around ¥1500.

North of Oike-dōri, behind the Kyoto Hotel, *Merry Island* (☎ 075-213-0214) is a good place for coffee or a light lunch. This place is best in warm weather when they open the front doors and the place takes on the air of a sidewalk cafe. The music adds the final touch, usually something Latin. The lunch set is a good bet for ¥800. It's open daily from 11.30 am to 11 pm.

Eastern Kyoto *Buttercups* (☎ 075-751-9537) is a favourite of the local ex-pat community and a great place for lunch, dinner or a cup of coffee. The menu is international, most of the dishes discovered by the friendly, bilingual owner on his world travels. Try the Mexican rice for ¥580 or the vegetarian gado-gado for ¥850. For dessert, try their homemade cakes, pies and cookies. This is a good place to meet local residents and get inside information on Kyoto. It's open from 10 am to 11 pm, closed Tuesday. Look for the plants and the whiteboard menu outside.

On Marutamachi-dōri, near the Kyoto Handicraft Center, *Zac Baran* (☎ 075-751-9748) is another spot popular with Kyoto ex-pats. It's good for a meal or just a cup of coffee, particularly if you like jazz, which is always playing (sometimes a little too loudly). They serve a variety of spaghetti dishes as well as a good daily lunch special. In the evening, the place becomes more of a bistro, serving beer and wine. It's open daily from noon to 4 am. Look for the picture of the Fabulous Furry Freak Brothers near the entrance. While you're there, you may want to check out *Second House Cake Works* upstairs for good cakes, etc.

French food in Japan tends to be overpriced and adulterated to suit Japanese taste. *Le Zephyr* (☎ 075-752-8118) is a great exception to this rule. Hidden down a narrow alley only two minutes walk north-east of Sanjō Keihan station, the friendly owner of the place serves up hearty portions of authentic French food for very reasonable prices. His lunch set at ¥800 is tough to beat and dinners start as low as ¥1500. For dessert, try his homemade ice cream – the best we've had anywhere. Le Zephyr is open daily from 11.30 am to 11 pm. Look for the blackboard outside with the day's specials.

Northern Kyoto *Speakeasy* (☎ 075-711-5277) is a foreigner's hangout in Shūgakuin, famous as the only place in town for a real western breakfast. They also serve good tuna melts, tacos and burgers. It's open from 7 am to 2 am, closed Wednesday. Look for the large US flag outside.

On Higashiōji-dōri a few hundred metres north of Imadegawa-dōri you'll find *Didi* (☎ 075-791-8226), a friendly little vegetarian restaurant serving good Indian lunch/dinner sets from ¥800 as well as great breakfast sets of pancakes, muffins etc for ¥500.

ENTERTAINMENT

Most of Kyoto's cultural entertainment is of an occasional nature, and you'll need to check with the TIC or a magazine like *Kansai Time Out* to find out whether anything interesting coincides with your visit. Regular cultural events are generally geared at the tourist market and tend to be expensive and, naturally, somewhat touristy.

While geisha entertainment is going to be well out of reach of all but the fabulously rich, Kyoto has a good variety of standard entertainment options such as bars, clubs and discos, all of which are good places to meet young Japanese.

Traditional Dance & Theatre

Gion Corner (☎ 075-561-1119) presents shows every evening at 7.40 and 8.40 pm between 1 March and 29 November; it's closed on 16 August.

You should think carefully about whether tourist-oriented events of this kind are your scene before forking out the ¥2800 entry charge. While you get a chance to see snippets of the tea ceremony, Koto music, flower arrangement, gagaku (court music), kyōgen (ancient comic plays), Kyōmai (Kyoto-style dance) and bunraku (puppet play), you will be doing so with a couple of camera and video toting tour groups, and the presentation is a little on the tacky side. On top of this, 50 minutes of entertainment for ¥2800 is a little steep by anyone's standards. That said, if this is your only opportunity to dip into Japan's traditional entertainments and you have the cash, do it by all means – many people come away very pleased with the experience.

Dance The Miyako Odori (Cherry Blossom Dance) takes place four times a day throughout April at the *Gion Kōbu Kaburen-jō Theatre*, which adjoins Gion Corner. Maiko (apprentice geisha) dress elaborately to perform a sequence of traditional dances in praise of the seasons. The performances start at 12.30, 2, 3.30 and 4.50 pm. The cheapest ticket is ¥1650 (non-reserved on the tatami mat) and the ¥4300 ticket includes participation in a tea ceremony.

A similar series of dances, Kamogawa Odori, takes place from 1 to 24 May and from 15 October until 7 November at *Pontochō Kaburen-jō Theatre* (☎ 075-221-2025). Ticket prices start at ¥1650 (for a non-reserved seat on the 2nd floor). The ¥4300 ticket also includes participation in a tea ceremony.

Performances of *bugaku* (court music and dance) are often held in Kyoto shrines during festival periods. The TIC can provide information on performances.

Kabuki The *Minami-za Theatre* (☎ 075-561-0160) in Gion in central Kyoto is the oldest kabuki theatre in Japan. The major event of the year is the Kao-mise Festival (1 to 26 December) which features Japan's finest kabuki actors. Other performances take place infrequently and on an irregular basis. Those interested should check with the TIC. The most likely months for performances are May, June and September.

Nō For performances of nō, the main theatres

are *Kanze Kaikan Nō Theatre* (☎ 075-771-6114), *Kongō Nō Stage* (☎ 075-221-3049), and *Kawamura Theatre* (☎ 075-451-4513). Takigi-Nō is an especially picturesque form of nō performed with lighting from blazing fires. In Kyoto, this takes place in the evenings of 1 and 2 June at Heian-jingū Shrine – tickets cost ¥2000 if you pay in advance (ask at the TIC for the location of ticket agencies) or pay ¥3300 at the entrance gate.

Musical Performances Musical performances featuring the koto, *shamisen* and *shakuhachi* are held in Kyoto on an irregular basis. The same is true of gagaku court music. Check with the TIC to see if any performances are scheduled to be held while you are in town.

Bars
Kyoto has a wide variety of bars, from exclusive Gion clubs where it's possible to spend ¥100,000 in a single evening to grungy gaijin bars. In summer, many hotels offer rooftop beer gardens with all-you-can-eat/drink deals and good views of the city. The best of these is the *Sunflower Hotel* (☎ 075-761-9111), which is on the very eastern end of Marutamachi-dōri, where admission to the beer garden costs ¥4000 and includes an all-you-can-eat barbecue and all the beer you can drink. It's a little expensive, but the view from the roof is the best in town.

In any season, the best place to start the evening is at *A-Bar*, an izakaya (combination bar and restaurant) with a log-cabin interior. There's a big menu to choose from and everything's cheap. The staff here are famous for opening beer bottles with chopsticks or whatever else is handy and it's only a matter of time until a flying beer cap causes someone a major injury. Until that time, the place is great – the manager often strips down to a small towel and hurls profanities at the customers, the customers dance on the tables, that sort of thing. The best part is when they add up the bill – you'll swear they've undercharged you by half. It's a little tough to find – look for the small black-and-white sign at the top of a flight of steps just past Ōsho Chinese restaurant.

One of Kyoto's most popular gaijin hangouts is the *Pig & Whistle*. Like its counterparts in Osaka, it's a British-style pub with darts, pint glasses and (of course) fish & chips. The pub's two main drawcards are Guinness on tap and its friendly bilingual manager, Ginzo. Drunken giants should watch their heads on the rowing boat suspended from the ceiling. It's on the 2nd floor of the Shobi building, opposite Keihan-Sanjō station.

Less British and more American in style is *Pub Africa*. It's not as good a place to meet people as the Pig & Whistle, mainly because the video screens showing movies tend to dominate everyone's attention, but it's still a good place for an early evening beer and something to eat. The menu is only in Japanese.

Bar, Isn't It?, part of a chain based in Osaka, is popular with young Japanese and foreign men desperately searching for ... something. It's huge, loud and often very crowded. All the drinks are ¥500 and there's a sake bar at one end where you can sample a large variety of sake from all over Japan. Simple bar food is also served for those who want to pad their stomachs before drinking. Perhaps the biggest attraction is the sign near the entrance which reads 'Don't shit down here'.

On the northern end of Kiyamachi-dōri, *Rub-a-Dub* is a funky little reggae bar with a shabby tropical look and good daiquiris. It's a good place for a quiet drink on weekdays, but on Friday and Saturday nights you'll have no choice but to bop along with the crowd. Look for the stairs heading down to the basement beside the popular Nagahama Ramen shop.

Teddy's is part club and part bar. Early in the evening it's a quiet place for a drink and a bite of Indonesian food in faux-tropical surroundings. Later, the tables are cleared away and the dancing starts, usually to dance hall reggae. On weekend nights there's a cover of ¥500. Most of the drinks here are just a shade more expensive than at other bars. It's in the Empire building on the 7th floor.

Near Kyoto University, *Post Coitus* is worth a visit, not only for its unusual name. The interior decorations are an experiment in radical minimalism (you'll see what we mean). The lack of decorations are intended to make you concentrate on the drink at hand, and this place has plenty to choose from – a real connoisseur's haven. If it's not on the drink list it probably doesn't exist. It's 150m north of the intersection of Higashiyama and Imadegawa, on the east side down a small side street (turn at Fujii paint store).

On a little alley off Kiyamachi-dōri, one street north of Sanjō-dōri, *Backgammon* is a Kyoto institution. Small, dark and loud, it's a place for serious drinking. This is where the strange people come late at night. Check out the crow's nest drinking area at the top of the ladder – if you don't want to climb down for the next round, they'll send it up to you with a special drink elevator. It's open until dawn and the lack of windows in the joint guarantees that the first light of day will be a bracing shock when you stumble out of the door.

Real late-nighters might want to check out *Step-Rampo*, a 7th floor bar overlooking Kawaramachi-dōri. This place doesn't really get going until around 2 am and it's been known to stay open until way past dawn, when the morning light casts a strange pall over the drunks left dangling from the bar. It's on Kawaramachi-dōri, one building north of the Hagen Daaz building. While you're in the there, you might want to poke your head into *Bar Amnesia* on the 5th floor.

Clubs

Yeah, you can dance the night away in the cultural heart of Japan and give the temples and shrines a miss the next day while you sleep off your hangover.

One of the most popular places for this kind of thing is *Metro* (☎ 075-752-4765). It's part disco, part live house and even hosts the occasional art exhibition. Every night is a different theme (pick up a schedule in Rub-a-Dub), so it's a good idea to check ahead to see what's going on. Some of the best parties are Latin night, Diamond Night Transvestite Cabaret and Non-hetero-At-The-Metro night. Weekends usually feature an admission charge of ¥1500 to ¥2000 (with one drink), while Wednesday and Thursday are usually free. It's actually inside the No 2 exit of Keihan-Muratamachi subway station.

Another choice for dancing is *Louisiana Mama's*, part of the famous Bar, Isn't It? chain. This place gets packed on weekend nights with hordes of young people doing intricately worked out dance routines on table tops – you'll wonder if they meet to practise during the day. It's down the alley across from the more northern of the two big pachinko parlours on Kawaramachi. Also, check out *Teddy's*, listed under Bars, for one more dance spot.

THINGS TO BUY

The TIC provides shopping maps and can help you track down specialist shops. *Old Kyoto: A Guide to Traditional Shops, Restaurants & Inns* (Kodansha, 1989) by Diane Durston, available at Maruzen bookstore, is useful for finding unusual traditional items sold (and often produced) by elegant shops with vintage character.

There are several crafts which are specific to Kyoto. *Kyō-ningyō* are display dolls, *kyō-shikki* is lacquerware with designs formed using gold or silver dust, *kyō-sensu* are ritual fans made from bamboo and Japanese paper, *kyō-yaki* are ceramics with elegant decorations, *zogan* is a damascene technique laying pure gold and silver onto figures engraved on brass, *nishijin-ori* is a special technique of silk textile weaving and *kyō-yūzen* is a form of silk-dyeing.

The heart of Kyoto's shopping district is around the intersection of Shijō-dōri and Kawaramachi-dōri. The blocks running north and west of here are packed with all sorts of stores selling both traditional and modern goods. Kyoto's largest department stores (Hankyū, Takashimaya, Daimaru and Fujii Daimaru) are grouped together in this area. The 6th floor of Takashimaya is a good place for deals on pottery and kitchenware.

A smaller shop worth a look in this neighbourhood is the *House of Kajinoha/ Morita Washi* (☎ 075-341-1419) which sells a fabulous variety of handmade washi (Japanese paper) for reasonable prices. Nearby, both Teramachi and Shinkyōgoku shopping arcades offer a mix of tacky souvenir shops and more up-market stores. One store in the Teramachi Arcade definitely worth a visit is *Nishiharu* (☎ 075-211-2849), a dealer in wood-block prints. All of the prints are accompanied by English explanations and the owner is happy to take the time to find something you really like. It's on the corner of Sanjō and Teramachi streets.

North of city hall, the area around Teramachi-dōri has a number of classic old Kyoto shops and is pleasant for strolling and window shopping. Three shops well worth a look are: *Ippō-dō* (☎ 075-211-4321), an old-fashioned teashop selling all sorts of tea, open from 9 am to 7 pm, closed Sunday; *Kakimoto* (☎ 075-211-3481), a shop dealing in exquisite washi, open from 9 am to 6 pm and closed Sunday; and *Unsodo* (☎ 075-231-3613), a shop specialising in wood-block prints, open from 9 am to 5.30 pm and closed Thursday.

In eastern Kyoto, the paved streets of Ninnen-zaka and Sannen-zaka (close to Kiyōmizu-dera Temple) are renowned for their crafts and antiques.

If you want to do all your shopping under one roof, the following places offer a wide selection of Kyoto handicrafts. The *Kyoto Craft Center* (☎ 075-561-9660) near the Maruyama-kōen Park, exhibits and sells handicrafts and is open from 10 am to 6 pm daily except Wednesday. The *Kyoto Handicraft Center* (☎ 075-761-5080), just north of the Heian-jingū Shrine, is a huge cooperative which sells, demonstrates and exhibits crafts and is open from 9.30 am to 6 pm (wood block prints are a good buy here).

If you're interested in seeing all the weird and wonderful foods required for cooking in Kyoto, wander through Nishiki-kōji market. It's in the centre of town, one block north of (and parallel to) Shijō-dōri, between the shopping arcade of Shinkyōgoku and Karasuma-dōri. This is a great place to visit on a rainy day or as a break from temple-hopping. The variety of different foods on display is staggering and the frequent cries of 'Irasshiamase!' (welcome) are heart-warming.

While you're in Nishiki market, have a look in the knife shop *Aritsugu* (☎ 075-221-1091) near the northern end of the market. Here, you can find some of the best kitchen knives available in the world, as well as a variety of other kitchenware. It's open daily 9 am to 5.30 pm.

For an even more impressive display of foodstuffs check out the basements of any of the big department stores on Shijō-dōri (perhaps Takashimaya has the largest selection). It's difficult to believe the variety of food on display, as well as some of the prices (check out the ¥10,000 melons or the Kobe beef, for example). In these basement food emporiums you can really get a feel for the wealth of modern Japan.

Finally, not far from Kyoto station, *Kungyoku-dō* (☎ 075-371-0162) is a shop which has dealt in incense, herbs, spices and fine woods for four centuries. It's a haven for the olfactory senses, and is opposite the gate of the Nishi Hongan-ji Temple. It's open from 9 am to 7 pm but is closed on the first and third Sunday of each month.

Markets

On the third Saturday of each month, there is a flea market and general get-together of foreigners at the YWCA Thrift Shop, Muromachi-dōri, Demizu-agaru, Kamikyo-ku, Kyoto 602.

On the 21st of each month, there is a market fair, Kōbō-san, at Tōji Temple. On the 25th of each month, there's another market fair, Tenjin-san, at Kitano Tenman-gū Shrine. Arrive early and prepare to bargain.

GETTING THERE & AWAY
Air

Kyoto is served by Osaka Itami airport, which handles mostly domestic traffic, and the new Kansai international airport (KIX) which handles most international flights. There are frequent flights between Tokyo and Osaka – flight time is about 70 minutes – but unless you are very lucky with airport

connections you'd probably find it as quick and more convenient to take the *shinkansen*. There are ample connections to and from both airports, though the trip to Kansai international airport can be both expensive and time consuming.

Train

Kyoto to Osaka If you are loaded with money, or have a Japan Rail Pass, you can take the JR shinkansen line between Kyoto and Shin-Osaka – the trip takes only 16 minutes (¥1350). To connect between Shin-Osaka and central Osaka, you can take either the JR Tōkaidō (Sanyō) line or the Mido-suji subway line to Osaka station.

Those without a JR pass or money to burn should take one of the two private lines which connect Osaka and Kyoto. The Hankyū Kyoto line runs between Kyoto (Kawaramachi station) and Osaka (Umeda station – next to JR Osaka station). The fastest trip takes 47 minutes and costs ¥380.

The Keihan line runs between the Demachiyanagi station in northern Kyoto and Osaka's Yodoyabashi station, on the Midosuji subway line (convenient for connections with Shin-Osaka, Osaka and Namba). In Kyoto, it also stops at Sanjō (its main station), Shijō and Shichijō stations. The fastest trip from Sanjō to Yodoyabashi takes 40 minutes and costs ¥390.

The Japan Rail Pass is also valid on the JR Tōkaidō (Sanyō) line which runs via Osaka. The trip between Kyoto station and Osaka station takes 30 minutes and is ¥530 for a one-way ticket.

Kyoto to Nara Unless you have a Japan Rail Pass, the best option is the Kintetsu line linking Kyoto and Nara (Kintetsu Nara station) in 33 minutes by limited express (tokkyū) (¥1090 one way). If you take a local or regular express train on this line, the ticket price drops to ¥590 for the 45 minute ride, but you will need to change at Yamato-Saidai-ji which is a five minute train ride from Kintetsu Nara station.

The JR Nara line connects Kyoto with Nara JR station in one hour (¥740 one way).

Kyoto to Tokyo The JR shinkansen line is the fastest and most frequent rail link. The hikari super-express takes two hours and 40 minutes from Tokyo station and a one-way ticket including surcharges costs ¥12,970.

Unless you're travelling on a Japan Rail Pass or are in an extreme hurry, you'll probably be looking for a cheaper way to make the trip. Travelling by local trains takes around eight hours and involves at least two (often three or four) changes along the way. The fare is ¥7830, and you should call in to the TIC for details on the schedules and where changes are necessary for the particular time you are travelling.

Bus

JR buses run four times a day between Osaka and Tokyo via Kyoto and Nagoya. Passengers change buses at Nagoya. Travel time for the express buses between Kyoto and Nagoya is about 2½ hours (¥2200). The journey between Nagoya and Tokyo takes about 6¼ hours (¥5000). Other companies competing with JR on the same route include Meihan and Nikkyū. All buses run from the same point.

The overnight bus (JR Dream Bus) runs between Tokyo and Kyoto (departures in both directions). The trip takes about eight hours and there are usually two departures, at 10 and 11 pm. Tickets are ¥8030 plus a reservation fee. You should be able to grab some sleep in the reclining seats. If you find sleep a bit of a struggle, you can console yourself with the thought that you are saving on accommodation and will be arriving at the crack of dawn to make good use of the day. Buses run either to Yaesu bus terminal close to Tokyo station or to Shinjuku station.

Other JR bus possibilities include Kanazawa (¥3990), Tottori (¥3800), Hiroshima (¥5500), Nagasaki (¥11,100), Kumamoto (¥10,500) and Fukuoka (¥9500).

Hitching

For long-distance hitching, the best bet is to head for the Kyoto-Minami Interchange of the Meishin expressway which is about four km south of Kyoto station. Take the Toku No 19 bus (make sure the kanji for 'special' (toku) precedes the number) from Kyoto station and get off when you reach the Meishin expressway signs.

From here you can hitch east towards Tokyo or west to southern Japan.

GETTING AROUND
The Airport
Osaka Itami Airport There are frequent airport limousine buses running between Osaka airport and Kyoto station (the Kyoto station airport bus stop is on the south side of the building in front of Vivre department store). Buses also run between the airport and various hotels around town, but on a less regular basis (check with your hotel). The journey should take around 55 minutes and the cost is ¥1260.

Kansai International Airport The fastest, most convenient way between KIX and Kyoto is the special 'Haruka' airport express which makes the trip in 75 minutes for ¥3430. All seats are reserved on this train but can usually be purchased at the airport or Kyoto station on the day of travel. If you're leaving from KIX at an especially busy time, you might want to stop into a local travel agent to pick up your train tickets in advance to be sure of getting a seat.

If you have time to spare, you can save some money by taking the Kanku Kaisoku (express) between the airport and Osaka station and taking a regular Shinkaisoku (limited express) to/from Kyoto. The total journey by this method takes about 90 minutes with good connections and costs ¥1800.

Another cheap option is to go by limousine bus between Keihan Tenmabashi station and the airport and take the Keihan line to/from Kyoto. This way costs ¥1690 and takes about two hours with good connections.

For those travelling on Japanese airlines (JAL and ANA), there is an advance check-in counter inside the JR ticket office in Kyoto station. To use this service, you must already hold a train ticket to the airport.

Remember that there is a departure tax at

KIX of ¥2600 which must be paid in yen. It's a good way to get rid of that last loose change (and also a good way to get stuck if you're not prepared for it).

Bus

Kyoto has an intricate network of bus routes which provides an efficient way of getting around at moderate cost. Many of the bus routes used by foreign visitors have announcements in English. The core timetable for buses is between 7 am and 9 pm, though a few run earlier or later.

The main bus terminals are Kyoto station, Keihan-Sanjō station, Karasuma-Shijō-station and Imadegawa subway station in the north of the city. The bus terminal at Kyoto station is on the north side of the station and has three main departure bays (departure points are indicated by the letter of the bay and number of stop within that bay).

The TIC's *Kyoto Transportation Guide* is a good map of the city's main bus lines, with a detailed explanation of the routes and a Japanese/English communication guide on the reverse side. Since this map is intended for tourists it is not exhaustive. Those who can read a little Japanese should get a copy of the regular Japanese bus map available at major bus stops throughout the city.

Bus stops throughout the city usually display a map of bus stops in the vicinity on the top section. On the bottom section there's a timetable for the buses serving that stop. Unfortunately, most of this information is written in Japanese, and non-speakers will simply have to ask locals waiting at the stop for help.

Entry to the bus is usually through the back door and exit is via the front door. Inner city buses charge a flat fare (¥220) which you drop into the clear plastic receptacle on top of the machine next to the driver. The machine gives change for ¥100 and ¥500 coins or ¥1000 notes, or you can ask the driver.

On buses serving the outer areas, you take a numbered ticket (*seiri-ken*) when entering. When you leave, an electronic board above the driver displays the fare corresponding to your ticket number.

To save time and money, you can buy a *kaisū-ken* (book of five tickets) for ¥1000 at bus centres or from the driver.

There's a one-day pass (*ichinichi jōsha-ken*), which is valid for unlimited travel on city buses and is available for ¥700 at bus centres and subway stations. A similar ticket which also allows for unlimited use of the subways costs ¥1200. A two-day pass (*futsuka jōshā-ken*) is also available and costs ¥2000. The passes can be picked up in subway stations and the City Information Office.

Bus No 59 is useful for travel between the sights of north-western Kyoto and Keihan-Sanjō station. Bus No 5 connects Kyoto station with the sights of eastern Kyoto.

Three-digit numbers written against a red background denote loop lines. Bus No 204 runs around the northern part of the city and Nos 205 and 206 circle the city via Kyoto station. Buses with route numbers on a blue background take other routes.

When heading for locations outside of the city centre, be careful which bus you board. *Kyoto city* buses are green, *Kyoto* buses are tan and *Keihan* buses are red and white.

Subway

The quickest way to travel between the north and the south of the city is to take the subway, which operates from 5.30 am to 11.30 pm. There are eight stops, though the most useful ones are those in the centre of town. The minimum fare is ¥200.

Taxi

Kyoto is well-endowed with taxis. Fares start at ¥630 for the first two km. The exception is MK Taxis (☎ 075-721-2237) which start at ¥580. If you have a choice, always take an MK Taxi – in addition to being cheaper, the drivers are scrupulously polite and can often speak a bit of English.

MK Taxi also provides tours of the city with English-speaking drivers. For a group of up to four people, prices start at ¥12,620 for a three hour tour. Another company offering a similar service is Kyōren Taxi Service (☎ 075-672-5111).

Cycling

Kyoto is a great city to explore on a bicycle; with the exception of outlying areas it's mostly flat and there is a new bike path running the length of the Kamogawa River.

An excellent deal is offered by the Green Flag Matsumo rental shop (☎ 075-381-4991). If you call a day in advance (or get someone from your hotel or the TIC to do so), they will deliver a bicycle to your lodgings (or any other arranged meeting place) for ¥500. After that, daily rental fees are only ¥100. It's open 9 am to 5 pm and closed on Wednesday.

At Sanjō Keihan station, Kitazawa Bicycle Shop (☎ 075-771-2272) rents out bicycles for ¥200 per hour and ¥1000 per day, with discounts for rentals over three days. It's a 200m walk north of the station next to the river on the east side. A passport is necessary for rental, though one will suffice for a group. It's open daily from 8 am to 5 pm. Arashiyama station has several places for bicycle rental. Nippon Rent-a-Cycle is near Nishioji station, one stop from Kyoto station. Ask for a map to the store at the TIC. If you take the train, the rental shop will reimburse you for your fare. Expect rental rates of around ¥1100 per day, but different rates apply depending on the kind of bicycle. Both Higashiyama and Utano youth hostels offer bicycle rental.

Lake Biwa-ko 琵琶湖

Lake Biwa-ko, Japan's largest freshwater lake, dominates Shiga Prefecture. The lake has a variety of attractions easily visited as day trips from Kyoto or as stop-offs when travelling to or from Tokyo. Ōtsu and Hikone are the major sightseeing centres. Mt Hiei-zan and Enryaku-ji Temple are covered under Northern Kyoto in the earlier Kyoto section of this chapter.

JNTO publishes a leaflet entitled *Lake Biwa, Ōtsu & Hikone*, which has useful mapping and concise information. The Kyoto TIC has more detailed information on transport, sights and events in this region.

If you want to stay overnight near the lake rather than staying in Kyoto, the main centres for accommodation are Omi-hachiman, Ōtsu and Hikone. There are youth hostels dotted around the lake, for example, at Ōmi-imazu (☎ 0740-25-3018), Ōmi-hachiman (☎ 0748-32-2938) and Ōtsu (☎ 0775-22-8009).

ŌTSU 大津

Ōtsu (population 260,000) developed from a 7th century imperial residence (the city was capital of Japan for a brief five years) into a lake port and major post station on the Tōkaidō highway between eastern and western Japan. It is now the capital of Shiga-ken.

The information office (☎ 0755-22-3830) at the JR Ōtsu station is open from 8.45 am to 5 pm daily. Some English is spoken and they have an excellent, free map of the area entitled *Biwako Otsu Guide Map*.

Mii-dera Temple 三井寺

Mii-dera Temple, formally known as Onjō-ji Temple, is a 10 minute walk from Keihan Hama-Ōtsu station. The temple, founded in the late 7th century, is the head branch of the Jimon branch of the Tendai school of Buddhism. It started its days as a branch of Enryaku-ji Temple on Mt Hiei-zan, but later the two fell into conflict, and Mii-dera was repeatedly razed by Enryaku-ji's warrior monks.

Admission costs ¥450. It's open from 8 am to 5 pm but closes half an hour earlier between November and March.

Special Events

The Ōtsu Matsuri Festival takes place on 9 and 10 October at Tenson-jinja Shrine, which is close to JR Ōtsu station. Ornate floats are displayed on the first day and paraded around the town on the second day.

Getting There & Away

From Kyoto, you can either take the JR Tōkaidō line from Kyoto station to Ōtsu station (10 minutes, ¥190) or travel on the

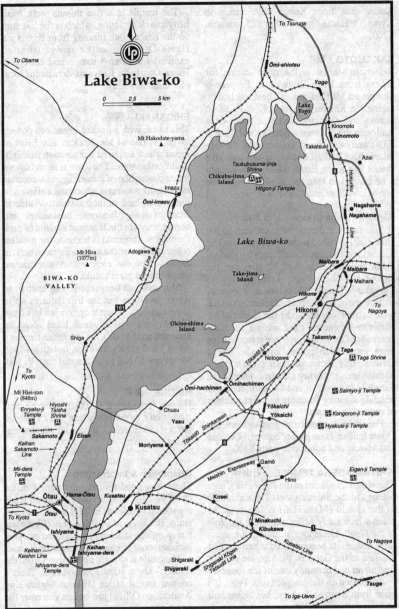

Lake Biwa-ko

0   2.5   5 km

To Obama

To Tsuruga

To Obama

Ōmi-shiotsu

Yogo

Lake Yogo

Kinomoto

Kinomoto

Takatsuki

Azai

Mt Hakodate-yama

Hokuriku Line

Tsukubusuma-jinja Shrine

Chikubu-jima Island

Hōgon-ji Temple

Imazu

Ōmi-imazu

Nagahama

Nagahama

Koseei Line

Lake Biwa-ko

Mt Hira (1077m)

Adogawa

Maibara

Maibara

Maihara

BIWA-KO VALLEY

Take-jima Island

Hikone

Hikone

161

To Nagoya

Okino-shima Island

Takamiya

Taga

Taga Shrine

Shiga

Tōkaidō Line

Notogawa

To Kyoto

Saimyo-ji Temple

Mt Hiei-zan (848m)

Ōmi-hachiman

Ōmihachiman

Yōkaichi

Yōkaichi

Kongoron-ji Temple

Enryaku-ji Temple

Hiyoshi Taisha Shrine

Chuzu

Yasu

Tōkaidō Shinkansen

Hyakusi-ji Temple

Sakamoto

Eizan

Keihan Sakamoto Line

Moriyama

8

Gamō

Mii-dera Temple

Meishin Expressway

Eigen-ji Temple

Hino

To Kyoto

Ōtsu

Ōtsu

Hama-Ōtsu

Kusatsu

Kusatsu

Kosei

Minakuchi

Kibukawa

To Kyoto

1

Ishiyama

Ishiyama

Keihan Keishin Line

Kusatsu Kōgen Tetsudō Line

To Nagoya

Keihan Ishiyama-dera Line

Ishiyama-dera Temple

Shigaraki

Shigaraki

Shigaraki Kōgen Tetsudō Line

To Iga-Ueno

To Tsuge

KANSAI REGION

Keihan line from Keihan-sanjō station in Kyoto to Hama-Ōtsu station (25 minutes, ¥300).

SAKAMOTO 坂本

Sakamoto station is the main station for access from Lake Biwa-ko to Enryaku-ji Temple on Mt Hiei-zan. It's best reached by taking the Keihan line from Kyoto's Sanjō station and changing trains at Hama-Ōtsu station to the Sakamoto bound local. Fare is ¥330 and with good connections the trip takes about half an hour. You can also take the JR line to the Eizan station in Sakamoto – be careful to take the Kosei (west of the lake) line (20 minutes, ¥310).

Hiyoshi Taisha Shrine 日吉大社

If you fancy a detour on your visit to Mt Hiei-zan, Hiyoshi Taisha (also known as Hie Taisha) is a 15 minute walk from the station. Dedicated to the deity of Mt Hiei-zan, the shrine became closely connected with Enryaku-ji Temple. Displayed in a separate hall are the *mikoshi*. (portable shrines) which were carried into Kyoto by the monks of Mt Hiei-zan whenever they wished to make demands of the emperor. Since it would have been gross sacrilege to harm the sacred shrines, this tactic of taking the shrines hostage proved highly effective. During the Sannō Matsuri on 13 and 14 April, there are mikoshi fighting festivals and a procession of mikoshi on boats.

The shrine is open from 9 am to 5 pm, but closes half an hour earlier between October and March, and admission costs ¥300.

ISHIYAMA-DERA TEMPLE 石山寺

This temple, founded in the 8th century, now belongs to the Shingon sect. The room next to the Hondō (Main Hall) is famed as the place where Lady Murasaki wrote the *Tale of the Genji*. Local tourist literature masterfully hedges its bets with the statement that the Tale of the Genji is 'perhaps the world's first novel and certainly one of the longest'.

Admission to the temple costs ¥400. It's open from 8 am to 5.15 pm but closes half an hour earlier in winter.

The temple is a five minute walk from Ishiyama-dera station, which is the last stop on the Keihan line running from Kyoto via Hama-Ōtsu. Take the *junkyū* (limited express) from Sanjō station and change at Hama-Ōtsu to the Ishiyama-dera bound local (40 minutes, ¥330).

SHIGARAKI 信楽

This town, with a limited interest to pottery lovers, is one of the Ancient Six Kilns of Japan which acquired a reputation for high-quality stoneware. The town is most famous for its production of *tanuki* figures – ceramic raccoon-like animals which are believed to bring good luck to their owners. Visible in front of many Japanese businesses and homes, they are the Japanese version of pink flamingos. Shigaraki is home to the greatest concentration of these figures anywhere in Japan – you can even eat in a restaurant shaped like a giant tanuki.

Shigaraki can be reached by JR train from Kyoto or Osaka but the trip requires up to three transfers. A better option is a bus from JR Ishiyama station which takes about an hour and costs ¥1000. On weekends there is a direct bus from Kyoto's Sanjō station which leaves at 9.40 and 11.25 am and costs ¥1300.

HIKONE 彦根

Hikone (population 99,000) is the second largest city in the prefecture and of special interest to visitors for its castle, which dominates the town.

Orientation & Information

There is a good tourist information office (☎ 0749-22-5540) on your left as you leave the station which has helpful maps and literature. The *Street Map & Guide to Hikone* has a map on one side and a suggested one-day bicycle tour of Hikone's sights on the reverse.

The castle is straight up the street from the station – about 10 minutes on foot. There's another tourist office (Hikone Sightseeing Association Office) just before you enter the castle grounds.

Hikone-jō Castle　彦根城

The castle was completed in 1622 by the Ii family who ruled as *daimyō* over Hikone. It is rightly considered one of the finest remaining castles in Japan – much of it is original – and there is a great view across the lake from the upper storeys. The castle is surrounded by more than 1000 cherry trees, making it a popular spot for spring-time *hanami* activities.

Admission costs ¥500 and includes entry to Genkyū-en Garden. Remember to hang onto your ticket if you plan to visit the garden. The castle is open from 8.30 am to 5 pm but closes half an hour earlier from November to March.

Next to the main gate of the castle is Hikone-jō Castle Museum. Items on display came from the Ii family and include armour, nō costumes, pottery and calligraphy. Admission costs ¥500 and it's open from 9 am to 4 pm.

Genkyū-en Garden, below the castle, is beautiful. Buy yourself a bag of fish food for ¥20 at the gate and copy the other visitors who save the bloated carp the effort of movement by lobbing morsels straight into their blubbery lips. It's a tough life being an ornamental carp in Japan! Entry to this garden is included in the admission ticket for the castle.

Other Attractions

If you have more time in Hikone, you can follow the cycling route in the *Street Map & Guide to Hikone*. The route passes through the old town to the west of the castle, then south-west via Ichiba (Market Street) to **Kawaramachi**. There you can take a look at a candle-maker's shop (this is also the bar and nightlife district for Hikone) and then crosses to the other side of the Seri River.

From there, you can cross the town and visit a couple of Zen temples in the south-east. The most interesting of these is **Ryōtan-ji Temple**, which has a fine Zen garden. Admission to the temple costs ¥300 and it's open from 9 am to 5 pm but closes an hour earlier between December and February.

Cruises

There are departures from Hikone to Chikubu-jima Island four times daily (¥3240, return – rather pricey given that it's only a 35 minute trip). There are also several daily departures to Take-jima Island (30 minutes, ¥1700).

Special Events

Hikone-jō Matsuri takes place at the castle on 3 November. Children dress up in the costume of feudal lords and parade around the area.

Getting There & Away

Hikone is only one hour (¥1090) from Kyoto on the JR Tōkaidō line. If you take the shinkansen, the best method is to ride from Kyoto to Maibara (25 minutes) and then backtrack from there on the JR Tōkaidō line to Hikone (10 minutes). Maibara is useful to travellers as a major rail junction for the JR Tōkaidō line, JR Hokuriku line and JR shinkansen line. From Osaka it takes one hour and 45 minutes (¥1850) on the Tōkaidō line to Hikone.

NAGAHAMA　長浜

Nagahama's main claim to fame is the Nagahama Hikiyama Matsuri held from 14 to 26 April. Costumed children perform Hikiyama kyōgen (comic drama) on top of a dozen festival floats which are decked out with elaborate ornamentation.

Nagahama is a 10 minute ride north of Maibara on the JR Hokuriku line. From Nagahama frequent boats make the 25 minute trip to Chikubu-jima Island.

CHIKUBU-JIMA ISLAND　竹生島

This tiny island is famed for its **Tsukubu-suma-jinja Shrine** and the **Hōgon-ji Temple** which is one of those included on the Kansai Kannon temple pilgrimage.

The island is connected by boat with Hama-Ōtsu, Hikone, Nagahama and Ōmi-imazu. Prices and departure times tend to vary so check them with the Kyoto TIC or the Hikone tourist information office.

KANSAI REGION

Osaka 大阪

Osaka and Kyoto represent the poles of the Japanese experience – Kyoto a reminder of Japan's elegant past, Osaka a bustling showcase of its present. While Kyotoites are nationally famous for their refined manners and cool demeanour, Osakans pride themselves on their down-to-earth manners and boisterous ways.

Nowhere is all this more evident than in the dialects of each city – real Kyoto-ben (dialect) is almost baroque in its formality, while Osaka-ben is as gritty as London cockney. So colourful is Osaka speech that aspiring Japanese comedians must do an apprenticeship here in order to learn it. For all these reasons, Osaka is the place to refresh yourself after an overdose of high culture in the old capital.

First and foremost, Osaka is a working city – so much so that locals commonly greet each other with the question, 'Moo kari makka?' ('Are you making any money?'). Without question, Osaka is making money. Last year Osaka recorded a gross domestic product greater than those of all but eight countries in the world (including such countries as Australia and Mexico). This remarkable economic success has its roots deep in the history of the city, for Osaka was the merchant capital of Japan long before Tokyo was even incorporated as a city.

This isn't to say that Osaka is an attractive city. Almost bombed flat in WWII, it appears an endless expanse of ugly concrete boxes punctuated by pachinko parlours and elevated highways. If you go looking for beauty, Osaka will surely disappoint. What Osaka offers is a chance to enjoy what ordinary Japanese enjoy – good food and drink in a rowdy atmosphere. The Osakans call it *kuidaore*, which means eat until you drop. Osaka presents ample opportunities to do just that, with thousands of restaurants lining its cramped streets. There are also stores of every sort, from thrift shops selling single shoes to the most elegant boutiques, and there are bars to rival the best Tokyo has to offer.

HISTORY

Osaka has been a major port and mercantile centre from the beginning of Japanese recorded history. It was also, for a brief period, the first capital of Japan (before the establishment of a permanent capital at Nara). During its early days, Osaka was Japan's centre for trade with Korea and China, a role which it shares today with Kobe and Yokohama. So important was Osaka as a window to the world that in the 6th century Prince Shotoku Taishi ordered Shitennō-ji Temple built near the Osaka Bay to impress visiting dignitaries from China.

Being a major centre for foreign trade, Osaka has always had a large foreign population. Indeed, Heian period censuses show the presence of large numbers of Korean and Chinese nationals living in the city. The cosmopolitan nature of the city can still be felt today, particularly in neighbouring Kobe, where many of the foreigners moved with the establishment of the port there.

In the late 16th century, Osaka rose to prominence as Toyotomi Hideyoshi, having unified all of Japan, chose Osaka as the site for his castle. Merchants set up around the castle and the city quickly grew into a busy economic centre. This was further encouraged by the Tokugawa shogunate which adopted a hands-off approach to the city, allowing merchants to prosper unmolested by government interference.

In the modern period, Tokyo has usurped Osaka's position as economic centre of Japan, and most of the companies formerly headquartered in Osaka have moved east. Nonetheless, with a GDP of US$391 billion, the city is still a vast economic powerhouse, as all the factories on the outskirts of the city will attest. Some have even gone so far as to suggest that in the event of a major earthquake in Tokyo, Osaka might once again become the capital of Japan.

ORIENTATION

Umeda, in Kita-ku, the northern ward, and Shinsaibashi and Namba, in Minami-ku, the southern ward, each have distinct features. Kita-ku is the business part of town with a

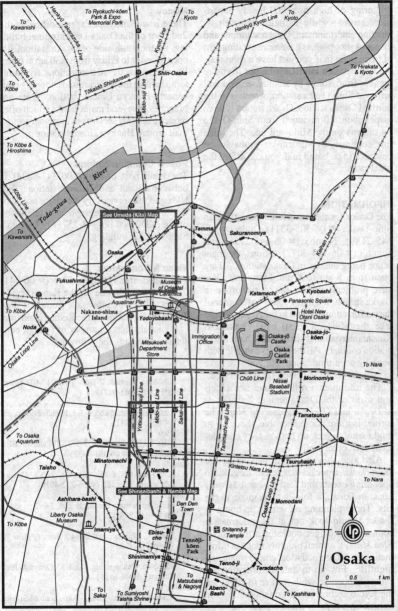

To Kawanishi

Hankyū Takarazuka Line

To Ryokuchi-kōen
Park & Expo
Memorial Park

To Kyoto

Kyoto Line

Hankyū Kyoto Line

To Kyoto

To Hirakata
& Kyoto

To Kōbe

Hankyū Kōbe Line

Tōkaidō Shinkansen

Midō-suji Line

Shin-Osaka

To Kōbe &
Hiroshima

Kōbe Line

River

Yodo-gawa

To Kawanishi

See Umeda (Kita) Map

Temma

Sakuranomiya

Keihan Line

Osaka

Fukushima

Museum
of Oriental
Ceramics

Aqualiner Pier

Katamachi

Kyobashi

Panasonic Square

To Kōbe

Nakano-shima
Island

Yodoyobashi

Hotel New
Otani Osaka

Noda

Osaka Loop Line

Mitsukoshi
Department
Store

Immigration
Office

Osaka-jō Castle

Osaka-jō-
kōen

Osaka
Castle
Park

To Nara

Chūō Line

Nissei
Baseball
Stadium

Morinomiya

Yotsubashi-suji Line

Midō-suji Line

Sakai-suji Line

Tanimachi-suji Line

Tamatsukuri

To Osaka
Aquarium

Minatomachi

Namba

Kintetsu Nara Line

Tsuruhashi

Taisho

To Nara

Ashihara-bashi

See Shinsaibashi & Namba Map

Den Den
Town

Momodani

Liberty Osaka
Museum

Imamiya

Ebisu-
cho

Osaka Loop Line

Shitennō-ji
Temple

To Kōbe

Tennōji-
kōen
Park

To Kashihara

Shinimamiya

Tennō-ji

Teradacho

Osaka

To
Sakai

To Sumiyoshi
Taisha Shrine

To Matsubara
& Nagoya

Abeno
Bashi

0   0.5   1 km

scattering of high-rises and trendy department stores, while Minami-ku, with its bustling entertainment, great restaurants and discount shopping, is a far more exciting part of town to be in if you just have a short stay.

Osaka station is in Umeda, but if you're coming from Tokyo by shinkansen you will arrive at Shin-Osaka station, which is to the north of Osaka station. Osaka station is three stops (about 10 minutes) from Shin-Osaka by subway on the Mido-suji line. The same line continues to Minami-ku, probably the best area to be based in if you can afford the hotel rates.

INFORMATION

The Osaka Tourist Association has offices in Shin-Osaka (☎ 06-305-3311), Osaka (☎ 06-345-2189), Namba (☎ 06-643-2125) and Tennōji (☎ 06-774-3077) stations, the main office being the one in Osaka station. All are open from 8 am to 8 pm. Many travellers have problems finding the tourist office in Osaka station. It's in the south-east corner of the station complex, and to find it you should take the Midōsuji (east) exit. Osaka and Kansai international airports also have information counters. All the offices can help with booking accommodation, but you will have to visit the office in person for this service.

The information offices have two excellent maps of the Osaka region, *Your Guide to Osaka* and *Osaka Sightseeing Map*. The former is more comprehensive, though you might want to pick up both as they complement each other well.

Also available and worth picking up are *Meet Osaka*, a pocket-size reference guide to upcoming events and festivals, and *Subway Lines in Osaka*, a fold-out rail guide to the city. Those planning on setting up house in Osaka should look out at the information counters and bigger bookstores for *Kansai Flea Market*, a small monthly that has information on accommodation, employment and nightlife. For up-to-date information on events happening while you're in town, see the Kyoto section for information on where to pick up a copy of *Kansai Time Out*.

Money

There is an American Express office on the 2nd floor of the Osaka Daiichiseimei building, on the south side of Osaka station. It's open Monday to Friday from 9.30 am to 6 pm. For international card transactions, try Sumitomo bank in the underground shopping mall beneath Hankyu Umeda station. There are branches of several major banks which offer money changing services in the underground mall around Hankyu Umeda station.

Post & Communications

The main post office (☎ 06-347-8034) is between Osaka and Umeda stations. For telex and fax services try the major hotels or the international telegraph and telephone office (KDD) (☎ 06-343-2571) in Umeda's Shin-Hanshin building.

Visas & Consulates

The Osaka immigration office (☎ 06-941-0771) is the main one for the Kansai region and is a three minute walk from exit 3 of Temmabashi station on the Keihan main line.

Osaka also has a number of foreign consulates, including the following:

Australia
    Chūō-ku, Shiromi, 2-1-61, Twin 21 MID Tower 33F (☎ 06-941-9271)
Austria
    Chūō-ku, Kyūtarō-chō, 4-1-3, Itochū-shōji co, nai (☎ 06-241-3011)
Belgium
    Kita-ku, Nishitenma, 5-9-3, Takahashi Biru Honkan 8F (☎ 06-361-9432)
Canada
    Chūō-ku, Nishi shinsaibashi, 2-2-3, Daisan Matsutoyo Biru 12F (☎ 06-212-4910)
China
    Nishi-ku, Utsubo honmachi-chō, 3-9-2 (☎ 06-445-9481)
Denmark
    Kita-ku, Dōjimahama, 2-1-40, Suntory Biru 3F (☎ 06-346-1285)
France
    Chūō-ku, Kitahama higashi, 4-33, Ōbayashi Biru 24F (☎ 06-946-6181)
India
    Chūō-ku, Kyūtarō-chō, 1-9-26, Senba I.S. Biru 10F (☎ 06-261-7299)

Italy

> Chūō-ku, Shiromi, 2-1-61, Twin 21 MID Tower 31F (☎ 06-949-2970)

UK

> Chūō-ku, Hakurō-chō, 3-5-1, Seikō Osaka Biru 19F (☎ 06-281-1616)

USA

> Kita-ku, Nishitenma, 2-11-5 (☎ 06-315-5900)

Bookshops

There are branches of Kinokuniya and Maruzen in Osaka, and the huge Books Asahiya in Umeda (about five minutes walk from Osaka station) has a reasonable selection of English-language books, as well as a limited selection of German publications on its 4th floor. Kinokuniya, which probably has the best selection of foreign books, is inside Hankyū Umeda station.

CENTRAL OSAKA
Osaka-jō Castle 大阪城

Osaka's foremost attraction is unfortunately a 1931 concrete reproduction of the original. The castle's exterior retains a certain grandeur but the interior looks like a barn with lifts. The original castle, completed in 1583, was a display of power on the part of Toyotomi Hideyoshi. After he achieved his goal of unifying Japan, 100,000 workers toiled for three years to construct an 'impregnable' granite castle. However, it was destroyed just 32 years later in 1615 by the armies of Tokugawa Ieyasu.

Within 10 years the castle had been rebuilt by the Tokugawa forces, but it was to suffer a further calamity when another generation of Tokugawas razed it to the ground rather than let it fall to the forces of the Meiji

KANSAI REGION

Osaka Castle, built in 1931, is a concrete reproduction; the original was completed in 1583.

Restoration in 1868. The interior of today's castle houses a museum of Toyotomi Hideyoshi memorabilia as well as displays relating the history of the castle. They are of marginal interest but the 8th floor provides a view over Osaka. The castle is open from 9 am to 5 pm daily and admission is ¥500.

On Sunday, you might want to check out the music scene which takes place along the road leading from the Morinomiya JR Loop Line stop to the park. Here, local bands gather to play music/offend the elderly in Osaka's version of the Tokyo Harajuku park scene. It's noisy and most of the music is pretty bad, but for people watching it can't be beat. It usually starts at noon and ends at 6 pm.

The Ōte-mon Gate, which is the entrance to the park, is about a 10 minute walk northeast of Tanimachi-yonchōme station on the Chūō and Tanimachi subway lines. From the JR Osaka Loop Line (Kanjo-sen) that circles the city, get off at Morinomiya station and look for the castle grounds a couple of minutes to the north-west. You enter through the back of the castle.

Shitennō-ji Temple　四天王寺

Shitennō-ji Temple, founded in 593, has the distinction of being one of the oldest Buddhist temples in Japan, but none of the present buildings are originals.

Most are the usual concrete reproductions, a notable exception being the big stone torii (entrance gate), quite an unusual feature for a Buddhist temple. It dates back to 1294, making it the oldest of its kind in Japan. Apart from the torii, there is little of real historical significance, and the absence of greenery in the raked-gravel grounds makes for a rather desolate atmosphere.

The temple is open from 9 am to 5 pm daily. Entry to the temple is free and the adjoining museum costs ¥200 (though it's of limited interest). It's most easily reached from Shitennōji-mae station on the Tanimachi subway line. Take the southern exit, cross to the left side of the road and take the small road that goes off at an angle away from the subway station. The entrance to the temple is on the left.

Tennōji-kōen Park　天王寺公園

About a 10 minute walk from the temple with which it partly shares its name, this park can be combined with a visit to Shitennō-ji Temple.

The park has a botanical garden, a zoo and a circular garden known as Keitaku-en. The latter is open from 9.30 am to 9 pm in July and August and closes at 5 pm the rest of the year. It's closed Monday. The park is a 10 minute walk from Tennō-ji station on the JR Osaka Loop Line (Kanjo-sen). To get there from the Shitennō-ji Temple, exit through the torii, turn left, then right, then left again into the main road and look for the park on your right.

Sumiyoshi Taisha Shrine　住吉大社

This shrine is dedicated to Shinto deities associated with the sea and sea travel, in commemoration of a safe passage to Korea by a 3rd century empress.

Having survived the bombing in WWII, the Sumiyoshi Taisha Shrine actually has a couple of buildings that date back to 1810. The shrine was founded in the early 3rd century and the buildings that can be seen today are faithful replicas of the originals. They offer a rare opportunity to see a Shinto shrine that predates the influence of Chinese Buddhist architectural styles.

The main buildings are roofed with a kind of thatch rather than the tiles on most later shrines. Other interesting features are a collection of more than 700 stone lanterns donated by seafarers and business people, a stone stage for performances of bugaku and court dancing and the attractive Taiko-bashi Bridge, an arched bridge with park surroundings.

The shrine is open every day from 6.30 am to 5 pm and admission is free. It's next to both Sumiyoshi-taisha station on the Nankai line and Sumiyoshi-tori-mae station on the Hankai line.

KITA-KU　キタ

There's not a lot to do in Kita-ku and if you've passed through the area on your arrival that might be enough to get a feel for what the northern part of town is about.

Umeda Sky Building

Just north-west of Osaka station, the Umeda Sky building is a twin-tower complex with the two towers joined at the top. Residents of Osaka are sharply divided about its appearance: some love its futuristic look while others find it an eyesore. What is certain is that the view from the top on a clear day is impressive.

There are two observation galleries, an outdoor one on the roof and an indoor one on the floor below. Getting to the top is half the fun as you take a glassed-in escalator for the final five storeys (definitely not for vertigo sufferers). There is also a Chinese restaurant and bar at the top where the prices reflect the choice location. The observation decks are open all year from 10 am to 10.30 pm and entry (including the white-knuckled escalator ride) costs ¥1000. Tickets for the observation decks can be purchased on the 3rd floor of the east tower.

The restaurant and bar can be reached for free by a conventional elevator. You can walk to the building through an underground passage which heads due north from Osaka or Umeda station, or take the JR Osaka Loop Line (Kanjo-sen) and get off at Fukushima station.

Umeda Chika Centre

This labyrinthine underground shopping arcade is so complex even long term residents have trouble finding their way around. After a few hours of wandering, you may wish you had brought a spool of thread to find your way back to your starting point. Nonetheless, getting lost is half the fun and you'll have a chance to check out every variety of store and restaurant. The complex links Osaka station with Umeda station and can be entered from either station.

Museum of Oriental Ceramics

With more than 1000 exhibits, this museum is said to have one of the finest collections of Chinese and Korean ceramics in the world. Opening hours are from 9.30 am to 5 pm daily (closed on Monday) and admission is ¥400.

To get to the museum, go to Yodoyabashi station on either the Mido-suji line or the Keihan line (different stations). Walk north to the river and cross to Nakano-shima Island. Turn right, pass the city hall on your left, bear left with the road and the museum is on the left.

Panasonic Square パナソニックスクエア

Billed as a 'Futuristic Electro-Fun Zone', Panasonic Square is a display forum for high-tech gadgetry developed by the Matsushita Electric Group of companies. It's very much hands-on and quite fun if you haven't already been to a similar place in Japan. Highlights include the Starforce virtual reality game and a CD jukebox that you enter and request songs from by punching in a number.

In the same building, on the 1st floor, there is an Internet 'square' where cyber-starved travellers can log on for the steep rate of ¥1000 per hour (10 am to 8 pm, closed Monday).

Panasonic Square is open daily from 10 am to 6 pm, and admission is ¥500. The easiest way to get there is to take the Keihan line to Kyōbashi station, take the southern exit, cross the river and turn right. Panasonic Square is on the 2nd floor of the Twin 21 Tower building.

MINAMI-KU ミナミ

This part of town south of Shinsaibashi subway station (on the Mido-suji line) is fun just to wander around but it really doesn't come into its own until night falls and the blaze of neon charges the atmosphere. North of Dōtomburi-dōri, between Midosuji-dōri and Sakaisuji-dōri, the narrow streets are crowded with hostess bars, discos and pubs. Expensive cars clog the streets, hostesses dressed in kimono and *geta* trot a few steps behind flushed businessmen, and young salarymen stagger around in drunken packs.

Amerika-Mura アメリカ村

Amerika-mura, or America village, is a compact enclave of trendy shops and restaurants, with a few discreet love hotels thrown

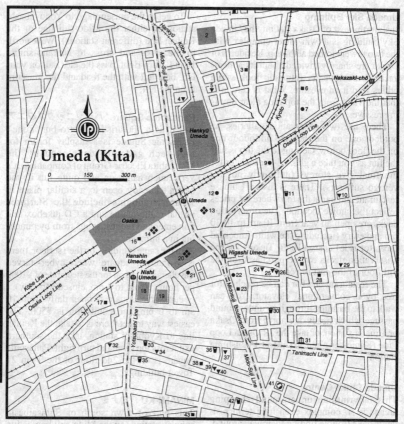

Umeda (Kita)

0   150   300 m

Hankyū Line
Kōbe Line
Mido-Suji Line
Kyoto Line
Nakazaki-chō
Osaka Loop Line
2
3
6
7
5
4
Hankyū Umeda
8
9
12
11
10
Umeda
13
Osaka
14
15
Hanshin Umeda
20
Higashi Umeda
27
29
16
Nishi Umeda
24 25 26
28
18   19
22
21
23
17
Midosuji Boulevard
30
Kōbe Line
Osaka Loop Line
Yotsubashi Line
31
32
33
34
36
37
Tanimachi Line
35
38   39   40
Mido-Suji Line
41
42
43

KANSAI REGION

in for good measure. Highlights include colourful graffiti, a massive Tower Records, the futuristic Wave complex, the ultra-kitsch Disney store (stock up on your Mickey Mice here) and the general ambience, courtesy of hordes of colourful Japanese teens living out the myth of *Amerika*.

In the middle of Amerika-mura is a small 'park' (all concrete) with benches. It's a good place to sit down for a while and watch the action. Amerika-mura is located one or two blocks west of Midosuji-dōri, bounded on the north by Suomachi-suji-dōri and the south by the Dōtomburi-gawa River.

Dōtomburi 道頓堀

You can start by exploring the wall-to-wall restaurants along the south bank of the Dōtomburi-gawa River, though don't restrict your gaze to ground level – almost every building has three or four floors of restaurants with prices ranging from reasonable to sky-high. South of Dōtomburi down to Namba station is a maze of colourful arcades with more restaurants, pachinko parlours, strip clubs, cinemas and who knows what else – take a camera. At night, Dōtomburi looks like a scene from the science-fiction movie *Blade Runner*.

PLACES TO STAY

1 Hotel Sunroute Umeda
ホテルサンルート梅田

2 Hotel Hankyū International
ホテル阪急インターナショナル

3 Osaka Tōkyū Hotel
大阪東急ホテル

6 Hotel Green Plaza Osaka
ホテルグリーンプラザ大阪

8 Hotel New Hankyū
新阪急ホテル

15 Osaka Terminal Hotel
大阪ターミナルホテル

17 Hotel Hanshin
ホテル阪神

18 Osaka Hilton Hotel
大阪ヒルトン

19 Osaka Dai-ichi Hotel
大阪第1ホテル

23 Umeda OS Hotel
梅田OSホテル

27 Hokke Club Osaka
法華クラブ大阪

28 Hotel Kansai
ホテル関西

38 Hotel New Central
ホテルニューセントラル

43 ANA Sheraton Hotel
全日空シェラトンホテル大阪

PLACES TO EAT

4 Isaribi
漁火

5 Hatago
旅篭

10 Herradura

24 Zakoba
ざこば寿司

25 Kamesushi
亀寿司

26 Nawasushi
縄寿司

29 Machapuchare

32 Shabu-zen
しゃぶ禅

34 Court Lodge

37 Canopy Restaurant

39 Maguro-tei
まぐろ亭

40 Kani Doraku
かに道楽

OTHER

7 Osaka Nō Theatre
大阪文楽劇場

9 A'cross Travel

11 Bar, Isn't It?

12 Hankyū Grand Building
阪急グランドビル

13 Hankyū Department Store
阪急デパート

14 Daimaru Department Store
大丸デパート

16 Central Post Office

20 Hanshin Department Store
阪神デパート

21 New Hankyū Building
新阪急ビル

22 Books Asahiya
朝日屋書店

30 Pig & Whistle Bar

31 Umeda Gallery of Modern Art
梅田近代美術館

33 Karma Bar

35 Underground Bar

36 Canopy Bar

41 American Consulate
アメリカ領事館

42 Bar, Isn't It

KANSAI REGION

National Bunraku Theatre 国立文楽劇場

Although bunraku, or puppet theatre, did not originate in Osaka, the art form was popularised here. The most famous bunraku playwright, Chikametsu Monzaemon (1653-1724), wrote plays set in Osaka concerning the classes that traditionally had no place in Japanese art: merchants and the denizens of the pleasure quarters. Not surprisingly, bunraku found an appreciative audience among these people and a theatre was established to put on the plays of Chikametsu in Dōtomburi. Today's theatre is an attempt to revive the fortunes of bunraku.

Performances are only held at certain times of the year: check with the tourist information offices. Tickets normally start at around ¥3500 and programme guides in English and earphones are available.

Osaka Human Rights Museum/Liberty Osaka

This museum, which goes by two names, is dedicated to the suffering of Japan's

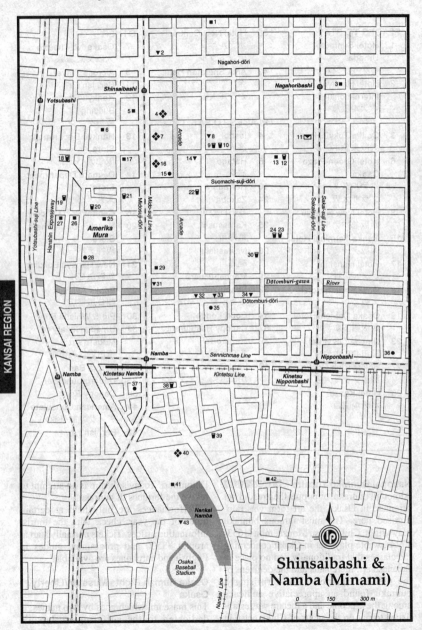

KANSAI REGION

Nagahori-dōri

Shinsaibashi

Yotsubashi

Nagahoribashi

Arcade

Suomachi-suji-dōri

Midōsuji-dōri

Yotsubashi-suji Line

Hanshin Expressway

Sakaisuji-dōri

Sakai-suji Line

Amerika Mura

Arcade

Dōtomburi-gawa   *River*

Dōtomburi-dōri

Namba   Sennichmae Line   Nipponbashi

Namba   Kintetsu Namba   Kintetsu Line   *Kinetsu Nipponbashi*

Mikdo-suji Line

Nankai Namba

Osaka Baseball Stadium

Nankai Line

0   150   300 m

Shinsaibashi & Namba (Minami)

PLACES TO STAY		
1	Hotel Do Sports Plaza ホテルドゥスポーツ プラザ	
3	Ark Hotel Osaka アークホテル	
5	Hotel Nikkō Osaka ホテル日航	
6	Hotel California ホテルカリフォルニア	
13	Asahi Plaza Hotel East Shinsaibashi 朝日プラザホテル	
17	New Shinsaibashi Hotel ニュー心斎橋ホテル	
25	Arrow Hotel アローホテル	
26	Capsule Hotel Asahi Plaza Shinsaibashi カプセルホテル朝日 プラザ心斎橋	
27	Asahi Plaza Hotel Amenity Shinsaibashi 朝日プラザホテル アメニティー心斎橋	
29	Holiday Inn Nanka Osaka ホリデーイン南海	

41	Nankai South Tower Hotel; Namba City 南海サウスタワー ホテル
42	Business Hotel Nissei ビジネスホテル ニッセイ

PLACES TO EAT	
2	Field of Farms
8	Nishiya にし家
14	Vlado's; Chico-n- Charlie's; Capricciosa
31	Shabu-zen しゃぶ禅
32	Zuboraya づぼらや
33	Kani Doraku かに道楽
34	Sawasdee
43	Hard Rock Cafe

OTHER	
4	Sogō Department Store そごうデパート
7	Daimaru Department Store 大丸デパート
9	Diva

10	Be-in Bar
11	Minami Post Office ミナミ郵便局
12	Murphy's
15	Athens Bookshop アテネ書房
16	Daimaru Department Store Annex 大丸デパート アネックス
18	Vinyl
19	Someplace Else
20	Grand Cafe
21	Uncle Steven's
22	Pig & Whistle
23	Nell's
24	Vino
28	Tower Records
30	Bar's Bar
35	Nakaza Theatre 中座
36	National Bunraku Theatre 国立文楽劇場
37	Shin Kabukiza Theatre 新歌舞伎座
38	Southside Blues & Co
39	Karapara
40	Takashimaya Department Store 高島屋デパート

KANSAI REGION

Burakumin people. The Burakumin were the outcasts in Japan's four-tiered caste system which was officially outlawed in 1879 under the Emancipation Edict issued by the newly restored Meiji government. Though legally freed from discrimination, the group still suffers today from unfair hiring practices as well as stigmas against marrying those of Burakumin ancestry. Exhibits on display document Burakumin professions like slaughterhouse work, drum making and shoe repair, all of which were considered unclean by the four 'respectable' castes. An English leaflet is available. The museum is open from 10 am to 5 pm every day except Monday. Admission is ¥250. Take the JR Osaka Loop Line (Kanjo-sen) to Ashihara-bashi station and walk south for five minutes.

OTHER ATTRACTIONS
Aqualiner River Cruises
アクアライナー水上バス
Sure, it's not Venice, but Osaka *does* have a few canals on which you can cruise the city, taking in the sights without any strain on the legs. It's a nice way to spend a day in the city

when it's just too hot for walking. There are guide tapes available to explain the sights upon request. Tours depart on the hour every day from 10 am to 4 pm with additional departures at 6 and 7 pm on weekends and holidays. Fare is ¥1800 for the one hour ride. Take the JR Osaka Loop Line (Kanjo-sen) to Osaka-jō Koen station and walk west toward the next bridge over from the station. Look for the sign to the Aqualiner Pier.

Osaka Aquarium　大阪海遊館

In the Osaka Harbor Village complex, this is one aquarium (and Japan has a glut of them) that is worth a visit. You start by taking an elevator to the top, before you begin a slow, winding descent on foot down a walkway which winds its way around the aquarium's giant main tank. Here, a variety of sharks and other fish share their quarters with the aquarium's star attractions, two enormous whale sharks. Even in the world's largest aquarium tank the fish look cramped and one can't help but feel sorry for them as they swim their way endlessly round and round. That said, they are an awesome sight, particularly when they swim right in front of you.

On the other side of the walkway are displays of life found on eight different ocean levels. The giant spider crabs in the Japan Ocean Deeps section look like something from another planet – very eerie. Presentations have both Japanese and English captions and an environment-friendly slant to them. The building itself is fascinating, with one reader writing in to suggest that with its two wings it looks like 'a large insect spreading its wings to fly'.

To get there, take the Chūō subway line to the last stop (Osaka-kō), and from here it's about a five minute walk to Tempō-zan Harbor Village (there's English signposting in the station), which is next to the aquarium. It's open daily from 10 am to 8 pm and entrance is ¥1950. Get there for opening time if you want to beat the crowds – on weekends and holidays long queues are the norm.

Suntory Museum

In Tempō-zan Harbor Village, the Suntory

Museum complex holds an IMAX 3-D theatre and art gallery with posters and glass artwork on display. Admission to the gallery is ¥950 and it's open daily from 10 am to 8 pm. The IMAX theatre has daily showings on the hour from 11 am to 7 pm for ¥1000.

Tempō-zan Contemporary Museum

This museum, also in Tempō-zan Harbor Village, has interesting displays of holographic art and optical illusions. It's worth a visit on a rainy day or for fans of this sort of art. It's open daily from 10 am to 7 pm and costs ¥1000. Check the *Meet Osaka* guide for details on current exhibits.

Expo Memorial Park　万国博記念公園

This park is the legacy of Expo '70, and houses a few interesting attractions such as the National Museum of Ethnology, Expo Land and a Japanese garden. Dominating the park is the Tower of the Sun, designed by Okamoto Taro. Its concrete and metal construction looks like the work of a child and has been described by one famous Japanologist as 'the ugliest thing ever made by the hands of man'. To get there take the Midosuji line to Senri Chūō station and change to bus Nos 114 or 115 to the park. Alternatively there is a monorail service from Senri-chūō that takes around five minutes and costs ¥200.

National Museum of Ethnology This museum features everyday items from cultures around the world and makes extensive use of audio-visual equipment. Admission is ¥400 and it is open from 10 am to 5 pm but is closed on Wednesday.

Sakai Nintoku Burial Mound
堺仁徳天皇稜

The history of Sakai's burial mound is a lot more interesting than its present reality. Today it merely looks like a mound. In its time, however, it is thought that some 800,000 workers laboured to fashion the final resting place of the 4th century Emperor Nintoku. To get to the mound, take the JR Hanwa line from Tennō-ji station in

Osaka to Mozu station, from where it is about a five minute walk.

Open Air Museum of Old Japanese Farmhouses

Here, *nine gasshō-zukuri* (thatch roof) farmhouses are on display in pleasant natural surroundings. Each of the farmhouses represents a different regional building style used in pre-industrial Japan. The surrounding park, **Ryokuchi-kōen**, is pleasant for strolling and picnics, particularly after time spent in the urban sprawl of downtown Osaka. An English pamphlet is available. Take the Mido-suji subway line to its northern terminus, Esaka station, and walk north to Ryokuchi-kōen Park. The park is open daily from 9.30 am to 5 pm April to October, and closes at 4 pm from November to March. Admission is ¥410.

SPECIAL EVENTS

The major festivals held in Osaka include the following:

Sumiyoshi Taisha Odori
1 to 3 January. Children stage traditional dances every 30 minutes from 10 am to 3 pm at Sumiyoshi Taisha Shrine.

Toka Ebisu
9 to 11 January. Huge crowds of more than a million people flock to the Imamiya Ebisu Shrine to receive bamboo branches hung with auspicious tokens. The shrine is near Imamiya Ebisu station on the Nankai line.

Doya Doya
14 January. Billed as a 'huge naked festival', this event involves a competition between young men, clad in little more than headbands and imitation Rolex wrist watches, to obtain the 'amulet of the cow god'. This talisman is said to bring a good harvest to farmers. The festival takes place at 3 pm at Shitennō-ji Temple.

Shōryō-e
22 April. Shitennō-ji Temple holds night time performances of bunraku.

Otaue Shinji
14 June. Women and girls dressed in traditional costume commemorate the establishment of the imperial rice fields. The festival is held at the Sumiyoshi Taisha Shrine.

Tenjin Matsuri
24 to 25 July. Processions of portable shrines and people in traditional attire start at Temmangu Shrine and end up in the Okawa River (in boats). As night falls the festival is marked with a huge fireworks display.

Danjiri Matsuri
14 to 15 September. Reportedly Osaka's wildest festival, a kind of running of the bulls except with festival floats *(danjiri)*, many weighing over 3000 kg. The danjiri are hauled through the streets by hundreds of people using ropes, and in all the excitement there have been a couple of deaths – take care/stand back. Check with the information office at Osaka station or the TIC in Kyoto, but generally the best place to see the action is west of Kishiwada station on the Nankai Honsen line (from Namba Nankai station).

PLACES TO STAY

The best place to stay when visiting Osaka is Kyoto. It's less than 20 minutes away by shinkansen, or around 40 minutes on the Keihan or Hankyū lines, there's a far better choice of accommodation (particularly in the budget bracket) and it's a much nicer place. Business hotels in Osaka are concentrated in the central area and the cheaper places are inconveniently further out.

Youth Hostels

Nagai Youth Hostel (☎ 06-699-5631) near the new stadium in Nagai is the nearest youth hostel to downtown Osaka. A bed in the dorm room is ¥2500, a private room is ¥3000, and a family room for up to four people is ¥3500 per person. There are also a limited number of private double rooms for ¥3000 per person. Sheet rental is ¥200. Take the Mido-suji subway line south from the centre of town to Nagai station and walk 10 minutes. The hostel is at the new stadium.

About 15 minutes from Kita-ku or 30 minutes from Minami-ku is the *Osaka-fu Hattori Ryokuchi Youth Hostel* (☎ 06-862-0600), where beds are ¥1800 (no membership necessary). A simple dinner is served for ¥850 and breakfast is ¥550. Take the Mido-suji line to Ryokuchi-kōen station and leave through the western exit. Enter the park and follow the path straight ahead past a fountain and around to the right alongside the pond. You will find the youth hostel is a little further on the right.

Not exactly a youth hostel, not exactly a hotel, *Shin-Osaka House* (06-391-3133) is an option as a base for those thinking of setting up shop in Osaka, or for those who intend longer stays but can't afford hotel accommodation. Weekly rates start at ¥10,500 and monthly rates from ¥35,000. It's a four minute walk from Shin-Osaka station. Call the owner for specific directions (he speaks some English).

Hotels – bottom end

The *Rinkai Hotel Dejimaten* (☎ 0722-41-3045), *Rinkai Hotel Kitamise* (☎ 0722-47-1111) and *Rinkai Hotel Ishizuten* (☎ 0722-44-0088) are close together and good for short or long-term stays; they should be cheaper by the month. At the Dejimaten, singles start at ¥4000, doubles ¥3400 per person. At the Ishizuten prices are the same and they also offer singles without a bath for ¥3600. The Kitamise is the most expensive of the three with single/double/twin prices of ¥5800/7000/8000 per person. Each of the hotels has cooking facilities and dining areas.

To get to the hotels, the best thing would be to call into one of the Osaka information counters and pick up a map. The hotels are a fair way out of town near Minato station on the Nankai line, which runs out of Namba station – take an express from platform 5 or 6 at Namba station, change to a Nankai line local train at Sakai and get off at the next stop, Minato station.

Hotels – middle

Minami Area The Minami area is probably the best place to be based; but, while it has a good selection of mid-range business hotels, it's also worth bearing in mind that Osaka is an important business centre, and there is often a squeeze on accommodation – particularly the smaller and less expensive places. It's wise to book ahead.

Worth a special mention is the wonderfully kitsch *Hotel California* (☎ 06-243-0333). The bar downstairs is a very Japanese interpretation of California style, complete with garish wooden marlin, parrots and vertical ducks hanging on the walls. The huge potted plants give the lounge the appropriate 'oasis' feel. The rooms are slightly larger than those in an average business hotel and prices start at ¥8000/11,000 for singles/doubles with bathroom. To get to the Hotel California, take the No 8 exit of Shinsaibashi station, turn right into the small street that runs off the main road next to the big Hotel Nikkō Osaka and the hotel is about 50m down on the left – you'll see the sign.

South-west of the Hotel California is the *Asahi Plaza Hotel Amenity Shinsaibashi* (☎ 06-212-5111), where singles/twins start from ¥7700/15,000. East of here is another Asahi hotel with mid-range rates: the *Asahi Plaza Hotel East Shinsaibashi* (☎ 06-241-1011) has singles/twins at ¥7400/14,200. In the Amerikamura area of Shinsaibashi is the *Arrow Hotel* (☎ 06-211-8441), a modern hotel with singles/twins/doubles for ¥7200/9200/8800.

Some other mid-range possibilities in Minami include:

Ark Hotel Osaka (☎ 06-252-5111) – prices for singles/twins/doubles start from ¥7500/13,000/12,000; next to Nagahoribashi subway station or 10 minutes walk east of Shinsaibashi subway station

Business Hotel Namba Plaza (☎ 06-641-3000) – singles cost from ¥6900; twins from ¥12,770; five minutes walk east of Nankai Namba station

Business Hotel Nissei (☎ 06-632-8111) – singles/twins/doubles cost ¥6300/13,000/11,000; next to Nankai Namba station

New Shinsaibashi Hotel (☎ 06-251-3711) – singles/twins/doubles cost ¥8650/13,100/11,950; five minutes walk from Shinsaibashi subway station

Osaka Station Area While this isn't the ideal place to be based, Osaka's efficient subway system means that you aren't far from the rest of town, and this area has the widest range of hotels to choose from.

Just north of Hankyū-Umeda station is the *Hotel Sunroute Umeda* (☎ 06-373-1111), where singles/twins/doubles start from ¥8400/15,000/13,900. Not far to the south of here, the *Hotel Green Plaza Osaka* (☎ 06-374-1515) has singles/twins/doubles from ¥8200/10,500/12,700. About five minutes south of Osaka station, near Books Asahiya, is the *Umeda OS Hotel* (☎ 06-312-1271). It has 208 single rooms from ¥8100 to ¥8400; twins are also available from ¥11,400. About five minutes walk east of the OS is the *Hotel Kansai* (☎ 06-312-7971), a cheaper business hotel, where singles/twins/doubles start from ¥5500/9200/8200. Close by is the *Hokke Club Osaka* (☎ 06-313-3171), another cheaper option with the luxury of a noon checkout (as opposed to the usual 10 am); singles/twins are ¥6700/10,600.

Hotels – top end

Osaka is brimming with upper-end accommodation. The most expensive hotel in town, and presumably the best, is the *Hotel Hankyū International* (☎ 06-377-2100), just north of Hankyū-Umeda station. Singles here range from ¥18,000 to ¥27,000, twins from ¥33,000 to ¥40,000 and doubles from ¥33,000 to ¥42,000, lower prices are, in effect, weekdays.

The following is a list of Osaka's major up-market hotels:

ANA-Sheraton Hotel (☎ 06-347-1112) – singles/doubles from ¥16,000/27,000; 10 minute walk south of Osaka station

Holiday Inn Nankai Osaka (☎ 06-213-8281) – singles/doubles from ¥15,000/20,000; five minutes north of Namba subway station

Hotel Hanshin (☎ 06-344-1661) – singles from ¥11,500; twins from ¥18,500; doubles from ¥16,500; Japanese-style rooms also available from ¥19,000; three minutes south of JR Osaka station

Hotel New Hankyū (☎ 06-372-5101) – singles/twins/doubles from ¥12,000/21,000/23,000; next to Hankyū-Umeda station

Hotel New Otani Osaka (☎ 06-941-1111) – singles/twins/doubles from ¥18,000/30,000/32,000; near Osaka-jō Kōen station on the JR Osaka loop line

Hotel Nikkō Osaka (☎ 06-244-1111) – singles/doubles from ¥17,000/28,500; above Shinsaibashi subway station

Hyatt Regency Osaka (☎ 06-612-1234) – singles/doubles from ¥19,000/24,000

Osaka Dai-Ichi Hotel (☎ 06-341-4411) – singles/twins/doubles from ¥13,600/23,000/27,200; three minutes south of JR Osaka station

Osaka Hilton Hotel (☎ 06-347-7111) – singles/doubles from ¥26,000/32,000; next to JR Osaka station

Osaka Tōkyū Hotel (☎ 06-373-2411) – singles/twins/doubles from ¥10,000/22,000/19,000; near Hankyū Umeda station

PLACES TO EAT

Osaka is a city where eating is taken seriously. Indeed, without many cultural attractions to vie for your attention, eating is the best way to have a good time here. Luckily, restaurants are plentiful, varied and cheap.

Kita

The backstreets and shopping arcades around JR Osaka and Hankyū Umeda station are bursting with restaurants. The stiff competition forces many of them to offer cheap lunch and dinner specials, including lots of all-you-can-eat deals. Most of the restaurants in Kita are located in the neighbourhoods south and west of the station. Don't be afraid to walk into one that looks good – Osakans are used to foreigners and will make a valiant effort at communication. The following places all offer good value and are pretty easy to find.

Starting at the northern end of Hankyū Umeda station, you can choose from two excellent robotayaki places (robotayaki is easy to order since all the food is laid out in front of you – just point at what you want).

Isaribi (☎ 06-373-2969) is downstairs at the north-west end of the station. Everything here is ¥300 except beer which is ¥600; it's open daily from 5 pm to 11.15 pm. On the other side of the station, just down a little side street, *Hatago* (☎ 06-373-3440) has a warm, country feel. The set menus are from ¥2500 but it's more fun to order a la carte by pointing at what you want. It's open from 5 to 11 pm. Look for the old wooden building.

Herradura (☎ 06-361-1011) is a good Mexican restaurant located just off a shopping arcade to the east of Hankyū Umeda station. They serve all the usual Mexican favourites including a platter of 12 taco shells and a variety of fillings for ¥2800. It's open every day except Monday from 5 to 11 pm.

A short walk east from Hanshin department store brings you to a neighbourhood which must have the highest concentration of sushi restaurants on the planet. *Nawasushi* (☎ 06-312-9891) offers good value (three pieces of sushi per order, usually around ¥400) in a pleasant atmosphere, and is open from 3 pm to midnight on weekdays and from noon to midnight on weekends. Just down the street, *Kamesushi* (☎ 06-312-3862) offers similar fare in slightly more spacious digs, and hours are the same as Nawasuhi. On the same street, downstairs *Zakoba* (☎ 06-312-0358) offers more up-market fare and atmosphere. Here, a jōnigiri moriawase (assortment set) of sushi goes for ¥3000. It's open daily from 5 to 11 pm.

Not far to the east of the sushi ghetto, *Machapuchare* (☎ 06-315-8169) serves filling sets of Nepalese food. Lunch sets, which usually include two kinds of curry and chai, go for ¥850. Lunch is served from 11.30 am to 2 pm, and dinner from 5.30 to 10 pm. It's closed Sunday.

In one of the narrow streets just south of the Osaka Ekimae Dai-San building, *Kani Doraku* (☎ 06-344-5091) serves anything to do with crab, with sets going from about ¥3000. It's open daily from 11 am to 11 pm. Look for the giant crab out front.

Nearby *Maguro-tei* (☎ 06-452-5863) is a modern, noisy, automatic sushi place which has an all-you-can-eat special on weekday evenings from 5 pm and all day on Sunday (¥1500 for men and ¥1000 for women). It's open daily from 11 am to 4 am (for those late night sushi cravings).

Court Lodge (☎ 06-342-5253) serves delicious and filling Sri Lankan food in a tiny keyhole of a restaurant not far from the Osaka Hilton. Lunch sets here start at ¥800. Look for the beer signs in the window. It's open daily from 11 am to 9 pm.

For delicious shabu-shabu in an elegant setting, try *Shabu-zen* (☎ 06-343-0250) on the 10th floor of the AX building not far from the Osaka Hilton. They serve full shabu sets from ¥3300. Lunch is served from 11 am to 2 pm and dinner from 5 to 11 pm.

For good lunches close to the station, head to the Osaka Hilton. On the 1st floor, just across from the reception desk, *The In Place* serves a curry buffet with six curries to choose from for ¥1700 including salad and dessert daily from 11.30 am to 2.30 pm. Downstairs, on level B2 in the Hankyu Plaza, *Victoria Station* (☎ 06-347-7470) has a good salad bar and steak menu starting at ¥1500.

Minami

The place to eat in Minami-ku is the restaurant-packed street of Dōtomburi-dōri. If you pick a place that is doing brisk business you are unlikely to be disappointed. Dōtomburi has a couple of famous Japanese restaurants whose extensive menus feature some very reasonably priced dishes. You can't miss *Kuidaore* (☎ 06-211-5300) as it has a lively mechanical clown posted outside its doors, attracting the attention of potential customers by beating a drum. The restaurant has eight floors serving almost every kind of Japanese food, and windows featuring a huge range of plastic replicas. Main-course meals cost from ¥1000. It's open daily from 11 am to 10 pm.

Down the road from the drum-pounding clown is a restaurant that sports a huge mechanical crab helplessly waving its pincers around. The *Kani Doraku* (☎ 06-211-8975) (*kani* is Japanese for 'crab') specialises in crab dishes and does all kinds of imaginative things to the unfortunate crustaceans. Most dishes are fairly expensive (¥3000 and up) although there are a few exceptions. It's open daily from 11 am to 11 pm.

Zuboraya (☎ 06-211-0181) is the place to go when you've worked up the nerve to try fugu (Japanese puffer fish). Their standard set of fugu prepared a variety of ways goes for ¥6000 – about the cheapest fugu set anywhere. Let your friends take the first bite. It's open daily from 11 am to 11.30 pm.

Dōtomburi also has a wide range of international restaurants including *Sawasdee* (☎ 06-212-2301), a small Thai restaurant with friendly staff and great food. Open from 11.30 am to 10 pm, closed Monday, it's on the 2nd floor of the Shibata building, not far from Kani Doraku. Look for the English sign at ground level.

Leaving Dōtomburi and heading north, you'll pass the Gurukas building just across the river on Midosuji-dōri. On the 6th floor of this building, *Shabu-zen* (☎ 06-213-2935) serves excellent shabu in an elegant setting. Courses start at ¥3000. It's open daily from 11 am to 11 pm.

There are some more good international restaurants located in the neighbourhood behind Daimaru department store. For delicious steaks, served with good wine or beer, head to *Vlado's* (☎ 06-244-4129). The lunch-time steak sets, starting at ¥970, are a good value. For dinner, try the Osaka course for ¥2900. The staff of Australian ex-pats can also help visitors find their way around the city. In the same building, try *Chico-n-Charlie's* (☎ 06-243-6025) for good Mexican food or *Capricciosa* (☎ 06-243-6020) for cheap, plentiful Italian food.

Not far north of Vlado's, in the neighbourhood behind Sogo department store, *Nishiya* (☎ 06-241-9221) serves Osaka udon noodles and a variety of hearty nabe (iron pot) dishes for reasonable prices. It's open daily from 11 am to 10 pm. Look for the traditional wooden building.

Located on the northern side of Nagahori-dōri, *Field of Farms* (☎ 06-253-0500) is a must for lovers of vegetarian cooking. It serves a buffet-style lunch for ¥900 and has an extensive, bilingual menu for dinner. It's open from 11.30 am to 2 pm for lunch, and 5.30 to 10.30 pm for dinner, closed Sunday. Look for the sign just after you cross Nagahori-dōri then climb down the steps two flights to B2.

Finally, and also an entertainment option, Osaka has its own branch of the *Hard Rock Cafe* (☎ 06-646-1470), with drinks and American-style eats. On weekdays it's open from 11 am to 11 pm, and on weekends from 11 am to 3 am. It's south of Nankai Namba station, in front of Osaka baseball stadium.

ENTERTAINMENT
Traditional Japanese Entertainment
You can check the National Bunraku Theatre (☎ 06-212-1122) described earlier for bunraku (Japanese puppet shows). Osaka Nō Hall (☎ 06-373-1726), a five minute walk

east of Osaka Station, holds nō shows about four times a month, some of which are free. There are also five *Manzai* (comic dialogue) theatres around the city with something going on most nights. It's also possible, if your timing is right, to take in some *rakugo* (comic monologue) performances held in small theatres in Osaka.

Unfortunately, none of these places have regularly scheduled shows. The best thing is to check with the tourist information offices about current shows, check the listings in the *Meet Osaka* guide or look in *Kansai Time Out*. Those who can read a little Japanese might want to look in *L Magazine Osaka* for up-to-date listings on these and other performances.

Bars & Clubs
A big Japanese city with a large foreign community, such as Osaka, is bound to have a lively nightlife – and it does. In the Kita area, check out *Underground* for their ¥300 weekday happy hour from 6 pm to 9 pm and occasional live music. It's in a basement not far from the Osaka Hilton. Look for the British Underground sign outside.

Nearby, *Karma* is popular with Japanese and foreigners alike. Look for the white canvas sign on the front of the building. A short walk east on the same street brings you to *Canopy* which serves drinks and food until dawn and is popular with ex-pats for a late night snack and drink. Look for the yellow-and-green sign.

Walking north toward the station again, you'll find the *Pig & Whistle*, a British-style pub which serves good fish & chips and imported beer (served as a set for ¥900 until 7 pm). A few minutes walk east of Hankyu department store brings you to *Bar, Isn't It?*, a large bar popular with the young, after-work crowd.

For more intense late-night action head south to the Minami District, particularly the backstreets of Shinsaibashi and Amerika-mura. You won't believe the number of people who flock here on a weekend night, and simply looking at them is half the fun. On the way to the bars, stop for a moment on any of the bridges over the Dōtomburi-gawa

River to take in the *Blade Runner* nightscape of the area.

Karapara is a good place to start your pub crawl, as you should be relatively sober to appreciate the awesome, futuristic look of the place (¥2.3 billion spent on decor). At the opposite end of the spectrum *Southside Blues & Co.* is a good place to enjoy blues and blues-influenced music in a mellow atmosphere. Touring foreign musicians sometimes stop in here for an informal jam session. There's also a grill for those who want to combine dinner and a drink.

North of the Dōtomburi-gawa River is another enclave thick with bars and restaurants. Located almost next to each other *Vino* and *Nell's* offer two intriguing options. While they're both good for a late night drink, Nell's has the more alternative crowd. A few blocks north *Murphy's* is an Irish pub for those in search of a well-mixed drink. Look for the plain concrete front and the low lights inside. On the same block is *Diva*, a karaoke place specialising in English songs (look hard for the sign written in English on street level outside, then take the elevator to the 6th floor). Close by, on the 2nd floor of a building across the street from Lawson

convenience store, *Vlado's Bar* is a good place for a drink or snack in the company of ex-pats.

When you're in the mood for something a little more trendy, head across Midosuji-dōri to Amerika-mura – a ghetto of clubs, bars and young people dressed in the latest fashions. *Uncle Steven's* is a Tex-Mex bar good for spicy food, music and beer. It's above Mosburger. *Grand Cafe* is a spacious, cool place which occasionally offers live music. *Someplace Else*, in a basement just across from the little 'park' in Amerika-mura, is very popular with ex-pats and gets pretty wild late at night when a lot of the hostesses and bartenders from other clubs knock off and stop in for a drink.

A block north of Someplace Else, on the same street, *Vinyl* is a good bar with unique '60s mod decor and an interesting clientele. A good place to hide from dawn is *Bar's Bar*, a classic hole-in-the-wall hidden down a small alley just north of the river. This is where the serious drinkers wind up when lesser mortals have gone home.

One last option that's worth a look-in is *Y-1 Bar* located near Shin-Osaka station. Take the Midosuji subway line to the Higashimikuni stop, go out exit No 4 and walk one block north and one and a half blocks east. It's in the Viva building on the 1st floor. This is another place to get some inside information on Osaka for those thinking of setting up digs here, as well as for those just passing through. It's open from 7 pm until dawn.

THINGS TO BUY

Osaka has almost as many shops as it does restaurants. For department store shopping look in the area around JR Osaka and Umeda stations. Most of the major department stores are represented. For cheaper, more interesting shopping, check out Amerika-mura in the Minami area of town.

For Osaka's local specialty, electronics, head to Den Den Town. Taking its name from the Japanese word for electricity (*denki*), Den Den Town is Osaka's version of Tokyo's Akihabara – an area of shops almost exclusively devoted to electronic goods. Make

The young and trendy can be found in the clubs and bars of the Amerika-mura area.

sure the manufacturer's receipt is included with your purchase. To avoid sales tax, check if the store has a 'Tax Free' sign outside and bring your passport. Take the Sakaisuji subway line to Ebisu-cho station and exit at No 1 or No 2 exits. Most stores are closed Wednesday.

GETTING THERE & AWAY
Air
Osaka is serviced by two airports: the old Itami airport which now handles mostly domestic traffic and the new Kansai international airport (KIX). Built on an artificial island south of Osaka city, KIX is Japan's first 24 hour airport and represents a major bid by city planners to make Osaka competitive with Tokyo as Japan's major air hub. Impressive as the new airport is, if you have a choice, try to get a flight into Itami as it's in Osaka city proper and much more convenient to both Kyoto and central Osaka.

Train
Osaka is the centre of an extensive rail network that sprawls across the Kansai region. Kōbe is a mere 30 minutes away, even quicker by shinkansen, while Kyoto and Nara are each about 45 minutes from Osaka.

Shinkansen services operate between Shin-Osaka station and Tokyo station (just under three hours, ¥13,480), Kyoto station (15 minutes, ¥1350), and Hakata in northern Kyūshū (about three hours, ¥14,310).

To get to Kyoto from Osaka the quickest route, other than the shinkansen, is with the private Hankyū line, departing from Umeda station. The trip takes around 40 minutes by limited express and costs ¥380. You can also take the Keihan line to Kyoto's Sanjō station from Yodoyabashi station on the Mido-suji subway line (45 minutes by limited express, ¥390). See the Kyoto Getting There & Away section for more information on other possible routings.

Osaka station to Nara takes about 40 minutes and costs ¥760. The private Kintetsu line also operates between Namba station and Nara station, taking about 30 minutes for ¥530. From Tennōji station, trains depart on the Hanwa line for destinations in southern Kansai including Wakayama city, Yoshino, Shirahama spa, Kushimoto and Shingu.

It is also possible to travel between Osaka and Kōya-san from Nankai Namba station via the private Nankai-Kōya line.

Boat
Osaka has a twice-monthly international ferry service to Shanghai in China. The ferries leave from the Osaka Nankō International Ferry Terminal, which can be reached by taking the 'New Tram' service from Suminoe-kōen station to Nankoguchi station. The price for a 2nd class tatami-style berth is ¥23,000. For further information about Shanghai-bound ferries you can ring the Nitchū Kokusai Ferry company (☎ 078-392-1021), though don't expect any English to be spoken. A better source of information on schedules and bookings would be the Kyoto TIC.

Ferries also depart from Nankō, Kanome-futō and Benten-futō piers for various destinations around Honshū, Kyūshū and Shikoku. For Beppu in Kyūshū (via Kōbe) the 2nd class fare is ¥6900; for Miyazaki in Kyūshū the 2nd class fare is ¥8230. Other possibilities in Kyūshū include Shinmoji in the north of the island near Shimonoseki and Shibushi in the south of the island. For Shikoku, the possibilities include Kōchi (¥4530), Matsuyama (¥4900, 2nd class), Takamatsu (¥5990, 2nd class) and Tokushima (¥1970, 2nd class). For detailed information on sailing schedules and bookings contact the TIC or call Kansai Kisen ferry company directly (in Japanese) at ☎ 06-614-6411.

GETTING AROUND
The Airport
Itami Airport There are frequent limousine buses running between the airport and various parts of Osaka. Buses run to/from Shin-Osaka station every 15 minutes from 8 am to 9.30 pm and cost ¥480. The trip takes around 25 minutes. Buses run at about the same frequency to/from Osaka and Namba stations (half an hour, ¥610).

There are also direct airport buses to and

KANSAI REGION

from Kyoto and Kōbe (see the Kyoto and Kōbe sections for details).

Kansai International Airport There are a variety of routes between KIX and Osaka. Limousine buses leave to/from Shin-Osaka, Osaka Umeda, Kyobashi, Tenmabashi, OCAT Namba, Uehonmachi, Tennō-ji and Nanko (Cosmo Square) stations. The fare is ¥1300 for most routes and the journeys take an average of 50 minutes depending on traffic conditions. The OCAT (Osaka City Air Terminal), located in Namba station, allows passengers on Japanese and some other airlines to check-in and deposit baggage before boarding trains to the airport. Check with your airline for details. There is a similar advance check-in service at Kobe Port Island (K-CAT) where you can catch a ferry to the airport (30 minutes, ¥2200). There is a similar service in Kyoto (check Kyoto section for details).

By train, the fastest way to and from the airport is the private Nankai express 'Rapit' which departs from Namba station on the Mido-suji subway line. The ride takes 30 minutes and costs ¥1370. Make a reservation at the station office or at a travel agent (same day ticket purchase is possible on all but the most crowded days). The limited airport express 'Haruka' operates between the airport and Shin-Osaka (45 minutes, ¥2930) and Tennō-ji station (30 minutes, ¥2230). Regular expresses called Kanku Kaisoku also operate between the airport and Osaka station (66 minutes, ¥1140), Kyōbashi station (75 minutes, ¥1140), Tennō-ji station (45 minutes, ¥1010) and JR Namba station (61 minutes, ¥1010). For the imaginative, you can take a ferry (35 minutes, ¥1650) from Osaka Tempozan Harbor Village which is reached from the last stop, Osakako, on the Chuo subway line.

Train

Osaka has a good subway network and, like Tokyo, a JR Loop Line (known in Japanese as the JR Kanjo-sen) that circles the city area. In fact, there should be no need to use any other form of transport while you are in

Osaka unless you stay out late and miss the last train. Subway and JR stations are clearly marked in English as well as hiragana and kanji so finding your way is relatively easy.

There are seven subway lines, but the one that most short-term visitors are likely to find most useful is the Mido-suji line, which runs north to south taking in the key areas of Shin-Osaka (shinkansen connection), Umeda (next to JR Osaka station) and Shinsaibashi/Namba, the main commercial and entertainment areas.

If you're going to be using the rail system a lot on any day, it might be worth considering a 'one-day free ticket'. For ¥850 you get unlimited travel on any subway, the so-called New Tram and the buses, but unfortunately you cannot use the JR line. You'd really need to be moving around all day to save any money but it might save the headache of working out fares and buying tickets. These tickets are available at the staffed ticket windows in most subway stations.

Bus

Osaka has a bus system though it is nowhere near as easy to use as the rail network. Japanese-language bus maps are available from the tourist offices.

Kōbe 神戸

More than two years have passed since the disastrous earthquake of January 17, 1995 struck Kōbe, levelling whole neighbourhoods and killing more than 6000 people. Though some evidence of the disaster is still visible, mostly in construction sites dotted around the city, visitors will be surprised to find that it's mostly business as usual in this pleasant city by the bay. In spite of all the damage wrought by the quake, Kōbe remains one of Japan's most attractive cities, owing largely to its location – perched on hills overlooking the sea. It's also small enough to negotiate on foot, most of the sights being within 30 minutes of the main train stations.

In many ways Kōbe can be likened to Nagasaki. Both cities are ports, have Chinese communities and in the late 19th century were settled by European traders. Both the Chinese and the European influences linger and can be found in the city's diverse restaurants and architectural styles. While some of the city's foreign population relocated after the quake, many have stayed on and continue to turn out some of the best food available in Japan.

All things considered, Kōbe makes a pleasant day trip from Osaka or Kyoto. For those planning a longer stay in Japan, Kōbe is undoubtedly one of the most livable cities in the country.

Orientation & Information

The two main entry points into Kōbe are Sannomiya and Shin-Kōbe stations. Shin-Kōbe station is where the shinkansen pauses, and is in the north-west of town. A subway runs from here to the Sannomiya station, which has frequent rail connections with Osaka and Kyoto. It's possible to walk between the two stations in around 15 minutes. Sannomiya (not Kōbe) station marks the city centre.

There are information counters in both Shin-Kōbe and Sannomiya stations. The main office is the one at Sannomiya (☎ 078-322-0220), where English is spoken and a variety of English-language publications are available. It's located on the south side of Sannomiya station. At the very least, it's worth picking up a copy of the *Kōbe Guide Map*, which is regularly updated and has listings of restaurants and sights. Both counters can assist with accommodation bookings.

Bookshops There's a branch of Maruzen near Nankinmachi (Chinatown). Also, and something of a rarity in Japan, Wantage Books is a second-hand English bookshop. It's just down the road from Shin-Kōbe station.

Kitano-chō 北野町

Kitano-chō is where most of Kōbe's foreign architecture can be found. There are also a number of places of religious worship in the area – a Russian Orthodox church, a mosque, a synagogue and a Catholic church.

There is no real need to go out of your way to visit Kitano-chō. As in Nagasaki, western-style homes are probably of limited appeal to westerners who grew up surrounded by them. This area can also get very busy with Japanese tourists on the weekends. The other thing to consider is the way the entry fees soon mount up.

Kōbe Municipal Museum
神戸市立博物館

Kōbe Municipal Museum has a collection of so-called Namban (literally 'southern barbarian') art and occasional special exhibits. Namban art is a school of painting that developed under the influence of early Jesuit missionaries in Japan, many of whom taught western painting techniques to Japanese students. Entry to the museum is ¥200 and it's open from 10 am to 4.30 pm, closed Monday.

Kōbe Phoenix Plaza
神戸フェニックスプラザ

This new hall is both an earthquake museum and a clearing house of information for Kōbe citizens affected by the quake. On the 1st floor there is a wide variety of displays documenting the earthquake and the fires which swept the city in its wake. There are also displays documenting the city's continuing efforts at reconstruction and plans for the future. The upstairs is geared mostly to citizens of Kōbe who are looking for work and housing. Some of the displays are accompanied by English explanations, but most of the videos are only in Japanese. It's open daily from 10 am to 7 pm and entry is free. It's just south of the main tourist information office at Sannomiya station. Look for the new glass building.

Chinatown 南京町

Known as 'Nankinmachi' by locals, Kōbe's Chinatown is no rival for Chinatowns elsewhere, but is a good place for a stroll and a quick bite to eat. As in the Chinatowns of Yokohama and Nagasaki, the Chinese food here should properly be called Japanese/Chinese food, as it has been Japanicised to

KANSAI REGION

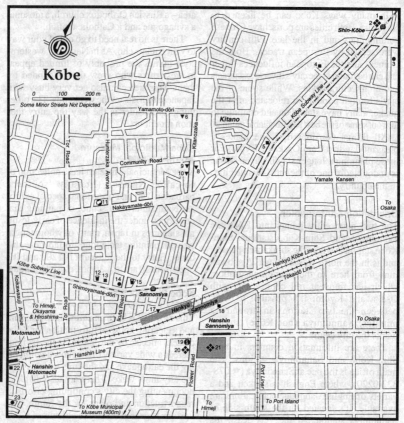

suit local tastes (the prices have also been
Japanicised).

Thus, the best bets are not the full-course
sit down meals offered by nearly all the
restaurants, but the small delicacies served
out front for take-away. Try the gyoza
(dumplings), butaman (pork buns) or the
shumai (another sort of dumpling). If you do
want a sit-down meal, the rule is the more
gaudy the facade, the higher the prices.
Nankinmachi is easy to find – starting from
Motomachi station, walk south on Koikawa-
suji-dōri for a few blocks until you see the
Chinese-style gate at the entrance to the street.

Port Island ポートアイランド

An artificial island, this is touted as one of
Kōbe's premier tourist destinations. A monorail (the Port Liner) does a circuit of the
island from Sannomiya station and stops at
the sights along the way for ¥240. Most of
these are little different from the usual tourist
traps to be found at any of Japan's major
tourist destinations.

Rokko Island 六甲アイランド

This artificial island was one of the hardest
hit areas in Kōbe, suffering from large scale
liquefaction of the landfill of which it was

PLACES TO STAY	PLACES TO EAT	3	Wantage Books
1 Shin-Kōbe Oriental Hotel 新神戸オリエンタルホテル	6 Wang Thai	11	Korean Consulate 大韓民国領事館
	7 Marrakech		
	8 Ju Ju 樹樹	12	Rub-a-Dub Reggae Bar
4 Green Hill Hotel 2 グリーンヒルホテル第2	9 Cookhouse Un Deux Trois	14	Tōkyū Hands 東急ハンズ
5 Green Hill Hotel 1 グリーンヒルホテル第1	10 Abait Faim	15	Bar, Isn't It?
	16 Ikariya いかりや	19	Tourist Information Office 観光案内所
13 Washington Hotel ワシントンホテル	17 Omoni おもに		
18 Sannomiya Terminal Hotel 三宮ターミナルホテル	OTHER	20	Kōbe Phoenix Plaza 神戸フェニックスプラザ
	2 OPA Shopping Centre & Hub OPA ショッピングセンター		
22 Kōbe Plaza Hotel 神戸プラザホテル		21	Sogō Department Store そごうデパート
		23	Maruzen 丸善

built. Most of the attractions which were in operation before the quake are still under reconstruction, and are probably of little interest to foreign travellers anyway. A monorail (the Rokko Liner) makes a loop around the island from JR Sumiyoshi station for ¥240, stopping at several points along the way.

Other Attractions

Featured prominently in all the tourist literature is 931m **Mt Rokko-san**. It's a pleasant trip by cablecar to the top costing ¥560. To get there, take bus No 25 from Rokko station on the Hankyū line. Get off the bus at the Rokko cablecar station. You can continue onwards on the Arima cablecar (¥700). This is also a good area for hiking; some people take the cablecar up and then hike down. Further up from the cablecar terminus is the **Herb Garden**, which gets good reports from locals and visitors alike. Further up again are good views of Kōbe Harbour and Port Island.

Fifteen minutes north of Motomachi station is the Japanese-style **Soraku-en Garden** with a pond and some old buildings. The garden is a pleasant enough place for a stroll. It is open from 9 am to 5 pm (closed on Thursday) and admission is ¥150.

Cruises

From 20 March to 25 December, cruises depart daily from Kōbe's Naka pier. They usually last a couple of hours and cost ¥3090. Possibilities include the Akashi Bay cruise (and a look at the Akashi Kaikyō Bridge, the world's longest suspension bridge), a cruise around the new Kansai airport project and an evening Osaka Bay cruise. Dinner cruises are also available with a variety of menus. For more information ring Luminous Kankō (☎ 078-333-8414).

Places to Stay

Youth Hostels The *Kōbe Tarumi Youth Hostel* (☎ 078-707-2133) has dormitory beds for ¥2800, single rooms for ¥5000 and twins for ¥4000 per person. They also serve breakfast for ¥500 and dinner for ¥800. Unfortunately, it's a bit far out of town. Take a San'in line train from Kōbe station and get off after six stops at Tarumi station. The hostel is an eight minute walk east along the road that parallels the south side of the railway tracks.

Hotels – middle Middle-range hotels in Kōbe are expensive even by Japanese standards. Unless you book ahead with one of the (marginally) cheaper places, you'll be hard-pressed to come up with anything under ¥7000 – and that's for a tiny single.

The Sannomiya station area has the greatest number of mid-range hotels. The *Green Hill Hotel 1* (☎ 078-222-1221) is about 10 minutes walk to the north (about equidistant between Shin-Kōbe and Sannomiya stations). It charges from ¥7000/13,500 for singles/twins. The *Green Hill Hotel 2* (☎ 078-222-0909) is further up the hill and down a side street. It has slightly bigger rooms at ¥8300/14,600.

About five minutes walk to the west of Sannomiya station, behind Motomachi station, is the *Kōbe Plaza Hotel* (☎ 078-332-1141), where singles range from ¥7200 to ¥8500 and twins range from ¥13,500 to ¥15,000.

Right on top of Sannomiya station, the *Sannomiya Terminal Hotel* (☎ 078-291-0001) has comfortable rooms with all the usual features from ¥9000/17,500.

Hotels – top-end Kōbe abounds in top-end accommodation. Close to Shin-Kōbe station is the *Shin-Kōbe Oriental Hotel* (☎ 078-291-1121) in a great gleaming tower building. Singles range from ¥13,000 to ¥22,000 and doubles from ¥23,000 to ¥33,000.

Near the waterfront, about 10 minutes walk south of Motomachi station, the *Hotel Okura Kōbe* (☎ 078-333-0111) has rooms from ¥14,000/24,000 for singles/doubles. About 10 minutes walk south-west of here, the *Kōbe Harbourland New Otani* (☎ 078-360-1111), part of the prestigious Otani chain, has singles from ¥10,000 to ¥16,000, twins from ¥26,000 to ¥35,000 and doubles from ¥30,000 to ¥45,000.

The Sheraton chain is represented over on Rokko Island, where you can find the *Kōbe Bay Sheraton Hotel* (☎ 078-857-7000). Singles start from ¥18,000, twins and doubles from ¥24,000.

Places to Eat

Kōbe is teeming with restaurants, and the best advice is to wander around the southern part of the Kitano-chō area and take a look at what's on offer. Kōbe's two main culinary attractions are Kōbe beef and ethnic restaurants – there are French and Italian restaurants in abundance. Lunch-time specials are probably the best way to sample Kōbe's culinary diversity; this is a tourist town, a fact that is reflected in dinner prices.

For Kōbe beef, *Ikariya* is your best bet. It's only a short walk north of Sannomiya station, there's a menu in English and they're fairly used to foreigners. Set menus of Kōbe beef are priced from ¥10,000.

For more economical fare, take a stroll up Kitano-zaka. Here you'll find *Abait Faim*, a good Italian restaurant with reasonable prices (and menus in English). A few doors up the road is *Cookhouse Un Deux Trois*, as you guessed, a French restaurant, with courses from ¥3000. On the other side of the road look out for *Ju Ju* (it means 'tree tree'), a very up-market Chinese restaurant.

The Sri Lankan restaurant *Court Lodge* is a great place for lunch or dinner in the Kitano-zaka area. They serve a variety of reasonably priced lunch and dinner sets, as well as good Sri Lankan tea. For a light snack try their godamba roti (a beef and potato concoction). The staff all speak English and an English menu is available. Other Kitano highlights, some of them long-running favourites, include *Wang Thai* for Thai food, and *Marrakech* for superb, if pricey, Moroccan food.

Down by Sannomiya station itself, there are two excellent choices. For authentic Korean cuisine in a warm atmosphere, try *Omoni*, under the tracks on the north side of the station. They also have an annex a few shops further west serving simpler meals. Slightly uphill from the station, the Indian restaurant *Ganesh Gar* serves tasty lunch sets from ¥850 and dinner sets from ¥2500. It's upstairs, but their sign is on street level.

For Chinese food, the natural choice is *Nankinmachi* (Chinatown) just south of Motomachi station. For a light lunch, you can choose from any of the restaurants serving take-away dumplings etc from stands in front of their stores. For sit down meals, most of the restaurants serve about the same standard sets. Take a look at the pictures and prices in their windows to choose one that fits your budget. Remember that the gaudier the facade the higher the prices, and the longer the line the better the food.

Entertainment

Kōbe has a relatively large foreign community and a number of bars that see mixed Japanese and foreign crowds. Across from Shin-Kōbe station, on the 2nd floor of the OPA shopping centre, *Hub* is a British-style pub popular on weekends.

Garage Paradise Bar is a little expensive (¥1000 cover), but it's an atmospheric, laid-back kind of place with live piano music, a good place for couples. *Bar, Isn't It?* is like its counterparts in Osaka and Kyoto – loud, lively and cheap. In addition to these, a walk around the small streets north of Sannomiya station will turn up any number of small bars, karaoke rooms and clubs.

Getting There & Away

Train Shin-Kōbe station is the shinkansen stop for trains to Kyoto, Osaka and Tokyo (three hours 13 minutes) or into western Japan and onto Fukuoka (two hours 54 minutes) in Kyūshū. Sannomiya station serves the JR line as well as two private lines, Hankyū and Hanshin railways. If you're in a hurry to or from Kyoto or Osaka, the best way is to take the JR Shinkaisoku limited express (to/from Kyoto, ¥1030, 50 minutes; to/from Osaka station ¥390, 21 minutes).

The private lines are cheaper if a little slower. Hankyū is the more convenient of the two. To or from Osaka's Umeda Hankyū station it costs ¥300 and takes 30 minutes by limited express. To or from Kyoto on the Hankyū line costs ¥590 and takes about an hour by limited express (change at Osaka's Jūso station).Trains also leave westward from Kōbe to the castle town of Himeji, Okayama City and western Honshu. The

Hankyu line is a cheap option as far as Himeji, beyond that you'll have to rely on JR.

Boat There are ferries from Kōbe to Shikoku, Kyūshū and Awaji-shima Island. There are two departure points for ferries: Naka Pier, next to the port tower, and Higashi-Kōbe Ferry Terminal. Basically, the former has ferries to Matsuyama and Imabari (Shikoku) and Ōita (Kyūshū), while the latter has ferries to Takamatsu (Shikoku). The lowest fares are Takamatsu ¥2370, Imabari ¥3600, Matsuyama ¥4430 and Ōita ¥5870. For information regarding departure times call Japan Travel-Phone (☎ 0120-444-800) or inquire at the TIC in Tokyo or Kyoto.

Osaka-Shanghai ferries also stop in Kōbe. For more information, see the Osaka Boat section.

Getting Around

Itami Osaka Airport It is possible to take a bus directly to or from Osaka's Itami airport (which serves mostly domestic traffic). The buses leave the airport every 20 minutes, and the 40 minute trip costs ¥720. They start and terminate at Kōbe's Sannomiya station.

Kansai International Airport There are a number of routes between Kōbe and KIX. By train, the fastest way is the JR Shinkaisoku to/from Osaka station, and the JR Kanku Kaisoku to/from the airport (total cost ¥1530, total time 90 minutes). There is also a direct limousine bus to/from the airport with departures about every half hour (70 minutes, ¥1800). The Kōbe bus stop is on the southern side of Sannomiya station.

There is the sea route, which is the fastest and most interesting way, although a little more expensive than the land routes. Jet shuttle boats make the trip between KIX and Kōbe's Port Island in 27 minutes for ¥2200 (one way). Buses run between the Port Island and Sannomiya and Shin-Kōbe stations (¥240/320, respectively). You'll also have to take a bus from the ferry terminal on the airport island to the passenger terminal for ¥180. If you're leaving from KIX don't forget to bring ¥2600 in cash for the airport departure tax.

Local Transport Kōbe is small enough to travel around on foot. JR, Kankyū and Hanshin railway lines run east to west across Kōbe, providing access to most of Kōbe's more distant sights. A subway line also connects Shin-Kōbe station with Sannomiya station (¥160). There is also a city loop bus service which makes a grand circle tour of most of the city's sightseeing spots (¥250 per ride, ¥650 for an all-day pass). The bus stops at both Sannomiya and Shin-Kōbe stations. Other city buses are also frequent and reliable, and because of the fairly low level of traffic, taxis are often a reasonable option in Kōbe.

Himeji 姫路

If you see no other castles in Japan you should at least make an effort to visit Himeji-jō Castle, unanimously acclaimed as the most splendid Japanese castle still standing. It is also known as Shirasagi, the 'White Egret', a title which derives from the castle's stately white form. The surrounding town itself has little to offer as a tourist attraction, but there are plenty of places to grab a meal on the way to the castle.

Himeji can easily be visited as a day trip from Kyoto. A couple of hours at the castle, plus the 10 to 15 minute walk from the station is all the time you need there. The only other attraction worth lingering for is Himeji's historical museum, which has some interesting exhibits on Japanese castles. Walk to the castle down one side of the main street and back on the other to see the statuary dotted along both sides.

On the way to Himeji, take a look out the train window at the soon-to-be-completed Akashi Kaikyō Suspension Bridge. Its 3910m span links the island of Honshū with Awaji-shima Island, making it the longest suspension bridge in the world. It comes into view on the south side of the train about 10 km west of Kobe.

Orientation & Information

There's a tourist information counter at the station (☎ 0792-85-3792). Between 10 am and 3 pm, English-speaking staff are on duty and can help with hotel/ryokan reservations and arranging guide service at the castle. The castle is straight up the main road from the station, and clearly visible to the north if you're simply passing through Himeji. If you have luggage with you, there are coin lockers at the station.

Himeji-jō Castle 姫路城
Himeji-jō Castle is the most magnificent of the handful of Japanese castles which survive in their original (non-concrete) form. Although there have been fortifications in Himeji since 1333, today's castle was built in 1580 by Toyotomi Hideyoshi and enlarged some 30 years later by Ikeda Terumasa. Ikeda was awarded the castle by Tokugawa Ieyasu when the latter's forces defeated the Toyotomi armies. In the following centuries the castle was home to 48 successive lords.

The castle has a five-storey main donjon and three smaller donjons, the entire structure being surrounded by moats and defensive walls punctuated with rectangular, circular and triangular openings for firing guns and shooting arrows at attackers. The walls of the donjon also feature *ishiotoshi* or openings that allowed defenders to pour boiling water or oil on to anyone that made it past the defensive slits and was thinking of scaling the walls. All things considered, visitors are recommended to pay the ¥500 admission charge and enter the castle by legitimate means.

Ask at the tourist information office or at the castle reception desk about English-speaking guides. The guide service is free and highly recommended by those we spoke to. It's best to call the castle (☎ 0792-85-1146) ahead of time to make an appointment.

It takes about 1½ hours to follow the arrow-marked route around the castle. The castle is open from 9 am to 6 pm (last entry 5 pm) in summer and it closes an hour earlier in winter.

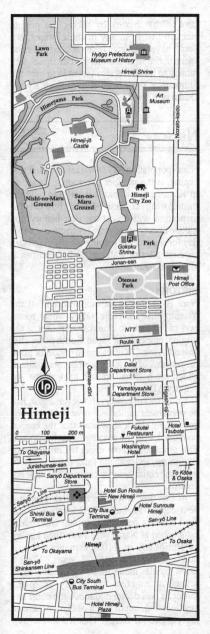

Hyōgo Prefectural Museum of History
県立歴史博物館

This well laid out museum has good displays on Himeji-jō Castle and other castles around Japan and, indeed, the whole world. At 11 am, and 2 and 3.30 pm you can try on a suit of samurai armour or a kimono. In the event of competition for this singular honour, the museum staff resolve the conflict by the drawing of lots. Tell the staff at the main reception desk that you'd like to participate and they'll take care of the details.

The museum is a five minute walk north of the castle. Admission is ¥200, and it's open from 10 am to 5 pm daily except Monday.

Shosha-zan Engyō-ji Temple
書写山円教寺

Around eight km north-east of Himeji station is this seldom visited (by western travellers at least) temple complex on Mt Shosha-zan. It's a well known pilgrimage spot and has been around for some 1000 years. Eight of the temple buildings and seven Buddha images have been designated important cultural properties. Take your time to explore the temple grounds which continue quite a way up the mountain from the cablecar stop. It's most beautiful here in the cherry blossom season (April) or maple leaf season (November) but in any season this is a good spot to escape the crowds.

To get there, take a No 6 or 8 bus from Himeji station (¥260). The trip takes around 25 minutes. Get off at Shosha, and board the cablecar (¥500 one way, ¥900 return) to the top. Entry to the temple area is ¥300, and the cablecar operates every 15 minutes between 8.30 am and 6 pm.

Special Events

The Mega-Kenka Festival, held on 14 and 15 October, involves a conflict between three mikoshi (portable shrines) which are battered against each other until one smashes. The festival is held about a five minute walk from Shirahamanomiya station (10 minutes from Himeji station on the Sanyō-Dentetsu line); just follow the crowds.

KANSAI REGION

Places to Stay

There *are* some places to stay in Himeji, but in general they are overpriced and have little to recommend them. Basing yourself elsewhere and visiting Himeji as a day trip is a far better option.

Seinen-no-Ie Youth Hostel (☎ 0792-93-2716) is a cheap but drab option. Per person rates are ¥1000 for the dorm room (no meals). Cooking and laundry facilities are available. Take bus No 37 bound for Himeji Port and get off at the Chūo Kōen Mae bus stop. The hostel is about 600m west of the stop past a Japanese garden. The tourist information office in Himeji station has maps.

In Himeji itself, the *Hotel Himeji Plaza* (☎ 0792-81-9000) is also close to the station and has singles/doubles from ¥5900/12,000. A cheaper though less attractive option is *Hotel Tsubota* (☎ 0792-81-2227) which has singles for ¥4500, and doubles for ¥8000. It's a plain concrete building about five minutes north of the station. The tourist information office has listings of additional lodgings and can help with directions and reservations.

Places to Eat

There is a food court in the underground mall at JR Himeji station with all the usual western and Japanese foods. There are also several bakeries in the mall for those wishing to take food along for picnics around the castle.

On the way to the castle, a good place to try Japanese kaiseki cuisine at a reasonable price is *Fukutei* (☎ 0792-23-0981). They serve a mini-kaiseki lunch for ¥1600 from 11 am to 2 pm every day except Thursday. Kaiseki dinners, served from 6 to 9.30 pm, start at ¥5000. It's located four streets north of Himeji station a block east of the shopping arcade.

Getting There & Away

The best way to Himeji from Kyoto, Osaka or Kōbe is the JR shinkaisoku (limited express) train. To/from Kyoto it costs ¥2160 and takes two hours. To/from Osaka it costs ¥1420 and takes 90 minutes. To/from Kobe it costs ¥930 and takes one hour. You can save a little money by taking the private Hankyū line from any of these places, but you'll have to change trains at least once and spend more time travelling. For those with money to burn, it's also possible to take the Shinkansen to or from Himeji from Kyoto, Osaka or Kōbe.

Nara 奈良

Nara (population 349,000), Japan's first real capital, is the number two tourist attraction in Kansai after Kyoto. Like Kyoto, Nara is uninspiring at first glance, but careful inspection will reveal the rich history and hidden beauty of the city. Try to choose a fine day for sightseeing – doing the sights in Nara requires a lot of walking, and it's no fun at all in bad weather.

HISTORY

Nara is located at the northern end of the Yamato plain, a fertile valley where members of the Yamato clan rose to power as the original emperors of Japan. South of the city, around Asuka, Kofun burial mounds mark the remains of these early emperors, some of which are believed to date back to the 3rd century AD.

Until the 7th century, however, Japan had no permanent capital as native Shinto taboos concerning death stipulated that the capital be moved with the passing of each emperor. This practice died out under the influence of Buddhism, and with the Taika reforms of 646 when the entire country came under imperial control.

At this time it was decreed that a permanent capital be built. Two locations were tried before a permanent capital was finally established at Nara (which was then known as Heijōkyō) in 710. Permanent status, however, lasted a mere 75 years. When a priest by the name of Dōkyō managed to seduce an empress and nearly usurp the throne, it was decided to move the court to a new location, out of reach of Nara's increasingly powerful clergy. This led to the new capital being established at Kyoto, where it remained until 1868.

Although brief, the Nara period was extraordinarily vigorous in its absorption of influences from China, a process that laid the foundations of Japanese culture and civilisation. The adoption of Buddhism as a national religion made a lasting impact on government, arts, literature and architecture. With the exception of an assault on the area by the Taira clan in the 12th century, Nara was subsequently spared the periodic bouts of destruction wreaked upon Kyoto, and a number of magnificent buildings have survived.

ORIENTATION

Nara retains the grid pattern of streets laid out in Chinese style during the 8th century. The two main train stations, JR Nara station and Kintetsu Nara station, are roughly in the middle of the city and Nara Park, which contains most of the important sights, is on the east side, against the bare flank of Mt Wakakusa-yama. Most of the other sights are south-west of the city and are best reached by buses which leave from both train stations. It's easy to cover the city centre and the major attractions in adjoining Nara-kōen Park on foot, though some may prefer to rent a bicycle.

INFORMATION

If you are heading to Nara from Kyoto, the TIC in Kyoto has extensive information. In Nara, the best source of information is the Nara City Tourist Center (☎ 0742-22-3900), which is open from 9 am to 9 pm. It's a short walk from JR Nara or Kintetsu Nara station. There's a plush lounge to relax in, a display of handicrafts, and helpful staff doling out stacks of maps and literature about transport, sights, accommodation, etc.

The TIC can also put you in touch with volunteer guides who speak English and other foreign languages – try to book ahead. Two of these services are the YMCA Goodwill Guides (☎ 0742-45-5920) and Nara Student Guides (☎ 0742-26-4753). These services are a pleasant way for a foreigner to meet the Japanese (often bright students keen to practise their foreign languages), but they are volunteers so you should offer to cover the day's expenses for your guide.

There are also information offices at both of Nara's train stations which stock maps and have staff who can answer basic questions. The JR Nara station office (☎ 0742-22-9821) is open from 8 am to 6 pm; the Kintetsu Nara station office (☎ 0742-24-4858) is open from 9 am to 5 pm. Ask at the Kintetsu Nara station information office about their cultural exchange programme which may be taking place during your visit.

At the Kyoto Tourist Information Center you can get a copy of the JNTO walking guide to Nara, *Walking Tour Courses in Nara*, which has maps and information on sights. They also have the red JNTO *Tourist Map of Kyoto & Nara* which is fairly useful. Nara tourist information offices have two very useful maps: the green *Japan, Nara City* map which is best for sightseeing within the city limits and the yellow *Japan, Nara Prefecture* which is best for outlying areas. They also have a black leaflet simply called *Nara* which gives an excellent overview of all the sights in the prefecture (look for the picture of Tōdai-ji Temple's Great Buddha on the cover). The main office also has comprehensive listings of places to stay and, time permitting, will help you with reservations (Nara receives thousands of tourists, but they're mostly day-trippers).

For a more academic look at Nara's sights, pick up a copy of *Historical Nara* by Herbert Plutschow (Japan Times, Tokyo, 1983).

PLANNING YOUR ITINERARY

If you're torn between Nara and Kyoto, it's probably safe to say that Nara is a more rewarding sightseeing destination. Nara is also small enough that it's quite possible to pack the most worthwhile sights into one full day. It's preferable, of course, if you can spend at least two days here, but this will depend on how much time you have for the Kansai region. Those with time to spare would best be served by allowing a day for Nara-kōen Park and another day for the

KANSAI REGION

sights in western and south-western Nara. A one-day visit would be best spent tramping around Nara-kōen Park; trying to fit in the more distant sights as well would probably be too exhausting.

NARA-KŌEN PARK AREA 奈良公園周辺

The park was created from wasteland in 1880 and covers a large area. The JNTO's leaflet called *Walking Tour Courses in Nara* includes a map for this area. Although walking time is estimated at two hours,

you'll need at least half a day to see a selection of the sights and a full day to see the lot.

The park is home to about 1200 deer which in old times were considered messengers of the gods and today enjoy the status of national treasures. They roam the park and surrounding areas in search of handouts from tourists, often descending on petrified children who have the misfortune to be carrying food. You can buy special biscuits (shika-sembei, ¥100) from vendors to feed the deer (don't eat them yourself, as we saw one misguided gaijin tourist doing). Although

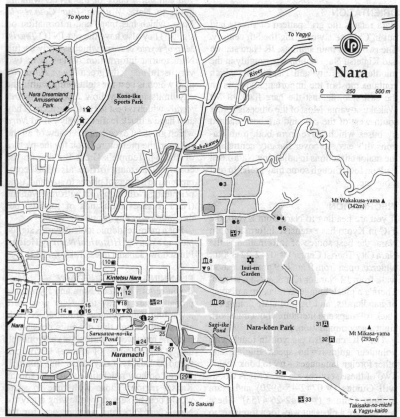

they look cute, these creatures have been spoilt rotten and can be a real menace, particularly during mating season.

Kōfuku-ji Temple 興福寺

This temple was transferred here from Kyoto in 710 as the main temple for the Fujiwara family. Although the original temple complex had 175 buildings, fires and destruction through power struggles have left only a dozen still standing. There are two pagodas, a three-storey one and a five-storey one, dating from 1143 and 1426 respectively.

The National Treasure Hall (Kokuhōkan) contains a variety of statues and art objects salvaged from previous structures. A descriptive leaflet is provided in English.

Admission to the Kokuhōkan costs ¥500 and it's open from 9 am to 4.30 pm.

Nara National Museum 奈良国立博物館

The Nara Koku-ritsu Hakubutsukan (Nara National Museum) is devoted to Buddhist art and is divided into two wings. The western gallery exhibits archaeological finds and the eastern gallery has displays of sculptures, paintings and calligraphy. The galleries are linked by an underground passage.

A special exhibition is held in May and the treasures of the Shōsō-in Hall, which holds the treasures of Tōdai-ji Temple, are displayed here from 21 October to 8 November. The exhibits include priceless items from the cultures along the Silk Road. If you are in

KANSAI REGION

PLACES TO STAY

- 1 Nara Youth Hostel
  奈良ユースホステル
- 2 Seishōnen Kaikan Youth Hostel
  青少年会館ユースホステル
- 10 Nara Green Hotel
  奈良グリーンホテル
- 13 Nara Kokusai Hotel
  奈良国際ホテル
- 14 Hotel Fujita Nara
  ホテルフジタ奈良
- 17 Ryokan Hakuho
  旅館白鳳
- 24 Minshuku Sakigake
  旅館さきがけ
- 25 Minshuku Yamaya
  民宿山屋
- 26 Hotel Sunroute Nara
  ホテルサンルート奈良
- 27 Nara Hotel
  奈良ホテル
- 28 Ryokan Seikan-sō
  旅館静観荘

- 29 Ryokan Matsumae
  旅館松前
- 30 Hotel Nara
  ホテル奈良

PLACES TO EAT

- 9 Sanshū
  三秀
- 11 Tsukihi-tei
  月日亭
- 12 Garden Yamato
  ガーデン大和
- 15 Subway
- 18 Udon-tei
  うどん亭
- 19 Yamazakiya
  山崎屋
- 20 Beni-e
  べに江

OTHER

- 3 Shōso-in Treasure Repository
  正倉院
- 4 Nigatsu-dō Hall
  二月堂

- 5 Sangatsu-dō Hall
  三月堂
- 6 Daibutsu-den
  大仏殿
- 7 Tōdai-ji Temple
  東大寺
- 8 Neiraku Art Museum
  寧楽美術館
- 16 Nara City Tourist Centre
  奈良市観光案内所
- 21 Kōfuku-ji Temple
  興福寺
- 22 Tourist Information Office
  観光案内所
- 23 Nara National Museum
  奈良国立美術館
- 31 Kasuga Taisha Shrine
  春日大社
- 32 Wakamiya-jinja Shrine
  若宮神社
- 33 Shin-Yakushi-ji Temple
  新薬師寺

Nara at these times, you should make a point of visiting the museum.

Regular admission to the museum costs ¥400 and special exhibitions cost ¥790. Hours are 9 am to 4.30 pm.

Neiraku Art Museum & Isui-en Garden
寧楽美術館

The art museum (Neiraku Bijutsukan) displays Chinese bronzes and Korean ceramics and bronzes. The garden, dating from the Meiji era, is beautifully laid out with abundant greenery and a fine view of Tōdai-ji Temple with the hills rising behind. For ¥450 you can enjoy a cup of tea on tatami mats overlooking the garden. You can also eat lunch in the nearby *Sanshū* restaurant while gazing at the garden. Check the Places to Eat section for details. It is highly recommended if you need a break.

Admission to the museum costs ¥600. The same ticket allows entry into the garden. It is open daily from 10 am to 4.30 pm in April, May, October and November, and closed Wednesday during the rest of the year.

TŌDAI-JI TEMPLE 東大寺

This temple is the star attraction in Nara. It is the largest wooden building in the world and houses the Great Buddha – one of the largest bronze images in the world. It also deserves a place in the record books for the largest concentration of tour groups, including hundreds of uniformed kids wearing yellow baseball caps being herded by guides with megaphones and banners.

On your way into the main hall you'll pass through the Nandaimon Gate which contains two fierce looking Niō guardians. These recently restored wooden images, carved in the 13th century by the sculptor Unkei, are considered some of the finest wooden sculptures in all of Japan.

Daibutsu-den Hall 大仏殿

The Daibutsu-den (Hall of the Great Buddha) is not remarkably ancient, being a reconstruction dating from 1709.

The Daibutsu, however, dates back to 746.

The Buddha represented here is the Dainichi Buddha, the cosmic Buddha believed to give rise to all worlds and their respective historical Buddhas. Each lotus leaf on which the Buddha sits represents one entire universe. Historians believe that Emperor Shōmu

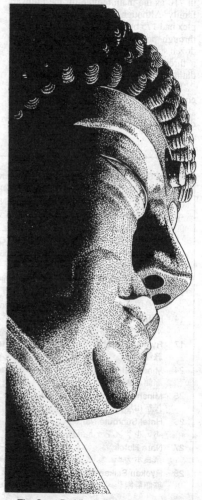

The Great Buddha in Tōdai-ji Temple, the largest wooden building in the world.

ordered the building of the Buddha both as a charm against smallpox which had ravaged Japan in preceding years and as a symbol of the power which he wielded over the country. Over the centuries the statue took quite a beating from earthquakes and fires, losing its head a couple of times in the process.

The present statue, rebuilt in the Edo period, stands just over 16m high and consists of 437 tonnes of bronze and 130 kg of gold. Big isn't necessarily beautiful, but it's still impressive – even more so if you consider that it is only two-thirds the size of the original.

As you circle the statue towards the back, you'll see a wooden column with a small hole at the base. Popular belief maintains that those who can squeeze through are ensured of enlightenment. You'll probably see a lot of disappointed, firmly wedged adults reluctantly giving way to streams of nimble kids making quick work of enlightenment. A hint for determined adults: it's a lot easier to go through with both arms held above your head.

Admission to the Daibutsu-den costs ¥400, and your ticket has a convenient list of the Daibutsu's vital statistics. Opening hours vary throughout the year. You might miss the crowds if you come early in the day or on weekdays in the winter. Opening hours are as follows: November to February from 8 am to 4.30 pm; March from 8 am to 5 pm; April to September from 7.30 am to 5.30 pm; October from 7.30 am to 5 pm.

Shōsō-in 正倉院

The Shōsō-in (Treasure Repository) is a short walk north of Daibutsu-den. If you discount the slight curve to the roof, the structure is reminiscent of a log cabin from North America. The building was used to house fabulous imperial treasures and its wooden construction allowed precise regulation of humidity through natural expansion and contraction. The treasures have been removed and are shown twice a year, in spring and autumn, at the Nara National Museum. The Shōsō-in building is open to the public at the same time.

Kaidan-in Hall 戒壇院

A short walk west of the entrance gate to the Daibutsu-den, you can visit this hall which was used for ordination ceremonies and is famous for its clay images of the Shi Tennō (Four Heavenly Guardians). The hall is open from 8 am to 4.30 pm and admission costs ¥400.

Nigatsu-dō & Sangatsu-dō Halls 二月堂・三月堂

If you walk east from the entrance to the Daibutsu-den, climb up a flight of stone steps, and continue to your left, you reach these two halls.

Nigatsu-dō Hall is famed for its Omizutori Festival (see the later section on Nara Special Events for details) and a splendid view across Nara which makes the climb up the hill worthwhile – particularly at dusk. The hall is open from 8 am to 4.30 pm. Admission is free.

A short walk south of Nigatsu-dō is Sangatsu-dō Hall which is the oldest building in the Tōdai-ji Temple complex. This hall contains a small collection of fine statues from the Nara period. Admission costs ¥400 and it's open from 8 am to 4.30 pm.

Kasuga Taisha Shrine 春日大社

This shrine was founded in the 8th century by the Fujiwara family and completely rebuilt every 20 years according to Shinto tradition, until the end of the 19th century. It lies at the foot of the hill in a pleasant wooded setting with herds of sacred deer awaiting hand-outs.

The approaches to the shrine are lined with hundreds of lanterns and there are many more hundreds in the shrine itself. The lantern festivals held twice a year at the shrine are a major attraction. For details about these and other festivals held at the nearby Wakamiya-jinja Shrine, see the later section on Nara Special Events.

The Hōmotsu-den (Treasure Hall) is just north of the entrance torii for the shrine. The hall displays Shinto ceremonial regalia and equipment used in bugaku, nō and gagaku performances. Admission costs ¥400 and it's open from 9 am to 4 pm.

KANSAI REGION

Takisaka-no-michi/Yagyū Kaidō Day Walk

Time: about three hours
Distance: about eight km
Major Sights: stone Buddhas, tea plantations, Shin-yakushu-ji Temple

Traipsing around dozens of temples in quick succession can be tiring for mind and body. If you've got half a day to spare, this walk in the forested hills around Nara is definitely recommended.

The Nara City Tourist Center can provide maps and transport details. The tourist centre doesn't have any English maps, but you can make do with the Japanese ones, which are more detailed anyway. Ask the staff to circle a few of the key points on the route and write down the names in romaji.

The Takisaka-michi is the old highway leading from the Yagyū area to Nara city (hence its other name, the Yagyū Kaidō). It is cobblestone for part of the way, but most of it is a dirt path which meanders through forests passing the occasional stone Buddhas and shrines by the wayside. Take an early bus from boarding bay 4 opposite Kintetsu station to Enjō-ji Temple. The ride takes about 30 minutes and costs ¥520. Bus Nos 100, 101 and 102 all go via Enjō-ji Temple and take another 17 minutes (and an extra ¥230) to reach Yagyū which is another possible place to start if you want a longer walk down the Takisaka-michi.

After arriving, you can visit Enjō-ji Temple or start the hike immediately. To find the trailhead, cross the road south of the temple and look for a wide path leading off into the woods. There are some confusing trail junctions, but if you stick to the signs leading to Nara you should have no problem (the signs are mounted on posts, with the word Nara written in Japanese as it appears at the beginning of this section). After passing through a small village you'll come to a teahouse which marks the halfway point of the hike. This is an ideal spot to stop for lunch (tea is free and *kusamochi* cakes are ¥130 each).

After the teahouse, the trail works its way downhill to a road which you must cross and after which you descend a stone flight of stairs. At the bottom of these you'll come to a circular wooden rest house, from which you should follow the path downhill alongside the stream. This is the walk's nicest section.

From here on, the best advice is to stick to the trail which parallels the stream. There are various shrines and stone Buddhas along the way. Tucked away on a side track, almost obscured by trees, is the Sunset Buddha, so named because the last rays of the sun light up its face. The trail comes out near Shin-yakushi-ji Temple. If you are exhausted by the time you reach the temple, the No 2 bus will take you back to the city centre. ■

TEMPLES SOUTH-WEST OF NARA

Shin-Yakushi-ji Temple 新薬師寺

This temple was founded by Empress Kōmyō in 747 in thanks for her husband's recovery from an eye disease. Most of the buildings were destroyed or have been reconstructed, but the present main hall dates from the 8th century. The hall contains sculptures of Yakushi Nyorai (Healing Buddha) and a set of 12 divine generals. Admission costs ¥500 and the temple is open from 9 am to 5 pm.

Hōryū-ji Temple 法隆寺

This temple was founded in 607 by Prince Shōtoku, considered by many the patron saint of Japanese Buddhism. Legend has it that Shōtoku, moments after birth, stood up and started praying. A statue in the treasure museum depicts this auspicious event. Hōryū-ji is a veritable shrine to Shōtoku and is renowned not only as the oldest temple in Japan, but also as a repository for some of the country's rarest treasures. Despite the usual fires and reconstructions in the history of the temple, several of the wooden buildings now remaining are believed to be the oldest of their kind in the world.

The layout of the temple is divided into two parts, Sai-in (West Temple) and Tō-in (East Temple); it is the Sai-in precinct that lays claim to being Japan's oldest temple.

The entrance ticket costing ¥1000 allows admission to the Sai-in Temple, Tō-in Temple and Great Treasure Hall. A detailed map is provided and a guidebook is available in English and several other languages. The JNTO leaflet called *Walking Tour Courses in Nara* includes a basic map for the area around Hōryū-ji Temple. From 11 March to 19 November the temple is open from 8 am to 5 pm; for the rest of the year until 4.30 pm.

The main approach to the temple proceeds from the south along a tree-lined avenue and continues through the Nandai-mon Gate and Chū-mon Gate before entering the **Sai-in precinct**. On your way in, you may want to take a short detour to the north-west corner of the temple grounds to see the 'grave' of Landon Warner, located near the Saien-dō Hall. While not his actual grave, this monument was built to honour the Harvard scholar who many Japanese believe was responsible for saving Kyoto and Nara from US bombing in WWII.

As you enter the Sai-in precinct, you'll see the **Kondō** (Main Hall) on your right, and a pagoda on your left. The Kondō houses several treasures, including the triad of the Buddha Sākyamuni with two attendant Bodhisattvas. Though it is one of Japan's great Buddhist treasures, it is dimly lit and barely visible (you may want to bring a flashlight). The pagoda rises gracefully in five finely tapered storeys. The inside walls are lined with clay images depicting scenes from the life of Buddha. Again, without a flashlight you won't be able to see much.

On the eastern side of the Sai-in Temple are the two concrete buildings of the **Daihōzō-den** (Great Treasure Hall), containing numerous treasures from Hōryū-ji Temple's long history. Renowned Buddhist artifacts in this hall include the Kudara Kannon and two miniature shrines: the Tamamushi Shrine and the Shrine of Lady Tachibana.

The **Tamamushi Shrine** is named for the insect (tamamushi or jewel-beetle) whose wings were used to decorate it. The colour in the original has faded, but an example of fresh tamamushi wings is on display and one can only imagine how the shrine must have looked when it was entirely covered with shimmering blue-green wings.

If you leave this hall and continue east

through the Tōdai-mon Gate you reach the **Tō-in**. The Yumedono (Hall of Dreams) in this temple is where Prince Shōtoku is believed to have meditated and been given help with problem sutras by a kindly, golden apparition.

At the rear of the Tō-in compound is the entrance to **Chūgū-ji Nunnery**, which is drab in appearance, but contains two famous art treasures: the serene statue of the Bodhisattva Miroku and a portion of the embroidered Tenjukoku (Land of Heavenly Longevity) mandala, which is believed to date from the 7th century and is the oldest remaining example of this art in Japan. Admission to this temple is ¥400 and it's open from 9 am to 4.30 pm.

To get to the Hōryū-ji Temple, take bus No 52, 60, 97 or 98 from either JR Nara station or Kintetsu Nara station and get off at the Hōryū-ji Mae stop (50 minutes, ¥720). You can also take the JR Kansai line from JR Nara station to Hōryū-ji station (15 minutes). A bus service shuttles the short distance between the station and Hōryū-ji Temple. On foot it takes about 25 minutes.

If you're hungry and can't wait to get back to Nara city to eat, try *Shōkodō* (☎ 0745-74-0908), just outside Hōryū-ji's main gate. Here, they serve excellent shigure udon (noodles with raw egg, nori, wasabi and grated radish) for ¥800. It's open every day 11 am to 5 pm. Look for the traditional wooden building.

Hōrin-ji Temple 法輪寺
Hōrin-ji Temple is about 10 minutes on foot from Chūgū-ji Nunnery. Unless you are a serious fan of Buddhist images, this temple may be of limited interest. In the drab, recently rebuilt Kondō (Main Hall) of the temple there are several images including a fine statue of Yakushi Nyorai (Healing Buddha) with a radiant smile. The pagoda was frazzled by lightning in 1944, but reconstructed in 1975. Admission costs ¥400 and an English leaflet is provided. It's open from 8 am to 5 pm daily but closes an hour earlier between December and February.

Hokki-ji Temple 法起寺

Hokki-ji Temple is a 10 minute walk from Hōrin-ji and instantly recognisable by its elegant three-storey pagoda, which dates back to the early 8th century and vies with the structures at Hōryū-ji Temple for the honour of being the oldest wooden building in the world. The temple has a cosy garden with a small pond. Admission costs ¥300. It's open from 9 am to 4 pm.

Jikō-in Temple 慈光院

Jikō-in Temple is about 25 minutes on foot from Hokki-ji. This Zen temple was founded in 1663 by Sekishu Katagiri who had studied at Daitoku-ji Temple in Kyoto and then devoted himself to Zen and the tea ceremony. Although the gardens and buildings are impressive, the ¥800 admission fee is a bit steep even with the free cup of **matcha** (powdered tea) thrown in. The view from the tearoom ranges over the garden to the encroaching urban sprawl. The temple is open from 9 am to 5 pm, and until 5.30 pm in the summer.

To return to Nara by bus, you should turn left when leaving the temple and go down the hill a short distance to the main road. Turn left again and walk about 100m along the road until you cross a bridge over a river. The bus stop is just beyond the bridge. Buses to the nearby Kintetsu Kōriyama station are more frequent than those to Nara, so if you're in a hurry the train from Kōriyama is the best bet.

Yakushi-ji Temple 薬師寺

Yakushi-ji was established by Emperor Temmu in 680. With the exception of the **East Pagoda**, the present buildings either date from the 13th century or are very recent reconstructions.

The main hall was rebuilt in 1976 and houses several images, including the famous Yakushi Triad (the Buddha Yakushi flanked by the Bodhisattvas of the sun and moon), dating from the 8th century. Originally gold, a fire in the 16th century turned the images an appealing mellow black.

The East Pagoda is a unique structure because it appears to have six storeys, but three of them are *mokoshi* (lean-to additions) which give a pleasing balance to its appearance. It is the only structure to have survived the ravages of time, and dates from 730.

Behind the East Pagoda is the **Tōin-dō** (East Hall), which houses the famous Shō-Kannon image, built in the 7th century showing obvious influences of Indian sculptural styles.

Admission costs ¥500 and a leaflet in English is provided. It's open from 8.30 am to 5 pm.

To get to Yakushi-ji, take bus No 52, 97 or 98 from either JR Nara station or Kintetsu Nara station and get off at the Yakushi-ji Higashiguchi stop (18 minutes, ¥230).

Tōshōdai-ji Temple 唐招提寺

This temple was established in 759 by the Chinese priest Ganjin (Jian Zhen), who had been recruited by Emperor Shōmu to reform

Dolls in Japan are often festival figures rather than simply being playthings for children.

Buddhism in Japan. Ganjin didn't have much luck with his travel arrangements from China to Japan: five attempts were thwarted by shipwreck, storms and bureaucracy. Despite being blinded by eye disease, he finally made it on the sixth attempt and spread his teachings to Japan. The lacquer sculpture in the Miei-dō Hall is a moving tribute to Ganjin: blind and rock steady. It is shown only once a year on 6 June – the anniversary of Ganjin's death (sixth day of the fifth month in the lunar calendar).

The Shin Hōzō (Treasure Hall) has some fine sculptures and images. Admission costs ¥100 and it's open during the same hours as the temple, but only from late March to late May, and from mid-September to early November.

Admission to the temple costs ¥300 and a detailed leaflet is provided in English, including a precise map of the extensive temple grounds. It's open from 8.30 am to 4.30 pm.

Tōshōdai-ji Temple is a 10 minute walk from Yakushi-ji Temple; see the preceding section for transport details from Nara.

SPECIAL EVENTS

Nara has plenty of festivals throughout the year. The following is a brief list of the more interesting ones. More extensive information is readily available from Nara tourist offices or from the TIC in Kyoto.

Yamayaki (Grass Burning Festival)
    15 January. To commemorate a feud many centuries ago between the monks of Tōdai-ji and Kōfuku-ji temples, Mt Wakakusa-yama is set alight at 6 pm with an accompanying display of fireworks. Arrive earlier to bag a good viewing position in Nara-kōen Park.
Mantōrō (Lantern Festival)
    2-4 February. Held at Kasuga Taisha Shrine at 6 pm, this is a festival renowned for its illumination with 3000 stone and bronze lanterns; a bugaku dance also takes place in the Apple Garden.
Omizutori (Water-Drawing Ceremony)
    1-14 March. The monks of Tōdai-ji Temple enter a special period of initiation during these days. On the evening of 12 March, they parade huge flaming torches around the balcony of Nigatsu-dō (in the temple grounds) and rain down embers on the spectators to purify them. The water-drawing ceremony is performed after midnight.

Kasuga Matsuri
    13 March. This ancient spring festival features a sacred horse, classical dancing (Yamato-mai) and elaborate costume.
Takigi Nō
    11-12 May. Open-air performances of nō held after dark by the light of blazing torches at Kōfuku-ji Temple and Kasuga Taisha Shrine.
Mantōrō (Lantern Festival)
    14-15 August. The same as the festival held in February.
Shika-no-Tsunokiri (Deer Antler Cutting)
    Sundays & national holidays in October. Those pesky deer in Nara-kōen Park are pursued in a type of elegant rodeo into the Roku-en (deer enclosure) close to Kasuga Taisha Shrine. They are then wrestled to the ground and their antlers sawn off. Tourist brochures hint that this is to avoid personal harm, though it's not clear whether they mean the deer fighting each other, or the deer mugging the tourists.
On Matsuri
    15 to 18 December. This festival, dating back to the Heian period, is held to ensure a bountiful harvest and to ward off disease. It takes place at Wakamiya-jinja Shrine (close to Kasuga Taisha Shrine) and features a procession of people dressed in ancient costume, classical dances, wrestling and performances of nō.

PLACES TO STAY

Although Nara is favoured as a day trip from Kyoto, accommodation can still be packed out for festivals, holidays and at weekends, so make reservations in advance if you plan to visit at these times. The Nara City Tourist Centre can help with reservations and has extensive lists of hotels, minshuku, pensions, ryokan and shukubō.

Youth Hostels

The *Seishōnen Kaikan Youth Hostel* (☎ 0742-22-5540) is a nondescript, concrete place with helpful staff. Dorm rooms are ¥2600 per person. They also have private double rooms for ¥3800 per person and triples for ¥3000 per person. It's a 30 minute uphill walk from the centre of town to the hostel. From JR Nara station you can take bus No 21 (in the direction of the Dreamland amusement park's south entrance) and get off at the Sahoyama-mae bus stop which is opposite the hostel. Buses run about twice an hour between 7 am and 9 pm.

The *Nara Youth Hostel* (☎ 0742-22-1334) is close to Kōno-ike Pond, a short walk from the other youth hostel. This is a ritzier hostel which *only* takes guests with a hostel membership card and charges ¥2500 per person per night. It is often booked out and swarming with schoolkids on excursions. From either JR or Kintetsu Nara station, take bus No 108 in the direction of Nara Dreamland amusement park and get off at the Yakyūjō-mae stop, which is in front of a baseball stadium beside the hostel.

Ryokan & Minshuku

The *Ryokan Seikan-sō* (☎ 0742-22-2670) has wooden architecture and a pleasant garden. It's a 15 minute walk south of Kintetsu Nara station. Prices for a Japanese-style room without bath start at ¥3800 per person.

The *Ryokan Hakuhoh* (☎ 0742-26-7891) is in the centre of town, just a five minute walk from JR Nara station. Prices for a Japanese-style room without bath start at ¥6500 per person.

The *Ryokan Matsumae* (☎ 0742-22-3686) is close to Nara-kōen Park. Prices for a Japanese-style room without bath start at ¥4500 per person.

There are some minshuku in the city centre. *Minshuku Sakigake* (☎ 0742-22-7252) is in an attractive, traditional style building and has rates of ¥5700 per person including two meals. Slightly cheaper than that is *Minshuku Yamaya* (☎ 0742-24-0045), which costs ¥4200 per person, with no meals. Don't expect English-speaking staff at either of these minshuku, though some English is spoken at each of the three ryokan listed above.

Shukubō

The Nara City Tourist Center has a list of temples offering lodgings. *Shin-Yakushi-ji Temple* (☎ 0742-22-3736), which is in a quiet area near Nara-kōen Park, offers lodging and breakfast from ¥4000 per person per night.

Hotels

The city centre has a few business hotels. The *Nara Green Hotel* (☎ 0742-26-7815) is a small place with singles from ¥6400, twins from ¥12,000 and doubles at ¥11,000. It's close to Kintetsu Nara station. *Nara Fujita Hotel* (☎ 0742-23-8111) is a nice hotel with singles for ¥9500 and doubles for ¥18,000. During off-peak times, they reduce their rates to ¥6000 and ¥10,000 but you must go through the Kintetsu Nara TIC to get this deal.

The *Nara Kokusai Hotel* (☎ 0742-26-6001) is close to JR Nara station and has a small number of singles at ¥7000; twin rooms here are expensive at ¥16,000. Close to the south-western corner of Nara-kōen Park, the *Hotel Sunroute Nara* (☎ 0742-22-5151) has singles from ¥8000 and doubles from ¥15,000.

Not far from the Hotel Sunroute Nara, the rambling *Hotel Nara* (☎ 0742-26-3300) is Nara's premier hotel. It has singles from ¥8000, twins from ¥14,800 and doubles from ¥15,500.

PLACES TO EAT

Nara is full of good restaurants, most of which are located in the central area near the two main train stations and the tourist offices. If you need help finding a place, the main tourist information office has lists of restaurants by category (Japanese, Chinese, western, etc) and can help with reservations and recommendations.

Western Cuisine

You'll find all the standard fast-food places around both train stations. *Subway*, just north of the main tourist information office, makes sandwiches perfect for picnics in Nara-kōen Park. *Garden Yamato* (☎ 0742-26-2260), just east of Kintetsu Nara station, offers courses of French cuisine from ¥1800 for lunch and ¥6000 for dinner. There is also a good steak house in Hotel Fujita Nara called *Steak House Ginza* (☎ 0742-23-8111) which serves set courses for lunch from ¥1000 to ¥3000 and dinners from ¥5000.

Japanese Cuisine

Nara is known for the full-course delights of kaiseki cuisine, which start at about ¥5000 for a basic version. This usually includes the local delicacy called narazuke, tart vegetables pickled in sake. A good place to try simple kaiseki and narazuke is *Yamazakiya* (☎ 0742-27-3751) in the arcade just to the south of Kintetsu Nara station, where set lunches start from ¥1350. There's also a shop in front of the restaurant which sells the pickles as souvenirs.

In the same arcade, close to the northern end on the second floor, is *Tsukihi-tei* (☎ 0742-23-5470) which serves simple kaiseki dishes at very reasonable prices. The tenshin bento is a very good bet at ¥1500. It includes sashimi, rice, vegetables, chawamushi and several other tidbits. Ordering is very easy as there are plastic food models in the window. Just downstairs is *Udon-tei* (☎ 0742-23-5471), which serves set noodle dishes. Try the goshiki (five colour) teishoku lunch for ¥1350.

Also in the arcade, the unusually named *Mamimumeiji* (☎ 0742-26-4586) serves good kushi katsu, skewers of fried meat and vegetables in set courses. The 'A set' of 10 skewers is ¥2000 and the 20-skewer 'B set' is ¥4000. It's only open for dinner from 5 to 10.30 pm and is closed Monday. Nearby is the restaurant *Beni-e* (☎ 0742-22-9439) which serves good tempura from ¥2000 for lunch and dinner. It's located a little back from the street behind a shoe store on the southern end of the arcade.

Perhaps the best place for lunch in all of Nara is *Sanshū* (☎ 0742-22-2173), located next to the beautiful Isui-en Garden in Nara-kōen Park. They serve a traditional Japanese dish made from grated yam, barley and rice. Guests sit on tatami mats enjoying the food while gazing out over the splendour of one of Nara's best gardens. Ordering is simple due to the choice of either the mugitoro gozen (without eel) for ¥1100 or the unatoro gozen (with eel) for ¥2200. Lunch is served every day except Tuesday from 11.30 am to 2 pm.

A short walk from Yakushi-ji or Toshodai-ji Temples in south-western Nara, *Van Kio* (☎ 0742-33-8942) is an interesting choice for those who happen to be in the neighbourhood. Here, they serve an unusual dish called suien mushi, which is made by steaming your choice of meat and vegetables with a red-hot ceramic disc inside a casserole dish. A suien mushi set with duck, seafood or beef costs ¥3300 and includes soup and salad. You may want to call ahead for detailed directions as it is a little tricky to find.

GETTING THERE & AWAY

Air

Nara is served by the new Kansai international airport.

Train

Nara to Kyoto Unless you have a Japan Rail Pass, the best option is the Kintetsu line (often indicated in English as the Kinki Nippon railway) linking Kyoto and Nara (Kintetsu Nara station) in 30 minutes by direct limited express (¥1090 one way). Ordinary trains take 45 minutes and cost ¥590. The JR Nara line connects Kyoto with JR Nara station (one hour, ¥680 one way).

Nara to Osaka The Kintetsu Nara line connects Osaka (Kintetsu Namba station) with Nara (Kintetsu Nara station) in half an hour by limited express (¥1030). Express and local trains take about 40 minutes and cost ¥530.

The JR Kansai line links Osaka (Tennō-ji station) and Nara (JR Nara station) via Hōryū-ji (50 minutes by express, ¥760).

Bus

There is an overnight bus service between Shinjuku in Tokyo and Nara which costs ¥8240 one way or ¥14,830 return. The bus leaves Nara at 10.50 pm and reaches the Tokyo next day at 6.20 am. The bus from Tokyo leaves at 11 pm and arrives in Nara the next day at 6.50 am. Check with the Nara City Tourist Office or the Tokyo TIC for further details.

GETTING AROUND
The Airport
There is a limousine service between Nara and the airport with departures roughly every hour in both directions. The trip takes 90 minutes and costs ¥1800. At Kansai international airport ask at the information counter, and in Nara go to the bus stop in front of Kintetsu Nara station (the same bus platform as the daily bus tours). Reservations are a good idea and can be made on ☎ 0742-22-5110. There are no direct train connections to the airport. By train, in either direction, take the JR line via Tennōji station in Osaka.

Bus
Nara has an excellent bus system geared to tourists and most of the buses have taped announcements in English. Outside Kintetsu station there's even a machine which gives advice in English for your destination. Just push the right destination button to find out your boarding terminal, bus number, ticket cost and departure time for the next bus.

Most of the area around Nara-kōen Park is covered by two circular bus routes. Bus No 1 runs counter-clockwise and bus No 2 runs clockwise. There's a ¥170 flat fare. You can easily see the main sights in the park on foot and use the bus as an option if you are pushed for time or get tired of walking.

The most useful buses for western and south-western Nara (Tōshōdai-ji Temple, Yakushi-ji Temple and Hōryū-ji Temple) are Nos 52 and 97, which have taped announcements in English and link all three destinations with the Kintetsu and JR stations. Buses run about every 30 minutes between 8 am and 5 pm, but are much less frequent outside these times.

From Kintetsu station, allow about 20 minutes and a fare of ¥230 for the trip to Tōshōdai-ji Temple and Yakushi-ji Temple; add another 30 minutes and an extra ¥500 if you continue to Hōryū-ji Temple. Times and fares are about the same from JR Nara station.

Those who don't like walking or making travel arrangements on their own might want to try an organised bus tour – a good way to pack a lot of sights into a limited amount of time. Nara Kōtsū (☎ 0742-22-5263) runs daily bus tours on a variety of routes, two of which include Nara city sights only and two which include more distant sights like Hōryū-ji Temple and the burial mounds around Asuka. With the exception of the Asuka route, an explanation tape in English is available. Prices for the all-day trips average ¥7000 for adults (which includes all temple fees and a tape recorder). Lunch at a Japanese restaurant on the route is optional (reserve when buying ticket). Nara Kōtsū has offices in JR Nara station and across the street from Kintetsu Nara station.

Taxi
Taxis are plentiful, but expensive. From JR station to either of the youth hostels costs about ¥1000.

Cycling
Nara is a convenient size for getting around on a bicycle. The Kintetsu Rent-a-Cycle Center (☎ 0742-24-3528) is close to the Nara City Tourist Center. From the centre, walk east down the main street to the first intersection, turn left into Konishi-dōri and walk about 70m until you see Supermarket Isokawa on your right. Opposite the supermarket is a small side street on your left – the bicycle rental centre is at the bottom of this street. Prices start at ¥900 for four hours or ¥1000 for the day on weekdays and ¥1100/1200 on weekends and holidays. There's a discount for two day rental.

Around Nara

Southern Nara Prefecture was the birthplace of imperial rule and is rich in historical sites which are easily accessible as day trips from Nara or Kyoto – provided that you make an early start. Of particular historical interest are the Kofun burial mounds which mark the graves of Japan's first emperors, concentrated mostly around Asuka and Sakurai. There are also several isolated temples which allow the traveller to escape the crowds which plague Nara's city centre. Farther afield, the mountaintop town of Yoshino makes a pleasant getaway, at least when it's not packed with drunken revellers admiring the town's famous cherry blossoms (April).

The Tourist Division of Nara Prefectural Government publishes an excellent, detailed map called *Japan: Nara Prefecture*. The Nara City Tourist Center should have copies of this map, which gives an overall view of the prefecture and has insets providing precise locations for temples and other sights.

Sakurai and Yamato-Yagi are two cities which are easily reached by rail and are useful as transport hubs for visiting sights in the surrounding region. Travelling from Nara to Yamato-Yagi station you will need to go west to Yamato-Saidaiji first, then change to the south-bound Kintetsu Kashihara line. The JR Sakurai line runs direct between Nara and Sakurai.

AROUND SAKURAI

There are a few interesting places to visit close to the town of Sakurai, which can be reached direct from Nara on the JR Sakurai line (30 minutes, ¥310). To reach Sakurai via Yamato-Yagi (for example, from Kyoto or Osaka), take the Kintetsu Osaka line.

Ōmiwa-jinja Shrine 大神神社

This shrine is just north of Sakurai and can be reached by bus from Sakurai station. You can also walk to the shrine from Miwa station which is one stop north of Sakurai on the JR Sakurai line. Ōmiwa-jinja boasts the highest torii in Japan (32.2m), and is one of Japan's oldest Shinto shrines. Mt Miwa-yama is considered sacred because it is the abode of the shrine's *kami* (spirit gods), and there is a trail for pilgrims to hike up the wooded slopes.

Tanzan-jinja Shrine 談山神社

Tanzan-jinja lies south of Sakurai, and can be reached in about 25 minutes by bus (Nos 1, 33 or 504, ¥440) from Sakurai station. It is tucked away in the forests of Mt Tōnomine, famous for their autumn colours. Enshrined

here is Nakatomi no Kamatari, patriarch of the Fujiwara line which effectively ruled Japan for nearly 500 years. Legend has it that Nakatomi met here secretly with prince Naka no Ōe over games of kickball to discuss the overthrow of the ruling Soga clan. This event is commemorated on the second Sunday in November by sombre priests playing a game of kickball – divine hackey-sack.

The central structure of the shrine is an attractive 13-storey pagoda best viewed against a backdrop of maple trees ablaze with autumn colours. There's a hiking trail from the shrine leading down through the forests in less than two hours to Asuka (Ishibutai-kofun Tomb).

Hase-dera Temple 長谷寺

Two stops east of Sakurai on the Kintetsu Osaka line is Hasedera station which is a 20 minute walk from Hase-dera Temple. After a long climb up endless steps, you enter the main hall and are rewarded with a splendid view from the gallery, which juts out on stilts over the mountainside. Inside the top hall, the huge Kannon image is well worth a look. Perhaps the best time to visit this temple is in the spring when the way is lined with blooming peony flowers. Admission is ¥400 and it's open daily from 8.30 am to 5 pm.

MURŌ-JI TEMPLE 室生寺

To visit Murō-ji Temple, you should return to Hasedera station and continue two stops further east down the Kintetsu Osaka line to Murōguchi-Ōno station. From there, it's a 15 minute ride by bus (No 25 or 702, ¥380).

The temple was founded in the 9th century and has strong connections with Esoteric Buddhism (the Shingon sect). Unlike other Shingon temples, women were never excluded from here, which lead to the nickname, 'the Woman's Koya'. The five-storey pagoda dates from the 8th or 9th century and is the smallest in Japan. It's a peaceful, secluded place in thick forest and worth a visit. It's open daily from 8 am to 4.30 pm and entry is ¥400.

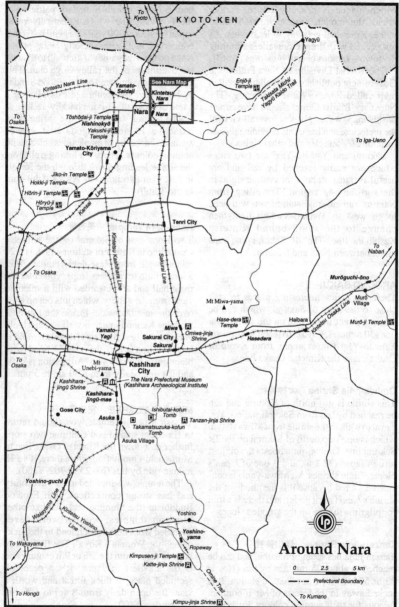

KYOTO-KEN

To Kyoto

Yagyū

See Nara Map

Enjō-ji Temple

Takhata Michi/ Yagyū Kaidō Trail

Kintetsu Nara Line

Yamato-Saidaiji

Kintetsu Nara

Nara

Nara

To Osaka

Tōshōdai-ji Temple
Nishinokyō
Yakushi-ji Temple

To Iga-Ueno

Yamato-Kōriyama City

Jiko-in Temple

Hokki-ji Temple

Hōrin-ji Temple

Hōryū-ji Temple

Kansai Line

Tenri City

To Nabari

Kintetsu Kashihara Line

Sakurai Line

Muroguchi-ōno

Mt Miwa-yama

Muro Village

To Osaka

Hase-dera Temple

Haibara

Muro-ji Temple

Kintetsu Osaka Line

Yamato-Yagi

Miwa

Sakurai City

Sakurai

Hasedera

Omiwa-jinja Shrine

Mt Unebi-yama

Kashihara City

The Nara Prefectural Museum
(Kashihara Archaeological Institute)

Kashihara-jingū Shrine

Kashihara-jingū-mae

Gose City

Asuka

Ishibutai-kofun Tomb

Tanzan-jinja Shrine

Takamatsuzuka-kofun Tomb

Asuka Village

Yoshino-guchi

Wakayama Line

Kintetsu Yoshino Line

To Osaka

Yoshino

To Wakayama

Yoshino-yama

Kimpusen-ji Temple

Ropeway

Katte-jinja Shrine

Ōmine Trail

To Hongū

Kimpu-jinja Shrine

To Kumano

Around Nara

0   2.5   5 km

····· Prefectural Boundary

IMAI-CHŌ
On the south-western edge of Yamato-Yagi is the small town of Imai-chō which (an extreme rarity for Japan) has preserved its houses virtually intact from the Edo period. This is a good place to see classic *machiya* (Japanese townhouse) architecture. It's a pleasant place to walk around and seven of the buildings are open to the public (10 am to noon, 1 to 5 pm, ¥170). To get there, take a train one stop south from Yamato-Yagi to Yagi-Nishiguchi. The town is a 10 minute walk south-west of the station.

KASHIHARA 橿原
Three stops south of Yamato-Yagi, on the Kintetsu Kashihara line, is Kashihara-jingū-mae station. There are a couple of interesting sights within easy walking distance, north-west of this station.

Nara Prefectural Museum
奈良県立橿原考古博物館
This museum, which houses the Kashihara Archaeological Institute, is a must for archaeology buffs interested in the rich pickings from digs in the region. It's open from 9 am to 4.30 pm, closed on Monday, and entry is ¥300.

Kashihara-jingū Shrine 橿原神宮
This shrine, at the foot of Mt Unebi-yama, dates back to 1889, when many of the buildings were moved here from the Kyoto Imperial Palace. The shrine buildings are built in the same style as those of Ise-Jingū's Grand Shrine (Japan's most sacred shrine) and are a good opportunity to see classical Shinto architecture without going all the way to Ise. The shrine is dedicated to Japan's mythical first emperor Jimmu, and an annual festival is held here on 11 February, the legendary date of Jimmu's enthronement. The vast, park-like grounds are pleasant for a stroll. The shrine is five minutes on foot from Kashihara-jingū-mae station.

ASUKA 飛鳥
One stop further south on the Kintetsu Kashihara line is Asuka station. You can rent bicycles here and head east to explore the area's temples, palace remains, tombs and strange stones. The best rental shop is Manyō Rent-a-Cycle (☎ 0744-54-3500) which rents bikes for ¥300 per hour or ¥1000 per day. They allow you to drop bikes off at Kashihara and Asuka-dera Temple, for those who want to do longer tours.

You can also take a bus from Kashihara-jingū-mae station which makes stops within walking distance of many of the sights. Those who want a more structured tour can try the Nara Kōtsū bus tour of the region which leaves from either JR Nara station or Kintetsu Nara station. See the Nara 'Getting Around' section for details.

Two tombs worth seeing are **Takamatsuzuka-kofun** and **Ishibutai-kofun** (*kofun* is 'tomb'). The former (excavated in 1972) is closed to the public, but has a museum (which is open from 9 am to 5 pm, closed Monday, entry ¥200) displaying a copy of the frescoes. History buffs will note that the entire tomb is done in the Chinese style of the time (T'ang), indicating the great degree to which early Japanese civilisation was influenced by continental culture. The Ishibutai-kofun is open to the public, but has no frescoes. It is said to have housed the remains of Soga no Umako but is now completely empty. Entry is from 9 am to 5 pm daily and tickets are ¥200.

The best museum in the area is **Asuka Historical Museum**, which has exhibits from regional digs. If you have time, take a look at **Asuka-dera Temple**, which dates from 596 and is considered the first true temple in all of Japan. Housed within is the oldest remaining image of Buddha in Japan – after more than 1300 years of venerable existence, you'll have to excuse its decidedly tatty appearance.

YOSHINO 吉野
Yoshino is Japan's top cherry blossom wonder. For a few weeks in spring (usually from 10 to 25 April), the blossoms of thousands of cherry trees form a floral carpet gradually ascending the mountainsides. It's definitely a sight worth seeing, but the narrow streets of Yoshino become jammed

tight with thousands of visitors and you'll have to be content with a day trip unless you've booked accommodation long in advance. Early morning or late afternoon on a weekday is a good time to escape the crowds. Another severe impediment to enjoyment of the peaceful setting is an irritating loud-speaker system which relentlessly pursues you with a Mickey Mouse voice turned up at volume to reverberate across the valley.

History

In early times the remote mountainous regions around Yoshino were considered the mysterious abode of the kami (spirit gods) and later became a centre for Shugendō, a Buddhist school which incorporated ancient Shamanistic rites, Shinto beliefs and ascetic Buddhist traditions. The school has its origin

in the banding together of Buddhist hermits who practised their faith deep in the moun-tains, though the legendary En-no-Gyōja, to whom powers of exorcism and magic are ascribed, is frequently referred to as the founder of the school.

Yoshino came to historical prominence in the years following Emperor Go-Daigo's efforts to wrest imperial rule from the Kamakura Shogunate. In 1333, Emperor Go-Daigo successfully toppled the Kama-kura Shogunate with the help of disgruntled generals. The return to imperial rule, known as the Kemmu Restoration, only lasted three years. Go-Daigo failed to reward his sup-porters adequately and he was ousted in a revolt by one of his generals, Ashikaga Takauji, who set up a rival emperor.

Go-Daigo beat a hasty retreat to the

Kofun Burial Mounds

The origins of the Japanese imperial line and the Japanese people in general are shrouded in mystery. Much of what we do know comes from large, earthen burial mounds scattered around the islands of Honshū, Kyūshū and Shikoku. These burial mounds, called *kofun*, served as tombs for members of Japan's early nobility, primarily members of the imperial household. The practice of building these mounds started quite suddenly in the 3rd century and died out gradually by the end of the 7th century. It was during this period that the forerunners of the present imperial family, the Yamato clan, were consolidating their power as rulers over Japan's warring rival factions.

The practice of kofun burial started in the region known today as Kinai, which encompasses Kyoto, Osaka and Nara. Early burial mounds were built on hilltops overlooking fertile land, usually in a round or keyhole shape. Along with the imperial corpse, a variety of both military and ceremonial items were buried, many of which were Chinese in origin, testifying to the extent to which early Japanese civilisation was influenced by continental culture. This influence was the result of frequent contact between Japan and Korean and Chinese cultures present on the Korean peninsula.

In the 4th century the practice of kofun burial spread along the inland sea to western Honshū, Shikoku and Kyūshū, and finally to regions in the west, near present-day Tokyo. Mounds of this period contain, along with the body, vast amounts of funerary objects, most of them continental in origin and military in nature. One mound, the Ōjin mausoleum in Ariyama, was found to contain about 3000 swords buried in a separate treasure mound. The richness of these tombs gives some indication of the absolute power held by these early emperors over the labour and resources of their societies.

Some of the largest mounds were built in the 5th century, including the tomb believed to house the remains of Emperor Nintoku, in southern Osaka. This keyhole-shaped mound is 28m high, 486m in length and covers an area of 32 hectares. The volume of material in this mound is said to be greater than that of the Great Pyramid of Cheops. The use of moats to surround and protect the central chamber also appeared during this period.

Under the influence of Buddhism, which favoured cremation over burial, the practice of kofun burial gradually died out and disappeared by the end of the 7th century.

Some of the best preserved mounds are located in Nara Prefecture, concentrated around the village of Asuka. Most interesting is the stone Ishibutai-kofun, said to house the remains of Soga no Umako, a 7th century noble. Its exposed stone burial chamber looks over the Nara plain and speaks of a time in Japanese history when the emperor held power over his subjects not unlike the power wielded by some of history's other great tomb builders, the pharaohs of ancient Egypt. ■

remote safety of Yoshino where he set up a rival court. Rivalry between the two courts continued for about 60 years, known as Nanbokuchō (Northern & Southern Courts period), until Ashikaga made a promise (which was not kept) that the imperial lines would alternate.

Orientation & Information

To walk from the top cablecar station to Kimpu-jinja should take about 75 minutes at an easy pace. Allow a couple of extra hours to see the sights, or take a picnic for a lazy afternoon under the cherry trees and stay longer.

The village is often clogged with traffic inching its way through the narrow streets past souvenir shops and restaurants, many of which have dining areas on balconies overlooking the valley. Two local specialties are *kuzu* (arrowroot starch) and washi (handmade paper).

For information, you can try the tourist booth on your right as you exit the station, or ask at a similar booth which is in front of the top cablecar station. The official tourist information office is about 400m further up the street, on your right just after the Zao-dō Hall. The staff don't speak much English but are quite helpful and have a specially prepared English/Japanese phrasebook to help foreign travellers.

Things to See

As you walk up the main street, pass through Kuro-mon Gate and then veer slightly to the right up some stone steps to Ni-ō-mon Gate. This brings you to the massive, wooden structure of the Zaō-dō Hall, which is the main building of **Kimpusen-ji Temple**. Said to be the second-largest wooden building in Japan (a claim made about several others), the main hall is most interesting for its unfinished wooden columns. For many centuries Kimpusen-ji has been one of the major centres for Shugendō and pilgrims often stopped here to pray for good fortune on the journey to Mt Ōmine-san. It's open from 8 am to 5 pm daily, and entry to the Zaō-dō Hall is ¥400.

About 500m further up the street you pass **Katte-jinja Shrine** on your right. The road forks uphill to the right, but keep to the left and follow the road until it twists up a hill to some shops. On your left, opposite the shops, there's a steep path leading up the mountain to **Kimpu-jinja Shrine**. Just past the shops, there's a bus stop (with infrequent buses to Kimpu-jinja) to your left on the Yoshino-ōmine driveway – good for motorised transport, but uninteresting as a walk.

There are plenty of streets or flights of steps leading off the main street to small temples and shrines. A short walk beyond the Kizō-in Temple Youth Hostel is the **Chikurin-in Temple** which provides expensive lodging and boasts a splendid garden said to be designed by the famous tea master Sen no Rikyū. You can visit the garden, with its ornamental pond and fine view across the valley, for ¥300. It's open daily from 8 am to 5 pm.

Yoshimizu-jinja Shrine, on a side street opposite the tourist office, has a good platform for blossom viewing.

Mt Ōmine-san Pilgrimage Trail

From Kimpu-jinja Shrine in Yoshino, there's a Shugendō pilgrimage trail running all the way via the ranges of sacred Mt Ōmine-san to coastal Kumano. During the Heian period, the pilgrimage became immensely popular with pilgrims and **yamabushi** (Shugendō priests) trekking from as far as Kyoto and undergoing austere rites en route. Pilgrims who contravened the rules or lacked sufficient faith were given a gentle lesson by being hung over a precipice by their heels. Between May and September many pilgrims still hike this route.

Women were barred from the entire route until as recently as the 1960s. Today, there are still points at either end of the route beyond which women definitely may not pass; any who do try are met with fierce resistance. The most popular part of the route is the climb up Mt Ōmine-san, which can be done either by walking all the way from Kimpu-jinja Shrine outside of Yoshino (about 30 km), or by taking a train and bus to the village of Dorogawa and starting from there. To get to Dorogawa, take the Kintetsu line from Kashihara-jingū-mae to Shimoichiguchi, then switch to a bus for the ride to Dorogawa. The bus takes two hours and costs ¥1330 (buses depart from Shimoichiguchi station at 9.15 am, and 1.15 and 5.45 pm). There are huts along the route for hikers to stay in, open from 1 May to 30 September.

I did the hike from Dorogawa, since it was October and the mountain huts along the trail from Yoshino were supposed to be closed. But if you are equipped with a good sleeping bag and a gas stove you can find shelter in some of the huts along the way from Yoshino to Dorogawa (even out of season).

From Dorogawa, the hike starts from an old cemetery (in summer there is bus service here, otherwise you have to walk about one hour from the town). Women are not permitted beyond this point. I passed some iron corrugated huts which are ... unmanned in the off-season and after a pleasant hike of about two hours I reached the junction with the trail coming from Yoshino. From Yoshino, it would take about eight hours of hiking to reach this point. I turned right here past a large shelter and continued along the route to Sanjō-ga-take, the main summit of Mt Ōmine-san.

After 15 minutes of hiking I met three middle-aged men from Sakai City, one of whom proved to be a sort of weekend yamabushi since he knew this mountain like the back of his hand. He recommended that we take a challenging route up the mountain rather than the usual pilgrim route. This turned out to be a real challenge, indeed. We walked on narrow ledges and pulled ourselves up iron chains dangling from rocks. I felt like a real yamabushi myself.

This route provides gorgeous views of the surrounding mountains, including Mt Hakken-san and Mt Inamura-ga-take. In late October and early November, my friend said, the foliage here is spectacular. About an hour later we arrived at the summit of Mt Sanjō-ga-take and enjoyed our bento lunches in front of a small shrine. There were also a lot of huts on the summit which are closed in the off-season.

We took the tourist route back to the foot of the mountain, I said goodbye to my new friends and then walked back to Dorogawa along the right side of the river. An hour later I arrived at my ryokan (Iroha Ryokan) and enjoyed a hot bath and delicious dinner before collapsing in my futon.

Ingo Westner

Places to Stay & Eat

The tourist information office in the centre of the village can organise accommodation or you can use the information booths outside Yoshino station or at the top cablecar

station. Many of the temples offer lodgings, but you'll be looking at a minimum of ¥10,000 including meals. A slightly cheaper alternative is provided by several minshuku.

The cheapest option, at ¥2600 per person per night, is *Kizo-in Temple* (☎ 07463-2-3014), which doubles as the local youth hostel and provides an excellent opportunity to stay in a temple. Several of the hostel rooms look out across the valley.

Kizō-in Temple is easy to find. Just after Katte-jinja Shrine, the road divides. Take the right-hand fork up the steep hill for about 300m until you reach the imposing temple gate at the crest of the hill on your left.

On the same fork of the road, near the fork itself, is the *Kokuminshukusha Yoshino Sansō* (☎ 07463-2-5051). It has a good reputation for its meals, and per-person costs including two meals are from ¥6500. *Chikurin-in Temple* (☎ 07463-2-8081) is an exquisite temple, famous for its garden, which now operates primarily as a ryokan. Both the present and the previous emperors have stayed here, and a look at the view afforded by some of the rooms explains why. To best enjoy the view, ask for a room on the northern or western sides of the building. Per person prices start at ¥15,000 including two meals. Reservations are essential for the cherry blossom season, a good idea at all other times.

The main street has dozens of restaurants and coffee shops. The former tend to close early after the day-trippers have left.

Getting There & Away

All rail connections to and from Yoshino run via Yoshino station. From the station you can reach the centre of Yoshino by simply walking uphill for 25 minutes or by taking a five minute cablecar ride (¥460 return).

From Kyoto you can take the train south on the Kintetsu Nara/Kashihara lines (they change halfway) to Kashihara-jingū-mae (50 minutes). At Kashihara-jingū-mae it's necessary to change to the Kintetsu Yoshino line for Yoshino station (40 minutes). You can do the whole trip in around two hours by regular express service. The ticket price is ¥1170 (almost double that for limited express service). It's possible to do the same trip from Nara by taking a train from Nara to Kashihara-jingū-mae station.

From Osaka (Abenobashi station close to Tennō-ji station) you can take the direct train on the Kintetsu Minami-Osaka line to Yoshino. Limited express services take one hour 12 minutes and costs ¥1780.

For rail connections to or from Wakayama Prefecture (for example, Mt Kōya-san), you can join the JR Wakayama line at Yoshino-guchi station.

IGA-UENO 伊賀上野

This rather drab town, an hour west of Nara by train, is dominated by a castle, which was once a base for ninja who were trained in martial and spiritual skills. The town also derives considerable literary and touristic clout from being the birthplace of Bashō, Japan's most celebrated haiku poet. In response to popular demands, the city elders have considerably installed a drop-in box for visitors' haiku poetry.

Orientation & Information

The sights are contained in Ueno-kōen Park – the castle is visible from the station – which

is a 12 minute walk north of Ueno-shi station. Use the walkway under the tracks, cross the road and continue uphill into the park.

There's an information office with maps and English leaflets just outside Ueno-shi station. If you have a large backpack which won't fit the lockers, you can pay ¥200 to deposit it at the Taki Sankō taxi stand next to the station and save yourself the trouble of lugging your load around the park.

The area around Iga-Ueno is famous as a ceramics centre which produced classic items for the tea ceremony. There's a pottery museum, Iga Shigaraki Kotōkan, right next to Ueno-shi station.

Iga is also famous for producing virtually all of Japan's *kumihimo*, braided cords made from silk as adornments for swords and, in modern times, as classy kimono accessories.

Ninja Yashiki House 忍者屋敷

The house originally belonged to a village leader and was moved here from Takayama village in the Iga district.

Pink-suited *kunoichi* (ninja girls) go through a quick and wooden routine demonstrating how to slip through revolving doors. The group of visitors is then handed over to an old man who reveals a concealed cupboard and then continues with perhaps the most

KANSAI REGION

Ninjutsu

Those who have read *Shogun* by James Clavell, watched a few martial arts movies or taken an interest in the Teenage Mutant Ninja Turtles will know about this martial art. Although the Japanese claim it as their own, it's more probable that it was adapted in ancient times from the *Sonshi*, a Chinese tactical manual, used in Shugendō for training *yamabushi* (mountain priests).

Ninjutsu (the art of stealth) was perfected after the 13th century as a means for the practitioners *(ninja)* to provide their lords with services such as assassination, stealthy thievery, sabotage and spying.

Two schools flourished during the 14th and 15th centuries, the Iga and Koga. Training took place in small family units. At one stage nearly 50 of these were active. Trainee ninja were taught the spiritual and physical skills of both overt and clandestine action along the lines of the Chinese theory of Yin and Yang. They developed tremendous agility in climbing, jumping and swimming, and could even sprint sideways and backwards.

To facilitate their spying and killing, they dressed in black for night operations and used a variety of gadgets. These included a collapsible bamboo stick for scaling walls, metal throwing stars *(shuriken)* and nasty little items called caltrops *(tennenbishi)* which had four spikes arranged to skewer the feet of pursuing enemies. ∎

impressive display when he deftly flips up a fake floorboard and retrieves a hidden sword in one rapid movement.

In the basement of the house is a museum with uniforms, martial implements and information in Japanese about *ninjutsu* (the art of ninja).

Admission costs ¥500 and it's open from 9 am to 5 pm but closed from 29 December to 1 January.

Ueno-jō Castle 上野城

This castle was built on the remains of a temple in 1608 by the lord of Iga and Ise, Todo Takatora. The present structure is a reconstruction from 1935. As you climb up steep stairs, there are exhibits of pottery, paintings, armour and ninja paraphernalia on each floor. It's worth a quick visit, particularly in the cherry blossom season and in combination with the Ninja House.

Admission to the castle costs ¥400. It's open from 9 am to 5 pm but closed from 29 December to 1 January.

Bashō Memorial Museum

Bashō Ou Kinekan (Bashō Memorial Museum) is a brick and concrete building displaying some of Bashō's literary works. Unless you are a Bashō fan, you can safely skip this.

Those interested in literary trivia might like to know that Bashō is also the name for the Japanese banana tree and the poet was given his name after a disciple had planted one as a present at the gate of his retreat.

Admission costs ¥150 and it's open from 8.30 am to 5 pm daily except Monday, Thursday afternoon and days following a national holiday.

Special Events

Ninja Matsuri takes place on the first Sunday in April in the park.

Ueno Tenjin Matsuri takes place at Sugiwara-jinja Shrine between 23 and 25 October. Dating from the 16th century, the festival features a parade of mikoshi (portable shrines) on ornate floats which are accompanied by fearsomely attired demons.

Getting There & Away

The best way to Iga-Ueno from Kyoto or Osaka is the JR line via Nara. From Nara station, there are expresses on the Kansai main line to Iga-Ueno station. Change trains at Iga-Ueno station to the Kintetsu local for the short trip down to Ueno-shi station (¥220). Since departures are fairly infrequent on this line, you may prefer to walk (30 minutes) or take a taxi down to Ueno-kōen Park. Kintetsu connections to Ueno run via Iga-kanbe station, south of the city. From there you have to change to the local for the 25 minute ride to Ueno-shi station. The total cost, by limited express, is ¥2500 from Nagoya and ¥2010 from Osaka.

Wakayama-ken 和歌山県

This remote and mountainous prefecture is on the south-western side of the Kii Peninsula. Wakayama is best known for its hot springs in the south and the mountaintop temple complex of Kōya-san in the north, one of the major centres of Buddhism in Japan. It's also the location of a historic pilgrim trail known as the Kumanokodō, which used to stretch from Osaka to three of Japan's most famous shrines in the south of the prefecture, known collectively as the Kumano Sanzan. In the summer, the beaches around Shirahama are popular with Japanese and the rugged coastline near Kushimoto at the southern tip of the prefecture is beautiful in any season.

Transport can be slow and infrequent, whether chugging along the coastline by rail or bussing through the remote, mountainous regions.

JNTO publishes a leaflet called *Shirahama & Wakayama Prefecture*, which gives concise details about sights and transport. Also, the International Exchange Section (☎ 0734-32-4111) of Wakayama Prefectural Government publishes *Welcome to Wakayama Prefecture* which has detailed mapping and information. Call in Japanese.

SHINGŪ 新宮

This town is nothing exceptional to look at, but functions as a useful transport hub for access to the three major Shinto shrines of the Kumano Sanzan (Kumano Hayatama Taisha, Kumano Hongū Taisha and Nachi Taisha). There's an information office (☎ 0735-22-2840) at the station where you can get tourist information, pick up maps and check bus or train schedules.

If you are killing time between trains or buses, you could visit the gaudy **Kumano Hayatama Taisha Shrine** which is a 15

minute walk north-west of Shingū station. The shrine's Boat Race Festival takes place on 15 and 16 October. The nearby Shinpokan Museum houses treasures accumulated by the shrine.

Kamikura Shrine is famous for its Oto Matsuri Festival on 6 February when over 1000 carrying torches ascend the slope to the shrine. The shrine is a 15 minute walk west of the station.

If you're looking for a place to stay, you could try the *Shingū Hayatama Youth Hostel* (☎ 0735-22-2309) which is a 15 minute walk

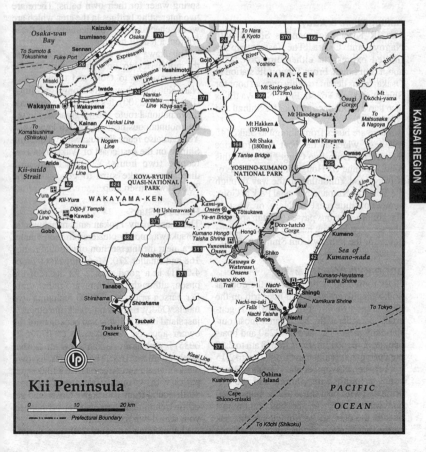

Kii Peninsula

0   10   20 km

Prefectural Boundary

KANSAI REGION

from the station, close to Kumano Hayatama Taisha Shrine. It's a relatively inexpensive youth hostel, with beds at ¥2500. Slightly more up-market is the *Hase Ryokan* (☎ 0735-22-2185) which is a two minute walk north-east of the station. Though billed as a ryokan, it feels like a minshuku. Per person prices including two meals are ¥6000 without a private bath and ¥7000 with a private bath. With no meals, prices are ¥4500/5500. Ask at the tourist information office for a map to both places. For dinner, you might try the *Daikichi* yakitori restaurant across from the station.

Getting There & Away

The JR Kisei line connects Shingū with Nagoya and Osaka. The fastest trip by limited express in either direction takes about four hours. From Tennoji JR station in Osaka, trains depart roughly once an hour for Shingū and cost ¥6380. From Nagoya trains also leave about once an hour for Shingū and cost ¥6550.

There are buses from Shingū to Shikō (45 minutes), which is the boat dock for trips through the Doro-kyō Gorge. Buses on this route continue via Hongū or the spa towns of Kawayu and Yunomine all the way through the Yoshino-Kumano National Park to Gōjō; some continue east to Nara or west to Hashimoto. The bus passes through spectacular scenery, but you need to allow over five hours for the journey from Shingū to Gōjō.

DORO-KYŌ GORGE 瀞峡

Glass-roofed boats depart from the dock at Shikō for the dramatic two hour trip on the Kitayama-gawa River through what is generally considered to be Japan's most outstanding gorge. The fare is ¥3280 and boats operate at regular intervals from 8 am to 2.50 pm during the summer and from 9 am to 2.15 pm between November and February. Buses connect Shikō with Shingū and are coordinated with boat times (42 minutes, ¥960 one way). Look for the bus station just outside the entrance to Shingū station. Ask at the bus station about special bus/boat

tickets which include round-trip bus fare from Shingū for ¥5100.

TOTSUKAWA ONSEN 十津川温泉

Totsukawa Onsen is a great place to enjoy an outdoor bath in pleasant surroundings. While actually part of southern Nara prefecture, it's been considered as part of the onsen group surrounding Hongū as the two are only a short distance apart. There are a variety of onsen around Totsukawa, the best of which is Kamiyu, a simple outdoor bath beside a mountain stream. Many of the minshuku in the area also use natural hot-spring water for their own baths. There are two interesting bridges in the area which are worth checking out, particularly for those without a fear of heights.

Totsukawa is not serviced by train. From the north (Kyoto or Osaka), take the JR Wakayama line to Gojō and transfer to a Nara Kōtsū bus bound for Hongū or Shingū (five hours, ¥3300). It's a long but scenic ride down national route 168 – a great way to see the mountainous heart of the Kii Peninsula. You can also reach Totsukawa by bus from Shingu on the east coast of Wakayama Prefecture (two hours, ¥2010). From both directions, make sure to get off at the Totsukawa Onsen stop.

Places to Stay

There are many ryokan and minshuku in Totsukawa, mostly clustered in the Hiratani area, near the intersection of national routes 168 and smaller 270. *Matsunoya* (☎ 07466-4-0111) is a good choice for its roof-top onsen, although the rooms are rather drab. Per person prices are ¥5000 including two meals. Oddly, there is no check-in counter – just stand in the hallway and beckon until the owner appears. *Totsukawasō* (☎ 07466-2-0035) is a pleasant ryokan a few km further north on route 168. The inn has its own outdoor onsen and prices start at ¥13,000 per person with two meals. Take any of the buses north-bound from Totuskawa Onsen and get off at Uenoji. You can also get off here on your way down from Gojō.

Out of town on route 270, just upriver

from Kamiyu onsen, the minshuku *Kawauso* (☎ 07466-4-0663) has rooms for ¥6700 per person with two meals. This is a quiet place right out in the middle of the forest, very convenient to Kamiyu Onsen. You'll have to walk an hour from town, take a taxi or call and ask the owner to come and pick you up.

Camping is also an option. There is a private camping ground about one km west of the village on route 270, which charges ¥500 per adult, but there seems little reason to stay here as you can camp for free just a few minutes walk up either of the rivers nearby. Note that there are *mamushi* (Japanese vipers) in the area and you should be careful when bushwhacking, especially in the evening when the snakes are most active.

Totsukawa ya-en Bridge

A *ya-en* is a bridge used to transport people and goods across frequently flooded mountain rivers. It's a wooden basket suspended from two wire cables with a hemp rope in the middle which one uses to pull the basket across the river. It's strictly a one-person affair, although friends on either side of the river can help by pulling the rope. The Totsukawa ya-en Bridge is located about a km west of Totsukawa village on route 270, just past the camping ground. It's free and open any time. Look for the yellow and red signs written in Japanese on both sides of the bridge warning about Japanese vipers. It's a five minute walk here from Totsukawa Onsen village. Ask at the local corner store for directions.

Tanise no Tsurubashi Bridge

This bridge stretches 297m from end to end over the Totsukawa river. It's in Uenoji, about 20 km north of the main part of Totsukawa village. Crossing the bridge is most exciting when others are also on the bridge, making it sway and vibrate over the river some 54m below. Most of the buses from Gojō in the north to Hongū and Shingū in the south make regular stops here to give passengers a chance to cross the bridge. Those coming from Totsukawa Onsen village can take any of the local buses north-

bound for Uenoji. There is no charge to cross the bridge.

Kamiyu Onsen

This is the onsen to visit when you're tired of built-up, touristy onsens. It's a *rotenburo* (outdoor, hot-spring bath) alongside a picturesque mountain stream. It's possible to spend all afternoon here, jumping into the river to cool down when the bath gets too hot. Unfortunately, as is often the case in Japan, the men's bath is nicer than the women's. If there's no-one around and all parties are amenable, just ask the owner to let everyone into the men's bath. Kamiyu Onsen is on route 270 about five km west of Totsukawa village. You can walk from town in about an hour or take a taxi for about ¥1000. It's open from 9.30 am to 8 pm every day except Monday and Friday when it closes at 5 pm. Admission is ¥500.

HONGŪ 本宮

Hongū itself isn't particularly interesting but it makes a good starting point for the onsen villages located nearby. Hongū is also home to one of the three sacred shrines of the Kumano Sanzen, **Kumano Hongū Taisha**. The approach to the shrine follows a tree-lined avenue up a steep flight of steps. While you're in Hongū you might want to try the local specialty, mehari sushi, which is rice wrapped in edible leaves. Look for stands outside many of the town's restaurants.

Nara Kōtsū and JR buses leave for Hongū from Gojō in the north and Shingū in the south. From Gojō, it's a scenic five hour ride (¥3900) and from Shingū it's a two hour ride (¥1950). Buses in both directions make stops at the three onsens listed below. Prices and times are about the same for all three stops. There are also regular local buses to the three onsens which leave from Hongū's main bus station.

YUNOMINE, WATARASE & KAWAYU ONSEN

These are three ancient spa towns popular with hot-spring enthusiasts. The best of these is Yunomine, a cosy little town nestled in a

KANSAI REGION

river valley. Kawayu, which means 'hot water river', is best in the winter when the entire river is turned into a giant onsen capable of accommodating about 1000 people. Watarase Onsen is the least atmospheric of the three, built to serve bus tour groups. It does, however, boast the largest rotenburo (outdoor, hot-spring bath) in Kansai, and may be worth a visit during the off-peak season. While all three onsen have ryokan and minshuku nearby, those on a tight budget might prefer to camp. The best place for this is on the riverbanks downstream from Watarase Onsen. See Hongū for transport details to these three onsen.

Yunomine Onsen　湯の峰温泉
Yunomine consists of a narrow main street with a river and hot springs running down the middle. There are numerous hotels and minshuku on the wooded slopes either side of the street. Most of the baths in town are inside ryokan or minshuku. Tsuboyu Onsen, however, is open to all and is definitely worth a try. It's right in the middle of town, inside a wooden shack on an island in the river. Buy a ticket (¥250) at the coffee shop just above the onsen. Entry is one group at a time, so if someone is already there, just sit on the bench outside and wait your turn. The water here is reputed to change colour seven times a day, and you'll certainly turn colour waiting for it to do so.

While you're there, you can try your hand at cooking some *onsen tamago* – eggs boiled in the hot water of an onsen. There is a pool of hot-spring water just downstream from Tsuboyu for cooking. The coffee shop sells bags of six eggs for ¥300. Put them in before you enter the bath and they should be done when you get out.

Yunomine has plenty of minshuku and ryokan to choose from. At the upper end of the village, *Yunotanisō* (☎ 07354-2-1620) has pleasant tatami rooms for ¥7000 per person with two meals. At the lower end of the village, *Minshuku Azumayasō* (☎ 07354-2-0238) has rooms for ¥8000 per person with two meals. When you call, be sure to specify that you want to stay in the minshuku, as they

also run a ryokan for three times the price. Both places have their own hot-spring baths.

Watarase Onsen
Watarase Onsen is built around a bend in the river a few km downstream from Yunomine Onsen. There is little to recommend this cluster of new, characterless buildings. If you are a big onsen fan, however, you can try the huge rotenburo (open-air baths) here for ¥700 from 9 am to 8 pm. Otherwise, continue on to Kawayu Onsen.

Kawayu Onsen　川湯温泉
Kawayu Onsen is in a flatter, less attractive valley than Yunomine Onsen. It's interesting, though, because the hot springs bubble out of the riverbed and there are numerous makeshift rotenburo dug out of the stones. You can spend all day here going back and forth between the baths and the river. Entrance is free and those shy about prancing around naked in public might want to bring a bathing suit. In the winter, from 1 November to 28 February, bulldozers are used to turn the river into a giant 1000 person rotenburo.

The cheapest place to stay in Kawayu is the drab *Kajika-sō* (☎ 07354-2-0518), a combined youth hostel and minshuku. Rates for the youth hostel are ¥4300 per night (plus ¥100 onsen tax) for members, ¥4600 for non-members. The minshuku is overpriced at ¥8000 per-person. Both rates include two meals.

Hotels in Kawayu, as in other Japanese onsen towns, tend to be expensive. *Pension Ashita-no-Mori* (☎ 07354-2-1525) is a pleasant wooden building where per-person costs are ¥10,000 with two meals. Almost next door, *Fujiya* (☎ 07354-2-0007) is a more up-market ryokan, where a tasteful room will set you back ¥18,000 or more with two meals.

NACHI-KATSUURA　那智・勝浦
This is a district, close to the southern tip of the Kii Peninsula, with several sights reached either from Nachi station or Kii-Katsuura station. The rocky coast around the area is quite lovely, but encroaching tourist development is starting to take its toll.

Nachi 那智

Nachi has several sights grouped around the sacred **Nachi-no-taki Falls**, Japan's highest waterfall, which has a drop of 133m. **Nachi Taisha Shrine**, one of the three great shrines of the Kii Peninsula, is near the waterfall as a natural homage to its kami. The way to the shrine is above the main parking lot for the falls. The shrine itself is gaudy and not really worth the long climb to reach it. If you are in the mood for a climb, however, a trail leaves from the shrine to two hidden waterfalls above the main falls. These are seldom visited by tourists and are worth a look. You can also pay ¥200 at the base of the falls to hike up to a viewpoint which affords a better view of the falls.

The Nachi-no-Hi Matsuri (Fire Festival) takes place at the falls on 14 July. During this lively event portable shrines (mikoshi) are brought down from the mountain and met by groups bearing flaming torches.

Buses from Nachi station to the waterfall take 20 minutes and cost ¥450. From Kii-Katsuura station buses take about 30 minutes and cost ¥580.

Kii-Katsuura 紀伊勝浦

This resort town offers cruises around local islets and the renowned Bōki-dō Cave spa, which was popular with nobility in the Edo period. The catch is that the spa is inside one of Japan's largest hotels – the expensive Hotel Urashima (☎ 07355-2-1011). The cave spa is open to visitors from noon to 10 pm, and admission costs ¥2000. It's on the spit of land across the harbour from the train station.

The town is famous for its seafood, particularly its fresh maguro (tuna) sushi and sashimi. *Katsuichi-no-maguro-ryōri* (☎ 07355-2-0830), a few blocks east of the station, is a good place to try the local fare. Full-set dinners go from ¥3500. It's closed Thursday.

The tourist office (☎ 07355-2-5311) is in front of the station.

Getting There & Away

A leisurely way of reaching the Kii Peninsula from Tokyo is the ferry between Tokyo Ferry Terminal (Ariake Pier in Toyocho) and Ukui Port close to Nachi. There's one sailing every second day (13 hours, from ¥9060). There is a connecting bus (20 minutes, ¥400) between Nachi station and Ukui Port.

The same ferry runs between Ukui Port and Kōchi on Shikoku in about eight hours. Fares start at ¥5560 for this section of the trip or ¥13,910 for the whole trip between Tokyo and Kōchi.

The JR Kisei line runs from Osaka's Tennōji station to Taiji in about four hours. Limited express fare is ¥6160. There is also direct service from Kyoto twice a day which takes about five hours and costs ¥7600.

TAIJI 太地

The earliest methods of whaling in Japan consisted simply of capturing whales that had become beached on the shore or trapped in bays. At the beginning of the 17th century, Taiji was one of the first communities to organise its whale hunting into a full-scale industry using hand harpooning and later, net whaling. The rest of the story leading to the virtual extinction of many species of whale is well known and those who love whales will certainly be saddened by a visit to Taiji.

Things to See

The **Whale Beach Park** (Kujira Hama-kōen) is about five minutes by bus from Taiji station. Admission costs ¥1030 and it's open from 8.30 am to 5 pm. The entry ticket admits you to the Whale Museum, Whalers Museum, Marine Aquarium and Tropical Botanical Garden. It's a two km walk from Taiji station to Whale Beach Park. You can also approach the park from Katsuura station by bus (20 minutes, ¥440).

Places to Stay

The *Taiji Youth Hostel* (☎ 07355-9-2636) is three km from the station: 45 minutes on foot or nine minutes by bus. Get off at the Kōen-mae stop. Nightly costs at the hostel are ¥2800. Breakfast and dinner are served for ¥500 and ¥800 respectively.

KANSAI REGION

KUSHIMOTO & CAPE SHIONO-MISAKI
串本・潮岬

Cape Shiono-misaki was an island off the southern tip of the Kii Peninsula until a sandbar formed connecting it to the mainland. Now, the sandbar is buried underneath the city of Kushimoto. The city itself is rather drab, but the cape is worth a look for its rugged, rocky coastline. It's also a short ferry ride from here to **Kii Ō-shima Island** (10 minutes, ¥170), which has a beautiful coastline and is a pleasant place to explore on foot.

Kushimoto is renowned for the Hashi-kui-iwa, a line of pillar-like rocks that have been imaginatively compared to a 'line of hooded monks' heading towards Kii Ō-shima Island. To take a look at the rocks, take a Shingū bound bus from Kushimoto station, and get off five minutes later at the Hashi-kui-iwa stop (¥130). For more local information contact the Kushimoto Tourist Association (☎ 07356-2-3171).

There are two youth hostels almost next to each other, on the tip of Cape Shiono-misaki. *Shiono-Misaki Youth Hostel* (☎ 07356-2-0570), with rates of ¥2800, is the cheaper of the two. *Misaki Lodge Youth Hostel* (☎ 07356-2-1474), with rates of ¥4550, has the better location. It's also a minshuku with large rooms looking right out over the Pacific for ¥7000 per-person including two meals. Take a Shiono-misaki bound bus from Kushimoto station (20 minutes) and get off at the last stop – Sugu-mae.

Kushimoto is one hour from Shirahama by JR limited express, 3½ hours from Tennō-ji in Osaka, and two hours from Shingū by bus.

SHIRAHAMA 白浜

Shirahama is one of Japan's top hot-spring resorts and comes complete with hectares of swish hotels, golf courses, cabarets, an Adventure World and so forth. This probably makes it rather more interesting for Japanese than for most foreigners. Nonetheless, the white sand beach for which the town is named is quite beautiful and may appeal to beach fans in the quieter times of June or September. The wonders of Shirahama are some distance from the station so you'll need to take a bus

or rent a bicycle if you arrive by rail. The bus ride to the city centre takes 17 minutes.

The Shirahama tourist information office (☎ 0739-42-2900) is in the station and open from 8.30 am to 5 pm. It's closed on Thursday. You could also try the Shirahama Tourist Association (☎ 0739-43-5511).

If you want to be independent, there's a bicycle rental place at the station – charges are ¥400 per hour or ¥1100 for the day.

Things to See & Do

Sakino-yu hot springs are built into the rocks of a point jutting out into the sea – the view is great. Come early in the day to beat the crowds. Take the bus from Shirahama station to Yuzaki bus stop (17 minutes), then walk for 10 minutes down to the seaside baths. Admission is free and the baths are segregated by sex. Sakino-yu is open from 7 am to 7 pm in the summer and from 8 am to 5 pm in the winter but is closed on Wednesday.

Shirahama Beach, the main beach in town, is famous for its white sand. If it reminds you of Australia don't be surprised – the town had to import sand from Australia after the original stuff washed away. This place is packed during July and August. In the off-peak season, it can actually be quite pleasant. The beach is difficult to miss as it dominates the west side of town. Exploring the town's other beaches to the north and west of this beach may yield quieter venues.

Overlooking the ocean on a point just south of town, **Isogi kōen Park** is a great place for a picnic away from the crowds of Shirahama. Bushwhack through the woods from the parking lot to the sea and you'll be rewarded with a great view of the Pacific and the rocky coast south of Shirahama. When big waves are rolling in it's spectacular. The park is a 20 minute walk south of the Sandaki bus stop.

At Tsubaki Onsen, two stops south of Shirahama on the JR line, there's the **Tsubaki Monkey Park**. The monkeys, some 250 of them, are described as being 'popular with visitors' and 'humorous'. You'd *have* to be humorous if you wanted to live there, deal with all the crowds and stay sane. If you want to contribute to the monkeys' happiness, bring some bananas.

Places to Stay

If you don't mind staying outside the town of Shirahama, the cheapest option is *Ohgigahama Youth Hostel* (☎ 0739-22-3433), which is close to some good beaches. The hostel is 10 minutes on foot from Kii-Tanabe station which is three stops (15 minutes) north of Shirahama station, or 30 minutes by bus from Shirahama station. From 1 July to 31 August the hostel charges ¥2200 per night, and ¥2000 throughout the rest of the year.

In Shirahama itself, there are several kokuminshukusha and minshuku. The best of these is the centrally located *Katsuya* (☎ 0739-42-3814), which is only a two minute walk from the main beach.

The place is built around a Japanese garden and has a small natural hot-spring bath and friendly owner. It's also cheap at ¥4500 per person, ¥7000 with meals.

The *A-Course* (☎ 0739-42-3680) minshuku is also pleasant and fairly close to the beach. It has its own onsen and costs ¥10,000 per person with two meals, ¥12,000 on weekends and holidays. Ask at the tourist information centre for a map to both places.

Getting There & Away

There are twice daily flights between Shirahama and Tokyo. The Kuroshio limited express on the JR Kisei line links Tennō-ji station in Osaka with Shirahama in two hours 15 minutes (¥4530).

There is a bus service from Kii-Tanabe station just north of Shirahama which runs inland to Hongū via Yunomine Onsen and Kawayu Onsen in three hours. It follows the Nakaheji road which has been used by pilgrims for centuries.

WAKAYAMA　和歌山

Wakayama, the prefectural capital, is a pleasant little city useful as a transport hub for travellers headed to other parts of the prefec-

ture. The new Kansai international airport is only 20 km to the north of Wakayama.

The city's main attraction is **Wakayama-jō Castle**, a 20 minute walk from Wakayama-shi station or JR Wakayama station.

The original castle was built in 1585 by Toyotomi Hideyoshi and razed by bombing in WWII. The present structure is a passable postwar reconstruction.

Admission is ¥300 and it's open 9 am to 4.30 pm every day.

Places to Stay & Eat

While Wakayama offers all the standard accommodation, those looking for a more relaxing atmosphere ought to head to the Shinwaka Ura area, a pleasant collection of minshuku and ryokan on a point south-west of the city.

Overlooking the beach *Bagus Cafe* (☎ 0734-44-2559) is one of the most unusual places in Kansai. Built in what looks like a cave, Bagus takes its name from the Indonesian word for 'hang-loose'.

It's open from 1 July to 28 August. It serves curry for ¥700 and a variety of drinks. Take bus No 7 from JR Wakayama station to the last stop, Shinwaka Ura (¥370), climb down the steps to the beach and look for the driftwood-framed entrance.

If you're in Wakayama on the three days around the full moon in September, check out the full-moon festival held here – best described as the Japanese Woodstock. Surfers may want to try the breaks around the point to the west of here.

Right above the Bagus Cafe, *Kimuraya* (☎ 0734-44-0155) is a friendly ryokan with a nice bath looking out over the bay.

Rooms start at ¥10,000 with two meals. Take bus No 7 from JR Wakayama station (¥370).

Nearby, in a beautiful old Japanese house, the Indonesian restaurant *Bulan Bintang* (☎ 0734-47-3958) serves nasi goreng (Indonesian-style fried rice), as well as the more traditional norigoren for ¥700. Indonesian coffee is good and strong at ¥300. It's open from 11 am to 8 pm every day except

Tuesday. Ask at Kimuraya ryokan for directions as it's a little tricky to find.

Close to JR Wakayama station is the restaurant *Ide* (☎ 0734-24-1689), a must for ramen lovers. Here, you can try the local specialty, shoyū ramen, for ¥450. Be careful, they call their ramen *chuka soba* and you should do the same or else risk being laughed out of the joint. It's open from 5 pm to midnight every day except Thursday. It's two blocks south and one block west of JR Wakayama station.

Getting There & Away

Osaka is connected by rail with Wakayama via the Nankai Honsen line which leaves from Shin-Osaka station (70 minutes, ¥2610 limited express, ¥1180 local) and the JR Hanwa line which leaves from Tennō-ji station (55 minutes, ¥2250 limited express, ¥820 local). The Nankai line is serviced by Wakayama-shi (Wakayama city) station, which is about two km to the west of Wakayama station, where JR Hanwa line trains pull in. The two stations are connected by the JR Kisei line, which starts at Wakayama-shi station. There is also a direct train from Kyoto to Wakayama which leaves twice daily (90 minutes, ¥3590).

To visit Kōya-san from Wakayama you can go by rail on the JR Wakayama line to Hashimoto (one hour 20 minutes, ¥800) and then continue on the Nankai Dentetsu line express to Gokurakubashi station and take the cablecar to the top (40 minutes, ¥800 for a combined ticket).

From Wakayama Port, there's a ferry service to Komatsushima on Shikoku. From Fuke Port, just north of Wakayama, there are ferries to Sumoto (Awaji-shima Island) and Tokushima on Shikoku.

MT KŌYA-SAN & KŌYA-SAN 高野山

Mt Kōya-san is a raised tableland covered with thick forests and surrounded by eight peaks in the northern region of Wakayama Prefecture.

The major attraction on this tableland is the monastic complex, known as Kōya-san, which is the headquarters of the Shingon school of Esoteric Buddhism. Though not quite the Shangri-la it's occasionally described as, it is one of the most rewarding places to visit in Japan, not just for the natural setting of the area, but also as an opportunity to stay in temples and get a glimpse of long-held traditions of Japanese religious life.

More than a million visitors come here annually so you should be prepared for congestion during peak holiday periods and festivals. Summer is a popular time to visit and escape from the lowland heat. You can miss large crowds by getting up really early for a stroll around the area before returning to take part in the morning religious service usually held around 6 am. Similarly, late-night strolls are most enjoyable for the peace and quiet they bring. Apart from the obvious attractions of spring and autumn foliage, some hardy visitors like to wander round Kōya-san, mingling with skiers and pilgrims in the winter snow.

Although you could visit Kōya-san in a day, it's much better to reduce the travel stress and allow two days. This is one of the best places in Japan to treat yourself and splurge on a stay at a shukubō (temple lodging).

History

The founder of the Shingon school of Esoteric Buddhism, Kūkai (known after his death as Kōbō Daishi), established a religious community here in 816. Kōbō Daishi travelled as a young priest to China and returned after two years to found the school. He is one of Japan's most famous religious figures and is revered as a Boddhisattva, scholar, inventor of the Japanese kana syllabary and as a calligrapher. He is believed to be simply resting in his tomb, not dead but meditating, awaiting the arrival of Miroku (Maitreya – Buddha of the Future).

Over the centuries, the temple complex grew in size and attracted many followers of the Jōdo (Pure Land) school of Buddhism. During the 11th century, it became popular with both nobles and commoners to leave hair or ashes from deceased relatives close to Kōbō Daishi's tomb, handy for his reawakening. This practice continues to be very popular today and accounts for the thousands of tombs around Okuno-in Temple.

In the 16th century, Oda Nobunaga asserted his power by slaughtering large numbers of monks at Kōya-san. The community subsequently suffered confiscation of lands and narrowly escaped invasion by Toyotomi Hideyoshi. At one stage, Kōya-san numbered about 1500 monasteries and many thousands of monks. The members of the community were divided into clergy (*gakuryō*), lay priests (*gyōnin*) and followers of Pure Land Buddhism (*hijiri*).

In the 17th century, the Tokugawa Shogunate smashed the economic power of the lay priests who managed considerable estates in the region. Their temples were destroyed, their leaders banished and the followers of Pure Land Buddhism were bluntly pressed into the Shingon school. During the Edo period, the government favoured the practice of Shinto and confiscated the lands that supported Kōya-san's monastic community. Women were barred from entry to Kōya-san until 1872.

Kōya-san is a thriving centre for Japanese Buddhism, with more than 110 temples remaining and a population of 7000. As the headquarters of the Shingon school, it numbers about 10 million members and presides over nearly 4000 temples all over Japan.

Orientation & Information

At the Kōyasan cablecar station there's a tourist information office where you can book temple lodgings.

The Kōya-san Tourist Association (☎ 0736-56-2616) has an office in the centre of town in front of the Senjuinbashi-mae bus stop. Some English is spoken and a detailed brochure and maps are provided. Both tourist offices are open from 8.30 am to 5.30 pm in summer and from 9 am to 4.30 pm in winter. If enlightenment is imminent and you'd like to tell the folks abroad, there's an international phone booth beside the office.

The precincts of Kōya-san are divided into the Garan (Sacred Precinct) in the west and Okuno-in Temple with its vast cemetery in the east.

Okuno-in Temple　奥の院

Any Buddhist worth their salt in Japan has had their remains or just a lock or two of hair interred here to ensure pole position when the Buddha of the Future and Kūkai return to the world.

The Tōrō-dō (Lantern Hall) is the main building, located at the northernmost end of the graveyard. It houses hundreds of lamps, including two believed to have been burning for more than 900 years. Behind the hall you can see the closed doors of the Gobyō, Kūkai's mausoleum.

As you walk away from the Lantern Hall, you will recross the Mimyo-no-hashi Bridge. Worshippers ladle water from the river and pour it over the Jizō statues as an offering for the dead. The inscribed wooden plaques in the river are in memory of aborted babies or for those who have met a watery death. Just below the Jizō statues there's a hall with a kitchen at the back where you can join tired, bedraggled pilgrims and brew your own tea.

Return along the main path for about 10 minutes, then take the path to the left and continue wandering through more hectares of tombs. Among these are two very unusual tombs which are worth a look. First, on your left, is the Shiro-ari (white ant) monument, built by pesticide companies in Japan to expiate their guilt for insect genocide. Further on down the path, just before you reach the giant car park, is a spaceship-shaped tomb dedicated to the employees of an aerospace company.

The best way to approach Okuno-in Temple is to walk or take the bus east to Ichi-no-hashi-mae bus stop. From here you cross Ichi-no-hashi Bridge and enter the cemetery grounds along a winding, cobbled path lined by tall cypress trees and thousands of tombs. As the trees close in and the mist swirls, it's a ghostly feeling, especially as night falls, to wander past all the monuments to shades from Japan's past. Fortunately, the stone lanterns are lit at night.

Buses return to the centre of town from the terminus just across from the concrete shopping complex.

KANSAI REGION

Kongōbu-ji Temple 金剛峯寺

This is the headquarters of the Shingon school and the residence of Kōya-san's abbot. The present structure dates from the 19th century and is definitely worth seeing. Unfortunately, it is under construction and the exterior of the building may be hidden from view until 1998.

The Ohiro-ma Room has ornate screens painted by Kanō Tanyu in the 16th century. The Yanagi-no-ma (Willow Room) has equally pretty screen paintings of willows, but the rather grisly distinction of being the place where Toyotomi Hideyoshi committed seppuku (ritual suicide by disembowelment).

The rock garden is interesting for the sheer number of rocks used in its composition, giving the effect of a throng of petrified worshippers eagerly listening to a monk's sermon. The moss garden, nearby, has seen better days as the moss is presently dry.

Admission is ¥350 and includes tea and rice cakes served beside the stone garden. It's open from 8 am to 5 pm in the summer and from 8.30 am to 4.30 pm in the winter.

Danjogaran 壇上伽藍

This is a temple complex of several halls and pagodas. The most important buildings are the Dai-tō (Great Pagoda) and Kondō (Main Hall). The Dai-tō, rebuilt in 1934 after a fire, has recently been repainted and many find it a little gaudy. This pagoda is said to be the centre of the lotus flower mandala formed by the eight mountains around Kōya-san. The nearby Sai-tō (Western Pagoda) was most recently rebuilt in 1834 and is pleasantly more subdued. Admission to all the buildings is ¥100 but little is gained by going inside.

Treasure Museum 霊宝館

The Reihōkan (Treasure Museum) has a compact display of Buddhist works of art, all collected in Kōya-san. There are some very

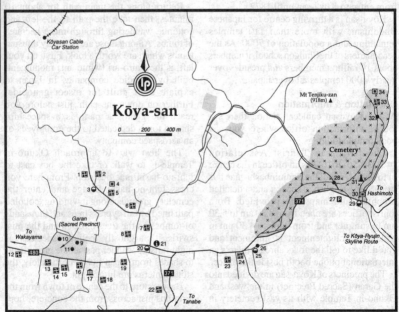

fine statues, painted scrolls and mandalas. Admission is ¥500 and it's open from 8.30 am to 5 pm during the summer but closes at 4.30 pm in the winter.

Tokugawa Mausoleum   徳川家霊台

Admission to the Tokugawa-ke Reidai (Tokugawa Mausoleum) is ¥100 and your view is from behind densely barred doors. It's not worth a special detour.

Special Events

Aoba-Matsuri is a festival held on 15 June to celebrate the birth of Kōbō Daishi.

Mandō-Kuyoe (Candle Festival) is held on 13 August. In remembrance of dead relatives, thousands of mourners light candles along the approaches to Okuno-in Temple.

Places to Stay

There are more than 50 temples offering lodgings and meals. Many of them have superb gardens and architecture. The temples have recently formed a group to fix prices and now all lodgings start at ¥9000 per person including two meals. Some may give a slight discount if you plead poverty or arrive in the low season. The only exception to this is the *Haryō-in Temple* (☎ 0736-56-2702) which functions as a kokuminshukusha and is one of the cheapest temple accommodations around. It's a couple of minutes on foot from the Isshi-guchi-mae bus stop. A room for the night, including two meals, costs ¥5100. When staying at a shukubō, you'll probably be asked to participate in either morning Buddhist prayer services (O-inori)

KANSAI REGION

1	Haryō-in Temple 巴陵院	12	Sainan-in Temple 西南院	23	Karukaya-do Temple 苅萱堂
2	Rengejō-in Temple 蓮華定院	13	Hōon-in Temple 報恩院	24	Eikō-in Temple 恵光院
3	Isshi-guchi-mae Bus Stop 一心口前バス停	14	Hōki-in Temple 宝亀院	25	Ichi-no-hashi-mae Bus Stop 一の橋前バス停
4	Tokugawa Mausoleum 徳川家霊台	15	Yōchi-in Temple 桜池院	26	Ichi-no-hashi Bridge 一の橋
5	Nan-in Temple 南院	16	Henjōson-in Temple 遍照尊院	27	Nakano-hashi Parking 中之橋駐車場
6	Fukuchi-in Temple 福智院	17	Reihōkan (Treasure Museum) 霊宝館	28	Nakano-hashi Bridge 中之橋
7	Ichijō-in Temple 一乗院	18	Jōju-in Temple 成就院	29	Okuno-in-mae Bus Stop 奥の院前バス停
8	Kongōbu-ji Temple 金剛峯寺	19	Tentoku-in Temple 天徳院	30	Spaceship Tomb
9	Dai-tō (Great) Pagoda 大塔	20	Senjuinbashi-mae Bus Stop 千手院橋前バス停	31	Shiro-ari Monument
10	Sai-tō (Western) Pagoda 西塔	21	Kōya-san Tourist Association Office 高野山観光協会	32	Mimyo-no-hashi Bridge
11	Kondō (Main Hall) 金堂	22	Kongōsanmai-in Temple 金剛三昧院	33	Okuno-in Temple & Lantern Hall 奥の院
				34	Kūkai's Mausoleum 空海の墓

or work (O-tsutome). While neither of these is mandatory, they provide a good chance to see the daily workings of a Japanese temple.

During high season and holidays you should make advance reservations through the Kōya-san Tourist Association or directly with the temples. If you arrive in Kōya-san after hours or you want to do things yourself, the following shukubō have English-speaking staff and are at the lower to middle end of the price spectrum.

Henjōson-in Temple (☎ 0736-56-2434) was once a youth hostel, but is now one of the nicer shukubō in town. Here you get a pleasant room with a garden view, tatami furnishings, an excellent vegetarian dinner served in your room and the use of a terrific, wooden (smooth cedar) tub in the men's bathroom. There's even a temple bar and barmaid! The temple is close to the Treasure Museum and if you take the bus you should get off at Reihōkan-mae bus stop.

Eikō-in Temple (☎ 0736-56-2514) is another good choice. It's run by a friendly bunch of young monks and the rooms look out on beautiful gardens. It's easy to think you're staying at a good ryokan here, at least until you're woken at 6.30 am for morning prayers! Rooms are ¥10,000, but discounts may be given for young travellers. This is also one of the two temples in town (the other is Kongōbu-ji Temple) where you can study zazen (sitting zen meditation). Call ahead to make arrangements. The temple is on the eastern side of town, near Ichi-no-hashi Bridge.

Places to Eat

The culinary speciality of Kōya-san is shōjin ryōri (vegetarian food) – no meat, fish, onions or garlic – which you can sample by ordering your evening meal at your temple lodgings. Two tasty tofu specialities are goma-tōfu (sesame tofu) and kōya-tōfu (local tofu). If you're just in town for the day, you can try shōjin ryōri at any of the temples which offer shukubō lodging. Ask at the Kōya-san Tourist Association office and they'll call ahead to make reservations. Most temples charge ¥3500 to ¥5000 for lunch.

There are various coffee shops dotted around town for breakfast – a convenient one is at the main crossroads close to the tourist office. For lunch you can try the *Nankai-shokudō*, where all the standard lunch items are represented by plastic food models in the window. Katsu-donburi (pork cutlet over rice) is ¥800. It's diagonally across from the main tourist office.

Getting There & Away

All rail connections to and from Mt Kōya-san run via Gokurakubashi which is at the base of the mountain. A cablecar provides frequent connection between the base and the top of the mountain (five minutes). Buses run on two routes from the top cablecar station via the centre of town to Ichi-no-hashi Bridge and Okuno-in Temple. The fare to the tourist office in the centre of town at Senjūin-bashi is ¥280. The final stop, Okuno-in, is ¥400.

From Osaka (Namba station) you can go direct by ordinary express on the Nankai Dentetsu line to Gokurakubashi station (one hour 30 minutes). Most visitors buy a combined rail and cablecar ticket to Kōya-san for ¥1210. For the slightly faster limited-express service with reserved seats you pay a supplement of ¥750.

From Wakayama you can go by rail on the JR Wakayama line to Hashimoto (one hour 20 minutes, ¥800) and then continue on the Nankai Dentetsu train to Gokurakubashi station (40 minutes, ¥800 for train and cablecar).

If you are heading into the Kii Peninsula, you should take the train from Gokurakubashi to Gojō. There are two buses a day between Gojō and Shingū (5½ hours, ¥3900) which travel down scenic route 168 via Totsukawa and Hongu onsens.

For rail connections to Yoshino, you must first travel from Mt Kōya-san (via Gokurakubashi) to Hashimoto and then continue on the JR Wakayama line to Yoshino-guchi station where you can change to the Yoshino Kintetsu line for a short trip to Yoshino station.

Getting Around

Apart from Okuno-in Temple, which is 40

minutes on foot from the centre of town, all the other sights in the Garan area are conveniently reached from the centre on foot. As you walk, look out for the street drain covers; they have a temple motif!

Bicycles are available for hire at ¥400 per hour or ¥1200 for the day. The Kōya-san Tourist Association Office has more details.

There are three convenient bus services. One links the cablecar station with Ichi-no-hashi Bridge, another runs between the cablecar station and Okuno-in, and one more runs between the cablecar station and Daimon Gate. The stop opposite the tourist office in the centre of town is called Senjuin-bashi-mae. An all-day bus pass is available for ¥800.

Shima-hantō Peninsula
志摩半島

The Ise-Shima region, on the Shima-hantō Peninsula, is most famous for Ise-jingū Grand Shrine, Japan's most sacred Shinto shrine. It also encompasses the tourist mecca of Toba and some fine beaches around Kashikojima Island. Most of the region is located within the boundaries of Ise-shima National Park, but this seems to have little effect on rapid tourist development of the area. Ise-Shima is easily reached from Nagoya, Kyoto or Osaka and makes a good two day trip.

JNTO publishes *Ise-Shima*, a leaflet providing basic mapping and concise travel information for the area. Information is also available at the tourist information office at the Kashikojima Kintetsu station. Minshuku and ryokan reservations can be made by the privately run tourist information office just outside the station.

SPECIAL EVENTS
The Hatsumōde Festival celebrates the new year between 1 and 3 January. Millions of worshippers pack the area and accommodation is booked out for months in advance.

The Kagurai-sai Festival is celebrated on 5 and 6 April at Ise-jingū Grand Shrine. This is a good chance to see performances of *kagura* (sacred dance), bugaku (sacred dance and music), nō and Shinto music.

Those in search of strange festivals might like to be around for the Hamajima Lobster Festival on 6 June when local folks prance around a giant paper lobster. Or else drop in on the Nakiri Waraji Festival which takes place on 5 September (during the typhoon season). An enormous *waraji* (straw sandal) is floated out to sea to protect the locals from the sea monster.

PLACES TO STAY
Ise and Toba are prime tourist centres so there's plenty of accommodation, but it's probably preferable to stay in the quieter, more attractive places of the Ise-Shima area, such as Kashikojima or Futamigaura, which are within easy reach of Ise by train or bus. Be aware that prices for all ryokan and minshuku go up on weekends and holidays.

Youth Hostels
Youth Hostel Taikōji (☎ 0596-43-2283) is a temple hostel in Futamigaura. Take a four minute bus ride from the station, then walk for five minutes. The price is ¥2400 per night.

Ise-Shima Youth Hostel (☎ 0599-55-0226) is close to Anagawa station (two stops north of Kashikojima) – seven minutes on foot. Members stay for ¥3100 and non-members for ¥3800.

Ryokan
The *Hoshide Ryokan* (☎ 0596-28-2377) is a quaint wooden ryokan with some nice traditional touches, seven minutes on foot from Ise-shi station. It's a member of the Japanese Inn Group and the friendly owners offer vegetarian and macrobiotic food. Prices range from ¥6500 to ¥10,000 per person depending on the room.

Ishiyama-sō (☎ 0599-52-1527) is a member of the Japanese Inn Group on an island in Ago-wan Bay. The owner picks you up at Kashikojima Pier in his boat and speeds you back in a couple of minutes to the ryokan.

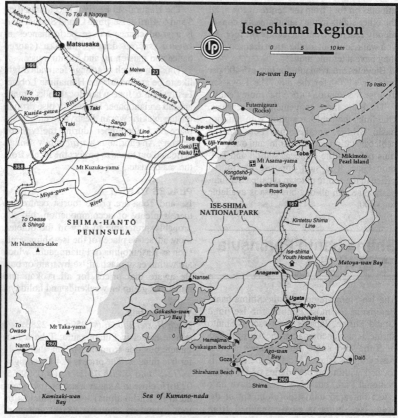

Ise-shima Region

KANSAI REGION

Singles/doubles cost ¥4500/9000. Some rooms have sliding doors less than a metre above the water. You can dip your toes in the water and watch the boats crossing the bay. Dinner is good value at ¥1500 for a large spread of seafood.

A ferry ride from the same pier brings you to Goza, a popular summer beach resort. In less crowded periods (basically anytime other than mid-July to the end of August), the numerous minshuku there provide cosy seaside lodging. *Shiojisō* (☎ 05998-8-3232) is the best of these, located just off the beach. Per-person prices are ¥7000, with two meals.

Those who don't mind spending a little extra for the ryokan experience might want to try *Yamada-kan* (☎ 0596-28-2532), an atmospheric old ryokan about 500m south of Ise-shi station, close to Ise-jingū Shrine. Per-person costs start at ¥10,000 with two meals.

Hotels

Just to the east of Ise-shi station, the *Ise City Hotel* (☎ 0596-28-2111) is a standard business hotel, with singles from ¥6500 and twins from ¥13,000.

Shima Kankō Hotel (☎ 0599-43-1211) sits above Kashikojima, commanding a panoramic view across Ago Bay. Its prices are commensurate with the view. Doubles start around ¥27,000 and Japanese-style rooms start a bit lower at ¥20,000. There are no single rooms. The hotel has Japanese and western restaurants both offering fine dining.

PLACES TO EAT

Seafood, the main speciality of the area, is best sampled at your minshuku or ryokan, as the cost of a seafood dinner at any of the restaurants in the area is likely to be more than the cost of a night's lodgings.

In Ise City there are a few fast-food places near Ise-shi station, but those in search of more traditional food should check out the arcade just north of the Naikū (Inner Shrine) of Ise-jingū Grand Shrine. *Nikōdōshiten* (☎ 0596-24-4409) is a good place to try some of the local specialities in a rough, roadhouse atmosphere. Ise-udon, thick noodles in a rich sauce, make a light lunch for ¥400. Ōasari, large steamed clams, are also tasty at ¥480. The restaurant is located about 100m north of the entrance to the arcade.

About 200m further on you can follow your nose to *Akafuku Honten* (☎ 0595-24-2154). Here, akafuku mochi, a kind of Japanese sweet, is served with tea for ¥330. Look for the large, steaming cauldrons and the queue out front.

GETTING THERE & AWAY

Ise is well endowed with direct rail connections for Nagoya, Osaka and Kyoto. For those without a Japan Rail Pass, the Kintetsu line is by far the most convenient way to go. Note that there are two stations in Ise City, Ise-shi station and Uji-Yamada station, which are only a few hundred metres apart.

From Nagoya, the limited express on the Kintetsu line takes 80 minutes to Uji-Yamada station, and takes another half hour to reach its terminus at Kashikojima. The fare is expensive (¥2630 one way to Ise-shi, ¥3410 to Kashikojima), but this is the quickest route. If you opt for JR services, your best bet is an express from Nagoya, which takes up to two hours and requires a change at Taki

for the short ride to Ise-shi station. It's ¥3980 one way on the express.

From Osaka (Uehonmachi station), the Kintetsu limited express takes about 1¾ hours to Uji-Yamada station and the one-way fare is ¥3480. The same train continues on to Toba arriving about 30 minutes later for ¥3730.

From Kyoto, the Kintetsu limited express takes two hours to Ise-shi station and continues for about an hour to reach its terminus at Kashikojima. The one-way fare from Kyoto to Ise-shi station costs ¥3450. To Kashikojima it costs ¥4230.

If you're taking JR from Kyoto or Osaka you'll have to change up to four times and pay ¥2160 from Kyoto and ¥3190 from Osaka. Inquire at the station office for transfer details.

ISE-JINGŪ GRAND SHRINE 伊勢神宮

Dating back to the 3rd century, Ise-jingū Grand Shrine is the most venerated Shinto shrine in Japan. Shinto tradition has dictated for centuries that the shrine buildings (about 200 of them) be replaced every 20 years with exact imitations built on adjacent sites according to ancient techniques – no nails, only wooden dowels and interlocking joints. Upon completion of the new buildings, the god of the shrine is ritually transferred to its new home in the Sengū No Gi ceremony, first witnessed by western eyes in 1953. The wood from the old shrine is then used to reconstruct the Torii gates at the shrine's entrance or is sent to shrines around Japan for use in rebuilding their structures. The present buildings were rebuilt in 1993 (for the 61st time) at a cost exceeding ¥5 billion.

The reason for this expensive periodic rebuilding is not clear. The official version holds that rebuilding the shrine every 20 years keeps alive traditional carpentry techniques. Perhaps the real reason goes back to pre-Buddhist Japanese taboos concerning death. Before the establishment of a permanent capital at Nara it was thought that the emperor's residence was defiled by death. This meant that the entire capital had to be razed and rebuilt with the passing of each

KANSAI REGION

emperor. This thinking may have carried over to the dwellings of Shinto gods resulting in the periodic reconstruction of the shrines which continues to this day.

Visitors to the shrine are often shocked to discover that the main shrine buildings are almost completely hidden from view. Only members of the imperial family and certain shrine priests are allowed to enter the sacred inner sanctum. This is unfortunate as the buildings are stunning examples of pre-Buddhist Japanese architecture. Don't despair, though, as determined neck craning over fences allows a decent view of the upper parts of the buildings. You can also get a good idea of the shrine's architecture by looking at any of the lesser shrines nearby which are exact replicas built on a smaller scale. The structure of the shrine is thought to derive from the structure of rice storehouses used in pre-Buddhist Japan. That the structure of these granaries would come to be used in shrine buildings says something about the importance of rice in Japanese culture.

There are two parts to the shrine – Gekū (Outer Shrine) and Naikū (Inner Shrine) – which are six km apart and linked by a frequent bus service. If you are in a hurry and can see only one of the shrines, the Naikū is by far the more impressive of the two. More than 100 other shrines are associated with the Grand Shrine.

No admission is charged and the shrines are open from sunrise to sunset. There are restrictions on photography and smoking.

Gekū 外宮

The Gekū (Outer Shrine) dates from the 5th century and enshrines the god of food, clothing and housing, Toyouke-no-Ōkami.

A stall at the entrance to the shrine provides a leaflet in English with a map. The main hall is approached along an avenue of tall trees and surrounded by closely fitted wooden fences which hide most of the buildings from sight.

Take some time to pause in front of the main sanctuary to observe an interesting Shinto ritual. While most pilgrims are content to pray outside the four walls surrounding the shrine, those with particularly urgent wishes can pay a fee (about ¥5000) and enter the outermost of four enclosures round the shrine. After consulting with a priest, the pilgrim is ritually purified with salt and then led into the enclosure. As the priest waits patiently by, the pilgrim goes through a long series of bows and prayers. The seriousness with which this is done gives some insight into reverence Japanese have for this shrine. While you're watching, take a look at the priest's footwear – perhaps the mother of all clogs.

From Ise-shi station or Uji-Yamada station it's a 12 minute walk down the main street to the shrine entrance. Frequent buses leave from stop No 11 opposite the shrine entrance and run to the Naikū (Inner Shrine) for ¥400 and Toba for ¥670. A similar bus service operates to and from Uji-Yamada station.

Naikū 内宮

The Naikū (Inner Shrine) is thought to date from the 3rd century and enshrines the sun goddess, Amaterasu-Ōmikami, who is considered the ancestral goddess of the imperial family and the guardian deity of the Japanese nation. Naikū is held in even higher reverence than Gekū because it houses the sacred mirror of the emperor, one of the three imperial regalia (the other two are the curved jewels and the sacred sword).

Since being enshrined here in the 3rd century, this mirror has not been seen by human eyes. Members of the imperial family technically have the right to see it, but apparently no-one has ever tried to do so. It stands on a wooden pedestal wrapped in a brocade bag. To insure that it is never sullied by human gaze, when this bag wears thin, it is simply placed inside another, resulting in what one writer has suggested must be the world's best collection of Japanese brocade weaving.

Speculation abounds as to what is inscribed on the back of the mirror and some have even suggested that it bears ancient Hebrew inscriptions. Unless a member of the imperial family can be convinced to sneak a peak, it is doubtful that this mystery will be solved any time soon.

A stall just before the entrance to the shrine provides the same English leaflet given out at Gekū. Next to this stall is the Uji-bashi Bridge which leads over the crystal clear Isuzu River into the shrine. One path leads to the right and passes Mitarashi, a place for pilgrims to purify themselves in the river before entering the shrine. This isn't easy, as the river is teeming with colourful carp awaiting handouts.

The path continues along an avenue lined with towering cryptomeria trees to the main hall. Photos are only allowed from the foot of the stone steps. Here too, you can only catch a glimpse of the structure as four rows of wooden fences obstruct the view. If you're tempted to jump the fence when nobody's around, think again – they're watching you on closed-circuit TV cameras not so cleverly disguised as trees!

A better view of the shrine can be had by walking along its front (western) side toward the separate Aramatsurinomiya shrine. Here, you can see a good bit of the shrine, and on a sunny days the cypress wood of the shrine gleams almost as brightly as the gold tips of its roof beams.

On your return to the bridge, take the path to your right and visit the sacred white horse which seems a little bored with its easy life – comfortable accommodation and plenty of fodder in return for a couple of monthly appearances at the shrine.

Buses run from Ise-shi station to the Naikū, take around 15 minutes and cost ¥400. Get off at Naikū-mae stop. From the shrine there are buses back to Ise-shi station via Gekū (15 minutes from bus stop No 2, ¥400). Buses also leave from bus stop No 1 to Toba (45 minutes, ¥1100) which run along the Ise-Shima Skyline Road via Kongōshō-ji Temple on the top of Mt Asama-yama. If you have time, take a look around the temple, which is famous for its Moon Bridge, a footprint of Buddha – he seems to have left plenty around Asia – and eerie rows of memorial poles adorned with paraphernalia from the deceased.

FUTAMIGAURA　二見浦

If you take the train from Ise towards Toba on the JR line, you might want to stop off at Futaminoura station (note the name difference) and take a detour of an hour or so out to Futamigaura. The big attractions are Futami Okitama-jinja shrine and the Meoto-iwa (Wedded Rocks). These two rocks are considered to be male and female and have been joined in matrimony by *shimenawa* (sacred ropes) which are renewed each year in a special festival on 5 January.

The rocks are a 20 minute walk from the station. The small town is packed with places to stay, restaurants and souvenir shops.

TOBA　鳥羽

Unless you have a strong interest in pearls or enjoy a real tourist circus, you can safely give this place a miss. The information office at the station has a map in English. You can dump your packs here or in the lockers at the aquarium or at Mikimoto Pearl Island. Storage charges are ¥250.

Buses run between Toba and Ise via Naikū and Gekū shrines. The JR line runs from Ise-shi station via Futamigaura to Toba and then on to Kashikojima.

There are ferry connections from Toba Port to Irako on the Atsumi Peninsula in Aichi Prefecture. The trip takes an hour and costs about ¥1030.

Mikimoto Pearl Island　ミキモト真珠島

This is the place to go if you want to know more about pearls than you ever wanted to know. There are copious explanations in English – a relative rarity in Japan.

The establishment is a monument to Kokichi Michimoto who devoted his life to producing cultured pearls and, after irritating a lot of oysters with a variety of objects, finally succeeded in 1893.

The demonstration halls show all the oyster tricks from growing and seeding to selection, drilling and threading of the finished product. The demonstrators' English vocabulary is limited to their set piece. It must be a very repetitive job, both threading pearls and reciting a text which has been learned by rote.

There is an observation room from which you can watch a boat put into view and drop off the *ama* (women divers) in their white outfits. There are several thousand ama still operating in these coastal areas – but despite valiant efforts by regional tourist organisations to make you think they're after pearls, they are actually after shellfish or seaweed. There is a taped commentary in English which tells you all about the divers and their watery ways. Just ask if you'd like the attendant to put in a tape in another language.

Admission is ¥1200 and it's open from 8.30 am to 5 pm in summer and from 9 am to 4 pm in winter.

Toba Aquarium 鳥羽水族館

This place – both expensive and crowded – is a last resort for a rainy day. There is a collection of unhealthy sea creatures kept in substandard conditions. There's an annex to the Toba Aquarium, a 100m or so walk along the waterfront.

Admission to the aquarium and annex is

¥2400, and it's open from 8 am to 5 pm from 21 March to 30 November; during the rest of the year it is open from 8.30 am to 4.30 pm.

AGO-WAN BAY & KASHIKOJIMA 英虞湾・賢島

Ago-wan Bay is a pleasant stretch of coastline, with sheltered inlets and small islands. It is a good place to see ama divers hard at work harvesting shellfish from the sea floor.

Kashikojima, an island in the bay, is the terminus of the Kintetsu line, only 40 minutes from Ise, and a good base for exploration of Ago-wan Bay. The island itself is probably of little interest to foreign travellers as it is dominated by large resort hotels. Those in search of peace and quiet might want to take a ferry to Goza on the other side of the bay.

From the station, it's a three minute walk down to the pier. A ferry runs between Kashikojima and Goza. The 25 minute ride spins you past oyster rafts along the coast.

Goza is a sleepy fishing community where the main attractions are the fish market, ama divers and Goza Shirahama beach, a long white sand beach on the south

Kumano Kodō – an Old Road for New Pilgrims

From the earliest times, the Japanese believed the wilds of the Kii Peninsula to be inhabited by *kami*, Shinto deities. When Buddhism swept Japan in the 6th century, these kami became *gongen* – manifestations of the Buddha or a Bodhisattva – in a syncretic faith known as *ryōbu*, or 'dual Shinto'. The area's three principal shrines, in contemporary south-eastern Wakayama Prefecture, are Hongū Taisha in Hongū, Hayatama Taisha in Shingū and Nachi Taisha in Nachi Katsuura. Together they are known as the Kumano Sansha – the three shrines of Kumano.

Japan's early emperors made pilgrimages into the area. The route they followed from Kyoto, via Osaka, Kii Tanabe and over the inner mountains of Wakayama, is known today as the Kumano Kodō – the Kumano old road. The retired emperor Go Shirakawa Jōko performed the pilgrimage no less than 33 times – each time with an entourage of about 1000 retainers and 200 horses. Over time, the popularity of this pilgrimage spread from nobles to common folk and yamabushi priests (wandering mountain ascetics). Indeed, it became so popular that the route was sometimes referred to as the *ari Kumano mōde* – the Kumano pilgrimage of ants. Eventually, the way was paved with stones and graded with well-laid flagstone steps.

Much of the southern route remains passable. A thick carpet of moss has grown over the stones, making for pleasant hiking. While it's possible to walk all the way from Kii Tanabe on the west coast of Wakayama to Nachi Taisha Shrine on the east coast, it's better to start from Hongū. From there, it's a two day hike over mountainous terrain to the shrine at Nachi, overlooking beautiful Nachi falls. There is a private camping ground midway, but many hikers opt to camp along the route at spots of their own choosing. Additional information about the Kumano Kodō is available from the Wakayama Tourist Board. ∎

side of town. The beach is mobbed in late July and early August but is quite nice at other times. After the beginning of August, there may be some *kurage* jellyfish in the water so ask the locals about conditions. There are bus connections between Goza and Ugata, which is close to Kashikojima, but the bus follows a new road, bypassing the scenic coastal road.

Shirahama camping ground is on a beach close to Goza, but like most camping grounds in Japan is a dismal affair. Unofficial camping is possible in some of the more sheltered bays for those willing to hike.

If you'd like to continue exploring the beaches, you can take a ferry from the pier at Goza to Hamajima (15 minutes, ¥300). **Hamajima** is a point of land on the other side of the bay which has several beaches within walking distance of the pier. If you don't find the first one to your liking, continue westward. All of the beaches here are likely to be less crowded than the beach at Goza.

SOUTH OF KASHIKOJIMA

If you want to continue down the Kii Peninsula, avoiding the tortuous road, the easiest way is to backtrack to Ise and then go by rail on the JR Kisei line.

The regions around Owase and Kumano offer good opportunities for hiking, but check locally for information on facilities and trails before you head into remote areas.

From Kumano, the railway crosses into Wakayama-ken and continues down to Shingū on its way round the Kii Peninsula.

Owase 尾鷲

The spectacular **Ōsugi Gorge** lies to the north of Owase, between Mt Hinodega-take and Mt Ōkōchi-yama. Owase has Japan's highest average rainfall at 4000mm.

The *Business Hotel Phoenix* (☎ 05972-2-8111) is close to Owase station – five minutes on foot. Rates are ¥5000/9000 for singles/doubles.

Kumano 熊野

Kumano can be used as a base to do the whitewater raft trip from Kamikitayama-mura to Doro-hatchō via the Doro-kyō Gorge. The *Kumano Seinen-no-ie Youth Hostel* (☎ 05978-9-0800) is cheap at ¥2100 per night (¥3500 with two meals) and is only an eight minute walk from the station. Note that it is closed from 29 December to 3 January.

Western Honshū　　　本州の西部

Western Honshū is known in Japanese as Chūgoku, or literally the 'middle lands' (the same kanji, incidentally, that the Chinese use to refer to China). Over time, the region acted as a major inroad for much of Japan's distinct Chinese and Korean influence. There are three main routes from the Kansai Region through the western end of Honshū to the island of Kyūshū. Most visitors choose the southern route through the San-yō region. This is a heavily industrialised and densely populated area with a number of important and interesting cities including Kurashiki and Hiroshima. The island-dotted waters of the Inland Sea, sandwiched between Honshū and Shikoku, are also reached from ports on the San-yō coast. As an additional reason for choosing this route, the Tokyo-Kyoto-Osaka-Hakata shinkansen rail route also runs along the San-yō coast.

The usual alternative to this route is the northern San-in coast. By Japanese standards, the north coast is comparatively uncrowded and rural. Although there are not as many large cities as on the southern route, the north coast route takes you to the historically interesting town of Hagi. Matsue, Izumo and Tsuwano are also interesting towns worth a stop. Despite the lower population density, travel along the San-in coast is likely to be slower, as the train services are less frequent and not so fast. Road travel, too, may be slower, as there are not the long stretches of expressway found along the southern coast. Still, as the traffic is lighter, the San-in coast is an excellent part of Japan to visit using your own transport.

Finally, there is the central route, a fast road route between Kyoto or Osaka and Shimonoseki at the western end of Honshū. The Chūgoku Expressway runs the full length of Western Honshū, more or less equidistant from the north and south coasts. Attractions along this route are comparatively limited and can usually be visited as side trips from the north or south coast

WESTERN HONSHŪ

HIGHLIGHTS

◆ Experience the Japanese countryside while staying at one of the International Villas in Okayama-ken

◆ Stroll the well-preserved warehouses and wonderful museums along the canal in Kurashiki

◆ Enjoy a half day trip to the charming fishing village of Tomo-no-Ura in Hiroshima-ken

◆ Visit the Peace Park and Peace Museum, and view the chilling A-Bomb dome in Hiroshima

◆ See the floating torii gate and Itsukushima-jinja Shrine on the island of Miyajima

◆ Rent a bicycle for the day and explore the pleasant and peaceful valley setting of Tsuwano in Yamaguchi-ken

◆ Spend a day strolling or pedalling through the streets of the historically rich pottery mecca of Hagi

◆ Ferry over to one of the myriad islands in the Inland Sea such as Shodo-shima, famed for its olive groves and spectacular Kanka-kei Gorge, and Ōmi-shima where 80% of the armour and helmets designated as National Treasures are displayed in Ōyamatsumi-jinja Shrine

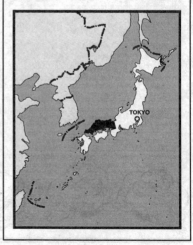

Momotarō – the Peach Boy

Okayama-ken and neighbouring Kagawa-ken on the island of Shikoku are linked with the legend of Momotarō, the tiny 'Peach Boy' who emerged from the stone of a peach and, backed up by a monkey, a pheasant and a dog, defeated a three-eyed, three-toed, people-eating demon. There are statues of Momotarō at JR Okayama station, and the main road of the town is named after him. Another statue of the boy stands at the end of the Kōraku-en Garden island in Okayama. Mega-shima Island, off Takamatsu in Shikoku, is said to be the site of the clash with the demon. Momotarō may actually have been a Yamato prince who was deified as Kibitsuhiko. His shrine, the Kibitsu-jinja, is visited on the Kibi Plain bicycle ride described in the Around Okayama section. ■

routes. Some of these central excursions, particularly the one to the mountain town of Takahashi, are well worth the trip.

GETTING THERE & AWAY

Although there are flights to a number of cities in the region and ferry connections between the major ports and surrounding islands, the shinkansen is the main means of getting to and through Western Honshū. Travelling from one end of the region to the other takes a little less than three hours by shinkansen.

Okayama-ken　岡山県

Okayama Prefecture includes the cities of Okayama and Kurashiki along with numerous other interesting towns and tourist attractions. The Seto-ōhashi Bridge forms the main road and rail link from Honshū to Shikoku.

International Villas

In a brave attempt to attract foreign visitors to the less frequently visited areas of the country, the Okayama Prefectural Government has established six International Villas scattered around the prefecture. They're small and well equipped and rates are ¥3500/6000 for single/double occupancy (¥500 less per person for students and subsequent stays). The villas have kitchen and cooking facilities, instructions in English on

where to shop locally or where to find local restaurants, and even bicycles for visitors' use.

The villas are located in: the mountain village of Fukiya; in Koshihata and Hattoji (where the villas are restored thatched-roof farm cottages); in Ushimado, overlooking the Inland Sea; on Shiraishi Island; and in Takebe, to the north of Okayama city. For reservations or more information contact the Okayama International Villa Group (at the Okayama International Center) by phone ☎ 086-256-2535 or fax 086-256-2576. Members of the staff speak English.

OKAYAMA　岡山

Okayama (population 593,000) is so close to the smaller, but touristically more attractive, town of Kurashiki that it's very easy to stay in one town and day-trip to the other. Although Okayama is not as interesting as Kurashiki, there are a number of important places to visit, including one of Japan's 'big three' gardens.

Orientation & Information

The town's main street, Momotarō-dōri, leads directly from the station to Okayama-jō Castle and Kōraku-en Garden. Tram lines run down the middle of the street.

JR Okayama station has a tourist information counter (☎ 086-222-2912) and the staff are helpful and can provide excellent English information about Okayama and Kurashiki. The Kinokuniya and Maruzen bookshops both have good English-language sections.

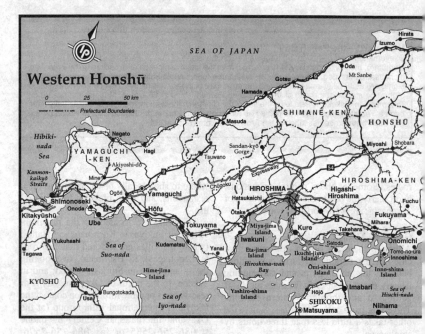

Kōraku-en Garden   後楽園

The Japanese penchant for rating and numbering things is apparent once again at this park, which is said to be one of the three finest in Japan. The other official members of the big three are the Kairaku-en Garden in Mito (Northern Honshū) and Kenroku-en Garden in Kanazawa (Central Honshū).

Constructed between 1687 and 1700, Kōraku-en is a stroll garden. (Kōraku-en means 'the garden for taking pleasure later', taken from the Chinese proverb that 'the lord must bear sorrow before the people and take pleasure after them'.) Part of its attraction in crowded Japan is the expanse of flat lawn but there are also attractive ponds, a hill in the centre, a curious tiny tea plantation and rice paddy and a neatly placed piece of 'borrowed scenery' in the shape of Okayama-jō Castle. Look for the nō stage, the pretty little Ryuten building where poetry composing contests were once held, and the nearby Yatsu-hashi zigzag bridge.

Opening hours are from 7.30 am to 6 pm in spring and summer and from 8 am to 5 pm in the autumn (fall) and winter months. Entry is ¥350 (see the 'combined entry' note in the Okayama-jō Castle section). An excellent English brochure describing the garden's attractions is available. You can rent rowing boats and swan-shaped paddle boats in the river channel between the garden and the castle.

From the station take the Higashi-yama tram to the Shiroshita stop (¥140) for the garden or castle. Alternatively take an Okaden bus from stand No 9 at the station to the Kōrakuen-mae bus stop (¥150).

Okayama-jō Castle   岡山城

U-jō (Crow Castle) was built in 1597 and it's said that its very striking black colour was a daimyō's jest at Himeji's pristine 'White Egret Castle'. Like many other great castles in Japan, U-jō was destroyed in WWII; only the small Tsukima-yagura (Moon-Viewing

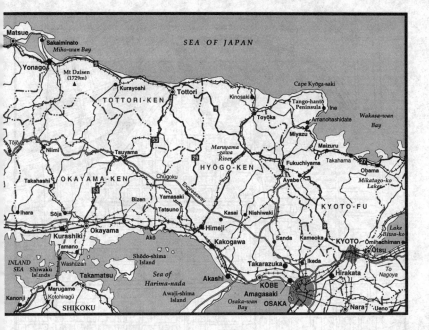

Turret) survived the war-time destruction. It was rebuilt in 1966, a modern reinforced concrete construction like most of the postwar reconstructions. Nevertheless, there is an interesting display inside and much of it is labelled in English.

Entrance to the castle costs ¥250 but you can get combined tickets to the castle plus the Orient Museum for ¥350; the castle plus Kōraku-en Garden for ¥480; or the castle, the garden and the Hayashibara Museum for ¥630. The castle is open from 9 am to 5 pm daily. See the Kōraku-en Garden section for information on getting to the castle.

Museums

Close to the castle's back entrance, quite near the corner of the moat, the **Hayashibara Museum of Art** houses a private collection of Japanese and Chinese artifacts. It's open daily from 9 am to 4.30 pm and entry is ¥300. Beside the main entrance to the Kōraku-en Garden is the good **Okayama Prefectural Museum** which has displays connected with local history. It's open from 9 am to 5 pm (closed on Monday) and entry is ¥200. Just north of the Kōraku-en Garden is the **Yumeji Art Museum**, displaying work by famed artist Yumeji Takehisa. It's open from 9 am to 5.30 pm (closed on Monday) and entry is ¥600.

Just north of the end of Momotarō-dōri, where the tram line turns south, is the excellent **Okayama Orient Museum**. The small collection of Middle Eastern art is beautifully displayed. Entry is ¥300 and it's closed on Monday. Behind this museum is the **Okayama Prefectural Museum of Art**, open from 9 am to 4.30 pm (closed on Monday); entry is ¥300.

Other Attractions

Only a block east of the station, the canal-like Nishi-gawa River, flanked by its gardens and sculptures, makes for a pleasant short stroll.

WESTERN HONSHŪ

Okayama

South-east of central Okayama is the **Tōko-en Garden**, which is easy to overlook in a town with one of the 'big three' gardens. It's worth trundling out on the tram to visit this small, attractive early-17th century garden just beyond the Asahi-gawa River. The garden is centred around a large pond, and it actually predates the Kōraku-en Garden by 70 years. It's open daily from 9 am to 5 pm and entry is ¥300. Beyond the Tōko-en Garden is the **Sōgen-ji Temple**, which also has a noted garden. Both the temple and the garden are open from 6 am to 6 pm and entry is ¥100.

Special Events
The Saidai-ji Eyō (Naked Festival) takes place from midnight on the third Saturday in February at the Kannon-in Temple in the Saidai-ji area. A large crowd of near-naked men fight for two sacred wooden sticks *(shingi)* while water is poured over them!

Places to Stay
Youth Hostels *Okayama Seinen-kaikan Youth Hostel* (☎ 086-252-0651) is west of the railway station and costs ¥2900.

Hotels One of the cheaper places around is the *Makibi Kaikan* (☎ 086-232-0511), just south of the station. It's on the 5th floor of an educational institute and only has 24 rooms, so it may be booked out. Singles/twins are ¥5200/8500. Perhaps the cheapest option in hotels is the *Eki Mae Business Hotel* (☎ 086-222-0073) with per person rates from ¥4000. Another less expensive business hotel not far from the station is the *Hotel Maira* (☎ 086-222-5601), which has singles/twins at ¥6700/12,000. The *Chisan Hotel* (☎ 086-225-1212) has singles from ¥7000. The *Okayama Castle Hotel* (☎ 086-234-5678) is east of the station and singles/doubles cost from ¥6200/10,500. Rooms at the luxurious *Granvia Hotel* (☎ 086-233-3131) beside the station begin at ¥12,000. Further down Momotarō-dōri is the *Washington Hotel* (☎ 086-231-9111) with singles from ¥7600.

In the quieter area west of the station, there are more hotels only a few minutes walk from the centre of things. The *Okayama Tower Hotel* has clean singles/doubles from ¥6680/12,700, the *New Station Hotel* (☎ 086-253-6655) charges ¥5200/9000 for singles/doubles and the *Dai Ichi Inn* (☎ 086-253-5311) has singles/twins from ¥6800/12,500.

Places to Eat
Okayama has a familiar collection of eating places in and around the railway station. The small street parallel to and immediately south of Momotarō-dōri has a varied collection of places to eat, including the popular *Mura Ichiban Robatayaki* (fully illustrated menu) and on the 2nd floor of the Communication building, the *Pizza & Salad St Moritz*.

Curiously, Okayama is brimming with Italian restaurants, from relatively inexpensive pizzerias through to pricey ristorante. There are two branches of the *Pizza Patio* in town, one close to the station and one over by the Hō-machi arcade. Both have an excellent selection of pizzas and pasta dishes, with prices

starting at around ¥700. The popular, woodsy (and delightfully no smoking) *Jolly Fox*, just north of the Chisan Hotel, has pastas, pizza and praiseworthy salads. Lunch specials are ¥950 and a set dinner course costs ¥2000. The friendly owner also runs a small bistro close to the castle. *Flumen Tempus*, a slightly more up-market dinner option, features home-made Italian pastas and fresh bread and cakes prepared by a New Zealand chef.

For sushi, it's worth heading over to the Omote-cho Arcade, where you'll find *Itcho*, a good sushi bar with affordable prices. Just down from here is another Italian place, *Ristorante Italiano*, and *Kirin City*, a snazzy bar with good counter lunches.

Popular bars with the local foreign community include *Hunters* and *Desperado*; both feature occasional live music. Another interesting option is *Bierstube*, a German establishment with a quote from Goethe on its frontage.

In summer, there's a beer garden on the roof of the *New Okayama Hotel*, which is just in front of the station. Take the elevator to floor R; a fully illustrated menu of snacks to go with your beer is provided. In the arcade behind the hotel is the *Sushi Land – Marine Polis*, a revolving sushi restaurant.

Getting There & Away
All Nippon Airways (ANA) flies to Okayama from Tokyo several times daily; the airport is about 40 minutes from the city by bus. Okayama is on the main shinkansen line, unlike nearby Kurashiki. By shinkansen it only takes about an hour to get from Osaka to Okayama (¥5750). Himeji is about halfway between the two cities.

See the Kurashiki section for details on travelling between Okayama and Kurashiki. When travelling west, it's quicker to transfer from the shinkansen at Okayama than at Shin-Kurashiki. You also change trains in Okayama if you're heading to the island of Shikoku, across the Seto-ōhashi Bridge.

Buses run from in front of the station, from the Tenmaya bus station in the Tenmaya department store and from the nearby Uno bus station.

Getting Around

Getting around Okayama is a breeze since the Higashi-yama tram route will take you to all the main attractions. There are only two tram routes, both starting from directly in front of the station. With your back to the station, the Higashi-yama tram route is the one on the right; the easily recognised *yama* is the second character on the front. Trams charge a standard ¥140 anywhere in town.

AROUND OKAYAMA

There are a number of places of interest in the Okayama-Kurashiki area including the pottery centre of Bizen, the Inland Sea, the Seto-ōhashi Bridge lookout at Washūzan and the enjoyable Kibi Plain bicycle route.

For those with time to venture out into the northern parts of the prefecture, there are several hot-spring resort areas worth seeking out including Okutsu Onsen, Yunogō Onsen, and Yubara Onsen (where there is a co-ed, 24 hour, free outdoor spring (roten-buro) on the banks of the Asahi River). Staff at the Okayama TIC can provide more information.

Kibi Plain Bicycle Route
吉備路サイクリングルート

An excellent way to spend half a day seeing a less visited part of Japan is to follow the Kibi Plain bicycle route. The route follows bicycle paths for most of its length and visits a number of temples, shrines and other sites. You can rent a bicycle *(renta saikaru)* at one JR station along the route and leave it at another (see aside).

Takamatsu-jō Castle & Ashimori
高松城・足守

Places of interest on the Kibi Plain, but not on the bicycle route, include the site of Takamatsu-jō Castle where Hideyoshi defeated the Lord of Shimizu. Hideyoshi hastened the siege by flooding the castle, and the remains of the great dykes can still be seen.

North-west of the Takamatsu-jō Castle site is Ashimori, with its well-preserved samurai residence and the lovely **Omizu-en Garden**, another stroll garden in the Enshū style. The castle is around 15 minutes on foot

north-east of Bitchū Takamatsu station on the JR Kibi line, but the samurai residence and the garden are some distance north of Ashimori station. The best way to get to Omizu-en is to take a bus to Ashimori-machi from outside Okayama station. The trip takes 40 minutes and costs ¥600.

Although there is little to be seen at the site of Takamatsu-jō Castle, it played a crucial part in the finale to the chaotic 'Country at War' century. In 1582, Hideyoshi besieged the castle on behalf of the ruthless Oda Nobunaga and agreed to allow the castle's defenders to surrender on condition that their commander, Lord Shimizu, committed suicide. On the very eve of this event, word came from Kyoto that Oda Nobunaga had been assassinated. Hideyoshi contrived to keep this news from the castle garrison and in the morning his unfortunate opponent killed himself. Hideyoshi then sprinted back to Kyoto and soon assumed command himself.

Bizen 備前

East of Okayama, on the JR Akō line, is the 700-year-old pottery region of Bizen, renowned for its unglazed Bizen-yaki pottery. High-quality examples of these wares, much prized by tea ceremony connoisseurs, are produced in wood-fired kilns and can get very expensive. At Imbe station, the drop-off point to explore the area, there is a tourist information counter (☎ 0869-64-1100) which can provide a good English pamphlet on the history of Bizen-yaki, though foreign-language assistance is limited at best.

On the 2nd floor of the station is the **Bizen Ceramic Crafts Museum** (open 9.30 am to 5.30 pm, closed Wednesday, free) and on the north side of the station are the **Okayama Prefectural Bizen Ceramics Art Museum** (9.30 am to 4.30 pm, closed Monday, ¥500), and the **Bizen Ceramics Center** (10 am to 4.30 pm, closed Monday, free), all of which display the pottery of the area.

There are several kilns in the area which, for around ¥3000, offer a chance to try your hand at making Bizen-yaki (reservations necessary). Try **Bishū Gama** (☎ 0869-64-1160), where some English is spoken, and in about two hours you can sculpt a masterpiece; you'll need to arrange to have your creation shipped to you after it's been fired. Another option is the **Bizen-yaki Traditional Pottery Center** (☎ 0869-64-1001) on the 3rd floor of Imbe station where there are workshops held on Saturday, Sunday and holidays from April to November.

North-east of Imbe is the **Shizutani Gakkō school** which was established in 1670. Picturesquely sited, encircled by a beautiful wall, and roofed with Bizen-yaki tiles, it was one of the first schools established specifically for commoners. It's quite

a way to the north of town, and locals recommend taking a taxi, which will set you back ¥2500 one way. Try hitching if you're really keen.

Seto-ōhashi Bridge Area
児島・鷲羽山・瀬戸大橋

From the peninsula south of Kurashiki and Okayama, the Seto-ōhashi Bridge connects Honshū (Japan's biggest island) with Shikoku (its fourth largest). The 12-km-long bridge (or more correctly bridges, since there

---

Kibi Plain Bicycle Route

To access this excellent cycling course, take a local JR Kibi line train from Okayama three stops to Bizen Ichinomiya, ride the 15 km route to Sōja, drop off your bike and take a JR Hakubi/San-yō line train back through Kurashiki to Okayama. Bicycles cost ¥200 per hour or ¥1000 for the whole day.

From the JR Bizen Ichinomiya station turn right, then right again to cross the railway line and in just 300m you reach the Kibitsuhiko-jinja Shrine, which fronts a large pond. From here you soon pick up the bicycle path following a canal through the fields until it rejoins the road just before the Fudenkai Temple. Just 200m further is the **Kibitsu-jinja Shrine**, where a wide flight of steps leads up to its attractive hilltop setting. Have your fortune told (in English) for ¥100 by the serve-yourself oracle in the courtyard. The shrine, built in 1425, is unusual in having both the oratory and main sanctum topped by a single roof. The legendary peach boy, Momotarō, is connected with the shrine.

Pedalling on, you pass the Koikui-jinja Shrine, also connected with the legendary figure Kibitsuhiko, and reach the huge 5th century **Tsukuriyama-kofun Burial Mound**, rising like a rounded hill from the

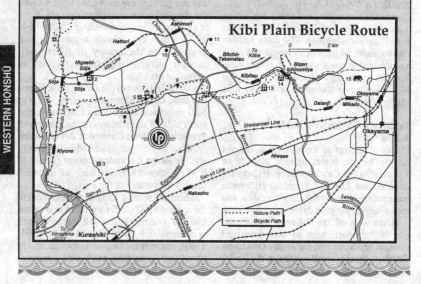

Kibi Plain Bicycle Route

are six of them stepping from island to island across the strait) was opened in 1988 and has considerably shortened travel time to Shikoku. The long span at the Honshū end is the world's longest double-level suspension bridge carrying both road and rail traffic.

The **Washū-zan Hill**, near the end of the peninsula, was long renowned as a lookout point over the Inland Sea. Now it looks out over the bridge as well. The best views are from the No 2 viewing platform at an elevation of 133m. Shitaden buses from Kurashiki

run direct to the platform in one hour 20 minutes and cost ¥790.

If you are particularly interested in taking a look at the bridge, the best way to do so is via a boat tour around it from **Kojima**. During the summer months (from March to November), boats depart approximately hourly between 9 am and 4 pm. Cruises last for around an hour and cost ¥1540. The cruise boats leave from just a couple of hundred metres to the south-east of Kojima station.

surrounding plain. You really need to be in a hot-air balloon or a helicopter to appreciate that it's really a 350m-long keyhole-shaped mound, not a natural hill. Just north of here is the birthplace of famous artist Sesshū (1420-1506). He was once a novice monk at the **Hōfuku-ji Temple**, three km north-west of JR Sōja station.

Finally, there are the foundation stones of the **Bitchū Kokubun-niji Convent**, the nearby **Kibiji Archaeological Museum** (closed on Monday), the excavated **Kōmorizuka Burial Mound** and the **Bitchū Kokobun-ji Temple** with its picturesque five-storey pagoda. From here it's a few more kilometres into Sōja.

There are countless drink-vending machines along the way, and occasionally the bicycle path passes close enough to a main road to divert for food. If you start early you can arrive in Sōja in time for lunch, or buy a sandwich from the *Little Mermaid* bakery near the station and eat on the train on your way back. If this bicycle ride appeals to you, you can easily plot others on the network of tracks that covers the area. A walking path also runs very close to the bicycle route. ∎

1	Hōfuku-ji Temple 宝福寺	6	Kōmorizuka Burial Mound こうもり塚古墳
2	Sōja Shrine 総社宮	7	Kibiji Archaeological Museum 吉備路郷土館
3	Anyo-ji Temple 安養寺	8	Bitchū Kokubun-niji Convent 備中国分尼寺跡
4	Sumotoriyama Burial Mound すもとり山古墳	9	Tsukuriyama-kofun Burial Mound 造山古墳
5	Bitchū Kokubun-ji Temple 備中国分寺		

10	Sesshū's Birthplace 雪舟誕生の地
11	Takamatsu-jō Castle Site 高松城址
12	Koikui-jinja Shrine 鯉喰神社
13	Kibitsu-jinja Shrine 吉備津神社
14	Kibitsuhiko-jinja Shrine 吉備津彦神社
15	Ikeda Zoo 池田動物園

WESTERN HONSHŪ

There's really nothing to linger in Kojima for. The **Seto-ōhashi Memorial Bridge Museum** is probably fascinating for bridge engineers, but for the average visitor the ¥510 admission charge is money better spent elsewhere. It's open from 9 am to 4.30 pm and closed Monday. Just to the north of the museum is the **Nozaki Residence**, the home of a late-Edo period salt merchant. Entry is ¥500 and the house is closed on Monday.

Places to Stay There are a good number of hotels, pensions and ryokan in the Kojima/ Washūzan area, but particularly well located is the *Washūzan Youth Hostel* (☎ 0864-79-9280), which is at the foot of the hill right at the end of the peninsula. It charges ¥2060, or ¥3350 with two meals, and buses run from in front of Kojima station. Ask for the *yūsu-hosuteru-mae basu-no-tei*. Those looking for up-market digs should ask at the Kojima station tourist information counter (☎ 0864-72-1289).

Getting There & Away Buses run to Kojima from Kurashiki and Okayama, and the JR Seto-ōhashi line from Okayama to Shikoku runs through Kojima station before crossing the bridge. Buses run from Kojima station to Washūzan in 20 minutes (¥240), but are not all that frequent. There's also the Shimotsui Narrow Gauge Railway which runs from Kojima (near the Seto-ōhashi Memorial Bridge Museum) at one end, via Washūzan station to Shimotsui station at the other. Shimotsui is an interesting little fishing port and ferries cross from here to Marugame on Shikoku.

KURASHIKI 倉敷

Kurashiki's claim to fame is a small quarter of picturesque buildings around a stretch of moat. There are a number of old black-tiled warehouses which have been converted into an eclectic collection of museums. Bridges arch over, willows dip into the water and the whole effect is quite delightful – it's hardly surprising that the town is a favourite with tourists. Kurashiki means 'warehouse village'.

In the feudal era, the warehouses were used to store rice brought by boat from the

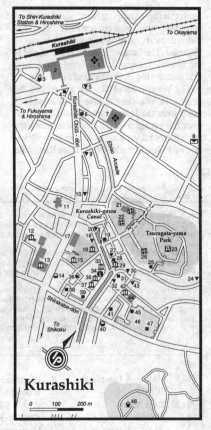

Kurashiki

0   100   200 m

surrounding rich farmlands. As this phase of Kurashiki's history faded, the town's importance as a textile centre increased and the Kurabō Textile Company expanded. Ōhara Keisaburō, the owner of the company, gathered together a significant collection of European art and, in the 1920s, opened the Ōhara Museum to display it. It was the first of a series of museums which have become the town's principal attraction and is still one of the finest.

Orientation & Information

As in so many other Japanese towns, the main street leads straight out from the

PLACES TO STAY

2 Kurashiki Terminal Hotel
倉敷ターミナル
ホテル
3 Young Inn
ヤングイン
4 Ryokan Ōguma
旅館おおぐま
6 Kurashiki Station Hotel
倉敷ステーション
ホテル
17 Kurashiki Kokusai Hotel
倉敷国際ホテル
25 Kamoi Minshuku
カモ井民宿
28 Tsurugata Inn & Restaurant
鶴形イン
31 Ryokan Kurashiki
旅館くらしき
36 Lady's Hotel
レディーズホテル
38 El Paso Inn
エルパソイン
39 Kawakami Minshuku
かわかみ民宿
41 Tokusan Kan Minshuku
特産館民宿
47 Kurashiki Ivy Square Hotel
倉敷アイビー
スクエア
48 Kurashiki Youth Hostel
倉敷ユースホステル

PLACES TO EAT

5 McDonald's
9 Domino Café
10 Rentenchi Italian Restaurant
煉天地
18 El Greco Café
20 Kiyū-tei Steakhouse
亀遊亭ステーキ
ハウス
24 Kanadean
27 Kamoi
カモ井
30 Mamakari-tei
ままかり亭
32 Coffee-Kan
珈琲館
43 Kana Izumi
かないずみ

OTHER

1 Mitsukoshi Department Store
三越百貨店
7 Tenmaya Department Store
天満屋百貨店
8 Post Office
郵便局
11 Ōhashi House
大橋家
12 Museum of Natural History
自然史博物館
13 Kurashiki City Art Museum
市立美術館
14 Mizushima Washūan Bus Stop
水島鷲羽山バス停
15 Ōhara Museum Annexe
大原美術館分館

16 Ōhara Museum of Art
大原美術館
19 Ōhara House
大原家
21 Kanryū-ji Temple
観竜寺
22 Seigan-ji Temple
誓願寺
23 Achi-jinja Shrine
阿智神社
26 Honei-ji Temple
本栄寺
29 Kurashiki Archaeological Museum
倉敷考古館
33 Kurashiki Ninagawa Museum
倉敷蜷川博物館
34 Tourist Information; Traveller's Rest Area
観光案内所
35 Kurashiki Museum of Folkcraft
倉敷民芸館
37 Japan Rural Toy Museum
日本郷土玩具館
40 Kojima Washūan Bus Stop
小島鷲羽山バス停
42 Torajirō Kojima Museum; Orient Museum
児島虎次郎記念館
44 Kurabō Memorial Hall
倉紡記念館
45 Ivy Academic Hall
アイビー館
46 Ivy Square
アイビースクエア

WESTERN HONSHŪ

railway station. It's about one km from the station to the old canal area. If you walk from the station, the very typical urban Japanese scenery is enough to make you wonder whether you are in the right town. But when you turn into the canal area, everything changes; Ivy Square is just beyond the canal. A number of shops along the main street, Kurashiki Chūō-dōri, sell Bizen-yaki pottery.

The staff at the station's information counter (☎ 086-426-8681) will make accommodation bookings, and there is also a helpful tourist information office near the bend in the canal. Most of the museums and galleries are closed on Monday and the number of visitors drops dramatically, so Monday is a good time to enjoy Kurashiki without the crowds (but also without the museums).

Don't be surprised if you have the fortune of running into Mr Sato, an eccentric white-haired gentleman (and retired English teacher) who frequents the canal area daily and has managed to stir up the local volunteer guide association with his unlicenced befriending of foreign visitors and his resounding tongue. Despite his persistence and vigour, he expects nothing in return for his guide services, except that you loan him an ear (or two).

Around the Canal

The museums and galleries which are the town's major attraction are concentrated along the banks of the canal. At times, the canal area can seem like rush hour at Tokyo station, so if you want to see how pleasant the area looks without throngs of tour groups, you should wander the canal banks early in the morning or on a Monday. It's not necessary to visit all of the museums; some are definitely more interesting than others.

Ōhara Museum of Art

This is undoubtedly Kurashiki's number one museum, housing the predominantly European art collection of the textile magnate Ōhara Keisaburō (1880-1943). Rodin, Matisse, Picasso, Pissarro, Monet, Cézanne, Renoir, El Greco, Toulouse-Lautrec, Gauguin, Degas and Munch are all represented here. The museum's neo-classical facade is Kurashiki's best known landmark, to which the constant procession of tour groups being photographed outside attests. Entry is a whopping ¥1000; opening hours are from 9 am to 5 pm and it's closed on Monday.

Your ticket also takes you to the museum's folk art and Chinese art collections and to the contemporary art collection, housed in a new building behind the main one. You have to exit the old building and walk down the street to enter the new gallery, where you will find works by Pollock, Rothko, de Kooning, Henry Moore and others.

Kurashiki Ninagawa Museum Between the Ōhara Museum and the tourist office is the interesting Kurashiki Ninagawa Museum, which houses a collection of Greek, Etruscan and Roman antiquities, together with more modern European marbles and other items. Entry is ¥800 and it's open from 9 am to 5 pm daily.

Kurashiki Museum of Folkcraft The folkcraft museum's impressive collection is mainly Japanese, but also includes furniture and other items from many other countries. The collection is housed in a rustic, attractive complex of linked kura (warehouses). Entry is ¥700 and it's open from 9 am to 4.15 pm (December to February) or 5 pm (March to November). It's closed on Monday.

Japan Rural Toy Museum This interesting little museum displays folkcraft toys from Japan and around the world. Japanese rural toys are also on sale. Entry is ¥310 and it's open from 8 am to 5 pm daily.

Kurashiki Archaeological Museum Just directly across the canal from the tourist office, this museum is a gem for archaeology buffs and those interested in bits of ancient pottery, but otherwise it's a bit dry. There are finds from burial mounds from the Kibi Plain and even an Inca room with some pre-Columbian pottery from Peru. Entry is ¥400 and it's open Tuesday to Sunday from 9 am to 4 pm.

Other Museums If you've not had your fill of museums there's also the Kurashiki City Museum of Natural History (¥100, open from 9 am to 5 pm, closed Monday) and the Kurashiki City Art Museum (¥200, same opening hours).

Ivy Square アイビースクエア

The Kurabō textile factories have moved on to more modern premises and the fine old Meiji-era red-brick factory buildings (dating from 1889 and remodelled in 1974) now house a hotel, restaurants, shops and yet more museums. Ivy Square, with its ivy-covered walls and open-air cafe, is the centre of the complex.

The **Torajirō Kojima Museum** displays work by the local artist who helped Ōhara establish his European collection, along with some fine pieces from the Middle East in the associated Orient Museum. The museums are open Tuesday to Sunday from 9 am to 5 pm and admission is ¥350.

The museum in the **Kurabō Memorial Hall** tells the story of Kurashiki's growth as a textile centre, while the curious **Ivy Academic Hall** (Ivy Gakkan) attempts to trace the development of western art through reproductions of notable paintings. The two are open from 9 am to 5 pm daily and a combined entry ticket costs ¥350.

Ōhashi House 大橋家住宅

The Ōhashi family were retainers to the Toyotomi family, who were on the losing side of the upheavals leading to the establishment of the Tokugawa Shogunate. The Ōhashi family abandoned its samurai status and eventually ended up in Kurashiki, where they became wealthy merchants and built this house in 1796. In its heyday it would have been a fine example of an upwardly mobile merchant's residence but today it's very worn and shabby. Entry is ¥500 and it's open from Tuesday to Sunday, 9 am to 5 pm.

Shrines & Temples

The Achi-jinja Shrine tops Tsurugata-yama Park, overlooking the old area of town. The Honei-ji Temple, Kanryū-ji Temple and the Seigan-ji Temple are also found in the park.

Places to Stay

Kurashiki is a great town for staying in a traditional Japanese inn and there's an ample selection of minshuku and ryokan.

Youth Hostels *Kurashiki Youth Hostel* (☎ 086-422-7355) is south of the canal area and costs ¥2800 per night (nonmembers add ¥600). It's a long climb to its hilltop location, but the view is great and the staff are very friendly. From the station you can take a bus to the shimin kaikan stop (¥150) and then walk about 15 minutes uphill to the hostel.

Minshuku & Ryokan There are several good-value minshuku conveniently close to the canal. The *Tokusan Kan* (☎ 086-425-3056) is near Ivy Square and offers a per person price with two meals from ¥7000. Right by the canal near the toy museum the simple *Kawakami Minshuku* (☎ 086-424-1221) is slightly cheaper at ¥6000.

The *Kamoi Minshuku* (☎ 086-422-4898) is easy to find (at the bottom of the steps to the Achi-jinja Shrine) and conveniently close to the canal area. Although this minshuku is new, it looks very traditional – an atmosphere enhanced by the antiques throughout the building. The cost per person, including two good meals in this pleasant minshuku, is ¥6000. The Kamoi also has a popular restaurant by the canal.

There are also more expensive ryokan around the canal. The canal-side *Tsuragata Inn Kurashiki* (☎ 086-424-1635) dates from 1744 and nightly charges in this tasteful ryokan range from ¥17,000 to ¥35,000. The ryokan's restaurant serves non-guests, mainly at lunch time, and there is also a cafe.

Also by the canal, the *Ryokan Kurashiki* (☎ 086-422-0730) is old, elegant and expensive, costing from ¥20,000 per person with two meals. Either of these ryokan would make a good introduction to staying at a fine traditional inn.

Most of the traditional ryokan and minshuku are around the canal area, an exception being the friendly *Ryokan Ohguma* (☎ 086-422-0250) which is near the station. It's to the right as you leave the station, down the

WESTERN HONSHŪ

small arcade which angles off the main road. It costs ¥4000 or ¥8000 per person with two meals.

Hotels The best places to look for hotels are around the popular canal area, or near the railway station.

Canal Area Part of the Ivy Square complex, the *Kurashiki Ivy Square Hotel* (☎ 086-422-0011) has singles at ¥6500 or ¥9000 with bath. Doubles and twins range from ¥10,800 to ¥12,800 without bath, ¥14,300 to ¥27,000 with bath. Rooms without a bath or shower have a toilet and sink only – there are large communal baths and showers.

Backing onto the Ōhara Museum is the expensive *Kurashiki Kokusai Hotel* (☎ 086-422-5141), with singles/doubles from ¥9900/18,700. There are also more expensive Japanese-style rooms in this popular and attractive hotel.

Also close to the canal is the stylish *El Paso Inn* (☎ 086-421-8282). It only has a couple of singles, but doubles range from ¥9900 and twins from ¥11,000. A real oddity in the canal area is the *Lady's Hotel* (☎ 086-422-1115); the sign announces this in English. It's a women-only hotel aimed specifically at young OLs (office ladies), which seems to involve painting the rooms pink or a lurid shade of green and dotting stuffed toys around the place. Per person rates begin at ¥4500.

Station Area The JR-operated *Hotel Kurashiki* (☎ 086-426-6111) is inside the station building and has singles from ¥8000 and twins from ¥14,000. The *Kurashiki Terminal Hotel* (☎ 086-426-1111) is immediately to the right as you come out of the station and the entrance is on the 9th floor. It's a typical business hotel with singles from ¥6500, and twins or doubles from ¥12,000.

The *Young Inn* (☎ 086-425-3411), behind the Terminal Hotel, has singles/twins without bath for ¥4000/7000, quite a bargain. There are also slightly more expensive rooms with bathroom in this vaguely hostel-like hotel.

The *Kurashiki Station Hotel* (☎ 086-425-2525) is a short distance along Kurashiki Chūō-dōri towards the canal. The entrance is around the side of the building, with reception on the 5th floor. The rooms in this older but cheaper business hotel are minute and utterly straightforward; singles cost from ¥5000 and doubles from ¥9000.

Places to Eat
If you plan to eat out in the canal area of Kurashiki, don't leave it too late. Many of the restaurants you may notice at lunch time will be closed by early evening. The hordes of day-trippers will have disappeared by then and many of the visitors actually staying in Kurashiki will be eating in their ryokan or minshuku.

Beside the canal is the *Kamoi Restaurant*, run by the same people as the popular Kamoi Minshuku. Plastic meals are on display and the restaurant closes early in the evening as well as all day on Monday. Not far from the Ryokan Kurashiki is *Mamakari-tei*, a cosy traditional spot named and famed for the local sardine-like fish they dish out daily (served both raw and cooked). If you're not a sardine lover, try the tōfu manjū (fried tofu patties). They have lunch sets from ¥1500 (11 am to 2 pm) and are open for dinner from 5 to 10 pm. At the northern end of the canal is *Kiyū-tei*, a steakhouse in an old traditional Japanese house. They have good set lunch meals for under ¥1000 and a fixed evening meal of soup, salad, steak, bread and coffee costs ¥2500.

Just back from the canal is *Kana Izumi*, a pleasant, modern restaurant with plastic meals in the window and a fully illustrated menu. You can get good tempura and noodles for ¥1650 and the restaurant stays open until 8 pm. There's a snack bar in Ivy Square and several restaurants in and near the square. A special treat, south-east of Tsurugata-yama Park, is *Kanadean*, a small place specialising in 'Asian' cuisine. It has milk tea and 15 kinds of spicy curries, with set meals starting at ¥1000. It's open from noon to 9.30 pm. Look out for the blue latticework windows and the blue sign.

There are also a number of places to eat along Kurashiki Chūō-dōri. *Domino* is a neat little place where you can get a good teishoku lunch for under ¥800. Not far away the *Rentenchi Italian Restaurant* has coffee for ¥300 and pasta dishes from ¥700. *El Greco* (you can't miss its ivy-clad walls), right by the canal and close to the Ōhara Museum, is a fashionable place to stop for tea or coffee and something sweet. The menu, in English on one side, offers ice cream for ¥450, cake for ¥400 and drinks for about the same. It's closed on Monday. Another great spot for coffee – and coffee only – is the cavernous tavern *Coffee-Kan*, just beside the Ryokan Kurashiki. It offers an amazing selection of home-roasted java and is truly one of the few places in Japan where the coffee and atmosphere are actually worth the money!

Getting There & Away

Kurashiki, only 16 km from Okayama, is not on the shinkansen line. Travelling westwards, it's usually faster to disembark at Okayama and take a San-yō line local train to Kurashiki. These operate several times an hour; the trip takes just over 15 minutes and costs ¥470. If you're eastbound, get off at the Shin-Kurashiki station, two stops on the San-yō line from Kurashiki.

To get to Washūzan and Shikoku from Kurashiki, you can either travel by train to Okayama and change trains there for Washūzan or take a bus (from outside the station or from the canal area stops shown on the map) direct to Kojima or Washūzan.

Getting Around

Walk – it's only 15 minutes on foot from the station to the canal area, where almost everything is within a few minutes stroll.

TAKAHASHI 高梁

Built along the banks of the Takahashi River, this pleasant small town, midway between Kurashiki and the central Chūgoku Expressway, gets few western visitors even though it has a temple with a very beautiful Zen garden and is overlooked by an atmospheric, even spooky, old castle.

Orientation & Information

While the town is Takahashi, the railway station is Bitchū-Takahashi, which is a bit confusing. The tourist information counter in the bus terminal beside the railway station (☎ 0886-21-0229) has some information in English as well as maps in Japanese. The Raikyū-ji Temple is about a km to the north of the station, on the east side of the tracks, though to get there you'll need to walk north on the west side and then cross over. Bitchū-Matsuyama-jō Castle is about five km north of the station, up a steep hillside. If you are not up to the hefty walk or cycle up there, a taxi should run you up for about ¥1500. There are bicycles for hire at the station for ¥200 per hour.

Raikyū-ji Temple 頼久寺

The classic Zen garden in this small temple is the work of the master designer Kobori Enshū and dates from 1604. A peaceful place to sit on the veranda and contemplate, it contains all the traditional elements of this style of garden, including stones in the form of turtle and crane islands, a series of topiary hedges to represent waves on the sea, and it even incorporates Mt Atago in the background as 'borrowed scenery'. A short English leaflet on the temple and garden's history is available and entry is ¥300. It is open from 9 am to 5 pm daily.

Bitchū-Matsuyama-jō Castle 備中松山城

High above Takahashi stands the highest castle in Japan (430m), a relic of an earlier period of castle construction when fortresses were designed to be hidden and inaccessible, unlike the later, much larger constructions designed to protect the surrounding lands. The road winds up the hill to a car park, from where you have a steep climb to the castle itself. On a dark and overcast day you can almost feel the inspiration for a film like Kurosawa's *Throne of Blood*. Entry to the castle is ¥300 and it is open daily from 9 am to 4 pm.

The castle was originally established in 1240 and in the following centuries was enlarged until it finally covered the whole mountain top. The castle fell into disrepair after the Meiji Restoration, but the townspeople took over its maintenance from 1929 and it was finally completely restored in the 1950s and has recently undergone further repairs and additions.

Other Attractions

Takahashi has some picturesque old samurai streets with traditional walls and gates, mainly in the area around Raikyū-ji Temple. Around 500m to the north of Raikyū-ji is the **Takahashi Samurai House Museum** (*bukeyashiki-kan*), a well-preserved samurai residence dating from the 1830s. It is open daily from 9 am to 5 pm and entry is ¥300. If you walk up to Raikyū-ji, you'll pass the **Local History Museum** (*kyōdō shiryō-kan*), a fine wooden Meiji structure dating from 1904. It has displays of items associated with the area's mercantile and agricultural past, and is open daily from 9 am to 5 pm; entry ¥300. The **Shōren-ji Temple**, directly east of the station, has unique terraced stone walls. It's open from 9 am to 5 pm and is free.

Places to Stay

The *Takehashi Youth Hostel* (☎ 0866-22-3149) costs ¥2600 and is about a km north of the station, just south of Raikyū-ji Temple.

The best alternative to the youth hostel, but for women only, is the terrifically atmospheric *Minshuku Jōrin-ji* (☎ 0866-22-3443), a temple with rooms with breakfast for ¥4500. It is a bit of a hike from the station, located just north of Shōren-ji Temple.

The *Business Hotel Takahashi* (☎ 0866-22-6766), just west of the station, has singles/twins at ¥5000/9000.

The *Takahashi-shi Cycling Terminal* (☎ 0866-22-0135) is a 20 minute bus trip from the JR station at the Wonderland amusement park. Accommodation at the terminal, including meals, is ¥5000. You can rent bicycles from the terminal for ¥400 for four hours, but think twice before setting out to ride up to the castle!

There are also several ryokan and minshuku in town worth a look. Just west of the station, the very attractive *Midori Ryokan*

(☎ 0866-22-2537) has per person room-only rates from ¥4200 or ¥8000 with two meals. The elegant *Aburaya Ryokan* (☎ 0866-22-3072), on the main road facing the river, costs ¥13,000 with two meals.

Places to Eat

Savoury Shikoku-style udon noodles can be found at *Sanukiya*, beside the canal, west of Raikyū-ji. Though there's no English menu, the choices are pretty straightforward and the staff can help you order. The special of the house is a hearty udon stew with duck meat called kamo nabe udon. There are also good ramen noodles at *Ajiya*, just north along the same street.

Also close by, on the main road facing the river, is *Nishimura*, a unique little cafe housed in an old sake warehouse which offers tea or coffee and delicious sweet jellies flavoured with citron fruit (yuzu). These delectable little sweets can be purchased as souvenirs nearby at *Enshūdō*, a local candy manufacturer in production since the Edo period!

Getting There & Away

Although Takahashi is not on any of the regular tourist routes through Western Honshū, it would not take a great effort to include it in an itinerary. The town is about 50 km north of Okayama or 60 km from Fukuyama. It's on the JR Hakubi line so a stop could be made when travelling between Okayama on the south coast and Yonago (near Matsue) on the north coast.

FUKIYA 吹屋

The beautifully situated village of Fukiya, north-west of Takahashi, was once a rich copper mining centre and has many attractive buildings from the latter years of the Edo period and the first years after the Meiji Restoration. One of the prefecture's International Villas is in the village. To get to Fukiya, take a JR limited express (*tokkyūD*) from Okayama to Bitchū-Takahashi station; from there it is about an hour by bus.

Hiroshima-ken

In addition to the primary attractions in Hiroshima City related to the horrific bombing in 1945, the prefecture has a number of other noteworthy places of interest including nearby Miyajima Island, with the famed Itsukushima-jinja Shrine, the quaint fishing village at Tomo-no-Ura, and a marathon temple walk in Onomichi.

FUKUYAMA 福山

Fukuyama (population 370,000) is a modern industrial town of little interest to the tourist, but its convenient situation on the Osaka-Hakata shinkansen route makes it a good jumping-off point for the pretty fishing port of Tomo-no-Ura or for Onomichi, which in turn is a jumping-off point for Inland Sea cruises. If you do have a few hours to spend in Fukuyama, you can visit the art gallery and museum and the reconstructed castle.

Orientation & Information

Most of the places of interest, as well as the hotels and restaurants, are close to the station. Route 2 runs parallel to the railway line, about half a km south. There is a tourist information and accommodation booking counter (☎ 0849-22-2869) in the busy, modern railway station.

Fukuyama-jō Castle

Fukuyama-jō Castle was built in 1619, torn down during the 'one realm, one castle' period, and reconstructed in 1966. It overlooks the railway station, which is only a couple of minutes walk away. As well as the imposing donjon of the castle itself, there are turrets, the fine Sujigane-Go-mon Gate and a bathhouse. The castle contains the usual collection of samurai armour and similar artifacts. It's open from 9 am to 4 pm, closed on Monday, and entry is ¥200.

Museum of Art & History Museum
美術館・歴史博物館

Immediately to the west of the castle hill are Fukuyama's Museum of Art (open from 9.30 am to 4.30 pm, closed Monday, entry ¥300) and the Hiroshima Prefectural History Museum (open from 9 am to 4.30 pm, closed Monday, entry ¥300).

Auto & Clock Museum 時計博物館

The Fukuyama Auto & Clock Museum, north of the town centre, charges an exorbitant ¥900 entry fee but the strange little collection makes an interesting change from the usual feudal artifacts. Anything old is a little strange in modern Japan so the 1950 Mazda motorcycle taxi looks particularly curious. The 1961 Datsun Fairlady sports car would have been no competition at all for a British sports car of that period – 30 years on how things have changed! The museum also houses waxwork figures of US presidents Abraham Lincoln and George Washington, James Dean, Elvis Presley, General Douglas MacArthur and a very dissolute-looking Commodore Matthew Perry.

Places to Stay

There are lots of business hotels close to the railway station. Two of the cheaper ones are the *Fukuyama Kokusai Hotel* (☎ 0849-24-2411) behind the station, with singles/twins for ¥5800/¥11,000, and the *Fukuyama New Kokusai Hotel* (☎ 0849-24-7000) in front, with single rooms only at ¥5400. The *Fukuyama Station Inn* (☎ 0849-25-3337) is one of the cheapest places around, with singles from ¥4700 and a small number of twins/doubles at ¥7800.

Immediately in front of the station is the *Fukuyama Tōbu Hotel* (☎ 0849-25-3181) with singles from ¥7000 and twins from ¥11,000. Nearby is the *New Castle Hotel* (☎ 0849-22-2121), at the very top of the Fukuyama hotel price range with rooms from ¥9000/18,000.

The *Fukuyama Castle Hotel* (☎ 0849-25-2111), directly behind the station, has singles from ¥6800 and twins from ¥11,500. The *Fukuyama Grand Hotel* (☎ 0849-21-5511) has singles from ¥8200, twins from ¥16,000 and a few doubles at ¥18,000.

WESTERN HONSHŪ

WESTERN HONSHŪ

Fukuyama

0   125   250 m

Places to Eat

The full complement of fast-food places can be found immediately south of the railway station. *Studebaker* is a Japanese-Italian restaurant curiously named after a US car manufacturer which went belly up in the early '60s. The menu features a selection of spaghetti, though for more authentic (and pricey) Italian food head for *Zuccheroe Sale*.

A good place to seek out a bite to eat is the 8th floor of the Tenmaya department store next to the station. It has several Japanese and Chinese eateries with good lunch-time sets. There are also good, cheap curries at *Naish Curry American* behind the store. The alleys either side of *McDonald's* harbour a good number of rāmen shops that do a busy lunch-time trade with the salaryman set and are worth checking out.

If you're heading out for a drink and a bite at night, try the tropical *Fujimoto Garden*, or if you're just drinking, there is the local gaijin hangout, the *Mondo Bar*. For a bit more style check out *Bar 333* or a little shot bar called *Key West*.

PLACES TO STAY

2 Fukuyama Grand
   Hotel
   福山グランドホテル

6 Fukuyama Castle
   Hotel
   福山キャッスル
   ホテル

7 Fukuyama Kokusai
   Hotel; Fukuyama
   Station Inn
   福山国際ホテル／
   福山ステーショ
   ンイン

8 Fukuyama Hotel
   福山ホテル

9 Fukuyama New
   Kokusai Hotel
   福山ニュー国際
   ホテル

10 New Castle Hotel
   ニューキャッスル
   ホテル

11 Fukuyama Tōbu
   Hotel
   福山東武ホテル

PLACES TO EAT

13 Studebaker
14 McDonald's
15 Zuccheroe Sale
17 Naish Curry
   American

OTHER

1 Gokoku Shrine
   護国神社

3 Fukuyama Museum
   of Art
   福山美術館

4 Hiroshima Prefectural
   History Museum
   広島県立歴史博物館

5 Fukuyama-jō Castle
   福山城

12 NTT

16 Tenmaya
   Department Store
   天満屋

18 Fujimoto Garden
   フジモトガーデン

19 Main Post Office
   中央郵便局

Getting There & Away

Fukuyama is on the main railway lines along the San-yō coast. If you are travelling between Fukuyama and Kurashiki, it's usually quicker to stick to the San-yō line all the way rather than travel from Fukuyama to Shin-Kurashiki station by shinkansen and transfer to the San-yō line there. There are frequent buses from the Fukuyama station area to Tomo-no-Ura. The trip takes around 30 minutes and costs ¥500.

TOMO-NO-URA　鞆の浦

The delightful fishing port of Tomo-no-Ura, with its numerous interesting temples and shrines, is just half an hour by bus south of Fukuyama. In feudal days, due to its central location on the Inland Sea, the port played an important role as host to fishing boats which would wait in the harbour to determine the next shift in the tides and winds before heading back out to sea.

Although gaijin visitors are infrequent, an English map and brochure is available and explanatory signs are dotted all around town. If you set aside a full day to travel from Kurashiki to Hiroshima you can spend a pleasant morning exploring Tomo-no-Ura, get back to Fukuyama for lunch, and visit Onomichi in the afternoon before continuing to Hiroshima.

Four km beyond Tomo-no-Ura is the Abuto Kannon Temple with superb Inland Sea views.

Cruises

Ferries run on a regular basis to Sensui-jima

Tomo-No-Ura Bicycle Tour

An excellent way to explore the narrow streets of Tomo-no-Ura and take in its temples and sights is by bicycle. Bicycles *(renta-saikaru)* are available near the ferry building and cost just ¥100 for two hours. The map shows an interesting circuit of the main attractions.

Right across the road from the ferry landing is the **Muronoki Song Monument** with a sad poem composed by a Korean emissary whose wife had died en route to Tomo-no-Ura. Climb the headland to the ruins of **Taigashima Castle**, where you will also find **Empuku-ji Temple** and a monument to the haiku poet Bashō.

Cross the headland to the harbour and continue until you reach the steps leading to the Museum of History (¥150). It's open from 9 am to 4.30 pm. This interesting and well-presented museum features a great model of the Sea Bream Fishing Festival. Back on the road, have a look in the nautical equipment shop on the corner and then head down towards the harbour to the **Shichikyō-ochi Ruins**. This one-time sake shop isn't a ruin at all but played a small part in the Meiji Restoration when a fleeing anti-shogunate group paused here long enough for one member of the group to compose a waka (31 syllable poem) extolling the virtues of the shop's sake.

Continue towards **Iou-ji Temple** – although it's easier to park your bicycle at the bottom of the steep hill and walk up. From the temple, steep steps lead to a fine view over the town from Taishiden Hill. Back on your bicycle, continue to **Hōsen-ji Temple**, originally founded in 1358. The Tengai pine tree in the grounds spreads to cover 600 sq metres. Just beyond the temple, the **Sasayaki** (Whispering Bridge) commemorates an illicit romance which, according to a local tourist brochure, resulted in the lovers being 'drowned into the sea'. Beside the bridge is the **Yamanaka Shikanosuke Monument**, where, after a failed vendetta, the hapless Shikanosuke had his 'head severed for inspection'.

The **Nunakuma-jinja Shrine** has a portable Nō stage used by Hideyoshi to enjoy performances during sieges. It has been designated as an Important National Treasure. The shrine itself is picturesquely sited, with a gentle flight of stairs leading up to it. **Ankoku-ji Temple** (entry ¥100) dates from 1270 and houses two wooden statues which are national treasures. It has a slightly tatty *kare-sansui* (waterless-stream garden) which was relaid in 1599.

From here you head back towards your starting point, pausing to take in 'eastern Japan's most scenic beauty' on the way. Whether it deserves the appellation or not you can decide for yourself, but that is how it seemed to a visiting Korean dignitary in 1711. The **Taichō-rō Guest House**, built in 1690 for visitors from Korea, is in the Fukuzen-ji Temple compound and the cheerful priest will usher you in and let you sit to admire the view of Kōgo, Benten and Sensui islands. ■

Island from the harbour area. The five minute trip costs ¥240 return. There are some quiet walking trails on the island.

If you can rustle up five interested parties, you can putter around the bay and Sensui-jima Island in a small boat for ¥6000. As well, boats will also take you south to the Abuto Kannon, which is at the foot of the Numakuma-hantō Peninsula, a trip that will set a party of five back about ¥9000. You'll need at least some Japanese, but try to track down Mr Miyake, a local fisherman who often takes people out touring and fishing (particularly during sea bream *(tai)* season in May and November). He can be reached on ☎ 0849-82-2278.

Special Events

The Tai-ami Sea Bream Fishing Festival takes place during the entire month of May.

Places to Stay

Rather than staying in Fukuyama, a night in Tomo-no-Ura, an altogether more picturesque location, would be a more pleasant experience. Right by the water, not far from the harbour, is the friendly *Taizan-kan* (☎ 0849-83-5045). Per person rates with two meals start at ¥16,000. The *Tomo Seaside Hotel* (☎ 0849-83-5111), near the bus terminal, has per person rates from ¥12,000 to ¥35,000, depending on how extravagantly you want to be fed.

Over on Sensui-jima Island there are a couple of options as well. The elegant *New Kinsui Kokusai Hotel* (☎ 0849-82-2111) costs from ¥20,000 with two meals, or for a cheaper alternative, try the *Kokuminshukusha Kaihin Hotel*. Costs here are around ¥6000 per person with two meals.

Getting There & Away

It's only 14 km from Fukuyama to Tomo-no-Ura; frequent buses from stand No 2 outside JR Fukuyama station take 30 minutes and cost ¥500.

ONOMICHI　尾道

Onomichi is an undistinguished-looking industrial town, hemmed in against the sea

To Fukuyama

Ferry to
Sensui-jima
Island

Benten
Island

Tomo Harbour

Ferry To
Hashiri Island

Tomo-no-Ura

Not to Scale

- - - - - - Bicycle Tour

by a backdrop of hills. Along the base of this backdrop is a fascinating temple walk. It's well signposted in English, and English brochures are available at the station inquiry desk. The walk itself is pleasant, although you'd have to be obsessed to want to visit all of the 30-odd temples and shrines (see aside).

Places to Stay

A lot of the nicer accommodation in Onomichi is very expensive, though there are a few business hotels with reasonable rates.

The old-style *Nishiyama Honkan* (☎ 0848-37-2480), has rates from ¥13,000 per person with two meals. The topnotch *Nishiyama Bekkan* (☎ 0848-37-3145) has exquisite grounds and ranges from ¥24,000. It's a fair distance to the east of JR Onomichi station. One of the cheaper ryokan in town is the *Yūshi Ryokan* (☎ 0848-37-2258), with rooms from ¥8000 with two meals. It's close by the Nishiyama Honkan, just south of the cablecar station.

1	Ankoku-ji Temple 安国寺	15	Jōkan-ji Temple 静観寺	29	Nautical Equipment Shop 船具店
2	Shōbō-ji Temple 正法寺	16	Sasayaki Bridge ささやき橋	30	Taisensuirō 対仙酔楼
3	Post Office 郵便局	17	Hōsen-ji Temple 法宣寺	31	Jōsen-ji Temple 浄泉寺
4	Jitokuin Temple 慈徳院	18	Pine Tree 天蓋の松	32	Fukuzen-ji Temple 福善寺
5	Zengyō-ji Temple 善行寺	19	Tomo-no-Ura Museum of History 鞆の浦歴史民俗資料歴	33	Muronoki Song Monument むろの木歌碑
6	Kogarasu-jinja Shrine 小鳥神社			34	Tomo Seaside Hotel 鞆シーサイドホテル
7	Hongan-ji Temple 本願寺	20	Tomo-jō Castle Ruins 鞆城跡	35	Ferry Landing 渡船場
8	Daikan-ji Temple 大観寺	21	Jizō-in Temple 地蔵院	36	Taizan-kan Ryokan 対山館
9	Nunakuma-jinja Shrine 沼名前神社	22	Nanzenbō-ji Temple 南禅坊寺	37	Bashō Monument 芭蕉の句碑
10	Komatsudera Temple 小松寺	23	Amida-ji Temple 阿弥陀寺	38	Empuku-ji Temple 円福寺
11	Kenshō-ji Temple 顕政寺	24	Myōen-ji Temple 明円寺	39	Taigashima Castle Ruins 大可島城跡
12	Myōren-ji Temple 妙連寺	25	Iou-ji Temple 医王寺	40	Yodohime-jinja Shrine 淀姫神社
13	Bus Terminal バスターミナル	26	Old Lighthouse 常夜灯		
14	Yamanaka Shikanosuke Monument 山中鹿之助	27	Iroha-maru Museum いろは丸展示館		
		28	Shichikyō-ochi Ruins 七卿落遺跡		

Alternatives to inn accommodation can be found in the *Sunroute Onomichi* (☎ 0848-25-3161), which has singles/twins at ¥7000/15,200, and the *Onomichi Dai-Ichi Hotel* (☎ 0848-23-4567), where rooms are ¥5000/10,500. Both of these hotels are just to the west of Onomichi station.

Getting There & Away

The Shin-Onomichi shinkansen station is three km north of the JR San-yō line station. Buses connect the two stations and also run straight to the cablecar station (¥170), but it's probably easier to reach Onomichi on the JR San-yō line and change to the shinkansen line either at Fukuyama (to the east) or Mihara (to the west). Hiroshima is one hour 30 minutes away on the San-yō line, and tickets cost ¥1420.

Ferries run from Onomichi to Setoda, the starting and finishing point for the popular Setoda-Hiroshima-Miyajima cruises. (See the Inland Sea section for details.) Ferries also operate from Onomichi to Imabari and Matsuyama, both on Shikoku.

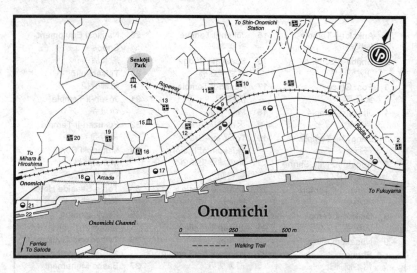

Onomichi

1	Saikoku-ji Temple 西国寺	9	Ropeway Station ロープウェイ山麓駅	16	Kibitsuhiko-jinja Shrine 吉備津彦神社
2	Jōdo-ji Temple 浄土寺	10	Fukuzen-ji Temple 福善寺	17	Watashibadōri Bus Stop 渡し場通りバス停
3	Jōdoji-shita Bus Stop 浄土寺下バス停	11	Jikan-ji Temple 慈観寺	18	Tsuchidshōshita Bus Stop 土堂小下バス停
4	Bōjiguchi Bus Stop 防地口バス停	12	Tennei-ji Temple 天寧寺	19	Kōmyō-ji Temple 光明寺
5	Jyōsen-ji Temple 浄泉寺	13	Senkō-ji Temple 千光寺	20	Jikō-ji Temple 持光寺
6	Rakutenjiguchi Bus Stop 楽天寺口バス停	14	City Museum of Art; Senkō-ji Hill Lookout 市立美術館／千光寺山展望台	21	Bus Terminal バスターミナル
7	Nishiyama Honkan 西山本館	15	Memorial Hall of Literature 文学記念室	22	Onomichi Pier 尾道駅前桟橋
8	Nagaeguchi Bus Stop 長江口バス停				

ONOMICHI TO HIROSHIMA
尾道から広島へ
Mihara 三原

Mihara is on the San-yō shinkansen line and is a convenient departure or arrival point for Setoda on Ikuchi-jima, other islands of the Inland Sea and for Shikoku. The harbour is directly south of the station, a couple of hundred metres away behind the Tenmaya department store. There is a TIC (☎ 0848-67-6074) in the modern JR station, open 10 am to 6 pm daily, which can provide a useful

Onomichi Temple Walk

Several of Onomichi's many temples were locations in films by famed (and local-born) movie director Ōbayashi Nobuhiko. His admirers spend a whole day seeking them out on an extended temple walk. But it is also possible to do a shorter version and avoid getting templed-out.

Take a bus from outside the station and continue for three stops to the Nagaeguchi stop, near the cablecar station. From there, you can follow the walk all the way to Jōdo-ji Temple, almost at the end of the route, then take a bus back to the station from the Jōdoji-shita bus stop.

A cablecar ascends to the top of Senkō-ji Hill, where there is a museum and fine views over the town. You can look down on **Senkō-ji Temple**, founded in 806, then walk to it along the Path of Literature where poets and authors have their works immortalised in stones beside the path. From the temple, continue downhill past the three-storey **Tennei-ji Temple**, originally built with five storeys in 1388 but rebuilt with three in 1692.

The walk continues past **Fukuzen-ji Temple**, dating from 1573, with its impressive gates carved with cranes and a dragon. **Saikoku-ji Temple** is entered through the Niō-mon ('two kings') Gate, which is hung with gigantic two-metre-long straw sandals. From there, a steep flight of steps leads up to the temple, overlooked by a red three-storey pagoda.

Jōdo-ji Temple has an unusual two-storey temple in its compound and a fine garden and teahouse moved here from Fushimi-jō Castle. The temple houses a number of important art works including a painting damaged by the fire which destroyed the temple in 1325.

For anyone who hasn't seen enough temples for one day, between the station and the cablecar are Kōmyō-ji and Jikō-ji Temples, both of which are of lesser interest. The nearby Onomichi Cultural Hall (Onomichi Bunka Kinen-kan) might also be of interest to some. It's open daily from 9 am to 5.30 pm and admission is ¥200. ■

and informative English brochure and map of the area.

Next to the north exit of the station are the ruins of **Mihara-jō Castle**. Slightly more interesting is the **furui-machi** ('old town'), which is a short walk to the right of the north exit. There are a considerable number of photogenic wooden houses, and if you continue further on and bear left, there is a string of small temples of minor interest.

Just to the south of town, **Mt Hitsuei-zan**, at 330m, provides good views of the area and is reportedly particularly beautiful in the cherry blossom season. Kure line buses run from Mihara station to the hill in around five minutes and cost ¥180.

Takehara 竹原

Takehara is on the coastal JR San-yō line or can be reached by boat from Omi-shima Island. There is also a convenient bus service from Mihara that takes one hour and costs ¥940. Takehara was an important centre for salt production in the Edo period and still retains some interesting Edo-period houses. The old part of town is north of the station

area. Follow the tree-lined avenue in front of the station, turn right into the main avenue about 200m up the road and follow it until you cross a river. A left turn here will take you up an attractive area with traditional-style homes, some of which are open to the public. **Shōren-ji Temple** is slightly north of this area and has an impressive 'bell gate', but little else to recommend it.

South of Takehara is **Ōkuno-jima Island**, which has the rather dubious distinction of harbouring the largest resort in Western Honshū. It's all you would expect of a large Japanese resort; boats run out to it from Takehara Harbour (five minutes walk south of the station) in 30 minutes and cost ¥1640.

Kure 呉

The giant battleship *Yamato*, sunk off Nagasaki on a suicide mission to Okinawa during WWII, was just one of the many naval vessels built in Kure. The town, virtually a suburb of Hiroshima, is still an important shipbuilding centre and there is a naval museum on nearby Eta-jima Island – although it takes a while to get there. The information booth in JR Kure station (☎ 0823-23-7845) has city maps, but only in Japanese. The Nikyu-kyō Gorge is 15 km north-east of Kure.

NORTHERN HIROSHIMA-KEN
Taishaku-kyō Gorge 帝釈峡

North of Onomichi, very close to the central Chūgoku Expressway, this 15 km limestone gorge could be a real chance to get off the beaten track. There are natural rock bridges, limestone caves and, for the Japanese, a major attraction in **Lake Shinryū-ko**, which has cruise boats.

Transport connections to the area are not as convenient as for most other attractions in this part of Japan, but this will be part of the fun for some. Probably the best means of transport is to take a bus direct from the Hiroshima bus centre. These buses take around two hours and cost ¥1750. Alternatively there are buses running to the area from both Bingo-Shōbara and Tōjō stations on the JR Geibi line. Tōjō station is closest (25 minutes by bus), but it is also a lot further from Hiroshima and not particularly convenient to anywhere else.

Sandan-kyō Gorge 三段峡

Sandan-kyō Gorge, about 70 km north-west of Hiroshima, is another area that you could get lost in for a few days. The gorge itself isn't as interesting as the one at Taishaku, but this is not an area that is likely to be overrun by tourists.

Buses run from Hiroshima station and the Hiroshima bus centre to Sandan-kyō station at the southern end of the 16-km-long gorge. The journey takes around two hours and costs ¥1240. Ordinary trains to JR Sandan-kyō station, the terminus of the Kabe line, take 2½ hours and cost ¥1090. A walking trail leads through the gorge.

HIROSHIMA 広島

Although it's a busy, prosperous, but not unattractive industrial city, visitors would have no real reason to leave the shinkansen in Hiroshima (population 1,090,000) were it not for that terrible instant on 6 August 1945 when the city became the world's first atomic bomb target. Hiroshima's Peace Memorial Park is a constant reminder of that tragic day and attracts a steady stream of visitors from all over the world.

The city's history dates back to 1589, when the feudal lord Mōri Terumoto named the city and established a castle there.

Orientation & Information

Hiroshima ('broad island') is a city built on a series of sandy islands on the delta of the Ōta-gawa River. JR Hiroshima station is east of the city centre and, although there are a number of hotels around the station, the central area, with its very lively entertainment district, is much more interesting. Peace Memorial Park and most of the atomic bomb reminders are at the northern end of an island immediately west of the city centre.

Hiroshima's main east-west avenue is Heiwa-dōri (Peace Blvd), but the busiest road (with the main tram lines from the station) is Aioi-dōri, which runs parallel to Heiwa-dōri. Just south of Aioi-dōri, and again parallel to it, is the busy Hon-dōri shopping arcade.

There is an information office in JR Hiroshima station (☎ 082-261-1877), open 9 am to 5 pm daily, where the English-speaking staff can make accommodation bookings. For the benefit of those arriving by sea, Ujina, Hiroshima's port, also has an information counter. Information can also be obtained from the tourist office in Peace Memorial Park (☎ 082-247-6738). Hiroshima is a major industrial centre with a Mitsubishi heavy industries plant and the main Mazda (Matsuda in Japanese) car plant. Inquire at the tourist office about factory visits.

A good source of information, especially for those planning a lengthier stay in Hiroshima, is *Signpost*, a locally produced magazine with news on clubs, movies, restaurants and so on. Those planning on a long-term stay in Hiroshima might want to get hold of a copy of *Hiroshima Attention Please*, a comprehensive guide to the city. It's available at Maruzen bookshop.

The big department stores are Mitsukoshi (closed on Monday), Tenmaya (closed on Tuesday), Fukuya (closed on Wednesday) and Sogo (closed on Thursday).

Books English-language books can be found in the Kinokuniya bookshop on the 6th floor of the Sogo department store or in the Maruzen bookshop, nearby in the shopping arcade and opposite Andersen's Restaurant. There is also a good used – and gaijin-run – foreign bookstore called the Book Nook where you can buy, sell and trade books. It's located out of the north exit of the JR station, about a 15 minute walk to the east.

John Hersey's *Hiroshima* (Penguin, 1946) is still the classic reporter's account of the bomb and its aftermath. In 1985 a new edition, available in paperback, followed up the original protagonists. Eleanor Coerr's children's book *Sadako & the Thousand Paper Cranes* tells the sad but inspiring story of a 12 year old girl's death from leukemia, contracted due to exposure to the bomb's radiation.

The A-Bomb Dome

The symbol of the destruction visited upon Hiroshima is the A-Bomb Dome (Gembaku Dōmu) just across the river from Peace Memorial Park. The building was previously the Industrial Promotion Hall until the bomb exploded almost directly above it and effectively put a stop to any further promotional activities. Its propped-up ruins have been left as an eternal reminder of the tragedy, floodlit at night and fronted with piles of the colourful origami cranes which have become a symbol of Hiroshima's plea that nuclear weapons should never again be used. The actual epicentre of the explosion was just south of the A-Bomb Dome, and is marked by a park.

The A-Bomb Dome is the only blast survivor left in ruins, but some of the damaged buildings were repaired and still stand. On Rijō, just 380m south-east of the epicentre,

---

The Hiroshima Bomb

Prior to the atomic bomb explosion, Hiroshima had not been bombed at all. This was a highly unusual situation, given that so many Japanese cities had been virtually flattened by repeated raids, and it is speculated that this was a deliberate policy in order to measure exactly how much damage the atomic bomb had done.

Dropped from the USAF B-29 *Enola Gay*, the bomb exploded at 8.15 am and approximately 75,000 people were killed almost immediately by the blast and subsequent fires. In comparison, all the bombing in WWII killed about 30,000 people in London and about another 30,000 in the rest of the UK. The Hiroshima death toll has probably now reached 200,000 as people continue to die from the radiation aftereffects. Even today, certain types of cancers still occur among Hiroshima's population in greater numbers than other comparable cities.

The first atomic explosion, the testing of a plutonium bomb, had taken place less than three weeks previously in the USA. The Hiroshima bomb used uranium, while the bomb dropped on Nagasaki three days later on 9 August used plutonium. On 2 September the Japanese surrendered. Ever since these events, there has been speculation as to whether it was necessary to drop the bomb, whether a demonstration of its capabilities could have prompted the Japanese surrender and whether a warning should have been given. Whether the Japanese would have resorted to using atomic weapons if they had invented them first has raised less speculation.

What is certain is that two bombs equivalent to a total of 38 kilotons of TNT brought Japan to its knees, despite a history of spectacular suicides which had shown that death was very often preferable to surrender. Also, the horrendous carnage at Okinawa had clearly shown that an invasion of the Japanese mainland was not going to be an easy task.

Today, nuclear weapons can have an explosive power equivalent to 50 megatons of TNT, over 1000 times greater than the Hiroshima and Nagasaki bombs combined. Given the devastating effects achieved by two relatively small nuclear bombs, why on earth do we still need thousands of much larger weapons just a button's push away?

Tony Wheeler

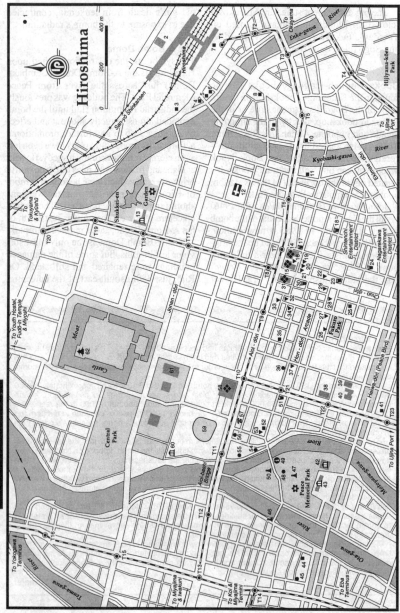

Hiroshima

PLACES TO STAY

2 Hiroshima Granvia
広島グランビア

3 Hotel New Hiroden
ホテルニュー
ヒロデン

4 Hiroshima Ekimae
Green Hotel
広島駅前グリーン
ホテル

5 Hotel Sun Palace
ホテルサンパレス

6 Hotel Yamato
ホテルやまと

7 Hiroshima Station
Hotel
広島ステーション
ホテル

8 Hiroshima City Hotel
広島シティホテル

9 Mikawa Ryokan
三河旅館

10 Hiroshima Intelligent
Annex
広島インテリ
ジェントアネックス

11 Hiroshima Central
Hotel
広島セントラル
ホテル

25 Sera Bekkan Ryokan
世羅別館

35 Hiroshima Kokusai
Hotel
広島国際ホテル

39 Hokke Club Hotel
法華クラブ広島

40 ANA Hotel Hiroshima
広島全日空ホテル

41 Hiroshima Tōkyū Inn
広島東急イン

44 Minshuku Ikedaya
民宿池田家

52 Hiroshima Green
Hotel
広島グリーンホテル

PLACES TO EAT

16 Tokugawa
Okonomiyaki
お好み焼き徳川

17 Kuimonoya; Ottimo;
Harry's Bar
くいものや／
オッティモ

19 Tonkatsu Tokugawa
とんかつ徳川

20 McDonald's

21 Capriciossa;
Namiki Junction
カプリチョーザ／
並木ジャンクション

22 Michan
みっちゃん

26 Mario Expresso

27 Kumar Indian
Restaurant

28 Okonomi-Mura
Village
お好み村

29 Chikara Soba
ちから

32 Rally's Steakhouse

33 Yōrō-no-Taki
養老の滝

34 Spaghetteria San
Mario

37 Andersen's Bakery &
Restaurant

53 California Cafe

OTHER

1 Pagoda of Peace
平和塔

12 World Peace
Memorial Cathedral
世界平和記念堂

13 Prefectural Art
Museum
県立美術館

14 Mitsukoshi
Department Store
三越百貨店

15 Tenmaya
Department Store
天満屋百貨店

18 Snappers

23 Kento's
ケントス

24 Top Five

30 Mac

31 Fukuya Department
Store
福屋百貨店

36 Maruzen Bookshop
丸善

38 Former Bank of
Japan Building
旧日本銀行

42 Peace Memorial Hall
平和記念館

43 Peace Memorial
Museum
平和記念資料館

45 Laundrette
コインランドリー

46 Korean A-Bomb
Memorial
韓国人原爆犠牲者
慰霊碑

47 Cenotaph
原爆慰霊碑

48 Peace Flame
平和の灯

49 Tourist Information
Office
観光案内所

50 Children's Peace
Memorial
原爆の子の像

51 Bar 13

54 Atomic Bomb
Epicentre
爆心地

55 A-Bomb Dome
原爆ドーム

56 ANA
全日空

WESTERN HONSHŪ

Key continued on next page

57	KDD (International Telephone)	T2	Enkobashi 猿猴橋	T13	Tokaichimachi 十日市町
58	Sogō Department Store; Sogō Bus Centre; Kinokuniya Bookshop そごう百貨店／そごうバスターミナル／紀伊国屋	T3	Matoba-chō 的場町	T14	Dobashi 土橋
		T4	Danbara Ohata-chō 段原大畑町	T15	Teramachi 寺町
		T5	Inarimachi 稲荷町	T16	Betsuin-mae 別院前
59	Hiroshima Carp's Baseball Stadium 広島市民球場	T6	Kanayama-chō 銀山町	T17	Jogakuin-mae 女学院前
		T7	Ebisu-chō 胡町	T18	Shukkeien-mae 縮景園前
60	Science & Culture Museum for Children こども文化科学館	T8	Hatchobori 八丁堀	T19	Katei Saibansho-mae 家庭裁判所前
		T9	Tatemachi 立町		
61	Hiroshima Museum of Art 広島美術館	T10	Kamiya-chō 紙屋町	T20	Hakushima Line Terminus 白島
62	Hiroshima-jō Castle 広島城	T11	Genbaku Dōmu-mae (A-Bomb Dome) 原爆ドーム前	T21	Hon-dōri 本通
				T22	Fukuromachi 袋町
TRAM STOPS		T12	Honkawa-chō 本川町	T23	Chuden-mae 中電前
T1	Hiroshima-ekimae 広島駅前				

the former Bank of Japan building looks rock solid; however, although the shell survived intact, the interior was totally destroyed and all 42 people in the bank at the time were killed. It was back in limited business two days later.

Peace Memorial Park

From the A-Bomb Dome, cross the T-shaped Aioi-bashi Bridge to Peace Memorial Park (Heiwa-kōen). It is thought that the T-shape may have been the actual aiming point used by the bombardier. If so, his aim was acute. The park is dotted with memorials including the cenotaph which contains the names of all the known victims of the bomb and frames the A-Bomb Dome across the river. The flame burning beneath the arched cenotaph is not designed to be eternal – when the last nuclear weapon on earth has been destroyed it will be extinguished.

Nearby is what for many is the most poignant memorial in the park – the Children's Peace Memorial inspired by leukemia victim Sadako. When she developed leukemia at 10 years of age she decided to fold 1000 paper cranes, the symbol of longevity and happiness in Japan, convinced that if she could achieve that target she would recover. She died having completed her 644th crane but children from her school folded another 356, with which she was buried. Her story inspired a nationwide bout of paper crane folding which continues to this day. Around the memorial are heaped not thousands but millions of cranes, regularly delivered by the boxload from schools all over Japan.

Just across the river from the park is a memorial to the bomb's Korean victims. Great numbers of Koreans were shipped from their homeland to work as slave labourers in Japanese factories during WWII, and more than one in 10 of those killed by the bomb was a Korean. The Korean memorial, erected long after the war (in 1970), carries a bitter reminder that no prayers were said for the Korean victims, and that despite the plethora of A-bomb monuments, not one had been erected in their memory.

A-Bomb Museum　平和記念資料館
Like its equivalent in Nagasaki, the A-bomb museum will win no awards for architectural inspiration, but its simple message is driven home with sledgehammer force. The exhibits tell the story of the bomb and the destruction it wrought on Hiroshima and its people. A model showing the town after the blast highlights the extent of the damage – seeing this, you might ponder what an insignificant little squib this bomb was, compared to the destructive potential of modern atomic weapons. The museum is open from 9 am to 5.30 pm (May to November), or 4.30 pm (December to April). Entry is ¥50.

Hiroshima-jō Castle　広島城
Also known as Ri-jō, or 'Carp Castle', Hiroshima-jō was originally constructed in 1589 but much of it was dismantled following the Meiji Restoration, leaving only the donjon, main gates and turrets. The remainder was totally destroyed by the bomb and rebuilt in modern ferro-concrete in 1958. There are some interesting displays including an informative and amusing video with some three-dimensional laser embellishments about the construction of the castle. It's open from 9 am to 4.30 pm (October to March) and closes an hour later between April and September; entry costs ¥300.

Shukkei-en Garden　縮景園
Modelled after Xihu (West Lake) in Hangzhou, China, the Shukkei-en Garden dates from 1620 but was badly damaged by the bomb. The garden's name literally means 'shrunk' or 'contracted view', and it attempts to re-create grand vistas in miniature. It may not be one of Japan's celebrated classic gardens, but it makes a pleasant stroll if you have time to spare. Entry is ¥250 and it's open from 9 am to 5.30 pm (4.30 pm from October to March).

Other Attractions
The **Hiroshima Museum of Art** (¥500, closed Monday) and the **Science & Culture Museum for Children** (free except for the planetarium) are both in Central Park just west of the castle. Hijiyama-kōen Park, directly south of JR Hiroshima station, is noted for its cherry blossoms in spring. The **Hiroshima City Museum of Contemporary Art** (¥300) is also in the park. To get to Hijiyama-kōen Park, take a No 5 tram from the station towards Ujina (Hiroshima's port) and get off at the Hijiyama-shita stop. The new **Hiroshima Prefectural Art Museum** (¥500, closed Monday), is next to Shukkei-en Garden.

Fudō-in Temple, directly north of the station and about half a km beyond the youth hostel, is one of the few old structures in Hiroshima which survived the bomb blast. **Mitaki-ji Temple** is north-west of the town centre.

Special Events
On 6 August paper lanterns are floated down the Ōta-gawa River towards the sea in memory of the bomb blast.

Places to Stay
Hiroshima has places to stay for a range of budgets, both around JR Hiroshima station and within walking distance of Peace Memorial Park.

Youth Hostels *Hiroshima Youth Hostel* (☎ 082-221-5343) is about two km north of the town centre; take a bus from platform 22 in front of the JR station or from platform 29 behind it. The hostel is very clearly marked and has a special price for foreigners of ¥1680.

Ryokan & Minshuku The *Mikawa Ryokan* (☎ 082-261-2719) is a short stroll from the JR Hiroshima station and has singles/doubles at ¥3500/6000, room only. Although the ryokan is convenient for train travellers,

WESTERN HONSHŪ

and staff are friendly, the rooms are very cramped and gloomy. In contrast, the *Minshuku Ikedaya* (☎ 082-231-3329) is modern, bright and cheerful. The nightly rate is ¥5000, room only. The helpful manager speaks good English and if your dirty washing is piling up, there's a laundrette on the corner of the road. The Ikedaya is on the other side of Peace Memorial Park in a quiet area but an easy walk via the park from the town centre. To get there, take tram No 6 or a Miyajima tram from the station and get off at the Dobashi stop.

There are a number of other budget places in the vicinity plus a compact enclave of colourful love hotels including one rejoicing in the name 'Hotel Adult'.

Hotels The hotels around the station and central Hiroshima areas include:

Station Area The *Hiroshima Station Hotel* (☎ 082-262-3201) is right in the station building and costs from ¥7500/12,500 for singles/doubles. *Hotel Yamato* (☎ 082-263-6222) is slightly cheaper at ¥6000/12,300 and is close to the station, overlooking the river. Next to it is the *Hotel Sun Palace* (☎ 082-264-6111) which is cheaper again at ¥5500/9000. Also near the station is the *Hiroshima Ekimae Green Hotel* (☎ 082-264-3939) with rooms at ¥6300/10,000.

The expensive *Hotel Granvia* (☎ 082-262-1111), directly behind the station, has singles/doubles from ¥9500/15,500. Other business hotels around the station area include the *Hotel New Hiroden* (☎ 082-263-3456), the *River Side Hotel* (☎ 082-227-1111), the *Hiroshima Central Hotel* (☎ 082-243-2222), the *Hiroshima Union Hotel* (☎ 082-263-7878) and the *Hiroshima City Hotel* (☎ 082-263-5111). All offer rates of around ¥6000 to ¥7000.

Central Hiroshima The *Hiroshima Kokusai Hotel* (☎ 082-248-2323) is right in the city centre and has rooms from ¥7000/12,500 for singles/doubles. The *Hiroshima Green Hotel* (☎ 082-248-3939) is on the edge of the city centre and close to the riverside and Peace Memorial Park; it costs from ¥6200/9200.

The *Hokke Club Hotel* (☎ 082-248-3371) has tiny rooms, but the noon check-in/checkout is a good deal. Singles/twins cost from ¥6500/10,500.

Directly behind the Hokke Club, on Heiwa-dōri, is the expensive *ANA Hotel Hiroshima* (☎ 082-241-1111) with singles from ¥9800, and twins and doubles from ¥20,000. It's probably the city's best hotel and during summer there's a rooftop beer garden. Across Heiwa-dōri from the ANA Hotel the *Hiroshima Tōkyū Inn* (☎ 082-244-0109) has rooms from ¥8700/16,000.

Hiroshima does have traditional Japanese ryokan but most are in modern, anonymous buildings. The *Sera Bekkan* (☎ 082-248-2251) is central and costs from ¥12,000 per person including two meals.

Places to Eat
Hiroshima is noted for its seafood, particularly oysters, and also Hiroshima-yaki, a local version of okonomi-yaki made with soba noodles and fried egg. Check out *Okonomiyaki-mura Village*, an amazing grouping of some 30 mini-restaurants on the 2nd, 3rd and 4th floors of the Shintenchi Plaza Building behind the Parco department store. All specialise in this tasty 'Japanese pizza' (most under ¥1000) and the boisterous atmosphere alone is worth taking a look – just wander around until you see one which looks appealing. A few have English on their menus and display photos of the choices. Other popular spots for Hiroshima-yaki include *Michan*, nearby on Chūō-dōri and *Tokugawa* behind the Mitsukoshi department store. There is good pasta at *Capriciossa*, next to McDonald's in the same area.

The very popular Mario chain of Italian restaurants serve pastas and pizza and are a great bet across the board for an inexpensive lunch or dinner. Across from Fukuro-machi Park is the local favourite *Mario Expresso*, and just off Hon-dōri arcade there is a *Spaghetteria San Mario*, of which there is another branch on the 2nd floor of the Sogo annex at the Peace Park end of Hon-dōri arcade.

A familiar assortment of fast-food outlets

can be found in the Hon-dōri shopping arcade. *Andersen's* on Hon-dōri is a popular restaurant complex with an excellent bakery section – a good place for an economical breakfast, watching the world pass by from the tables in the front window. There are a variety of other restaurant sections in the Andersen's complex and close by is the peculiar *California Café*, a cafe/bar run from inside an enormous modern mobile home (RV).

The *Kumar Indian Restaurant*, only a couple of blocks south of Hon-dōri, has excellent curries, tandoori and the like. Lunch-time teishokus cost between ¥800 and ¥1100. Main courses are typically ¥1100, and the menu is in English. The other Indian restaurant to look out for in the arcade area is *Tandoor* (☎ 082-247-5622), which also has good lunch-time specials.

Also in the popular 'ethnic' department is *Kuimonoya* with hybrid Asian cuisine prepared by a Thai chef. It has a great dinner course for ¥2800, and the restaurant can be found on the 2nd floor of the Apple 2 building, which also houses Harry's Bar (see the Entertainment section). The 5th floor of the same building also has the excellent Italian restaurant *Ottimo*, though this place is a bit pricey – figure on spending around ¥3500 to ¥5000 per person for dinner.

Just north of the Hon-dōri arcade, near the Kokusai Hotel, *Yōrō-no-Taki* is an excellent, boisterous robatayaki with cheap draught beer. Across the road is *Rally's* steakhouse. This whole area is great for seeking out good Japanese restaurants, and probably the best advice is to wander around the arcades looking at the window displays of restaurants until you find one you like. Look out for *Chikara*, a very interesting soba shop with very economical prices, and *Tonkatsu Tokugawa*, a snazzy place with a good selection of breaded-pork cutlet dishes. Back down on Aioi-dōri is a branch of the *Suehiro* steak restaurant chain, always a reliable, if slightly expensive, option.

Entertainment

Like any large Japanese city, Hiroshima has its fair share of boozing establishments –

somewhere in the vicinity of 4000 in this case. Shintenchi and Nagarekawa are the entertainment districts and they make for an interesting evening stroll. If you want to avoid the hostess scene, look out for shot bars – there are a fair number of them about.

The foreign community in Hiroshima has a number of trusty bars to hang out in; two of the most popular are Mac and Snappers. *Mac* is a tiny, mellow place on the 4th floor of a building near the corner of Chūō-dōri and one of the streets running into the arcade area; there's an English sign at ground level. It has an astoundingly wide selection of CDs and LPs, and the cheerful owners, Mac and Yumi, will regale you with 'pick a song...any song'. They've probably got it.

On the more boisterous, biker-friendly side, *Snappers*, run by Mitch, a Harley-riding Tasmanian, attracts a slightly more raucous clientele and is known to get wild in the wee hours. Another option is *Harry's Bar* in the basement of the Apple 2 building, much more up-market in appearance than Mac and Snappers. As the sign outside notifies prospective customers, it's '15% off drink prices for foreigners'; reverse discrimination, of course, but then a cheap beer is a cheap beer.

Other nightlife options in Hiroshima include the shot bar *Top Five*, and *Bar 13*, with a wide selection of beer from around the world (look for the American flag outside). There is a branch of *Kento's*, the live 'oldies but goodies' standby, and also the country-western bar *Clementine's* (where line-dancing customers don cowboy hats and drink Budweiser!). For live music, check out *Jakara*, featuring jazz-fusion bands, or *Namiki Junction* for standard rock.

Getting There & Away

Air There are frequent flights between Hiroshima and other parts of Japan. Flights to Tokyo (Haneda) take around one hour 20 minutes and cost ¥21,600 one way, ¥39,060 return. Flights from Sapporo take two hours five minutes and cost ¥33,600 one way. Okinawa is one hour 40 minutes away and flights cost ¥26,600.

An American in Hiroshima

A ride in a Japanese taxi can prove to be a cultural experience. From white-gloved cabbies and auto-open/close doors to complimentary breath mints for the ride. Then there's Hiroshima, where perhaps Japan's only gaijin taxi driver has been cruising the streets since the summer of 1995 and naturally gaining plenty of attention.

After discovering his job as a long-distance delivery driver was keeping him away from his family, American Stephen Outlaw-Spruell took a friend's advice and began driving a cab for Hiroshima's Tsubame Kōtsū. His meter soon became a hit with locals and visitors and these days his unique charter tours around the city are in high demand with Japanese and fellow gaijin alike.

Beside the appeal of being foreign, and speaking English, he takes a different approach to his fares. Unlike standard Japanese taxi tours, where the drivers simply drop customers in front of attractions to fend for themselves, Outlaw-Spruell stays by his clients' side, providing sight-by-sight historical tidbits and unique insight (he says he has been contacted on several occasions by A-Bomb survivors who wish him to pass on their stories to others).

Outlaw-Spruell offers a three hour tour taking in the city's main attractions, and also a six to eight hour route including nearby Miyajima and other less-travelled areas. Though the price is not cheap (¥5200 per hour), split between up to five people it can be a worthwhile and enlightening way to discover Hiroshima. Outlaw-Spruell can be reached at Tsubame Kōtsū on ☎ 082-222-8180; or fax ☎ 082-228-5200. He is also listed with JTB offices around the world. ■

Train Hiroshima has long been an important railway junction, one of the factors which led to it being the prime atomic bomb target in WWII. Today it is an important stop on the Tokyo-Osaka-Hakata shinkansen route, with some services originating or terminating in Hiroshima. By shinkansen, it takes about 4½ to five hours to reach Hiroshima from Tokyo (¥11,120 plus a tokkyū charge of ¥6580), 1½ to two hours from Kyoto and slightly less from Hakata.

The JR San-yō line passes through Hiroshima and onwards down to Shimonoseki, hugging the coastline for much of the way. If you're travelling this way, the ordinary local services move along fairly quickly and are the best way to visit the nearby attractions of Miya-jima Island and Iwakuni.

Bus Long-distance buses run from the shinkansen exit of Hiroshima station, although there is also a bus terminal on the 3rd floor of Sogo department store. Buses between Hiroshima and Tokyo take around 12 hours and cost ¥11,840; they run from the JR bus terminal next to Tokyo station. Buses to and from Nagoya take around eight hours and cost ¥7700. There are also buses to and

from Kyoto (¥5500), Fukuoka (¥4430) and Nagasaki (¥6500).

Boat Hiroshima is an important port with a variety of Inland Sea cruises as well as connections to other cities. The Hiroshima to Matsuyama ferry and hydrofoil services are a popular way of getting to or from Shikoku. (See the Matsuyama section in the Shikoku chapter for details.) Ferries also operate to Beppu on Kyūshū and to Imabari on Shikoku. For information on the Imabari service (in Japanese) ring Hiroshima-Imabari Kōsoku-sen (☎ 082-254-7555); tickets cost ¥4360. For information on the Beppu service, ring Hirobetsu Kisen (☎ 082-253-0909); economy class tickets are ¥4000.

Getting Around

The Airport Hiroshima's airport is conveniently close to the south-west of town and trams do the trip in around 30 minutes (¥200).

Bus Buses are more difficult to use than the trams as they are not numbered and place names are in kanji only, but the stands outside the station are clearly numbered.

Take a bus from stand No 1 to the airport, No 2 to the port.

Tram Hiroshima has an easy-to-use tram (streetcar) service which will get you pretty well anywhere you want to go for a flat fare of ¥130 (¥90 on the short No 9 route). There is even a tram which runs all the way to the Miyajima Port for ¥250. The tram routes are shown on the Hiroshima map. Note that the tram colours have no connection with the routes – it's popularly rumoured that Hiroshima ended up with its rainbow variety of trams by buying up other cities' old trams as they closed down their tram services. If you have to change trams to get to your destination, you should ask for a transfer ticket (norikaeken) as you leave the tram and pay an additional ¥50.

MIYA-JIMA ISLAND 宮島
Correctly known as Itsuku-shima, Miyajima Island is easily reached from Hiroshima. The famous 'floating' torii of the Itsukushima-jinja Shrine is one of the most photographed tourist attractions in Japan and, with the island's Mt Misen as a backdrop, is classified as one of Japan's 'three best views'. The other two are the sandspit at Amanohashidate (northern coast of Western Honshū) and the islands of Matsushima-wan Bay (near Sendai, Northern Honshū). Apart from the shrine, the island has some other interesting temples, some good walks and remarkably tame deer which even wander the streets of the small town. Look out for the signs warning of the dangers of fraternising with the horned varieties.

Orientation & Information
There's an information counter (☎ 082-944-2011) in the ferry building. Turn right as you emerge from the building and follow the waterfront to get to the shrine and the centre of the island's small town. The shopping street, packed with souvenir outlets and restaurants, is a block back from the waterfront.

Itsukushima-jinja Shrine 厳島神社
The shrine, which gives the island its real name, dates from the 6th century and in its present form from 1168. Its pier-like construction is a result of the island's holy status. Commoners were not allowed to set foot on the island and had to approach the shrine by boat, entering through the floating torii out in the bay. Much of the time, however, the shrine and torii are surrounded not by water but by mud. The view of the torii, which is immortalised in thousands of travel brochures, requires a high tide.

The shrine is open from 6.30 am to sunset and entry is ¥300. On one side of the floating shrine is a floating nō stage built by a Mōri lord. The orange torii, dating from 1875 in its present form, is often floodlit at night. A 'son et lumière' is sometimes performed from 8.30 to 9 pm, particularly in summer. You can hear it on headphones in English as well as Japanese for ¥300.

The treasure house, west of the shrine, is open from 8 am to 5 pm and entry is ¥300. The collection of painted sutra scrolls dating from the 12th century is not usually on display and the exhibits are not of great interest except, perhaps, to the scholarly.

Temples & Other Buildings
Topping the hill immediately east of the Itsukushima-jinja Shrine is the Senjō-kaku (Pavilion of 1000 Mats) built in 1587 by Hideyoshi. This huge and atmospheric hall is constructed with equally massive timber pillars and beams and the ceiling is hung with paintings. It looks out on a colourful five-storey pagoda dating from 1407. The Senjō-kaku should have been painted to match but was left unfinished when Hideyoshi died.

Miya-jima has numerous other temples including the Daigan-ji just west of the shrine, which is dedicated to the god of music and dates from 1201. The colourful and glossy Daishō-in Temple is just behind the town and can be visited on the way down Mt Misen. This is a temple with everything – statues, gates, pools, carp, you name it. The rituals performed at the main Itsukushima-jinja Shrine are also administered by the

Daigan-ji. West of Itsukushima-jinja Shrine is the picturesque Tahō-tō Pagoda.

Miya-jima History & Folklore Museum
歴史民俗資料館

This interesting museum combines a 19th century merchant's home with exhibits concerning trade in the Edo period, a variety of displays connected with the island and a fine garden. The museum is open from 8.30 am to 4.30 pm and there's an excellent and informative brochure in English. Entry is ¥250.

Mt Misen & Other Walks 弥山

The ascent of 530m Mt Misen is the island's finest walk; the uphill part of the round trip can be avoided by taking the two stage cablecar for ¥900 one way, ¥1600 return. It leaves you about a 15 minute walk from the top. Around the cablecar station there are monkeys as well as deer. On the way to the top look for the giant pot said to have been used by Kōbō Daishi (774-835) and kept simmering ever since! It's in the smaller building beside the main temple hall, also said to have been used by the founder of the Shingon sect.

There are superb views from the summit and a variety of routes leading back down. The descent takes a good hour and walking paths also lead to other high points on the island, or you can just follow the gentle stroll through Momiji-dani (Maple Valley), which leads to the cablecar station.

Other Attractions

There's an aquarium, a popular beach, a seaside park and, across from the ferry landing, a display of local crafts in the Hall of Industrial Traditions.

Special Events

Island festivals include fire-walking rites by the island's monks on 15 April and 15 November, a fireworks display on 14 August and the Kangensai Boat Festival on 16 June.

Places to Stay & Eat

There is no inexpensive accommodation on Miya-jima Island, although the *Miyajima-guchi Youth Hostel* (☎ 0829-56-1444) is near

the ferry terminal and JR Miyajima-guchi station on the mainland. It costs ¥2630.

If you can afford to stay on the island, it's well worthwhile: you'll be able to enjoy the island in the evening, minus the day-trip hordes. The *Kokuminshukusha Miyajima Lodge* (☎ 0829-44-0430) is west of the shrine and has rooms from ¥8500 per person including meals. At the large and pleasant *Iwasō Ryokan* (☎ 0829-44-2233) or at the *Miyajima Grand Hotel* (☎ 0829-44-2411) you can count on at least ¥20,000 per person with meals. There are a number of fairly expensive hotels and ryokan along the water-

PLACES TO STAY		2	Hall of Industrial Traditions (Handicraft Display); Post Office 伝統産業会館	18	Itsukushima-jinja Shrine 厳島神社
4	Miyajima Royal Hotel 宮島ロイヤルホテル			19	Nō Stage 能舞台
6	Pension Miyajima ペンション宮島	3	Tokuju-ji Temple 徳寿寺	20	Daigan-ji Temple 大願寺
9	Kamefuku Hotel ホテルかめ福	5	Zonkō-ji Temple 存光寺	21	Kiyomori Shrine 清盛神社
11	Kinsuikan Hotel 錦水館	7	Shinkō-ji Temple 真光寺	22	Treasure House 宝物館
15	Miyajima Grand Hotel 宮島グランドホテル	8	Castle Ruins 城跡	23	Miyajima History & Folklore Museum 歴史民俗資料館
16	Iwasō Ryokan 岩惣	10	Konju-in Temple 金寿院	24	Tahō-tō Pagoda 多宝塔
26	Kokuminshukusha Miyajima Lodge 国民宿舎宮島ロッジ	12	Kōmyō-in Temple 光明院	25	Aquarium 水族館
		13	Senjō-kaku Pavilion 千畳閣	27	Ōmoto Shrine 大元神社
OTHER		14	Five Storeyed Pagoda 五重塔	28	Daishō-in Temple 大聖院
1	Miyajima Pier 宮島港	17	Floating Torii 大鳥居		

front, that includes the *Kamefuku Hotel* (☎ 0829-44-2111), the *Kinsuikan Hotel* (☎ 0829-44-2133) and the *Miyajima Royal Hotel* (☎ 0829-44-2191).

A more moderately priced alternative is the friendly and very pleasant *Pension Miyajima* (☎ 0829-44-0039), which is just back from the ferry landing. Rooms with bathroom cost ¥10,000 per person with two superb meals included. Although there are many restaurants and cafes on Miya-jima Island, most of them cater to the day-trippers and close early in the evening.

Getting There & Away
The mainland ferry terminal for Miya-jima Island is near the Miyajima-guchi station on the JR San-yō line between Hiroshima and Iwakuni. Miyajima trams from Hiroshima terminate at the Hiroden-Miyajima stop by the ferry terminal. The tram (55 minutes, ¥250) takes longer than the train (25 minutes,

¥390) but runs more frequently and can be boarded in central Hiroshima. On some trams you may have to transfer at the Hiroden-Hiroshima stop.

From the terminal, ferries shuttle across to Miya-jima Island in just 10 minutes for ¥170. One of the ferries is operated by JR so Japan Rail Pass holders should make sure they use this one. Ferry services also operate to Miya-jima Island direct from Hiroshima. High-speed ferries (¥1440) do the trip there and back eight times daily and take just over 20 minutes from Hiroshima's Ujina Port. The SKK (Seto Naikai-kisen) Inland Sea cruise on the *Akinada* starts and finishes at Miyajima; the Miyajima to Hiroshima leg costs ¥1480.

Getting Around
Bicycles can be rented from the ferry building or you can walk. A free bus operates from in front of the Iwasō Ryokan to the Mt Misen cablecar station.

WESTERN HONSHŪ

The Inland Sea
瀬戸内海

The Inland Sea is bounded by the major islands of Honshū, Kyūshū and Shikoku. Four narrow channels connect the Inland Sea with the ocean. To the north the Kanmon Straits separate Honshū from Kyūshū and lead to the Sea of Japan; to the south, leading to the Pacific, the Hoya Straits separate Kyūshū from Shikoku; at the other end of Shikoku the Naruto Straits and Kitan Straits flow each side of Awaji-shima Island, which almost connects Shikoku to Honshū.

For the visitor, the most interesting area of the Inland Sea is the island-crowded stretch from Hiroshima east to Takamatsu and Okayama. There are said to be more than 3000 islands, depending on what you define as an island! There are a number of ways of seeing the Inland Sea. One is to simply travel through it as there are numerous ferry services crisscrossing the sea or even running its full length, such as the service from Osaka on Honshū to Oita, near Beppu, on Kyūshū. Alternatively, but more expensively, there are Inland Sea cruises ranging from short day trips to longer overnight cruises. Also, you can visit single islands in the Inland Sea for a first-hand experience of a part of Japan which, though rapidly changing, is still quite different from the fast-moving metropolitan centres.

Information
Brochures, maps and general tourist information are readily available but Donald Richie's *The Inland Sea*, originally published in 1971 and now available in paperback, makes an excellent introduction to the region. Although much of the Inland Sea's slow-moving and easy-going atmosphere has disappeared since his book was published (and indeed he emphasised its rapidly changing nature even at that time), it still provides some fascinating insights. High points of the book include his encounter with a yakuza priest at the Oyamatsumi-jinja

Shrine on Ōmi-shima Island, his demolition job of the Kōsan-ji Temple at Setoda, the amusing search for a stone cat on Kitagishima and the wistful tale of the prostitutes of Kinoe on Osakikami-jima.

Cruises
Miya-jima to Setoda The popular SKK (Seto Naikai-kisen; ☎ 082-321-5111) cruises between Miya-jima and Setoda on Ikuchi-jima Island or on to Onomichi offer the easiest (though rather touristy) way of seeing one of the finest stretches of the Inland Sea. Day cruises offered by SKK are seasonal (most halt services in the winter months) and typically offer routes between Onomichi, Setoda, Ōmi-shima Island, Kure and Miya-jima. Prices vary between ¥7000 and ¥12,000, and also depend on whether you take lunch on board or not.

SKK has numerous other ships operating, including day cruises from Hiroshima to Etajima, Miya-jima and Eno-shima islands.

The Japan Travel Bureau (JTB) and other tour operators also have a variety of overnight cruises from Osaka. Check with local TICs for details on times and current prices.

ŌMI-SHIMA ISLAND 大三島
This hilly rather than mountainous island boasts the mountain god's **Ōyamatsumi-jinja Shrine**, which once commanded much respect from the Inland Sea's pirates. In fact, the pirates were more like a local navy than real pirates but, until Hideyoshi brought them to heel, they wielded real power in these parts. Along the way, an armour collection was built up in the shrine's treasure house, including more than half the armour in Japan; 80% of the armour and helmets designated as National Treasures are held here. Entry to the treasure house is ¥800, open 8.30 am to 4.30 pm, but despite the importance of the collection, saturation soon sets in and it's probably of more interest to those with a specific interest in Japanese military accoutrements than to the average visitor.

In an adjacent building is a boat used by Emperor Hirohito in his marine science investigations, together with a somewhat tatty natural history exhibit. The shrine's history is actually one of the most ancient in Japan, ranking with the shrines at Ise and Izumo.

Miyaura Port is a 15 minute walk from the shrine. The *Omi-shima Suigun* restaurant is near the shrine.

Getting There & Away

The *Akinada* cruise from Hiroshima visits Ōmi-shima but you can also get there by ferry service from Onomichi, Mihara or Setoda on the neighbouring island of Ikuchi-jima, and also from Takehara, further west on the Honshū coast.

IKUCHI-JIMA ISLAND 生口島

At Setoda, the main town on the island, Ikuchi-jima is actually linked to neighbouring Takane-jima by a bridge. The town is noted for the **Kōsan-ji Temple**, a wonderful exercise in kitsch. Local steel-tube magnate Kanemoto Kōzō devoted a large slab of his considerable fortune from 1935 on to re-creating numerous important temples and shrines all in this one spot and all in grateful homage to his mother. If you haven't got time to visit the originals, this is an interesting substitute.

Entry is ¥1000 which includes the 1000 Buddhas Cave, the art museum and the treasure house. It costs another ¥200 to visit Kanemoto Kōzō's mother's quarters. The extraordinary 1000 Buddhas Cave includes an introductory 'hell', very Tiger Balm Garden-like with its tableaux of the damned being mangled, chopped, fried and generally hard done by. From there you follow winding tunnels and spiral stairs lined with 1000 Buddhas. One sour note at this temple is the poor Australian emu penned up in far too small an enclosure by the main entrance.

To get to the temple, turn right as you leave the boat landing then left up the shop-lined 600m-long street. The **Setoda History & Folklore Museum** is at the start of this street and entry is free. Halfway up the same street you can turn left towards a temple on the hillside; around the back of this temple and

much further up the hill is the **Kōjō-ji Temple**, dating from 1403, with a three-storey pagoda and fine views over the island. You can also get there by turning left from the pier (towards the bridge) and heading straight up the hill.

Places to Stay

The *Ikuchi-jima Tarumi Youth Hostel* (☎ 08452-7-3137) costs ¥2500 (nonmembers add ¥1000), or ¥4000/5000 respectively with two meals. The *Setoda Youth Hostel* (☎ 08452-7-0224) is a short walk from the dock and offers similar prices.

Getting There & Away

You can get to Ikuchi-jima Island by the regular cruise from Hiroshima or by ferries from Mihara or Onomichi on Honshū. Mihara has the widest range of services, some continuing on to Ōmi-shima Island and Imabari on Shikoku. It pays to shop around at the harbour area. Fares range from ¥300 to ¥1400, depending on the speed and luxury of the ferry. No matter how you want to travel, you shouldn't have to wait more than an hour.

INNO-SHIMA ISLAND 因島

Famed for its flowers and abundance of fruit, Inno-shima Island is connected by bridge to Mukai-shima Island and on to Onomichi. The island has an interesting pirate castle (entry ¥310, open 8.30 am to 5 pm).

SHIWAKU ISLANDS 塩飽諸島

North of Marugame on Shikoku are the scattered Shiwaku Islands, once the haunt of daring pirates and seafarers. Hon-jima is a larger island just west of the Seto-ōhashi Bridge with some fine old buildings and interesting sites. From Marugame port, the island can be reached by ferry in 35 minutes (¥450).

SHŌDO-SHIMA ISLAND 小豆島

Famed for its vast olive groves and the location for the Japanese film classic *Twenty Four Eyes*, Shōdo-shima Island translates literally as 'island of small beans'. It offers a

WESTERN HONSHŪ

number of interesting places to visit and makes an enjoyable short escape from big-city Japan. The second largest island in the Inland Sea, Shōdo-shima even has a miniature version of neighbouring Shikoku's 88 Temple Circuit. Though Shōdo-shima can't muster 88 temples, the itinerary is padded out with a number of other notable sites.

Orientation & Information

Tonoshō, at the western end of the island, is the usual arrival point from Takamatsu, Uno or Okayama and makes a good base from which to explore the island. Fukuda in the north-east and Sakate in the south-east are other busy ports. If you arrive on Shōdo-shima Island from Takamatsu (the most popular jumping-off point) you'll find an information office just inside the ferry building.

Coastal Area

The island's olive-growing activities are commemorated at Olive Park on the south coast. Nearby is the **Shōdo-shima Folk Museum**, open 9 am to 4.30 pm, closed Monday (¥300). The end of the peninsula to the south of Ikeda is marked by the **Jizōzaki Lighthouse** and offers fine views over the Inland Sea. Just north of Sakate is the turn-off to the small village of **Tanoura**, site of the village school in the book *Twenty Four Eyes* and the later film of the same name. There's a distinct feeling that this was Shōdo-shima Island's sole brush with fame; the real school and its movie set version are both open for inspection (¥650 combined ticket). A statue of the teacher and her pupils (the movie version) stands outside the Tonoshō ferry terminal.

South of Fukuda, on the eastern side of the island, huge rocks cut for Osaka-jō Castle now lie jumbled down a cliffside at **Iwagatani**. The unused rocks are classified as *zanseki* (rocks left over) or *zannen ishi* (rocks which were sorry not to be in time for shipment) and each bears the seal of the general responsible for their quarrying and dispatch. The north-eastern corner of the island is still one big quarry to this day. More

unshipped castle rocks can be seen on the northern coast at **Omi**, along with the site of a shipyard used by Hideyoshi.

Central Mountains

The **Kanka-kei Cablecar** is the main attraction in the central mountains, making a spectacular trip up through the Kanka-kei Gorge in the shadow of Mt Hoshigajō-yama (¥600 one way, ¥1150 return). There's a walking track if you really want to walk one way. Around the eastern side of the mountain the island's tenuous connection with Greece (they both grow olives) is celebrated in the **Olive Sanctuary** where there's even a fake mini-Parthenon.

As you descend towards Tonoshō (rented scooters are allowed to travel down this road but not up it; perhaps it's too steep) you pass the Choshi-kei Gorge's **monkey mountain** (open 8 am to 5 pm, ¥360) where wild monkeys come for a daily feed. Beside the car park is a restaurant offering *somen nagashi* noodles for ¥500. (A bowl of noodles is dropped into a sort of water race-track which swirls around a circular channel in the middle of the table. You intercept them with your chopsticks as they come by!)

Near Tonoshō is the **Hosho-in Temple** with its huge and ancient juniper tree.

Special Events

The Shikoku-mura Village at Yashima, just outside Takamatsu on Shikoku, has a village kabuki theatre from Shōdo-shima. Farmers' kabuki performances are still held on the island: on 3 May at Tonoshō and on 10 October at Ikeda.

Places to Stay & Eat

Shōdo-shima Olive Youth Hostel (☎ 0879-82-6161) is on the south coast, just beyond Olive Park and the folk museum heading towards Kusakabe and Sakate. Nightly costs are ¥3100 (nonmembers add ¥1000) or an additional ¥1600 including two meals. The *Uchinomi-chō Cycling Terminal* (☎ 0879-82-1099) in Sakate has nightly rates of ¥2780, or ¥5150 with two meals, and rents bikes; ¥510 for four hours and ¥50 per extra

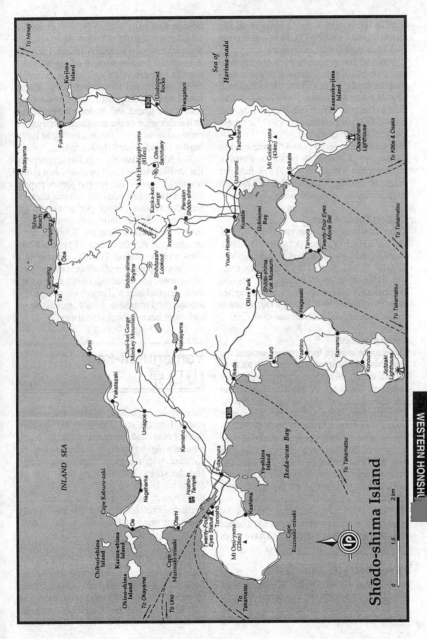

Sea of Harima-nada

To Himeji

Kōjima Island

Unshipped Rocks

Iwagatani

Nadayama

Fukuda

Mt Hoshigajō-yama (816m)

Olive Sanctuary

Tachibana

Kazenoko-jima Island

Mt Goishi-yama (434m)

Okadōhana Lighthouse

To Kōbe & Osaka

Silver Beach

Camping

Ōbe

Kanka-kei Gorge

Pension Shōdo-shima

Uchinomi

Sakate

Tai

Camping

Shōdo-shima Skyline

Inotani

Shidōzashi Lookout

Kusabe

Uchinomi Bay

Twenty-Four Eyes Movie Set

Tanoura

To Takamatsu

Ōmi

Chōsi-kei Gorge Monkey Mountain

Nakayama

Youth Hostel

Olive Park

Shōdo-shima Folk Museum

Nagasaki

To Takamatsu

Yakatazaki

Ikeda

Murō

Yoshino

Kamano

Jizōzaki Lighthouse

Konoura

Umaoe

136

Cape Kaburu-zaki

INLAND SEA

Kamisho

Yo-shima Island

Ikeda-wan Bay

To Takamatsu

Chiburi-shima Island

Kazura-shima Island

Nagahama

Oe

Hōsho-in Temple

Futagoura

Kashima

Okino-shima Island

To Okayama

To Uno

To Takamatsu

Cape Murosaki-mitsaki

Ōtami

Tonoshō

Twenty-Four Eyes Statue

Mt Ōmi-yama (226m)

Cape Kuroaki-mitsaki

Shōdo-shima Island

0   1.5   3 km

hour. In Ikeda there is the *Kokuminshukusha Shōdo-shima* (☎ 0879-75-1115) which costs ¥4000, or ¥6000 with two meals.

Tonoshō has a variety of hotels, ryokan and minshuku, particularly along the road running straight back from the waterfront. The *Maruse Minshuku* (☎ 0879-62-2385), next to the post office is neat and tidy, and costs ¥4000 per person, plus ¥500 for breakfast and ¥1500 for dinner.

North of the youth hostel, on the road to Inotani, are a couple of pensions. *Pension Shōdoshima* (☎ 0879-82-0181) has per person costs of ¥3700 (no bath), ¥4800 (with bath), or ¥8000 with bath and two meals.

Getting There & Away

There is a variety of ferry services from Honshū and Shikoku to various ports on the island. Popular jumping-off points include Uno on Honshū (trains go to Uno from Okayama) and Takamatsu on Shikoku. The regular Takamatsu to Tonoshō high-speed ferries take 35 minutes and cost ¥1000. Regular ferries take around an hour and cost ¥500.

Getting Around

There are plenty of bus services around the island and a host of bus tours (¥3000 to ¥5000) which seem to set off with every ferry arrival at Tonoshō. Alternatively, you can rent cars from a couple of agencies by the Tonoshō ferry terminal or motor scooters from Ryōbi Rent-a-Bike (☎ 0879-62-6578). The scooter agency operates out of a container near the ferry terminal; the daily hire cost is ¥2990 including fuel. The island is small enough to explore in a day if you start early, although a circuit of the coast and a mountain excursion will clock up well over 100 km. With adequate time, touring by bicycle presents a great way to see the island and there are several places which have bikes for rent.

AWAJI-SHIMA ISLAND　淡路島

Awaji-shima Island, the Inland Sea's largest island, forms the region's eastern boundary and almost connects Honshū with Shikoku. At the Shikoku end, the **Naruto-ōhashi Bridge** spans the Naruto Straits across the well-known **Naruto Whirlpools** to connect Shikoku with Awaji-shima Island. (See the Around Tokushima section of the Shikoku chapter.) At the other end of the island, a bridge is planned to connect Awaji-shima Island with Akashi, near Kōbe. The northern part of the island will be long remembered as the epicentre of the massive January 1995 earthquake which claimed over 6000 lives, mostly in and around the Kōbe area.

The island is densely populated, relatively flat and has some good beaches. It was the original home of the *ningyō jōruri* puppet theatre which preceded the development of bunraku theatre. Short performances are given several times daily in the small puppet theatre in Fukura. Near the Kōshien ferry terminal, at the **Onokoro Ai-rando-Kōen Park** (¥800, closed Tuesday), there is a bizarre grouping of replica world sightseeing attractions (constructed one twenty-fifth their original size). They include the Taj Mahal, the Parthenon, Pisa's leaning tower and other international favourites.

Yamaguchi-ken 山口県

Yamaguchi Prefecture, marking the western end of Honshū, straddles both the southern San-yō coast and the northern San-in coast. Southern highlights of the prefecture include Iwakuni, with the great Kintai-kyō Bridge, and the shrine and 'floating torii' gate on Miyajima-Island, while Shimonoseki acts as the gateway to Kyūshū and Korea. The northern stretch includes the historically important town of Hagi and in the central mountains the vast Akiyoshi-dai Cave.

IWAKUNI　岩国

The five-arched Kintai-kyō Bridge is Iwakuni's major attraction, although the town also has a US military base (an 'unattraction' perhaps?) and a number of points of interest in the Kikko-kōen Park.

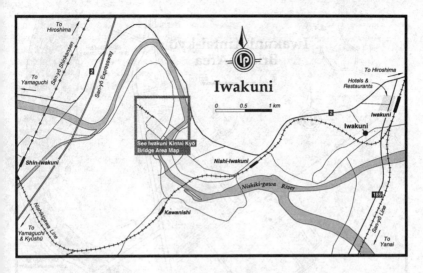

Iwakuni

Orientation & Information

Iwakuni has three widely separated areas, which can, at first, be somewhat confusing for visitors. To the far west of the town centre is the Shin-Iwakuni shinkansen station, totally separate from the rest of town. In the central area is the old part of town with the bridge, the samurai quarter, the castle and all the other tourist attractions. To the east, in the modern part of town, the JR Iwakuni station has a helpful information centre (☎ 0827-21-6050) as well as hotels, restaurants, bars and other conveniences. There is also a TIC just downriver from the bridge. Tune your radio to 1575 AM for the US military radio station.

Kintai-kyō Bridge   錦帯橋

Also known as the 'Brocade Sash Bridge', the Kintai-kyō Bridge was built in 1673 and washed away by a flood in 1950. It was authentically rebuilt in 1953, albeit with some cunningly concealed steel reinforcements. The bridge is immediately recognisable by the five extremely steep arches. In the feudal era only samurai could use the bridge, which connected their side of the river with the rest of the town; commoners

had to cross the river by boat. Today visitors have to pay a ¥210 toll to walk across and back. The ticket office at the entrance to the bridge also sells an all-inclusive ticket *(setto-ken)* for ¥820 that covers the bridge (¥210), the return cablecar (ropeway) trip (¥520) and Iwakuni-jō Castle (¥260), which is a saving of ¥170 if you plan to visit all three.

The bridge and castle are also brightly flood-lit nightly until 10 pm, making an interesting photo opportunity (bring a tripod, or improvise).

Samurai Quarter & Iwakuni Historical Museum

Some traces remain of the old samurai quarter by the bridge. The area is overlooked by Iwakuni-jō Castle and, beside the castle cablecar, is the Iwakuni Historical Museum with its extensive collection of samurai armour and equipment. It's said to be one of the best collections in Japan, but since only a small part of it is displayed at one time (and very little is labelled in English) it is unlikely to impress those already suffering from feudal-artifact overload. Entry is an expensive ¥500 and it's open from 9 am to 5 pm.

The old samurai quarter is now part of

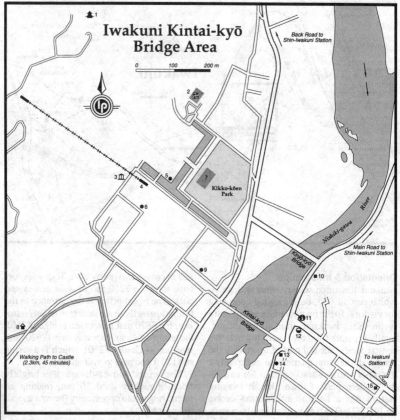

Iwakuni Kintai-kyō Bridge Area

0   100   200 m

Kikko-kōen Park

Nishiki-gawa River

Back Road to Shin-Iwakuni Station

Main Road to Shin-Iwakuni Station

Kintai-kyō Bridge

Walking Path to Castle (2.3km, 45 minutes)

To Iwakuni Station

1	Iwakuni-jō Castle 岩国城	7	Chōkokan Library 徴古館	12	Bus Stop バス停
2	Fukkō Temple	8	Youth Hostel ユースホステル	13	Shiratame Ryokan 白為旅館
3	Iwakuni Historical Museum 岩国歴史美術館	9	Nagaya-mon Gate 長屋門	14	Iwakuni Sightseeing Centre 岩国観光センター
4	Cablecar Station ケーブルカー駅	10	Iwakuni Kokusai Kankō Hotel 岩国国際観光ホテル	15	Hangetsu-an 半月庵
5	Kinun-kaku Pavilion 錦雲閣	11	Iwakuni Visitor's Centre 岩国ビジターズ センター		
6	Mekata House 目加田家旧宅				

Kikko-kōen Park and includes some picturesque moats and remnants of the feudal buildings such as the Kagawa Nagaya-mon Gate, a fine old samurai gateway. Beside the moat, close to the cablecar station, is the Kinun-kaku Pavilion. Look for the swan houses in the moat. Also beside the cablecar car park is the Mekata House, a fine old samurai home. The Chokokan Library houses documents from the samurai period.

Iwakuni-jō Castle 岩国城

The original castle was built between 1603 and 1608 but stood for only seven years before the daimyō was forced to dismantle it and move down to the riverside. It was rebuilt in 1960 during Japan's great castle reconstruction movement; but modern Japanese castles were built for tourism, not warfare, so it now stands photogenically on the edge of the hillside, a short distance in front of its former hidden location. The well beside the path indicates where it was originally built.

You can get to the castle by cablecar or by the road (walking only) from beside the youth hostel. The cablecar costs ¥300 one way, or ¥520 return, but see the Kintai-kyō Bridge entry for the all-inclusive ticket.

Special Events

Traditional cormorant fishing (*ukai*) takes place at the Kintai-kyō Bridge every night from June to August except when rain makes the water muddy or on full-moon nights. For about ¥3500 you can catch your own dinner. Sightseeing boats operate on the Nishiki-gawa River during the fishing.

Places to Stay

Youth Hostels The *Iwakuni Youth Hostel* (☎ 0827-43-1092) is close to most of the attractions on the samurai side of the bridge. There are 106 beds and costs per night are ¥2580, or ¥4160 with two meals (nonmembers add ¥500).

Ryokan If you were to stay in Iwakuni, the only real incentive to do so would be to stay in one of the traditional ryokan near the Kintai-kyō Bridge. One of the cheaper of these is the *Hangetsu-an* (☎ 0827-41-0021), which has rates from ¥8500 per person with two meals. Costs at the nearby *Shiratame Ryokan* (☎ 0827-41-0074) are higher, with rooms at ¥15,000 per person with two meals.

Hotels The *Ogiya Station Hotel* at Shin-Iwakuni shinkansen station has rooms for ¥5000/10,000 but is a long way from anywhere. Around JR Iwakuni station, there's a choice of business hotels. The *Iwakuni Kinsui Hotel* (☎ 0827-22-2311) is right beside the station and has singles/twins for ¥7700/13,200. *City Hotel Andoh* (☎ 0827-22-0110) is only a couple of minutes walk from the station and has singles/doubles from ¥5500/9000. The *A-1 Hotel* (☎ 0827-21-2244) is not much further away and has clean, tidy, well-equipped rooms from ¥5830/12,460 for singles/doubles.

Places to Eat

There are several small restaurants and cafes around the bridge and a wide variety of restaurants, bars and fast-food outlets around the station area.

Getting There & Away

Iwakuni is only 44 km from Hiroshima, connected by shinkansen to the Shin-Iwakuni station (17 minutes, ¥1540), or regular JR San-yō line trains (44 minutes, ¥720) to the central JR Iwakuni station.

Getting Around

The Kintai-kyō Bridge is almost equidistant from the two main stations, about five km from either. Buses shuttle back and forth between JR Iwakuni station and the bridge (¥240) and Shin-Iwakuni station and the bridge (¥270).

YAMAGUCHI 山口

During the tumultuous Muromachi (Country at War) period from 1467 to 1573, Yamaguchi (population 129,000) prospered as an alternative capital to chaotic Kyoto. In 1550, the Jesuit missionary Francis Xavier paused for two months in Yamaguchi on his way to

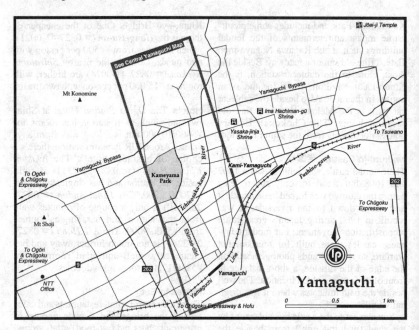

the imperial capital but quickly returned to the safety of this provincial centre when he was unable even to find the emperor in Kyoto! In the following centuries, Yamaguchi took turns with Hagi as the provincial capital and, like Hagi, Yamaguchi played an important part in the Meiji Restoration. Today it's a pleasantly peaceful town with a number of interesting attractions.

Orientation & Information

Ekimae-dōri is the main shopping street, running straight up from the station and crossing the main shopping arcade before it reaches Route 9. There's an information counter (☎ 0839-33-0090, open 9 am to 5 pm) on the 2nd floor of the railway station with some useful English brochures.

Xavier Memorial Chapel
ザビエル記念聖堂
The Xavier Memorial Chapel overlooks the town centre from a hilltop in Marugame

Park; this church was built in 1952 to commemorate the 400th anniversary of Francis Xavier's visit to the city. It recently burned down under mysterious circumstances, although it was slated to re-open in early 1998.

Art Gallery & Museums
At the foot of the hill stands the Yamaguchi Prefectural Art Museum (open from 9 am to 4.30 pm, closed Monday, entry ¥190), where frequent special exhibitions are held. Just north is the Yamaguchi Prefectural Museum, which has the same opening hours and costs ¥130. The Yamaguchi History Museum is just off Route 9; it's open from 9 am to 5 pm (closed on Monday) and costs ¥100.

Kōzan-kōen Park & Rurikō-ji Pagoda
香山公園・瑠璃光寺五重塔
Further north again from the town centre is Kōzan-kōen Park, where the Rurikō-ji five-storey pagoda, dating from 1404, is picturesquely sited beside a small lake. A small

museum has photos and details of all 40 Japanese five-storey pagodas, plus a map indicating where they're located. It's open daily from 9 am to 5 pm and entry is ¥200.

The Rurikō-ji Temple, with which the pagoda is associated, is also in the park and was moved here from a small village. The park's teahouse was also moved here – the Yamaguchi daimyō held secret talks in the house under the pretext of holding a tea ceremony. The park is also the site of Tōshun-ji Temple and the graves of the Mōri lords.

Jōei-ji Temple　常栄寺

The Jōei-ji Temple, three km north-east of the JR station, was originally built as a house and is notable for its beautiful Zen garden designed by the painter Sesshū. Visitors bring bentō (boxed lunches) and sit on the veranda to eat while admiring the garden. Entry to the garden is ¥300; it's open daily from 8 am to 5 pm.

Other Attractions

North of Route 9, the **Ichinosaka-kawa River** has a particularly pretty stretch, lined with cherry trees. Naturally they're at their best during the blossoming time in spring, but they're also lovely on summer evenings when large fireflies flit through the trees.

During the annual Gion Matsuri Festival in late July, the Sagi-mai Egret Dance is held in the **Yasaka-jinja Shrine**. The interesting **Ima Hachiman-gū Shrine** has a unique local architectural style that encompasses the gate, oratory and main hall under the same roof. The **Yamaguchi Dai-jingū Shrine** was a western branch of the great Ise-jingū Shrine in the Kansai District.

Places to Stay

Yamaguchi Youth Hostel (☎ 0839-28-0057) is about four km from Miyano station (two stops east of Yamaguchi), and has 30 beds at ¥2500 per night (nonmembers add ¥700). From Miyano station you can catch a bus (¥220) to Miyano Onsen and get off at the last stop; the hostel is a five minute walk to the north. A JR bus also stops at Okuyuda bus stop, which is a 15 minute walk to the hostel.

You can rent bicycles there and a bicycle tour map is available.

The *Fukuya Ryokan* (☎ 0839-22-0531), just up Ekimae-dōri from the station, is popular, conveniently central and reasonably priced at ¥6000 per person with two meals.

There's the usual assortment of modern business hotels around the station area including the *Sun Route Kokusai Hotel Yamaguchi* (☎ 0839-23-3610), which has rooms from ¥6200/12,500 for singles/doubles. A short distance from the station down Ekimae-dōri the *Yamaguchi Kankō Hotel* (☎ 0839-22-0356) and the *Taiyō-dō Ryokan* (☎ 0839-22-0897) both have rooms with two meals included from between ¥6000 and ¥7000.

Yuda Onsen, a 10 minute bus trip from the station, has a number of traditional ryokan including the expensive but historically interesting *Matsudaya Hotel* (☎ 0839-22-0125), which has rooms from ¥18,000 to ¥39,000 per person with meals.

Places to Eat

The arcade off Ekimae-dōri has lots of restaurants, coffee bars and fast-food places. Just a couple of doors down from the Fukuya Ryokan is *Yamabuki* (☎ 0839-22-1462), a pleasant old soba shop where you can eat well for ¥500.

There are a number of good places along Ekimae-dōri. *Shiva* has excellent Indian food and curries (lunch specials from ¥800, fully illustrated menu) and is open until 9 pm. Across the street is *Ikoi* with Japanese fare and plastic food to choose from, while further up is *Jardin*, a good little bakery/patisserie. At the top of the road, the *Green Park* restaurant is worth a try.

Getting There & Away

Yamaguchi is only 15 minutes by train (¥230) on the Yamaguchi line from the main shinkansen line station at Ogōri. JR buses run between Yamaguchi and Hagi, taking one hour 10 minutes and costing ¥1600.

Getting Around

Bicycles can be rented from the railway station and since the town's attractions are somewhat scattered (it's eight km just to the Jōei-ji Temple and back) and the traffic is not too chaotic, this is a good idea. The first two hours cost ¥310 or it's ¥820 for a day.

AROUND YAMAGUCHI

Ogōri 小郡

Ogōri, only 10 km south-west of Yamaguchi, is of no particular interest except as a place to change trains. It's at the junction of the San-yō Osaka-Hakata shinkansen line with the JR Yamaguchi line, which continues to Tsuwano and Masuda on the San-in coast.

Hōfu 防府

The **Hōfu Tenman-gū Shrine**, about a 10 minute walk north of Hōfu station, originally dates from 904 AD and is rated highly along with Dazaifu's (near Fukuoka on Kyūshū) Tenman-gū Shrine. It's open from 9 am to 4.30 pm daily and entry is ¥200. Close by is the **Suōkokubun-ji Temple**, a structure that is said to date back originally to 741.

Not far east of Hōfu Tenman-gū Shrine, the **Mōri Hontei Villa** dates from the Meiji era and has a famous Sesshū painting on display. The extensive villa gardens (3300 sq metres) are very picturesque. It's open from 9 am to 4 pm, closed on Sunday and charges an expensive ¥700 entry.

Three km north of the station is the **Tsuki-no-Katsura-no-tei Garden**, a beautiful if diminutive Zen rock garden. The scattered rocks include one in the shape of a crescent moon (the *tsuki* of the garden's name means 'moon' in Japanese). The garden is open daily from 9.30 am to 4.30 pm and entry is ¥300.

Hōfu is about 20 minutes from Ogōri on the San-yō line and tickets cost ¥310.

Chōmon-kyō Gorge 長門峡

The Chōmon-kyō Gorge is on the Abugawa River, and extends about 10 km north from Chōmon-kyō station, about 20 km north-east of Yamaguchi.

SHIMONOSEKI 下関

Shimonoseki (population 270,000) is a featureless, modern city, but for travellers it's also an important crossroads, a place through

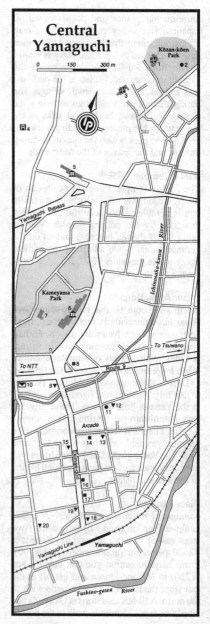

Central Yamaguchi

PLACES TO STAY
8   Sun Route Kokusai
     Hotel Yamaguchi
     サンルート国際
     ホテル山口
14   Fukuya Ryokan
     福屋旅館
16   Taiyō-dō Ryokan
     太陽堂旅館
17   Yamaguchi Kankō
     Hotel
     山口観光ホテル

PLACES TO EAT
9   Green Park
     Restaurant
12   Lotteria

13   Yamabuki Noodle
     Shop
     そば処やまぶき
15   Jardin Patisserie
     ジャルダン洋菓子店
18   Shiva
19   Ikoi
     いこい
20   Churamu

OTHER
1   Rurikō-ji Temple
     瑠璃光寺
2   Five Storeyed
     Pagoda
     五重塔
3   Tōshun-ji Temple
     洞春寺

4   Yamaguchi
     Dai-jingū Shrine
     山口大神宮
5   Yamaguchi History
     Museum
     山口市歴史民俗
     資料館
6   Yamaguchi
     Prefectural Art
     Museum
     山口県立美術館
7   Xavier Memorial
     Chapel
     ザビエル記念聖堂
10   Post Office
     郵便局
11   Japan Travel Bureau
     (JTB)

which many people pass and few pause. At the extreme western tip of Honshū only a narrow strait separates Shimonoseki from the island of Kyūshū. The expressway crosses the Kanmon Straits by the Kanmon Bridge, while another road, the shinkansen railway line and the JR railway line all tunnel underneath. The town is also an important connection to South Korea, with a daily ferry service to and from Pusan. Despite Shimonoseki's reputation as a place to pass through as rapidly as possible, there are a number of points of minor interest.

Information

There's a tourist information office in both the JR Shimonoseki station (☎ 0832-32-8383) and the shinkansen station. Beside the station is the large Sea Mall Shimonoseki shopping centre and just east is the new Kaikyō Yume Tower; here a ¥600 ticket gets you to the 30th floor observatory where you can take in an impressive 360° view of the surrounding scenery.

If you're arriving from Korea, note that the bank in the ferry terminal is only open from 9 to 9.30 am after the ferry arrival, but there are branches of the Tokyo-Mitsubishi and Yamaguchi banks near the station. Those arriving on a weekend should make sure they bring some Japanese yen with them. If you need a visa for Korea, the Korean consulate is about a km south of the station, beyond the ferry terminal.

Akama-jingū Shrine 赤間神宮

The bright red/orange Akama-jingū Shrine is dedicated to the child-emperor Antoku who died in 1185 in the naval battle of Dan-no-Ura. The battle took place in the Kanmon Straits which are overlooked by the shrine. In the Hōichi Hall stands a statue of 'Earless Hōichi', hero of a traditional ghost story retold by Lafcadio Hearn. The shrine is about three km east of the station, en route to Mt Hino-yama. Get off the bus at the Akamajingu-mae bus stop.

Mt Hino-yama 火の山

About five km north-east of JR Shimonoseki station there are superb views over the Kanmon Straits from the top of 268m Mt Hino-yama. The km-long Kanmon Bridge is right at your feet, ships shuttle back and forth

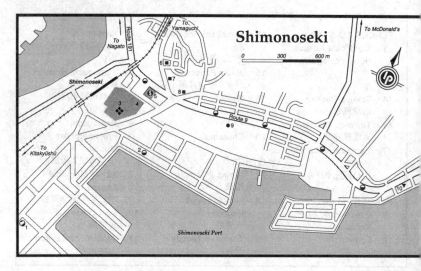

through this narrow but important waterway and at night, the views of the city are wonderful. You can walk, drive or travel by cablecar to the top. The cablecar costs ¥200 one way, ¥400 return. Take a Ropeway-mae bus to the Mimosurogawa bus stop near the cablecar station or a Kokuminshukusha-mae bus right to the top – these depart hourly from stand No 3 at the station.

Sumiyoshi-jinja Shrine　住吉神社
The Sumiyoshi-jinja Shrine, dating from 1370, is north of Mt Hino-yama, near the Shin-Shimonoseki station. It's open from 9 am to 4 pm daily but closed from 8 to 15 December.

Aquarium　下関水族館
Shimonoseki's aquarium is not a must-see, and unless you've got a lot of extra time you could give it a miss. There's a dolphin and sea-lion show as well as fish, penguins and other sea creatures (some crammed into tanks or enclosures far too small for them). An unfortunate giant leatherback turtle is squeezed into a small circular pool into which visitors toss coins; perhaps it can eventually buy its freedom.

On the hilltop overlooking the complex, a concrete 'whale' houses exhibitions showing all the reasons the Japanese give for slaughtering whales. The aquarium is south-east of the centre, just past the big Ferris wheel marking Marine Leisureland. In Japanese, aquarium is *suizokukan* and buses run from the station to the Suizokukan-mae bus stop. The aquarium is open from 9 am to 5 pm and entry is ¥500.

Chōfu　長府
If you have any time in Shimonoseki, a trip up to Chōfu to stroll around the streets would be the best way of utilising it. It is the old castle town area (jōka-machi) and, while little remains of the old coastal castle itself, there are old earth walls and samurai gates in Chōfu, along with a museum and some important temples and shrines. The **Kōzan-ji Temple** has a Zen-style hall dating from 1327 and the Chōfu Museum (9 am to 5 pm, closed Monday, ¥200) is also in the temple grounds. Other interesting temples and shrines include the Kakuon-ji Temple, the Iminomiya-jinja Shrine and the Nogi-jinja Shrine.

Buses run fairly frequently up Route 9 from Shimonoseki station to Chōfu (¥330).

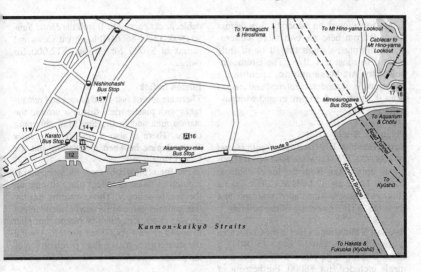

PLACES TO STAY

- **4** Shimonoseki
  Tōkyū Inn; Tokyo-
  Mitsubishi Bank
  下関東急イン／
  東京三菱銀行
- **6** Shimonoseki Station
  Hotel
  下関ステーション
  ホテル
- **7** Hotel Thirty Eight
  ホテル38下関
- **8** Shimonoseki Green
  Hotel
  下関グリーンホテル
- **12** Shimonoseki Grand
  Hotel
  下関グランドホテル

17 Hotel San-yō
  山陽ホテル
18 Hinoyama Youth
  Hostel
  下関火の山ユース
  ホテル

PLACES TO EAT

- **10** Sunday's Sun;
  Jolly Pasta
- **11** Kitagawa
  喜多川
- **14** Rosan-tei
  魯山亭
- **15** Nakao
  なかお

OTHER

- **1** Korean Consulate
  大韓民国領事館
- **2** Pusan Ferry
  Terminal
- **3** Sea Mall Shopping
  Centre
  シーモール下関
- **5** Yamaguchi Bank
  山口銀行
- **9** Kaikyō Yume Tower
  海峡ゆめタワー
- **13** Former British
  Consulate (Museum)
  旧英国領事館
- **16** Akama-jingū Shrine
  赤間神宮

WESTERN HONSHŪ

Two bus stops service the area: Matsubara to the south and Jōshita-machi to the north – the latter is the more convenient of the two. Check with the TIC at the JR station for maps of Chōfu.

Other Attractions

Across the road from the Grand Hotel in central Shimonoseki and by the Karato bus stop, is the Meiji-era former **British consulate building** of 1906. It's open from 9 am to

5 pm and closed on Monday. Just across Route 9 from here are two more western-style buildings, though they'll be of little interest to most travellers. The **Shimonoseki City Art Museumhino**, opposite the aquarium, is of moderate interest and is open from 9.30 am to 4.30 pm, closed Monday; entry is ¥200.

Places to Stay

Youth Hostels The *Hinoyama Youth Hostel* (☎ 0832-22-3753) is at the base of Mt Hino-yama, only 100m from the lower cablecar station. There are 52 beds at ¥2575. Take a Hino-yama bus from the station; you can't miss the huge 'YH' sign on top of the building.

Ryokan & Minshuku Over in the Chōfu area is the *Chōfu Ryokan* (☎ 0832-45-0404), a rustic-looking little place with rooms, two meals included, for ¥8000. Further out of town still, in the Hino-yama area are several kokuminshukusha (people's lodges) with costs of ¥6500 per person with two meals. They are clustered around the waterfront. Try the *Kaikan-sō* (☎ 0832-23-0108).

Hotels A number of business hotels can be found close to the station, including the *Hotel Thirty Eight* (☎ 0832-23-1138), only a couple of minutes walk away with singles from ¥4900 and twins from ¥8600. Close by is the pricier *Shimonoseki Station Hotel* (☎ 0832-32-3511) with singles/doubles from ¥5800/8300.

Cross the road from the station and turn right to reach the *Shimonoseki Green Hotel* (☎ 0832-31-1007) which has rooms at ¥5800/7200. Right next to the station is the *Shimonoseki Tōkyū Inn* (☎ 0832-23-0285) with singles from ¥6500, and twins from ¥11,500.

A couple of km from the JR station, the *Shimonoseki Grand Hotel* (☎ 0832-31-5000) has a wide variety of western and Japanese-style singles from ¥8000 and twins from ¥14,000. Reception is on the 8th floor and there are superb views over the strait from this 7th, 8th and 9th floor hotel. Even further from the station, just below the

cablecar car park, you'll find the *Hotel San-yō* (☎ 0832-32-8666). It has great views and rooms at ¥7000 for singles, ¥12,000 for twins.

Places to Eat

There are lots of fast-food places and restaurants with plastic meal displays around the station area and in the Sea Mall shopping centre. There is also a *Sunday's Sun/Jolly Pasta* duplex between the station and the Grand Hotel.

For fugu (blowfish) fans, Shimonoseki is reputed to be an excellent place to dine on the deadly delicacy. Those wanting to play this gourmet game of Russian roulette might try *Rosan-tei*, *Kitagawa* or *Nakao*, but plan to spend at least ¥6000 per person. Around the station giant plastic fugu perch on top of the phone boxes.

Getting There & Away

Train Shinkansen trains stop at the Shin-Shimonoseki station, two stops from the JR Shimonoseki station in the town centre. There are frequent trains and buses between the two stations. By shinkansen, it's half an hour to Hakata, 40 to 80 minutes to Hiroshima and three to four hours to Osaka. The easiest way to cross over to Kyūshū is to take a train from the Shin-Shimonoseki station to Moji-ko and Kitakyūshū.

Car From Shimonoseki, the bridge and tunnel connect roads in Honshū with Kyūshū. Eastbound travellers can take Route 191 along the northern San-in coast, Route 2 along the southern San-yō coast or the Chūgoku Expressway through Central Honshū.

Ferry within Japan Ferries run regularly from early morning to late at night from the Karato area of Shimonoseki to Moji-ko on Kyūshū. From Kokura in Kitakyūshū there are ferries to Kōbe, Osaka and Tokyo on Honshū and to Matsuyama on Shikoku.

Ferry to Korea The Kampu Ferry Service (☎ 0832-24-3000) operates the Shimonoseki-Pusan ferry service from the terminal a few minutes walk from the station. Head up to the 2nd floor of this enormous desolate building for bookings. The office closes between noon and 1 pm for lunch. There are daily departures of the *Kampu* or the *Pukwan* at 6 pm from Shimonoseki and Pusan, arriving at the other end at 8.30 am (the next morning). You can board from 3 pm. Arrive early to allow ample time to clear customs and immigration. One-way fares start from ¥6800 for students and continue up through ¥8500 for an open, tatami-mat area, ¥10,500 (six berth cabin), ¥12,000 (four berth cabin) and ¥14,000 (two berth cabin). There's a 10% discount on return fares.

This route is used by many long-term western visitors to Japan, particularly those involved in English teaching, and as such expect to have your passport rigorously inspected.

Hitching If you're hitching out of Shimonoseki, you'll need to get on the expressway. There's a complicated mass of junctions north of the youth hostel and Mt Hino-yama. Roads diverge in a variety of directions – to Kyūshū by the tunnel or bridge, to Hiroshima by the Chūgoku Expressway and to Yamaguchi by Routes 2 and 9.

SHIMONOSEKI TO HAGI

There's some good coastal scenery, small fishing villages and interesting countryside along the coast road between Shimonoseki and Hagi, which is at the western extremity of Honshū.

Ōmi-shima Island, with its scenic, rocky coast, is immediately north of **Nagato** (population 28,000) and connected to the mainland by a bridge. The island is part of the Kita Nagato Coastal Park which extends eastwards beyond Hagi.

AKIYOSHI-DAI 秋芳洞

The rolling Akiyoshi-dai Tablelands are about halfway between Yamaguchi on the southern San-yō coast and Hagi on the northern San-in coast. The green fields are dotted with curious rock spires and beneath this picturesque plateau are hundreds of limestone caverns, the largest of which, Akiyoshi-dō Cave, is open to the public.

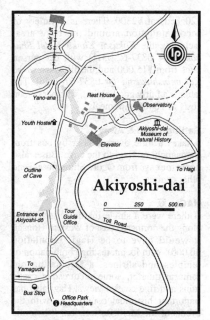

The Akiyoshi-dō Cave is of interest principally for its size; the stalagmites and stalactites are not particularly noteworthy. In all, the cave extends about 10 km, a river flows through it and a pathway runs through for about a km. At the mid-point of the cave walk you can take an elevator up to the surface where there is a lookout over the surrounding country. There are entrances to the cave at both ends of the pathway as well as at the elevator, and buses run between the two ends if you do not want to retrace your steps. The cave is open from 8.30 am to 4.30 pm daily; entry is ¥1240.

The **Akiyoshi-dai Museum of Natural History** has exhibits concerning the cave and the surrounding area.

Places to Stay

The *Akiyoshi-dai Youth Hostel* (☎ 0837-62-0341) is close to the cave entrance and has

WESTERN HONSHŪ

120 beds at ¥2300. There is a variety of accommodation around the cave area, including the *Kokusai Kankō Hotel Shuhokan* (☎ 0837-62-0311) with per person rates from ¥15,000 and the *Wakatakesanso Kokuminshukusha* (☎ 0837-62-0126). The latter is a fairly good option, with per person costs of ¥6400 with meals.

Getting There & Away

It takes a little over an hour by bus from Yamaguchi or Hagi to the cave. Buses also run to the cave from Ogōri, Shimonoseki and other centres.

HAGI 萩

If there were a single reason for travelling along the northern coast of Western Honshū it would have to be Hagi (population 50,000), with its interesting combination of temples and shrines, a fascinating old samurai quarter, some picturesque castle ruins and fine coastal views. Hagi also has important historical connections with the events of the Meiji Restoration. It is ironic that the town's claim to fame is its role in propelling Japan directly from the feudal to the modern era while its attractions are principally its feudal past. Hagi is also noted for its fine pottery.

History

Hagi in Honshū and Kagoshima in Kyūshū were the two centres of unrest which played the major part in the events leading up to the Meiji Restoration. Japan's long period of isolation from the outside world under Tokugawan rule had, by about the mid-19th century, created tensions approaching breaking point. The rigid stratification of society had resulted in an oppressed peasantry, while the progressive elements of the nobility realised Japan had slipped far behind the rapidly industrialising European nations and the USA. The arrival of Commodore Perry brought matters to a humiliating head as the 'barbarians' simply dictated their terms to the helpless Japanese.

Japan could not stand up against the west if it did not adopt western technology, and this essential modernisation could not take place under the feudal shogunate. Restoring the emperor to power, even if only as a figurehead, was the route the progressive samurai chose and Shōin Yoshida of Hagi was one of the leaders in this movement. On the surface, he was also a complete failure. In 1854, in order to study the ways of the west first hand, he attempted to leave Japan on Perry's ship, only to be handed over to the authorities and imprisoned in Edo (Tokyo).

When he returned to Hagi he hatched a plot to kill a shogunate official, but talked about it so much that word leaked out to his enemies. He was arrested again and in 1859, at the age of 29, he was executed. Fortunately, while Shōin was a failure when it came to action he was a complete success when it came to inspiration and in 1865 his followers led a militia of peasants and samurai which overturned the Chōshū Government of Hagi. The western powers supported the new blood in Hagi and Kagoshima and when the shogunate army moved against the new government in Hagi, it was defeated. That the downfall of the shogunate had come at the hands of an army, not just of samurai but of peasants as well, was further proof of the changes taking place.

In late 1867, the forces of Kagoshima and Hagi routed the shogunate, the emperor was restored to nominal power and in early 1868, the capital was shifted from Kyoto to Tokyo, as Edo soon became known. To this day, Hagi remains an important site for visitors interested in the history of modern Japan and Shōin Yoshida 'lives on' at the Shōin-jinja Shrine.

Orientation & Information

Hagi consists of three parts. Western and central Hagi are effectively an island created by the Hashimoto-gawa and Matsumoto-gawa rivers, while eastern Hagi (with the major JR station, Higashi-Hagi) lies on the eastern bank of the Matsumoto-gawa River.

The main road through central Hagi starts from JR Hagi station and runs north, past the bus station in the centre of town. There's a wide variety of shops along Tamachi arcade,

CHARLOTTE HINDLE

ALEX THOMPSON

A: Wall-to-wall restaurants, Dōtomburi area, Osaka
B: Falls at Akame, Mie

TONY WHEELER

MASON FLORENCE

RICHARD I'ANSON

ALAN HOLTZMAN

TONY WHEELER

CHARLOTTE HINDLE

<table>
<tr><td>A</td><td>B</td></tr>
<tr><td>C</td><td>D</td></tr>
<tr><td>E</td><td>F</td></tr>
</table>

A: Drying octopus
B: Autumn colours, Kitayama, Kyoto
C: Sumiyoshi-jinja Shrine, Osaka
D: Prayer rope
E: Nishi Hongan-ji Temple, Kyoto
F: Bullet train

close to the bus station. West of this central area is the old samurai quarter of Jokamachi, with its picturesque streets and interesting old buildings. More interesting old buildings can be found in Horiuchi to the north-west and Teremachi to the north-east of Jokamachi.

Hagi's tourist information office (☎ 0835-25-1750) is open daily from 9 am to 5 pm and has good English literature, but it's a little difficult to find. On the main road through town, just south of the bus station, is Nagasaki Chanmen, an outlet of the Japanese fast-noodle chain which looks a bit like a New England church building. Across the road from it is a bank-type building and the tourist office is in the back of that building. There's also an information counter beside Higashi-Hagi station.

Hagi Pottery & Kilns 萩焼窯

Connoisseurs of Japanese pottery rank Hagi-yaki, the pottery of Hagi, second only to Kyoto's raku-yaki. As in other pottery centres in Japan, the craft came from Korea when Korean potters were brought back after Hideyoshi's unsuccessful invasion in the late 1500s. There are a number of shops and kilns where you can see the pottery being made and browse through the finished products. Hagi-yaki is noted for its fine glazes and delicate pastel colours. The small notch in the base of each piece is also a reminder of the pottery's long history. In the feudal era only samurai were permitted to use the pottery, but by cutting a tiny notch in some pieces, the potters 'spoilt' their work and this pottery could then be used by the common folk.

The Shizuki Kiln in Horiuchi has particularly fine pieces. The western end of Hagi has several interesting pottery kilns near Shizuki-kōen Park. Hagi-yaki pottery can also be inspected in the Hagi-yaki Togei Kaikan Museum near the park; there's a big souvenir area downstairs.

Castle Ruins & Shizuki-kōen Park 萩城址・指月公園

There's not much of the old Hagi-jō Castle to see, apart from the typically imposing outer walls and its surrounding moat. The castle was built in 1604 but dismantled in 1874 during the Meiji Restoration; since Hagi played a leading part in the end of the feudal era and the downfall of the shogunate, it was appropriate that the town also led the way in the removal of feudal symbols.

Now the grounds are a pleasant park with the Shizukiyama-jinja Shrine, Hananoe Teahouse and other buildings. From the castle ruins you can climb the hillside to the 143m peak of Mt Shizuki-yama. The castle is open daily from 8 am to 4.30 pm and entry is ¥200; the entry ticket also covers the Mōri House. Also in the park is the small Hagi Shiryōkan Museum, open daily from 9 am to 4.30 pm with an entry fee of ¥350.

Sekichō-kōen Park 石彫公園

About five minutes walk to the west of Shizuki-kōen is this new park with its collection of sculptural works from around the world (the park's name means 'sculpture park'). It's open daily and entry is free at the moment.

Mōri House 毛利家

South of the park is Mōri House, a row (terrace) house where samurai soldiers were once barracked. It's open daily and the same ticket covers entry to the castle ruins. There's an interesting Christian cemetery to the south of the samurai house.

Jokamachi, Horiuchi & Teremachi 春若町・堀内・寺町

Between the modern town centre and the moat that separates western Hagi from central Hagi is the old samurai residential area with many streets lined by whitewashed walls. This area is fascinating to wander around and there are a number of interesting houses and temples, particularly in the area known as Jokamachi. Teremachi is noted particularly for its many fine old temples.

Kikuya House The Kikuya family were merchants rather than samurai but their wealth and special connections allowed

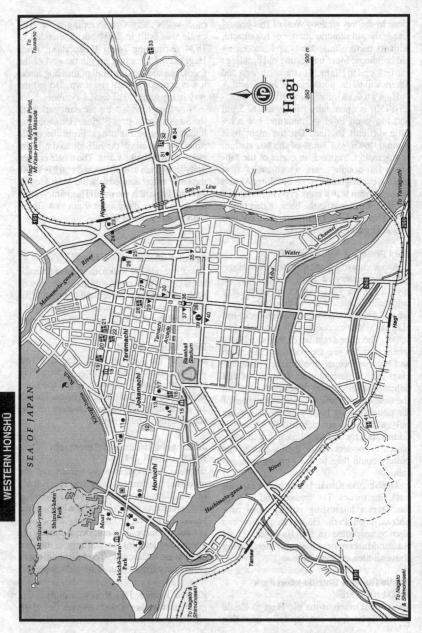

WESTERN HONSHŪ

SEA OF JAPAN

Hagi

500 m

0   250

To Tsuwano

To Hagi Pension, Myōjin-ike Pond,
Mt Kasa-yama & Masuda

To Yamaguchi

Matsumoto-gawa River

Higashi-Hagi

San-in Line

Channel

Water

Aiba

Hagi

Kikugahama Road

Teramachi

Jōkamachi

Tamachi Arcade

Baseball
Stadium

Horiuchi

River

San-in Line

Mt Shizuki-yama

Shizuki-kōen Park

Moat

Sekichō-kōen Park

Hashimoto-gawa

Tamae

To Nagato &
Shimonoseki

To Nagato
& Shimonoseki

them to build a house well above their station. The house dates from 1604 and has a fine gate, attractive gardens and there are numerous examples of construction details and materials which would normally have been forbidden to the merchant class. Entry to the house is ¥500 and it is open daily from 9 am to 5 pm. Tea-bowl enthusiasts may also find the **Ishii Chawan Museum** interesting. The museum is open from 9 am to 5 pm, closed on Tuesday; entry is ¥500.

Other Houses Nearby is Kido Takayoshi House (open from 9 am to 5 pm) and Takasugi Shinsaku House, which is still a private residence. Takasugi was a student of Shōin Yoshida and played a key role in the events leading up to the Meiji Restoration. Interesting houses in the Horiuchi area include the Masuda and Sufu houses.

Kumaya Art Museum The art museum in Jokamachi has a small collection including tea bowls, screens and other items in a series of small warehouses dating from 1768. The Kumaya family handled the trading and commercial operations of Hagi's ruling Mori family. Opening hours are from 9 am to 5 pm. Entry is ¥500.

Other Buildings The Horiuchi and Teremachi areas are dotted with temples and shrines and if you simply wander around the area you will pass by many of them. The **Fukuhara Gate** is one of the finest of the samurai gates in Horiuchi. Nearby is the **Tomb of Tenjuin**, dedicated to Terumoto Mori, the founder of the Mori dynasty. There are numerous old temples in the Teremachi area including the two-storey Kaicho-ji Temple, the Hōfuku-ji with its Jizō statues (the Buddha for travellers and the souls of departed children), the Jonen-ji Temple with its gate carvings and the Baizo-in Temple with its Buddha statues. The large Kyotoku-ji Temple has a fine garden.

Tōkō-ji Temple 東光寺

East of the river stands this pretty temple with the tombs of five Mori lords. The odd-numbered lords (apart from number one) were buried here; the even-numbered ones at the Daishō-in Temple. The stone walkways on the hillside behind the temple are flanked by almost 500 stone lanterns erected by the lord's servants. It's open daily from 8.30 am to 5 pm and entry is ¥200.

Shōin-jinja Shrine 松陰神社

West of the Tōkō-ji Temple is this Meiji-era shrine to Shōin Yoshida, an important force in the Meiji Restoration. Events from his life are illustrated in the nearby **Shōin Yoshida Rekishikan** (Shōin Yoshida History Hall) which is open from 9 am to 5 pm daily, ¥650. Just south of the shrine is the **Itō Hirobumi House**, the early home of the four-term prime minister who was a follower of Shōin Yoshida and later drafted the Meiji Constitution. There are a number of other places connected with Shōin Yoshida in the vicinity including his tomb near the Toko-ji Temple and his school (the Shōkasonjuku) in the shrine grounds.

Daishō-in Temple 大照院

South of the centre, near the JR Hagi station, this funerary temple was the resting place for the first two Mori generations and after that, all even-numbered generations of the Mori lords. Like the better known and more visited Tōkō-ji Temple, it has pathways lined by stone lanterns erected by the Mori lord's faithful retainers. The original Mori lord's grave is accompanied by the graves of seven of his principal retainers, all of whom committed *seppuku* (ritual suicide) after their lord died. An eighth grave is that of a retainer to one of the retainers who also joined in the festivities. The shogunate quickly banned similar excessive displays of samurai loyalty. The temple is open daily from 8 am to 5 pm and entry is ¥200.

Myōjin-ike Pond & Mt Kasa-yama 明神池・笠山

A couple of km east of the town, the Myōjin-ike Pond is actually connected to the sea and shelters a variety of saltwater fish. The road beside this small lagoon continues to the top of Mt Kasa-yama, a small extinct volcano cone from where there are fine views along the coast. Buses running from Hagi to Mt Kasa-yama take around 15 minutes and cost ¥240.

Other Attractions

At the south-eastern end of the Hagi 'island', carp can be seen swimming in the roadside **Aiba water channel**. East of the town and close to the main road to Masuda, is the **Hagi Hansharo**, an old reverberating furnace dating from 1858 which was used to make gun and ship parts.

Places to Stay

Hagi Youth Hostel (☎ 0838-22-0733) is south of the castle at the western end of the town, has 120 beds at ¥2600 per night (nonmembers add ¥300) and has rental bicycles. The hostel is closed from mid-January to mid-February. Tamae is the nearest JR station.

There are ryokan and minshuku in town with affordable prices. Close to the park again is *Kokuminshukusha Jō-en* (☎ 0838-22-3939) with rooms from ¥8000 including two meals. Over the river from Higashi-Hagi station is the *Nakamura Ryokan* (☎ 0838-22-0303), with per person costs from ¥8000 to ¥15,000 with two meals.

Pension Hagi (☎ 0838-28-0071) is a pleasant, modern pension 10 km east of town in the fishing port of Nagato-Ohi (pronounced *oy*). The pension is just back from the main road and costs ¥6300 per person including breakfast. JR Nagato-Ohi station is two stops from Higashi-Hagi and the pension's owner, Eukio Yamazaki, who learnt his excellent English in Papua New Guinea, will meet you at the station.

The *Hagi Royal Hotel* (☎ 0838-25-9595) is right by the Higashi-Hagi station and has rooms from ¥8000 (add ¥1000 for breakfast and ¥4000 for dinner). Cheaper hotels in the same area include the *Riverside Hotel* (☎ 0838-22-1195), with good rooms from ¥5000/15,000, and the *Hagi Travel Inn* (☎ 0838-25-2640), just across the river from the Higashi-Hagi station, with rooms for ¥5000/10,000. Just across the road from the Travel Inn is the *Hotel Orange* (☎ 0838-25-5880) with singles/twins from ¥4500/8000.

Places to Eat

There are many restaurants in the central area around the bus station, including a couple of nice cake and pastry places – *Kobeya* and *Gateaux Koube*. Just south-west of the station is *Hagi-ko*, which has lots of plastic meals to help you make your selection – spaghetti, noodles and other dishes cost ¥400 to ¥800.

A couple of places worth looking out for, both in the east of town, are *Restaurant & Tea Room Shizuki* and *Restaurant & Tea Room Kōdai*. The former, in a Tudor fronted building, has French cuisine and although a lot of it is pretty expensive, there are some good set lunches and dinners. The latter is well known for its Hagi cuisine and has a pricey (¥2000) but excellent special lunch.

Akashi is east of the centre, on the main through route, and has good teishoku meals. There are some fast-food specialists, including one of the *Nagasaki Chanmen* noodle restaurants across from the building with the tourist office.

Getting There & Away

The JR San-in line runs along the north coast through Tottori, Matsue, Masuda and Hagi to Shimonoseki. The faster expresses take four hours to or from Matsue.

JR buses to Hagi take 1½ hours from Ogōri, south of Hagi on the Tokyo-Osaka-Hakata shinkansen line. The buses go via Akiyoshi-dai, take one hour 10 minutes and cost ¥1900; there are also buses from Yamaguchi. Buses also operate between Tsuwano and Hagi, taking a little under two hours.

Getting Around

Hagi is a good place to explore on a bicycle and there are plenty of bicycle rental places, including one at the youth hostel and several around the castle and JR Higashi-Hagi station.

Shimane-ken　島根県

Along the northern San-in coastline of the Sea of Japan, Shimane Prefecture has several important places worth getting to, as well as a slew of less travelled areas including the spectacular Oki Islands. Tsuwano, one of Japan's many 'little Kyotos'; Matsue, where writer Lafcadio Hearn lived and produced some of his best known works; and the great shrine at Izumo should not be missed by those in this part of the country.

TSUWANO　津和野

In the far western reaches of Shimane Prefecture, about 40 km east of Hagi, is Tsuwano, a pleasant and relaxing mountain town with some fine castle ruins, interesting old buildings and a wonderful collection of carp swimming in the roadside water channels (the some 65,000 of these colourful fish outnumber the local population by tenfold!). The town is noted as a place to get to by the superb old steam-train service from Ogōri and as a place to explore by bicycle, of which there are quite a phenomenal number for rent.

Orientation & Information

Tsuwano is a long, narrow town wedged into a deep north-south valley. The Tsuwano-kawa River, JR Yamaguchi line and main road all run down the middle of the valley. The staff at the tourist information office (☎ 08567-2-1144) by the railway station are very helpful and have excellent English information on hand. The number of souvenir shops (and bicycles) around town are a clear indicator of just how popular Tsuwano is as a tourist destination.

Tsuwano-jō Castle   津和野城

The ruins of Tsuwano-jō Castle seem to brood over the valley, the broken stone walls draping along the ridge. The castle was originally constructed in 1325 and remained in use until the Meiji Restoration. A short chair lift takes you up the hillside for ¥450 (return trip), from where there's a further 15 minute walk to the castle ruins. At the top there is a splendid view over the town and surrounding mountains. If you've got the energy and time, it is possible to follow a trail on foot all the way up from the Taikodani-Inari-jinja Shrine.

Taikodani-Inari-jinja Shrine
太鼓谷稲荷神社

Just below the castle chair-lift station, this brightly painted shrine is one of the largest Inari shrines in Japan. You can walk up to it from the main road through a 'tunnel' created by over 1100 red torii gates. Festivals are held here on 15 May and 15 November each year. The annual Sagi Mai Festival (Heron Dance Festival) is performed on 20 and 27 July at the Yasaka-jinja Shrine, near the start of the torii tunnel.

Tonomachi District
殿町・養老館・郷土館

Only the walls and some fine old gates remain from the former samurai quarter of Tonomachi. 'Ditches' (the word used in the local tourist brochure) is too plain a word to apply to the water channels that run alongside this picturesque road: the crystal-clear water in the channels is home to tens of

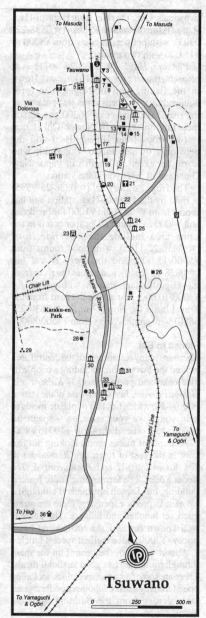

Tsuwano

PLACES TO STAY

1 Hotel Sun Route
ホテルサンルート

8 Hoshi Ryokan
星旅館

12 Hiroshimaya
Minshuku
広島屋

14 Meigetsu Ryokan
明月

16 Tsuwano Grand Hotel
津和野グランド
ホテル

19 Tsuwano Kankō Hotel
津和野観光ホテル
新宿

26 Kokuminshukusha
Aonesansō
国民宿舎青根山荘

27 Wakasagi-no-Yado
Minshuku
民宿わかさぎの宿

36 Tsuwano Youth
Hostel
津和野ユース
ホステル

PLACES TO EAT

3 Hinokuma
ひのくま

7 Shō-kyoto
小京都

10 Furusato
ふるさと

13 Sekishin-tei
石心亭

17 Waraji-ya
わらじ屋

OTHER

2 TIC
観光案内所

4 Chapel of St Mary
マリア聖堂

5 Komyō-ji Temple
光明寺

6 Tsuwano Industry
Museum
産業資料館

9 Post Office
郵便局

11 Katsushika Hokusai
Museum
葛飾北斎美術館

15 Hashimoto Sake
Brewery
橋本酒店

18 Yōmei-ji Zen Temple
永明寺

20 Bus Station
バスターミナル

21 Catholic Church
津和野カトリック
教会

22 Yōrōkan Museum
養老館

23 Taikodani-Inari
Yōrō-kan-jinja Shrine
太鼓谷稲成神社

24 Kyōdo-kan Museum
津和野町立郷土館

25 Musée de Morijuku
杜塾美術館

28 Dento Kōgeisha
Paper Making Centre
津和野伝統工芸舎

29 Tsuwano-jō Castle
Ruins
津和野城跡

30 Jingasa Museum
津和野陣笠民芸館

31 Itahashi Antique Doll
Museum
板橋アンティック
ドール美術館

32 Sekishukan Museum
和紙会館

33 Mori Ōgai House
森鴎外旧宅

34 Mori Ōgai Memorial
Museum
森鴎外記念館

35 Nishi Amane House
西周旧宅

thousands of large and healthy carp. It's said that these goldfish were bred to provide a potential source of food should the town ever be besieged. The feared attack never came and the fish have thrived.

At the northern end of the street is the **Catholic church**, a reminder that Nagasaki Christians were once exiled here. At the other end of Tonomachi, just north of the river, is the **Yōrō-kan**. This was a school for young samurai in the late Edo period, a relatively innovative idea at that time. The

building now houses the **Minzoku Shiryō-kan**, an interesting little folk art museum with all sorts of farming and cooking equipment. It's open from 8.30 am to 5 pm daily and entry is ¥200.

Across the river is the **Kyōdo-kan**, a small local history museum with some displays concerning the Christian exiles. Hours are from 8.30 am to 5 pm and entry is ¥350, but it's not of great interest. Down near the post office, is the **Katsushika Hokusai Museum** (open 9.30 am to 5 pm daily, ¥450) featuring a collection by the master Edo-period painter Hokusai and his disciples.

Chapel of St Mary マリア聖堂
The tiny Maria-Seido Chapel dates from 1948 when a German priest built it as a memorial to the exiled Catholics who died in the final period of Christian persecution before the anti-Christian laws were repealed in 1872. Tsuwano's own **Via Dolorosa** leads along the side of the valley from the chapel with markers for the stations of the cross. At the end of this winding pathway through the forest, a road leads down by the **Yōmei-ji Zen Temple** which dates from 1420. It is open from 8.30 am to 5 pm, entry is ¥300. The tomb of Mori Ōgai (see Other Attractions section) is at the temple.

Other Attractions
The beautiful former residences of Nishi Amane, who played an important part in the Meiji Restoration Government, and Mori Ōgai, a highly regarded novelist, are in the south of the town and definitely worth checking out. In back of the latter is the **Mori Ōgai Memorial Museum** (open 9 am to 4.45 pm, closed Monday, ¥500), a striking modern building which houses many of the writer's personal effects. Entry to the grounds of his residence only (which is far more interesting than the museum) is ¥100. Nearby is the **Sekishukan**, also known as the Washi Kaikan, a museum relating to washi (handmade paper) where you can watch the process of paper making and pick up some fine souvenirs. Entry is free.

The **Itahashi Antique Doll Museum** houses an astounding collection of fine European antique dolls, though the ¥800 entry fee keeps most without a penchant for such away. Perhaps more interesting (and still with a bit of European flavour) is the **Musée de Morijuku** (open daily from 9 am to 5 pm – foreigners pay a discounted ¥300 entry fee). Housed in an old farmhouse, there is a room of Goya etchings and paintings by local artists. Make sure to see the pinhole camera feature on the 2nd floor (the proprietor will gladly show you).

The **Dento Kogeisha** centre also has paper-making displays. Across the road from it is **Jingasa** with a museum of old items and costumes used in the annual Heron Dance Festival. The **Tsuwano Industry Museum** is right by the station and displays local crafts including paper making and sake brewing. It's open daily. There are a number of sake breweries in town, some of which you can stop in for tastings. Try **Hashimoto**, midway between the Catholic church and Katsushika Hokusai Museum. Here Mr Toba, one of the resident staff, can answer your questions in English while you sample the local brew.

South of the town is the **Washibara Hachiman-gū Shrine**, about four km from the station. Archery contests on horseback are held here on 2 April.

Special Events
The Sagi Mai (Heron Dance) Festival is a major annual festival held in July. Lighted lanterns are floated down the river in August.

Places to Stay
The information counter outside the railway station will help with bookings for the town's many minshuku and ryokan.

Youth Hostels The *Tsuwano Youth Hostel* (☎ 08567-2-0373) has 28 beds at ¥2800 (nonmembers add ¥1000), and breakfast is available for ¥600. The hostel is a couple of km south of the station, beside a small temple.

Minshuku & Ryokan The *Wakasagi-no-Yado Minshuku* (☎ 08567-2-1146) is not in the town centre but it's a pleasant, friendly and frequently recommended place at ¥6600 per person with two meals. They'll even pick you up at the station. Other similarly priced minshuku and ryokan include the *Hoshi Ryokan* (☎ 08567-2-0136) with costs of ¥6000, and *Hiroshimaya Minshuku* (☎ 08567-2-0204), at ¥5500. Both are centrally located and also include two meals. The *Meigetsu Ryokan* (☎ 08567-2-0685) is a traditional and more expensive ryokan with costs from ¥10,000 to ¥20,000. This is a place where by request you may get to try Tsuwano's famine food – carp!

Across the river and away from the centre is the government-run *Kokuminshukusha Aonesansō* (☎ 08567-2-0436), which costs ¥6600 including two meals.

Hotels Hotels in town include the *Sun Route* (☎ 08567-2-3232), a bland modern hotel overlooking the town from the eastern slope of the valley, with singles from ¥6800 to ¥9800 and twins from ¥10,600 to ¥24,600. *Tsuwano Kankō Hotel* is right in the centre of town while the *Tsuwano Grand Hotel* (☎ 08567-2-0888) is on the eastern valley side by Route 9; rates here are expensive at around ¥12,000 per person with two meals.

Places to Eat

If you're not eating at a minshuku or ryokan there are several restaurants and cafes around town, some of which serve the local speciality, uzume-meishi, a tasty rice-based stew with local sansai (mountain vegetables), tofu, carrots and nori (seaweed). A couple of places to sample the dish are *Sekishin-tei* near the Meigetsu Ryokan and *Furusato* across from the post office.

For a simple lunch-time meal there are a good number of places not far from the station. *Shō-kyoto* has curries, katsudon and coffee. *Hinokuma* has simple Japanese cooking, and the rustic *Waraji-ya* serves noodles and such in a traditional shop with an irori (open fireplace).

There are also a number of good noodle shops with plastic food displays around the small shrine by the bridge in the centre of town.

Getting There & Away

The JR Yamaguchi line runs from Ogōri on the south coast through Yamaguchi to Tsuwano and on to Masuda on the north coast. It takes about one hour 15 minutes by limited express from Ogōri to Tsuwano and about 30 minutes from Masuda to Tsuwano. A bus to Tsuwano from Hagi takes nearly two hours and an overnight bus from Osaka takes about eight hours.

During the late April to early May Golden Week holiday, from 20 July to 31 August and on certain other Sundays and national holidays, a popular steam locomotive service operates between Ogōri and Tsuwano. It takes two hours each way and you should book well ahead.

Getting Around

Tsuwano is packed with bicycle rental places and rates start from ¥400 for two hours, with a maximum of ¥800 for a day.

MASUDA 益田

Masuda is a modern industrial town with two temples, the Mampuku-ji and the Iko-ji. Both have notable gardens said to have been designed by the famed painter Sesshū, whose tomb is also in the vicinity. The temples are about 10 minutes by bus from the JR station.

Masuda is the junction for the JR Yamaguchi line, which runs between Ogōri, Yamaguchi, Tsuwano and Masuda, and the JR San-in line, which runs from Shimonoseki, through Hagi and Masuda before continuing along the coast. Masuda is about 30 minutes from Tsuwano, one hour from Higashi-Hagi and two hours and 10 minutes from Izumo.

IZUMO 出雲

Only 33 km west of Matsue and just north of Izumo itself, the small town of Izumo Taisha has one major attraction – the great Izumo Taisha Shrine.

Orientation & Information

The Izumo Taisha Shrine is actually several km north-west of the central area of Izumo. There's no real reason to visit central Izumo, since the shrine area, more or less one main street running straight up to the shrine, has two railway stations and a range of (generally expensive) accommodation and restaurants. There's a tourist information office (☎ 0853-53-2298) on the main street near the shrine entrance.

Izumo Taisha Shrine 出雲大社

Although this is the oldest Shinto shrine in Japan and is second in importance only to the shrines of Ise, the actual buildings are not that old. The main shrine dates from 1744, the other important buildings only from 1874. Nevertheless, the wooded grounds are pleasant to wander through and the shrine itself enjoys the 'borrowed scenery' of the Yakumo Hill as a backdrop. Okuninushi, to whom the shrine is dedicated, is *kami* (spirit god) of, among other things, marriage. So visitors to the shrine summon the deity by clapping four times rather than the normal two – twice for themselves and twice for their partner or partners to be.

The Haiden (Hall of Worship) is the first building inside the entrance torii and huge *shimenawa* (twisted straw ropes) hang over the entry. The main building is the largest shrine in Japan but the Honden (Main Hall) cannot be entered. The shrine compound is flanked by *jūku-sha*, long shelters where Japan's eight million kami (Shinto spirit gods) stay when they make their annual visit to Izumo.

On the south-eastern side of the compound is the Shinko-den (Treasure House) (open from 8 am to 4.30 pm, ¥150) which has a collection of shrine paraphernalia. Behind the main shrine building in the north-western corner is the former Shōkokan (Treasure Hall) with a large collection of images of Okuninushi in the form of Daikoku, a cheerful chubby character standing on two or three rice bales with a sack over his shoulder and a mallet in his hand. Usually his equally happy son Ebisu stands beside him with a fish tucked under his arm.

Cape Hino-misaki　日御埼

It's less than 10 km from the Izumo Taisha Shrine to Cape Hino-misaki where you'll find a picturesque lighthouse, some fine views and an ancient shrine. On the way, you pass the pleasant **Inasano-hama Beach**, a good swimming beach just two km from Izumo Taisha station on the private Ichihata line. Buses run regularly from the station out to the cape, via the beach, in just over half an hour.

The **Hinomisaki-jinja Shrine** is near the cape bus terminus. From the cablecar park, coastal paths lead north and south offering

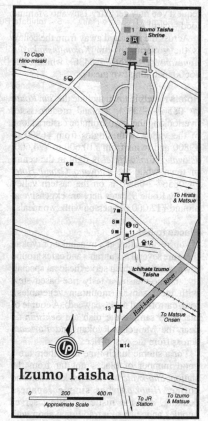

Izumo Taisha

fine views, particularly from the top of the lighthouse (open from 9 am to 4 pm, entry ¥150). Beyond the cape is **Owashihama** and then **Uryū**, two picturesque little fishing villages where you can stay in minshuku.

Special Events

The lunar calendar month corresponding to October is known throughout Japan as Kannazuki (Month without Gods). In Izumo, however, it is known as Kan-arizuki (Month with Gods) for this is the month when all the Shinto gods congregate for an annual get-together at the Izumo Taishi Shrine. In

1	Former Treasure Hall 彰古館	5	Ichibata Bus Terminal 一畑バス停	10	Information Centre 観光案内所
2	Izumo Taisha Shrine Main Hall (Honden) 本殿	6	Inabaya Ryokan いなばや旅館	11	Katō Ryokan 加藤旅館
3	Haiden (Hall of Worship) 拝殿	7	Takenoya Ryokan 竹野屋旅館	12	Ebisuya Youth Hostel えびすやユース ホステル
4	Treasure House 宝物殿	8	Satobara Ryokan 藤原旅館	13	Otorii Gate 大鳥居
		9	Hotel Matsuya ホテル松屋	14	Izumo Ryokan 出雲旅館

accordance with the ancient calendar, an important festival takes place here from 11 to 17 October. The month of October is also a popular time for weddings at the shrine.

Places to Stay & Eat

There's no imperative reason to stay overnight in Izumo Taisha since it's easy to day-trip there from Matsue or simply pause there while travelling along the coast. If you do want to stop, there are a host of places along the main street of Izumo Taisha, which runs down from the shrine to the two railway stations.

The *Ebisuya Youth Hostel* (☎ 0853-53-2157) is just off the main street and costs ¥2800 (nonmembers add ¥1000). Breakfast and dinner cost ¥600 and ¥1000 respectively. On the street nearby is the *Katō Ryokan* (☎ 0853-53-2214) with Japanese-style rooms from ¥10,000 per person including excellent meals. Other places along the main street include the *Hotel Matsuya* at ¥6200, the *Inabaya Ryokan* (☎ 0853-53-3180) with rooms including two meals from ¥10,000 to ¥28,000, the classy *Takenoya Ryokan* (☎ 0853-53-3131) at ¥12,000 to ¥35,000 and the *Satobara Ryokan* (☎ 0853-53-2009) at ¥12,000.

Izumo's soba gets high praise, particularly in the dish known as warigo, buckwheat noodles over which you pour a broth. There are a number of noodle shops along the main street.

Getting There & Away

Izumo Taisha has two railway stations, the JR one at the end of the street leading down from the shrine and the private Ichihata line station about halfway up the street. The Ichihata line starts from Matsue-onsen station in Matsue and runs on the northern side of Lake Shinji-ko to Izumo Taisha station. The JR line runs from JR Matsue station to JR Izumo station, where you transfer to an Izumo Taisha train. The private-line service also requires a change of train, at Kawato, but is more frequent (more than 20 services a day) and also takes you closer to the shrine. The private-line trip takes less than an hour and passes by rows of trees grown as windbreaks.

Izumo has an airport with JAS flights to and from Tokyo.

MATSUE 松江

Matsue (population 143,000) straddles the Ōhashi-gawa River, which connects Lake Shinji-ko to Lake Nakanoumi-ko and then the sea. A compact area in the north of the town includes almost all of Matsue's important sites: an original castle, a fine example of a samurai residence, the former home of writer Lafcadio Hearn and a delightful teahouse and garden.

Information

The tourist information office (☎ 0852-21-4034) at the JR station (on the left as you leave the station, just past Mr Donut) has a surprising amount of information in English and the staff are helpful. It's open daily from 9.30 am to 6 pm.

WESTERN HONSHŪ

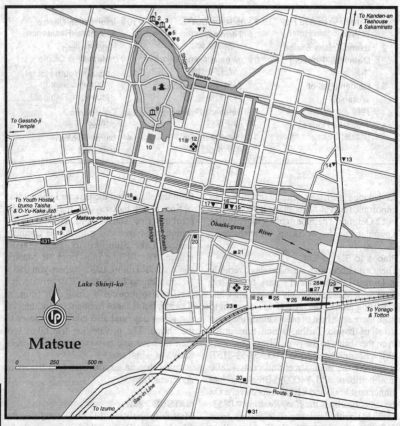

To Kanden-an
Teahouse
& Sakaminato

Shiomi

Nawate

To Gesshō-ji
Temple

To Youth Hostel,
Izumo Taisha
& O-Yu-Kake Jizo

Matsue-onsen

431

Lake Shinji-ko

Matsue

0   250   500 m

To Izumo

Sen-in Line

Ōhashi-gawa   River

Matsue-ōhashi
Bridge

To Yonago
& Totton

Route 9

Matsue

Matsue-jō Castle 松江城

Matsue's castle is not huge or imposing but it is original, dating from 1611. Modern Japan has so many rebuilt castles, externally authentic-looking but internally totally modern, that it can almost be a shock to step inside one where the construction is real wood, not modern concrete. It's open from 8.30 am to 5 pm and entry is ¥500, though with a 'universal pass' combined ticket to the castle, Buke Yashiki Samurai Residence and Lafcadio Hearn Memorial Museum (¥800), you can save ¥200.

The regional museum (Matsue Kyodo-kan) is within the castle precinct and is open from 8.30 am to 4.30 pm; entry is free. The road alongside the moat on the north-eastern side of the castle is known as the Shiomi Nawate, at one time a narrow lane through the old samurai quarter. The high tile-topped walls still remain from that era and there are a number of places of interest. A No 1 or 2 bus from outside the JR station will get you to the castle.

Lafcadio Hearn Residence 小泉八雲旧宅

At the northern end of the Shiomi Nawate is the Lafcadio Hearn Memorial Museum and

PLACES TO STAY		PLACES TO EAT		5	Buke Yashiki
16	Washington Hotel ワシントンホテル	4	Yakumo-an 八雲庵		Samurai Residence 武家屋敷
18	Suimei-sō Hotel 水明荘	6	Yakumo-an Bekkan 八雲庵別館	8	Matsue-jō Castle 松江城
19	Ichihata Hotel ホテル一畑	7	Meimei-an 明々庵	9	Matsue Cultural Museum; Regional
20	Young Inn Matsue ヤングイン松江	13	McDonald's		Museum 松江郷土館
21	Daiei Business Hotel ダイエービジネス ホテル	14	KFC	10	Prefecture Hall 県庁
		15	Benkei Robatayaki 弁慶	11	Matsue Prefectural Product & Craft
23	Business Ishida Hotel ビジネス石田ホテル	17	Kawa-kyo かわきょう		Centre 物産観光館
25	Green Hotel Matsue グリーンホテル松江	26	Mr Donut	12	Ichihata Department Store
27	Matsue Tōkyū Inn 松江東急イン	**OTHER**			一畑デパート
28	Matsue Urban Hotel 松江アーバンホテル	1	Lafcadio Hearn Memorial Museum 小泉八雲記念館	22	Yayoi Department Store やよいデパート
30	Business Hotel Lake Inn ホテルレークイン	2	Lafcadio Hearn Residence 小泉八雲旧宅	24	Japan Travel Bureau (JTB)
		3	Tanabe Art Museum 田部美術館	29	Post Office 松江中央郵便局
				31	Laundrette コインランドリー

next to it is his former home. Hearn was a British writer (although he was born in Greece in 1850, educated in France and the UK and lived in the USA from 1869) who came to Japan in 1890 and was to remain there for the rest of his life. His first book on Japan, *Glimpses of Unfamiliar Japan*, is a classic, providing an insight into the country at that time. The Japanese have a great interest in the outsider's view of their country so Hearn's pretty little house is an important attraction, despite the fact that he only lived in Matsue for just over a year. Hearn's adopted Japanese name is Koizumi Yakumo. While you're admiring the garden you can read his essay *In a Japanese Garden*, describing how it looked a century ago. Entry to the house is ¥200 and it's open daily from 9 am to 4.30 pm.

Lafcadio Hearn Memorial Museum 小泉八雲記念館

Next to the writer's home is his museum (the Koizumi Yakumo Memorial Museum) with displays about his life, his writing and his residence in Matsue. Of the many interesting Hearn possessions on display behind glass, there are a stack of Japanese newspapers on which Hearn had written simple words and phrases to teach his son English. Entry is ¥250 and the museum is open from 8.30 am to 4.30 pm. The museum has an English brochure and map showing various points of interest around the town mentioned in his writings.

Tanabe Art Museum 田部美術館

This museum principally displays family items from the many generations of the region's Tanabe clan, particularly tea bowls and other tea ceremony paraphernalia. Opening hours are 9 am to 4.30 pm, closed Monday. Entry is ¥500.

Buke Yashiki Samurai Residence
武家屋敷

The Buke Yashiki is a well-preserved middle Edo-period samurai residence built in 1730. There's a good English description leaflet of the various rooms and their uses in this large but somewhat spartan residence. This was not the home of a wealthy samurai. Entry is ¥250 and opening hours are from 8.30 am to 5 pm.

Meimei-an Teahouse 明々庵

A little further south is the turn-off to the delightful Meimei-an Teahouse with its well-kept gardens and fine views to Matsue-jō Castle. The teahouse was built in 1779 and was moved to its present site in 1966. Look for the steep steps up from the road to the thatched-roof building. Entry is ¥200 and it's open from 9 am to 5 pm. Here you can sample some tea with sweets for ¥350.

Other Attractions

The **Kanden-an Teahouse** is about a 20 minute drive north-east of the centre. It dates from 1792 and is one of the finest teahouses in Japan. It's open from 9.30 am to 4 pm, closed Thursday.

About a km west of the castle is the **Gesshō-ji Temple**, which was converted from an ordinary temple to a family temple for Matsue's Matsudaira clan in 1664 but dismantled during the Meiji Restoration. The graves of nine generations of the clan remain and family effects are displayed in the treasure house.

Matsue has its own onsen (hot spring) area, just north of the lake near Matsue-onsen station on the Ichihata-Dentetsu line. There are a number of hotels and ryokan in the area and a popular 'hell', a very hot spring known as the **O-Yu-Kake Jizō**. The sunset views over **Lake Shinji-ko** are fine and best appreciated from the Matsue-ōhashi Bridge. The **Matsue Folk Art Center**, across

from the Ichihata Hotel in the onsen area by the lake, displays regional crafts. The **Matsue Prefectural Product & Craft Center** is another regional craft centre, just south of the castle in the town centre.

Places to Stay

Youth Hostels *Matsue Youth Hostel* (☎ 0852-36-8620) is about five km from the centre of town in Kososhimachi, on the northern side of the lake at the first station you come to along the Ichihata line from Matsue-onsen station. There are 50 beds at ¥2800 a night (nonmembers add ¥500).

Budget Accommodation The *Pension Tobita* (☎ 0852-36-6933) in Hamasadamachi is in the same direction as the youth hostel and has Japanese and western-style rooms at ¥6000 per person with breakfast only, ¥7000 with two meals.

As usual, there are a lot of business hotels around the station including the unbusiness-like *Business Ishida* (no English sign; ☎ 0852-21-5931) in Teramachi, a simple Japanese-style hotel with tatami-mat rooms and shared bathrooms at ¥3800 per person. It's good value and conveniently close to the station: just continue walking past the tourist information office through the bicycle and car parks and it's right beside the elevated railway lines, just past the first road you cross.

Other possibilities, all with shared bathrooms, include the *Daiei Business Hotel* (☎ 0852-24-1515) down by the river with rooms from ¥3800 and the *Business Hotel Lake Inn* (☎ 0852-21-2424), behind the station on the corner of Route 9, with singles/twins at ¥4500/8000. Not far from the Daiei Business Hotel is the *Young Inn Matsue* (☎ 0852-22-2000). It's a small place with an English sign and a limited number of twins at ¥3090.

Hotels More expensive hotels include the *Matsue Tōkyū Inn* (☎ 0852-27-0109) just across the road from the station. This popular chain hotel has singles from ¥7600, doubles and twins from ¥14,600. Also in front of the station, the *Green Hotel Matsue* (☎ 0852-27-

3000) has singles from ¥5700 and twins from ¥9600 to ¥10,400. The *Matsue Urban Hotel* is a cheaper place behind the Tōkyū Inn with singles/twins from ¥5000/9000.

The *Matsue Washington Hotel* (☎ 0852-22-4111) is across the river from the JR station but still convenient to the town centre. Singles start at ¥7000, twins ¥14,400.

Places to Eat

If you're wandering the Shiomi Nawate, the old samurai street in the shadow of the castle, pause for lunch at the *Yakumo-an Restaurant*, next to the samurai house. It's a delightfully genteel noodle house with a pond full of very healthy-looking carp. Noodle dishes range from ¥500 to ¥750 for Niku udon or Niku soba. Warigo-style noodles cost ¥600; they're a local speciality. There is also a pleasant tea house annex by the same name just on the other side of the samurai house with a tea and sweets set for ¥550.

Matsue's kyodo ryōri, or regional cuisine, includes 'seven exotic dishes from Lake Shinji'. They are:

Suzuki or *hosho yaki* – steam baked paper-wrapped bass
Shirauo – whitebait tempura or sashimi
Amasagi – sweet tempura or teriyaki
Shijimi – tiny shellfish in miso soup
Moroge ebi – steamed shrimp
Koi – baked carp
Unagi – broiled freshwater eel

Kawa-kyo, near the Washington Hotel north of the river, offers these seven local specialities on an English menu with prices from ¥250 (shijimi) to ¥1500 (hosho yaki).

There are a number of *Benkei* yakitori (grilled-food restaurants) around town: there's a particularly good one with an illustrated menu near the Washington Hotel in Higashihonmachi. The tourist office at the station can give you a list of good local restaurants including numerous Izumo soba specialists.

Restaurants with plastic meal replicas and the usual fast-food places can be found in the station area. There's a *Mr Donut* in the station

and a *Dom Dom* burger place in the nearby Yayoi department store, where there's also an excellent basement supermarket.

Getting There & Away

Matsue is on the JR San-in line which runs along the north coast. It takes a little over 2½ hours to travel via Yonago to Kurashiki on the south coast. See the previous Izumo section for information on the two railway lines running west from Matsue. Matsue is also a jumping-off point for the Oki Islands (see the Oki Islands section later for details).

Yonago is the airport for Matsue. There are ANA flights to Tokyo and JAS flights to the Oki Islands.

Getting Around

Airport buses run between Matsue-onsen station and the airport, taking about 40 minutes. Tour buses leave from stand No 8 in front of JR Matsue station. Other bus routes include Matsue-onsen (No 1), Kaga (No 4), Izumo (No 6) and Yonago (No 7). You pick up a ticket on entering the bus and the relevant fare for your starting point is displayed as you leave.

Matsue is a good place to explore by bicycle: these can be hired at the Matsue and Matsue-onsen stations for ¥600 for two hours, ¥100 per additional hour or ¥1000 per day.

AROUND MATSUE & IZUMO

There are a number of places of interest in the vicinity of Matsue and neighbouring Izumo.

Lake Shinji-ko　宍道湖

Sunset over the Yomega-shima islet in Lake Shinji-ko is a photographer's favourite and the lake also provides the region's seven favourite local delicacies (see Matsue's Places to Eat section). At the western end of the lake, the garden in the Gakuen-ji Temple in Hirata is noted for its autumn colours.

At the south-western corner of the lake, the town of Shinji has the *Yakumo Honjin* (☎ 0852-66-0136), one of the finest ryokan in Japan. Parts of the inn are 250 years old but if you stay here (from ¥15,000 per night) ask for the old wing or you'll end up in the modern air-conditioned one. Casual visitors can have a look around for ¥300.

Shimane-hantō Peninsula 島根半島

North of Matsue, the coastline of the Shimane-hantō Peninsula has some spectacular scenery, particularly around Kaga, where Kaga-no-Kukedo is a cave you can enter by boat.

Fudoki-no-Oka & Shrines 風土記の丘

Five km south of Matsue, around the village of Yakumo-mura, there are interesting shrines and important archaeological finds. Fudoki Hill is a 1st century AD archaeological site with finds displayed in the Fudoki-no-Oka Shiryōkan (Archaeological Museum), which is open from 9 am to 5 pm, closed Monday. Nearby is the **Okadayama Tumuli**, an ancient burial mound. Haniwa pottery

figures were found here, similar to those of Miyazaki on Kyūshū.

West of Fudoki-no-Oka is the ancient **Kamosu-jinja Shrine**, dedicated to Izanami, the mother of the Japanese archipelago. The shrine's Honden (Main Hall) dates from 1346. A little further west is the **Yaegaki-jinja Shrine** which is dedicated to the gods of marriage and commemorates a princess's rescue from an eight-headed serpent. The events are illustrated in fine 12th century wall paintings and the shrine sells erotic amulets to ensure fruitful marriages! There's a pretty little wood with shrines and ponds close by.

Fudoki-no-Oka is best visited on the way back from Bessho if you're going there. Get off at the Fudoki-no-Oka Iriguchi bus stop, walk to the archaeological centre and on to the two shrines, then take another bus to Matsue from the Yaegaki-danchi Iriguchi bus stop, north of the Yaegaki-jinja Shrine.

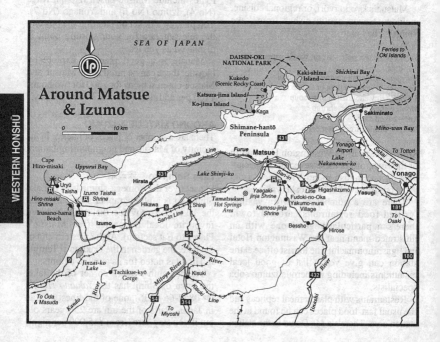

Bessho 別所

About 15 minutes south of Fudoki-no-Oka is Bessho, which features the **Abe Eishiro Museum**, dedicated to the craftsman credited with revitalising the making of paper by hand. The museum is open from 9 am to 4.30 pm and you can also visit paper-making workshops in the village. A bus from stand No 3 at the JR Matsue station will get you to Bessho; it stops at Fudoki-no-Oka on the way back.

Yasugi 安来

East of Matsue on Lake Nakanoumi-ko is Yasugi. The **Kiyomizu Temple** has a beautiful three-storey pagoda and an important 11-faced statue of Kannon, the goddess of mercy. The **Adachi Art Museum** in Yasugi has a magnificent, photogenic garden and a beautifully illustrated English pamphlet (it's the least you would expect for the exorbitant entry fee of ¥2300 – foreigners, however, are entitled to a half price ticket, but you'll need to show your passport).

Tachikue-kyō Gorge 立久恵峡

Immediately south of Izumo is this km-long, steep-sided gorge. It takes 30 minutes by bus to the gorge station from Izumo.

Mt Sanbe-san 三瓶山

Mt Sanbe is inland from Ōda and reaches 1126m; its four separate peaks are known as the Father, the Mother, the Child and the Grandchild. It's part of the Daisen-Oki National Park and a popular skiing centre during the winter. Buses leave for Ōda from Izumo.

It takes about an hour to climb Mt Sanbe from Sanbe Onsen. Buses regularly make the 20 km run from Ōda to Sanbe Onsen. Lake Ukinunonoike is near the hot springs.

If you follow the Go-gawa River southwest from Mt Sanbe, the Dangyo-kei Gorge is six km south of Inbara and there's a four km walking track along the ravine.

OKI ISLANDS 隠岐諸島

Directly north of Matsue, the Oki Islands, with their spectacular scenery and steep cliffs, are strictly for those who want to get away from it all. At one time, they were used to exile political prisoners and daimyō (on one occasion the emperor himself) who came out on the losing side of political squabbles. The islands consist of the larger Dōgo Island and the three smaller Dōzen Islands plus associated smaller islands. The seven-km-long cliffs of the Oki Kuniga coast of Nishino-shima Island, at times falling 250m sheer into the sea, are particularly noteworthy. The Kokobun-ji Temple on Dōgo Island dates from the 8th century. Bullfights are an attraction during the summer months on Dōgo Island.

Places to Stay

The islands have numerous minshuku and other accommodation.

On Dōgo Island the *Okino-shima Youth Hostel* (☎ 08512-7-4321) costs ¥2260 or ¥3840 with two meals (nonmembers add ¥700). The *Oki Plaza Hotel* (☎ 08512-2-0111) has twins at ¥8000.

On Chiburi-jima Island the minshuku *Kanishima* (☎ 08514-8-2355) costs ¥7000 including two meals and the *Hashine Ryokan* (☎ 08514-8-2351) has per person rates from ¥7000 with two meals.

On Nishino-shima Island there is the *Seaside Hotel Tsurumaru* (☎ 08514-6-1111) which has Japanese-style rooms with two meals at ¥12,000 per person.

On Nakano-shima Island the *Marine Port Hotel* (☎ 08514-2-0033) has per person rates with two meals of ¥9000.

Getting There & Away

There are ferry services to the Oki Islands from Shichirui or Sakaiminato. From Matsue, it's an hour by bus to Shichirui then 2½ hours by ferry. JAS flights operate to the islands from Yonago, Izumo and Osaka.

YONAGO 米子

Yonago is an important railway junction connecting the north and south coasts and, as such, is a place to pass through rather than

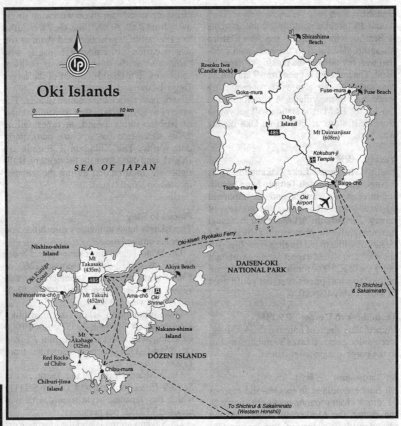

Oki Islands

0   5   10 km

SEA OF JAPAN

Shirashima Beach

Rosoku Iwa (Candle Rock)

Goka-mura

Fuse-mura Fuse Beach

Dōgo Island

485

Mt Daimanjisar (608m)

Kokubun-ji Temple

Tsuma-mura

Saigo-chō

Oki Airport

Oki-kisen Ryokaku Ferry

DAISEN-OKI NATIONAL PARK

To Shichirui & Sakaiminato

Nishino-shima Island

Mt Takasaki (435m)

Akiya Beach

485

Oki Kuniga Coast

Nishinoshima-chō

Mt Takuhi (452m)

Ama-chō Oki Shrine

Nakano-shima Island

Mt Akahage (325m)

DŌZEN ISLANDS

Red Rocks of Chibu

Chibu-mura

Chiburi-jima Island

To Shichirui & Sakaiminato (Western Honshū)

visit. From Yonago airport, there are flights to and from Osaka and Tokyo and on to the Oki Islands.

Tottori-ken 鳥取県

Though perhaps the least enticing prefecture in western Japan, Tottori has a couple of attractions worth checking out if you are travelling the San-in coast of the Sea of Japan. The Tottori sand dunes are the most commonly associated landmark in the region

and the steep slopes of beautiful Mt Daisen are popular with hikers.

TOTTORI 鳥取

Tottori (population 142,000) is a large, busy town some distance back from the coast. The main coast road passes through Tottori's northern fringe in a blizzard of car dealers, pachinko parlours and fast-food outlets. The town's main attraction is its famous sand dunes. There's a helpful tourist information booth inside the station (☎ 0857-22-8111) with English pamphlets and maps.

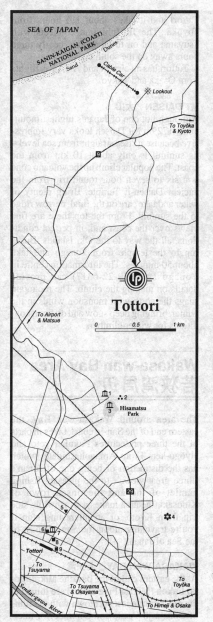

1　Prefectural Museum
　　県立博物館

2　Tottori-jō Castle Ruins
　　鳥取城跡

3　Jinpū-kaku Villa & Museum
　　仁風閣

4　Kannon-in Garden
　　観音院

5　Flags Restaurant/Café
　　フラッグス

6　Tottori Green Hotel Morris
　　鳥取ホテルグリーンモリス

7　Folkcraft Museum
　　民芸美術館

8　Hotel Taihei
　　ホテル太平

9　Washington Hotel
　　ワシントンホテル

WESTERN HONSHŪ

The Dunes　砂丘

Used as the film location for Teshigahara Hiroshi's classic 1964 movie *Woman in the Dunes*, the Tottori sand dunes are on the coast a couple of km from the city. There's a viewing point on a hillside overlooking the dunes, along with a huge car park and the usual assortment of tourist amenities. The dunes stretch for over 10 km along the coast and, at some points, can be a couple of km wide. The section where the dunes are highest is popular with parachutists who stand at the edge, fill their chutes with the incoming sea breezes and leap off the dune top to sail down towards the sea.

From Tottori station, take a bus for the 20 minute ride (¥270) out to Tottori-sakyū, as the dunes are known in Japanese. The bus stop for the dunes is *sakyū-sentā* ('Dunes Center').

About a km south-west of the lookout it is possible to rent good bicycles at the Tottori Cycling Terminal *(saikinguru tāminaru)* for ¥300 for four hours. Buses on their way to the dunes stop at the terminal – ask for *kodomo-no-kuni iriguchi* ('Children's World entrance').

Other Attractions

Tottori's other attractions are mainly concentrated in a compact little group about 1.5 km north-east of the station. Only the foundations remain of **Tottori-jō Castle**, which overlooked the town from the hillside. Below the castle walls is the European-style **Jinpū-kaku Villa**, dating from 1906-07. The villa is now used as a museum; entry is ¥150 and it's open from 9 am to 5 pm, closed on Monday. Across from this building is the modern **Tottori Prefectural Museum** (entry ¥180). Tottori also has an interesting little **Folkcraft Museum** near the JR station, with folkcraft items from Japan, Korea, China and even Europe. It's open from 10 am to 5 pm (closed on Wednesday) and entry is ¥500. East of the station is the 17th century **Kannon-in Garden**, open daily from 9 am to 5 pm. Entry is ¥600.

Dune-parachuting is not the only seaside sporting activity around Tottori. A few km west of the town there's a popular surfing break, packed with Japanese surfies on weekends. There are other breaks along this coast.

Places to Stay & Eat

One of the cheaper places around is the *Tottori Green Hotel Morris* (☎ 0857-22-2331; the English sign outside simply says Hotel Morris), which has rooms from ¥5000 to ¥13,100. The *Hotel Taihei* (☎ 0857-29-1111) has singles from ¥5300 and twins at ¥9500. The *Tottori Washington Hotel* (☎ 0857-27-8111), next to the railway station, has singles from ¥6700 to ¥7200 and doubles or twins for ¥13,500.

There are plenty of restaurants (with the usual plastic food displays) around the station including a *Mr Donut*. A few streets north from the station on the left is *Flags*, a good little pizzeria open from 11 am to 10 pm daily. There is also a coffee shop next door run under the same name, open 7.30 am to 10 pm. A wide selection of fast-food joints also operate along Route 9, the main road through town.

Getting There & Away

The coastal JR San-in line runs through Tottori and it takes about 1½ hours from Toyōka. The JR Inbi line connects with Tsuyama and on to Okayama, nearly three hours away on the south coast.

Tottori has an airport and ANA has flights from Osaka and Tokyo.

MT DAISEN 大山

Although not one of Japan's highest mountains, 1729m Mt Daisen looks very impressive because it rises straight from sea level – its summit is only about 10 km from the coast. The popular climb up the volcano cone is a six to seven hour round trip from the ancient Daisen-ji Temple. Bring plenty of water and take care on the final, narrow ridge to the summit. From the top there are fine views over the coast and, in perfect conditions, all the way to the Oki Islands. Buses run to the temple from Yonago and take about 50 minutes. The information centre in Yonago (☎ 0859-22-6317) can provide details on making the climb. The mountain snags the north-west monsoon winds in the winter, bringing deep snow and difficult conditions for winter climbers.

Wakasa-wan Bay Area 若狭湾周辺

The area around Wakasa-wan Bay, the eastern end of the San-in coast, takes in parts of the three prefectures Fukui, Kyoto and Hyōgo-ken. From Amanohashidate, which has the distinction of being one of Japan's 'three great views', to the pleasant fishing hamlet of Ine and the onsen town of Kinosaki, the area makes a worthwhile side trip from Kyoto, or an interesting stop if you're travelling along the San-in coast of the Sea of Japan.

WAKASA-WAN BAY 若狭湾

At the eastern end of the bay, the **Mikatago-ko Lakes** (Mikata Five Lakes) are joined to the sea. **Obama** is a port town with the ruins of Obama-jō Castle and a number of interesting old temples including the Myōtsū-ji, the Mantoku-ji and the Jingū-ji. Tour buses operate from the JR Obama station and there are also boat trips around the picturesque Sotomo coastline with its inlets, arches and caves, just north of Obama. Continuing around the bay, more interesting coastal scenery can be reached by boat trips from Wakasa-Takahama. From Maizuru there are regular ferry services to Otaru in Hokkaidō. Ferries also run to Otaru from Tsuruga, at the other end of Wakasa-wan Bay (see the Fukui-ken section of the Central Honshū chapter).

AMANOHASHIDATE　天橋立

Amanohashidate (Bridge to Heaven) is rated as one of Japan's 'three great views', along with Miya-jima Island (near Hiroshima) and the islands of Matsushima-wan Bay (near Sendai). The 'bridge' is really a 'pier', a tree-covered sandspit 3.5 km long with just a couple of narrow channels preventing it from cutting off the top of Miyazu-wan Bay as a separate lake.

The town of Amanohashidate consists of two separate parts, one at each end of the spit. At the southern end there are a number of hotels, ryokan, restaurants, a popular temple and the JR Amanohashidate station. At the other end, a funicular railway (¥260 one way) and a chair lift run up the hillside to the Kasamutsu-kōen Park vantage point from where the view is reputed to be most pleasing. From here, incidentally, you're supposed to view the sandspit by turning your back to it, bending over and observing it framed between your legs! There's another hilltop viewpoint at the southern end of the spit.

A bridge and swing bridge cross the two channels at the southern end of the spit and cycling along the spit is a popular activity.

Places to Stay

There's an information counter at the railway station. The *Amanohashidate Youth Hostel* (☎ 07722-7-0121) is at Ichinomiya, close to the funicular to the lookout point. To get there take a Tankai bus from the JR Amano-hashidate station and get off at the Jinja-mae bus stop, from where it's a 10 minute walk.

The nightly cost is ¥2700 or ¥4000 with two meals. The *Amanohashidate Kankōkaikan Youth Hostel* (☎ 07722-7-0046) is also near the park and has similar rates to the Amanohashidate Youth Hostel.

There are a number of ryokan and hotels, generally fairly expensive, near the station at the other end of the 'bridge'. The *Toriko Ryokan* (☎ 07722-2-0010) costs from ¥6500 or ¥12,000 per person including two meals. The *Shoehino Ryokan* is similarly priced. Other places include the *Hotel Taikyo* and the *Hotel Monju-sō*.

Getting There & Away

The coastal JR Miyazu line connects Obama with Amanohashidate and on to Toyōka where you change to the JR San-in line for Tottori. It takes about three hours by limited express from Kyoto, half an hour longer by tour bus.

Getting Around

You can cross the 'bridge to heaven' on foot, bicycle or on a motorcycle of less than 125cc capacity. Bicycles can be hired at a number of places for ¥400 for two hours or ¥1600 a day. Tour boats also operate across Miyazu-wan Bay.

TANGO-HANTŌ PENINSULA　丹後半島

Travelling westward, Amanohashidate marks the start of the Tango-hantō Peninsula, jutting north into the Sea of Japan. A coast road runs around the peninsula, passing a number of small scenic fishing ports. The village of **Ine**, on a perfect little bay, is particularly interesting, with (funaya) houses built right out over the water and boats drawn in under them as if in a carport.

From the hilltop Funaya-no-Sato Park, where there is a tourist information office (☎ 0772-32-0277) with Japanese maps and brochures, there's a fine view over the harbour. Below the park Ine-wan Meguri frequent tour boats putter around the bay (30 minute rides cost ¥650; there are no services in January and February). There are several fine minshuku in the town including *Yoza-sō* (☎ 0772-32-0278). Per person rates here start at ¥8000 with two meals. Buses reach Ine in about an hour from Amanohashidate (¥1100).

At the end of the peninsula, a large car park and restaurant mark the start of the one hour round-trip walk to the **Cape Kyōgasaki Lighthouse**. There are some pleasant coastal views though the lighthouse is nothing special.

KINOSAKI 城崎

In the north part of Hyōgo Prefecture, the little onsen town of Kinosaki makes a pleasant overnight excursion. The road around the Tango-hantō Peninsula rejoins the main coast before the city of Toyōka, which is linked to Kyoto by the JR San-in line. Toyōka itself is not worth more than a quick look from the train window, but Kinosaki, two stops on, is a laid-back place to roam around and soak in hot springs. The **Gokuraku-ji Temple** has a good miniature rock landscape garden, and the **Gembu-dō Caves** are one stop south on the San-in line. Take a stroll north from the station until you hit the stream that runs through the town. If you follow this for a couple of hundred metres away from the Maruyama River, you should be able to find Gokuraku-ji Temple on the left, around 100m south of the stream.

The Gembu-dō Caves are not a major event, but they might make a pleasant excursion. From the east exit of Gembudō station, it's necessary to take a five minute ride (¥190) across the Maruyama River to Gembudō-kōen Park. The caves are a couple of hundred metres south of the ferry drop-off point.

Kinosaki's biggest attraction is its hot-spring bathhouses, of which there are six

open to the public (¥300 each). Guests staying in town stroll the canal from bath to bath donning *yukata* (summer kimono) and *geta* (wooden sandals). Most of the ryokan and hotels in town also have their own private baths *(uchi-yu)*, but also provide their guests with free tickets to the ones outside *(soto-yu)*. In addition to the allure of the baths here, savoury crab from the Sea of Japan is a speciality in Kinosaki during the winter months.

Places to Stay There is a slew of mostly expensive accommodation in town, though if you don't mind paying a bit of money, Kinosaki is a great place to experience a night in a traditional Japanese inn. The ultimate of inns here is the classic *Nishimura Honkan Ryokan* (☎ 0796-32-2211), but expect to shell out in excess of ¥28,000! Other more affordable options where some English is spoken are *Tsutaya* (☎ 0796-32-2511) along the canal, as well as *Mikuniya* (☎ 0796-32-2414), in front of the JR Kinosaki station. Both have per person rates with two meals from ¥15,000. *Yutōya* (☎ 0796-32-2121) costs from ¥16,000.

There is a tourist information centre (☎ 0796-32-3663) in the JR Kinosaki station, and also a ryokan reservation centre (☎ 0796-32-4141) which can provide more choices and make bookings (Japanese only).

Getting There & Away Trains run to Kinosaki from Kyoto in around two hours 40 minutes. From Amanohashidate, change trains at Toyōka (about 1½ hours on the JR Miyazu line) to the San-in line to go to Kinosaki or the Gembu-dō Caves.

Northern Honshū (Tōhoku) 本州の北部

The northern part of Honshū, known in Japanese as Tōhoku, comprises Fukushima, Miyagi, Iwate, Aomori, Akita and Yamagata prefectures. This chapter begins with Fukushima, then moves north along the east side of Tōhoku, continues round the northern tip, and descends the west side to include Niigata-ken and Sado-ga-shima Island.

For those who want to see traditional rural life and enjoy vast areas of unspoilt natural scenery, the relative 'backwardness' of this mostly mountainous region provides a strong incentive to visit.

The major cities, few in number, generally merit no more than a cursory stop before heading off into the back country, which offers hikes in volcanic and mountainous regions or along spectacular rocky coastlines. Tōhoku has scores of hot springs tucked away in the mountains and there are also cultural sights such as temples, festivals and folkcrafts. Several excellent ski resorts benefit from the long and severe winters with their accompanying heavy snowfalls.

The region was originally inhabited by a people known in previous centuries as the Ezo. The Ezo are believed to have been related to the Ainu, who now only remain on Hokkaidō. Although the Ezo were conquered and pushed back during the Kamakura period, it wasn't until the 17th century that the area came under complete government control.

During the Meiji era, the region suffered from years of neglect. This trend was only reversed after WWII, with a drive for development based heavily on industrial growth. Despite this, the region retains a strong reliance on agriculture and many Japanese still consider it as a place in the back of beyond – an economic laggard compared to the rest of Japan.

INFORMATION

Since Tōhoku is less travelled by foreigners and sources of information are less common

HIGHLIGHTS

- ◆ Explore the hiking trails and gorgeous lake scenery around Mt Bandai-san
- ◆ Experience the peaceful beauty of Miyagi-ken's Kinkazan island
- ◆ Visit the historic town of Hiraizumi, home to some of Tōhoku's finest temples
- ◆ Take in the hikes around Lake Tozawa-ko and the seclusion of Nyūtō Onsen
- ◆ Stroll around Kakunodate, a small town with well-preserved samurai homes and scenic tree-lined streets
- ◆ View Dewa Sanzan, a trio of sacred peaks that have drawn Buddhist pilgrims for more than 1400 years
- ◆ Enjoy the attractive seascapes, sleepy fishing villages and colourful festivals of Sado-ga-Shima island

outside major cities, you may well find your queries are answered more easily by phoning Japan Travel-Phone, toll free on ☎ 0120-44-4800 between 9 am and 5 pm.

Exploring Tōhoku (Weatherhill, 1982) by

NORTHERN HONSHŪ

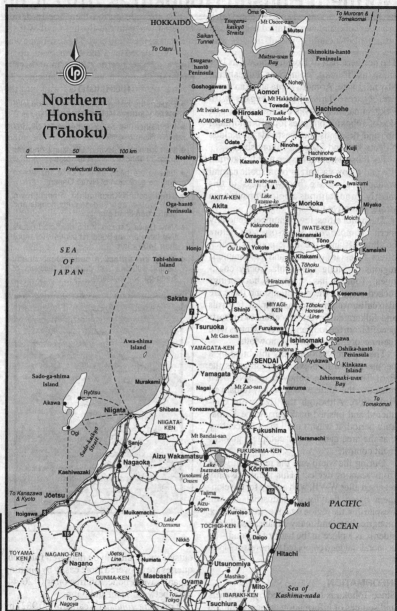

Northern
Honshū
(Tōhoku)

0   50   100 km

- - - - - - Prefectural Boundary

HOKKAIDŌ

To Otaru

SEA
OF
JAPAN

Tsugaru-
kaikyō
Straits

Seikan
Tunnel

Ōma
Mt Osore-zan ▲

Mutsu

Mutsu-wan
Bay

Shimokita-hantō
Peninsula

Tsugaru-
hantō
Peninsula

Goshogawara

Noheji

Mt Iwaki-san ▲

HIROSAKI

Aomori

▲ Mt Hakkōda-san

Hachinohe

AOMORI-KEN

Towada

Lake
Towada-ko

Ōdate

Ninohe

Hachinohe
Expressway

Kuji

Noshiro

Kazuno

Ryūsen-dō
Cave

Iwaizumi

Oga

Mt Iwate-san ▲

Morioka

Miyako

Oga-hantō
Peninsula

Akita

AKITA-KEN

Lake
Tazawa-ko

IWATE-KEN

Moichi

Kakunodate

Hanamaki

Tōno

Tobi-shima
Island

Ōmagari

Yokote

Kitakami

Kamaishi

Honjo

Ōu Line

Tōhoku
Line

Sakata

13

Hiraizumi

Kesennuma

Shinjō

MIYAGI-
KEN

Tōhoku
Honsen
Line

7

Tsuruoka

Awa-shima
Island

▲ Mt Gas-san

Furukawa

Ishinomaki

Onagawa

YAMAGATA-KEN

Matsushima

Oshika-hantō
Peninsula

SENDAI

Ayukawa

Kinkazan
Island

Sado-ga-shima
Island

Yamagata

Ishinomaki-wan
Bay

Ryōtsu

Murakami

Nagai

Mt Zaō-san ▲

Iwanuma

To
Tomakomai

Aikawa

Shibata

Niigata

Yonezawa

Fukushima

Haramachi

Ogi

Sanjo

NIIGATA-
KEN

49

Mt Bandai-san ▲

FUKUSHIMA-KEN

Kashiwazaki

Nagaoka

Aizu Wakamatsu

Lake
Inawashiro-ko

Kōriyama

Jōetsu

Yunokami
Onsen

Tajima

To Kanazawa
& Kyoto

Itoigawa

8

Muikamachi

Lake
Ozenuma

Aizu-
kōgen

Kuroiso

49

Iwaki

PACIFIC

OCEAN

Nikkō

Daigo

TOYAMA-
KEN

18

NAGANO-KEN

Jōetsu
Line

TOCHIGI-KEN

Hitachi

Nagano

Numata

GUNMA-KEN

Maebashi

Oyama

Mashiko

Utsunomiya

Mito

To
Nagoya

To
Tokyo

IBARAKI-KEN

Tsuchiura

Sea of
Kashima-nada

Jan Brown is a guide to the region which provides solid and very detailed background information including useful indices with place names in *kanji*.

For some literary refreshment en route you could dip into *The Narrow Road to the Deep North & Other Travel Sketches* (Penguin, 1970), which contains classic haiku penned by Bashō (1644-94), perhaps the most famous Japanese poet, on his travels in Tōhoku and elsewhere. To bring yourself up to date, you could also read *The Narrow Road to the Deep North: Journey into Lost Japan* (Jonathan Cape, 1990) by Lesley Downer. This is a well-written account of a walk which retraced one of Bashō's trips through the central and southern parts of Tōhoku.

The Japan National Tourist Organization (JNTO) publishes a glossy brochure entitled *Tōhoku* that includes a map and brief details for sights, festivals and transport in the prefecture. JNTO also publishes leaflets for separate parts of Tōhoku and these are mentioned in the appropriate places in this chapter.

GETTING AROUND

Transport in the region focuses on three major railway lines: two of these run north-south down the east and west coasts and the third snakes down between them in the centre. The JR Tōhoku shinkansen line links Tokyo (Ueno) with Morioka in the lightning time of 3½ hours.

Exploration of the remoter parts of Tōhoku, particularly if you're following an east-west route, requires a greater amount of time chugging patiently along local railway lines or winding up mountains on local bus services.

Fukushima-ken

AIZU WAKAMATSU 会津若松

During feudal times, this castle town developed into a stronghold for the Aizu clan. The clan later remained loyal to the shogunate

during the Edo period then briefly defied imperial forces in the Boshin Civil War (at the start of the Meiji era). The resistance was swiftly crushed and the town went up in flames – the heroic 'last stand of the samurai', complete with mass suicides by young warriors, has found its way into the annals of Japanese history and attracts many Japanese visitors to Aizu Wakamatsu.

Two bus lines conveniently circle from Aizu Wakamatsu station around the main sights – one clockwise and the other anti-clockwise. Bicycle rental is also available at the station.

Information

The Aizu Wakamatsu tourist information office (☎ 0242-32-0688) is in the View Plaza of JR Aizu Wakamatsu station. Large, detailed maps of the area in English are available – excellent for orientation. The office is open from 10 am to 6 pm, 10 am to 5 pm on Sunday. If you want to visit nearby sake museums and breweries (tastings available!) or a hall exhibiting local lacquerware, the English-speaking staff can give you directions.

JNTO publishes a leaflet entitled *Aizu Wakamatsu & Bandai*, which has maps and brief details of sights, transport and accommodation in Aizu Wakamatsu and the surrounding region.

Iimori-yama Hill 飯盛山

This hill is renowned as the spot where teenage members of the Byakkotai (White Tigers Band) retreated from the imperial forces and committed ritual suicide in 1868. The standard account of this tragedy maintains that the youngsters killed themselves after they looked down from the hilltop and saw the town and its castle go up in flames; another version maintains that it was just the town that was alight – the Meiji government did not get around to torching the castle until 1874.

The graves of 19 Byakkotai members are lined up on the hill – one member of the group survived his suicide attempt and is reported to have felt ashamed for the rest of his life. The event has received attention not only from Japanese admirers of loyalty, but also from foreigners with similar sentiments. Close to the graves are two monuments, one from a German military attaché and another from Italian fascists. Some of the inscriptions were erased by the US military occupation force after WWII, but were later restored.

Apart from a **museum** housing Byakkotai memorabilia, there's also the **Sazae-dō Hall**, a hexagonal building dating from the 18th century, which has an intricate set of stairs arranged as a double spiral. Admission to the hall costs ¥300 and it's open from 8 am to sunset. Just down the steps is the outlet to an irrigation channel leading to Lake Inawashiro-ko. Built in the mid-17th century, it required three years of effort by some 55,000 labourers, but its main claim to fame is that it was used by the Byakkotai as an escape route during their battle with the imperials.

The hill is a 15 minute bus ride from the railway station and can be climbed on foot – or use the hillside elevator (¥250). The No 15 bus stops at Iimori-yama (¥210) before going on in the direction of Tsuraga-jō Castle.

Oyaku-en Garden 御薬園
This is a splendid garden complete with tea arbour, large central pond (with huge carp) and a section devoted to the cultivation of medicinal herbs, as encouraged by former Aizu lords.

In the souvenir shop you can sample herbal tea, and packets of *daimyō* herbal brew are on sale.

Admission costs ¥300 and opening hours are from 8 am to 5 pm (April to October) and 8.30 am to 4.30 pm (November to March). The garden is a 15 minute bus ride from the station – get off at the Oyaku-en Iriguchi bus stop.

Aizu Buke-yashiki (Samurai House) 会津武家屋敷
Aizu Buke-yashiki is an interesting, large-scale reconstruction of the lifestyle of opulent samurai in the Edo period. An English leaflet and map are provided for you to guide yourself around dozens of rooms,

which range from the kitchen to the principal residence. The toilet has a special sandbox for medical advisers to inspect their lord's daily deeds! The complex is open from 8.30 am to 5.30 pm (April to October) and 9 am to 4.30 pm (November to March). Admission costs ¥800. To reach the residence, take the No 3 bus from the railway station to Higashiyama Onsen for 15 minutes and get off at the Buke-yashiki-mae bus stop (¥280).

Tsuruga-jō Castle 鶴ヶ城
The present castle is a reconstruction from 1965 and contains a historical museum. Admission costs ¥400 and it's open from 8.30 am to 5 pm. Take the No 14 bus from the station and get off at Tsuruga-jō Kitaguchi (¥200). After touring the castle you could take the No 14 bus onward to Iimori-yama Hill.

Aizu Aki Matsuri Festival 会津秋まつり
This festival, held from 22 to 24 September, features a large parade with participants dressed as daimyō and their retainers, and there are performances of folk dances.

Places to Stay & Eat
The tourist information office has lists of ryokan and minshuku accommodation and can help with reservations, though they may charge you a ¥515 service fee.

Just south of Aizu Wakamatsu station is the *Eki-mae Fuji Grand Hotel* (☎ 0242-24-1111), which has singles from ¥4800 and not-too-cramped twins for ¥9800. A few blocks east, the *Green Hotel Aizu* (☎ 0242-24-5181), has singles/twins for ¥5500/9600. Also nearby, and a bit more refined, is the *Aizu Wakamatsu Washington Hotel* (☎ 0242-22-6111) where singles start at ¥7200 and twins/doubles are ¥14,500/13,000.

Across from the Aizu Washington Hotel, the *Mikuni Ryokan* (☎ 0242-24-9015) has reasonable per-person rates of ¥6000 including two meals. Another Japanese-style option is the *Kadoya Ryokan* (☎ 0242-22-1730), which is just south of the Eki-mae Fuji Grand Hotel in a quiet residential neighbourhood with old buildings. Per-person rates are also ¥6000 with two meals.

The *Aizu-no-Sato Youth Hostel* (☎ 0241-27-2054) is a 10 minute walk from Shiokawa station, which is 10 km from Aizu Wakamatsu and a little closer to Kitakata. Rates are ¥2000 to ¥2200 depending on the time of year. Bicycle rental is available at the hostel, which is also part of a liquor store: maybe you can get a good deal on a case of beer.

Aizu Wakamatsu is pretty grim on the restaurant front. There aren't too many choices, and a lot of places close early. The station area is particularly barren, which is unfortunate given that a lot of accommodation is around here. If you're in this area, there's a nice little restaurant in the railway station that serves set lunches and dinners. Portions are generous for the money and the menu is all pictures for easy ordering.

The main eating and drinking area is located around Nanokomachi-dōri, about 20 minutes walk south of the railway station along the main road, Chūō-dōri. There are a few sushi places here and several *izakaya* to choose from, and numerous tiny bars stacked atop one another in multi-storey pub buildings.

Getting There & Away
From Tokyo (Ueno), the quickest route is to take the JR Tōhoku *shinkansen* line to Kōriyama then change to the JR Ban-etsu-Saisen line to Aizu Wakamatsu – total time for the trip is about 2½ hours; total cost is ¥8900.

Local trains run between Aizu Wakamatsu and Niigata on the JR Ban-etsu-Saisen line, take 2¼ hours and cost ¥2160.

From Nikkō, there's the option of combining train rides from Shimo-Imaichi to Kinugawa Onsen on the Tōbu Kinugawa line, then changing to the Aizu-Kinugawa line. To get a closer look at the countryside and rural architecture in the valleys on this route, you can also take buses part of the way from Kinugawa Onsen before hopping back onto the train.

KITAKATA AREA 喜多方周辺
Kitakata, just 20 minutes by train from Aizu Wakamatsu, is famed for its thousands of *kura*, or mud-walled storehouses, which come in all sorts of colour schemes and function not only as storehouses, but also as living quarters, shops and workshops. Some are also still used as sake breweries, a few of which will let you in to peer at the production process.

The information office at the station can provide a (somewhat dated) map in English which outlines walking routes – allow three hours at an easy pace. Bicycle rental is also

---

Targeting Tourists' Tastebuds
As it stood, Kitakata was already an attractive little town, with its well-preserved traditional inns, sake breweries and *kura* (storehouses). But as Japan soared toward the peak of its mid-1980s economic boom, locals felt the town needed something more to draw in tourist dollars. Enter the now-renowned 'Kitakata Rāmen'.

This was not exactly a new trick – you can't swing a dead cat in Japan without hitting someplace touting its 'famous' variety of the ubiquitous soup noodle dish. The Kitakata version got its start at the Genraiken restaurant, and featured a clear pork soup base and special wavy noodles designed to 'catch' as much broth as possible.

Not the stuff of culinary fantasy perhaps. But the recipe seems to have struck a chord with Japanese tourists and Kitakata is now home to a staggering 120 rāmen shops. Although it earned a place on Japan's tourist maps for its rich collection of kura, mention Kitakata to your average Japanese and their first response will likely be 'rāmen!'

If you want to try the original, Genraiken is a 10-minute walk from the station. Another top spot with locals is the Shanghai rāmen shop, a tiny no-frills affair. Staff at the Kitakata tourist information shop will gladly show you how to get to either place. ■

available near the station (¥250 per hour) and a horse-drawn tourist carriage (a sort of double-decker 'kuramobile') does the rounds in two hours (¥1300) – Japanese commentary only.

Brick-built, western-style kura can be seen at the tiny town of **Mitsuya**, nine km north of Kitakata (15 minutes by bus from Kitakata station) on Route 121. Take the bus for Negoya and get off at the Mitsuya stop (¥350). Buses run six times a day between 6.30 am and 5.45 pm.

The community of **Sugiyama**, six km further north from Mitsuya, is almost solid with kura, all of which are still in private hands. The appropriate bus stop is Jirikyoku-mae (¥450).

Six km south-west of Kitakata (25 minutes by bus from Kitakata station; ¥450) is the **Kumano-jinja Shrine**, renowned for its Nagatoko Hall which was built more than 900 years ago and has neither walls nor doors – more than 40 massive columns support the roof. The bus stop for the shrine is Shingu. There are six buses daily between 6.45 am and 5.45 pm.

LAKE INAWASHIRO-KO　猪苗代湖

This is a large lake – the fourth largest in Japan – and is popular with the Japanese as a place to take ferry rides and go camping. However, it's really nothing special, and the town of Inawashiro is best used as a staging post to visit the more scenic area around Mt Bandai-san.

Close to Inawashiro-ko (10 minutes by bus from Inawashiro station) is **Noguchi Hideyo Memorial Hall** (Noguchi Hideyo Kinenkan), which honours Noguchi Hideyo, a medical pioneer famed for his research into snake poison, syphilis and yellow fever – the latter disease ironically ended his own life at the age of 52 in Africa. Admission costs ¥400. It's open daily from 8.30 am to 4.45 pm (April to October) and 9 am to 4 pm (November to March). To get there, take the bus to Aizu-Wakamatsu via Nagahama and get off at the Noguchi Hideyo Kinenkan stop (¥280).

Close to this memorial hall is **Aizu Minzokukan**, a folk museum which includes

two farmhouses from the Edo period, a mill, and a candle-making shop. Admission costs ¥500 and it's open daily – except Thursday – from 8 am to 5 pm (April to October) and 8.30 am to 4.30 pm (November to March).

About 12 km further west along the lake is **Naga-hama Beach**, which is accessible by bus (¥430) from Inawashiro station. This place isn't really worth a visit as the beach is cluttered with trash and with pedal-boats shaped like swans, snails and the like.

Getting There & Away

JR trains run between Aizu-Wakamatsu and Inawashiro station in about 30 minutes (¥460). There are also buses from Aizu-Wakamatsu station that run via Naga-hama (45 minutes, ¥850) to Inawashiro station (one hour, ¥1100). From Inawashiro station there are fairly frequent buses to the Inawashiro-ko area and up to Bandai-kōgen Plateau.

MT BANDAI-SAN & BANDAI-KŌGEN PLATEAU　磐梯山・磐梯高原

Bandai-san erupted on 15 July 1888 and destroyed dozens of villages and their inhabitants. At the same time it completely rearranged the landscape, creating a plateau and damming local rivers which then formed numerous lakes and ponds. Now a national park, the whole area offers spectacular scenery with ample scope for walks or long hikes.

The most popular walk, sometimes jammed with hikers from end to end, takes about an hour and follows a trail between a series of lakes known as **Goshikinuma** (Five Coloured Lakes). The trailheads for the Goshikinuma walk are at Goshikinuma Iriguchi and at Bandai-kōgen-eki, the main transport hub on the edge of Lake Hibara-ko. As can be expected of a main transport hub, Bandai-kōgen-eki is geared to the tourist circus with souvenir shops, restaurants and a vast asphalt expanse to accommodate tour buses. Along with the pleasure boat rides there are various walking trails on the eastern side of the lake. Nearby are several other lakes, including **Lake Onagawa-ko** and

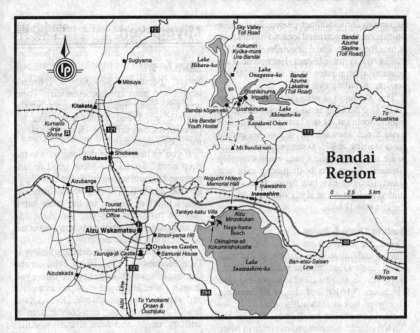

Lake Akimoto-ko, which also offer walks along their shores.

Ura Bandai Youth Hostel is very close to Goshikinuma Iriguchi and makes a convenient base for extended hikes. The hostel has maps in Japanese outlining routes and approximate times for hikes in the areas.

The most popular hiking destination is Bandai-san, which can be climbed in a day if you start as early as possible and allow up to nine hours. A popular route for this hike starts from Kawakami Onsen (about 10 minutes by bus from the youth hostel) and climbs up to Bandai-san, looping around the rim of the crater before descending to Bandai-kōgen-eki bus stop.

Places to Stay & Eat

There's a tourist information office at Idemitsu, between Goshikinuma Iriguchi and Bandai-kōgen-eki, but if you need help with booking accommodation (and you don't speak Japanese) it's probably easier to use the tourist office in Aizu Wakamatsu, which has English-speaking staff.

The *Ura Bandai Youth Hostel* (☎ 0241-32-2811) is a little the worse for wear, but it's in a quiet spot next to one of the trailheads for the Goshikinuma walk. It's also a good base for longer mountain hikes. The staff can provide maps and basic information for hikes in the area. Bicycle rental is also available. The hostel is closed from 1 December to 31 March. A bed for the night is ¥2600. Meals are available, but they are not recommended.

To get there take the bus bound for Bandai-kōgen-eki from Inawashiro station and get off 30 minutes later at the Goshikinuma Iriguchi bus stop (¥720). The hostel is seven minutes on foot from the bus stop, along the Goshikinuma trail.

Near the Goshikinuma Iriguchi bus stop, the *Resort Hotel Goshikinuma* (☎ 0241-32-3023) looks more like a public housing block than a resort, but has comfortable rooms with two meals for ¥8500 per person. For a more up-market stay you need look no further than across the street. The *Fraser Hotel* (☎ 0241-32-3470) is an elegant European-style pension where rates start at ¥16,500 per person, including two meals.

The *Kokumin Kyūka-mura Ura-Bandai* (☎ 0241-32-2421) is in a somewhat more remote location, at the last stop on the bus route from Inawashiro. It has per-person costs starting at ¥7500 with two meals. Just to the south of it is the *Kyūka-mura Camping Ground*. To get to both places take the Bandai-kōgen-eki bus from Inawashiro station and get off at Kyūka-mura, which is the last stop (¥840).

Getting There & Away

There are buses from Aizu Wakamatsu station and Inawashiro station to the trailheads for the Goshikinuma walk. Buses from Aizu Wakamatsu to Bandai-kōgen-eki take 1½ hours (¥1610) and almost all require a change of bus at Inawashiro station. Buses from Inawashiro to Bandai-kōgen-eki (¥840) take 25 minutes and run once to twice an hour from 7 am to 7 pm. Buses from Aizu-Wakamatsu run less frequently.

Between Bandai-kōgen-eki and Fukushima there is a bus service along two scenic toll roads – Bandai Azuma Lakeline and Bandai Azuma Skyline. The trip provides great views of the mountains and is highly recommended if you are a fan of volcanic panoramas.

The bus makes a scheduled stop (30 minutes) at Jōdodaira, a superb viewpoint, where you can climb to the top of Mt Azumakofuji (1705m) in 10 minutes and, if you still feel energetic, scramble down to the bottom of the crater. Across the road is Mt Issaikyō-yama, which belches steam in dramatic contrast to its passive neighbour – a steepish climb of 45 minutes is needed to reach the top with its sweeping views.

The bus fare between Fukushima and Bandai-kōgen-eki is ¥2780; the trip takes about three hours. There are two to three buses a day in each direction. The service only operates between late April and late October.

Miyagi-ken　宮城県

SENDAI　仙台

Sendai (population 980,000) is Tōhoku's largest and most cosmopolitan city. There aren't too many sights around town, but the city's clean, broad boulevards make for pleasant enough strolling – it's good at least for an overnight stay.

If you've been hiking the long road to the deep north, Sendai has some good restaurants and a couple of nightlife options (don't get too excited). Those coming from the bright lights of Tokyo, on the other hand, may be better off skipping the place and heading straight to nearby Matsushima or the coastal towns further north.

The dominant figure in Sendai's history is Date Masamune (1567-1636), who earned the nickname Dokuganryū ('one-eyed dragon') after he caught smallpox as a child and went blind in his right eye. Date adopted Sendai as his base and, in a combination of military might and administrative skills, became one of the most powerful feudal lords in Japan. An accomplished artist and scholar, Date also raised Sendai to the status of cultural centre of the Tōhoku region.

Unfortunately, there's not much evidence of high culture these days. During WWII, Sendai was demolished by Allied bombing, and the city was later rebuilt with streets and avenues laid out in a grid pattern.

Orientation

Sendai station is within easy walking distance of the city centre, and the grid layout of the streets makes orientation relatively simple. From the station, the broad sweep of Aoba-dōri, lined with many of the major department stores, banks and hotels, leads west to Aoba-yama Hill. The main shopping areas are along the mall-like Ichibanchō-dōri and Chūō-dōri – confusingly, the latter is also known as Clis Road. Kokubunchō-dōri, west of Ichibanchō-dōri, is the largest entertainment district in Tōhoku, with thousands of bars and eateries.

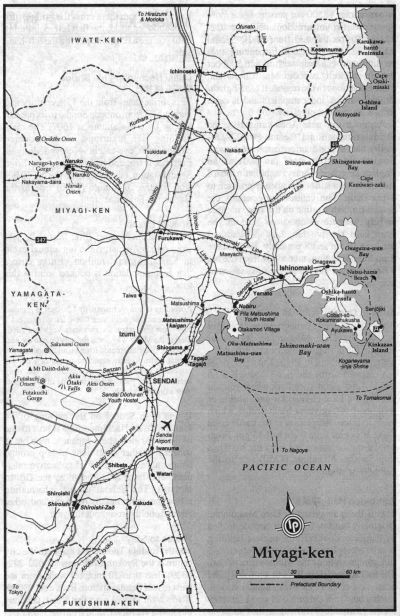

Miyagi-ken

0   30   60 km

Prefectural Boundary

Information

Sendai tourist information office (☎ 022-222-3269), on the 2nd floor of JR Sendai station, usually has English-speaking staff on duty who can help with inquiries about the city as well as about Matsushima and other attractions in the region. It has English-language maps and pamphlets and is open from 8.30 am to 8 pm daily.

Across town, near Aoba-yama Hill, the Sendai International Center (☎ 022-224-1919) has a good information desk with English-speaking staff, as well as an English-language library, a bulletin board and CNN broadcasts. It's open from 9 am to 8 pm daily. The centre also operates the Sendai English Hotline on the same number to help with travel questions (and maybe even help resolve language difficulties) between 10 am and 8 pm daily. To get there from Sendai station, take a bus from the No 9 bus stop and get off at the Kokusaisenta-mae stop.

Aoba-jō Castle 青葉城跡

Aoba-jō Castle was built on Aoba-yama Hill in 1602 by Date Masamune. Its partial destruction during the Meiji era was completed by bombing in 1945. The castle ruins – a restored turret and that's about it – lie inside Aoba-yama-kōen Park where you can pause for a look at Gokoku-jinja Shrine or walk south to Yagiyama-bashi Bridge, which leads to a zoo. Admission to the castle costs ¥400. It's open from 9 am to 4.15 pm. From Sendai station, take a bus from the No 9 bus stop for the 20 minute (¥250) ride to the Aoba-jōshi stop.

Zuihō-den Hall 瑞鳳殿

This is the mausoleum of Date Masamune. Originally built in 1637, but later destroyed by bombing in WWII, the present building is an exact replica – faithful to the ornate and sumptuous style of the Momoyama period. The hall is open from 9 am to 4 pm daily and admission costs ¥515. From Sendai station, catch a bus from either No 11 or 12 bus stop for the 15 minute (¥180) ride to the Otamaya-

bashi stop. From there cross the bridge, turn right and then make the first left, continuing until you see a flagstone path on the left-hand side.

Ōsaki Hachiman-jinja Shrine 大崎八幡神社

This shrine dates from the 12th century and was moved from outside Sendai to its present site by Date Masamune in 1607. The main building is a luxurious, black-lacquered edifice with eye-catching carved designs. Entrance is free and it closes at sunset. From Sendai station, take a bus from the No 10 bus stop for the 20 minute (¥220) ride to the Hachiman-jinja-mae stop.

Special Events

The Tanabata Matsuri (Star Festival), held from 6 to 8 August, is the big annual event in Sendai. Several million visitors ensure that accommodation is booked solid at this time.

According to a myth (originally Chinese), a princess and a peasant shepherd were forbidden to meet, but 7 July – the time when the two stars Vega and Altair meet in the Milky Way – was the only time in the year when the two star-crossed lovers could sneak a tryst. Sendai seems to have stretched the dates a bit, but celebrates in grand style by decorating the main streets, holding parades and rounding off the events with a fireworks finale.

If you're in Sendai on the evening of 14 January, Osaki Hachiman-jinja is host to one of those parades where Japanese men brave subzero weather conditions to hop around almost naked in a show of collective madness. The festival is known as the **Donto Matsuri**. The Sendai tourist information office has more details on these and other festivals held throughout the year.

Places to Stay

Youth Hostels The closest hostel to the city centre is the *Ryokan Chitoseya* (☎ 022-222-6329), less than 20 minutes walk from the west exit of Sendai station. Beds cost ¥3000. If you want to give your feet a rest, take any bus going via Miyamachi from the No 17 bus

TONY WHEELER

TONY WHEELER

MASON FLORENCE

CHRIS TAYLOR

TONY WHEELER

JEFF WILLIAMS

A	B
C	D
E	F

A: Boats, Hiroshima River
B: Cemetery, Onomichi
C: Drying persimmons, Wakasa Bay
D: Itsukushima-jinja Shrine, Miyajima

E: Paper cranes, Peace Memorial
   Park, Hiroshima
F: Genbaku Dome, Hiroshima

MASON FLORENCE

NICKO GONCHAROFF

MASON FLORENCE

NICKO GONCHAROFF

NICKO GONCHAROFF

A	D
B	
C	E

A: Tarai traditional boat,
   Sado-ga-shima Island
B: Fern, Shirakami Mountains,
   Aomori

C: White rocks of Matsushima
D: 1400-year-old staircase,
   Mt Haguro-san, Dewa Sanzan
E: Trail marker, Aomori

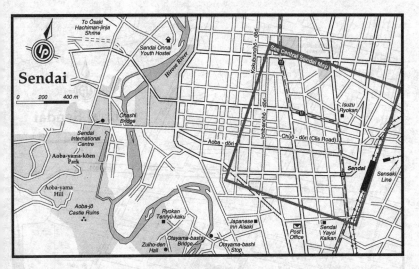

Sendai

To Ōsaki
Hachiman-jinja
Shrine

Sendai Onnai
Youth Hostel

Hirose River

Ōhashi
Bridge

Sendai
International
Centre

Aoba-yama-kōen
Park

Aoba-yama
Hill

Aoba-jō
Castle Ruins

Ryokan
Tenryū-kaku

Zuihō-den
Hall

Otayama-bashi
Bridge

Otayama-bashi
Stop

Japanese
Inn Aisaki

Kokubunchō - dōri

See Central Sendai Map

Ichibanchō - dōri

Aoba - dōri

Chūō - dōri

Isuzu
Ryokan

Chūō - dōri (Clis Road)

Sendai

Senseki
Line

Post
Office

Sendai
Yayoi
Kaikan

0   200   400 m

stop at Sendai station, and get off at
Miyamachi Ni-chome. The hostel is tucked
down a small side street near the bus stop.

Sendai Dōchu-an Youth Hostel (☎ 022-
247-0511), about five km south of Sendai in
an old farmhouse, has a high reputation for
hospitality to foreigners – it's twinned with
a youth hostel in Meiringen, Switzerland.
Bicycle rental is available and there may still
be a discount on the price of accommodation
for foreigners. The hostel enforces a strict
no-smoking policy inside the building.
Nightly rates are ¥3100.

From Sendai station, take the subway to
Tomizawa station then walk for eight
minutes to the hostel. Alternatively, you can
walk to the hostel in 18 minutes from
Nagamachi JR station, which is one stop
south of Sendai station. If you get lost, the
hostel manager can give you directions over
the phone.

Sendai Onnai Youth Hostel (☎ 022-234-
3922) is in the northern part of the city. Take
a bus bound for Shihei-chō (the No 24 stop,
in front of the Sendai Hotel, opposite the
station) and after about 15 minutes get off at
the Tōhokukai Byō-in Shigakubu-mae stop
(¥180). The hostel is two minutes walk away.

A bed for the night is ¥2500 and bicycle
rental is available at reasonable rates.

Ryokan *Japanese Inn Aisaki* (☎ 022-264-
0700), a member of the Japanese Inn Group,
is behind the post office, a 15 minute walk
from Sendai station. It's a friendly place with
meals available. Prices for singles/doubles
start at ¥4500/8400 without meals. Just
below the entrance to Zuihō-den Hall, the
Ryokan Tenryū-kaku (☎ 022-222-9957) is in
a peaceful setting surrounded by trees and
greenery. Rooms with two meals start at
¥6500 per person. The ryokan also has an
onsen spa to wash away the strains of the
day's sightseeing.

Hotels This constitutes the bulk of Sendai's
accommodation – the city centre is packed
with business hotels. One of the cheapest is
the small *Business Hotel Yamato* (☎ 022-
267-6961). It has singles/twins/doubles at
¥6000/10,000/9000. Further south of the
station the *Sendai Yayoi Kaikan* (☎ 022-227-
9515) looks a bit past its prime, but rooms
are cheap at ¥6000/10,000 for singles/twins.
On the intersection of Chūō-dōri and Higashi

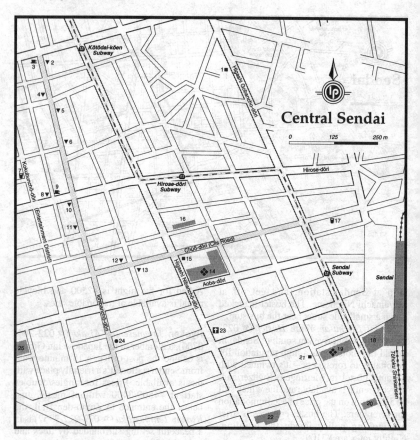

Central Sendai

0   125   250 m

Nibanchō-dōri, a very central location, is the *Tokyo Dai-Ichi Hotel Sendai* (☎ 022-262-1355), with singles from ¥6800 and twins from ¥13,800.

There are many centrally located up-market alternatives to these cheaper business hotels. Right next to the station, the *Hotel Metropolitan Sendai* (☎ 022-268-2525) has singles from ¥10,000 and doubles from ¥21,000. Equally classy and around 10 minutes walk from the station is the *Sendai Kokusai Hotel* (☎ 022-268-1112). It has singles from ¥11,000 and doubles from ¥18,000.

Places to Eat

Finding a place to eat in Sendai is easy. Just steer yourself in the direction of the shopping arcade streets of Chūō-dōri and Ichibanchō-dōri and you'll find dozens of restaurants, ranging from fast-food pasta and sushi spots to up-market Japanese and French restaurants. The Sendai tourist information office can give you a map with some 60 different dining choices on it.

Among the more affordable options is *Pronto*, a coffee shop chain that also dishes up affordable pasta: prices range from ¥580 to ¥780 per dish, and the coffee is only ¥160

PLACES TO STAY

1 Hotel Hokke Club
Sendai
ホテル法華クラブ

15 Tokyo Dai-Ichi Hotel
Sendai
東京第一ホテル仙台

16 Hotel Century Sendai
ホテルセンチュリー
仙台

18 Hotel Metropolitan
Sendai
ホテル
メトロポリタン仙台

20 Hotel Sun Route
Sendai
ホテルサンルート
仙台

21 Business Hotel
Yamato
ビジネスホテル
ヤマト

22 Sendai Kokusai Hotel
仙台国際ホテル

25 Sendai Tōkyū Hotel
仙台東急ホテル

PLACES TO EAT

2 Hagen Daaz Ice
Cream Shop

3 La Terrasse Coffee
Shop

4 Santake
さん竹

5 Genroku-Zushi
元禄寿司

6 Bali Bali Yakiniku
House
バリバリ焼肉

8 Yoshinoya
吉の屋

9 Doutor Coffee;
Tonton Rāmen
とんとんラーメン

10 Mr Donut

11 McDonald's

12 Pronto

13 Vino Il Salotto

OTHER

7 Simon's Bar

14 Daiei Department
Store
ダイエー

17 Vilevan Bar

19 Seiyō Department
Store
仙台セイヨー

23 Eastern Orthodox
Church
ハリストス正教会

24 Maruzen Bookstore
丸善書店

a cup. The Japanese *gyūdon* (beef on rice) chain *Yoshinoya* has a branch up on Hirose-dōri – good economical fare. For high quality rāmen head over to *Tonton Rāmen*. Prices here start at ¥500 and don't go above ¥850 for huge bowls of noodles.

For some slightly more up-market Japanese cooking, check out *Santake*, a pleasant place with good tempura and udon dishes from ¥900 to ¥1600. There's plenty to choose from at the lower end of the menu. Further south on Ichibanchō-dōri is *Bali Bali Yakiniku House*, a do-it-yourself Japanese/Korean-style barbecue. Figure on around ¥2000 per person, excluding drinks. For more authentic Italian food, *Vino Il Salotto* is worth checking out. The English menu has pasta dishes from ¥850, and the restaurant often has good deals on wine (¥1000 for all you could drink in 90 minutes when we were in town last). There are lots of other international restaurants in this area as well.

Entertainment

Sendai just wouldn't be a Japanese city if it didn't have its own famous nightlife area. In this case it's clustered around the northern end of Kokubunchō-dōri. It makes for an interesting evening stroll, but there probably isn't much that the average traveller could afford there. Interesting places that we stumbled across include *Sherlock Holmes*, *Baron Potato*, *Popeye the Hōrensō* (*hōrensō* means spinach), *Madame Lee Phone 63-5575* (yes, it's a bar), *Fancy Pub Spunky Sugar* and, the one place that probably sums the area up most succinctly, *Member's Bar Rip Off*.

For a couple of affordable beers the best option is probably *Vilevan* (pronounced vi-leh van), at the station end of Chūō-dōri. It was formerly called the Village Vanguard, but apparently the original New York establishment got wind of this, and suggested a name change. It's a laid-back jazz bar, with live acts occasionally performing on the

NORTHERN HONSHŪ

A Question of Delicacy

Japanese cuisine is known for using ingredients, such as seaweed or fermented soybeans, that many foreign palates might not categorise as 'food'. But for sheer inedibility, few dishes can rival the lowly sea squirt, known to Japanese as the *hoya*. Only the most hardened tastebuds could believe that humans were meant to eat this flabby, red-orange, primitive sea creature.

Hoya are harvested only along Japan's northern Pacific coast, and are especially prevalent on the shores of Miyagi and Iwate prefectures. This is also where you'll find the country's few hoya aficionados, people who will tell you with a straight face that this dish – which tastes like rubber dipped in ammonia – is a delicacy.

Hoya is served raw in vinegar, with a few slices of cucumber on the side to soften the blow. Fans claim that it goes well with sake. Feel free to try it for yourself at the local sushi or seafood restaurant. Just don't say you weren't warned. ■

---

weekends, and the reverse-discrimination foreigner discounts on the draught beer (¥300 for a draught Heineken!) make this a very affordable place to knock a few cold ones back. In Kokubunchō-dōri, one bar that occasionally gets foreign customers and isn't a member's rip-off affair is *Simon's Bar*. Beers are ¥400, pretty cheap by Japanese bar standards, and there's no service charge if you're willing to stand at the bar (sitting at a table will cost you ¥300 per person, again relatively reasonable).

Getting There & Away
Air From Sendai airport there are flights to Osaka, Sapporo airport (New Chitose airport), Nagoya, Fukuoka, Komatsu (Kanazawa) and Okinawa. To get to and from Tokyo, the shinkansen is so fast, it's not really sensible to take a plane. International destinations include Seoul, Pusan, Guam, Saipan and Singapore.

Train The JR Tōhoku shinkansen line takes two hours by the Yamabiko service or 2½ by the Aoba service between Tokyo (Ueno) and Sendai (¥10,390). Trains run about once every 20 minutes. The JR Tōhoku shinkansen line also connects Fukushima with Sendai in 26 minutes and continues north to Morioka in 50 minutes.

The JR Senzan line connects Sendai with Yamagata in one hour. The JR Senseki line links Sendai with Matsushima in 40 minutes.

Bus The Tōhoku Kyūkō (express night bus) runs between Tokyo (Tokyo station) and Sendai (7¾ hours, ¥6100) and reservations are necessary. There are also night buses between Sendai and Osaka (12¼ hours, ¥11,700) and day buses to Niigata, Tsuruoka and other Tōhoku destinations.

Boat Sendai is a major port with daily ferries operating to Tomakomai (Hokkaidō). The trip takes just under 15 hours and a second class berth is ¥8850 (1st class, ¥17,720). There are also ferries operating every second day to Nagoya (21 hours, ¥9580). Japanese speakers can make reservations on ☎ 022-263-9877 or in Tokyo on ☎ 033-564-4161.

To get to Sendai-futō Pier from Sendai station, take the JR Senseki line to Tagajō station and then a 10 minute taxi ride.

Getting Around
The Airport Sendai airport is a 40 minute bus ride (¥890) south of Sendai. Buses leave approximately every 30 minutes from 7 am to 5.30 pm from the No 15 bus stop at Sendai station.

Bus Sendai has a huge – and initially confusing – network of bus services. Most of the sights can be reached by bus direct from Sendai railway station. The tourist information office provides a leaflet in Japanese and English with relevant bus numbers, bus destinations and the names of the appropriate bus stops: definitely worth picking up. If you're having trouble with the bus system, a call to the Sendai English Hotline (☎ 022-224-1919) can probably set you straight.

Subway The present subway system runs from Izumi Chūō in the north to Tomizawa in the south. Pricing is according to sections, from ¥200 to ¥280, but few short-term visitors are likely to need to use it as it's not really useful for sightseeing. An extension of the subway is planned to run from east to west.

AKIU ONSEN 秋保温泉
This hot-spring resort, 50 minutes by bus west of Sendai, is a good base for sidetrips further into the mountains to see **Akiu Ōtaki Falls** and, further still, **Futakuchi Gorge** with its rock columns known as Banji-iwa. There are hiking trails along the river valley and there's a trail leading from Futakuchi Onsen to the summit of **Mt Daitō-dake** (about a three hour walk). There are numerous hotels and also minshuku scattered throughout this area. The *Banjisan-sō* (☎ 022-399-2775) is fairly close to trailheads for Mt Daitō-dake, Futakuchi Gorge and the Akiu Visitors Center, where you can pick up hiking maps. Rooms with two meals range from ¥8000 to ¥12,000 per person. It's at Futakuchi Onsen, around 30 minutes by bus past Akiu Onsen. Staff at the Sendai tourist information office can also help book accommodation in the Akiu area. Buses leave from the No 8 bus stop outside Sendai station and cost ¥770 to Akiu Onsen, ¥1090 to Futakuchi Onsen.

MATSUSHIMA 松島
Matsushima and the islands in Matsushima-wan Bay are meant to constitute one of the *Nihon sankei*, or 'three great sights' of Japan – the other two are the floating *torii* of Miya-jima Island and the sandspit at Amanohashidate. Besides the islands, there's also a lot of unprepossessing industrial scenery. Bashō (yes, Bashō was here too!) was reportedly so entranced by the surroundings in the 17th century that his flow of words was reduced

to simply: 'Matsushima, Ah! Matsushima! Matsushima!'

It's certainly a picturesque place which merits a half-day visit, but there are also impressive and less-touristed seascapes further east.

Orientation & Information
Just to confuse things, there's a Matsushima station on the Tōhoku line, but the station that's more convenient to the sights and the harbour is Matsushima-kaigan, which is on the Senseki line. From Matsushima-kaigan station, it's only around 500m to the harbour where boats leave for cruises around the bay. Sights are all within easy walking distance.

The Matsushima Information Center (☎ 022-354-4053) is on your right as you exit the station, and has a few English-language pamphlets and maps. The staff don't speak English, but can help you book accommodation using a bilingual card that lets you indicate your requirements. You can also leave your luggage here for the day (¥200 per piece). The office is open from 8.30 am to 6.30 pm.

Zuigan-ji Temple 瑞巌寺
Though founded in 828, the present buildings of Zuigan-ji were constructed in 1606 by Date Masamune to serve as a family temple. This is one of Tōhoku's finest Zen temples and well worth a visit to see the painted screens and interior carvings of the main hall and the Seiryūden (Treasure Hall), which contains works of art associated with the Date family.

Admission costs ¥600 and includes an English leaflet. The temple is open from 8 am to 5 pm from April to mid-September, though for the rest of the year opening hours vary almost month by month; the core opening hours are from 8 am to 3.30 pm. The temple is five minutes on foot from the cruise-boat piers and is approached along an avenue lined with tall cedars.

Godai-dō Hall 五大堂
This is a small wooden temple reached by two bridges. The interior of the hall

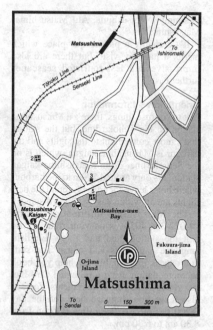

1 Sakuragawa Ryokan
   桜川旅館

2 Zuigan-ji Temple
   瑞巌寺

3 Matsushima Kankō Hotel
   (Ryokan Matsushima-jō)
   松島観光ホテル

4 Matsushima Century Hotel
   松島センチュリーホテル

5 Godai-dō Hall
   五大堂

6 Matsushima Cruise Boats
   松島遊覧船

7 Kanran-tei Pavilion
   観瀾亭

8 Matsushima Tourist Information
   松島観光案内所

9 Aquarium
   マリンピア松島水族館

is only opened once every 33 years – so you will probably have to be content with the weatherbeaten exterior and the view out to sea.

Kanran-tei Pavilion 観瀾亭

This pavilion is about five minutes on foot from the dock; bear left after leaving the boat. Kanran-tei is claimed to have been presented to the Date family by Toyotomi Hideyoshi in the late 16th century and served as a genteel venue for tea ceremonies and moon-viewing. The garden includes a small museum housing a collection of relics from the Date family.

Admission to the pavilion costs ¥200 and includes entrance to the museum. It's open from 8.30 am to 5 pm (April to October) but closes 30 minutes earlier during the rest of the year.

Fukuura-jima Island 福浦島

This island is connected to the mainland by a 252m-long red wooden bridge, just south of the Matsushima Century Hotel It has been made into a botanical garden, with a walking trail that winds around the island in a leisurely 30 minutes. Admission is ¥150 and the island is open from 8 am to 5 pm.

Special Events

Seafood lovers will appreciate the Matsushima Oyster Festival, which is held on the first Sunday in February – fresh oysters are sold near the boat dock.

The Tōrō Nagashi Festival, held on 15 August, honours the souls of the departed with the Bon ritual of floating lighted lanterns out to sea. A fireworks display adds zip to the occasion.

Places to Stay

Most of the accommodation in Matsushima is very pricey so you won't find anything under ¥8000 per person, including two meals. One of the cheaper places in town is the *Sakuragawa Ryokan* (☎ 022-354-2513) where ¥8000 per person buys you a nicely furnished room and two sumptuous meals. It's about a two minute walk from the

Takagimachi station, just one stop past Matsushima-kaigan. From Matsushima-kaigan station it will take you around 20 minutes to get there on foot. Most of the luxury hotels charge at least ¥20,000 per person. One exception is the *Matsushima Century Hotel* (☎ 0223-354-4111), which has twins for ¥12,000. But before you get too excited, this price buys you a view of the car park rather than the sea. If you want to splash out, one of the most unique choices is probably the *Matsushima Kankō Hotel* (☎ 0223-54-2121), which is a ryokan that looks like a castle – not a very authentic one admittedly. Costs here range from ¥10,000 to ¥30,000 per person with two meals. This hotel is also called the *Ryokan Matsushima-jō*, just to make things confusing.

Cheaper options can be found in the town of Nobiru, in Oku-Matsushima (see the following section).

Getting There & Away

Train The easy way to get to Matsushima is by train from Sendai. Trains run on the Senseki line, take around 40 minutes and cost ¥390. There are only around two services an hour to Matsushima, though there are three as far as Shiogama. This is important because travelling by train to Shiogama and then travelling onwards by boat to Matsushima is a popular way of reaching the latter, taking in one of Japan's most self-celebrated strips of coastline on the way. The train fare to Shiogama is ¥310.

Boat Shiogama itself is not particularly noteworthy, though it's a thriving fishing port and has a celebrated festival every 5 August, with a parade of colourful boats decked out with streamers and banners. The cruises to Matsushima are what is important for most visitors. The harbour is around 10 minutes on foot from Hon-Shiogama station – turn right at the station exit.

Cruises between Shiogama and Matsushima usually take about 50 minutes and operate from 8 am to 4 pm. There are hourly departures between April and November, less frequent departures during the rest of the

year, and the one-way fare costs ¥1400. The loudspeakers on the boat are cunningly placed so that there is no escape from the full-blast Japanese commentary – unless you leap overboard.

Cruises also set forth from Matsushima itself: ¥1400 for a 45-minute loop through the pine-covered islets. Before shelling out for your ticket, be advised that you will likely share your journey with about 100 seagulls and an equal number of frenzied tourists who eagerly feed the birds fried shrimp crackers (sold on board the boats). The end result is that unless it's a slow day, you'll have a hard time seeing any of the scenery unless you sit in the enclosed cabin: not a great way to get a feeling for one of Japan's three great sights.

OKU-MATSUSHIMA 奥松島

On the eastern curve of Matsushima-wan Bay, Oku-Matsushima is less touristed and offers several hiking trails for exploration by bicycle or on foot.

In order to reach Oku-Matsushima from Matsushima-kaigan, take the JR Senseki line six stops east (two stops by rapid express) to Nobiru station. From Nobiru station, it's a 10 minute bus ride (take the bus to Muro-hama) to Otakamori village where a 20 minute climb up the hill provides a fine panorama of the bay. In summer the buses leave about once an hour from 8 am to 5 pm, but during the rest of the year there are only five departures a day. As Otakamori is only around five km from Nobiru, it may be quicker and easier to rent a bicycle at the Pila Matsushima Youth Hostel (see Places to Stay, below). The hostel can also provide directions for the hiking trails.

Places to Stay

The *Pila Matsushima Youth Hostel* (☎ 0225-88-2220) has been newly renovated and is quite comfortable, but quite expensive at ¥3500 for a bed. Bicycle rental is available. The hostel is closed from 5 to 12 July. From Nobiru station, walk across the bridge and toward the ocean for about 10 minutes until you reach an intersection with a blue youth hostel sign pointing down the road to the right. From there it's about 800m. If you're lucky enough to catch one of the infrequent buses to Murohama Beach, just tell the driver 'youth hostel' and he'll let you off there. Staff at the information centre in the JR Nobiru station can give you a map to the hostel.

There are a couple of other options fairly close to Nobiru station. *Minshuku Bōyō-sō* (☎ 0225-88-2159) is a clean, spacious place with per-person costs from ¥6500 with two meals. It's in a western-style blue and white building near the intersection with the youth hostel sign. Just behind Boyo-sō is another minshuku which has similar prices.

Oshika-hantō Peninsula
牡鹿半島

AYUKAWA 鮎川
Ayukawa was once a major whaling centre and now relies on other types of fishing and tourism. Its main purpose for the visitor is as a jumping off point for exploring Kinkazan Island. Boats leave from the pier opposite the bus station.

Places to Stay
An excellent place to stay is *Cobalt-sō Kokuminshukusha* (☎ 0225-45-2281). This modern people's lodge is in a superb position on a forested hilltop opposite Kinkazan Island. For ¥6500 you get two meals and a well-maintained room. A variety of seafood is included in the evening meal. There is no bus service here, but you can call the lodge from Ayukawa and they will send a van to pick you up.

In Ayukawa itself there are several minshuku, mostly along the road at the back of town that slopes uphill. All charge ¥6000 per night, including two meals. Right near the bus station is the *Grand Hotel Oshika* (☎ 0225-45-2126), but unless every other place is full and you're desperate, it's probably not worth the ¥14,000 they'll charge you for their most basic twin.

Getting There & Away
The main gateway to this beautiful, secluded peninsula is **Ishinomaki**, from where you can get buses to Ayukawa, at the tip of the peninsula. From Ayukawa you can get a ferry to scenic Kinkazan Island, arguably the highlight of any visit to Oshika-hantō.

The ride down the peninsula is particularly enjoyable as the bus repeatedly climbs across forested hills before dropping down into bays and inlets where tiny fishing villages are surrounded by mounds of seashells and the ocean is full of rafts and poles for oyster and seaweed cultivation. Ishinomaki is about 30 minutes from Matsushima-kaigan by limited express on the JR Senseki line. It can also be reached via the Ishinomaki line from Ichinoseki on the Tōhoku line.

From Ishinomaki station there are around seven buses a day between 9 am and 6 pm to Ayukawa (90 minutes, ¥1430). From Ayukawa departures are between 6 am and 5 pm.

KINKAZAN ISLAND 金華山
For those in search of peace and quiet, an overnight stay on Kinkazan Island is recommended. The island features a pyramid-shaped mountain (445m), an impressive shrine, a handful of houses around the boat dock, no cars, droves of deer and monkeys and mostly untended trails. Most Japanese visitors seem to be day-trippers – this means the island is virtually deserted in the early morning and late afternoon.

The island is considered one of the three holiest places in Tōhoku – women were banned until late last century. On the first and second Sunday in October, there's a deer-horn cutting ceremony to stop the deer from causing injury to each other during the mating season.

From the boat dock, it's a steep 20 minute walk up the road to **Koganeyama-jinja Shrine**, which has several attractive buildings in its forested precincts. Below the shrine are grassy expanses where crows delight in hitchhiking on the back of deer while the deer cadge titbits from visitors.

A steep trail leads from the shrine up the

thickly forested slopes, via several wayside shrines, to the summit in about 50 minutes. From the shrine at the summit, there are magnificent views out to sea and across to the peninsula. On the eastern shore of the island is **Senjōjiki** or '1000 Tatami Mats Rock', a large formation of white, level rock.

A map of the island on green paper is provided by the shrine or the ticket window at the Kinkazan ferry pier. It has neither contour lines nor scale and its only use is to demonstrate that there *are* trails and to provide the kanji for various places on the island (this may be useful when you come across one of the weatherbeaten trail markers). Hiking around the island is a great way to find some peace and solitude as some areas are deserted, so be prepared to find a few of the trails almost fully overgrown. The hike around the southern half of the island, up to the summit and then back down to the pier, covers around 16 km, so be sure to stock up on up on food and drink at the dock or at the shrine shop. If you get lost, head downhill towards the sea – there's a dirt road or trail circling the entire island along the shore.

Places to Stay & Eat

The *Koganeyama-jinja Shrine* (☎ 022-545-2264), 15 minutes on foot up the steep hill from the dock, has rooms with two meals for ¥9000 per person. Advance reservations are recommended. You can supplement the meals with food purchased from the shop outside the shrine – careful, the deer can mug the unwary! If you get up before 6 am you may be allowed to attend morning prayers.

About 10 minutes walk south of the ferry pier is the *Minshuku Shiokaze* (☎ 022-545-2244), which has per-person rates of ¥6000, including two meals. You must book in advance, as the owners actually live in Ayukawa and only come out to Kinkazan if they have customers.

Getting There & Away

Ferries depart Ayukawa hourly between 8 am and 3.30 pm. The return ferry departs hourly between 9 am and 4 pm. The trip takes 25 minutes one way and costs ¥880.

A variation in routing is provided by the ferry – a high-speed catamaran – between Kinkazan Island and Onagawa, which is the eastern gateway to the peninsula. There are four daily departures in both directions; the first ferry leaves between 9 and 10 am and the last leaves between 2 and 3 pm (half an hour, ¥1600 one way, ¥3020 return). Some of the ferries have open-air fantail decks, which make for a pleasant ride. Sailings from Kinkazan are timed so that you can catch trains from Onagawa station to Ishinomaki.

ONAGAWA 女川

This fishing town serves as another access point for Kinkazan Island. Onagawa is also the terminus for the JR Ishinomaki line, 30 minutes from Ishinomaki (¥310) where you can either catch a train south-west towards Sendai or west towards Furukawa (a change of train may be necessary, en route, at Kogota).

From the station, walk straight for about 100m, turn right and walk another 200m to the pier. The ferry ticket office is down a side street opposite the pier, little more than a hole in the wall on the right-hand side, next to the Sunkus convenience store.

KESENNUMA 気仙沼

From Onagawa a road winds north along the rugged coastline past the eroded rock formations of **Cape Kamiwari-zaki** (there's a camping ground nearby) and eventually up to Kesennuma and the Karakuwa-hantō Peninsula.

Kesennuma serves as a base to visit the **Karakuwa-hantō Peninsula** and **Ō-shima Island**, which is 30 minutes by boat (¥250) from Kesennuma Port. Ferries leave every 30 to 60 minutes from 7 am to 7 pm. The port, 10 minutes by bus from Kesennuma station, is also worth a morning visit to witness the busy fish market – Kesennuma is the largest fishing town in the prefecture.

At the tip of Karakuwa-hantō Peninsula, one hour by bus from Kesennuma, is **Cape O-saki**, which has a camping ground, a kokuminshukusha, the small Osaki-jinja Shrine, a tourist information office and the

Tsunami Museum (Tsunami Hakubutsukan). The museum demonstrates the horrifying effects of the *tsunami* or tidal wave with simulated earthquakes, films and scary wind effects.

Places to Stay & Eat

Karakuwa Youth Hostel (☎ 0226-32-2490) is on the peninsula and can be reached by bus or boat from Kesennuma in about an hour. Special guest rooms and bicycle rental are also available. Dorm beds cost ¥2800. From Kesennuma station, take a bus for 10 minutes to the Basu-senkyō-annaisho (bus and ferry information centre), where you can catch a bus to Cape O-saki and, after about 40 minutes, get off at the Ezokari stop. The bus and ferry information centre is right near Kesennuma Port, where there are also boats for Kosaba-ko, which stop at a pier about 15 minutes walk from the hostel. Alternatively, take the train to Shishiori Karakuwa station (one stop north of Kesennuma), where there are also buses to Cape O-saki that pass by Ezokari.

The *Kokuminshukusha Karakuwa-sō* (☎ 0226-32-3174) is located at Cape O-saki, one hour by bus from Kesennuma. Per-person rates with two meals (seafood, of course) are ¥6500. The appropriate bus stop is Kokuminshukusha-mae. You can also take a bus (40 minutes) from Shishiori Karakuwa station, on the JR Ōfunato line. Advance reservations are recommended.

Getting There & Away

Kesennuma is reached from Ichinoseki (Iwate-ken) by train on the JR Ōfunato line in about 1¾ hours. It's also possible to get there from Ishinomaki by travelling to Maeyachi on the Ishinomaki line and then changing there to the Kesennuma line to Kesennuma. Total travel time is around 2½ hours, but be prepared for long waits between trains.

NARUKO ONSEN 鳴子温泉

This is a major hot-spring resort in the northwestern corner of Miyagi-ken. The entrance to **Narugo-kyō Gorge** can be reached by a five minute taxi ride from Naruko station, in the direction of Nakayama-daira. It's around three km away, so walking shouldn't be a great strain (follow Route 44 west from the station). From the entrance there is a four km walk along the river valley to Nakayama-daira. From Naruko station, there is a bus service (three to four buses a day) which heads north for 30 minutes to reach more hot springs at **Onikōbe Onsen** which is also a popular ski resort in winter.

There are dozens of ryokan and hotels in the area, most of which are fairly expensive. One of the cheaper options at Naruko Onsen is *Ryokan Eisen* (☎ 0229-83-3007), which has per-person rates starting at ¥6000, including two meals. It's on the opposite side of the river from the railway station. After crossing Naruko-bashi, turn right and head down the road along the river: the ryokan is on the left-hand side. Close to the station, *Ubanoyu* (☎ 0229-83-2314) has rooms from ¥8000, again with two meals. If you're staying for a longer period, they have rooms with kitchens. From the railway station turn left and the ryokan is just past the second street on the left-hand side.

Naruko Onsen is one hour by train from Furukawa on the JR Rikuu-tōsen line.

Iwate-ken 岩手県

HIRAIZUMI

Of the few cultural sights in Tōhoku, Hiraizumi is one that definitely merits a visit.

From 1089 to 1189, three generations of the Fujiwara family created a political and cultural centre in Hiraizumi which was claimed to approach the grandeur and sophistication of Kyoto. This short century of fame and prosperity was brought to an end when the last Fujiwara leader, Fujiwara Yasuhira, held so much wealth and power that he incurred the distrust of Minamoto Yoritomo, who ordered the annihilation of the Fujiwara clan and the destruction of Hiraizumi.

Only a couple of the original temple buildings now remain as the rest have been restored or added to over the centuries.

Iwate-ken

0   20   40 km

--- Prefectural Boundary

Orientation & Information

Hiraizumi is now a small town and orientation is straightforward. Some of the sights in the area, such as Geibikei-kyō Gorge, are best reached by buses leaving from Ichinoseki station: frequent bus services between Ichinoseki and Hiraizumi means this is not a problem.

The tourist information office (☎ 0191-46-2111) is in the waiting room at Hiraizumi station, and while staff don't speak much English, they have English pamphlets and maps on hand and are willing to help you book accommodation. JNTO publishes a leaflet entitled *Sendai, Matsushima & Hiraizumi*, which has a schematic map of Hiraizumi and brief details for sights, access and accommodation.

Chūson-ji Temple 中尊寺

Chūson-ji was originally established in 850, but it was the first lord of the Fujiwara clan who decided in the early 12th century to expand the site into a complex with more than 40 temples and hundreds of residences for priests. A massive fire in 1337 destroyed most of the complex – even so, what you can see now is still most impressive.

The steep approach to the temple follows a long, tree-lined avenue past the Hondō (Main Hall) to an enclosed area with the splendid Konjiki-dō (Golden Hall) and several ancillary buildings.

Golden Hall Built in 1124, the Konjiki-dō is small but packed with gold ornamentation, black lacquerwork and inlaid mother-of-pearl. The centrepiece of the hall is a statue of Amida with attendants. Beneath the three side altars are the mummified remains of three generations of the Fujiwara family. The fourth and last lord of the family, Fujiwara Yasuhira, was beheaded at the order of Minamoto Yoritomo, who further required the severed head to be sent to Kyoto for inspection before returning it for interment next to the coffin of Yasuhira's father.

Admission costs ¥800 – the ticket is also valid for admission to Kyōzō Sutra Treasury and Sankōzō Treasury. It is open daily from 8 am to 5 pm and 8.30 am to 4.30 pm from November to March.

Kyōzō Sutra Treasury Built in 1108, this is the oldest structure in the temple complex. The original collection of more than 5000 sutras was damaged by fire and the remains of the collection have been transferred to the Sankōzō Treasury.

Sankōzō Treasury This building houses temple treasures including the coffins and funeral finery of the Fujiwara clan, scrolls, swords of the Fujiwara clan and images transferred from halls and temples that no longer exist.

Mōtsū-ji Temple 毛越寺
Originally established in 850, this temple once rivalled Chūson-ji in size and fame. All that remains now are foundation stones and the attractive Jōdo (Paradise) Garden which gives a good impression of the luxurious, sophisticated lifestyle of the Heian period. The temple and gardens attract large numbers of visitors for Jōgyōdō Hatsuka-yasai, a performance of ancient dances, on 20 January, and for the Iris Festival, which is held from late June to mid-July, when the irises bloom.

Admission to the garden costs ¥500 and it is open from 8.30 am to 5 pm, closing 30 minutes earlier from December to March. Those staying at the youth hostel in the grounds do not have to pay for admission.

Takadachi Gikei-dō Hall 高館義経堂
This is a small memorial honouring Minamoto Yoshitsune, a member of the powerful Minamoto family, who grew up with and trained under the Fujiwara clan. Yoshitsune left Hiraizumi to fight side by side with his brother Yoritomo in their battles against the rival Taira family. But soon after, the two brothers had a serious falling out, and Yoshitsune fled to seek shelter in Hiraizumi. The third Fujiwara leader resisted Yoritomo's decrees to have his brother killed, but the fourth, Yasuhira, turned on Yoshitsune. At Takadachi, Yoshitsune was attacked. Seeing no way out, he killed his family and then himself to escape the shame of capture and execution. For performing his dirty work, Minamoto Yoritomo rewarded Yasuhira by killing him and attacking Hiraizumi, ending the Fujiwara reign.

Admission to the hall is ¥200 and it is open daily from 8.30 am to 5 pm. It is located at the top of a small hill which has fine views of the Kitakami River and the fields and hills beyond.

Takkoku-no-Iwaya Cave 達谷窟
A few km south-west of Mōtsū-ji Temple is a temple built in a cave and dedicated to Bishamonten, the Buddhist guardian deity of warriors. The present structure is a reproduction dating from 1961.

The cave is open from 8 am to 5 pm but closes half an hour earlier from November to March. Admission costs ¥200. The cave can be reached in 10 minutes by taxi (¥1500) or you can cycle if you like.

Genbikei-kyō Gorge 巌美渓
This small gorge can easily be explored on foot and you can see where the river has carved elaborate shapes out of the rocks. Buses leave frequently from the No 9 bus

Hiraizumi

```
0    0.5    1 km
```

To Morioka
To Sendai

Koromo River
Kitakami River
Tōhoku Expressway
Tōhoku Honsen Line
Hiraizumi

1	Kyōzō Sutra Treasury 経蔵
2	Golden Hall 金色堂
3	Sankōzō Treasury 讃こう蔵
4	Chūon-ji Temple 中尊寺
5	Takadachi Gikei-dō Hall 高館義経堂
6	Minshuku Yoshitsune-sō 民宿義経荘
7	Hiraizumi Folklore Museum 平泉郷土館
8	Mōtsū-ji Temple 毛越寺
9	Mōtsū Youth Hostel 毛越寺ユースホステル
10	Asadaya Ryokan 朝田屋旅館

Geibikei-kyō Gorge 猊鼻渓

This is a much more impressive gorge than Genbikei-kyō. The best way to reach it is to take a 40 minute bus ride (¥610) from Ichinoseki station to the Geibikei-kyō Iriguchi stop, which is the entrance to the gorge – buses leave once an hour from 7 am to 6.30 pm. Or you can take the train to Geibikei station, on the JR Ōfunato line (30 minutes from Ichinoseki).

Between April and November, there are flat-bottomed boats with singing boatmen ferrying their passengers up and down the river between the sheer cliffs of the gorge. The trip takes 1½ hours and costs ¥1300. Boats depart hourly between 8.30 am and 4 pm.

Special Events

The Spring Fujiwara Festival, held from 1 to 5 May, features a costume procession, folk dances and performances of nō. A similar Autumn Fujiwara Festival takes place from 1 to 3 November. See the Mōtsū-ji Temple section for the two festivals held there each year.

Places to Stay

Mōtsū-ji Youth Hostel (☎ 0191-46-2331) is part of Mōtsū-ji Temple and a pleasantly peaceful place to stay – guests are not charged admission to the gardens. The temple is eight minutes on foot from Hiraizumi station. Beds are ¥2700.

About 15 minutes north of the station, near Takadachi Gikei-dō Hall, is *Minshuku Yoshitsune-sō* (☎ 0191-46-4355), a quiet little place with rooms for ¥6500 per person with two meals. Rates without meals are ¥4000. From here it's only about five minutes to the entrance of Chūson-ji Temple. If you want accommodation right next to the railway station, there's *Asadaya Ryokan* (☎ 0191-46-2316), where a room and two meals costs ¥8500 per person.

Getting There & Away

To reach Hiraizumi from Sendai, take a JR Tōhoku shinkansen to Ichinoseki (35 minutes), then the bus which goes via Hiraizumi station to Chūson-ji Temple (26

stop at Ichinoseki station. The ride takes around 20 minutes and costs ¥480. Get off at the Genbikei bus stop.

minutes, ¥340). You can also take a JR Tōhoku Honsen line train from Sendai to Hiraizumi station, but a change of trains is usually necessary at Ichinoseki and the trip takes about two hours.

Morioka to Ichinoseki on the JR Tōhoku shinkansen line takes 43 minutes. Trains between Ichinoseki and Morioka on the JR Tōhoku Honsen line are less frequent and take about 1¾ hours.

Getting Around

Buses run from Ichinoseki station via Hiraizumi station to Chūson-ji Temple every 20 or 30 minutes from 7 am to around 8 pm. The ride from Hiraizumi station to the temple takes 10 minutes and costs ¥140. On foot it's about 20 minutes: take the road east of the railroad tracks as it's much quieter. From the station, Mōtsū-ji Temple is an easy 10 minute walk. Bicycle rental is available outside the station at ¥500 for two hours and ¥200 for every additional hour. The office is on the right side as you exit the station and is open from 8 am to 5 pm.

TŌNO 遠野

Tōno excited attention at the beginning of this century when a collection of regional folk tales were compiled by Kunio Yanagida and then published under the title *Tōno Monogatari*. During the '70s, this work was translated into English by Robert Morse under the title *The Legends of Tōno* – it should still be available in specialist foreign-language bookshops like Kinokuniya or Maruzen in Tokyo. The tales cover a racy collection of topics from supernatural beings and weird occurrences to the strange ways of the rustic folk in traditional Japan.

The present city of Tōno was formed out of a merger of eight villages in the '50s and is not uniformly interesting – just a few sights scattered around the more appealing rural fringes. The region still has some examples of the local style of farmhouse, known as *magariya*, where farmfolk and their prized horses lived under one roof – but in different sections.

Information

The tourist information office in Morioka has details about Tōno. The Tōno tourist information office (☎ 0198-62-3030) is outside JR Tōno station. The staff can provide an English brochure entitled *Come & See Traditional Japan in Tōno*, which has full details of transport, accommodation and sights. It also includes an accurate map for cycling routes on a scale of 1:70,000. Bicycle rental is available at this office and also at the youth hostel.

Once you've picked up your brochure and decided on your mode of transport, you might want to see the first two sights in the centre of town and then head for the more appealing sights on the rural fringes – such as the **Water Mill** (Suisha), which still functions, about 10 km north-east of Tōno station.

Tōno Municipal Museum 遠野市立博物館

The 3rd and 4th floors of the building house the museum. There are exhibits of folklore and traditional life and a variety of audio-visual and visual presentations of the legends of Tōno. The museum is about 500m south of the station. Admission costs ¥300; a combined ticket for the nearby Tōno Folk Village is discounted to ¥500. The museum is open daily from 9 am to 5 pm, closed on the last day of every month and, from November to March, closed Monday as well.

Tōno Folk Village 遠野昔話村

This 'village', a couple of minutes on foot from the museum, consists of a restored ryokan, an exhibition hall for folk art and items connected with the local legends. A couple of souvenir shops sell local crafts. Admission to the village costs ¥300; a combined ticket for the nearby Tōno Municipal Museum is discounted to ¥500. Opening hours are the same as for the Tōno Municipal Museum.

Fukusen-ji Temple 福泉寺

This temple lies north-east of Tōno station, about 30 minutes by bicycle. Founded in 1912, its major claim to fame is the wooden Fukusen-ji Kannon statue – 17m high – which is claimed to be the tallest of its type

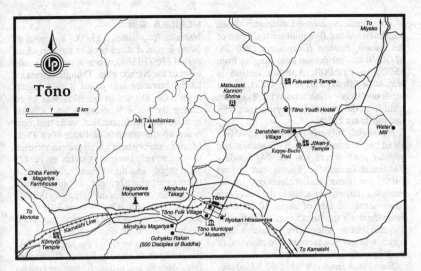

Tōno

0   1   2 km

Mt Takashimizu

To Miyako

Matsuzaki Kannon Shrine

Fukusen-ji Temple

Tōno Youth Hostel

Denshōen Folk Village

Jōken-ji Temple

Kappa-Buchi Pool

Water Mill

Chiba Family Magariya Farmhouse

Haguroiwa Monuments

Minshuku Takagi

Tōno

To Morioka

Kamaishi Line

Minshuku Magariya

Tōno Folk Village

Gohyaku Rakan (500 Disciples of Buddha)

Tōno Municipal Museum

Ryokan Hirasawaya

Kōmyō-ji Temple

To Kamaishi

in Japan. Admission costs ¥300. If you're not cycling, take a bus bound for Sakanoshita and get off at Fusenji (¥370). There are around eight to nine departures daily.

Jōken-ji Temple & Kappa-Buchi Pool 常堅寺・カッパ淵

Jōken-ji is about two km south of Fukusen-ji. Outside the temple is a distinctive lion statue; inside the temple is a famous image which some believe will cure their illness if they rub the part on its body which corresponds to the part where their own body ailment is.

Behind the temple is a stream and the Kappa-Buchi Pool. *Kappa* are considered to be mischievous, mythical creatures but legend has it that the kappa in this pool once put out a fire in the temple. The lion statue was erected as a gesture of thanks to honour the kappa. See the Folklore & Gods section in the Facts about the Country chapter for more details about kappa.

Also in this vicinity is **Denshōen**, a small folk village where you can see an old magariya farmhouse, a water wheel, a wooden kura (storehouse) and various traditional farming implements and exhibits. Admission is ¥200 and it's open from 9 am to 4.30 pm.

There are around four buses servicing Jōken-ji from Tōno station: the ride takes 15 minutes (¥290) and the appropriate stop is Denshōen.

Gohyaku Rakan 五百羅漢

On a wooded hillside, about three km southwest of Tōno station, are the Gohyaku Rakan (500 Disciples of Buddha). These rock carvings were fashioned by a priest to console the spirits of those who died in a disastrous famine in 1754.

Chiba Family Magariya Farmhouse 千葉家曲り家農家

Just over 10 km west of Tōno station is this magariya which has been restored to give an impression of the traditional lifestyle of a wealthy farming family of the 18th century. The farmhouse is open from 8 am to 5 pm and admission costs ¥300. Unless you want to fork out several thousand yen for the taxi ride, you'll probably have to cycle here as there's not much in the way of bus service.

Places to Stay & Eat

The tourist information office can help with booking accommodation – there are a couple

NORTHERN HONSHŪ

of hotels and ryokan and at least a dozen minshuku. About five minutes walk east of the station, *Ryokan Hirasawaya* (☎ 0198-62-3060) has per-person rates ranging from ¥5000 to ¥12,000. Another option is *Minshuku Takaki* (☎ 0198-62-4273), a fairly small two-storey affair around three minutes walk from the station. Per-person rates with two meals are ¥6500.

Minshuku Magariya (☎ 0198-62-4564), about two km south-west of the station, is a popular place where you can stay inside a traditional farmhouse. Prices start around ¥9800 per person and include two meals. From the station, take a bus to the bus centre (Basu-senta), a ride of about 10 minutes. From there it's another 15 minutes on foot to the minshuku. Alternatively, take a taxi, which will get you there in five minutes, or walk in around 30 minutes.

Tōno Youth Hostel (☎ 0198-62-8736) provides a base for cycling or walking around the area. From Tōno station, take a bus bound for Sakanoshita and get off at the Nitagai stop (about 12 minutes). From there it's 10 minutes on foot to the hostel. Bicycle rental is available at the hostel, and a bed for the night is ¥3000.

Getting There & Away

Train On the JR Kamaishi line, it takes an hour to get from Tōno to Hanamaki (which is on the JR Tōhoku line) and an hour to Shin-Hanamaki (which is on the Tōhoku shinkansen line).

Bus There are two buses daily from Morioka to Kamaishi that go via Tōno. Buses leave from the No 8 bus stop at Morioka station, take two hours to Tōno, and cost ¥1890.

Getting Around

The sights in Tōno can't be adequately covered on foot and the bus services can be inconvenient. The best method is either to take a taxi or, even better, rent a bicycle for the day at the tourist information office. The cycling course map in the tourist brochure is accurate and detailed in its coverage of three different routes.

MORIOKA 盛岡

Morioka (population 235,000) is capital of Iwate-ken, and dates back to the early Edo period (1600-1868), when it was the castle town of the Nambu clan. Though Morioka's tourist literature still paints it as a 'castle town', the fortress in question was razed during the Meiji Restoration, and all that remains are the foundation walls that now make up the grounds of Iwate-kōen Park. Morioka simply isn't a high priority destination. Genuinely interesting sights are in very short supply, and the tourism bureau has had to resort to hyping bridges, old buildings and even a cherry tree that has sprung up through a rock. That said, it's a pleasant little place, with riverside pathways and a few nice shops scattered about, so don't panic if you find yourself having to spend the night here. As the terminus of the JR Tōhoku shinkansen line, Morioka is also a useful staging post for visiting the northern part of Tōhoku, and there are plenty of accommodation options around the city.

Orientation & Information

The Kita Tōhoku tourist information counter (☎ 0196-25-2090) is inside the Train Square coffee shop at the south exit of Morioka station on the 2nd floor. There should be at least one English speaker on hand, and there is a good supply of information material. It's open from 8.30 am to 7.30 pm.

The Iwate International Plaza (☎ 0196-54-8900), about 15 minutes walk south-east of the station, has an information counter with English-speaking staff who can help answer questions, though the centre is aimed more at long-term residents. The centre is open 10 am to 9 pm Tuesday to Friday, and 10 am to 5 pm on weekends. It is closed on Monday.

The city centre is east of the station, on the other side of the Kitakami-gawa River. Ō-dōri, which heads from this point through Iwate-kōen Park, is the main shopping street. From the station, it only takes around an hour to stroll around town and get a feel for the place.

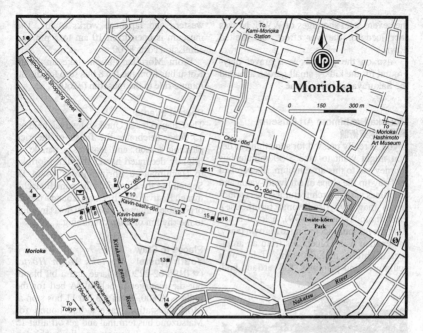

Morioka

PLACES TO STAY
3 Morioka New City
   Hotel
   盛岡ニューシティー
   ホテル
4 Hotel Metropolitan
   Morioka
   ホテル
   メトロポリタン盛岡
6 Morioka City Hotel
   盛岡シティーホテル
8 Hotel Rich
   ホテルリッチ盛岡
9 Takahashi Ryokan
   高橋旅館

13 Ryokan Kumagai
   熊谷旅館
15 Hotel Carina
   ホテルカリーナ
16 Hotel New Carina
   ホテルニュー
   カリーナ

PLACES TO EAT
7 Koiwai Regley
10 Chinese Restaurant
   中国飯店
12 Molton Curry House
   カレーハウス
   モルトン

OTHER
1 Nambu Antique
   Design Prints
   小野染彩所
2 Kōgensha Craft Shop
   光原社
5 Post Office
   郵便局
11 Doutor Coffee
14 Iwate International
   Plaza
   岩手県立国際交流
   プラザ
17 Iwate Bank
   岩手銀行

NORTHERN HONSHŪ

Iwate-kōen Park 岩手公園

This park, in the centre of town, is where Morioka-jō Castle once stood. Today there's nothing left but the moss-clad walls. At the

highest point of the park you'll find a large, ungainly granite block that used to support a large steel sculpture of one of the Nambu clan lords on horseback. However, during the severe steel shortages of WWII, he was sacrificed for the war effort, and melted down.

Also on the grounds is a gravel playground for the kids, a small garden area and the Sakurayama-jinja Shrine.

Morioka Hashimoto Art Museum
盛岡橋本美術館

If you're really pressed for something to do, you might want to take a 30 minute bus journey out to this art museum. It's perched halfway up the slope of Mt Iwate-yama and combines various architectural styles including a magariya (traditional farmhouse). Hashimoto Yaoji (1903-79), a local artist, built the museum according to his own fancy, rather than using blueprints from an architect. Exhibits include some of his own sculptures and paintings, folk art and both

The Chagu-Chagu Umakko festival in Morioka celebrates the end of the rice-planting season.

western and Japanese works of art. The museum is open from 10 am to 5 pm and admission costs ¥700.

From Morioka station, take an Iwate Kōtsū bus from the No 8 bus stop for the 30 minute ride to the museum (¥260).

Special Events
The Chagu-Chagu Umakko festival, held on 15 June, celebrates the finish of the rice planting season, and features a parade of brightly decorated horses through Morioka to Hachiman-gū Shrine. From 14 to 16 September the city holds the annual Hachimangū Festival, which centres around a parade of portable shrines and colourful floats moving to the rhythm of *taiko* drumming.

Places to Stay
Youth Hostel *Morioka Youth Hostel* (☎ 0196-62-2220) is large and a bit bland, but the manager is helpful. A bed for the night is ¥2800. From the No 11 bus stop at Morioka station, take a bus bound for Matsuzono bus terminal and get off after 15 minutes at the Takamatsu-no-ike-guchi stop (¥210). It's a three minute walk from here to the hostel. There are three to four buses an hour from 7 am to 7 pm.

Ryokan The *Ryokan Kumagai* (☎ 0196-51-3020), a member of the Japanese Inn Group, is in a nice building about 15 minutes on foot from the railway station. Singles/doubles start from ¥4500/8000; triples from ¥10,000.

Hotels Morioka has no shortage of business hotels. Affordable options close to the station include the *Morioka City Hotel* (☎ 0196-51-3030), which has singles from ¥6100 and doubles from ¥7800, and the *Morioka New City Hotel* (☎ 0196-54-5161), with singles/doubles at ¥6100/7800.

The *Hotel Rich* (☎ 0196-25-2611) is right next to the Kaiun-bashi Bridge just a couple of minutes from the station. Singles start from ¥6500 and doubles from ¥13,000. For affordable doubles, try the *Hotel Carina* (☎ 0196-24-1111), which has singles for

¥7000 and doubles/twins for ¥8000/10,000. The *Hotel New Carina*, across the street, has slightly higher rates, but newer rooms as well. Next door to the station is the *Hotel Metropolitan Morioka* (☎ 0196-25-1211), a considerably classier place with singles from ¥7500 to ¥8500 and twins from ¥15,500 to ¥20,500.

Places to Eat

Ō-dōri (and the side streets running off it) is the best place to look for a meal. The section by Iwate-kōen Park has a number of restaurants and noodle shops with reasonable prices, but you'll have to make do without an English menu. A few more yakitori and robatayaki places are tucked down the side streets. Near the Kitakami-gawa River end of Ō-dōri is a Chinese restaurant, though the food is actually a mix of Chinese, Korean and Japanese dishes. It's basic, hearty fare, with set meals from ¥650 to ¥1000 and dishes from ¥500 to ¥800. It even has an English sign, and is imaginatively called *Chinese Restaurant*. Down near Kaiunbashi-dōri is a tiny Japanese-style curry place, *Molton Curry House*. There's no English menu, but some of the items are pictured. In any case, if you ask for 'beef curry' or 'chicken curry', that's what you'll get, along with a salad, soup and coffee or ice cream for dessert, all for around ¥800 to ¥900. Other specialities include 'Popeye Curry' (curry with spinach, egg and potato) and 'Indo Curry', a truly fiery blend served with naan bread or saffron rice.

For a good deal on coffee try the awkwardly named *Koiwai Regley*, a bakery/restaurant right near the station. A two-cup pot of quite good coffee is ¥380. Food is mainly western-style and uses ingredients from the renowned Koiwai farm, which is outside the city near Mt Iwate-san. Lunch sets are pretty good value and range from ¥700 to ¥1000.

Finally, beer drinkers may be interested in a chance to taste a locally made Ginga Kōgen Beer, at the time of writing Tōhoku's only microbrew. The brewery has its own bar, conveniently located in the railway station, on the ground floor near the north exit. The beer is quite good and at ¥480 for a 300 ml glass, the prices are comparable to what you'd pay in most bars for run-of-the-mill brands like Asahi or Kirin.

Things to Buy

The Morioka region is famous for the production of Nanbu Tetsubin (Nanbu Ironware), which includes items such as tea kettles, flower pots and wind chimes. One of the best places to look for these items is the New Nanbu Craft Studio, located across the Nakatsu River. It's in a small traditional building (the English sign out front says Workshop Kamasada), and has affordable gift items alongside kettles and cookware that cost as much as a small car.

For hand-woven and dyed fabrics, check out Nanbu Antique Design Prints, which has an impressive selection: even the emperor himself came by to do some window shopping. Nearby is the attractive Zaimoku-cho, a former street of lumber shops that now houses numerous craft shops. Among these, Kōgensha wins the prize for atmosphere: in addition to tastefully displayed pottery, lacquerware and fabrics, this little complex houses a coffee shop and a garden looking out over the river: even avowed shopping-haters could enjoy a stop at this place.

Getting There & Away

Train From Morioka to Tokyo (Ueno) on the JR Tōhoku shinkansen line, the fastest trains take a mere 2¾ hours. If you are heading further north to Aomori by train, you should change to the JR Tōhoku line for the 2½ hour trip.

Lake Tazawa-ko, just west of Morioka, is reached via the JR Tazawa-ko line (40 minutes by limited express). To visit the Hachimantai area, north-west of Morioka, take the JR Hanawa line to either Obuke station or Hachimantai station, then continue by bus. There are also buses from Morioka station direct to Hachimantai Chōjō (see below). To reach Miyako, on the eastern coast of Tōhoku, take the JR Yamada line.

Bus The bus terminal at the railway station is well organised and has abundant English signs and a directory showing which buses leave from what stop, as well as journey times and fares. Popular destinations served include Mt Iwate-san, Miyako, Ryūsen-dō Cave and Towado-ko and Tazawa-ko lakes. See the following sections on these places for details.

Getting Around

The city is small enough to comfortably navigate on foot. Buses for local destinations leave from the station. There are also departures from the bus terminal, close to Iwate-kōen Park, but the facilities at the railway station are far better suited to travellers.

MT IWATE-SAN

The volcanic peak of Iwate-san (2039m) is a very dominating landmark north-west of Morioka, and a popular destination for hikers. There are several different routes to the top, all of which take around eight to nine hours round trip. The Kita Tōhoku tourist information counter can supply you with photocopies of an English-language chapter on hiking in Iwate that details the different approaches. One popular option is to take a bus from Morioka station north-west to **Amihari Onsen** (65 minutes, ¥1120), which is the start of one of the main trails to the summit. Buses leave five times daily from the No 10 bus stop. This allows you to use the chair lift at Amihari ski area, which saves some 1300m of vertical ascent. There is no shortage of accommodation at Amihari Onsen, if you want to soak your weary legs in a soothing spa at the end of the day.

MIYAKO 宮古

Miyako is a small city in the centre of the Rikuchū-kaigan National Park, a 180 km stretch of interesting rock formations and seascapes along the eastern coastline of Tōhoku from Kesennuma in the south to Kuji in the north.

Information

Miyako tourist information office (☎ 0193-62-3574) is on your right as you exit the station. The staff speak a little English and can provide maps and train timetables. Both the Miyako and Morioka tourist offices can provide you with an English-language pamphlet on Miyako that includes a fairly useful map of the town.

Jōdoga-hama Beach 浄土ヶ浜

This is a very attractive beach with white sand, dividing rock formations and a series of walking trails through the forests of pine trees on the steep slopes leading down to the beach.

From the concrete souvenir centre opposite the bus stop, a path leads down to the dock for excursion boats. A 40 minute boat trip (¥1200) to a few rock formations should be enough to introduce you to the loudspeakers and gluttonous seagulls.

You can skip the boat excursion and escape some of the crowds by leaving the tarmac road beyond the bus stop and climbing up trails into the hills where there are good views across the beach.

There are buses every 30 minutes to one hour connecting the beach with Miyako station (15 minutes, ¥170).

There are also daily excursion boats running up the coast from Jōdoga-hama to various fishing villages like Masaki and Ōtanabe. Though this might be a fun way to get up the coast, as an outing it's a bit expensive (¥2000 to ¥3000) and the loudspeakers and seagull feeders usually ensure that it's not very relaxing either.

Places to Stay

Suehiro-kan Youth Hostel (☎ 0193-62-1555) is just three minutes on foot from Miyako station. Walk straight out of the station exit and continue 30m to the intersection with the main street, turn right and walk about 20m to the hostel, which is on the right-hand side of the street – there's a youth hostel sign next to the door. A bed for the night is ¥2800.

Further down the main street is *Kumayasu Ryokan* (☎ 0193-62-3545), which has a reputation for serving outstanding seafood. Per-person costs with two meals range from

¥8240 to ¥15,000. If you don't mind a longer walk (15 minutes from the station), *Sawadaya Chūōkan* (☎ 0193-62-2968) is more affordable at ¥6000 per person including two meals. The exterior of this drab two-storey structure wins no points for style, but the rooms are comfortable enough.

Getting There & Away

Train Morioka is linked with Miyako on the JR Yamada line (2¼ hours), which continues south from Miyako down the coast for another 75 minutes to Kamaishi.

The JR Kita-Rias line runs north from Miyako along the coastline to Kuji in about 1¾ hours – the scenery is mostly obscured by tunnels.

Bus Buses between Morioka and Miyako stations leave once to twice an hour from 6 am to 8 pm (2¼ hours, ¥1950). There are several bus departures daily linking Miyako with Kamaishi via the southern coastline of Rikuchū-kaigan National Park.

RYŪSEN-DŌ CAVE   龍泉洞

Close to Iwaizumi (north-west of Miyako) is Ryūsen-dō Cave, one of the three largest stalactite caves in Japan. It contains a huge underground lake (said to be the one of the clearest in the world) which is 120m deep. Admission to the cave is ¥820, which also includes entry to the adjacent Ryūsen Shindō, in which a number of stone tools and earthenware were found, some of which are on display.

From either Morioka or Miyako, take the JR Yamada line to Moichi station, where you change to the Iwaizumi line for the 55 minute ride to Iwaizumi station. From the station it's a 10 minute bus trip to the cave (¥190). Buses leave every one to two hours. There are four to six buses daily from the No 1 bus stop at Morioka station direct to the cave (2½ hours, ¥2540). From Miyako, take a train on the Sanriku Tetsudo line 30 minutes north to Omoto, where you can change to a bus for the 50 minute ride to the cave (¥580).

Aomori-ken   青森県

HACHINOHE   八戸

Travellers to Hokkaidō can take the ferry from Hachinohe-kō Port to either Tomakomai or Muroran. The ferry for Tomakomai leaves twice daily at 1 and 10 pm. The trip takes about nine hours and 1st/2nd class tickets are ¥7800/3900.

The ferry for Muroran departs twice daily at 5.45 am and 5.30 pm. The trip takes about eight hours and the fares are the same as for the Tomakomai ferries.

Hachinohe-kō Port is around 20 minutes by bus from Hon-Hachinohe station on the JR Tōhoku Honsen line. Hachinohe is 70 minutes from Morioka by limited express (¥3690), and one hour from Aomori (¥2820). Local trains to Aomori take 1¾ hours and cost ¥1390.

SHIMOKITA-HANTŌ PENINSULA
下北半島

Looking like a giant axe poised at the top of Honshū, this peninsula is still fairly isolated, and has long stretches of sparsely inhabited coastline and remote mountain valleys. The main draw is **Mt Osore-zan**, a barren volcanic mountain that has for centuries been considered one of Japan's most sacred places. **Entsū-ji Temple**, founded on the slopes of Osore-zan in the 9th century, is a destination for those seeking to commune with the dead, especially parents who have lost their children to the great beyond. With its craggy, sulphur-strewn rocks, hissing vapour, and ravens swarming about, it's an appropriate setting. Even the name, Osore, means fear or dread. Entry to the mountain via the temple costs ¥500, and opening hours are 6 am to 6 pm.

On the western edge of Shimokita-hantō is scenic **Hotokegaura**, a three-km stretch of coastline dotted with 100m tall cliffs. Water and wind have carved delicate patterns into the rock faces. Locals claim that some of these natural statues bear a resemblance to the Buddha. Boats running from Wakinosawa

NORTHERN HONSHŪ

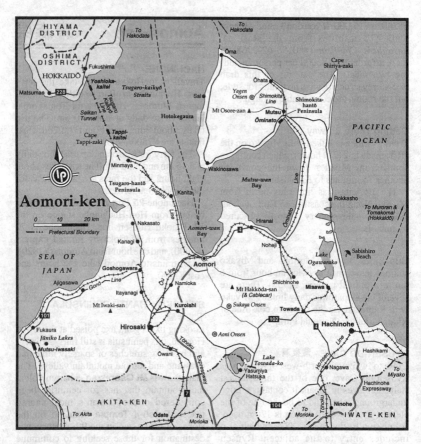

at the southern side of the peninsula cruise past Hotokegaura on their way to the fishing village of Sai. See the Getting Around section below for more information. There are also several hot-spring resorts and numerous little fishing villages dotting the peninsula.

Orientation & Information

Access to Shimokita-hantō is via the town of Noheji, at the base of the peninsula. The main transport and accommodation hub on Shimokita-hantō is Mutsu. However, Mutsu is kind of a dump so you may want to explore

some of the other options available (see Places to Stay below). Confusingly, the railway station for Mutsu is Tanabu station, which is on the privately owned Shimokita-Kotsu line.

North of Mutsu is Ōhata, where you can get buses to Yagen Onsen, a hot-spring resort area up in the hills. To the east is Cape Shiriya-zaki, to the west is Ōma, the northernmost point on Honshū. At the bottom tip of the 'axe blade' of the peninsula is Wakinosawa, which is linked to Aomori by ferry in 90 minutes.

The information office inside Mutsu bus

terminal can help with transport information and leaflets in Japanese. The tourist information offices in Aomori can supply you with some English information, but not much that's of any practical use.

Special Events

Osore-zan Taisai, a festival held from 20 to 24 July, attracts huge crowds of visitors keen to consult *itako* or 'mediums'. The itako are blind women who act for the visitors and make contact with dead family members. A similar, but smaller, festival is held from 9 to 11 October.

Places to Stay & Eat

The staff at the information office inside Mutsu bus terminal don't speak English, but they will do their best to help you to book some accommodation. There are plenty of minshuku and ryokan in the drab confines of Mutsu. To find them, walk either north or south from the Tanabu station for about 10 minutes.

Of the two youth hostels on the peninsula, *Wakinosawa Youth Hostel* (☎ 0175-44-2341) is well placed for an excursion along Hotokegaura, the spectacular western coast of the peninsula, and for the ferry connection to Aomori. It's about 10 minutes on foot from the Wakinosawa bus stop, and 15 minutes from the ferry pier. Bicycle rental is available. Beds cost ¥2800.

Shiriyazaki Youth Hostel (☎ 0175-47-2941) is in a more remote location, about four km south of Cape Shiriya-zaki. Beds are ¥2800, and the hostel is only open from 1 April to 31 October. From Mutsu, there are five to six buses a day to the bus stop at Shiriya (50 minutes, ¥1240). From the bus stop it's a five minute walk to the hostel.

Other accommodation is spread out around the peninsula. Just north of Ōhata station, *Minshuku Matsunoki* (☎ 0175-34-2467) has per-person rates of ¥6000, including two meals. On the northern coast, between Ōhata and Ōma, is Shimofuro Onsen, where you will find *Minshuku Maruyama* (☎ 0175-36-2217), a pleasant place facing the sea, also with rates of ¥6000.

It's five minutes on foot from the Shimofuro Onsen-mae bus stop.

More up-market accommodation is available at Yagen Onsen, mainly in the form of places like the *Hotel New Yagen* (☎ 0175-34-3311), which charges ¥9000 to ¥30,000 per person with two meals.

Getting There & Away

Train The JR Ōminato line connects Noheji with Shimokita, where it intersects with the Shimokita-Kotsu line, before terminating at Ōminato. There are four direct trains daily between Aomori and Shimokita station (1¾ hours), where you can change to a Shimokita-Kotsu train for the seven minute ride to Tanabu station (Mutsu). The entire journey costs ¥1290. If you don't catch a direct train, you'll need to change at Noheji. The Shimokita line continues north past Tanabu, terminating at Ōhata.

Bus There are buses every one to two hours between Aomori and Mutsu bus terminal via Noheji (2¾ hours, ¥2470). Buses leave Aomori from the bus terminal next to the Aspam Building. From Noheji the trip takes 1½ hours and costs ¥1420.

Boat Ferries link Aomori with Wakinosawa in 40 minutes (¥2500). There are two departures daily, in the morning and afternoon. The ferries then continue past Wakinosawa up the coast of the peninsula to Sai. Boats sail from the Aomori harbour passenger ferry terminal, just north of Aomori station.

From Ōma, there are ferries to Hakodate on Hokkaidō. There are two to three sailings a day, depending on the season. The trip takes just over 1½ hours and the cheapest passenger fare is ¥1000. Between April and October there are also ferries between Ōhata and Muroran on Hokkaidō. The trip takes four hours and 1st/2nd class tickets cost ¥2800/1400.

Getting Around

You can catch buses to nearly all destinations on the peninsula from the Mutsu bus terminal. Some buses also pass by Tanabu station before heading out of Mutsu. Buses to Mt Osore-zan leave every 60 to 90 minutes (one hour, ¥730). This service only operates from April to November. There are eight buses a day that run along the northern shore, passing Ōhata, Shimofuro Onsen and Ōma before terminating at Sai (2¼ hours, ¥2220). The ride from Mutsu to Ōma takes 1¾ hours and costs ¥1840. The ride to Shimofuro Onsen from Mutsu takes one hour (¥1060).

To get to Yagen Onsen, first take a bus or train to Ōhata, from where there are two to five buses making the 30 minute ride (¥630) to the hot-spring resort.

JR operates eight buses a day between Mutsu and Wakinosawa (1½ hours, ¥1760), where you can then take a ferry to Aomori. Ferries coming from Aomori stop in Wakinosawa before continuing up to Sai via the Hotokegaura coastline. There are two departures to Sai daily, at 10.35 am and 4.10 pm. The trip to Sai takes 1½ hours and costs ¥2600.

AOMORI 青森

Aomori (population 288,000) is the prefectural capital and an important centre for shipping and fishing. It was bombed heavily during WWII and has since been completely rebuilt – as a result, its architecture is not all that appealing. Although the city is showing signs of prosperity, it's somewhat out of Japan's economic mainstream, and thus retains a sleepy, fishing town quality.

Aomori is a useful transport hub for visits to Lake Towada-ko, the scenic region around Mt Hakkōda-san, and the Shimokita-hantō and Tsugaru-hantō peninsulas.

Information

There's a tourist information office, where limited English is spoken, near the south exit of the railway station. They cannot help with making accommodation bookings, but can at least provide lists of ryokan and hotels in town, as well as some good English-language maps and pamphlets. There is also tourist information counter on the ground floor of the distinctive Aspam Building, but

aside from offering a few scattered leaflets, it's not good for much.

Things to See

The prime reason for a visit to Aomori would be the Nebuta Matsuri Festival (see Special Events later). Those interested in folkcrafts could visit the **Aomori Prefectural Folklore Museum**, which also displays archaeological exhibits. This museum is a 10 minute bus ride from the station. From the No 4 bus stop, take a bus bound for Aoyogi Keiyu Tōbu Eigyosho, and get off at Honcho-go-chome (¥160).

The **Munakata Shikō Memorial Museum** houses a collection of wood-block prints, paintings and calligraphy by Munakata Shikō, an Aomori native whose art and wit won him fame both in Japan and abroad. The museum, designed in consultation with Munakata just prior to his death, has only around 30 paintings and prints, in line with his request that visitors not face sensory overload. To reach the museum, take a bus from JR Aomori station bound for Tsutsui and get off after about 15 minutes at the Chūō Shimin Sentā-mae stop (¥190). From the bus stop, walk back to the intersection, turn left and walk around 200m. The museum is on the left.

Special Events

The Nebuta Matsuri, held in Aomori from 2 to 7 August, is renowned throughout Tōhoku and Japan for its parades of colossal illuminated floats accompanied by thousands of dancers. There are a number of stories as to how the festival originated. The most dramatic is the tale of Sakanoue Tamuramaro, a 7th century general who was sent by the imperial palace to quash a rebellion by the native Ezo tribe. The crafty Tamuramaro is said to have used giant lanterns, along with drums and flutes, to lure the unsuspecting Ezo from their redoubts, after which they were swiftly subdued.

Aomori can be a difficult place to book accommodation even in off-peak periods, so if you're planning to come to see Nebuta you'll need to reserve a room well in advance, or plan to commute from a nearby town like Hirosaki. Hotel rates are often higher during festival time.

Places to Stay

Aomori is a popular place to break one's journey between Tokyo and Hokkaidō, and

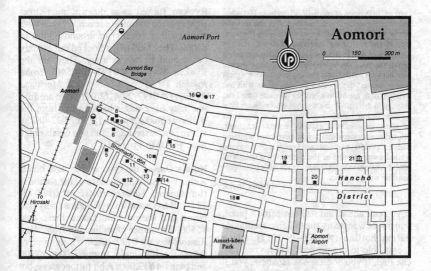

PLACES TO STAY

5 Hotel New
   Aomori-kan
   ホテルニュー青森館

6 Aomori Grand Hotel
   青森グランドホテル

7 Iroha Ryokan
   いろは旅館

8 Ryokan Nanjō
   旅館南條

9 Maruhisa Ryokan
   まるひさ旅館

10 Hotel Sunroute
   ホテルサンルート
   青森

11 Aomori Sunrise Hotel
   青森サンライズ
   ホテル

12 Aomori Kokusai Hotel
   青森国際ホテル

15 Hotel JAL City
   Aomori
   ホテル JAL シティ
   青森

18 Aomori Dai-Ichi Hotel
   青森第一ホテル

19 Takko Ryokan
   田子旅館

20 Hotel Shibata
   ホテルシバタ

PLACES TO EAT

4 Fish & Fresh Food
   Market
   市場団地

13 Kakigen
   柿源

OTHER

1 Aomori Harbour
   Passenger Ferry
   Terminal
   青森港旅客船
   ターミナル

2 JR Bus Station
   JR バスのりば

3 Aomori City Buses
   青森市バスノリバ

14 Caffeol Coffee Shop

16 Buses to Mutsu
   下北交通バスのりば

17 Aspam Building

21 Aomori Prefectural
   Folklore Museum
   青森県立郷土館

NORTHERN HONSHŪ

in the peak seasons it's not that uncommon for *all* accommodation in town to be booked out. Book ahead to be sure.

> I arrived in Aomori at around 7.30 pm from Hakodate and started ringing around the ryokan ... and then the hotels. An hour and a half later I was ringing Hirosaki, then Morioka. Nothing. It seemed as if every hotel in Tōhoku was full. In the end I slept with the tramps on one of the bus stop benches across from the station. Not that I got much sleep. Passing drunks took a great deal of interest in the down-and-out gaijin, with one trying to drag me off to a brothel. The one time I did manage to drift off, I was woken up 10 minutes later by a deaf-mute toothless old granny who, by means of some impressively expressive body language, offered me services that might have been tempting had she been 50 years younger. I politely declined and whiled away the rest of the night with a delightful hobbit-like old man who regaled me with incomprehensible *rakugo* stories.
>
> **Chris Taylor**

If you call ahead and still can't find a place, you might want to try the toll-free accommodation hotline (☎ 0120-39-1717), which seems able to dig up beds that no one else can find. If you don't speak Japanese, you'll need to enlist the help of someone who can. Should you arrive in town with nothing booked, hit the streets: there are lots of hotels and a determined search in person can often yield success where phone queries have failed.

Ryokan Tucked away down a quiet street right near the station are several ryokan with costs (without meals) of around ¥3500 to ¥4000. They tend to get booked out quickly but should be worth a try. They are the *Ryokan Nanjō* (☎ 0177-22-6540), *Iroha Ryokan* (☎ 0177-22-8689) and *Maruhisa Ryokan* (☎ 0177-22-4166). If these are full, you may have better luck further from the station at *Takko Ryokan* (☎ 0177-22-4825), where per-person rates with two meals range from ¥6000 to ¥10,000.

Hotels One of the cheaper business hotels within easy striking distance of the station is the *Aomori Sunrise Hotel* (☎ 0177-73-7211). It has mainly single rooms (only five twins and four doubles), and these cost ¥5500. The rather glum looking *Hotel New Aomori-kan* (☎ 0177-22-2865), in front of the station, has singles from ¥6300 to ¥7300 and twins at ¥12,000. A bit further away, but also cheaper, is the *Hotel Shibata* (☎ 0177-75-1451) where singles/twins are ¥5700/10,400.

The *Aomori Dai-Ichi Hotel* (☎ 0177-75-4311) is also a bit further from the station and has singles from ¥5800 to ¥6500 and twins from ¥11,000 to ¥12,000. Slightly more up-market is the *Aomori Kokusai Hotel* (☎ 0177-22-4321), where singles/twins cost from ¥7000/13,000. Probably the nicest place in town is the new *Hotel JAL City Aomori* (☎ 0177-32-2580) where singles start at ¥8200 and twins at ¥14,000. At the time of writing the hotel also had doubles at ¥11,000, very good value for money. It might be worth checking to see if this price is still available.

Places to Eat
Shinmachi-dōri, the main shopping street, runs east from the station and has some good sushi shops, seafood restaurants and a couple of fast-food places. One spot worth visiting is *Kakigen*, which specialises in scallops, an

Dressed in *hanten*, a short workmen's coat

Aomori speciality. There's no English menu, but you can ask for hotate yaki teishoku (grilled scallop set dinner) or hotate sashi teishoku (raw scallop set). There's also the mouth-watering hotate bata yaki teishoku (scallops grilled with butter). All cost ¥1200, and there are other seafood dishes available as well.

Seafood lovers may also want to venture into the fish and fresh food market, just south of the station, where there are good deals to be had on seafood, rāmen and set lunches, as long as you don't mind hunting around the seafood stalls.

Getting There & Away

Air JAS operates frequent flights to Nagoya, Osaka, Tokyo and Sapporo. There are also international flights to Seoul (Korean Airlines) and Khabarovsk (Aeroflot). From Aomori station, buses leave once to twice an hour for the 35 minute ride (¥550) to Aomori airport, just south of the city.

Train Aomori is connected with Hokkaidō by the JR Tsugaru Kaikyō line which runs via the Seikan Tunnel beneath the Tsugaru Kaikyō Straits to Hakodate in two hours (¥6050). But you might as well take one of the rapid trains (*kaisoku*), which do the trip in 2½ hours for the cost of a local train (¥3090). Taking a rapid train also gives you the option of trying the unique Seikan Tunnel tour. For details see the introductory Getting There & Away section of the Hokkaidō chapter.

The JR Tōhoku Honsen line links Aomori with Morioka in just over two hours by limited express (¥5850). From Morioka, you can zip back to Tokyo in 3½ hours on the shinkansen.

The JR Ōu line runs from Aomori via Hirosaki to Akita, then continues down to Yamagata and Fukushima. From Akita, the JR Uetsu Honsen line runs to Niigata.

Bus JR operates a nightly bus to Tokyo (9½ hours, ¥10,000), and several buses daily to Morioka (three hours, ¥3100) and Sendai (five hours, ¥5600). Buses leave from the JR

bus terminal, near the north end of Aomori station.

Between mid-April and mid-November JR runs between four and seven buses a day from Aomori to Lake Towada-ko (three hours, ¥2830). One hour out of Aomori, the bus reaches Hakkōda cablecar (ropeway), then continues through a string of hot-spring hamlets to the lake.

For a visit to Mt Osore-zan (Shimokita-hantō Peninsula), you can take a direct bus from Aomori (Aspam Building) via Noheji to the Mutsu bus terminal in 2¾ hours.

Boat There's a hydrofoil service linking Aomori with Hakodate on Hokkaidō in 1¾ hours. There are one to two sailings a day from the Aomori harbour passenger ferry terminal, a 10 minute walk north of the station. The one-way fare during the week is ¥5040, but it jumps to ¥6300 on weekends.

Those with more time than money might opt for the regular ferry service, which takes 3¾ hours but costs only ¥1400 for a 2nd class ticket (1st class is ¥3500). As the ferries also haul vehicles, there are frequent departures, at least nine sailings daily. There are two ferries a day to Muroran (Hokkaidō). The trip takes seven hours and tickets cost ¥3400/6800 for 2nd/1st class. The ferry pier, on the western side of the city, is a 10-minute taxi ride from Aomori station. There is no bus service to the pier.

For a ferry connection to Shimokita-hantō Peninsula, you could take the one hour trip (¥2500) between Aomori and Wakinosawa. Ferries leave from the Aomori harbour passenger ferry terminal.

MT HAKKŌDA-SAN 八甲田山

Just south of Aomori is a scenic region around Hakkōda-san that is popular with hikers, hot-spring enthusiasts and skiers.

A bus service from Aomori reaches Hakkōda cablecar in one hour and then continues to Lake Towada-ko. The cablecar whisks you up to the summit of Mt Tamoyachi-yama in nine minutes (¥1650 return). From there you can follow a network of hiking trails. Some trails in this area are covered in *Hiking in Japan* by Paul Hunt. The tourist information offices in Aomori have copies of a pamphlet that has a 'North Hakkoda Mountain Range Ski Route Map' on the reverse side. The map has English place names, contour lines and trails. One particularly nice route starts from the cablecar, scales the three peaks of Akakura-dake, Ido-dake and Ōdake, and then winds its way down to Sukayu Onsen, which is about 10 minutes by bus beyond the cablecar station, in the direction of Lake Towada-ko. The hike is eight km in length and can be done in a leisurely four hours.

With the cablecar to speed things along, Hakkōda-san can easily be done as a day trip from Aomori. There is accommodation near the bottom of the cablecar station, though none in the budget category. The *Yamagoya Hakkodasanso* (☎ 0177-28-1512) is a rustic place with per-person rates, including two meals, of ¥10,000. If you make the hike to Sukayu Onsen and want to spend the night, the *Kokuminshukusha Sukayu* (☎ 0177-38-6400) is right at the end of the trail and has per-person rates with two meals of around ¥6500.

To get to the cablecar station, take a JR bus from Aomori station bound for Lake Towada-ko and get off at the Hakkoda Ropeway-eki bus stop (¥1050). Buses run four to seven times daily between mid-April and mid-November. In winter, buses to Sukayu Onsen run past the ropeway stop, then continue another 10 minutes to the Sukayu terminus.

TSUGARU-HANTŌ PENINSULA
津軽半島

The tip of this peninsula above Aomori can be visited by taking the JR Tsugaru line from Aomori station to Minmaya. The trip takes between 1¾ and two hours (¥1090). You'll almost certainly need to change trains at Kanita. From Minmaya, buses run six times daily between 6.30 am and 5 pm along the coastline to **Cape Tappi-zaki** (35 minutes, ¥660), which has superb views across the Tsugaru Straits. Two of the buses continue

10 minutes further down to the road to the Tappi Lighthouse.

Having come all the way out here, you may want to at least stay the night. If so you can try *Minshuku Masukawa-sō* (☎ 0174-37-2520), which is a two minute walk from Minmaya station. Per-person rates with two meals (fresh seafood dinners) are ¥6000.

HIROSAKI 弘前

Founded in the 17th century, the castle town of Hirosaki (population 174,000) developed into one of the leading cultural centres in Tōhoku. With the exception of its dreary modern centre – which can be avoided – it has retained much of its original architecture, including a large portion of its castle area, temple districts and even a few buildings from the Meiji era. Hirosaki is recommended for its pleasing atmosphere and a collection of sights that can be covered in one day at an easy walking pace.

Orientation & Information

The main station is JR Hirosaki station. All bus connections for destinations outside Hirosaki are made at Hirosaki bus terminal, a concrete monster of a building just a few minutes up the street from the JR station. Hirosaki is compact in size and easily covered on foot. To give yourself a quick start – and avoid the drab town centre – take a bus or a taxi from the station for a 15 minute ride to Neputa-mura, where you can start your circuit of the castle and the other sights.

The information office (☎ 0172-32-0524) is on your right as you exit the station. Be sure to pick up the English brochure entitled *Hirosaki City: Castle Town of Cherry Blossoms and Apples*, which lists sights, festivals, accommodation and has an excellent map. Staff at the office don't speak English, but will try to help you book accommodation. Just near the southern gate of Hirosaki-kōen Park is the Hirosaki Sightseeing Information Center (☎ 0172-37-5501), which has maps and leaflets for Hirosaki and other destinations in Aomori. Both informa-

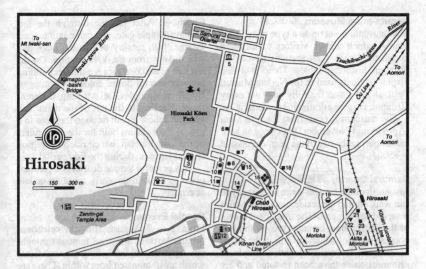

Hirosaki

PLACES TO STAY		PLACES TO EAT		8	Tanakaya
2	Hirosaki Youth Hostel 弘前ユースホステル	14	Kagi-no-Hana かぎのはな		Lacquerware Store 田中屋
6	Ishiba Ryokan 石場旅館	20	Aisaka 笹宝寿し	9	Aomori Ginkō Kinenkan Memorial Hall
7	Hirosaki Grand Hotel 弘前グランドホテル	22	Yamauta Live House やまうたライブ		青森銀行記念館
10	Edogawa Ryokan 江戸川旅館		ハウス	12	Saishō-in Temple 最勝院
11	Kobori Ryokan 小堀旅館			13	Gojū-no-tō Pagoda 塔
18	Tsukasa Residential Hotel ツカサレジデン シャルホテル		OTHER	15	Biru-tei Pub びいる亭
		1	Chōshō-ji Temple 長勝寺	16	Nakasan Department Store
21	City Hirosaki Hotel シティ弘前ホテル	3	Hirosaki Sightseeing Information Centre 弘前観光会		中三デパート
23	Business Hotel Shinjuku ビジネスホテル新宿	4	Hirosaki-jō Castle 弘前城	17	Gloria Jean's
		5	Neputa-mura Museum 津軽藩ねぶた村	19	Hirosaki Bus Terminal 弘前バスターミナル

tion offices are open daily from 9 am to 6 pm, 9 am to 5 pm in winter.

And, just in case you were wondering, the neon-coloured building that looks to be sporting a gigantic colander is the Nakasan department store. Fits right in, doesn't it?

Neputa-mura Museum ねぷた村

This museum is set up as a type of 'village' (*mura*) which allows visitors to follow a circuit through several sections devoted to different historical topics. There is a fine display of floats used in the Neputa Matsuri Festival and a man dutifully pops out every 10 minutes to give a drumming demonstration.

The museum is open from 9 am to 5 pm (April to mid-November) but closes an hour earlier during the rest of the year. Admission is ¥500.

Samurai Quarter 津軽藩武家屋敷

Just north of the Neputa-mura Museum, you can walk around the residential district once reserved for samurai. The traditional layout of the district now contains mostly modern houses (some of which are still in the hands of samurai descendants), but a couple of samurai houses have been restored and are periodically opened to the public.

Hirosaki-jō Castle 弘前城

Construction of the castle was completed in 1611, but it was burnt down in 1627 after being struck by lightning. One of the castle's corner towers was rebuilt in 1810 and now houses a small museum of samurai weaponry and garments. Admission is ¥200 and the museum is open from 9 am to 5 pm from April to late November. The castle grounds have been turned into a splendid park that attracts huge crowds for *hanami* (flower viewing) celebrations during the April cherry blossom season. There are more than 5000 sakura trees in the park. The ramparts across from the castle tower offer nice views of Mt Iwaki-san.

Saishō-in Temple 最勝院

About a 15 minute walk south of the castle, this temple is worth a visit to see the Gojū-no-tō Pagoda, a splendid five-storey example constructed in 1667.

Chōshō-ji Temple 長勝寺

About 20 minutes on foot, west of the pagoda, you come to an avenue – flanked by temples on either side – which leads to Chōshō-ji. After passing through the impressive temple gate, you can continue past a large, 14th century bell to the main hall which dates from the 17th century. On the left side of the courtyard is a smaller building housing several dozen colourful statues of Buddhist disciples, all striking different poses. Keeping to the left of the main hall, you can follow a path through the trees to a row of mausoleums built for the early rulers of the Tsugaru clan, which ruled the region around Hirosaki during the Edo period.

This peaceful temple district is a pleasant place to walk in the early morning or late afternoon.

Special Events

From 1 to 7 August, Hirosaki celebrates Neputa Matsuri, a festival famous throughout Japan for its beautifully painted floats which are illuminated from within. These are paraded in the evenings on different routes through the town to the accompaniment of flutes and drums. Like its more rowdy counterpart held in Aomori, this festival attracts thousands of visitors – book accommodation well in advance if you plan to visit at this time.

Places to Stay

Youth Hostel The *Hirosaki Youth Hostel* (☎ 0172-33-7066) is in a good location for the sights, and while a bit drab, is set back from the street so it's fairly quiet. From Hirosaki station, take a bus from bus stop No 3 and get off after about 15 minutes at the Daigaku-byōin stop (¥170). If you're taking a bus from the bus terminal, buses leave from stop Nos 9 and 10. Walk straight up the street for five minutes and the hostel is on your left down an alley: look out for a small white sign with green letters and a red arrow. Nightly costs are ¥2800.

Ryokan There are several options not far from Hirosaki-kōen Park, a convenient location for taking in the sights. *Kobori Ryokan* (☎ 0172-32-5111) is in a large traditional-style building, and has per-person rates starting at ¥8000, including two meals. Just around the corner is *Edogawa Ryokan*

(☎ 0172-32-4092), which is in a less appealing three-storey modern structure, but the rooms are comfortable. Per-person rates with two meals start at ¥8500. A few blocks north, *Ishiba Ryokan* (☎ 0172-32-9118) is a bit more up-market, with prices starting at ¥9000.

Hotels One of the best economy options in town is the *Tsukasa Residential Hotel* (☎ 0172-37-0111). This place used to be a 'weekly mansion', playing host only to longer-term business guests. Now it also acts as a standard hotel, and rooms are clean, fairly spacious and comfortable. Singles are ¥5000 to ¥6000 and twins/doubles are ¥8000 to ¥10,000, good value for money.

There are a few business hotels in the station area, although this is not a particularly good part of town to be based in. The *City Hirosaki Hotel* (☎ 0172-37-0109), right in front of the station, is the most expensive of the lot, with singles from ¥7500 and twins from ¥15,000. Smaller and slightly cheaper is the *Business Hotel Shinjuku* (☎ 0172-32-8484) which has 19 singles at ¥6500 and just three doubles at ¥11,000.

The *Hirosaki Grand Hotel* (☎ 0172-32-1515) is more centrally located and has singles from ¥5500 to ¥6500 and twins from ¥10,000 to ¥14,000.

Places to Eat

The two best areas to go hunting for a meal are around the station and up and down Kajimachi, the town's diminutive drinking and dining district. A good place to sample the local cuisine (mountain vegetables, river fish and so on) is *Kagi-no-Hana*, which has good teishoku (set meals) from ¥1600. It's hidden on the bottom floor of a black concrete and steel building. Look for the vertical sign that says 'East Buil2'; the entrance is on the left-hand side.

Those not easily cowed by chefs with attitude might venture into *Aisaka*, a little sushi place not far from the station. The owner/chef can be rather surly, and doesn't have time for menus, orders for out-of-season seafood, and other modern violations of sushi tradition. Your best bet is to just go in and order a sushi set: ask for *nigiri-zushi*. Prices range from ¥1000 to ¥2000 – not all that cheap but it is excellent sushi.

For a less painful ordering process head to the 7th floor of the *Nakasan Department Store* (the colander building) where there are several places with decent food, reasonable prices and lots of point-and-choose food displays and picture menus.

Just across the river from Nakasan is *Gloria Jean's*, a relaxing spot to have a good, though expensive, cup of coffee. Cyberspace fans might want to try their Internet deal, which gives you one hour of online time (64,000 bps!) for ¥1500, which includes a cup of coffee.

Entertainment

If you want to combine food and entertainment then why not splurge on a visit to *Yamauta Live House* (☎ 0172-36-1835), a large plaster and wood building just five minutes on foot from the station. The place is run by a family which serves the drinks and food, then picks up three-stringed musical instruments, known as *tsugaru jamisen*, and launches into local music. There is an extensive menu. If you order one of the teishoku and a couple of beers, you can expect to pay around ¥2500. The restaurant is open from 5 to 11 pm, and there are usually two sets of music a night. It's closed one night a week, but the night is not fixed, so you may want to call ahead.

If you're just looking for a beer, *Biru-tei Pub* on Kajimachi has more than 240 brands to choose from, more than a dozen of them on tap. Going through the lot would use up the family fortune for several generations, but a few cold ones shouldn't set you back more than ¥2000, including table charge.

Getting There & Away

Train Hirosaki is connected with Aomori on the JR Ōu line (35 minutes by limited express, ¥1360), or 50 minutes by local train (¥640). On the same line, trains south from Hirosaki to Akita take about two hours by limited express (¥3810).

Bus The bus terminal is about five minutes walk from Hirosaki station, on the ground floor of the Ito Yokado department store car park. Between mid-April and early November, there are between three and six buses a day from Hirosaki bus terminal to Lake Towada-ko. The trip takes 2¼ hours and costs ¥2310.

Morioka is linked with Hirosaki by an hourly JR bus service which takes 2¼ hours (¥2880). From mid-April to late October, there are two buses a day from the Hirosaki bus terminal to Mt Iwaki-san (75 minutes, ¥1500).

AONI ONSEN 青荷温泉
The bus from Hirosaki to Lake Towada-ko climbs through the mountains and passes a series of remote hot-spring hamlets. One is Aoni Onsen (☎ 0172-54-8588), a rustic group of ryokan that prefer oil lamps to electricity and serve wholesome mountain food. To get there you'll have to get off the bus at Aoni Onsen Iriguchi then walk about an hour up the track. Advance reservations are necessary and you should expect to pay around ¥6500 per person which includes two meals.

Buses leave Hirosaki bus terminal for Towada three to six times a day, depending on the season. The fare for the 70 minute ride is ¥1140. From Aoni Onsen Iriguchi it's about one hour by bus to Lake Towada-ko.

MT IWAKI-SAN 岩木山
Soaring above Hirosaki is the sacred volcano of Iwaki-san, which is a popular climb for both pilgrims and hikers.

From mid-April to late October, there are two buses a day (usually in the morning) from the Hirosaki bus terminal to Iwaki-san. The trip takes 75 minutes (¥1500) to Hachigōme at the foot of the cablecar to the summit. After a seven minute ride (¥380, one way) on the cablecar, it takes another 45 minutes to climb to the summit (1625m). This route is the shortest and easiest – the youth hostel in Hirosaki has maps showing other climbing routes and times.

Akita-ken

LAKE TOWADA-KO 十和田湖
This is a large crater lake with impressive scenery. It is rated by Japanese as the top tourist spot in Tōhoku which means you can expect lots of company!

Nenoguchi, a small tourist outpost on the eastern shore of the lake, marks the entrance to the **Oirase Valley**. The 3½ hour hike up this valley to Ishigedō (refreshment centre and bus stop) is the most enjoyable thing to do around the lake. You can, of course, do the hike in the opposite direction. The path winds through thick deciduous forest following the Oirase-gawa River, with its mossy boulders, plunging waterfalls and tumbling tracts of white water. Early morning might be the best time to do the hike, particularly if you visit during the peak viewing season in autumn.

The other main tourist spot on the lake, **Yasumiya**, is an accommodation centre and has numerous boat tours of the lake, which are not really worth the time or money. One practical route is the one hour cruise between Yasumiya and Nenoguchi. Boats leave once to twice an hour between 8 am and 4 pm and the one-way fare is ¥1300. The boat cruises only run from mid-April to early November.

During the same period there are frequent buses which link the valley with Aomori and Hirosaki.

Places to Stay
Hakubutsukan Youth Hostel (☎ 0176-75-2002) is tucked away *inside* the Grand Hotel, a few hundred metres from the pier at Yasumiya. Beds are ¥3000, which is a bit steep, but nothing compared to what the hotel guests are shelling out.

In Hatsuka, about five minutes by bus west of Yasumiya, the *Towada Youth Hostel* (☎ 0176-75-2603) is one of the cheapest options in the area, with beds for ¥2200. Bicycle rental is also available. The hostel is only open from 1 May to 31 October. Buses to the JR station at Towada Minami run past

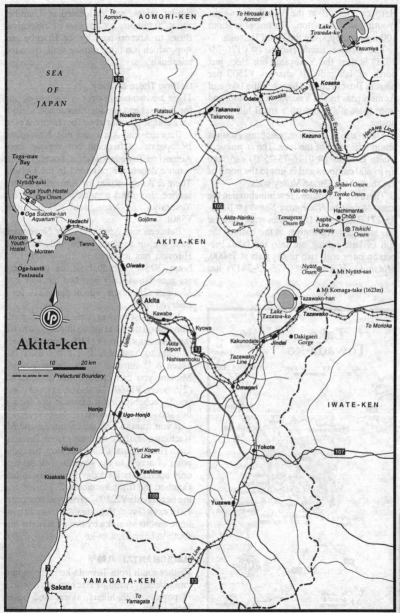

Hatsuka. Get off at the Yusu-hosteru-mae (youth hostel) bus stop. The hostel is about 100m south, opposite the Hotel Hatsuka.

The *Oirase Youth Hostel* (☎ 0176-74-2031) is near the Yakeyama bus stop, just north of Ishigedo. It charges ¥2500 per person. Buses running between the lake and Aomori pass by the Yakeyama bus stop, and from there it's 200m up a small hill to the hostel.

There are at least four camping grounds around the edge of the lake. The *Nenoguchi Camp Ground* (☎ 0176-75-2503) can take up to 800 campers and is just to the north of the start of the Oirase Valley walk.

There are also quite a few minshuku in the area. *Minshuku Himemasu Sansō* (☎ 0176-75-2717) is around 15 minutes walk from the bus station in Yasumiya, at the base of the spit of land jutting out into the lake. Per-person rates with two meals start at ¥6000. *Minshuku Hōkasō* (☎ 0176-75-2417) has

similar prices, and is located in Utarube, about 20 minutes by bus east of Yasumiya. Buses to Aomori pass by the Utarube bus stop, which is a three minute walk from the minshuku.

Getting There & Away

There are two bus centres in Yasumiya, one for JR buses and one for other services. Both are a couple of minutes on foot from the pier.

Between mid-April and mid-November, JR operates a frequent bus service from Aomori to Towada-ko (three hours, ¥2830) – more details are provided in the Getting There & Away section for Aomori. This bus service also offers a quick way to get from Yasumiya and Nenoguchi (27 minutes, ¥580).

Between mid-April and early November, there are up to three buses daily between Hirosaki bus terminal to Towada-ko (2¼ hours, ¥2310). Throughout the year, there are nine buses daily between the lake and Morioka (2¼ hours, ¥2380 plus ¥210 for a reserved seat).

The nearest railway station is at Towada Minami, on the JR Hanawa line. Buses make the one hour trip (¥1110) from Towada Minami to Yasumiya five times daily between 8.45 am and 4 pm. From Towada Minami you can catch trains to Morioka (2½ hours, ¥1760). However, in most cases you'll probably find it easier to opt for the bus services listed above.

If you want to visit the region around Mt Hachimantai, there are buses from Towada-ko to Hachimantai Chōjō bus stop, the main point of access to the summit. This service only operates twice a day from May to late October; the trip takes about 2½ hours and the ticket costs ¥2210 – a reserved seat costs ¥210 extra. From Hachimantai you can continue east to Morioka by bus or take the bus south to Lake Tazawa-ko.

HACHIMANTAI 八幡平

Further south from Towada-ko is the mountain plateau region of Hachimantai, which is popular with hikers, skiers and onsen enthusiasts.

The Aspite Line Highway, open from late April to November, runs east to west across the plateau. Transport connections revolve around Hachimantai Chōjō, the main access point and car park for the summit. Although the views are nice, the walks around the ponds on the summit only take an hour or so and are rather tame. The hike to Hachimantai peak is around 30 minutes, as is the Onuma walking trail, which takes in several ponds and some marshland. Longer hikes are possible over a couple of days, for example, from nearby **Tōshichi Onsen** to Mt Iwate-san.

West of the summit, the road winds along the Aspite Line Highway past a number of hot-spring resorts before joining Route 341, which leads south to Lake Tazawa-ko and north towards Towada-ko.

The best place to pick up information on Hachimantai is the Kita Tōhoku tourist information counter at the Morioka JR station. Tourist offices in Akita, Tazawa-ko and Towada-ko can supply you with maps and pamphlets, although most of these will only be in Japanese.

Places to Stay & Eat
Yuki-no-Koya (☎ 0186-31-2118) is a member of the Toho network and functions as an alternative youth hostel and mountain lodge – it has been highly recommended by some travellers. Prices start at ¥4500 per person including two excellent meals.

The lodge is located at Shibari Onsen, which is on Route 341, just north of the turn-off for the Aspite Line Highway to Hachimantai. From Hachimantai station on the JR Hanawa line it's a 24 minute bus ride to the Shibari Onsen bus stop: between April and October there are five to six buses running from Hachimantai station to Tamagawa Onsen which pass by Shibari Onsen. Buses running between Towada-ko and Hachimantai also pass by Shibari Onsen.

Those thinking of tackling the hike from Tōshichi Onsen to Iwate-san might want to consider starting (or finishing) their trek at the *Tōshichi Onsen Saiun-sō* (☎ 0195-78-3962), which has per-person rates from ¥10,000 with two meals. It's only open from late April to late October. Frequent buses running from Hachimantai Chōjō to the terminus at Hachimantai Horai-sō pass by Tōshichi Onsen.

Hachimantai Youth Hostel (☎ 0195-78-2031) is east of the summit, 23 minutes by bus to Hachimantai Kankō Hoteru-mae bus stop. If you're coming by bus from Obuke station, the ride to this stop takes about 50 minutes. A bed for the night is ¥2500 (¥2800 from October to April). Guests have access to nearby onsen baths.

Getting There & Away
From Morioka, there are buses which take about two hours (¥1300) to Hachimantai Chōjō bus stop – this service only operates between late April and October. Another option is to take the train on the JR Hanawa line from Morioka to Obuke or Hachimantai stations, then change to the bus service. After stopping at Hachimantai Chōjō, the bus continues to the terminus at Hachimantai Horai-sō. Buses leave from the No 4 bus stop at Morioka station, and there are seven to eight departures between 7.30 am and 1.30 pm.

For bus connections with Towada-ko, see the earlier Getting There & Away section for that lake.

A bus service connects Hachimantai via Tamagawa Onsen with Lake Tazawa-ko in about 2½ hours (¥1960). There are three departures daily between late April and late October: service is suspended during the rest of the year.

TAMAGAWA ONSEN 玉川温泉
This hot-spring resort, 41 km north of Lake Tazawa-ko on Route 341, has a variety of hot springs, baths and treatments. A paved path leads up the ravine through the steam and bubbling vents to open-air baths. Serious soakers who'd like to organise a stay have but one option, the *Tamagawa Onsen Ryokan* (☎ 0187-49-2352), which has rates ranging from ¥7000 to ¥15,000 per person, including two meals.

Buses from Tazawa-ko station run to Tamagawa Onsen three to four times daily between mid-April and late October. The ride takes 1½ hours and costs ¥1390. Most buses continue onward to Hachimantai Chōjō (one hour).

LAKE TAZAWA-KO AREA 田沢湖周辺

Tazawa-ko is the deepest lake in Japan and a popular place for Japanese tourists keen on watersports. The foreign traveller may find more enjoyment by using the lake as a staging point for hikes along the trails of Mt Komaga-take and perhaps combining these with a stay in one of the isolated hot-spring ryokan scattered around Nyūtō Onsen.

Orientation & Information

The main access point to the area is Tazawa-ko station, which is 15 minutes by bus to the east side of the lake, known as Tazawa-kohan. The tourist information office is directly opposite the main exit of the station and next to the bus terminal. You can get maps and leaflets and the staff will help with accommodation bookings. There is also a helpful bilingual sign listing current bus departure times for destinations such as Nyūtō Onsen and Hachimantai. If you're planning on doing any hiking in the area, there's one map of the area that has trails clearly marked. The only English is on the cover: *Lake Sports Country Tazawako*. But you can still use it to match up the kanji against trail markers, and the staff at the tourist centre may be willing to pencil in the English names of some of the peaks.

The bus station at Tazawa-kohan also has an information office where you pick up maps and pamphlets. Even if they don't want to stay, prospective hikers may want to visit the nearby youth hostel to request a look at the plastic folder with its detailed hiking maps.

Things to Do

The lake offers boat excursions, swimming beaches, row boats and a road around the lake shore which can be followed by bus, car or on a bicycle rented at Tazawa-kohan. If you're interested in hiking around **Mt Komaga-take** (1623m) there are several different approaches.

The easiest way to start would be to take a bus from Lake Tazawa-ko for the 50 minute ride (¥790) to Komagatake-Hachigōme (Komagatake Eighth Station). From there it takes about an hour to climb up to the summit area where you can choose trails circling several peaks. One trail leads across to the peak of Nyūtō-san from where you can hike down to **Nyūtō Onsen**. This is an all-day trek, so make sure you are properly prepared. The bus service operates from June to October only – during July and August there are departures once to twice an hour and during the rest of the time the service only operates on Saturday, Sunday and national holidays. From Tazawako station take a bus to Kōgen Onsen, where you can change for buses to Komagatake-Hachigōme. If the bus service isn't running, buses running up to Nyūtō Onsen stop at Komagatake Tozan-guchi. From here it's a seven km walk to the Eighth Station.

Hot-spring enthusiasts will want to try some of the places around Nyūtō Onsen which is 40 minutes by bus from Lake Tazawa-ko. From these ryokan you can also climb up to Nyūtō-san (1477m), a round trip of eight to 10 km, depending on where you start out.

Places to Stay

The staff in the information office at Tazawako station don't speak much English, but will try to help with accommodation bookings.

Tazawako Youth Hostel (☎ 0187-43-1281) is about five minutes on foot from the bus station at Tazawa-kohan. If you're arriving by bus, ask to get off at the Kōen Iriguchi bus stop which is virtually opposite the hostel's front door. A bed for the night costs ¥2800, and bicycle rental is available. Close by, in the south of Tazawa-kohan, is the *Tazawa-ko Camping Ground*, which is open from 1 May to 31 October, and charges ¥400 per person. Tent rental ranges from ¥800 to ¥1100 and spartan cabins are available for ¥2000 to ¥3000.

To really get away from it all, you can stay in one of the hot-spring ryokan around Nyūtō

Onsen: most of them are at least one km on foot from the nearest bus stop. There are half a dozen to choose from. *Tsurunoyu Onsen Ryokan* (☎ 0187-46-2814), *Kuroyu Onsen Ryokan* (☎ 0187-46-2214), and *Magoroku Onsen Ryokan* (☎ 0187-46-2244) are rustic, traditional places with a variety of open-air baths. Prices for accommodation and two meals start around ¥8500. Some of the ryokan close from early November until late April, and all are quite popular, so it would be best to call in advance. From 1 April to 30 November, there are around six buses daily between Tazawa-ko station and Nyūtō Onsen (55 minutes, ¥730). To get to Tsurunoyu, get off at Tsurunoyu Onsen kyūdō-guchi: from there it's a 20 minute walk down a wooded trail to the ryokan. The Kuroyu and Magoroku Onsen ryokans are about one km from the Nyūtō Onsen terminus. The trailhead is across the road from the bus stop.

Getting There & Away

Train Local trains take about one hour between Morioka and Tazawa-ko station on the JR Tazawa-ko line. Kakunodate, a short distance south-west of Lake Tazawa-ko, is reached in 20 minutes by local train on the same line. Connections to Akita take about 1½ hours and usually require a change to the JR Ōu line at Omagari. A new shinkansen line between Akita and Morioka was set to open in March 1997, which will offer travellers a considerably quicker trip, though for a substantially higher fare.

Bus Between late April and late October a bus service connects Lake Tazawa-ko via Tamagawa Onsen with Hachimantai in about 2½ hours (¥1960). There are three to four buses daily. From Hachimantai you can catch a bus north to Lake Towada-ko or east to Morioka.

From Tazawako station there are buses approximately once every 1½ hours to Kakunodate (25 minutes, ¥480). Departures before 3 pm continue on to Akita (two hours, ¥1600).

KAKUNODATE 角館

This small town with its well-preserved samurai district and avenues of cherry trees is well worth a visit. You can cover the main sights in a few hours or devote a lazy day to browsing around town. There are half a dozen samurai houses open to the public along a couple of the main streets north-west of Kakunodate station – 15 minutes on foot. The **cherry tree promenade** beside the river is a major tourist attraction when the trees bloom in April.

Just outside Kakunodate, about 25 minutes away by bus or train (Jindai station), is **Dakigaeri Gorge** with a pleasant four km nature trail.

Orientation & Information

JNTO publishes a leaflet entitled *Kakunodate & Lake Tazawa-ko, Akita & Oga Peninsula*, which has a map of Kakunodate and brief details of the sights.

The tourist information office (☎ 0187-54-2995) is on your right as you leave the station, in a small building that also houses a pleasant coffee shop. The friendly staff can help with reservations and provide a detailed English-language map with lists of sights, restaurants and accommodation. The office may be moved after the new Akita shinkansen line begins service (scheduled for March 1997): at the time of writing staff weren't sure what would happen, but you should still have little problem finding it.

The town is small and easily covered on foot in three or four hours. Bicycle rental is available at a small shop near the station. Rates range from ¥200 to ¥300 per hour depending on the condition of the bicycle. The shop has a sign advertising ¥100-per-hour bicycles, but these somehow seem to always be rented out.

Kawarada-ke House & Samurai Shiryōkan 河原田家

The interior of the house can be viewed from a path leading through the garden. Next door is the Samurai Shiryōkan, a cramped museum with an interesting assortment of martial equipment. Admission is ¥300 and it's open from 8.30 am to 4.30 pm.

Denshōkan Museum 伝承館

This museum houses exhibits of armour, calligraphy and ceramics and there is also a large section housing tools and products of the cherry-bark craft. In a room to the side an artisan demonstrates the craft.

The museum is open daily from 9 am to 5 pm (April to November) and closes 30 minutes earlier and all day Thursday during the rest of the year. Admission costs ¥300. A discount ticket is available for ¥720 that allows access to the Denshōkan, Ishiguro-ke and the nearby Hirafuku Memorial Art Museum, which displays various folkcrafts from around the region.

Aoyagi-ke House 青柳家

Aoyagi-ke is actually a conglomeration of mini-museums. One focuses on folk art, another exhibits heirlooms from the Aoyagi family and a 'new-fangled gadget' museum displays all the things that seemed so modern in the Meiji era. Admission costs ¥500. It's open from 8.30 am to 5 pm from April to November and 9 am to 4 pm from December to March.

Ishiguro-ke House 石黒家

This is a fine example of a samurai house with a sweeping thatched roof and meticulously laid out gardens. The friendly ladies at the front desk lend foreign visitors a file with English information. The house is open from 9 am to 5 pm and admission costs ¥300. It is closed from 1 December to 15 April.

Special Events

From 7 to 9 September, Kakunodate celebrates the Hikiyama Festival in which participants haul enormous seven-tonne wooden carts or *yama* around, seeking out narrow streets where they can crash into each other.

Places to Stay

The tourist information office (☎ 0187-54-2995) at the station can help with reservations and provide a list of places to stay.

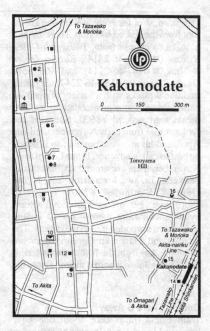

A long-time favourite with foreign visitors is *Minshuku Hyakusui-en* (☎ 0187-55-5715), an old house 15 minutes on foot from the station. Excellent meals are served around an *irori* (open hearth). The owner believes that beer and sake should flow freely and guests are seated next to each other so there's less isolation and more chat. Prices start around ¥7000 per person without meals or from ¥9800 with two meals.

If that's a bit beyond your budget, you can hike up to *Sakura-no-Sato* (☎ 0187-55-5652), a minshuku in a traditional two-storey building set on a quiet street in the northern part of town. Rooms with two meals are a reasonable ¥5700, and the staff at the tourist office can help call ahead to make sure there's room before you start your trek.

The *Ishikawa Ryokan* (☎ 0187-54-2030) is slightly closer to the station and has per-person costs of around ¥9500 with two meals. The only real business hotel in town is the *Kakunodate Plaza Hotel* (☎ 0187-54-2727),

PLACES TO STAY	OTHER	
1 Sakura-no-Sato Minshuku 桜の里	2 Ishiguro-ke House 石黒家	8 Odana-ke House 小田野家
9 Kakunodate Plaza Hotel 角館プラザホテル	3 Aoyagi-ke House 青柳家	10 Post Office 郵便局
11 Minshuku Hyakusui-en 百穂苑	4 Denshōkan Museum 伝承館	13 Fujiki Denshirō Shōten Store 藤木伝四郎商店
12 Ishikawa Ryokan 石川旅館	5 Iwahashi-ke House 岩橋家	15 Rent-a-Cycle
14 Ryokan Yamaya 旅館やまや	6 Matsumoto Samurai House 松本家	16 Bus Station 羽後交通バス ターミナル
	7 Kawarada-ke House 河原田家	

a rather weathered place with singles at ¥4500 and twins at ¥8500. It does, however, boast Kakunodate's only revolving restaurant as well as what must be the town's most garish lobby.

Things to Buy

Kakunodate is renowned for *kabazaiku*, a craft which uses cherry bark to cover household or decorative items. You can see the production process in the Denshōkan Museum and there are numerous shops selling the finished products. The canny merchants of Kakunodate have got just about everything covered with the bark – from cigarette lighters to *geta* (sandals) and even tissue boxes for the lady who has everything in her boudoir! The tea caddies are attractive and it's worth spending a bit more on the genuine article made entirely from wood, rather than buying the cheaper version which has an inner core made from tin. Locals say the best shop in town for high quality kabazaiku is Fujiki Denshirō Shōten, which has its own workshop nearby, though it sells products from other artisans as well.

Getting There & Away

Train Trains on the JR Tazawa-ko line connect Kakunodate with Tazawa-ko station (access to Lake Tazawa-ko) in about 20 minutes and continue to Morioka in about 45 minutes. Connections to Akita take about an hour and usually require a change to the JR Ōu line at Omagari. After April 1997, travellers will also probably be able to use the new shinkansen service linking Akita and Morioka. Fares had not been set at the time of writing, but don't expect any bargains.

Bus The bus station in Kakunodate is north of the railway station, about 10 minutes on foot. There are seven buses daily to Akita between 6 am and 3.30 pm – the trip takes 1½ hours (¥1300). Buses run to Tazawako station in about 30 minutes (¥480). There are six departures daily between 7.30 am and 5.30 pm.

AKITA 秋田

Akita (population 302,000), the prefectural capital, is a large commercial and industrial city. It has few sights of special interest to foreign travellers and is best used as a staging point for visits to Kakunodate, Lake Tazawako or the Oga-hantō Peninsula. The tourist information office at the station provides maps and details of transport and sightseeing.

If you have time to kill, it's just 10 minutes on foot from the station to **Senshū-kōen Park**, which was once the site of Kubota-jō

Akita

1 Osumi-yagura Tower
   御隅櫓
2 Hirano Masakichi Art Museum
   平野政吉美術館
3 Hotel Hawaii Eki-mae
   ホテルハワイ駅前
4 Hotel Metropolitan Akita
   ホテルメトロポリタン秋田
5 Kohama Ryokan
   小浜旅館
6 Hotel Hawaii Shin Honten
   ホテルハワイ新本店
7 Hotel Hawaii Lagoon
   ホテルハワイラグーン
8 Akarengakan Folklore Museum
   赤れんが郷土館

Castle. The park provides the locals with greenery and contains the castle ruins. At the northern end is the **Osumi-yagura Tower**, a reconstruction of one of the eight turrets of Kubota-jō, the top of which offers a nice view of the city. Admission is ¥100 and it's open daily from 9 am to 4.30 pm.

Special Events
From 4 to 7 August, Akita celebrates the Kantō Matsuri, which is one of the most famous festivals in Tōhoku. During the festival, there's a parade with more than 160 men balancing giant poles, hung with illuminated lanterns, on their heads, chins, hips and shoulders. The poles can be 10m long and weigh 60 kg.

Places to Stay
Kohama Ryokan (☎ 0188-32-5739), a member of the Japanese Inn Group, is five minutes on foot from Akita station. Prices for singles/doubles start at ¥4500/8500; triples start from ¥12,750.

Akita is also home to a dull selection of business hotels. For a relatively cheap overnighter close to the station, the *Hotel Hawaii Eki-mae* (☎ 0188-33-1111) has a lot of singles (more than 300 of them) from ¥4000 to ¥5700, twins from ¥5500 to ¥9000, and six doubles for ¥6800. You'll probably need to book ahead for the cheaper rooms. The hotel's brethren, the *Hotel Hawaii Lagoon* (☎ 0188-33-1112) and the *Hotel Hawaii Shin Honten)* (☎ 0188-33-1110), have slightly nicer rooms at slightly higher prices. Don't expect any hula skirts though. The *Hotel Metropolitan Akita* (☎ 0188-31-2222) next door to the station, is one of the better hotels in town, and has singles/twins from ¥7500/15,000.

Places to Eat
The local food specialities include two types of hotpot – kiritanpo (made with rice cakes and chicken) and shottsuru (made from a local fish). Just 15 minutes walk west of the station is *Kawabata-dōri*, the main street for eateries, which is said by tourist brochures to be packed with 'more than 1000' pubs, restaurants and bars. Some of these must be well hidden.

Getting There & Away

Air There are flights between Akita and Fukuoka, Nagoya, Osaka, Sapporo and Tokyo. Akita's airport is well south of the town, 50 minutes by bus (¥870) from JR Akita station.

Train At the time of writing a new shinkansen line to Akita was due to open in March 1997, a source of great excitement for the city's government and residents. The new service will cut travel time between Akita and Tokyo to four hours. The line will run from Morioka via Tazawa-ko and Kakunodate. At the time of writing JR had not yet determined exact travel times and fares. Local service along the JR Tazawa-ko line will continue. Local trains to Kakunodate take around two hours, to Lake Tazawa-ko 2½ hours.

The JR Uetsu line connects Akita with Niigata in four hours. The JR Oga line links Akita with the Oga-hantō Peninsula (Oga station) in about an hour.

Bus A convenient bus service runs from Akita station via Kakunodate to Tazawako station. There are five departures daily between 8.45 am and 4.30 pm. The two hour ride costs ¥1600. There are also buses to Oga Aquarium on the Oga-hantō Peninsula.

OGA-HANTŌ PENINSULA 男鹿半島

This peninsula juts out for about 20 km and is worth visiting to see the contrasts between its rugged coastline and grassy slopes. Most transport to and from the peninsula shuts down between November and late April as do the sights.

The **Oga Suizoku-kan Aquarium** is the largest in northern Japan and has a huge variety of fishy species on display. Admission is ¥950 and it's open from 8.30 am to 4.30 pm, closing at 6 pm in the summer. A 50 minute boat cruise (¥1650) operates along the spectacular coastline between the aquarium and Monzen. There are three to five sailings daily between late April and late October.

At the northern tip of the peninsula, **Cape Nyūdō-zaki** has wide cliff-top lawns, fine sea views and, to complete the picture, a striped lighthouse.

Special Events

A curious festival called Namahage is celebrated here on 31 December. The *namahage* are men dressed as fearsome demons complete with a straw cape over the body, a terrifying mask over the face and carrying a wooden pail and knife. The demons roam around villages and visit houses where there are children to admonish them against idleness. The house owners do their bit to welcome the demons and mollify the threats by giving the namahage rice cakes and sake.

This type of festival is common in northern Japan, but Oga-hantō's version is particularly famous.

Places to Stay & Eat

Monzen Youth Hostel (☎ 0185-27-2823) is part of a temple and a useful base for exploring the peninsula. From Akita, take the train on the JR Oga line to Oga station, then change to a bus to reach the bus terminus at Monzen; from there it's a seven minute walk to the hostel. A bed for the night is ¥3000. Bicycle rental is available.

Oga Youth Hostel (☎ 0185-33-3125) is right next to the sea at Oga Onsen, one of the gateways for visits to the peninsula. A bed for the night is ¥2800. From Akita, take the train on the JR Oga line to Hadachi station; then take a 50 minute bus ride to Oga Onsen and get off at the Oga Grand Hoteru-mae stop – the hostel is 200m down the street, above the seashore. There is also a direct bus which takes just under two hours from Akita station to Oga Onsen.

Right near the Oga Youth Hostel is the *Kokuminshukusha Oga* (☎ 0185-33-3181), a popular 'people's lodge' with per-person rates of ¥6640, including two meals.

Minshuku accommodation is grouped mostly around Toga-wan Bay, just north of the Oga Aquarium. Per-person rates with two meals start at ¥6000. Monzen has the lion's share of Oga-Hantō's ryokan, and prices start at ¥8000 to ¥9000 per person, again with two meals.

Getting There & Away

Frequent trains on the JR Oga line connect Akita with the peninsula in about an hour (¥720). From here, a typical route would involve a bus to Monzen (35 minutes, ¥540), followed by an excursion boat to the Oga Aquarium. There are buses from the aquarium to Oga Onsen (15 minutes, ¥340), at which point you may be able to catch a bus back to Akita (two hours, ¥1040), though there's only one a day. However, there are fairly frequent buses from Oga Onsen to the JR station at Hadachi, where you can catch trains back to Akita. There is also a direct bus daily between Akita and Oga Aquarium. Akita direct bus services only operate from April to late October.

From the Hadachi station, which is one stop before Oga station, you can catch buses to Oga Onsen, Cape Nyūdō-zaki and Oga Aquarium.

Yamagata-ken   山形県

SAKATA 酒田

This large port city (population 100,000) has a couple of interesting sights and is a useful staging point for boat trips on the Mogami-gawa River or an island hop to Tobi-shima Island.

The **Homma Art Museum** is a couple of minutes on foot from the station. In the museum grounds is an impressive residence of the Homma family and a delightful rock garden. Entry is ¥600, and the museum is open from 9 am to 4.30 pm, except Monday.

The **Domon Ken Memorial Museum** contains the photographs of the renowned Japanese photographer, Domon Ken. Domon Ken believed that photography should be involved with social issues, and his photographs often provide a sensitive insight into the underside of Japanese life in the postwar years. The museum is a 15 minute

(¥150) bus ride to the south of town from Sakata station. Take a bus bound for Jūrizuka and get off at the Domon Ken Kinenkan-mae stop. Entry to the museum is ¥410; it's open from 9 am to 4.30 pm, and closed on Monday, except for July and August, when it's open daily.

From 15 to 17 February, the Kuromori Kabuki Festival features performances of *kabuki* by farmers.

Places to Stay

There's business hotel accommodation in the station area at the *Hotel Alpha One Sakata* (☎ 0234-22-6111), which has singles at ¥5350 to ¥6250 and twins/doubles at ¥12,000/11,200. The *Sakata Tōkyū Inn* (☎ 0234-26-0109) is a bit more expensive at ¥6600/12,100 for singles/doubles. For cheaper accommodation, you'll have to walk 10 minutes into the centre of town, where you'll find the *Sakata Park Hotel* (☎ 0234-22-0033). The singles/doubles here are ¥4500/8800.

Getting There & Away

Sakata is on the JR Uetsu line: 1½ hours by limited express north to Akita or 2½ hours by limited express south to Niigata. Trains from Sakata to Tsuruoka take around 45 minutes: you'll need to change trains at Amarume. There are flights from Shonai airport (40 minutes away by bus) to Tokyo, Osaka and Sapporo. For details on the airport bus, see the Tsuruoka Getting There & Away section.

TOBI-SHIMA ISLAND 飛島

Ferries leave from Sakata-kō Port to Tobi-shima, a mere speck of a thing, some 2½ sq km in size. The main attractions are rugged cliffs, sea caves, black-tailed gulls and other feathered friends and, reportedly, excellent fishing. You can also organise boat trips out to smaller islands.

There are more than a dozen ryokan and minshuku. The *Sawaguchi Ryokan* (☎ 0234-95-2246) is also the island's youth hostel – seven minutes on foot from the ferry pier. Rates vary from ¥2200 to ¥2400 (without

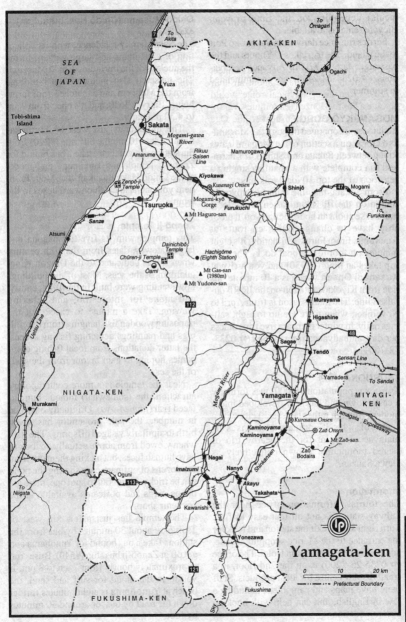

SEA
OF
JAPAN

AKITA-KEN

To Ōmagari

To Akita

Ogachi

Yuza

Ōu Line

13

Tobi-shima
Island

Sakata

Mogami-gawa
River

Mamurogawa

47 Mogami

Amarume

Rikuu
Saisen
Line

Kiyokawa
Kusanagi Onsen

Shinjō

Ōu
Line

Furukawa

Zenpō-ji
Temple

Mogami-kyō
Gorge

Furukuchi

Tsuruoka

▲ Mt Haguro-san

Sanze

Dainichibō
Temple

Atsumi

Chūren-ji Temple

Hachigōme
(Eighth Station)

Obanazawa

Ōami

▲ Mt Gas-san
(1980m)

Murayama

▲ Mt Yudono-san

112

Higashine

Uetsu Line

Sagae

Tendō

Sensan Line

7

Yamadera

To Sendai

NIIGATA-KEN

Mogami River

Yamagata

48

MIYAGI-
KEN

Murakami

Kurosawa Onsen

Yamagata
Expressway

Kaminoyama
Kaminoyama

Zaō Onsen

▲ Mt Zaō-san

Nagai

Shinkansen

Zaō
Bodaira

Imaizumi

Nanyō

To
Niigata

Oguni

113

Akayu

Yonezaka Line

Takahata

Kawanishi

Yonezawa

121

Sky Valley Toll Road

To
Fukushima

FUKUSHIMA-KEN

Yamagata-ken

0   10   20 km

Prefectural Boundary

meals) depending on the time of year. Bicycle rental is available.

Ferries run once daily from Sakata-kō Port to the island. The trip takes 1½ hours and the passenger fare is ¥2000. Advance reservations (☎ 0234-24-2454) are recommended in summer.

MOGAMI-KYŌ GORGE 最上峡

Boat tours are operated through the Mogami-kyō Gorge on a section of the Mogami-gawa River between Sakata and Shinjō. It's harmless fun complete with a boatman singing a selection of the top 10 local folk hits.

From Sakata, take the train to Furukuchi station on the JR Rikuu-saisen line – local trains take about an hour, though you'll probably have to change trains en route at Amarume. From Furukuchi station, it's eight minutes on foot to the boat dock. The boat trip takes an hour (¥1930) and you arrive at **Kusanagi Onsen** which is a 10 minute bus ride from Kiyokawa station on the JR Rikuu-saisen line. The main season is from April to November, when there are up to eight sailings daily. In winter there are five trips or less per day, and advance reservations (☎ 0233-72-2001) are required.

TSURUOKA 鶴岡

Tsuruoka (population 99,000) was formerly a castle town and has now developed into a modern (though rather laid-back) city with a couple of sights. It's primary interest is as the main access point for the nearby trio of sacred mountains, known collectively as Dewa Sanzan.

Information

The tourist information office near the railway station is not all that easy to find. Turn right as you exit the station and look for the entrance to the Marica shopping arcade, adjacent to the Washington Hotel. The office (☎ 0235-23-2200) is on the 2nd floor, in a small display centre for local products. Staff there have maps and pamphlets, including a few in English, and can help with booking accommodation.

Chidō Museum (Chidō Hakabutsukan) 致道館

The Sakai family residence, with its collection of craft items and large garden, forms the nucleus of the intriguing Chidō Museum. The museum also includes two buildings from the Meiji era and a thatched-roof farmhouse. Entry is ¥620, and it's open from 9 am to 4.30 pm daily.

The museum is just west of Tsuruoka-kōen Park, a 10 minute bus ride (¥220) from the station. To get there, take a bus bound for Zenpō-ji Temple and Yunohama, and get off at the Chidō Hakabutsukan-mae stop. From here you can also catch onward buses to the temple.

Zenpō-ji Temple 善宝寺

This temple, with its five-tier pagoda and large gateway, dates from the 10th century when it was dedicated to the Dragon King, guardian of the seas. Most of the buildings now standing were built in the 19th century, and make for interesting and relaxing viewing. Take a minute to check out the imposing wooden fish hanging from the ceilings and paintings depicting fishing scenes, the latter donations from local fishing companies hoping to gain favour from the gods of the seas.

Near the temple is a more contemporary attraction, the (somewhat) famous human-faced fish (*jinmen-gyo*). Originally only one in number, the sole progenitor has given birth to similarly visaged offspring. The fish, when viewed from above actually do look to have human faces, but picking them out from the dozens of ordinary carp sharing the pond can be tricky. If you fail to spot one, there are phone cards and postcards available at the souvenir shop.

The temple lies just a few km west of Tsuruoka, about 30 minutes by bus from the station. Take a bus bound for Yunohama and get off at Zenpō-ji bus stop (¥540). Buses run approximately hourly from 7 am to 8 pm. If you're in the mood for surf and sand, the beach at **Yunohama** is eight minutes further down the road by bus, or around 30 minutes by foot.

Special Events

Tsuruoka's most well-known festival is the Tenjin Matsuri, also known as the Bakemono (masked faces) Matsuri. For three days people stroll around in masks and costume, serving sake to passers by and keeping an eye out for friends and acquaintances. The object is to make it through all three days without anyone recognising you. The festival is held 23 to 25 March.

On 15 July, the Dewa Sanzan Hana Matsuri is held on the peak of Mt Haguro-san. Portable shrines are carried to the shrine at the top and flowers presented to visitors. The Hassaku Festival takes place on Mt Haguro-san from 31 August to 1 September. *Yamabushi* (mountain priests) perform ancient rites for a bountiful harvest.

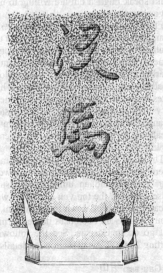

Rice cake offerings are part of the ancient rites performed by priests at the Hassaku Festival.

Places to Stay & Eat

Tsuruoka Youth Hostel (☎ 0235-73-3205) is not in a convenient location. It's a 15 minute walk from Sanze station, which is three stops south-west of JR Tsuruoka station. A bed for the night is ¥2600. The hostel is closed from 27 May to 5 July and from 1 November to 31 March.

Business hotel accommodation around the station includes the *Tsuruoka Washington Hotel* (☎ 0235-25-0111), directly in front of the station, with singles/twins from ¥6000/10,000; and the *Tokyo Dai-Ichi Hotel Tsuruoka* (☎ 0235-24-7611), where singles range from ¥6400 to ¥7500 and twins from ¥12,000 to ¥15,000.

If you feel like staying long enough to take in some of Tsuruoka's sights, then you might want to try out the *Tsuruoka Hotel* (☎ 0235-22-1135), a traditional Japanese inn in the centre of town. Rooms with two meals are pretty good value at ¥8500 per person, and the hotel's location is convenient for visiting Chidō Museum, Tsuruoka Park and several other local attractions. To get there, take one of the city loop buses to the Uchikawa Dōri stop, then walk back up the street, across the intersection, and halfway down the next block. The hotel is on the right-hand side of the street. Look for the English sign saying 'Japanese style Tsuruoka Hotel'.

Getting There & Away

Air Flights from the nearby Shonai airport link Tsuruoka and Sakata with Tokyo, Osaka and Sapporo. Bus departures are timed to coincide with flights. From Tsuruoka station the ride to the airport takes 30 minutes and costs ¥690. From Sakata station the ride takes 40 minutes and costs ¥740.

Train Tsuruoka is on the JR Uetsu line with connections north to Akita in 1¾ hours by limited express (¥3690) or connections south to Niigata in 2¼ hours by limited express (¥4310). Taking the train to Yamagata or Sendai usually requires three changes, one at the very least. It is far more convenient to take the bus.

Bus Buses are run by the Shōnai Kōtsū Bus Company. The main terminal is a five minute walk west of the railway station (on the right-hand side as you exit the station). All buses pass by the station, so you only need go to the terminal if you want to assure yourself of a seat for a longer ride, say to Yamagata or Sendai.

Buses between Tsuruoka and Yamagata take 2¼ hours and cost ¥2000. Between mid-July and 31 October the buses run via the Yudonosan Hotel, which provides access to Mt Yudono-san. There are around 10 departures daily, though services can often be cut back during the winter months, when snowdrifts along the road to Yamagata get as high as eight metres. There are frequent buses to Sendai (three hours, ¥2500).

For details on buses to Haguro-san and Gas-san, see the Dewa Sanzan Getting There & Away section below.

DEWA SANZAN 出羽三山

Dewa Sanzan (Three Mountains of Dewa) is the collective title for three sacred peaks – Mt Haguro-san, Mt Gas-san and Mt Yudono-san – that have been worshipped for centuries by yamabushi (mountain priests) and followers of the Shugendō sect. (See the Shugendō section under Religion in the Facts about the Country chapter.) During the pilgrimage seasons you can see many pilgrims (equipped with wooden staff, sandals and straw hat) and the occasional yamabushi (equipped with conch shell, check jacket and voluminous white pantaloons) stomping along mountain trails or sitting under icy waterfalls as part of the arduous exercises intended to train both body and spirit. You can also see plenty of older pilgrims happy to take advantage of bus services and other labour-saving devices.

Theoretically, if you hiked at a military pace and timed the buses perfectly, you might be able to cover all three peaks in one day. However, this would leave you no time to enjoy the scenery, and chances of missing a key bus connection are good. So if you want to tackle all three mountains it's best to spend at least two days doing it.

Mt Haguro-san 羽黒山

This mountain has several attractions and easy access, thus ensuring a steady flow of visitors. From Tsuruoka station buses run to the Haguro centre bus station in Tōge, a village consisting mainly of shukubō (temple lodgings), at the base of the mountain. The orthodox approach to the shrine on the summit requires the pilgrim to climb hundreds of steps from here but the less tiring approach is to take the bus to the top. However, the climb is well worth the trouble and can be done at a very leisurely pace in about 50 minutes – take your time and enjoy the woods.

The Haguro centre bus station has a small information office that has English-language pamphlets and can help book accommodation. The English pamphlet contains a rather abstract 'guide map' which might serve better as wall art, but combined with a Japanese map it may be of some use. The staff don't speak English but are willing to help out as best they can.

From the Haguro centre bus station, walk straight ahead through an entrance gate and continue across a bridge into beautiful cryptomeria woods with trees forming a canopy overhead. En route you pass a marvellous, weatherbeaten, five-storey **pagoda** which dates from the 14th century. Then comes a very long slog up hundreds of stone steps arranged in steep sections. Pause halfway at a teahouse for refreshment and a view across the hills to the sea.

The scene at the top is a slight anticlimax. There are several shrines, often crowded with visitors, and an uninspiring history museum. From the top you can either walk or catch a bus back down to the bottom. In summer there are two buses in the morning that go on to Gas-san. See the following Getting There & Away section for details.

Mt Gas-san 月山

Mt Gas-san (1980m), the highest of the three sacred peaks, attracts pilgrims to **Gassanjinja Shrine** on the peak itself. The peak is usually accessed from the trailhead at Hachigōme (the Eighth Station on Gas-san). The trail passes through the alpine plateau of Midagahara to the Ninth Station (Kyūgōme) in 1¾ hours and then requires an uphill grind for 70 minutes to the shrine. The trail

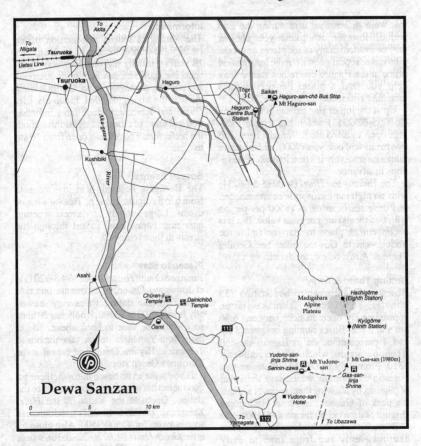

Dewa Sanzan

between Hachigōme and Gassan-jinja Shrine is only open from 1 July to 10 October.

The descent down the other side to **Yudono-san-jinja Shrine** takes another 2½ hours. After about 40 minutes of this descent, you also have the choice of taking the trail to Ubazawa, the main ski resort on Gas-san, which has its own cablecar.

Mt Yudono-san 湯殿山

The mountain is approached via a three km toll road from Yudono-san Hotel to Sennin-zawa trailhead (see Getting There & Away

below). The shrine is then a 10 minute hike further up the mountain.

The sacred shrine on this mountain, **Yudono-san-jinja**, is not a building but a large orange rock continuously lapped by water from a hot spring. The ¥300 admission gains you admission to the inner sanctum where you perform a barefoot circuit of the rock, paddling through the cascading water.

Places to Stay

There are more than 30 shukubō in the town of Tōge, at the base of Mt Haguro-san. This is a lot, but it's a far cry from the 300 or so that were in business here during the Edo period. However, as a tourist your choices may be limited: many of the places only take pilgrims or repeat guests, but the information office at the Haguro centre bus station may help you find a place. Per-person rates including two meals are around ¥7000.

Up at the top of Haguro-san is the *Saikan* (☎ 0235-62-2357) which has temple lodgings open to all visitors. A night here with two meals will cost you ¥7000, and to ensure things go smoothly it's best to make reservations in advance.

The *Yudono-san Hotel* (☎ 0235-54-6231) wins no high marks for style or atmosphere, and the rates (starting at ¥8500 per person with two meals) are not great value. But it is a convenient place to start or finish the Yudono-san to Gas-san hike. See Getting There & Away, below, for details.

Getting There & Away
Buses to Haguro centre bus station (35 minutes, ¥630) leave Tsuruoka station approximately once an hour between 6.30 am and 8 pm. Buses running between 8 am and 4 pm continue on to Haguro-san-chō (Haguro summit), which costs an additional ¥310. From July to October, there are two buses in the morning which save the sweat of pilgrims by allowing them to travel towards the peak of Gas-san, as far as Hachigōme (Eighth Station) in 50 minutes (¥1190).

Buses between the Yudono-san Hotel and Tsuruoka only run from June to early November. There are four buses daily in either direction (80 minutes, ¥1530). The last bus from Yudono-san leaves around 4.30 pm. Buses stop at the Yudono-san Hotel and then continue three km up the road to the trailhead at Sennin-zawa.

YAMAGATA 山形
Yamagata (population 251,000) is the prefectural capital and a thriving industrial city. For the foreign traveller, the city is not a sightseeing destination but a useful gateway to the sacred mountains of Dewa Sanzan, Yama-dera Temple and the skiing and hiking region around Zaō Onsen.

Information
The Yamagata tourist information office (☎ 0236-31-7865), located in the Yamagata JR station, usually has one or two English-speaking staff who can help with questions and booking accommodation. Useful leaflets include the highly detailed *Yamagata City Guide* and *Yamagata* which have information and maps of cities and sights throughout the prefecture. The office is open from 10 am to 6 pm.

Special Events
The Hanagasa Festival, held in Yamagata from 6 to 8 August, is one of Tōhoku's major events. Large crowds of dancers wearing *hanagasa* (straw hats) cavort through the streets in the evenings.

Places to Stay
Yamagata Youth Hostel (☎ 0236-88-3201) is at Kurosawa Onsen, a 25 minute bus ride from Yamagata station. Rates vary seasonally from ¥2600 to ¥2700. It only has 20 beds so it would be wise to book ahead. To get there from Yamagata station, take the bus to Takamatsu-Hiyama Onsen and get off at the Kurosawa Onsen stop.

If you want to be based in town, there's a good selection of business hotels close to the station. Opposite the station is the *Hotel Yamagata* (☎ 0236-42-2111), which has singles/twins for ¥5500/9500. Also close by is the *Green Hotel* (☎ 0236-22-2636), where singles range from ¥5600 to ¥5800 and twins come in at ¥9600. For much more plush accommodation, there's the *Hotel Metropolitan Yamagata* (☎ 0236-28-1111) which is part of the JR station. Singles start at ¥8800 and twins at ¥16,000.

Getting There & Away
Air There are flights from Yamagata to Fukuoka, Kansai, Nagoya, Osaka, Sapporo and Tokyo. Buses run from Yamagata station to the airport (Yamagata Kūkō) in 40 minutes (¥650). Departures are approximately once an hour and are timed to coincide with flights.

Train The JR Tōhoku shinkansen line was extended to Yamagata in 1992, making the travel time between Yamagata and Tokyo around 2½ hours. The cost is ¥5670 plus a ¥5140 shinkansen surcharge.

The JR Senzan line runs from Yamagata via Yamadera to Sendai in about 70 minutes.

The JR Yonesaka line links Yamagata with Niigata in 3¼ hours by limited express. A change to the JR Uetsu line is usually necessary at Sakamachi.

Tsuruoka is connected with Yamagata via the JR Ōu line, JR Rikuu-saisen line and JR Uetsu line in about three hours. There are one or two direct trains to Sakata: you will need to get off at Amarume to change for a local train to Tsuruoka. Better yet, take the bus.

The JR Ōu line runs north from Yamagata along the centre of Tōhoku to Ōmagari (with easy access to the region around Lake Tazawa-ko) in 2½ hours by limited express.

Bus Buses originate at the Yamagata Kōtsu bus station, but then stop at Yamagata station before heading out. There are frequent buses from Yamagata to Zaō Onsen (45 minutes, ¥770), and less frequent ones to Yama-dera and Yonezawa. Buses to Sendai leave every 20 to 30 minutes from 7 am to 9 pm and cost ¥1000. There are frequent buses between Tsuruoka and Yamagata (2¼ hours, ¥2000). Between mid-July and 31 October the buses run via the Yudono-san Hotel, which provides access to Mt Yudono-san.

The Tohoku Express Bus Company runs one bus daily and one nightly to Tokyo (Ueno, Asakusa) from the Shōkō bus station, two streets east of Yamagata station. The one-way fare is ¥6300. Day buses take nearly six hours, night buses 9½ hours.

MT ZAŌ-SAN 蔵王山
The region around this mountain is very popular with skiers in the winter (the main skiing season is from December to April) and it is a pleasant hiking destination at other times of the year. The main ski resorts are centred around **Zaō Onsen** and **Zaō Bodaira**. There is an extensive network of ropeways and lifts, and night skiing is available until 9 pm.

During summer you can make your way up to **Okama**, a volcano crater-lake (caldera) atop Zaō-san, considered by the Japanese to be the area's premier sight. The most convenient access is via the Karita Chūsha-jō (Karita car park), where a chair lift takes you to the top in six minutes (¥620). From there it's three minutes to the Okama overlook. There are numerous trails around the area, including a good one hour walk over to Jizōsancho-eki, from where you can hike or catch a chair lift (¥1300) down to Zaō Onsen. Like all mountain resorts in summer, this one is packed with visitors during July-August.

Information
Zaō Onsen tourist information office (☎ 0236-94-9328) has maps, and advice on transport and accommodation.

Places to Stay & Eat
There are plenty of minshuku, pensions and ryokan, but advance reservations are essential if you visit during the peak season or during weekends. You might want to try one of the two minshuku at Zaō Onsen: *Lodge Chitoseya* (☎ 0236-94-9145) or *Yūgiri-Sō* (☎ 0236-94-9253), which have prices starting around ¥7000 per person including two meals.

At Zaō Bōdaira, you could try *Pension Alm* (☎ 0236-79-2256) or *Pension Ishii* (☎ 0236-79-2772), which have prices starting around ¥8000 per person including two meals.

Getting There & Away
There is a frequent bus service from Yamagata station to Zaō Onsen (45 minutes, ¥770). Buses also run to Zaō Onsen from Kaminoyama station, just south of Yamagata. To cope with demand during the winter – more than a million visitors – there is a regular bus service direct from Tokyo. Between April and November there are two buses daily that connect Yamagata via Zaō Onsen with Karita Chūsha-jō (1½ hours, ¥1500). Departures from Yamagata are in the morning, from Karita in the early afternoon.

YAMADERA 山寺

Yamadera's main attraction is **Yama-dera Temple** (also known as Risshaku-ji Temple) which was founded here in 860 as a branch of the Enryaku-ji Temple near Kyoto. The temple is actually a cluster of buildings and shrines laid out on wooded slopes. From the railway station, walk straight to the three-way intersection, turn right, then left at the bridge. After crossing the bridge, a short walk to either the right or left will bring you to stone steps that lead up to the temple area. Walking to the right will bring you to Konponchū-dō Hall, a national treasure. From there continue past the Treasure Museum and, after paying your ¥300 entry fee, start a steep climb up hundreds of steps through the trees to the Niō-mon Gate. The trail continues a short distance uphill to the Okuno-in (Inner Sanctuary); trails lead off on either side to small shrines and lookout points. The temple area is open from 8 am to 5 pm. There's not much in the way of tourist information available at the railway station, but there's a map of the area on a large sign just opposite the railway station exit.

Pension Yamadera (☎ 0236-95-2240) is just a one minute walk from the station and has rooms with two meals for ¥8000 per person, ¥8500 for rooms with attached bath. Directly opposite the railway station at the three-way intersection the *Yamadera Hotel* (☎ 0236-95-2216) is a traditional Japanese inn with per-person rates of ¥8500, with two meals.

Trains on the JR Senzan line link Yamagata with Yamadera station in 15 minutes (¥230) and then take another hour to Sendai (¥800).

YONEZAWA 米沢

During the 17th century, the Uesugi clan built their castle in this town which later developed into a major centre for silk weaving. The town's production of rayon textiles has now eclipsed that of silk. It's a quiet, unpretentious place, worth a brief stopover if you are passing through this part of the prefecture.

Things to See

A 10 minute bus ride from JR Yonezawa station, **Matsugasaki-kōen Park** contains the castle ruins and the Uesugi-jinja Shrine. The shrine's Keishō-den (Treasure House) displays armour and works of art belonging to many generations of the Uesugi family.

Just south of the shrine is the **Uesugi Kinenkan** (Uesugi Memorial Hall), which is a fine residence from the Meiji era with more relics from the Uesugi family.

The **Uesugi-ke Byō Mausoleum** is further west from the park, about 15 minutes on foot. A dozen generations of the Uesugi clan are entombed here in a gloomy row of individual mausoleums overshadowed by tall trees.

Places to Stay

There's not much in the way of budget accommodation in Yonezawa, and even most of the business hotels are a fair trudge from the station. The *Hotel Otowaya* (☎ 0238-22-0124), an atmospheric, vaguely castle-like building, is in front of the station. Singles range from ¥5300 and there are expensive twins available from ¥13,000. The *Yonezawa Station Hotel* (☎ 0238-21-4111) is a couple of minutes walk from the station, and has singles/twins at ¥4500/8000.

Getting There & Away

The JR Ōu line connects Yonezawa with Yamagata in 45 minutes (¥800) and trains run east from Yonezawa on the same line to Fukushima (45 minutes, ¥720). The JR Yonesaka line links Yonezawa with Niigata via the JR Uetsu line.

Niigata-ken 新潟県

NIIGATA 新潟

Niigata (population 436,000), the capital of the prefecture, is an important industrial centre and major transport hub. The city itself has few sights and most foreign visitors use Niigata as a gateway for Sado-ga-shima Island.

Information

The tourist information office (☎ 025-241-7914) is on your left as you exit on the

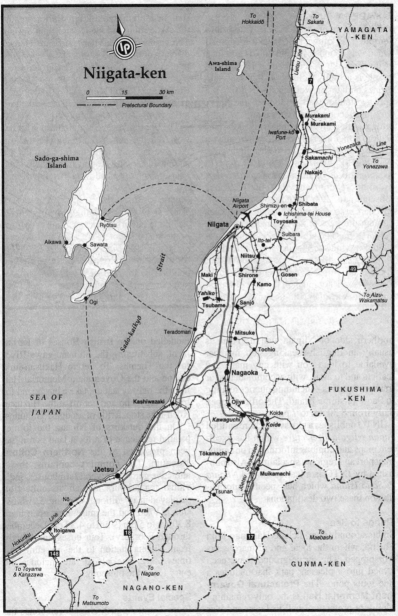

northern side of Niigata station. There is usually an English-speaking staff member available to load you with city maps and leaflets and to assist with accommodation or transport queries – including queries relating to Sado-ga-shima Island. The office is open daily from 8.30 am to 7 pm.

JNTO publishes a glossy brochure entitled *Japan Niigata Prefecture* which has excellent maps and copious information on sights, transport and regional specialities. Also published by JNTO is a leaflet entitled *Niigata & Sado Island* which has specific information on these two destinations.

Things to See

Sights around town include **Hakusan-jinja Shrine**, where the local god of marriage is worshipped. The shrine grounds have been turned into a pleasant park that includes a fine lotus pond. The **Prefectural Government Memorial Hall** is the only remaining Meiji-era prefectural hall in Japan and was modelled on the British Houses of Parliament, substituting the Shinano-gawa River for the Thames. To get to Hakusan-jinja Shrine and the Government Memorial Hall from the railway station, take a bus bound for Irifune-eigyosho and get off at the Hakusan Kōen-mae stop, a ride of around 15 minutes.

On the outskirts of Niigata the former palatial residence of a local land baron has been preserved as the **Northern Culture Museum**. The complex contains, in its attractive gardens, several farmhouses, individual tea arbours and an art collection displayed in a traditional warehouse. Admission is ¥700 and the museum is open from 8.30 am to 5 pm (9 am to 4.30 pm December through February). Tour buses run directly from Niigata station to the museum four times daily. The ¥1570 fare includes the entry fee to the museum.

Special Events

From 7 to 9 August, Niigata celebrates the

PLACES TO STAY	OTHER	
4 Niigata Ōnoya Ryokan 新潟大野屋旅館	1 Sado Kisen Ship Company (Ferries for Sado-ga-Shima) 佐渡汽船（佐渡ヶ島 ゆきフェリー）	6 Prefectural Government Memorial Hall 新潟県政記念館
9 Shin Ōnoya Ryokan 新大野屋旅館		7 Rainbow Tower レインボータワー
10 Niigata Green Hotel 新潟グリーンホテル	2 Niigata Prefectural Art Museum 新潟県立美術館	8 Central Post Office 中央郵便局
11 Hotel Kawai ホテルカワイ	3 Nihon-kai Tower 日本海タワー	13 Bus Terminal バスターミナル
12 Niigata Tōkyū Inn 新潟東急イン	5 Hakusan-jinja Shrine 白山神社	14 Tourist Information Office 観光案内所

Niigata Matsuri Festival, the major annual bash with boat parades, thousands of folk dancers, a costume parade and a bumper fireworks display.

Places to Stay

The tourist information office can suggest and book accommodation to suit most budgets. There are plenty of business hotels around the station. The *Niigata Green Hotel* (☎ 025-246-0341) has singles from ¥4800; the *Hotel Kawai* (☎ 025-241-3391) has similar rates. The *Niigata Tōkyū Inn* (☎ 025-243-0109) has more up-market rooms at ¥6800/13,000 for singles/twins.

For ryokan accommodation near the station, there's the *Shin Ohnoya Ryokan* (☎ 025-247-9271), which has rooms starting at around ¥4500 per person without meals. If you're looking for something a little less basic, you might try the *Niigata Ohnoya Ryokan* (☎ 025-229-2951), which is on the northern side of the Shinano-gawa River near the Furumachi shopping district. Per-person rates including two meals range from ¥10,000 to ¥20,000.

Getting There & Away

Air Niigata has flights to Khabarovsk, (Russia) which connect with departures on the Trans-Siberian Railway. There are also flights to Irkutsk and Vladivostok. The Aero-flot office (☎ 025-244-5935) is a couple of minutes on foot from the station. Korean Airlines (☎ 025-244-3311) operates flights between Niigata and Seoul.

Flights link Niigata with Ryōtsu on Sado-ga-shima in 25 minutes (¥7120). There are also flights to Fukuoka, Hakodate, Hiroshima, Nagoya, Osaka, Sapporo and Tokyo.

Niigata airport lies north-east of Niigata, 25 minutes by bus from Niigata station. Buses leave every half hour from the station between 7 am and 6.30 pm, and the fare is ¥320.

Train Niigata is connected with Tokyo (Ueno station) by the JR Jōetsu shinkansen line in two hours (¥10,080).

Travelling north, Niigata is linked via the JR Uetsu line with Tsuruoka (two hours) and Akita (four hours). Travelling south-west on the JR Hokuriku line, it takes four hours to Kanazawa, and direct trains also continue to Kyoto and Osaka.

Bus There are several long-distance buses daily to Tokyo (Ikebukuro) (¥5150, five hours) and a night bus to Kyoto (8¼, hours¥8750) and Osaka (9¼ hours, ¥9270).

Boat The Shin-Nihonkai ferry from Niigata to Otaru (Hokkaidō) is excellent value at ¥5150 for a 2nd class ticket (1st class is ¥10,300). The trip takes 18 hours and there

NORTHERN HONSHŪ

are six sailings a week. The appropriate port is Niigata-kō: take the bus to Rinko Nichome and get off at Suehirobashi, a ride of about 20 minutes from Niigata station.

There are frequent ferries and hydrofoils to Ryōtsu on Sado-ga-shima from the Sado Kisen terminal, which is 15 minutes by bus (¥170) from the station. For more information see the Getting There & Away section for Sado-ga-shima.

SADO-GA-SHIMA ISLAND 佐渡島

In medieval times, this was a place of exile for intellectuals who had fallen out of favour with the government. Among those banished here were Emperor Juntoku, and Nichiren, the founder of one of the most influential sects of Buddhism in Japan. When gold was discovered near Aikawa in 1601, there was a sudden influx of gold-diggers – often vagrants shipped from the mainland as prisoners and made to work like slaves. Today the island relies on fishing, rice farming and tourism.

The southern and northern mountain ranges of this island are connected by a flat, fertile plain. The best season to visit is between late April and early November – during the winter, the weather can be foul, much of the accommodation is closed and transport is reduced to a minimum.

It is possible to do a two day tour which hits all the sights, but the real attractions of the island are its unhurried pace of life and natural scenery. A minimum of three or four days is recommended to visit the rocky coastline and remote fishing villages, or to wander inland to the mountains and their temples.

Information

The Sado Kisen Ferry Company (☎ 025-245-1234) publishes an English booklet which has excellent timetables, some sightseeing and transport information and a good map. These are available at the ferry terminal offices in Niigata and Ryōtsu. They also have island bus timetables, though only in Japanese. Staff at the Niigata office can also help with booking accommodation.

The Niigata Kōtsū Information Center (☎ 0259-27-3141) is in front of the pier at Ryōtsu. It has timetables for tour buses and local buses, but little English is spoken. Operating hours are from 5.30 am to 8.40 pm. Over in Sawata, the Sado information centre (☎ 0259-52-3163) provides pamphlets, books and advice for foreign visitors. It's open from 10 am to 7 pm from Monday to Friday but is closed weekends and holidays.

The Sado Association publishes a glossy brochure entitled *Japan Sado Island* which has information on sights and transport, and an excellent map. JNTO publishes a leaflet entitled *Niigata & Sado Island*, which has specific information for these two destinations.

Ryōtsu 両津

This is the main town and tourist resort and a base to pick up information before travelling to more interesting places on the island. The business and restaurant part of town is a 10 minute walk north of the terminal.

Sawata 佐和田

The town of Sawata, 16 km south-west of Ryōtsu, is on the main road between Ryōtsu and Aikawa. If you get off the bus at Shimonagaki, about one km east of the town, you can then walk for about 30 minutes up into the hills to **Myōshō-ji Temple**. This temple, set in dilapidated grounds, belongs to the Nichiren sect. From the shrine at the top of the steps, a pleasant path leads through the woods to rice paddies. Buses between Ryōtsu and Sawata run once to twice an hour from 6.30 am to 8 pm, take 50 minutes, and cost ¥530.

Aikawa 相川

From a tiny hamlet, Aikawa developed almost overnight into a boom town when gold was discovered nearby in 1601. Gold mining continued to the end of the Edo period and the town once numbered 100,000 inhabitants. The mine was closed in 1867 – now the town's population has dwindled to a few thousand and its main source of income is tourism.

From Aikawa bus terminal, you can either walk for 40 minutes up a steep mountain or

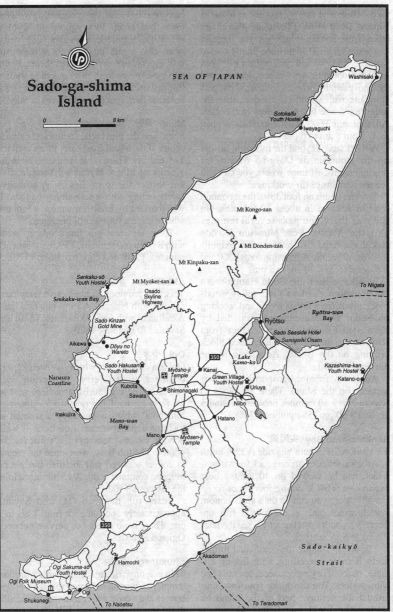

Sado-ga-shima Island

0   4   8 km

SEA OF JAPAN

Washisaki

Sotokaifu Youth Hostel
Iwayaguchi

▲ Mt Kongo-zan

▲ Mt Donden-zan

▲ Mt Kinpaku-zan

Senkaku-sō Youth Hostel
▲ Mt Myoker-san
Senkaku-wan Bay
Osado Skyline Highway

To Niigata

Sado Kinzan Gold Mine
Aikawa
Dōyu no Wareto
Ryōtsu-wan Bay
Ryōtsu
Sado Seaside Hotel
Sumiyoshi Onsen

Sado Hakusan Youth Hostel
Lake Kamo-ko
350
Myōsho-ji Temple
Kanai
Green Village Youth Hostel
Kazashima-kan Youth Hostel
Katano-o

Nanaura Coastline
Kubota
Sawata
Shimonagaki
Uriuya
Niibo

Inakujira
Mano-wan Bay
Hatano

Mano
Myōsen-ji Temple

Sado-kaikyō Strait

350

Akadomari

Hamochi
Ogi Sakuma-sō Youth Hostel
Ogi Folk Museum
Shukunegi
Ogi
To Naoetsu
To Teradomari

NORTHERN HONSHŪ

take a 10 minute ride by taxi or bus to **Sado Kinzan Gold Mine**. (There are also direct buses from Ryōtsu which get you there in 1¼ hours for ¥820.) The mine finally ceased working in 1989 and one section has been turned into a museum. Visitors descend into the chilly depths, where mechanical puppets complete with sound effects dramatise the tough existence led by miners in the past. Admission is ¥600 and the museum is open daily from 8 am to 6 pm.

A short walk beyond the museum, further up the mountain, is Dōyu-no-Wareto, the original open-cast mine where you can still see the remains of the workings.

You can return on foot down the mountain road to Aikawa in about 30 minutes. On the way there you pass several temples and the **Aikawa Folk Museum** (Kyōdo Hakubutsukan), which has more exhibits from the old mine. Admission costs ¥300 and it is open from 8.30 am to 5 pm.

In Aikawa itself the **Sado Hanga-mura Art Museum** displays (and sells) woodblock prints from artists living and working on Sado. The museum was founded by Takahashi Shinchi, an art teacher from Ryōtsu who helped revitalise wood-block printing on the island. Admission to the museum is ¥300.

Aikawa is a major transport hub for bus services on the island. There are buses to Ryōtsu every 30 minutes between around 5 am and 8.30 pm (55 minutes, ¥740).

Senkaku-wan Bay 尖閣湾

This bay, a 20 minute bus ride (¥320) north of Aikawa, features striking rock formations, which can be viewed on 40 minute boat excursions (¥640), sailing four times daily. For ¥10 more you can go on a glass-bottom vessel, which sails as soon as it fills up. There's a youth hostel nearby – see the later Places to Stay section.

The scenery along the coast road further north is more interesting, with fishing villages, racks of drying seaweed, sea mist and calm waters. You can make your own tour around the northern part of the island by taking the local bus from Aikawa to Iwayaguchi (¥970), then connecting with the local bus from Iwayaguchi to Ryōtsu (¥1140). The full trip takes about 3½ hours. Note that while buses from Aikawa to Iwayaguchi run every 1½ hours, there are only two buses a day from Iwayaguchi to Ryōtsu (the last one leaves at 3 pm). There's a youth hostel at Iwayaguchi – see Places to Stay.

Mano 真野

Mano was the provincial capital and cultural centre of the island from early times until the 14th century. There are several temples in the vicinity of Mano. **Myōsen-ji Temple**, five km east of the town, lies in an attractive forest setting with a five-storey pagoda. It was founded by Endo Tamemori, a samurai who became a follower of Nichiren.

There are local bus lines linking Mano with Ryōtsu (40 minutes, ¥590), Sawata (15 minutes, ¥240) and Ogi (one hour, ¥770).

Akadomari 赤泊

This port provides an alternative ferry connection with Niigata. A local bus line links Akadomari with Ogi (35 minutes, ¥530) and Sawata (70 minutes, ¥870).

Ogi 小木

Ogi is a drowsy port which has been kept in business by the ferry connection with Naoetsu. The big tourist attraction, next to the ferry terminal, is a ride in a *taraibune* or 'tub boat' which is poled by a woman in traditional fisherwoman's costume – well, nobody wears it nowadays, it's just for the photos. The tub boats were once the means to collect seaweed and shellfish but are no longer a common sight. A 15 minute spin in the tub costs ¥500.

Buses run between Ogi and Sawata approximately once an hour from 7 am to 7 pm. There is no direct bus service between Ogi and Ryōtsu.

Shukunegi 宿根木

This is a tiny fishing village with a drowsy temple, a few weatherbeaten rows of wooden houses and a cove where a couple of old tubs moulder away. On the hill, just at the entrance to the village, you should definitely pop in to see the quirky **Ogi Folk Museum** (Ogi Minzoku Hakubutsukan) with its random (and dusty) collection of dolls, clocks, tools, ceramics, old TVs, radios, projectors and even thermos flasks! The museum is open from 8 am to 4 pm and admission costs ¥400.

There is an infrequent bus service running west from Ogi via Shukunegi (¥260) to the museum, though since it's only four km, you may prefer walking to waiting for the next bus.

Organised Tours

Teiki kankō (sightseeing buses) have neatly packaged itineraries – ultra-convenient, sanitised, hectic and brassy. Tickets and departures are arranged at Sado Kisen offices or tourist information offices where you can pick up the appropriate *teiki kankō jikokuhyō* (sightseeing bus timetable). The one itinerary that merits a recommendation is the Skyline Course because it follows the spectacular Osado Skyline Highway from Ryōtsu to Aikawa – there is no local transport alternative for this particular highway. The trip takes about three hours and costs ¥3700.

Special Events

The booklet published in English by the Sado Kisen Ferry Company has a detailed list and brief descriptions for many of the festivals on the island. There seem to be

festivals happening almost every week, although some seem specially engineered for tourists. The island is famed for its *okesa* (folk dances), *ondeko* (demon drum dances) and *tsuburosashi* (a phallic dance with two goddesses). Following is a brief selection.

Sado Geinō Matsuri Festival
  Held in Mano from 28 to 29 April with ondeko, folk songs and performances of tsuburosashi.
Kōzan Festival
  Held in Aikawa from 25 to 27 July with okesa, ondeko and fireworks.
Ogi Matsuri Festival
  Held in Ogi from 28 to 30 August and features lion dances, folk songs and tub-boat frolics.
Mano Matsuri Festival
  Held in Mano from 15 to 16 October and includes performances of local art forms and lion dances.

As a special favour to tourists, between April and November there are nightly performances of okesa and ondeko dances in Ryōtsu, Aikawa, Ogi and Sawata. The tourist information office in Sawata has exact details.

Places to Stay

The island is well furnished with minshuku, ryokan, kokuminshukusha, hotels and youth hostels. There are several camping grounds as well. You can get help with booking accommodation from the tourist information offices and the Sado Kisen Ferry Company offices at the ferry terminals. Booking your

---

Three Days of Dancing & Drumming

Along with its scenery, one of Sado's biggest draws for foreign visitors is the Earth Celebration, a three-day music, dance and art festival held during the third week in August. Performances range from African dance to traditional Japanese to Irish folk music, and dance and music workshops are offered (though these often require at least basic Japanese-language ability). The focal point of the festival is performances by the Kodo Drummers, who live in a small village north of Ogi, and have built up a large and loyal following in Japan, and to some extent, abroad. Travellers, expats living in Japan and Japanese all rave about the festival, and everyone seems to feel it's worth the fairly high ticket prices.

Evening performances usually cost around ¥4000, and there are various package deals available. It's highly recommended you buy tickets (and arrange accommodation) in advance. Concert tickets are available through the advance ticket services run by JR East, Ticket Saison and Ticket Pia. Workshops must be booked directly through the organisers, Kodo (☎ 0259-86-3630; fax 86-3631), who can also provide you with brochures and other information. ■

accommodation in advance (even if it means doing it in Niigata or Naoetsu before boarding) is highly recommended in the hectic summer months.

Youth Hostels These can be found all over the island, making it possible to really see Sado on a budget. Most have only around 20 beds, so it's important to book in advance.

Sado Belle Mer Youth Hostel (☎ 0259-75-2011) is in the touristy area of Senkaku-wan Bay, close to Aikawa. The building has recently been refurbished, so beds are a bit more expensive at ¥3100. From Aikawa, take the Kaifu-sen bus line for the 20 minute ride north to the Himezu bus stop: from there it's a five minute walk in the direction of the shore. *Sado Hakusan Youth Hostel* (☎ 0259-52-4422) is inland in a farming area. Beds are ¥2400 per person. Take the bus from Ryōtsu bound for Aikawa, but get off after about 40 minutes at Kubota (about two km west of Sawata). Then it's a 25 minute walk up the side street opposite the bus stop. If you phone the hostel, they'll fetch you at the bus stop. Guests can use a nearby hot spring.

Sotokaifu Youth Hostel (☎ 0259-78-2911) is in a tiny fishing hamlet in the middle of nowhere run by a friendly family. Rates are around ¥2300 per person. To get there from Ryōtsu, take the Sotokaifu-sen bus line which runs via Washisaki, continues round the northern tip of the island and deposits you at the Iwayaguchi bus stop – in front of the hostel door. This service operates two or three times a day (1¾ hours, ¥1140) – late April to late November only. There are more frequent buses to Iwayaguchi from Aikawa (1½ hours, ¥970).

Ogi Sakuma-sō Youth Hostel (☎ 0259-86-2565) is 20 minutes on foot from Ogi, in the far south of the island. Beds cost ¥2400. It is only open between March and November and guests can use a nearby hot spring. *Kazashima-kan Youth Hostel* (☎ 0259-29-2003) also charges ¥2400 for a bed and is on the south-eastern side of the island. From Ryōtsu, take the Higashi Kaigan-sen bus line to Katano-o and then be sure to get off at the Yūsu-hosuteru-mae bus stop.

Newly opened, the *Green Village Youth Hostel* (☎ 0259-22-2719) is a cheerful little spot in the hills west of Ryōtsu. Beds are ¥2800. From Ryōtsu take a bus bound for Sawata and get off after about 10 minutes at the Uriuya stop.

Minshuku There are dozens of minshuku, and by some sort of mutual commercial agreement, prices at all of them are a uniform ¥7000, which includes two meals. Most of the minshuku are clustered along the Nanaura coastline, a 15 minute bus ride south of Aikawa. The staff at *Nanaura-sō* (☎ 0259-76-2735) speak some English, and several of the rooms have balconies overlooking the ocean. From Aikawa, take the Nanaura Kaigan-sen bus line and get off at Nagatemisaki-iriguchi. A few bus stops north is *Takimoto* (☎ 0259-74-3103), which has, among other amenities, a bath with an ocean view. It's just next to the Ōura-nishi bus stop on the Nanaura Kaigan-sen bus line. Both minshuku can also be reached by bus from Sawata (25 minutes), which is the southern terminus for the Nanaura Kaigan-sen line. Note that only buses on this line go along the Nanaura coast: the Honsen line, which also links Sawata and Aikawa, has much more frequent service but follows an inland road which won't get you to the minshuku.

One of Sado's most popular minshuku with Japanese tourists is *Kunimisō* (☎ 0259-22-2316), which is set in an inland valley about 15 minutes by bus from Ryōtsu (close to the Green Village Youth Hostel). The minshuku's popularity is said to stem in part from its impressive collection of Bunya puppets, which the owner often opens for guests. To get there from Ryōtsu take a bus bound for Sawata. After about 10 minutes get off at the Uriuya stop.

If you're taking the ferry from Naoetsu to Ogi, you can try *Sakaya* (☎ 0259-86-2535). Rooms are pretty basic but clean, and the minshuku is conveniently located: a few minutes walk east of the Ogi ferry terminal.

Hotels Most of Sado's hotels are near Ryōtsu, and many charge criminally high rates. One exception is the *Sado Seaside Hotel* (☎ 0259-27-7211), at Sumiyoshi Onsen, about two km (25 minutes on foot) from Ryōtsu Port. A free shuttle service is available to and from the port, and for the dance and music performances in Ryōtsu in the evening. The hotel has its own hot-spring bath which you can use any time. Seafood dinners are a speciality and per-person costs with meals start at around ¥10,000.

Getting There & Away
Air Flights link Ryōtsu on Sado-ga-shima with Niigata in 25 minutes (¥7210). There are three to four flights daily.

Boat The Sado Kisen ferry company runs both regular passenger/car ferries and hydrofoils between Niigata and Ryōtsu. Fares on the regular ferries range from ¥2030 for a 2nd class ticket to ¥4060 for a plush seat in the 1st class lounge. There are between five and six departures daily.

The hydrofoil (also known as the 'jet foil') zips across in a mere hour, but costs a hefty ¥5960. There are at least six departures daily between April and early November; just two or three during the rest of the year.

From Naoetsu (south-west of Niigata), there are ferry and hydrofoil services to Ogi, in the south-west part of the island. Between April and late November, there are four or more ferry departures daily; during the rest of the year the service is considerably reduced. Fares are the same as for the Niigata-Ryōtsu service. From the bus terminal next to the Naoetsu JR station, it's a 10 minute bus ride (¥150) to the port.

From Teradomari (a short distance below Niigata), there is a ferry service to Akadomari, on the southern edge of Sado-ga-shima. Second class tickets cost ¥1390 and the trip takes two hours. There are two or three departures daily depending on the season, and service is suspended between mid-January and 1 February.

Getting Around
Bus Local buses are fine on the main routes – between Ryōtsu and Aikawa, for example. However, services to other parts of the island are often restricted to two or three a day. If you plan to make extended use of local buses, a vital piece of paper is the Sado-ga-shima Basu Jikokuhyō, the island's bus timetable (in Japanese) which is available from bus terminals and tourist information offices. The timetable has a map showing the numbered bus routes for you to match up to the individual timetables. During the summer extra bus departures are added to handle the flow of tourists, but in the winter months service is sharply scaled back.

Car This might make sense for a small group since it frees the visitor from the hectic schedules of tour buses and the infrequency of local buses. Sado Kisen Ferry Company in Ryōtsu provides car rental (☎ 0259-27-5195) at prices from ¥10,100 for 24 hours. See the company's magazine for more details.

Cycling This is quite feasible and an enjoyable way to potter around off the beaten track. Unfortunately some places charge exorbitant rates, as much as ¥800 for the first hour (¥100 for each hour thereafter). The tourist information offices can provide details for bicycle rental in Ryōtsu, Aikawa and Ogi.

Hokkaidō   北海道

Hokkaidō (population 5,689,000) is the northernmost and second largest of Japan's islands. Although it accounts for over one fifth of Japan's land area, only 5% of the Japanese population lives there. The real beauty of the place lies in the wilderness regions where – in contrast to Honshū – there are no cultural monuments, but superb opportunities for outdoor activities such as hiking, camping, skiing, relaxing in hot springs and observing wildlife.

HISTORY & DEVELOPMENT

Until the Edo period, Hokkaidō, or Ezo as it was known prior to the Meiji Restoration, was a backwater in the currents of Japanese history. The island was largely left to its indigenous inhabitants, notably the Ainu, a people who are postulated by certain experts to be of Siberian origin, though there is still not enough evidence to prove this theory.

In the 16th century, the Matsumae clan arrived from Honshū, establishing a foothold on the south-western tip of the island. The rest of Hokkaidō continued to be the domain of the Ainu, who lived as hunters and gatherers.

The Meiji Restoration of 1868 saw a major policy shift in Japan's approach to its northernmost island. A colonial office was established to encourage settlers from other parts of Japan, and the new name Hokkaidō (literally the 'North Sea Road') was formally adopted. Foreign advisers were called in to help with the development of the island: Sapporo's grid-like layout was planned by a US architect, and US agricultural experts also introduced farm architecture, which has endured as a characteristic of Hokkaidō's landscape.

Hokkaidō's sparsely populated landmass has made it an important agricultural base and it is now Japan's largest food producer. Wheat, potatoes, corn, rice and dairy farming make up the bulk of production. The island is also home to forestry and pulp & paper industries, as well as fishing and mining.

In the past decade Hokkaidō has become

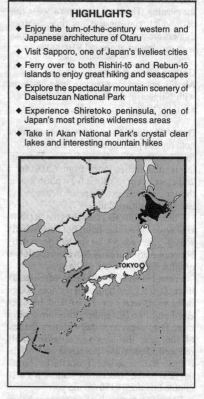

HIGHLIGHTS

◆ Enjoy the turn-of-the-century western and Japanese architecture of Otaru

◆ Visit Sapporo, one of Japan's liveliest cities

◆ Ferry over to both Rishiri-tō and Rebun-tō islands to enjoy great hiking and seascapes

◆ Explore the spectacular mountain scenery of Daisetsuzan National Park

◆ Experience Shiretoko peninsula, one of Japan's most pristine wilderness areas

◆ Take in Akan National Park's crystal clear lakes and interesting mountain hikes

a top destination for Japanese tourists. The business they bring is a major source of income, particularly for remote communities that would otherwise find it hard to make a living from more traditional sectors such as fishing or agriculture.

WHEN TO GO

Although only a small segment of Japan's population calls Hokkaidō home, at peak

Japan's 'Northern Territories'

The collapse of the Soviet Union sent cartographers scurrying to redraw the newly independent fragments of ex-Soviet territory. One Soviet possession they haven't had to worry about, however, is a group of islands formerly belonging to Japan and occupied by the Soviet Union on 3 September 1945. The disputed islands are Kunashiri-tō, Etorofu-tō, Shikotan-tō and Habamaisho-tō, and their control gave the Soviet Union – and today, Russia – access to one of the richest fishing grounds in the world.

Arguably what the Russians need today – much more than fish – is Japanese investment. There's no doubt that conceding the islands to their former custodians would lead to a grateful flood of Japanese yen. But national pride still takes precedence and Russia's official line is one of no compromises. Similarly, Japan will accept nothing less than unconditional return of the islands. Recent Russian offers to develop the disputed territory in cooperation with Japan have met with a frosty response.

There has been some progress. Russia has made it easier for Japanese to visit relatives or family graves on the islands and, in return, Japan has eased some immigration restrictions on Russian visitors. But Tokyo still refuses to pledge any meaningful economic assistance until the islands are returned, and Russia vows that the islands will remain Russian.

In Japan, emotions run hottest in Hokkaidō; hardly surprising given that the nearest of the disputed islands is a mere four km off Cape Nosappu-misaki, just east of the town of Nemuro. Hokkaidō is the scene of annual rallies and signature collecting drives. Neither is likely to cut any ice with Russia, where the economic malaise is generating widespread nationalist fervour. ■

travel times it can seem like the rest of the country has come up to join them. The island attracts hikers and campers from May to October, but the real crunch comes in June, July and August. September is also popular, as people come up to see the leaves turn colour. While transport services are more frequent and extensive at this time of year, it also can be difficult to escape the hordes, as well as find accommodation – a tent is a good idea. However, it's often possible to skirt the crowds and enjoy the last of the autumn weather from October to early November. After that, winter sets in for five months of heavy snowfall and subzero temperatures. Skiers then form the bulk of the tourists, many of whom head for the ski resorts of Niseko or Furano, though some skip skiing to see Sapporo's Ice Festival in February. Whatever time of year you visit, don't underestimate the weather – take proper clothing to stay warm and dry.

PLANNING YOUR ITINERARY

Even if you only want to skim the surface of Hokkaidō, the absolute minimum would be a week. There is no pressing need to spend more than a day or two in Sapporo – to pick up information, organise transport, make bookings and change money – before heading for remote parts. If you cut out a visit to Rishiri-Rebun-Sarobetsu National Park, you could visit the other four national parks at a comfortable pace in a fortnight. If you include this park, you'll need an extra week. It would also be easy to spend a full week or so exploring just one area, such as Daisetsu-zan National Park.

To keep to a comfortable and enjoyable itinerary, it's best to remember that the less time you have available, the less you should try and pack into it – otherwise the transport costs simply soar and the fun factor plummets. It is also essential that you check the operating dates for transport services, as they vary each year. They can be ascertained from timetables or by consulting the information sources given in this chapter.

INFORMATION

The relevant sources of information for Hokkaidō are given under the Sapporo section of this chapter. Bear in mind that you can always use the Japan Travel-Phone, a nationwide toll-free phone service provided by the Japan National Tourist Organisation

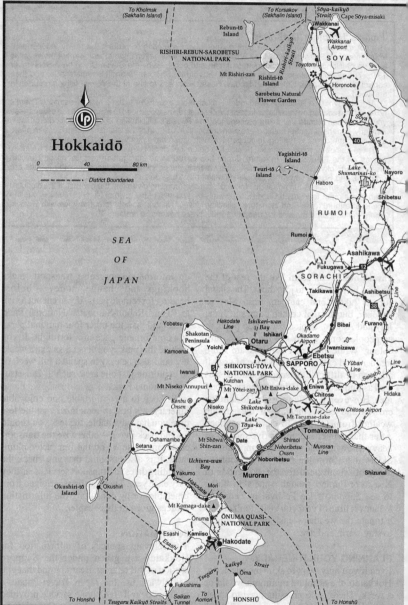

Hokkaidō

0   40   80 km

District Boundaries

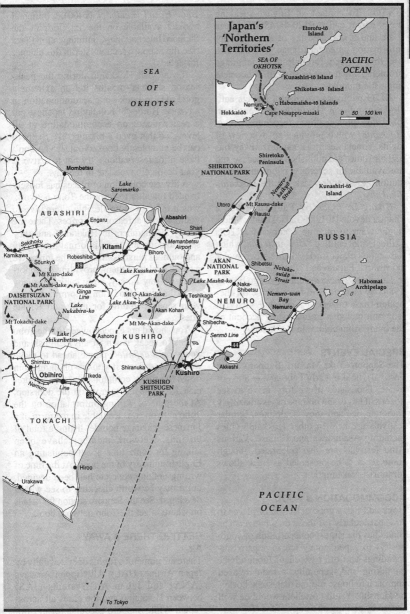

Japan's 'Northern Territories'

SEA OF OKHOTSK

PACIFIC OCEAN

Etorofu-tō Island

Kunashiri-tō Island

Shikotan-tō Island

Nemuro

○ Habomaisho-tō Islands

Hokkaidō

Cape Nosappu-misaki

0   50   100 km

SEA

OF

OKHOTSK

Mombetsu

Lake Saromarko

SHIRETOKO NATIONAL PARK

Shiretoko Peninsula

Nemuro-kaikyō Strait

Kunashiri-tō Island

ABASHIRI

Engaru

Sekihoku Line

Kamikawa

Sōunkyō

▲ Mt Kuro-dake

Robeshibe

Kitami

Bihoro

Abashiri

Shari

Utoro

Mt Rausu-dake

Rausu

RUSSIA

39

Memanbetsu Airport

Shibetsu

Notuke-suidō Strait

Habomai Archipelago

Mt Asahi-dake ▲

Furusato-Ginga Line

Lake Kussharo-ko

AKAN NATIONAL PARK

Lake Mashū-ko

Naka-Shibetsu

DAISETSUZAN NATIONAL PARK

Mt O-Akan-dake

Teshikaga

Lake Akan-ko

Nemuro-wan Bay

Nemuro

Lake Nukabira-ko

Akan Kohan

●

NEMURO

Mt Tokachi-dake

Mt Me-Akan-dake ▲

Shibecha

Lake Shikaribetsu-ko

Ashoro

KUSHIRO

Senmō Line

44

Shimizu

Shiranuka

Shibetsu

Obihiro

Ikeda

Kushiro

Akkeshi

Nemuro Line

38

KUSHIRO SHITSUGEN PARK

TOKACHI

Hiroo

PACIFIC OCEAN

Urakawa

To Tokyo

(JNTO). To contact an English-speaking travel expert call ☎ 0120-44-4800 between 9 am and 5 pm, any day of the week, for information on eastern Japan. You can also use this service for help with language problems when you're stuck in a hopeless linguistic muddle.

JNTO publishes two useful leaflets entitled *Sapporo & Vicinity* and *Southern Hokkaidō* plus a glossy brochure, *Japan Hokkaidō*, which provides an overview of sights. Timetables for Hokkaidō railway, bus and air routes are published in Japanese and are available in several versions at railway station newsstands – ask for the *Hokkaidō Jikokuhyō*.

Hiking in Japan by Paul Hunt has a chapter devoted to hikes in Hokkaidō. Skiers might want to pick up a copy of JNTO's skiing leaflet entitled *Skiing in Japan*, which has some details for Hokkaidō's two major ski resorts: Furano and Niseko.

Unbeaten Tracks in Japan (Virago Books, 1984) by Isabella Bird recounts the off-the-beaten-track travels of a doughty Victorian lady and includes an interesting account of the dying Ainu culture in Hokkaidō.

SPECIAL EVENTS

The Sapporo Yuki Matsuri (Sapporo Snow Festival), held in early February, is a major event. Thousands of visitors arrive to see dozens of large, and in some cases amazingly elaborate, ice and snow sculptures. Similar festivals are held in other Hokkaidō cities including Asahikawa and Chitose. Various Ainu festivals are also celebrated, though some seem to be presented as freak shows for tourist consumption.

ACCOMMODATION & FOOD

Hokkaidō has a good selection of places to stay, particularly for those on a budget. The island has the largest concentration of youth hostels in Japan; many are in superb surroundings and offer excellent food, advice on hiking and, generally, a more relaxed approach to house routine than some hostels on Honshū. Youth hostellers would be well served by picking up a copy of the *Hokkaidō*

Youth Hostel Handbook (¥400), a bilingual booklet available on the 1st floor of the Sapporo International Communication Plaza (see the Sapporo section later in this chapter for details).

If you visit Hokkaidō during the peak-season summer months it's an extremely good idea to book your accommodation in advance. Hordes of holidaying Japanese put a real squeeze on accommodation at all levels, so that even a big city like Sapporo can be completely booked out. If you don't have prior reservations, try not to arrive at your destination too late in the day.

A diverse collection of places has loosely banded together to form the Toho network, which offers a more flexible alternative to youth hostels at reasonable prices. There are nearly 80 members in Hokkaidō and they seem to concentrate on informal hospitality and outdoor pursuits. Many of the inns have a rustic quality to them, providing an opportunity to stay in, say, a log cabin. In many cases the accommodation is dormitory style, with separate rooms for male and female guests.

You should not expect owners of the Toho places to speak much (if any) English and you should *definitely* phone ahead to make reservations. Even if you are phoning from down the street, common courtesy is appreciated – don't just turn up on the doorstep. At the time of writing, information on the Toho network was available in the form of a Japanese-language booklet listing a total of 90 inns. Network members have been talking for some time about publishing an English summary of the book. At the time of writing nothing concrete had been decided, but it may be worth checking to see what's developed. See the Sapporo section for details on where to get the Toho network book.

GETTING THERE & AWAY
Air

There are numerous flights operated daily by Japan Airlines (JAL), All Nippon Airways (ANA) and Japan Air Systems (JAS) between Hokkaidō and the cities all across Japan. While Sapporo accounts for most of the traffic, smaller cities such as Asahikawa, Hakodate, Kushiro and Wakkanai also have flights to Tokyo and Osaka and other Honshū destinations.

The main airport for Sapporo is New Chitose airport, which is about 40 km south of the city. Sapporo has a subsidiary airport at Okadama, about 10 km north of the city. Ask, if you're not certain, which airport is stated on your ticket.

Train

Two of the fastest rail connections from Tokyo are the Hokutosei Express, which is a direct sleeper to Sapporo in 16 hours, and a combination of the shinkansen to Morioka followed by a limited express (*tokkyū*) via Aomori and Hakodate to Sapporo in 11 hours. There is also a sleeper service from Osaka (21 hours).

The trains cross from Honshū to Hokkaidō via the Seikan Tunnel, the world's longest undersea tunnel, which is an eerie 53.85 km in length. Travellers who can't stand the idea of being underground, and under the sea, for so long can take a ferry from Aomori.

JR offers special round-trip deals to Hokkaidō which include a return ticket plus unlimited travel on JR buses and trains while you're there. For example, a 14 day pass of this kind commencing in Tokyo costs ¥40,360 and there are more permutations

available. For details of these discount tickets check with travel agencies, JR Travel Service Centres (found in major JR stations – see the Tickets & Reservations section in the Getting Around chapter), or call the JR East-Infoline in Tokyo on ☎ 3423-0111. The JR East-Infoline service is available from 10 am to 6 pm, Monday to Friday, but not on holidays.

Boat

If you have the time, the cheapest way to visit Hokkaidō is on one of the many long-distance ferries from Honshū – if you travel overnight, you also save on accommodation costs. The main ferry ports on Hokkaidō are Otaru, Hakodate, Muroran, Tomakomai and Kushiro. These are connected with ports on Honshū such as Tokyo, Niigata, Nagoya, Sendai, Maizuru and Tsuruga. From Northern Honshū (Tōhoku) there are short-hop ferry routes to several of the major ports on Hokkaidō.

Sakhalin Ferry From late April to early September regularly scheduled ferries run between Otaru and Kholmsk on Russia's Sakhalin Island. During the same period there is also ferry service between Wakkanai and the Sakhalin port of Korsakov. Schedule and fare details can be found in the Otaru and Wakkanai Getting There & Away sections.

Seikan Tunnel Tour

Fancy spending two hours in a concrete tube at the bottom of the ocean? If the idea appeals, you may want to try JR's **Seikan Tunnel Tour**, conducted at the Yoshioka-kaitei station, located 145m below sea level.

The tour takes you through a maze of service corridors and passageways, quickly showing the immensity of this tunnel, which is the world's longest. Staff use bicycles and even cars to make their rounds. Longer tours include some of the tunnel's unique features, such as a 600m-long cablecar link to the shore of Hokkaido and a narrow passageway between the railway tracks that gives visitors a worm's eye view of trains roaring past.

Travellers travelling from Hokkaidō to Aomori take the tour at the Tappi-kaitei station, which is also underwater, just before the tunnel reaches the Tsugaru-hantō Peninsula. The tour costs ¥820 and you'll need to take a rapid train (kaisoku) from either Aomori or Hakodate. Limited express trains don't stop at the tunnel stations. Depending on the time when the next train comes to pick you up, tours last from one to 2½ hours. The tour is given in Japanese only, but infrastructure freaks should find enough to keep them entertained. ■

Most tourists who make this trip go with a tour group. Doing it alone is possible, but will require time and a healthy dose of patience. In addition to a Russian visa, you'll need to get an invitation letter from a hotel or tourist organisation in Sakhalin, plus a letter of permission from the captain of the ship on which you plan to sail. One place to get this bureaucratic ball of red tape rolling is the Japan-Russia Friendship Association (☎ 011-737-6221) which can handle queries on visas and other documents. For information on tours, call Polar Star Japan (☎ 011-271-2466).

GETTING AROUND

When planning a route around Hokkaidō, it's essential to remember the time (and expense) required because of the sheer size of the place. By way of illustration: the train journey from Hakodate, in the extreme south-west, to Wakkanai, at the northern-most tip, will take around 10 hours by limited express; a flight from Sapporo to Wakkanai takes only 50 minutes, but the one-way fare is ¥14,850.

Air

A network of internal flights radiating from Sapporo makes it easier for those in a hurry to bridge the large distances on Hokkaidō. Destinations include Hakodate, Kushiro and Wakkanai. Flights depart from both New Chitose and Okadama airports, so be sure to check when you buy your ticket to see which airport you'll be flying out of.

The Airport New Chitose airport, the main airport for Sapporo and Hokkaidō, is just a few minutes by bus from the actual city of Chitose, an expanding industrial centre. The airport has its own railway station and bus centre. The information desk and car rentals counter are next to the exit on the 1st floor of the airport terminal. Ask at the information desk for a brochure called *Chitose*. It's in English and Japanese, and includes useful phone numbers, details of bus services and maps of the region. The bus centre is outside the exit.

Sapporo is a 35 minute train ride (¥1030) by limited express on the JR Chitose line. There are convenient bus services to various destinations on Hokkaidō. Some useful ones include Sapporo (70 minutes, ¥800), Lake Shikotsu-ko (45 minutes), Lake Tōya-ko (2¼ hours), Noboribetsu Onsen (70 minutes) and Niseko (three hours). Buses to Lake Tōya-ko and Noboribetsu Onsen only run from June to October.

Buses link Sapporo with Okadama airport in 25 minutes (¥300).

Train

The rail network on Hokkaidō has a couple of major lines with fast and frequent services, while the remainder have mainly slow or infrequent trains. Most unprofitable lines have been phased out in favour of buses – several lines shown on old maps are no longer in operation.

Hokkaido's long distances mean that rail fares can eat up a large part of your budget. However, for some destinations JR offers discounted return tickets that may ease the pain somewhat. One example is the 'S-kippu' (S-ticket). This is usually valid for four days from the time you start your outbound trip and offers savings of 20% to 40% compared with two one-way tickets. For a few of the longer routes, notably Sapporo-Wakkanai, the validity period is extended to six days. If there are two of you, then you can try the 'S-kippu-four', which is valid for three months. There are other types of ticket packages, such as area passes that allow you unlimited rail travel within a certain section of Hokkaido. These aren't often that useful, however, as many local destinations are accessible only by bus. It's difficult to sort out all the different fare options unless you speak Japanese or can find an English-speaking travel agent. If you're in Sapporo, staff at the International Communication Plaza may be able to help out.

Also, on a couple of routes JR Hokkaido offers a discounted limited express surcharge if you go without a reserved seat. For example, between Hakodate and Sapporo, the surcharge without a reserved seat is

¥1240, while that for a reserved seat is ¥2970. This discount surcharge is also offered between Sapporo and Asahikawa.

Bus

Hokkaido's bus network is far more extensive than that of the railway, so if you're planning to cover a lot of ground, you'll likely be doing do much of it by bus. Intracity buses are usually almost as quick as the trains, tend to run more often and cost less. However, buses to more remote regions tend to run infrequently, or only during the peak tourist season, and fares are often expensive.

Car Rental

If you can afford the extra expense, or can find passengers to share the costs, driving is highly recommended as it cuts out the problems with the slow or infrequent public transport. It also provides you with the mobility to reach remote areas at your own pace. Rates for smaller cars start around ¥7800 for 24 hours, but bear in mind the expressway tolls and fuel costs. Most of the large cities have car rental agencies such as Nippon or Budget Rent-a-Car. Mazda Rent-a-Car (☎ 0120-01-5656) generally offers slightly cheaper rates and does not charge for mileage, which can make for significant savings in Hokkaidō. The company also sometimes has special deals and offers discounts to travellers who have stayed at Toho network inns.

Bicycle

This is a popular mode of transportation; many of the roads around the coastline have low gradients and there are plenty of cycling terminals and youth hostels which cater for cyclists.

Hitching

The residents on Hokkaidō, and even tourists passing through, seem happy to oblige with a ride. In more remote regions, and especially during the off season for tourism, there may simply be a lack of traffic. If you ask around, it's sometimes possible to arrange a ride with other guests at youth hostels – the hostel manager usually knows who's going where.

HAKODATE 函館

Hakodate (population 313,000), a convenient gateway for Hokkaidō, is a laid-back kind of place with something of an historical heritage. It was one of the first foreign trading ports to be opened up under the terms of the Kanagawa Treaty of 1854 and a small foreign community took root here.

It's worth spending a day here to ride the trams (introduced in 1913) or stroll around the Motomachi district with its assortment of Western-style buildings. In fine weather the summit of Mt Hakodate-yama offers fine views across the city, day or night.

Orientation

Hakodate is fairly spread out. The western part of the city, within easy reach of Hakodate station by tram and bus, is the area with the bulk of the historical sights and is spread out below the slopes of Mt Hakodate-yama. Several km east of the station is the sprawling city centre and the mildly interesting remains of Goryōkaku fort.

Information

The Hakodate Tourist Information Office (☎ 0138-23-5440) is to the right as you exit the station. It's open from 9 am to 7 pm, but closes at 5 pm in winter. The office has plenty of detailed maps and brochures in English, and can also help with finding accommodation.

JNTO publishes a leaflet entitled *Southern Hokkaidō* which has a basic map and details on the sights, transport and accommodation in Hakodate.

Mt Hakodate-yama 函館山

Fine views of Hakodate can be enjoyed from the summit of this mountain, preferably on a clear night. A cablecar (the Japanese call these 'ropeways') whisks you up to the top in a few minutes and relieves you of ¥1130 for the return trip. Operating hours are from 10 am to 10 pm (26 April to 31 October), and 10 am to 9 pm (1 November to 25 April).

To reach the cablecar station from JR Hakodate station, take tram Nos 2 or 5 and get off at the Jyūjigai tram stop (about a six minute ride). The base station is then a seven

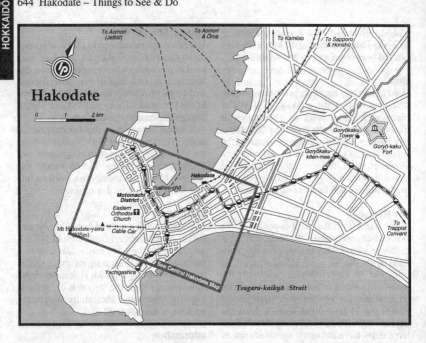

minute walk uphill. From Hakodate station, you can take a bus (20 minutes, ¥360) directly to the summit, but this service is suspended from late October until late April.

If you feel fit, there's a mountain trail winding up the mountain, though it's closed from late November to late April.

Motomachi District 元町

This district, at the base of Mt Hakodate-yama, has retained several Western-style buildings from the turn of the century and is a pleasant place to stroll around.

The easiest building to recognise is the Eastern Orthodox Church, an attractive reconstruction dating from 1916 (the original was constructed in 1859). Entry is free. From May to November the church is open from 10 am to 5 pm (4 pm the rest of the year); it's closed from noon to 1 pm. Other sights in Motomachi worth checking out include the Chinese Memorial Hall (a bit pricey at ¥500) and the Foreigner's Cemetery.

To reach Motomachi, take tram No 5 from Hakodate station to the Suehiro-chō tram stop (¥200) and then walk uphill for about 10 minutes.

Goryō-kaku Fort 五稜郭

Japan's first western-style fort was built here in 1864 in the shape of a five pointed star. Five years later, forces loyal to the Tokugawa Shogunate held out for just seven days before surrendering to the attacking troops of the Meiji Restoration. All that's left now are the outer walls, and the grounds have been made into a park with the obligatory squads of cherry trees. Inside the grounds, keen historians or militarists can pay ¥100 admission to visit the Hakodate Museum which displays the hardware used in the battle and the inevitable blood-stained uniforms.

Close to the park's entrance is the Goryō-kaku Tower, which provides a bird's-eye view of the ruins and the surrounding area.

The tower is open daily from 8 am to 8 pm from April to October, and from 9 am to 6 pm the rest of the year; admission is ¥520. For a bottom-up perspective, you can rent a rowboat for the two km circuit around the moat (¥1000 for 45 minutes). Be careful not to get your oars tangled in the lily pads.

To reach the fort, take tram No 2 or 5 for a 15 minute ride (¥220) to the Goryōkaku-kōen-mae tram stop. From there, it's a 10 minute walk to the fort.

Trappist Convent トラピスト修道院
This convent, founded in 1898, is on the outskirts of Hakodate, close to Yunokawa Onsen. Visitors come to see the architecture and gardens, but the real drawcard is the shop which sells delicious home-made biscuits, sweets and butter.

From Hakodate train station, take bus No 19 or No 39 for the 35 minute ride to the Yunokawa-danchi-kitaguchi bus stop (¥260). From there, it's a 15 minute walk to the convent. Hakodate Bus Company bus No 10-2 stops at Trapistine-mae, right in front of the convent (¥290). Note that the one day, open transport tickets are not valid for these buses.

Yachigashira Onsen Spa 谷地頭温泉
This enormous spa, accommodating some 600 bathers, is not a major attraction, but is an inexpensive opportunity to take a look at Japanese onsen culture. Entry is just ¥340 and the spa can be reached by tram from Hakodate station. Get off at Yachigashira, the final stop (¥220). From 1 April to 31 October it's open from 6 am to 9.30 pm (from 7 am to 9.30 pm the rest of the year); it's closed on the 2nd and 4th Friday of every month and over New Year.

Market
If you're an early bird, the good *asa-ichi* ('morning market') is open from 5 am to noon; closed on Sunday. Most of the real action is over by 7 am; from then on it's mostly aimed at tourists. It's a two minute walk south from the west exit of Hakodate station.

Special Events
In mid-May, the festival of Hakodate Goryōkaku Matsuri features a parade with townsfolk dressed in the uniforms of the soldiers who took part in the Meiji Restoration battle of 1868.

Places to Stay
During the busy summer months, Hakodate is swamped with Japanese tourists heading northwards to other parts of Hokkaidō, and accommodation can be hard to find. If you don't have a reservation, it's a good idea to call into the tourist information office next to the station – the staff here will know which ryokan, minshuku or hotels, if any, have vacancies. They will also ring ahead and make same-day reservations for you.

Minshuku *Minshuku Tabiji* (☎ 0138-26-7652) is a pleasant, well-run place and also a member of the Toho network. Prices start at ¥5800 per person including two meals or ¥3500 without meals. One block further west is the *Niceday Inn* (☎ 0138-22-5919), which has a special rate for foreigners of ¥3000 per person, without meals. The rooms are a bit cramped, but staff are friendly and the owner speaks English.

Close to the Hōrai-chō tram stop is the *Minshuku Ryokan Nagashima* (☎ 0138-26-2101), a small ryokan with only 13 rooms. Per-person costs are ¥6500 with two meals. Around the next corner is the *Hakodate Youth Guesthouse* (☎ 0138-26-7892). It's not an official youth hostel and rooms are either doubles or triples. Per-person costs are ¥3500 except during 1 July to 30 September, when they rise to ¥4500.

Hotels One of the cheapest hotels close to the station is the *Business Hotel New Ōte* (☎ 0138-23-4561). It has singles from ¥5000 to ¥5500 and twins from ¥9000 to ¥10,000. The *Aqua Garden Hotel* (☎ 0138-23-2200) has singles/twins at ¥6000/12,000 and, to the north of the station, the *Hakodate Plaza Hotel* (☎ 0138-22-0121) has singles for ¥6500, twins for ¥11,000 and doubles for ¥10,000.

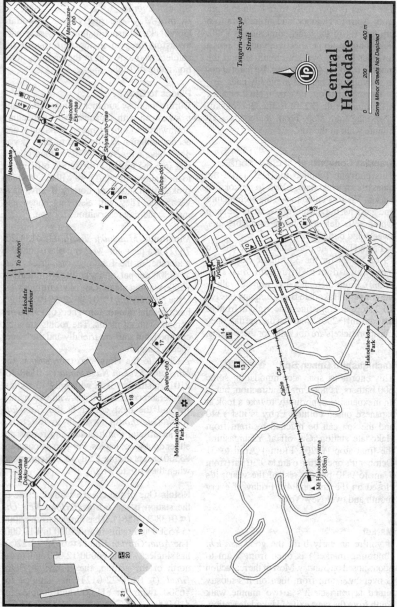

Central Hakodate

0   200   400 m

Some Minor Streets Not Depicted

PLACES TO STAY

1 Hakodate Plaza
Hotel
函館プラザホテル

4 Hakodate Harbour
View Hotel
函館ハーバー
ビューホテル

5 Business Hotel New
Ōte
ビジネスホテル
ニュー大手

6 Aqua Garden Hotel
アクアガーデン
ホテル

7 Hakodate Kokusai
Hotel
函館国際ホテル

8 Minshuku Tabiji
民宿旅路

9 Niceday Inn
ナイスデイイン

11 Minishuku Ryokan
Nagashima
民宿旅館長島

12 Hakodate Youth
Guesthouse
函館ユースゲスト
ハウス

PLACES TO EAT

2 Hisago Sushi
ひさご寿司

3 The Don Restaurant

10 Indo Curry Koike
小いけ

16 Hakodate Kaisen
Club
はこだて海鮮倶楽部

OTHER

13 Eastern Orthodox
Church
ハリストス正教会

14 Higashi Hongan-ji
Temple
東本願寺

15 Jetfoil Terminal
ジェットフォイル
乗り場

17 Kanemori
Warehouse
金森美術館

18 Chinese Memorial
Hall
中華会館

19 Old Russian
Consulate
旧ロシア領事館

20 Kōryū-ji Temple
高竜寺

21 Foreigner's Cemetry
外人墓地

More up-market station area options include the *Hakodate Kokusai Hotel* (☎ 0138-23-5151), where singles range from ¥10,000 to ¥15,000 and twins from ¥20,000 to ¥30,000. A bit more reasonable is the *Hakodate Harbour View Hotel* (☎ 0138-22-0111), with singles/twins/doubles at ¥9000/18,000 /13,000.

North of Hakodate If you want to stay out of Hakodate in some fine scenery, you could consider *Exander Ōnuma Youth Hostel* (☎ 0138-67-3419) – see the section on Ōnuma.

Places to Eat

The station area doesn't offer a great deal in the way of restaurants, though there are a few rāmen shops and fast-food barns on the main street running out from the station. Near the station *The Don* restaurant is a tiny place

specialising in *donburi* (meat or seafood atop a heaping bowl of rice). Prices start at ¥400 and sometimes there are special deals that make things even cheaper. Photos tacked up on the wall and in the front window aid in ordering.

For something a little more up-market, try *Hisago Sushi*, a sushi restaurant that is popular with Japanese tourists. Sushi platters range from ¥1500 to ¥2500, but of course prices can go much higher if you sit at the sushi bar and point at will.

One of Hakodate's culinary landmarks is *Indo Curry Koike*, which dishes up delicious curry, perfected after 60 years of effort on the part of the founder, Koike-san. Specialities include scallop curry and jumbo pork cutlet curry, and prices range from ¥550 to ¥800. It's located in the western part of town, a few blocks south of the Jyūjigai intersection.

At the foot of the mountain, in the

Motomachi district, there are plenty of trendy eateries in converted western-style buildings. There are also a few along the water, near the jetfoil terminal. The *Hakodate Kaisen Club*, located on the second floor of a wooden Hakodate Nishi-Hatoba shopping/restaurant complex, has a nice outdoor deck, and beers are almost reasonable at ¥350. You can't eat outside, though this is just as well as the food is overpriced.

Getting There & Away
Air ANA and JAL connect Hakodate airport with Nagoya, Osaka, Sendai and Tokyo.

Train Hakodate is connected with Aomori by the JR Tsugaru Kaikyō line, which runs via the Seikan Tunnel beneath the Tsugaru Kaikyō Straits to Hakodate in two hours by limited express. The fare is ¥3090, plus ¥2150 limited express surcharge. Almost as fast, and much cheaper, is the rapid train (*kaisoku*) service, which does the trip in 2½ hours and costs only ¥3090. This train also gives you the option of taking the Seikan Tunnel Tour. See the Getting There & Away section in the introduction to this chapter for details.

Limited express sleeper services from Ueno in Tokyo (they continue on to Sapporo) take 14 hours and 20 minutes (¥14,220). A combination of limited express and shinkansen (as far as Morioka) from Tokyo takes around seven to eight hours and costs ¥17,830 plus express surcharges.

There is a limited express service available between Osaka and Hakodate. Like the Ueno-Sapporo service it is a sleeper train and takes 17 hours and 30 minutes (¥16,480).

Sapporo is linked with Hakodate in 3¾ hours by limited express via New Chitose airport and Tomakomai. The fare is ¥8420, or ¥6690 if you don't opt for a reserved seat.

Bus An afternoon bus service links Hakodate with Sapporo (6½ hours, ¥4600). There is also an overnight bus that leaves at 11.55 pm and arrives at 6.30 am. Buses leave from, and arrive in, Hakodate at the Hakodate Harbour View Hotel.

Boat Ferries link Hakodate with Aomori and Ōma, both in Aomori prefecture in northern Honshū. The most convenient service is the jetfoil which links Hakodate with Aomori in 1¾ hours. The fare is ¥5040 during the week and ¥6300 on weekends. The terminal is about one km south-west of Hakodate station, not far from the Jyūjigai tram stop.

From Hakodate port there are two to three ferries a day to Ōma (1¾ hours, ¥1000) and at least nine sailings daily to Aomori (3¾ hours, ¥1400). Unfortunately, Hakodate-kō Port is not convenient for access to the city centre. The taxi ride to the JR station costs around ¥1500. The closest bus stop, Hokudai-mae, is a seven minute walk from the ferry terminal; from there you can catch bus Nos 1, 17 or 19 to the station (¥250).

Getting Around
The Airport A bus service links Hakodate airport with the city in around 20 minutes (¥290). Buses leave once to twice an hour from in front of the Harbour View Hotel, near to the JR Hakodate station.

Bus & Tram One day (¥1000) and two day (¥1700) open tickets, which entitle you to unlimited city bus and tram travel, are available from the tourist information office or on buses or trams. The tickets are not valid for travel on Hakodate Bus Company buses, which leave from the platform closest to the street at Hakodate station. This is no problem, as the city transport services are more than sufficient and even include the bus service to the top of Mt Hakodate-yama.

ŌNUMA　大沼
This small town, just north of Hakodate, is the gateway to **Ōnuma Quasi National Park**, which contains a trio of lakes beneath Mt Komaga-dake, the volcano that formed the lakes when it erupted. There are several camping grounds on the shores of the lakes, as well as a network of hiking trails.

The main lakes, **Lake Ōnuma** and **Lake Konuma**, meaning 'big' lake and 'little' lake respectively, are really one big lake separated by a road and rail bridge. There are cruise boats that take in both lakes in about 30 minutes (¥820), leaving every 40 minutes from the pier around 500m north-west of the Ōnuma-kōen station. Cruises operate from May to October only.

Places to Stay

Exandar Ōnuma Youth Hostel (☎ 0138-67-3419) is a 10 minute walk south of JR Ōnuma-kōen station. Walk out of the station and follow the road for a couple of hundred metres before taking the first right. The hostel is on the left-hand side shortly after you cross the railway tracks. Bicycles can be rented from the hostel and there are hot springs near by. The owner is an avid canoeing fan and runs canoe tours from the hostel. Beds are ¥2800 and the hostel is closed from 13 November to 12 December.

Minshuku Itō-sō (☎ 0138-67-2522) has rates starting at around ¥6500 per person including two meals. To get there walk out from the station for a few hundred metres and continue through the first intersection. The minshuku is a little further down the road on the right side.

Those who don't mind spending a little extra can try the *Pension Haine* (☎ 0138-67-3618) which is around a five to 10 minute walk from the station on the way to the youth hostel, and is also on the left-hand side. Per-person costs range from ¥7800 to ¥8500 with two meals.

The nearest camping ground to the station is the *Ōmura Camping Ground*. It's only about 600m from the station, a bit further on from the pier.

Getting There & Away

Ōnuma-kōen station is about 40 minutes to one hour by local train from Hakodate on the JR Hakodate line and tickets cost ¥520. You may have to change trains at Ōnuma station. A limited express will get you there in a mere 20 minutes, but costs ¥1740. There are also five buses daily between Hakodate station to Ōnuma-kōen station (one hour, ¥700). From Hakodate, buses leave from the Hakodate Bus Company platform in front of the station.

ESASHI & OKUSHIRI-TŌ ISLAND
江差・奥尻島

Esashi is a major fishing town, 67 km west of Hakodate. The town is renowned for its annual festival, Ubagami Taisha Matsuri, which is held from 9 to 11 August and features a parade of more than a dozen ornate floats. Okushiri-tō Island is a sleepy place with small fishing villages, beautiful coastline scenery and only a few touristy sights cluttering up the view. Ferries link Esashi with Okushiri, the main town on the island, in just over two hours.

In mid-1993 Okushiri-tō was devastated by a major earthquake that measured 8.1 on the Richter scale. The ensuing tsunami washed away many coastal homes and claimed some 400 lives. Although the island is basically back in business, don't be surprised if some places look a little worse for wear.

Places to Stay

There are plenty of minshuku near the ferry pier in Okushiri. *Minshuku Honobono-sō* (☎ 01397-2-3395) is a three minute walk from the pier and has rooms with two meals for ¥6000 per person. *Minshuku Hemmi* (☎ 01397-2-2020), about five minutes from the pier, costs around ¥5000 per person with two meals. There are also places to stay in Aonae, a fishing village on the southern tip of the island. At the opposite end of the island, near Cape Inaho-misaki, is *Minshuku Inaho* (☎ 01397-2-2230), which also charges around ¥6000 per person, including two meals. If you arrive in town too late to catch the last ferry to Okushiri-tō, there are also minshuku and ryokan in Esashi with similar rates.

Getting There & Away

There are six buses daily linking Hakodate with Esashi (2¼ hours, ¥1700). By train from Hakodate it takes about three hours (infrequent service) on the JR Esashi line.

From Esashi, ferries depart twice daily (once a day in winter) to Okushiri-tō. The trip takes 2¼ hours and costs ¥2060 for a second class ticket. The last ferry from

Esashi leaves at 1 pm. Between late April and October another ferry service operates from Okushiri to Setana, further north of Esashi. Ferries depart once or twice daily and the trip takes 1¾ hours (¥1540). From Setana there is a bus service to Oshamanbe (1¾ hours, ¥1240) which is on the JR Hakodate line.

If time is more precious than money, you can also fly directly to Okushiri-tō from either Sapporo (¥37,600 round trip) or Hakodate (¥20,940).

NISEKO ニセコ

Niseko lies between Mt Yōtei-zan and Mt Niseko Annupuri and functions as a year-round ski resort. It is one of Hokkaidō's prime ski resorts during winter and a hiking base during summer and autumn. Numerous hot springs in the area are also popular. The staff at the International Communication Plaza in Sapporo (☎ 011-211-3678) can supply you with information on other activities in the area, such as white water rafting, and how to get to them.

Places to Stay & Eat

Most places in Niseko are hard to reach by public transport, except in winter when there are frequent direct buses to the area's ski slopes.

Niseko Annupuri Youth Hostel (☎ 0136-58-2084) is located near the Annupuri Kokusai skiing ground and has beds for ¥3100. To get there, from Niseko station take a bus bound for Konbu Onsen and get off at the Annupuri Kokusai ski-jō stop. From there it's about seven minutes on foot to the hostel. *Niseko Kōgen Youth Hostel* (☎ 0136-44-1171) is in a nice rural setting, but is harder to reach. Take a bus from Niseko station bound for Konbu Onsen and, after around six minutes, get off at the Fujiyama stop. Walk back 20m to the intersection and turn right. The hostel is about one km down the road on the left-hand side. Bike rental is available at the hostel and the manager speaks some English; you may be able to call ahead and have them pick you up at the bus stop. Buses from Niseko station to Konbu

Onsen run seven times daily in summer and more frequently in winter.

Niseko Ambishiasu (Ambitious) (☎ 0136-44-3011), a member of the Toho network, is five minutes by car from Niseko station and, if you speak enough Japanese to get the message across or can find someone to speak on your behalf, the owners will come and pick you up at the station; rates are ¥4000 with two meals (¥4300 in winter).

One of the largest concentrations of accommodation in the Niseko area is at Hirafu ski resort (Hirafu station is one stop north of Niseko). *Hirafu Sansō* (☎ 0136-22-0285) is near the Hirafu ski lifts and charges ¥5000 per person, including two meals. Nearby, *Mountain Jam* (☎ 0136-23-2020) is a pension with rates of around ¥7500 for the same deal. In winter there are shuttle buses to the ski resort from Hirafu station, as well as buses running from Kutchan station (one stop north of Hirafu). There is no bus service in summer.

Getting There & Away

Although it's a year-round resort, Niseko suffers from poor public transportation links in the summer and most accommodation and activities are aimed at people with vehicles. Before you go, it would be a good idea to check with the tourist information office about what transport options are available. Winter is a different story: there are frequent direct buses to the area's ski resorts from Sapporo and New Chitose airport, as well as shuttle buses from the railway stations at Niseko, Hirafu and Kutchan.

Niseko is 2¾ hours from Sapporo on the JR Hakodate line; tickets cost ¥2060 to Niseko and slightly less to Kutchan and Hirafu. You may have to change trains at Otaru, especially in summer. In winter there are special ski trains that make the trip far more quickly, but cost about twice as much.

In winter there are regular bus services connecting the Niseko ski resorts with Sapporo and New Chitose airport (three hours, ¥2000). In summer buses run from Otaru to Niseko station in just under two hours (¥1300).

OTARU 小樽

Otaru (population 162,200) is a ferry port
with services south to Honshū and, in
summer, to Russia's Sakhalin island. The
town's importance as a port in the early
development of Hokkaidō has left a small
legacy of old western-style buildings and an
attractive canal area. While it bustles with
port activity, Otaru is still small enough to
tackle on foot. It's a good place to spend a
leisurely day strolling around and admiring
the architecture.

Information

The tourist information office (☎ 0134-29-
1333), at the entrance to JR Otaru station, is
open from 10 am to 6 pm daily, except on
Saturday and Sunday, when the opening
hours are from 9.30 am to 5.30 pm. The *Otaru
Handy Map* is a helpful English-language

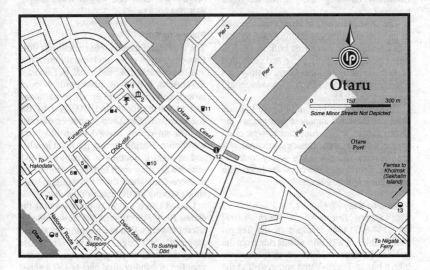

1	Takinami マンジャーレ Takinami	5	Otaru Green Hotel 小樽グリーンホテル
		6	New Green Hotel ニューグリーン ホテル
2	Otaru Municipal Museum 小樽市博物館	7	Otaru Kokusai Hotel 小樽国際ホテル
3	Uminekoya Coffee Shop 海猫屋	8	Bus Station バスターミナル
4	Ebiya Ryokan 海老屋旅館	9	Business Hotel New Minato ビジネスホテル ニューみなと

10	Kito Ryokan キト旅館
11	Otaru Beer Pub 小樽ビール
12	Tourist Information Booth 観光案内所
13	Otaru Sakhalin Ferry Terminal 小樽サハリン フェリーターミナル

pamphlet with several maps and information about Otaru sights, transportation and accommodation.

Things to See

Most of the attractions in town are east of Otaru station, close to the harbour, and consist of Japanese and western-style buildings dating back from early this century. Rated highly are the Ex-Nippon Yūsen Company building and the Mitsui Bank building.

The **Otaru Municipal Museum** is housed in an almost Chinese-looking building that was a warehouse when first built in 1893. It now houses a tastefully presented collection of items relating to local Otaru history. It's open from 9.30 am to 5 pm (closed Monday) and entry is ¥100.

Perhaps the best known of Otaru's attractions, at least for Japanese tourists, is the **Otaru Canal**, which runs east to west close to the harbour area. Beside the canal is a granite path with gas lamps – very romantic at dusk. Sections of the canal are lined with photogenic old buildings.

Places to Stay

The *Otaru Tengu-Yama Youth Hostel* (☎ 0134-34-1474) is close to the Tengu-Yama cablecar, a 10 minute bus ride from the station. Beds are ¥2600. From the station, take a bus to Tengu-Yama and get off at the last stop.

There are several ryokan scattered around town which, while not particularly interesting, are a pleasant alternative to business hotels. *Ebiya Ryokan* (☎ 0134-22-2317) is located in a quiet area, not far from the Otaru Canal and the old western buildings. Per-person rates with two meals range from ¥6500 to ¥7800. Also just a few streets away from the canal is *Kito Ryokan* (☎ 0134-22-2803) which has rates of ¥8000 for the same deal.

On the business hotel front, one of the cheapest places around is the *Otaru Green Hotel* (☎ 0134-33-0333). It's just four minutes on foot from Otaru station; prices for singles/doubles start at ¥3500/ 7000. Just across the road is the *New Green Hotel*

(☎ 0134-33-6100) with singles at ¥5000 and twins at ¥9400. Also close to the station is the *Business Hotel New Minato* (☎ 0134-32-3710), where singles start from ¥4200 and twins from ¥5200.

An interesting, and more expensive, alternative to all these is a night at the *Otaru Grand Hotel Classic* (☎ 0134-22-6500), which occupies one of the nicer, renovated, western-style buildings. This little slice of history will cost you ¥9350 for a single, ¥18,700 for a twin.

Places to Eat

The area along the canal has numerous little European-style cafes and restaurants. Just one street back from the canal is *Takinami Restaurant*, a relaxing place with wooden rafters, ceiling fans and excellent pasta and fish set lunches for around ¥900. Nearby, the *Uminekoya Coffee Shop* is another exercise in pleasant decor, housed in an old brick warehouse. During the day it has set lunches and at night it doubles as a pub. Raw fish aficionados may want to take a stroll along Sushiya-dōri, where there is a string of sushi shops serving up the catch of the day.

One of Otaru's most popular spots is the *Otaru Beer Pub*, one of the new breed of microbreweries that are popping up around Japan. It's in a large, renovated warehouse along the canal where you can quaff several varieties of hand-crafted beer (¥450 a glass) amid solid wood furnishings and gleaming copper beer vats, with jazz music tinkling in the background. The menu (there's an English version) consists mostly of German-style food, and dinner for two with a few beers will probably run to around ¥5000. It's not a lunch option, however, as the doors don't open until 3 pm.

Getting There & Away

Train Otaru is 30 minutes by rapid train from Sapporo on the JR Hakodate line. Local trains take around 50 minutes. Tickets for either cost ¥610.

Bus A very frequent bus service runs directly between Otaru and Sapporo from in front of

Sapporo station. It takes around 50 minutes and costs ¥550.

Boat Long-distance ferries link Otaru with ports on Honshū such as Niigata (19 hours, ¥5150), Tsuruga (21 hours, ¥7290) and Maizuru (29 hours, ¥6590). All fares are for the cheapest second-class berths. Ferries leave from the Shin Nihonkai Ferry Terminal. To get there from Otaru station, take the Marine-go tourist bus to Katsunai-futō Pier (¥180).

Sakhalin Ferry Between late April and early September there is a limited ferry service between Otaru and the Russian port town of Kholmsk on Sakhalin island. There are only a few scheduled sailings each month, though extra departures are sometimes added. The cheapest one-way/round trip fare is ¥38,000/ 54,000, which buys you a berth in an eight person room. Slightly cheaper is a route that runs from Otaru to Kholmsk and on to Wakkanai. For more information on making the trip to Sakhalin, see the Getting There & Away section in the introduction to this chapter.

Getting Around
The main part of town is small enough to comfortably negotiate on foot, but you can also use the Otaru Marine-go tourist bus service, which makes a loop through the city taking in most of the sights, as well as the Shin Nihonkai Ferry Terminal. There is a flat fare of ¥190 and one-day passes are available for ¥700.

SAPPORO　札幌
Sapporo (population 1.75 million) is Hokkaidō's administrative hub, main population centre and a lively, prosperous city. The friendly locals and cosmopolitan flavour of the city, with its sweeping tree-lined boulevards, make it well worth a night or two. There may not be a wealth of 'sights', but there's plenty to do day and night. Like Hiroshima in western Honshū, Sapporo presents a good chance to take a peek at modern Japan without feeling squeezed by the pressing crowds that prevail in cities like Tokyo and Osaka.

Orientation
Sapporo is one of the only cities in Japan where it's almost possible to find places by their addresses. The reason is the precise grid pattern of the blocks, which are named and numbered according to compass points (north, east, south, west). The centre point is near the Sapporo TV Tower. The street names reflect this pattern, with the exception of the major Ō-dōri. Thus the major artery, West 3-4, runs north to south between the West 3 and West 4 blocks. Addresses are also given in terms of blocks: for example Sapporo's famous Tokei-dai Clocktower is located at North 1, West 2. See the orientation map to get an idea of the grid layout.

From Sapporo station, West 3-4 makes a beeline straight through the administrative, commercial and entertainment areas of the city, crossing the huge Ō-dōri on the way. The area between the station and Ō-dōri is mainly administrative. This is where you'll find the airline companies, banks and so on. South of Ō-dōri is a shopping district, with large numbers of department stores and restaurants. Between the South 4 and South 9 blocks is the Susukino entertainment area, which looks rather dull by day, but comes to life at night. It's the largest entertainment area north of Tokyo and, besides the usual soaplands, peep shows, discos and shot bars, there are some very good restaurants in the area.

Information
Sapporo has several tourist offices with helpful English-speaking staff. The municipal government also produces a wide range of English-language pamphlets and maps.

The information counters are run by the Sapporo International Communication Plaza Foundation. The one most travellers will likely hit first is the Lilac Paseo International Information Corner (☎ 011-213-5062) in JR Sapporo station. It's open daily from 9 am to 5 pm, closed the second and fourth Wednesday of every month. The staff here have a wide range of maps and information on Sapporo and the rest of Hokkaidō – at the very least pick up a copy of the excellent

Traveller's Sapporo visitor's handbook and map. Although the staff are not authorised to book accommodation, they can make recommendations according to your budget. The office is in the west concourse of the station, inside the JR Ticket & Travel Office.

The Sapporo International Communication Plaza (☎ 011-211-3678) is on the 1st and 3rd floors of the MN building, just opposite the clocktower, and caters to the needs of tourists both in Sapporo and further afield around Hokkaidō. Large folders crammed with information on Hokkaidō are available and well worth taking a look at if you're heading off to more remote parts of the island. Hiking and cycling maps are also available. Staff can also help those planning a long-term stay in Sapporo.

There is a notice board with messages, teaching advertisements and invitations to 'Free Talk Parties'. There's also a selection of foreign newspapers and magazines to read in the comfort of the large lounge. It is also possible to organise youth hostel membership on the 1st floor. The offices are open daily from 9.30 am to 5 pm except for New Year's day.

If you plan to spend some time in Sapporo, pick up copies of *Monthly Hokkaidō* or *What's On in Sapporo* for listings of events.

Other offices around town include the Sapporo Tourist Association (☎ 011-211-3341) and the Sapporo City Government's tourist section (☎ 011-211-2376); both have English-speaking staff. There is also an information counter in the Ōdōri subway station, located near Exit 14.

Visas & Consulates Sapporo has a few consulates:

Australia
Australian Consulate, North 1, West 3 (on the 5th floor of the Daiwa Bank building) (☎ 011-242-4381)
China
Consulate General of the People's Republic of China, South 13, West 23 (☎ 011-563-5563)
Russia
Consulate General of the Russian Federation, South 14, West 12 (☎ 011-561-3171)

South Korea
Consulate General of the Republic of Korea, North 3, West 21 (☎ 011-621-0288)
USA
Consulate General of the United States, North 1, West 28 (☎ 011-641-1115)

Books Sapporo has branches of both Maruzen and Kinokuniya bookshops in the Chūō shopping district. Kinokuniya has a small selection of foreign books on its 2nd floor. The 4th floor selection of foreign books in Maruzen, however, is much more extensive and is the best place north of Tokyo to pick up reading material.

The Sapporo Library has around 2300 English-language titles on its 2nd floor. It also has copies of English-language newspapers. It has slightly bewildering opening hours, but basically is open from 9 am to 5 pm, except for Tuesday, when it's open from 1 pm to 5.15 pm, and on Monday when it's closed all day. It's located at South 22, West 13. To get there, take the tram to the Toshokan-mae stop.

Botanical Garden 植物園
The Botanical Garden, run by Hokkaido University, has more than 5000 varieties of Hokkaidō's flora on 14 hectares and provides a relaxing spot for a stroll, or an afternoon nap on one of the well kept lawns.

In the garden grounds near the main gate is a small **Ainu Museum** with a good collection of tools, clothing, household utensils and the like. The display cases hold around 200 out of the 2000 items that are in the care of Hokkaido University. Many of them are from Sakhalin – keep an eye out for the mock balalaika and the salmon-skin boots. There are English captions for all the exhibits, making it well worth a visit.

The garden is open daily from 9 am to 4 pm (29 April to 3 November), but closes half an hour earlier from October to early November, when it's also closed on Monday. Admission is ¥400. Between 4 November and 28 April, only the greenhouse is open (10 am to 3 pm); admission is ¥150 and it is closed on Sunday.

Tokei-dai Clocktower　時計台

The Tokei-dai Clocktower was constructed in 1878 and has now become a cherished landmark for Sapporo residents and a useful orientation point for visitors. It's not particularly stunning, but you can enter the building and wander around a small museum of local history. If you're wondering why such an unimposing little structure should attract a constant stream of amateur photographers, it's because the clocktower is considered *the* symbol of Sapporo and no self-respecting Japanese would go home from a trip to the city without a picture of themselves posed in front of it.

At the time of writing the clocktower was closed for renovation and was not due to re-open until September 1998.

Sapporo Beer Garden & Museum
サッポロビールビヤガーデン・博物館

The Sapporo Beer Garden and Museum are on the site of the original Sapporo Brewery. Dating back to 1876, it was the first brewery to be established in Japan. Tours of the museum are free. If there's a large number of you, make reservations in advance (☎ 011-731-4368). The tours, lasting about 80 minutes, are given throughout the year from 9 am to 3.40 pm (until 4.40 pm from June to August).

The cavernous beer 'garden' (it's actually a hall) offers the opportunity for some serious drinking and pigging out – look out for the 'all you can eat and drink' offers, starting at around ¥3500. The standard dish is 'Ghengis-Khan Barbecue' – prices for other dishes on the menu start at around ¥1000 and a mug of draught beer costs ¥450. The beer garden is open from 11.30 am to 9 pm, and reservations are recommended though not essential (☎ 011-742-1531).

The beer garden is about 10 minutes on foot from the Higashi-Kuyakusho-mae subway station on the Toho line. You can also get there by taking a Higashi 88 (Factory Line) bus from in front of the Gobankan Seibu department store, close to JR Sapporo station.

TV Tower　テレビ塔

This prominent landmark in Ōdōri-kōen Park provides good views of Sapporo from its 90m-high viewing platform. From May to September it's open from 9 am to 9 pm; through the rest of the year it's open from 9.30 am to 6.30 pm. Entry is ¥700. If you don't feel like paying this rather steep fee, you can get a view that's almost as good, free of charge, by going up to observation deck on the 19th floor of the City Office building (*shiyakusho*), just across the street from the TV tower. It's open from 10 am to 4 pm Monday to Friday (unless it's a public holiday or the weather is particularly poor), but is closed during winter. There's a little coffee shop up here and you can take your food or drink outside to the observation deck.

Museums

The Hokkaidō **Museum of Modern Art** has a collection of modern art from overseas (mainly France), as well as works by local artists. Special exhibitions are also frequently held. The museum is open from 10 am to 4.30 pm. Between 23 November and 31 March it is closed on Monday and public

Sapporo beer can be sampled at the Sapporo Beer Garden & Museum.

Sapporo

To Ishikari

North 7

North 6

Hakodate Line

North 5

North 4

North 3

North 2

North 1

To Otaru

To Asahikawa

Botanical
Garden

Nanboku Line

Toho Line

West 14 West 13 West 12 West 11 West 10 West 9 West 8 West 7 West 6 West 5 West 4 West 3 West 2 West 1 East 1

Ōdori-kōen Park

Odori Odori

Nishi-Juitchōme

Tozai Line

Tanuki - kōji   Arcade

Susukino

Hosui
Susukino

South 1

South 2

South 3

South 4

South 5

South 6

South 7

South 8

South 9

South 10

To Muroran

To Tomakomai

Nakajima-kōen

Nakajima-kōen
Park

Toyohira-gawa

River

Sapporo

0   200   400 m

Some Minor Streets Not Depicted

PLACES TO STAY

1 Hotel Hokkueikan
   ホテル北榮館
2 Yugiri Ryokan
   夕霧旅館
3 Sapporo House
   Youth Hostel
   札幌ハウスユース
   ホステル
4 Sapporo Washington
   Hotel 2
   札幌第2ワシントン
   ホテル
5 Keiō Plaza Hotel
   Sapporo
   京王プラザホテル
   札幌
7 Nakamuraya Ryokan
   中村屋旅館
8 Hotel Center Park
   ホテルセンター
   パーク
9 Hotel Sapporo
   Garden Palace
   ホテル札幌ガーデン
   パレス
11 KKR Sapporo Hotel
    ホテルKKR札幌
12 Sapporo Washington
    Hotel 1
    札幌ワシントン
    ホテル
18 Hotel New Ōtani
    Sapporo
    ホテルニュー
    オータニ札幌
40 Susukino Green
    Hotel I
    すすきのグリーン
    ホテル
45 Tōkyū Inn
    東急イン
46 Susukino Green
    Hotel II
    すすきのグリーン
    ホテルII

47 Sapporo International
    Inn Nada
    札幌インターナショ
    ナルイン灘
49 Business Hotel
    Shintō
    ビジネスホテル新東
51 Sapporo Central
    Hotel
    札幌セントラル
    ホテル
52 Susukino Green III
    すすきのグリーン
    ホテルIII
56 Hotel Sunlight
    ホテルサンライト
57 Sapporo Oriental
    Hotel
    札幌オリエンタル
    ホテル
59 Hotel Paco Sapporo
    ホテルパコ札幌

PLACES TO EAT

27 Café D'or
28 Ristorante
    Cha-Cha-Cha
29 American Foods
    Restaurant
33 Taj Mahal
35 Delhi
36 Doutor Coffee
39 KFC
41 Yoshinoya
    吉野屋
42 Tsubohachi
    つぼ八
43 Rāmen Yokochō
    Alley
    ラーメン横丁
48 Hōran Rāmen Shop
    芳蘭ラーメン
50 Tokei-dai Rāmen
    Shop
    時計台ラーメン

58 Kirin Beer Hall
    キリンビール園

OTHER

6 Hokkaido University
   Ainu Museum
   北方民族資料館
10 Immigration Office
    札幌出入国管理局
13 ANA; Qantas; Cathay
    Pacific
    伊藤加藤ビル
14 Sapporo Station Bus
    Terminal; Sogō
    Department Store
    札幌バス
    ターミナル／
    そごうデパート
15 Sapporo Central Post
    Office
    札幌中央郵便局
16 Tōkyū Department
    Store
    東急デパート
17 American Express
    Office
    アメリカン
    エクスプレス
19 Sapporo International
    Communication
    Plaza
    札幌国際コミュニ
    ケーションプラザ
20 Tokei-dai Clocktower
    時計台
21 Chūō Bus Company
    Station
    中央バスターミナル
22 Ōdōri Post Office
    大通り郵便局
23 TV Tower
    テレビ塔
24 Kinokuniya Books
    紀伊国屋書店

Key continued on following page

25	Maruzen Books 丸善	31	Parco Department Store パルコデパート	44	Robinson's Department Store ロビンソン札幌
26	Mitsukoshi Department Store 三越デパート	32	Virgin Megastore CD & Video	53	Al's Bar
30	Gaijin Bar 不良外人の巣	34	Tower Records	54	Rad Brothers Bar
		37	Suntory Shot Bar Brosto	55	King Xmhu (Disco) キングシェムー ディスコ
		38	Blues Alley		

holidays; entry is ¥250 or higher if there's a special exhibit on.

The nearby **Migishi Kotaro Museum of Modern Art** is devoted to the works of the Sapporo artist of the same name (1903-34). It's probably only of interest to those with a special interest in the development of Japanese modern art. Its opening hours are the same as those of the Museum of Modern Art and entry is ¥250. Both museums are around a five minute walk just north of Nishi-jūhatchōme subway station on the Tōzai line. Take exit No 3.

See the Botanical Garden entry above for details on the Ainu Museum there.

An interesting, off-beat option is the **Sapporo Salmon Museum**, where you can learn everything you every possibly wanted to know about these frisky fish. To get there, you'll have to take the Nanboku subway line to the terminus at Makomanai and then change to city bus Minami 95, 96, 97 or 98. Get off at the Makomanai kyōgijō-mae stop and walk for five minutes. The museum is open from 9.15 am to 4.45 pm daily except for Mondays. Admission is free.

Special Events

The Sapporo Yuki Matsuri (Sapporo Ice Festival), held in Ōdōri-kōen Park in early February, is probably Hokkaidō's major annual event. Since 1950 when the festival was first held, it has developed into a mass display of snow sculptures, many of which are very intricate buildings complete with internal illumination. If you plan to visit at this time, you should book accommodation well in advance or take a course in igloo construction.

The Sapporo Summer Festival (21 July to August 20) kicks off with the setting up of beer gardens in Ōdōri-kōen Park, and actually comprises numerous smaller events such as concerts and international gatherings. Among these is the Pacific Music Festival, which was started by famed conductor Leonard Bernstein.

Places to Stay

Youth Hostels Although there are three hostels in Sapporo, only one, *Sapporo House* (☎ 011-726-4235), has convenient access, being only a 10 minute walk from the station. It's not a memorable place to stay – drab and prison-like. Beds are ¥2670.

Sapporo Miyagaoka Youth Hostel (☎ 011-611-9016) is close to Maruyama-kōen Park in the west of Sapporo, but it's only open from July to late September. Beds are ¥3050. Take the Tōzai subway line to Maruyama kōen and then bus Nos 14 or 15 to Sōgō-gurando-mae, which is a two minute walk from the hostel.

Sapporo Lions Youth Hostel (☎ 011-611-4709) is further west, close to the Miyanomori Ski Jump, and charges ¥3200 for a bed. To get there, take the Tōzai line to Maruyama kōen and then change to the No 14 bus. Get off at the Miyanomori-shanze-mae stop and walk for seven minutes.

Toho Network The *Sapporo International Inn Nada* (☎ 011-551-5882) is probably the most popular budget place to stay in

Sapporo. It's close to the Susukino entertainment area and has no curfew, making it an ideal base for a late night foray into Hokkaidō's most happening nightclub district. Costs are ¥3500 per head, though this will probably mean sharing a room. Breakfast is available for ¥600 and there's a heating charge of ¥200 during winter. It's around a 10 minute walk west from Susukino subway station.

Nada's owner is the founder of the Toho network so, even if staying elsewhere, those planning to do some further travel around Hokkaidō should call in and pick up a copy of the Toho network book (¥200). There have been plans for several years now to produce an English-language summary of the booklet: maybe by the time you stop by it will be available.

Ryokan The most popular place with foreigners is the *Yugiri Ryokan* (☎ 011-716-5482), which has per-head costs of around ¥3500 (depending on the room). The management (mainly in the form of one overworked old woman) don't speak English but seem to have reconciled themselves to the ways of visiting gaijin and try hard to please. It's a five minute walk north-west of the station, close to Hokkaidō University.

Nakamuraya Ryokan (☎ 011-241-2111) is a member of the Japanese Inn Group. Prices are relatively high at around ¥7000/13,000 for singles/doubles and ¥18,000 for triples, though discounts are sometimes available on polite request. The ryokan is a seven minute walk south-west of the station.

Hotels Despite the fact that Sapporo has more than 100 hotels, during summer *everything* gets booked out very quickly. It's wise to book ahead before arriving here. If you are having problems finding somewhere with vacancies, give the Business Hotel Reservation Center (☎ 011-221-0909) a phone call, although you will need Japanese or the help of a Japanese speaker to get any sense out of them. If you still can't find anything, you might try asking staff at the International Communication Plaza to suggest some

hotels in one of Sapporo's suburbs, such as Makomanai.

Station/Ō-dōri Area If you're targeting Sapporo's nightlife you may be better off staying down in the Susukino district. But the area between the station and Ō-dōri is convenient for access to transportation and some sights, and also smells better in the morning.

One of the cheaper options around here is the *Hotel Hokkueikan* (☎ 011-716-0156), about a 10 minute walk north of the station. Singles/doubles are ¥5000/10,000. The staff speak English, and the International Communication Plaza tourist centres often steer travellers to this place: mention their name and you'll probably get a discount.

Two streets south of the station is the *KKR Sapporo* (011-231-6711), a government-subsidised hotel with fairly spacious rooms. Singles range from ¥5500 to ¥7000, twins from ¥9000 to ¥14,000 and doubles are ¥11,000. This place is very popular, so you'll probably need to book ahead. A bit cheaper, and looking it, is the *Hotel Center Park* (☎ 011-512-3121) which has singles at ¥6000 and twins/doubles from ¥9000/7000.

Just a couple of minutes from the station, the *Sapporo Washington Hotel 1* (☎ 011-251-3211) has singles from ¥5900, twins from ¥13,200 and doubles at ¥15,500. It would be a good idea to book ahead for one of the cheaper singles. Singles at the nearby *Sapporo Washington Hotel 2* (☎ 011-222-3311) are more expensive at ¥9030; doubles start at ¥17,000. In this same class, and perhaps better value for money, is the *Hotel Sapporo Garden Palace* (☎ 011-261-5311), where singles range from ¥6300 to ¥9300 and twins/doubles start at ¥11,600/13,600.

The station area also has some of Sapporo's top-class hotels. The opulent *Hotel New Ōtani Sapporo* (☎ 011-222-1111) has singles from ¥14,000 and doubles from ¥25,000. Similar high standards can be found at the *Keiō Plaza Hotel Sapporo* (☎ 011-271-0111), which has singles from ¥14,000 to ¥15,000 and doubles/twins at ¥25,000.

Susukino Area There are dozens upon dozens of hotels in the Susukino area which is a fun part of town to be based in. One of the cheapest is the *Sapporo Central Hotel* (☎ 011-512-3121), a reasonably small hotel that tends to get booked out quickly. Singles are ¥6000, while doubles range from ¥7000 to ¥9000. Nearby, the *Business Hotel Shintō* (☎ 011-512-6611) has singles/twins at ¥6000/10,000. In this same neighbourhood, the *Sapporo Oriental Hotel* (☎ 011-521-5050) has similar rates, as does the *Hotel Sunlight* (☎ 011-562-3111). A bit further south from here, near Nakajima-kōen Park, is the *Hotel Paco Sapporo* (☎ 011-562-8585) which is a bit newer and has singles at ¥8000 and twins/doubles at ¥12,000/11,000.

There are three Green Hotels in the Susukino area. The cheapest is the *Susukino Green Hotel 1* (☎ 011-511-4111) which has singles/twins at ¥6000/15,000. The *Susukino Green Hotel 2* (☎ 011-511-9111) charges ¥7500/14,000 for singles/twins and looks to be the most spacious of the three. Singles at the *Susukino Green Hotel 3* (☎ 011-511-4111) are ¥8000 and twins ¥15,000.

Places to Eat

Sapporo is a big city and there's a lot to choose from in the dining category. As you'd expect, the fast-food huts are well represented, mainly in Susukino and the shopping district just to the north.

Hokkaidō is famous for its rāmen noodles, and there are rāmen shops all over the city. Many of them have photographs of the dishes outside, which makes ordering slightly easier. You'll usually have a choice of broth: miso, shōyu (soy sauce) and shio (salt). Most shops also have a large choice of toppings. If you're having problems ordering, just ask for miso rāmen (or shōyu or shio rāmen), the basic, no-frills (and cheapest) option. A good spot to try these is *Rāmen Yokochō*, an alleyway crammed with some two dozen shops to choose from. Other good places are *Tokei-dai Rāmen* and *Hōran Ramen*. Of course, if you've been travelling in Japan for some time already, you may

want nothing to do with rāmen. But the Sapporo version really is quite tasty.

For 'Genghis-Khan Barbecue' you can try the Sapporo Beer Garden or the *Kirin Beer Hall*, which has a similar set-up on it's 2nd/3rd floor 'Spacecraft' dining hall, which seats up to 560 people. For ¥3000 you get all the vegetables and lamb you can grill and all the beer, whisky or soft drinks you can quaff in 100 minutes: good, fattening fun.

Sapporo has some good Indian cuisine in the *Delhi Restaurant* and the *Taj Mahal*, both in the Chūō shopping district. The latter is part of a Japanese chain and, while the food is good, it's fairly expensive. The best deals are its lunch-time specials. Delhi Palace, on the other hand, has an Indian cook, authentic dishes and is inexpensive by Japanese standards – you can get a set dinner with a draught beer for around ¥2000.

There are also plenty of western-style restaurants to choose from. The *American Foods Restaurant* has good barbecue and Mexican food; two burritos and salad for ¥800 last time we were in town. *Ristorante Cha-Cha-Cha* doesn't sound very Italian, but it's a pleasant enough spot with decent pasta dishes from around ¥900.

Entertainment

Susukino is wall-to-wall bars, karaoke parlours and kinky soaplands. That said, most of this kind of action is prohibitively expensive and probably of little interest for visiting westerners. This doesn't mean you should shun Susukino altogether though – there are loads of great places to eat and quite a few bars that serve as watering holes for local gaijin.

The best thing to do is to ask around for the latest 'in' spot. At the time of writing, one of the more popular bars in town was *Al's*. Look out for the English sign outside and head down into the basement. It has usually has a cover charge of around ¥2500, which gets you a handful of 'Al dollar bills' to buy some drinks with. There are also drinking specials, such as ¥2000 for all you can drink on Monday nights. Just down the street *Rad Brothers* stays open from 6 pm to 6 am daily and, by all accounts, is hopping almost every night. Suntory whiskey at ¥300 a glass doesn't hurt.

For those seeking something just a bit more low-key, there's the *Gaijin Bar* and *Saltimbanco*, two tiny but comfortable places in a little ramshackle wooden building near the Tanuki-Kōji Arcade. They're easy to miss so keep an eye out for the lighted sign on the sidewalk out front.

Suntory Shot Bar Brosto has almost no personality, but makes up for it with a decent happy hour from 6.30 to 8 pm, and fairly cheap beer and whiskey at all times.

One place that has to be mentioned, even if it would probably break the average traveller's budget, is *King Xmhu* (everyone calls it 'King Moo's'), Sapporo's answer to *Juliana's* in Tokyo. This is an opulent disco if ever there was one. The cover charges vary from night to night, but hover around ¥4000, though some evenings there are discounts for those age 25 and over.

Even if you don't go to the disco (emphasis on techno beat), just wander down and take a look at the exterior. King Xmhu himself, massively carved in stone, presides wearily bemused over the neon of Susukino. The interior is no less fabulous – glowing demons with lasers for eyes leer over the dance floor.

Getting There & Away

Air Sapporo has flight connections with most of the major cities on Honshū and even Okinawa. There are more than 20 flights daily from Tokyo – the basic one-way fare is ¥24,520. The principal airlines offering services to Hokkaidō are JAS, ANA and JAL. Air Nippon Kōku (ANK) also operates on internal routes for Hokkaidō. See the later Getting Around section for details on transport to/from the airport.

There are several international airlines with offices in Sapporo: Cathay Pacific (☎ 0120-355-747); Continental Micronesia (☎ 011-221-4091); Korean Air (☎ 011-210 3311) and Qantas Airways (☎ 011-242-4151). The Cathay Pacific and Qantas offices are upstairs from the ANA ticket offices opposite JR Sapporo station. See the

Getting There & Away chapter for details on international flights to and from Sapporo.

Train Two of the fastest rail connections from Tokyo include the Hokutosei Express, a direct sleeper to Sapporo in 16 hours, and a combination of the shinkansen to Morioka followed by a limited express via Aomori and Hakodate to Sapporo in 11 hours. In the case of the former, if you are using a Japan Rail Pass, you will have to pay the sleeper supplement. This is a popular service and it only runs three times daily, so book ahead. The sleeper trip costs ¥13,790 with a ¥3590 surcharge. The shinkansen/limited express trip costs ¥21,890.

From Sapporo to Hakodate, it takes 3¾ hours by limited express via New Chitose airport and Tomakomai. The fare is ¥8420, or ¥6690 if you don't purchase a reserved seat.

The trip from Sapporo to Otaru on the JR Hakodate line takes about 30 minutes by rapid train or 50 minutes by local (¥610). There are frequent trains running north-east on the JR Hakodate line to Asahikawa in 90 minutes (limited express). From Sapporo to Wakkanai, there's a sleeper service that leaves Sapporo around 10 pm and arrives in Wakkanai around 6 am, nicely timed to take the early ferry across to Rishiri-tō or Rebun-tō islands. If you're travelling on a Japan Rail Pass, you'll need to pay about ¥7400 in supplementary charges.

Bus Sapporo is linked with the rest of Hokkaidō by an extensive network of long-distance bus services such as those for Wakkanai (6¼ hours, ¥5650), Asahikawa (two hours, ¥1900), Kushiro (6¼ hours, ¥5500), Kitami (4¾ hours, ¥5100) and Hakodate (5¼ hours, ¥4600). There are also night buses to Kushiro and Hakodate which take slightly longer. The night bus option is worth considering if you are backtracking, short on time or wish to save money on accommodation costs. However, it isn't exactly restful and if you aren't backtracking you may lose out on some spectacular scenery.

Getting Around

The Airport The main airport for Sapporo is New Chitose airport, a 35 minute train ride (¥1030) or 70 minute bus ride (¥800) south of the city. Sapporo has a subsidiary airport at Okadama, which is a 25 minute bus ride (¥300) north of the city. Buses leave every 20 minutes or so from in front of the ANA ticket offices, opposite Sapporo station.

Bus & Tram There are several bus terminals in Sapporo, but the main one is next to the station, adjacent to the Sogo department store. Access is via the underground shopping plaza, from where you ascend to the platforms which are at ground level.

City buses operate according to a system that is very common in Japan. Enter by the centre door and take a token as you do so. Exit by the front door and calculate your fare by matching the number on your ticket with price indicated next to the same number on the board over the driver's seat.

There is a single tram line that heads west from Ō-dōri, turns south and then loops back to Susukino. You probably won't need to use it, but if you do, there is a flat fare of ¥170.

Subway This is the most efficient way to get around Sapporo. There are three lines, the two most useful being the Nanboku line, which runs on a north-south axis and the Tōzai line, which runs on an east-west axis. Fares start at ¥180 and special one-day passes are also available for ¥750; there are also passes for ¥950 which are valid for Sapporo's buses and trams.

ASAHIKAWA 旭川

Asahikawa (population 360,000) is an unimpressive urban sprawl and the second largest city on Hokkaidō. The city had its origins in the Meiji period as a farmer militia settlement and has since developed into a major industrial centre. For the traveller, its importance is largely as a transport hub: to the north, it's a long haul to Wakkanai; and to the south, there are the attractions of Daisetsuzan National Park.

Information

There's an information counter in the station (☎ 0166-22-6704), though only Japanese is spoken. The staff here have pamphlets on Asahikawa and Daisetsuzan National Park, and can help with finding accommodation if the worst happens and you get stranded in Asahikawa.

Things to See

There's not a great deal to see in town, although there are some attractions that can be reached by bus. The **Yūkara Ori Folkcraft Museum** has beautiful examples of dyed textiles from around the world and through the ages. Admission is ¥400 and it's open from 9 am to 5 pm daily from April to September and closed on Monday the rest of the year. The museum has a free shuttle that runs once an hour from its gallery shop, which is located about 10 minutes on foot from the station. Head straight out from the station along the pedestrian mall (Japan's first!) for six blocks, turn left and continue three more blocks. The shop is in a somewhat traditional looking plaster and brick building on the left-hand side. Staff at the tourist information counter will draw the route on a map for you.

The **Kawamura Kaneto Ainu Memorial Museum** is north-west of the city centre and is fairly touristy. It sometimes has Ainu dance displays. The museum is open from 9 am to 6 pm daily and entry is ¥500. Take bus No 24 from the No 14 bus stop, which is next to the Seibu department store 'B' building. The 15 minute ride to the museum costs ¥160; get off at the Ainu Kinenkan-mae bus stop.

Places to Stay

Asahikawa Youth Hostel (☎ 0166-61-2751) is four km from the station. You can either take a 15 minute bus ride or hop in a taxi (¥1150). Buses bound for Kannondai-kōen Park or Inosawa leave from next to the Malsa department store; get off at the Inosawa Yuriana Yōchien-mae stop, a 15 minute ride from the station. Bicycle rental is available at the hostel and there are hot springs near by. Beds cost ¥3100.

A three minute walk from the station is the *Asahikawa Green Hotel Bekkan* (☎ 0166-26-1414), which has singles for ¥5000 to ¥5350 and twins for ¥8850. Not far away, and somewhat nicer, is the *Asahikawa Prince Hotel* (☎ 0166-22-5155) with singles from ¥5300 to ¥6100 and doubles from ¥11,400 to ¥16,500.

Going considerably up-market, the *Asahikawa Terminal Hotel* (☎ 0166-24-0111), right next to the station, has singles/twins from ¥6500/13,500.

Getting There & Away

Air Asahikawa has flights to Fukuoka, Kansai, Nagoya and Tokyo. An airport bus service, timed to coincide with flight arrivals and departures, runs between the airport and Asahikawa station in 35 minutes (¥550).

Train Asahikawa is linked with Sapporo in 1½ hours by limited express on the JR Hakodate line. The price is ¥2370 with a ¥2250 limited express surcharge. However, if you don't require a reserved seat, the surcharge is only ¥1240. The JR Furano line connects Asahikawa with Furano in 1¼ hours (¥1020). The JR Sōya line runs north to Wakkanai – the trip takes just under four hours (¥6380).

Bus Bus tickets for most destinations can be bought from the Dōhoku bus company booking office directly opposite the railway station. Buses leave and arrive in front of the station, though some depart from bus stops scattered around the nearby department stores.

There are several bus services running from Asahikawa into Daisetsuzan National Park. One service runs twice daily (three times daily from mid-June to mid-October) to the hot springs resort of Asahidake Onsen. Buses leave from bus stop No 4 in front of the station. The ride takes 1½ hours and, believe it or not, is free (see the Asahidake Onsen Getting There & Away section for details).

From mid-June to late October, Dōhoku buses run approximately once an hour from Asahikawa via Kamikawa to Sōunkyō. The trip takes 1¾ hours and the ticket costs ¥1800.

A frequent bus service also operates between Sapporo and Asahikawa (two hours, ¥1900). Other bus services include Wakkanai (4¾ hours, ¥4300) and Furano (1½ hours, ¥850).

WAKKANAI 稚内

This windswept port on the northernmost fringe of Hokkaidō is the access point for Rishiri-tō and Rebun-tō islands. Wakkanai station has an information counter where you can ask for maps and ferry timetables. From the station, it's a 10 minute walk to the ferry terminal.

Unless your transport arrangements strand you there overnight, there's no compelling reason to stay in Wakkanai. If you do find yourself here with time on your hands, you could head up to **Wakkanai Kōen Park**, which sits atop the grassy hill a few blocks west of the railway station. A miniature gondola takes you up to the top, where there's a kiddy park, several scattered monuments, a number of walking trails and an observation tower that gives fine views of northern Hokkaido and, on clear days, Sakhalin Island. The tower is open from late April to November and February to March. The ride to the top costs ¥400.

Twenty-seven km east of Wakkanai lies **Cape Sōya-misaki**, the northernmost point of Japan. There's actually not a great deal to see and you should only make the trip if you like the idea of reaching the very top of the country. Aside from a landmark and a few souvenir shops there's the Sōya Peace Park, which has some interesting memorials. One is dedicated to the victims of Korean Airlines flight 007, which was shot down by a Soviet fighter jet off the Sakhalin coast in 1988. Buses run four times daily between the Wakkanai bus terminal and Cape Sōya-misaki. The ride takes 50 minutes and the fare is ¥1290.

Places to Stay

Youth Hostels *Wakkanai Moshiripa Youth Hostel* (☎ 0162-24-0180) is a five minute walk from Wakkanai station and eight minutes on foot from the Wakkanai-kō Port. Bicycle rental is available. It's closed for three weeks in both January and April and also from 18 November to 18 December. Beds are ¥3100 or ¥3800 if you want your own room. *Wakkanai Youth Hostel* (☎ 0162-23-7162) is a 12 minute walk from the Minami Wakkanai station, one stop before the terminus at Wakkanai. From Wakkanai station you can also take a bus bound for Midori-roku-chōme and get off after about 12 minutes at the Minami shōgakkō stop. The hostel is up on a hilltop and offers good views when the weather is clear. Bicycle rental is available. Beds cost between ¥2000 and ¥2800, depending on how many people you want to share your room with.

Ryokan Down the small street just to the right of the station is *Ryokan Saihate* (☎ 0162-23-3556), a well maintained little place that has per-person rates from ¥5500, including two meals. Right next to it is *Ryokan Tsubaki* (☎ 0162-23-4754) which looks a bit more tattered and has similar rates.

A bit further from the station is *Ryokan Kanno* (☎ 0162-23-3587), a traditionally run place that once played host to the visiting Showa emperor. Housed in a grimy concrete block, it doesn't look like much from the outside, but the rooms are spacious and comfortable, the staff friendly and the seafood dinners delicious. Per-person rates with two meals start at ¥6000. To get there, walk straight out from the station for three blocks, turn left at the light and continue for two more blocks. The ryokan is on the right-hand side of the street.

Hotels Next to Wakkanai station is the *Hotel Katsumiya* (☎ 0162-23-5595), a pleasant little place that's run like an Japanese inn. Singles/doubles are ¥6000/10,000, unless you want dinner and breakfast as well, in which case it's a flat rate of ¥10,000 per

person. To the right of the station, just past Ryokan Tsubaki, is the *Wakkanai Station Hotel* (☎ 0162-23-2111), a spartan place with singles/doubles at ¥5000/10,000.

Getting There & Away

Air There are two ways to fly with ANK from Sapporo to Wakkanai – both take about an hour. There is one daily flight from Sapporo's New Chitose airport and two daily flights from Sapporo's Okadama airport. Make sure you know which airport you are going to be using. The one-way fare is ¥14,850 from Okadama, ¥15,700 from Chitose. Wakkanai also has direct flights to Tokyo and Osaka. A bus service runs from Wakkanai station to the airport in 30 minutes (¥560). Buses leave from the bus terminal, about 40m north of the station.

Train There are two (rather slow) express trains a day between Sapporo and Wakkanai (six hours, ¥8240), as well as a sleeper service (¥14,420) that leaves Sapporo at 10 pm and arrives in Wakkanai at 6 am, in time for the early ferry across to Rishiri-tō or Rebun-tō islands. There are ways to make this trip cheaper. There is a return 'night and day ticket' (¥17,980) which allows you to travel one way via sleeper and the other by express. A return 'S-kippu' ticket, for express trains originating out of Sapporo, costs ¥11,760 and is valid for six days from the time you start your outbound leg. There is one train daily between Wakkanai and Asahikawa (four hours, ¥6380). JR Hokkaido also offers S-kippu discount tickets for this route.

Bus A bus service runs twice daily between Sapporo to Wakkanai in 6¼ hours and costs ¥5650. There is also one bus a day to Asahikawa (four hours, ¥4300). Buses arrive at and leave from the bus terminal, just north of Wakkanai station.

Boat Wakkanai is linked by ferries with Rishiri-tō and Rebun-tō. The ferry to Oshidomari on Rishiri-tō Island departs up to four times daily (between June and the end of August) and takes 1¾ hours; the cheapest passenger ticket is ¥1850. From Oshidomari there are two to three ferries a day to Kafuka on Rebun-tō (40 minutes, ¥1240) – these are linked to the arrivals/departures of the Wakkanai service. Between 1 June and 30 September there are also two ferries a day between Kutsugata (Rishiri-tō) and Kafuka.

There are direct ferries from Wakkanai to Rebun-tō (Kafuka) three to four times daily (five times daily between June and the end of August); the ride takes two hours (¥2060).

The port at Wakkanai is a 10 minute walk from the station – turn right as you exit the station, head past the towering Wakkanai ANA Hotel, and turn right again for the ferry pier.

Sakhalin Ferry Between late April and early September there is a regularly scheduled ferry service which links Wakkanai with Korsakov on Sakhalin Island (Russia). There are only one to two sailings a month, except for August, when there are five departures. The trip takes 9½ hours and the cheapest one-way/return fare is ¥32,000/45,000. There is also the possibility of going from Wakkanai to Sakhalin and then returning by way of Otaru. For more information on travelling to Sakhalin, see the Getting There & Away section in the introduction to this chapter.

Rishiri-Rebun-Sarobetsu National Park
利尻礼文サロベツ 国立公園

The Rishiri-Rebun-Sarobetsu National Park is made up of the two islands of Rishiri-tō and Rebun-tō, but also includes a 27 km strip of coast on the mainland of Hokkaidō known as the Sarobetsu Plain.

If you have the time, a visit to Rishiri-tō and Rebun-tō is a must. The best weather for hiking is during the tourist season which lasts from June to late September. You should plan on spending a minimum of four days if you want to visit both islands at an easy pace, including a hike or two.

RISHIRI-TŌ ISLAND   利尻島
This is an island dominated by the volcanic peak of Mt Rishiri-zan (1721m) which soars majestically out of the sea. A road circles the island and a bus service links the small fishing communities. The main activity for visitors is hiking on the various trails and lakes below the summit of the mountain. Providing you have warm clothes and proper footwear, the hike to the summit can be comfortably completed in a full day. Oshidomari and Kutsugata are the main ports for the island.

Information
Information booths at the ferry terminals provide maps and information on transport, sights and hiking, as well as booking accommodation. The booths open for the arrival or departure of ferries.

Mt Rishiri-zan Hike   利尻山ハイク
There are three trails to the summit (1721m). The most reliable ones lead from Oshidomari and Kutsugata. The third trail starts from Oniwaki, on the south side of the island, but is restricted to technical climbing. The Oshidomari route trailhead is three km from Oshidomari proper, while the Kutsugata route begins about three km outside Kutsugata town. There is no bus service to the trailheads. You may be able to arrange a ride if you're staying at a minshuku or youth hostel. Otherwise it's either walk, hitch or take a taxi.

Prepare properly for a mountain hike, aim for an early start and allow at least 10 hours for the ascent and descent. Advice and maps in Japanese (excellent hiking details with contour lines) are available from the information booths at the ports and from the youth hostels.

Just below the summit is Rishiridake-yamagoya, an unstaffed mountain hut, which perches on the edge of a precipice and provides

HOKKAIDŌ

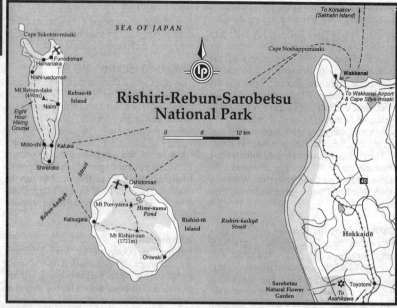

the bare minimum for a roof over your head. Take your own food (purchase it from shops in the ports) and water. If you stay here, be warned that it's bloody cold at night and the wind contributes generously to the drop in temperatures. If you can't sleep, the night views are absolutely amazing and, providing the clarity holds, the views during the day extend as far as Sakhalin Island (Russia). There is severe erosion on the sections between the mountain hut and the summit, and rockslides sometimes occur after heavy rain, so hike with care.

If you don't feel like hiking to the summit, there are several enjoyable hikes which are less strenuous. One of these follows the trail from Oshidomari for an hour towards the summit, but branches left in thick forest, about 10 minutes after reaching a group of A-frame chalets at the end of a paved road. This trail leads to Hime-numa Pond in 1¾ hours with the option of a 30 minute side trip to Mt Pon-yama.

Places to Stay

Camping Grounds There are five camping grounds spread out around Rishiri-tō and all of them are free (unless you need to rent a tent or cabin). The one at Kutsugata Misaki Kōen Park has received good reviews and is also the easiest to reach, being less than one km from Kutsugata. Others are located at Rishiri-cho Shinrin Kōen Park, Senbōshi Misaki Kōen Park and Numa-ura Pond. There is also a camping ground near the trailhead for the Oshidomari route up to Mt Rishiri-zan, but it's not recommended: one couple was so unimpressed upon seeing it that they turned around and hiked the five km back to Oshidomari.

Youth Hostels The *Rishiri Green Hill Youth Hostel* (☎ 01638-2-2507) is a five minute bus ride or about a 25 minute walk from Oshidomari-kō Port. The appropriate stop is Gurin Hiru Yusu-hoseteru-mae. Bicycle and scooter rental is available. Beds are ¥2500.

Minshuku Most of these are located in Oshidomari and Kutsugata, though there are also one or two in Oniwaki, on the south side of the island. *Pension Herasan-no-Ie* (☎ 01638-2-2361) is a five minute walk from the Oshidomari ferry pier. It looks pretty run down from the outside, but the rooms are well maintained and some have nice sea views. Per-person rates are ¥7000 with two meals.

Close by, the *Pension Misaki* (☎ 01638-2-1659) is a bit more basic, but is also cheaper at ¥6000 per person including two meals. Both places bill themselves as 'Japanese-style pensions', a fancier way of saying 'minshuku'. Walk out from the ferry pier to the main road, turn right and walk until the road curves to the left. Herasan-no-Ie is straight ahead, on top of a small hill, while Misaki is down the small road to the right, opposite the fishing boat wharf.

In Kutsugata, about 10 minutes from the ferry pier (near the town's main intersection), is *Minshuku Kutsugata-sō* (☎ 01638-4-2038), a fairly basic place with per-person rates of ¥6500 including two meals. Across the street from it, *Minshuku Nagiri-sō* (☎ 01638-4-2233) charges the same price for the same standards and service.

Getting There & Away
Air It's a 15 minute hop with ANK from Wakkanai and the round-trip ticket costs ¥14,120 – there are two flights daily during the peak summer season. The information office (☎ 01638-2-1770) at Rishiri Kūkō airfield is open from 9 am to 5 pm. The island bus runs by the airport: the stop (kūko-mae) is a 15 minute walk from the terminal. If you book a room in advance and can manage to let them know when your flight arrives, staff at minshuku or the youth hostel may come meet you at the airport. From Oshidmari a taxi to the airport costs ¥1200.

Boat For details of the service from Oshidomari via Kafuka (Rebun-tō) to Wakkanai, see the Getting There & Away section for Wakkanai.

Getting Around
Bus There are two bus lines, one each running clockwise and anticlockwise around the island. There are six buses daily in either direction which complete the circuit of the island in 1¾ hours (¥2100). The trip from Oshidomari to Kutsugata (travelling anticlockwise) takes 30 minutes and costs ¥690.

Bicycle Cycling is a great way to get around the island and bicycles are available for rental at the youth hostels. You can complete a leisurely circuit (53 km) of the island in about five hours. There is a cycling path between Oshidomari and Kutsugata.

REBUN-TŌ ISLAND 礼文島
In contrast to the conical heights of its neighbour, Rebun-tō is a low, arrow-shaped island which has one major road down the east coast. The main attractions of the island are the hiking trails which follow routes along the west coast past remote fishing communities. The terrain is more varied than that of Rishiri, making Rebun a better place if you want to spend several days trying different hiking routes and distances. Between June and August, the island's alpine flowers – over 300 species – pull out all the stops for a floral extravaganza: a memorable experience. Unfortunately, almost every species of tour group from Japan also seems to be on the island at this time as well. Things start to quieten down around mid-September.

Kafuka and Funadomari are the main communities and ports, at the southern and northern ends of the island, respectively.

Hiking
The classic hike down the entire length of the western coast is known as the *hachijikan haikingu Kōsu* (eight hour hiking course). It's a marvellous hike across grassy cliff tops, fields of dwarf bamboo, forests of conifers, deserted, rocky beaches and remote harbours with clusters of fishing shacks and racks of seaweed. There doesn't seem to be much sense in following the example of many Japanese hikers who turn it into an endurance race – complete with certificate of survival!

If you have the extra day, or simply want to pack less into the day, it would be more enjoyable to break the hike into two, four hour sections (*yonjikan haikingu Kōsu*).

The eight hour hike runs from Cape Sukoton-misaki on the northern tip, down to Moto-chi near the southern tip. The four hour hiking course starts at Cape Sukoton-misaki, runs down to Nishi-uedomari and then heads up to the bus stop at Hamanaka. Another variation would be to start at Nishi-uedomari and hike down to Moto-chi. You can follow the trails in either direction – most people seem to hike from north to south – but make sure you have arranged transport, and keep your timetable flexible to avoid spoiling things with the rush of a forced march.

Another popular hike is from Nairo, halfway down the east coast, to the top of Mt Rebun-dake. The peak is a tiddler at 490m, but it's a pleasant 3½ hour return hike.

Information & Preparation All the youth hostels and other places to stay on the island provide information on hiking and transport to trailheads. Youth hostels may also assign hikers to groups.

Although the eight hour hike is not a death-defying feat, it has some tricky stretches, including steep slopes of loose scree and several km of boulder-hopping along beaches, which can become very nasty in the unpredictable weather of these northern regions. Much of the trail is several hours away from human habitation and, for the most part, those who slip off a cliff or twist an ankle will require rescue by boat. There's no need to be paranoid, but this is the reason why group hiking is encouraged. Beware of being marshalled into large groups because things can then become too regimented. The best group size is four.

You'll need proper footwear, warm clothes and some form of rainwear. The hostels often provide packed lunches which some hikers affectionately refer to as 'the hinomaru bento' (Japanese flag box lunch) – an aluminium container of rice with a red pickled plum stuck in the centre. Another Japanese hiking staple is *onigiri* – rice

wrapped in dried seaweed with a titbit of plum, salmon or pickles stuffed in the middle. Take water or soft drinks with you. Do *not* drink the water from the streams. During the '30s, foxes were introduced from the Kurile Islands (Russia) and their faeces now contaminates the streams – it may be tapeworm gunk or something else.

Rebun Youth Hostel in Kafuka has an excellent folder in English entitled *Hiking Maps of Rebun*. The author details seven hikes and grades them according to difficulty. A really useful point is the inclusion of place names in kanji and romaji. The book is not for sale, but you can look through it and make notes, sketch maps and compile lists of place names.

Places to Stay
The information booth at the port can help you to find accommodation. There are many minshuku, a couple of hotels and a trio of youth hostels on the island.

Youth Hostels The *Rebun Youth Hostel* (☎ 01638-6-1608) in Kafuka is a very friendly place, about 25 minutes on foot from Kafuka-kō Port. If you phone ahead, they'll pick you up at the port and give you a lift back there. You can also take a bus bound for Cape Sukoton-misaki or Nishi-uedomari and get off after five minutes at the Yusu-mae stop. A bed costs ¥2600 and bicycle rental is available.

Momoiwa-sō Youth Hostel (☎ 01638-6-1421) has earned a reputation as one of Japan's rowdier youth hostels: big group activities by day, and singing and dancing late into the night. It's a 15 minute bus ride from Kafuka-kō Port. Take the bus bound for Moto-chi and get off at the Momoiwa Iriguchi stop; the hostel is about a seven minute walk from there, conveniently close to one of the trailheads for the eight hour hike. The hostel also often has someone waiting when ferries dock: look out for the guy in tie-dyes vigorously waving the Momoiwa-sō banner. It's open from 1 June to 30 September only. Beds are ¥2600.

Rebun-tō Funadomari Youth Hostel

(☎ 01638-7-2717) is a five minute walk from the Funadomari-honcho bus stop, which is a 40 minute ride from Kafuka (¥860). Like the other hostels, staff here will come get you at the pier if you book in advance. It's open from 10 May to 15 October only. Beds are ¥2600.

Minshuku & Ryokan These are spread out pretty evenly among Kafuka, Moto-chi, Shiretoko and Funodomari. *Kamome-sō* (☎ 01638-6-1973) is about 10 minutes on foot from the Kafuka ferry pier. Follow the road along the water until it ends at a three-way intersection: the minshuku is on the corner to the right. Per-person rates with two meals are ¥6000. *Nakamura Ryokan* (☎ 01638-7-2693) is located in the town of Funadomari and has similar rates.

If you want to get further out you can try *Minshuku Sukoton Misaki* (☎ 01638-7-2878), a rustic spot perched at the very northern tip of the island. Rates are ¥7000 per person with meals. At the opposite end of Rebun-tō, in the fishing hamlet of Shiretoko, is *Minshuku Shiretoko* (☎ 01638-6-1335), a clean, friendly place with rates of ¥7000 per person with meals. Some of the rooms have great views across the water to Mt Rishiri-zan.

Getting There & Away
Air ANK gets you to Rebun-tō in 20 minutes from Wakkanai and the round-trip ticket costs ¥16,100. There is one flight a day; two during the peak summer season. The information office (☎ 01638-7-2175) at Rebun-tō airfield is open from 9 am to 5 pm. The closest bus stop to the airport is kūko-shita, about a 15 minute walk from the terminal. A taxi from Kafuka costs the exorbitant sum of ¥7000, but if you book a room in advance the minshuku or hostel should be able to come and meet your flight.

Boat For details of the service from Kafuka providing connections to Oshidomari (Rishiri-tō) and to Wakkanai, see the Getting There & Away section for Wakkanai.

Getting Around
Most of the time you'll be getting around the island on foot. Youth hostels and other accommodation will usually help with your transport arrangements on arrival or departure. Taxis are available, but careful attention to the bus timetables should be enough to get you to the key points for hiking. The youth hostels and some of the minshuku also have bicycles to rent.

The main bus service follows the island's one major road from Kafuka in the south to Cape Sukoton-misaki in the north (one hour, ¥1130). En route it passes Funadomari and the Kūkō-shita (airport) bus stop. Some buses turn off after Fundomari and head to Nishi-uedomari. Buses run on this route up to six times daily: four go to Cape Sukoton-misaki, two to Nishi-uedomari. There are also three to five buses daily from Kafuka to Moto-chi and from Kafuka to Shiretoko. Be sure to pick up a copy of the island's bus timetable at the information office in Kafuka-kō Port.

SAROBETSU GENSEI-KAEN GARDEN
サロベツ原生花園
The Sarobetsu Gensei-kaen Garden (Natural Flower Garden) is basically a tourist information office with a series of wooden walkways across swamps. It is the best known part of the Sarobetsu Plain, which lies a short distance south of Wakkanai, and is a vast swampy region famous for its flora. From June to late July, tourists come here for the vistas of flowers – mainly rhododendrons, irises and lilies.

During the flowering season, from June to September, there are six buses running daily from Toyotomi station to the garden in 14 minutes (¥400). From October to May the service is reduced to four buses a day.

There is minshuku accommodation in the town of Toyotomi, as well as at Toyotomi Onsen, a 15 minute bus ride from Toyotomi station. Per-person rates with two meals start at around ¥6000.

There are eight trains a day to Toyotomi from Wakkanai, a ride of about 45 minutes.

YAGISHIRI-TŌ & TEURI-TŌ ISLANDS
焼尻島・天売島

Yagishiri-tō and neighbouring Teuri-tō lie off the west coast of Hokkaidō and are popular with hikers, naturalists and birdwatchers, who take boat trips out to the islands during the summer months.

Excursion boats leave from Haboro and take 80 minutes (¥1500) to Yagishiri-tō before continuing for the 20 minute trip (¥690) to Teuri-tō. There is also a fast ferry service that does the whole trip in about an hour, but costs nearly twice as much and only operates between late April and November.

There is minshuku and hotel accommodation in Haboro, as well as in Horonobe and Rumoi, the closest large towns to the north and south respectively.

A bus service connects Haboro with Horonobe, just south of the Sarobetsu Plain, and Rumoi, on the coast west of Asahikawa. Buses run up to 10 times daily. The ride from Horonobe to Haboro takes around two hours (¥1500); from Haboro down to Rumoi it's another 1½ hours (¥1150). Both Horonobe and Rumoi are accessible by rail.

Daisetsuzan National Park 大雪山国立公園

This is Japan's largest national park (2309 sq km), consisting of several mountain groups, volcanoes, lakes and forests. It also includes Mt Asahi-dake which at 2290m is Hokkaidō's highest peak. The park is spectacular hiking and skiing territory and the main hiking access points are Sōunkyō, Asahidake Onsen, Tenninkyō Onsen, Furano and Tokachidake Onsen. You can pick up maps and information (in English) about the park in Sapporo or try the local tourist information offices. Only a couple of hikes on the more well trodden trails have been mentioned here, but there are many more routes leading to more remote regions if you have several days, or even a week, to spare.

Those planning to take a look at the park should bear in mind that at least a few days are needed to get away from the tourist areas. It's dubious whether it's worth just heading up to Sōunkyō for an overnight trip. If you have limited time, Asahidake Onsen is a less touristy spot for a quick look at the park. Tokachidake Onsen is more remote and makes a good base for those looking to escape the crowds (a key consideration in summer and early autumn).

The main gateways to the park are Asahikawa and Kamikawa in the north, Kitami in the east and Obihiro in the south. Bus services through the park are restricted to routes between Kitami and Kamikawa (continuing to Asahikawa) via Sōunkyō, and a service between Asahikawa and Tenninkyō Onsen via Asahidake Onsen.

The tourist information counters at Asahikawa, Sōunkyō and Asahidake Onsen can provide you with basic maps of the park and lists of accommodation options. One of the most useful is 'Daisetsuzan National Park Sōunkyō' which has English (and Korean) text, a hiking map and a table showing times for various hikes starting from Sōunkyō. Stores in Sōunkyō and Asahidake Onsen also sell *Daisetsuzan Attack* (¥1200), a very detailed map of the park in Japanese.

KAMIKAWA 上川

Kamikawa is a useful gateway to Sōunkyō in Daisetsuzan National Park. This small town is not an attraction in itself and there's no real need to stay here. However, if you've missed the last bus to Sōunkyō, a night here isn't the worst of fates.

Places to Stay

Directly opposite the station *Kyōya Ryokan* (☎ 01658-2-1305) isn't in the most attractive of buildings, but rates are fairly reasonable at ¥5500 per person, including two meals. Offering the same rates and a bit more character is *Minshuku Saito* (☎ 01658-2-1095). It's in an interesting old wooden structure down a small sidestreet to the right of the station.

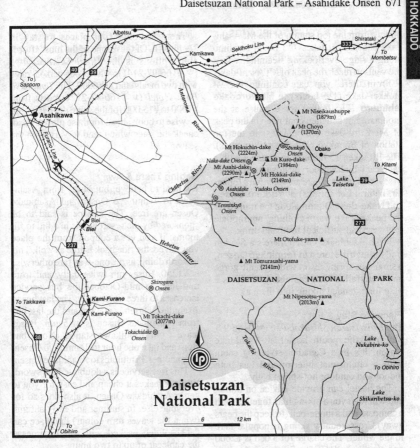

Daisetsuzan National Park

Getting There & Away

Local trains from Asahikawa take about 70 minutes to Kamikawa on the JR Sekihoku line (¥1020). Buses from Asahikawa stop in Kamikawa before continuing on to Sōunkyō. Service is approximately hourly from 8 am to 6 pm, and the ride from Kamikawa to Sōunkyō takes 32 minutes (¥750).

ASAHIDAKE ONSEN 旭岳温泉

This relatively small hot-spring resort consists of some 10 hotels and several houses surrounded by forest at the foot of **Mt Asahi-dake**. The nearby cablecar runs in two stages

(12 minutes, ¥1300) to a point within easy hiking distance of the peak. During the peak hiking seasons, cablecars and lifts operate from as early as 6 am until as late as 7.30 pm. Though Asahidake Onsen is not all that developed, it can get quite crowded, especially given the unbeatably low bus fares (see Getting There & Away later in this section).

Hiking

There are dozens of hiking options in this region. The most popular hike follows trails from the Mt Asahi-dake cablecar via several peaks to **Sōunkyō** – allow seven to eight hours. From the top station of the Mt Asahi-dake cablecar, it takes 1¾ hours to climb along a ridge overlooking steaming, volcanic vents to reach the peak of Mt Asahi-dake.

From there, you can continue via Mt Hokkai-dake (1½ hours) to **Mt Kurodake Ishimuro** (1½ hours) for a pause at the mountain hut and then continue via the peak of Mt Kuro-dake (30 minutes) to the top station of Sōunkyō chair lift (40 minutes). The lift takes 15 minutes to connect with a cablecar which whisks you down to Sōunkyō in seven minutes. There are *rotenburo* (open-air, natural hot springs) at **Yudoku Onsen** and **Naka-dake Onsen** along the trails over the peaks. Take warm clothing, appropriate footwear and sufficient food and drink.

From Asahidake Onsen there's a 5½ km trail through the forest to **Tenninkyō Onsen**, a small hot-spring resort with a scenic gorge and waterfall, which can also be used as a base for extended hiking into the park.

Places to Stay & Eat

The *Daisetsuzan Shirakaba-sō* (☎ 0166-97-2246) is the youth hostel at Asahidake Onsen. It's in a Canadian-style log cabin with a tatami-mat interior and has both indoor and outdoor hot-spring baths.

The hostel can provide advice on hiking and will loan you a hiking map together with a compass and a jingle-bell (to keep the bears away).Cross-country skiing is popular here in the winter. The charge for a bed is ¥2600 and there's a ¥150 fee for using the hot-spring baths. Those coming in from Asahikawa by bus would be better off getting off at the Kampu-jō-mae stop before Asahidake – the hostel is across the road.

Another accommodation option is the *Asahidake Park Hotel* (☎ 0166-97-2136), a delightfully eccentric little building that looks nothing like a hotel. Per-person costs with two meals start from ¥8500. Another atmospheric place is the *Lodge Nutapu-Kaushipe* (☎ 0166-97-2150). Per-person costs with two meals are ¥6500, and the lodge has a rotenburo. Both of these places are below the cable-car station on the road to Asahikawa.

There are only four places to stay in Tenninkyō. Of these, one of the most affordable options is the *Hotel Shikishima-sō* (☎ 0166-97-2141), where per-person rates with two meals start at ¥6000. The *Tenninkyō Park Hotel* (☎ 0166-97-2121) costs from ¥7000 to ¥15,000 for the same deal. It would be wise to book ahead for these places. Also, check the rates which tend to vary with the season.

Getting There & Away

It's hard to believe, but buses from Asahikawa to Tenninkyō Onsen and Asahidake Onsen are free. The service is said to be sponsored by the resort hotels in a bid to fill rooms: if you get a coupon from the place you stayed, the ride back is free as well. This is worth doing, as the one-way fare otherwise is ¥1250. Buses run twice daily, and from mid-June to mid-October the bus service increases to three times daily. The last bus to Asahidake Onsen is at 3 pm and the last bus from Asahidake Onsen is at 5 pm. Buses leave from Asahikawa station (No 4 bus stop) and take one hour to Tenninkyō Onsen, plus another 35 minutes to Asahidake Onsen.

This free service is a double-edged sword. While it makes it cheap and easy for you to get to Asahidake Onsen, it also does so for everyone else. In summer and early autumn (when the leaves turn colour) the place can get absolutely packed, with waiting times at the cablecar of up to two hours.

SŌUNKYŌ   層雲峡温泉

Sōunkyō is the tourist hub of the park and consists of Sōunkyō Onsen, a hot-spring resort, and Sōun-kyō Gorge itself (*kyō* means gorge in Japanese). For hikers, the gorge may seem a secondary attraction and rather tame compared to the role of Sōunkyō Onsen as a gateway for hikes into the interior of the park. Sōunkyō Onsen sees a steady stream of tourists, but has still managed to retain a degree of charm: the few hulking tour group hotels have been hidden away atop a small hill, separated from the low buildings that make up the main town area.

Information

The Kankō Centre next to the bus stop has several different kinds of maps and can also help book accommodation. The latter may be useful if you arrive at a busy time of year. No English is spoken.

Sōun-kyō Gorge　層雲峡

The gorge stretches for about eight km beyond Sōunkyō Onsen and is renowned for its waterfalls – Ryūsei-no-Taki and Ginga-no-Taki are the main ones – and for two sections of perpendicular columns of rock which give an enclosed feeling, hence their names – Ōbako (Big Box) and Kobako (Little Box).

Since the view from the road is restricted by tunnels, a separate walking/cycling path has been constructed and local entrepreneurs derive a sizeable income from bicycle rental at ¥1500 per day, ¥2000 for mountain bikes. You could also speed things up by taking a taxi or bus to Ōbako and walking back in a couple of hours. Buses run two to three times daily (35 minutes, ¥340).

Hiking Routes

The combination of a cablecar (seven minutes, ¥800) and a chair lift (15 minutes, ¥280) provides fast access to Mt Kuro-dake for hikers and sightseers (even those wearing high heeled shoes, one tourist pamphlet notes happily). Discounts are given to youth hostellers and for return tickets.

The most popular hike is the one to Mt Asahi-dake from either Sōunkyō or Asahi-dake Onsen – see the section on Asahidake Onsen for details. You can arrange to leave your baggage at either end and pick it up later after making the tedious loop back through Asahikawa by bus, or simply restrict your baggage to the minimum required for an overnight stay and return on foot by a different trail.

You can also do simple day hikes from the top of the lift station. The hike to the nearest peak, Mt Kuro-dake, takes about one hour. Adding on a trip to the next big peak, Mt Hokkai-dake, will stretch total walking time to around six hours.

Places to Stay & Eat

There are two youth hostels at Sōunkyō. *Ginsen Youth Hostel* (☎ 01658-5-3003) is part of the Ginsen Kaku Hotel; check in at the hotel front desk. A bed costs ¥2800. The *Sōunkyō Youth Hostel* (☎ 01658-5-3418) is about a 10 minute walk from the bus station, wedged in between (and dwarfed by) the Prince and Daisetsuzan Hotels. The hostel has information on trails in the park, organises hikes and rents out gloves, snow boots and other items you may need to brave the elements.

Apart from the youth hostel, there are a number of hotels and minshuku. The *Kitakawa Minshuku* (☎ 01658-5-3515) costs ¥6000 per person with two meals. *Yamagoya Minshuku* (☎ 01658-5-3325) is a cosy little spot down the street from the Ginsen-kaku Hotel, with per-person rates with two meals of ¥6500.

Sōunkyō is one of those Japanese tourist towns where everyone eats in their hotel or minshuku, but there are a few places that serve up basic fare (noodles and so on). The restaurant at the cablecar station serves up a good cup of coffee and a nice view of town.

Getting There & Away

Buses run from Sōunkyō approximately once an hour to Kamikawa (32 minutes, ¥750), continuing on to Asahikawa (two hours, ¥1800). There are up to four buses daily to Kitami (two hours, ¥2450) and two a day to Kushiro (five hours, ¥4700). The Kushiro buses run via Akan Kohan (3¼ hours, ¥3200), in Akan National Park. There are also two buses a day to Obihiro (2½ hours, ¥2200), which follow a scenic route via Lake Nukabira-ko.

FURANO　富良野

This is one of Japan's most famous ski resorts with over a dozen ski lifts and excellent facilities for powder skiing considered by some to be among the best in the world.

The JR Furano line links Asahikawa with Furano in 1¼ hours (¥1020). There is also a railway line from Sapporo via Takikawa to Furano. Limited express trains take 3¼ hours (¥4620), however, these usually only run on weekends and holidays, except during the ski season when service is more frequent. If you're going skiing, check with travel agents about rail/accommodation packages, which can often save you some money.

Frequent buses also connect Furano with Asahikawa (1½ hours, ¥850) and Sapporo (2½ hours, ¥2000).

Places to Stay

There are plenty of minshuku, ryokan, hotels and pensions – the information counter at Furano station can provide help with accommodation. For an inexpensive place to stay, you could try *Furano White Youth Hostel* (☎ 0167-23-4807) which is a 10 minute bus ride from Furano station. In winter take a bus bound for the *suki-jō* (skiing ground) and get off at the last stop – the youth hostel is 150m from the stop. In summer take a bus bound for Goryo and get off at the Kisen stop, which is around 200m from the hostel. Buses leave from Furano station. The hostel is closed from 6 to 24 April and from 31 October to 9 December (these dates seem to vary each year, so call ahead). Rates are ¥3000.

Suzuki Ryokan (☎ 0167-22-3852) is a five minute walk from Furano station. Per-person rates with two meals start at around ¥5000. If you're planning a winter ski trip to Furano, it would be best to arrange accommodation in advance through a travel agent, who will probably get you better deals than if you booked directly.

TOKACHIDAKE & SHIROGANE ONSEN
十勝岳・白金温泉

A short distance north-east of Furano are the remote hot-spring villages of Tokachidake Onsen and Shirogane Onsen, which make good crowd-free bases for hiking and skiing. You can climb **Mt Tokachi-dake** in a day; some trails extend as far as Tenninkyō Onsen or Mt Asahi-dake, though these require between three and four days of hiking.

Tokachidake only has three places to stay, although none of them are particularly cheap. Probably the most reasonable option is *Kokuminshukusha Kamihoro-sō* (☎ 0167-

45-2970) where per-person rates, including two meals, start at ¥7000. An inexpensive place to stay at Shirogane Onsen is *Shirogane Center* (☎ 0166-94-3131), a youth hostel with rates at ¥2300. There's a ¥150 fee for using the hot-spring bath. It's one minute on foot from the Shirogane Onsen bus stop. Also in the same area is *Onsen Minshuku Rindo* (☎ 0166-94-3036), which has per-person rates of ¥6500, including two meals.

From Kami Furano station on the JR Furano line, it's a 45 minute bus ride (¥490) to Tokachidake Onsen – up to three buses run daily. From Biei station on the JR Furano line, it's a 30 minute bus ride (¥600) to Shirogane Onsen – up to four buses run daily. There are also up to four direct buses daily to Shirogane Onsen from Asahikawa (1¼ hours, ¥1100).

KITAMI 北見

Along with its distinction of being Japan's top onion producer, this small agricultural city is a useful transport hub for eastern Hokkaido. To the west is Sōunkyō Onsen, to the north-east is Abashiri and Shiretoko National Park, and to the south is Akan National Park. There's no reason to stay in Kitami, but if you're going to any of these destinations you may well find yourself making bus or train connections here. From Kitami station, it's one hour by local train on the JR Sekihoku line east to Abashiri. Trains to Abashiri run via Bihoro, where you can catch a bus for Kawayu Onsen in the eastern section of Akan National Park.

The bus terminal is on the left as you exit the station. Buses connect Kitami with Abashiri (70 minutes, ¥1430), Bihoro (40 minutes, ¥800), Akan Kohan (1½ hours, ¥1800) and Kushiro (three hours, ¥3300). Buses to Sōunkyō Onsen take two hours and cost ¥2450.

If you find yourself with time to kill in Kitami, you can wander over to the **Okhotsk Beer Factory**, the city's very own microbrewery. It's a 15 minute walk north-west of the station. The tourist information office next to the JR ticket counter in the station can give you an English map with the factory listed on it. The beer is tasty and a half-litre mug costs ¥600 to ¥700, depending on the type of brew.

Should too many frosty mugs lead you to miss the last bus, there are plenty of hotels near the station. The *New Kitami Hotel* (☎ 0157-24-2157) has singles from ¥3500 and twins for ¥8200, but may scare off all but the most serious budget travellers. The *Kitami Dai-Ichi Hotel* (☎ 0157-25-7337) is more expensive, with singles/twins at ¥5500/11,000, but should also offer a better night's sleep.

ABASHIRI 網走

Abashiri (population 44,000) is mainly of interest to travellers as a transport hub for access to Shari and the Shiretoko Peninsula. The town is primarily a harbour, though the harbour itself is closed from December to March each year due to ice floes. Abashiri is also the site of a maximum security prison – there's even a **Prison Museum** you can visit on Mt Tento-san, though entry is a little steep at ¥1030. (The museum is a prison dating from the Meiji era, but has long since been replaced by the maximum security facility: if it's live prisoners you're after, you're out of luck.)

The tourist information office in Abashiri station has details about the few sights around Abashiri that can be reached by bus. There's a lookout on **Mt Tento-san**, about four km from the station, which also features the **Museum of Ice Floes** (Okhotsk Ryūhyō-kan) (¥500) and **The Museum of Northern Peoples** (¥250), which displays items from the culture of native tribes from northern Eurasia and North America. About one hour by bus west of Abashiri is **Lake Saroma-ko**, known for it's beautiful floral and marsh scenery.

Places to Stay & Eat

Close to the station, on the left-hand side, is *Hotel Misono* (☎ 0152-43-3312), which has basic singles/twins for ¥5000/9000. Also opposite the station, but to the right, is *Hotel Shinbashi* (☎ 0152-43-4307), a Japanese-style hotel with singles at ¥6000 and doubles at ¥11,000.

The nearest youth hostel is the recently opened *Abashiri Ryūhyō-no-Oka* (☎ 0152-43-8558) located in the northern part of the city. To get there take a bus bound for Futatsu-iwa and get off after eight minutes at Meiji-iriguchi. From there it's a 10 minute walk. Beds are ¥3100 and bicycle rental is available.

If you do venture out to Lake Saroma-ko, the *Saroma Kohan Youth Hostel* (☎ 0158-76-2515) is located at Hama-Saroma, a one hour bus ride from Abashiri station. Nightly rates are ¥2800.

Getting There & Away

Memanbetsu airport links Abashiri with Sapporo, Fukuoka, Nagoya, Osaka and Tokyo. Buses run from Abashiri station to the airport in 25 minutes (¥720). Between 1 July and 30 September there is one bus daily from the airport via Abashiri to Utoro Onsen, in Shiretoko National Park (two hours, ¥2600).

Abashiri is the terminus for the JR Sekihoku line which runs across the centre of Hokkaidō to Asahikawa – the fastest trains take about 3¾ hours (¥7100). It is also the terminus for the JR Senmō line which runs via Shari to Kushiro. From Abashiri to Shari takes 48 minutes by local train (¥790). There are also local buses to Shari (one hour, ¥1050), but departures aren't that frequent and you may have to change buses at Jūhachi-sen. If it's between June and September, you can also take the Memanbetsu Airport-Utoro bus, which runs via Abashiri station.

Shiretoko National Park
知床国立公園

This remote park (386 sq km) features a peninsula with a range of volcanic peaks leading out to the rugged cliffs around Cape Shiretoko-misaki. It has seen little development and remains one of the most pristine wilderness areas in Japan. Roads run along each side of the peninsula, but they peter out well before the tip, which can be viewed as part of a long boat excursion from Utoro. Another road crosses the peninsula from

Rausu to Utoro. Transport is restricted to infrequent buses and bicycle rental; hitching is also a viable option. The main season for visitors is from mid-June to mid-September – most of the hikes are not recommended outside this season.

From Shari, the gateway to the peninsula, there is an efficient bus service to the resort town of Utoro Onsen, home to most of the area's accommodation. However, as Iwaobetsu Youth Hostel is more convenient as a base for hiking, details about sights and hiking on the peninsula are concentrated in the Iwaobetsu section below.

SHARI　斜里

Unless you miss the last bus there's no reason to stay in this slightly run-down town, as accommodation in the park is only an hour's ride away. A tourist information office at Shari station can provide timetables and leaflets in Japanese, though it's only open from 11 am to 5 pm.

Places to Stay

Staff at the tourist information office can give you a map showing accommodation in Shari and Utoro, and can help book rooms in Shari. The *Shari Youth Hostel* (☎ 01522-3-2220) is just a five minute walk from Shari station – walk straight out from the station to the first intersection, turn left, left again at the next road and, after crossing the railroad tracks, look for the hostel on the left. Per-person costs are ¥2600. The hostel is closed from November to late May.

Green Onsen (☎ 01522-3-2239) is a small minshuku located about a five minute walk along the road leading straight out from the station. Cross the first intersection and then look for the minshuku on the right. Per-person rates with two meals are ¥6500. In the same area, but on the left side of the street, is *Matsumaya Ryokan* (☎ 01522-3-2239) which has similar rates.

Getting There & Away

Shari is connected to Abashiri and Kushiro by the JR Senmō line. The ride to Abashiri takes 48 minutes by local train. To Kushiro it's about 2½ hours.

The bus centre is to your left as you exit the station. Between late April and November there are up to eight buses daily from Shari to Utoro Onsen (¥1420), but only three or four continue to Iwaobetsu – the full trip from Shari to Iwaobetsu takes 70 minutes (¥1700). From November to late April service is reduced to four buses a day: service to Iwaobetsu is suspended during this time.

UTORO　ウトロ

Utoro is the only town of any size on the northern side of the Shiretoko peninsula. Unless you're staying at the Iwaobetsu Youth Hostel, this is probably where you'll find your accommodation. There's a tourist information office in the front section of the bus centre which can supply you with maps and help you to book hotels, though not minshuku.

Between May and early September, two boat excursions operate from Utoro: one runs once daily out to the soaring cliffs of

Cape Shiretoko-misaki (3¾ hours, ¥6000); and the other runs up to five times daily for a short cruise along the coastline as far as Kamuiwakka-no-Taki Falls (90 minutes, ¥2400). Short of hiking for several days, the boat cruise is the only way to catch a glimpse of the tip of the peninsula. That said, your money might be better spent on bus fares to the trailheads or bicycle rental.

Places to Stay

The youth hostel in Utoro is run by *Shiretoko Yūhi-no-Ataru-ie Hotel* (☎ 01522-4-2034). Rates are ¥3100 and you can use the hot-spring bath in the hotel. It's located on a hill overlooking town, beyond the Shiretoko Prince Hotel. Between May and October there's a shuttle bus service that meets incoming buses from Shari which will take you to the hostel. Otherwise it's a 15 minute walk uphill from the bus terminal.

There are minshuku aplenty along the main road through town. Opposite the bus terminal is *Minshuku Taiyō* (☎ 01522-4-2939), which charges only ¥4000 per person, two meals included. The owners say they haven't changed the price since they opened 15 years ago. Next door is *Minshuku Peleke* (☎ 01522-4-2236), a more up-market place that charges ¥6500 per person with two meals. Just down the street, on the same side as the bus terminal, is *Bon's Home* (☎ 01522-4-2271), a member of the Toho Network. Dormitory-style accommodation costs ¥4500 per person, including two meals. It's closed from late October to late December.

The *Shiretoko Campground* is located near the youth hostel and charges ¥300 per person for a tent site.

Getting There & Away

The Utoro bus terminal is the transport hub for the park. This station is also sometimes referred to as Utoro Onsen. Between late April and mid-October buses run three times daily along the northern side of the peninsula, passing the Shiretoko National Park Nature Center, the Iwaobetsu Youth Hostel, Shiretoko Goko lakes, and Kamuiwakka Falls before terminating at Shiretoko-ōhashi

Bridge. The trip from Utoro to Shiretoko-ōhashi takes 45 minutes and costs a hefty ¥1020. From mid-October to late April buses run only as far as the Nature Center. From July to mid-October there are also buses twice daily to Rausu via Shiretoko-toge Pass (50 minutes, ¥1260).

From 1 July to 30 September there is one bus a day between Utoro and Akan Kohan in Akan National Park, running via Shari, Kawayu Onsen and Teshikaga. The full trip takes four hours and costs ¥5300.

IWAOBETSU　岩尾別

Iwaobetsu is a hamlet, further up the coast from Utoro, and the *Shiretoko Iwaobetsu Youth Hostel* (☎ 01522-4-2311) deserves recommendation as a friendly and convenient base for exploring the peninsula. The hostel runs 'briefing' sessions to outline hikes and trips available; organised outings are also arranged, including multi-day trips around the peninsula (you'll need to call well in advance for these). The hostel rents out mountain bikes, albeit at a budget-blowing rate of ¥2000 per day.

The hostel is closed from 25 October until 29 April. (It opens from 1 February to 25 March, but only for those who have signed up for a special three-day winter hiking tour) Per-person costs are ¥2800.

From late April to 31 October there are three buses daily from Utoro which run by the hostel. If you've missed the bus from Utoro, either hitch (it's only nine km) or phone the cheery and long-suffering hostel manager who has been known to fetch stranded foreigners.

A road almost opposite the youth hostel leads four km uphill to Iwaobetsu Onsen, which lies at the start of the trail up Mt Rausu-dake. The *Hotel Chi-no-Hate* (☎ 01522-4-2331) here is a bit frayed at the edges and isn't particularly cheap (from ¥8500 per person with two meals). Still, it's worth wandering up here for the rotenburo (open-air baths) just below the hotel's car park. Nearby, at the trailhead for Mt Rausu-dake, is *Kinoshita Goya* (05122-4-2824) a wooden mountain hut that's only open from

June to September and offers extremely basic accommodation for ¥1500 a night. There's also an outside hot spring. If possible, it would be best to book ahead.

SHIRETOKO PENINSULA

About 10 minutes by bus from Iwaobetsu Youth Hostel are the **Shiretoko Goko** (Shiretoko Five Lakes), where wooden walkways have been laid out for visitors to stroll around the lakes in an hour or so.

Another 30 minutes by bus down the dirt road towards the tip of the peninsula, you come to the spectacular rotenburo which form part of **Kamuiwakka-no-Taki Falls**. It takes about 20 minutes to climb up through the warm waters of the stream until you come to cascades of hot water emptying into a succession of pools. (Rubber-soled sandals or deck shoes are highly recommended for this hike.) Bathers simply strip off (although many bring bathing suits), soak in the pools and enjoy the superb panorama across the ocean. Near the trailhead is an old man who does a brilliant business renting out straw sandals at ¥500 a pop – exorbitant to be sure, but you'll find it's worth every yen if you haven't brought adequate footwear. Buses to the falls are spaced about three hours apart, which will give you time to relax and enjoy the waters.

Warning: Bear Activity

Shiretoko Peninsula is home to around 600 brown bears, one of the largest communities in Japan. Park pamphlets warn visitors that once they enter Shiretoko National Park, they should assume bears can appear at any time. Favourite bear haunts include Shiretoko Goko Lakes and Kamuiwakka-no-Taki Falls.

Hikers are strongly advised not to go into the forest in the early morning or at dusk, and to avoid hiking alone. Carrying a bell or some other noise-making device is also recommended. Bear activity picks up noticeably during early autumn, when the creatures are actively foraging for food ahead of their winter hibernation. Visitors should be especially cautious at this time. ∎

There are several hikes on the peninsula, and Iwaobetsu Youth Hostel can provide more detailed advice on routes, trail conditions and the organisation of transport. Proper footwear and warm clothes are essential.

The hike to the top of **Mt Rausu-dake** (1661m) starts from the hotel at Iwaobetsu Onsen. There's only one bus a day out to the hotel, so you'll probably have to walk for an hour up the road from Iwaobetsu Youth Hostel to reach the start of the trail – allow 4½ hours from there to reach the top at a comfortable pace.

The hike to the summit of **Mt Iō-zan** (1562m) starts about 500m beyond the Shiretoko-ōhashi Bridge and requires about eight hours for the return trip.

There is also a shorter hike to Lake Rausu-ko, near **Shiretoko-toge Pass**. The trailhead is several kilometres south of the pass, on the way to Rausu. The hike takes about four hours there and back and takes you through virtually untouched wilderness. Buses run twice a day between Utoro and Rausu via the pass, which also offers great views of the mountains and Kunashiri Island, the closest of Japan's 'northern territories', currently still in Russian hands.

RAUSU 羅臼

This is a small fishing village that grew wealthy on herring fishing, though things seemed to have quietened down quite a bit. There's not much reason to come here unless you're planning to hike around the peninsula or feel like taking an alternate route out of Shiretoko. From Rausu there are four to six buses daily to Kushiro (3½ hours, ¥4650).

Places to Stay

Rausu Youth Hostel (☎ 01538-7-2145) is about a 10 minute walk from the terminus of the Utoro-Rausu bus. It only gets a one-star rating from the Japan Youth Hostel Association, so don't expect much. Nightly costs are ¥2400. In the same part of town is *Takashimaya Ryokan* (☎ 01538-7-2145), which has per-person rates of ¥6500, including two meals.

Akan National Park
阿寒国立公園

This large park (905 sq km) in eastern Hokkaidō contains several volcanic peaks, some large caldera lakes and extensive forests. The gorgeous scenery attracts some five million visitors a year, but in late spring and early autumn the crowds really thin out, giving ample opportunity to actually commune with nature rather than tour groups. There aren't many chances for extended hiking, but there are several interesting day hike options.

The main gateways on the fringe of the park are Kitami and Bihoro in the north and Kushiro in the south. The major centres inside the park are the towns of Kawayu Onsen and Akan Kohan. The small town of Teshikaga lies outside the park proper, but is a useful transport hub.

The only efficient and speedy transport in the park is provided by Akan Bus Company sightseeing buses. The running recorded commentary gets a bit tiresome, but the ride brings you past all the major sights and through beautiful scenery – on clear days there are outstanding views of the park's mountains and lakes. Most bus services run only between May and late October. Kushiro would be a convenient place to rent a car – ask at the tourist information office in Kushiro station. There are also car rental offices at Kushiro airport. The JR Senmō line runs from Shari to Kushiro, though trains aren't too frequent.

KAWAYU ONSEN   川湯温泉

This pleasant little hot-spring resort is a convenient base for visiting the nearby sights of Lake Kussharo-ko, Mt Iō-zan and Lake Mashū-ko. The town itself is centred around a small park and bordered on all sides by

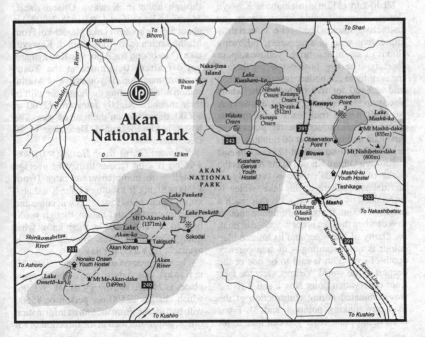

forest. Even the pint-sized bus terminal sits amidst a grove of trees.

There's a tourist information office, about a five minute walk through the park from the bus terminal, which has maps of the town and the area around Lake Kussharo-ko and Lake Mashū-ko. Staff can also help book accommodation, but charge a fee for doing so. The Akan National Park Visitor Centre is near the bus terminal and has an English-language pamphlet with basic information on the park, as well as more detailed hiking and nature guides in Japanese.

Things to See

About three km from Kawayu Onsen is **Lake Kussharo-ko**, the largest inland lake in Hokkaidō and a popular spot for swimming and camping. At **Sunayu Onsen** on the eastern shore a few small hot springs warm the sand on the beach, while at **Wakoto Onsen** on the southern shore there are hot springs bubbling into open-air pools.

Mt Iō-zan (512m), just outside Kawayu Onsen, is unmistakable for its steam and distinctive smell. The scene is certainly impressive with hissing vents, billowing clouds of steam and bright yellow sulphur deposits. The egg business is big here – crates of them are boiled over the vents and sold at ¥400 for five (although the whole place provides a free eggy whiff, anyway). A beautiful nature trail leads from the bus centre for 2½ km through dwarf pines to the mountain and takes about 40 minutes.

Lake Mashū-ko is about 15 km south-east of Kawayu Onsen. Known to the Ainu as the 'Lake of the Gods', there is certainly an unusual atmosphere to this lake, which is surrounded by steep rock walls that reach a height of 300m. If you are fortunate enough to visit when the lake is not wreathed in mist, the clarity of the water and its intense blue colour is quite startling – its transparency depth of over 35m is said to be one of the deepest in the world. Visitors view the lake from observation point Nos 1 and 3 (No 2 was eliminated during construction of the road now linking points 1 and 3). From observation point No 1 you can hike to **Mt**

Mashū-dake (855m), the craggy volcanic peak that lords over the eastern shore of the lake. Allow about six hours for the return trip and walk with care: a major earthquake in 1993 dislodged a lot of the rock along the narrow crater ridge, making an already tricky hike even more precarious.

Observation point Nos 1 and 3 can be reached by bus from Kawayu Onsen. Buses also run from Mashū station to observation point No 1. See the Getting There & Away section later for details.

If you have the time, a bicycle is a good way to see some of the closer sights such as Lake Kussharo-ko, Sunayu Onsen and Mt Iō-zan. Mashū-ko observation point No 1 is a 15 km ride from Kawayu Onsen, but be forewarned that it's a pretty steep climb. You can rent bicycles at the bus terminal (¥750 for two hours, ¥1200 for five hours).

Places to Stay

There are two youth hostels in the area, though none in Kawayu Onsen itself. *Mashū-ko Youth Hostel* (☎ 01548-2-3098) is about 5½ km south of Lake Mashū-ko. From Mashū station (two stops south of Kawayu) take a bus bound for Bihoro or Kawayu and get off after 10 minutes at the Yūsu-hosuteru-mae stop. If you arrive at Mashū station after 4 pm, ring the hostel for a lift in their minibus. Nightly rates are ¥2700 to ¥3000, depending on the time of year. The hostel is closed from 1 December to 20 December.

Kussharo-Genya Youth Hostel (☎ 01548-4-2609) is a bit fancier than your average hostel, with commensurate rates (from ¥3500 a night). It's south of Lake Kussharo-ko, off Route 243. Hostel staff will come and pick you up at Mashū station, though you'll need to call ahead and let them know what time your train arrives. Bicycle rental is available for ¥2000 per day.

There are numerous hotels and minshuku in Kawayu Onsen itself. One of the cheapest places is *Minshuku Nire* (☎ 01548-3-2506) which charges ¥3500 per person or ¥5500 with two meals. From the tourist information office, follow the road in the direction of Mt

Iō-zan. After about 10 minutes you'll reach an intersection at the edge of town, just before the road sign for Iō-zan and Lake Mashū-ko. The minshuku is down a driveway to the left, in the shadow of the glaring green and white Kozan-so Hotel.

In Nibushi Onsen, four km from Kawayu Onsen and on the shore of Lake Kussharo-ko, is *Onsen Minshuku Nibushi-no-Sato* (☎ 01548-3-2294) a casual place with a log-cabin feel to it. The laid-back owner will pick you up and take you back to the Kawayu Onsen bus terminal, and also rents mountain bikes for ¥1800 per day, so you can get around on your own. Per-person rates with two meals range from ¥6500 to ¥7500. There's also a nice indoor hot-spring bath with a view of the lake.

Getting There & Away

The JR Senmō line links Kawayu station with Shari in 55 minutes and with Kushiro in 1½ hours. Kawayu Onsen bus terminal is a 10 minute bus ride (¥270) from Kawayu station. Bus departures are timed to meet the trains.

From Kawayu Onsen bus terminal there are up to four buses a day to Bihoro (1¾ hours, ¥2640) and two buses daily to Kushiro (2½ hours, ¥2760). The Bihoro service runs via scenic Bihoro pass and only operates from May to October.

Between May and October a sightseeing bus service operates four times daily from Kawayu Onsen via the main sights in the park to Akan Kohan (2½ hours, ¥3190). The bus makes stops of around 20 minutes each at Mt Iō-zan and Lake Mashū-ko observation point No 1. The ride from Kawayu Onsen to observation point No 3 takes 45 minutes and costs ¥900. There are also buses to observation point No 1 from Mashū station (25 minutes, ¥720). Both services run past the stop for the Mashū-ko Youth Hostel which is south of the lake on the road to Teshikaga.

There are five buses a day running directly between Kawayu Onsen and Mashū station (35 minutes, ¥780).

Buses to Bihoro run past Nibushi, Sunayu and Wakoto onsens.

TESHIKAGA 弟子屈

Teshikaga lies just outside the park and is a convenient transport hub, though there's no reason to stay here. Teshikaga (also referred to as Mashū Onsen) serves as the midpoint of the sightseeing bus route between Kawayu Onsen and Akan Kohan. It's also on the JR Senmō line; the station name is Mashū.

You can catch buses from Mashū station to the No 1 observation point at Lake Mashū-ko. This station is also the best place to get off if you're headed to either the Mashū-ko or Kussharo-Genya Youth Hostels (see the preceding Places to Stay section).

Between Lake Akan-ko and Teshikaga is a particularly scenic stretch on Route 241, with an outstanding lookout at **Sokodai**, which overlooks Lake Penketō and Lake Panketō.

AKAN KOHAN 阿寒湖畔

Unlike it's counterpart at Kawayu Onsen, this hot-spring resort on the edge of **Lake Akan-ko** has done little to try and blend in with its surroundings. You can safely skip the boat trips (¥1100) on the lake and the 'authentic' Ainu village tours, but the town is still a good base for doing some interesting mountain hikes in the area.

On the eastern side of town is the Lake Akan tourism information office (0154-67-3200) where you can pick up English-language pamphlets on the park, including excellent alpine trail guides for Mt O-Akan-dake and Mt Me-Akan-dake. The office can also help with booking accommodation, and is open daily from 9 am to 5 pm. Further east, at the edge of town, is the national park's Akan-kohan Visitor Centre, which has park leaflets, hiking maps and exhibits on area flora and fauna. The centre also has tanks where you can come face to face with *marimo*, a globe-shaped algae which is peculiar to the lake. These green fuzzballs can take 200 years to grow to the size of a baseball: interesting items, but severely overdone as a tourist attraction. Hours are 9 am to 5 pm daily.

Behind the centre is a scenic nature trail which leads through the woods to **Bokke** (a collection of spluttering mudholes beside the lake) and then returns via the lake shore to town.

Hiking

Mt O-Akan-dake (1371m) is about six km north of the town. The hiking trail starts at Takiguchi. The ascent takes a fairly arduous 3½ hours and the descent about 2½. From the peak there are fine views of Lake Penketō and Lake Panketō, and in summer the top is covered with alpine wildflowers. On clear days one can see as far as Daisetsuzan National Park.

Mt Me-Akan-dake (1499m) is an active volcano and the highest mountain in the park. If you intend to climb this peak, keep a close watch on the weather as it can change very fast. When hiking around the crater, watch out for the noxious effects of the sulphur fumes from the vents. There are several approaches, but unless you have a car the most convenient way is via the trailheads near the beautiful Onnetō-ko lake. One leads up from Nonaka Onsen (near the Nonaka Onsen Youth Hostel) and the other from the southern edge of Lake Onnetō-ko. The ascent from either trailhead takes around two hours and the descent about 1½ hours. From 1 July to 20 October buses run three to four times daily from Akan Kohan via Nonaka Onsen to the lake (¥1130).

For an excellent short hike, try the climb up to the observation platform on Mt Hakutō-zan, where you get fine views of the lake and the surrounding peaks: it's a great place for a picnic, or at least a cold beer. The trail starts at the Akan Kohan Skiing Ground, about one km south of town. The ascent from the ski ground takes about an hour, winding through birch and fir forests and past several groups of bubbling sulphur hot springs.

Places to Stay & Eat

Youth Hostels The *Akan Angel Youth Hostel* (☎ 0154-67-2309) is a 12 minute walk from the bus terminal at Akan Kohan. If you phone ahead, the owner may offer to fetch you and will give you a lift to the terminal when you leave. He can also provide advice on hiking in the area and often takes groups himself.

Bicycle rental and a hot-spring bath (¥150 additional fee) are also available. Nightly costs are ¥2600.

The *Nonaka Onsen Youth Hostel* (☎ 01562-9-7454), about 20 km south-west of Lake Akan-ko, is in a beautiful setting, and provides a base for climbing Mt Me-Akan-dake. Buses run from Akan Kohan to Nonaka Onsen three to four times daily between 1 July and 20 October, but after that you'll have to arrange your own transport. For an additional fee of ¥75 you can use the hot-spring bath. Nightly rates are ¥2500. The hostel is closed from 6 to 13 November.

Minshuku & Hotels There are around a dozen minshuku in Akan Kohan and the tourist office has maps showing their locations. Two of the very best places to stay are in the western side of town. *Minshuku Kiri* (☎ 0154-67-2755) is an attractive place with per-person costs of ¥5500, including two meals. It's opposite the Akan Grand Hotel on the road that runs alongside Lake Akan-ko: look for the woodblock-print style sign. A bit further down the road, on the opposite side of the street, is *Yamaguchi* (☎ 0154-67-2555), which has clean rooms, friendly staff, hot-spring baths and even a bilingual mynah bird to greet and harass guests.

Akan Kohan has numerous up-market resort hotels. Per-person rates with two meals start at ¥12,000 to ¥14,000 in summer and drop to ¥7000 to ¥8000 in winter. Among the best choices in this category are the *New Akan Hotel* (☎ 0154-67-2121) and the *Hotel Akanko-sō* (☎ 0154-67-2231).

Getting There & Away

See the Kawayu Onsen Getting There & Away section for details of the park sightseeing bus service. From Akan Kohan Bus Centre there are several buses daily to Kitami (1½ hours, ¥1800) and Asahikawa (5 hours, ¥4500). The latter run via Sōunkyō in Daisetsuzan National Park (3¼ hours, ¥3200). There are up to five buses daily to Kushiro (2¼ hours, ¥2600) which go via Kushiro airport. From 1 July to 30 September there is also one bus daily to Utoro Onsen

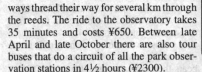

in Shiretoko National Park (four hours, ¥5300). Between mid-July and mid-August there is a bus service connecting Akan Kohan and Obihiro.

KUSHIRO 釧路

Kushiro (population 205,000) is the industrial and economic centre of eastern Hokkaidō and one of the main gateways to Akan National Park.

If you have time to spare, you might want to visit the nearby **Kushiro Shitsugen National Park** (also referred to as Kushiro Marshlands Park), a swampy area famed for its flora and dwindling numbers of *tanchō-zuru* (red-crested white cranes). Frequent buses run from in front of the Akan Bus terminal (next to the station) to the Kushiro Marsh Observatory, where wooden walk-

Spotting a red-crested white crane (tanchō-zuru) is regarded as a good omen. Approximately 400 birds now inhabit Kushiro Shitsugen National Park.

ways thread their way for several km through the reeds. The ride to the observatory takes 35 minutes and costs ¥650. Between late April and late October there are also tour buses that do a circuit of all the park observation stations in 4½ hours (¥2300).

There is a tourist information counter in Kushiro station, next to the JR ticket counter, that can supply you with information on Kushiro Shitsugen and maps detailing the sparse offering of sights in the city itself.

Places to Stay & Eat

The *Kushiro Makiba Youth Hostel* (☎ 0154-23-0852) is a 15 minute walk from the station. Turn left out of the station, walk eastwards for 900m and take the first railroad crossing after the bridge. Follow this road for around 500m and look out for a small park on your left. The youth hostel is just after the park. The tourist office at the station can give you a hand-drawn map showing the way. Nightly costs are ¥2300, and alcohol and smoking are strictly verboten. The hostel is closed from 10 November to 20 January.

Kushiro Youth Hostel (☎ 0154-41-1676) is a 15 minute bus ride from the station, near Harutori Kōen Park. Take a No 27 or No 30 bus, get off at the Yūsu Hosuteru-mae stop and from there it's a two minute walk. It's marginally cheaper than most Japanese youth hostels – ¥1800 to ¥2000 depending on the time of year. It's closed from 16 January to 25 January and from 16 to 19 May.

The *Ryokan Kawatani* (☎ 0154-23-8221) is about 500m east of the station on the road that runs parallel to the train tracks – look out for the ryokan just before the bridge. It has per-person costs of ¥5500 with two meals.

Opposite the station is the *Kushiro Tōei Hotel* (☎ 0154-23-2121), a fairly up-market business hotel with singles/twins from ¥6000/12,000. Cheaper and a bit shabbier is the *Eki-mae Hotel Adachi* (☎ 0154-22-3111) with has singles/twins from ¥5500/8500.

If you don't mind dropping ¥17,000 for a twin room, you can stay at one of the silliest looking hotels in Japan, the *Kushiro Castle Hotel* (☎ 0154-43-2111), which looks like the result of a spat between two kindergarten architects. It overlooks the Kyukushiro-gawa River about 15 minutes on foot from the station: you can't miss it.

If you have the time to wander over to the river, the Fisherman's Wharf complex (which bears the perplexing moniker of 'MOO') is a nice place to get a bite to eat or have a drink. The restaurants on the first floor have some good set lunch deals and, if the weather is nice, you can buy your lunch to take outside and eat at the tables along the wharf.

Getting There & Away

Air Flights connect Kushiro with Sapporo (40 minutes, ¥14,050) and Tokyo (1¾ hours, ¥24,250). Kushiro airport is a 50 minute bus ride (¥890) from Kushiro station.

Train The JR Senmō line runs north through Akan National Park to Shari (2½ hours, ¥2680). The JR Nemuro line runs west to Sapporo (five hours by limited express). The fare to Sapporo is ¥5970 with a ¥2970 limited express surcharge. Sapporo also has a night service to Kushiro that leaves at around 11 pm (check for the latest time), arriving at around 6 am in Kushiro. A sleeper berth will cost you ¥14,620; otherwise the fare is the same as the limited express. At the time of writing JR was planning to introduce a new high-speed train in early 1997 which will cut travel time to Sapporo to 3¾ hours.

Bus Buses leave from terminals at Kushiro station (to the left as you exit the station) and the fisherman's wharf MOO complex. There are up to five buses daily to Akan Kohan (2¼ hours, ¥2600) and two daily to Kawayu Onsen (two hours, ¥2760). Up to four buses run daily to Rausu (3½ hours, ¥4650) on the Shiretoko Peninsula. Buses to Sapporo leave three times a day: the trip takes 6¼ hours and costs ¥5500. There is also a night bus that leaves around 11.30 pm, arriving in Sapporo at 6 am. The night service leaves from the MOO terminal and does not stop at Kushiro station.

Boat A regular ferry service connects Kushiro with Tokyo in 34 hours – the cheap-est passenger fare is ¥14,420. Kushiro Nishi-kō Port (also known simply as the *ferii tāminaru)* is a 15 minute bus ride (¥300) west of Kushiro station. Buses run from the Akan Bus terminal next to the station on days when there are departures or arrivals. Alternatively, the ferry terminal is just over 500m south of Shin Fuji station, one stop west of Kushiro station.

TOMAKOMAI 苫小牧

This is a city renowned for its multitude of paper-making factories – it's Japan's leading paper manufacturing centre. This doesn't exactly commend the place to the average foreign traveller and Tomakomai's main point of interest is its port, which is the hub for ferry links with Honshū.

Places to Stay

Tomakomai is within easy reach of other more interesting destinations so, unless you have an early morning ferry or arrive late at night, there shouldn't be any need to stay here. The nearest youth hostel is the *Utanai-ko Youth Hostel* (☎ 0144-58-2153) which is by the shore of Lake Utanai-ko, a popular spot for birdwatching. This is one of Japan's cheaper youth hostels with rates of ¥1450 from 1 May to 31 October and ¥1600 from 1 November to 30 April. From Tomakomai station it's a 30 minute bus ride in the direction of New Chitose airport or Chitose. Get off at the Utanai-ko Yūsu Hosuteru-mae stop – from there it's a 10 minute walk in the direction of the lake.

Most of the business hotel accommodation around the station is fairly expensive. The *Tomakomai New Station Hotel* (☎ 0144-33-0333) in front of the station has singles at ¥7000 and twins at ¥13,500. On the street behind it, the *Tomakomai Green Hotel* (☎ 0144-32-1122) has singles at ¥6300, twins at ¥12,000, and doubles at ¥9800.

Getting There & Away

The JR Chitose line links Tomakomai with Sapporo in 1¼ hours (¥1380) by local train. The limited express does it in 44 minutes for an additional ¥1630. Tomakomai to Hakodate takes 2¾ by limited express.

Buses run three to four times a day between Tomakomai and Lake Shikotsu-ko in 45 minutes (¥630). There are also three to five buses daily from Tomakomai to Noboribetsu Onsen (1¼ hours, ¥1050) and buses every one to two hours to Shiraoi (45 minutes).

Ferry services link Tomakomai with Sendai (15 hours, ¥8850), Nagoya (39 hours, ¥15,450), Tokyo (32 hours, ¥11,840) and Hachinohe (nine hours, ¥3900). The Tomakomai ferry terminal is a 15 minute bus ride south-east of Tomakomai station.

SHIRAOI 白老

The big attraction in this small town is the reconstructed **Ainu village**, known as 'Poroto Kotan', and the **Ainu Minzoku Hakubutsukan** which is an excellent museum of Ainu culture in a modern building inside the village. Shiraoi is only around 1½ hours from Sapporo by limited express and is easily visited as a day trip.

The museum exhibits are labelled in both Japanese and English and the museum guide (¥400) is also available in both languages. Admission costs ¥515 and the museum is open from 8 am to 5.30 pm, April to October, and from 8.30 am to 4.30 pm, November to March. The village is a 10 minute walk from JR Shiraoi station – turn left when you walk out of the south side of the station. Most bus services drop passengers off at the Poroto Kotan bus stop opposite the approach road to the village.

Getting There & Away

Shiraoi is on the JR Muroran line, 25 minutes from Noboribetsu station (¥340) and 30 minutes from Tomakomai (¥450). Buses between Shiraoi and Tomakomai are marginally cheaper and make the trip in 45 minutes. A limited express from Sapporo makes the trip in just over one hour and costs ¥2720. The Chūō and Donan bus companies both operate services between Sapporo and Shiraoi (two hours, ¥1400): round trip discount tickets are available.

Shikotsu-Tōya National Park
支笏洞爺国立公園

Shikotsu-Tōya National Park (983 sq km) encompasses Lake Shikotsu-ko, Lake Tōya-ko and Noboribetsu Onsen. The lakes have the added attractions of mountain hikes or close-up encounters with volcanoes, while Noboribetsu Onsen will appeal to hot-spring enthusiasts. Fast and easy access to the park from Sapporo or New Chitose airport makes it a favourite with visitors who have only a short time to spend in Hokkaidō.

JNTO publishes a leaflet entitled *Southern Hokkaidō* which provides a map of the park with information on sights, transport and accommodation.

LAKE SHIKOTSU-KO 支笏湖

Lake Shikotsu-ko is a caldera lake surrounded by several volcanoes. It's Japan's second deepest lake after Lake Tazawa-ko in Akita-ken. The main centre for transport and information is **Shikotsu Kohan**, which consists of a bus terminal, a visitor centre, a pier for boat excursions and assorted souvenir shops, restaurants and places to stay.

The visitor information office (☎ 01232-5-2453), located in the park just downhill from the bus terminal, is open from 9.30 am to 4.30 pm and has maps and other information. From the boat pier, there are rather tame sightseeing cruises which stop off at a couple of places around the lake before returning to the pier (30 minutes, ¥930).

If you cross the bridge on your far left as you walk down to the lake shore, you can follow a nature trail around the forested slopes for an hour or so. There's no bus service around the lake, but you can bicycle to various destinations, or even take on the full circuit (50 km). The youth hostel rents bicycles for ¥400 per hour or ¥1500 per day. Mountain bikes are available for ¥2000 per day.

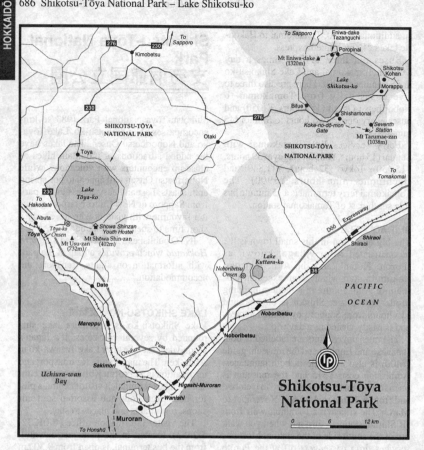

Shikotsu-Tōya National Park

Hiking

The mountain hikes are perhaps the most interesting activities to do around the lake. The youth hostel or tourist information office can give more advice on access, routes and timings.

Mt Eniwa-dake (1320m) lies on the north-west side of the lake. The start of the trail is about 10 minutes on foot from the Eniwa Tozan-guchi bus stop near Poropinai. It takes about 3½ hours to hike to the summit, where there is a fine panorama of the surrounding lakes and peaks. Don't bother with this hike if it rains – some of the steeper sections of

the trail become dangerously slippery. Buses from Shitkotsu Kohan to Sapporo pass by the Eniwa Tozan-guchi stop.

Mt Tarumae-zan (1038m) lies on the southern side of the lake and offers the rugged delights of wandering around the crater of an active volcano. The crater is an easy 40 minute hike from the seventh station, which can be reached from Shikotsu Kohan in three hours on foot – or in 20 minutes by taxi (around ¥3500). There is no bus service. From the crater, you can either return to the seventh station or follow the trail north-west down the mountain for 2½ hours to Kokeno-dōmon, a mossy gorge, which is 10 minutes from the car park at Shishamonai on the lake shore. From Shishamonai you'll have to walk or hitch the 15 km to Shikotsu Kohan.

Places to Stay & Eat

There are over a dozen minshuku, ryokan and hotels on the edge of the lake; camping grounds are also available at Morappu, Poropinai and Bifue. The tourist information office can help with booking accommodation.

Shikotsu-ko Youth Hostel (☎ 0123-25-2311) is at Shikotsu Kohan, just a couple of minutes from the bus terminal there. It's a friendly place and has family rooms, as well as the usual dormitory-style accommodation. Bicycle rental and a hot-spring bath (additional fee of ¥150) are also available. Staff at the hostel can offer advice on hiking and bicycling routes, and may be able to help with organising transport to trailheads. Nightly rates are ¥2600 (¥2800 from 1 July to 30 September). The hostel is closed from 1 to 10 December and from 16 to 19 May. From the bus terminal go left across the parking lot where you'll see the youth hostel sign and driveway.

Just behind the bus terminal is *Shikotsu-sō* (☎ 0123-25-2718) a cheerful little minshuku with per-person rates of ¥5800, including two meals. Tucked away in the little alley behind Shikotsu-sō is the *Log Bear* (☎ 0123-25-2738), a log cabin bed & breakfast with per-person rates of ¥5000.

Out at Morappu, about 10 minutes by car, is *Lapland* (☎ 0123-25-2239), a great little log cabin with nice views of the lake. It's a member of the Toho network and accommodation is mostly dormitory-style, though for ¥1000 extra per person you can have your own room if need be. The owners, a quite friendly young couple, will pick you up and take you back to the bus terminal, or to mountain trailheads. Nightly rates are ¥4800 per person, with two meals. Smoking is not allowed anywhere inside the lodge.

There are numerous little restaurants in Shikotsu Kohan serving up ramen or set meals (teishoku). The Log Bear also doubles

as a coffee shop: the atmosphere is nice, but the prices (¥1100 for a plate of chicken curry) are a bit hard to take.

The camping ground at Poropinai is the only one accessible by public transportation. Site charges are ¥300 per person and tent rental rates start at ¥1200. It's located around 500m from the Poropinai bus stop, which is served by buses running between Shikotsu Kohan and Sapporo.

Getting There & Away

The bus service from Sapporo (Hokkaidō Chūō bus from Sapporo station) to Lake Shikotsu-ko takes 80 minutes (¥1200). There are six buses daily between 1 June and 31 October, but only three a day during the rest of the year. Other bus services run from New Chitose airport (45 minutes, ¥830) and Tomakomai (45 minutes, ¥630). From the airport, buses leave from stop Nos 3 and 35. From either the airport or Tomakomai you can connect with buses to Noboribetsu Onsen. These latter services aren't too frequent, so it would be best to get an early start.

NOBORIBETSU ONSEN　登別温泉

This is perhaps the most popular hot-spring resort in Hokkaidō with an array of brutally ugly hotels and at least 11 different types of hot-spring water to soothe ailments or simply invigorate. It is also Japan's most productive hot-spring source, churning out some 10,000 tonnes of piping hot water daily. The resort is fairly small and worth a visit if you are fascinated by hot springs. Avoid holiday periods, however, when every hotel or hostel in town is packed.

The bus terminal is halfway up the main street. A couple of minutes further up the street there's a tourist office (☎ 0143-84-3311) on your left, where you can pick up a helpful English brochure that includes a map clearly showing accommodation and sights, most of which are accessible on foot from the main street.

Dai-Ichi Takimoto-kan　第一滝本館

The Dai-Ichi Takimoto-kan is a luxury hotel boasting one of the largest bath complexes in Japan. Guests of the hotel are allowed to use the bath free of charge (it costs enough to stay there anyway), but visitors are admitted on payment of a large admission fee.

Plan to make the most of your ticket by spending half a day or longer wandering from floor to floor trying out all the mineral pools (very hot!), waterfalls, walking pools, cold pools (freezing!), jacuzzi, steam room, outdoor pool (with bar) and the swimming pool with its water slide. There are separate sections for men and women, but the swimming pool and water slide are mixed – swimwear is required.

Admission costs ¥2000 and you must enter between 9 am and 3 pm. Take a towel. The entrance to the bath section is at the top of the main street, just past the ramp leading to the hotel's lobby on the right.

Hell Valley　地獄谷

A five minute walk further up the hill from the Dai-Ichi Takimoto-kan, you reach the entrance to Hell Valley (Jigokudani), a valley of volcanic activity. A pathway leads up the valley close to steaming and sulphurous vents with streams of hot water bubbling out of vivid red, yellow and brown rocks.

If you continue up the valley and bear left, you cross a road and come out on a point overlooking **Oyu-numa Pond** with its water bubbling violently and steam rising from the sickly coloured surface. If you have time to continue, the area is crisscrossed by a network of hiking trails. The English-language brochure available at the tourist information office lists several walking routes varying from 40 to 80 minutes in duration.

Lake Kuttara-ko　倶多楽湖

About six km from Noboribetsu Onsen is this small caldera lake with exceptionally clear water which turns an intense blue on fine days. There is no bus service, so if you don't have your own vehicle you'll have to either walk or hitch. The road to the lake starts near a small visitor centre located at the entrance to Hell Valley hot springs.

Places to Stay & Eat

Youth Hostels *Akashiya-sō Youth Hostel* (☎ 0143-84-2616) is a couple of minutes' walk downhill from the bus terminal and on your left after the fire station. Nightly rates are ¥2800 and a hot-spring bath (open 24 hours a day) is available for an additional fee of ¥100. Only breakfast is available (¥600).

Kanefuku Youth Hostel (☎ 0143-84-2565) is a 15 minute walk further down the road from Akashiya-sō, on the right-hand side of the road. If you're taking the bus from JR Noribetsu station, get off at the Kōseinenkin byōin-mae stop. Nightly rates are ¥2600. The hostel doesn't have a hot-spring bath, but does offer home-made ice cream.

Ryokan *Ryokan Hanaya* (☎ 0143-84-2521), a member of the Japanese Inn Group, is next to the Hanaya-mae bus stop about a 10 minute walk downhill from the bus terminal. It's quite a nice spot with many rooms overlooking the river. Singles/doubles start from ¥5500/10,000 and triples from ¥15,000, not including meals.

Not as elegant, but more affordable, is the *JR Seiran-sō* (0143-84-2009) where spacious rooms (including your own sink) cost ¥3290 per person, or ¥5720 including meals. This is probably one of the best deals in town. The hotel is just below and behind the bus terminal, across a small red bridge.

Hotels If you're in the mood for luxury there are many resort hotels from which to choose. Those wanting to stay in the *Dai-Ichi Takimoto-kan* (☎ 0143-84-2111) (see the above entry on the hotel's onsen facilities) are looking at spending ¥12,000 to ¥45,000 with two meals. At the northern end of town the *Noboribetsu Prince Hotel* (☎ 0143-84-2255) is a member of Japan's most distinguished resort hotel chain. Per-person rates with two meals start at ¥10,000 and soar to ¥70,000.

Getting There & Away

There are direct buses between Sapporo and Noboribetsu Onsen (1¾ hours, ¥1800), as well as buses running via Tomakomai (2½ hours). From Noboribetsu Onsen, buses leave from the bus terminal and from in front of the Chuo Bus Company office, located directly across the street.

Between June and late October there are three buses daily to New Chitose airport (one hour, ¥1300). During the rest of the year there is only one bus a day.

If you're headed to Lake Shikotsu-ko, the fastest way is to take a bus to New Chitose airport and change for frequent buses from there to Shikotsu Kohan. You can also take a bus to Tomakomai station (1¼ hours, ¥1050) and change there for buses to Shikotsu Kohan (40 minutes, ¥630). However, the latter bus service only runs four times a day, which means risking a lengthy stopover in not-so-scenic downtown Tomakomai. See the Lake Tōyako Getting There & Away section below for details on bus service between the lake and Noboribetsu Onsen.

There are buses once to twice an hour to Muroran (1½ hours, ¥700).

From Noboribetsu station on the JR Muroran line, it's a 17 minute bus ride to Noboribetsu Onsen. Buses leave approximately once an hour and the fare is ¥320.

LAKE TŌYA-KO 洞爺湖

Although Lake Tōya-ko is a large and attractive lake, most foreign visitors who come here concentrate on seeing the 'upstart' volcanoes near by. The centre of activity for the lake is **Tōya-ko Onsen**, a hot-spring resort on the south shore of the lake.

Mt Shōwa Shin-zan & Mt Usu-zan
昭和新山・有珠山

In 1943, after a series of earthquakes, Mt Shōwa Shin-zan was first formed as an upstart dimple in some vegetable fields and then continued to surge upwards for two more years to reach its present height (402m). It is still an awesome sight as it sits there, hissing and issuing steam and keeping the locals guessing about its next move.

At the base of the mountain is a large car park with some irritating tourist facilities. At the lower end of the car park, hidden behind

the souvenir shops, is the **Masao Mimatsu Memorial Museum**. It's an intriguing museum which displays many items collected by the postmaster who actually owned the ground that turned into a volcano. For many years the old man kept possession of his land, but finally let it pass into the hands of the government.

Among all the photos and paintings, look out for the articles which were taken from English newspapers. Apparently, the Japanese government was keen to hush up the volcanic eruption which it thought might be misinterpreted by the people as a bad omen and thereby hamper the progress of WWII. The postmaster was even requested to find a way to shield the volcanic glare or extinguish it so that the volcano couldn't be used by enemy aircrew for orientation! Admission to the museum costs ¥300 and it's open from 8 am to 5 pm.

At the top end of the car park is the cablecar for Mt Usu-zan, which operates from May to the end of September. The ride takes six minutes and the return ticket costs ¥1450. Those who stay at the Shōwa Shinzan Youth Hostel are eligible for a 10% discount.

Mt Usu-zan (732m) is a frisky volcano which has erupted frequently and was the force behind the creation of Mt Shōwa Shinzan. The last eruption in 1977 destroyed the previous cablecar and rained down rocks and some 30 cm of volcanic ash onto Tōya-ko Onsen. From the top station of the cablecar, there are superb views across the lake to the cone of Mt Yōtei-zan. A short trail leads up to a lookout where you can look into the desolate crater and keep an eye on the emission of smoke and fumes.

Getting There & Away The volcanoes are a 15 minute (¥320) bus ride south-east of Tōya-ko Onsen and about three km from Shōwa Shin-zan Youth Hostel. From Tōyako Onsen take a Tōnan bus to Shōwa Shin-zan and get off at the last stop. Between May and late October buses run hourly between 9 am and 5 pm.

Tōya-ko Onsen Attractions

If you have time to spare after seeing the volcanoes, Tōya-ko Onsen itself is not completely devoid of sights and things to do.

On the floor above the bus terminal is the somewhat dusty **Volcano Science Museum** which charges ¥600 for admission to displays explaining the origins and activities of volcanoes with special emphasis on Mt Usuzan. Visitors can sit in a special room and experience the visual and aural fury of an eruption – the 16-woofer speakers will certainly clean your ears out! It's open from 9 am to 5 pm.

Another diversion available is a boat cruise out to **Naka-jima Island** in the middle of the lake. There's not a great deal out there, but it gives you a chance to see wild Ezo deer and perhaps visit the **Lake Tōya Forest Museum**. The latter is rather dull, with a couple of stuffed Ezo deer and slide shows featuring the changing of the seasons in the lake area. Boats out to the island leave every 30 minutes and cost ¥1300. During the summer, there are fireworks displays every evening.

Across from the bus terminal is a motorcycle shop that has bicycle rental at the extortionate rate of ¥900 for two hours, or ¥2000 for a full day. For ambitious cyclists, there's a 37 km cycling course around the lake.

Places to Stay

Shōwa Shin-zan Youth Hostel (☎ 0142-75-2283) is at the beginning of the steep road leading uphill to Mt Usu-zan and Mt Shōwa Shin-zan. To get there take an eight minute bus ride from Tōya-ko Onsen to the Tozanguchi stop. For an additional fee of ¥150 you can use the hot-spring bath. Bicycle and scooter rental is also available – a convenient way to pop into Tōya-ko Onsen for the evening fireworks display or to pedal around the lake. The hostel has been recently renovated, so nightly rates are a bit higher than average at ¥3000.

Tōya-ko Onsen is overrun with resort hotels along the lakefront, where per-person rates start at around ¥15,000. There are some more affordable options right near the bus terminal, however. Probably the best is the *KKR Tōya Suimei-sō* (☎ 0142-75-2826), which has large rooms, hot spring water baths, excellent food and per-person rates from ¥7300 to ¥8300, including two meals. To get there, turn right as you exit the bus station, take a right at the intersection and walk uphill about 50m. The hotel is on the right side of the street.

One street down from the bus terminal is the spartan *Green Hotel* (☎ 0142-75-3030), where per-person rates (without meals) start at ¥4000. Across the street, looking a bit tattered, is the *Hotel Grand Tōya* (☎ 0142-75-2288), which costs ¥5000 per person, again not including meals.

There are a few camping grounds around the lake, none of which are very convenient unless you have your own transportation. *Takinoue Camping Ground* (☎ 0142-66-2121) is on the south-west side of the lake, about 30 minutes by bus from Tōya-ko Onsen. Ten minutes further along the road is *Nakatōya Camping Ground* (☎ 0142-66-2121) on the eastern edge of the lake. Site costs at both places are ¥300 per person and tent rental is available. Takinoue is open from June through August; Nakatōya for July and August only. Both Takinoue and Nakatōya can be reached by taking a bus bound for Tōya-mura: the respective bus stops are Higashi Kohan and Nakatōya. There are only two buses a day, both running in the afternoon.

Getting There & Away

From Sapporo, unless you're on a Japan Rail Pass, probably the best way to reach Tōya-ko Onsen is by direct bus from in front of Sapporo station. There are six buses daily. The trip takes 2¾ hours and costs ¥2650. There are also two buses a day connecting Tōya-ko Onsen with Hakodate (3½ hours, ¥2750) and frequent services from Muroran that take two hours and cost ¥1150.

Limited express trains from Sapporo take one hour and 50 minutes and cost ¥5650. Limited express trains from Hakodate reach Tōya station in 1½ hours and cost ¥5240.

Buses run once to twice an hour from in front of Tōya station to Tōya-ko Onsen in around 15 minutes and cost ¥310.

Between 1 June and late October, a bus service operates five times daily from Tōya-ko Onsen via Orofure pass to Noboribetsu Onsen (1¼ hours, ¥1500). One departure a day stops at Shōwa Shin-zan: this ride takes 2¼ hours. Between late October and 31 May service is reduced to one bus a day. Between June and October, three of these buses continue past Noboribetsu Onsen to New Chitose airport. The total time for the trip is 2½ hours and the fare is ¥2100. Many of the buses from Tōya-ko Onsen to Sapporo or Noburibetsu Onsen require 'advance reservations' – just try and buy your ticket a few hours ahead and staff at the counter should be satisfied.

MURORAN 室蘭
Muroran (population 117,000) is a huge industrial hub, not worth a special visit unless you want to tour factories or use one of the city's handy ferry links with Honshū.

Places to Stay
Muroran Youth Hostel (☎ 0143-44-3357) is a 15 minute walk from Wanishi station (three stops east of Muroran station). From Wanishi station, turn left and head down the road along the tracks until you see a youth hostel sign pointing down the street to the right; from there it's about one km The hostel is closed from 16 to 25 January and from 16 to 19 May, and charges ¥2800.

Most of Muroran's business hotel accommodation is clustered around Muroran station. Next to Muroran station is the *Business Hotel Million* (☎ 0143-24-6511) which has singles from ¥4500. About 500m south of Muroran station (down Route 36) is the *Hotel Bayside* (☎ 0143-24-8090) which has singles at ¥4800 and twins at ¥8600.

Getting There & Away
Train A direct limited express between Muroran and Hakodate on the JR Muroran line takes 2¼ hours (¥6050); the loop north to Sapporo takes 1¾ hours (¥4620).

Boat Ferry services link Muroran with Hachinohe (eight hours, ¥3900) and Aomori (seven hours, ¥3400). Muroran-futō Pier is a three minute walk from Muroran station.

Shikoku 四国

In Japan's feudal past, the island of Shikoku (population 4,195,000) was divided into four *(shi)* regions *(koku)*, which today have become four prefectures. Although Shikoku is Japan's fourth largest island, it's predominantly rural and very much off the standard tourist track.

In addition to the Ritsurin-kōen Garden in Takamatsu and the four castles (Kōchi, Marugame, Matsuyama and Uwa-jima) that managed to survive both the Meiji Restoration and WWII, there are a variety of attractions, both natural and hand-built, which for those with time make Shikoku a worthwhile excursion (those with an abundance of time might even consider setting off on Kōbō Daishi's 88 Temple Circuit of the island!). The construction of the Seto-ōhashi Bridge linking Shikoku with Honshū has made the island much more accessible.

The island is set to become even more accessible with the construction of two more bridges: one to the east, from Naruto to Akashi (near Kōbe) via Awaji-shima Island; and the other to the west, island hopping from Imabari to Onomichi. Both bridges are slated to open in 1998.

GETTING THERE & AWAY

Air services connect major cities in Shikoku with Tokyo, Osaka and other centres on Honshū.

Numerous ferries ply the waters of the Seto Inland Sea (Seto-nai-kai), linking Shikoku with the Inland Sea islands and with ports on the San-yō coast of Honshū. Takamatsu and Matsuyama are particularly busy Shikoku ports, though there are many others.

The opening of the Seto-ōhashi Bridge in 1988 simplified access to the island and there are frequent train services from Okayama to Takamatsu and Matsu-yama as well as direct bus services to several Shikoku cities from Osaka and Tokyo.

HIGHLIGHTS

◆ Spend a morning or afternoon strolling through the exquisite Ritsurin-kōen Garden in Takamatsu

◆ Spectacular views from Yashima plateau, and the Pond of Blood, where samurais rinsed their swords

◆ Travel to Kotohira and hike up the 800-odd granite steps to pay homage at the sacred Kompira-san Shrine in Kagawa-ken

◆ Dance and revel in the madness during Tokushima's Awa Odori Festival held annually in August

◆ Soak in the tubs at the ancient public bathhouse in Matsuyama's famed Dōgo Onsen spa area

◆ Stroll down thoughtfully preserved Edo-era Yokaichi street in picturesque Uchiko in Ehime-ken

◆ Explore the deep gorges, abundant nature and vine suspension bridge in the secluded Iya region in Tokushima-ken

◆ Rid yourself of all human desires by setting out on the island's monumental 88 Temple Circuit

TOKYO

The 88 Temple Circuit

Japan's best known pilgrimage is Kōbō Daishi's 88 Temple Circuit of Shikoku. Kūkai (774-835), known as Kōbō Daishi after his death, is the most revered of Japan's saints. He founded the Shingon Buddhist sect in 807 after a visit to China. Shingon, often referred to as Esoteric Buddhism, is related to Tantric Buddhism, with its mystic rituals and multi-armed deities.

Kōbō Daishi was born in Shikoku, and it is said he personally selected the 88 temples which make up the circuit. Today, most pilgrims on the circuit travel by tour bus but some still walk – set aside about two months and be prepared to walk over 1500 km if you want to join them. Some of the temples are only a few hundred metres apart and you can walk to five or six in a day. However, at the other extreme, it can be 100 km between temples. Oliver Statler's book *Japanese Pilgrimage* follows the temple circuit.

Individually, none of the temples is exceptionally interesting; it's the whole circuit that counts. The 88 temples represent the same number of evil human passions defined by the Buddhist doctrine and completing the circuit is said to rid one of these. The route begins in Tokushima and is generally made clockwise. The pilgrims, known as *henro*, wear white robes *(hakui)*, carry a staff *(otsue)* and often top the ensemble with a straw hat *(kasa)*. Temple circuiters stamp their robes with the temples' red seals.

Local TIC's can provide more information on making the pilgrimage. About half of the temples have lodging facilities for pilgrims for about ¥4000 per person including two meals. ■

Kagawa-ken   香川県

Formerly known as Sanuki, Kagawa Prefecture is the smallest of Shikoku's four island regions and sits on the north-western coast overlooking the Seto Inland Sea and the Sea of Harima-Nada. Highlights of this region include the beautiful Ritsurin-kōen Garden and the remarkable Shikoku-mura Village (both at Takamatsu) and also the celebrated Kompira-san shrine at Kotohira. Kagawa prefecture also encompasses rural Shōdoshima Island (see Western Honshū section).

TAKAMATSU   高松

Takamatsu (population 330,000) was founded during the rule of Toyotomi Hideyoshi (1537-98) as the castle town of the feudal lord of Kagawa. At that time, Takamatsu was known as Sanuki. The town was virtually destroyed in WWII but rapidly rebounded. The completion of the Seto-ōhashi Bridge reinforced Takamatsu's importance as a major arrival point on Shikoku.

Despite the new rail link, it remains an important port for Inland Sea ferry services, particularly to popular Shōdo-shima Island. The town features an important garden, and the nearby Shikoku-mura Village Museum,

while the famed Kotohira-gū Shrine is an easy day trip.

Orientation & Information

Takamatsu is surprisingly sprawling; it's a two km walk to Ritsurin-kōen Garden from JR Takamatsu station. There's an information centre outside the station (☎ 0878-51-2009) where the English-speaking staff can provide useful leaflets and maps. There's another information counter at the east entrance to Ritsurin-kōen Park that can help with booking accommodation. Equidistant from these two, on the north-west corner of Chūō-kōen Park, is the very praiseworthy Kagawa International Exchange Center (I-PAL KAGAWA). This remarkable resource centre has a message board, a well-stocked library of foreign books and magazines, self-service international phones and fax, satellite English news broadcasts, and access to the Internet. It's open from 9 am to 6 pm Tuesday through Sunday, and also offers a 24 hour recorded information service (☎ 0878-39-2300). Once connected, dial ☎ 774 for tourist information, ☎ 775 for information on sightseeing spots, or ☎ 782 for information on local events.

The ferry terminal buildings are beside JR Takamatsu station. Chūō-dōri, the main road in Takamatsu, leads out from the station,

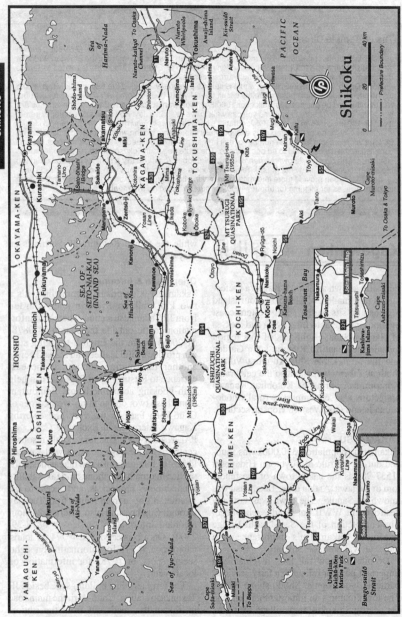

SHIKOKU

with the private Kotoden Chikkō station almost immediately on the left. A busy shopping arcade extends across Chūō-dōri and then runs parallel to it, passing through the entertainment district. The main shopping area is further south, near the Kotoden Kawaramachi station. Beside the Takamatsu City Museum of Art, the Miyawaki Shoten bookstore has a wide selection of English books and magazines on the 5th floor.

Ritsurin-kōen Garden 栗林公園

Although not one of Japan's 'big three' gardens, Ritsurin-kōen could easily be a contender for that list. The garden, which was first made in the mid-1600s, winds around a series of ponds with lookouts, tearooms, bridges and islands. The garden actually took more than a century to complete and was used as a villa garden for more than 200 years prior to the Meiji Restoration. In one direction, Mt Shiun forms a backdrop to the garden but in the other direction, there is some much less impressive 'borrowed scenery' in the form of dull modern buildings.

In the garden, the Sanuki Folkcraft Museum displays local crafts. The feudal-era Kikugetsu-tei Teahouse, also known as the Chrysanthemum Moon Pavilion, offers Japanese tea and sweets for ¥510, and there are several other small teahouses inside the park including the very lovely thatch-roofed Higurashi-tei Teahouse. Entry to the garden is ¥350 and it's open from sunrise to sunset. You can get there by Kotoden or JR train, but the easiest way is by a Kotoden bus (¥220) from platform No 2 at the JR Takamatsu station.

Takamatsu-jō Castle 高松城

There's very little left of Takamatsu Castle, which is just a stone's throw from the JR Takamatsu and Kotoden stations. The castle grounds, which now form the pleasant Tamamo Park, are only one-ninth their original size. When the castle was constructed in 1588, the moats on three sides were filled with sea water while the sea itself formed the fourth side of the castle. Entry is ¥150, and it's open from 8.30 am to 6 pm April through September; otherwise it closes at 5 pm.

Yashima 屋島

The 292m-high table-top plateau of Yashima stands five km east of the centre of Takamatsu. Today, it's the site of the Yashima-ji Temple (No 84 on the temple circuit) and offers fine views over the surrounding countryside and the Inland Sea, but in the 12th century it was the site of titanic struggles between the Genji and Heike clans. The temple's treasure-house collection relates to the battle. Just behind the treasure house is the Pond of Blood, where the victorious warriors washed the blood from their swords, staining the water red.

A funicular railway runs up to the top of Yashima Hill from the left of the shrine at the bottom. The cost is ¥700 one way or ¥1300 return. At the top you can rent a bicycle (¥300, plus a ¥1000 deposit) to pedal around the attractions – it's a long walk otherwise.

The two best ways of getting to Yashima are by Kotoden train or bus. From Kotoden Chikkō station it takes around 20 minutes (¥260) to Kotoden Yashima station. From here you can take the cablecar to the top. Kotoden buses run directly to the top from in front of JR Takamatsu station, take around 30 minutes and cost ¥740.

Shikoku-mura Village

At the bottom of Yashima Hill is an excellent village museum with old buildings brought from all over Shikoku and neighbouring islands. There are explanations in English of the many buildings and their history. Highlights include a traditional vine suspension bridge (though actually reinforced with steel cables, it certainly looks the part). There are other such bridges in Shikoku, the best known of which crosses the Iya-kei Gorge.

Shōdo-shima Island is famed for its traditional farmers' kabuki performances; the village's fine kabuki stage came from that island. Other interesting buildings include a border guardhouse from the Tokugawa era (a time when travel was tightly restricted), and a bark steaming hut that was used in papermaking. There's also a water-powered rice hulling machine and a fine old stone storehouse. Entry is ¥800; the small museum in the village costs an extra ¥100. The village is open from 8.30 am to 4.30 pm (5 pm in the winter months).

If you want to skip Yashima, you can visit Shikoku-mura directly: it's north of Yashima station and takes around seven minutes on foot.

Other Attractions
Just offshore from Yashima is **Megi-jima Island**, also known as Oniga-shima or 'Demon Island'. Several homes on the island are surrounded by Ōte, high stone walls built to protect the house from waves, wind and ocean spray. It was here that Momotarō, the legendary 'Peach Boy', met and conquered the horrible demon. You can tour the caves where the demon was said to have hidden. See the Western Honshū chapter for the Momotarō story.

The caves are open from 8.30 am to 5 pm and entry is ¥500. Boats run to Megi-jima Island from the ferry area next to Takamatsu station, take 20 minutes and cost ¥320. There are several minshuku and a couple of campsites on the island to accommodate those who come to fish or to swim in summer.

Places to Stay
Youth Hostel The *Takamatsu Yashima-sansō Youth Hostel* (☎ 0878-41-2318) is a five minutes walk north-east of Kotoden Yashima station. The hostel charges ¥2680 per night (non-members ¥3710).

Hotels There are a number of budget business hotels a stone's throw from JR Takamatsu station. The *Pearl Hotel* (☎ 0878-22-3382), is small, clean and quite acceptable with rooms from ¥5000 for singles and ¥9600 for doubles or twins. Nearby is the *Station Hotel* (☎ 0878-21-6989) with singles from ¥6000 and doubles or twins from ¥13,000.

Two of the cheapest places around are the *Business Hotel Japan* (☎ 0878-51-8689), south of the station in the shopping and entertainment district, and the *Business Hotel Marukyu* (☎ 0878-51-7305), which is south-west of Takamatsu station. Both are small and at the grotty end of the business hotel spectrum, but offer singles/twins for ¥4000/7000.

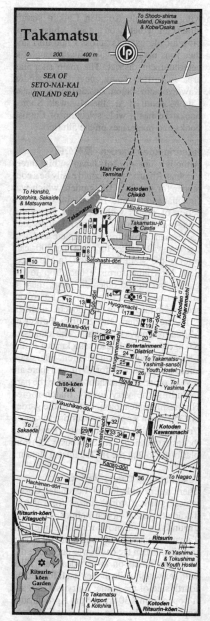

SHIKOKU

PLACES TO STAY

3 Station Hotel
ステーションホテル

4 Pearl Hotel
高松パールホテル

6 Takamatsu Grand
Hotel
高松グランドホテル

8 Takamatsu Terminal
Hotel
高松ターミナル
ホテル

9 Hotel New Frontier
ホテルニュー
フロンティア

10 Century Hotel
高松センチュリー
ホテル

11 Business Hotel
Marukyu
ビジネスホテル丸久

13 Takamatsu
Tōkyū Inn
高松東急イン

17 Hotel Kawaroku
ほてる川六

25 Business Hotel
Japan
ビジネスホテル
ジャパン

26 Royal Park Hotel
ロイヤルパーク
ホテル

27 Takamatsu
Washington Hotel
高松ワシントン
ホテル

34 Tokiwa Honkan
常盤本館

37 Keiō Plaza Hotel
京王プラザホテル

PLACES TO EAT

2 Mr Donut

12 Tenkatsu
天勝本店

15 McDonald's

18 Kawa Fuku
川福本店

19 Grill Yama
グリル山

20 Kanaizumi
かな泉

23 Italian Tomato

24 Goemon
五右衛門

29 Milano no
Okazuya-san
ミラノのおかず
屋さん

30 Milk Doll

31 La Provence

32 McDonald's

33 Spice Kingdom

35 Mr Donut

OTHER

1 Tourist Information
Office
観光案内所

5 ANA
全日空

7 JAL
日航

14 Post Office
高松郵便局

16 Mitsukoshi
Department Store
三越百貨店

21 Takamatsu City
Museum of Art
高松市美術館

22 Miyawaki Shoten
Bookshop

28 I-Pal Kagawa
アイパル香川

36 NTT

A few minutes walk from the station, the *Takamatsu Terminal Hotel* (☎ 0878-22-3731) is a small, clean place with singles from ¥6000 and twins from ¥10,000. Close by, the *Hotel New Frontier* (☎ 0878-51-1088) offers similar standards for ¥6000/10,000 for singles/twins.

The *Takamatsu Grand Hotel* (☎ 0878-51-5757), on top of the Kotoden Chikkō station, overlooks the Takamatsu Castle grounds and is conveniently situated only a few steps from JR Takamatsu station. It's a little more up-market and singles/twins cost from ¥7000/12,500.

The *Takamatsu Tōkyū Inn* (☎ 0878-21-0109) is a popular chain hotel on Chūō-dōri, just beyond the arcade, and has singles/doubles from ¥7700/14,000. Much further down Chūō-dōri, almost at the Ritsurin-kōen Garden, is the *Keiō Plaza Hotel* (☎ 0878-34-5511) with singles/twins from ¥7300/13,500.

In the entertainment district, the *Royal Park Hotel* (☎ 0878-23-2222) has singles/doubles from ¥10,000/18,000. A few steps away is the *Takamatsu Washington Hotel* (☎ 0878-22-7111). It has singles/twins from ¥7500/15,500.

Ryokan Takamatsu has a couple of expensive, but centrally located ryokan. *Hotel Kawaroku* (☎ 0878-21-5666) is south of the shopping arcade, just off Chūō-dōri. Rooms cost from ¥7000/12,000 for singles/doubles without meals and from ¥14,000 per person with meals.

Near the Kotoden Kawaramachi station is the traditional *Tokiwa Honkan* (☎ 0878-61-5577), which costs from ¥15,000 to ¥20,000 per person including two meals.

Places to Eat

Every larger railway station in Shikoku seems to have an *Andersen's* bakery, also known as *Willie Winkie*. The one at JR Takamatsu station is good for an economical breakfast, though there's nowhere to sit down. Across the road is a *Mister Donut* and there are a number of other restaurants nearby. The Kotoden Kawaramachi station is also a centre for a variety of cheap eats.

A trip to Takamatsu would not be complete without slurping back some of the the region's prized (and amazingly inexpensive) sanuki udon noodles. Though there are seemingly endless places to sample the fare, one of the best in town is *Sakaeda*, where for under ¥ 300 you can stuff yourself with tasty noodles, served hot or cold. The restaurant has counter service only and though there is no English menu, the choices are simple (noodles, either plain or with a slice of sweet fried tofu, tempura or wakame seaweed). Once you get your bowl of noodles – *shō* (small), *chū* (medium) or *dai* (large) – you can add broth, and condiments such as sliced spring onions, ginger and tempura chips to your liking. It's open Monday to Saturday until 5 pm, but is basically a lunch spot. Once the day's batch of fresh noodles are sold out they close up shop, so get there early. Other good places to sample sanuki udon are *Goemon* (not far from the Washington Hotel) and *Sanuki Udon* (just outside JR Takamatsu station).

The best selection of restaurants is found along the shopping arcade in the entertainment district. *Kawa-Fuku* is a pleasant restaurant offering good sanuki udon, tempura and other dishes from around ¥1000

– try the gyūdon (beef with rice), which comes with a bowl of udon for ¥880. Just beyond Kawa-Fuku is the *Grill Yama*, which offers a variety of grilled meat dishes at up-market prices (from ¥1500). *Kanaizumi*, a block east on Ferry-dōri, specialises in sanuki udon – you may see them being made in the window.

In and around the arcade near Kotoden Kawaramachi station there are a variety of good restaurants to choose from. The funky and popular *Milk Doll* has reasonable lunch and dinner specials (as well as an astounding collection of *manga* (Japanese comic books) and just west of here there is the fine French restaurant *La Provence* with a superb set lunch for ¥1800 and dinners from ¥4800. The Indian food at *Spice Kingdom* is also good and nearby is the stylish Italian restaurant *Milano no Okazuya-san*, across from the Cinema Hall Soleil. More affordable Italian fare is available at a branch of the popular *Italian Tomato* restaurant chain on Bijutsukan-dōri.

A few doors beyond the end of the Hyogomachi arcade west of Chūō-dōri, you'll find *Tenkatsu*, a popular restaurant with a central bar surrounding a large fish tank in which you can see your order swimming about before it's scooped out and prepared.

If you're out at Yashima at lunch time, head for *Zaigo Udon*, right beside the Shikoku-mura Village car park. There are also places to eat near the cable car station.

Getting There & Away

Air Japan Air Systems (JAS) has flights to and from Fukuoka and Tokyo; All Nippon Airways (ANA) has flights to and from Osaka and Tokyo.

Train The Seto-ōhashi Bridge has brought Takamatsu much closer to the main island of Honshū. From Tokyo, you can take the shinkansen to Okayama, change trains there and be in Takamatsu in five hours. The Okayama-Takamatsu section takes about an hour of those five.

From Takamatsu, the JR Kōtoku line runs south-east to Tokushima and the JR Yosan line runs west to Matsuyama. The Yosan line branches off at Tadotsu and becomes the Dosan line, turning south-west to Kotohira and Kōchi. The private Kotoden line also runs direct to Kotohira.

Bus Direct buses operate between Tokyo-Nagoya-Osaka and Takamatsu. From Tokyo the JR 'Dream Takamatsu Gō' or Keiō-tēto 'Hello Bridge' bus services cost ¥10,300 one way, taking about 10½ hours. From Nagoya JR buses take about seven hours (¥7000), and from Osaka, the Hankyū 'Sanuki Express' takes around four hours (¥4500).

Boat Takamatsu is an important ferry terminus with services to several ports in the Inland Sea, and Honshū, including Kōbe (4½ hours) and Osaka (5½ hours) costing ¥2400. There is also a speedboat service to Osaka (Tempōzan) taking less than three hours for ¥6000. Uno, to the south of Okayama, used to be the main connection point to Takamatsu prior to the construction of the bridge. It's still a quick way to make the Honshū-Shikoku trip (about one hour, ¥380) since Uno-Okayama trains connect with the ferry departures. Takamatsu is also the easiest jumping-off point for visiting attractive Shōdo-shima Island.

Getting Around

Takamatsu airport is 16 km from the city and the bus, which departs from outside JR Takamatsu station, takes about half an hour.

Takamatsu has a local bus service, but for most visitors the major attractions (principally the Ritsurin-kōen Garden and also Yashima), can be easily reached on the JR Kōtoku line or the more frequent Kotoden line service. The main Kotoden junction is Kawaramachi, although the line ends at the Chikkō station, just across from JR Takamatsu station.

WEST OF TAKAMATSU

Sakaide 坂出

Sakaide, a port city on the JR Yosan line, has little of interest for the traveller except perhaps for the views over the Inland Sea from the southern end of the Seto-ōhashi Bridge.

Marugame 丸亀

On the JR Yosan line, just 25 minutes west of Takamatsu and close to the southern end of the Seto-ōhashi Bridge, **Marugame-jō Castle** (dating from 1597) has one of only 12 original wooden donjon left out of more than 5000 in Japan, and stepped stone walls towering over 50m high. The castle is about a km south of the JR station.

Other attractions include the picturesque **Nakazu Banshō-en Garden** (9.30 am to 5 pm daily). The ¥1000 ticket includes entry to the **Marugame Art Gallery** which features a collection of impressionist art. At the **Uchiwa Museum** (9.30 am to 5 pm, entry free, closed Monday), there are displays and crafting demonstrations of traditional Japanese paper fans (*uchiwa*). It is said that Marugame is responsible for about 90% of the country's uchiwa fan output, making it a logical place to pick one up.

The Takamatsu TIC can provide an English pamphlet and more information on Marugame. The Shiwaku Islands (see the Inland Sea section of the Western Honshū chapter) are also reached from here.

Zentsū-ji Temple 善通寺

The Zentsū-ji, No 75 on Kōbō Daishi's (Kūkai) 88 Temple Circuit, is said to have been founded in 813 AD and boasts a magnificent five-storey pagoda and lovely giant camphor trees. The Mieidō Hall here was Kōbō Daishi's birthplace so it has particular importance and for ¥500 visitors can venture into the basement and traverse a 100m long passageway in pitch darkness. By moving along with your left hand pressed on the left hand wall (which is painted with mandalas, angels and lotus flowers) you are said to be safely following Buddha's way. The same ticket allows you entrance to a small museum housing temple treasures such as scrolls and a remarkable sceptre both made and brought back from China by Kūkai himself. The temple is one station north of Kotohira on the JR Dosan line.

Kanonji 観音寺

Kanonji (population 45,000) is noted for the

Zenigata, the 350m diameter outline of a square-holed coin dating from the 1600s. The coin's outline and four kanji characters are formed by trenches which, it is said, were dug by the local population as a warning to their feudal lord not to waste the taxes they were forced to pay him. The huge coin is beside the sea, at the foot of Kotohiki Hill in Kotohiki Park, 1½ km north-west of Kanonji station. Also in the park is **Kanonji-jinne-in Temple** and the **Sekai-no-Koin-kan**, or World Coin Museum. The latter has coins of varying age from over 100 countries; it's open from 9 am to 5 pm, closed Monday, and entry is ¥300.

Kanonji can be reached by train from JR Takamatsu station in around 50 minutes. If you're travelling between Takamatsu and Matsuyama you could fit in a visit to both Kanonji and Kotohira provided you set off early enough. Buses run between Kotohira and Kanonji seven times daily between 7 am and 6 pm and cost ¥900.

KOTOHIRA 琴平

The Kompira-san Shrine at Kotohira is one of Shikoku's major attractions and for anyone in this part of Japan it shouldn't be missed, despite the huge number of pilgrims and tourists who flock here daily.

Orientation & Information

Kotohira is small enough to make orientation quite straightforward. The busy shopping arcade continues on until it reaches the shrine entranceway, lined with the inevitable souvenir shops. Those seeking to truly immerse themselves in the Japanese experience might, (as every Japanese visitor seems to do) buy a walking stick at one of the shops for the trek up to the shrine.

There is an information centre in the NTT building (look for the NTT sign) along the main road between JR Kotohira station and Kotoden Kotohira station. Though no English is spoken, the friendly staff can provide a well-illustrated English pamphlet on the shrine and information on possible accommodation.

Kompira-san Shrine 金刀比羅宮

Kompira-san or, more correctly, Kotohira-gū, was originally a temple dedicated to the guardian of mariners but became a shrine after the Meiji Restoration. Its hilltop position gives superb views over the surrounding country and there are some interesting reminders of its maritime connections.

An enormous fuss is made about how strenuous the climb is to the top but, if you've got this far in Japan, you've probably seen a few long ascents to shrines already; this one isn't the most horrific to be found. If you really blanch at the thought of climbing all those steps (nearly 800 of them) you can dish out ¥4000 and be carried up in a palanquin – the carriers wait at the bottom. Worse than the steps are the countless tour guides who, bawling out over their megaphones, can totally spoil the tranquil atmosphere.

As you trudge up to the shrine, you might like to reflect how this is another of Japan's misplaced shrines. On Omishima Island in the Inland Sea, the Oyamazumi-jinja Shrine is dedicated to the mountain god. Here, a hill-top shrine is venerated by seafarers!

The first notable landmark on the long climb is the Ō-mon Gate. Just to the right, beyond the gate, the **Hōmotsu-kan treasure house** is open from 8.30 am to 5 pm; entry is ¥200. Nearby you will find five traditional candy vendors at tables shaded by large umbrellas. A symbol of ancient times, these Gonin Byakushō (Five Farmers) are the descendants of the original (and only five) farmers who were permitted to trade within the grounds of the shrine. A little further uphill is the reception hall known as the Shoin with the same ¥200 entry fee and similar opening hours to the treasure house. Built in 1659, it has some interesting screen paintings and a small garden.

Continuing the ascent, you eventually reach the large Asahino Yashiro (Shrine of the Rising Sun). The hall, built in 1837 and dedicated to the sun goddess Amaterasu, is noted for its ornate woodcarving. From here, the short final ascent brings you to the Gohonsha (Main Hall) and the Ema-dō Pavilion, the latter crowded with maritime offerings. Exhibits range from pictures of ships, both old and new, to models and even

SHIKOKU

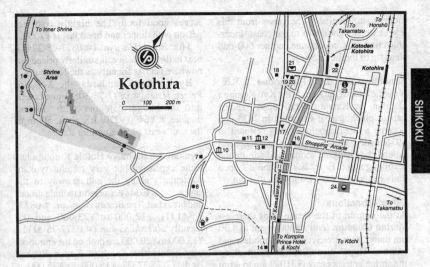

Kotohira

0   100   200 m

To Inner Shrine

Shrine
Area

To Takamatsu

To Honshū

Kotoden
Kotohira

Kotohira

Shopping Arcade

Kamakura-gawa River

To Takamatsu

To Kōchi

To Kompira
Prince Hotel
& Kōchi

PLACES TO STAY

7   Kotohira Grand Hotel
琴平グランドホテル
9   Kotohira Seinen-no-
le Youth Hostel
琴平青年の家
ユースホステル
11   Shikishima-kan
敷島館
13   Bizenya Ryokan
備前屋
14   Kotohira Kadan
Ryokan
琴平花壇旅館
16   Kotobuki Ryokan
ことぶき旅館
18   Kotohira Royal Hotel
琴平ロイヤルホテル
20   Hotel Maruya
ホテルまるや

PLACES TO EAT

17   Tako Sushi
たこ寿司
19   Shōhachi Noodle
Restaurant
将八うどん

OTHER

1   Gohonsha Main Hall
金毘羅宮本殿
2   Ema-dō Pavilion
絵馬堂
3   Asahino Yashiro
(Shrine of the Rising
Sun)
旭社
4   Shoin (Reception
Hall)
書院
5   Hōmotsu-kan
Treasure House
宝物館

6   Ō-mon Gate
大門
8   Kanamaru-za Kabuki
Playhouse
金丸座
10   Marine Museum
海の科学館
12   Kinryō-no-Sato Sake
Museum
金陵の里
15   Saya-bashi Covered
Bridge
鞘橋
21   Post Office
琴平郵便局
22   Takadōrō Lantern
Tower
高灯籠
23   Tourist Information
Office; NTT
観光案内所
24   Bus Station
バス停留所

modern ship engines. The views from this level extend right down to the coast. Incurable climbers can continue another 600-odd steps up to the Inner Shrine.

Kanamaru-za Kabuki Playhouse 金丸座

Near the base of the steps is the Kyū Kompira Ōshibai, or Kanamaru-za, Japan's oldest kabuki playhouse. It was built in 1835 and became a cinema before being restored in 1976. Inside, you can wander backstage and around the changing rooms, and admire the revolving stage. Entry is ¥300 and it's open daily except Tuesday from 9 am to 4 pm.

Other Attractions

At the bottom of the shrine steps there's a **Marine Museum** (entry ¥400, 9 am to 4.30 pm daily) with a variety of ship models and exhibits. There's also a **Sake Museum** along the shrine entranceway (¥310, 9 am to 4 pm daily). At the southern end of the town, past the bus station and just before the Kotohira Kadan Ryokan, is the wooden **Saya-bashi covered bridge**. Note the curious **Takadōrō lantern tower** beside Kotoden Kotohira station. The 27.6m tower was lit in times of trouble in the past. About a 10 to 15 minute walk south of the shrine entrance is the **Shikoku Festival Village**, which exhibits artefacts and photographs relating to the festivals of Shikoku. Entry to the village area is free but there's not a lot to see; entrance to the museum itself is a somewhat steep ¥800. It's open daily from 9 am to 4.30 pm.

Places to Stay

Kotohira has expensive hotels and ryokan, some moderately priced minshuku and a youth hostel.

Youth Hostel The *Kotohira Seinen-no-Ie Youth Hostel* (☎ 0877-73-3836) costs ¥2300 (plus ¥200 for non-members) and is near the kabuki playhouse.

Minshuku & Budget Hotels *Kotobuki Ryokan* (☎ 0877-73-3872) is right by the riverside on the shopping arcade. It's conveniently situated, clean, comfortable and

serves good food. The nightly cost per person with dinner and breakfast is ¥7000.

The *Hotel Maruya* (☎ 0877-75-2241), next to the post office, is similarly priced but nowhere near as friendly as the Kotobuki.

By Kotohira standards, the *Kompira Prince Hotel* (☎ 0877-73-3051) just creeps into the budget category with singles/doubles at ¥6490/9270. It's about 500m to the south-east of JR Kotohira station.

Ryokan & Expensive Hotels Kotohira has some expensive but very tasteful ryokan, particularly along the entranceway to the shrine steps. Costs per person include dinner and breakfast. The *Bizenya Ryokan* (☎ 0877-75-4131), ¥12,000 to ¥23,000 and the friendly *Shikishima-kan* (☎ 0877-75-5111), ¥13,000 to ¥20,000 are both on the entranceway, while the *Kotohira Kadan Ryokan* (☎ 0877-75-3232), ¥15,000 to ¥25,000 is just beyond the Saya-bashi covered bridge.

Hotels include the *Kotohira Grand Hotel* (☎ 0877-75-3232) (from ¥13,000 with two meals) near the bottom of the steps up to the shrine and (in the same price range) the grand and glossy *Kotohira Royal Hotel* (☎ 0877-75-1000) near the post office.

Places to Eat

Many of the restaurants in Kotohira cater for day-trip visitors and close early. There are a couple of reasonably priced places with udon, katsudon and so on just north of Kotoden Kotohira station (on the left side of the road). Just over the bridge at the end of the shopping arcade and to the right is *Taco-sushi* (*taco* is 'octopus' in Japanese, not a Mexican treat), a quaint little sushi place that won't break the budget and which serves other dishes besides octopus. Look for the big red friendly octopus painted above the door.

Up near the entrance to the shrine, many of the souvenir shops do udon lunches. They are a little expensive, but cheaper choices are available for under ¥1000.

Getting There & Away

The JR Dosan line branches off the Yosan line at Tadotsu and continues through

Kotohira and south to Kōchi. There is also a direct Takamatsu to Kotohira private Kotoden line. On either line, the journey takes around an hour from Takamatsu.

Tokushima-ken 徳島県

From the vivacious Awa Odori Festival and the mighty whirlpools of the Naruto Channel, to the pristine scenery of the Iya and Ōboke Gorges and sacred Mt Tsurugi, Tokushima Prefecture has a number of note-worthy attractions.

TOKUSHIMA 徳島

Tokushima (population 268,000), on Shi-koku's east coast, is a pleasant modern city and the traditional starting point for pilgrims heading off on the 88 Temple Circuit. Apart from the annual Awa Odori Festival in August and traditional Awa puppet theatre, there are several places in and around town where visitors can observe (and try their hand at) traditional crafts such as indigo dyeing, papermaking, bamboo work and pottery.

Orientation & Information

Orientation in Tokushima is very easy since it's neatly defined by two hills. One, with the castle ruins, rises up directly behind the station. From in front of the station, the main street, Shinmachibashi-dōri, heads south-west across the river to the cablecar station at the base of Mt Bizan. The entertainment district and main shopping arcade is west of the river and south of the main street.

Though there's a small tourist information booth outside JR Tokushima station, the information centre at the Tokushima Prefecture International Exchange Association (TOPIA) (☎ 0866-85-3303) is a better place to get started. There are helpful English-speaking staff and a good variety of pamphlets as well as facilities including a library, satellite TV, computers, and an information/message board. From inside the JR station building, take the elevator up to the 6th floor of Clement Plaza. There's also an

international phone by the entrance, it is open daily from 10 am to 6 pm.

Mt Bizan 眉山

A broad avenue with a central parade of palm trees runs south-west from the station to the foot of Mt Bizan, also known as Mt Otaki. There's a cablecar (¥500 one way, ¥800 return) and a four km toll road to the 280m high summit from where there are fine views over the city and the Inland Sea. You can walk down in 15 minutes.

Bizan Park also has a 25m Peace Pagoda, erected in 1958 as a memorial to local sol-diers who perished in Burma during WWII, and a Wenceslão de Morães Museum (open 9 am to 5 pm, 9.30 to 4 pm from October through March, closed Tuesday, ¥200). Morães, a Portuguese naval officer, lived in Japan from 1893 until his death in 1929 and produced a multi-volume study of Japan.

Tokushima-Chūō-kōen Park
徳島中央公園

Less than half a km north-east of the railway station, the ruins of Tokushima-jō Castle, built in 1586, stand in Tokushima-Chūō-kōen Park. In the park you will also find the attractively landscaped Senshūkaku-tien Garden, which dates from the Momoyama period (entry ¥50) and the Tokushima-jō Castle Museum (9.30 am to 4.30 pm, closed Monday, ¥300).

Awa Puppet Theatre

For hundreds of years, Jōruri puppet theatre (Ningyō Jōruri) thrived in the farming com-munities in and around Tokushima as a popular form of amusement (while the rich were being entertained with the likes of Kabuki). Gradually the region's multitude of puppet theatres dwindled and today one of the last remaining local puppet dramas can be seen at the **Awa no Jūrobei Yashiki** (☎ 0886-65-2202). At the former residence of Jūrobei, whose tragic Edo-era life story forms the material for the plot (Keisei Awa no Naruto), a 30 minute puppet show is performed by local women.

Shows take place Saturday at 3 pm and Sunday and holidays at 10 am and 3 pm (¥350 entry fee). A two minute walk from

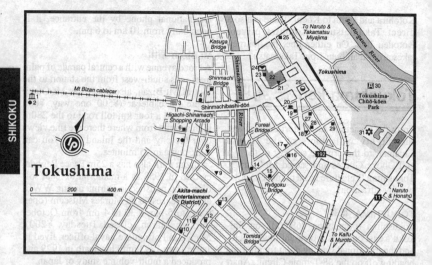

PLACES TO STAY

5 Business Hotel New
Tōyō
ビジネスホテル
ニュー東洋

6 Washington Hotel
ワシントンホテル

15 City Hotel Hamaya
シティホテルはまや

16 Marston Green
Hotel
ホテルマーストン
グリーン

19 AWA Kankō Hotel
阿波観光ホテル

23 Tōkyū Inn
東急イン

25 Grand Palace Hotel
ホテルグランド
パレス徳島

27 Station Hotel
ステーションホテル

28 Astoria Hotel
アストリアホテル

29 Aivis Hotel
エイヴィスホテル

32 Park Hotel
パークホテル

PLACES TO EAT

8 Nishi-Moto
西本

9 Hashimoto
橋本

17 Sanuki Udon
さぬきうどん

18 Takashima
たかしま

21 Mr Donut

OTHER

1 Wenceslão de
Morães Museum
モラエス記念館

2 Peace Pagoda
平和塔

3 Cablecar Station
眉山ケーブルカー駅

4 JAS
日本エアシステム

7 Dancing Clock
阿波おどり時計

10 Paradise

11 Mars

12 Warehouse

13 Dominos; Ray
Charles

14 Boat Rental
貸しボート

20 Copa Cafe/Bar

22 Sogō Department
Store
そごう百貨店

24 Post Office
徳島郵便局

26 Bus Station
バスターミナル

30 Gokoku Shrine
護国神社

31 Senshūkaku-teien
Garden
徳島城表御殿庭園

here is the **Awa Deko Ningyō Kaikan** (Awa Puppet Hall), where puppets are on display and demonstrations of their manufacture and use can be seen (open 8.30 am to 5 pm daily, ¥400). To get there take a bus from JR Tokushima station bound for Miyajima, across the Yoshino River to the Jūrobei Yashiki-mae bus stop (about 25 minutes, ¥270).

Other Attractions

There are some **rowboats** for hire on the Shinmachi-gawa River. Just south of here, near the entertainment district, is the **dancing clock**. This is a curious contraption featuring figurines that perform the local Awa Odori dance; they pop up out of an otherwise ordinary bus stop five times a day.

Among other traditional crafts, Tokushima is famed for both deep-blue **indigo-dyed cloth** (*aizome*) and **handmade rice paper** (washi). There are several places in and around the city where you can catch demonstrations by craftspeople, and even try your hand at the arts (reservations recommended). For dyeing try *Furushō Some Kōjō* (☎ 0886-22-3028) or the *Aizumi Historical Museum Ai no Yakata* (☎ 0886-92-6317). For traditional paper, head out for the exhibits, demonstrations and hands-on opportunities at *Awagami Factory* (☎ 0883-42-6120) near

JR Awa Yamakawa station. Pottery buffs should check into the local **Ōtani-yaki wares**. Detailed information on these and more places can be obtained through TOPIA.

For those who want to get a taste of such arts but don't have the time to make it out to the various factories, there is always **ASTY Tokushima** (☎ 0886-24-5111) a unique facility which has potted highlights of regional culture under one roof for the benefit of short-term visitors. It houses both the 'Experience Tokushima Area,' where you can catch a taste of Awa Odori dances and local puppet drama, and the 'Tokushima Industrial Arts Village' where you can watch and undertake in a variety of traditional arts.

Special Events

One of the premier good time festivals in Japan, the annual Awa Odori Festival from 12 to 15 August brings people from all over to the streets of Tokushima where, in traditional costume the dancing and mayhem last into the wee hours of the morning!

Places to Stay

Hostel *Tokushima Youth Hostel* (☎ 0886-63-1505) is by the beach some distance out of town and costs ¥2500.

Dancing Fools

Every 12 to 15 August the streets of Tokushima, an otherwise placid city, play host to one of the biggest and best good-time events in Japan, the Awa Odori Dance Carnival. The annual event is the largest and most famous 'bon' dance in Japan and attracts tens of thousands of people annually. For four nights straight the revelry continues as men, women and children donning yukata (summer kimono) take to the streets to dance to the samba-like rhythm of the theme song 'yoshikono', accompanied by the sounds of shamisen (three-stringed guitars), taiko drums and fue flutes.

As at Rio's Carnival or the Mardi Gras in New Orleans, the paraders dance in groups (ren), waving their hands, shuffling their feet and chanting a phrase which says it all:

The dancing fools
And the watching fools
Are foolish the same
So why not dance?

There are several groups which delight in having gaijin join their pack and the staff at TOPIA (☎ 0886-56-3303) can provide details. If you're not lucky enough to be there for the real thing in August, you can always see and try the dance throughout the year at the local Civic Centre, by Sogō in the Amico Building (8 to 8.40 pm, ¥600, closed Tuesday). ■

SHIKOKU

Hotels Hotels close to the railway station include the *Station Hotel* (☎ 0886-52-8181) and the *Astoria Hotel* (☎ 0886-53-6151), both with singles/doubles at ¥6000/11,000. The *Aivis Hotel* has similar rates. There are more expensive places like the *AWA Kankō Hotel* (☎ 0886-22-5161) with rooms from ¥7200/14,000; the *Grand Palace Hotel* (☎ 0886-26-1111), with rooms from ¥8000/15,000; and the *Tōkyū Inn* (☎ 0886-26-0109) with rooms from ¥7800/14,500.

Close to the river, in a pleasant and quieter area of town, you'll find the *City Hotel Hamaya* (☎ 0886-22-3411). Although a member of the Japanese Inn Group, it's really just a small business hotel. Singles/doubles with bathroom cost from ¥5500/9100, or from ¥4500/8100 without bathroom. Across the river, the *Business Hotel New Tōyō* (☎ 0886-25-8181), has singles for ¥5100 and twins from ¥9800.

Close to the City Hotel Hamaya is the glossy *Marston Green Hotel* (☎ 0886-54-1777), which really does have a green-tiled exterior. Singles/doubles start from ¥6800/11,500, and in summer there's a beer garden on the 9th floor. Across the river, on the edge of the entertainment district, is the *Washington Hotel* (☎ 0886-53-7111). Singles here range from ¥8000, twins/doubles from ¥17,000.

Places to Eat

If you're just passing through Tokushima, you can pop down to the basement of Clement Plaza inside the station and raid the expansive delicatessen area for a wide range of cheap snacks.

Like any big city, there are a number of fast-food places, but for more interesting dining you're going to have to do some digging. A two minute walk from the station is *Copa*, a neat little cafe. Its menu features, of all things, fresh bagels! It's open from 7.30 am to 5 pm. In the evening it becomes a bar. Across the street, at the intersection with Route 192, is *Takashima*, another cosy little spot where the friendly couple behind the counter whip up good coffee and tasty sandwiches.

Another place worth checking out is an izakaya, *Nishi-Moto*. It's a lively place with

reasonable prices and is open from 11.30 am to 11 pm, closed on Wednesday. *Hashimoto*, a popular soba place with prices from ¥500, has several branches in town, one near the dancing clock and another near the Shinmachibashi bridge. If you missed out on Takamatsu's special udon, there are good noodles at *Sanuki Udon* across from the Marston Green Hotel.

Entertainment

For nightlife head to the Akita-machi area where there is an array of gaijin-friendly watering holes with such cultured names as *Warehouse*, *Mars*, *Drug Store*, *Dominos* and *Ray Charles*. For live blues and soul music, check out *Paradise* in the same area, just a few minutes on foot from the dancing clock.

Getting There & Away

Air JAS connects Tokushima with Osaka and Tokyo.

Train & Bus Tokushima is less than 1½ hours from Takamatsu by limited express train (tokkyū). There are also railway lines west to Ikeda on the JR Dosan line (which runs between Tadotsu and Kōchi) and south along the coastal Mugi line as far as Kaifu from where you will have to take a bus to continue to Kōchi.

Boat Ferries connect Tokushima with Tokyo, Osaka and Kōbe on Honshū, with Kokura on Kyūshū, and with various smaller ports. It only takes two hours to Kōbe by hydrofoil.

Getting Around

It's easy to get around Tokushima on foot; from the railway station to the Mt Bizan cablecar station is only 700m. Bicycles can be rented from the underground bicycle park in front of the station.

AROUND TOKUSHIMA
Naruto Whirlpools 鳴門の渦潮

At the change of tide, the water whisks through the narrow Naruto Channel with such velocity that ferocious whirlpools are created. Boats venture out into the channel, which separates Shikoku from nearby Awaji-shima Island, and travel under the modern Naruto-ōhashi Bridge to inspect the whirlpools close up. Brochures on the boat trips (¥1500, or ¥2000 in a fancy glass-bottom boat) available at the JR Tokushima station information centres give details of tide times (ask for *naruto-no-uzu-shio*). The whirls generally occur four times a day, and going between 11 am and noon you stand a good chance of seeing them.

There's a fine view over the channel from **Naruto-kōen Park** at the Shikoku end of the bridge and you can save the walk up to the top of the lookout by taking a long, ¥200 escalator ride. Getting to the bridge by public transport can be time consuming although it's not a great distance. From Tokushima, take a train to JR Naruto station (40 minutes, ¥310) and a bus from there to the bridge (20 minutes but running infrequently, ¥300). It might be better to take a bus directly from Tokushima bus station. Ferries also run to the park from Awaji-shima Island.

Dochū Sand Pillars 土柱

About 35 km directly west of Tokushima is Dochū, where erosion has formed a large grouping of curious sand pillars standing about 15m high. Reached via JR Anabuki station, it is said that pillars of this size are only found at two other places on Earth (in the US Rocky Mountains and the European Alps).

Mt Tsurugi-san 剣山

'Sword' peak (Mt Tsurugi-san) is actually gently rounded rather than sharp edged and, at 1955m, is the second highest mountain in Shikoku. A chair lift takes you to a point from which it is a leisurely 40 minute walk to the summit. Keeping a long tradition of mountain worship, a festival is held annually on 1 August at the Ōtsurugi-jinji Shrine at the summit. From April through October it is possible to stay at the Tsurugi-jinja Lodge (☎ 0886-67-5244) or the Kokumin Shukusha Tsurugi-sansō Lodge (☎ 0883-67-5150).

South of Tokushima

The JR Mugi line runs south as far as Kaifu

from where you can continue by bus to Cape Muroto-misaki and on to Kōchi. There are great views as you travel south along the **Anan Coast**. At Hiwasa, turtles come ashore to lay their eggs in the **Ohama-kōen Park** in late July and early August and submarine rides can be had on the Blue Marine (¥1400) from Shishikui. As you cross into Kōchi-ken, there is good surfing at Shirahama and Ikumi beaches, scuba diving at Kannoura and Muroto, and whale-watching tours from Sakihama Port.

KOTOHIRA TO KŌCHI

Although Kotohira is in Kagawa-ken and Kōchi is in Kōchi-ken, part of the distance between the two towns is in Tokushima-ken. The railway and road follow the Yoshino River Gorge much of the way, and the scenery is often spectacular.

Ōboke & Koboke 小歩危・大歩危

The scenery on the eight km gorge of the Yoshino River between these two is particularly spectacular. From the starting point near the Restaurant Ōboke-kyō, about a 20 minute walk from Ōboke station on the JR Dosan line, there are half-hour-long boat rides down the gentle rapids toward Koboke and back (¥1000).

Iya-kei Gorge 祖谷渓

If you've seen the vine suspension bridge at the Shikoku-mura Village near Takamatsu, you might be interested in seeing its archetype, the **Kazura-bashi Bridge** which crosses the Iya-kei Gorge. At one time, many river gorges in the mountainous interior of Shikoku were crossed by similar bridges and until recently the Kazura-bashi Bridge was the only one left (the increase in tourists, however, has lately spawned a small comeback of these bridges).

The vines on the bridge have to be totally replaced every three years. There's a charge of ¥500 to cross the bridge which (despite the safety cables underneath) is not for the faint-hearted. It's open daily from sunrise to sunset; there's a miniature replica on the platform at Ōboke station.

For those with time to explore the region in further depth, there is some spectacular scenery away from the throngs of tourists in the area around the bridge. Particularly noteworthy are the deep canyons between the village of Icchyu and JR Iya-guchi station. There are also popular mid-gorge hot-spring baths at Iya-onsen.

From the Ōboke JR station, it's 12 km (¥860) to the bridge, but buses are infrequent and take an hour. Buses from Awa-Ikeda station (further to the north on the Dosan line) may be more frequent. They take around one hour and 15 minutes and cost ¥1200.

There are several minshuku in the area and an excellent camping ground (¥350 per person) not far upriver on the exit side of the Kazura-bashi Bridge.

Iya, considered by the Japanese to be one of the 'three hidden regions', is romanticised in long-term Japan resident Alex Kerr's fascinating book *Lost Japan* (Lonely Planet, 1996). In 1973 Kerr bought an old thatch-roofed farmhouse (kayabuki) here in the small hamlet of Tsuri, and has since been thoughtfully restoring the home and roof back to its original brilliance.

Jōfuku-ji & Buraku-ji Temples
浄福寺・武楽寺

Further south towards Kōchi, and actually in Kōchi-ken, the Jōfuku-ji has a *Youth Hostel* (☎ 0887-74-0301) with nightly costs of ¥3190 (non-members add ¥1000). On the JR Toyonaga station platform, there's a sign in English directing people to the hostel. The next stop is Ōtaguchi, from where it's a 40 minute walk to the Buraku-ji. The main hall there dates from 1151 AD.

Kōchi-ken   高知県

The largest of Shikoku's four prefectures, Kōchi-ken spans the entire Pacific coastline from Cape Muroto-misaki to Cape Ashizuri-misaki and is blessed with an abundance of flora and fauna and a warm southern climate. It is a popular domain for outdoor sports, from diving, surfing and whale watching on the seaside to canoeing, rafting, and camping along the 192 km Shimanto-gawa River – the last undammed, naturally flowing river in Japan.

KŌCHI 高知

Kōchi (population 317,000) was the castle town of what used to be known as the Tosa Province, and the small but original castle still stands. Like Kagoshima in Kyūshū and Hagi in Western Honshū, the town can lay claim to having played an important role in the Meiji Restoration.

Orientation & Information

Harimayabashi-dōri, the main street in Kōchi, has a tram line down the centre, runs north-south, and crosses the main shopping arcade and the other main street near Harimaya-bashi Bridge. The bridge (apart from some purely decorative railings) has long gone but the citizens of Kōchi still recall a famous ditty about a bald monk buying a hair band at the bridge, presumably for a female friend. Apart from the castle, most of Kōchi's other attractions are all some distance from the town centre.

The information office at JR Kōchi station (☎ 0888-82-7777) is open daily from 9 am to 5 pm. Just outside the station and to the left, there are excellent brochures in English, and there is usually a helpful staff member around who speaks good English.

Sakamoto Ryōma 坂本竜馬

Although it was the progressive samurai of Kagoshima and Hagi who played the major part in the dramatic events of the Meiji Restoration, the citizens of Kōchi claim it was their boy, Sakamoto Ryōma, who brought the two sides together. Unhappy with the rigid class structure institutionalised under Tokugawa rule, Sakamoto sought exile in Nagasaki, where he ran a trading company and helped build the powerful alliances that prompted the collapse of the shogunate. His assassination in Kyoto in 1867, when he was just 32 years old, cemented his romantic/tragic image and he appears, looking distinctly sour, on countless postcards and other tourist memorabilia in Kōchi. There's a notable statue of Sakamoto at Katsura-hama Beach.

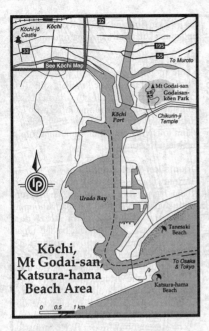

Kōchi,
Mt Godai-san,
Katsura-hama
Beach Area

0   0.5   1 km

Dogs & Roosters

The Kōchi area is noted for its fighting dogs and long-tailed roosters. The mastiff-like dogs are ranked like sumo wrestlers and even wear similar aprons. You can see demonstration fights at Katsura-hama Beach, and buy toy fighting dogs from the souvenir shops. Breeders have persuaded the long-tailed rooster (Onaga-dori) to produce tail feathers up to 10m long! You can see them at the Chōbikei Center in Nankoku City (¥500), out towards Kōchi airport and also at the Ryūga-dō Cave.

Kōchi-jō Castle 高知城

Kōchi's castle may not be one of the great castles of Japan but it is a real survivor, not a postwar concrete reconstruction, and the lovely grounds are great for a stroll. Although a construction on the site dates back to the 14th century, the present castle was built between 1601 and 1611, burnt down in 1727 and rebuilt in 1753. By this time, the peace of the Tokugawa period was well established and castles were scarcely necessary except as a symbol of a feudal lord's power. The Kōchi lord therefore rebuilt the castle with his living quarters (the Kaitokukan) on the ground floor, with doors opening into the garden. Kōchi-jō, therefore, is not a gloomy castle, as those which were strongly fortified against enemy attack tended to be.

At the bottom of the castle hill is the well-preserved Ōte-mon Gate. Inside the castle there is a small museum with exhibits relating to Sakamoto Ryōma, and from the castle there's a fine view over the town. The castle is open from 9 am to 5 pm and entry is ¥350. There's a very informative brochure on the castle available in English.

Godaisan-kōen Park & Chikurin-ji Temple 五台山公園・竹林寺

The hilltop Chikurin-ji and Kōchi's botanical garden are both in Godaisan-kōen Park, several km from the town centre. The temple is No 31 on the Shikoku temple circuit, and there's an attractive five-storey pagoda at the top of the hill. The temple's treasure house has an interesting collection of old statues, some of them looking very Indian or Tantric, and is worth a look. The ¥400 entry fee also covers the temple garden. On the other side of the car park is the Makino Botanical Garden and greenhouse, admission is ¥350.

To get to the park and temple take a bus, marked 'to the temple' (in English) from the Toden Seibu bus station next to the Seibu department store at the Harimaya-bashi junction. The journey takes about 20 minutes and the bus stops outside the temple steps. Buses run about once an hour until 5 pm and the fare is ¥320.

Katsura-hama Beach 桂浜

Only the Japanese could make a big deal out of a beach which is liberally dotted with large and permanent looking signs proclaiming 'No Swimming'. Nevertheless, Katsura-hama Beach is a popular 13 km excursion from Kōchi. Apart from the sand, there's the statue of Sakamoto Ryōma, an aquarium, a

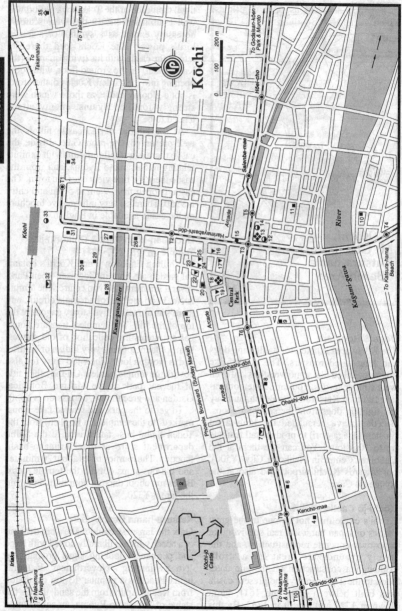

SHIKOKU

Kōchi

shell display and demonstration dog fights, which are held twice daily in the Tosa Tōken Center.

Five minutes walk west of Katsura-hama Beach is the **Sakamoto Ryōma Memorial Museum**, which tells the local hero's life

PLACES TO STAY

3 Orient Hotel Kōchi
   オリエントホテル
   高知

4 Kōchi Green Kaikan
   高知グリーン会館

5 Sansuien Hotel
   三翠園ホテル

6 Hotel New Hankyū
   高知新阪急ホテル

8 Kōchi Sunrise Hotel
   高知サンライズ
   ホテル

9 Hotel Tosa
   ホテル土佐

10 Aki Hotel
   民宿あき

11 Kōchi Business Hotel
   Honkan
   高知ビジネスホテル
   本館

21 Washington Hotel
   高知ワシントン
   ホテル

26 Kōchi Green Hotel
   高知グリーンホテル

27 Hotel Takasago
   ホテル高砂

28 Tosa Gyoen Ryokan
   土佐御苑旅館

29 Business Hotel City
   Kōchi
   ビジネスホテル
   シティ高知

30 Sun Route Hotel
   サンルートホテル

31 Kōchi Hotel
   高知ホテル

34 Dai-ichi Hotel
   第一ホテル

35 Kōchi Ekimae Youth
   Hostel
   高知駅前ユース
   ホステル

PLACES TO EAT

16 Tsukasa
   料亭司

17 Tsukasa
   料亭司

19 Tsukasa
   料亭司

20 Cafe Mousse

22 Murasaki Robatayaki
   むらさき炉端焼き

23 Baffone

24 Okonomiyaki
   Yakisoba Hakobe
   お好み焼き焼きそば
   はこべ

25 Tosahan
   土佐藩

OTHER

1 Anraku-ji Temple
   安楽寺

2 Prefectural Museum -
   Kōchi History
   Museum
   高知郷土文化会

7 Post Office
   郵便局

12 Katsura-hama Bus
   Stop
   かつら浜バス停

13 Seibu Department
   Store
   西武デパート

14 Toden-Seibu Bus
   Station
   とでん西武バス
   ターミナル

15 Harimaya-bashi
   Bridge
   はりまや橋

18 Daimaru Department
   Store
   大丸百貨店

32 Main Post Office
   高知中央郵便局

33 Kōchi Bus Station (to
   Katsura-hama Beach
   & Matsuyama)
   バスターミナル
   （松山行き他）

TRAM STOPS

T1 Kōchi-eki
   こうちえきまえ

T2 Hasuike-machi
   はすいけまち

T3 Harimaya-bashi
   はりまやばし

T4 Umenotsuji
   うめのつじ

T5 Toden-Seibu
   とでんせいぶまえ

T6 Horizume
   ほりづめ

T7 Ōhashi-dōri
   おおはしどおり

T8 Kōchijō-mae
   こうちじょまえ

T9 Kenchō-mae
   けんちょうまえ

T10 Grand-dōri
   グランドどおり

story in miniature dioramas. It's open daily from 9 am to 4.30 pm, and entry is ¥350.

Buses make the 30 minute run from Kōchi bus station to Katsura-hama every hour (¥610); there's also a bus stop on the southeast corner of Chūō-kōn Park (¥560).

Market

If you're in Kōchi on Sunday, visit the popular and colourful street market along Phoenix Blvd, the road which leads to Kōchi-jō Castle. The market has everything from fruit, vegetables and goldfish to large stones for use in gardens.

Places to Stay

Youth Hostel *Kōchi Ekimae Youth Hostel* (☎ 0888-83-5086) is only a few minutes walk east of the railway station and costs ¥2800 (non-members add ¥1000).

Budget Hotels For very basic accommodation, try the *Kōchi Business Hotel Honkan* (☎ 0888-83-0221). It has singles from ¥4000 and twins from ¥7000. At the *Hotel Tosa* (☎ 0888-25-3332), not far from the Horizume tram stop, rooms also start at ¥4000. Just south of the Kencho-mae tram stop, the *Kōchi Green Kaikan* (☎ 0888-25-2701) has singles at ¥5500 and twins at ¥10,000.

Another cheapie is the *Business Hotel City Kōchi* (☎ 0888-72-2121), close to the station, which has singles from ¥5300, twins at ¥9000 and doubles at ¥8500. The *Kōchi Green Hotel* (☎ 0888-22-1800) is another straightforward, cheaper hotel that's not too far from the station. Singles are ¥6100, and twins and doubles range from ¥9800.

Expensive Hotels The *Washington Hotel* (☎ 0888-23-6111), on Phoenix Blvd, is conveniently central and close to the castle. Rooms cost from ¥7700/15,800 for singles/doubles.

The pleasant *Orient Hotel Kōchi* (☎ 0888-22-6565) is south of the castle and on the tram line. Rooms for one cost from ¥6900, for two from ¥11,500. The *Kōchi Sunrise Hotel* (☎ 0888-22-1281) charges from

¥6600/12,600 for singles/doubles. Not far from the station is the *Hotel Takasago* (☎ 0888-22-1288), with similar prices.

The large *Sansuien Hotel* (☎ 0888-22-0131), south of the castle, includes some old buildings from the Kōchi daimyō's grounds. Costs per person range from ¥15,000, including meals.

Places to Eat

Kōchi's best restaurants are clustered around the Daimaru department store near the Harimaya-bashi Bridge end of the shopping arcade.

Here you'll find at least three branches of *Tsukasa*, a popular Japanese Tosa-ryōri restaurant displaying plastic meals from tempura to sashimi and offering fixed-price specials and friendly service. On the 2nd and 3rd floors of a building just off the arcade there's a branch of the *Murasaki Robatayaki*, easily recognisable by its thatched-house motif.

Baffone, a cosy little open air cafe, has homemade pizza, pasta and salads and though the daily menu is posted in Japanese, the owner can speak good English and will let you know what's cooking. *Okonomiyaki Yakisoba Hakobe* offers the very popular 'cook it yourself' omelette dish known as okonomiyaki.

Cruel Cuisine

Being cruel to your food is a Japanese tradition – you know the fish is fresh if it squeals when you eat it – and Takamatsu is certainly a centre for it. A prized dish here is *sugata-zukuri* – sea bream sliced seconds before it's placed in front of you. If you're quick with the chopsticks you can get the first mouthfuls down before it dies. I ate one night at Tenkatsu, where the bar encloses a large tank of fish and other sea life. When a customer ordered octopus, the unfortunate creature was scooped out of the tank and four tentacles were hacked off. Then, still living, but less than complete, the octopus was tossed back into the tank to crawl forlornly off to a corner.

Tony Wheeler

Getting There & Away

Air ANA connects Kōchi with Osaka, Tokyo and Miyazaki in Kyūshū. Air Nippon Koku (ANK) also flies between Kōchi and Osaka while JAS flies to Fukuoka, Nagoya and Osaka.

Train Kōchi is on the JR Dosan line which runs from the north coast of Shikoku through Kotohira. It takes about 2½ hours by limited express from Takamatsu. From Kōchi, rail services continue westward to just beyond Kubokawa where the line splits south-west to Nakamura and north-west to Uwajima. From Uwajima, you can continue north to Matsuyama but this is a long and circuitous route.

Bus Travel between Kōchi and Matsuyama is faster by bus. These depart hourly from outside the bus station near the JR Kōchi station. If you want to travel right around the south coast, either west around Cape Ashizuri-misaki to Uwajima or east around Cape Muroto-misaki to Tokushima, you will have to travel by bus as the railway lines do not extend all the way.

Boat Kōchi is connected by ferry to Osaka (around nine hours, ¥4,530) and Tokyo (about 21 hours, ¥16,000).

Getting Around

The tram service (¥180) running north-south from the station intersects the east-west tram route at the Harimaya-bashi junction. Ask for a *norikaeken* (transfer ticket) if you have to transfer there. You can easily reach the castle on foot, though for the town's other attractions you must take a bus.

AROUND KŌCHI

Apart from Katsura-hama Beach, there are a number of other interesting places easily reached from Kōchi.

Ryūga-dō Cave 竜河洞

This limestone cave (one of the best three in Japan!) has characteristic stalactites and stalagmites plus traces of prehistoric habitation. You can also see the famed long-tailed roost-ers (Onaga-dori) here. A bus bound for Odochi will get you to the cave in about an hour; entry is ¥1000.

Aki 安芸

Further east is Aki, where Iwasaki Yatarō, founder of the giant Mitsubishi conglomerate, was born in 1834. His thatch-roofed house is well preserved; phone ☎ 0887-34-1111 if you want to see it. There are some old samurai streets around the castle remains.

Ino-chō Paper Museum 伊野町立紙の博物館

In Ino, just four stations west of Kōchi on the JR line, the Ino-chō Paper Museum has demonstrations of traditional Tosa paper making. The museum is open from 9 am to 5 pm daily except Monday; entry is ¥300.

Across the road from here there is a large camping ground (¥100 per person) on the banks of the Niyodo-gawa River, and a few km north on Route 194 is the **Culture Resort Ino** (☎ 0888-92-1001) an impressive modern complex, housing paper making facilities, three restored *kura* (traditional grain warehouses), a hotel, a restaurant and top-notch hot-spring baths. The resort is charming and not unreasonably priced (about ¥10,000 per person with two meals), though campers and day-trippers can indulge in the bathing facilities only (all kindly labelled in English) for ¥700. Ask for a pamphlet on the resort (also known as Cour aux Dons) at the JR Kōchi station TIC.

CAPE MUROTO-MISAKI 室戸岬

Cape Muroto-misaki, south-east of Kōchi, has a lighthouse topping its wild cliffscape. The **Higashi-dera Temple** here is No 24 on the Shikoku temple circuit. Just north of Muroto is a chain of black-sand beaches known by local surfers as **Little Hawaii**. There's youth hostel accommodation on the cape at the *Hotumisaki-ji Youth Hostel* (☎ 0887-23-2488), where nightly costs are ¥2800 (non-members add ¥800), and for ¥1500 extra includes dinner and breakfast.

SHIKOKU

SHIKOKU

Getting There & Away

You can reach the cape by bus from Kōchi and can continue right round to Tokushima on the east coast. The Tosa Dentetsu buses for Cape Muroto-misaki run from the Harimaya-bashi intersection in central Kōchi. The journey takes around two hours and 20 minutes and costs ¥2770. For those continuing on to Tokushima, the JR Mugi line runs around the east coast from Tokushima as far as Kaifu.

CAPE ASHIZURI-MISAKI

South-west of Kōchi, Cape Ashizuri-misaki, like Cape Muroto-misaki, is a wild and picturesque promontory ending at a lighthouse. As well as the coastal road, there's the scenic central **Skyline Road**. Cape Ashizuri also has a temple (the Kongōfuku-ji, No 38 on the temple circuit) which, like the one at Cape Muroto, has its own youth hostel (☎ 0880-88-0038). Nightly costs including two meals are ¥4100 (non-members add ¥1000), though the hostel is only open certain days in a month; call in advance. The *Ashizuri Kokuminshukusha* (☎ 0880-88-0301) costs from ¥6600 per person with two meals. Just

in front of the lodge is a small tourist information booth with English maps of the area and there is also a statue beside here of legendary local boy John Manjirō.

The cape's main attractions, including **Kongōfuku-ji Temple** and a wooded 'romance walk', are all within easy walking distance of the Ashizuri-misaki bus centre.

From Tosashimizu, at the northern end of the cape, ferries operate to Kōbe on Honshū. From Kōchi, there is a railway as far as **Nakamura**, the usual point of access for the cape. From Nakamura station there is regular bus service taking about an hour to the tip of the cape for ¥1930. Travel from Nakamura around the cape and on to Uwajima is by bus.

Nakamura is also the best place to organise a trip to explore the very beautiful **Shimanto-gawa River**. The friendly staff at the TIC in front of JR Nakamura station can provide information on river boat trips, camping and outdoor activities.

NORTH-WEST TO UWAJIMA
宇和島方面へ

From Tosashimizu, the road continues around the southern coast of Shikoku to Uwajima

---

Manjirō the Hero

Nearly every corner of Shikoku boasts a local hero, but perhaps most extraordinary of them all is Kōchi-born John Manjirō.

His real name was Nakahama Manjirō. In 1841, while helping out on a fishing boat, a violent storm swept 14-year-old Manjirō and four others onto the desolate shores of Tori-shima Island, some 600 km off Tokyo Bay. They were rescued five months later by a US whaler, which gave them safe passage to Hawaii.

In Hawaii the ship's captain invited Manjirō to return to his home in Massachusetts. There the boy spent the next four years learning English, navigation and the ways of the west. His skills took him back to sea and around the world. In 1851, 10 years after he left, Manjirō returned to Japan, where he was interrogated (Japan's National Seclusion policy forbade overseas travel) but allowed to return to Kōchi.

When Commodore Perry's 'black ships' arrived in 1853, Manjirō was summoned to Edo to advise the Shōgun. He was later the chief translator for the Harris Treaty negotiations of 1858, and subsequently published Japan's first English-language phrase book, *Shortcut to Anglo-American Conversation*. He returned to the US in 1860 as part of a Japanese delegation, and after the Meiji Restoration in 1867 he took up a post at the Kaisei School for Western Learning (which later became part of Tokyo University).

Manjirō is remembered as a man whose destiny took him from the simple life of a teenage fisherman to becoming one of Japan's first true statesmen. At Cape Ashizuri-misaki, a large statue stands in his honour; there is also a museum dedicated to his achievements. ∎

in Ehime-ken. The scenery is particularly attractive through **Tatsukushi**, where there is a **coral museum** (¥300) and a **shell museum** (¥500). **Sightseeing boats** and glass-bottom boats operate from the town (¥850).

Sukumo has a fine harbour and the *Sukumo Youth Hostel* (☎ 0880-64-0233). You can take boats out to remote Okino-shima Island from Sukumo.

Sukumo is less than an hour by bus from Nakamura by the direct road although much longer around the coast via the cape. On to Uwajima takes about two hours. From Sukumo, ferries make the three hour crossing several times daily to Saeki on Kyūshū.

There are several popular **dive sites** in the area, but most notably at Nishi-umi and Kashiwa-jima; there is also good diving on Okino-shima.

Ehime-ken 愛媛県

Occupying the north-western region of Shikoku and famed for its oranges and cultured pearls, highlights in Ehime-ken include Matsuyama Castle and Dōgo Onsen, 1982m high Mt Ishizuchi-san, as well as the pleasant towns of Uwajima and Uchiko.

MATSUYAMA 松山
Shikoku's largest city, Matsuyama, is a busy north coast town (population 443,000) and an important transport hub with frequent ferry links to Hiroshima. Matsuyama's major attractions are its castle, one of the finest survivors from the feudal era, and the Dōgo Onsen hot-springs area with its magnificent old public bath.

Orientation & Information
The JR Matsuyama station is west of the town centre and the castle hill. The town centre is immediately south of the castle and close to Matsuyama City station (Shi-eki) of the private Iyo-tetsudō line. The Ichiban-chō tram stop, Mitsukoshi department store and nearby Okaidō shopping arcade are important

landmarks in the town centre. Dōgo Onsen is east of town while the port at Takahama is north of the town centre and the JR station.

English-language books can be found on the 4th floor of the Kinokuniya bookshop, which is near the Matsuyama City station. Matsuyama is noted for its deep-blue textiles known as Iyo-kasuri. Tobe-yaki is a locally produced pottery.

Information counters can be found at JR Matsuyama station and at the ferry terminal for arrivals from Hiroshima. The main information counter is the JR Matsuyama station branch (☎ 0899-31-3914); it's open from 8.30 am to 7.30 pm. The Dōgo Onsen also has a tourist information office beside the tram terminus, at the entrance to the arcade which leads to the old public bath.

Matsuyama-jō Castle 松山城
Picturesquely sited atop a hill which virtually erupts in the middle of the town, Matsuyama-jō is one of Japan's finest original surviving castles. It only squeaks in with the 'original' label as it was restored just before the end of the Edo period. In the early years of the Meiji Restoration, rebuilding feudal symbols was definitely not a high priority.

The castle was built in 1602-03 with five storeys, but burnt down and was rebuilt in 1642 with three storeys. In 1784, it was struck by lightning and burnt down again, though, in those peaceful and slow-moving Edo years, it took until 1820 for a decision to be made to rebuild it and until 1854 for the reconstruction to be completed! It was completely restored between 1968 and 1986.

You don't even have to climb the steep hill up to the castle; a cablecar and/or chair lift will whisk you up there for ¥400 return. Entry to the castle costs ¥350.

Shiki-dō 子規堂
Matsuyama claims to be the capital of haiku poetry, and just south of Matsuyama City station (Shi-eki) in the grounds of the Shoshu-ji Temple is a replica of the house of haiku poet Shiki Masaoka (1867-1902). The Shiki Memorial Museum in Dōgo Park is also dedicated to the poet.

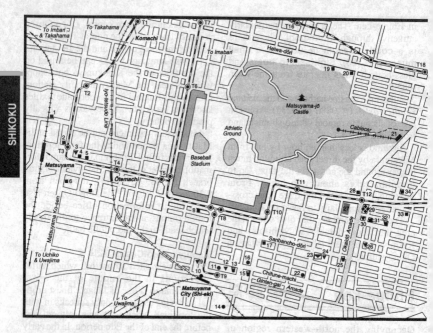

PLACES TO STAY	20	Business Hotel New	9	Mr Donut
1	Hotel Sun Route		Kashima	12	Atom Boy Sushi
	Matsuyama		ビジネスホテル		Restaurant
	ホテルサンルート松山		ニューかしま		アトム寿司
2	Terminal Hotel	27	ANA Hotel	13	Munchen Beer Hall
	Matsuyama		Matsuyama	15	Kirin City Pub
	ターミナルホテル松山		全日空ホテル松山	24	Restaurant Goshiki
4	Hotel New Kajiwara	28	Matsuyama		五志喜
	ホテルニューカジワラ		Tōkyū Inn	25	Piccadilly Circus Bar
5	City Hotel American		松山東急イン	26	Spice House
	シティホテル	33	Hotel Top Inn		スパイス王国
	アメリカン		ホテルトップイン	30	Murasaki
6	Central Hotel	34	Matsuyama		むらさき
	セントラルホテル		International Hotel	31	Pound House Coffee
7	Hotel Nisshin		国際ホテル松山		Bar
	ホテル日進	39	Matsuyama Youth	32	Bar Icarus
8	Tokyo Dai-Ichi Hotel		Hostel		
	東京第一ホテル		松山ユースホステル	OTHER	
17	Chateau-tel Matsuyama	41	Minshuku Miyoshi	10	ANA; JAS; Sogō
18	Hotel Heiwa		民宿みよし		Department Store
	ホテル平和				全日空／
19	Business Hotel Taihei	PLACES TO EAT			日本エアシステム／
	ビジネスホテル泰平	3	Nakanoka		そごうデパート
			中野家	11	New Grand Building

SHIKOKU

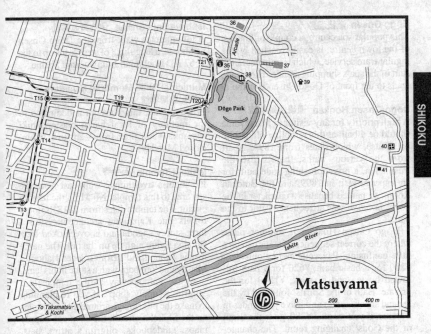

Matsuyama

0   200   400 m

To Takamatsu
& Kochi

Dōgo Park

Ishite River

Dōgo Onsen 道後温泉

This popular spa centre, a couple of km east of the town centre, is easily reached by the regular tram service, which terminates at the start of the spa's shopping arcade. The arcade leads to the front of Dōgo Onsen Honkan.

Dōgo Onsen Honkan 道後温泉本館

A high priority for any visitor to Matsuyama should be a bath at this rambling old public bathhouse, which dates from 1894. Apart from the various baths, there's also the Yūshinden, a private bathing suite built for an imperial visit in 1899, and the Botchan Room, so named because a character in the novel *Botchan* was a frequent visitor to the baths.

Dōgo Onsen Honkan is another place where the correct sequence of steps can be a little confusing. Pay your money outside – ¥280 for a basic bath; ¥620 for a bath followed by tea and a snack; ¥1240 for the private 'Bath of the Spirits' followed by the tea and snack – enter and leave your shoes in a locker. If you've paid ¥280, go to the 'Bath of the Gods' changing room. The change-rooms are signposted in English so you won't wander into the wrong one and shock anybody, though if you're male, you may be slightly surprised to find matronly ladies looking after the male changing room. You'd be even more surprised if you took the wrong exit when heading for the bath in summer as only a cane blind separates the changing room from the street!

If you've paid ¥620 or ¥1240, first go upstairs to the balcony and get your yukata (dressing gown), then return to the appropriate changing room. You can leave valuables upstairs in the charge of the attendants who dispense the yukata. After your bath, those destined for upstairs can don their yukata and retire to the veranda to sip tea and look down on onsen visitors clip-clopping by in yukata and geta.

Though the baths can get quite crowded, especially over weekends and holidays, around dinner time is perhaps the least crowded time to go as most tourists will be dining in their respective inns.

Isaniwa-jinja Shrine 伊佐爾波神社

A few minutes walk from the Dōgo Onsen bathhouse, a long flight of steps leads up to the 1667 AD Hachiman Isaniwa-jinja Shrine.

Municipal Shiki Memorial Museum 子規記念博物館

In Dōgo Park, this museum is dedicated to the memory of local haiku master Shiki Masaoka (¥300, open from 9 am, to 4.30 pm, closed Monday).

Ishite-ji Temple 石手寺

It's about a five-minute walk east from the spa area to this temple, No 51 on the temple circuit. The temple dates from 1318, is noted for its fine Kamakura architecture, has a three-storey pagoda and is overlooked by a Buddha figure high up on the hill. The name means 'stone hand', from a legend about a Matsuyama lord born with a stone in his hand.

At the entranceway to the temple is a 'pilgrim's supply shop'. If you're planning to make the pilgrimage around all 88 temples on the Shikoku circuit, the shop can supply maps, guidebooks, pilgrim's attire, hats, bells and staffs; in fact everything for the complete pilgrim. Matsuyama has seven other circuit temples.

Places to Stay

Matsuyama has three accommodation areas – around the JR station (business hotels); the centre (business hotels and more expensive hotels); and Dōgo Onsen (ryokan and Japanese-style hotels).

Youth Hostel *Matsuyama Youth Hostel* (☎ 0899-33-6366), near the Isaniwa-jinja Shrine in Dōgo Onsen, costs ¥2600 a night (non-members add ¥500). Breakfast and dinner here respectively cost ¥500 and ¥1000.

Hotels Some of the hotels in the following areas are:

Matsuyama Station Area The *Central Hotel* (☎ 0899-41-4358) is a cheaper business hotel with singles/twins from ¥4800/ 8500.

Other hotels within a stone's throw of the

station include the *Hotel New Kajiwara* (☎ 0899-41-0402) with singles/twins from ¥5100/8500 and the *City Hotel American* (☎ 0899-33-6660), which is next door and has singles from ¥4500.

The *Hotel Sun Route Matsuyama* (☎ 0899-33-2811), has singles from ¥5500 and doubles or twins from ¥10,000. Next door to the station, the *Terminal Hotel Matsuyama* (☎ 0899-47-5388) has singles at ¥5500 and twins at ¥10,000. The *Hotel Nisshin* (☎ 0899-46-3111) is a slightly longer walk from the station and has singles/doubles from ¥5500/11,000.

Central Matsuyama The *Tokyo Dai Ichi Hotel* (☎ 0899-47-4411) is on the station side of the town centre and has singles from ¥6600, doubles or twins from ¥12,000. Rooms at the *Chateau-teru Matsuyama* (☎ 0899-46-2111) range from ¥6000 for singles and ¥11,000 for twins.

The *ANA Hotel Matsuyama* (☎ 0899-33-5511) near the Ichiban-chō tram stop has singles from ¥6000, and twins from ¥11,000. Just across the road is the *Matsuyama Tokyū Inn* (☎ 0899-41-0109), where singles range from ¥7000 to ¥12,000, twins and doubles from ¥15,000 to ¥20,000.

Immediately north of the castle hill is a quieter area, conveniently connected to the town centre by a tram line. One of the hotels in this area is the curiously old-fashioned *Business Hotel Taihei* (☎ 0899-43-3560), with rooms from ¥5500/10,000; others are the *Hotel Heiwa* (☎ 0899-21-3515) and the *Business Hotel New Kashima* (☎ 0899-47-2100) with singles/twins from ¥5800/9100. Take a tram to Tetsubō-chō tram stop and walk south to the main road to find them.

Dōgo Onsen Area For Japanese tourists, Dōgo Onsen, east of the town centre, is the big attraction and there are numerous Japanese-style hotels and ryokan in the area. Most of them are quite pricey, but *Minshuku Miyoshi* (☎ 0899-77-2581), behind the petrol station near Ishite-ji Temple, is an exception at around ¥7000 per person with two meals. The *Funaya Ryokan* (☎ 0899-47-0278) is one of the best of the onsen ryokan but count on around ¥20,000 upwards per person, including meals.

Places to Eat

The long Ginten-gai and Okai-dō shopping arcade in central Matsuyama has a variety of restaurants including fast food. There's good Japanese-style fast food just across from Matsuyama station at *Nakanoka*, a 24 hour gyūdon specialist. The arcade leading from the Dōgo Onsen tram stop to the Dōgo Onsen Honkan bath-house also has a number of restaurants with plastic meal replicas.

Next to the post office in the town centre, *Restaurant Goshiki* offers somen noodles and other dishes. Although there are plastic models in the window and an illustrated menu showing the multi-coloured noodles, this is another place where the artistically scrawled sign looks nothing like the printed kanji. Somen and tempura cost ¥850 and you can buy noodles in packets (one colour or mixed) to take home. The area around the Okai-dō arcade is one of the best places to seek out a more interesting meal. One place worth checking out is the basement *Spice House*, a cosy Indian place with Indian chefs and reasonable prices – main courses from ¥1100. Also close by, look out for *Pound House*, a coffee bar with a delicious selection of cakes at ¥350.

For a cold beer and not bad pub food there are a couple of places near the Matsuyama City station. *Kirin City Pub* is near the Kinokuniya bookshop. Directly opposite the station is *Munchen*, a pseudo-German beer hall. Also in this area is the inexpensive revolving sushi shop *Atom Boy*.

For straight drinking, *Piccadilly Circus* calls itself a 'British antique bar', and is decked out with all kinds of British paraphernalia. Cheaper and less pretentious is *Bar Icarus*, just down the road from the Pound House Coffee Bar. During summer, Matsuyama has a large number of rooftop beer gardens. Try the Sogō department store, the Matsuyama ANA Hotel or the Chateau Teru Matsuyama's *Terrace Garden*.

Getting There & Away

Air ANA connects Matsuyama with Osaka, Nagoya and Tokyo (both Narita international airport and Haneda airport). JAS has connections to Fukuoka, Miyazaki and Kagoshima, all in Kyūshū. JAL also flies to Tokyo.

Train & Bus The north coast JR Yosan line connects Matsuyama with Takamatsu and there are also services across the Seto-ōhashi Bridge to Honshū. Matsuyama to Okayama takes three hours and 15 minutes. Another line runs south-west from Matsuyama to Uwajima and then east to Kōchi, though this is a rather circuitous route – it's faster to take a bus directly to Kōchi. There are also direct buses which run from Osaka and Tokyo.

Boat There are frequent ferry and hydrofoil connections with Hiroshima. Take the Iyo-tetsudō private railway line from Matsuyama City (Shi-eki) or Ōtemachi station right to the end of the line at Takahama (¥350 from Ōtemachi). From Takahama, a connecting bus whisks you the remaining distance to Matsuyama Kankō-kō Port. The hydrofoils zip across to Hiroshima in just over one hour for ¥5700 but there's not much to see en route – the view is much better from the regular ferries. Some services go via Kure, south-west of Hiroshima. The ferry takes from 2¾ to three hours (depending on the port in Matsuyama) and costs ¥4490 1st class and ¥2130 2nd class to Hiroshima from Matsuyama Kankō-kō.

Other ferries operate to and from Matsuyama and Beppu, Kokura and Oita on Kyūshū as well as Iwakuni, Kure, Mihara, Onomichi and Yanai on Honshū, but check which of the Matsuyama ports services operate from. From Matsuyama Kankō-kō, a hydrofoil zips across to Ocho (¥2660), Kinoe (¥3070), Omishima (¥3310), Setoda (¥4530), and Onomichi (¥4950).

Getting Around

Matsuyama has the private Iyo-tetsudō railway line and a tram service. The railway line is mainly useful for getting to and from the port for Hiroshima ferries.

The tram services cost a flat ¥170 any-

where in town. There's a loop line and major termini at Dōgo Onsen and outside the Matsuyama City station. The Ichiban-chō stop outside the Mitsukoshi department store and ANA Hotel is a good central stopping point. Tram numbers and routes are:

Tram No	Route
1 & 2	The Loop
3	Matsuyama City Station (Shi-eki)-Dōgo Onsen
5	JR Matsuyama Station-Dōgo Onsen
6	Kiya-chō-Dōgo Onsen

AROUND MATSUYAMA
Mt Ishizuchi-san 石鎚山

Mt Ishizuchi-san (1982m), the highest mountain in Shikoku (indeed in all western Japan), is easily reached from Matsuyama. It's also a holy mountain and many pilgrim climbers make the hike, particularly during the July-August climbing season. In winter it's snow-capped.

From Matsuyama, you can take a bus to Tsuchigoya, south-east of the mountain. Or you can take a bus from the JR Iyo Saijō station on the Yosan line to the Nishi-no-kawa cable-car station on the northern side. This route passes through the scenic Omogo-kei Gorge, an attraction in its own right. Out of season, bus services to the mountain are infrequent. You can climb up one way and down the other or even make a complete circuit from Nishi-no-kawa to the summit, down to Tsuchigoya and then back to Nishi-no-kawa. Allow all day and an early start for the circuit.

The cablecar takes five minutes and costs ¥900 one way or ¥1700 return. The ride can be followed by an chair lift (¥200 one way, ¥350 return), which slightly shortens the walk to Jōju, where the Ishizuchi-jinja Shrine offers good views of the mountain. From Jōju, it's 3½ km to the top, first gently downhill through forest, then uphill through forest, across a more open area and finally a steep and rocky ascent. Although there's a path, and often steps, all the way to the top, the fun way to make the final ascent is up a series of *kusari*, heavy chains draped down the very steep rock faces. Clambering up these chains is the approved pilgrimage method. The actual summit, reached by climbing along a sharp ridge, is a little beyond the mountain hut on the top.

Imabari 今治

This industrial city is of no particular interest apart from its position beside the most island-crowded area of the Inland Sea. At this point, whirlpools rather like those at Naruto (see the Around Tokushima section earlier) form in the narrow channel separating Shikoku from Ō-shima Island.

There are numerous ferry services connecting Imabari with ports on Honshū including Hiroshima, Kōbe, Mihara, Niigata, Onomichi, Takehara and various ports on islands of the Inland Sea.

UCHIKO 内子

Halfway between Matsuyama and Uwajima, and on the JR Yosan line, the charming and photogenic little town of Uchiko has a street lined with old buildings dating from the late Edo period and the early years following the Meiji Restoration. At that time, Uchiko was an important centre for the production of the vegetable wax known as *rō*, and some of the houses along Yōkaichi, the town's old street, belonged to merchants who made their fortunes from producing the wax.

Orientation & Information

Many places on Yōkaichi are closed on Monday. There's a map with *some* English outside the JR station but very little else in Uchiko is labelled in English. Yōkaichi is a 20 minute walk to the north of Uchiko station. There is a tourist information counter (☎ 0893-44-2111) on the 3rd floor of City Hall (on the main thoroughfare through the town) with English-speaking staff who can provide an English pamphlet on local attractions.

Yōkaichi 八日市

Uchiko's picturesque old street, which extends for about a km, has a number of interesting old buildings along with museums, souvenir and craft shops and teahouses. At the start of the street is an old sake brewery, across from which is the **Moribun Amazake Chaya Teahouse** (*amazake* is a sweet sake). Here you

can sample the local brew and see their small 'museum' of sake and soy sauce production on the 2nd floor. A bit further along the street, the house of **Ōmori Rōsoku** is still engaged in traditional candle production. Here you can buy and see these rō wax candles being made by Mr. Ōmori, a fifth-generation (and Uchiko's sole remaining) candlemaker. Continuing up the hill, there is the **Machi-ya Shiryōkan Museum** (open daily 9 am to 4.30 pm, free entry) a rustic 1790s merchant house which was thoughtfully restored in 1987. Be sure to remove your shoes before heading up to the 2nd floor.

As the road makes a slight bend, there come into view several well-preserved Edo-era buildings such as the **Ōmura Residence** and the **Hon-Hagi-tei House**, a fine example of a wealthy merchant's private home (only the finely groomed garden is open for viewing). Further down is the exquisite **Kami-Hagi-tei** (entry ¥400, open daily from 9 am to 4.30 pm) a wax merchant's house within a large complex of wax making-related buildings which can be self-toured. Towards the end of the street there is a traditional umbrella maker's shop near the **Sokō-kan Museum** (¥150, open daily from 9 am to 4.30 pm).

A few minutes walk from Yōkaichi, across from the Hachiman-jinja Shrine, is the interesting **Akinai-to-Kurashi Hakubutsu-kan Museum**, exhibiting historical materials, and wax figures portraying a typical merchant scene of the Taishō-era (1912-26). Entry is ¥200, open daily from 9 am to 4.30 pm.

Uchiko-za Theatre 内子座

The Uchiko-za is an old kabuki theatre, originally built in 1915 and restored in the mid-80s, where there are still occasional performances held. Entry is ¥300, open daily from 9 am to 4.30 pm.

Places to Stay

There are a couple of nice and reasonable ryokan not far from the main sights in town. *Shin Machi-sō Ryokan* (☎ 0893-44-2021) has per person rates at ¥8000, while the *Matsunoya Ryokan* (☎ 0893-44-2161) costs ¥12,000. Prices include dinner and breakfast.

Places to Eat

There are a few small restaurants along Yōkaichi. *Sōgen* is an atmospheric little spot in the back of a craft shop with noodles and curry, and across the street and just south of here *Inakappe* serves up good udon and mountain vegetables.

Getting There & Away

Uchiko can be reached by bus or train from Matsuyama and Uwajima. Ordinary train services from Matsuyama only take an hour. You need at least a few hours to explore Yōkaichi.

Getting Around

Yōkaichi is just over one km from the JR Uchiko station; if you're stopping off the train and your time is limited, consider taking a taxi. The bus station is closer to Yōkaichi.

Ikazaki 五十崎

Just over the hill from Ryūō-kōen Park in Uchiko is the pleasant little town of Ikazaki, a nice detour for those with a bit of extra time to explore. There is an interesting **kite museum** and a **traditional paper making factory** where you can observe and even try your hand at the craft for ¥500. Reservations are recommended; call the Tenjin-san-shi Kōjō, (☎ 0893-44-2002), closed Sunday.

UCHIKO TO UWAJIMA

Only 20 km south-west of Uchiko, there are more interesting old houses and shops near the river in **Ōzu**, including the **Garyū-sansō** (closed Wednesday, entry ¥200), a wealthy trader's house built early this century. Traditional cormorant fishing (*ukai*) takes place in the river during summer. The *Ōzu Kyōdokan Youth Hostel* (☎ 0893-24-2258) has nightly rates of ¥2800. It's in the south-west of town, over the river next to the Ōzu-jō Castle ruins.

Ten km south-west of Ōzu is **Yawatahama**, from where ferry services operate to Beppu and Usuki on Kyūshū – the crossing to either port takes about three hours. Yawatahama-kō Port is a 10 minute bus ride north of Yawatahama station.

Cape Sada-misaki extends about 50 km

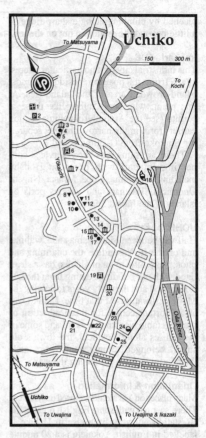

towards Kyūshū, and from Misaki, near the end of the cape, ferries make the crossing to Saganoseki (near Oita and Beppu) in just over an hour (¥700) and to Beppu (¥1250).

UWAJIMA 宇和島

Uwajima (population 68,000) is a relatively quiet and peaceful place with a small but original castle, the remnants of a fine garden, some pleasant temples and a notorious sex shrine! It makes a very interesting pause between Kōchi and Matsuyama although an afternoon or a morning is long enough for a reasonable look around.

SHIKOKU

1	Kōshō-ji Temple 高昌寺	10	Ōmura Residence 大村家	18	Uchiko-bashi Bus Station 内子橋バス停留所
2	Tour Bus Parking 観光バス駐車場	11	Inakappe 田舎っぺ	19	Hachiman-jinja Shrine 八幡神社
3	Sokō-kan Museum 素巧館	12	Kawasemi かわせみ	20	Akinai-to-Kurashi Hakubutsu-kan Museum 商いとくらし博物館
4	Traditional Umbrella Maker 和傘製造	13	Atarashi-ya Craft Shop あたらし屋	21	Uchiko-za Kabuki Theatre 内子座
5	Stone Lantern 常夜灯	14	Moribun Amazake Chaya Teahouse 森文あま酒茶屋	22	Matsunoya Ryokan 松乃家
6	Inari Shrine 稲荷神社	15	Machi-ya Shiryōkan Museum 町屋資料館	23	Shin Machi-sō Ryokan 新町荘
7	Kami-Haga-tei House 上芳我邸	16	Ōmori Rōsoku Candle Maker 大森和蝋燭店	24	Bus Terminal 内子バスターミナル
8	Sōgen Noodle Shop; Craft Shop 創玄	17	Moribun Brewery 森文酒醸造所	25	City Hall; TIC 観光案内所
9	Hon-Haga-tei House 本芳我邸				

Orientation & Information

There is an information office (☎ 0895-22-3934) across the road from JR Uwajima station. It is open daily from 8.30 am to 5 pm and the English-speaking staff are very helpful.

Uwajima is a centre for cultured pearls: the tourist information office can tell you about shops dealing in them.

Uwajima-jō Castle 宇和島城

Uwajima-jō was never a great castle but it's an interesting 'little' three storeyed one and, dating from 1665, is an original, not a reconstruction. It once stood by the sea and although land reclamation has moved the sea well back, there are still good views over the town.

Inside the castle there are photos of its recent restoration and of other castles in Japan and overseas. Entry is ¥200 and it's open from 6 am to 5 pm daily (until 6.30 pm in summer).

Taga-jinja Shrine & Sex Museum 多賀神社

Once upon a time, many Shinto shrines had a connection to fertility rites but this aspect was comprehensively purged when puritanism was imported from the west following the Meiji Restoration. Nevertheless, a handful of holdouts survived and Uwajima's Taga Shrine is certainly one of them – it's totally dedicated to sex. There's a tree trunk phallus and various other bits and pieces around the temple grounds, but the three storey sex museum is the temple's major attraction.

Inside, it's packed floor to ceiling with everything from explicit Peruvian pottery to Greek vases, from the illustrated Kama Sutra to Tibetan Tantric sculptures, from South Pacific fertility gods to a showcase full of leather S&M gear, and from early Japanese *shunga* (pornographic prints) to their European Victorian equivalents, not to mention modern porno magazines. Saturation soon

SHIKOKU

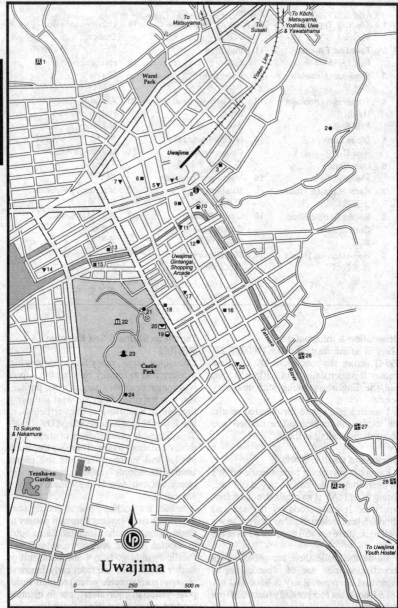

To Matsuyama

To Kōchi,
Matsuyama,
Yoshida, Uwa
& Yawatahama

To Susaki

Yosan Line

Warei
Park

Uwajima

2

3

7 6 5 4

8

9 10

11

13 12

15 14

Uwajima
Gintengai
Shopping
Arcade

17

22 21 18

23 20 19 16

Castle
Park

24

Tatsuno River

26

To Sukumo
& Nakamura

27

Tensha-en
Garden

30

29 28

To Uwajima
Youth Hostel

Uwajima

0   250   500 m

PLACES TO STAY	7 Scratch Bakery Craft	21 Samurai Gate Kōri
3 Terminal Hotel	11 Hozumitei	Family
ターミナルホテル	ほずみ亭	武家門
6 Shirakabe Business	14 Funahei	22 Castle Museum
Hotel	舟平	宇和島城資料館
ビジネスホテル白壁	17 Restaurant Itariya	23 Donjon of Uwajima-jō
9 Kokusai Hotel	伊太利屋	Castle
国際ホテル	25 Gansui	宇和島城
10 Grand Hotel	丸水	24 Naboritachi Gate
グランドホテル		のぼりたち門
13 Park Hotel	**OTHER**	26 Seigōzen-ji Temple
パークホテル	1 Taga-jinja Shrine;	西江寺
15 Minshuku Mihara	Sex Museum	27 Ryūgesan Tōkaku-ji
民宿みはら	多賀神社	Temple
16 Dai-ichi Hotel	2 Municipal Bullfighting	東閑寺
第一ホテル	Ring	28 Kongōsan Dairyū-ji
18 Business Hotel	私営闘牛場	Temple
Heiwa-sō	8 Tourist Information	大竜寺
ビジネスホテル	Office	29 Uwatsuhiko-jinja
平和荘	観光案内所	Shrine
	12 NTT	宇和津彦神社
PLACES TO EAT	19 Bus Centre	30 Municipal Date
4 Tomiya	バスセンター	Museum
とみや	20 Post Office	市立伊達博物館
5 Kadoya	宇和島郵便局	
かどや		

sets in; it's open daily 8 am to 5 pm, entry is ¥800.

Temples & Shrines
In the south-eastern part of town, a number of old temples and a shrine can be found by the canal. They include the Seigōzen-ji Temple, the Ryūgesan Tōkaku-ji Temple, the Kongōsan Dairyū-ji Temple with its old tombs and the Uwatsuhiko-jinja Shrine.

Bullfights 市営闘牛場
Tōgyū is a sort of bovine sumo wrestling where one animal tries to shove the other out of the ring (actually, victory is achieved by forcing the other animal to its knees or forcing it to turn and flee from the ring). Fights are held occasionally at Uwajima's municipal bullfighting ring. You might be

lucky enough to hook up with a Japanese tour group that has paid for a special performance, but otherwise fights are held on four particular dates each year: 2 January; second Sunday of April; 24 July; and 14 August. Tickets are ¥3,000.

Other Attractions
The **Tensha-en Gardens** are definitely not among Japan's classic gardens; they look distinctly worn and thin compared to the well-tended lushness of most Japanese gardens. They are open daily from 8.30 am to 4.30 pm and entry is ¥300.

The **Municipal Date Museum** has a collection that includes a portrait of Toyotomi Hideyoshi and items connected with the Date lords. It's open from 9 am to 4.30 pm, closed Monday, and entry is ¥200.

Places to Stay

Youth Hostel The *Uwajima Youth Hostel* (☎ 0895-22-7177) is a long walk south of the town centre: when you get to the temples overlooking the town, it's another 650m uphill climb. From Uwatsuhiko-jinja Shrine, the hostel is a 1¼ km walk, but there are fine views back down to the town. The hostel charges ¥2500 per night.

Hotels & Minshuku The friendly *Minshuku Mihara* (☎ 0895-25-5384) is good value at ¥6000 including two meals.

The *Grand Hotel* (☎ 0895-24-3911) is just south of the station and has singles from ¥4700, twins from ¥9200 and a few doubles from ¥8200. The *Kokusai Hotel* (☎ 0895-25-0111), across the road from the Grand, is an expensive place with Japanese-style rooms pulling in per-person costs of ¥13,000 upwards with two meals. The *Dai-ichi Hotel* (☎ 0895-25-0001) is near the south-eastern end of the arcade and is more affordable with singles/twins at ¥5200/10,300.

One of the cheapest options in town is the *Business Hotel Heiwa-sō* (☎ 0895-22-7711), where singles are ¥3000. It's a small place, and definitely at the shabby end of the business hotel spectrum, but it's cheap. It's over by Uwajima-jō Castle opposite the post office. There is also the friendly *Shirakabe Business Hotel* (☎ 0895-22-3585) where some English is spoken and singles cost ¥4300.

Places to Eat

Remarkably, Uwajima is free of fast-food chains, having only an *Andersen's* bakery in the station and a burger place in the arcade. The arcade is principally inhabited by coffee bars, and the entertainment district, with many places to eat, sprawls on both sides.

Kadoya, one of the restaurants along the road by the station, is a friendly place with plastic replica meals in the window and some interesting dishes. *Tomiya*, a restaurant on the same stretch of road but closer to the station, has more variety – choose from the plastic display outside. Almost next door is *M House*, a pizza and coffee place.

South of the station in the arcade area you might want to drop into *Restaurant Itariya*, a little pizzeria that throws in a few generic pasta dishes for good measure – prices range from around ¥650.

Finally, for a decent snack, on your way to the Sex Museum (or you might prefer a snack afterwards) look out for *Scratch Bakery Craft* (yes, English sign). It has pretty good pastries.

Getting There & Away

You can reach Uwajima by train from Matsuyama (via Uchiko and Uno), a one hour and 40 minute trip by limited express. From Kōchi, it takes 3¾ to 4½ hours by limited express via Kubokawa, where you change trains. If you want to head further south and to Cape Ashizuri-misaki, you'll have to resort to buses as the railway line from Kōchi terminates at Nakamura.

Direct bus services operate to Osaka from Uwajima, and there is also a ferry connection to Beppu on Kyūshū which travels via Yawatahama.

Getting Around

Uwajima is a good place to explore by bicycle since it's quiet and the traffic is not too bad. The tourist office across from Uwajima station has bicycles for hire for ¥100 an hour.

Kyūshū　　　　　　　　　　　　　九州

Kyūshū (population 14.5 million) is the third largest and southernmost of the four major islands of Japan. Although isolated from the Japanese mainstream on Central Honshū, it has been an important entry point for foreign influence and culture. Kyūshū is the closest island to Korea and China, and it was from Kyūshū that the Yamato tribe extended their power to Honshū. Some of the earliest evidence of Japanese civilisation can be seen at the archaeological excavations around Miyazaki and at the many ancient stone carvings in the Usuki area. More recently Kyūshū was for many centuries the sole link to European civilisation. During the long period of isolation from the west, the Dutch settlement at Nagasaki in Kyūshū was Japan's only connection to the outside world.

For visitors, Nagasaki is one of Kyūshū's prime attractions, due to its European-influenced history and its atomic tragedy. In the north, Fukuoka/Hakata is a major international arrival point and the terminus for the *shinkansen* (ultra-fast train) line from Tokyo. In the centre of the island there is the massive volcanic caldera of Mt Aso, while more volcanic activity can be witnessed in the south at Sakurajima. Larger towns like Kagoshima and Kumamoto offer fine gardens and magnificent castles, while Beppu is one of Japan's major hot-spring centres. There are some good walking opportunities, particularly along the Kirishima volcano chain.

The climate is milder than in other parts of Japan, and the people of Kyūshū are reputed to be hard drinkers and outstandingly friendly – a visit to a local bar may provide proof of both theories.

GETTING THERE & AWAY
Air
See the introductory Getting Around chapter for details of fares and routes. There are major airports at Beppu/Ōita, Fukuoka, Kagoshima, Kumamoto, Miyazaki and Nagasaki. Fukuoka is the major international gateway

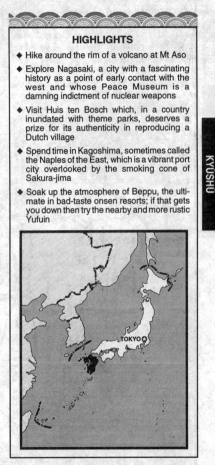

HIGHLIGHTS

◆ Hike around the rim of a volcano at Mt Aso

◆ Explore Nagasaki, a city with a fascinating history as a point of early contact with the west and whose Peace Museum is a damning indictment of nuclear weapons

◆ Visit Huis ten Bosch which, in a country inundated with theme parks, deserves a prize for its authenticity in reproducing a Dutch village

◆ Spend time in Kagoshima, sometimes called the Naples of the East, which is a vibrant port city overlooked by the smoking cone of Sakura-jima

◆ Soak up the atmosphere of Beppu, the ultimate in bad-taste onsen resorts; if that gets you down then try the nearby and more rustic Yufuin

for Kyūshū. There are also flights to islands off the coast of Kyūshū and to the islands south-west of Kagoshima down to Okinawa.

Train
The shinkansen line from Tokyo and Osaka crosses to Kyūshū from Shimonoseki and

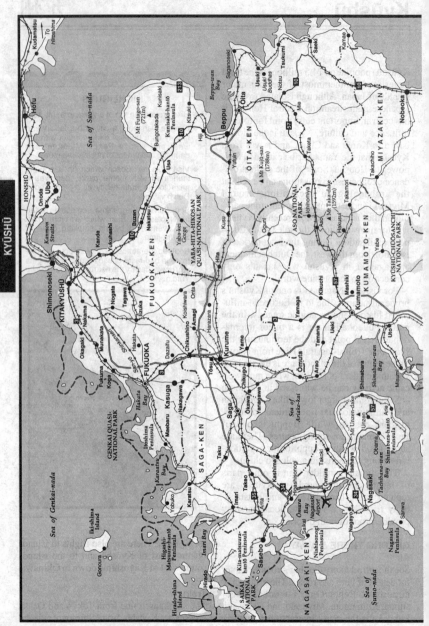

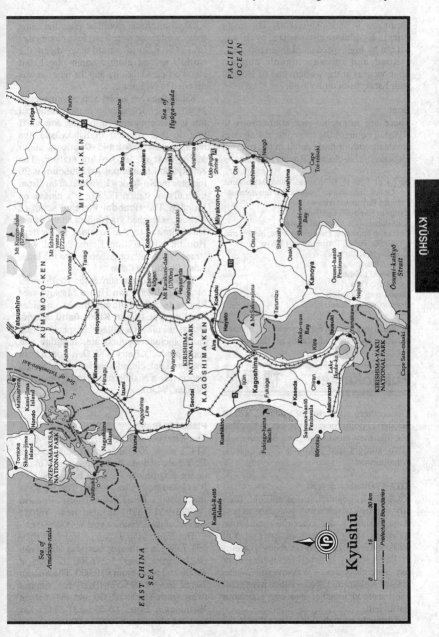

KYŪSHŪ

Kyūshū

terminates in Fukuoka/Hakata. The major cities in Kyūshū are all connected by railway but not by high-speed shinkansen service.

Road and railway tunnels connect Shimonoseki at the western end of Honshū with Kitakyūshū on Kyūshū.

Boat

There are numerous sea connections to Kyūshū; some of the more interesting ones are dealt with in more detail in the relevant sections of this chapter. Routes include:

Beppu or Ōita to Hiroshima, Kōbe, Matsuyama, Osaka, Takamatsu, Uwajima and Yawatahama
Fukuoka/Hakata to Okinawa
Hyūga to Kawasaki and Osaka
Kagoshima to Okinawa and Osaka
Kokura to Hitakatsu, Izumiotsu, Kōbe, Matsuyama, Osaka, Pusan, Tokushima and Tokyo
Kunisaki to Tokuyama
Saeki to Sukumo
Saganoseki to Misaki
Shibushi to Osaka
Takedazu to Tokuyama
Usuki to Yawatahama

In addition, local ferry services operate between Kyūshū and islands off the coast.

Fukuoka-ken 福岡県

The northern prefecture of Fukuoka will be the arrival point for most visitors to Kyūshū, whether they cross over from Shimonoseki or fly straight into Fukuoka city's international airport.

KITAKYŪSHŪ 北九州

Kitakyūshū (population one million), literally 'North Kyūshū City', is a place to pass through quickly; this industrial conurbation sprawling along the north-eastern corner of the island is unlikely to be anybody's favourite Japanese city. In actual fact it consists of five separate cities – Wakamatsu, Yahata, Tobata, Kokura and Moji – which have gradually merged together into one enormous traffic jam.

Curiously enough, one of the cities in the Kitakyūshū cluster would be a familiar name today worldwide were it not for a cloudy day in 1945. Kokura would have been the world's second atomic bomb target, but cloud obscured the city and the mission was diverted to Nagasaki.

Kitakyūshū has achieved pre-eminence in Japanese semiconductor manufacture but this is scarcely a reason to hang around. If you do find yourself in Kitakyūshū, the reconstructed **Kokura-jō Castle** is about 500m west of JR Kokura station. The **Kitakyūshū Municipal Art Museum** is 20 minutes by No 40 or 41 Nishitetsu bus from the railway station (¥230); it's closed on Monday. The **Hiraodai Plateau**, south of Kokura, is reached via Ishihara and is somewhat similar to Akiyoshidai in western Honshū with rolling fields dotted with strange rock outcrops; there's also the limestone **Senbutsu Cave**.

Those who opt to stay at the youth hostel or at the Hotel Town House Matsuya (see Places to Stay below) should consider heading out to the **Kitakyūshū Mingei Mura**, or Folk Arts Village. Displays of folk crafts include lacquerware, furniture and paper products. Entry is ¥500. It's open from 9 am to 5 pm; closed Monday. From Yahata station take a Nishitetsu bus to Jizō-mae (36 minutes, ¥430).

Places to Stay

The *Kitakyūshū Youth Hostel* (☎ 093-681-8142), about 20 minutes walk (uphill) from JR Yahata station (20 minutes from Kokura on the Kagoshima line), has beds at ¥2600. It's closed from 5 to 14 June. The Japanese Inn Group's *Hotel Town House Matsuya* (☎ 093-661-7890) is also near Yahata station; singles/doubles cost ¥5000/8800.

The *Kitakyūshū Dai Ichi Hotel* (☎ 093-551-7331) is a cheaper business hotel with singles from ¥6000 to ¥6500, doubles at ¥8000 and twins from ¥10,000. The *Kokura Tōkyū Inn* (☎ 093-521-0109) has singles/twins from ¥6500/10,000 and the *Kokura Washington Hotel* (☎ 093-531-3111) has singles/twins from ¥7000/14,000.

Getting There & Away

Train The simplest means of getting from Kitakyūshū to Shimonoseki in Honshū, or vice versa, is to take a JR train through the tunnel under the Kanmon Straits. The first railway station on the Kitakyūshū side is Moji, but Kokura is more central.

Hitching Kitakyūshū is one long, sprawling urban mess, unpleasant to drive through and nearly impossible to hitch out of. Travellers hitching to Honshū can either try the Kanmon tunnel entrance near JR Moji station or cross to Shimonoseki on the Honshū side and start from there. Hitching further into Kyūshū is probably best accomplished by getting well out of Kitakyūshū before you start.

Boat There are regular ferry services between Kokura and Kōbe, Matsuyama, Osaka, Tokyo and other Honshū ports.

FUKUOKA/HAKATA　福岡／博多

Fukuoka/Hakata (population 1.2 million) is the biggest city in Kyūshū. It was originally two separate towns – the lordly Fukuoka to the west of the Naka-gawa River and the common folks' Hakata to the east. When the two merged in 1889, the label Fukuoka was applied to both towns, but subsequent development has chiefly been in Hakata and many residents refer to the town by that name. The airport is known as Fukuoka, the railway terminus as Hakata.

Although there are no compelling tourist attractions in Fukuoka, it's a pleasant place and easy to get around. The city gives a real impression of energy and movement. It feels very cosmopolitan and, comparatively speaking, there seem to be many gaijin (foreigners). Nearby areas of interest include the fine coastal scenery beyond Karatsu to the west and the interesting temples and shrines of Dazaifu, only a few km south.

Orientation

There are two important areas in central Fukuoka – Hakata and Tenjin. JR Hakata station is the transport terminus for the city and is surrounded by hotels and offices. The railway station is flanked by the Fukuoka Kōtsū bus centre on one side and the Hakata post office on the other. Separating Hakata and Tenjin to the west is the Naka-gawa River, now the site of a rather impressive mall complex, Canal City.

Tenjin is the business and shopping centre, its focus along Watanabe-dōri. Underneath this busy street is Tenjin-chika-gai, a crowded underground shopping mall which extends for 400m. The Tenjin bus centre here is close to the terminus of the private Nishitetsu Ōmuta line. Slightly to the north, just off Shōwa-dōri, is the restaurant and entertainment district of Oyafuko-dōri.

Sandwiched between JR Hakata station and the shopping centre, on an island in the Naka-gawa River, is Nakasu, the businessmen's entertainment centre of the city. It's a maze of restaurants, strip clubs, hostess bars, cinemas and department stores.

Information

Tourist Office The tourist information office (☎ 092-431-3003) in JR Hakata station is open from 9 am to 7 pm daily and has information and maps in English. The office is more or less in the centre of the main floor.

The Fukuoka International Association Rainbow Plaza (☎ 092-733-2220 is on the 8th floor of the IMS building in Tenjin. Rainbow also has videos on Japan, books, magazines and a noticeboard with events, accommodation and jobs.

Foreign Consulates For travellers going on to South Korea there's a Korean consulate (☎ 092-771-0461) west of Tenjin, very near the Akasaka subway station. Other consulates include: Australia (☎ 092-734-5055); Canada (☎ 092-752-6055); China (☎ 092-713-1121); the UK (☎ 092-476-2525); and the USA (☎ 092-751-9331).

Bookshops On the 6th floor of the IMS building is a branch of Maruzen with a small collection of English books. Kinokuniya, on the 6th floor of the Tenjin Core building, has an excellent selection of English-language books.

KYŪSHŪ

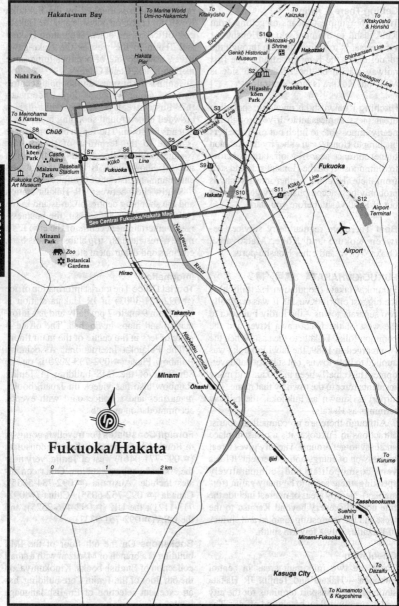

Fukuoka/Hakata

SUBWAY STATIONS
HAKOZAKI LINE

S1　Hakozaki-miya-mae
　　箱崎宮前

S2　Maidashi-Kyūaibyōin-mae
　　馬出九大病院前

S3　Chiyo-Kenchō-guchi
　　千代県庁口

S4　Gofuku-machi
　　呉服町

S5　Nakasu-Kawabata
　　中洲川端

KŪKŌ LINE

S5　Nakasu-Kawabata
　　中洲川端

S6　Tenjin
　　天神

S7　Akasaka
　　赤坂

S8　Ōhori-kōen
　　大濠公園駅

S9　Gion
　　祇園駅

S10　Hakata
　　博多駅

S11　Higashi-Hie
　　東比恵

S12　Fukuoka-Kūkō
　　福岡空港

Shrines & Temples

Shōfuku-ji Temple is a Zen temple originally founded in 1195 by Eisai, who introduced Zen doctrines to Japan and who is also credited with introducing tea. The temple was badly damaged during WWII and only occupies a quarter of its former area. It's within walking distance of JR Hakata station; don't confuse it with Sōfuku-ji Temple, a little further away.

Also within walking distance of JR Hakata station is **Sumiyoshi-jinja Shrine**, one of the oldest in Kyūshū; the main shrine was restored in 1623. **Kushida Shrine**, near

the Hakata-gawa River opposite the south-eastern end of Nakasu Island, is the starting point for the Hakata Yamagasa float race in July. **Hakozaki-gū Shrine** has a stone anchor retrieved from the Mongol invasion attempt. To get there, take the Hakozaki subway line to Hakozaki-miya-mae.

Fukuoka-jō Castle & Ōhori-kōen Park

Only the walls of Fukuoka-jō Castle remain in what is now Maizuru Park, but the castle's hilltop site provides fine views of the city. Ōhori-kōen Park is adjacent to the castle grounds and has a traditional (though recently constructed) Japanese garden, **Nihon-teien Garden**, on its southern side. The garden has a ¥200 entry charge and is closed Monday. The **Fukuoka City Art Museum** is also in the park and is open from 9.30 am to 5.30 pm daily except Monday; admission is ¥200. You can get to the castle site by bus No 13 from Tenjin or by the subway to Ōhori-kōen station.

Other Attractions

The red-brick building on Shōwa-dōri, close to the west bank of the river, is of English design and dates from 1909. It serves as an annex of the **Fukuoka City Historical Museum**, which is in a new building west of the town centre.

Higashi-kōen Park is north-east of JR Hakata station, en route to the Hakozaki-gū Shrine. In the park is the **Genkō Historical Museum** (entry ¥300), also known as the Anti-Mongol Hall. It displays items related to the abortive Mongolian invasions, but there's little in the way of English captioning. To get there, take a JR train one stop from Hakata to Yoshizuka or take the subway towards Kaizuka and get off at the Maidashi-Kyūdaibyōin-mae stop. Between Yoshizuka station and the museum is a large statue of Nichiren (1222-84) who predicted the invasion.

West of the city centre and clearly visible from many parts of town is the **Fukuoka Tower**. Like other Japanese towers elsewhere, you can take an elevator up to a viewing platform and view the Fukuoka skyline. The tower is open from 9.30 am to

KYŪSHŪ

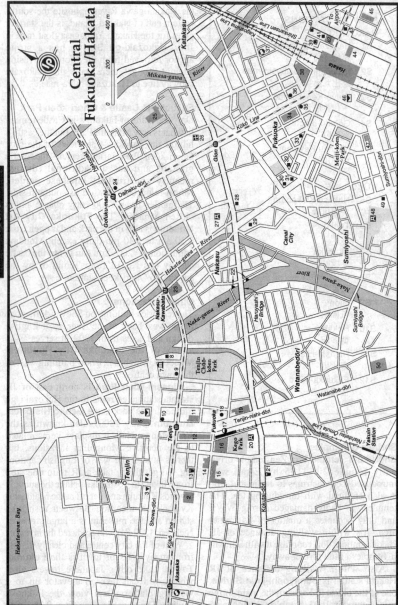

Central
Fukuoka/Hakata

0   200   400 m

PLACES TO STAY

2 Nishitetsu Grand Hotel
西鉄グランドホテル

8 Hakata Tōkyū Hotel
博多東急ホテル

28 Capsule Inn Hakata
カプスルイン博多

29 Sauna Wellbe
サウナウェルビー

30 Mitsui Urban Hotel
三井アーバンホテル

31 Chisan Hotel Hakata
チサンホテル博多

32 Business Hotel Royal
ビジネスホテル
ロイヤル

33 Hakata Business Hotel
博多ビジネスホテル

34 Hotel Nikkō
ホテル日航

39 Green Hotel 2
グリーンホテル2

40 Green Hotel 1
グリーンホテル1

41 Sun Life Hotel 1
サンライフホテル1

42 Hotel Centraza Hakata;
Gourmet City
ホテルセントラーザ

43 Sun Life Hotel 2
サンライフホテル2

44 Hotel Clio Court
ホテルクリオコート

47 ANA Hotel Hakata
日空ホテル博多

49 Hokke Club Hakata
ホテルクラブ博多

50 Hotel New Otani
ホテルニューオタニ

PLACES TO EAT

3 Nanak

4 Taiwan Yatai
台湾屋台

22 Food Stalls
屋台

OTHER

1 Korean Consulate
韓国領事館

5 Matsuya Ladies
松屋レディース

6 Main Post Office
中央郵便局

7 Former Historical Museum
元祖長浜屋

9 Thai International Airways
泰国航空

10 ANA

11 Tenjin Core Building
天神コア

12 Iwataya Department Store
天神岩田屋

13 Blue Note (Jazz Bar)

14 NHK

15 NTT

16 Solaria Plaza

17 Tenjin Bus Centre
天神バスセンター

18 IMS Building
IMS ビル

19 Daimaru Department Store
大丸

20 Kego-jinja Shrine
警国神社

21 DJ Bar Roots

23 Tamaya Department Store
玉屋

24 JAL

25 Shōfuku-ji Temple
聖福寺

26 Tocho-ji Temple

27 Kushida Shrine
櫛田神社

35 ANA

36 JAS

37 UK Consulate
英国領事館

38 Fukuoka Kōtsū Bus Centre
福岡交通バスセンター

45 NTT

46 Hakata Post Office
博多郵便局

48 Sumiyoshi-jinja Shrine
住吉神社

KYUSHU

9 pm and entry is ¥800. Next to the tower is Momochi-kōen Park and beach. It's a popular spot for swimming. Get to this area by the Kūkō subway and get off at Fujisaki station.

Fukuoka's **zoo** and **botanical gardens** are south of Fukuoka-jō Castle in Minami Park. To get there, take bus No 56 (for Hibaru-eigyosho) or bus Nos 41 or 43 (for Dobutsu-en-yuki) from stop No 10 in the Tenjin bus centre. **Marine World Umi-no-Nakamichi** is a seaside amusement park and swimming pool reached by ferry across Hakata Bay from Hakata Pier.

Special Events

If you're in town on 3 January you can head

out to Hakozaki-gū Shrine and see young men in loincloths chasing a wooden ball. The Hakata Yamagasa Festival, the city's major annual event, is held from 1 to 15 July; seven groups of men race through the city carrying huge floats which weigh about a tonne. The floats are displayed around the city from 1 to 14 July.

A major sumo tournament is held in Kyūshū in mid-November and, in early December, the Fukuoka Marathon, one of the world's most important marathons, attracts world-class runners from many countries.

Places to Stay

Budget Accommodation Fukuoka itself has no youth hostel, but there is one in nearby Dazaifu, within easy commuting distance of the city (see the Dazaifu Places to Stay section). The information counter in JR Hakata station has a list of inexpensive hotel accommodation in Fukuoka and can make reservations.

If you've wanted to try a capsule hotel (for which you have to be male) then head for *Sauna Wellbe* (☎ 092-291-1009), which is north of Hakata and near the Nakasu Island entertainment district. A sign outside also announces 'Daiwa Club' in English. Your very own capsule costs ¥3910 for the night and there's a large bath, sauna, massage room, restaurant, bar, TV room and other amenities. Just around the corner is the *Capsule Inn Hakata* (☎ 092-281-2244), where capsules cost ¥3090. Some travellers have found these places to be unfriendly.

Hotels There are numerous business hotels around the city centre, particularly around JR Hakata station. The *Green Hotel 1* and *Green Hotel 2* (☎ 092-451-4111) are two of about 10 hotels directly behind the railway station. They both have singles/doubles from ¥6400/8600.

Other hotels behind the station include three *Sun Life* hotels (☎ 092-473-7112). All three have singles/doubles from ¥7300/12,000. The *Hotel Clio Court* (☎ 092-472-1111) is an altogether more up-market business hotel, with singles from ¥11,000 and doubles

and twins from ¥30,000. Facing the Clio Court is the *Hotel Centraza Hakata* (☎ 092-461-0111), another expensive hotel; prices here are from ¥10,500/17,000 for singles/doubles.

The *Mitsui Urban Hotel* (☎ 092-451-5111), five blocks from JR Hakata station along Daihaku-dōri, has singles/doubles from ¥7500/14,000; the rooms are typically minute. Next door is the similarly priced *Chisan Hotel Hakata* (☎ 092-411-3211). The smaller *Hakata Business Hotel* (☎ 092-431-0737) has singles/doubles from ¥6200/9500 and the *Business Hotel Royal* (☎ 092-441-8448), near the Chisan and Mitsui Urban hotels, has singles/doubles from ¥5200/7600.

The *ANA Hotel Hakata* (☎ 092-471-7111), on the left as you leave JR Hakata station, is one of the best places in town, with singles/doubles from ¥12,000/21,000.

Places to Eat

The busy JR Hakata station offers a great number of places to eat, including the full assortment of fast-food joints, department stores and restaurant streets. The station itself has two underground restaurant malls, both with a bewildering array of restaurants.

Behind the railway station, under the Hotel Centraza Hakata, is *Gourmet City*, with two basement floors of restaurants offering Chinese, Japanese and European food and desserts. Lunch time features some excellent teishoku (set lunch) bargains, and it's open until 11 pm. There are plenty of restaurants, bars, shops and bakeries around the Suehiro Inn.

Another good place to check out at lunch time is Canal City. This ultra-slick development has a great selection of basement restaurants. Get there early if you don't want to queue. Good places for a meal include *Ninnikuya* (international cuisine – ninniku is garlic), *Kohinoor* (Indian), *Tonkatsu Wakō* and *Ichiran* (budget rāmen – noodles). There's also a branch of *Pronto*, the budget coffee specialists, and the *Kirin Beer Theatre*, which also has izakaya-style (Japanese pub) food. Canal City has more up-market dining in the section beneath the Washington Hotel:

NICKO GONCHAROFF

NICKO GONCHAROFF

MASON FLORENCE

A: Mt O-Akan-dake, from Lake Mashūro, Akan National Park
B: Vapour seeps from 54-year-old Mt Showa-shinzan
C: Ainu girl, Nibudani, Hokkaidō

MASON FLORENCE

MASON FLORENCE

MASON FLORENCE

MASON FLORENCE

TONY WHEELER

A	B
C	D
E	

A: Autumn colours, Central Shikoku
B: Harvest season, Central Shikoku
C: Vine bridge, Iyadani-kei Gorge, Tokushima-ken
D: Grandmother's little helper
E: Taga-jinja phallus, Uwajima

La Cucina is a superb Italian restaurant with lunch specials at around ¥800.

Fukuoka is renowned for its *yatai*, or streetside food stalls (there are around 300 of them). Come nightfall, the riverside area is swarming with these brightly lit places. The most popular ones have long queues. It's pointless making suggestions – take a stroll along the Naka-gawa River and drop in to one of these places for a meal of rāmen, yakitori (chicken kebabs) or tempura (depends on the stall) from around ¥400. The yatai represent a good opportunity to try Fukuoka's famous rāmen dish – Hakata rāmen. The Nakasu Island entertainment district is another good place to try Hakata rāmen – just look for the rāmen photographs at the entrances to restaurants. This area also has a number of fast-food outlets.

Oyafuko-dōri was once the chic, happening part of town, but since the opening of Canal City it has started to look tired. Still, there are several good restaurants here, including *Taiwan Yatai*, a small but friendly place which does Taiwanese/Chinese food at very reasonable prices. Just up the road from here is *Taj*, an Indian restaurant whose Japanese sign announces *essuniku kāri senmon*, or the 'ethnic curry specialist' – prices are from ¥700. *Nanak* is a branch of the Indian chain; it's on the corner of Shōwa-dōri.

Entertainment

Nakasu Island is one of the busiest entertainment districts in Japan with several thousand bars, restaurants and clubs. However, it's not really the place to go unless you are on a company expense account. Elsewhere around town, there are quite a number of bars that are popular with young Japanese and resident gaijin; the difficult thing is finding them. Drop into *DJ Bar Roots* (☎ 092-711-1705) and chat to the folks there. It's a 2nd floor bar and has a happy hour from 7 to 9 pm from Monday to Thursday when drinks are half price. Other popular bars around town include *Happy Cock* (on Tenjin-nishi-dōri), *Cross Up* and *Mikey's*.

Jazz aficionados will be interested to know that Fukuoka has a *Blue Note* (092-715-6666).

Acts lined up to play at the time of writing included Wayne Shorter, Joe Sample, Dee Dee Jackson and The Three Degrees. Ticket prices range from ¥8500 for international acts, but include food and drink coupons.

Things to Buy

Clay Hakata dolls depicting women, children, samurai and geisha are a popular Fukuoka craft. Hakata *obi*, the silk sashes worn with a kimono, are another typical craft of the region. Try the Iwataya department store in Tenjin for these and other items.

Getting There & Away

Air Fukuoka is an international gateway to Japan with flights to and from Australia, New Zealand, Hong Kong, South Korea, China, the Philippines, Thailand, Malaysia, Indonesia, Taiwan and the USA. There are also internal flights to other centres in Japan including more than 50 flights a day to Tokyo Haneda airport (1¾ hours, ¥26,600); there are also four flights a day to Narita international airport. Flights to Osaka (¥15,450) take just over an hour.

Train & Bus JR Hakata station is the western terminus of the 1177 km Tokyo-Osaka-Hakata shinkansen service. There are 21 services a day to/from Tokyo (five to six hours, ¥21,300), 56 to/from Osaka (2½ to three hours, ¥14,310) and 62 to/from Hiroshima (one to two hours, ¥8530). Prices are slightly higher for the Nozomi super express.

JR lines also fan out from Hakata to other centres in Kyūshū. The Nippō line runs through Hakata, Beppu, Miyazaki and Kagoshima; the Kagoshima line runs through Hakata, Kumamoto, Yatsushiro and Kagoshima; and both the Nagasaki and Sasebo lines run from Hakata to Saga and Sasebo or Hakata to Nagasaki. From Tenjin station the Nishitetsu Ōmuta line operates through Tenjin, Dazaifu, Kurume, Yanagawa and Ōmuta. You can also travel by road or train to Karatsu and continue from there to Nagasaki by train.

Buses depart from the Kōtsū bus centre near JR Hakata station and from the Tenjin

KYŪSHŪ

bus centre. There are buses to Tokyo (15 hours, ¥15,000), Osaka (9½ hours, ¥10,000), Nagoya (12 hours, ¥10,500) and many destinations around Kyūshū.

Boat There are ferry services from Fukuoka to Okinawa, to Iki-shima Island and other islands off Kyūshū. Ferries operate between the Tokyo ferry terminal and Kokura harbour, taking around 36 hours, and also between Osaka and Shinmonshi harbour, taking around 12 hours.

Fukuoka also has an international high-speed hydrofoil service connecting the city with Pusan in Korea daily. The hydrofoil is run by JR Kyūshū (☎ 095-281-2315); tickets cost ¥12,400 one way, ¥21,500 return, and the journey takes just under three hours. The Camellia line (☎ 092-262-2323) also runs a ferry service to Pusan, but it takes around 15 hours. Tickets range from ¥8500 to ¥18,000.

Getting Around
The Airport Fukuoka airport is conveniently close to the city centre, a contrast with most airports around Japan. Airport buses take about 15 minutes to JR Hakata station (¥240) or 30 minutes to Tenjin (¥270). But most people use the subway system, which takes just five minutes to Hakata station (¥220) and 11 minutes to Tenjin station (¥220). Taxis cost from around ¥1000.

The airport has three terminals – No 3 is for international flights, No 2 is for JAL and JAS flights to Tokyo (both Haneda and Narita airports) and to Okinawa, and No 1 is for all other domestic flights.

Train There are two subway lines in Fukuoka. The Kūkō (Airport) line runs from Fukuoka airport to Meinohama, via Hakata and Tenjin stations. The Hakozaki line runs from Nakasu-Kawabata station to Kaizuka. Fares around town are ¥220 and tickets can be bought at automatic vending machines which have clear English instructions.

Bus City and long-distance bus services operate from the Kōtsū bus centre at JR Hakata station and the Tenjin bus centre at Tenjin.

The Nishitetsu bus company covers most tourist attractions around the city within its ¥170 fare zone; ¥700 one-day passes are available.

DAZAIFU 太宰府
Dazaifu, with its superb shrine and interesting temples, is almost close enough to be a suburb of Fukuoka. You could take a day trip to Dazaifu or, as most budget travellers do, stay there and skip Fukuoka altogether.

Dazaifu was the governmental centre of Kyūshū during the Kofun period (300-710) and through the Heian period (794-1185). Dazaifu was also important as the chief port for commercial and cultural contacts with China. It diminished in importance from the 16th century, and is now dwarfed by its huge neighbour Fukuoka.

Information
The information office (☎ 092-925-1880) outside Nishitetsu-Dazaifu station, near the entranceway to the Temman-gū Shrine, has helpful staff and an excellent English brochure and map.

Temman-gū Shrine 天満宮
The poet and scholar Sugawara-no-Michizane (845-903) was an important personage in the Kyoto court until he fell foul of political intrigue and was exiled to distant Dazaifu, where he died two years later. Subsequent disasters which struck Kyoto were blamed on his unfair dismissal and he became deified as Temman Tenjin or Kankō, the god of culture and scholars. His great shrine and burial place attracts countless visitors.

The brightly painted orange shrine is entered via a picturesque arched bridge. Behind the shrine building is the Kankō Historical Museum (entry ¥200) with dioramas showing events in Tenjin's life. The treasure house has artifacts connected with his life and the history of the shrine. The shrine's Honden (Main Hall) was rebuilt in 1583.

Kōmyō-ji Temple 光明寺
In this small temple the Ittekikaino-niwa Garden is a breathtakingly beautiful example of a Zen garden and a peaceful contrast to the

Dazaifu

0   250   500 m

1	Kankō Historical Museum 観光歴史資料館	
2	Temman-gū Shrine 天満宮	
3	Treasure House 宝物殿	
4	Five-Arched Bridge 五孔橋	
5	Tourist Information; Bicycle Rental レンタサイクル	
6	Kōmyō-ji Temple; Ittekikaino-niwa Garden 光明寺	
7	Kyūshū Historical Museum 九州歴史資料館	
8	Post Office 郵便局	
9	Dazaifu City Office 市役所	
10	Kanzeon-ji Treasure House 宝蔵	
11	Kanzeon-ji Temple 観世音寺	
12	Kaidan-in Temple 戒壇院	
13	Dazaifu Exhibition Hall 太宰府展示館	
14	Tofurō Ruins 都府楼跡	
15	Enoki-sha 榎社	

crowds in the nearby shrine. Entry is ¥200. It is open daily from 9 am to 5 pm.

Kaidan-in & Kanzeon-ji Temples
戒壇院・観世音寺

Now a Zen Buddhist temple, the Kaidan-in dates from 761 AD and was one of the most important monasteries in Japan. The adjacent Kanzeon-ji Temple dates from 746 AD but only the great 697 AD bell, said to be the oldest in Japan, remains from the original construction.

Kanzeonji Treasure Hall

This treasure hall has a wonderful collection of statuary, most of it of wood, dating from the 10th to 12th centuries and of impressive size. The style of some of the pieces is more Indian or Tibetan than Japanese. The display is open from 9 am to 5 pm and entry is ¥400. It's closed on Monday.

Other Attractions

The **Dazaifu Exhibition Hall** displays finds

from local archaeological excavations and is open daily from 9 am to 4.30 pm except Monday. Nearby are the **Tofurō ruins**, foundations of the buildings dating from the era when Dazaifu governed all of Kyūshū. Enoki-sha is where Sugawara-no-Michizane died. His body was transported from here to its burial place, now the shrine, on the ox cart which appears in so many local depictions. The **Kyūshū Historical Museum**, near the shrine, is open from 9.30 am to 4.30 pm daily except Monday; admission is free.

Places to Stay
The *Dazaifu Youth Hostel* (☎ 092-922-8740) is actually in one of the Dazaifu temples; it has only 24 beds and charges ¥2800 per night. *Ryokan* (traditional Japanese inns) and other accommodation can be found in the nearby town of Futsukaichi Onsen.

Getting There & Away
Train & Bus A Nishitetsu line train will take you to Futsukaichi station from Tenjin in Fukuoka in 20 to 30 minutes. From Futsukaichi, you'll have to change for the two-station ride to Nishitetsu-Dazaifu station. The trip costs ¥360 and takes around 40 minutes all up.

Getting Around
Bicycles can be rented from the information office next to Nishitetsu-Dazaifu station for ¥200 for one hour.

AROUND FUKUOKA-KEN
Anti-Mongol Wall　元寇防塁跡
Fukuoka and the north-west coast of Kyūshū secured their place in Japanese history books when the Mongol leader Kublai Khan invaded Japan in 1274 and 1281. The invaders were defeated on their first try and before the second attempt, a three-metre-high 'anti-Mongol wall' was built along the coast. It proved unnecessary as a *kamikaze* or 'divine wind' in the form of a typhoon wiped out the invader's fleet. In the final desperate days of WWII, the Japanese tried to create their own divine wind with kamikaze suicide pilots.

The wall extended for 20 km and some short stretches have been excavated at the Genkō fort north of Imajuku near Imazu-wan Bay. To get to the wall, take a Nishinoura bus from the Fukuoka Kōtsū bus centre and get off at Midōrimachi; the wall is known as the *bōheki*. Other stretches of anti-Mongol wall can be seen at Iki-no-Matsubara, back toward the city near the Odo Yacht Harbour, and at Nishijin, closer again toward the city centre.

Genkai Quasi-National Park
The Genkō fort wall at Imajuku is in the Genkai Quasi-National Park and the nearby Obaru Beach offers surprisingly good swimming although there are even better beaches further west. **Keya-no-Oto** (Great Cave of Keya) is at the western end of the Itoshima Peninsula. It's a popular tourist attraction and buses run there directly from the Fukuoka Kōtsū bus centre, taking about 1½ hours.

Kurume　久留米
The town of Kurume, south of Dazaifu, is noted for its crafts including paper making, bamboo work and tie-dyed textiles. Pottery is also produced in nearby towns. The **Ishibashi Bunka Center** is a Bridgestone-sponsored art museum (open from 10 am to 5 pm daily, closed Monday; ¥300) and the town also has the Bairin-ji Temple and the Suiten-gū Shrine, both of which are just west of JR Kurume station. It takes about half an hour to get to Kurume from Fukuoka, either on the JR Kagoshima line or the Nishitetsu line.

Yanagawa　柳川
Yanagawa, south-west of Kurume, is a peaceful old castle town noted for its many moats and canals. Regular canal trips are made around the waterways (¥1500). The town has some interesting old buildings including a teahouse and a museum. Yanagawa has a range of accommodation including a youth hostel – *Runowaru Youth Hostel* (☎ 0944-62-2423). A train from Kurume to Yanagawa on the Nishitetsu-Ōmuta line takes about 20 minutes.

Saga-ken 佐賀県

KARATSU 唐津

The small city of Karatsu (population 80,000) has a reconstructed castle and a superb display of the floats used in the annual Karatsu Okunchi Festival. Only 50 km south-west of Fukuoka, it makes a good jumping-off point for visits to the picturesque Higashi-Matsuura-hantō Peninsula. Potters in Karatsu turn out primitive but well-respected pottery with clear connections to the Korean designs first introduced into Japan. The sandy beach east of Karatsu at Niji-no-Matsuura draws crowds in summer.

Karatsu-jō Castle 唐津城

Although it's just a modern reconstruction, the castle looks great, perched on a hill overlooking the sea. Inside, there's a museum with archaeological and pottery displays; opening hours are from 9 am to 4.30 pm daily and admission is ¥300.

Okunchi Festival Floats 曳山展示場

The 14 floats used in the Karatsu Okunchi Festival are displayed in the Hikiyama Festival Float Exhibition Hall beside the Karatsu-jinja Shrine. The festival is believed to have started in the 1660s with floats from each of the 17 areas of the city. From 1819, the design of the floats was standardised; previously a new float had been built each year. The Aka-jishi (Red Lion) float was the first to take a permanent design. Others include a turtle, samurai helmets, bream, a dragon and a chicken. The display, which includes a video about the festival parade, is open from 9 am to 5 pm daily and entry is ¥200.

Other Attractions

There are a number of pottery kilns where you can see local potters at work as well as pottery shops along the street between the railway station and the town centre. The most famous kiln is that of **Nakazato**

Tarōemon. There is also a gallery at this kiln. It's about five minutes walk to the south-east of Karatsu station. A popular cycling track cuts through the pine trees planted behind the five km long **Niji-no-Matsubara Beach**.

Special Events

The wonderful Karatsu Okunchi Festival takes place from 2 to 4 November when 14 superb floats are drawn through the town.

Places to Stay

The *Karatsu City Hotel* (☎ 0955-72-1100) is a big, modern hotel right behind the railway station. Singles/doubles start from ¥6800/13,000. Most other hotels and ryokan are along the Niji-no-Matsuura Beach and are fairly expensive. One of the very cheapest is the *Kokuminshukusha Niji-no-Matsubara Hotel* (☎ 0955-73-9111); singles/twins cost ¥6000/10,000. North of here on the beachfront, the expensive *Ryokan Yōyōkaku* (☎ 0955-72-7181) has rooms ranging from ¥15,000 to ¥40,000 with two meals.

Getting There & Away

From Fukuoka take the Kūkō subway line from Hakata or Tenjin to the end of the line and continue on the JR Chikuhi line. It takes about one hour 20 minutes to reach Karatsu and costs ¥950. You can continue from Karatsu to Nagasaki by taking the JR Karatsu line to Saga and the JR Nagasaki line from there.

Getting Around

Bicycles can be rented from JR Karatsu station or from Seto Cycle, just across the bridge from the castle towards Niji-no-Matsuura Beach. A circuit of the Higashi-Matsuura-hantō Peninsula would make a good day trip from Karatsu in a rental car.

HIGASHI-MATSUURA-HANTŌ PENINSULA 東松浦半島

Karatsu is at the base of the Higashi-Matsuura-hantō with its dramatic coastline and interesting little fishing ports.

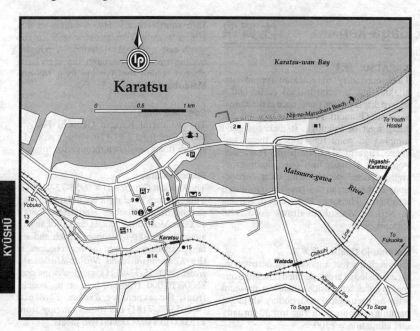

1	Kokuminshukusha Niji-no-Matsubara Hotel 虹の松原	6	NTT	11	Kinsho-ji Temple 近松寺
2	Ryokan Yōyōkaku 旅館洋洋館	7	Karatsu-jinja Shrine 唐津神社	12	France's Bakery フランスベーカリー
3	Karatsu-jō Castle 唐津城	8	Showa Bus Station 昭和バスセンター	13	Kojiro Kiln 小次廊窯
4	Car Park 駐車場	9	Hikiyama Festival Float Exhibition Hall 曳山展示場	14	Karatsu City Hotel 唐津シティホテル
5	Main Post Office 中央郵便局	10	Tourist Information Centre 観光案内所	15	Nakazato Tarōemon Kiln 中里太郎石街門窯

Yobuko 呼子

This busy little fishing port has a wonderful early-morning market for fish and produce. A series of ryokan, charging from around ¥7000 per person, line a narrow lane running beside the waterfront; rooms look straight out onto the bay. Shōwa buses from Karatsu take around 40 minutes and cost ¥620.

Hatomizaki Underwater Observatory 玄海海中公園

A pier leads out to this underwater observatory

where you can see different species of local fish attracted to the observatory by regular feeding. Entry is ¥515; it's open from 9 am to 6 pm daily. From Yobuko, Shōwa buses take around 20 minutes and cost ¥330.

Nagoya Castle　名護屋城址

En route between Yobuko and Hatomizaki, buses stop at this now ruined castle, from which Hideyoshi launched his unsuccessful invasions of Korea.

POTTERY TOWNS

Imari and Arita are the major pottery towns of Saga-ken. From the early 17th century, pottery was produced in this area using captive Korean potters. The work was done in Arita and nearby Ōkawachiyama and the Korean experts were zealously guarded so that the secrets of their craft did not slip out. Pottery from this area, with its brightly coloured glazes, is still highly esteemed in Japan.

Imari　伊万里

Although Imari is the name commonly associated with the pottery from this area, it is actually produced in Ōkawachiyama and Arita. Ōkawachiyama, where 20 pottery kilns operate today, is a 15 minute bus ride (¥250) from the JR Imari station. The nearby **Nabeshima Hanyō-kōen Park** shows the techniques and living conditions in a feudal-era pottery.

The *Imari Grand Hotel* (☎ 0955-22-2811) is around 200m south-west of Imari station and has singles/twins for ¥4800/9600. Imari is about an hour by bus from Karatsu (¥870), a little less by train on the JR Chikuhi line.

Arita　有田

It was at Arita that kaolin clay was discovered in 1615 by Ri Sampei, a naturalised Korean potter, permitting the manufacture of fine porcelain for the first time. By the mid-17th century it was being exported to Europe.

Arita is a sprawling town, and less interesting than Imari. The **Kyūshū Ceramic Art Museum** is well worth a visit if you want an overview of the development of ceramic arts in Kyūshū. Entry is ¥200. It's open from 9 am to 4.30 pm; closed Monday. Of more specialised interest is **Rekishi Minzoku Shiryōkan** (Folk History Museum), and the **Arita Tōji Bijutsukan** (Arita Ceramic Art Museum) is also near by; both have the same opening hours as the Kyūshū Ceramic Museum and entry for each is ¥100.

For the full treatment, join the Japanese package tours at the **Arita Porcelain Park**. Essentially it's a theme park centred around Arita porcelain, with kilns, a porcelain history museum and a baroque porcelain palace where you can find paintings and special porcelain exhibits on display. Entry is ¥2500. It's open daily from 9 am to 4.30 pm. Shuttle buses go from Arita station (10 minutes, ¥210).

Pottery connoisseurs are sure to find the **Imaizumi Imaemon Gallery** (open from 9 am to 5 pm daily except Sunday), the **Sakaida Kakiemon Kiln** (open from 9 am to 5 pm) and the Genemon Kiln (open Monday to Saturday from 8 am to 5.30 pm) very interesting.

Arita is about 25 minutes from Imari on the Matsuura line. Alternatively, there are direct buses running from the Tenjin bus centre in Fukuoka (one hour 55 minutes, ¥1900).

Islands off Kyūshū's North-West Coast

Five larger and many smaller islands lie to the north-west of Kyūshū and are accessible from Fukuoka, Sasebo and Nagasaki. Tsushima Island, the largest of the group, is in the strait midway between Japan and Korea and is actually closer to Pusan than to Fukuoka. These are islands strictly for those who want to get far away from it all; foreign visitors are very rare. Some of the islands are part of Saga-ken, while other islands are part of Nagasaki-ken.

PLACES TO STAY

Tsu-shima has the *Tsushima Seizan-ji Youth Hostel* (☎ 09205-2-0444), which has 16 beds

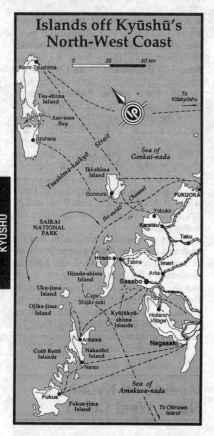

Islands off Kyūshū's North-West Coast

Tsu-shima cost ¥4600 and ¥6500 respectively, and take less than one hour. Ordinary services cost ¥3520 to Tsu-shima and ¥1890 to Iki-shima and take just over two hours.

TSU-SHIMA ISLAND 対馬

The mountainous island of Tsu-shima, 682 sq km in area, is actually two islands: the narrow neck of land connecting the two parts was channelled through during the 16th century. The port of **Izuhara** is the island's main town and has a fort originally built by Toyotomi Hideyoshi during an expedition to Korea in 1592. The island has seen a more recent conflict when the Czar's fleet was utterly routed by the Japanese during the Russo-Japanese War in 1905. The conflict took place in the Tsushima Straits, between Tsu-shima and Iki-shima islands.

Tsu-shima has a number of small towns and a road runs most of its length. **Aso-wan Bay**, the almost totally enclosed bay between the north and south islands, has many islets and inlets.

IKI-SHIMA ISLAND 壱岐

Iki-shima, with an area of 138 sq km, is south of Tsu-shima and much closer to Fukuoka. Iki-shima is an attractive island with fine beaches; it's also relatively flat and a good place for cycling. **Gonoura** is the main port and Toyotomi Hideyoshi also built a fort there.

HIRADO-SHIMA ISLAND 平戸島

The island of Hirado-shima, close to Sasebo and actually joined to Kyūshū by a bridge from Hirado-guchi, has had an interesting European history. Portuguese ships first landed on Hirado-shima in 1549 and, a year later, St Francis Xavier paid a visit to the island (after his expulsion from Kagoshima).

It was not until 1584 that the Portuguese formally established a trading post on the island but they were soon followed by the Dutch (in 1609) and the British (in 1613). Relations between the British and Dutch became so acrimonious that in 1618, the Japanese had to restore law and order on the island. In 1621, the British abandoned Japan

and costs ¥2000. There are also quite a few *minshuku* (family-run guest houses) and ryokan on Tsu-shima, Hirado-shima and Fukue-jima islands.

GETTING THERE & AWAY

Air There are a number of local air services to the islands. ANK flies between Fukuoka and Iki-shima Island for ¥6000, Fukuoka and Tsu-shima Island for ¥9080 and Nagasaki and Iki-shima Island for ¥8830.

Boat

Jetfoil services from Hakata to Iki-shima and

and turned their full attention to India. Things were not easy for the Europeans during the anti-Christian period in Japan and today there is very little trace of the European trading operations. The main town, **Hirado**, was burnt down in 1906.

Hirado-shima has some older buildings including a **museum** in the residence of the Matsuura, who ruled the island from the 11th to the 19th centuries. There are fine views over the Gotō Rettō Islands from **Cape Shijiki-zaki** and the western coast of the island is particularly attractive. From Kashimae, half an hour by bus from Sasebo, regular boats operate to Hirado-shima via the Kyūjūkyū-shima Islands.

GOTŌ RETTŌ ISLANDS　五島列島

The two main islands in the Gotō Rettō group are **Fukue-jima** and **Nakadōri**, but there are three other medium-sized islands, squeezed between the two large ones, plus over 100 small islands and islets. At one time, the islands were a refuge for Japanese Christians fleeing the Edo government's anti-Christian repression; today the main attraction is the natural beauty of the mountainous islands.

Fukue, the fishing port on the island of the same name, is the main town in the group. **Ishida-jō Castle** in the town was burnt down

in 1614 and rebuilt in 1849. Along with Hirado-shima and a strip of the Kyūshū coast, the Gotō Rettō Islands are part of the Saikai National Park.

KYŪJŪKYŪ-SHIMA ISLANDS　九十九島

Between Hirado-shima and the Kyūshū coast are the 170-odd Kyūjūkyū-shima Islands; although the name actually means '99 islands'. Cruise boats operate around the islands from Sasebo.

Nagasaki-ken　長崎県

NAGASAKI　長崎

Nagasaki (population 450,000) is a busy and colourful city but its unfortunate fate as the second atomic bomb target obscures its fascinating early history of contact with the Portuguese and Dutch. Even after Commodore Perry's historic visit to Japan, Nagasaki remained one of the major contact points with the west. Despite the popular image of Nagasaki as a totally modern city rising from an atomic wasteland, there are many reminders of its earlier history and European contact. The bomb actually missed its intended target towards the south of the city

The Atomic Explosion

When the USAF B-29 bomber *Bock's Car* set off from Tinian in the Marianas on 9 August 1945 to drop the second atomic bomb on Japan, the target was Kokura on the north-eastern coast of Kyūshū. Fortunately for Kokura it was a cloudy day and, despite flying over the city three times, the bomber's crew could not sight the target, so a course was set for the secondary target, Nagasaki.

The B-29 arrived over Nagasaki at 10.58 am but again visibility was obscured by cloud. When a momentary gap appeared in the cloud cover, the Mitsubishi Arms Works, not the intended Mitsubishi shipyard, was sighted and became the target. The 4.5 ton 'Fat Man' bomb had an explosive power equivalent to 22 kilotons of TNT, far more than the 13 kilotons of Hiroshima's 'Little Boy'. Afterwards, the aircraft turned south and flew to Okinawa, arriving there with its fuel supply almost exhausted.

The explosion took place at 11.02 am, at an altitude of 500m, completely devastating the Urakami suburb of northern Nagasaki and killing 75,000 of Nagasaki's 240,000 population. Another 75,000 were injured and it is estimated that that number again have subsequently died as a result of the blast. Anybody out in the open within two km of the epicentre suffered severe burns from the heat of the explosion; even four km away exposed bare skin was burnt. Everything within a one km radius of the explosion was destroyed and the resultant fires burnt out almost everything within a four km radius. A third of the city was wiped out. ■

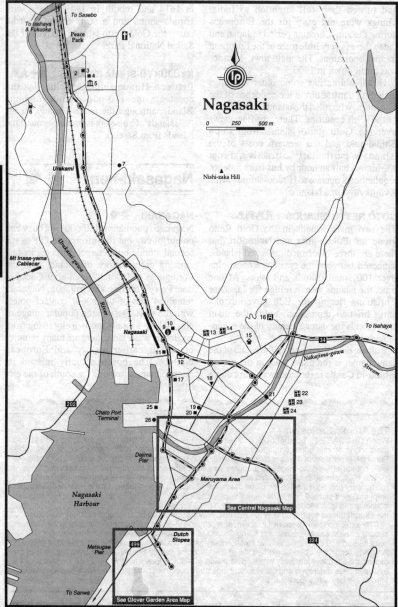

Nagasaki

0   250   500 m

To Sasebo

To Isahaya
& Fukuoka

Peace Park

Urakami

Urakami-gawa

Mt Inasa-yama
Cablecar

River

Nagasaki

Nishi-zaka Hill

To Isahaya

Nakajima-gawa

Stream

202

Chato Port
Terminal

Dejima
Pier

Nagasaki
Harbour

Maruyama Area

See Central Nagasaki Map

Matsugae Pier

499

Dutch
Slopes

To Sanwa

See Glover Garden Area Map

324

34

and scored a near direct hit on the largest Catholic church in Japan.

History

Nagasaki has the most varied history of any city in Japan, much of it tied up with the dramatic events of the 'Christian Century'. The accidental arrival of an off-course Portuguese ship at Tanega-shima Island in 1542 signalled the start of Nagasaki's long period as Japan's principal connection with the west.

The first visitors were soon followed by the great missionary St Francis Xavier in 1560 and, although his visit was brief, these Portuguese contacts were to have far-reaching effects. The primitive guns introduced by the Portuguese soon revolutionised warfare in Japan, forcing the construction of new and stronger castles and bringing to an end the anarchy and chaos of the 'Country at War' century.

Among the first Japanese to be converted to Christianity by the visitors was a minor *daimyō* (regional lord) in north-western Kyūshū. Under his auspices, Nagasaki, established in 1571, soon became the main arrival point for Portuguese trade ships. Although the Portuguese principally acted as intermediaries between China and Japan, the trade was mutually profitable, and Nagasaki quickly became a fashionable and wealthy city.

By 1587, Japanese authorities had begun to perceive the growing influence of Christianity as a threat. Jesuit missionaries were expelled and a policy of persecution was soon implemented. In 1597, 26 European

KYŪSHŪ

PLACES TO STAY	PLACES TO EAT		
3 Volks Hotel In Park フォルクスホテル	18 Harbin ハルビン	13	Fukusai-ji Zen Temple 福済寺
4 Park Side Hotel パークサイドホテル	**OTHER**	14	Shōuku-ji Temple 聖福寺
6 Minshuku Tanpopo 民宿タンポポ	1 Urakami Cathedral 浦上天主堂	16	Suwa-jinja Shrine 諏訪神社
10 Nishi-Kyūshū Dai-Ichi Hotel; Capsule Inn Nagasaki 西九州第一ホテル／カプセルイン長崎	2 Hypocentre (Epicentre) Park 原爆落下中心地	19	NTT
		21	Megane-bashi Bridge 眼鏡橋
	5 A-Bomb Museum 長崎国際文化会館	22	Kōku-ji Temple 興福寺
11 Hotel New Nagasaki ホテルニュー長崎	7 One-Legged Torii 片足鳥居	23	Ema-ji Temple 絵馬寺
15 Nagasaki Youth Hostel 長崎ユースホステル	8 26 Martyrs Memorial 二十六聖人殉教地	24	Chosho-ji Temple 長照寺
17 Terada Inn 寺田屋	9 Prefectural Tourist Federation; Ken-ei Bus Station 観光案内所／県営バスターミナル	26	Harbour Cruise Office 観光船大波止発着所
20 Sakamoto-ya Bekkan 坂本屋			
25 Newport Business Hotel ビジネスホテルニューポート	12 Post Office 郵便局		

and Japanese Christians were crucified in Nagasaki and in 1614 the religion was banned. Suspected Christians were rounded up, tortured and killed; the Japanese wives and children of foreigners were deported; and the Catholic Portuguese and Spanish traders were expelled in favour of the Protestant Dutch, who were perceived as being more interested in trade and less in religion.

The Shimabara peasant uprising of 1637 – perceived as a Christian uprising at the time – was the final chapter in the events of the 'Christian Century'. All subsequent contact with foreigners was banned and no Japanese were allowed to travel overseas. The one small loophole in this ruling was the closely watched Dutch enclave at Dejima Island near Nagasaki. Through this small outpost a trickle of western science and progress continued to filter into Japan, and from 1720, when Dutch books were once again permitted to enter the country, Nagasaki became an important scientific and artistic centre. When Nagasaki reopened to the west in 1859, it quickly re-established itself as a major economic force, particularly for shipbuilding, and it was this industry which made Nagasaki an atomic target in the closing days of WWII.

Orientation & Information

The Hamano-machi arcade and the Maruyama entertainment area form the focus of Nagasaki's central city area, about a km south of the railway station. Further south are the Chinatown, Dutch Slopes and Glover Garden areas. Nagasaki is relatively compact and it's quite feasible to walk from the central area all the way south to Glover Garden. The atomic bomb epicentre is in the suburb of Urakami, about 2½ km north of JR Nagasaki station.

The tourist information office (☎ 0958-23-3631) in JR Nagasaki station can assist with finding accommodation, although you may have to be a little bit persistent. The Nagasaki Prefectural Tourist Federation (☎ 0958-26-9407) is opposite (the walkway leads into the prefectural office building at the upstairs level, through the exhibition of local crafts and manufactures). An information computer in the station displays information (in Japanese and English) about attractions, hotels and restaurants and even prints out a map.

A-Bomb Site 原爆落下中心地

Urakami, the epicentre of the atomic explosion, is today a prosperous, peaceful suburb with modern shops, restaurants, cafes and even a couple of love hotels just a few steps from the epicentre. Nuclear ruin seems a long way away. The Matsuyama tram stop, the eighth stop north of JR Urakami station on tram routes 1 or 3, is near the site.

The Epicentre The Hypocentre Park has a black stone column marking the exact point above which the bomb exploded. Nearby are bomb-blasted relics including a section of the wall of the Urakami Cathedral and a buckled water tower.

A-Bomb Museum The new Gembaku Shiryōkan, or A-Bomb Museum, opened in April 1996, and is a vast improvement on the old International Cultural Center. Everybody should visit this reminder of the horror of nuclear destruction – it is quite a chilling experience. Entry is ¥200. It is open daily from 8.30 am to 5 pm.

Peace Park North of the Hypocentre Park is Heiwa-kōen (Peace Park) presided over by the Nagasaki Peace Statue, which – good intentions aside – is a monstrosity of immense proportions. At the time of the explosion, the park was the site of the Urakami Prison and every occupant of the prison – prisoners and warders – was killed instantly. An annual antinuclear protest is held at the park on 9 August.

Urakami Cathedral The original Urakami Cathedral, the largest church in the east, was completed in 1914 and flattened in 1945. Relics from the cathedral are displayed in the Hypocentre Park. The replacement cathedral was completed in 1959.

Other Relics The 'One-legged Torii' (a *torii* is an entranceway to a Shinto shrine) is 850m south-east of the epicentre. The blast knocked down one side of the entrance arch to the Sanno Shinto-gū Shrine but the other leg still stands to this day.

Dr Nagai Takashi devoted himself to the treatment of bomb victims until he himself died in 1951 from the after effects of the bomb; his small hut is preserved as a memorial.

Nagasaki Station Area

26 Martyrs Memorial A few minutes' walk from JR Nagasaki station on Nishi-zaka Hill is a memorial wall with reliefs of the 26 Christians crucified in 1597. In this, Japan's most brutal crackdown on Christianity, six of those crucified were Spanish friars, the other 20 were Japanese and the two youngest were boys aged 12 and 13. The memorial dates from 1962 and behind it is an interesting museum with displays about Christianity in the area; entry is ¥250. The museum is open from 9 am to 6 pm daily (closes an hour earlier from December to February).

Fukusai-ji Zen Temple Although Fukusai-ji is not on any list of architectural or cultural gems, this unique construction, also known as the Nagasaki Kannon Universal Temple, shouldn't be missed. In fact you can't miss it, since the temple building is in the form of a huge turtle, carrying on its back an 18m-high figure of the goddess Kannon. It faces JR Nagasaki station from near the 26 Martyrs Memorial. Inside, a Foucault Pendulum (a device which demonstrates the rotation of the earth on its tilted axis) hangs from near the top of the hollow statue. Only St Petersburg and Paris have larger examples of these pendulums.

The original temple was built in 1628 but was completely burnt down by the A-bomb fire. The replacement, totally unlike the original of course, was built in 1979. A bell tolls from the temple at 11.02 am daily, the exact time of the explosion. Entry is ¥200.

Shōfuku-ji Temple Shōfuku-ji, not to be confused with Sōfuku-ji Temple, is near the Nagasaki Youth Hostel and JR Nagasaki station. The temple gardens are particularly pleasant and contain an arched stone gate dating from 1657 and moved here from the old Jingū-ji Temple outside the city in 1886. The main building, of typical Chinese style, was reconstructed in 1715. Almost adjacent to the temple is the Kanzan-ji Temple, with the biggest camphor tree in Nagasaki.

Suwa-jinja Shrine 諏訪神社

The Okunchi Festival (7-9 October), with its dragon dance, is Nagasaki's most important annual celebration and is centred at this shrine. The Suwa-jinja Shrine was originally established in 1555, and although it is mostly new, its wooded hilltop setting is attractive. Tram lines 3, 4 and 5 all run to the Suwa-jinja-mae stop, close to the shrine.

Sōfuku-ji Temple 崇福寺

An Ōbaku (the third largest Zen sect after Rinzai and Sōtō) temple, and one of Nagasaki's most important, the Sōfuku-ji dates from 1629 and has a fine gateway which was built in China and brought to Japan for reassembling in 1696. Inside the temple, you can admire a great bell from 1647 and a huge cauldron used to prepare food for victims of a famine in 1680. The temple is open from 8 am to 5 pm and entry is ¥150.

Temple Row

The path between Sōfuku-ji and Kōfuku-ji temples is lined with a series of lesser temples. Just down the road from Sōfuku-ji, steep steps lead up to **Daijo-ji**, behind the huge Kowloon Restaurant. The entrance is the most interesting part; it's now used as a preschool.

Almost at the bottom of the road, turn right and take a few steps to the **Hosshin-ji Temple bell**. Cast in 1483, it's the oldest temple bell in Nagasaki. Climb up the stairs to the large Kuroganemochi tree at the entrance to Daion-ji Temple. Follow the road to the left of the temple to the grave of Matsudaira Zushonokami. He had been magistrate of Nagasaki for a year when, in 1808, the British warship HMS *Phaeton*

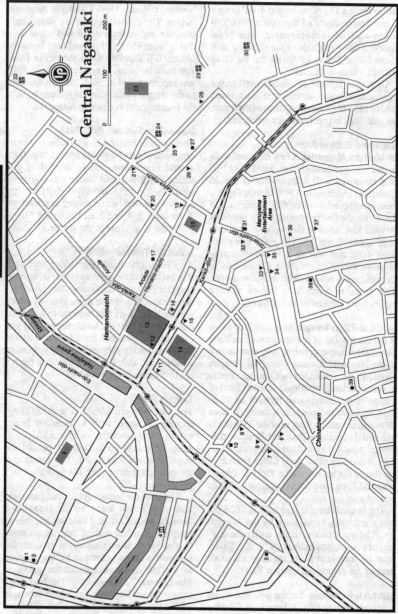

Central Nagasaki

0   100   200 m

KYŪSHŪ

KYŪSHŪ

sailed into Nagasaki Harbour and seized two Dutch hostages. The British and Dutch were on opposite sides in the Napoleonic War at that time. Unable to oppose the British, Zushonokami capitulated to their demands for supplies, then committed *seppuku* (suicide by disembowelment).

A short distance further on, turn down the path to **Kotai-ji Temple**; it's a favourite with local artists and has a notable bell dating from 1702. Again, the grounds are used by a pre-school. Continuing towards Kōfuku-ji, you come to **Chosho-ji** and **Ema-ji** temples, both pleasant escapes from the hustle of modern Japan. Nagasaki's temple row does not end with the Kōfuku-ji, there are several temples beyond it. Only the major temples at the beginning and end of the row charge admission.

Kōfuku-ji Temple 興福寺

The final temple along the temple-row walk, Kōfuku-ji dates from the 1620s and has always had strong Chinese connections. The temple is noted for its lawns and cycad palms and for the Chinese-influenced architecture of the main hall. Like the Sōfuku-ji, it is an Ōbaku Zen temple. Opening hours are from 8 am to 5 pm; entry is ¥200.

Megane-bashi Bridge 眼鏡橋中島川

Parallel to the temple row is the Nakajima-gawa Stream, crossed by a picturesque collection of bridges. At one time, each bridge was the distinct entranceway to a separate temple. The best known of the bridges is Megane-bashi (Spectacles Bridge), so called because if the water is at the right height, the arches and their reflection in the water come together to create a 'spectacles' effect. The double-arched stone bridge was built in 1634 but in 1982 a typhoon flood washed away all the bridges along the stream. The Megane-bashi has been meticulously rebuilt.

Maruyama Area 丸山周辺
The Shian-bashi tram stop marks the site of the Shian-bashi Bridge over which pleasure seekers would cross into the Maruyama quarter. The bridge and the elegant old brothels are long gone but this is still the entertainment area of Nagasaki. During Japan's long period of isolation from the west, the Dutch – cordoned off at their Dejima trading post – were only allowed contact with Japanese trading partners and courtesans. It's said that fortunes were made as much from smuggling as from the world's oldest profession.

In between the bars, restaurants and clubs, Maruyama still has a few reminders of those old days. A walk up from Shian-bashi to where the first road forks leads to the Fukusaya Castella Cake Shop, an old *kasutera* (sponge cake) shop where the cake recipe is said to have come from the Portuguese. An elegantly wrapped package of this traditional Nagasaki delicacy costs from ¥600.

Turn left at this junction, pass the police post and you come to the driveway entrance to Kagetsu, now an elegant and expensive restaurant, but at one time an even more elegant and expensive brothel.

Dejima Museum 出島資料館
The old Dutch trading enclave is long gone, swallowed up by new buildings and land reclamation to the point where it is now well inland from the sea. From the mid-17th century until 1855, this small isolated community was Japan's only contact with the western world and fortunes were made by traders here in the exchange of Japanese crafts for western medicine and technology. The small museum near the old site of Dejima has exhibits on the Dutch and other foreign contact with Nagasaki. It's open from 9 am to 5 pm daily except Monday;

entry is free. Across the road in the museum yard is an outdoor model of Dejima. Attempts to reconstruct the trading post have fallen foul of local landowners.

Chinatown Area 新地
Theoretically, during Japan's long period of seclusion, Chinese traders were just as circumscribed in their movements as the Dutch, but in practice, they were relatively free to come and go from their compound. Only a couple of buildings remain from the old area, but Nagasaki still has an energetic Chinese community which has had a great influence on Nagasaki's culture, festivals and cuisine.

Dutch Slopes オランダ坂
The gently inclined flagstoned streets known as the Dutch Slopes or 'Oranda-zaka' were once lined with wooden Dutch houses. To reach them, take a tram to the Shimin-Byōin-mae stop or walk there from the Dejima Museum or Glover Garden.

Confucian Shrine & Historical Museum of China 孔子廟・中国歴代博物館
Behind the gaudily coloured Confucian Shrine is the Historical Museum of China with exhibits on loan from the Beijing Museum of History. The original building dates from 1893 but was destroyed in the fires following the A-bomb explosion. The Confucian Shrine, near the Dutch Slopes, is also known as the Kōshi-myō-tojinkan; entry is ¥515. It's open daily. To get to the museum and shrine, see under Glover Garden, following.

Glover Garden グラバー園
At the southern end of Nagasaki, a number of the former homes of the city's pioneering Meiji period (1868-1912) European residents have been reassembled in this hillside garden. The series of moving stairways up the hill, plus the fountains, goldfish and announcements, give it the air of a cultural Disneyland, but the houses are attractive, the history is interesting, and the views across Nagasaki are superb.

The garden takes its name from Thomas

Glover (1838-1911), the best known of the expatriate community. This amazingly energetic Scot seemed to have time to dabble in half a dozen fields at once. Glover's arms-importing operations played an important part in the Meiji Restoration; he built the first railway line in Japan and he even helped establish the first modern shipyard from which Nagasaki's Mitsubishi shipyard is a direct descendant.

The best way to explore the hillside garden is to take the walkways to the top and then walk back downhill. At the top of the park is the **Mitsubishi No 2 Dock building** with displays about the city's important shipyard. Going down the hill you come to the **Walker House**, the **Ringer and Alt houses** and finally the **Glover House**.

Halfway down the hill, above the Glover House, is the renowned statue of the Japanese opera singer Miura Tamaki. The statue is often referred to as Madame Butterfly although, of course, she was a purely fictitious character. Puccini, the Italian composer of *Madame Butterfly*, is also honoured here with a relief made, so the inscription goes, of Italian marble. You exit the garden through the **Nagasaki Traditional Performing Arts Museum**, which has a display of dragons and floats used in the colourful Okunchi Festival.

Entry is ¥600. The park is open from 8 am to 6 pm (March to November) and from 8.30 am to 5 pm (December to February). Glover Garden, the Historical Museum of China and the Ōura Church (see below) are all near the end of tram Route 5; get off at the Ōura-Tenshudō-shita tram stop.

Ōura Catholic Church 大浦天主堂

Just below Glover Garden is this prettily situated church, built between 1864 and 1865 for Nagasaki's new foreign community. Soon after its opening, a group of Japanese came to the church and announced that Christianity had been maintained among the Urakami community throughout the 250 years it had been banned in Japan. Unfortunately, despite Japan's newly opened doors to the west, Christianity was still banned for the Japanese and when this news leaked out, thousands of Urakami residents were exiled to other parts of Japan, where many of them died before Christianity was finally legalised in 1872. The church is dedicated to the 26 Christians crucified in 1597 and has beautiful stained-glass windows. It's open from 8 am to 5.45 pm (8.30 am to 4.45 pm in winter) and entry is ¥250.

Jūrokuban-kan Mansion 十六番館

The Jūrokuban-kan Mansion near the garden has displays depicting Nagasaki's Dutch and Portuguese history in an 1860 building used by the first US diplomatic mission to the city. Entry is ¥500; it's open daily from 8.30 am to 5 pm.

History Museum 歴史民俗資料館

Housed in the 1908 Hong Kong & Shanghai Bank building near the Ōura Church, this museum has a mildly interesting collection of historical items. Some of them relate to telegraph lines, a subject of limited interest to the average punter. The old bank was the point from which Japan was first linked with the outside world by telegraph, via Shanghai, in 1871.

Mt Inasa-yama Lookout 稲佐山展望台

From the western side of the harbour, a cablecar ascends to the top of 332m-high Mt Inasa-yama, offering superb views over Nagasaki, particularly at night. It costs ¥550 one way and the cablecar operates every 20 minutes from 9 am to 10 pm in summer and from 9 am to 5 pm in winter. Bus Nos 3 or 4 leave from outside JR Nagasaki station; get off at the Ropeway-mae stop. For the return trip, take a No 30 or No 40 bus.

Siebold House シーボルト邸

Near Shin-Nakagawamachi tram stop is the site of Dr Siebold's house. The doctor is credited with being an important force behind the introduction of western medicine and scientific learning to Japan between 1823 and 1829.

KYŪSHŪ

Special Events

Nagasaki's major annual event is the Okunchi Festival (7-9 October), featuring Chinese-influenced dragon dances and parades. The festival centres around the Suwa-jinja Shrine (although tourists are not allowed in there) and there are displays concerning the festival at the Glover Garden.

Places to Stay

Nagasaki has a wide range of accommodation possibilities, from the love hotels clustered around the A-bomb site to the more up-market hotels of the Glover Garden area.

Youth Hostels There are three youth hostels in Nagasaki. The *Nagasaki Youth Hostel* (☎ 0958-23-5032) has 122 beds at ¥2800 and is within walking distance of JR Nagasaki station; it's well signposted in English. It's closed from 29 December to 3 January.

The *Oranda-zaka Youth Hostel* (☎ 0958-22-2730) is south of the centre on the hilly Dutch Slopes street and can be reached by

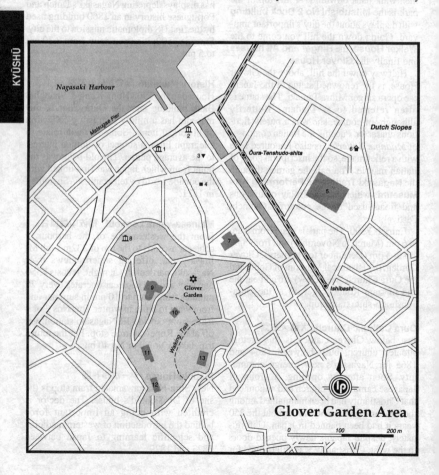

Glover Garden Area

tram No 5; get off at the Shimin-Byōin-mae stop. Beds are ¥2400.

The *Uragami-ga-Oka Youth Hostel* (☎ 0958-47-8473) is around 10 minutes west of Ōhashi and Matsuyama tram stops. There are 56 beds at ¥3000.

Minshuku & Ryokan Central Nagasaki, obviously the best place to be based, has a couple of affordable ryokan. Pick of the pack is *Nishiki-sō* (☎ 0958-26-6371), a delightful, creaky old building with fabulous views over Nagasaki. It's close to Maruyama-kōen Park and per person costs are ¥4000. *Miyuki-sō* (☎ 0958-21-3487), five minutes north of the Maruyama entertainment district, has singles/doubles for ¥3800/8000. Slightly more expensive, but still a great deal, the clean and friendly *Fukumoto Ryokan* (☎ 0958-21-0478) has singles/doubles for ¥4500/9000.

Minshuku Tanpopo (☎ 0958-61-6230), a Japanese Inn Group member, is north of JR Nagasaki station and near the A-bomb site. Get off at the Matsuyama tram stop or JR Urakami station, cross the river, and walk to the street with a petrol station. Follow that street, turn left at the first junction and take the right side of the fork. Rooms are ¥4000 (singles) or ¥3500 per person in double or triple rooms.

The more expensive options include the *Terada Inn* (☎ 0958-22-6178), five minutes walk south of JR Nagasaki station; it has rooms from ¥8000. To get there, take the first left after Gotō-machi tram stop, turn left again and look out for it on the left. South of JR Nagasaki station in the central city area, the *Sakamoto-ya Bekkan* (☎ 0958-26-8211) is an old and very well-kept place costing from ¥14,000 to ¥44,000 per person including meals.

Hotels Hotels in Nagasaki include the following:

Nagasaki Station Area There are less business hotels around the station area than you generally find in other Japanese cities. Just opposite the station, the *Nishi-kyūshū Dai-Ichi Hotel* (☎ 0958-21-1711) charges from ¥6200/9600 for singles/doubles. For a cramped cheapie, directly behind the Nishi-kyūshū Dai-Ichi Hotel is the *Capsule Inn Nagasaki* (☎ 0958-21-1099). A capsule for the night is ¥2800. For basic business hotel accommodation, try the *Business Royal Hotel* (☎ 0958-27-0488), which has singles at ¥5500 and twins at ¥9800. The expensive *Hotel New Nagasaki* (☎ 0958-26-8000) has doubles and twins from ¥23,000.

Central Nagasaki Near the Maruyama

KYŪSHŪ

1	History Museum 歴史民俗資料館	5	Confucian Shrine; Historical Museum of China 孔子廟	9	Glover House グラバー邸
2	Telegraph Office Museum Annex (Site of Sagarimatsu Customs House) 郵便局資料館	6	Oranda-zaka Youth Hostel オランダ坂ユースホステル	10	Walker House ワーカ邸
3	Shikai-rō 四海楼	7	Ōura Catholic Church 大浦天主堂	11	Ringer House リンガ邸
4	Nagasaki Tōkyū Hotel 長崎東急ホテル	8	Nagasaki Traditional Performing Arts Museum 十六番館	12	Alt House オルト邸
				13	Mitsubishi No 2 Dock Building 旧三菱第2ドックハウス

entertainment area, the central *Holiday Inn* (☎ 0958-28-1234) has singles/doubles from ¥8500/16,000. The *Nagasaki Grand Hotel* (☎ 0985-23-1234) is also close to the central entertainment and business areas and has singles from ¥9000 to ¥9500, doubles and twins from ¥15,000 to ¥23,000 as well as a very popular beer garden.

A little further back towards the harbour is the *Harbour Inn Nagasaki* (☎ 0958-27-1111). This is a comfortable, modern, business hotel with singles/doubles from ¥6570/11,330. Next door is the *Hotel Ibis* (☎ 0958-24-2171), another economical business hotel, with singles/doubles at ¥5700/10,000. Closer again to the harbour is the *Newport Business Hotel* (☎ 0958-21-0221), with singles from ¥4900, doubles and twins from ¥9000. Reception is on the 4th floor.

South of the Holiday Inn, where the entertainment area merges into the Chinatown area, is the *Nagasaki Washington Hotel* (☎ 0958-28-1211). Rooms cost from ¥7800 to ¥25,500 in this more expensive business hotel.

Glover Garden Area The *Nagasaki Tōkyū Hotel* (☎ 0958-25-1501), just below Glover Garden, is typical of the more expensive hotels in the Tōkyū chain. Singles cost from ¥11,000 to ¥12,000, doubles from ¥20,000.

Places to Eat

Like Yokohama and Kōbe, Nagasaki has the reputation of being a culinary crossroads. The city's diverse influences come together in shippoku-ryōri, a banquet-style offering (generally you need at least four diners) that rolls together Chinese, Japanese and Portuguese influences. Champon, the local rāmen speciality, is less expensive but probably overrated unless you're a fan of shredded cabbage. Sara-udon is the stir-fried equivalent.

Hamano-machi The best area for ferreting out restaurants is not on the Hamano-machi arcade, but on the sidestreets that run north of it. The *Garde Pizza House*, a block north of the arcade, has no less than 54 varieties of pizza on offer – all at ¥700/1050/1400 for small/medium/large. The restaurant has an English menu. If it looks boarded up during the day, try it again in the evening.

Around the corner from Garde Pizza is *Bharata Restaurant*, an Indian restaurant on the 2nd floor of the Yasaka St building. It can be hard to find even though the name is in English outside. It offers excellent South Indian thalis for ¥1250 or tandoori and curry dishes from ¥800. Bharata is closed on Monday. Back on Kankō-dōri, opposite a KFC, is *Nanak* (☎ 0958-27-7900), another fine Indian restaurant with friendly Indian staff. The Bombay Course, a combination of tandoori, curry, butter naan, salad and a drink, is a good deal at ¥2300.

Nearby, on Kajiya-machi, is *Ginrei Restaurant* (☎ 0958-21-2073), a well-known western-style restaurant (look for the ivy outside) that has recently been treated to a face lift. It specialises in steaks, but curries and so on are also available at prices from around ¥800.

The *Hamakatsu Restaurant* serves a variety of local specialities including a relatively inexpensive shippoku, although that still means a cost of about ¥4500 per person. There's an illustrated menu and the downstairs area is cheaper than upstairs. A little further up the street is the huge Chinese *Kowloon Restaurant*.

Maruyama In among the pachinko parlours and bars along Shianbashi-dōri you'll find an *Italian Tomato* pasta specialist (dishes from ¥1000) and the *Izakaya Tai Shōgun* (☎ 0958-25-7887). For the latter you will need to be able to find your way around a Japanese izakaya menu (see the Food section in the Facts for the Visitor chapter), but adventurous souls will find the effort worth it. Most dishes range from ¥500 to ¥700.

At the end of Shianbashi-dōri the road forks; turn left, walk past the police post and at the far end of the square is the entrance to *Kagetsu* (☎ 0958-22-0191), a shippoku restaurant with a history that stretches back to 1642. At one time it was a high-class brothel. Today it's still high-class; count on ¥20,000 per person.

The *Fukusaya Castella Cake Shop* was established in 1624. It's in a charming traditional building, and sells its handmade cakes in gift-ready packaging. The best of the cakes – castella ichi-gō or ōranda kēki ichi-gō – cost ¥1400, but there are also cheaper versions.

Chinatown During Japan's long period of isolation from the west, Nagasaki was a conduit not only for Dutch trade and culture but also for the trade and culture of the Chinese. Today that influence can be seen in the city's many Chinese temples and restaurants. The food is not exactly authentic, but it's still good.

Popular Chinese restaurants around the Nagasaki Washington Hotel include *Saiko, Kyōka-en, Chūka-en* and *Kōzan-rō*. These places tend to be on the pricey side, so if you're trying to keep your costs down look out for some of the smaller restaurants operating in the Chinatown area.

The *Shikai-rō Restaurant* is a Nagasaki institution; it's a huge building which is able to accommodate over 1000 diners on five floors. The restaurant claims to be the creator of the popular champon noodles. There's an English menu but last orders are taken at 8 pm.

Other Areas There are a number of interesting possibilities in other areas of the city, particularly between Hamano-machi and JR Nagasaki station. *Harbin Restaurant* is a Russian/French restaurant with an English menu, white tablecloths, heavy cutlery, dark wood and excellent food. At lunch time you can select from a long menu offering a starter, main course, bread and butter and tea or coffee all for ¥1300 to ¥1600 – a real bargain. At night, main courses cost from ¥1700 to ¥5000.

Things to Buy

There are displays of local crafts and products directly opposite JR Nagasaki station on the same floor as the Prefectural Tourist Federation. You'll find lots of shops along the busy Hamano-machi shopping arcade. For Japanese visitors, the Portuguese-influenced kasutera sponge cake is *the* present to take back from Nagasaki, and Fukusaya is the place to buy it – see Maruyama in Nagasaki's Places to Eat section for details.

Please ignore Nagasaki's tortoise-shell crafts: turtles need their shells more than humans do.

Getting There & Away

Air There are flights between Nagasaki and Kagoshima, Tokyo (Haneda airport), Osaka and Okinawa as well as flights to and from a variety of lesser locations.

Train By local train, it takes about 2½ to three hours from Hakata to Nagasaki on the JR Nagasaki line. The fare is ¥2470; add ¥1650 if you want to travel by limited express (*tokkyū*). Kyoto to Nagasaki takes about six hours (with a change at Hakata, the terminus for the shinkansen). To get to Kumamoto from Nagasaki, take a JR Nagasaki main line train north to JR Tōsu station (two hours) and a Kagoshima main line train from there (one hour).

Bus Regular buses operate between Nagasaki and Kumamoto. The three hour trip costs ¥3600 but note the following section about the interesting route via the Shimabara-hantō Peninsula. From the Ken-ei bus station opposite JR Nagasaki station, buses go to Unzen (two hours 20 minutes, ¥1750) from stand No 3 (express buses from stand No 2), Shimabara (two hours, ¥1850) from stand No 5, Sasebo (1½ hours, ¥1400) from stand No 2, Fukuoka (three hours, ¥2900) from stand No 8, Kumamoto (three hours, ¥3600) and Kokura (Kitakyūshū) from stand No 6 and sightseeing buses from stand No 12.

Night buses for Osaka, Kōbe and Nagoya leave from both the Ken-ei bus station and the Nagasaki Highway bus station next to the Irie-machi tram stop. There are also buses running to Sasebo and the Holland Village from here.

Hitching Hitching out of Nagasaki is easier if you take a train or bus to Isahaya and start from there.

Getting Around

The Airport Nagasaki's airport is about 40 km from the city and is situated on an artificial island. Buses to the airport (one hour,

KYŪSHŪ

¥1150) operate from stand No 4 in the Ken-ei bus station opposite JR Nagasaki station.

Bus Buses cover a greater area (reaching more of the sights) but are, of course, much harder to decipher than the trams. Nagasaki is compact enough to explore on foot.

Tram The best way of getting around Nagasaki is on the excellent and easy to use tram service. There are four colour-coded routes numbered 1, 3, 4 and 5 (there's no No 2 for some reason). Most stops are signposted in English. It costs ¥100 to travel anywhere in town or you can get a ¥500 all-day pass for unlimited travel. The passes are available from the shop beside the station information counter, from the Prefectural Tourist Federation across the road or from major hotels. On a one-ride ticket you can only transfer to another line at the Tsukimachi stop. The trams stop around 11 pm.

HUIS TEN BOSCH　ハウステンボス

An hour north of Nagasaki, near the town of Sasebo, the development that began as the Biopark and grew into Nagasaki Holland Village has now expanded into Huis ten Bosch, an environment-friendly Dutch town covering 158 hectares. It's easy to scoff at sights like this which whiff of the Japanese theme park obsession but, one thing is certain, the developers have spared no expense.

The idea was to create an 'eco-city' with a Dutch theme (the Nagasaki, Dejima connection). The result is a sanitised version of the Netherlands with a round-the-clock, computer-controlled energy conservation and waste recycling system. Like 40% of the Netherlands, the town is built on reclaimed land. Dutch expertise was employed in building dykes and creating six km of canals; they are renewed and cleansed using locks in combination with the ocean tides.

Huis ten Bosch (pronounced 'house-ten-bosh') means House in the Woods. It is the name of the Dutch royal family's residence, a complete replica of which is the centrepiece of the town. Although this *is* a theme park, there are houses with price tags from

US$570,000 to US$3,570,000; by 1998 the developers plan to have accommodation for 10,000 people. The town also has banks, travel agencies, a post office, hospital and a university (with 20 Dutch foreign-exchange students studying Japanese).

The town divides into Breukelen, with its windmills, castle and also the East-India Company attraction; Nieuwstad, with its amazing Mysterious Escher building complete with a 3D movie using MC Escher graphics and, among other attractions, the Horizon Theatre, which re-creates a Dutch fairy tale about the sea; Museumstad, which has five museums; Binnenstad, which is the shopping and entertainment area, and even has a cheese market; Utrecht, the restaurant area with a plaza with the 105m Domtoren, a replica of the Netherlands' tallest church tower; Spakenburg, with its Great Voyage Theatre, Tall Ship Museum and Porcelain Museum along with some fine restaurants; and finally Paleis Huis ten Bosch and the Forest Park.

Nagasaki Holland Village is still running. It's a 40 minute shuttle cruiser ride (¥600 including entry to the village) from Huis ten Bosch. Five minutes by bus from Holland Village is the Biopark. It's open from 9 am to 5.30 pm (6.30 pm during the summer); entry is ¥1250.

Costs

If you just want to wander around and take a look at the place, a general 'passport' costs ¥3900, ¥3200 for children. This will get you into the free attractions, but there aren't too many of these. A Prince 10 passport gives you 10 'stars' (entry to most attractions is two to four stars) and costs ¥4800, ¥4000 for children. A King 30 gives you 30 stars, which would cover just about everything, and costs ¥5600. Finally, the Great Voyage passport gives you 35 stars, and a cruise shuttle ride and entry to Holland Village for ¥6200.

Places to Stay

It's actually possible to stay in Huis ten Bosch – if you have the money. There's talk of having a camping ground available by the time it is completely finished in 1998, but in the meantime, the town's hotels are probably too expensive for most travellers. They include the *Hotel Europe*, with standard double rooms from ¥35,000; *Hotel Den Haag*, with economy doubles from ¥31,000; *Hotel Amsterdam*, with standard triples from ¥38,000; and *Forest Villa*, with four-person cottages from ¥53,000. Bookings can be made by ringing NHV Hotels (☎ 0956-27-0270).

Places to Eat
There's an enormous range of places to eat in Huis ten Bosch. Possibilities range from burgers to excellent Italian, Indian and Dutch cuisine. *Patisserie*, in Utrecht, is devoted to cheesecakes.

Getting There & Away
Both trains and buses take a little over an hour from Nagasaki, leave approximately once an hour, and cost around ¥1300 one way or ¥2400 return. Buses run from the Ken-en bus station opposite the railway station. There are also direct buses from Kumamoto and Fukuoka, as well as a special Huis ten Bosch train from Fukuoka. From Nagasaki airport there is a direct ferry to Huis ten Bosch (45 minutes, ¥1400).

Getting Around
Huis ten Bosch has the full complement of olde worlde transport: boats cruising the canals, 'classical buses' trundling the streets, horse carts cantering here and there, as well as bicycle hire for ¥1000 per day.

Shimabara-hantō Peninsula
島原半島

A popular route to or from Nagasaki is via the Shimabara-hantō Peninsula using the regular car ferry service between Shimabara and Misumi, south of Kumamoto. Bus services connect with the ferry, and tour buses also operate directly between Nagasaki and

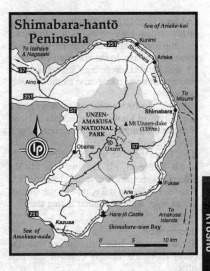

Kumamoto. The major attractions on the peninsula are Unzen and Shimabara itself.

It was the uprising on the Shimabara Peninsula (1637-38) which led to the suppression of Christianity in Japan and the country's subsequent two centuries of seclusion from the west. The peasant rebels made their final valiant stand against overwhelming odds (37,000 versus 120,000) at Hara-jō Castle, almost at the southern tip of the peninsula. The warlords even chartered a Dutch man-of-war to bombard the hapless rebels, who held out for 80 days but were eventually slaughtered. Little remains of the castle.

In June 1991, 1359m Mt Unzen-dake erupted after laying dormant for 199 years. The explosion left at least 38 people dead. Nearby villages were evacuated and the lava flow reached the outskirts of Shimabara. The once popular ascent of Mt Fugen was still prohibited at the time of writing.

UNZEN 雲仙
The Japanese enthusiasm for hot springs runs riot once again in this onsen town. Unfortunately the bubbling and spurting 'hells' or *jigoku* are marred by the spaghetti tangle of pipes taking the hot water to hotels

and spas. (Jigoku are hot springs for looking at rather than bathing in.) A few centuries ago, the boiling hot water was put to a much more sinister use. In the era when Christianity was banned, dropping Christians into a boiling pool was a favourite method of execution.

In the late 19th century, Unzen became a popular resort for western residents of Hong Kong and Shanghai, and its acclaimed golf course (the oldest in Japan) dates from that time. From the town there are popular walks to Mt Kinugasa, Mt Takaiwa and Mt Yadake. Outside the town, reached via the Nita Pass, is Mt Fugen-dake, part of the Unzen-dake range, with its popular hiking trail.

Information
There's a tourist information office with displays about the vicinity opposite the post office.

Places to Stay
Unzen has numerous hotels and ryokan (most of them very pricey) and two kokuminshukusha (people's lodges) with nightly costs from around ¥7000 including dinner and breakfast. They are the *Seiun-sō* (☎ 0957-73-3273) and also the *Yurin-sō* (☎ 0957-73-3355). *Unzen Kokumin Kyūka Mura* (☎ 0957-74-9131) has rooms with two meals for ¥7500 per person.

The *Unzen Kankō Hotel* (☎ 0957-73-3263) dates back to the '30s, when it was a summer retreat for expatriate gaijin. It still has character. Rates of around ¥17,000 with meals apply.

Getting There & Away
Bus Direct buses between Nagasaki and Unzen take less than 2½ hours and cost ¥1750. Buses run more frequently from the town of Isahaya, which is 40 minutes by train (¥560) from Nagasaki on the Nagasaki line. From Isahaya, buses take 1½ hours and cost ¥1200. From Unzen, it takes 50 minutes by bus to Shimabara. The bus to Nita Pass, the starting point for the Mt Fugen walk, operates regularly from the Unzen bus station (30 minutes, ¥300). There's a ¥700 toll fee for

cars. The No 262 Nagasaki-Kumamoto tour bus goes via Unzen.

MT FUGEN WALK　普賢岳
The Mt Fugen walk is no longer feasible since the volcano became active again in 1991. It is still possible, though, to head up to the summit of 1333m Mt Myōken by cablecar (¥1200 return). It may be worth asking the tourist information offices in Nagasaki and Unzen whether walks in the area have again been declared safe, but the chances are that it will be some time before this happens.

SHIMABARA　島原
Shimabara is the port for ferries to Misumi, south of Kumamoto, and has a rebuilt castle and other attractions. The ferry terminal has an information desk.

Shimabara-jō Castle　島原城
The castle, originally built in 1624, played a part in the Shimabara Rebellion in 1637-38 and was rebuilt in 1964 during Japan's nationwide spate of castle reconstruction. It houses a museum of items connected with the Christian uprising. There's also a small sculpture museum in the watch tower with works by Seibo Kitamura, who sculpted the Nagasaki Peace Statue. Entry is ¥300.

Other Attractions
In the Teppo-chō District, north-west of the castle, is a *buke yashiki*, or samurai house. Just south of the town centre, near the Shimatetsu bus station, are carp streams with lots of colourful goldfish. Also south of the town centre, in the Kōtō-ji Temple, is the **Nehan Zō**, or 'Nirvana Statue'. It's the longest reclining Buddha statue in Japan, though by Thai or Burmese reclining-Buddha standards, eight metres isn't all that long.

Places to Stay
The *Shimabara Youth Hostel* (☎ 0957-62-4451) costs ¥2500 per person. There's also a variety of hotels. The *Ajisai Inn* (☎ 0957-64-

1101) has singles/doubles from ¥5600/8200. It's just south of the castle.

Getting There & Away
Train & Bus You can reach Shimabara from Nagasaki by bus via Unzen or by rail via Isahaya. JR trains on the Nagasaki line run to Isahaya, where you then connect up with the private Shimabara Tetsudō line to Shimabara. Trains from Isahaya take one hour and cost ¥1280. Shimabara Tetsudō station is a few hundred metres to the east of the castle.

Boat Ferries run 13 to 17 times a day to Misumi and take about an hour. The fare is ¥830 per person or ¥2370 to ¥4840 for a car and driver. From Misumi it's 50 minutes by train or 1½ hours by bus to Kumamoto. Ferries also run to the Amakusa Islands from Shimabara.

Kumamoto-ken 熊本県

KUMAMOTO 熊本
Kumamoto (population 565,000) has one of Japan's finest reconstructed (as opposed to original) castles plus a contender for Japan's 'best garden' title. Add a few lesser temples and shrines, a very active entertainment area and a convenient location whether you're travelling up, down or across the island and a pause in Kyūshū's third largest city becomes a very worthwhile proposition.

Orientation & Information
The JR station is some distance south of Kumamoto's city centre, where you'll find not only offices, banks, hotels, restaurants and the entertainment area but also the big Kumamoto Kōtsū bus centre, the castle and other attractions.

The tourist information office (☎ 096-352-3743) is in front of JR Kumamoto station. Kinokuniya and Nagasaki Books are good bookshops in the central arcades. The Nippon Telegraph & Telephone (NTT) office, for long-distance phone calls, is

Shimabara

0   250   500 m

KYŪSHŪ

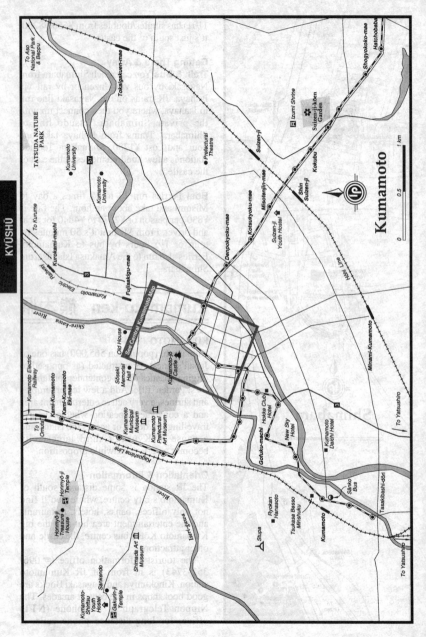

Kumamoto

beside the Kumamoto Kōtsū bus centre. Just south of Kumamoto-jō Castle is the Kumamoto City International Centre, which has CNN news (better than nothing) and recent English magazines – a good place to while away an afternoon if you've been out in the backwoods for a while.

Kumamoto-jō Castle　熊本城

Kumamoto's castle dominates the centre of town. Like many other Japanese castles, it looks superb at night. Although Kumamoto-jō is a modern reproduction, the lack of authenticity is compensated for by the castle's sheer size and its numerous interesting exhibits and displays. These include a section of the ceremonial boat in which a daimyō and his followers made their regular voyage to the court of Edo.

Kumamoto-jō, built between 1601 and 1607, was once one of the great castles of feudal Japan. Its architect, Katō Kiyomasa, was considered a master of castle design and some of his ingenious engineering, including slots for dropping stones and other missiles onto attackers, can be seen in the reconstruction. In its prime, the castle had 120 wells, 49 turrets, 18 turret gates, 29 castle gates and a circumference around the outer walls of more than five km.

The steep outer walls with their backward curve were known as *musha-gaeshi* or *nezumi-gaeshi*, which meant that not even a mouse could climb them. The main donjon was entered through the *kuragari mon ato*, or 'gate of dark passage'. Nevertheless, in 1877, during the turmoil of the Satsuma Rebellion, a postscript to the Meiji Restoration, the castle was besieged and burnt in one of the final stands made by samurai warriors against the new order. The rebel samurai held out for 55 days before finally being overcome. (See the Kagoshima section for more on the rebellion and its leader, Saigō Takamori.)

Entry to the castle grounds is ¥200, plus another ¥300 for entry into the castle itself. It's open daily from 8.30 am to 5.30 pm in summer and from 8.30 am to 4.30 pm in winter.

Museums

Beyond the castle are the Kumamoto Prefectural Art Museum (¥250), the Kumamoto Municipal Museum (¥100) and the Kumamoto Traditional Crafts Center (¥190). All of them are open from 9 am to 5 pm and are closed on Monday. The Municipal Museum has a 3D relief map of part of southern Kyūshū. It's quite interesting to see the configuration of Mt Fugen on the Shimabara-hantō Peninsula, Mt Aso and the many other peaks. The crafts centre has an interesting collection of odds and ends including porcelains.

Suizen-ji-kōen Garden　水前寺公園

This fine and relatively extensive garden originated with a temple in 1632. The stroll garden imitates the 53 stations of the Tōkaidō (the old road that linked Tokyo and Kyoto), and the miniature Mt Fuji is instantly recognisable. The Kokin Denju-no-Ma Teahouse was moved here from Kyoto in 1912, and although the building itself is somewhat shoddy, the views across the ornamental lake show the garden at its finest. Turn the other way and you will see the garden at its worst – it's been invaded by souvenir stalls.

The garden is open from 7.30 am to 6 pm from March to October and from 8.30 am to 5 pm the rest of the year; entry is ¥200. The garden actually remains open after hours and entry is then free but only the north gate is open. A Route 2 tram will take you there from JR Kumamoto station or you can take a Route 2 or 3 tram from the central area. Get off at the Suizenji-kōen-mae stop.

Honmyō-ji Temple　本妙寺

To the north-west of the centre, on the hills sloping up from the river, is the temple and mausoleum of Katō Kiyomasa, the architect of Kumamoto's great castle. A steep flight of steps leads up to the mausoleum which was designed to be at the same height as the castle's donjon. There's a treasure house with exhibits concerning Kiyomasa (open from 9 am to 4.30 pm daily except Monday; entry is ¥300). Steps continue up the hill to

KYŪSHŪ

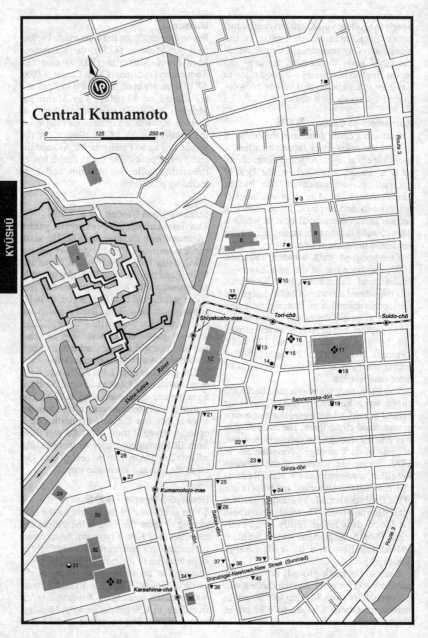

Central Kumamoto

0   125   250 m

KYŪSHŪ

PLACES TO STAY
1 Ryokan Saekya
   栄屋旅館
2 Maruko Hotel
   丸小旅館
6 Kumamoto Castle
   Hotel
   熊本ホテル
   キャッスル
8 Tsukasa Honten
   Hotel
   司本店ホテル
29 Kumamoto Kankō
   Hotel
   熊本観光ホテル
32 Kumamoto
   Kōtsū Centre Hotel
   熊本交通センター
   ホテル
35 Kumamoto Tōkyū Inn
   熊本東急イン

PLACES TO EAT
3 Capricciosa
9 Mr Donut
15 KFC
20 Swiss Konditerei
21 Baden Baden

22 Yatai
   自由市場
24 Blue Seal Ice Cream
25 Deutsche Hand-
   Made Sausage
34 Lotteria
36 Yōrōnotaki
   養老の滝
37 Higokko Robatayaki
   肥後っ子
38 Kyōya Noodle Shop
   京屋そば
39 McDonald's
40 KFC

OTHER
4 Kumamoto
   Traditional Crafts
   Centre
   熊本伝統工芸館
5 Kumamoto-jō Castle
   熊本城
7 Nagasaki Books
   長崎書店
10 Rock Balloon
11 Post Office
   郵便局

12 Municipal Office;
   City Hall
   市役所
13 Bar Jail
14 Tower Records
16 Parco Department
   Store; Body Shop
   パルコ
17 Tsuruya Department
   Store
   鶴屋
18 Lafcadio Hearn
   House
19 Shark Attack
23 Kinokuniya Bookshop
   紀伊国屋書店
26 Suntory Shot Bar
27 JAL
28 Kumamoto City
   International Centre
   国際交流会館
30 NTT
31 Kumamoto
   Kōtsū Bus Centre
   熊本交通バス
   センター
33 Iwataya Isetan
   Department Store
   岩田屋伊勢丹

another temple and then a final steep flight leads to the very top, from where there are good views over the town.

Writers' Homes

Right in the centre of town, behind the Tsuruya department store, is the former home of writer Lafcadio Hearn (Koizumi Yagumo). Entry is free but it's not as interesting as his first Japanese residence in Matsue (see Matsue in the Western Honshū chapter). The former home of the Meiji-era novelist Natsume Sōseki is preserved as the Sōseki Memorial Hall. It's just north of the castle and the Traditional Crafts Center.

Tatsuda Nature Park 立田自然公園

The Tatsuda Nature Park with the 1646 Taishō-ji Temple and a famous teahouse is north-east of the centre. The grave of Hosokawa Gracia (1563-1600) is in the temple grounds. She was an early convert to Christianity but her husband had her killed to prevent his enemies from capturing her. To get there, take a Kusunoki-danchi-Musashigaoka-danchi line bus from platform 28 at the Kotsū bus centre to the Tatsuda Shizen-kōen-iriguchi stop.

The **International Folk Art Museum** is half an hour by bus from central Kumamoto or 15 minutes beyond the Tatsuda Park and displays crafts from all over the world.

Other Attractions

Continue up the hill beyond the cheap ryokan and minshuku near JR Kumamoto station, past the large collection of love hotels and you eventually reach the **pagoda** topping the hill. The effort of the climb is rewarded with superb views over the town. Also on this side of town, north of the pagoda and south of the Honmyō-ji Temple, is the privately owned **Shimada Art Museum** (open from 9 am to 5 pm; closed Wednesday).

Places to Stay

Youth Hostels Kumamoto has two hostels. The *Suizen-ji Youth Hostel* (☎ 096-371-9193) is about halfway between the town centre and Suizen-ji-kōen Garden and costs ¥2800 per night. The Misotenjin-mae stop on tram Routes 2 or 3 is close by. The *Kumamoto-Shiritsu Youth Hostel* (☎ 096-352-2441) is west of town, across the Iseri-gawa River, and costs ¥1600 or ¥1800 depending on the time of year. A bus from platform 36 at the Kumamoto Kōtsū bus centre will take you there. It's closed from 28 December to 3 January.

Ryokan & Minshuku The Japanese Inn Group's representative in Kumamoto, the *Minshuku Ryokan Kajita* (☎ 096-353-1546), is run by a family who seem to wish they were doing something else, but other than that it's an OK place to be based for a night or two. Japanese-style rooms without bath cost ¥4000/7600 for singles/doubles. From Kumamoto station, take a bus to the Shinmachi stop; from there it's a five minute walk.

The *Maruko Hotel* (☎ 096-353-1241) is in the town centre, north-east of the castle, and has 47 rooms, nearly all of them Japanese style, from ¥6500/12,000 for singles/doubles. The hotel has been around for 100 years, which makes it one of Kumamoto's oldest. From JR Kumamoto station, take a Route 2 tram and get off at the Tetori-Honcho stop. There's a prominent sign from the covered arcade. One block north of the Maruko Hotel is the pleasant *Ryokan Saekya*

(☎ 096-353-5181), where singles/doubles cost ¥7500/15,000.

Hotels The *Kumamoto Station Hotel* (☎ 096-325-2001) is about two minutes walk from the station, just across the first small river. It's a typical modern business hotel with Japanese and western-style rooms from ¥6000/10,600 for singles/doubles.

The *Hokke Club Hotel* (☎ 096-322-5001), between the railway station and the centre, is another typical business hotel with singles from ¥6300 to ¥6700 and doubles or twins from ¥8800. The *Kumamoto Kōtsū Centre Hotel* (☎ 096-354-1111) is centrally located right above the Kumamoto Kōtsū bus centre and has singles from ¥5700. Reception is on the 3rd floor. Also in the centre of town, the *Kumamoto Tōkyū Inn* (☎ 096-322-0109) is part of the popular Tōkyū chain and has singles/doubles from ¥7300/10,300.

More expensive hotels include the *New Sky Hotel* (☎ 096-354-2111) about midway between the railway station and the town centre. This efficiently run and well-equipped modern hotel has both Japanese and western-style rooms which cost from ¥9500/19,000 for singles/doubles. Overlooking the castle, the *Kumamoto Castle Hotel* (☎ 096-326-3311) has singles from ¥8800 to ¥14,000 and doubles from ¥15,500 to ¥24,000.

Places to Eat

The station area is not particularly good for restaurants, but if you're out this way the best selection is in the station itself. The 2nd floor has a good range of tempura, rāmen and generic western-style restaurants, all with plastic replicas gracing the window spaces. Over in the central part of town, the best advice is to strike off into the side streets that run off the arcades. For the unadventurous, the central arcades carry all the familiar fast-food options.

Just off the Shinshigai arcade is the *Higokko Robatayaki* where you can sit at the bar and select from a wide range of kebabs. The chef will grill the kebabs right in front of you and pass them over the counter on a long paddle, rather like the one used for removing pizzas from a pizza oven. Each spit costs around ¥300 to ¥500.

Just south of this place is *Yōrōnotaki*, a link in a huge and very successful izakaya chain. It has an excellent illustrated menu with everything from pizza to sushi, and prices are very reasonable. Another popular chain with a Kumamoto branch is *Capricciosa*. This chain has its detractors, but the massive servings of Italian food at reasonable prices mean there are queues outside every lunch and dinner time.

Back down the Shimotori arcade is *Kōran-tei*, an excellent Chinese restaurant with some good teishoku deals at lunch time. Try the roast-pork noodle soup (chashū men) for ¥600. Due west of here is *Baden Baden*, a noisy beer hall with a huge selection of izakaya and pub food at good prices. The nearby *Yatai Restaurant* (the kanji (script) announces it as the 'free market') is a youth oriented yaki-niku (fried meat) setup, with reggae music and pitchers of beer.

For the gourmet, Kumamoto's local specialities are raw horsemeat (ba-sushi) and fried lotus root (karashi-renkon), both of which can be sampled in Kumamoto's numerous izakaya. You might also try *Itchō*, in the Kumamoto Castle Hotel. It's an unusually good hotel restaurant with a huge range of local specialities.

Entertainment

Kumamoto has a sprinkling of gaijin haunts if you are in need of a few drinks and some conversation. *Bar Jail*, just west of the northern end of Shimotori arcade, is a peculiarly narrow place with an upstairs area for playing pool, darts and so on, and a box downstairs for dancing in. *Rock Balloon* is a grungier establishment – graffiti and loud sounds. Draught beers cost ¥500 and there's no cover charge. For something unusual, track down *Shark Attack*. It's the only bar we've come across in Japan that has sand (the stuff you usually find on beaches). Monday is movie night. It's on the 8th floor of the Anty Rashon building, which has a couple of hundred other bars in it.

Things to Buy

The Kumamoto Traditional Crafts Center displays local crafts and shows how they're made. *Higo zōgan*, black steel with silver and gold inlaid patterns wrought into a chrysanthemum-like shape, is a renowned local craft. These items range from around ¥5000, though what you'd do with one is hard to say. Another curious local product is the *ohanake kintai*, which is a tiny red head with a little red protruding tongue, the whole affair topped with a black dunce's cap – don't travel without one. Entry to the crafts centre's downstairs shop area is free but it costs ¥190 to see the upstairs exhibits. The tourist office map identifies the centre as the *Industrial Art Museum*; it's just north of the Kumamoto Castle Hotel.

Getting There & Away

There are flights to Kumamoto from Tokyo, Osaka, Nagoya and Naha (Okinawa). The JR Kagoshima line between Hakata and Nishi-Kagoshima runs through Kumamoto and there is also a JR line to Miyazaki on the south-eastern coast. Buses depart from the Kōtsū bus centre for Hakata, taking just over 1½ hours.

See the Shimabara-hantō Peninsula section for details on travel to Nagasaki via Misumi, Shimabara and Unzen. Kumamoto is a popular gateway to Mt Aso (see that section for transport details and the Beppu section for travel across Kyūshū via Mt Aso to Beppu).

Getting Around

The Airport The airport bus service takes nearly an hour between the airport and JR Kumamoto station. It costs ¥670.

Tram Kumamoto has an effective tram service which will get you to most places of interest. On boarding the tram you take a ticket with your starting tram stop number. When you finish your trip a display panel at the front indicates the fare for each starting point. From the railway station to the castle/town centre costs ¥140. Alternatively you can get a ¥500 one-day pass for unlimited travel.

KYŪSHŪ

There are two tram routes. Route 2 starts from near JR Kumamoto station, runs through the town centre and out past the Suizen-ji-kōen Garden. Route 3 starts to the north, near Kami-Kumamoto station and merges with Route 2 just before the centre. Services are frequent, particularly on Route 2.

MT ASO AREA 阿蘇山周辺

In the centre of Kyūshū, halfway from Kumamoto to Beppu, is the gigantic Mt Aso volcano caldera. There have been a series of eruptions over the past 30 million years but the explosion which formed the outer crater about 100,000 years ago must have been a big one. It's around 24 km across the original crater from north to south, 18 km east to west and 80 km in circumference. Inside this huge outer crater there are towns, roads, railways, farms, 100,000 people and a number of smaller volcanoes, some of them still active.

Orientation & Information

Highway Routes 57, 265 and 325 make a circuit of the outer caldera and the JR Hōhi line runs across the northern section. Aso is the main town in the crater but there are other towns including Takamori on the southern side. All the roads running into the centre of the crater and to the five 'modern' peaks within the one huge, ancient, outer peak are toll roads. There's a very helpful and informative tourist office at JR Aso station.

Five Mountains of Aso

Aso-gogaku (Five Mountains of Aso) are the five smaller mountains within the outer rim. They are Mt Eboshi-dake (1337m), Mt Nishima-dake (1238m), Mt Naka-dake (1216m), Mt Neko-dake (1408m) and Mt Taka-dake (1592m). Mt Naka-dake is currently the active volcano in this group. Mt Neko-dake, furthest to the east, is instantly recognisable from its craggy peak but Mt Taka-dake, between Neko-dake and Naka-dake, is the highest.

Mt Naka-dake 中岳

Recently Mt Naka-dake has been very active indeed. The cablecar to the summit of Naka-dake was closed from August 1989 to March 1990 due to eruptions and it had only been opened for a few weeks when the volcano erupted again in April 1990, spewing dust and ash over a large area to the north.

In 1958, when a totally unexpected eruption killed 12 onlookers, concrete 'bomb shelters' were built around the rim for sightseers to take shelter in an emergency. Nevertheless, an eruption in 1979 killed three visitors over a km from the cone in an area which was thought to be safe. This eruption destroyed the cablecar which used to run up the north-eastern slope of the cone, and, although the supports still stand, the cablecar has never been replaced.

When Mt Naka-dake is not misbehaving, the cablecar whisks you up to the summit in just four minutes (¥410 each way). There are departures every eight minutes. The walk to the top takes less than half an hour. The 100m-deep crater varies in width from 400m to 1100m and there's a walk around the southern edge of the crater rim.

Mt Aso Walks

There are plenty of interesting walks around Mt Aso. You can walk all the way to the Aso-nishi cablecar station from the Aso Youth Hostel in about three hours, but for much of the way you'll be forced out onto the side of the road, where there is little protection from careering tour buses and cars. From the top of the cablecar run you can walk around the crater rim to the peak of Mt Naka-dake and on to the top of Mt Taka-dake. From there you can descend either to Sensui-kyō, the bottom station of the cablecar run on the north-eastern side of Naka-dake, or to the road which runs between Taka-dake and Neko-dake. Either road will then take you to Miyaji, the next railway station east from Aso. The direct descent to Sensui-kyō is very steep, so it's easier to continue back from Taka-dake to the Naka-dake rim and then follow the old cablecar route down to Sensui-kyō.

Allow four or five hours from the Aso-nishi cablecar station to Sensui-kyō. Buses

MASON FLORENCE

MASON FLORENCE

MASON FLORENCE

ANTHONY WEERSING

A: Kirishima National Park
B: New Year's offerings,
   Aoshima-jinja Shrine, Kyūshū

C: Monkey with a Coke habit, Beppu
D: Shrine, Kyūshū

MASON FLORENCE

TONY WHEELER

MASON FLORENCE

MASON FLORENCE

MASON FLORENCE

MARTIN MOOS

A	B
C	D
E	F

A: Aftermath of Mt Unzen eruption, 1993
B: Chinoike Jigoku, Beppu
C: Sunrise near Mt Aso
D: A 'wild horse' on Cape Toi, Kyūshū
E: Walking in Aso-kuju National Park
F: Habu snakes, Naha

down to Miyaji are irregular and the downhill walk takes about 1½ hours.

Shorter walks include the interesting ascent of Mt Kijima-dake from the Aso Volcanic Museum. From the top you can descend to the top of the ski lift on the ski field just east of the museum. You can also climb to the top of Mt Eboshi-dake and any of these peaks offer superb views over the whole Aso area. The outer rim of the ancient crater also gives good views from a number of points. Shiroyami-tempodai, a lookout on the Yamanami Highway as it leaves the crater, is one good point; Daikanbō near Uchinomaki Onsen is another.

Aso Volcanic Museum 阿蘇火山博物館

Despite the usual shortage of non-Japanese labelling, the Aso Volcanic Museum will undoubtedly fill a few gaps in the average person's knowledge of volcanoes. There are displays, models and natural history exhibits. An entertaining selection of videos shows various volcanoes around the world strutting their stuff while another film shows what the Aso volcano can do along with scenes of the Aso region through the seasons and local festivals. Entry is ¥820. The museum is open from 9 am to 5 pm daily.

Kusasenri & Mt Komezuka
草千里・米塚山

In front of the museum is the Kusasenri meadow (literally '1000 km of grass'), a grassy meadow in the flattened crater of an ancient volcano. There are two lakes in the meadow. Just off the road which runs from the museum down to the town of Aso is the perfectly shaped small cone of Mt Komezuka, another extinct volcano. The name means 'rice mound', presumably because that's what it looks like.

Aso-jinja Shrine 阿蘇神社

Aso-jinja Shrine is a 20 minute walk north of JR Miyaji station and is dedicated to the 12 gods of Mt Aso.

Places to Stay & Eat

There are over 50 places to stay around Mt Aso including a youth hostel, a collection of places (many of them pensions) at Uchinomaki Onsen, north of Aso, and pensions at Tochinoki Onsen (to the west of the caldera) and the village of Takamori (to the south).

Aso The *Aso Youth Hostel* (☎ 0967-34-0804) is a 15 to 20 minute walk or a three minute bus ride from JR Aso station and costs ¥2000. There's a camping ground further along the road from the hostel. *Aso No Fumoto* (☎ 0967-32-0264) is a good minshuku, conveniently close to JR Aso station, which costs ¥6600 per person with meals, ¥4000 without. *Kokuminshukusha Aso* (☎ 0967-34-0111) is just one minute from the station and costs ¥5800 with meals, ¥3500 without. Similar rates prevail at the *Kokuminshukusha Nakamura* (☎ 0967-34-0317).

Takamori The *Murataya Ryokan Youth Hostel* (☎ 09676-2-0066) costs ¥2600 or ¥2800 depending on the time of year, and is right in Takamori. The *Minami Aso Kokumin Kyūkamura* (☎ 09676-2-2111), a national vacation village, costs from ¥6500 per person with two meals, and from ¥5200 without; it's crowded in July and August.

Just outside Takamori, on the southern side of the ancient crater, is a *pension mura* (pension village) with prices around ¥8000 per person including dinner and breakfast. Pensions include the *Wonderland* (☎ 0967-62-3040), *Cream House* (☎ 0967-62-3090) and *Flower Garden* (☎ 0967-62-3021). (The others don't have their names in English but they're all in one convenient little clump.)

Just out of Takamori towards the kokumin kyūkamura is *Dengaku-no-Sato*, an old farmhouse restaurant where you cook your own kebab-like dengaku on individual hibachi barbecues. The restaurant closes at 7.30 pm and the set meal teishoku is good value for around ¥1600.

Other Places The *YMCA & Youth Hostel Aso Camp* (☎ 0967-35-0124) is near JR Akamizu station, the third stop west of JR Aso station. The cost per night is ¥2000. *Minami Aso Kokuminshukusha* (☎ 0967-67-0078) is near

KYŪSHŪ

KYŪSHŪ

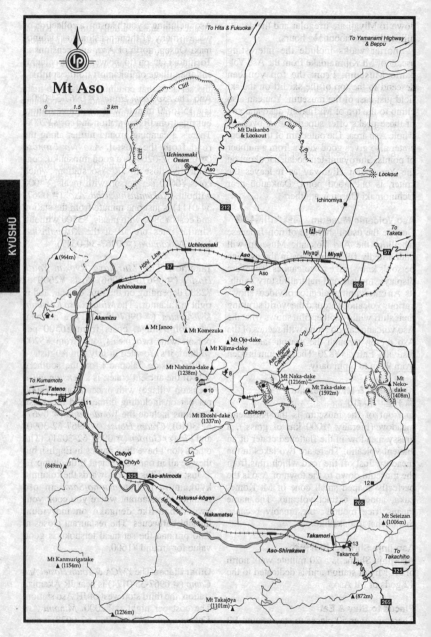

To Hita & Fukuoka

To Yamanami Highway
& Beppu

Mt Aso

0   1.5   3 km

Cliff

Cliff

Mt Daikanbō
& Lookout

Cliff

Uchinomaki
Onsen

Aso

Lookout

212

Ichinomiya

To
Taketa

Hōhi Line

Uchinomaki

Aso

Miyagi   Miyaji

57

57

Aso

Ichinokawa

▲ (964m)

③ ⓢ

ⓢ 4

Akamizu

265

Aso

⛩ 2

▲ Mt Janoo   ▲ Mt Komezuka

Mt Ojo-dake

▲ Mt Kijima-dake

Aso Higashi
Cablecar

ⓢ 5

To Kumamoto

Tateno

Mt Nishima-dake
(1238m)   ▲

⛩ 8
9

● 10

Mt Naka-dake
(1216m)   Mt Taka-dake
(1592m)

Mt Neko-
dake
(1408m)

11

7   Cablecar

Mt Eboshi-dake
(1337m)

6

▲ (849m)

Chōyō

Chōyō

Aso-shimoda

325

Hakusui-kōgen

Minamiaso

Railway

Nakamatsu

12 ■

Mt Seieizan
▲ (1006m)

265

Takamori

Aso-Shirakawa

13
Takamori

To
Takachiho

▲ Mt Kanmurigatake
(1154m)

325

▲ (872m)

265

Mt Takajōya
(1101m)   ▲

▲ (1236m)

1 Aso-jinja Shrine
   阿蘇神社

2 Aso Youth Hostel
   阿蘇ユースホステル

3 Akamizu Hot Springs
   赤水温泉

4 YMCA & Youth Hostel Aso Camp

5 Sensui-kyō
   仙酔峡

6 Mt Naka-dake Crater
   中岳

7 Aso-nishi Cablecar Station
   阿蘇西ロープウェイ乗り場

8 Ski Field
   スキー場

9 Aso Volcanic Museum
   阿蘇火山博物館

10 Kusasenri Meadow
   草千里

11 Tochinoki Onsen
   とちのき温泉

12 Takamori Pension Village
   高森ペンション村

13 Murataya Ryokan Youth Hostel
   むらたや旅館ユースホステル

the Aso-shimoda private railway station, the fourth stop west of Takamori. Rooms cost from ¥3800 without meals.

Getting There & Away

The JR Hōhi line operates between Kumamoto and Beppu via Aso. From JR Aso station there are buses to the Aso-nishi cablecar station. From Kumamoto to Aso, local trains take 1½ hours (¥930), while limited express trains take one hour and cost ¥2030. The Beppu-Aso limited express service costs ¥2800 and takes 2½ hours. Note that there are only three limited express services a day. To get to Takamori on the southern side of the crater, transfer from the JR Hōhi line to the Minamiaso private railway line at Tateno.

From March to November the *Aso Boy* steam train makes a daily run from Kumamoto to Aso, terminating at Miyaji station. The one-way fare is ¥1730.

Buses from Beppu to Aso take 2½ to three hours and cost ¥3000, plus another ¥1100 for the services that continue to the Aso-nishi cablecar station. From Takamori, buses continue south to the mountain resort of Takachiho (1½ hours, ¥1280). It's a scenic route.

Getting Around

Buses operate approximately hourly from JR Aso station via the Aso Youth Hostel to the Aso-higashi cablecar station on the slopes of Mt Naka-dake. The trip takes 30 minutes up, 25 minutes down and costs ¥420. There are less frequent services between Miyaji and Sensui-kyō on the northern side of Mt Naka-dake.

Buses also operate between Aso and Takamori. Cars can be rented at Aso and at Uchinomaki, one stop west of JR Aso station.

SOUTH OF KUMAMOTO
Yatsushiro 八代

The castle town of Yatsushiro, directly south of Kumamoto, was where Hosokawa Tadoki retired. The powerful daimyō is chiefly remembered in Japan for having his Christian wife killed to stop her falling into the hands of his enemies. Near the castle ruins is the 1688 Shohinken house and garden. The town's Korean-influenced Koda-yaki pottery is admired by pottery experts.

Hinagu & Minamata 日奈久・水俣

Further south along the coast at Hinagu there are fine views out towards the Amakusa Islands. To the north is the port of Minamata which became infamous in the late '60s and early '70s when it was discovered that the high incidence of illness and birth defects in the town were caused by mercury poisoning. A local factory had dumped waste containing high levels of mercury into the sea and this had contaminated the fish eaten by local residents. The company's ruthless efforts to suppress the story focused worldwide attention on the town.

KYŪSHŪ

Hitoyoshi 人吉

Directly south of Yatsushiro toward the Kirishima volcano chain, the town of Hitoyoshi is noted for the 18 km boat trip down the rapids of the Kuma-gawa River. There are a variety of trips taking from about 2½ hours, ending at Osakahama and costing ¥2700 per person. The boat trips shut down between November and February, and even for the rest of the year there are only three to four services a day on weekdays. The weekends are more lively, with seven to eight services daily. The boat departure point is about 1½ km south-east of the railway station, directly across the river from the ruins of Hitoyoshi-jō Castle. Ask for *kuma-gawa kudari*.

Getting There & Away From Kumamoto it's half an hour on the JR Kagoshima line to Yatsushiro then one hour on the JR Hisatsu line to Hitoyoshi. From Hitoyoshi, it's a little over 1½ hours on the Hisatsu line and then the JR Kitto line to Kobayashi, from where buses run to Ebino in the Kirishima National Park.

AMAKUSA ISLANDS 天草諸島

South of the Shimabara-hantō Peninsula are the Amakusa Islands. The islands were a stronghold of Christianity during Japan's Christian Century and the grinding poverty here was a major factor in the Shimabara Rebellion of 1637-38. It's still one of the more backward regions of Japan.

Hondo is the main town on the islands and has a museum relating to the Christian era. Tomioka, where the Nagasaki ferries berth, has castle ruins and a museum. This west coast area is particularly interesting.

There are ferry services from various places in Nagasaki-ken (including Mogi near Nagasaki and Shimabara on the Shimabara Peninsula) and from the Kumamoto-ken coast (including Yatsushiro and Minamata). In addition, the Amakusa Five Bridges link the island directly with Misumi, south-west of Kumamoto.

Kagoshima-ken 鹿児島県

Kyūshū's southernmost prefecture has the large city of Kagoshima, overlooked by the ominous volcano of Sakurajima across Kinkō-wan Bay. To the south is the Satsuma-hantō Peninsula, while the north has the Kirishima National Park with its superb volcanoes.

KIRISHIMA NATIONAL PARK 霧島国立公園

The day walk from Ebino-kōgen Village on the Ebino-kōgen Plateau to the summits of a string of volcanoes is one of the finest volcanic hikes in Japan. It's about 15 km from the summit of Mt Karakuni-dake to the summit of Mt Takachiho-no-mine and there's superb scenery all the way. If your time or energy is limited there are shorter alternatives such as a pleasant lake stroll on the plateau or a walk up and down Mt Karakuni-dake or Mt Takachiho. The area is also noted for its spring wildflowers and has fine hot springs and the impressive 75m Senriga-taki Waterfall.

Orientation & Information

There are tourist information offices with maps and some information in English at Ebino-kōgen Village and at Takachiho-gawara, the two ends of the volcano walk. There are restaurant facilities at both ends of the walk as well, but Ebino-kōgen has most of the hotels, camping facilities and the like. Kobayashi to the north and Hayashida, just to the south, are the main towns near Ebino-kōgen.

Ebino-kōgen Walk えびの高原

The Ebino-kōgen lake circuit is a pleasantly relaxed stroll around a series of volcanic lakes – **Lake Rokkannon** has the most intense colour, a deep blue-green. Across the road from Lake Fudou, at the base of Mt Karakuni-dake, is a steaming **jigoku**. From there you can make the stiff climb to the 1700m summit of **Mt Karakuni-dake**, skirting the edge of the volcano's deep crater

Ebino Kōgen/Kirishima

KIRISHIMA - YAKU NATIONAL PARK

KAGOSHIMA-KEN

MIYAZAKI-KEN

before arriving at the high point on the eastern side. There are good views back over Ebino-kōgen Plateau, but the view to the south is superb, taking in the perfectly circular caldera lake of Onami-ike, the rounded Mt Shinmoe-dake and the perfect cone of Mt Takachiho-no-mine. On a clear day, you can see right down to Kagoshima and the smoking cone of Sakurajima.

Longer Walks
The views across the almost lunar landscape from any of the volcano summits is otherworldly. If you have time you can continue from Mt Karakuni-dake to Mt Shishiko, Mt Shinmoe-dake, Mt Naka-dake and then Takachiho-gawara, from where you can make the ascent of Mt Takachiho-no-mine. Close up, Takachiho is a decidedly ugly looking volcano with a huge, gaping crater. Legends relate that Ninigi-no-mikoto, a descendant of the sun goddess, arrived in Japan on the summit of this mountain.

Places to Stay
Ebino-kōgen Village has a good choice of accommodation, including the expensive *Ebino-kōgen Hotel* (☎ 0984-33-1155), with rooms from ¥10,000, and a kokuminshu-kusha, *Ebino-Kōgen-sō* (☎ 0984-33-0161), with accommodation from ¥6500 per person including two meals. Just north-east of the centre is the *Ebino-kōgen Rotenburo* with basic but cheap huts around a popular series of open-air hot-spring baths. There's also a camping ground. More accommodation can be found at Hayashida Onsen, between Ebino-kōgen and the Kirishima-jingū Shrine.

Getting There & Away
JR Kobayashi station to the north of Ebino-kōgen and Kirishima-jinja station to the south are the main railway junctions. From Miyazaki or Kumamoto take a JR Ebino-gō limited express train to Kobayashi on the JR Kitto line, from where buses operate to Ebino. From Kagoshima (around one hour)

or Miyazaki (1½ hours) you can take a JR Nippō limited express to Kirishima-jingū station. From there infrequent buses operate to Takachiho-gawara (about 45 minutes) and Ebino-kōgen (¥550).

A direct bus to Ebino-kōgen is probably the best way to go. The two main approaches are Kagoshima and Miyazaki. Buses arrive and depart from Ebino-kōgen (the village on the Ebino-kōgen Plateau, not to be confused with the town of Ebino down on the plains). From Nishi-Kagoshima station most buses run to Hayashida Onsen (two hours, ¥1260), one stop short of Ebino-kōgen. Miyazaki is not much better: just three buses a day go through to Ebino-kōgen (2½ hours, ¥2570).

There are good views of the volcano scenery from buses driving along the Kirishima Skyline road.

KIRISHIMA-JINGŪ SHRINE 霧島神宮

The bright orange Kirishima-jingū Shrine is colourful and beautifully located, with fine views down towards Kagoshima and the smoking cone of Sakurajima, but otherwise not of great interest. It originally dates from the 6th century, although the present shrine was built in 1715. It is dedicated to Ninigi-no-mikoto, who made his legendary landing in Japan on the summit of Mt Takachiho.

The shrine can be visited en route to the park from Kagoshima or Miyazaki; see the preceding Kirishima National Park section for transport details. The shrine is about 15 minutes by bus from Kirishima-jingū station and it's another 50 minutes by bus to the Ebino-kōgen Plateau.

KAGOSHIMA 鹿児島

Known to the Japanese as the Naples of Japan, Kagoshima (population 536,000) is the southernmost major city in Kyūshū and a warm, sunny and relaxed place – at least as long as Kagoshima's very own Vesuvius, Sakurajima, is behaving itself. Just a stone's throw from Kagoshima, across Kinkō-wan Bay, is the huge cone of Sakurajima, an active volcano. 'Dustfall' brings out the umbrellas in Kagoshima as frequently as rainfall in other parts of the world.

History

Kagoshima's history has been dominated by a single family, the Shimazu clan, who held sway there for 29 generations and nearly 700 years until the Meiji Restoration. The Kagoshima region, known as Satsuma, was always receptive to outside contact and for many years was an important centre for trade with China. St Francis Xavier first arrived here in 1549, making Kagoshima one of Japan's earliest contact points with Christianity and the west.

The Shimazu family's interests were not confined to trade, however. In the 16th century their power extended throughout Kyūshū and they also gained control of the islands of Okinawa, where they treated the people so oppressively that the Okinawans have regarded the mainland Japanese with suspicion ever since.

During the 19th century as the Tokugawa Shogunate increasingly proved its inability to respond to the challenge of the industrialised west, the Shimazu were already looking further afield: in the 1850s, the Shimazu established the country's first western-style manufacturing operation. Then, in 1865, the family smuggled 17 young men out of the country to study western technology first-hand in the UK. In conjunction with the Mori clan of Hagi (see the Hagi section in the Western Honshū chapter) the Shimazu played a leading part in the Meiji Restoration.

Orientation & Information

Kagoshima sprawls north-south along the bayside and has two major JR stations, Nishi-Kagoshima to the south and Kagoshima to the north. The town centre is between the two stations, and accommodation is evenly distributed between here and the Nishi-Kagoshima station area. Iso-teien Garden, the town's principal attraction, is north of Kagoshima station but most other things to do are around the centre, particularly on the hillside that forms a backdrop to the city. While these hills provide one clear landmark, the city's other great landmark, the smoking Sakurajima volcano, is even more evident.

The tourist information office (☎ 099-253-2500) in the Nishi-Kagoshima station car park is open from 8.30 am to 5 pm daily and has a surprising amount of information in English, if you ask for it. Also in front of the station is the curious stepped column with 17 people perched on it, commemorating the 17 Kagoshima students who defied the 'no going overseas' rules. The main post office is right beside the station.

The Tenmonkan-dōri tram stop, where the lively Tenmonkan-dōri shopping and entertainment arcade crosses the tram lines, marks the town centre. There's another tourist office (☎ 099-222-2500) at JR Kagoshima station, and the Kagoshima Prefectural Tourist Office (☎ 099-223-5771), on the 4th floor of the Sangyo Kaikan building, is between the centre and JR Kagoshima station.

Iso-teien Garden　磯庭園

The Shimazu family not only dominated Kagoshima's history, they also left the city its principal attraction, the beautiful bayside Iso-teien Garden. The 19th Shimazu lord laid the garden out in 1660, incorporating one of the most impressive pieces of 'borrowed scenery' to be found anywhere in Japan – the fuming cone of Sakurajima.

Although the garden is not as well kept and immaculate as tourist literature would have you believe, it is pleasant to wander through. Look for the stream where the 21st Shimazu lord once held poem parties – the participants had to compose a poem before the next cup of sake floated down the stream to them.

The garden contains the Shimazu Villa, the family home of the powerful Shimazu clan. Above the garden and reached by a cablecar (¥280 one way) is the Isoyama recreation ground, which has great views over the city. Look for the large rock on the hillside overlooking the garden, into which are carved two Chinese characters proclaiming it 'a big rock'.

The garden is north of the centre (10 minutes by Hayashida line bus No 11 from the stop outside JR Kagoshima station) and open daily from 8.30 am to 5.30 pm, except in winter, when it closes half an hour earlier. Entry is ¥800.

Shōko Shūseikan Museum　尚古集成館

This museum, adjacent to Iso-teien Garden, is housed in the building established in the 1850s as Japan's first factory. At one time the factory employed 1200 workers. Exhibits relate to the Shimazu family and to the factory's activities but only a few items are labelled in English. Entry is included in the garden admission fee and opening hours are the same.

Other Museums

The **City Art Museum** has a small permanent collection principally dedicated to the works of local artists but also including paintings by European impressionists along with regular special exhibitions. Entry is ¥200. The **Kagoshima Prefectural Museum of Culture** is on the former site of Tsurumaru-jō Castle: the walls and the impressive moat are all that remain of the 1602 castle. The

Saigō Takamori
Although the Great Saigō had played a leading part in the Meiji Restoration in 1868, in 1877 he changed his mind – possibly because he felt the curtailment of samurai power and status had gone too far – and led the ill-fated Satsuma or Seinan Rebellion. Kumamoto's magnificent castle was burnt down during the rebellion but when defeat became inevitable, Saigō eventually retreated to Kagoshima and committed seppuku. Despite his mixed status as both a hero and villain of the restoration, Saigō is still a great figure in Satsuma's history and indeed in the history of Japan. His square-headed features and bulky appearance are instantly recognisable and Kagoshima has a famous Saigō statue, as does Ueno-kōen Park in Tokyo. ■

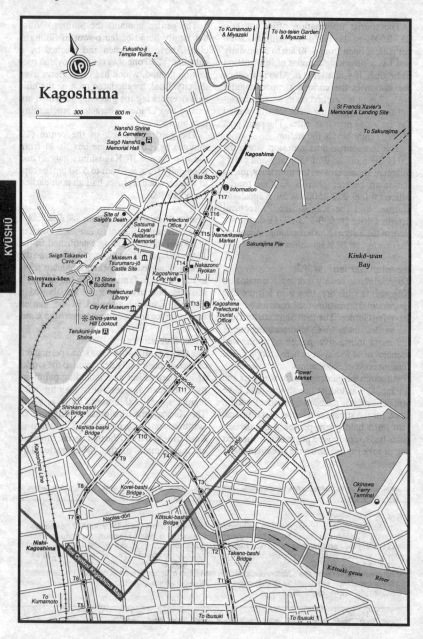

Kagoshima

0   300   600 m

To Kumamoto
& Miyazaki

To Iso-teien Garden
& Miyazaki

Fukusho-ji
Temple Ruins

St Francis Xavier's
Memorial & Landing Site

Nanshū Shrine
& Cemetery

Saigō Nanshū
Memorial Hall

Kagoshima

To Sakurajima

Bus Stop

Information

T17

Site of
Saigō's Death

Satsuma
Loyal
Retainers'
Memorial

Prefectural
Office

T16

T15

Namerikawa
Market

Sakurajima Pier

Saigō Takamori
Cave

Museum &
Tsurumaru-jō
Castle Site

T14

Nakazono
Ryokan

Kinkō-wan
Bay

Shiroyama-kōen
Park

13 Stone
Buddhas

Prefectural
Library

Kagoshima
City Hall

City Art Museum

Shiro-yama
Hill Lookout

Terukuni-jinja
Shrine

T13

Kagoshima
Prefectural
Tourist
Office

T12

Flower
Market

Tenmonkan-dōri

T11

Shinkan-bashi
Bridge

Nishida-bashi
Bridge

T10

Perin-dōri

T9

T4

Kagoshima Line

T8

Korai-bashi
Bridge

T3

Okinawa
Ferry
Terminal

T7

Naples-dōri

Kōtsuki-bashi
Bridge

Nishi-
Kagoshima

See Central Kagoshima Map

T2

Takeno-bashi
Bridge

Kōtsuki-gawa   River

T6

T1

To
Kumamoto

T5

To Ibusuki

To Ibusuki

KYŪSHŪ

TRAM STOPS	T6	Miyako-dōri	T12	Izuro-dōri
Route 1		都通り		いづろ通り
T1 Kōtsū-kyoku	T7	Nishi Kagoshima	T13	Asahi-dōri
交通局		Station		朝日通り
T2 Takenohashi		西鹿児島駅前	T14	City Hall
竹の橋	T8	Takamibashi		市役所前
T3 Shinyashiki		高見橋	T15	Prefectural Office
新屋敷	T9	Kajya-machi		県庁前
T4 City Hospital		鍛冶屋町	T16	Sakurajima
市立病院前				Sanbashi-dōri
	Route 1 & 2			桜島桟橋通り
Route 2	T10	Takami-baba	T17	Kagoshima Station
T5 Nakasu-dōri		高見馬場		鹿児島駅前
中洲通り	T11	Tenmonkan-dōri		
		天文館通り		

KYŪSHŪ

museum has displays on Kagoshima's history with special emphasis on the Satsuma period and entry is ¥260. The gallery and the museum are both open from 9 am to 4.30 pm daily except Monday.

The **Kagoshima Prefectural Museum** covers natural history and science, and has an interesting exhibit on the Sakurajima volcano, tracing its history and eruptions. Entry is ¥200.

Saigō Takamori 西郷隆盛

There are numerous reminders of Saigō Takamori's importance in Kagoshima, including a large statue of him near the City Art Museum. In true Japanese fashion, there's a sign showing you where to stand in order to get yourself and the statue in the same photograph. The cave where he hid and the place where he eventually committed suicide are on Shiro-yama Hill. Further north are the Nanshū Shrine; the Saigō Nanshū Memorial Hall (entrance ¥100; closed on Monday), where displays tell of the failed rebellion; and the Nanshu-bochi Cemetery, which contains the graves of more than 2000 of Saigō's followers.

St Francis Xavier フランシスザビエル

There are a number of memorials to St Francis Xavier around the city, including a church and a memorial park near the city centre. Near the waterfront, north of JR Kagoshima station and towards the Iso-teien Garden, is a memorial at his supposed landing spot.

Kōtsuki-gawa River 甲突川

Kagoshima enjoys twin-city status with Naples in Italy and Perth in Australia. The street running perpendicular to the Nishi-Kagoshima station starts as Naples-dōri and changes to Perth-dōri after it crosses the Kōtsuki-gawa River. There's a very pleasant riverside walk from near the station. Start at the attractive 18th century stone Nishida Bridge and walk south; there are four other attractive bridges along the way.

The statue of Ōkubo Toshimichi, another important local personage in the events of the Meiji Restoration (he became the prime minister in the new government), is by the tramline road. Further south is the site of Saigō's home and the 'Statue of Hat', appropriately named after the statue's only item of apparel.

Morning Market 朝市

Kagoshima's *asa ichi*, or morning market, operates daily (except Sunday) in front of Nishi Kagoshima station from 6 am to around noon. It's a raucous, lively event and worth taking a look at. There's another morning market up at the main JR station, but the Nishi-Kagoshima station market is the better one to visit.

Other Attractions

Behind the Kagoshima Prefectural Museum is the **Terukuni-jinja Shrine**, dedicated to Shimazu Nariakira, the 28th Shimazu lord who was responsible for building Japan's first factory and introducing modern western technology to the area. He also designed Japan's rising sun flag. Continue up the hillside behind the shrine and you eventually reach the lookout in **Shiroyama-kōen Park**, which has fine views over the city and across to Sakurajima.

North of the memorial are the remains of the **Fukusho-ji Temple**, once the Shimazu family temple. **Iso-hama Beach**, near the Iso-teien Garden, is the town's popular summer getaway. The **Ijinkan** or 'foreigners' residence', also near Iso-teien Garden, was used by British engineers brought to Japan to help set up the factory at Shōko Shuseikan. **Tagayama Park**, between Iso-teien Garden and Kagoshima station, has a noted statue of Admiral Togo, who defeated the Czar's fleet in the Russo-Japanese war of 1905.

Some distance south of Kagoshima is the **Hirakawa Zoological Park**, which has a koala collection. It's open daily, except Tuesday, from 9 am to 5 pm (the koala section closes at 4 pm) and costs ¥200 entry.

Special Events

One of Kagoshima's more unusual events is the late July *Umbrella Burning Festival*. Boys burn umbrellas on the banks of the Kōtsuki-gawa River in honour of the Soga brothers, though why they do this isn't exactly clear.

Places to Stay

Youth Hostel The only youth hostel close to Kagoshima is the *Sakurajima Youth Hostel*. To get there you have to take the ferry across the bay (see the following Sakurajima section for details).

Ryokan The Japanese Inn Group's *Nakazono Ryokan* (☎ 099-226-5125) is a superb place to be based. It's close to JR Nishi-Kagoshima station and the Sakurajima pier, and is clearly signposted in English. The friendly Mr Nakazono will give you sightseeing tips for Kagoshima. Rates are ¥4000/7600 for Japanese-style rooms without bath.

Hotels Around Nishi-Kagoshima station, the cheapest hotel (only 22 singles) is the *Business Hotel Suzuya* (☎ 099-258-2385), where singles cost ¥4320. The *Silk Inn Kagoshima* (☎ 099-258-1221) has singles/doubles from ¥5800/9500. Alternatively, turn left immediately out of the station, pass the post office and take the first left across the railway tracks to the *Business Hotel Union* (☎ 099-253-5800). It's a friendly place with rooms at ¥5500/ 9000 but definitely at the tatty and worn-out end of the business hotel spectrum and for emergency accommodation only. Nearby is the *City Hotel Kagoshima* (☎ 099-258-0331), with rooms starting at ¥5500.

In central Kagoshima is the *Business Hotel Nichisenren* (☎ 099-225-6161), which has singles from ¥3500 and twins from ¥7000, but don't expect anything more than the basics. Another cheapie is just south of the Mitsukoshi department store: the *Business Hotel Satsuma* (☎ 099-226-1351) has singles with/without bath for ¥4600/3500 and twins for ¥7900/6400.

By the tramline and also quite close to the Tenmonkan-dōri shopping arcade, the *Kagoshima Hayashida Hotel* (☎ 099-224-4111) is an important central meeting point and has singles/doubles from ¥7500/10,500. The hotel features a large central garden atrium. Across the road is the *New Central Hotel* (☎ 099-224-5551), where singles/doubles range from ¥5700/9300 – it comes complete with a bunny-girl bar on the top floor. Another central option, right in the heart of all the entertainment action, is the *City Hotel Tenmonkan* (☎ 099-223-7181), which has singles at ¥6000 and doubles at ¥12,000.

More up-market options include the *Station Hotel New Kagoshima* (☎ 099-253-5353), with singles/doubles at ¥6500/12,000; and the *Kagoshima Tōkyū Inn* (☎ 099-253-3692), with singles/doubles from ¥7700/14,000.

Places to Eat

Most restaurants are in and around Tenmonkan. In the Tenmonkan arcade itself restaurants are few, but there are a few good patisseries: *Toit Vert* and *Boulangerie*. You'll also find the usual fast-food barns, including a branch of *Subway* in this area.

Akachōchin is an izakaya of wildly exaggerated cheerfulness – the welcomes are bawled out so loudly that new arrivals reel back at the door. The menu is in Japanese only, though some dishes are illustrated and most are in the ¥250 to ¥500 range. Look for the octopus over the entrance. There's another branch of this popular izakaya near Nishi-Kagoshima station.

Kumasotei (☎ 099-222-6356) is a favourite for its Satsuma cuisine. There is an English menu with set lunches from ¥2000 to ¥5000 and set dinners from ¥3000 to ¥20,000. The ¥4000 dinner gives you a taste of all the most popular Satsuma specialities.

Other places in this central area include *Casa Salone* for good value Italian fare, *Wakana* with a variety of meals (all with plastic versions on display), *Roman Yakata* for Italian dishes, *La Sei* for French dishes and *Le Ciel de Paris*, a pleasant little patisserie/coffee bar. For fairly ordinary Indian fare (this is not the best of their branches), look out also for *Nanak*.

Kagoshima is renowned for its rāmen, the soup stock for which is made with a secret recipe. You can try it at *Zabon Rāmen*, which is just around the corner from the Kagoshima Hayashida Hotel. A bowl of Kagoshima's famous noodles will set you back ¥700. Generally you buy a ticket for your meal at the vending machine just inside the door, but the friendly staff will do it for you if you look confused. Zabon rāmen is the No 2 button. Further down the same street is another famous noodle shop – *Kuruiwa Rāmen*.

Although the Tenmonkan area reigns supreme, there are also a few restaurants around the Nishi-Kagoshima station area, including an old railway carriage converted into a restaurant called the *Vesuvio* (an appropriate name, given the Naples-Vesuvius versus Kagoshima-Sakurajima connections). Pizza and spaghetti feature heavily on the menu. There are also a few fast-food places like *Mr Donut* in this area.

Entertainment

There's a lot happening in Tenmonkan – shot bars, discos, bunny bars, peep shows, karaoke boxes and hide-away coffee shops – but little is accessible to visiting gaijin. For a quiet drink that isn't going to clean out your wallet, try *Namusete*, a basement reggae bar around the corner from the Kagoshima Hayashida Hotel. Downstairs from the *Suntory Shot Bar* (a very staid place), is a small group of bars; a couple are popular with the foreign community.

Things to Buy

Satsuma specialities include a variation on the *ningyō* (Japanese doll), cards printed with inks produced from Sakurajima volcanic ash, Satsuma *kiriki* (cut glass) and nifty little wooden fish on wheels. Satsuma-yaki porcelain is also highly valued. All these things can

Satsuma

Kagoshima's cuisine speciality is known as Satsuma, the food of the Satsuma region. Satsuma dishes include: *tonkotsu*, which is pork ribs seasoned with miso and black sugar then boiled until they're on the point of falling apart; *kibinago*, a sardine-like fish which is usually prepared as sashimi with vinegared miso sauce; *satsuma-age*, a fried fish sausage; *satsuma jiru*, a chicken miso soup; *torisashi*, which is raw chicken with soy sauce; *katsuo no tataki*, which is sliced bonito; *katsuo no shioka*, which is salted bonito intestines; and *sakezushi*, a mixed seafood sushi.

Kagoshima rāmen is the region's renowned noodle dish. *Shōchū*, the Kagoshima firewater, comes in many forms, including *imo-shōchū*, made from sweet potatoes. There's also a local sweet-potato ice cream. ■

KYŪSHŪ

KYŪSHŪ

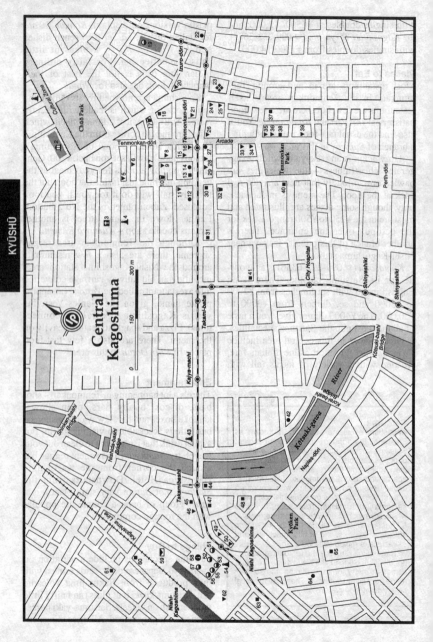

Central
Kagoshima

0   150   300 m

KYŪSHŪ

PLACES TO STAY

13 Kagoshima
Hayashida Hotel
かごしま林田ホテル

18 Business Hotel
Nichisenren
ビジネスホテル
日専連

30 New Central Hotel;
ANA
ニューセントラル
ホテル

31 Kagoshima
Washington Hotel
ワシントンホテル

37 Business Hotel
Satsuma
ビジネスホテル薩摩

38 Kagoshima Kankō
Hotel
鹿児島観光ホテル

40 City Hotel
Tenmonkan
シティホテル天文館

41 Hokke Club
Kagoshima
法華クラブ鹿児島

44 Kagoshima Tōkyū
Inn
鹿児島東急イン

45 Hotel Taisei Annexe
ホテルタイセイ
アネックス

47 Station Hotel New
Kagoshima
ステーションホテル
ニューカゴシマ

48 Kagoshima Gasthof
鹿児島ガストフ

60 City Hotel Kagoshima
シティホテル鹿児島

61 Business Hotel Union
ビジネスホテル
ユニオン

63 Business Hotel
Suzuya
ビジネスホテル
すずや

65 Silk Inn Kagoshima
シルクイン鹿児島

PLACES TO EAT

5 Le Ciel de Paris

6 Kumasotei
熊襲亭

7 Casa Salone

8 Roman Yakata
ロマンヤカタ

9 Wakana
吾愛人

11 KFC

15 Zabon Rāmen
ざぼんラーメン

16 Nanak

20 Dom Dom
Hamburgers

21 Mr Donut

24 KFC

25 McDonald's

26 Toit Vert
天文館トワベール

28 Lotteria

29 Vie de France Bakery

33 Boulangerie

34 Mujaki
天文館むじゃき

35 Seafood Restaurant
Paeriya
巴絵里屋

36 Bali Bali Yakiniku
House
バリバリ焼肉ハウス

39 Akachōchin
あかちょうちん

46 Italian Tomato

49 Satsuma
薩摩レストラン

50 Mr Donut

62 Vesuvio

OTHER

1 Saigō Takamori
Statue
西郷隆盛銅像

2 Kagoshima
Prefectural Museum
県立博物館

3 St Francis Xavier
Church
ザビエル教会

4 St Francis Xavier
Memorial
ザビエル記念碑

10 Namusete Bar

12 JAL
日本航空

14 JTB

17 T-Bone Bar

19 Yamakataya
Department Store;
Bus Station
山形屋

22 Izuro (Stone Lantern)
石灯籠

23 Mitsukoshi
Department Store
三越

27 Tower Records

32 Suntory Shot Bar

42 Site of Saigo House
西郷旧居

43 Statue of Ōkubo
Toshimichi
大久保誕生地

51 Hayashida Sangyo
Kōtsū (Kirishima);
Minami
Kyūhū Kosoku
(Miyazaki)
林田産業交通
(至霧島)

52 City Bus
(Kagoshima City)
シティバス
(鹿児島市)

Key continued on following page

53	Kagoshima Kōtsū (Chiran, Ibusuki)	鹿児島交通
54	17 Young Pioneers Statues	若き薩摩の群像
55	Hayashida Sangyo Kōtsū (Ebino, Kirishima)	林田産業交通 (至えびの)
56	JR Bus (Sakurajima)	JRバス (至桜島)
57	Kagoshima Kōtsū; City Bus (Sightseeing Buses)	鹿児島交通 (観光バス)
58	Tourist Information Office	観光案内所
59	Post Office	郵便局
64	Morning Market	朝市

be bought in the Kagoshima specialities store (☎ 0992-25-6120), north of Tenmonkan.

Local crafts are also displayed in the same building as the Kagoshima Prefectural Tourist Office (see Orientation & Information in this for its location). Mitsukoshi, Yamakataya and Takashimaya are the main department stores, and all are good places to seek out souvenir items.

Getting There & Away

Air Kagoshima's airport has international connections with Hong Kong and Seoul, as well as domestic flights to Tokyo, Osaka, Nagoya and a variety of other places in Honshū and Kyūshū. Kagoshima is the major jumping-off point for flights to the South-West Islands and also has connections with the Kagoshima-ken islands and Naha on Okinawa. (See the Okinawa & the South-West Islands chapter for more details.)

Train Both Nishi-Kagoshima and Kagoshima stations are arrival and departure points for other areas of Japan. While Nishi-

Kagoshima station is close to a greater choice of accommodation, Kagoshima station is closer to Iso-teien Garden and the Sakurajima ferry. The stations are about equal distance north and south of the town centre.

It takes about 4½ hours by train from Fukuoka/Hakata via Kumamoto to Kagoshima on the JR Kagoshima line. The local train fare is ¥5150; add ¥2560 for the limited express service. The JR Nippō line connects Kagoshima with Kokura on the north-eastern tip of Kyūshū for ¥7210, plus ¥2780 for limited express. Nippō line trains operate via Miyazaki and Beppu.

Trains also run south from Kagoshima to the popular hot-spring resort of Ibusuki, taking about one hour 10 minutes.

Bus Hayashida buses to Kirishima and Ebino-kōgen go from the Takashimaya department store in the centre. A good way of exploring Chiran and Ibusuki, south of Kagoshima, is by rented car, but you can also get there by bus from bus stop No 10 at Nishi-Kagoshima station. Buses also run from Nishi-Kagoshima station to other places near and far, including the following:

Destination	Bus Stop	Duration	Fare
Miyazaki	No 8	2½ hours	¥2700
Kumamoto	No 17	3½ hours	¥3600
Fukuoka	No 16	4½ hours	¥5300
Osaka	No 8	12½ hours	¥12,000
Kyoto	No 16	13½ hours	¥12,600
Nagoya	No 16	14½ hours	¥14,000

There are also daily tours to Ibusuki and Chiran, among other places, from bus stop No 4. Most of the tours will be unlikely to be of interest to most western visitors but, as an example of what's on offer, at 10.10 am daily a bus heads off to Chiran, whizzes you around the sights and then does the same thing in Ibusuki, ending the day with a soak in a hot spring (which you'll probably need after all that running around). All this for a mere ¥3950.

Boat Ferries shuttle across the bay to Sakurajima and also further afield to a number of the South-West Islands, including

Okinawa. For ferries to Okinawa, bookings can be made with travel agents, but you can also contact the Queen Coral Marikku Line (☎ 099-225-1551), which has daily ferries to Okinawa via Amami Ō-shima, Tokuno-shima, Okino-Erabu-jima and Yoron-jima. The trip takes around 25 hours and costs ¥11,840 in 2nd class. The Akebono Maru company (☎ 0992-46-4141) does exactly the same routing daily for the same price.

Getting Around
The Airport Buses operate between Nishi-Kagoshima station (bus stop No 7) and the airport every 20 minutes, stopping off at Tenmonkan on the way; the 40 km trip takes a bit less than an hour and costs ¥1200.

Bus There is a comprehensive city bus network, though you won't need it for most of Kagoshima's sights. For information on the one-day unlimited travel pass, see the Tram entry.

Tram As in Nagasaki and Kumamoto, the tram service in Kagoshima is easy to understand, operates frequently and is the best way of getting around town. You can pay by the trip (¥160) or get a one-day unlimited travel pass for ¥500. The pass can also be used on city buses, and can be bought at the Nishi-Kagoshima station tourist information booth.

There are two tram routes. Route 1 starts from Kagoshima station, goes through the centre and on past the suburb of Korimoto to Taniyama. Route 2 follows the same route through the centre, then diverges at Takami-baba to Nishi-Kagoshima station and terminates at Korimoto.

SAKURAJIMA　桜島
Dominating the skyline from Kagoshima is the brooding cone of this decidedly over-active volcano. In fact, Sakurajima is so active that the Japanese differentiate between its mere eruptions (since 1955 there has been an almost continuous stream of smoke and ash) and real explosions, which have occurred in 1914, 1915, 1946, 1955 and

1960. The most violent eruption was in 1914, when the volcano poured out over three billion tonnes of lava, overwhelming numerous villages and converting Sakurajima from an island to a peninsula. The flow totally filled in the 400m-wide and 70m-deep strait which had separated the volcano from the mainland and extended the island further west towards Kagoshima.

Sakurajima actually has three peaks – Kita-dake (1117m), Naka-dake (1060m) and Minami-dake (1040m) – but at present only Minami is active. While some parts of Sakurajima are covered in deep volcanic ash or crumbling lava, other places have exceptionally fertile soil, and some huge *daikon* (radishes) weighing up to 35 kg are grown. Sakurajima is also known for its tiny oranges, only three cm in diameter, but at ¥500 each even the Japanese find them expensive.

Sakurajima Visitors' Center
桜島ビジターセンター
The tourist information office near the ferry terminal has a variety of exhibits about the

KYŪSHŪ

Japan hosts one tenth of the world's active volcanoes. Minami-dake, one of Sakurajima's three cones, is amongst the most active.

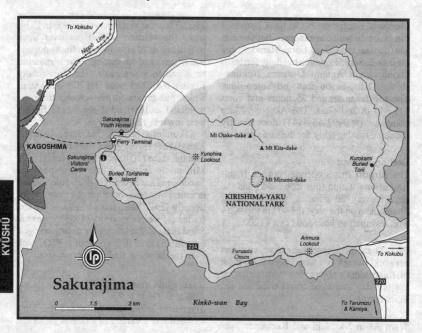

KYŪSHŪ

volcano, its eruptions and its natural history. The working model showing the volcano's growth over the years is the centre's main attraction. The centre is open from 9 am to 5 pm daily except Monday and entry is free.

Lookouts 展望台

Although visitors are not permitted to climb the volcano there are several good lookout points. The Yunohira lookout is high on the side of the volcano and offers good views up the forbidding, barren slopes and down across the bay to Kagoshima. The Arimura lava lookout is east of Furusato Onsen; there are walkways across a small corner of the immense lava flow and the lookout points offer a glimpse of the immense outpouring that linked the island to the mainland in 1914. The An-ei lava flow lies to the west, the 1914 Taisho lava flow to the east.

Other Attractions

A complete circuit of the volcano is 38 km.

South of the tourist information office is **Buried Torishima Island**, where the 1914 Taisho lava flow totally engulfed the small island which had been half a km offshore. On the way down the mountainside the lava swallowed three villages, destroying over 1000 homes.

Continuing anticlockwise around the island, you come to the monument to writer Hayashi Fumiko, the hot springs at Furusato Onsen and then the **Arimura Lava Lookout**. At the **Kurokami Buried Torii**, only the top of a shrine's entrance torii emerges from the volcanic ash – another reminder of the 1914 eruption.

Organised Tours

Three hour sightseeing bus tours operate twice daily from the ferry terminal and cost ¥1700. This is one of the few tour buses that holders of JR passes may use free of charge. JR buses also operate from the Sakurajima ferry terminal up to the Arimura lookout for ¥330.

Places to Stay

The *Sakurajima Youth Hostel* (☎ 099-293-2150) is near the ferry terminal and tourist information office and has beds at ¥1850 or ¥2050, depending on the season. The ferry service is so quick that it's possible to stay here and commute to Kagoshima.

Getting There & Away

The passenger and car ferry service shuttles back and forth between Kagoshima and Sakurajima. The trip takes 15 minutes and costs ¥150 per person, payable at the Sakurajima end. From Kagoshima station or the Sakurajima Sambashi-dōri tram stop, the ferry terminal is a short walk through the Nameriwaka market area.

Getting Around

Getting around Sakurajima without your own transport can be difficult. You can rent bicycles from near the ferry terminal but a complete circuit of the volcano would be quite a push, even without the climbs to the various lookouts.

Satsuma-Hantō Peninsula

Satsuma-hantō Peninsula 薩摩半島

The Satsuma-hantō Peninsula, south of Kagoshima, has fine rural scenery, an unusual kamikaze pilots' museum, the hot-spring resort of Ibusuki, the conical peak of Mt Kaimon-dake, and Chiran, with its well preserved samurai street. On the other side of Kinkō-wan Bay is Cape Sata-misaki, the southernmost point on the main islands of Japan.

GETTING AROUND

Using public transport around the region is time-consuming, although it is possible to make a complete loop of the peninsula by train and bus through Kagoshima, Chiran, Ibusuki, Mt Kaimon-dake, Makurazaki, Bōnotsu, Fukiage-hama and back to Kagoshima. The Ibusuki-Makurazaki JR line runs south from Kagoshima to Ibusuki then turns west to Makurazaki. You can continue on from there by bus and eventually make your way back to Kagoshima.

This is, however, a place where renting a car can be useful. Alternatively, there are tour buses which operate from Kagoshima via Chiran to Ibusuki and then from Ibusuki back to Kagoshima via Chiran and Tarumizu on the opposite side of the bay. There's a Yamakawa-Nejime ferry service across the southern end of the bay.

CHIRAN 知覧

South of Kagoshima, Chiran is a worthwhile place to pause en route to Ibusuki. This interesting little town has a well preserved samurai street with a fine collection of samurai houses and gardens, plus a fascinating memorial and museum to WWII's kamikaze pilots. Chiran was one of the major bases from which the hapless pilots made their suicidal and less than totally successful attacks on Allied shipping.

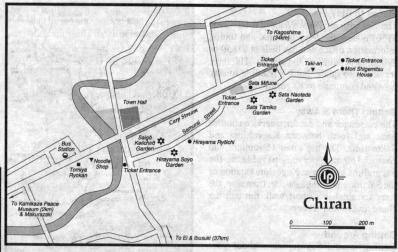

Samurai Street 武家屋敷街

The seven houses along Chiran's samurai street are noted for their finely preserved gardens, where you'll find all the standard features of formal garden design. Look for the use of 'borrowed scenery', particularly in No 6 (the houses are numbered on the brochure you pick up at the street entry point), where the garden is not so impressive but the 'borrowed' hill is focused wonderfully.

Notice how each of the gardens feature a 'mountain', backed by a tall hedge and always in the left corner when viewed with the house to your back; this feature is particularly evident in Nos 1, 4 and 5.

Traditionally, the outhouses were placed just inside the front gate, where an occupant could eavesdrop on comments from passersby. House No 3 has a good example of this. The water features are always imitated by sand or gravel except in No 7, the Mori Shigemitsu House, where real water is used. This house is particularly well preserved and dates from 1741.

Between houses No 3 and No 4/5 is the thatched-roof building of Futatsuya Minke, now used as a souvenir stand. Along the main road, parallel to the samurai street, is a well-stocked carp stream.

Entry to the samurai street houses is ¥310, payable at one of the entry points. The houses and gardens are open daily from 9 am to 5.30 pm.

Kamikaze Peace Museum 特攻平和会館

A more modern version of the samurai is commemorated in the Tokkō Heiwa Kaikan (Kamikaze Peace Museum) at the western end of town. There's a distinctly weird feeling to this comprehensive collection of aircraft, models, mementoes and photos of the young, fresh-faced pilots who enjoyed the dubious honour of flying in the Special Attack Corps. Unfortunately, there's hardly a word in English, apart from the message that they did it for the dream of 'peace and prosperity'. Crashing your aircraft into a battleship seems a strange way of ensuring peace and prosperity. Not only that, the bare statistics indicate that, far from achieving the aim of 'a battleship for every aircraft', only minor ships were sunk at the cost of over 1000 aircraft and, of course, their pilots. The museum is open daily from 9 am to 4.30 pm and entry is ¥310.

Chiran History Museum 知覧資料館

The exhibits at the history museum relate mainly to the samurai homes and, but for the absence of English explanations, would probably be a very educational experience. It's open daily from 9 am to 5 pm and entry is ¥205.

Places to Stay & Eat

Most visitors take a day trip to Chiran or stop there en route between Kagoshima and Ibusuki. If you want to stay overnight, the *Tomiya Ryokan* (☎ 0993-83-4313) is on the main street opposite the bus station, and has rooms from ¥8300. Also opposite the bus station is a *noodle shop* which is good for a cheap lunch. *Taki-An* on the samurai street is a rather more traditional place with a nice garden where you can sit on *tatami* mats to eat a bowl of pleasantly up-market soba noodles at ¥650.

Getting There & Away

Kagoshima Kōtsū buses to Chiran and Ibusuki run from stop No 10 at the Nishi-Kagoshima station or from the Yamakataya bus station at the Yamakataya department store in central Kagoshima. Chiran is 35 km from Kagoshima. The bus takes about one hour 20 minutes and the fare is ¥860.

IBUSUKI 指宿

At the south-eastern end of the Satsuma-hantō Peninsula, 50 km from Kagoshima, is the hot-spring resort of Ibusuki, a good base from which to explore other parts of the peninsula. The staff at the JR Ibusuki station information counter are very helpful.

Hot Springs

For onsen connoisseurs, Ibusuki has two renowned hot springs. On the beach in front of the Ginsho Hotel you can pay ¥710 for the somewhat dubious pleasure of being buried up to your neck in hot sand produced by steam rising up through the beach from somewhere in the bowels of the earth.

You pay at the entrance (the fee includes a *yukata* – like a bath robe – and towel),

change in the changing rooms then wander down to the beach where the burial ladies are waiting, shovel in hand. Those unused to real onsen heat may find the experience too hot to bear and quickly retreat to the baths to wash the sand off. You can take part in this ritual between 8.30 am and 9 pm from April to October and between 8.30 am and 8 pm from November to March.

Other Attractions

The town's modern art gallery is next to the Ibusuki Kankō Hotel and is open from 8 am to 5.30 pm daily. There are fine views over Ibusuki and along the coast from the 214m summit of Mt Uomi-dake.

Places to Stay & Eat

Ibusuki has two hostels. The *Ibusuki Youth Hostel* (☎ 0993-22-2758/2271) is just north of the station and costs ¥2600. The ryokan-style *Tamaya Youth Hostel* (☎ 0993-22-3553) is near the sand baths and costs ¥2000 or ¥2200, depending on the season.

The Japanese Inn Group representative in Ibusuki is the *New Yunohama-sō* (☎ 0993-23-3088), which has Japanese-style rooms with/without bathroom for ¥4000/3000. It's just 10 minutes walk from Ibusuki station in the direction of the beach. The English sign outside announces 'New'. *Minshuku Marutomi* (☎ 0993-22-5579) is a small but popular place, close to the town centre and just a stone's throw from the sand baths. The cost per person, including two meals, is ¥7000.

On the other side of Uomi-dake is the *Ibusuki Kokumin Kyūka Mura* (☎ 0993-22-3211), a large people's lodge that charges ¥8000 for rooms with two meals.

More expensive hotels and ryokan include *Ryokan Syūsuien* (☎ 0993-23-4141), which has a restaurant with a very high reputation and rooms from ¥24,000 to ¥100,000, and the *Ginsho Hotel*, which charges ¥20,000 with two meals.

Ibusuki has many other restaurants to choose from, especially around the JR station. There is also a good supermarket on the road leading straight out from the station.

KYŪSHŪ

Getting There & Away

Ibusuki is about 1½ hours from Kagoshima by bus; see the Chiran section for details. Trains operate from Nishi-Kagoshima station on the JR Makurazaki line. They take one hour 15 minutes and cost ¥800.

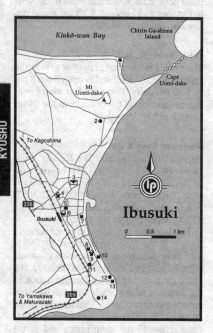

OTHER SATSUMA-HANTŌ PENINSULA ATTRACTIONS

Lake Ikeda-ko, west of Ibusuki, is a beautiful volcanic caldera lake inhabited by giant eels weighing up to 15 kg. Heading west along the coast you come to **Cape Nagasakibana** from where the offshore islands, including the smoking cone of Iwo-jima, can be seen on a clear day. The beautifully symmetrical 922m cone of **Mt Kaimon-dake** can be climbed in about two hours from the Kaimondake bus stop.

At the south-western end of the peninsula is **Makurazaki**, a busy fishing port and the terminus for the railway line from Kagoshima. Just beyond Mazurazaki is **Bōnotsu**, a pretty little fishing village which was an unofficial trading link with the outside world via Okinawa during Japan's two centuries of seclusion. North of Bōnotsu is **Fukiage-hama**, where the long beach is used for an annual summer sand-castle construction competition. The *Fukiage-hama Youth Hostel* (☎ 099-292-3455) costs ¥2400, depending on the season.

CAPE SATA-MISAKI 佐多岬

The southernmost point on the main islands of Japan is marked by the oldest lighthouse in Japan. You can reach Cape Sata-misaki from the Kagoshima side of Kinkō-wan Bay either by going around the northern end of

PLACES TO STAY	9 Tamaya Youth Hostel 玉屋ユースホステル	OTHER
1 Ibusuki Kokumin Kyūka Mura 指宿国民休暇村	10 Ginsho Hotel; Sand Bath 旅館吟松	2 Baseball Stadium 野球場
4 Ibusuki Youth Hostel 指宿ユースホステル	11 Ryokan Shūuien 秀水園旅館	3 Post Office 郵便局
7 New Yunohama-sō ニュー湯ノ浜荘	13 Ibusuki Kankō Hotel; Jungle Bath 指宿観光ホテル	5 Supermarket スーパーマーケット
8 Minshuku Marutomi 民宿まるとみ		6 Bus Station バスターミナル
		12 Ibusuki Art Gallery 指宿美術館
		14 Ginsho Pottery 吟松窯

Within the map:

Kinkō-wan Bay

Chirin Ga-shima Island

Mt Uomi-dake

Cape Uomi-dake

To Kagoshima

226

Ibusuki

Ibusuki

0   0.5   1 km

To Yamakawa & Makurazaki

269

KYŪSHŪ

the bay, taking the ferry from Kagoshima to Sakurajima or by taking the ferry from Yamakawa, south of Ibusuki, to Nejime, near Cape Sata-misaki. An eight km bicycle track leads down to the end of the cape.

Miyazaki-ken 宮崎県

OBI 飫肥

Only five km from the coast, the pretty little castle town of Obi has some interesting buildings around its old castle site. From 1587, the wealthy Ito clan ruled from the castle for 14 generations, surviving the 'one kingdom one castle' ruling in 1615. The clan eventually moved out in 1869 when the Meiji Restoration ended the feudal period.

Obi Castle 飫肥城

Although only the walls of the actual castle remain, the grounds contain a number of interesting buildings. The ¥500 entry fee includes all these buildings and Yōshōkan House just outside the castle entrance. Opening hours are from 9.30 am to 5 pm.

1	Matsuo-no-Maru House 松尾の丸
2	Tanoue Hachiman-jinja Shrine 田上八幡神社
3	Obi Castle Museum 資料館
4	Shintoku-dō School 振徳堂
5	Ōte-mon Gate 大手門
6	Yōshōkan House 豫章館
7	Ōtemon Chaya 大手門茶屋
8	Obi-ten オビテンレストラン
9	Merchant's Museum 商家資料館
10	Bus Station バスターミナル
11	Post Office 郵便局

KYŪSHŪ

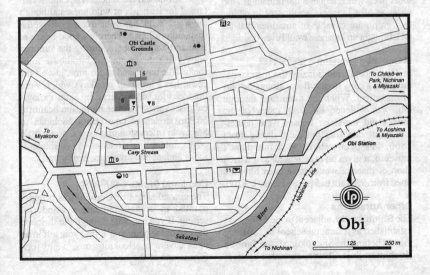

Obi

Yōshōkan House When the Obi lord was forced to abandon his castle after the Meiji Restoration, he moved down the hill to the Yōshōkan, formerly the residence of the clan's chief retainer. It stands just outside the castle entrance and has a large garden incorporating Mt Atago as 'borrowed scenery'. Beyond this house you enter the castle proper through the impressive Ōte-mon Gate.

Obi Castle Museum The castle museum has a collection relating to the Ito clan's long rule over Obi and includes everything from weapons and armour to clothing and household equipment.

Matsuo-no-Maru House Matsuo-no-Maru, the lord's private residence, has been reconstructed and there's an excellent descriptive leaflet of this quite extensive house. There's even a room with a window specifically placed for comfortable viewing of the autumn moon. When the lord visited the toilet at the far end of the house, he was accompanied by three pages – one to lead the way, one to carry water for the lord to wash his hands and one to fan him during the summer months! Look for the English sign on the toilet itself which requests 'no urinating!', the absence of a Japanese equivalent implying that gaijin are capable of atrocities that no well brought up Japanese would even consider.

Merchant's Museum   商家資料館
In Hommachi, traditionally the merchants' quarters, a carp stream flows alongside part of one street. When the main road through Obi was widened in 1980, many of the town's old merchant houses were demolished but one fine building, dating from 1866, has been rebuilt as a merchant's museum; it gives an excellent idea of what a shop of that era would have been like. It's open from 9.30 am to 5 pm and entry is ¥100.

Other Attractions
The **Shintōku-do**, adjacent to the castle, was established as a samurai school in 1801. Up the hill behind the Shintōkudo is the **Tanoue Hachiman-jinja Shrine**, shrouded by trees

and reached by a steep flight of steps. On the western side of the river, the **Ioshi-jinja Shrine** has a pleasant garden and the Ito family mausoleum. The **Chikkō-en Park** is on the eastern side of town, near the railway station.

Places to Eat
The entranceway to the castle is flanked by the *Obi-ten Restaurant* to the right, with up-market Japanese cooking featuring mountain vegetables, and the *Ōtemon Chaya* to the left, a friendly and unassuming noodle shop. Featured on the menu of the latter are tsukimi soba (literally 'moon-viewing soba') and curry udon.

Getting There & Away
The JR Nichinan line runs through Obi and Aoshima to Miyazaki. Miyazaki to Obi costs ¥800 and takes around an hour. Route 222 from Miyakono-jō to Obi and Nichinan on the coast is a superb mountain road, twisting and winding as it climbs over the hills.

CAPE TOI-MISAKI & NICHINAN-KAIGAN COAST   都井岬・日南海岸
Like Cape Sata, the views over the ocean from Cape Toi-misaki are superb. The cape is also famed for its herds of wild horses although the word 'wild' has to be treated with some suspicion in Japan. There's a good beach at Ishinami-kaigan where, during the summer only, you can stay in old farmhouse minshuku. The tiny island of Kō-jima, just off the coast, has a group of monkeys which were the focus for some interesting anthropological discoveries. Further north, the beautiful 50 km stretch of coast from Nichinan to Miyazaki offers stunning views, pretty little coves, interesting stretches of 'washboard' rocks and, at holiday times, heavy traffic.

Udo-jingū Shrine   鵜戸神宮
The coastal shrine of Udo-jingū is brightly painted in orange and has a wonderful setting. If you continue through the shrine to the end of the path, you'll find yourself in an open cavern overlooking some weird rock formations at the ocean's edge. A popular

sport is to buy five round clay pebbles for ¥100 and try to get them into a shallow depression on top of one of the rocks. Succeeding at this task is supposed to make your wish come true. Generally wishes are concerned with marriage and childbirth because, as a Japanese pamphlet explains, 'Udo is the god of marriage and easy childbirth'; the god is probably not too good at granting less domestic wishes. Buses bound for Nichinan from the Miyazaki Kōtsu bus station take around one hour 20 minutes to get to the shrine and cost ¥1340.

Aoshima 青島

This popular beach resort, about 10 km south of Miyazaki, is a tourist trap famed for the small island covered in betel palms, fringed by 'washboard' rock formations and connected to the mainland by a causeway. Due to the prevailing warm currents, the only place you'll find warmer water in Japan is much further south in the Okinawa Islands.

On the island is **Aoshima-jinj Shrine**, the **Tropical Botanical Garden** (¥200) and **Children's World** (¥600). The island shrine is connected to the mainland by a bridge and is only around five minutes walk from Aoshima station.

Places to Stay The *Aoshima Youth Hostel* (☎ 0985-65-1657) is near the railway tracks and costs ¥2200 or ¥2400, depending on the season. The *Aoshima Kokuminshukusha* (☎ 0985-65-1533) has Japanese-style rooms starting from ¥7000 with two meals. Aoshima also has a wide variety of hotels, most of them aimed at Japanese tourists with lots of money to throw around.

Getting There & Away Aoshima is on the JR Nichinan-Miyazaki line and less than half an hour away from JR Miyazaki station by train.

MIYAZAKI 宮崎

Miyazaki (population 290,000) is a reasonably large city with an important shrine and a pleasant park. Due to the warm offshore currents, the town has a balmy climate. The

area around Miyazaki played an important part in early Japanese civilisation and some interesting excavations can be seen in Saitobaru, 27 km north.

Orientation & Information

JR Miyazaki station is immediately east of the town centre. Most hotels (including the up-market riverside ones) and the youth hostel are reasonably close to the station. The main bus station is south of the Ōyodo-gawa River; the town's two principal attractions – Miyazaki-jingū Shrine and Heiwadai-kōen Park – are several km north.

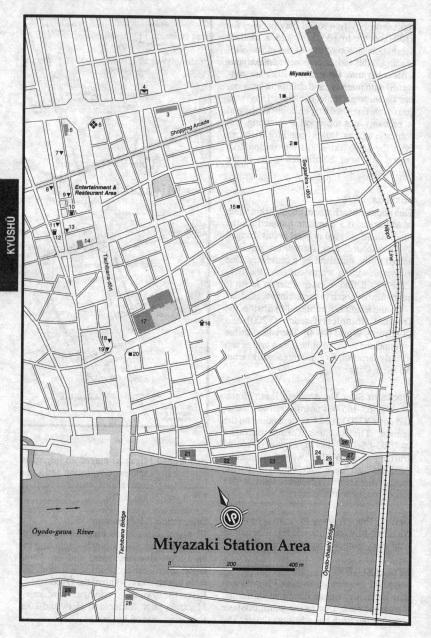

Miyazaki Station Area

Óyodo-gawa River

0   200   400 m

PLACES TO STAY

1 Shinshū Ryokan
新洲旅館
2 Miyazaki Hotel
Oriental
宮崎オリエンタル
ホテル
14 Miyazaki Washington
Hotel
宮崎ワシントン
ホテル
15 Business Hotel
Family
ビジネスホテル
ファミリー
16 Fujin Kaikan Youth
Hostel
婦人会館ユース
ホステル
20 Hotel Bigman
ホテルビッグマン
21 Kandabashi Hotel
ホテル神田橋

22 Miyazaki Plaza Hotel
宮崎プラザホテル
23 Miyazaki Kankō Hotel
宮崎観光ホテル
24 Ronkotei Hotel
ホテル監江亭
25 KKR Hotel
KKR ホテル
26 Miyazaki Grand Hotel
宮崎グランドホテル
27 Phoenix Hotel
ホテルフェニックス
28 Hotel Sunlight
ホテルサンライト
29 Sun Route Hotel
サンルートホテル

PLACES TO EAT

7 Italian Tomato
8 Mr Donut
9 Tommy's

11 Meiji-ya
明治屋
13 Den Den
でんでん
18 Mos Burgers
19 Suginoko
杉の子

OTHER

3 NTT
4 Main Post Office
中央郵便局
5 Yamakataya
Department Store
山形屋
6 ANA; JAS
10 Loose Bar
12 Suntory Shot Bar;
Time
17 Prefectural Office
宮崎県庁

KYŪSHŪ

There is a tourist information office (☎ 0985-22-6469) in JR Miyazaki station that can help find accommodation and one in the prefectural office (☎ 0985-25-4676), where you will also find a display of local products. The prefectural tourist office is just off Tachibana-dōri, Miyazaki's main boulevard.

Miyazaki-jingū Shrine & Museum
宮崎神宮・宮崎県総合博物館

The Miyazaki Shrine is dedicated to the Emperor Jimmu, the semimythical first emperor of Japan and founder of the Yamoto court. At the northern end of the shrine grounds is the Miyazaki Prefectural Museum with displays relating to local history and archaeological finds. Entry to the museum is ¥155 and it's open from 9 am to 4.30 pm daily except Monday. Also worth a look is the Minka-en, with its collection of traditional-style Kyūshū homes. It's also closed on Monday.

The shrine is about 2½ km north of JR Miyazaki station or a 15 minute walk from Miyazaki-jingū station, one stop north. From the station, the shrine is easy to find. Just look out for the big torii gate. Bus No 1 also runs to the shrine.

Heiwadai-kōen Park 平和台公園

The *heiwa* or 'peace' park has as its centrepiece a 36m-high tower constructed in 1940, a time when peace in Japan was about to disappear. Standing in front of the tower and clapping your hands produces a strange echo.

The Haniwa Garden in the park is dotted with reproductions of the curious clay *haniwa* figures which have been excavated from burial mounds in the region. You can buy small and large examples of these often rather amusing figures from a shop in the Haniwa Garden or from the park's main shopping complex. Small figures cost as little as ¥800 but the large ones are in the ¥10,000 to ¥20,000 bracket.

The Haniwa Garden is about 1½ km north of the Miyazaki Shrine but the museum, in the northern corner of the shrine grounds, is only a couple of minutes walk from the southern corner of the park. Bus No 8 runs to the park from outside JR Miyazaki station (¥270).

Special Events

On 3 April there is a samurai horse riding event at Miyazaki-jingū Shrine. Mid-April's Furusato Festival has around 10,000 participants in traditional attire dancing to local folk songs on Tachibana-dōri. A similar event takes place in late July, with *mikoshi* (portable shrines) being carried through the streets. In late July, Miyazaki is host to Kyūshū's largest fireworks show. Most locals seem to rate the major event of the year as the Dunlop Phoenix Golf Tournament, which is held in mid-November and attracts golfers from all over the world.

Places to Stay

The *Fujin Kaikan Youth Hostel* (☎ 0985-24-5785) is within easy walking distance of Miyazaki station and costs ¥2300. There are only 26 beds in the hostel, so it would be wise to book ahead.

A reasonably inexpensive ryokan is the *Shinshū Ryokan* (☎ 0982-24-4008), just across the road from the station, a few doors down on the right in the arcade. There's no English sign, but you can't miss it. Rooms without meals are ¥4800.

Across the road from the station, the *Miyazaki Oriental Hotel* (☎ 0985-27-3111) is a straightforward business hotel with singles from ¥5900 and doubles and twins from ¥9500.

Hotel Bigman (☎ 0985-27-2111) (what a great name!) is further west along the road from the youth hostel. It has singles/doubles from ¥5700/9500. When it comes to good names, the proprietors didn't stop at the hotel title; the Bigman also has the *Coffee House Realips*!

Most of the more expensive hotels are clustered along the riverside between the Tachibana Bridge and the Ōyodo-ōhashi Bridge. The *Miyazaki Plaza Hotel* (☎ 0985-

27-1111/2727) has doubles/twins from ¥13,500/14,000. Next to it is the *Miyazaki Kankō Hotel* (☎ 0985-27-1212) with singles from ¥7000 to ¥16,000 and doubles and twins from ¥14,000 to ¥120,000. Other riverside hotels include the *Kandabashi Hotel* (☎ 0985-25-5511), an expensive place with doubles and twins from ¥16,000. One place outside the riverside hotel strip is the *Miyazaki Washington Hotel* (☎ 0985-28-9111), which is in the town centre and entertainment area and has singles/twins from ¥7000/13,000.

Places to Eat

In the station area, the best place is in the arcade, where there are dozens of rāmen shops with plastic displays outside. There are also some fast-food barns dotted around, but by no means as many as you might expect of such a large town. Head right up the arcade and into the entertainment area for the best range of restaurants.

Suginoko (☎ 0985-22-5798) specialises in Miyazaki cuisine with its emphasis on locally grown vegetables. Although the menu is in Japanese only, there is a brief description in English posted downstairs and simply asking for the teishoku (the set meal of the day) will get you something interesting. A lunch-time 'hanashobu course' (mainly tempura) is ¥1500, a 'hamayu course' (mainly sushi) is ¥2500. At night the set meals cost from ¥3800 to ¥6000.

In the heart of the entertainment district, look out for *Meiji-ya*, a lively izakaya with a locomotive exterior. You'll hear it as you come down the street; speakers outside the restaurant blast out the puffing and whistling sounds of a labouring little steam train. Nearby is *Den Den*, a classy *kushiage* (boiled meat on sticks) restaurant that's not as expensive as it looks. *Tommy's* is an American diner – in other words it may be OK for a watery beer and a hamburger.

The *Miyazaki Hotel Oriental* has a good quality Chinese restaurant on its ground floor. It even serves dim sum, which are rare in this part of the world. The riverside *Phoenix Hotel* has a rooftop beer garden in the summer months with good views over the city. The Miyazaki station is known for its shiitake ekiben, a boxed lunch featuring mushroom.

Entertainment

Locals claim that Miyazaki has some 3500 bars and, after taking a stroll through the entertainment area, you won't find this too difficult to believe; it's packed with boozing establishments from basement level upwards. For a quiet, inexpensive beer head over to the *Suntory Shot Bar*, where a draught beer costs ¥380. The master-san speaks some English – ask him for his 'special'.

Getting There & Away

Air Miyazaki is connected with Tokyo (¥27,050), Osaka (¥16,950), Okinawa (¥22,850) and other centres by air.

Train The JR Nippō line runs from Kokura (5½ hours, ¥5360) in the north through Miyazaki to Kagoshima (2½ hours, ¥2160) in the west. If you're coming from Kagoshima, you may have to change trains in Kokubu. There are also train connections to Kumamoto (4½ hours, ¥5460), Fukuoka (Hakata) (5½ hours, ¥8860) and south through Obi to Nichinan.

Bus The Miyazaki Kōtsū city bus station is south of the Ōyodo-gawa River in Miya-ko, near JR Minami-Miyazaki station, and this is where most buses originate. There is also a second bus station opposite the Miyazaki station, which has buses to Saitobaru. Take a bus No 10 down the coast to Aoshima and Nichinan or a Cape Toi Express for Cape Toi-misaki. Buses also go from here to Ebino-kōgen in the Kirishima National Park, taking about two hours 15 minutes, to Fukuoka, Kagoshima and other centres. You can connect with many of the bus services along Tachibana-dōri, but figuring out just which stop you're meant to be standing at is not that easy. If you don't read Japanese you'll probably save yourself some frustration by heading down to the south bus station.

It is also possible to get long-distance buses from the Miyazaki bus station to Kagoshima (2½ hours, ¥2700), Fukuoka (five hours, ¥6000) and to Osaka (12½ hours, ¥11,500). Osaka buses run only once a day and do the trip by night.

Boat There are ferry services linking Miyazaki with Osaka. They take around 16½ hours, and 2nd class tickets cost ¥8230. For reservations in Miyazaki, contact Seacom (☎ 0985-29-8311). Seacom can also be reached in Osaka (☎ 06-311-1533).

Getting Around

The Airport Miyazaki's airport is conveniently situated about 20 minutes by bus from JR Miyazaki station. Buses run every 20 minutes from the Miyazaki Kōtsū bus station opposite the main railway station and head to the airport via the south bus station (¥360).

Bus Although bus services start and finish at the Miya-kō city bus station near JR Minami-Miyazaki station, many of them run along Tachibana-dōri in the centre, including No 1 to the Miyazaki-jingū Shrine and No 8 to Heiwadai-kōen Park. Miyazaki-Eigyosho, the other bus station, is near JR Miyazaki station.

Tours from the Miya-kō city bus station are operated by the Miyazaki Kōtsū bus company and cover not only the sights in town but sights along the coast to Aoshima and the Udo-jingū Shrine. The all-day tours cost about ¥5000.

SEAGAIA

The Seagaia Ocean Dome is a miraculous thing – a kind of Rendezvous with Rama water amusement park. It may not be, as the hype has it, a 'paradise within a paradise', but the idea of putting a 140m white sand beach and a splash of ocean under a huge dome is mind-boggling. It's almost as if the Japanese obsession with germ-free fun and amusement parks finds its apotheosis here – a completely controlled 'natural' environment.

Seagaia is a great place to bring kids. Entry is ¥4200. It's open from 9 am to 10 pm daily. Buses run from JR Miyazaki station (35 minutes, ¥530).

SAITOBARU　西都原

If the haniwa pottery figures in Miyazaki piqued your interest in the region's archaeology, then head north 27 km to the **Saitobaru Burial Mounds Park**, where several sq km of fields and forest are dotted with over 300 burial mounds (*kofun*). The 4th to 7th century AD mounds range from insignificant little bumps to hillocks large enough to appear natural creations. They also vary in shape, some being circular, some square, others a curious keyhole shape. Many are numbered with small signs, though any information is in Japanese. There's an interesting small museum with displays about the burial mounds and the finds that have been made, including swords, armour, jewellery, haniwa pottery figures and much more. Another exhibit shows items from the 18th century Edo period.

Entry to the museum is ¥155 and it is open from 9 am to 4.30 pm daily except Monday.

The park area is always open. Buses run to Saitobaru from the Miyazaki Kōtsu bus station next to Miyazaki station, and the one hour trip costs ¥950. If you want to explore the mound-dotted countryside you're either going to need your own transport or plan to walk a lot. Saitobaru is just outside the town of Saito.

TAKACHIHO　高千穂

The mountain resort town of Takachiho is about midway between Nobeoka on the coast and Mt Aso in the centre of Kyūshū. It's famed for its beautiful gorge and for a number of interesting shrines. There's a helpful tourist information counter by the tiny railway station.

Takachiho-kyō Gorge　高千穂峡

Takachiho's beautiful gorge, with its waterfalls, overhanging rocks and sheer walls, is the town's major attraction. There's a one km walk alongside the gorge, or you can inspect it from below in a rowboat, rented for a pricey ¥1000 for 40 minutes. The gorge is about two km from the centre, a ¥750 to ¥800 ride by taxi. You can walk it in just over half an hour.

Takachiho-jinja Shrine　高千穂神社

Takachiho-jinja shrine, about a km from JR Takachiho station, is set in a grove of cryptomeria. The local *iwato kagura* dances (see the Takachiho Legends aside in this section) are performed from 8 to 9 pm each evening, and entry is ¥500.

Amano Iwato-jinja Shrine　天岩戸神社

The Iwato-gawa River splits Amano Iwato-jinja Shrine into two parts. The main shrine, Nishi Hongū, is on the west bank of the river; while on the east bank is Higashi Hongū, at the actual cave where the sun goddess is alleged to have hidden and been lured out by the first performance of the iwato kagura dance. From the main shrine it's a 15 minute walk to the cave. The shrine is eight km from Takachiho. Buses leave every 45 minutes from the bus station and cost ¥340; a taxi would cost around ¥1500.

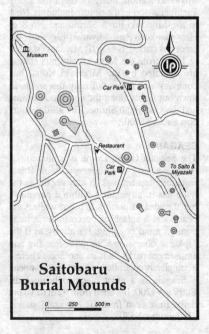

Saitobaru
Burial Mounds

0　250　500 m

Amano Yasugawara Cave 天安河原洞

A beautiful short walk from the Amano Iwato-jinja Shrine beside a picture-postcard stretch of stream takes you to the Amano Yasugawara cave. There, it is said, the gods conferred on how they could persuade the sun goddess to leave her hiding place and thus bring light back to the world. Visitors pile stones into small cairns all around the cave entrance.

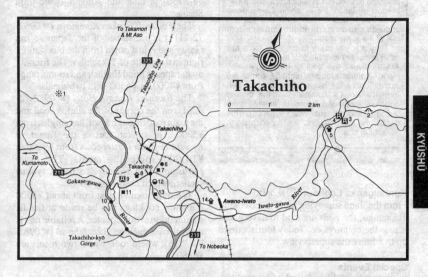

KYŪSHŪ

PLACES TO STAY

- 5 Iwato Furusato Youth Hostel
  岩戸ふるさとユースホステル
- 7 Business Hotel Kanaya
  かなやホテル
- 8 Yamatoya Ryokan; Youth Hostel
  旅館大和屋／ユースホステル
- 11 Kokuminshukusha Takachiho-sō
  国民宿舎高千穂荘
- 13 Folkcraft Ryokan Kaminoya
  民芸旅館上ノ屋
- 14 Takachiho Youth Hostel
  高千穂ユースホステル

OTHER

- 1 Kunimigaoka Lookout
  国見が丘
- 2 Amano Yasugawara Cave
  天安川原
- 3 Amano Iwato-jinja Shrine - Higashi Hongū
  天岩戸神社東本宮
- 4 Amano Iwato-jinja Shrine - Nishi Hongū
  天岩戸神社西本宮
- 6 City Hall
  市役所
- 9 Takachiho-jinja Shrine
  高千穂神社
- 10 Takachiho-kyō Gorge Bridge
  高千穂大橋
- 12 Bus Station
  バスターミナル

Takachiho Legends

Ninigi-no-mikoto, a descendant of the sun goddess Amaterasu, is said to have made landfall in Japan on top of Mt Takachiho in southern Kyūshū. Or at least that's what's said in most of Japan; in Takachiho the residents insist that it was in their town that the sun goddess' grandson arrived, not atop the mountain of the same name.

They also lay claim to the sites for a few other important mythological events, including Ama-no-Iwato, the 'boulder door of heaven'. Here Amaterasu hid and night fell across the world. To lure her out, another goddess performed a dance so comically lewd that the sun goddess was soon forced to emerge from hiding to find out what was happening. That dance, the iwato kagura, is still performed in Takachiho today. ■

Kunimigaoka Lookout 国見ヶ丘

From the 'land surveying bluff' overlooking Takachiho, the gods are said to have gazed across the countryside. Today tourists drive up to admire the superb view.

Special Events

Important iwato kagura festivals are held on 3 May, 23 September and 3 November at the Amano Iwato-jinja Shrine. There are also all-night performances in farmhouses from the end of November to early February and a visit can be arranged by inquiring at the shrine. A short dance performance takes place every night at the Takachiho-jinja Shrine.

Places to Stay

Takachiho has plenty of places to stay: the list at JR Takachiho station information counter includes more than 20 hotels, ryokan and pensions and another 20 minshuku. Despite this plethora of accommodation, every place in town can be booked out at peak holiday periods.

There are three youth hostels in the area, each costing ¥2500 a night. Right in the town centre, the *Yamatoya Ryokan & Youth Hostel* (☎ 0982-72-2243/3808) is immediately

recognisable by the huge figure painted on the front. The *Takachiho Youth Hostel* (☎ 0982-72-5192) is a couple of km from the centre, near the JR Amano-Iwato station. The *Iwato Furusato Youth Hostel* (☎ 0982-74-8750) is near the Amano Iwato-jinja Shrine.

The *Folkcraft Ryokan Kaminoya* (☎ 0982-72-2111) is a member of the Japanese Inn Group and is just down from the bus station, right in the centre of Takachiho. The friendly owner speaks good English and rooms range from ¥4000, or ¥6500 with two meals.

The *Business Kanaya Hotel* (☎ 0982-72-3261), on the corner of the station road and the main road through town, has singles from ¥5000. The ryokan part of the *Yamatoya Ryokan & Youth Hostel* costs from ¥9500 to ¥14,000, including meals. The *Iwato Furusato Youth Hostel* also has a ryokan section, which costs from ¥6000.

The minshuku all cost from about ¥5500 a night – bookings can be made at the JR station information counter. A reliable one is the *Kokuminshukusha Takachiho-sō* (☎ 0982-72-3255), where rooms with two meals are ¥6850.

Places to Eat

Many visitors just eat in their ryokan or minshuku, but Takachiho has plenty of restaurants. Opposite the Folkcraft Ryokan is *Kencha's*, a cheerful little yakitori (grill restaurant specialising in chicken dishes) marked by a bamboo frontage, banners, flags, signs, lanterns and a cavepeople cartoon across the top. The yakitori is nothing short of fabulous.

Getting There & Away

The private Takachiho Tetsudō line runs inland from Nobeoka on the coast, taking just over 1½ hours and costing ¥1300. Alternatively, there are bus services to Takachiho: buses take about three hours 15 minutes from Kumamoto, 3½ hours from Fukuoka (¥3910), 1½ hours from Nobeoka (¥1650) or less than an hour from Takamori (¥1280) near Mt Aso.

KYŪSHŪ

Getting Around

Although you can walk to the gorge and the Takachiho-jinja Shrine, the other sites are some distance from town and public transport is a problem. Regular tours leave from the bus station: the 'A Course' (¥1100) covers everything, while the 'B Course' (¥750) misses the Amano Iwato-jinja Shrine.

Ōita-ken 大分県

Ōita Prefecture offers an insight into the Japanese onsen (hot-spring) mania at both its best (Yufuin) and worst (Beppu). The region also bears some traces of Japan's earliest civilisations, particularly on the Kunisaki Peninsula and around Usuki.

BEPPU 別府

Beppu (population 140,000) is the Las Vegas of spa resort towns, a place where bad taste is almost requisite. Many Kyūshū travellers end up in Beppu and most come away disappointed. Beppu is not only onsen fever at its worst, it's also Japanese tourism at its most kitsch. If you're trying to develop an appreciation and understanding of onsen, you are not going to find it here. Beppu can be fun – just don't take it seriously.

Information

The JR Beppu station concourse has a tourist information counter (☎ 0977-24-2838), with maps and other information, but Beppu also has a Foreign Tourist Information Office (☎ 0977-23-1119) a few blocks from the station on the 2nd floor of the Furosen building, which is actually an onsen. The office has information sheets, maps and other useful material in English and has helpful English-speaking personnel.

The JR Beppu station area is very convenient for visitors. Facilities include a choice of accommodation, restaurants, banks, travel agencies and, of course, the railway station and other transport facilities. Beppu is, however, a sprawling town and the hot-spring areas are spread out, often some distance from the town centre. The adjacent town of Ōita is virtually contiguous with Beppu, and although it lacks any notable attractions, it could be an alternative place to stay.

Hot Springs

Beppu has two sorts of hot springs and there are lots of statistics about the more than 100 million litres of hot water they pump out every day. The jigoku are hot springs for looking at. The onsen are hot springs for bathing in.

The Hells Beppu's most hyped attraction is the 'hells' or jigoku, a collection of hot springs where the water bubbles forth from underground, often with unusual results. Admission to each hell is ¥400, or you can get a booklet of tickets for ¥2000 which covers all except one hell. The only real reason to visit all of them would be if you had a passion to see Japanese tourism at its absolute worst – car parks overflowing with tour buses, enthusiastic flag-waving tour guides, souvenir stands, the lot. Jigoku tour buses depart regularly from the JR Beppu station bus stop and cost ¥2700.

The hells are in two groups – seven at Kannawa, about eight km north-west of the station, and two more several km away. In the Kannawa group, the **Umi Jigoku** (Sea Hell), with its large expanse of gently steaming blue water, and the **Shiraike Jigoku** (White Pond Hell) are worth a look. **Kinryū Jigoku** (Golden Dragon Hell) and **Kamado Jigoku** (Oven Hell) have a dragon figure and a demon figure overlooking the pond. Skip the **Oniyama Jigoku** (Devil's Mountain Hell), where crocodiles are kept in miserable concrete pens, and the **Yama Jigoku** (Mountain Hell), where a variety of animals are kept under miserable conditions.

The smaller group has the **Chinoike Jigoku** (Blood Pool Hell), with its photogenically red water, and the **Tatsumaki Jigoku** (Waterspout Hell), where a geyser performs regularly. The former is worth a visit, but the latter can be skipped (there's too much concrete and too little natural beauty). The final hell, and the one not included in the group

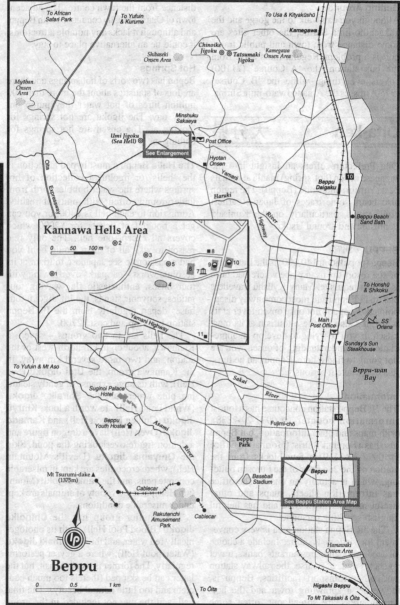

KYUSHŪ

To African
Safari Park

To Yufuin
& Kurume

To Usa & Kitakyūshū

Kamegawa

Chinoike
Jigoku

Tatsumaki
Jigoku

Kamegawa
Onsen Area

Shibaseki
Onsen Area

Myōban
Onsen
Area

Minshuku
Sakaeya

Umi Jigoku
(Sea Hell)

Post Office

See Enlargement

Hyotan
Onsen

Yamani

Beppu
Daigaku

Haruki

Ōita
Expressway

Highway

River

Beppu Beach
Sand Bath

Kannawa Hells Area

2

0   50   100 m

3

1

5

8

6   7   9   10

4

Yamani Highway

11

To Honshū
& Shikoku

Main
Post Office

SS
Oriana

Sunday's Sun
Steakhouse

To Yufuin & Mt Aso

Sakai

River

Beppu-wan
Bay

Suginoi Palace
Hotel

Beppu
Youth Hostel

Fujimi-chō

Beppu
Park

Asami

River

Baseball
Stadium

Beppu

See Beppu Station Area Map

Mt Tsurumi-dake
(1375m)

Cablecar

Cablecar

Rakutenchi
Amusement
Park

Hamawaki
Onsen Area

Beppu

0   0.5   1 km

To Yufuin & Mt Aso

To Ōita

Higashi Beppu

To Mt Takasaki & Ōita

1	Yama Jigoku (Mountain Hell) 山地獄
2	Kamado Jigoku (Oven Hell) かまど地獄
3	Oniyama Jigoku (Devil's Mountain Hell) 鬼山地獄
4	Shiraike Jigoku (White Pond Hell) 白池地獄
5	Kinryū Jigoku (Golden Dragon Hell) 金龍地獄
6	Hotel Ashiya ホテルあしや
7	Hinokan Sex Museum 秘宝館
8	Rakurakuen Ryokan 楽々園旅館
9	Kamenoi Bus Station (Buses to Chinoike Jigoku) 亀の井バスターミナル (至血の池地獄)
10	Kamenoi Bus Station (Buses to Beppu Station) 亀の井バスターミナル(至別府駅)
11	Oishi Hotel 大石ホテル

admission ticket, is the **Hon Bōzu Jigoku** (Monk's Hell). It has a collection of hiccupping and belching hot mud pools and is up the long hill from the main group of hells.

From the bus stop at JR Beppu station, bus Nos 16, 17, 41 and 43 go to the main group of hells at Kannawa. There are half a dozen buses an hour but the round trip costs virtually the same as an unlimited travel day pass. The No 26 bus continues to the smaller Chinoike/Tatsumaki group and returns to the station in a loop.

Onsen Ostensibly, it's sitting back and relaxing in the warm spring water that's Beppu's main attraction, and scattered around the town are eight onsen areas. Onsen enthusiasts spend their time in Beppu moving from one bath to another. Costs range from ¥200 to ¥600. Bring your own soap and towel.

The Beppu onsen area is in the town centre area near JR Beppu station. Among the most popular is **Takegawara Onsen** (¥610), which dates from the Meiji era and includes a sand bath. Here, the heat from the spring rises up through the sand and patrons lie down in a shallow trench and are buried up to their necks in the super-heated sand.

In the south-eastern part of town, near the road to Ōita, is the **Hamawaki onsen area**, with the popular old Hamawaki Koto Bath. North of the town, the **Kannawa onsen area** (near the major group of hells) is one of the most popular onsen areas in Beppu. There are also many ryokan and minshuku in this area.

The quieter **Shibaseki onsen area** is near the smaller group of hells, close to a mountain stream. Also north of JR Beppu station, near Kamegawa station, is the **Kamegawa onsen area** where the Hamada Bath is particularly popular. The **Beppu Municipal Beach Sand Bath** (¥600) is two km south of the Kamegawa onsen area. In the hills north-west of the town centre is the **Myōban onsen area**.

Hinokan Sex Museum 秘宝館

All that lolling around in hot water must have some sort of sensual side to it, so a sex museum seems just the thing for Beppu. It's

A wide range of cultural exhibits is on display at the Hinokan Sex Museum.

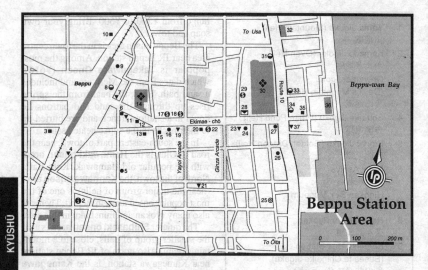

Beppu Station Area

0   100   200 m

in among the Kannawa hells, beside the large Indian temple relief opposite the Hotel Ashiya. Inside you'll find a bizarre collection ranging from 'positions' models and illustrations to a large collection of wooden phalluses (some very large indeed).

Erotic art on display ranges from Papua New Guinean fertility figures to Tibetan Tantric ones. There are life-size models which plunge into copulatory action at the press of a button, including one of Snow White having a lot of fun with the Seven Dwarfs. Another button lights up the windows of a model apartment building to reveal something happening in every room, including one room with tiny figures of Popeye and Olive Oil on a rotating bed. Entry costs a hefty ¥1500 and opening hours are from 9 am to 11 pm daily.

Mt Takasaki Monkey Park
高崎山自然動物園
A couple of km beyond Beppu towards Ōita, tribes of monkeys descend to the park at the foot of Mt Takasaki for a daily feed. It's said that the monkeys got into the habit of appearing for a free meal in the 1950s when a local farmer decided that feeding them was more

economical than allowing them simply to take his crops. The monkeys are in three distinct tribes – the largest has about 1000 members, the other two have 500 and 400. Each tribe has its own appointed feeding time during the day.

Admission to the park is ¥500 and Ōita Kōtsū buses from the Kitahama bus station operate to the Mt Takasaki park entrance (shared with the Marine Palace Aquarium) every 20 minutes.

Other Attractions
West of the station area, a cablecar carries visitors to the 1375m summit of **Mt Tsurumi-dake** but you can also walk to the top. It's a popular launching point for hang-gliders. The 12 km long **Yufugawa Ravine** is sandwiched between Mt Tsurumi-dake and Mt Yufu-dake (see the Yufuin section). The two mountains rise from the Tsukahara Plateau, also known as Matsuzuka or 'Pine Mound'.

There's a large **African safari park** 18 km north-west of Beppu (entrance is ¥2200, plus another ¥450 for the safari bus); in town itself is **Rakutenchi Amusement Park** (¥1500). **Utopia Shidaka** is another amusement park about 12 km from the town centre.

KYŪSHŪ

PLACES TO STAY

1　Kamenoi Hotel
　　亀の井ホテル
3　Business Hotel
　　Kagetsu
　　ビジネスホテル花月
6　New Hayashi Hotel
　　ニューハヤシホテル
10　Beppu Dai-Ichi Hotel
　　別府第一ホテル
12　Kiyomizu-sō Hotel
　　清水荘
13　Minshuku Kokage
　　民宿こかげ
15　Hotel New Kimekiya
　　ホテルニュー
　　きめきや
20　Green Hotel
　　グリーンホテル
35　Hanabishi Hotel
　　花菱ホテル
36　Seifu Hotel
　　清風ホテル

PLACES TO EAT

4　KFC
7　Bentō Shop
　　吉四六弁当
11　Jūoku-ya
　　十徳屋

19　Marui Shokudō
　　まるい食堂
21　Kani Ryōri
　　カニ料理屋
23　Tairitsu Honten
　　Noodle Shop
　　大陸ラーメン
37　Royal Host
　　Restaurant

OTHER

2　Foreign Tourist
　　Information Office
　　外国人旅行者観光
　　案内所
5　Laundry
　　コインランドリー
8　Beppu Station Bus
　　Stop
　　別府駅バス停
9　Car Rental Office
　　駅前レンタカー
14　Kintetsu Department
　　Store
　　近鉄百貨店
16　Scala-za Cinema
　　スカラ座
17　Iyo Bank
　　伊予銀行

18　Beppu Shinyo Bank
　　別府信用金庫
22　Fukuoka City Bank
　　福岡市銀行
24　Cinema
　　別府オスカー
25　Takegawara Onsen
　　竹瓦温泉
26　JTB
27　Robata & Beer Pub
　　ろばたやきビアパブ
28　Post Office
　　郵便局
29　Ōita Bank
　　大分銀行
30　Cosmopia Shopping
　　Centre; Tokiwa
　　Department Store
　　コスモピア／
　　常盤百貨店
31　Airport Bus Stop
　　空港バス停
32　Beppu Tower
　　別府タワー
33　Kamenoi Bus Station
　　亀の井バス停
34　Kitahama Bus Station
　　北浜バス停

The **Marine Palace Aquarium** (¥1050) is by the seafront, sharing the same car park as the monkey park at Mt Takasaki.

Places to Stay

Although places to stay are scattered around Beppu, they are concentrated around the south-west of town (Suginoi Hotel area), around JR Beppu station and in the Kannawa hot-springs area.

Around Suginoi The huge *Suginoi Palace Hotel* (☎ 0977-24-1141) overlooks Beppu from its hillside location but you'll pay for the view: rooms range from ¥15,000 to ¥36,000.

The *Beppu Youth Hostel* (☎ 0977-23-4116) costs ¥2600 a night and is very close to the Suginoi Hotel. To get to the hostel, take a No 4 bus (departing hourly from Beppu station's western exit) or a No 14 bus (departing half hourly) and get off at the Kankaiji-bashi bus stop.

Around Beppu Station The *Minshuku Kokage* (☎ 0977-23-1753), a member of the Japanese Inn Group, is just a few minutes walk from Beppu station. It's a particularly friendly minshuku, used to dealing with the vagaries of gaijin clients, and has rooms at ¥3000/4000 per person without/with bathroom. There's a spacious bath upstairs and a laundry costing ¥100 each for a load of washing and drying. If the Kokage is full, just around the corner is the slightly down at heel *Kiyomizu-sō* (☎ 0977-23-0221), where rooms range from ¥4000.

The *Business Hotel Star* (☎ 0977-25-1188) is right behind JR Beppu station and has very basic rooms at ¥4000 for singles, ¥7000 for twins and doubles. The *Beppu Dai Ichi Hotel* (☎ 0977-24-6311), also behind the station, has singles/doubles at ¥4500/8000.

The *New Hayashi Hotel* (☎ 0977-24-5252) has singles/doubles at ¥4500/8400. Down the road is the *Green Hotel* (☎ 0977-25-2244), with singles/doubles at ¥4500/8000. The beach area is also crowded with hotels but most of them are very expensive.

Kannawa Jigoku Area There are a number of minshuku and ryokan around the Kannawa hot springs, including the big *Hotel Ashiya* (☎ 0977-67-7711), which is right in among the jigoku.

Also close to the Kannawa jigoku is the *Rakurakuen Ryokan* (☎ 0977-67-2682) which costs from ¥6500 to ¥10,000 per person and has a variety of baths to try. Up the road from the jigoku, behind the small post office, is *Minshuku Saekya* (☎ 0977-66-6234). It costs ¥4500 per person (room only) or ¥8000 with breakfast and dinner. This popular minshuku is in an interesting old building and your food is cooked using hot-springs heat.

Places to Eat
Beppu is renowned for its freshwater fish, for its fugu (globefish) and for the wild vegetables grown in the mountains further inland. If you're game for the fugu experience, you can do it in style at *Fugu Matsu* (☎ 0977-21-1717). Fugu sushi courses cost ¥3000.

For predictable izakaya food, *Jūtoku-ya* is close to the station and has an enormous range of dishes on its illustrated menu, all at very reasonable prices. It's also a good place for a couple of beers with snacks.

The area around the Minshuku Kokage is good for yakitori restaurants; most of them

have dishes ranging from ¥200 to ¥400 as well as beer on tap. Just off the Yayoi arcade, look out for *Kani Ryōri*, which specialises in crab but also has other, less expensive items on its menu. You can't miss this place as it has an enormous crab suspended over the doorway. Back on Ekimae-chō, between the two arcades, there's an excellent little *rāmen shop*, and on the same side of the road, closer to the station, is the *Marui Shokudō*, a good place for inexpensive tonkatsu and katsudon (pork cutlet dishes).

The station and vicinity is the place to seek out fast-food outfits: don't panic – they're all represented. If you're looking for somewhere for a drink in the evening, try *Cocktail Vague*, just around the corner from the station.

Getting There & Away
Air There are flights to Ōita airport from Tokyo, Osaka, Nagoya, Kagoshima and Okinawa. It's even possible to fly direct to Seoul.

Train From Fukuoka/Hakata via Kokura in Kitakyūshū it takes about 2½ hours on the JR Nippō line to Beppu. The basic *futsū* fare is ¥3190, while the limited express service costs an additional ¥2150. The line continues on down the coast to Miyazaki. The JR Hōhi line runs from Beppu to Kumamoto via Mt Aso; it takes about 2½ hours to Aso and another hour down to Kumamoto.

Bus The Yamanami Highway bus No 266 links Beppu and Kumamoto with a side trip to Mt Aso. The journey between Beppu and Mt Aso takes about three hours, another hour from Mt Aso to Kumamoto.

Boat The Kansai Kisen ferry service (☎ 0977-22-1311) does a daily run between Beppu and Osaka (17 hours, ¥6900), stopping en route at Kōbe (14 to 15 hours, ¥6900) and Matsuyama (4½ hours, ¥2400). Late evening boats to western Honshū should pass through the Inland Sea during daylight hours the next morning.

Getting Around

The Airport Hovercraft run from Ōita and Beppu (¥2700) to Ōita airport, which is 40 km around the bay from Beppu. The airport bus service takes about an hour (¥1700) and leaves from the stop outside the Cosmopia shopping centre.

Bus There are four local bus companies, of which Kamenoi is the largest. Most buses are numbered, but Ōita Kōtsū buses for the Mt Takasaki monkey park and Ōita are not. An unlimited travel 'My Beppu Free' pass for Kamenoi buses comes in two varieties: the 'mini pass' version, which covers all the local attractions, including the hells, for ¥900; and the 'wide pass', which goes further afield and is ¥1600 for one day or ¥2400 for two. The passes are available at the JR Beppu station information counter and at the Beppu Youth Hostel.

A variety of bus tours operate from the Kitahama bus station including tours to the Kannawa hot springs, the African safari park and other attractions.

USUKI 臼杵

About five km from Usuki is a collection of some superb 10th to 13th century **Buddha images**. More than 60 images lie in a series of niches in a ravine. Some are complete statues, whereas others have only the heads remaining, but many are in wonderful condition, even with paintwork still intact. The **Dainichi Buddha head** is the most impressive and important of the Usuki images. There are various other stone Buddha images at sites around Ōita Prefecture, such as Motomachi, Magari and Takase, but the Usuki ones are the most numerous and most interesting. Entry to the ravine is ¥520 and it's open from 8.30 am to sunset. There's a choice of restaurants at the site. The town of Usuki is about 40 km south-east of Beppu; trains take a little under one hour and cost ¥1400. It's then a 20 minute bus ride (¥300) to the ravine site; alternatively, you could walk the few km from the Kami-Usuki station.

YUFUIN 湯布院

If Beppu is the hot-spring resort scene at its glitzy worst, then Yufuin is its genteel relation. About 25 km inland from Beppu, Yufuin makes a pleasant stop between Beppu and Mt Aso and has an interesting variety of baths to sample, including some fine *rotenburo* (open-air baths).

Information

The tourist information office in front of the railway station has some information in English. Change money in Beppu, as there's no place to do it readily in Yufuin. There are onsen festivals in April and May.

Things to See & Do

As in Beppu, making a pilgrimage from one onsen to another is a popular activity in Yufuin. The difference is that in Yufuin you get some rustic peace and quiet to do it in. The Kinrinko and Makinote rotenburo are special attractions. **Lake Kinrin-ko** is fed by hot springs, so it's warm all year round. Shitan-yu is a thatched bathhouse (¥100) on the northern shore of the lake.

The town has a number of interesting temples and shrines including the **Kozenin-ji**, **Bussan-ji** and **Bukko-ji** temples. Yufuin is also noted for its arts and handicrafts, which can be seen at the **Mingei-mura Folk Art Village** (8.10 am to 5.30 pm daily, ¥610) and in a number of shops and galleries.

The double-peaked 1583m **Mt Yufu-dake** volcano overlooks Yufuin and takes about one hour to climb. Take a bus from the Kamenoi bus station to Yufu Tozanguchi, about 20 minutes away on the Beppu-Yufuin bus route.

Places to Stay & Eat

Yufuin has many minshuku, ryokan and pensions, including the popular *Pension Yufuin* (☎ 0977-85-3311), which costs from ¥9500 per person, including two meals. It's a typically Japanese 'rural western' guest house fantasy. *Kokuminshukusha Yufu Sansō* (☎ 0977-84-2105) costs from ¥6500 per person, including two meals. It's next to the morning market, very close to Yufuin station.

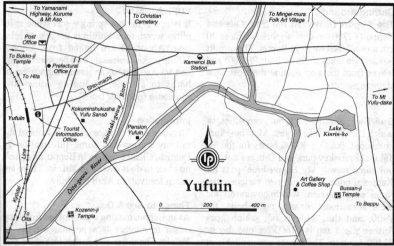

Most of the ryokan around town are high-class places with very high costs.

Getting There & Away

Buses go to Yufuin from the JR Beppu station bus stop every hour and the one hour trip costs ¥980. The JR Kyūdai line runs to Yufuin from Ōita (one hour 10 minutes, ¥800). Continuing beyond Yufuin is not always easy. Kyūshū Kokusai Kankō (KKC) buses go to Mt Aso and Kumamoto but not year round.

BEPPU TO MT ASO
別府から阿蘇山方面へ
Yamanami Highway やまなみハイウェイ

The picturesque Yamanami Highway extends 63 km from the Mt Aso region to near Yufuin; from there, the Ōita Expressway runs to Beppu on the east coast. There's a ¥1850 toll to drive along this scenic road, however, tour buses operating between Kumamoto, Aso and Beppu, or the reverse, also use this route. The road crosses a high plateau and passes numerous mountain peaks, including **Mt Kujū-san** (1788m), the highest point in Kyūshū.

Taketa 竹田

South of Yufuin, near the town of Taketa, are the **Oka-jō Castle ruins**, which have a truly magnificent ridge-top position. The ruins are about two km from JR Bungo-Taketa station; take a Taketa Kōtsū bus (¥140) there and walk back into town. Taketa has some interesting old buildings, reminders of the Christian period and a museum (no English). Bungo-Taketa is on the JR Hōhi line between Ōita and Mt Aso. From Mt Aso to Taketa, it takes just under an hour by train or bus; from there it's just over an hour by train to Ōita – a little longer by bus.

KUNISAKI-HANTŌ PENINSULA
国東半島

Immediately north of Beppu, the Kunisaki-hantō Peninsula bulges eastwards from the Kyūshū coast. The region is noted for its early Buddhist influence, including some rock-carved images which are related to the better known ones at Usuki.

Usa 宇佐

In the early post-WWII era, when 'Made in Japan' was no recommendation at all, it's said that companies would register in Usa so they could proclaim that their goods were 'Made in USA'! The town is better known for its bright orange **Usa-jinja Shrine**, the original of which dated back over 1000 years. The current shrine is much newer and connected with Hachiman, the god of war. The treasure house costs ¥300 to enter, but the shrine is free. It's a 10 minute (¥240) bus ride from town.

Getting There & Away From Beppu station, the Nichirin service on the JR Nippō line runs hourly to Usa (35 minutes, ¥1820).

Other Attractions

The Kunisaki-hantō Peninsula is said to have more than half of all the stone Buddhas in Japan. The 11th century **Fuki-ji Temple** in Bungotakada is the oldest wooden structure in Kyūshū and one of the oldest wooden temples in Japan. Entry is ¥300. Take an Ōita

Kunisaki-hantō Peninsula

Kōtsū bus from Usa station to Fuki-ji (40 minutes, ¥770).

Right in the centre of the peninsula, near the summit of Mt Futago-san, is **Futago-ji Temple**, dedicated to Fudomyo-o, the god of fire. It's open from 8.30 am to 4 pm daily; entry is ¥200. It's difficult to get to using public transport.

Carved into a cliff behind the Taizo Temple, two km south of **Maki Ōdō**, are two large Buddha images; a six-metre-high figure of the Dainichi Buddha and an eight-metre-high figure of Fudō-Myō-o. These are known as the **Kumano Magaibutsu** and are the largest Buddhist images of this type in Japan. Other stone statues, thought to be from the Heian period of 1000 to 1100 AD, can be seen in Maki Ōdō. You can get there via the same bus as the one to Fuki-ji Temple from Usa station (one hour 50 minutes, ¥1600).

Getting Around

The easiest way to tour the peninsula is on the daily five to seven hour bus tours from Beppu or Nakatsu. Beppu's Ōita airport is on the peninsula, about 40 km from Beppu. Ōita Kōtsū buses from Usa station do a loop around the main attractions of the peninsula.

NORTHERN ŌITA-KEN
大分県の北部
Nakatsu 中津

In the far north of Ōita-ken on the JR Nippō line is Nakatsu, a small town that is noted most of all for its picturesque castle. **Nakatsu-jō Castle**, originally dating from 1588, is a modern reconstruction but it still looks good. There are exhibitions of samurai armour and weapons in the castle. The castle is open from 9 am to 5 pm daily; entry is ¥300. It's about one km north-west of the station.

Nakatsu has accommodation, but it's probably best just to stop over en route between Fukuoka and Beppu. The *Hotel Sunroute* (☎ 0979-24-7111) is just behind the station, and has singles/twins from ¥5830/13,860. Close by is the *Hotel Sunrise* (☎ 0979-24-3355) and the *Nakatsu Oriental Hotel* (☎ 0979-24-8111), both of which have singles/twins from about ¥5000/9000. The

KYŪSHŪ

Hiyoshi Ryokan (☎ 0979-22-7310) is north of the station and has rooms from ¥6500.

Yaba-kei Gorge 耶馬渓

From Nakatsu, Route 212 turns inland and runs through the picturesque Yaba-kei Gorge. The gorge extends for about 10 km, beginning about 16 km from Nakatsu. The **Ao-no-Dōmon** (Ao Tunnel), at the start of the gorge, was originally cut over a 30 year period by a hard-working monk in order to make the Rankan-ji Temple more accessible.

Smaller gorges join the main one, and there are frequent buses up the gorge road from Nakatsu. A 35 km cycling track follows a now disused railway line. You can rent bicycles (two hours for ¥360) and stay at the *Yabakei Cycling Terminal* (☎ 0979-54-2655), which costs ¥5000 with two meals. The *Yamaguniya Youth Hostel* (☎ 0979-52-2008) costs ¥2800 per night.

From Nakatsu station Ōita-kōtsū buses do the 40 minute trip to Ao-no-Dōmon for ¥580.

For the cycling terminal Ōita Kōtsu Hida-bound buses do the trip in around 55 minutes and cost ¥930.

Hita Area 日田

Further inland from the Yaba-kei Gorge is Hita, a quiet country town and onsen resort where cormorant fishing (*ukai*) takes place in the river from May to October. Just across the prefectural border in Fukuoka-ken you can also see cormorant fishing in **Harazara**, another hot-spring resort.

North of Hita, towards Koishiwara, is **Onta**, a small village renowned for its curious pottery. The **Onta-yaki Togeikan Museum** has a display of the local product. Koishiwara also has a pottery tradition dating back to the era when Korean potters were first brought to Kyūshū.

Hita is on the JR Kyūdai line between Ōita (two hours) and Kurume (one hour). By bus it takes about 40 minutes to travel from Hita to Onta.

Okinawa & the South-West Islands
沖縄 · 南西諸島

The South-West Islands, or Nansei-shotō as they are known in Japanese, meander for more than 1000 km in the direction their name suggests from the southern tip of Kyūshū to Yonaguni-jima Island, just a strenuous stone's throw (a little over 100 km) from the east coast of Taiwan.

The northern half of the Nansei-shotō group falls within Kagoshima-ken and includes the Ōsumi-shotō Islands and the Amami-shotō Islands.

The four island groups which form the southern half of the Nansei-shotō Islands comprise Okinawa-ken. Of these, the most important islands – and those that attract the most visitors – are the Okinawa (or Ryūkyū) Islands to the north and the Yaeyama Islands to the south.

Okinawa, the hub of the island chain, is referred to as *hontō* – main island – and its key role in the closing months of WWII holds a continuing fascination for visitors. But for natural beauty and deeper insights into Okinawan culture, you must continue on to the *ritō* – 'outer islands'. Kume-jima Island, for example, is famed for its unspoilt beauty; Taketomi-jima is a tiny island with a picture-postcard village; and Iriomote-jima Island is Japan's last wilderness, cloaked in dense tropical jungle. Prime scuba-diving sites are found around the Kerama-rettō Islands and around Iriomote-jima.

In between the Okinawa Islands and the Yaeyama Islands are the Miyako Islands; 350 km to the east of Okinawa are the isolated Daito Islands.

A warm climate, fine beaches, excellent scuba diving and traces of traditional culture are the prime attractions for visitors to Nansei-shotō. But don't think of these islands as forgotten backwaters with a mere handful of visitors – both ANA and JAL fly tourists to Okinawa from mainland Japan by the 747-load and even the local flights from

HIGHLIGHTS

- ◆ Explore Naha's Kokusai-dōri, a sunny, relaxed stretch of bars, steak restaurants and souvenir shopping which is great fun by day or night
- ◆ Visit Shuri-jō Castle, a beautifully executed re-creation of the traditional seat of Ryūkyū power
- ◆ Hire a car, or take local buses, to the war memorial sites of southern Okinawa, enjoying the rural and seaside scenery along the way
- ◆ Dive off Ishigaki and its neighbouring islands
- ◆ Spend time in Iriomote to see Japan's only pocket of jungle wilderness

Okinawa to other islands in the chain are by 737s. Despite having survived centuries of mainland exploitation, and then horrific destruction during the closing months of WWII, the traditional ways of these islands may not survive the onslaught of mass tourism.

809

KYŪSHŪ

KAGOSHIMA

PACIFIC
OCEAN

Tanega-shima
Kuro-shima
ŌSUMI-SHOTŌ
ISLANDS

Kuchino-
Erabu-jima   Yaku-shima

Kuchino-shima
Nakano-shima
Gaja-jima   Suanose-jima
TOKARA   Taira-shima   Akuseki-jima
ISLANDS
Takara-jima   Kikai-shima

Naze   Amami-
ōshima
AMAMI-SHOTŌ   Kakeroma-shima
ISLANDS   Yoro-shima   Uke-jima

EAST   Yokoate-jima   Tokuno-shima
CHINA
SEA   Okino-Erabu-jima
Yoron-jima

Iheya-jima
Izena-jima
Ie-jima   Nago
OKINAWA   Okinawa
ISLANDS   Okinawa City   Island
Aguni-jima   Naha
Zamami-jima   Tokashi-
Kume-jima   ki-jima
Kerama-rettō
Tonaki-shima   Islands

**South-West
Islands**

0   100   200 km

Hirara
MIYAKO   Miyako-jima
ISLANDS   Irabu-jima
Shimoji-jima
Tarama-shima
YAEYAMA
ISLANDS   Ishigaki-jima
Ishigaki   Taketomi-jima
Iriomote-jima   Kuro-shima
Kohama-jima
Hateruma-jima
Yonaguni-jima

KAGOSHIMA-KEN   OKINAWA-KEN

HISTORY

The islands of the Nansei-shotō chain look like stepping stones from Japan to Taiwan, and they have long been a bridge between Japanese and Chinese culture. For the often unfortunate residents of the islands this has sometimes resulted in being squeezed and pulled from both sides. More recently Okinawa was the scene for some of the most violent and tragic action in the closing months of WWII.

For centuries, the islands formed a border zone between Chinese and Japanese suzerainty. In 1372 an Okinawan king initiated tributes to the Chinese court; this was to remain the practice for 500 years.

In the 15th century the whole island of Okinawa was united under the rule of the Shō dynasty and the capital shifted from Urasoe to Shuri, where it was to remain until the Meiji Restoration. The period from 1477 to 1525 is remembered as a golden age of Okinawan history. By the 17th century, however, Japanese power was on the ascendancy. The Okinawans found themselves under a new ruler when the Satsuma kingdom of southern Kyūshū invaded in 1609. From this time the islands were controlled with an iron fist and taxed and exploited greedily. In 1879 the islands were formally made a prefecture under Meiji rule.

After being treated as foreign subjects by the Satsuma regime, the Okinawans were pushed to become 'real' Japanese. They paid a heavy price for this new role when they were trapped between the relentless US hammer and the fanatically resistant Japanese anvil in the closing stages of WWII.

US bombing started in October 1944. On 1 April 1945, US troops landed on the island. The Japanese made an all-out stand. It took 82 horrendous days for the island to be captured. Not until 22 June was the conquest complete, by which time 13,000 US soldiers and, according to some estimates, a quarter of a million Japanese had died. Many of the Japanese casualties were civilians and there are terrible tales of mass suicides by mothers clutching their children and leaping to their

The Okinawan Problem

Compared to the rest of Japan, Okinawa is a tiny place, amounting to just 0.6% of the nation's total landmass. Curious then that 75% of Japan's US military bases should be crowded onto the island. Military bases account for over 20% of Okinawa's land.

Okinawan resentment at being a de facto US colony came to a head in September 1995, when three US soldiers abducted a 12-year-old girl, drove her to a field in a rented car and raped her. Sentencing of the soldiers to jail terms of 6½ to seven years was widely seen as inadequate and did little to quell public anger. A protest rally in October 1995 drew crowds of 850,000 people. US promises in late 1996 to return some 20% of the military-owned land were received with little enthusiasm when they refused to lower troop numbers.

Okinawan anger is directed not just at the US but at 'mainland' Japan, which many Okinawans claim habitually deals out losing hands to the Ryūkyū islanders. Some islanders have been heard to wonder aloud whether greater autonomy, or even independence altogether, isn't the best way forward. In a poll held in 1995, over 46% of correspondents claimed to see themselves as Uchimanchu – the name Ryūkyū islanders use to refer to themselves; a further 31% saw themselves as both Uchimanchu and Japanese; just 12% saw themselves as Japanese.

The issue of US bases has perhaps hastened a political awakening in a part of Japan that many see as experiencing a 'renaissance'. Okinawan music has made significant inroads into the Japanese mainstream music industry, its writers and artists are gaining attention, and some Japanese, tired of big city life in mainland Japan, are starting to look south longingly at Okinawa. Many young Japanese are moving to Okinawa, where they claim life is more relaxed and relationships more intimate. It is with new-found confidence and pride that Okinawans are starting to stand up and ask the central government in Tokyo to share some of the burden of US bases if they are to remain in Japan. ■

deaths off cliff tops to avoid capture by the foreigners whom, they had been led to believe, were barbarians.

The Japanese commanders committed *seppuku* ('ritual suicide'), but a final horror remained. The underground naval headquarters at Tomigusuku were so well hidden they were not discovered until three weeks after the US victory. The underground corridors contained the bodies of 4000 naval officers and men, all of whom had committed suicide.

Okinawa became a major US military base during the cold war. Sovereignty of the island was finally returned to Japan in 1972, but even today a strong US military presence persists on Okinawa. The rape of a Japanese schoolgirl by US marines in 1995 brought anger about the US military presence to a head. There has been talk of reducing US military numbers on the island.

CLIMATE

The climate of the Nansei-shotō Islands is much warmer than that of the Japanese main islands, and Okinawa is virtually a tropical getaway. November to April is considered to be the best season, May and June can bring heavy rain, July to August is not only very hot but also very crowded, while September and October is the typhoon season.

Although the winter months (November to March) are cooler, the crowds are lighter and for divers underwater visibility is at its best.

GETTING THERE & AWAY

Okinawa is the travel hub of the Nansei-shotō chain. There are numerous flights and shipping services to Naha, the main city on Okinawa, from Kagoshima at the southern end of Kyūshū and from many other cities, including Tokyo.

Some shipping services stop at islands on the way to Okinawa. There are also connecting flights and ships from Okinawa to other islands further down the chain. See the sections on individual islands later in this chapter for details.

Travellers who show their YHA membership card when buying boat tickets will get coupons for free meals on board.

OKINAWA & SOUTH-WEST ISLANDS

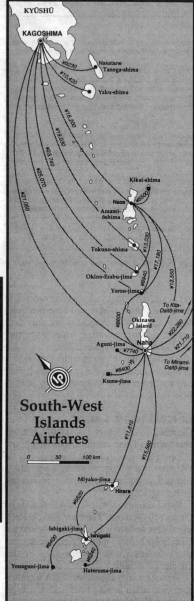

KYŪSHŪ

KAGOSHIMA

¥9230
¥10,420

Nakatane
Tanega-shima

Yaku-shima

¥16,200

¥19,030

¥23,740

¥25,070

¥21,060

Kikai-shima

Naze ¥6500
Amami-
ōshima

¥13,030

Tokuno-shima

¥17,180

Okino-Erabu-jima ¥6940 ¥13,550

Yoron-jima

To Kita-
Daitō-jima

¥8600

Okinawa
Island

¥22,280

Aguni-jima ¥7740 Naha ¥21,710

To Minami-
Daitō-jima

¥6400

Kume-jima

**South-West
Islands
Airfares**

0   50   100 km

¥11,810

¥15,560

Miyako-jima

Hirara

Ishigaki-jima

¥6400 Ishigaki

¥6940

Yonaguni-jima

Hateruma-jima

Ōsumi-shotō Islands
大隅諸島

The northernmost island group of the Nansei-shotō chain is the Ōsumi-shotō Islands. Tanega-shima and Yaku-shima, the two main islands of the group, are less than 100 km from Kagoshima at the southern end of Kyūshū. The islands, one flat and long, the other high and round, are about as different as two islands could be. South of these two main islands are the smaller, scattered Tokara Islands.

GETTING THERE & AWAY
Ferry services and JAS flights connect Kagoshima with the two main islands – 3½ hours by ferry to Tanega-shima, 4½ hours to Yaku-shima. Boats operate between Cape Shimama-zaki at the southern end of Tanega-shima and Kamiyaku on Yaku-shima.

TANEGA-SHIMA ISLAND 種子島
Tanega-shima's low-lying terrain is mainly devoted to agriculture. The island is about 55 km long and the port of **Nishino-omote** (population 26,000) is the main town. The island has an important place in Japanese history, for this was where a Portuguese ship first made landfall in Japan in 1543. The introduction of modern European firearms from this first contact played an important part in bringing the disastrous 'Country at War' or Muromachi period to a close.

YAKU-SHIMA ISLAND 屋久島
In contrast to Tanega-shima's flatness, volcanic Yaku-shima rises to the 1935m peak of **Mt Miyanoura-dake**, the highest point in southern Japan. Mt Kuromi, the island's second-highest peak, is only slightly lower at 1836m. The island is just 25 km in diameter, but the towering terrain catches every inbound rain cloud, giving the island one of the wettest climates in Japan.

Kamiyaku, on the north-east coast, is the main port; a road runs around the island, passing through Anbō and Yaku. From Anbō

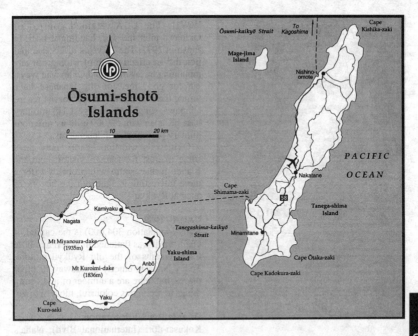

you can take a taxi up the slopes of the mountain and walk past a waterfall and through an ancient cedar forest.

Amami-shotō Islands
奄美諸島

There are five main islands in the Amami-shotō group. From Kagoshima to Amami-ōshima, the largest island in the group, is about 180 km. The islands are predominantly agricultural (producing bananas, papayas, pineapples and sugar cane) and have a sub-tropical climate, clear water and good beaches.

GETTING THERE & AWAY
There are JAS flights from Kagoshima to all five main islands. Air Nippon Koku (ANK) also flies between Kagoshima and Amami-

ōshima, and Amami-ōshima and Okinawa. South-West Airlines (SWAL) links Yoron-jima Island with Okinawa. Ferry services stop at Amami-ōshima en route from Kagoshima to Okinawa. Kagoshima to Naze on Amami-ōshima takes about 12 hours by ferry; Osaka to Naze takes 25 hours.

AMAMI-ŌSHIMA ISLAND 奄美大島
This 40-km-long island, also known simply as Ōshima Island, has a highly convoluted coastline with the almost enclosed Bay of Setouchi separating it from the nearby Kakeroma-jima Island. Naze is the main port.

OTHER ISLANDS
The island of **Kikai-shima** is east of Amami-ōshima, while the other three main islands lie like stepping stones in a direct line from Amami-ōshima to Okinawa. From north to south they are Tokuno-shima Island, Okino-Erabu-jima Island and Yoron-jima Island.

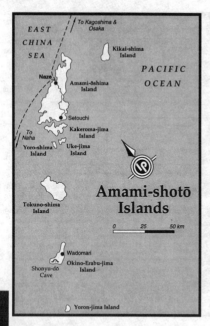

EAST
CHINA
SEA

To Kagoshima &
Osaka

PACIFIC
OCEAN

Kikai-shima
Island

Naze

Amami-ōshima
Island

Setouchi

To
Naha

Kakeroma-jima
Island

Yoro-shima
Island

Uke-jima
Island

Tokuno-shima
Island

**Amami-shotō
Islands**

0   25   50 km

Wadomari

Okino-Erabu-jima
Island

Shonyu-dō
Cave

Yoron-jima Island

Tokuno-shima is the largest island after Amami-ōshima, but **Okino-Erabu-jima** is probably the most interesting island, with its coral reefs and thatched-roof rice barns. The **Shonyu-dō Cave** stretches for over two km and is one of the most important limestone caves in Japan. China and Wadomari are the main ports on Okino-Erabu-jima. Tiny **Yoro-shima Island**, just south of Amami-ōshima, also has coral reefs.

There are youth hostels on Okino-Erabu-jima (☎ 09979-2-2024) and Yoron-jima (☎ 0997-97-2273).

Okinawa Island   沖縄

Okinawa is the largest and most important island in the Nansei-shotō chain. Its architecture once displayed its cultural differences with mainland Japan, but almost all traces of the old architecture were obliterated in

WWII. The USA retained control of Okinawa after the war, handing it back to Japan in 1972. The 26 years of US occupation did an effective job of wiping out any remaining traces of the old Okinawan ways, but for good measure the Japanese have turned the island into a major tourist resort. Okinawa still has the biggest US military base in Japan with 50,000 military and non-military personnel and dependents.

Okinawa's wartime history may have some interest for foreign visitors, but the islands further south will probably offer a more interesting insight into the history of ancient Ryūkyū.

NAHA   那覇
Naha (population 304,000) is the capital of Okinawa; it was flattened in WWII and little trace remains of the old Ryūkyū culture. Today Naha is chiefly a gateway to other places, but there are a number of interesting things to see in this colourful, modern town.

Orientation & Information
Kokusai-dōri (International Blvd), Naha's main street, is 1.5 busy km of hotels, bars, restaurants and shops. The airport is only three km west of Naha while a similar distance east is Shuri, the erstwhile Okinawan capital and the site of some renovated ruins.

The airport tourist information office (☎ 098-857-6884) is not open for all flights. The tourist information office (☎ 098-866-7515) in town is in the Palette Kumoji building at the south-west end of Kokusai-dōri. Neither office has English-speaking staff; a reflection of how few foreign tourists make it down into this neck of the woods.

If you're intending to explore Okinawa and other islands, particularly with a rented car, get a copy of *Okinawa by Road* (Kume Publishing, 1989, ¥1550) which should be available at some bookshops in Naha. Be sure not to confuse the English edition with the similar-looking and more readily available Japanese-language version.

You can quickly get your fill of the US forces radio on 648 kHz AM – the ads are amazingly awful.

OKINAWA & SOUTH-WEST ISLANDS

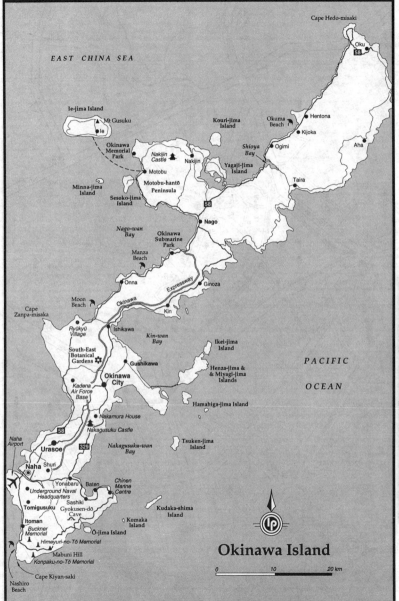

EAST CHINA SEA

Cape Hedo-misaki

Oku
58

Ie-jima Island

Mt Gusuku

Ie

Kouri-jima
Island

Okuma
Beach

Hentona

Kijoka

Aha

Okinawa
Memorial
Park

Nakijin
Castle

Nakijin

Shioya
Bay

Ogimi

Motobu

Yagaji-jima
Island

Minna-jima
Island

Motobu-hantō
Peninsula

Taira

Sesoko-jima
Island

58

Nago

Nago-wan
Bay

Okinawa
Submarine
Park

Manza
Beach

Onna

Expressway

Ginoza

Moon
Beach

Okinawa

Kin

Cape
Zanpa-misaki

Ryūkyū
Village

Ishikawa

Kin-wan
Bay

Ikei-jima
Island

South-East
Botanical
Gardens

Gushikawa

Okinawa
City

Henza-jima &
& Miyagi-jima
Islands

PACIFIC

OCEAN

Kadena
Air Force
Base

Hamahiga-jima Island

Nakamura House

Naha
Airport

Nakagusuku Castle

58

Urasoe

329

Shuri

Nakagusuku-wan
Bay

Tsuken-jima
Island

Naha

Yonabaru

Baten

Chinen
Marine
Centre

Underground Naval
Headquarters

Sashiki

Tomigusuku

Gyokusen-dō
Cave

Kudaka-shima
Island

Itoman

Buckner
Memorial

Komaka
Island

Himeyuri-no-Tō Memorial

Ō-jima Island

Mabuni Hill

Konpaku-no-Tō Memorial

Cape Kiyan-saki

Nashiro
Beach

Okinawa Island

0   10   20 km

OKINAWA & SOUTH-WEST ISLANDS

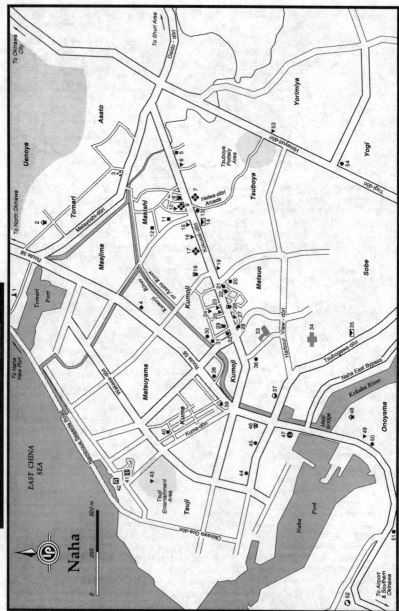

PLACES TO STAY

2 Harumi Youth Hostel
晴海荘ユース
ホステル

5 Nansei Kankō Hotel
南西観光ホテル

11 Hotel Sankyo;
Dragon's Den;
Post Office
ホテルサンキョー

12 Narumi Ryokan
なるみ

20 Naha Grand Hotel
那覇グランドホテル

21 Hotel Kokusai Plaza
ホテル国際プラザ

22 Hotel New Okinawa
ホテルニュー沖縄

31 Hotel Maruki
ホテルまるき

34 Okinawa
Harbourview Hotel
沖縄ハーバービュー
ホテル

39 Oceanview Hotel
オーシャンビュー
ホテル

40 Okinawa Washington
Hotel
沖縄ワシントン
ホテル

48 Okinawa
International Youth
Hostel
沖縄国際ユース
ホステル

PLACES TO EAT

6 Rawhide

10 Subway
(Sandwiches)

15 Grand Canyon
Steakhouse

16 Jin Jin
じんじん

19 Shakey's Pizza

23 Italian Tomato

24 Kotori
ことり

25 Ynangii
ゆなんぎい

27 Doutor Coffee

43 Teahouse of the
August Moon
秋月の茶屋

49 Naha Soba
那覇そば

53 McDonald's

OTHER

1 Commodore Perry
Memorial
ペルリ提督上陸
記念碑

3 Sōgen-ji Gates
崇元院石門

4 Nissan Rent-a-Car
ニッサンレンタカー

7 Kokusai Shopping
Centre
国際ショッピング
センター

8 Art of Noise

9 Mitsukoshi
Department Store;
Naha Tower
三越

13 Festival Building;
Tower Records

14 Post Office; Tacos-ya
郵便局／タコス屋

17 Yatakaya
Department Store
山形屋

18 Bar Dick

26 Sugar Hill

28 Javy Building
JAVY ビル

29 Ynangii
ゆなんぎい

30 JAL
日本航空

32 JAS
日本エアシステム

33 Okinawa Prefectural
Office
沖縄県庁

35 Main Post Office
中央郵便局

36 Naha City Office
那覇市役所

37 Bus Station
那覇バスターミナル

38 ANA
全日空

41 Gokoku-ji Temple
護国寺

42 Naminoue-gū Shrine
波上宮

44 Nippon Rent-a-Car
ニッポンレンタカー

45 Japaren Rent-a-Car
ジャパンレンタカー

46 KDD (International
Telephone Office)

47 Tourist Office
観光案内所

50 Toyota Rent-a-Car
トヨタレンタカー

51 SWAL
西南航空

52 US Consulate
アメリカ領事館

54 Immigration Office
那覇警察署

OKINAWA & SOUTH-WEST ISLANDS

Central Naha

Kokusai-dōri, with its curious mix of restaurants, army surplus stores, bars, souvenir shops and hotels, makes an interesting walk day or night. It's very much the heart of Naha. Turning south off Kokusai-dōri opposite the Mitsukoshi department store leads you to the Heiwa-dōri shopping arcade, which has the distinct flavour of an Asian market.

If you continue to the east end of Kokusai-dōri, a right turn takes you towards Shuri, while a left turn quickly brings you to the reconstructed gates of **Sōgen-ji Temple**. These stone gates once led to the 16th century temple of the Ryūkyū kings, but like almost everything else in Naha, it was destroyed in WWII. Continue beyond the gates and almost at the waterfront is the **Commodore Perry Memorial**, commemorating his 1853 landing in Naha (prior to his arrival in Tokyo). Nearby is a foreigners' cemetery.

Tsuboya Area 壺屋

Continue along the Heiwa-dōri shopping arcade, taking the left fork at the junction, and a short walk beyond the arcade will bring you to the Tsuboya pottery area. If you miss it simply continue in the same direction until you hit the big Himeyuri-dōri and Tsuboya is across the road from McDonald's.

About 20 traditional pottery workshops still operate in this compact area, a centre for ceramic production since 1682. You can peer into many of the small workshops and there are numerous shops selling popular Okinawan products such as the *shiisā* ('lion roof guardians') or the containers for serving *awamori*, the local firewater. The **Tsuboya Pottery Centre** (Tsuboya Toki Kaikan) is open from 9 am to 6 pm and has items from all the kilns.

Waterfront Temples

Kume-dōri runs from Kokusai-dōri straight through to the waterfront, where the hilltop Naminoue-gū Shrine and the Gokoku-ji and Kōshi-byō temples are picturesquely sited overlooking the sea and the red-light district. The buildings are unexceptional modern reconstructions and the neat little bay they

overlook has been totally ruined by the highway flyover which runs straight across it. Okinawan road building often seems to make no concessions for natural features. The Tsuji entertainment area was once a brothel quarter; now it features clubs, bars and some noted restaurants, together with a collection of colourful love hotels and US-style steakhouses. As Japanese red-light areas go, it's decidedly lacking in atmosphere.

Shuri Area 首里

Prior to the Meiji Restoration, Shuri was the capital of Okinawa; that title passed to Naha in 1879. Shuri's temples, shrines, tombs and castle were all destroyed in WWII. Some reconstructions and repairs have been made, but it's a pale shadow of the former city.

Shuri is about 2.5 km from the east end of Kokusai-dōri. Bus Nos 12, 13, 14 and 17 (¥170) run directly to the entrance *(shurijō kōen iriguchi)* of the Shurijō-kōen Park, which contains most of what's left of the old Ryūkyū royal capital. At the entrance is a building with a restaurant and information booth.

Shurijō-kōen Park Entry to the park itself is free, but there's a hefty charge for Shuri Castle. Just up from the entrance to the park is the reconstructed old residence of the Okinawan royal family, **Shuri-jo Castle**. The original was destroyed in the WWII Battle of Okinawa. The castle was only opened in early 1993, so don't expect much in the way of historical atmosphere. All the same, the reconstruction work has been carried out with meticulous attention to detail and there are several exhibition halls with interesting historical displays. The result is undoubtedly Naha's prime tourist attraction. The castle is open from 9 am to 5 pm and entry is a rather steep ¥800.

The castle's walls have numerous gates that are of minor interest. The pick of them is the Chinese-influenced **Shureino-mon Gate**. The ceremonial entrance to Shuri Castle, it was originally built nearly 500 years ago and was rebuilt in 1958. It's considered to be *the* symbol of Okinawa, so there's a constant

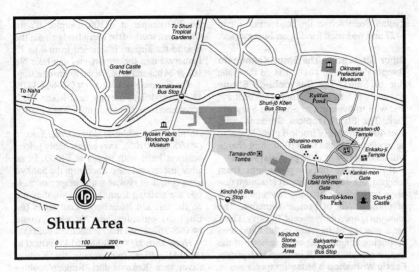

Shuri Area

0   100   200 m

Labels in map:
- To Shuri Tropical Gardens
- Grand Castle Hotel
- Okinawa Prefectural Museum
- Yamakawa Bus Stop
- Ryūtan Pond
- To Naha
- Shuri-jō Kōen Bus Stop
- Benzaiten-dō Temple
- Ryūsen Fabric Workshop & Museum
- Shureino-mon Gate
- Enkaku-ji Temple
- Tamau-dōn Tombs
- Kankai-mon Gate
- Sonohiyan Utaki Ishi-mon Gate
- Kinchō-jō Bus Stop
- Shurijō-kōen Park
- Shuri-jō Castle
- Kinjōchō Stone Street Area
- Sakiyama-Inguchi Bus Stop

stream of tour groups and school parties lining up to be photographed in front of it. A couple of young women in traditional Okinawan costume stand ready to make guest appearances in the photos, for a suitable fee.

Also worth checking out is the 15th to 16th century **Kankai-mon Gate** with its traditional Okinawan design. It was rebuilt right after the war. The Kyukei-mon Gate, built in 1508, has also been restored. The third large gate, the Keisei-mon, was originally built in 1546.

There are a couple of temples on the park grounds, but don't expect too much from them – they look a little the worse for wear. The **Benzaiten-dō Temple** is in the middle of Enkan Pond, just down from Shuri Castle. It was originally built in 1502, rebuilt in 1609 after being destroyed, and rebuilt again in 1968 after being burnt out during WWII. Cross the road to the rather bedraggled remnants of the **Enkaku-ji Temple**. This temple dates from 1492, but it too was destroyed in the Battle of Okinawa. All that remains is the outer gate, a bridge leading over a lotus pond, and the steps beyond the pond leading to the main gate. Engaku-ji has an entrance fee of ¥160.

In the far west of the park, the wartime destruction also did not spare the **Tamau-dōn Tombs**, which date from 1501, but have been restored. Traditionally, bodies were first placed in the central chamber. When the flesh had decayed the bones were removed, cleaned and permanently interred – kings and queens to the left, princes and princesses to the right. Shiisā look down on the courtyard from the central tower and both sides. Entry is ¥200 and opening hours are from 8.30 am to 6 pm in summer and 8.30 am to 5.30 pm in winter.

Kinjōchō Stone St At one time the 15th century Kinjōchō-no-Ishitatamimichi ran for 10 km from Shuri to the port at Naha. Now there's just one stretch of a couple of hundred metres, plus a few side lanes, but the steep and narrow path with its old stone walls and ornate gateways is very picturesque.

Prefectural Museum The museum's displays are connected with Okinawan lifestyle and culture and include some exhibits on the Battle of Okinawa and a large model of Shuri Castle. Entry to the museum is ¥200 and it's open from 9 am to 5 pm except Monday. The

Ryūtan Pond across the road was built in 1427 and was used for dragon-boat races.

Other Attractions The **Shuri Kannon-dō Temple** dates from 1618; it is on the Naha side of Shuri. The **Sueyoshi-gū Shrine** originally dates from the mid-15th century; it is well to the north of Shuri, in Sueyoshi Park. The **Shuri Tropical Gardens**, with over 400 varieties of tropical plant life, may be worth a look, but the ¥1030 entry charge will no doubt deter most potential visitors.

Housed in a building brought from Ishigaki, the **Japan Folkcraft Museum** displays traditional crafts and has a collection of photographs of prewar Okinawa. The museum is open daily except Tuesday. There are a number of factories in the Shuri area producing Bingata, the most famous of the traditional fabrics of Okinawa. The **Ryūsen Fabric Workshop & Museum** specialises in Ryūsen, an expensive material rather similar to Bingata.

Special Events
Popular local festivals include the colourful Geisha Horse Festival (Jiriuma), during which young women ride wooden horses in a parade starting from the Teahouse of the August Moon in the Tsuji entertainment district. The festival usually takes place in March. The Hārii dragon boat races take place in early May, particularly in Itoman and Naha. In August the Tsunahiki Festival takes place in various locations, but particularly in Itoman, Naha and Yonabaru – huge teams contest a tug-of-war using a gigantic rope (up to a metre thick).

Places to Stay
The information desk at Naha airport may be able to help you find accommodation, but it is unlikely. Okinawa's hotels tend to be scattered around Naha, and there are many along Kokusai-dōri which is probably the best area to be based.

Youth Hostels Naha has two youth hostels. The *Okinawa International Youth Hostel* (☎ 098-857-0073) is the largest, with room

for 200 people at ¥3100 a night. It's in Onoyama, south of the Meiji Bridge, near the road to the airport. It's closed from 8 to 18 January. From the airport you can take No 101 or 24 bus and get off at the Kōen-mae stop.

The *Harumi Youth Hostel* (☎ 098-867-3218/ 4422), is north of the city, near Route 58. It accommodates 38 people at ¥2900 a night.

Hotels Just off Kokusai-dōri is *Hotel Sankyo* (☎ 098-867-0105), a very reasonably priced business hotel with rooms at ¥4000. In an alley just around the corner from the Sankyo are a couple of ryokan with cheaper rates. If you are walking from the Sankyo, they are on the left and have fluorescent signs (no English) outside. The *Narumi Ryokan* (☎ 098-267-2138) has rooms from ¥3200.

Hotel Maruki (☎ 098-862-6135) is next to the JAL office, overlooking the Kumoji River near Kokusai-dōri. Singles/doubles start at ¥5400/9600. *Hotel Yagi* (☎ 098-862-3008) is near the bus station and is similarly priced.

There are plenty of moderately priced places along Kokusai-dōri, including the *Hotel Kokusai Plaza* (☎ 098-862-4243), where singles/doubles cost from ¥6000/9500. Right behind it is the similarly priced *Naha Grand Hotel* (☎ 098-862-6161), with singles from ¥6000 to ¥7000 and doubles for ¥11,000. Around the corner is the *Hotel New Okinawa* (☎ 098-867-7200), with rooms from ¥4800.

Other possibilities include the *Okinawa Washington Hotel* (☎ 098-869-2511), which is away from the city centre, halfway between Kokusai-dōri and the waterfront. This popular chain hotel has singles/doubles from ¥6700/13,000. The *Nansei Kankō Hotel* (☎ 098-862-7144) is right on Kokusai-dōri and has singles/twins from ¥7500/13,000. The very big and glossy *Oceanview Hotel* (☎ 098-853-2112) is on Route 58 and prices start from ¥9700/15,000 for singles/twins – no doubles are available.

Places to Eat
Perhaps due to the US military presence, Naha has just about every variety of fast-

food restaurant available in Japan, many of them in duplicate or triplicate. Along Kokusai-dōri alone you'll find *McDonald's*, *KFC*, *Mos Burger*, *Lotteria*, *Mister Donut*, *Shakey's Pizza*, *A&W Burgers*, *Dom Dom Hamburger* and a few others. *Subway* is the place for sandwiches, *Italian Tomato* is a pasta chain with prices from ¥800 to ¥1200, and across the road is a *Doutor coffee shop*, an excellent stop for breakfast.

Okinawa is said to have the best-priced steaks in Japan. This hardly means bargain prices, but the thing to do if you're a Japanese tourist in Naha is to dine out on steak and seafood. *Rawhide* is one of the long-runners, but the food is a bit tired these days. The *Grand Canyon Steakhouse* is a newer place where you can enjoy your meal in surroundings with more ambience. There are many more on Kokusai-dōri and in the Tsuji area, near the Naminoue-gū Shrine, where you can choose from *Restaurant George*, *Jackie's Steakhouse*, *Restaurant Stateside*, *Restaurant Texas*, *Restaurant 88* and others. These restaurants offer steaks from around ¥1300 up; they also have delicacies like pizza and tacos.

The *Teahouse of the August Moon* (☎ 098-868-2945) is another Tsuji restaurant. It's not particularly cheap (courses from ¥5000), but it's a good place to try some traditional local cuisine. You can do the same at cheaper prices on Kokusai-dōri at *Yūnangii* (☎ 098-867-3765). Evening courses range from ¥2200 to ¥2800, but you can also order à la carte – try the Okinawa soba at ¥480. A selection of awamori is on sale for ¥500 a glass or ¥2500 a bottle. There's no English sign outside, but the sign is written in white hiragana on a brown board, and there's a white lantern too. Farther up Kokusai-dōri, near the Grand Canyon Steakhouse, is *Jin-Jin* (☎ 098-866-6559), an Okinawan izakaya. No concessions are made to stray gaijin, but if you can make your way around a Japanese menu this place is a lot of fun.

Entertainment

The explosion of bars all over Japan in the last few years is nowhere more evident than in Naha. It seems as if every street running off Kokusai-dōri harbours a couple of hidden-away drinking spots.

Next to the Hotel Sankyo is the *Dragon's Den*, a funky little reggae bar that's open from 9 am until late. Other bars on or just off Kokusai-dōri include *Art of Noise*, *Rock Bar*, the interestingly named *Bar Dick* and the trendy *Q's Bar*. There are dozens more to choose from. Most places are friendlier than bars in mainland Japan.

For livelier places with some room to move around in, try *Sugar Hill*, a spacious club with a huge collection of music, and the *'80s Club* on the 8th floor of the Festival building opposite Mitsukoshi department store on Kokusai-dōri. Sugar Hill costs ¥1000 entry (with a drink ticket) before 10 pm, ¥1500 after. The '80s Club, which as its name suggests is an '80s-style disco, has an entry charge of ¥3500.

Things to Buy

Okinawa is renowned for its pottery and fabrics. Tsuboya pottery owes its origins to Chinese influences, as opposed to the Korean techniques which form the basis of most other Japanese pottery. Much of the pottery is in the form of storage vessels, but look for the shiisā (guardian lion figures) which can be seen perched on the rooftops of many traditional Okinawan buildings. Shiisā usually come in pairs, one with the mouth open, the other with the mouth closed.

Okinawa also has its own distinctive textiles, particularly the brightly coloured Bingata fabrics made in Shuri. Other fabrics made on Okinawa or other islands in the chain include Bashōfu (from northern Okinawa), Jōfu (from Miyako), Kasuri (from southern Okinawa), Minsā (from Taketomi), Ryūsen and Tsumugi (from Kume). Another popular Okinawan product is awamori which has an alcohol content of 30% to 60%. Drink with care! Real daredevils might want to look out for the version that comes with a small habu snake coiled in the bottom of the bottle. Most of the bars around town will have a bottle tucked away if you want to try a glass.

Getting There & Away

Air Direct flights to Okinawa include Northwest Orient from the USA, Continental from Guam, JAL from Hong Kong and China Airlines from Taipei. JAL, ANA, ANK, JAS and South-West Airlines (SWAL) connects major cities on the main Japanese islands with Naha, including Fukuoka (1½ hours, ¥28,350), Kagoshima (1½ hours, ¥21,050), Nagoya (two hours, ¥32,750), Osaka (two hours, ¥29,100), Hiroshima (two hours, ¥26,600), Tokyo (2½ hours, ¥34,900) and a number of other centres. SWAL has the most connections to the other South-West Islands. See the South-West Islands Airfares chart for inter-island details.

Airlines with offices in Naha include ANA or ANK (☎ 098-866-5111), JAS (☎ 098-867-8111), JAL (☎ 098-862-3311) and SWAL (☎ 098-857-4961). All the offices can be found in the city centre except for SWAL, which is across the Meiji Bridge towards the airport. There are plenty of travel agencies in central Naha, particularly on Kokusai-dōri, which can handle bookings.

Boat Various operators have shipping services to Naha from Tokyo, Nagoya, Osaka, Kōbe, Kagoshima and other ports. The schedules are complex and there is a wide variety of fares. From Tokyo it takes about 50 hours (¥19,670 to ¥39,350), from Osaka about 36 hours (¥15,450 to ¥38,620), from Kōbe about 40 hours (¥15,000 to ¥40,000) and from Kagoshima about 24 hours (¥11,840 to ¥29,610). Shipping companies include Arimura Sangyo, Kansai Kisen, Oshima Unyu, Ryūkyū Kaiun (RKK) and Terukuni Yusen. The frequency of services varies from eight to 10 a month from Tokyo to more than 30 a month from Kagoshima.

There are three ports in Naha, which can be confusing. From Naha Port (Naha-kō) ferries head north to Hakata and Yoron-jima Island. From Naha New Port (Naha Shin-kō) there are ferries to Fukuoka/Hakata, Kagoshima, Kōbe, Osaka and Tokyo and also to Miyako and Ishigaki islands. From Tomari Port, ferries operate to a number of the smaller islands including Kume, Aguni and the Daito Islands.

The Arimura Sangyō shipping company (☎ 098-869-1320 in Naha, 03-3562-2091 in Tokyo), operates a weekly ferry service between Okinawa and Taiwan. Boats depart from Naha Port on Thursday or Friday and from Keelung (or sometimes Kaohsiung) in Taiwan on Sunday. The service generally operates directly between Naha and either Keelung or Kaohsiung, but it occasionally (check beforehand) stops at Miyako and Ishigaki. The trip takes about 16 to 19 hours and costs range between ¥15,300 (economy class) and ¥24,300 (1st class).

Getting Around

The Airport The busy Naha airport is only three km from the town centre – 10 minutes by taxi for ¥800 to ¥1100 or 12 minutes by bus No 24 or 102 for ¥190. The buses run three to six times an hour (7 am to 10 pm) via the main bus station and then down Kokusai-dōri. The airport has three widely spaced terminals: international, domestic 1 (for mainland Japan) and domestic 2 (for the South-West Islands).

Bus The bus system is relatively easy to use. For local town buses, you simply dump ¥190 into a slot next to the driver as you enter. For longer trips you collect a ticket showing your starting point as you board and pay the appropriate fare as you disembark; a board at the front shows the various starting numbers and the equivalent fares. Buses run from Naha to destinations all over the island.

There are many bus tours around the island, particularly to the war sites in the south.

Car & Motorcycle Okinawa is a good place to get around in a rented vehicle since the traffic is not too heavy and the northern end of the island is lightly populated and has poor public transport. There are numerous rental companies in Naha with cars from around ¥5300 per day plus ¥1500 insurance. Convertibles are very popular. Try Japaren (☎ 0988-61-3900), Nippon Rent-a-Car (☎ 0988-68-4554) or Toyota Rent-a-Car (☎ 098-857-0100), among others.

A number of places rent scooters and

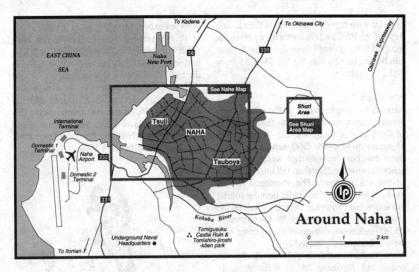

Around Naha

motorcycles. A 50cc scooter costs from ¥3300 for the day; a 250cc motorcycle ¥10,000. Try Sea Rental Bikes (☎ 0988-64-5116) or Trade (☎ 0988-63-0908), close to Mitsukoshi department store on Kokusai-dōri.

SOUTHERN OKINAWA

The area south of Naha was the scene of some of the heaviest fighting during the closing days of the Battle of Okinawa. There are a number of reminders of those terrible days, as well as some other places of interest in this densely populated part of the island.

The initial US landing on Okinawa took place north of Naha at Kadena and Chatan beaches on 1 April 1945. By 20 April, US forces had captured the northern part of the island and the area south of their landing place to Naha. The rest of the island was not captured until 21 June.

Underground Naval Headquarters
旧海軍司令部壕

About five km directly south of Naha is the underground naval headquarters where 4000 men committed suicide as the battle for Okinawa drew to its prolonged and bloody conclusion. Only 200m of the 1.5 km of

tunnels are open, but you can wander through the maze of corridors, see the commander's final words on the wall of his room and inspect the holes and scars in other walls from the grenade blasts which killed many of the men. In Japanese the headquarters are known as *kyū kaigun shireibugō*, though the sign from the main road simply reads 'Kaigungo Park'. Entry is ¥410 and it's open from 8.30 am to 5 pm. To get there take bus No 33 or 101 from the Naha bus station to the Tomigusuku-kōen-mae stop (25 minutes, ¥220), a 10 minute walk from the site.

Nearby is the Tomishiro-jiroshi-kōen Park with pleasant views of Naha, though there is very little trace of Tomigusuku Castle, after which the park was named. Entry is ¥520.

Itoman Area 糸満

The fisherfolks' Hakugin-dō Shrine is in this port town, 12 km south of Naha. You can also check out the Kōchi family tombs here, while just south is Nashiro Beach and the Lieutenant General Buckner Memorial, in memory of the US commander who was killed here by stray shrapnel in the final days of the Battle of Okinawa. The site of Gushikawa Castle at Cape Kiyan-saki is now popular with hang-gliders, but in the closing days of the Battle of Okinawa many civilians jumped to their death from the cliffs. Itoman can be reached by bus No 33, 34 or 35 from Naha bus station.

War Sites

Around the southern end of the island are a series of sites connected with the final days of the Battle of Okinawa. On 19 June 1945 at **Himeyuri-no-Tō**, 200 schoolgirls and their teachers committed suicide in the school grounds rather than fall into the hands of the US military. The memorial to this event is now one of the most popular tourist attractions in Okinawa. Directly south on the coast is the **Konpaku-no-Tō Memorial** to 35,000 unknown victims of the fighting who were subsequently buried here.

At **Mabuni-no-Oka** (Mabuni Hill), the remaining Japanese forces were virtually pushed into the sea. In their underground hideaway the commanders committed seppuku ('ritual suicide') on 23 June 1945, while above ground the US forces already had complete control of the island. Memorials from every prefecture in Japan dot the hillside and the **Peace Memorial Museum** tells the gruesome story of the struggle. One reader recommended looking out in particular for the 'brooding half-grey sphere' that is a memorial to the Korean labourers and comfort women who lost their lives in the war. The hill area is open daily from 9 am to

4.30 pm except Monday; entry is ¥100. Also at this extensive site is the **Peace Hall** (¥520), a seven sided tower built in 1978 and housing a 16m-high Buddha statue. Behind the hall is a **Peace Art Museum**.

Taking public transport to the sites is time consuming. From the Naha bus terminal bus Nos 32, 34, 35, 89 and 100 run to Itoman (30 to 40 minutes, ¥470), where you must change to a bus No 82 or 85 to the Peace Park entrance (20 minutes, ¥350).

By the end of the Battle of Okinawa, most of the survivors were those too old or young to fight or commit suicide.

The War & Okinawa

The Battle of Okinawa is still a controversial subject. The Okinawans had long felt they had got a tough deal from mainland Japan. Back in the Satsuma days they were exploited and looked down upon by the mainlanders. In the struggle for Okinawa during WWII they were expendable, a people to be used in order to delay the barbarian invasion of the mainland. The Okinawans paid a terrible price for that delay, as far more Okinawan civilians died than mainland military personnel.

Masahide Ota's *The Battle of Okinawa* (Kume Publishing, 1984) gives some interesting insights into the relentless ferocity of the struggle, but I came out of the underground naval headquarters pondering the sheer idiotic futility of it all. What I felt was anger at the stupidity, rather than sorrow for the deaths. If you're searching for reasons why the decision was made to nuke Nagasaki and Hiroshima, perhaps what happened in Okinawa will supply some answers.

Tony Wheeler

Habu Snakes

Any discussion of the South-West Islands eventually gets around to 'deadly *habu* snakes'. Perhaps it's a reflection of Japan's severe shortage of real dangers, but you could easily get the impression that the poor habu is the world's most dangerous snake and that they're waiting behind every tree, shrub, bush or bar stool on the islands. They're neither so deadly nor so prolific; in fact the most likely place to see one is at a mongoose versus habu fight put on for tourists. Nevertheless, it's probably not a good idea to go stomping through the bushes barefoot. Do stomp though, the vibrations will scare any snakes away. ■

Gyokusen-dō Cave   玉泉洞

Japan has plenty of limestone caves, but for those who can't get enough of stalactites and stalagmites there are more here. Nearly a km of the cave is open to visitors from 9 am to 5, 5.30 or 6 pm (depending on the time of year). Entry is ¥730. When you leave the cave you can continue straight in to the Gyokusen-dō Habu Park (¥520) and see the unfortunate 'deadly' habu suffering the traditional defeat by a mongoose. Bus No 54 from Naha bus station takes around one hour (¥460) to reach the cave, while bus Nos 51 and 52 drop you further from the cave (a 15 minute walk versus five minutes), but depart from Naha much more frequently.

Other Attractions

Just beyond the Mabuni Hill memorials is the Okinawa Coral Museum. Coral is much nicer where it belongs – underwater. Continuing north on Route 15, you'll find Himeyuri Park, which specialises in cactus. Turn east on Route 76 to reach Tomori-no-Ojishi, where a large stone shiisā overlooks a reservoir. This particular shiisā dates back to at least 1689; a popular image from the Battle of Okinawa shows a US soldier sheltering behind it while watching with binoculars.

Tiny Ō-jima Island is linked to the main island by bridge and has good beaches, as has Nibaru Beach a little further north. The island can be reached directly by bus from the Naha bus station by taking No 52, which takes around one hour and costs ¥550.

North of Ō-jima is the Chinen Marine Leisure Centre. This place is popular with

Japanese tourists for the glass-bottomed boat cruises, although 'cruise' is perhaps too grand a term; for ¥720 you get exactly 15 minutes to peer underwater, while ¥1030 will get you 25 minutes. There are also boats from here to Kudaka-jima Island and minute Komaka-jima Island, which is encircled by fine beaches. The leisure centre can be reached by bus Nos 37 and 38 from the Naha bus station for ¥710.

CENTRAL OKINAWA

Central Okinawa (north of Naha through Okinawa City to Ishikawa) is heavily populated, but beyond this area the island is much less crowded. The US military bases are principally in the southern part of central Okinawa and the resorts are in the northern part. Dotted around this stretch of Okinawa is an amazing number of artificial tourist attractions where many thousands of yen could be squandered on entry fees.

Urasoe   浦添

Urasoe, eight km north of Naha, was the early capital of the Ryūkyū kingdom, and today its two main attractions are the Yōdore Royal Tombs, dating back to the 13th century, and Jōseki-kōen Park. The latter contains the ruins of the original castle residence of the Okinawan royal family and costs ¥310 entry. The tombs date back to the 13th century and are about a 20 minute walk from the park; ask for Urasoe Yōdore. The No 56 bus runs to Urasoe Jōseki-kōen Park from the Naha bus station for ¥330.

Nakagusuku Castle 中城城跡

North of Naha, the lovely hilltop ruins of **Nakagusuku Castle** have a wonderful position overlooking the coast. The castle was built in 1448, predating stone construction of this type on the mainland by 80 years. The castle was destroyed in 1458 in a bizarre episode of feudal manoeuvring known as the Amawari Rebellion. When Gosamaru, the Nakagusuku lord, heard that Amawari, another Okinawan lord, was plotting a rebellion against the king he mobilised his troops. The scheming Amawari then convinced the king that it was Gosamaru who was planning to revolt, so the hapless Nakagusuku ruler committed suicide.

There's no sign pointing out the castle site. Look for the entrance gate with a field in front of it and the inevitable tourist activity. To get there by public transport from Naha, take a bus to Futenma and from there bus No 58. It's open from 8.30 am to 5.30 pm and entry is ¥300.

Nakamura House 中村家

A half km up the road from the castle is probably the best preserved traditional Okinawan house on the island. The Nakamura family's origins in the area can be traced back to the 15th century, but the foundations of this house date from around 1720. The construction is typical of a well off farming family's residence at that time. Originally, the roof would have been thatched, but it was later roofed with traditional red tiles. As you explore this interesting and surprisingly comfortable-looking home, notice the substantial stone pig pens, the elevated storage area (to deter rats) and the trees grown as typhoon windbreaks. The house is open from 9 am to 5.30 pm and entry is ¥300. It's a 10 minute walk up from Nakagusuku Castle; bus No 58 passes by the house.

Okinawa City 沖縄市

Okinawa City is the US military centre on Okinawa, centred around the Kadena Air Force Base which was the initial target of the US invasion at the end of WWII. The prewar village has mushroomed to a population of

Bullfighting
Battles between opposing bulls, where one tries to push the other out of the ring (rather like sumō wrestlers) are known as *tōgyū* in Japan. The custom is found in a long sweep of islands all the way from Indonesia to Japan. There are about a dozen tōgyū stadiums in Okinawa, the most important ones being the Agena Stadium in Gushikawa and the Kankō Stadium in Okinawa City. The most important fights are held in May and November, but they take place a couple of times a month year-round. The bulls for Okinawa tōgyū events are bred on Kuroshima Island, near Iriomote-jima. ■

over 100,000. The city has all the hallmarks of American influence, from pizzerias to army surplus stores. There's even an *A&W Burgers* outlet where you can order from your car over an intercom and your food is brought out to you – shades of American drive-ins of the '50s. The Tuttle Bookstore at the Plaza House shopping mall is the best English-language bookshop on Okinawa.

Attractions around Okinawa City, some of them decidedly artificial, include the **Moromi Folkcraft Museum**, the **Koza-yaki Pottery Factory**, **Okinawa Children's Land**, the Tonan or **South-East Botanical Gardens** and the Agena and Katsuren Castle sites. Bullfights, where one bull tries to push another out of a ring, are held on Sunday at **Gushikawa**, near Okinawa Children's Land. The South-East Botanical Gardens are popular with Japanese tourists, but are a hassle to get to by public transport from Naha. Buses run from Okinawa City, and the Gardens are open from 9 am to 6 pm; entry is ¥720.

Bus Nos 21, 22, 23, 24, 25, 26, 31, 63, 77 and 90 all run to Okinawa City from Naha in around one hour and 20 minutes (¥700).

Okinawa City to Nago

Enthusiasts of castle ruins can find more of them at the **Iha Castle** site near Ishikawa and at the **Zakimi Castle** site on the west coast, north of Kadena. In the Zakimi Castle

Park the **Yomitan Museum** displays local farming equipment.

The Okinawan resort strip starts from **Zampa Beach** on Cape Zampa-misaki. The **Ryūkyū Village** (8.30 am to 5 pm daily, ¥600) offers yet another opportunity to see a re-creation of Okinawan farming life, and yet another snake park where, for the amusement of tourists, those 'deadly' habu lose out (once again) to those plucky mongooses. More beach life can be found at the Ramada Renaissance Resort, Moon Beach and Manza Beach, while just before Nago the **Okinawa Submarine Park**, where you can actually descend into the ocean depths in a submarine called *Moglyn* for ¥9800.

As well as the expensive resort hotels along this coast, there is also the *Maeda-misaki Youth Hostel* (☎ 0989-64-2497) near the Ryūkyū Village. Bus No 20 from Naha runs along the west coast past all these sites to Nago. It takes about one hour and 20 minutes to get to the Ryūkyū Village or Moon Beach; one hour and 40 minutes to Manza Beach; and two hours to the submarine park.

NAGO 名護

If you're spending a couple of days exploring Okinawa then Nago (population 51,000) is a good overnight stop; it's about two-thirds of the way up the island. There are fine views over the town and the coast from the castle hill, although little trace remains of the castle itself. In spring the cherry blossoms on the hill are particularly good. A fine old banyan tree, the **Himpun Gajumara**, is a useful landmark in the centre of town. You can find out all about traditional farming (which is fast-disappearing on Okinawa) at the **Nago Museum**. The museum is close to the banyan tree and is open from 10 am to 6 pm; entry is ¥100.

Places to Stay & Eat

The *Hotel Nago Castle* (☎ 0980-52-5954) is a clean, pleasant place close to the centre of town, with singles for ¥4500 and breakfast available for ¥500. It has a popular restaurant that does a mixture of generic western and Japanese dishes. The *Hotel 21st Century*

(☎ 0980-53-2655) has singles/twins from ¥5500/9000. It's further north up Route 58. Close by, on the beach, is the *Hotel Yugafuin Okinawa* (☎ 0980-53-0031), where rooms start at ¥7000.

Shinzan Shokudō is a famous Nago noodle shop that has been running for 60 years. Nago has many fast-food outlets – a *McDonald's* and *A&W Burgers* mark the southern entry to town. There's also the usual plethora of bars, snack bars and so on in the entertainment area.

Getting There & Away

Nago is the junction town for buses to northern Okinawa or to the Motobu-hantō Peninsula. From Okinawa City bus station, bus Nos 20 and 21 make the 62 km trip in about 2½ hours for ¥1700.

MOTOBU-HANTŌ PENINSULA 本部半島

Jutting out to the north-west of Nago, the hilly Motobu-hantō Peninsula has several points of interest, as well as ferry services to nearby Ie-jima Island.

Okinawa Memorial Park 海洋博覧会記念公園

The site of the 1975 International Ocean Exposition has a cluster of tourist attractions, most of which can be bypassed. Entry to the park itself is free, but the individual attractions charge entry fees. The aquarium (¥620) is claimed to be one of the largest in the world and the sharks and rays in the big tank, particularly the huge whale shark, are indeed impressive, although the tank is very crowded.

Aquapolis (¥510) is a rusting and faded vision of a floating city of the future where the main news is that there will still be a demand for tacky souvenirs. There's also the Oceanic Culture Museum (¥160), the Museum of Okinawa (¥150), the Native Okinawan Village (free), the Tropical Dream Centre, with orchid and other flower displays around the curious circular spiral tower (¥620), and a dolphin show (free). The park also has a beach and an amusement park.

The park is open from 9.30 am to 5.30, 6

or 7 pm depending on the season; it's closed on Thursday. Individual attractions close half an hour earlier. On Sunday and holidays, three No 93 buses run directly from Naha to the park; on other days you will have to take a bus to Nago and from there take a No 70 bus on the Motobu Peninsula Bise line (¥700). Shuttle buses run around the surprisingly sprawling park and cost ¥100.

Nakijin Castle Site 今帰仁城跡

Winding over a hilltop, the 14th century walls of Nakijin Castle may not be as neat as Nakagusuku, but they look terrific. From the summit of the hill there are superb views out to sea. Entry is ¥150; bus No 66 operates from Nago and bus No 65 from the Okinawa Memorial Park. The castle site is open daily from 8 am to 6 pm.

Other Attractions

The **Yambaru Wildlife Park** and **Izumi Pineapple Garden** are other peninsula sites. There are also two islands connected to the peninsula by road. To the south is **Sesoko-jima Island**, which has good beaches on the western side, as well as camping facilities. Bus No 76 takes around 55 minutes from Nago. From the bus stop it's around a 20 minute walk to the west side beaches (the island is only eight sq km). To the north of the peninsula is Yagaji-jima Island, which has little in the way of interest.

Three km west of Sesoko-jima is tiny Minna-jima Island (0.56 sq km), with fabulous beaches (again, like Sesoko-jima, the best ones are to the west). The only drawback of this island is that you can expect it to be packed with day-trippers from the expensive resorts in the high season, while out of season it's difficult to get to. Ferries run from Motobu Port just south of the Sesoko bridge.

Ie-jima Island 伊江島

North-west of the Motobu-hantō Peninsula, Ie-jima Island has a wonderful view from the top of **Mt Gusuku**. It's around a 45 minute walk from the pier. The truly indolent might consider a taxi, which should cost around ¥600. Around a five minute walk to the south

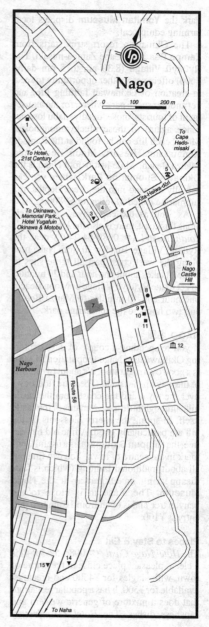

OKINAWA & SOUTH-WEST ISLANDS

PLACES TO STAY		9	Shinzan Shokudō 新山食堂	5	NTT
1	Hotel Nago Castle ホテル 名護キャッスル	14	McDonald's	6	Nago Cross Roads 名護十字路
10	Hotel Okura ホテルおおくら	15	A&W Burgers	7	Bowling Alley 北ボーリング場
11	Shiroyama Hotel 城山ホテル		**OTHER**	8	Banyan Tree バンヤンの樹
		2	Bus Stop; Oki-Mart Supermarket バス停／ おきマートスーパー	12	Museum 名護博物館
	PLACES TO EAT			13	Post Office 郵便局
3	Dom Dom	4	Market 市場		

of the pier is a monument to the American war correspondent Ernie Pyle, who was killed on the island during the early days of the Battle of Okinawa. Also possibly worth checking out is the **Jimamuraya Sightseeing Park**, not far to the north of the Ernie Pyle monument. It has an entry charge of ¥300.

Those planning a longer stay on the island can hire tents at the *Iejima Seishōnen Ryokō Mura* (Youth Travel Village). Alternatively, the *Marco Polo Pension*, around 300m to the north of the pier has rooms for ¥6800 with two meals included. The *Hill Top Hotel*, a nondescript white building, is about a 15 minute walk in the same direction and has similar rates.

Ferries make the 30 minute trip to the island from Motobu Port five times daily for ¥570. Buses around the eight km by three km island are irregular, but bicycles, scooters and cars can be rented.

NORTHERN OKINAWA 沖縄の北部

The northern part of Okinawa is lightly populated and comparatively wild and rugged. A road runs around the coast, making this an interesting loop trip, but buses are infrequent and do not continue all the way along the east coast.

West Coast to Cape Hedo-misaki
西海岸から平戸岬へ

Route 58 north from Nago has virtually con-

verted Shioya Bay into an enclosed lake. The village of **Kijoka** is noted for its traditional houses and for the production of the very rare cloth known as Bashōfu. You should make an advance appointment if you want to visit the Kijoka Bashōfu Weaving Workshop. Further north there's an expensive resort at **Okuma Beach** (rates range from ¥14,000), while the town of Hentona has shops, minshuku and other facilities.

Cape Hedo-misaki marks the northern end of Okinawa. The rocky point is liberally sprinkled with cigarette ends and soft-drink cans. Nevertheless, it's a scenic spot backed by hills, with rocks rising from the dense greenery. Bus No 67 (¥930) travels along the coast from Nago, but you have to continue north from Hentona on bus no 69 (¥640).

East Coast 東海岸

From Cape Hedo-misaki, the road continues to **Oku**, the termination point for buses travelling up the west coast via the cape. The English sign 'Hotel' at the beginning of the village leads you, 50m further on, to the cheap and cheerful *Oku Ryokan*. Then, 200m further along, another sign 'Wellcomes' you to *Lodging Okuyanbaruso*.

There are good beaches around Oku. For the next 15 km the road stays very close to the coastline, with more fine-looking beaches, but frequent warnings of current and tide dangers for swimmers, divers and

OKINAWA & SOUTH-WEST ISLANDS

snorkellers. **Aha** is a picturesque village which still has some traditional thatched-roof houses.

ISLANDS AROUND OKINAWA

Apart from the islands just a stone's throw from the Okinawan coast, there are three other island groups a little further away.

Iheya-jima & Izena-jima Islands
伊平屋島・伊是名島

North of Okinawa, these two islands have good beaches and snorkelling and a number of hotels and minshuku. A daily ferry runs from Motobu's port to Izena (1½ hours) and to Iheya (another 20 minutes).

Kerama-rettō Islands 慶良間諸島

There are about 20 islands in this group west of Okinawa, only four of them inhabited. The islands have fine beaches, some good walks, great lookouts and some of the finest scuba diving in Japan. Ferries from Naha take one to 1½ hours; flights are also available.

Kume-jima Island 久米島

Further west of the Kerama-rettō Islands is beautiful Kume-jima Island, with its superb scenery, excellent beaches and the long curving sweep of sandbank at **Sky Holiday Reef**, just east of the island. The Uezu House is a samurai-style home dating from 1726.

There are ryokan and minshuku on the island, particularly near **Iifu Beach**. There are also several resort hotels, such as *Resort Kume Island* (☎ 098-985-8001), where rooms cost from ¥13,000 per person with two meals. Day trips can be made from Iifu Beach to Sky Holiday Reef.

From Naha, ferries to the island take approximately 3½ hours (¥2600), and SWAL has regular daily flights, taking 35 minutes at a cost of ¥5360.

You can get around the island by rented car, scooter or bicycle.

Miyako Islands
宮古列島

About 300 km south-west of Okinawa, directly en route to the Yaeyama Islands, is the small Miyako group, comprising Miyako-jima Island itself and, a few km to the west, Irabu-jima and Shimoji-jima Islands, plus a scattering of smaller islands. Each year the very low spring tide reveals the huge Yaebishi reef, north of Ikema-jima Island.

MIYAKO-JIMA ISLAND 宮古島

Like the other Okinawa islands, Miyako-jima offers beaches and diving and, since it escaped the destruction rained down upon Okinawa during WWII, some traces of Ryūkyū culture and architecture remain.

Hirara, the main town on Miyako-jima, is compact and easy to get around.

Hirara 平良

There are a few minor attractions in Hirara (population 33,000), but the operative word is indeed 'minor'. They are hardly worth the effort on a hot, sticky day. Near the waterfront, just north of the ferry terminal, is the **Nakasone Toimiyā**, the mausoleum of a 15th century Miyakoan hero who not only conquered the Yaeyama Islands to the south, but also prevented an invasion from the north. There's another impressively large mausoleum cut into the hillside just beyond it.

Continuing north along the coast road you'll find the **Jintōzeiseki** (Tax Stone), a 1.4m-high stone more or less plonked down in someone's front garden. During the heavy-handed rule of the Satsumas (the Satsuma Kingdom invaded from Kagoshima on Kyūshū in the 15th century), anyone taller than this stone was required to pay taxes.

Other sights in the town include the Kaiser Wilhelm or **Hakuai Monument**, presented to the island in 1878 as a gesture of gratitude for the rescue of the crew of a typhoon-wrecked German merchant ship. The **Harimizu Utaki Shrine**, a small structure devoted to local gods, is close to the ferry terminal.

Beaches & Diving

Miyako-jima has its share of good beaches and diving spots. Try the beaches along the southern and northern coasts or Yonaha Mae-hama Beach on the south-west coast, reputed to be the finest beach in Japan. The Tōkyū Resort is located here. Kurima-jima Island can be reached by ferry from Yonaha Mae-hama Port in just 10 minutes. Immediately north of Hirara is Sunayama (Sand Mountain) Beach. Ikema-jima Island is two km off Cape Nishi-Henna-misaki, the northernmost point of Miyako-jima, and can be reached by ferry from the town of Karimata.

Japanese triathletes flock to Miyako in April each year for the Strongman Challenge, which involves a three km swim, a 136 km bicycle race and a 42 km marathon. Miyako-jima is also a popular scuba-diving centre and there are a number of dive operators on the island.

Cape Higashi-Henna-misaki 東平安名岬

At the south-eastern end of the island this long, narrow and quite spectacular peninsula ends with a picturesquely placed lighthouse overlooking the rocky coastline.

Other Attractions

The **Hisamatsu-goyushi Monument** in the village of Hisamatsu, a few km south-west of Hirara, commemorates the fishermen who spotted the Russian fleet steaming north during the Russo-Japanese War of 1904-05. Admiral Tōgō was able to intercept them north of Kyūshū (see the Tsu-shima Island section in the Kyūshū chapter).

The **Hirara Tropical Botanical Gardens** are four km east of Hirara in Onoyama. They are open from 8.30 am to 5 pm (noon on Saturday), closed Sunday and public holidays, and are free. Just south of the botanical gardens, the **Hirashi Sōgō Museum** has an eclectic range of items on display. It's open

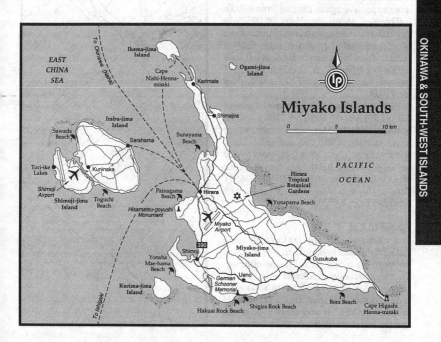

OKINAWA & SOUTH-WEST ISLANDS

from 9 am to 4.30 pm daily, except Monday, and costs ¥300.

Places to Stay

Hirara's minshuku and ryokan are the cheapest places to base yourself. Generally prices range from ¥5000 to ¥6000 with two meals thrown in. There are quite a few places about, but they're a bit difficult to find if you can't read Japanese. Try the *Minshuku Shichifuku-sō* (☎ 09807-2-3316), which has rooms with two meals for ¥5500, or the *Ryokan Uruma-sō* (☎ 09807-2-3113), up near the harbour terminal, which has rooms without meals for ¥5000.

There are also plenty of business hotels in Hirara, though finding them in the town's maze of narrow backstreets is not always that easy. Centrally located hotels with rooms from around ¥5000 (or cheaper) include the *Port Hotel* (☎ 09807-2-9820) and the *Hotel Urizun* (☎ 09807-2-4410). The *Hotel Kyowa* is near the waterfront, overlooking the Harimizu Utaki Shrine, but rooms here are more expensive again, ranging from ¥7000.

The *New Marakatsu Hotel* (☎ 09807-2-9936) is a rambling, slightly tatty place down an entrance alley from the main road in Hirara. There's no sign in English but look for the big letter 'K' in a circle at the top of the hotel sign. Singles are ¥7000 and doubles are ¥10,000.

Elsewhere on the island is the expensive *Tōkyū Resort* (☎ 09807-6-2109), on the beautiful Yonaha Mae-hama Beach, where prices start from ¥13,750 and reach astronomical rates. There are a few places to stay on neighbouring Irabu-jima, including the *Minshuku Katera-sō* (☎ 09807-8-3654), close to Toguchi Beach. It has rooms with breakfast from ¥4500.

Places to Eat

For chain-restaurant izakaya snacks, *Tsubohachi* has a good selection of the usual dishes with a colour menu for easy ordering. The sign outside proclaims it a 'Casual House'. Most dishes are ¥300 to ¥500.

Just down the road from Tsubohachi (towards the KFC) is a couple of sushi places that are popular with locals. Look out for the

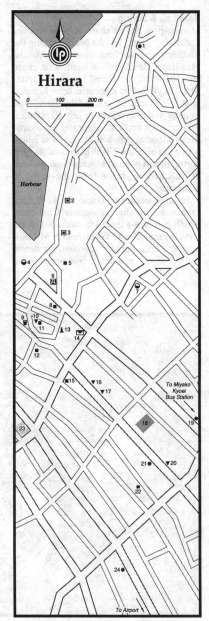

Hirara

0   100   200 m

Harbour

To Miyako Kyoei Bus Station

To Airport

PLACES TO STAY		16	Tsubohachi つぼ八	9	Jammin' Reggae Bar じゃみんレゲエバー
5	Hotel Kyowa ホテル共和	17	Mos Burger	13	Kaiser Wilhelm Hakuai Monument ドイツ皇帝博愛 記念碑
8	Ryokan Uruma-sō 旅館うるま荘	20	Nomura 野村レストラン		
11	Port Hotel ポート観光ホテル	**OTHER**		14	Post Office 郵便局
12	Hotel Urizun ホテルうりずん	1	Jintōzeiseki 人頭税石	19	Sankyū Rent-a-Bike サンキューレンタ バイク
15	Grand Hotel グランドホテル	2	Mausoleum 和利真良豊見之墓		
18	New Marukatsu Hotel ホテルニュー丸勝	3	Nakasone Toimiyā Mausoleum 仲宗根豊見之墓	21	Tomihama Motorcycle Rental とみはまモーター サイクルレンタル
22	Minshuku Shichifuku-sō 民宿七福荘	4	Ferry Terminal 平良港ターミナル		
		6	Harimizu Utaki Shrine	23	Market 平良市公設市場
PLACES TO EAT			張水御嶽神社	24	Marutama Motorcycle Rental まるたまモーター サイクルレンタル
10	Rakkii ラッキー食堂	7	Yachiyo Bus Station 八千代 バスターミナル		

blue nori curtains outside and the blonde wood exteriors. Just behind the Ryokan Uruma-sō is *Rakkii* (☎ 09807-2-7928), a sushi place with a good local reputation, where you can eat from around ¥1000.

Fast-food places around the centre of town include a *Mos Burger*, next door to Tsubohachi, and a *KFC* just down the road from it. There are also lots of red-lantern bars and 24 hour coffee shops; the latter are good for a set breakfast or 'morning service'.

The people of Miyako have a reputation for being outgoing and friendly – to the point where Hirara's Izzatu (west side) entertainment area is said to have more bars (relative to its population) than any other town in Japan. If you want to meet some friendly young locals, try *Jammin'*, a funky little reggae bar, not far from the Ryokan Uruma-sō.

Things to Buy

Jōfu fabric is Miyako-jima's traditional textile. It was once used to make tax payments.

Getting There & Away

Air SWAL flies from Naha on Okinawa to Miyako-jima Island about 10 times daily (45 minutes on a 737, one hour and 10 minutes on a YS-11, ¥11,810). SWAL also flies from Miyako-jima to Ishigaki-jima (35 minutes, ¥6820) and there is a direct flight between Tokyo and Miyako-jima (two hours and 50 minutes, ¥42,070).

Boat There are ferries from Naha every two to five days, taking about 10 hours and costing ¥3810. Most services continue to Ishigaki-jima, taking another six hours.

Getting Around

The Airport A taxi from the airport to Hirara costs around ¥600, but the airport is so close to the town you can walk it in 20 minutes.

Bus Miyako-jima has a comprehensive bus network. Bus Nos 1, 2, 3, 4, 7 and 8 run to the north of the island; while Nos 10, 11, 12,

13 and 15 go south towards Cape Higashi-Henna-misaki.

Motorcycle There is a number of motorcycle rental places around town with scooters for hire at ¥3000 a day, bigger bikes at ¥6000. Try the two Honda dealers shown on the map (Tomihama and Marutama), or Sankyū (☎ 09807-2-2204), a dealer with a wide range of bikes to choose from. Bicycles and cars can also be rented.

IRABU-JIMA & SHIMOJI-JIMA ISLANDS 伊良部島・下地島

If you fly over Shimoji-jima Island (between Okinawa and Ishigaki) have a look at the airport runway. It seems to be out of all proportion to the size of the island and the number of flights it gets. This is because JAL and ANA use it for 747 pilot training.

Irabu-jima and Shimoji-jima, linked by six bridges, are pleasantly rural islands with fields of sugar cane. **Sawada** and **Toguchi** are two good beaches on Irabu-jima Island. On Shimoji-jima the **Tōri-ike Lakes** are linked to the sea by hidden tunnels.

Getting There & Away

SWAL has a daily flight from Naha on Okinawa to Shimoji-jima, but most visitors arrive on the regular 15 minute, ¥400 ferry crossing between Hirara on Miyako-jima and Sarahama on Irabu-jima. There are two agencies selling tickets for boats in the ferry terminal.

Yaeyama Islands
八重山列島

At the far south-western end of the Nansei-shotō chain are the islands of the Yaeyama group, consisting of two main islands (Ishigaki-jima and Iriomote-jima) and a scattering of smaller islands between and beyond the two main ones. There are some fine dive sites around the islands, particularly on Yonaguni-jima Island, the westernmost

point in Japan, and Hateruma-jima Island, the southernmost point. Although there are many Japanese visitors to the islands, most of them, in true Japanese fashion, are day-trippers. Come nightfall on Iriomote-jima or Taketomi-jima most of the tourists will have scuttled back to their hotels on Ishigaki-jima.

ISHIGAKI-JIMA ISLAND 石垣島

Ishigaki-jima Island is the major flight destination for the Yaeyama island group, and boat services fan out from its harbour to the other islands. There are few sights in the town of Ishigaki itself and for most visitors it's mainly of interest as a jumping-off point to the other islands. Ishigaki-jima is about 400 km south-west of Okinawa Island.

Orientation & Information

Ishigaki town's focus is its busy harbour. As for the rest of town – you can stroll around it in a few minutes. Parallel to the main street are two shopping arcades. If you plan to take supplies to the outer islands you'll find a better choice in the arcades than at the places around the harbour. There are several interesting places to visit outside Ishigaki town, such as lovely Mt Omoto-dake and the Tamatorizeki-tembōdai Viewing Platform.

Miyara Dōnchi House

Although the South-West Islands never really had samurai, this is essentially a samurai house. It dates from 1819 and is the only one left in the whole island chain. The building itself is run-down and the garden is poorly maintained, but it's still a worthwhile excursion. Entry is ¥100; it's closed on Tuesday.

Torin-ji Temple 桃林寺

Founded in 1614, this Zen temple is the most important on the island. 'Sentry' boxes flank the gates and statues dating from 1737 (said to be the guardian deities of the islands) can be seen in the dim interiors. Immediately adjacent to the temple is the 1787 Gongen-dō Shrine. The original shrine was built in 1614, but destroyed in a flood in 1771. Every month, from the 15th to the 19th, if you get up very early, you can see Zen meditation being practised here from 5.30 am to 6.30 am. The temple is about a 15 minute walk from the harbour.

Mt Omoto-dake 於茂登岳
Mt Omoto-dake (526m) in the centre of the island is the highest point in Okinawa Prefecture. Mt Banna-dake, five km from town, is only 230m high, but has fine views and the Banna-dake Shinlin-kōen Botanical Garden (entry free).

The **Fusaki Kannon-dō Temple** dates from 1701 and from its hilltop position, about six km north-west of the town, there are good views towards Taketomi-jima and Iriomote-jima. Entry to the temple is free, but unless you hire a bicycle you'll have to take a taxi out there for around ¥1100. Close by is the Tōjin-baka Tomb, a Chinese grave site. At the northern end of the island is Cape Hirakubo-saki and a lighthouse.

Yaeyama Minzoku-en Village
The Yaeyama Minzoku-en Village, which faces Nagura-wan Bay about halfway to Kabira-wan Bay, should tell you everything you need to know about Yaeyama weaving and Yaeyama pottery. It's about 20 minutes by bus from Ishigaki town. Entry is ¥500 and it's open daily from 9 am to 6 pm. Bus Nos 5, 6 and 7 pass the museum en route to Kabira-wan Bay.

Tamatorizeki-tembōdai Viewing Platform
A little over halfway up the east coast of Ishigaki-jima is the Tamatorizeki-tenbōdai Viewing Platform, which provides great coastal views, and is a short walk from some fine, untouched beaches. Bus No 9 goes there from the Ishigaki bus terminal for ¥720. The trip takes around an hour. Get off at the Tamatori bus stop.

Other Attractions
The small **Yaeyama Museum** is very close to the harbour in Ishigaki town and has displays relating to the islands, including coffin palanquins, or *gau*, dugout canoes and other

old boats. Entry is ¥100 and it's open daily from 9 am to 4.30 pm except Monday.

The **Ishigakike-teien Garden** in town follows the regular garden construction conventions, complete with volcanic rocks, but there's not much garden to see. Although it is private, you should be able to see the garden if you ask politely.

Beaches & Diving
There are a number of popular beaches around the island, including Kabira-wan Bay with its fine sandy and sheltered beach, collection of places to stay and black-pearl industry. It can be reached by bus Nos 5, 6 and 7 from the Ishigaki bus station for ¥570.

There are a number of dive shops on Ishigaki-jima, including Aquamarine (☎ 09808-2-0863). However, as you might expect, in Japan diving doesn't come cheap. Rental of equipment for the day averages around ¥15,000. If you're looking at lessons as well (in Japanese), count on forking out ¥85,000 upwards for a beginner's course. For those with diving licences, boat dive trips with lunch included are around ¥12,000. Other popular beach activities, all with expensive price tags on them, include windsurfing and parasailing.

Places to Stay
Ishigaki is a compact little town and there are plenty of places to stay within a couple of minutes walk of the harbour. Other accommodation can be found scattered around the island.

The *Yashima Ryokan Youth Hostel* (☎ 09808-2-3157) is close to the centre of town and costs ¥2300 per night. It's a little tricky to find. Walk past the Yaeyama Museum and take the first left; the hostel is on the right-hand side of the third lane to the left in a slightly decrepit looking white building. The *Trek Ishigaki-jima Youth Hostel* (☎ 09808-6-8257) is on the east coast of the island and also costs ¥2300.

Besides the youth hostel, the cheapest accommodation in town is over on the second of the three narrow alleyways that run parallel to the main road before you come to the two shopping arcades. Here you'll find

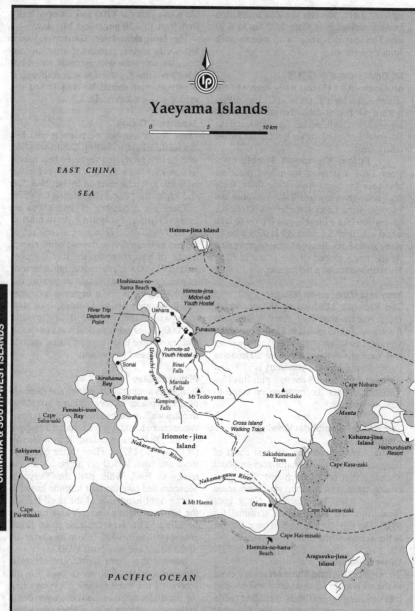

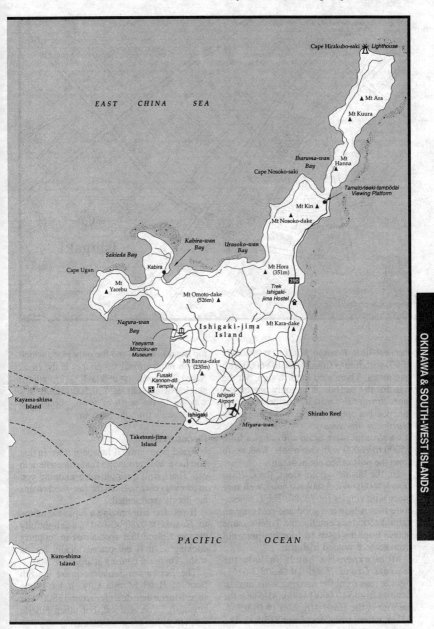

EAST CHINA SEA

Cape Hirakubo-saki ✳ Lighthouse

▲ Mt Ara

▲ Mt Kuura

Ibaruma-wan Bay

Mt Hanna ▲

Cape Nosoko-saki

Tamatorieeki-tembōdai Viewing Platform

Mt Kin ▲

▲ Mt Nosoko-dake

Kabira-wan Bay

Urasoko-wan Bay

Sakieda Bay

Kabira ●

Mt Hora ▲ (351m)

390

Trek Ishigaki-jima Hostel

Cape Ugan

Mt ▲ Yarebu

Mt Omoto-dake (526m) ▲

Nagura-wan Bay

Ishigaki-jima Island

▲ Mt Kara-dake

Yaeyama Minzoku-en Museum

Mt Banna-dake (230m) ▲

Fusaki Kannon-dō Temple

Ishigaki Airport

Kayama-shima Island

● Ishigaki

Miyara-wan

Shiraho Reef

Taketomi-jima Island

PACIFIC OCEAN

Kuro-shima Island

OKINAWA & SOUTH-WEST ISLANDS

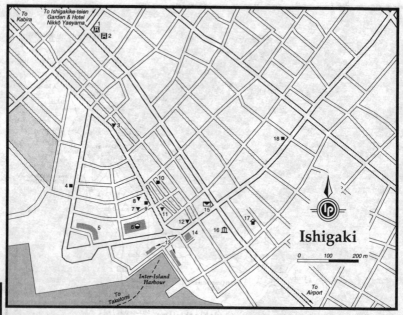

the neat little *Pension Mitake* (☎ 09808-2-4993) with rooms from ¥5000 to ¥6000 with two meals. There's no English sign, but the sign for the pension is the only one on the lane, so you can't miss it. Another relatively inexpensive option worth considering is the *Minshuku Yaeyama-sō* (☎ 09808-2-3231). It's a pleasant place again with singles from ¥5000 to ¥6000 with two meals. Walk north from the post office about 400m.

On the business hotel front, the *Ō-Hara Hotel* (☎ 09808-2-3380) is a quiet, well kept place with singles for ¥6500. The Japanese-style rooms here are good and cost only an extra ¥150. Incidentally, the hotel's name comes from the town on Iriomote-jima, not from some wayward Irishman.

More expensive hotels include the *Ishigaki Grand Hotel* (☎ 09808-2-6161) right across from the harbour, with singles/doubles from ¥10,000/14,000. Also near the harbour is the *Hotel Miyahira* (☎ 09808-2-6111), where twins cost from ¥15,500. The top hotel in town (and the only place which has an international telephone) is the *Hotel Nikkō Yaeyama* (☎ 09808-3-3311), where singles/twins start at ¥10,500/18,500. It's way up in the north of town, about a 25 minute walk from the harbour.

Places to Eat

Ishigaki is an unusual Japanese town in that you have walk around to find somewhere to eat. There isn't a restaurant beckoning you in on every corner. Even the fast-food chains are poorly represented.

If you feel like braving a Japanese menu, try *Hanaki* (☎ 09808-2-0805), a delightfully cluttered place that specialises in 'country cooking', but is celebrated locally for its sushi. There are courses at around ¥2500.

The *Restaurant Seahorse* is on the 8th floor of Hotel Marina City. It has some superb lunch time deals for around ¥800. The emphasis is on seafood, but other generic western dishes are available.

Other possibilities include a couple of Chinese restaurants, both close to the Ō-Hara Hotel: the *Pekin Ryōri Restaurant* and the *Taimon Restaurant*. The former is a tiny place opposite the docks and the Taimon is a bigger place with a sign outside in English proclaiming 'Chinese Restaurant'.

Getting There & Away
Air SWAL has more than 10 flights a day between Naha (Okinawa Island) and Ishigaki (one hour, ¥15,560) and three between Miyako-jima and Ishigaki-jima (30 minutes, ¥6400). ANK operate less frequent services between Naha and Ishigaki. SWAL flies from Ishigaki to the tiny Yonaguni-jima and Hateruma-jima islands. There are controversial plans to extend the Ishigaki airport runway which would result in the destruction of the beautiful coral reefs in the adjacent bay at Shiraho.

Boat There are ferry services every two to five days directly between Naha and Ishigaki (13 hours, ¥5250) or via Miyako-jima. Miyako-jima to Ishigaki takes about six hours and costs ¥2000. The Okinawa to Taiwan ferry service occasionally operates

via Ishigaki, but not often (see Naha, Getting There & Away for details).

Ishigaki is the centre for all the Yaeyama Islands' ferry services and the small harbour is a hive of activity. The ferry company offices are along the two sides of the harbour and there are often several operators, at a variety of prices, to a given destination.

Getting Around
A taxi between the airport and town costs about ¥700; there is no convenient bus service. Bus services fan out from Ishigaki town, the station is across the road from the harbour. A bus to Kabira costs ¥510, and to the top end of the island costs ¥950. Car rental is available at the airport and in town, and bicycles can also be rented in town; the going rate is ¥500 per hour or ¥1500 per day. For motorcycle rental, contact Sankyū (☎ 09808-2-5528), an established agent with a good selection of bikes from ¥2500 per day.

TAKETOMI-JIMA ISLAND 竹富島
Only a 10 minute boat ride from Ishigaki is the popular but relaxed little island of Taketomi-jima. It's noted for its beaches and the pretty little flower-bedecked village in the centre of the island. Even if you only

come over for a day trip, don't forget to bring a towel and your bathing costume. There's excellent swimming at Koindo-hama beach, about a 20 minute walk from the harbour area.

Orientation & Information

Taketomi-jima is a pancake-flat island with its village in the middle. From Taketomi Village, the roads fan out to various places around the edge. A perimeter road following the 10 km coastline is supposedly on the drawing board, but apart from a section around the north-western quadrant it fortunately hasn't come to much. The tourist information office has a coral and shell display.

Taketomi Village　竹富村

Akayama Oka is a tiny lookout atop an even tinier hillock but, on this otherwise flat island, it offers good views over the red-tiled roofs. Look for the walls of coral and rock and the angry guardian lion figures (shiisā) on the rooftops. The other observation point is the Nobukuru lookout, at the northern end of the village, on top of someone's house. It costs ¥100.

The **Kihōin Shūshūkan** is a small private museum with a diverse collection of local items and a ¥300 entry price. **Taketomi Mingeikan** is a local craft centre where you can see the island's Minsā belts and other local textiles being produced. Opposite the craft centre is the **Nishitō Utaki Shrine**, dedicated to a 16th century ruler of the Yaeyama Islands.

Beaches

Most of the island is fringed with beach, but the water is generally very shallow. At several places you can look for star sand (*hoshisuna*), tiny grains of sand with a distinctive star shape. They're actually the dried skeletons of tiny creatures. Although you are requested not to souvenir more than a few grains (where do you put them?), it's sold by the bucketful at shops and at Ishigaki airport. The map shows good star-sand hunting points. Around Cape Kondoi-misaki on the western side of the island you'll find star sand and the best swimming spot on the island.

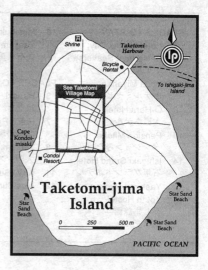

Places to Stay & Eat

The *Takana Ryokan & Youth Hostel* (☎ 09808-5-2151) is opposite the post office. Costs per night are ¥2300 for the hostel and from ¥5500 with two meals for the ryokan section. The *Nohara-sō* is cheaper, however, with rooms for ¥4000 with two meals. Close by, the *Shinda-sō* offers similar standards for ¥4500, as does the *Minshuku Mizumiya* (☎ 09808-5-2250) across the road. Accommodation is not difficult to find on Taketomi, as many of the traditional houses around the island are minshuku or ryokan.

There are also a few restaurants and coffee bars scattered around, though the island is by no means a gourmet paradise. *Chirorin-mura*, a rustic little snack bar about 600m south of the post office, is a good place for a lunch-time bowl of noodles for ¥500. Beer barrels and tree stumps are used as stools at the tables and bar.

Getting There & Away

The best deal for getting to the island is with the Yaeyama Kankō travel service, whose boats do the 10 minute run approximately every 30 minutes for ¥570.

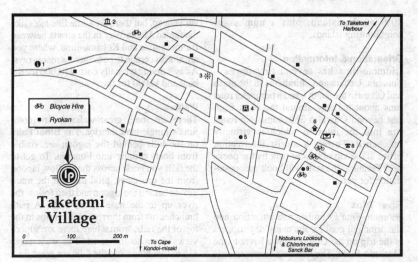

Taketomi Village

0   100   200 m

To Cape
Kondoi-misaki

To
Nobukuru Lookout
& Chirorin-mura
Sanck Bar

To Taketomi
Harbour

🚲 Bicycle Hire

■ Ryokan

1 Tourist Information
   観光案内所
2 Kihōin Shūhūan
   喜宝院蒐集館
3 Akayama Oka Lookout
   赤山丘展望台
4 Nishitō Utaki
   西塘御嶽神社
5 Taketomi Mingeikan
   竹富民芸館
6 Takana Ryokan; Youth Hostel
   高那旅館／ユースホステル
7 Post Office
   郵便局
8 NTT
9 Oxcart Rides
   水牛カート乗り場

Getting Around

The island is small enough to get around most of it on foot if the weather isn't too muggy. Otherwise, there are numerous bicycle rental places on the island, including one near the docks. Bikes cost ¥200 an hour

or ¥1000 a day and are great for exploring the tiny island's sandy roads. You can also hire tandem bicycles and motor scooters. For Japanese visitors, a popular activity is taking a tour of the island in a cart drawn by water buffalo. The cost is ¥1000 for 50 minutes, which is about what it takes to trundle around the island's points of interest.

IRIOMOTE-JIMA ISLAND 西表島

Dense jungle blankets much of Iriomote-jima, an island which could well qualify as Japan's last frontier. Trekking through the interior, you may find leeches, which in Japan is probably good enough for the 'wilderness' tag. The island's major attractions are fine beaches, rivers and waterfalls, and the Iriomote wildcat. Similar in size (and appearance) to a domestic cat, the Iriomote wildcat is nocturnal and rarely seen. The picturesque road signs alerting drivers to its possible presence are, however, quite common.

Much easier to find are the curious sakishimasuo trees with their twisting, ribbon-like root buttresses. You will find them all over the island, but particularly along the coast about five km north of Ōhara. The Iriomote National Park includes about

OKINAWA & SOUTH-WEST ISLANDS

80% of the island, plus a number of neighbouring islands.

Orientation & Information

Iriomote-jima has several tiny towns – Funaura, Uehara and Shirahama in the north and Ōhara in the south – and a perimeter road runs about halfway around the coast from just beyond Ōhara to Shirahama. No roads run into the interior, which is virtually untouched. There's a tourist information office at the top of the car park by the docks near Funaura; the staff will book accommodation for you.

River Trips

Iriomote-jima's number one attraction and the principal goal for the many day-trippers is the trip up the Urauchi-gawa River to the **Mariudo Falls**. The winding brown river is indeed a lot like a tiny stretch of the Amazon and, from where the boat stops, you have about a 1½ hour round trip walk to the Mariudo Falls and on to the long, rapids-like **Kampira Falls**. There are some good swimming places around the falls. From the falls a walking track continues right across the island. The river trip costs ¥1440. Boats operate from 9 am to 4 pm, but they need a minimum of four passengers to set off. There will probably be less waiting around if you get here in the morning, when most of the day-trippers turn up.

From close to the Ōhara docks it is also possible to take river cruises up Iriomote's second-largest river, the **Nakama-gawa River**. The cruises last for around one hour and 20 minutes through lush jungle-like vegetation and cost ¥1240.

Beaches & Diving

There are some fine beaches around the island and star sand can be found at Hoshisuna-no-Hama (Star Sand Beach). Sonai, beyond the Urauchi-gawa River towards Shirahama, also has a pleasant beach and some good places to stay. Haemita-no-Hama Beach, south of Ōhara, is said to be the best beach on the island.

Diving around Iriomote-jima certainly

isn't cheap, but there are some fine sites like the famed Manta Way in the straits between Iriomote-jima and Kohama-jima, where you are almost certain to come across manta rays. A day's diving typically costs ¥10,000 for the boat and ¥5000 for the gear.

Walks

There are some great walks in Iriomote-jima's jungle-clad interior. The **Binai Falls** on the hills behind the lagoon are visible from boats coming into Funaura. To get to the falls you wade across the shallow lagoon from the causeway, plod through the mangroves behind the lagoon and then follow the river up to the base of the falls. A path branches off from the river and climbs to the top of the falls, from where there are superb views down to the coast. The walk takes 1½ to two hours and the falls are great for a cooling dip, but bring salt or matches to get rid of leeches.

From the Kampira Falls at the end of the Urauchi-gawa River trip you can continue on the cross-island trail to **Ōhara**. The walk takes about eight hours and is particularly popular in the spring, when the many trekkers manage to lay a confusing network of false trails.

Places to Stay & Eat

Iriomote-jima has many ryokan, minshuku and pensions, each one lining up its minibus to meet incoming boats at Funaura. The staff at the Funaura Harbour information office will make bookings. The best places are found along the coast west of the harbour towards the Hoshisuna-no-Hama Beach or further west near the Urauchi-gawa River.

The *Irumote-sō Youth Hostel* (☎ 09808-5-6255) has a great hillside location near Funaura Harbour, good facilities, great food and a dive shop. The nightly cost is ¥2700. Continuing west along the coast from Funaura you soon come to the *Iriomote-jima Midori-sō Youth Hostel* (☎ 09808-5-6526/6253), which costs ¥2500 per night.

If you don't want a youth hostel and you want to be close to Funaura Harbour, there's a good choice of places. *Minshuku Kampira-sō* (☎ 09808-5-6508) has per-person costs from as little as ¥3500 with two meals. Not far away is *Uehara-kan* (☎ 09808-5-6516), a white box-like building, where per-person costs with two meals are ¥5000.

Plonked in between Ōhara and Haemita-no-Hama Beach, the best rated strip of sand on the island, is the *Minshuku Iketaya* (☎ 09808-5-5255), where rooms are ¥5000 with two meals. *Robinson's Inn* is a pleasant coffee bar on the main junction in Uehara, a km along the road from Funaura Harbour.

Close to the Minshuku Kampira-sō, look out for the *Riverside Garden Urauchi*, a rustic restaurant that looks like it has been snatched from Ko Pha-Ngan in Thailand. The food has a vegetarian influence.

Getting There & Away

A variety of boats operate between Ishigaki and Iriomote, most to Funaura, which is the place to get the Urauchi-gawa River Cruise, rather than Ōhara. Occasionally there are services to Shirahama. The trip typically takes from 40 minutes to one hour on the faster craft. The slower and less frequent ferries are cheaper.

Boats run out to Funaura from the Shinzato Kankō travel service four times a day at 8.30 and 11 am and 1.30 and 4 pm. The same boat returns from Funaura at 9.20 am, noon and 2.30 and 5 pm. Tickets cost ¥1800. The Yaeyama Kankō travel service offers the same deal for ¥2060.

Getting Around

Many of the minshuku and the youth hostels rent bicycles (¥200 per hour, ¥1200 per day) and scooters (¥600, ¥3000). Cars can also be rented: try Iriomote Rent-a-Car (☎ 09808-5-5303). There's a regular bus service between Ōhara and Shirahama at the two ends of the island's single road. A bus all the way from one end to the other takes nearly an hour and costs ¥960; a bus from Funaura Harbour to the Urauchi-gawa River costs ¥220.

ISLANDS AROUND IRIOMOTE
西表島周辺の島々

Directly north of Iriomote-jima, clearly visible from Funaura, tiny **Hatoma-jima**

Island has a handful of minshuku and some very fine beaches and snorkelling.

Close to the east coast of Iriomote-jima, the small island of **Kohama-jima** has a sprinkling of minshuku, the rather expensive Haimurubushi Resort (where rates start at ¥21,200) and superb scuba diving, particularly in **Manta Way**. Boats operate there from Ishigaki. Minshukus on the island are generally around ¥4500 with two meals included. Clustered together in the centre of the island are three such places: the *Minshuku Ufudaki-sō* (☎ 09808-5-3243); the *Kayama-sō* (☎ 09808-5-3236); and the *Nagata-sō* (☎ 09808-5-3250). From the Ishigaki harbour there are four operators, including Yaeyama Kankō offering seven boats a day to the island for ¥1000. The trip takes 25 to 30 minutes.

There are also regular services to the smaller Kuro-shima Island, directly south of Kohama. It's renowned as the place where bulls are raised for Okinawa's bullfights (*tōgyū*), but it's also got good diving and a couple of pensions and minshuku. The *Minshuku Kuroshima* (☎ 09808-5-4251) is south-east of the harbour and has rooms from ¥4500 with two meals. The Yaeyama Kankō travel service has five ferries a day from Ishigaki for ¥1100 and, as the trip only takes around 40 minutes, it's possible to do it as a day trip. The Shinzato Kankō ticket office has four boats a day to Kuro-shima. Boats leave at 9 am, noon, and 2 and 4.30 pm. They return at 9.40 am and 12.40, 4.40 and 5.10 pm. Tickets cost ¥1500.

YONAGUNI-JIMA ISLAND 与那国島

Yonaguni-jima Island is 100 km west of Iriomote-jima and Ishigaki-jima, and only 110 km from the east coast of Taiwan. The hilly island is just 11 km long and there are fine views from the top of 231m **Mt Urabu**. It's said that on a clear day you can see the mountains of Taiwan from Yonaguni. The island is renowned for its strong sake and its jumbo-sized moths known as *yonagunisan*. Traditional houses on the island have thatched roofs, but tiled roofs are becoming the norm.

There's not a lot to see in Yonaguni, but it has a reputation among some young Okinawans as being a mysterious place, perhaps because it's so far from the mainland and so close to Taiwan. The coastline is marked with some great rock formations, much like those on the east coast of Taiwan. The most famous of these is **Tachigami-iwa Rock** (literally the 'standing-god rock') on the south-east coast. Another famous rock formation is the **Sanninu-dai** (or Gunkan-iwa) **Rock** on the south-west coast. For Japanese this rock is famously evocative of virility (you'll see why). Of interest mainly to Japanese on tours of the island is the **Iri-saki Rock**, a rock carved with an inscription proclaiming it the westernmost point of Japan.

Yunaguni Island's airport is about 10 minutes by taxi from the main town of **Sonai**. There's not a great deal of interest in town, but you might want to check out the **Yunaguni Minzoku Shiryōkan**, with its cluttered displays of items from Yunaguni's history. It's free and open daily from 8.30 am to 6 pm. Also worth checking out is the **Yunaguni Traditional Crafts Centre** in the east of town, where you can see locals working on traditional looms, probably for the benefit of the occasional tourist.

Places to Stay

There are a few hotels and minshuku in Sonai and a couple of places over near Japan's westernmost rock. In terms of both economy and atmosphere, number one is *Minshuku Omoro* (☎ 09808-7-2419), an interesting little place with rooms for ¥4000 with two meals. It's just south of the Minzoku Shiryōkan. Just up the road from the Minzoku Shiryōkan is the *Hotel Irifune* (☎ 09808-7-2311), which even sports an English sign (and a picture of a rampant marlin) outside. It has rooms with two meals included for ¥6000. There are plenty of other places besides these if you care to look around.

Getting There & Away

SWAL flies to Yonaguni-jima from Ishigaki twice daily; the 40 minute flight costs ¥6400 one way. The Fukuyama ferry service (☎ 09808-7-2555) has two boats a week from Ishigaki to Yunaguni at a cost of ¥3400. The trip takes six hours.

Getting Around

Don't expect much in the way of public transport in this neck of the woods. Basically there isn't any, although the island is rumoured to have four public buses running somewhere everyday. Fortunately there are bikes for hire at an average cost of ¥2500 per day. A four hour taxi romp around the island will set you back a cool ¥15,000. Car hire is also available at the airport and in Sonai.

HATERUMA-JIMA ISLAND ハテルマ島

Directly south of Iriomote-jima is tiny Hateruma-jima Island, only five km long and the southernmost point of Japan. Like the westernmost rock on Yunaguni-jima Island, Hateruma-jima sports a **southernmost rock**. There are a few minshuku on the island, but you can also visit as a day-tripper. The Shinzato Kankō company on the harbour in Ishigaki has at least three boats a day at 8.40 and 11 am and 3.40 pm. The same boat heads back to Ishigaki at 9.50 am, 12.40 and 4.50 pm. The return trip is ¥3880. SWAL flights from Ishigaki take 20 minutes and cost ¥6240.

Glossary

aimai – ambiguous and unclear talk, not coming to the point.

Ainu – indigenous people of Hokkaidō; only small numbers remain.

aka-chōchin – red-lantern; working man's pub marked by red lanterns outside.

akirame – to relinquish; resignation.

amakudari – 'descent from heaven'; a retiring civil servant who then goes to work for a private corporation which he formerly dealt with.

ANA – All Nippon Airways

annai-jo – information office.

Arahitogami – living god, the emperor.

arubaito – from the German *arbeit*, meaning 'to work', adapted into Japanese to refer to part-time work; often contracted to *baito*.

ayu – sweetfish caught during *ukai* (cormorant fishing).

baito – from *arbeit*, the German word for 'work'; a part time job or an illegal immigrant worker.

bangasa – rain umbrella made from oiled paper.

banzai – literally '10,000 years', *banzai* means 'hurrah' or 'hurray'; in the west this exclamation is, for the most part, associated with WWII, although its more modern use is quite peaceful.

basho – sumo wrestling tournament.

basho-gara – literally 'the character of a place', fitting to the particular conditions or circumstances.

bentō – boxed lunch, usually of rice and fish, which is often sold for train journeys.

bonsai – the art of growing miniature trees by careful pruning of the branches and roots.

boso-zoku – hot car or motorcycle gangs, usually noisy but harmless.

bottle-keep – system where you buy a whole bottle of liquor in a bar and they keep it for you to drink on subsequent visits. Real entertainers may have bottles stored at numerous bars around town.

bugaku – dance pieces played by court orchestras in ancient Japan.

bunraku – classical puppet theatre using huge puppets to portray dramas similar to *kabuki*.

burakumin – literally 'village people', the *burakumin* were traditionally outcasts associated with lowly occupations such as leather work.

bushidō – 'Way of the Warrior', set of values followed by the samurai.

butsudan – Buddhist altar in Japanese homes.

carp – carp *(koi)* are considered to be a brave, tenacious and vigorous fish, and *koinobori* – carp windsocks – are flown in honour of sons whom it is hoped will inherit a carp's virtues. Many towns and villages have carp ponds or channels teeming with colourful ornamental *nishiki-goi* carp.

chanelah – fashionable young woman with a predilection for name brands, in particular Chanel products.

chaniwa – tea garden.

chanoyu – tea ceremony.

charm – small dish of peanuts or other snack food served, often unrequested, with a drink at a bar – and charged for.

chimpira – *yakuza* understudy; usually used pejoratively of a male with yakuza aspirations.

chizu – map.

chō – city area (for large cities) between a *ku* (ward) and *chōme* in size; also a street.

chōchin – paper lantern.

chōme – city area of a few blocks.

chōnan – oldest son.

chu – loyalty.

crane – cranes *(tsuru)* are a symbol of longevity and are often reproduced in *origami* and represented in traditional gardens.

daifuku – literally 'great happiness'; sticky rice cakes filled with red bean paste and eaten on festive occasions.

daimyō – regional lords under the shōguns.

danchi – public apartments.

dantai – a group (such as the ubiquitous Japanese tourist group).

deru kui wa utareru – 'the nail that sticks up gets hammered down'; popular Japanese proverb which is more or less the opposite of the western 'the squeaky wheel gets the oil'.

donko – name for local trains in country areas.

eboshi – black, triangular samurai hat.

eki – railway station.

ekiben – *bentō* lunch box bought at a railway station.

ema – small votive plaques hung in shrine precincts as petitions for assistance from the resident deities.

engawa – traditional veranda from a Japanese house overlooking the garden.

enka – often referred to as the Japanese equivalent of country & western music, these are folk ballads about love and human suffering that are popular among the older generation.

enryō – individual restraint and reserve.

ero-guro – erotic and grotesque *manga*.

fu – urban prefecture.

fude – brush used for calligraphy.

fugu – poisonous blowfish or pufferfish.

fundoshi – loincloth or breechcloth; traditional male garment consisting of a wide belt and a cloth drawn over the genitals and between the buttocks. Usually seen only at festivals or on sumo wrestlers.

furigana – Japanese script used to give pronunciation for *kanji*.

furii-kippu – one day open ticket.

fusuma – sliding screen.

futon – traditional quilt-like mattress which is rolled up and stowed away during the day.

futsū – literally 'ordinary'; a basic stopping-all-stations train.

gagaku – music of the imperial court.

gaijin – literally 'outside people'; foreigners.

gaman – to endure.

gasshō-zukuri – 'hands in prayer' architectural style.

gei-no-kai – the 'world of art and talent';

usually refers to TV where there's not much of either.

geisha – not a prostitute but a 'refined person'; a woman versed in the arts and dramas who entertains guests.

genkan – foyer area where shoes are removed or replaced when entering or leaving a building.

geta – traditional wooden sandals.

giri – social obligations.

giri-ninjō – combination of social obligations and personal values; the two are often in conflict.

go – board game in which players alternately place white and black counters down, with the object of surrounding the opponent and making further moves impossible; probably originating in China, where it is known as *weiqi*.

hachimaki – headband worn as a symbol of resolve; *kamikaze* pilots wore them in WWII, students wear them to exams.

haiku – 17 syllable poems.

haitaku – a hired taxi.

hakurai – literally 'brought by ship'; foreign or imported goods.

hanami – cherry blossom viewing.

haniwa – earthenware figures found in Kofun period tombs.

hanko – stamp or seal used to authenticate any document; in Japan your *hanko* carries much more weight than your signature.

harakiri – belly cutting; common name for *seppuku* or ritual suicide.

hara-kyū – acupuncture.

hashi – chopsticks.

heiwa – peace.

henro – pilgrims on the Shikoku 88 Temple Circuit.

higasa – sunshade umbrella.

hiragana – phonetic syllabary used to write Japanese words.

ichi-go – square wooden sake 'cups' holding 180 ml.

IDC – International Digital Communications

ike-ike onna – literally 'go-go girl'; young Japanese women who favour died brown hair, boutique suntans and bright lipstick.

ijime – bullying or teasing; problem in the Japanese school system.

ikebana – art of flower arrangement.

irezumi – a tattoo or the art of tattooing. Japanese tattoos are usually much more complex and artistic than their western counterparts. Traditionally they are worn by *yakuza* (Japanese Mafia members), but are becomingly less popular because of the attached stigma.

itadakimasu – before-meals expression; literally 'I will receive'.

ITJ – International Telecom Japan

ittaikan – feeling of unity, of being one type.

izakaya – Japanese version of a pub; beer and sake and lots of snacks available in a rustic, boisterous setting.

JAL – Japan Airlines

JAS – Japan Air Systems

jiage-ya – specialists used by developers to persuade recalcitrant landowners to sell up.

jigoku – 'hells' or hot springs for looking at.

jika-tabi – split-toe boots traditionally worn by Japanese carpenters and builders, which have recently become fashionable attire.

jikokuhyō – the book of timetables.

jitensha – bicycle.

JNTO – Japan National Tourist Organization

JR – Japan Railways

JTB – Japan Travel Bureau

jujitsu – martial art from which *judō* was derived.

juku – cramming schools.

JYHA – Japan Youth Hostel Association

kabuki – form of Japanese theatre based on popular legends and characterised by elaborate costumes, stylised acting and the use of male actors for all roles.

kachi-gumi – the 'victory group' who refuse to believe Japan lost WWII.

kaikan – hotel-style accommodation sponsored by government; literally 'meeting hall'.

kaiseki – Japanese cuisine which obeys very strict rules of etiquette for every detail of the meal and the diner's surroundings.

kaisha – a company, firm.

kaisoku – rapid train.

kaisū-ken – discount bus tickets.

kakizome – New Year's resolutions.

kamban-musume – 'shop sign girl'; girl who stands outside a shop or business to lure customers in.

kambu – management.

kami – Shinto gods; spirits of natural phenomena.

kamidana – Shinto altar in Japanese homes.

kamikaze – 'divine wind'; typhoon that sunk Kublai Khan's 13th century invasion fleet and the name adopted by suicide pilots in the waning days of WWII.

kampai – 'Cheers!'

kampō – Chinese herbal medicines that were dominant in Japan until the 19th century, when western pharmaceuticals were introduced.

kana – the two phonetic syllabaries, *hiragana* and *katakana*.

kanji – literally 'Chinese script'; Chinese ideographic script used for writing Japanese.

Kannon – Buddhist goddess of mercy (Sanskrit: Avalokiteshvara).

kannushi – chief priest of a Shinto shrine.

karakasa – oiled paper umbrella.

karaoke – bars where you sing along with taped music (usually mournful folk ballads); literally 'empty orchestra'.

karōshi – 'death by overwork'; the recently recognised phenomenon of overworked businessmen falling dead on urban streets.

kasa – umbrella.

katakana – phonetic syllabary used to write foreign words.

katamichi – one-way ticket.

katana – Japanese sword.

KDD – Kokusai Denshin Denwa (International Telephone & Telegraph)

keigo – honorific language used to show respect to elders.

ken – prefecture.

kendō – oldest martial art; literally 'the way of the sword'.

ki – life force, will.

kimono – brightly coloured, robe-like traditional outer garment.

kin'en-sha – nonsmoking carriage.

kissaten – coffee shop.

kōban – police box; the officers in this local police station keep a careful eye on their district.

ko garu – 'high school girl'; in particular junior *ike-ike onna* (see above) wannabes.

koinobori – carp banners and windsocks; the colourful fish pennants which wave over countless homes in Japan in late April and early May are for Boys' Day, the final holiday of Golden Week. These days Boys' Day has become Children's Day and the windsocks don't necessarily simply fly in honour of the household's sons.

kokki – Japanese national flag.

kokuminkyūka-mura – national vacation villages; a form of inexpensive accommodation set up by the government to ensure that all citizens have access to low-cost holiday accommodation.

kokuminshukusha – peoples' lodges; an inexpensive form of accommodation.

kokutetsu – Japanese word for Japan Railways (JR); literally, 'national iron'.

Komeitō – Clean Government Party; third-largest political party.

kone – personal connections.

kotatsu – heated table with a quilt or cover over it to keep the legs and lower body warm.

koto – 13-stringed instrument that is played flat on the floor.

kura – mud-walled storehouses.

kyakuma – drawing room of a home, where guests are met.

kyōiku mama – literally 'education mother'; a woman who pushes her kids through the Japanese education process.

kyujinrui – 'old breed'; opposite of *shinjinrui*.

kyūkō – ordinary express train (faster than a *futsū*, only stopping at certain stations).

live house – nightclub or bar where live music is performed.

machi – city area (for large cities) between a *ku* (ward) and *chōme* (area of a few blocks) in size; also street or area.

maiko – apprentice *geisha*.

mama-san – woman who manages a bar or club.

maneki-neko – beckoning cat figure frequently seen in restaurants and bars; it's supposed to attract customers and trade.

manga – Japanese comics.

matsuri – festival.

meinichi – the 'deathday' or anniversary of someone's death.

meishi – business card; very important in Japan.

mentsu – face.

miai-kekkon – arranged marriage; now rare.

mibun – social rank.

miko – shrine maidens.

mikoshi – portable shrines carried around by hordes of sweaty, half-naked salarymen during festivals.

minshuku – the Japanese equivalent of a B&B; family-run budget accommodation.

miso-shiru – bean-paste soup.

MITI – Ministry of International Trade & Industry

mitsubachi – accommodation for motorcycle tourers.

mizu-shōbai – see *water trade*.

mochi – pounded rice made into cakes and eaten at festive occasions.

mōfu – blanket.

morning service – *mōningu sābisu*; a light breakfast served until 10 am in many *kissaten*; often simply referred to as *mōningu* by customers.

mukō – 'over there'; anywhere outside Japan.

mura – village.

nagashi – folk singers and musicians who wander from bar to bar.

nagashi-somen – flowing noodles.

nengajō – New Year cards.

new humans – the younger generation, brought up in more affluent times than their parents and consequently less respectful of the frugal values of the postwar generation.

N'EX – Narita Express

NHK – Nihon Hōsō Kyōkai (Japan Broadcasting Corporation)

Nihon or **Nippon** – Japanese word for Japan; literally 'source of the sun'.

nihonga – term for Japanese-style painting.

ningyō – Japanese doll.

ninja – practitioners of *ninjutsu*.

ninjō – debt; fellow feeling; that which is universally right.

ninjutsu – 'the art of stealth'.

nō – classical Japanese drama performed on a bare stage.

noren – cloth hung as a sunshade, typically carrying the name of the shop or premise; indicates that a restaurant is open for business.

norikae – to change buses or trains; make a connection.

norikae-ken – transfer ticket (trams and buses).

NTT – Nippon Telegraph & Telephone Corporation

o- – prefix used to show respect to anything it is applied to. See *san*.

o-bāsan – grandmotherly type; an old woman.

obi – sash or belt worn with a kimono.

o-cha – tea.

ofuku – return ticket.

o-furo – traditional Japanese bath.

o-jōsan – young college-age women of conservative taste and aspirations.

OL – 'office lady'; female employee of a large firm; usually a clerical worker – pronounced *ō-eru*.

omake – an extra bonus or premium when you buy something.

ombu – 'carrying on the back'; getting someone else to bear the expense, pick up the tab. Also the custom of carrying a baby strapped to the back.

o-miai – arranged marriage; rare in modern Japan.

o-miyage – the souvenir gifts which Japanese must bring back from any trip.

on – favour.

onnagata – male actor playing a woman's role (usually in *kabuki*).

onsen – mineral bath/spa area, usually with accommodation.

origami – art of paper folding.

oshibori – hot towels provided in restaurants.

o-tsumami – bar snacks or *charms*.

oyabun/kobun – teacher/pupil or senior/junior relationship.

pachinko – vertical pinball game which is a Japanese craze (estimated to take in over ¥6 trillion a year) and a major source of tax evasion, yakuza funds, etc.

pinku saron – 'pink saloon'; seedy hostess bars.

puripeido kādo – 'prepaid card'; a sort of reverse credit card: you buy a magnetically coded card for a given amount and it can be used for certain purchases until spent. The prepaid phonecards are the most widespread but there are many others such as Prepaid Highway Cards for use on toll roads.

rakugo – Japanese raconteurs, kind of stand-up comics.

robatayaki – *yakitori* with a deliberately rustic, friendly, homey atmosphere; see also *izakaya*.

romaji – Japanese roman script.

rōnin – 'masterless samurai'; students who must resit university entrance exams.

rotemburo – open-air baths.

Ryōbu Shinto – literally 'two parts Shinto'; a sect that harmonises the Shingon Buddhist sect with the Shinto of Ise-jingū Shrine.

ryokan – traditional Japanese inn.

sadō – tea ceremony, literally 'way of tea'

saisen-bako – offering box at Shinto shrines.

sakazuki – sake cups.

sakoku – Japan's period of national seclusion.

sakura – cherry blossoms.

salaryman – standard male employee of a large firm.

sama – even more respectful suffix than *san* (see below); used in instances such as *o-kyaku-sama* – the 'honoured guest'.

samurai – warrior class.

san – suffix which shows respect to the person it is applied to; see also *o*, the equivalent prefix. Both can occasionally be used together as *o-kyaku-san*, where *kyaku* is the word for guest or customer.

san-sō – mountain cottage.

satori – Zen concept of enlightenment.

seku-hara – sexual harassment.

sembei – soy-flavoured crispy rice biscuits often sold in tourist areas.

sempai – one's elder or senior at school or work.

GLOSSARY

sensei – generally translates as 'teacher' but has wider reference. Politicians are *sensei* through their power rather than their teaching ability.

sentō – public baths.

seppuku – ritual suicide by disembowelment.

setto – set meal.

shamisen – three-stringed banjo-like instrument.

shi – city (to distinguish cities with prefectures of the same name).

shiken-jigoku – 'examination hell'; the enormously important and stressful entrance exams to various levels of the Japanese education system.

shikki – lacquerware.

shinjinrui – 'new species'; young people who do not believe in the standard pattern of Japanese life. Opposite of *kyujinrui*.

shinjū – double suicide by lovers.

shinkansen – ultra fast 'bullet' trains; literally 'new trunk line', since new railway lines were laid for the high speed trains.

shitamachi – traditionally the low-lying, less affluent parts of Tokyo.

shodō – Japanese calligraphy; literally the 'way of writing'.

shōgi – an Oriental version of chess in which each player has 20 pieces and the object is to capture your opponent's king.

shogun – military ruler of old Japan.

shōji – sliding rice-paper screens.

shōjin ryōri – vegetarian meals (especially at temple lodgings).

shūji – the 'practice of letters'; a lesser form of *shodō*.

shukubō – temple lodgings.

shunga – explicit erotic prints; literally 'spring pictures', the season of spring being a popular Chinese and Japanese euphemism for sexuality.

shuntō – spring labour offensive; an annual 'strike'.

shūyū-ken – excursion train ticket.

soapland – Japanese euphemism for bathhouses that offer sexual services.

soba – buckwheat noodles.

sōgō shōsha – integrated trading houses, like the old *zaibatsu*.

sokaiya – *yakuza* who seek extortion money from companies by threatening to influence proceedings at annual general meetings.

soroban – an abacus.

sukebe – lewd in thought and deed; can be a compliment in the right context (eg, among male drinking partners), but generally shouldn't be used lightly; English equivalent would be something like 'sleaze bag'.

sumi-e – black-ink brush paintings.

sumo – Japanese wrestling.

Suzuki – the most common Japanese family name, equivalent to Smith in English.

tabi – split-toed Japanese socks used when wearing *geta*.

tachi-shōben – men urinating in public are a familiar sight in Japan. It's the cause of some academic discussion over Japanese concepts of private places (strict rules apply) and public ones (anything goes); insiders (your friends don't care) and outsiders (whether they care doesn't matter); and even rural environments (we're all farmers at heart) versus urban ones (even in the city).

tadaima – 'now' or 'present'; a traditional greeting called out when one returns home.

tako – kites.

tanin – outsider, stranger, someone not connected with the current situation.

tanka – poems of 31 syllables.

tanuki – racoon or dog-like folklore character frequently represented in ceramic figures.

tarento – 'talent'; referring to musical performers generally notable for their lack of it.

tatami – tightly woven floor matting on which shoes are never worn. Traditionally, room size is defined by the number of tatami mats.

tatemae – 'face'; how you act in public, your public position.

TCAT – Tokyo City Air Terminal

teiki-ken – discount commuter passes.

teishoku – set meal.

tekitō – suitable or appropriate.

tennō – heavenly king, the emperor.

TIC – Tourist Information Center

to – metropolis.

tokkuri – sake flask.

tokkyū – limited express; faster than an ordinary express (*kyūkō*) train.

tokonoma – alcove in a house in which flowers may be displayed or a scroll hung.

torii – entrance gate to a Shinto shrine.

tsukiai – after work socialising by salarymen.

tsunami – huge 'tidal' waves caused by an earthquake.

uchi – literally 'one's own house' but has other meanings relating to 'belonging' and 'being part of'.

ukai – fishing with trained cormorants.

ukiyo-e – wood-block prints; literally 'pictures of the floating world'.

umeboshi – pickled plums; thought to aid digestion and often served with rice in bentō lunch sets.

wa – harmony, team spirit; also the old *kanji* used to denote Japan, and still used in Chinese and Japanese as a prefix to indicate things of Japanese origin; see *wafuku*.

wabi – enjoyment of peace and tranquillity.

wafuku – Japanese-style clothing.

waka – 31 syllable poem.

wanko – lacquerware bowls.

waribashi – disposable wooden chopsticks.

warikan – custom of sharing the bill (among good friends).

washi – Japanese paper.

water trade – entertainment, bars, prostitution, etc; called *mizu-shōbai*.

yakitori – chicken kebabs.

yakitori-ya – restaurant specialising in *yakitori*.

yakuza – Japanese mafia.

yamabushi – mountain priests (Shugendō Buddhism practitioners).

yama-goya – mountain huts.

yamato – a term of much debated origins that refers to the Japanese world, particularly in contrast to things Chinese.

yamato damashii – Japanese spirit, a term with parallels to the German *Volksgeist*; it was harnessed by the militarist government of the '30s and '40s and was identified with unquestioning loyalty to the emperor.

yamato-e – traditional Japanese-style painting.

yanquis – tastelessly dressed males with dyed hair and a cellular phone.

yatai – festival floats/hawker stalls.

YCAT – Yokohama City Air Terminal

yenjoy girl – unmarried woman with time and cash to spare.

yōfuku – western-style clothing.

Yomiuri Giants – *the* Japanese baseball team; although there are 12 big league teams over 50% of the population back the Giants.

yukata – rather like a dressing gown, worn for lounging or casual use; standard issue for bathing in ryokan.

zabuton – small cushions for sitting on (used in *tatami* rooms).

zaibatsu – industrial conglomerates; the term arose prior to WWII but the Japanese economy is still dominated by huge firms like Mitsui, Marubeni or Mitsubishi which are involved in many different industries.

Index

ABBREVIATIONS

MAPS

852

TEXT

Map references are in **bold** type.

Castles

Gardens

Thanks to the many travellers who wrote in with helpful hints, useful advice and funny and interesting stories.

Wilf Aldridge, JF Alonso-Llorente, Jamie Anderson, Yuriko Aoki, Chris Bain, Paul Bakker, Russell Banks, Alison Barbour, Gordon Bartram, Jon Batchelor, David Beattie, Bruce Beck, Sara Benson, Kathryn Bignell, Gordon Black, Mark Blacker, Werner Blumeuthal, Jorn Borup, David Bottomly, Sharon Boyle, Michel Bruneau, Jonathan Buchanan, Lone Burnett, Phillip Byderarken, Bonnie Carpenter, R Chambers, A Chan & M Greenwood, Jan Chouljian, Keiko Chuurne, Andrew Clarke, Kimberly Daly, Ann Daniels, Elaine Davis, Leroy Demery Jnr, NS Doyle, Pieter Droppert, Ellen Eedgeman, Blake Engelhard, Carla Fantini, Douglas Farm, V Faulkner, Gary Fishman, Anne Fromage, Mathias Fuchs, Adolfo Garcia, Robert Garing, GP Gervat, Terry Gibbs, Margaret Gordon, Martin Goyette, Eva Grootens, Steven Haynie, Cameron Hays, Eric Heide, Susan Henderson, Thomas Hensel, Lisa Hirst, Rowan Hooper, Sharyn Horowitz, Kimi Howell, Lars Hylander, Iizuka Izumi, A Jackson, Eric Johnson, Wendy Jones, Jackie Keating, Edward Kent, Ryoko Kita, Nic Klar, Ralf Kohl, Lise Kuhr, Gino Laan, Steve Lansford, George Lee, L Lees, John Lepore, Cheri Letkeman, Terri Lituchy, Mary Logan, Barry Lowden, Christine Lutz, Roger Lyman, Brent Madison, George Maeda, Greg Marlow, Christian & Mayumi Masing, Robert Mason, Debbie Matsuda, Gudrun Mattes, Terry McGlynn, David McIntyre, David Mead, I Michiko, Yoshida Michio, Derek Miller, Rahul Moodgal, Treasa Ni Mhiochain, Barbara Northend, Kenneth O'Connell, Mike O'Loughlin, H O'Sullivan, Maumi & Eugene Orwell, T Parnell, Steve Pav, Kenneth Pechter, Marion Penaud, R Peters, Anthony Philip, Sue Pickett, Julio Piernoni, Brent Pitman, Clemenz Portmann, Steffen Preuss, Alex Proudfoot, George Pyper, Aaron Quigley, Michael Rakower, Paolo Rapisarda, Etienne Raynaud, A Reboul, Jason Reeve, Manfred Roedig, Stephen Ryberg, Damien Sams, Robert Shanks, Paul Sharkey, Hagay Shemesh, Andrew Shuttleworth, Mark Skridulaitis, Carolyn Snider, Lars & Tirra Stenstedt, Richard Stump, Jemma Sussman, Cyril Suszckiewicz, Frank Suzzoni, Glenn Sweitzer, Tony Szeles, Kawahara Takamasa, Kinman Tam, Tan Hwee Meing, AC Tennant, Robert Thomason, Janice & Brian Thorburn, Kristin Torgerson, Marie Turner, Narelle Turnock, Hans van der Veen, Erik Ven der Molen, Daniel Vollmer, Jen Volpe, Nick Wagner, Gina Wales, Peter Ward, David Werner, David Whitmer, David Wilkinson, Alan Williams, Tim Williams, Nicola Wilson, Robert Wivchar, Nick & Jan Wooller, Pam Wornath, Edward Wright, Neal Yanover, Elena Yap, Morohashi Yoshiharu, Francesco Zavarese

LONELY PLANET PHRASEBOOKS

Building bridges,
Breaking barriers,
Beyond babble-on

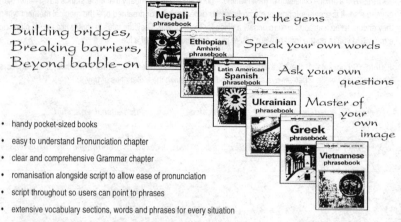

Listen for the gems

Speak your own words

Ask your own questions

Master of your own image

- handy pocket-sized books
- easy to understand Pronunciation chapter
- clear and comprehensive Grammar chapter
- romanisation alongside script to allow ease of pronunciation
- script throughout so users can point to phrases
- extensive vocabulary sections, words and phrases for every situation
- full of cultural information and tips for the traveller

'...vital for a real DIY spirit and attitude in language learning' – Backpacker

'the phrasebooks have good cultural backgrounders and offer solid advice for challenging situations in remote locations' – San Francisco Examiner

'...they are unbeatable for their coverage of the world's more obscure languages' – The Geographical Magazine

---

Arabic (Egyptian)
Arabic (Moroccan)
Australia
  Australian English, Aboriginal and
  Torres Strait languages
Baltic States
  Estonian, Latvian, Lithuanian
Bengali
Brazilian
Burmese
Cantonese
Central Asia
Central Europe
  Czech, French, German, Hungarian,
  Italian and Slovak
Eastern Europe
  Bulgarian, Czech, Hungarian, Polish,
  Romanian and Slovak
Ethiopian (Amharic)
Fijian
French
German
Greek

Hindi/Urdu
Indonesian
Italian
Japanese
Korean
Lao
Latin American Spanish
Malay
Mandarin
Mediterranean Europe
  Albanian, Croatian, Greek,
  Italian, Macedonian, Maltese,
  Serbian and Slovene
Mongolian
Nepali
Papua New Guinea
Pilipino (Tagalog)
Quechua
Russian
Scandinavian Europe
  Danish, Finnish, Icelandic, Norwegian
  and Swedish

South-East Asia
  Burmese, Indonesian, Khmer, Lao,
  Malay, Tagalog (Pilipino), Thai and
  Vietnamese
Spanish (Castilian)
  Basque, Catalan and Galician
Sri Lanka
Swahili
Thai
Thai Hill Tribes
Tibetan
Turkish
Ukrainian
USA
  US English, Vernacular,
  Native American languages ,and
  Hawaiian
Vietnamese
Western Europe
  Basque, Catalan, Dutch, French,
  German, Irish, Italian, Portuguese,
  Scottish Gaelic, Spanish (Castilian)
  and Welsh

LONELY PLANET JOURNEYS

JOURNEYS is a unique collection of travel writing – published by the company that understands travel better than anyone else. It is a series for anyone who has ever experienced – or dreamed of – the magical moment when they encountered a strange culture or saw a place for the first time. They are tales to read while you're planning a trip, while you're on the road or while you're in an armchair, in front of a fire.

JOURNEYS books catch the spirit of a place, illuminate a culture, recount a crazy adventure, or introduce a fascinating way of life. They always entertain, and always enrich the experience of travel.

'Idiosyncratic, entertaininingly diverse and unexpected . . . from an international writership'
– The Australian

'Books which offer a closer look at the people and culture of a destination, and enrich travel experiences'
– American Bookseller

LOST JAPAN
Alex Kerr

Originally written in Japanese, this passionate, vividly personal book draws on the author's experiences in Japan over thirty years. Alex Kerr takes us on a backstage tour, as he explores the ritualised world of Kabuki, retraces his initiation into Tokyo's boardrooms during the heady Bubble Years, tells how he stumbled on a hidden valley that became his home . . . and exposes the environmental and cultural destruction that is the other face of contemporary Japan.

Alex Kerr is an American who lives in Japan. He majored in Japanese studies at Yale, collects Japanese art and has founded his own art-dealing business. Simultaneously 'a foreigner' and 'an insider', Alex Kerr brings a unique perspective to writing about contemporary Japan.

Winner of Japan's 1994 Shincho Gakugei Literature Prize.

'This deeply personal witness to Japan's wilful loss of its traditional culture is at the same time an immensely valuable evaluation of just what that culture was' **– Donald Ritchie, Japan Times**

'Brilliantly combines essays and autobiography, chronicling Kerr's love affair with Japan' **– The Times**

LONELY PLANET TRAVEL ATLASES

Lonely Planet has long been famous for the number and quality of its guidebook maps. Now we've gone one step further and produced a handy companion series: Lonely Planet travel atlases – maps of a country produced in book form.

Unlike other maps, which look good but lead travellers astray, our travel atlases have been researched on the road by Lonely Planet's experienced team of writers. All details are carefully checked to ensure the atlas corresponds with the equivalent Lonely Planet guidebook.

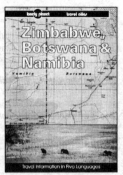

The handy atlas format means no holes, wrinkles, torn sections or constant folding and unfolding. These atlases can survive long periods on the road, unlike cumbersome fold-out maps. The comprehensive index ensures easy reference.

- full-colour throughout
- maps researched and checked by Lonely Planet authors
- place names correspond with Lonely Planet guidebooks
  – no confusing spelling differences
- legend and travelling information in English, French, German, Japanese and Spanish
- size: 230 x 160 mm

Available now:
Chile & Easter Island • Egypt • India & Bangladesh • Israel & the Palestinian Territories •Jordan, Syria & Lebanon • Kenya • Laos • Portugal • South Africa, Lesotho & Swaziland • Thailand • Turkey • Vietnam • Zimbabwe, Botswana & Namibia

LONELY PLANET TV SERIES & VIDEOS

Lonely Planet travel guides have been brought to life on television screens around the world. Like our guides, the programmes are based on the joy of independent travel, and look honestly at some of the most exciting, picturesque and frustrating places in the world. Each show is presented by one of three travellers from Australia, England or the USA and combines an innovative mixture of video, Super-8 film, atmospheric soundscapes and original music.

Videos of each episode – containing additional footage not shown on television – are available from good book and video shops, but the availability of individual videos varies with regional screening schedules.

Video destinations include: Alaska • American Rockies • Australia – The South-East • Baja California & the Copper Canyon • Brazil • Central Asia • Chile & Easter Island • Corsica, Sicily & Sardinia – The Mediterranean Islands • East Africa (Tanzania & Zanzibar) • Ecuador & the Galapagos Islands • Greenland & Iceland • Indonesia • Israel & the Sinai Desert • Jamaica • Japan • La Ruta Maya • Morocco • New York • North India • Pacific Islands (Fiji, Solomon Islands & Vanuatu) • South India • South West China • Turkey • Vietnam • West Africa • Zimbabwe, Botswana & Namibia

The Lonely Planet TV series is produced by:
Pilot Productions
The Old Studio
18 Middle Row
London W10 5AT UK

For video availability and ordering information contact your nearest Lonely Planet office.

Music from the TV series is available on CD & cassette.

PLANET TALK

Lonely Planet's FREE quarterly newsletter

We love hearing from you and think you'd like to hear from us.

When...is the right time to see reindeer in Finland?
Where...can you hear the best palm-wine music in Ghana?
How...do you get from Asunción to Areguá by steam train?
What...is the best way to see India?

For the answer to these and many other questions read PLANET TALK.

Every issue is packed with up-to-date travel news and advice including:

- a letter from Lonely Planet co-founders Tony and Maureen Wheeler
- go behind the scenes on the road with a Lonely Planet author
- feature article on an important and topical travel issue
- a selection of recent letters from travellers
- details on forthcoming Lonely Planet promotions
- complete list of Lonely Planet products

To join our mailing list contact any Lonely Planet office.

Also available: Lonely Planet T-shirts. 100% heavyweight cotton.

LONELY PLANET ONLINE

Get the latest travel information before you leave or while you're on the road

Whether you've just begun planning your next trip, or you're chasing down specific info on currency regulations or visa requirements, check out Lonely Planet Online for up-to-the minute travel information.

As well as travel profiles of your favourite destinations (including maps and photos), you'll find current reports from our researchers and other travellers, updates on health and visas, travel advisories, and discussion of the ecological and political issues you need to be aware of as you travel.

There's also an online travellers' forum where you can share your experience of life on the road, meet travel companions and ask other travellers for their recommendations and advice. We also have plenty of links to other online sites useful to independent travellers.

And of course we have a complete and up-to-date list of all Lonely Planet travel products including guides, phrasebooks, atlases, Journeys and videos and a simple online ordering facility if you can't find the book you want elsewhere.

www.lonelyplanet.com
or
AOL keyword: lp

LONELY PLANET PRODUCTS

Lonely Planet is known worldwide for publishing practical, reliable and no-nonsense travel information in our guides and on our web site. The Lonely Planet list covers just about every accessible part of the world. Currently there are nine series: *travel guides, shoestring guides, walking guides, city guides, phrasebooks, audio packs, travel atlases, Journeys – a unique collection of travel writing and Pisces Books - diving and snorkeling guides.*

EUROPE

Amsterdam • Andalucia • Austria • Baltic States phrasebook • Berlin • Britain • Canary Islands• Central Europe on a shoestring • Central Europe phrasebook • Czech & Slovak Republics • Denmark • Dublin • Eastern Europe on a shoestring • Eastern Europe phrasebook • Estonia, Latvia & Lithuania • Europe • Finland • France • French phrasebook • Germany • German phrasebook • Greece • Greek phrasebook • Hungary • Iceland, Greenland & the Faroe Islands • Ireland • Italian phrasebook • Italy • Lisbon • London • Mediterranean Europe on a shoestring • Mediterranean Europe phrasebook • Paris • Poland • Portugal • Portugal travel atlas • Prague • Romania & Moldova • Russia, Ukraine & Belarus • Russian phrasebook • Scandinavian & Baltic Europe on a shoestring • Scandinavian Europe phrasebook • Slovenia • Spain • Spanish phrasebook • St Petersburg • Switzerland •Trekking in Spain • Ukrainian phrasebook • Vienna • Walking in Britain • Walking in Italy • Walking in Switzerland • Western Europe on a shoestring • Western Europe phrasebook

Travel Literature: The Olive Grove: Travels in Greece

NORTH AMERICA

Alaska • Backpacking in Alaska • Baja California • California & Nevada • Canada • Chicago • Deep South• Florida • Hawaii • Honolulu • Los Angeles • Mexico • Mexico City • Miami • New England • New Orleans • New York City • New York, New Jersey & Pennsylvania • Pacific Northwest USA • Rocky Mountain States • San Francisco • Seattle • Southwest USA • USA phrasebook • Washington, DC & the Capital Region

Travel Literature: Drive thru America

CENTRAL AMERICA & THE CARIBBEAN

• Bahamas and Turks & Caicos • Bermuda • Central America on a shoestring • Costa Rica • Cuba • Eastern Caribbean • Guatemala, Belize & Yucatán: La Ruta Maya • Jamaica • Panama

Travel Literature Green Dreams: Travels in Central America

SOUTH AMERICA

Argentina, Uruguay & Paraguay • Bolivia • Brazil • Brazilian phrasebook • Buenos Aires • Chile & Easter Island • Chile & Easter Island travel atlas • Colombia Ecuador & the Galápagos Islands • Latin American Spanish phrasebook • Peru • Quechua phrasebook • Rio de Janeiro • South America on a shoestring • Trekking in the Patagonian Andes • Venezuela

Travel Literature: Full Circle: A South American Journey

ISLANDS OF THE INDIAN OCEAN

Madagascar & Comoros • Maldives • Mauritius, Réunion & Seychelles

AFRICA

Africa - the South • Africa on a shoestring • Arabic (Moroccan) phrasebook • Cairo • Cape Town • Central Africa • East Africa • Egypt • Egypt travel atlas• Ethiopian (Amharic) phrasebook • The Gambia & Senegal • Kenya • Kenya travel atlas • Malawi, Mozambique & Zambia • Morocco • North Africa • South Africa, Lesotho & Swaziland • South Africa, Lesotho & Swaziland travel atlas • Swahili phrasebook • Tunisia • Trekking in East Africa • West Africa • Zimbabwe, Botswana & Namibia • Zimbabwe, Botswana & Namibia travel atlas

Travel Literature: Mali Blues • The Rainbird: A Central African Journey • Songs to an African Sunset: A Zimbabwean Story

MAIL ORDER

Lonely Planet products are distributed worldwide. They are also available by mail order from Lonely Planet, so if you have difficulty finding a title please write to us. North American and South American residents should write to 150 Linden St, Oakland CA 94607, USA; European and African residents should write to 10a Spring Place, London NW5 3BH; and residents of other countries to PO Box 617, Hawthorn, Victoria 3122, Australia.

NORTH-EAST ASIA

Beijing • Bhutan • Cantonese phrasebook • China • Hong Kong • Hong Kong, Macau & Guangzhou • Japan • Japanese phrasebook • Japanese audio pack • Korea • Korean phrasebook • Kyoto • Mandarin phrasebook • Mongolia • Mongolian phrasebook • North-East Asia on a shoestring • Seoul • South-West China • Taiwan • Tibet • Tibet phrasebook • Tokyo

Travel Literature: Lost Japan

MIDDLE EAST & CENTRAL ASIA

Arab Gulf States • Arabic (Egyptian) phrasebook • Central Asia • Central Asia phrasebook • Iran • Israel & the Palestinian Territories • Israel & the Palestinian Territories travel atlas • Istanbul • Jerusalem • Jordan & Syria • Jordan, Syria & Lebanon travel atlas • Lebanon • Middle East • Turkey • Turkish phrasebook • Turkey travel atlas • Yemen

Travel Literature: The Gates of Damascus • Kingdom of the Film Stars: Journey into Jordan

ALSO AVAILABLE:

Brief Encounters • Travel with Children • Traveller's Tales • Not the Only Planet

INDIAN SUBCONTINENT

Bangladesh • Bengali phrasebook • Bhutan • Delhi • Goa • Hindi/Urdu phrasebook • India • India & Bangladesh travel atlas • Indian Himalaya • Karakoram Highway • Nepal • Nepali phrasebook • Pakistan • Rajasthan • South India • Sri Lanka • Sri Lanka phrasebook • Trekking in the Indian Himalaya • Trekking in the Karakoram & Hindukush • Trekking in the Nepal Himalaya

Travel Literature: In Rajasthan • Shopping for Buddhas

SOUTH-EAST ASIA

Bali & Lombok • Bangkok • Burmese phrasebook • Cambodia • Ho Chi Minh City • Indonesia • Indonesian phrasebook • Indonesian audio pack • Indonesia's Eastern Islands • Jakarta • Java • Laos • Lao phrasebook • Laos travel atlas • Malay phrasebook • Malaysia, Singapore & Brunei • Myanmar (Burma) • Philippines • Pilipino phrasebook • Singapore • South-East Asia on a shoestring • South-East Asia phrasebook • South-West China • Thailand • Thailand's Islands & Beaches • Thailand travel atlas • Thai phrasebook • Thai audio pack • Thai Hill Tribes phrasebook • Vietnam • Vietnamese phrasebook • Vietnam travel atlas

AUSTRALIA & THE PACIFIC

Australia • Australian phrasebook • Bushwalking in Australia • Bushwalking in Papua New Guinea • Fiji • Fijian phrasebook • Islands of Australia's Great Barrier Reef • Melbourne • Micronesia • New Caledonia • New South Wales • New Zealand • Northern Territory • Outback Australia • Papua New Guinea • Papua New Guinea phrasebook • Queensland • Rarotonga & the Cook Islands • Samoa • Solomon Islands • South Australia • Sydney • Tahiti & French Polynesia • Tasmania • Tonga • Tramping in New Zealand • Vanuatu • Victoria • Western Australia

Travel Literature: Islands in the Clouds • Sean & David's Long Drive

ANTARCTICA

Antarctica

THE LONELY PLANET STORY

Lonely Planet published its first book in 1973 in response to the numerous 'How did you do it?' questions Maureen and Tony Wheeler were asked after driving, busing, hitching, sailing and railing their way from England to Australia.

Written at a kitchen table and hand collated, trimmed and stapled, *Across Asia on the Cheap* became an instant local bestseller, inspiring thoughts of another book.

Eighteen months in South-East Asia resulted in their second guide, *South-East Asia on a shoestring*, which they put together in a backstreet Chinese hotel in Singapore in 1975. The 'yellow bible', as it quickly became known to backpackers around the world, soon became *the* guide to the region. It has sold well over half a million copies and is now in its 9th edition, still retaining its familiar yellow cover.

Today there are over 350 titles, including travel guides, walking guides, language kits & phrasebooks, travel atlases and travel literature. The company is the largest independent travel publisher in the world. Although Lonely Planet initially specialised in guides to Asia, today there are few corners of the globe that have not been covered.

The emphasis continues to be on travel for independent travellers. Tony and Maureen still travel for several months of each year and play an active part in the writing, updating and quality control of Lonely Planet's guides.

They have been joined by over 80 authors and 200 staff at our offices in Melbourne (Australia), Oakland (USA), London (UK) and Paris (France). Travellers themselves also make a valuable contribution to the guides through the feedback we receive in thousands of letters each year and on our web site.

The people at Lonely Planet strongly believe that travellers can make a positive contribution to the countries they visit, both through their appreciation of the countries' culture, wildlife and natural features, and through the money they spend. In addition, the company makes a direct contribution to the countries and regions it covers. Since 1986 a percentage of the income from each book has been donated to ventures such as famine relief in Africa; aid projects in India; agricultural projects in Central America; Greenpeace's efforts to halt French nuclear testing in the Pacific; and Amnesty International.

'I hope we send people out with the right attitude about travel. You realise when you travel that there are so many different perspectives about the world, so we hope these books will make people more interested in what they see. Guidebooks can't really guide people. All you can do is point them in the right direction.'

– Tony Wheeler

lonely planet

LONELY PLANET PUBLICATIONS

Australia
PO Box 617, Hawthorn 3122, Victoria
tel: (03) 9819 1877 fax: (03) 9819 6459
e-mail: talk2us@lonelyplanet.com.au

USA
150 Linden St
Oakland, CA 94607
tel: (510) 893 8555 TOLL FREE: 800 275-8555
fax: (510) 893 8572
e-mail: info@lonelyplanet.com

UK
10a Spring Place,
London NW5 3BH
tel: (0171) 428 4800 fax: (0171) 428 4828
e-mail: go@lonelyplanet.co.uk

France:
1 rue du Dahomey, 75011 Paris
tel: 01 55 25 33 00 fax: 01 55 25 33 01
e-mail: bip@lonelyplanet.fr

World Wide Web: http://www.lonelyplanet.com
or *AOL keyword: lp*